The final march past of Lieutenant Colonel C.V. Lilley, MC, CD., after he handed the reins of office (change of command) to Colonel J.P. Beer, MBE, CD.
The Cadet Parade Commander: Cadet Lieutenant Colonel Alexander Malczynski of The 2290 British Columbia Regiment (Duke of Connaught's Own) Cadet Corps. August 1976. LCol Lilley commanded the camp longer than any other CO.

'FORM THREE RANKS
ON THE ROAD!'

A novel

by

CORDELL CROSS

Published by:
Aggie Blinkhorn Organization Inc.
P.O. Box 88549
101 - 13753 72nd Avenue
Surrey, B.C., Canada
V3W 0X1

ISBN 0-9696248-1-6

Cover art by Peter Lynde - Ganges, B.C.

FOR MARY, WILLIAM, NORMAN, JOAN, RAY, CHRIS, STEVE AND RUSS

ROBORE ET VIGILANTIBUS — BY STRENGTH AND WATCHFULNESS

I NTRODUCTION

This book is about young boys attending the Vernon Army Cadet Camp in British Columbia. The camp is one of many across this great country, and thank God these institutions still exist. They are the guiding learning centres for responsible youth.

For years, the Members of Parliament forming the Government of Canada, and the Official Opposition, supported Navy, Army and Air Force cadet camps with fierce guardianship, thus ensuring their preservation. After all, the *drop-in-the bucket* costs out of the defence budget for maintaining these camps as well as a strong cadet organization was nothing compared to the billions of dollars spent fighting youth crime.

But when Pierre E. Trudeau entered the scene with his Minister of Defence, Paul Hellyer, tragic, illogical changes were made to the Canadian Forces. Deep in the bowels of this transformation, deceitful, disreputable *modifications* were made to these splendid and precious Navy, Army and Air force youth establishments. Cadet training was *changed*, and many cadet camps were closed. The press wasn't really cognizant of most of the horrific *mutations* Trudeau made to Canada, especially the cadet organizations, because his *dazzling* method of creating diversions, kept the media immersed in *other* matters for which this country has, and will suffer, for a long to time to come.

The citizens of this fine nation still don't realize the damage done to Canada's military, but what bothers me most of all, is the fact that succeeding governments have allowed Trudeau clones to continue his wicked policy of nearly eliminating a tried and tested exceptional youth-training movement. And now when the country is thoroughly called upon to supply people capable of handling peace-keeping in various places in the world, the *troops* we send, lack the fundamental training they would otherwise have received in cadets or advanced military establishments, such as the militia and the regular force.

What is the reason for this? Try this on for size. Millions upon millions of Canadians that benefited from cadet training in the past, have had their minds *diverted* by so many federal and provincial *problems*, they don't know if they're coming or going. As a result, they are not aware of what the government is doing with regard to cadet training and cadet summer camps, with the aid and *advice* of the ever-changing Minister of Defence and his or her (totally uninterested in cadet matters) *Chief* of Defence Staff.

Well, that is now going to change. At first it was thought that the various leagues could halt the carnage, but it would appear the *social* aspects cannot be erased, and *certain* individuals in the leagues accept anything for an answer. This in itself is a shame, and I would ask the leagues to accept a little more responsibility and voice their concern far more strongly when dealing with the *robots* in Ottawa. If this entails a slight change to their various charters, then so be it.

Over the past six months, a fellow by the name of Douglas Verdun has formed an organization called **CADETS (CANADIAN AWARENESS for the DISCI-PLINE, EDUCATION, AND TRAINING of CADETS, SOCIETY)** Eventually a branch will open in every province. Unlike the three Leagues, this organization will **aim its will** at Members of Parliament who seem to have lost sight of the fact that there are **six million concerned Canadians,** who have had enough of cadet camp closures and inferior cadet training.

Members of (CADETS) will not attend cocktail parties, and if past general officers wish to get involved, they must first cure themselves of the 'old boy network' syndrome, which in itself is a total farce. Having a drink with the *boys* doesn't work anymore. The Chairman, Mr. Verdun, will simply take aim at politicians pocketbooks. They can either do the right thing in the House and collect their salary, or go home, and like the rest of us Canadians, work hard for their money.

Those of you who wish to get involved, send a postage paid return envelope to **CADETS - Suite 108 - 7231 120th Street, Delta, B.C. V4C 6P5.** Membership is $10.00 per year, and corporate memberships and donations are welcome.

This organization has had enough of DNDs game-playing policies with cadets. As Mr. Verdun says, "There has been an abundance of 'white papers' on cadet matters. We're going to ensure that the only white papers the Minister of Defence and his Chief of Defence Staff introduce and use, are the ones in their toilets."

***

Normally the foreword of a book is written to introduce the story in the pages that follow and it can be written by someone other than the author. Unfortunately, I have to do a little more than just present the story. Also, I would have dearly loved to have someone other than me write the foreword, particularly someone from Defence Headquarters. If I asked *people* there, they would be too busy counting their fat salaries and personally auditing their up-coming pensions. I believe also that a typical deplorable reply would be, "Don't bother me about cadets and cadet camps. If such organizations exists, they would be the last thing on my mind."

You see, as I type this, cadet budgets are being cut across the country and the real meaning of the word 'army' is slyly and slowly being squeezed out of the words, 'army cadets.' Yes, the minister and his Chief of Defence Staff are *doing the dirty*. The same thing is also happening with the navy and air force cadets. I'm therefore going to look after a little *business* in this foreword, and a great deal of *business* in my Author's Notes at the end of the book.

When my first novel, **'Stand By Your Beds!'** was published, an acquaintance of mine said, "It's a little dated, isn't it?"

At first I agreed with him, however after considering his statement, I fully understand how wrong he really is. You see, my friend finds it difficult to comprehend how we, the general public, have allowed the military brass and politicians to guilefully and secretively separate the real meaning of the words' **army**, **navy** and **air force** from the word, **cadets**. My first novel dealt with army cadets. Not civilian cadets, scout cadets, lumber cadets, fisher-people cadets, horse-riding cadets, skateboard cadets, computer cadets, etc.

So realistically, my friend is wrong. He also doesn't seem to understand that while youngsters haven't changed, the sexual intellectuals who control the cadet movement have, and as such he naively believes the status quo of the steadfast cadet system has been properly maintained.

Now, whether or not he falsely believes this and looks the other way to protect his certain position, like many in Ottawa, I don't know. What I do know, is that the novel isn't dated. If the meanings of the words, **army**, **navy** and **air force** are to be applied to the word **cadets**, then nothing should have changed. However, if the meanings of the words **army**, **navy** and **air force** have changed at the regular force and militia levels, then that's an entirely different matter altogether. That means the total picture of Canada's *so-called* armed forces has changed. If this is the case, my comments in, **'Stand By Your Beds!'** were indeed dated.

I've made up my mind that is exactly what's happened. It is completely possible the training, equipment and leadership offered the cadet movement today, mirrors that which is used in the regular force and militia. As such, perhaps I can't blame those in Ottawa, regardless of their rank, or for that matter, those at the lower levels, because they simply don't know what the words, army, navy and air force, stand for. They've been molded by those who came before them and the mold is set. It's a shame what brain-washing has done with the 'me' generation.

However, if I'm wrong, then those responsible for this current *monstrosity*, must be held accountable.

***

Many people have asked, "Why write about cadets attending camp? Why not write about what takes place in the Camp Headquarters Building, the Supply Stores, Officers' Mess, Sergeants' Mess, Camp Hospital, the Military Police building, weapons stores, and so forth?" If I did that, my readers would fall asleep within the first five pages.

Camp Vernon is a cadet camp. Certainly, there are lots of stories about officers and non-commissioned officers, however, the heartbeat of The Vernon Army Cadet Camp is its cadets. They are young and in many cases away from home for the first time. It's better that I write about their life in the barracks, and their trials and tribulations. Without them, there wouldn't be a Headquarters Building, Supply Stores, etc., and I feel many people have forgotten that fact.

Also, once again, I would remind parents that the image of their youngsters inside the house, is not necessarily the same outside. It's close, mind you, however, try to remember when you were teenagers. Did your parents always know what you were up to?

If there were no sinners, there would be no saints. Thank God for youth and innocence. Without young people, our world would be such a forlorn place.

***

In my last novel, **'Stand By Your Beds!'** seven teenage boys from British Columbia attend the Vernon Army Cadet Camp for six weeks during the summer of 1953. In order to survive the rigors of camp, they form a mutual protective society between themselves, called the Musketeers. This agency works well, and when they leave camp to return home, the improvement in their bearing, deportment and knowledge is most evident due to the training and guidance they received from regular force personnel.

'Form Three Ranks On The Road!' is the continuation of that story in 1956, but not the end of the tale. You see, this tale can never end because the seven really personify all army cadets - past, part of the present, and I hope, the future.

There have been a million or so similar experiences by other boys, and now girls, participating in this once-great movement and attending camps across Canada.

It doesn't seem to matter what year we're talking about, when a young person is away from home in a strange environment, time and space are unimportant. What is important is the genuineness of the exercise, the comradeship, the challenge, self-improvement and the memories.

When I was a youngster, I can always recall people advising me, "If you're going to do something right, do it right the first time." That advice stuck in my mind when I joined army cadets, I was prepared to do it right, and I had help. The authenticity of experience I received came from doing the real thing. After all, I was an army cadet, not a quasi-army cadet. My instructors were real instructors in the army. My clothes didn't make me look like a garage mechanic. Although I was only fourteen, I could drive tanks and other vehicles. I could operate the then-present day radio sets in my sleep. I learned safe firearms training from regular force and militia personnel. I could even earn trades pay. If I joined the militia, or regular force, my qualifications moved with me and counted for something. The authenticity of experience I received was important to the politicians, the military brass and little old me.

Now, let's look at the authenticity of experience of present day **army** cadets. The politicians don't give a damn about Canada's military, particularly cadets. The regular force and militia have all but nearly abandoned cadets. Sure, I hear that these organizations bend over backwards, but that's just pure bunk. The people who state that these establishments assist, have been brainwashed. Had they been around in the *real* days, they would understand what the word assistance means.

The cadet uniform looks like a reject from the prison system, safe firearms training is a thing of the past, and as for regular force instructors and equipment, they just do not exist. **Military authenticity has gone, and if the present situation persists, it will not be too long before army cadets are a thing of the past in Canada.** What will remain is a skeleton of what was probably the finest youth training program in the world.

I really feel proud of present-day *cadets*, but I feel sorry for them as well. Although they don't have to put up with the type of jeers and remarks thrown at cadets during the hippie era, current cadets are still on the receiving end of ignorant civilian peer observation. Still, they are keen enough to get involved. They wear the *uniform* nobly to show their equals that they're seeking self-improvement through training, yet everyone lets them down by presenting them with a contrived effort of sub-standard knowledge in a still-deteriorating scheme.

You see, the army cadet organization is the whipping boy of the regular force and the militia, as the militia is also the whipping boy of the regular force. As for the regular force, the *people* who administer it, just do not have the brains to understand that every politician from the Prime Minister down, wipes their feet on it's image. Oh sorry, let me rephrase that. The Chief of Defence Staff understands that the force is used as a doormat, but since his position is *political*, he doesn't have to get involved to protect what image is left.

Recently, I attended a meeting of the British Columbia branch of the Army Cadet League of Canada. The meeting was held at the Grouse Mountain Cadet Camp, a wonderful facility that is supported by the league.

During that meeting, I saw charts galore on the diminishing numbers of army cadets in Canada, but more so in British Columbia. I also heard the military-types explain what they're attempting to do to stem the tide of disappearing youngsters.

Their enthusiasm was most sincere, and I admire them for it, but unfortunately, I've heard the same thing for the past twenty years. The words are the same, the action is the same, nothing is happening.

Reading between the lines, I understand their hands are tied. Tied so tightly by the bungling bureaucratic group of military civil servants in Ottawa, the system is nearly beyond repair.

Now, let me say this again to all you voters out there. Canada is spending billions and billions of dollars trying to stop youth crime. If a small portion of these funds were spent on revamping the cadet system in Canada, the result would be worth a hundred times as much as what is being squandered via the other route.

We really have a problem in this country. A near-perfect youth scheme has been almost decimated by bleeding heart politicians and the military brass. Unless something is done about it, and done soon, it will take a miracle to repair the damage, if it's not too late already. Even the skeleton will eventually turn into dust.

Please get involved. Please say to the politicians and uniformed civil servants who only worry about shuffling paper, looking after their pensions and collecting fat salaries, that safe firearms training, trades training and good strong military-style training with discipline, is actually good for youngsters.

To the military brass for whom I hold nothing but pity, come down from your ivory tower, roll up your sleeves, get some sweat on your brows and get the army, navy and air force cadet programs on the right path once again. When it comes to matters of the military, open up your mouths and speak up to the politicians. **LET YOURSELVES BE HEARD! THAT'S WHAT YOU'RE PAID TO DO, DO IT!** Please stop waiting until one year prior to retirement before you voice what small concerns you have. If enough small concerns are heard, then perhaps someone will put them all together and make the *problem* a big concern.

How the Chief of the Defence Staff and his hordes of 'yes men' can look themselves in the mirror, I don't know. They all understand what is wrong, but they wait until retirement, or one year prior, to *articulate* their apprehension. Any fool knows it is too late by then, because the new 'yes' man/woman is in place, and the cycle continues.

Their excuse for not speaking up, is usually, "As loyal *soldier-persons, sailor-persons*, and *air-persons*, our job is to take orders, and that's exactly what we intend to do. As parliament dictates, we will protect the image of our bisexual, tri-sexual, homosexual and heterosexual forces. We are here but to serve."

ISN'T THAT JUST BLODY WONDERFUL. THE LESSONS OF THE BATTLE AT GALLIPOLI STILL HAVEN'T BEEN LEARNED.

***

'Stand By Your Beds!' took place in 1953. **'Form Three Ranks On The Road!'** takes place in 1956. In 1954, cadets Douglas Brice and Wayne Banks attended the Signals course at Camp Vernon along with their friends, Rothstein, Jackson, East, Danyluk and 'Bergie.' The year 1954 will be covered in my upcoming novel, **'Next Stop, Vernon!'** In 1955, the group of them attended the Driver Mechanics course at the same camp. The antics these lads get themselves into that year, will be set out in, **'Rubber Gears Next Year!'** which is soon to be written.

In 1956 Bergie joined the regular force and a cadet by the name of Cunningham became the new seventh Musketeer. The seven of them decided they would attend Vernon for the last time and take the new-fashioned Senior Leader Instructor's Course. This course was designed specifically to train cadets in the art of *all* instruction, including drill and it conveyed to senior cadets the importance of developing good leadership habits, particularly, traits and types of leaders, leadership techniques, appropriate leadership styles, problem solving and decision making, team building, and the management of time. (I would like to point out here that like everything else, someone later interfered with this course. The present Cadet Leader Instructor's Course is a mere shadow of the original summer program. IBT (Instructor's Basic Training) which the seven took in 1953, was replaced with a course known as Senior Leader, which subsequently was changed to Cadet Leader).

You know the reasons for the changes, don't you? The changes were made to simply make changes. If the wheel ain't broken, fix it anyway.

Cadets who were accepted to attend the Senior Leaders Instructor's Course didn't realize that the course content was heavy...very heavy. They spent the first three weeks training and during the last three weeks, the course's top students were attached as acting *Corporals* to the Senior Leader companies. At the company training level, this move included trading places with the regular force Corporals associated with each platoon.

Although there weren't too many average students attending this course, following the intense three week program, those who didn't set high priorities for themselves were attached to Signals, Driver Mechanics, the camp hospital, headquarters building, mess halls, canteens, supply stores, Provost and most other agencies and cadres the camp housed.

The cadets who weren't posted to training companies, became, as Danyluk stated, "Hut-sluts! Those pongoes are just glorified hut-sluts. They could be doing what we're doing, but they didn't answer the sound of the bell. Ain't that right, *Cunnilingus?*"

Moose's friend, Gordie (the gambler) Cunningham, also referred to as *Cunnilingus, Cuntingham,* or *Cunner,* had nearly topped the course but now he was wondering why he'd worked so hard. Someone had told him that the cadets in Driver Mechanics and Signals had more money than the 'foot-plodding soldiers' of Senior Leaders.

"Jesus, Moose, use your head. That's where I should be. With a deck of cards I could clean them all out."

"Yeah, and they serve turkey in their mess halls on Sundays," said East, another Musketeer.

***

Now, let's go back to the City of Vernon in the year 1956. The town and the people who live there are wonderful. The weather is great, and the air has a marvelous blossom scent to it. The lakes are blue, and church bells still compete with the roosters by echoing their calls in the nearby hills every Sunday morning.

The Year, 1956, is exciting. On Broadway, shows such as, *Auntie Mame and My Fair Lady* are making it big. Long lines of people are at the movies watching, *Around the World in 80 Days, Friendly Persuasion, Giant, The King and I, and The Ten Commandments.* In 1956 the book, *Peyton Place,* became a giant seller, along with, *The Search for Bridey Murphy.* Television is really catching on with, *Kraft Theatre,*

$64,000.00 Question, Father Knows Best, Amos 'n' Andy, and Talent Scouts.

At the camp, nothing much has changed since 1953, except a new parade square has been constructed and a small drive-in has been built across the highway from the Provost shack. It doesn't have any seats or tables inside, but outside there are a few picnic tables close to the ordering window. It sells burgers and fries by the ton, especially to Cadet Jack East. Well, not just Jack, because Danyluk is usually there trying to catch one of Hop Sing's girls buying a burger. Although he *questions* many, probably hundreds, he never finds one who works at Hop Sing's Laundry.

This didn't bother him because Danyluk works on the percentage system. For every nine girls that say, "GET LOST YOU CREEP!" OR "TAKE OFF YOU ANIMAL!" one eventually succumbs to his *wondrous* charms. As usual, Danyluk has more *women* than he can handle.

Did I say Danyluk's wondrous charms? I must be getting old.

At the end of the first three weeks of training, we must consider that although the famous seven, plus a new friend, *know all the ropes* - when fourteen hundred cadets get together, there are new knots devised daily, as Brice, Banks, Danyluk, Rothstein, East, Jackson, Cunningham and Simon discover.

Although they are used to dishing out the ropes, they are about to get wound up in them.

The thought of hearing Regular Force Sergeants bellowing **"FORM THREE RANKS ON THE ROAD!"** at 0530 hours in the morning and continuing throughout the day, still makes me shudder.

These days I smile when I think of it. But I sure as hell didn't then. The only people who had anything resembling smiles on their faces, was a cadet named Danyluk and a certain Sergeant Simpson.

In Simpson's case, it was probably a gas pain because he'd spent too much time in the Sergeants' Mess the night before. As for Danyluk, he grimaced as he hopped back and forth because he didn't have time to take his morning pee.

Ah, the memories.   Cordell Cross - 7 July, 1993.

EDICATION

"FORM THREE RANKS ON THE ROAD!' is dedicated to all Royal Canadian Army cadets, Sea cadets and Air cadets - past, present and *future.*

It is also dedicated to the thousands of officers, senior and junior non- commissioned officers, privates, **parents, relatives and friends,** who were there, are there and will be there, to guide these boys and girls through this *nonconformist* responsible-youth movement called, **cadets**.

***

There is a man in Vancouver who is a living legend in the entertainment industry - particularly radio. I want to take this opportunity to thank Red Robinson for the clean-cut superior entertainment and fun he has always provided us with, starting in the 50s and continuing today.

It would be hard to imagine what the 50s and 60s would have been like if Red Robinson hadn't been a part of it, because to us teenagers, he personified the enchantment of that wonderful era.

As Red puts it. *"All of a sudden, those of us who were teenagers began to have a voice. As we became aware of the changes in our bodies and of the opposite sex, we also discovered a new kind of music and developed a new set of values. Through rock 'n' roll, we saw ourselves the way we were - not as others saw us. It was a time of change, an exciting time to be alive and growing up. Almost every day, a new record was released, a new fad in clothes emerged, and there was something new and exciting for teenagers in North America to talk about."*

Red, thanks very much for being a part of it all. I've just finished reading your book **'ROCKBOUND'** and I couldn't put it down. I'm going to read it again, and again. You've written it from the heart and thank God you kept those hundreds of pictures. What a book. Undoubtedly it is the Bible of the rock 'n' roll period.

To my readers, I want to say this. If you're interested in the 50s and 60s - the music, the entertainment, the kids and the times, do yourself a big favour. Send $19.95 plus GST and $3.00 postage, to, Red Robinson Management Ltd., 401 - 68 Water Street, Vancouver, B.C. V6B 1A4, and ask to receive a copy of **'ROCK-BOUND.'** You'll thank me for recommending it; as I can't thank Red enough for writing it. (This isn't a paid commercial. On second thought, Red, you can buy me a beer.)

Seriously, buy the book. It's something you'll cherish and want to read and look at, always. Also, it's a limited edition.

***

Writing **'FORM THREE RANKS ON THE ROAD!'** was fun and I want to thank all those thousands of people who informed me of their experiences in cadets and at camp during the *real* years. One Vancouver dentist even recognized his picture. He served as a cadet in the Loyal Edmonton Regiment.

Speaking of photographs. In **'Stand By Your Beds!'** the sharp-looking cadet leading the Irish Fusiliers' band, is non other than Brigadier General Daryl M. Dean. Congratulations Daryl and all other Canadian officers and non-commissioned officers who got their start as cadets at the Vernon Army Cadet Camp. Without prejudice, I must ask: **Have any of you taken the time to review the present plight of army cadet training?** No? Give it a try and smell the roses!

I also thank a fine professional soldier, Colonel J.P. (Jake) Beer. After an outstanding regular force career in the Canadian Forces, Colonel Beer commanded VACC during the '70s. Under his direction the word 'army' in army cadet training was well protected and maintained. During the late '70s and early '80s, Colonel Beer also commanded Canada's army cadet Bisley contingents. To this day, many world-class shooters are still wondering how they got a shellacking from a group of fifteen and sixteen year olds. Congratulations, Colonel.

Recently a member of The Army Cadet League of Canada (British Columbia Branch) asked me what I would do to straighten out the mess of the army cadet program in Canada.

I told him, if I had a hand in army cadet training, I would call up Colonel Beer and ask him to go to Ottawa. There, with a hand-chosen, highly-trained team of **regular force officers**, he would assess the specifications that led to the ill-drawn Course Training Standards for the army cadet level-training programs, as well as the Course Training Standards for army cadet summer camp programs and CIL (Cadet Instructor's List) officer training.

This would certainly be nice, but I'm not holding my breath. If I did that, I'd end up like the rest of them in Ottawa, dead from the ass up. I discuss this matter at length in the back of this book.

My thanks go out to a fine friend, E. Wane Banks; Brigadier, The Honourable H. P. Bell-Irving, OC, DSO, OBE, ED, CD; General Doug Anderson; Colonel Les Deane; Colonel Robert Lyon; Colonel & Mrs. Michael Warrington; Major Gordon Cunningham; Ray Glover; Major Roy Rigby-Jones; Viola and Eric Clark; William T. Ratcliffe; and especially Ken Gourley for their gracious support. Ken, thanks for your input. You're a genius.

Needless to say, these people do not necessarily agree with me insofar as my thoughts on *those* in Ottawa are concerned. I have no idea how they conceive the scene in Ottawa.

Also, I want to thank a fine gentleman for just being a great part of the British Columbia scene. Murray Goldman, you supplied the 'best threads' that everyone wanted. Not only did you prevented us from being naked, your in-store and on-the-air personality, kept Vancouver laughing. You deserve the country's highest medal (The Order Of Canada) for the way you have always unselfishly offered your time and money for community, provincial and national *projects*.

As far as fine haberdashery is concerned, undoubtedly, you've more than kept up with the times because I still join the happy throngs heading to your stores. Thanks Murray.

***

At a recent cocktail party, I thought I recognized one of the above voices. It was Colonel Deane. He was protecting half a crumpet and a cup of tea.

"Cross, get over here!"

Shaking in my boots, I marched over and snapped to attention. "Er, you wish to see me, Colonel Deane, sir."

"I most certainly do, Mr. Cross. I read your book, **'Stand By Your Beds!'**"

Now I knew I was in trouble. I cleared my throat. "Ahem, er, that was very good of you, sir. I hope you enjoyed it?"

"That's beside the point, Cross. How long have you been affiliated with the *system?*"

"I was too nervous to answer. This chap was my platoon officer in Vernon in 1955. It was difficult to get away with anything when he was around, but we did. "Er, bah, er...abah, er..."

He answered for me. "Not long enough, Cross. How do you spell the name of the Irish Fusiliers headdress?"

I could relax now, because I knew the answer. Sticking out my chest, I replied, C.A.R.A.B.I.N.E.E.R., sir."

"Wrong, Mr. Cross! For your information, it's spelled, C.A.U.B.E.E.N."

"But, sir, I thought it was a carabineer."

"You know what thought did, don't you, Cross? Don't answer that! The Irish Fusiliers wear *caubeens*, is that clear?"

"Yes, sir!"

"I CAN'T HEAR YOU, CROSS!"

"YES, SIR!"

After I was dismissed and crawled away, I heard him say to someone, "Good man, that Cross."

His associate replied, "But Colonel, he was in the British Columbia Regiment."

The Colonel chuckled. "I know. That's why he misspelled, *caubeen*. An officer from any other regiment would have known the difference."

***

To a certain Doctor Moose Danyluk who wrote me a ten page letter, informing me that since **'Stand By Your Beds!'** was published, his regular patients can't get through to him on his telephone. Apparently the lines are always tied up with women calling to ask if he's the Dr. Danyluk who was a cadet in Vernon.

I received similar letters from a Dr. Danyluk in Calgary, one in Lethbridge, one in Medicine Hat, one in Prince George, one in Winnipeg and finally one in Toronto. I never realized that the name, Danyluk, is so popular.

My apologies, Moose, but just look at all the new fans you have. I'm one of your biggest fans. Thanks just for being there.

Also, to all those other Doctor Danyluks - think of the many new patients you're going to acquire.

***

I tip my hat to the fine employees of the Vernon Daily News, the Vernon Museum, and the Vernon Library. Thank you very much for your wonderful cooperation in providing photographs and other valuable information.

Most of these photographs were taken by Major Cam LeBlond, and Doug Kermode. Cheers gentlemen on a job well done.

It wouldn't be fair if I left out thanking the most important people of all. The delightful and admirable, past and present townsfolk of Vernon.

Thank you for being with *us* from the first day. These days Ottawa doesn't make too many sound decisions, but it sure did when it chose Vernon, to house 'The Camp.' I'm sorry you don't see cadets in town very often. In the 50s, 60s and 70s, hundreds of cadets visited town seven days a week. Perhaps someday, the present situation will reverse itself.

***

The use of reference material is most essential when writing a novel like this. I had the opportunity of using, 'ROCKBOUND' by Red Robinson. 'BITS & PIECES (VOL. 1/NO. 6C).' 'The Art Of Leadership' by Professor Lin Bothwell, and 'A Study Of Organizational Leadership' Edited by the Associates, Office of Military Leadership, Unites States Military Academy. My thanks to the authors.

***

Oh, I almost forgot. The other day, I was having a drink with Gordie Cunningham at Chardonnays Restaurant on the corner of Howe and Hastings Streets in Vancouver. Chardonnays is the local watering hole of writers, stockbrokers, entrepreneurs, multi-millionaires and President Bill Clinton when he visits town. Although President Bill doesn't visit often, Gordie sits in for him and keeps the seat warm.

Gordie left Clinton's special chair for a minute, walked over next to me and smiled. At least I think it was a smile. It could have been a gas pain. "Hey *Corky*, wanna toss for a drink?"

I can't beat Gordie at tossing coins, so I had to think quickly. "Er, no thanks, Gord, I'm broke. What's on your mind?"

When it comes to money, 'the gambler' doesn't waste any time getting to the point. "When's your new novel, **'Form Three Ranks On The Road!'** coming out?"

Cunningham took a silver dollar out of my ear as he asked.

"Very soon. It's just being edited. Right now, I'm working on the Introduction and the Dedication."

"Oh yeah? Do you think your readers would like to buy my sure fire method of calculating odds in Black Jack, etc.?" As he asked, a newcomer came into the bar and *eyed* Clinton's *stool*. "DON'T EVEN THINK OF SITTING THERE!" yelled Gordie.

"Sure, if the price is right."

"The price is always right when the *gambler* sets it. Tell them to send six bucks to, Gordie Cunningham's Sure Fire Method, care of your address. You give me the dough and I'll send 'em the system."

What could I say; he had hold of my wrist. "Er, all right. Six bucks, eh? But, er, you don't need the money?"

Cunningham relaxed his grip, lit up a smoke and burped. "I know, but it'll be pocket change when I attend the Vernon Army Cadet Camp Reunion in July 1994. You're organizing the show on behalf of Major Roy Rigby-Jones and the British Columbia Army Cadet League, aren't you?"

How the hell did he know that? "Yes, there's information on the last page of the book. It runs from July 22nd to the 24th, 1994."

He got up and casually strolled over to 'Clinton's stool.' "Ya wanna sit in this distinguished chair for a minute? I'll give ya permission."

"Er, no thanks, Gordie, I've gotta go."

So that's how our conversation went. My address is PO Box 88549, 101 - 13753 72nd Avenue, Surrey, B.C. V3W 0X1. For six bucks, he'll send you the system. You can thank him at the Vernon Army Cadet Camp's 1994 Reunion, but don't start gambling with him. He never loses, as thousands of you have learned.

***

To Hop Sing, we always knew Hop Sing's was a fine laundry and nothing else.

***

Last but not least. Thanks Val Wilson and her firm, **Val Wilson Ink**, for editing, 'Form Three Ranks On The Road!'

In addition to being a perfectionist, Val is such a wonderful understanding person. I still can't get over our last meeting, when she spoke ever so gently.

"MY GOD, CORDELL, WHEN YOU WENT TO SCHOOL, DID YOU TAKE ENGLISH?"

Picking up my manuscript from the floor, I replied, "Never, I always drank Red Rose."

Val, thanks for putting all of those other manuscripts aside and editing mine first. Your expertise could be used in Ottawa.

God's Country
(a repeat from 'Stand By Your Beds!')

If a person ever wanted to visit what is referred to as God's Country, all one would have to do is travel to the City of Vernon in British Columbia, Canada.

Nestled against lakes, mountains and rolling hills, Vernon, for some reason, has kept its early village charm probably more than the other two beautiful cities in the Okanagan Valley, Penticton and Kelowna.

Named after the Vernon brothers, Forbes-George and Charles Vernon, in approximately 1887, this steadily growing city can boast about having two of the most spectacular lakes in the world right on its doorstep, Kalamalka Lake and Okanagan Lake.

In bygone days, the city was the end of the line for steamers that moved both freight and passengers on the lakes that caress the shores of what the Duke of Connaught referred to as, "The most magnificent setting I have ever seen. Absolutely stunning!"

Kalamalka Lake is the smaller of the two. At the Lookout above the lake, there used to be a sign which read, Kalamalka Means Lake of Many Colors. It indeed may mean that, but officially it was named after Kalamalka, an elder in the Okanagan Indian Band.

The population of Vernon in 1956 was approximately nine-thousand friendly people. Then, like today, they were closely tied to 'The Camp' as they referred to it.

'The Camp' has been a part of Vernon for eighty-one years, starting when a Drill Hall was built in 1912. That Drill Hall marked the beginning of the 'Mission Hill' Camp, which Ottawa officially established in 1915. Canadian soldiers trained there in two World Wars.

Not many years after the Second World War, it was designated as a summer training camp for Royal Canadian Army Cadets.

These days, it is used during the summer by cadets and at various times throughout the year, by personnel from the militia and the regular force.

EVERYMAN

MEN ARE FOUR

He who Knows
And Knows He Knows
He is wise
Follow Him

He who Knows
And Knows Not He Knows
He is asleep
Wake Him

He who Knows Not
And Knows Not He Knows Not
He is a fool
Shun Him

He who Knows Not
And Knows He Knows Not
He is a child
Teach Him

                                                 Anon

CHAPTER I

"DOUG, THERE'S GOTTA BE A SAFER WAY OF MAKING POCKET MONEY THAN SETTIN' PINS! IF THE LAST PIN THAT JUMPED WAS A RAZOR, I'D HAVE A TWO-INCH BALD SPOT JUST OVER THE MIDDLE OF MY FOREHEAD," Wayne Banks screamed to his buddy, Douglas Brice who was setting pins beside him at the Commodore Lanes on Granville Street in downtown Vancouver. The hot, stuffy bowling alley was packed with league bowlers who offered brief, dispassionate sympathy for the 'hidden' people behind the pins at the other end.

Douglas could spare little time to look at his friend. Each was setting two lanes and on league night, the bowling balls came hot and heavy.

"WHY DON'T YOU TAKE OFF THE STEEL JOCKSTRAP YOU DESIGNED AND PLACE IT OVER YOUR HEAD?"

A ball with the velocity of a bullet smashed and split the pins in one of Wayne's lanes. The 'setter' managed to bring his feet up just in time, otherwise he might have needed the invention to which his chum referred. Without smiling Wayne rushed into the lane-well closest to Douglas and yelled, "YOU PONGO! YOU KNOW THAT CONTRAPTION DIDN'T WORK. I'M STILL PUTTING OINTMENT ON MY NUTS FROM WEARING IT TO SCHOOL THAT DAY!" Banks could only glance at Douglas for a fraction of a second. No sooner had he set his pins, another 'jet' ball was on its way.

Douglas was now sitting up on the lane-divider, his arms around his knees which were drawn up into his chest. His bowlers were finished and he didn't have to help his buddy because this was the last frame. "ARE YOU TAKING IT TO VERNON WITH YOU?"

Wayne gave the 'thumbs up' to his bowlers who were figuring out their last scores. Breathlessly he jumped up and sat next to Douglas.

The noise had subsided considerably. "Am I taking *what* to Vernon?" asked Wayne.

Brice was still trying to catch his breath as well. "The steel jockstrap."

Wayne bit into half a sandwich he hadn't had time to eat earlier. Quickly swallowing, he replied, "Yeah, Danyluk wants it but I don't know what for. It's too small for him. He'd need a jockstrap the size of a bowling ball."

They both snickered before Douglas asked. "Why did you wear that thing to school, anyway?"

Wayne slapped Douglas on the back as they walked up the centre isle towards the front counter and the cold refreshing water of the Men's washroom.

"Because of that last fight I had with Albert Snider. He kicked me in the nuts before I planted one on him, remember? Every time I see him, I know he's gonna try and nail me again."

With cupped hands full of icy water, they soaked their faces and hair. It didn't matter if half the liquid ended up on their shirts and pants' - five hours of sweat was washed away, and once again both teenagers felt renewed.

It took Douglas only about three seconds to comb his hair, but when Wayne held a tail-comb in his hand, the world stopped turning. Douglas grew impatient; five minutes of watching this 'Hollywood' episode in the mirror, was all he could handle.

"Jesus, Wayne, you looked like Presley four minutes ago. Even *his* hair isn't as perfect as yours."

The *King's clone* completed the final touch, put his comb back into his right rear pants pocket, and headed for the door. He glanced back once to check that every hair was in place. "Yeah, I know, and just think, tomorrow I gotta lose this mop before we head for Vernon."

At the front counter, two bottles of Kik Kola disappeared quickly as they waited for their money. Wayne held his cold empty bottle against his forehead. "I really needed that."

"That's seven dollars for you, and seven dollars for you," said the cashier, placing the money into two piles without looking up. It was quickly swept away and pocketed by the boys. They signed receipts for their pay and let the swinging doors close behind them.

Douglas stopped to tie a shoelace as they climbed the stairs to the road above. The fresh air was a relief and Granville Street on a Thursday night was vibrant and alive with traffic and pedestrians. Most of the many movie theatres had queues around the block, and the restaurants were full. The crowds made it tough to maneuver, and everyone was dodging each other as the two boys walked south.

"I've told you Wayne, you gotta stay away from Albert Snider. The guy's tough and he's twice our size. Also, he's eighteen."

Wayne turned to glimpse the legs of a passing girl. "Well, we'll be eighteen in a couple of months. That idiot's a bully. I'm sick and tired of him putting on the act in front of the dames." They had paused in front of a restaurant where the sounds of Elvis Presley's, *Don't Be Cruel*, blared from the juke-box.

"Besides, I beat him, didn't I?"

Douglas was now walking backwards looking at the same girl. "Yeah, you beat him all right, but one day he'll come out of nowhere and kick you in the nuts before you have a chance to protect yourself. He's dirty that way."

Heading west on Davie Street, Wayne looked up and rolled his eyes back. "Do I look worried? Listen, we leave for Vernon the day after tomorrow, I won't have to concern myself with him for another two months. By the way, have you got all your kit ready?"

Douglas nodded. "Yeah, I've got *my* kit ready. Don't forget there's a meeting for all NCOs (non-commissioned officers) in the Drill Hall tomorrow night. Colonel Mikulitch wants to make certain that we conduct ourselves properly on the train, and while we're in Vernon."

Wayne smiled. "Are Lyons and Foster going to Vernon?" He was referring to another couple of friends who had been going to the Vernon Army Cadet Camp with them for three years.

Douglas put his arm around Wayne's shoulders. "No, they're both bound for Wainwright with the regiment. You know, that's where *we* should be going. I think the regiment's a bit peeved with the fact that we aren't with them. Look at the money we're missing?"

"I agree, but you tell that to Debbie and Diane." Wayne was thinking of their girlfriends who lived in Vernon. The boys had been going around with them since their first year at cadet camp. "Anyway, what's Colonel Mikulitch concerned about? A train trip's a train trip. Jeez, that guy worries a lot."

Douglas chuckled. "Mikulitch might be right because Danyluk's going to Vernon and you know when Danyluk and Cunningham go anywhere, anything can happen."

He was referring to a recent weekend training exercise in the Nanaimo Military Camp on Vancouver Island, where another friend, Gordie Cunningham, had been invited to join the regimental sergeants and officers in a Saturday night poker game. The brass had heard of Cunningham's card-playing expertise, but didn't believe it. They thought they'd take a few dollars off *the kid*, just to teach him a lesson. Six hours and twenty-two hundred dollars later, they believed it, all right. Cunningham had left camp in the middle of the night, and was on the first morning ferry to Vancouver. When the banks opened on Monday morning, Gordie was at the head of the line. He cashed the cheques and bought a new car.

"You got that right," replied Wayne. "Every twenty minutes, that Goddamned Cunningham kept rushing into the shack, shaking me to wake me up, then he'd push a pile of bills and cheques under my pillow. I said to him, 'Cunnilingus, what the hell's going on?'"

"What did *he* say?"

"He said, 'I'm cleaning the bastards out...they deserve it. I promise I won't bug ya again until my cab arrives, then I'll take the dough. Go back to sleep.'"

Both boys laughed heartily as Wayne continued his story. The smile on his face was proud, like the Chinese cook in the Blackhawks comic books.

"Wow, did he ever nail them! I heard Mr. Patterson (the Regimental Sergeant-Major) shouting, 'WHERE'S THAT GODDAMNED CUNNINGHAM?! HE DIDN'T GIVE US A CHANCE TO GET OUR MONEY BACK! WHO THE HELL SAID WE COULD FLEECE HIM LIKE A LAMB?!'"

Wayne roared out laughing and slapped Douglas on the back. "Some lamb! The old boys will never forget that night. They hadn't heard of Gordie's motto: 'Never be afraid of getting in the pit with the piranhas and the snakes.'"

Douglas' smile lit up his face. "Yeah, and that was the morning they couldn't find Danyluk, either. He'd spent the night entertaining the nurses in the field next to the tuberculosis hospital. Probably charming a few of the female patients, too." (The large hospital of the Nanaimo Military Camp had ceased to be used by the military and had been converted into a TB hospital. Today, it is used by headquarters' staff and houses militia personnel on weekends and summer courses.)

Wayne shook his head. "He's a lucky creep, that Danyluk. Have you noticed when we're in the tanks, there's a hundred arms hanging out the windows of the hospital waving for his tank to come over. All you can hear is, 'OH MOOSEY...MOOSE, BRING YOUR TANK OVER HERE, YOU BIG SOLDIER-BOY!'"

"And he does," said Douglas. "The guy doesn't care about SOPs (Standard Operating Procedures) when there's women in the offing. When five tanks are heading down a road, it's really odd to see one pull away, rolling towards the hospital. Grass or no grass, he parks it right in front of their windows, stands up in his seat and screams, 'HERE I AM, LADIES! FORGET THE REST AND TRY THE BEST!' He even shuts off his radio. The remainder of us have to listen to the Troop Leader's cursing. 'WHERE'S TWO-ALPHA...WHERE IN HELL IS TWO-ALPHA? DANYLUK, WHERE THE DEVIL ARE YOU?'"

By the time Douglas and Wayne got within two blocks of their homes, both boys' stomachs were sore from laughing so hard. Whenever they needed a good laugh after setting pins, all they had to do was think of their friend Danyluk. Life wouldn't be the same without him. Danyluk was the biggest of the group and would crawl a mile on his knees over a trail of broken glass, if a girl was at the other end. She could be fat, thin, tall, short, washed, unwashed, single, married, attached, unattached, pimples, no pimples, her own teeth, dentures, gums, no gums, just bone. Actually, any girl that walked, and even then, she didn't really *have* to walk.

Not that all of the guys weren't exactly the same way, however, for them there were some limitations. In Danyluk's case, if a girl accepted him for what he was, he would definitely become her knight in shining *skin*.

Many cadets steered clear of Danyluk, saying, "He's not normal." "There he is, there's the guy who struts to the shower with his towel draped over his customary morning hard-on." "He's got two heads to think with, and his real brains are at the end of his wang!"

"So what's wrong with that?" another would ask.

"Nothing, except that fifteen minutes later when he leaves the shower with a soaking wet towel, it's still hung over the same erection."

Even with all of Danyluk's shortcomings, or in his case, *longcomings*, he was the greatest to Douglas, Wayne and their friends, East, Jackson, Cunningham, Rothstein, and Bergie. After all, Moose Danyluk was an integral part of their assemblage of Musketeers, a group formed in 1953 to ensure survival at Vernon. Musketeers are Musketeers. They went to bat for one another. That's why they were all going to Vernon. That, plus the fact they had been told by their girlfriends they had *better* attend. But this would be their last year at the Vernon Army Cadet Camp, and as Danyluk and Cunningham had both stated on the last parade night before summer break, "We'd better make the most of it."

"That's right, Moose," said Cunningham. "You take the dames, and I'll take the money."

Danyluk rubbed his hands together. "Hey, Cunner, my dames have got moolah, too."

When Cunningham heard that statement, the expression on his face changed. Danyluk seemed to have the best of both worlds and it would be impossible for him to imitate Danyluk's lady's man performance, or duplicate his *novel* anatomy. No one except Danyluk had those qualifications. It was rumored that when Danyluk wore his uniform, he tucked his penis into his puttees!

"You mean your dames moo?" That was the only rebuttal Cunningham could think of.

"Many an old cow has still got soft udders and a ride left," mused Danyluk, getting the last word.

When they split up to go home, Wayne and Douglas waved to each other. "I'LL PHONE YOU TOMORROW AND SEE YOU AT THE ARMORIES...ALRIGHT?"

Wayne turned around. "O.K., DOUG. IS THE MEETING IN CIVVIES?"

Douglas cupped his hands to his mouth. "YEAH, CIVVIES...SEE YA!"

The early July night air was warm as Douglas strolled the two blocks home. As he walked, he hummed, *Don't Be Cruel*, and thought how great it was to have a buddy like Wayne. They had been inseparable friends for years, now this would be their last year in Vernon. Wayne was talking about getting a job as a waiter or bus-boy with CPR ferries. Douglas had decided to attend the University of British Columbia and tried to talk Wayne into going with him. But, his friend was fed up with school and wanted to make a few bucks.

"Doug, don't keep buggin' me about school. I'll go back when I'm good and ready."

As he turned his key in the lock and opened the door, he heard his mother. "Is that you, Doug?"

"Yeah, it's me, Mom," he replied, walking up the stairs to his room. He heard his dog, Colonel, jump off his bed to meet him on the upstairs landing, tail wagging like a swift metronome.

"Was it busy at the bowling alley tonight?" asked his mother from inside her room.

With two paws on Douglas, Colonel was standing on his hind legs. "We made seven bucks each!"

"Seven dollars? You must be tired. Oh well, you can sleep in tomorrow. No more school, Doug. Are you going to take Colonel for a walk?"

Douglas nodded to the dog, who nodded back, tail swinging. "If I didn't, he'd probably kick me out of bed. I'll be back shortly, Mom."

"O.K., son. I've left you a snack on the kitchen table. Good night, Doug."

"Thanks, good night, Mom."

If the old Beatty Street Drill Hall in Vancouver could talk, it could tell stories to make the most indifferent people perk up their ears and listen, spellbound.

Completed at the turn of the century and now renowned as one of Vancouver's finest historical landmarks, the Drill Hall has always been the meeting place of young men and women eager to defend the principles of freedom with their lives. It has housed patriots going off to four wars, and the thousands upon thousands of troops and cadets who trained under its roof all learned and understood the meaning of the regimental family and pride of country.

(Although quite unconventional, I bring to the reader's attention that during the hippie era, Pierre Trudeau turned these national heritage buildings into summer homes for traveling youth. At one point, Vancouver's longshoremen, God bless them, upon hearing certain *travellers* were urinating in the corners and on the walls of the building, and hanging up pictures of Chairman Mao, threatened to march and clear them out. I mentioned in the Foreword, Trudeau did his best to eliminate the military traditions of our great country.)

As Wayne and Douglas got off the bus and walked up Beatty Street towards the Drill Hall, Danyluk, East and Cunningham were coming out of the bus depot across from the armouries. The boys, all about the same age, had been chewing the fat in the Honey Dew Café. Danyluk carried his portable radio and as usual, it was turned up. Dean Martin was singing, *Memories Are Made Of This.*

Just before the group teamed up at the corner, East and Cunningham were deep into a conversation that had started in the bus depot.

"Oh, yeah? Listen Cunningham, I put my money on the counter. Danyluk saw me put my money on the counter. Moose, didn't you see me put my money on the counter?"

Danyluk had the radio to his ear, but he heard the question. "Nope!"

East was furious. "That's bullshit! I was the first up with my money. You guys say *your* money was there? I didn't see your money! Then you walk out and leave me with the bill. You creeps left nothin' on the counter!"

Cunningham smiled slyly. "That was our money you paid her with."

East stopped in his tracks and turned Cunningham's shoulders towards him. They were nose to nose. "BULLLLSHHHITT! O.K., O.K., THEN! HOW COME YOU ASKED THE WAITRESS IF SHE'D LIKE TO FLIP DOUBLE OR NOTHING FOR THE BILL? I'LL TELL YOU WHY, BECAUSE YOU HAD NO MONEY AND YOU KNEW YOU WERE GOING TO TAKE ME TO THE CLEANERS, THAT'S WHY!"

Danyluk herded the two across the street, towards Douglas and Wayne. Now Cunningham was getting loud.

"WHO THE HELL DROVE US HERE? I DID! WHO HAD TO BUY THE GAS TO GET US HERE? I DID!"

That comment really disturbed East. "WHAT? I GAVE DANYLUK TWO BUCKS TO GIVE TO YOU. IT WAS A BUCK FROM ME AND A BUCK FROM HIM. MOOSE, YOU STILL OWE ME A BUCK! JESUS, CUNNINGHAM, EVERY TIME I'M WITH YOU I LOSE MY SHIRT. IS THERE NO JUSTICE? HOW ABOUT NAILING THE IRISH, THE WESTIES, OR THE SEAFORTHS INSTEAD OF YOUR BROTHERS IN ARMS!"

The group was together now, and Wayne couldn't resist getting into the conversation. "He can't, it's against his religion."

East was back to normal, eating a chocolate bar and smiling. "Oh yeah? And what religion is that?"

Cunningham rubbed his right hand forefinger and thumb together. "I'm a Nevadian. We follow the Robin Hood principles of taking from the rich and giving to the poor."

"When was the last time you gave money to the poor, Cunningham?"

Cunningham walked slightly ahead of the rest, heading towards the giant Drill Hall doors. He cocked his head when he replied. "Jacky, my lad, it happened two minutes ago in the Honey Dew. I'm poor, ain't I?"

"Jesus Cunner, how much money do you want? Maybe you used to be poor, but since you met us, there's no need for you to appear on the *Sixty-Four-Thousand Dollar Question*. Just look at you. You wear nice duds, you drive a new car and your girlfriend always looks like she's bought out Woodward's Department Store. I've never been so broke since I met ya."

Smiling, Cunningham took out his tail-comb, and carefully pulled it through his hair. "Come off it, Jack, you're always exaggerating things." Then he flipped up the left cuff of his suede jacket. "How do you like my new watch? It's a Jean d'Eve."

East's eyes grew wider. "Where's my Timex...the one you won off me in that stuke game. The one when you even took my shoes?"

"What shoes? I gave then back to you, didn't I?"

"Yeah, only because there was a hole in one of them."

A serious look came over Danyluk's face. "You won my Timex, too, you creep!"

Cunningham turned and put a hand on a shoulder of each of the *gamblers*. "Guys, guys, let's not argue over such trivial matters. Moose, I won your radio off you as well, but you've still got it, haven't you?"

"Yeah, you handed it back, but I've got to shine your boots and do your kit for the first three weeks in Vernon."

"There you are then, Moose. How much fairer can I be?"

That statement got them all snickering as they prepared to enter the Drill Hall.

The old red-brick building resembled a castle. Three stories above the giant arched doorway, two mock circular ramparts with slits, could have hidden archers, ready to ward off foolish invaders. At ground level, two old cannons were separated by the length of the building, and a Ram tank sat to the right of the entrance.

The giant doors didn't have to be opened to gain entry. A smaller inset door allowed the boys to move inside into a large entrance-way before they stepped onto the parade square.

Although friends on the outside, attitudes changed the minute they entered the armouries. At least another twenty cadets were already inside, immaculately dressed and spotlessly clean. They came to attention when Cadet Regimental Sergeant-Major Brice and four WO2s (Warrant Officer Second Class) walked in.

The Drill Hall on Beatty Street is common to other armouries. A familiar military smell fills the nostrils of all who enter. The odor is probably a combination of gasoline, oil, grease, paint, gunpowder, cleaning supplies, and moth balls.

Two tanks stood inside along with some jeeps and other vehicles. One was a Sherman, the other a small light recce (reconnaissance) tank.

Some cadets were fooling around inside the tanks, but came out quickly when the five senior cadets appeared.

Brice stood to attention for a fraction of a second. All smiles and thoughts about the previous conversation had disappeared. "Thank you," he said, responding to their coming to attention. "Is the Commanding Officer here?"

A young Sergeant remained at attention. "Yes, sir! He has asked that we join him in the Cadet Orderly Room when everyone's here."

Douglas took a small roll-call book out of the back pocket of his jeans. "Thank you, Sergeant Alexander. I'm not going to fall everyone in, just answer your name when it's called. Sergeant-Major Banks!"

Banks snapped to attention. "Sir!"

"Sergeant-Major East!"

Jack East snapped to attention. "Sir!"

The roll-call took about three minutes to complete. Then Douglas said, "All right, gentlemen, follow me into the Orderly Room and keep the noise down."

Cunningham said, "I've got to get to a phone and call my bookie. There's a horse in the sixth that I really like."

"What's the nag's name?" Wayne asked.

"Hoof Hearted," Gordie replied, walking toward the orderly room door.

Wayne couldn't believe the name. "Who farted?"

"Don't look at me," said a grinning Danyluk. He hadn't heard Cunningham's answer. "If anyone did, it was East, the beast."

That remark further upset an already angry East. "UP YOUR NOSE, MOOSE! THE NEXT TIME YOU WANT ME TO CLEAR OUT THE SHOWER ROOM, YOU FART, BECAUSE I WONT!"

Gordie set Wayne straight. "Not who farted, Hoof Hearted!"

Douglas got everyone back on track. "Gordie, you can phone your bookie after the meeting. Also, there's only about eight chairs in there so most of you will have to remain standing."

Colonel Mikulitch was wearing a business suit and was sitting at his desk writing when the cadets started peeling into the office. He was a man of about fifty years of age who had actually been a Colonel during the Second World War. Although he was paid at the rank of Captain, the Commanding Officer of the British Columbia Regiment (DCO) and cadet authorities allowed him to wear his original rank when he wore his uniform.

The room was fairly large with an old fireplace opposite the entrance door, and an array of desks sporadically spaced throughout. Pictures of Queen Elizabeth and the Prince Consort graced the wall above the fireplace.

Only senior cadets and officers were allowed to enter this room at will. All others had to be invited in. It was the nerve-center of the 2290 British Columbia Regiment Cadet Corps (Duke of Connaught's Own) a cadet corps of over two-hundred-and-fifty cadets. It was also the first room Douglas Brice had entered when he joined. The measuring tape was still on the wall. Cadets had to be five-foot-two-inches to join. His friend, David Flater, had given him four pieces of cardboard to stick in the heels of his shoes, so he would meet the minimum height requirements.

The Colonel smiled and stood up. "Ah, Mr. Brice, and Sergeant-Majors. I see everyone is here. Good! Just relax. I have issued some instructions which I want followed when you are at the train station, on the train, and in Vernon." He passed them to Cunningham who handed a set to each of the cadets.

"Now, most of this is self-explanatory. There have been complaints about the way certain cadet corps conduct themselves while on the trai..."

The Colonel didn't complete his statement. He suddenly paused, looking up and around the room with a puzzled look on his face.

"Is it my imagination, or am I really hearing Kay Starr singing, *Rock And Roll Waltz?*" He was now staring at Danyluk. For that matter, so was everyone else.

Danyluk's face turned a bright shade of pink as he glanced at Douglas. The radio was in Moose's right hand and although he had turned it off, for some reason it had turned itself back on and Kay Starr's powerful voice filled the office.

Brice glared at Danyluk. "Sergeant-Major Danyluk, would you, er...turn it off, please?"

Danyluk's face expressed his embarrassment. "Er, sorry, sir." He turned it on and off again and gave it a smack. "Ssssorry, sir."

The Colonel smiled and continued. "Now where was I? Oh, yes...there have been complaints about the way certain cadet corps are conducting themselves while they are on the train...and I..."

"ONE, TWO, THREE O'CLOCK, FOUR O'CLOCK, ROCK! FIVE, SIX, SEVEN O'CLOCK, EIGHT O'CLOCK ROCK! NINE, TEN, ELEVEN O'CLOCK, TWELVE O'CLOCK ROCK! WE'RE GOING TO ROCK, AROUND THE CLOCK TONIGHT..."

In addition to nearly having a heart attack and falling off his chair, Danyluk's hands were shaking just as much as he was shaking the radio, trying to turn the infernal thing off. Everyone in the room had burst into laughter, the Colonel included.

"SON OF A BITCH! Oh, sorry, sir. I...er...*loaned* it to Sergeant-Major Cunningham, and it hasn't been *quite* the same since."

Tears streamed down Cunningham's cheeks, when Brice gently took Danyluk by the arm and led him out the door as the sounds of Bill Haley and the Comets echoed through the armouries.

"HI, I'M RED ROBINSON AND YOU'RE LISTENING TO..." the

announcer's voice suddenly stopped.

For the next hour, Danyluk's face felt like fire as he listened to Colonel Mikulitch and RSM Brice discuss the deportment of BCR cadets while they were away. Although the radio had been placed outside the door, two more times the radio started by itself and the meeting's participants had to listen to Moose's cussing as he excused himself to try to turn off Mitch Miller and his orchestra performing, *The Yellow Rose of Texas.*

Following their talk, Colonel Mikulitch shook each cadet's hand and wished him the best of luck.

Before they left the armouries, Douglas reiterated the importance of proper military etiquette while traveling. He also made certain the Cadet Sergeants present had the telephone numbers of the cadets attending the summer training session at Vernon. The Sergeants would telephone their list to pass along important information.

Needless to say, the comments made at the Honey Dew Café following the meeting, were of an entirely different nature. Danyluk's nerves were still on edge.

"Cunningham, you pongo, you did that on purpose. You knew bloody well that the radio would go off during the meeting. I felt like a real asshole in there."

Gordie wasn't sympathetic. "Moose, Moose, calm down, just calm down. I forgot to tell you that I dropped the radio by accident. It wasn't even working when I gave it back to you."

"YOU CREEP! YOU DIDN'T TELL ME THAT! YOU MADE ME PROMISE TO DO YOUR KIT FOR THE FIRST THREE WEEKS IN VERNON! WELL, YOU KNOW WHAT YOU CAN DO CUNNER...OLD MOOSE IS GOING TO LOOK AFTER HIMSELF...THAT'S IT!"

"No, no, Moose, a deal is a deal." Then Cunningham managed to quickly change the subject by pointing out to Danyluk that a girl sitting on the counter across from him was giving him the eye.

"That broad is hot for you, Moose. Look at the way she licks her lips after she takes a bite of her burger."

Instantly, Danyluk forgot about the radio, got up with his drink in hand, and moved to the seat next to the young lady.

Placing his mouth next to her ear, he whispered, "You can't take your eyes off me, can you, sweetheart? Is your body moaning and groaning to entwine itself with my muscular frame and highly stimulated solidified groin?"

The girl didn't quite know what hit her as she finished chewing her mouthful of burger and backed her head away from his nose. Her initial expression of fright turned into a smile. "BUG OFF, YOU NUT!"

Moose really looked hurt. But not for long, because Colonel Mikulitch walked in. When he saw the officer, Danyluk nodded, smiled and walked back to his seat, sipping his Honey Dew.

"Ah, Sergeant-Major Danyluk, I see you've met my daughter, Susan?"

After Moose sprayed a mouthful of Honey Dew all over the counter, a few slaps on his back helped him recover from his sudden fit of coughing.

"Er, your *daughter*, sir?"

Susan smiled. "Yes, dad, we've just met. He was explaining to me how he was in some sort of wrestling match and had hurt his groin."

Only two people weren't laughing. Danyluk and the Colonel. Moose had cowed into his 'humbler than thou pose,' and the Colonel had an inquiring look on his face. But not for long. He had heard the stories of this one-man-stud-farm, so he paid his daughter's bill and hustled her out of the restaurant.

"Good night, boys...have a fine time."

All of them, except Danyluk, replied, "Thank you, sir."

When it was 'safe' to talk, Moose glared at Cunningham. "You rotten creep! You knew all along that was his daughter, didn't you?"

"Moose, I..."

"SON OF A BITCH! You had me goin' at the Colonel's daughter! If she tells him, I'm ruined...that's it...ruined, finished, Kaput. It'll be back to Lance Corporal in charge of blank files and right wheels."

Cunningham sat there smiling. "She won't tell him. But I might, unless you do my kit."

Danyluk nodded. "Oh, all right, but Jesus you're starting to remind of me of Bergie." Bergie was still a very good friend of theirs, but couldn't attend Vernon this year because he had joined the Regular Force. This would be the first time in four years that the boys wouldn't have their buddy Bergie with them.

When it was time to leave, East had to wait because he had ordered two burgers to take out. He'd eat them in Cunningham's car on the way home. As he waited at the counter, the others paid their bills and told him they would wait outside. Moments later, a heavily perspiring East rushed out in a panic, his head and eyes searching for someone in particular.

"Where is he? The rotten bastard!"

"Who?" Douglas asked.

"CUNNINGHAM!" Puffed East.

"He's gone to get his car. Why?"

"Why? He told the cashier to put his bill on mine! I had to pay his bill! DAMN IT, HE GOT ME AGAIN!"

CHAPTER II

Cadets jammed the Canadian National Railway Station on Main Street in Vancouver; young men all eagerly awaiting the opportunity of boarding the train to Vernon. A civilian onlooker would suspect the Third World War had broken out, to see the private cars, taxis and buses unloading uniformed *soldiers,* all plugging the entrance-way of the pungent-smelling, engine-smoke-filled station.

This year, the loading arrangement wasn't as formal as in the past. Cadets were not formed up in three ranks. As a result, they were allowed to talk to their parents and friends who had come to see them off. Every square foot of the depot was filled with duffel-bags, suitcases, *soldiers,* and their relatives and acquaintances.

As teenagers get older, for some timeless reason, they tend to pull away from their parents, especially with their peers present. These army cadets were no different. Older cadets arrived at the station on their own, however, the younger ones generally led an entourage of throngs of relatives and friends. As usual, dads were assigned the job of carrying the heavy duffel-bags, and mothers appeared apprehensive about losing 'Johnny' for six whole weeks. Their faces expressed their thoughts. Who would look after him, cook his meals, wash his clothes, make certain he brushed his teeth and took a bath, or shower, etc.? What if he was in an accident and was rushed to the hospital wearing dirty underwear?

Little did the mothers realize that in most cases, Johnny's washed or unwashed undershorts would probably get *ripped off* the line in the drying room at camp during the first week and replaced with a dirty pair, or no pair at all. Johnny might not be wearing *any* undershorts until he had enough money to buy some new ones, or *found* a pair laying around in the drying room.

"Now make sure you take your vitamins, every day. Don't forget to wash behind your ears and, if you get homesick, pick up the telephone. If there are nasty boys in your room, ask to change rooms. Make sure you change your underwear and socks every day. I've packed two pairs of pajamas...the ones with the soccer players and the ones with the Mounties. If you need money, just call, and daddy and I will wire it to you. I've packed you some roast chicken to eat on the train. Even if you don't like army food, be sure to eat. Tell the army-men that the food is bad if you don't like it, then they'll change it to your liking. Now, are you sure you've got your hankies? Aunt Ethel will be here after she parks the car. She wants to kiss you good-bye. Here's five dollars, dear. Don't tell your father I gave it to you."

Usually the cadet looked around sheepishly, making certain his friends hadn't heard his mother's comments.

"Uh, thanks, Mom, but, uh...not so loud."

Their fathers didn't seem to worry about such matters. "Listen, son, just make sure you don't get any girls pregnant, and don't keep calling home, collect. I was in the army, I know what it's all about. Why, I can remember the time...you're too young, otherwise I'd tell you. Stay close to Ralph, he's a good buddy and you might need him if you get into a fight. Speaking of fights, did I tell you about the time? No, I can't tell you, you're not old enough. But one day I will. Don't wash your crotch with Sergeants' Soap, it'll take the skin off your nuts. Here's a ten-spot, don't tell your mother I gave it to you."

"Gee, thanks Dad. Don't worry, I'll be okay."

"That's the chip off the old block. Keep your nose clean, Son."

"I will, Dad, oh, oh, here comes Aunt Ethel."

It seemed everyone had an Aunt Ethel, and Aunt Ethels are loud. They also carry handkerchiefs to dry their tears.

"OH, JUNIOR, YOU LOOK SO MATURE IN YOUR UNIFORM. I WISH MY HERBERT HAD JOINED CADETS. YOU REMEMBER YOUR COUSIN, HERBERT, HE WAS THE ONE WHO STUCK A PEA UP YOUR NOSE WHEN YOU WERE A TINY TOT. IT TOOK THE DOCTORS TWO HOURS TO GET THE PEA OUT...AND YOU WERE CRYING AND CRYING. HERE, LET ME TAKE THAT PIECE OF LINT OFF YOUR HAT...THERE THAT'S BETTER. OH, I'VE GOT TO GIVE YOU A KISS AND A GREAT BIG HUG. THERE YOU ARE...OH, YOU ARE BIG AND STRONG. NOW EVERYBODY, LET'S ALL GET TOGETHER FOR A PICTURE."

The faces of the boys stung the same crimson as the lipstick marks planted by their aunts, but ensuing whispers made up for any embarrassment.

"Here, Junior, take this ten dollars. Shhh, don't tell anyone. Oh, to think not too long ago I used to change your diapers. You're so handsome in your uniform."

"Gee, thanks, Aunt Ethel...you're great!"

Parents and aunts weren't the only ones creating a fuss. Girlfriends also flooded the station. Usually, they were quiet and shy, saying nothing at all but standing close to their loved ones; their silence lasting only until they got tired of being ignored by their 'man' and outdone by Ethel.

"You won't meet anyone while you're away, will you? Hey, are you listening to me? I said, you won't meet any other girls, will you?"

"Naahh...you know there's only two important things in my life. You and the B.C. Lions."

Tears would well up in the girls' eyes. "I'll write to you every day, will you do the same with me?"

"Sure, great...hey, there's Shotsey. HEY, SHOTSEY, I'M OVER HERE!"

"Are you listening to me...I love you."

"Uh, yeah, you bet I'm listening. HEY SHOTSEY, I THOUGHT YOU HAD CHICKEN POX?"

The Shotsies were all over the place, with their own girls trailing behind. They'd whisper low and cup their hands around their friend's ear.

"It wasn't chicken pox, it was measles. Jesus, it was hell, but there was this nurse who rubbed this crap all over me, and her fingers were like Heaven."

Then the girls would take hold of their 'loved one's' hands, and pass on more good will. "I saved this baby-sitting, don't tell anyone I gave it to you."

A slight grin lit up the faces of the recipients. "Wow, five dollars...thanks."

It was hard to hear a conversation in the station because of the throngs, and the humorous Aunt Ethels.

Cadet Regimental Sergeant-Major Douglas Brice and three of the four other British Columbia Regiment Cadet WO2s were wrapped up with two other friends whom they hadn't seen for months: Cadet Regimental Sergeant-Major Harvey Rothstein and Cadet Staff-Sergeant Earl Jackson. These two brought the Musketeer total up to seven once again, and since they all didn't live in Vancouver, they had lots of news to catch up on.

Douglas looked at Wayne. "Sergeant-Major Banks, have you seen Sergeant-Major Danyluk?"

Wayne shook his head as his eyes scanned the interior of the station. To find Danyluk, all he had to do was look for a covey of girls.

"Yes, sir. He's, er, saying good-bye to his 'relatives' over in the corner."

Just then, a young-looking cadet from the 72nd Seaforth Highlanders Cadet Corps came up to him and stood at attention.

"Sir, can I speak to you for a minute, please?"

Wayne tucked his drill cane under his arm and looked down at the lad. "Yes, what is it?"

The boy took some papers out of his tunic pocket. "Sir!" he said, very seriously, "That WO3 (Warrant Officer 3rd class) over there, in your regiment...I think his name is Warrant Johnston, said you would show me which of these is my masturbation papers, sir. He told me I can't get on the train without them."

Maintaining a staid face, but dying to laugh, Wayne casually glanced over at Johnston. Johnston, however, was now looking the other way.

"Oh, he did, did he? Er, well, yes...well, I'm really not the one who knows what they look like." Wayne perused the bustling room again. "Ah, there's the one you should be asking. That Sergeant-Major is in your regiment...his name is Sergeant-Major Ashbough. Go and ask him. And listen, while you're at it, he's got the left-handed monkey wrench that we need for adjusting and painting the skyhook. Pick it up from Sergeant-Major Ashbough and give it to Warrant Johnston. At the same time, ask him where the *striped paint* is!"

The cadet was still at attention. "YES, SIR!" He turned around smartly, his kilt swirling. He was last seen marching over to the Seaforth Sergeant-Major.

After the cadet left, Wayne strolled over to Johnston, who couldn't hide his smile of utter mischief.

"I couldn't help it, sir. For some reason, he reminded me of myself three years ago."

Banks grinned. "I remember that, Johnston, and I also remember you didn't like it, either."

Johnston's face was still lit up. "It's all a part of growing up, sir. He'll probably do the same in the future."

A voice boomed over the loudspeakers. "WOULD ALL CADETS FORM UP IN THREE RANKS, PLEASE. THAT MEANS EVERYONE! PARENTS AND FRIENDS: PLEASE GO TO THE REAR!"

Now it was handkerchief, kissing, hugging and panic time.

All of the Aunt Ethels, mothers and fathers, and other relatives and friends smothered their 'Johnnys' with last farewells.

"Remember, be good and do what you're told. We'll send you a parcel of more fried chicken. Don't forget to obey all of the army-men up there."

The words, "All right, all right, Mom," could be heard throughout the station, along with all of the girlfriends' comments. "I'll put lipstick marks on my letters and S.W.A.K., on the envelopes...do you hear me? Do you know that S.W.A.K., means 'sealed with a kiss,' well, do you?"

"Yeah, sure, sure, yeah, that's nice. HEY SHOTSEY, GET NEXT TO ME!"

Slowly but surely, five hundred cadets formed up in snakes of three ranks and the building fell relatively quiet except for a boisterous discussion now going on in one of the corners.

"Sshhh, not so loud. She's my mother's friend, and so is she." Danyluk was trying to calm someone down. He was like a ballet dancer flitting from girl to girl, and covering their mouths with his hands.

"I AM NOT YOUR MOTHER'S FRIEND, I'M YOUR GIRLFRIEND! I DON'T EVEN KNOW YOUR MOTHER!"

"YOU CAN'T BE HIS GIRLFRIEND...I'M HIS GIRL!"

Another one of the four girls spoke up. "YOU HUSSY, MOOSE IS MY BOYFRIEND. LOOK, I'M WEARING HIS RING!"

"OH YEAH...WELL LOOK AT THIS RING. I'M THE ONE WEARING HIS MOTHER'S RING. SAY, THEY LOOK THE SAME. WHY DID YOUR MOTHER HAVE TWO RINGS THE SAME, MOOSE?"

Moose was still fluttering around on his toes. "Ah, well you see girls, er, um. I've really got to go."

"TWO RINGS? WHY ALL FOUR OF US HAVE GOT THE SAME TYPE OF RING. YOU LOWDOWN LOUSE, MOOSE DANYLUK. JUST WAIT UNTIL YOU GET BACK!"

Moose didn't turn around. His original slow pace broke into a mad run until he found a blank file in the ranks. He shrugged to those around him as if he didn't know what the girls' problems were, then straining his neck, he tried to find out who was saying, "What a lucky stiff. He's got four of 'em. I'll betcha he couldn't even handle *one*."

While instructions blared over the loudspeakers, the four girls were still going at it, the shrill of their *voices* heard everywhere.

The one in pigtails said, "AT LEAST I GAVE HIM TEN DOLLARS. YOU LOOK LIKE YOU'VE NEVER HAD A DOLLAR TO YOUR NAME."

That statement angered the 'girl' in bobbysox. Heavily chewing a wad of gum, she replied, "OH YEAH, I GAVE HIM TWENTY DOLLARS. AT LEAST I EARNED MINE STANDING UP!"

The third one was taking the curlers out of her hair, "I GAVE HIM SOME MONEY TOO!"

The fourth one with Minnie Mouse lips, was upset as well. "SO DID I!"

Rothstein tapped Jackson on the arm. "Earl, it's no wonder why Danyluk's rich, he's got a harem."

Earl smiled. "You bet, but a side-show wouldn't take them as freaks." Then he glanced over at Cunningham, and added, "Just take a look at Cunningham's face. He can't take his eyes off Moose. I can see by his expression, he'll have it all by the time we reach Vernon."

Rothstein smiled and nodded. He knew Earl was referring to Danyluk's new found riches.

East had overheard them. "Good, then he can start paying me back for the meals he sucked me into paying for. That creep! Jesus, he's got gall. Just ten minutes ago he came over and asked me what snacks I brought with me. He said, 'What goodies have *we* got for the train?'"

After the roll was called, it wasn't long before the endless parade of cadets marched past the barrier, and onto the platform to board the train. Parents and friends had to wait until the cadets were on the train before they were allowed on the platform to proffer their final good-byes. As usual, tears flowed and parcels of 'goodies from home' were passed along with advice to outstretched hands.

"YOUR DAD AND I WILL VISIT YOU IN THE FIRST WEEK OF AUGUST!"

"YEAH, OKAY, THANKS MOM. MAKE SURE YOU FEED GEORGE THE TURTLE. OH, AND TELL MR. MCKAY I STILL WANT TO DELIVER HIS GROCERIES WHEN I GET BACK!"

"DID YOU PACK YOUR TOOTHPASTE?"

"YEAH, BUT I NEED WASHING SOAP!"

"I THOUGHT THEY DID YOUR LAUNDRY FOR YOU?"

"NOT FROM WHAT I HEAR, MOM."

The dads usually stood behind their wives, giving the thumbs up sign to their sons. Although mothers did all the talking, occasionally a father spoke.

"I WISH I WAS GOING WITH YOU!" Then, after a disgusting look from his wife. "Oh sorry, dear. You know, I was only trying to...?"

Other dads offered sound advice, probably recalling their own past experience. "DON'T FORGET TO ASK FOR RUBBERS!"

"DAD, IT DOESN'T RAIN VERY MUCH IN VERNON!"

"I'M NOT TALKING ABOUT RAIN, SON...I'M TALKING ABOUT...!"

A quick wink. "GOTCHA, DAD! YEAH, I'LL GET 'EM!"

"Henry, what did you say?" asked the boy's mother, giving her husband a confused look.

The father returned his son's wink. "It's man-talk, honey...you wouldn't understand."

In Danyluk's area of the platform, the tone was different.

"I FEEL LIKE GETTING ON THIS TRAIN AND CLUBBING YOU, YOU SNEAK!"

"GIVE ME MY MONEY BACK!"

"MOVE ASIDE, YOU TROLLOP, AND MAKE WAY FOR HIS REAL GIRLFRIEND!"

Danyluk didn't know what to say. He really didn't want to be at the window. "NOW, GIRLS, SETTLE DOWN! JUST TRY TO UNDERSTAND...?"

"I'LL UNDERSTAND, YOU FREELOADER! AND TO THINK, YOU TALKED ME INTO LETTING YOU STAY OVERNIGHT!"

"ME, TOO, YOU PARASITE!"

"NOW I KNOW WHY YOU SPENT MORE TIME WITH MY MOTHER! I'LL BET SHE'S WEARING ONE OF THESE RINGS AS WELL!"

"FOUR RINGS...I'LL FOUR RINGS YOU! YOU BLOODSUCKING CASANOVA!"

Danyluk, with his upper body half out the window, cringed from the onslaught of their *fond* good-byes.

Inside the train, the usual mayhem prevailed. The aisles of each car were plugged with luggage and parcels. Smaller cadets had been placed in the lower berths, and the bigger boys, usually being senior, were relegated to upper berths. This really ticked them off, having no window and having to use a ladder.

All the Musketeers had upper berths across from one another, except Cunningham, who had talked another senior cadet into exchanging berths. Every year on the train to Vernon, he made certain his berth was in the middle of the car. That way, officers walking the aisle wouldn't notice the poker or stuke games taking place.

Douglas took off his uniform and put on civvy P. T. shorts and a T-shirt. Totally oblivious to the noise around him, he lay on his bed, with his hands behind his head. This was it. The last year of Vernon. Although this was his fourth departure, the trip always reminded him of the first time. Lyons wasn't here with his LPB (Lyons' personal bar) and the cadets didn't seem as rowdy for some reason. This year, his mother couldn't come with him to the station because she was working. They had said their farewells to each other when she left the house that morning. It was probably just as well, because parents weren't expected to see senior cadets off.

"Look after yourself, Doug and say hello to Diane for me."

"I will, Mom. Make sure Colonel doesn't go running off." Major, his first dog, had been killed by a car during his first year at camp.

"I'll promise you that, Doug. Write to me, or give me a call once in awhile."

"I will, Mom. Are you going to try and visit?" For the past three years, he had wanted his mother to see how beautiful the Okanagan Valley was.

Never having the opportunity to visit Vernon and very much wanting to do so, his mother managed a lost smile. "I'll do the best I can. It's not easy getting time off. I'll see what I can do. Well, I've got to go now, son." She put down her shopping bag and gave Douglas a hug. "I don't think I'll ever get used to you going away in a uniform. It's different when you wear civilian clothes. The uniform just reminds me too much of saying good-bye to your brother during the war."

"I understand, Mom."

His mother stroked his face and then cupped his hands in hers. "Good-bye, son."

"Good-bye, Mom."

Douglas stayed at the door for a few seconds. Mary Brice closed the gate and wiped her eyes before walking away. Douglas had been too young to understand his mother's feelings when she'd gone to the train station with his brother, Norman, during the war. Times were different then; most of the wives and mothers watching the trains roll out of sight never knew if they would see their loved ones again. He understood now, though, yet it was always difficult for him to fully comprehend the sadness of the war years.

After he closed the door, Colonel came over, wagging his tail. Like his canine predecessor in 1953, he knew his master was going away. Douglas stroked the dog's ears. Although excited about leaving, saying good-bye was something he could never get accustomed to. His current mood didn't last long because the telephone rang. It was Wayne.

"Doug, what time do you want me to come over?"

"Why not come over now? We leave in another couple of hours...we can share the cab fee."

"O.K., I'll be there in three-quarters of an hour."

"Wayne, is your dad going to the station?"

"What, are you out of your mind? Senior cadets don't have parents see them off at the station. Don't you remember the year he gave me a bear hug in front of everyone?"

Douglas winced and grinned. "Yeah, that was hilarious. He thought it was funnier than hell. The only person who didn't laugh was you."

"Can you blame me? I get a bear hug in front of seven hundred cadets. Once was enough, Dougie old buddy. Besides, he's working...so's my sister, Valerie. I'll see ya shortly."

The thought of Wayne's predicament had Douglas chuckling when he hung up the phone. Seconds later he grabbed Colonel's leash to take him for a walk along the beach. For some reason, the dog stayed closer to him this time.

Douglas Brice was awakened from his trance on the train by a 72nd Seaforth Highlanders of Canada cadet, bellowing, "SERGEANT-MAJOR BANKS?"

"I'M OVER HERE!" he heard Wayne answer.

The cadet fought his way through the aisle and snapped to attention before he looked up at the berth.

"Sergeant-Major Ashbough sends his compliments and says he knows nothing about the masturbation clause in the joining instructions. I told him I was going to ask an officer, but he said if I do that I might be put off the train. You know, not understanding what it means?"

Wayne's head was sticking out of the curtains. Although Douglas was smiling across the aisle, his friend kept a straight face.

"I'm sorry, I thought the Sergeant-Major would know about such things. I'll tell you what to do. Go to the very last car on this train and ask for Sergeant-Major Heppner. He's in the Canadian Scottish Regiment. What happened to the left-handed screwdriver you were going to get?"

The young cadet looked at his notes. He had written down, screwdriver, striped paint, and sky-hook.

He shrugged. "He don't know nothin' about those, either!"

"Well, ask Sergeant-Major Heppner about those, too."

"YES, SIR!" The cadet smartly turned to his right, picking up his left foot and slamming it down. With kilt swinging, he headed away to the last car on the train.

Wayne split his gut after the cadet was out of sight.

Douglas said, "Jesus, Wayne, that kid's going to be at it all night. Let Johnston sort it out."

No sooner had he spoke, another cadet came near. "SERGEANT-MAJOR BANKS?"

Wayne popped his head out. "YES, I'M UP HERE!"

This freckled-faced fellow was a Duke. (In the British Columbia Regiment [DCO]). His surname was Russell and he too had a concerned look on his perspiring face. "Sir, Sergeant-Major Ashbough of the Seaforths has informed me if you don't give me a pornographic picture, they won't accept my joining instructions at camp."

"HE SAID WHAT?"

The cadet started again. "He said if you don't...!"

"I heard you, Russell. Go to the last car on this train and ask for Sergeant-Major Heppner."

"YES, SIR!" Russell turned smartly to his right and headed away.

Wayne was now laughing out loud. "That bastard Ashbough got us back with one of our guys."

Douglas joined in the fun. "I pity Heppner. He's a great guy and he's going to wonder what we're up to."

Banks was putting on his running shoes. "Oh, he knows the ropes. He'll just pass the guys along to someone else. Hey, maybe someone in the Irish, or the 15th or 43rd Field?"

The voices coming in with the smoke from the platform were loud when the train started to pull away. Outstretched arms shook offered hands and bags of food were passed up. Shortly, all windows were slammed shut and the train started picking up speed. The throngs remaining on the platform watched listlessly as it wound its way out of sight.

As the train picked up speed, a conductor entered the Musketeer's car. "THIS CAR IN THE DINING ROOM IN TEN MINUTES. THIS CAR IN THE DINING ROOM IN TEN MINUTES!"

Cunningham rushed over to Douglas' berth. He was wearing only his undershorts and had an unlit cigar tucked behind his ear. "Doug, what's the dress in the dining room?"

"It's casual, but not that casual."

Cunningham rushed back to his berth muttering. "I had to undress. I just cleaned out a guy in the 15th Field Regiment and he accused me of pocketing cards. He learned I wasn't."

East and Danyluk came over. East was chomping on a chicken-leg. "Christ, Cunningham's started already. Have you seen the steady steam of 'customers' coming and going from his berth? One Irish cadet just lost his watch to him."

Danyluk was pale, not saying anything.

As a good friend, Wayne was concerned. Danyluk never looked this sad. Not even last year when, in the middle of the night, someone used a clothes-peg to attach the end of Moose's foreskin to his upper sheet. That morning, the Sergeant who stood at the entrance of the barracks and *ordered* all occupants to, "STAND BY YOUR BEDS!" didn't have to flip over mattresses and pull down blankets to get Danyluk out of bed. When Moose threw back his upper sheet and blanket, he went with them. His piercing scream quickly got everyone standing by their beds. Wayne had had to cheer him up then as well.

"Look at it this way," he had said. "If anyone thought they could beat your record for having the biggest foreskin in the world, they would be wrong. You've just added another inch."

Moose stopped rubbing his crotch. "Hey, you're right! No one could top this!"

But that was then. This time, Moose obviously had another problem. "What's the matter, Moose?" asked Banks.

Moose answered with an apprehensive look on his face. "What do you mean, what's the matter? I just lost four of 'em, now what am I going to do when I get back?"

Wayne smiled sympathetically and smacked Danyluk on the back. "Try and think on the bright side, Moose. Just think of the grand opportunity this allows for getting new dames. You're a man of the world. You know a change is better than a rest, don'tcha? I'll bet you were getting tired of them, anyway?"

The frown slowly disappeared from Danyluk's face and a victorious smile appeared. "Hey, yeah, youse is right! And more dough, too!"

"*And* they can take you to better restaurants," offered East.

Danyluk put his arm around East's shoulder and they headed towards the dining car. "Yeah, and the new dames can buy me the grub I like." Moose was back to his old 'self.'

Although Colonel Mikulitch had instructed the senior NCOs of the British Columbia Regiment to ensure that cadets were controlled on the train, it really wouldn't have been fair for them to subdue all the excitement and pranks that took place. After all, senior cadets in the *old days* didn't interfere with the fun cadets got into when leaving home for *their* first extended period of time. Besides, all of the senior cadets knew about the Okanagan's weather and *treatment* the first-timers would face when the train pulled into the Vernon station. Still, they would keep watch and if antics hurt the reputation of the regimental family, they would step in. Pride in the regiment counted above all.

"Can I have two portions?" asked East, when the waiter mentioned the roast beef was exceptionally good.

Four of the seven Musketeers were sitting at the same table, with Danyluk and East across the aisle with some senior cadets from the Westminster Regiment. (now the Royal Westminster Regiment). Cunningham had decided to sit with some Irish Senior NCOs. He had a coin rolling in his fingers and was taking it out of their ears, hair, or making it disappear completely. His audience loved it and didn't notice the deck of cards present and ready to be picked up next.

"No, only one portion per passenger," the waiter replied.

"How thick is it cut?"

"What do I look like, the bloody chef? What'll it be Mac?"

East finally settled on one portion, but asked the waiter if the chef could put an extra piece on his plate. When the food arrived, not only did he have less soup than Danyluk, he only had half as much roast beef.

"LOOK, THERE'S A TWENTY DOLLAR BILL ON THE FLOOR!" yelled East, before Danyluk retorted, "GET YOUR COTTIN-PICKIN' FINGERS OFF MY PLATE!" Moose wasn't about to fall for East's old trick, again.

East wore an embarrassed smile as he watched every morsel of food slip down Danyluk's throat. If he saw a chance for a quick grab, he'd try it. Unfortunately for East, all of the Musketeers knew of his lust for good culinary fare, so when East was around, one eye was always kept glued to their plates. Even if the victuals weren't that great, his table companions had to remain on guard.

"Has anyone heard if Sergeant Beckford is back in camp this year?" Douglas asked anyone within earshot.

Harvey Rothstein was blankly staring out the window at the passing lights. His meal was still untouched and he let out a long sigh. "I've heard he is. It's going to be good working with him again. I think all of us missed him when we took Signals and Driver-Mech." With that said, his eyes once again returned to the images reflecting in the window.

Douglas and Wayne knew something was wrong; their eyes displayed the concern they felt for their friend. The cadet sitting with them wasn't the normal Rothie Rothstein. Something was amiss because he hadn't said much since boarding.

"What's the matter, Rothie? What's troubling you?" Douglas asked.

Rothstein sighed again and kept his eyes on the window for about ten seconds before answering Douglas in an almost inaudible voice.

"My Mom's sick. I don't know if I should have come to camp or not. She's had two operations in the past year, and I'm really worried."

There was silence at the table. Eyes were meeting eyes, but Rothie's eyes just looked down. Clearing his throat, Douglas said, "I'm sorry, pal. What does the doctor say?"

"I think my dad knows the truth, but neither he nor the doctor has told any one of us. My older sister's going to phone the doctor tomorrow to demand the facts. Jesus, we're not kids anymore, we should know if it's serious." A tear rolled down his face and he quickly wiped it away. The next minute he said, "Excuse me, please," and left the table.

Normally East would have made his move and taken Rothie's seat. After all, an unfinished meal was sitting there. However, he'd overheard the conversation and was sombre like the rest of them.

Danyluk moved over and sat in Rothie's chair. Usually it was Moose who perked everyone up when they were down, but not this time. Rothstein was a best friend and like everyone else, Moose didn't have any answers. He hadn't had any solutions for Rothstein the previous year, either.

"His mom's been sick for a while. If you guys can remember, last year Rothie got a telegram that his mother was put in hospital. It really broke his heart. I walked with him up to the Lookout overlooking the lake and it took me four hours to cheer him up."

It was quiet for a minute or so. East had even stopped eating, pushing his plate away.

"What's wrong with her?" asked Wayne.

Danyluk took a deep breath. "Rothie told me last year his mom had gone for an x-ray and they'd discovered a shadow on her left lung. She doesn't smoke or anything like that, but if it's lasted this long, it's serious."

Wayne's eyes met Douglas's. "What are we going to do?"

Douglas's fingers were entwined on the table and he was circling his thumbs. "I'm afraid there's not much we can do but try to assure him that everything's going to work out all right. What I think we should do is try to keep him busy. What car is that officer in? Er, the one who's wearing the yellow wheel on his right upper arm?"

East knew. "He's in the second car from the front."

"Good, Wayne you come with me. We'll see the rest of you back at our car in a few minutes, okay?"

No one answered. The five split up, with Wayne and Douglas walking forward on the train. They found the officer lying on his lower berth going over a nominal roll.

"Excuse me, sir...I'm Mr. Brice from the BCRs, and this is Sergeant-Major Banks. Would it be possible for us to talk with you for a minute?"

The officer had removed his tie and his shoes and appeared quite relaxed. He immediately put down his papers and sat up. "Yes, boys...what can I do for you?"

The conversation lasted about twenty minutes, then both boys thanked the officer, stood up and returned to their car. It was relatively quiet, except for the poker game in Cunningham's berth. Rothie had closed his curtains so they didn't know what he was doing. The two of them crawled up to Wayne's berth. Douglas took out some papers he had to fill out to attend UBC (University of British Columbia) and Wayne reviewed the 'jobs list' of Canadian Pacific Steamships. Two minutes later they heard the officer's voice.

"IS SERGEANT-MAJOR ROTHSTEIN IN THIS CAR?"

Rothie's curtains opened. His eyes were red. "Yes,...yes, sir. I'm Sergeant-Major Rothstein."

"Ah, good. Sergeant-Major, we're tasking some senior cadets to assist us in the paperwork before we arrive in Vernon. Your name was picked out of a hat and I've got a very important job for you to take on. Are you willing?"

Rothstein thought for a moment. "Er, certainly, sir. What would you like me to do?"

The officer stood on the lower berth while he talked to Harvey. "Well, Sergeant-Major, you see this nominal roll.....?"

The officer only stayed about ten minutes, then Rothstein jumped down and stuck his head through the curtains of Wayne's berth. "I won't see much of you guys on this trip. I've got to check and ensure that everyone on board has their joining instructions and that the spelling of their names and addresses is correct. Wow, this could take until tomorrow. Can I start with you guys?"

"Sure, Rothie," Wayne replied. "Holy cow; you poor creep. How did you get stuck with that job?"

Rothstein smiled. His face was brighter now. "I'm not sure, but I've got an idea. Get your joining instructions out!"

The last time the other Musketeers saw the *volunteer*, he was heading towards the front car yelling, "I'LL BE BACK, GET YOUR JOINING INSTRUCTIONS READY!"

As Rothstein left, a joyful voice rang out from Cunningham's berth. "STUKE! YOU BASTARD! I'LL JUST TAKE THAT POT!"

Naturally, it was his voice. At least fifteen cadets were crammed in, and cigar smoke was billowing out. In addition to selling cigars, Cunningham also had a few 'mickies' of the dark and dirty (rum) on hand.

"WHAT DO YOU MEAN FIFTY-CENTS IS TOO MUCH FOR A SWIG? OH, ALL RIGHT, GO AND GET A PAPER CUP FROM THE JON. WHAT DO YOU IRISH THINK I'VE GOT...MUNG MOUTH? JUST LEAVE YOUR MONEY HERE...IT'LL BE SAFE WITH ME! O.K., GENTS, BETS DOWN!"

"Excuse me, are you Sergeant-Major Cunningham?" asked a small 72nd Seaforth cadet. A slight BCR cadet stood next to him.

Cunningham's head complete with a smoking cigar turned towards the cadet, but he didn't take his eyes off the cards. The bellow of smoke blown in the young fellow's face started him coughing as he tried to disperse the clouds with his hands.

"Sergeant-Major Heppner says...(gasp...cough)...that you can provide me with masturbation papers, and my friend here with a pornographic picture."

The *gambler* dealt the cards without missing a beat, laughing to himself that these two (a BCR and a Seaforth) were now *friends*.

"OH, HE DID, DID HE? WELL, I PASSED ALL THE INFORMATION ON TO SERGEANT-MAJOR ROTHSTEIN. HE'S SOMEWHERE ON THE TRAIN, GO AND SEE HIM! NOW, DON'T LET HIM PASS THE BUCK, HE'S GOT ALL THE PAPERS, PICTURES, AND INFORMATION YOU NEED. IS THAT CLEAR?"

"Yes, sir," they answered in unison, appearing a little tired.

"I CAN'T HEAR YOU!"

"YES, SIR!"

"Good, now away you go." Then the *gambler* returned to his game. "COME ON...GIVE ME AN ACE! YES, YES, YES!"

Douglas and Wayne heard the 72nd Seaforth spokesman talking as the two cadets left the car. "Damn these senior NCOs, they keep passing the buck!"

The other said, "What about the striped paint?"

"Oops, well Sergeant-Major Rothstein will probably have that too."

East, Jackson, and Danyluk had joined Wayne and Douglas in Wayne's berth. East was eating a banana and as he spoke, small pieces of white pulp shot from his mouth.

"Heppner sent them back, eh?"

Danyluk got hit in the eye with a piece of flying banana. "Christ, Jack, chew your food first before you talk, will ya?" Then he started laughing. "Those guys are going to be mad when they find out."

"They may never discover the truth," Jackson replied. "The poor bastards."

"LISTEN ASSHOLE, I'M ALREADY DOWN TO MY SHORTS, AND I DON'T MAKE A HABIT OF HIDING CARDS IN MY CROTCH! CHRIST, YOU IRISH ARE SOMETHING ELSE! GET YOUR MONEY IN THERE!"

Cunningham's voice was loud and obnoxious. His berth was really the only place of action in the Musketeer's car. Nothing much was happening in other berths. Some cadets were reading comic books, or shining their boots. Others cupped their hands on the windows, wondering were the hell they were. The train had stopped a few times picking up other cadets, and now the engineer was pouring on the coals. The swaying of the train made everyone sleepy and one by one each of the Musketeers had gone to his individual berth, drawn his curtains and were lost in his own thoughts.

Moose lay on his back with his legs crossed in the air and his hands behind his head. His mind was working a mile a minute as he listened to the sound of the Four Aces sing, *Love Is a Many Splendored Thing.*

"Damn it," he mumbled, thinking of his situation. 'What a body Alice's got. Then bloody Thelma, Hilda, and Olive had to turn up and ruin the whole thing. Son of a bitch! How in the hell did they get to meet each other, anyway? Who the hell gave them the time I would be at the station? I know they all knew I was leaving, but to have four of them there...damn, damn, damn. Oh, well, I know I can sweet-talk Hilda into ridin' the wind again, but lovely Alice...oh, what a body. I know what I'll do, I'll send them each a box of chocolates with a picture of me in my uniform. No, the candy would just give them pimples. Not that three of them haven't got pimples, anyway. Jesus, Thelma's got pimples all over her. But not Alice, her skin is as pure and smooth as the driven snow. Blast, I'll really miss her...and her money. I know what I'll do, I'll phone her when the train stops for ten minutes. When she finds the Moose calling, she'll forget about the other girls. I'll tell her she got the original ring. Damn it, I can't do that either...they all look the same. I know what I'll do, I'll tell Alice my mother wore all four rings but she had a favourite one and that's the one I gave to her. Nah, she'd never believe me. Son of a bitch, who tipped the other three off? Christ, it could have been worse. What if all the girls from the west side had turned up? Phyllis' breath would have knocked them all out. If I've told her once, I've told her a thousand times, chew a mint or somethin' or get your teeth fixed. No wonder she never smiles when she takes me out to my favourite restaurant. I betcha that's also the reason she always wants to turn out the lights. Jesus, that's weird, because Beulah likes the lights on. What a body that Beulah's got. It's just about as great as Mable's. Nah, there's no bazookas like Beulah's bazookas.'

Jack East hadn't yet taken off his uniform. He was in his berth undressing and eating a salmon sandwich his mother had packed for him. He had neatly rolled up his puttees and placed them in his boots in the net hammock that was swinging to and fro. He placed his weights (used for holding the bottom of the pants evenly over the puttees) over the tops of his boots and hung up his uniform. It, too, was swaying from the movement of the train. He then lay on his back, slipped on a pair of P.T. shorts, then sat up and put on a T-shirt.

Nothing much ever bothered Jack. He was a strong kid with not an ounce of fat on him, and he had jet black hair. His dad called him lazy, but Jack knew that wasn't the case at all. He did things in his own way and in his own time. Sure the other guys ribbed him about his eating habits, but what the hell, he thought, that's what food is for.

'It's too bad Rothie's mom is sick,' he thought to himself. 'He's such a great buddy. Although we don't get to see him all of the time, Rothie is nearly as much a Duke as we are. Jesus, why does life have to be so hellish? Why does there have to be so much pain and suffering? I wonder what Rothie's going to do if his mom dies? Maybe a new drug will come on the market. Yes, that's it, maybe a new drug is on the way and it will cure Mrs. Rothstein. Oh, wouldn't that be great! Rothie and his mom and dad and sisters and brothers together again. I'll ask the Medical Officer at Vernon if new drugs are being developed. Then I'll check with the drug stores in town. Surely the druggists will know? Rothie's mom doesn't deserve this. When she invited me over for supper I didn't know what hit me.'

"Mom, I'd like you to meet the one and only Jack East. The guys call him East the Beast."

"Harvey, don't talk that way," she said, holding out her hand. "No one should be called a beast. Hello, Jack!"

Jack was shy. "Mrs. Rothstein."

"No, not Mrs. Rothstein...you call me Rose. There are no formalities in this house. Now, what do you like to eat?"

Harvey started laughing. "Mom, this is one guy you don't have to ask that question. That's the reason they call him East the Beast. If it's cooked, he'll eat it."

Jack was also laughing. "I'll even eat it if it isn't cooked, Mrs. Rothst...Rose."

After three helpings of dinner, they all went bowling, and after that, Mr. Rothstein took both boys to see his dry-cleaning plant.

"Rose and I started out on a shoestring, but we have thirty employees now and we're still growing. Someday, Harvey, you'll be managing this with your brothers and sisters."

"But Dad, I've decided I want to teach math."

"So the dry-cleaning business isn't good enough for you?"

"Aw, let's not go into that again, Dad. Sure I like the dry-cleaning business, but I want to teach. I'm a good instructor, aren't I Jack?"

"He's one of the best instructors, sir. Harvey is a natural-born teacher."

"Well, son, as long as you know what you want and you do it well, I guess that's all that matters. What are you going to do, Jack?"

"I really don't know, sir. I've thought about becoming a chef, but everyone says I'd eat all of my creations."

Mr. Rothstein belly-laughed. "You become a chef, Jack. Don't you worry about what the others say."

As the train turned a sharp bend, Jack was lost in memories, smiling and thinking of the evening he had enjoyed with the Rothsteins. They were a close family and he loved every minute of being with them. When it came time to leave, Sid Rothstein placed a small package in his hands.

"It's a little gift from me and Rose. Wear them when you take the girlfriend out to dinner."

While Sid was driving him home, Jack peaked into the small box. It was a set of cufflinks. The inscription read, 'Get rid of your woes, let Sid clean your cloes.'

"Er, sir...Sid, thank you for these cufflinks. I, er...are you sure the spelling's right?"

Although Sid Rothstein was concentrating on maneuvering an icy road, he chuckled. "You see what happens when you give the job to your son? When Harvey was only ten, I sent him to the factory that makes them. I said order 500 sets and tell the guy what inscription I wanted on them. Jack, those cufflinks mean more to me now than Harvey will ever know. Since then, we've given away thousands of sets and we keep the same wording."

Jack East was still smiling as he got under the sheets and turned out his light. He had told Mrs. Rothstein that she was undoubtedly the best cook in the whole, wide world.

"Now are you certain you don't want any more?" she had asked.

"Er, Mrs. Roth...Rose, I've already gone back three times."

Rose laughed. "So, you're afraid your stomach will burst?"

"Well, oh alright, just one more helping."

Jack's light was off, but not Earl Jackson's. His curtains were open and he was in deep thought, sitting on the edge of his berth, legs dangling into the aisle, as he polished his cap badge and his brass. Danyluk's radio was on in the next berth and Earl was humming along with Gogi Grant singing her hit single, *Wayward Wind*. He kept time to the song with his cleaning brush.

'I hope my mom's going to be all right. The new wheelchair should be better for her, but who's going to help her get in the groceries? What a fighter she is. I don't know if I could put up with being in a wheelchair, day after day. Yet she picks up my clothes and does the laundry. Why do I insist on dropping my clothes all over the house? What's with me? Mom's got enough on her mind without having to pick up after me all the time. I don't do that in Vernon, why the hell do I do it at home? Oh well, I'm not dropping too much stuff these days. Maybe I am maturing, who knows? This should be a great course. I'm looking forward to working with Sergeant Beckford again. I wonder if Danyluk is looking forward to working with Sergeant Simpson again? I'll bet he doesn't know that Simpson's back. The past two years were fun, but it wasn't the same without Beckford and Simpson. Driver Mech was also great, but I don't think Beckford and Simpson will ever forget that we gave the finger to the guard when we drove past the parade square, day after day. Us guys, the real guard, gave them all the finger. Oh well, that's tradition and I bet the guard got into deep shit for mooning us. Then again, maybe not, because we did the same thing when we were the guard. I wonder if mom got those papers in the mail to UVIC? (University of Victoria) Damn it, I forgot to ask her.' "HEY MOOSE, TURN UP THAT SONG, PRESLEY'S GREAT!"

There were seven-hundred different memories and thoughts going through the cadets' heads on the train. For the younger cadets, this was their first trip away for such a long period of time. What if they failed the course, or got homesick? Some were homesick now but kept up a brave front. The older boys had told them of Vernon. What to do and what not to do. Keep your nose clean and your mouth shut and you may survive. Don't hang your wet clothing in the drying room if you want to keep it. Don't leave anything laying around if you want to keep it. Sergeants are gods; they can make no mistakes. They may be incorrect once in a while but they're never wrong. Don't drink too much at mug-up, you may wet the bed. Don't ever play cards with a BCR NCO by the name of Cunningham...he'll clean you out.

One young cadet was just dozing off, when suddenly a grim thought made him sit right up. 'That BCR cadet who took my money tonight had a name tag on his shorts that read, 'Chandler.' He must be one of Cunningham's students? Say, how come when I last saw him, his name tag read, Miller? Jesus, I wonder if I've been caught by the famous Cunningham? I'd better not mention it, I'd be the laughing stock of the cadet corps.'

The cadet was right. He *had* been caught by the prominent 'Cunningham.' Earlier in his *career*, Cunningham had learned that his name was feared when it came to a game of *chance*. He'd actually heard a 'Westie' Senior NCO passing information along. "Don't gamble with a BCR cadet by the name of Cunningham. He'll have your dough in no time. There's rumors that he even hides cards in his shorts."

To increase *business*, Cunningham had six name tags made. They read: Miller, Chandler, Rammington-Smythe, Gandhi, West, and Zaholuk.

Wayne, too, was in a melancholy mood as he perused the CPR Ferries jobs list. "You know, Doug, I think we had more fun when we didn't have rank!"

"I know, buddy, I know what you mean. I think the same way when I see these guys having a ball. They don't have any responsibility at all. Do you remember when we got on the train in 1953? Do you remember Lyons and Genova going at it? That Sergeant actually hit Genova in the nose, thinking it was Lyons. I've never laughed so much in my life when Lyons kept stepping on the guy's hand. Did I tell you that every time I see that Sergeant, oh what the hell's his name...anyway, he tells me his hand is still sore."

Wayne smiled and nodded. "I'm going to miss Bergie. I think Moose will, too. Why the hell did he have to go and join the Regular Force? After all, he was a Musketeer...and we don't split..."

Douglas knew the mood his friend was in. It was uncanny how they thought the same way, at times. Like himself, Wayne was watching the younger cadets having a ball. For most of them, this was their first trip away from home. Friendships were forming that would last for years, and the foundation for that kind of camaraderie would be laid in Vernon where there are no parents to solve problems...only friends.

Since 1953, the seven had taken on the world and won, and now Bergie had left the group. Although Jackson lived in Victoria, when he wanted to discuss something, he was on the phone, and then on the next ferry. But this past year was different. It hadn't just happened overnight; something was building up in all of them. The personal friendship of all those years was changing, but not in a way that was immediately noticeable; no, it was more subtle than that. For years, the group was inseparable, particularly he and Wayne. The change started when the phone calls became less frequent and instead of getting together four or five nights a week, it became three, then two. Gradually, each of them in his own way was acquiring new and different interests.

"It's coming to an end, Wayne. Remember Sergeant Beckford saying, 'Keep the memories, but don't let them ruin your life. You'll lose tomorrow if you do that. Only fools constantly look back. Live for the moment, cherish the past, but strive for the future.' I really didn't know what he meant then, but I do now. It's frightening, in a way. You and I are going our own ways, and, well...all of us will eventually split up. Damn it, Wayne, come to UBC with me? Why, we could have a ball, and..."

"I can't, Doug. I was going to quit school last year but you talked me out of it. I'm just fed up with it all. You and I are different in the sense that I want to get out of the house and see the world. I want to get out on my own and do my own thing."

"What brought this on all of a sudden? Why the sudden change right this minute?"

Wayne began looking through the CPR jobs list again. "It's not a sudden change, you know that? I don't know what it is. It's been building up slowly. My dad asked me the same thing, but he's being posted to a new town up north and I really don't feel like going with him. There's a giant new world out there and I want to discover and experience it. You know, I'm the only one in the group that sneaks in the beer parlors for a few beers. You guys won't join me in case you get caught. I even go up to Sadie's bootleggin' joint for a drink."

"Wayne, it's not that we don't want to go with you. For some reason people accept you as being older. When it comes time to check I.D.s, they bypass you and head straight for us."

"That's another thing, Doug. I think we've overstayed our welcome in cadets. I know we can serve until we're nineteen, but now I feel like a kid when I wear the uniform. I don't mind wearing my militia uniform, but I wear my raincoat over my cadet uniform until I get to the armouries."

"Jesus, Wayne, what if the senior NCOs that brought us along had thought like you? Do you think the 2290 would have survived? Hey, we're just filling a gap. The British Columbia Regiment and the 2290 will be around long after we're gone. The thousands who came before us left it intact for us. It's been a major part of our lives. What the hell do you think we'd be like if we hadn't joined...and now you're ashamed of the uniform?"

Wayne stopped looking at the list. Instead, he stared at the blanket while Douglas talked. Now, he slowly raised his head and their eyes met. "I'm not ashamed of the uniform."

"What is it then?"

"I don't know. I've done my share of protecting the heritage. Christ, the cadet corps is bigger and better now than it's ever been. The badge means a lot to me, it's just that...well...oh let's get off the subject."

Douglas watched as Wayne grabbed the jobs list again and ran his finger down the slate of 'opportunities'. He also saw the look of determination in Wayne's eyes.

"I'm going to miss you, buddy. We've been closer than brothers. You kept telling me that dames would split us up...they haven't."

Wayne threw the paper aside and yawned. "LET'S GET OFF THE SUBJECT! Neither of us is dead, we'll still see each other. I'll be over at your house. Let's just make the most out of this last year. I'll bet you, right this minute, Diane and Debbie are planning for the first dance at the arena. Are you still serious about Diane?"

Douglas nodded.

"Will you get married?"

"Wayne, I've only got thirty bucks to my name. How the hell can I get married?" They both laughed, then Wayne said, "Diane's probably got a few dollars stashed away?"

"Yeah, and I think that's for her education. I'm not like Danyluk, you know?"

"Then when will you get married? After you've finished UBC?"

Douglas took a deep breath and let it out slowly. "To tell you the truth, I don't even know if I'll finish UBC. I'm also leaning towards going into the forces as an officer."

"AS A WHAT? For a moment I thought you said, *officer?*"

"I did say officer. I don't think Laidlaw and Denver are happy being ORs." (Other Ranks - two friends who joined up recently) "It takes years for promotion and although it might look glamorous on the outside, I sure as hell don't believe it's that way on the inside. I'm even thinking about taking my commission with the regiment, next year."

Wayne put on his exasperated look. "Christ, Corporal Brice is now too good to be Corporal Brice...he wants to be Second Lieutenant Brice. You talk about me not wanting to wear a cadet uniform? There's nothing wrong with being a Corporal in the regiment, you know? You can move up the ranks and become a Sergeant, maybe even make RSM, who knows? What about the fact that you wanted to go back to Vernon as a driver?"

"It's not that, Wayne. I enjoy being a Corporal in the Regiment, however, if I join the Regular Force, I think having a commission will be an asset. I might change my mind again and go to Vernon as a Corporal, I'm not too sure. What about you? Are you at least staying in the regiment for a while?"

Wayne shook his head and picked up the jobs list again. "No, if I get a job on the ferries, I won't be able to parade on Tuesdays and Thursdays. Also, I wouldn't be able to make any of the weekend exercises. Damn it, I'm going to miss everything. I'll miss you, I'll miss the regiment...Bergie's gone, and..."

Wayne never had the chance to finish because a young male voice interrupted him.

"SERGEANT-MAJOR BANKS, SIR! MAY WE PLEASE SPEAK TO YOU, SIR?"

Wayne recognized the voice and winced. The voice coming from the aisle was that of the 72nd Seaforth cadet and his *new-found* friend.

"You again. What is it now?"

"WELL SIR, SERGEANT-MAJOR ROTHSTEIN SAYS HE IS TOO BUSY AND THAT HE PASSED EVERYTHING CONCERNING MASTURBATION PAPERS AND PORNOGRAPHIC PICTURES TO YOU, SIR!"

Even though Danyluk's radio was up full, Wayne could hear Cunningham. "HAAA, I'M GLAD HE DIDN'T COME BACK TO ME!" Followed by, "THERE'S TWO DOLLARS MISSING FROM THE POT! WHO TOOK THE TWO DOLLARS? OH, YOU DID, OKAY...DEAL! DON'T SNEAK A LOOK AT THE CARDS, JUST DEAL!"

Wayne finally gave in. The cadets had won. "OKAY, YOU GUYS, COME WITH ME...WE'RE GOING TO HAVE A LITTLE TALK ABOUT THE BIRDS AND THE BEES."

The two tired-looking cadets were surprised to see the Sergeant-Major jump down, put his arms on their shoulders, and edge them towards the car's smoking room.

Danyluk yelled. "THERE'S NO DOUBT IN MY MIND, THOSE TWO ANKLE-BITERS ARE GOING TO BECOME LIFE INSURANCE SALESMEN! I'VE NEVER SEEN SO MUCH PERSISTENCE SINCE HILDA KEPT SAYING, NO!"

"DID HILDA WIN?" asked Earl.

"NONE OF THEM WIN WHEN THE OL' MOOSE WANTS TO SLIP 'EM TWENTY POUNDS OF SAUSAGE MEAT!"

East's curtains opened. He had been asleep, but he thought he heard someone mentioning food. "WHO'S GOT WHAT...SAUSAGES?"

Danyluk roared out laughing. "OH GO BACK TO SLEEP, YOU CRAVING PONGO!"

East didn't let it rest there. "YOU USED TO SAY THIRTY-TWO POUNDS!"

"MY BODY'S SHRINKING WITH OLD AGE," Danyluk shot back. "AT LEAST IT'S BETTER THAN SIX OUNCES!"

"UP YOUR ASS, DANYLUK!"

Just then, two small and weary cadets came walking through the aisle, heading towards their car. The Seaforth cadet was still doing the talking. "Don't tell me you knew it all along, Russell. That's one word I'm never going to forget. Wait till I write my mom and dad and tell 'em what *masturbation* means."

Russell agreed. "Yeah, and what *pornography* means, too! But what about the striped paint and the left-handed screwdriver?"

"What about them?"

"Well, we haven't got them yet!"

Exhaustion showed on the Seaforth cadet's face. "Well, you get 'em, I've had it!"

Wayne crawled up. "I had to clue them in."

Douglas agreed. "You should have let Johnston do that. He started it."

"Ha, ha, ha. Noooo, Dougie, old boy. I've got Johnston out looking for the Last Post! That's one even *he* hasn't heard of."

"You're cruel, Wayne."

Danyluk added: "Not as cruel as Bergie. I'll never forgive that bastard for cutting my shitter pole. Do you guys remember how I got my own back, last year?"

The sound of clapping hands came from all directions, including the 'cardroom.' Everyone knew how Danyluk got even with Bergie. It was the event of the summer. After a full day's driving, everyone had been totally beat as the convoy pulled up in Glenemma to bivouac for the night. Bergie had fallen asleep instantly, and so soundly, he didn't wake up as Danyluk slowly pulled him in his sleeping bag towards the shitter. Moose wasn't as cruel as Bergie was, because he left him on the edge of the trench. He at least gave Bergie a fighting chance. But not for long because, one hour later, Bergie rolled over in his sleep. Did he *ever* roll over!

"WHAT THE...JESUS CHRIST ,WHERE THE HELL AM I? OH MY GOD, IS THIS JUST A BAD DREAM? MOOSE, YOU ROTTEN PRICK! GIVE ME A HAND TO GET OUT OF THIS BAG! I CAN'T EVEN MOVE!"

"YOU'VE GOT TO BE JOKING, BERGIE. HAVE FUN AT THE WATER TRUCK!"

Danyluk had jumped down from his berth and was now in the middle of the aisle gloating and subconsciously dancing to the tune on his radio. Red Robinson was playing a flashback called *Sh-Boom*, by the Crew Cuts.

"That disc-jockey, Red Robinson, has to be the greatest. Did I tell you guys that Red and I are like this." He entwined the first and second fingers of his right hand. "He's real George."

East stuck his head out of the curtains. He couldn't stand it when he thought Moose was *exaggerating*.

"BULLSHIT! YOU DON'T KNOW RED ROBINSON!"

Moose edged himself onto Jack's berth. "OH, REALLY? I SUPPOSE YOU DIDN'T KNOW THAT RED AND I WENT TO DIFFERENT SCHOOLS TOGETHER!"

Danyluk's statement jolted East. "No, I didn't. You didn't tell me that. Gee, so you really do know him. What's he like?"

"Youse, of all people, know I don't like bragging, but Red's really just one of the guys. Why just last week, Red and I went on a trip visiting different locations at the same time. He was at the Georgia Auditorium, and I was at the Cave Supper club."

East was enthralled. "Wow, I'd sure like to meet him; his radio show is mint!"

"Well, just stick with me, Jacky my old son, and I'll talk to my buddy Red about ya. Although he's busy, if I ask him, he may just sign an autograph for you. How's them apples?"

Danyluk had pulled one over on East again. "Wow, Moose. Okay, let's do it when we get back?"

Moose jumped down and headed for Cunningham's berth. "Maybe. Now if my boots could be made to look like yours...I..."

"Go take a hike, Moose. I'd like Red's autograph, but I ain't doin' your boots!"

Douglas left Wayne's berth and headed for bed, laughing to himself. Moose and East were great and he'd miss them, as well. As he crawled between the sheets, he heard Cunningham's voice. "GET YOUR NOSE OUT OF MY EAR AND STOP WHISPERING. WHAT WAS THAT? SCREW YOU, MOOSE...MONEY TALKS! I DON'T GIVE A DAMN HOW MANY RED ROBINSON AUTO-GRAPHS YOU CAN GET ME! I CAN'T DEPOSIT THEM IN THE BANK!"

As Douglas went to sleep, he tried to understand why everything couldn't just remain the same. So many things had changed. He never thought he'd ever miss Edwin Shanks. Edwin was one of the Irish Fusilier cadets who bugged them their first year at Vernon. He had a taken a particular disliking to Bergie and Danyluk. Probably, it was because he found out who organized the party that moved him and his sleeping bunkmate out onto the parade square in the middle of the night. Although he'd pleaded with Genova to box Bergie in the ring and had told every-one he hated Bergie's guts, after he lost the match, he and Bergie became close friends. For the past two years, Edwin Shanks had been a close friend of all the musketeers. He'd even turn up at the BCR's armoury on parade nights and invite everyone down to the Irish's Gilford Street Armoury for coffee on *their* parade nights.

Now Shanks had joined the Regular Force with Bergie. They had both enlisted in the RCEME and were closer than brothers.

As Douglas rolled over on his side, he thought to himself what a hell of a nice guy Edwin Shanks was.

"BREAKFAST IS READY IN THE DINING CAR. OCCUPANTS OF THIS CAR ARE TO BE THERE IN TWENTY MINUTES! BREAKFAST IS READY IN THE DINING CAR!"

Douglas unbuttoned his curtains and watched the Conductor stride through the car. Most guys were already up and the porter was making up the beds. The car was relatively quiet except for the noise in the middle.

"OF COURSE IT'S A NEW DECK, YOU FRUMP! ARE YOU ACCUSING ME OF BRINGING BACK THE DECK WE USED THREE HOURS AGO? ALL RIGHT...LET'S DEAL! YOU...GET YOUR HANDS AWAY FROM THE POT! SLIDE THEM BACK A LITTLE...I'M WATCHIN' YA!"

Wayne's berth had been made up and he was in the lower berth, just staring out the window. "So, you're awake at last?" Get washed up, we're nearly in God's country again."

Stretching, Douglas asked, "Does it look hot out there?"

"Hot isn't the word for it. Jack's in between cars with the half-door open. He says the air is blistering his face."

Breakfast was the same for everyone: bacon and eggs, toast and coffee. Rothstein, however, ordered a cheese omelette. His eyes were still a little red, but his mood had changed. He was again the old *Rothie* they knew so well.

"Jesus, if I had to look at another nominal roll, I'd jump out the window first. I didn't finish the job until one o'clock in the morning. Half the cadets were asleep with their curtains closed and I had to find them. One guy told me to 'eff' off and see him in the morning. Can you imagine that kind of language? I thought he was talking in his sleep. When I told him my name was Sergeant-Major Rothstein, he said, 'I don't care if it's General George Kitching...just 'eff' off!' His buddy told me the guy was mad and tired because he'd lost twenty five-bucks to: 'SOME BCR CREEP BY THE NAME OF ZAHOLUK!' Those Irish have no respect."

Six of the Musketeers were sitting at two tables adjacent to each other. East and Danyluk were sitting with, of all people, the 72nd Seaforth cadet and his pal, Russell.

"So youse now knows what masturbation means?" asked Danyluk.

Both cadets smiled and looked a little embarrassed. "Yes, sir...we learned about it the hard way."

Danyluk laughed. "Little play on words there, eh?"

The cadets did not know what he meant, so they didn't respond. Two minutes later, another tired-looking cadet stood at their table. "Hey, you guys, I can't find the NCO who knows about masturbation papers. What did you say his name was?"

Russell said, "Johnston, Warrant Johnston!" The smiling duo had *sucked* in someone else and the game was on again.

"STAND IN THE AISLE WITH YOUR DUFFEL-BAGS ON YOUR LEFT SIDE! TAKE OFF YOUR TUNICS AND TIES AND ROLL UP YOUR SLEEVES. YOU WILL CARRY YOUR BAGS IN YOUR LEFT HAND. MAKE CERTAIN YOU DIDN'T LEAVE ANYTHING BEHIND! YOU WILL EXIT FROM THAT DOOR! IS THAT CLEAR?" the Regular Force Sergeant bellowed as he walked the aisle pointing to the proper doorway.

"Yes, Sergeant!"

"I CAN'T HEAR YOU!"

"YES, SERGEANT!"

"MOVE NOW!" he ordered, as two Regular Force Corporals came in from the other door and started moving up the aisle, herding everyone off.

"YOU! GET THOSE CARDS PUT AWAY! WHAT WAS THAT? NO, I HAVEN'T GOT TIME FOR A QUICK GAME FOR BIG BUCKS! GET YOUR ASS IN GEAR, MAN! WHERE THE HELL DO YOU THINK YOU ARE...IN LAS VEGAS? WELL, DO YOU?"

Cunningham's response was fast. "NO, SERGEANT!"

The train had arrived in Vernon where the cadets were quickly unloaded and formed into three ranks with their backs to the sun. The sun's rays were blistering, but this didn't seem to deter the welcoming committee. Girls and their parents were everywhere. Some were waving and others were yelling out names to attract their *loved ones*.

The Musketeers' girls were no exception. They were together in a group, making most of the noise. Diane and Debbie were feverishly trying to point out their boys, as were Danyluk's girl Alma, and East, Jackson and Rothstein's girlfriends.

Douglas took a deep breath. "Wayne, just smell that air. It's great to be back in God's Country."

Perspiration was already forming on Wayne's forehead, below his beret. "Trust you to say that, when it's over a hundred degrees in the shade. Still, you're right. It's great to be back."

The girls had shy looks on their faces, just like the boys.

"MOOSE, YOU BIG HANDSOME LUG...I LOVE YA!" Alma screamed.

"I KNOW YOU DO!" he replied. "HEY, DID I LEAVE ANY OF MY SILK GAUNCH AT YOUR HOUSE?"

Alma blushed. "IS THAT YOUR WAY OF SAYING YOU LOVE ME?"

Moose pushed out his chest. "POSSIBLY. IT DEPENDS?"

"IT DEPENDS ON WHAT?"

"IT DEPENDS ON WHETHER YOU'LL TREAT ME IN THE MANNER TO WHICH I'VE BECOME ACCUSTOMED?"

"YOU KNOW I WILL, YOU GIGANTIC, MAGNIFICENT BEAST!"

Moose blew her a kiss and held out both of his arms. "THEN I LOVE YA!"

Danyluk should have paid a little more attention to the Sergeant in the Royal Canadian Regiment. Sergeants aren't particularly happy if romantic statements are made and they're not included.

"YOU! YES, YOU! KEEP YOU MOUTH SHUT! I'LL TELL YOU WHEN YOU CAN OPEN IT! IS THAT CLEAR?"

"YES, SERGEANT!"

"IS THAT YOUR GIRLFRIEND?"

"YES, SERGEANT!"

"CHRIST, SHE MUST HAVE ROCKS IN HER HEAD! HAVE YOU GOT LOTS OF MONEY, OR SOMETHING?"

East couldn't resist the opportunity. "OR SOMETHING, SERGEANT!"

The Sergeant shook his head and was still giving Danyluk a piercing stare when he decided to move them out.

"PICK UP YOUR GEAR! THIS MOB, ATTEN...TION! MOVE TO THE RIGHT IN THREES, RIGHT TURN...BY THE RIGHT, QUICK MARCH!"

The silent signal Douglas gave Diane was more than plain to her. He would call her as soon as he had the chance. Debbie understood Wayne's 'message' as well.

The Musketeers were fortunate again this year. Their railway car had been near the front of the train. This meant they did not have to wait for the trucks to return to pick them up. There were only enough trucks to pick up half the cadets, and occupants of the front railway cars were transported to camp first.

"THIS MOB, HALT! STAND STILL! I SAID, STAND STILL! YOU, QUIT SCRATCHING YOUR ASS! PLACE YOUR GEAR DOWN BUT KEEP YOUR HANDS ON IT! TRUCKS NUMBER FOUR AND FIVE ARE OURS. PEELING

OFF FROM THE RIGHT IN SINGLE FILE, QUICK MARCH!"

Slowly, but routinely, the trucks filled up. Some cadets were sitting, and some had to stand. A good majority of them made *quiet* signals to the local civilians.

Alma and the girls were standing next to their boys' truck. "MOOSE, THANK YOU EVER SO MUCH FOR SENDING ME YOUR MOTHER'S RING. I'LL CHERISH IT ALWAYS!"

East looked over. "You rotten creep, Danyluk. Even Alma?"

Although Danyluk wasn't supposed to reply, he did anyway. "IT'S ONE OF A KIND, BABE. SHE TOLD ME TO GIVE IT TO THE GIRL OF MY DREAMS!"

"OH MOOSE, YOU BIG HUNKA LOVE!"

The Sergeant didn't think Moose was a big hunk of love. "YOU, I THOUGHT I TOLD YOU TO KEEP QUIET! DID I NOT?"

"YES, SERGEANT!"

"JUMP DOWN HERE!"

Moose began picking up his kit-bag. "LEAVE YOUR KIT UP THERE! NOW, YOUNG FELLOW, WHEN I SAY KEEP QUIET, I MEAN JUST THAT. GET DOWN AND GIVE ME THIRTY! I'LL DO THE COUNTING!"

Moose hated those last words.

"One, two, three, four, five, six, six, six, seven, seven, eight, nine, ten, ten, ten, eleven"

Sixty push-ups later, Moose was wasted, and it was so hot, his hands felt burnt.

"I hope this guy ain't one of our instructors!" he whispered to Wayne. "I hate those guys who count that way."

Wayne smiled. "That's the way you count when you dish it out at the Drill Hall!"

"Yeah, but I'm not on the receiving end then."

"OH, YOU LOOKED SO HANDSOME AND ROUGH WHEN YOU DID THOSE PUSHUPS, MOOSE!" Alma bellowed.

Although the heat and the exercise had Danyluk perspiring heavily, he turned sideways and flexed his arms in a he-man pose.

Girls galore screamed out instructions as the trucks pulled away, heading for the camp. The guys in the vehicles couldn't react because this Sergeant wanted quiet, and he got it. He stood by the tailgate in the Musketeers' truck, his eyes scanning them constantly. Needless to say, Danyluk looked like an angel...an angel with a defiant smile on his face. However it turned to one of surrender when his eyes met the Sergeant's, and *his* 'smile' of challenge. Moose knew full well that even in a crowded three-ton-truck, room can always be made for pushups. Sergeants can make room for pushups anywhere.

The trucks didn't take the usual round-about way to the camp this year. Instead, they drove through the city, past the Allison Hotel, Highway 97, and the Silver Grill Cafe before turning left and heading up the west road which runs parallel to the main highway.

At the top, they turned left to Highway 97, turned right, past the guardroom and parade square, before finally turning left at the top of the camp. Approximately twelve minutes after leaving the station, the convoy stopped on the road outside the camp hospital.

All occupants of the trucks, except Cunningham, scanned the camp. He couldn't have cared less what the camp looked like; he was too busy reading Friday's closing prices of the Vancouver Stock Market. "Jesus, Cruiser Copper's up

2 1/2 cents a share. Let me see, I've got eight thousand shares, times two-and-a-half cents...?"

Rows upon rows of black tarpaper huts lined the east side of the highway. Sprinklers throwing out mists of water had been put there recently, in an attempt to turn the coarse brown 'grass' into green lawns. Those sprinklers would be on all summer, but only a few of the areas would actually turn green. The sun didn't allow much compromise.

Danyluk leaned over and whispered in East's ear. "Did you notice that Hop Sing's got himself a new sign?"

"What did it say?" asked East.

"Things are looking up, Jacky. It said, 'Our staff will be 'preased' to serve you. If you 'rook' and you can't find it, just ask!' I wonder if 'rook' meant, look or fuck? HAAA! HA! HA.! Whatever it meant, I'm going to be in there 'rooking.'"

The Sergeant jumped down and assisted the driver in opening the tailgates. East was out first. "So what do *you* think 'rook' means?"

Danyluk jumped down next. "It means he's got more dames. Youse can bet your life I'm goin' in there to rook. There's no doubt I'll be preased. And if I don't see it, I'm going to ask for it! This ain't gonna be my bashful year!"

East laughed. "Jesus, Moose, you've never been bashful in your life."

The Sergeant marched in front of a cadet. "RIGHT! PICK UP YOUR GEAR AND FORM THREE RANKS ON THE ROAD! COME ON NOW, LOOK ALIVE! YOU! YOU HORRIBLE LOOKING EXCUSE FOR A WALKING TALKING HUMAN BEING...WHAT'S YOUR NAME AND WHO TIED YOUR PUTTEES?"

The cadet didn't realize at first that the Sergeant was talking to him. When the Sergeant's nose was in his face, he instantly stood to attention and replied, "Lampman, and I tied them, Sergeant!"

"I CAN'T HEAR YOU!"

"LAMPMAN, AND I TIED THEM, SERGEANT!"

"WHO THE HELL IS LAMPMAN, YOUR MAN-SERVANT?"

"NO...THAT'S MY NAME, SERGEANT!"

"WHAT REGIMENT ARE YOU IN, LAMPMAN?"

"THE WESTMINSTER REGIMENT, SERGEANT!"

"IS THERE A FAINT POSSIBILITY THAT YOU'VE RECENTLY TRAINED WITH THE CHELSEA PENSIONERS?"

"NO, SERGEANT, JUST THE WESTIES!"

A 'gas pain' hit the Sergeant's face. "DO YOU HAVE AN EXTREME CASE OF GOUT, LAMPMAN?"

"NO, SERGEANT! WHAT'S GOUT?"

"WHAT'S GOUT? WHAT'S GOUT? WHERE'S THAT INTELLIGENT-LOOKING CADET THAT DID THE PUSHUPS?"

Danyluk grabbed East's arm. "This bastard's going to nail me again I can feel it. Quickly, quickly, what the hell is gout?"

East's mind worked fast, but not that fast. He put his hand to the side of his mouth and whispered, "It's a Mediterranean soup made with chick-peas and curry."

Danyluk immediately stood at attention and stuck his chest out. "IT'S A MEDITERRANEAN SOUP MADE WITH CHICK-PEAS AND CURRY, SERGEANT!"

The Sergeant crossed his eyes in disbelief. "A WHAT? ARE YOU TELLING

ME THIS POOR EXCUSE FOR A WELL-TRAINED SOLDIER HAS POURED
FUCKING MEDITERRANEAN SOUP MADE WITH CHICK-PEAS AND
CURRY DOWN HIS PUTTEES?"

"I, ER...UM...WELL, HE, ER...HE'S A WESTIE, HE COULD HAVE, ER...!"

"GIVE ME THIRTY...I'LL DO THE COUNTING! AND YOU...YOU WITH
THE SWOLLEN ANKLES, GIVE ME THIRTY AS WELL!"

When Danyluk and his 'partner' had completed their pushups, the Sergeant
dressed the ranks and proceeded to explain the upcoming medical procedure.

"WHEN I FALL YOU OUT, YOU WILL SIT ON THE 'GRASS' AND
TAKE OFF YOUR PUTTEES, BOOTS, SOCKS, AND TIES! YOU WILL
LEAVE YOUR BAGS EXACTLY WHERE THEY ARE NOW. YOU WILL
ENTER THE BUILDING IN SINGLE FILE AND KEEP THOSE ARTICLES OF
CLOTHING WITH YOU! INSIDE, YOU WILL BE MEDICALLY EXAMINED
AND IF YOU DON'T KNOW THE MEANING OF THE WORD 'GOUT' I SUG-
GEST YOU ASK THE DOCTOR! ARE THERE ANY QUESTIONS?"

The thunderous response, "NO, SERGEANT! echoed between the huts.

"RIGHT! THIS MOB, ATTEN...TION! FALL...OUT!"

Danyluk bounced next to East. They were both taking the small stones off the
bottoms of their feet.

"Thanks very much, Jack. For some reason I've got the feeling this Sergeant
Mack is now going to be my 'buddy' all summer."

"It was the best I could do on such short notice, Moose. Actually, I was close.
Rothie says it's an Eskimo dish, served with grated raw fish, called grout. It was
introduced to them by..."

That's all Danyluk needed. "SERGEANT MACK! YOU ASKED ME A
SERIOUS QUESTION, AND I GAVE YOUSE A SERIOUS ANSWER. I MAY
HAVE BEEN SLIGHTLY OFF IN MY GEOGRAPHICAL DESCRIPTION,
HOWEVER I DID ATTEMPT TO CORRECTLY ANSWER YOUR QUESTION!"

Sergeant Mack placed his large pace-stick under his arm and listened intently.
"Oh, is that right? I didn't know that? How far were you out, geographically?"

Danyluk was on the spot again. He looked at East who whispered, "About six
thousand miles."

In a low voice Moose replied. "About six thousand miles."

"HOW MANY?"

"A MERE SIX THOUSAND MILES, SERGEANT!"

Another gas pain formed on the Sergeant's face as he thought for a moment.
"IS THAT ALL? RIGHT! GET DOWN AND GIVE ME A MERE SIXTY...I'LL
DO THE COUNTING AND I'LL BE SLIGHTLY OFF, AS WELL!"

Jackson was the first one to enter the south end of the building. A long line-up
trailed behind him. After his name was checked off by a clerk, he entered a room
and had his feet, teeth, eyes, ears, and throat checked by medical orderlies and
Nursing Sisters. Moving along to another room, he was asked to remove his shirt
and pants. A medical orderly probed his chest with a stethoscope and then he had
his weight and height checked. Before leaving the building, a medical doctor asked
him to drop his undershorts and cough.

"WHAT'S GOUT, SIR?"

He had caught the doctor by surprise. "Please don't yell in here. Gout? It's a
paroxysmal disease with inflammation of the smaller joints. You don't have gout.
Next!"

"Thank *you*, sir!" Jackson proudly left the north end of the building. After he had walked down the stairs and turned the corner, he spotted Danyluk going in the other end. "Moose, hey, Moose. It's not a food at all. Gout is a disease that effects people with small wangs. If you've got a small joint, you could have gout! It's caused by too much peroxide. You know, the stuff those weirdos dye their hair with?"

Moose's face lit up. "Thanks, Earl. SERGEANT MACK! WHEN I RETURN, I WILL BE IN A BETTER POSITION TO INFORM YOU OF THE REAL MEANING OF THE WORD, GOUT!"

As Danyluk progressed through the 'sausage machine' and finally made it to checkpoint 'cough' it was hard for the cadets outside the hospital not to hear the Medical Officer.

"GOUT? WHAT'S THIS BIG CONCERN ABOUT GOUT? YOU DON'T HAVE GOUT!"

"SIR, I KNOW I DON'T HAVE GOUT, I WAS BORN THIS WAY. WHAT ABOUT THAT POOR BUGGER WHO WAS IN FRONT OF ME? IF ANYONE'S GOT IT, HE HAS, RIGHT?"

"HE DOESN'T HAVE GOUT, EITHER!"

"HE DOESN'T? YOU COULD HAVE FOOLED ME, SIR! EVEN WITH A STIFF, HE'D HAVE GOUT, SIR!"

East was next. After he coughed, he asked, "WHAT'S GOUT, SIR?"

"DON'T YELL IN HERE! WHY IS EVERYBODY YELLING? IT'S A PAROXYSMAL DISEASE WITH INFLAMMATION OF THE SMALLER JOINTS! WHAT'S THAT? NO, YOU'RE WRONG YOUNG MAN, I DON'T CARE WHAT YOUR FRIEND CADET ROTHSTEIN SAID! IT ISN'T FOOD! NEXT!"

While six of the Musketeers were putting on their boots, they heard the Medical Officer screaming to his administrative assistant.

"CAPTAIN SHORT, WHAT THE HELL IS GOING ON IN THERE? WHY IS EVERY CADET ASKING ME WHAT GOUT IS?"

"SIR, THEY'RE NOT TALKING ABOUT THE MEDICAL TERMINOLOGY, THEY'RE TALKING ABOUT SOME SORT OF SOUP OR STEW MADE WITH TURKEY AND BEANS IN THE MIDDLE EAST!"

"YOU MEAN THERE IS A MEAL CALLED GOUT?"

"APPARENTLY, SIR! THAT'S WHAT THESE CADETS ARE SAYING."

The Medical Officer's head appeared out the window. "Where's that boy? Oh, there you are. I may have been wrong. Your friend may be right." His head then disappeared, but not his voice. "JUST BLOODY-WELL COUGH AND DON'T ASK ME WHAT GOUT IS! WHAT'S THAT? NO, YOU HAVEN'T GOT IT, AND I DON'T HAVE TIME FOR A QUICK GAME OF POKER!"

By the time all of the cadets had been through the MIR (Medical Inspection Room) the doctor was asked about gout, 437 times. Although he didn't know it at the time, it would be the last time he would prescribe two aspirins and a glass of water to Sergeant Mack of the Royal Canadian Regiment, as he had the day before. Sergeant Mack had gotten his own back...or, as 'they' say, 'killed two birds with one stone.' Sergeants have wonderful ways of getting even when they are given the wrong diagnosis. The Sergeant took the two aspirins, but to be on the safe side, he made a trip to see a civilian doctor in town. It was then that he was informed he had symptoms of gout.

To this very day, the Medical Officer actually believes there are two meanings to the word gout. But of course there aren't. Jack East was thinking of the word 'kraut' as in sauerkraut and everyone knows, except the doctor, that sauerkraut is not an Eskimo meal. As far as Danyluk, Jackson, and hundreds of others were concerned, gout described something else entirely and the word was about to be used extensively throughout the summer. Although Danyluk tried a few times to explain to the Sergeant the real meaning of the word gout, the Sergeant took pity on him and refused to listen. It's doubtful whether Danyluk could have completed six thousand pushups anyway.

"NOW THAT THAT'S OVER WITH, DOES ANYONE HAVE ANY QUESTIONS?"

"NO, SERGEANT!"

"RIGHT! WE'RE NOW GOING TO BOARD THE TRUCKS AGAIN AND DRIVE OVER TO THE UPPER CAMP WHERE YOU WILL RECEIVE YOUR SUMMER CLOTHING AND EQUIPMENT! IS THAT CLEAR?"

"YES, SERGEANT!"

"NOW, I WANT YOU TO GET YOUR JOINING INSTRUCTIONS READY TO HAND IN. NOW REMEMBER, GENTLEMEN, AND I USE THE TERM LOOSELY, I AM THE ONLY ONE WHO WILL DO THE TALKING. YOU WILL DO THE LISTENING! IS THAT CLEAR?"

"YES, SERGEANT!"

"GOOD, THIS MOB, ATTEN...TION! MOVE TO THE RIGHT IN THREES, RIGHT TURN! BY THE LEFT..." The Sergeant stopped his order and walked over to a 72nd Seaforth cadet who was whispering to his friend.

"WHAT DID YOU SAY TO HIM?"

The cadet appeared a little nervous, but he had his chin up and was ready to take on the world. "I, er, I mentioned a new word to him, Sergeant."

"I CAN'T HEAR YOU!"

"I MENTIONED A NEW WORD TO HIM, SERGEANT!" the cadet replied, pointing to his friend, Russell.

"WAS IT GOUT?"

"NO, SERGEANT! IT WAS PROPHYLACTIC PAINT. WE'VE GOTTA REQUEST THE STUFF WHEN WE HAND IN OUR JOINING INSTRUCTIONS!"

"PROPHYLACTIC PAINT? WHY IN THE WORLD WOULD YOU REQUEST THAT?"

"SO WE CAN COVER UP THE MARKS ON THE LEFT-HANDED SCREWDRIVER AND THE SKY-HOOK, SERGEANT!"

There was laughter throughout the ranks, but the straight-faced 'life insurance salesman' and his *friend* weren't laughing. Prophylactic is a big and serious word and he was thankful the good Warrant Officer had suggested the 'advice.'

The Sergeant slowly walked over to the staid cadet. A smile, not a full smile, just a part of one appeared on the Sergeant's face.

"Well, yes, you just may need it." But, just between you, your friend, and me, who asked you to get it?"

"CADET WARRANT OFFICER JOHNSTON, SERGEANT!"

A full smile now crossed the Sergeant's face. "He did, did he? Is this Cadet Warrant Johnston here in this little group?"

"YES, SERGEANT!"

"Could you point out this *walking dictionary* for me?"

"CERTAINLY, SERGEANT! THAT'S WARRANT JOHNSTON RIGHT THERE. HE'S BEEN TRYING TO HELP US OUT, ISN'T THAT RIGHT, RUSSELL?"

Russell nodded. "I'M IN HIS SQUADRON IN VANCOUVER, SERGEANT AND HE'S ONE OF THE BEST."

"Oh, so that's him there? Isn't that wonderful? Right there? One of the best, eh? Well, thank you, boys."

Cadet Warrant Johnston had turned to his right like everyone else. His back was to the Sergeant, however, every nerve-ending in his body could feel the full impact of the Sergeant's eyes scanning him like an x-ray machine.

Sergeant Mack marched smartly to Johnston's side, and halted.

"THIS MOB...BY THE LEFT, QUICK MARCH! LEFT, RIGHT, LEFT, RIGHT! GET YOUR CHINS UP! YOU! YES, YOU! GET YOUR SHOULDERS BACK, MAN! YOU LOOK LIKE ONE OF THOSE HOMO BALLET DANCERS! ISN'T THAT RIGHT...JOHNSTON?"

The Sergeant had now 'introduced' himself to Johnston without even looking at him. Johnston's only worry now was how formal the 'introduction' was going to get.

"YES, SERGEANT, HE DOES!"

"LEFT, RIGHT, LEFT, RIGHT...GET YOUR ARMS UP THERE! DON'T DRAG YOUR BAG, THAT MAN! Don't agree with me on everything I say, Johnston. You didn't see him, I did. Isn't that right?"

"YES, SERGEANT!"

"DO YOU KNOW HOW TO SPELL, 'BALLET,' JOHNSTON?"

Johnston's eyes reached for the sky. Not his head, just his eyes. "YES, SERGEANT! I THINK SO!"

"Wonderful. That's just bloomin' wonderful! LEFT, RIGHT LEFT, RIGHT!"

The ride to the upper camp on the other side of the highway was bumpy and dusty. Like the rides of years past, dust covered the cadets from head to toe. For those who were sweating, it was worse because the grit became caked on their faces, arms, and hands.

"HEY, YOUSE PONGOES SWEATIN' IN KILTS ARE GONNA HAVE MUD ALL OVER YOUR BALLS!" Danyluk remarked.

A Canadian Scottish Cadet Senior NCO didn't appreciate Moose's statement.

"I THINK YOU'VE GOT IT ALL WRONG! UNLIKE YOU SLOBS IN THE DUKES, WE SCOTTISH DON'T SWEAT, WE PERSPIRE!"

Danyluk joined in the laughter which rang out from unseen faces, lost in clouds of dust.

When the vehicles arrived at the large supply-stores hangar and the cadets jumped down, other trucks were leaving and cadets were all over the place. The noise was deafening.

"FORM THREE RANKS...QUICKLY NOW, QUICKLY! YOU...GET YOUR FINGER OUT OF YOUR NOSE AND FALL IN!"

The cadet the Sergeant was looking at didn't have his finger up his nose, but Sergeants have a way with words that starts everyone moving quickly.

"PLACE YOUR BAGS NEXT TO YOU ON YOUR RIGHT SIDE AND LAY YOUR TUNICS AND TIES ON THEM!" The Sergeant then moved in front of a cadet from the Rocky Mountain Rangers and said, "ARE YOU THE ONE WHO ASKED WHICH SIDE IS YOUR RIGHT SIDE?"

The embarrassed cadet didn't know what to say. "ER, NO, NOT ME, SERGEANT!" He gained some control of himself when he noticed another gas pain on the Sergeant's face. "IT WAS THAT GUY THERE IN THE BRITISH COLUMBIA DRAGOONS!"

The Sergeant chuckled, then took his pace-stick out from under his armpit. "GET YOUR JOINING INSTRUCTIONS READY! WHEN I FALL YOU OUT, YOU WILL GO TO A TABLE THAT HAS THE INITIALS OF YOUR LAST NAME! IS THAT CLEAR? GIVE YOUR FIRST NAME LAST, AND YOUR LAST NAME FIRST!"

"YES, SERGEANT!"

"WHERE'S THAT WALKING DICTIONARY, WARRANT OFFICER JOHNSTON?"

"Here, Sergeant."

"WHERE THE HELL IS HERE?"

"HERE, SERGEANT...IN THE REAR RANK!"

"AH YES, THERE YOU ARE! RIGHT! YOU COME WITH ME!"

Johnston had a bit of a smile on his face as he *crept* out and stood to attention in front of the Sergeant. Before he marched Johnston into the hangar, the Sergeant called the rest to attention and had them fall out.

Within minutes, Johnston was back, lining up at 'his' table. In his right hand, he carried a large gallon paint tin. The label read, PROPHYLACTIC PAINT, and the liquid in the tin was very heavy.

"YOU'RE IN CHARGE OF THAT TODAY, JOHNSTON, AND IT TAKES A LOT OF RESPONSIBILITY TO HANDLE THE JOB. WHERE YOU GO, THE TIN GOES, IS THAT CLEAR?"

"YES, SERGEANT!"

Laughter echoed throughout the area. Sergeant Mack even had a smile on his face, as did Johnston. But Johnston's smile wouldn't last long though, as he found out later.

Wayne leaned over to Douglas. "Can you believe that? They must have gotten fed up with cadets requesting it last year. They've made up a tin."

The grin on Douglas' face was broad. "You mean, tins." He pointed over to another group. "Those three just came out, each carrying one as well."

Wayne took off his glasses and peered through the crowd. Three cadets in a row had come out of the large hangar carrying all their gear, plus big heavy containers of the 'sexy' stuff.

"You and your big mouth," he heard one 'painter' say to the other.

It took over an hour to issue the necessary uniforms and equipment the cadets would require for the next six weeks. The storesmen who 'threw' the items at the cadets must have had strong throats because not one of them was hoarse from all of their yelling.

"BOOTS, AMMUNITION, BLACK, FOR THE USE OF!"

"SHIRTS, KHAKI, COTTON, FOR THE USE OF!"

"PANTS, KHAKI, COTTON, FOR THE USE OF!"

"PUTTEES, WOOL, KHAKI, FOR THE USE OF!"

"BLANKETS, WOOL, MARK TWO, FOR THE USE OF!"

"WASH-BASIN, STAINLESS STEEL, MARK FOUR, FOR THE USE OF!"

East was furious. "They've issued me a new pair of boots. I don't need new boots, my boots are the best here."

Douglas agreed, but understood why another pair was necessary. "Jack, I told you before we left, you've got rubber soles on your boots. Those are tank boots; they want leather soles here."

Jack was really peeved. "Jesus, now I've got to iron and bone these. Look at the size of the bloody pepples on these boots. It'll take me weeks to have them looking like my other pair."

Danyluk laughed. Not too long ago, he had taken his boots to a shoemaker and had had them 'built up' with three extra soles with hob-nails and blakies. "Ya shoulda took 'em to my shoemaker, Jacky."

"How the hell could I do that, Moose? That God damned Cunningham's got all my money?"

Moose continued. "Yeah, I know he has. If Cunningham was a storesman, he'd say, "MONEY, EAST'S, PAPER, EASY, FOR THE USE OF!""

"Oh, go screw yourself, Moose!"

The ride back to the lower camp went quickly and when the trucks finally stopped outside barracks B-33, dust and dirt covered the ponchos and blankets the cadets had used to 'load' their clothing and equipment. Within minutes they were formed up in three ranks on the road, and the trucks left immediately, with Sergeant Mack.

Instantly, a giant of a man appeared from within the black-tarpapered H-hut. He was immaculately dressed in a bush uniform, and like Sergeant Mack, he *also* carried a large black pace-stick under his left arm.

"WELL, WELL, WELL!" he 'commented' as he walked down the steps and stood in front of approximately 130 weary, dust-covered 'Santa Clauses.'

"WHO SAID YOU COULD STAND EASY?"

Sergeant Beckford grinned as he walked the entire distance of the front of the 'mob's' first rank, his eyes pausing for a fraction of a second on those he knew.

"THIS GROUP...STAND EASY!" he ordered, before he marched to the centre of the front rank.

"MY NAME IS SERGEANT BECKFORD! MY REGIMENT IS THE PRINCESS PATRICIA'S CANADIAN LIGHT INFANTRY. YOU WILL REFER TO ME AS SERGEANT, NOT SIR!

"I AM LIKE ALL OTHER SERGEANTS...I AM NEVER WRONG! ONCE IN A WHILE I AM INCORRECT...VERY RARELY, MIND YOU, BUT I AM NEVER WRONG!

"YOU WILL NOTICE MY DRESS. THIS UNIFORM HAS BEEN SOAPED, STARCHED, AND IRONED BY MYSELF. IT HAS TAKEN ME THOUSANDS OF HOURS TO GET MY BOOTS LOOKING LIKE THIS! THOSE WERE MY OFF-DUTY HOURS. ALSO DURING MY OFF-DUTY HOURS, I PREPARE LECTURES, I STUDY, I READ ORDERS...ALL ORDERS, I CHECK ON MY MEN, I CHECK ON THEIR QUARTERS, I READ THEIR FILES, I UNDERSTAND THEIR HABITS, THEIR STRENGTHS, THEIR WEAKNESSES, THEIR DESIRES! YOU SEE, THAT IS MY JOB. WHEN ONE OF MY MEN HAS A PROBLEM, THAT PROBLEM IS ALSO MINE. WHEN PEOPLE DON'T PASS TESTS, I HAVEN'T TAUGHT THEM PROPERLY. WHEN A 'BAD APPLE' REARS HIS UGLY HEAD AND PERFORMS ACTIONS THAT ARE CONTRARY TO GOOD JUDGMENT AND DISCI-PLINE, I HAVEN'T MADE HIM UNDERSTAND WHAT IS EXPECTED OF

HIM. DO YOU SEE THESE THREE STRIPES?"

"Yes, Sergeant!"

"NOT GOOD ENOUGH! I CAN'T HEAR YOU!"

"YES, SERGEANT!"

"EACH STRIPE REPRESENTS ONE OF MY THREE DEGREES. YES, I HAVE THREE DEGREES AND I INTEND TO EVEN FURTHER MY EDUCATION! I RECEIVED MY B.A. AT LIDDELL, MY MASTERS AT WARRINGTON, AND MY DOCTORATE IN PHILOSOPHY, AT PROUSE! SO YOU SEE, I AM AN EDUCATED MAN...AND CONTRARY TO WHAT SOME OF YOU ARE NOW THINKING...MY PARENTS WERE MARRIED!"

Many chuckles filtered throughout the ranks, as the Sergeant continued.

"IN SHORT, MY JOB AS A SERGEANT IS TO PROPERLY TRAIN YOU PEOPLE. NOTICE I USED THE WORD *PROPERLY*? PROPERLY IS A VERY IMPORTANT WORD AS FAR AS I AM CONCERNED. IF I DO NOT DO MY JOB SKILLFULLY, YOU WON'T EITHER. IF I DO NOT SET AN EXAMPLE, NEITHER WILL YOU! IF I TREAT YOU UNFAIRLY, YOU WILL DO THE SAME TO OTHER PEOPLE UNDER YOUR COMMAND.

"SO YOU SEE, I HAVE A VERY BIG TASK CUT OUT FOR ME. ONE THAT I DO NOT TAKE LIGHTLY AND AM WELL LOOKING FORWARD TO!

"NOW, WHEN I ASK IF THERE ARE ANY QUESTIONS, THOSE OF YOU WHO HAVE A QUESTION WILL SMARTLY SNAP TO ATTENTION. THAT MEANS YOU WILL PICK YOUR LEFT FOOT SIX INCHES OFF THE GROUND, TOES POINTING DOWN AND PARALLEL WITH THE LEFT KNEE, AND YOU WILL SLAM YOUR FOOT DOWN, FEET AT A THIRTY-DEGREE ANGLE. AT THAT TIME, YOUR ARMS WILL BE STIFFLY BY YOUR SIDES, ALL FINGERS TOUCHING YOUR PANTS, THUMB ON THE SEAM. THERE WILL BE NO DAYLIGHT BETWEEN THE ARMS AND YOUR BODY. YOUR CHIN WILL BE UP, YOUR CHEST OUT AND YOUR EYES WILL LOCK ON AN OBJECT DIRECTLY AHEAD OF YOU AT EYE LEVEL. I DON'T LIKE TO SEE EYES MOVE. AT THAT POINT, YOU WILL EXTEND YOUR LEFT FOREARM SO THAT IT IS EVEN WITH YOUR WAIST AND PARALLEL TO THE GROUND. YOUR FINGERS WILL BE EXTENDED, THUMB ON TOP, THE 'CHOP' PORTION OF YOUR HAND LEVEL WITH THE GROUND! ARE THERE ANY QUESTIONS?"

One cadet carried out the action the Sergeant had 'suggested.'

Sergeant Beckford moved to a position in front of the 'man.'

"YES, DANYLUK?"

Danyluk was really proud that the Sergeant had remembered his name. "SERGEANT, I..."

"DID YOU MOVE YOUR EYES, DANYLUK?"

"ER, I DON'T THINK..."

"YES YOU DID! DON'T MOVE THEM AGAIN! I DON'T EVEN WANT TO SEE YOU BLINK! IS THAT CLEAR?"

"YES, SERGEANT!"

"NOW, WHAT IS YOUR QUESTION?"

Danyluk's stance and eyes were perfect. "SERGEANT, I HAVE NEVER HEARD OF THE UNIVERSITIES YOU JUST MENTIONED!"

Beckford was now nose to nose with Danyluk. "WHAT UNIVERSITIES ARE YOU TALKING ABOUT? I NEVER MENTIONED ANYTHING ABOUT UNI-

VERSITIES!"

"YOU DID, SERGEANT! YOU SAID, LIDDELL, WARRINGTON, AND PROUSE!"

"I DID NOT MENTION UNIVERSITIES! ARE YOU SAYING I'M WRONG, DANYLUK?"

"NO, SERGEANT...PERHAPS A LITTLE INCORRECT?"

"NEVER, DANYLUK! THOSE WERE NAMES OF INDIVIDUALS THAT I TRAINED! PARTICULAR PEOPLE WHO REQUIRED, SHOULD I SAY, A LITTLE EXTRA ATTENTION! SO MUCH ATTENTION THAT EACH ONE EARNED ME A DEGREE! YOU ASSUMED, DIDN'T YOU DANYLUK?"

"I, er, well, DAMN IT, um..."

A small gas pain appeared on Beckford's face. "IF I'VE TOLD YOU ONCE, I'VE TOLD YOU A THOUSAND TIMES, NEVER ASSUME! IS THAT CLEAR?"

"YES, SERGEANT!"

The Sergeant noticed East whispering to Jackson. "WHAT WAS THAT, EAST?"

East snapped to attention, eyes to his front, arms placed stiffly by his sides. "Nothing important, Sergeant!"

"THEN IF IT'S NOT IMPORTANT, YOU CAN SHARE IT WITH US!"

East started fidgeting and mumbled something.

"SPEAK UP, MAN!"

"I SAID, DANYLUK ALSO HAS A DEGREE, SERGEANT!"

All eyes were on East, including Danyluk's. Even though he was standing at attention, Moose gave East the finger, and moved his mouth without making a sound. East read his lips. Silently, Danyluk had bellowed, "YOU PONGO!"

The Sergeant's curiosity had been aroused. "HE DOES, DOES HE? AND JUST WHAT DOES HE HAVE A DEGREE IN?"

"HE HAS HIS MASTERS IN BATION, SERGEANT!"

Although other cadet companies were marching and driving by, the sounds of laughter originating from Alpha Company drowned out any other racket. East and Danyluk both winced; East when he screamed it out, and Danyluk when he heard his name being divulged by his friend.

Sergeant Beckford grasped the moment. "MASTERS IN BATION? SO, YOU TOOK A REPETITIVE, HIGHLY STIMULATING COURSE, DID YOU, DANYLUK?"

Danyluk stood to attention and glared at East before smiling and answering the Sergeant.

"WELL, ER...I, ER...I PERSONALLY FOUND THE COURSE BORING, SERGEANT, BUT HE...!" Danyluk glanced at East. "BUT OTHERS, SEEM TO HAVE THOROUGHLY ENJOYED IT. EAST IN PARTICULAR, SERGEANT. HE EVEN TOOK THE SCHOOL'S MEN'S MOTTO TO HEART."

"MEN'S MOTTO? WHAT WAS THE SCHOOL'S MEN'S MOTTO?"

Moose cleared his throat. "Our men's motto was, E wetnius cum plurdicinus."

Both a frown and a gas pain surfaced on Sergeant Beckford's face, when he asked, "Oh, we have a Latin scholar with us. SPEAK UP! WHAT IS IT AGAIN?"

"E WETNIUS CUM PLURDICINUS, SERGEANT!"

Which means?"

Danyluk mumbled something and stood at ease.

"SPEAK UP, MAN! WHAT DOES IT MEAN IN THE QUEEN'S ENG-LISH?"

Danyluk smiled, snapped to attention again and filled his lungs before he spoke. "IF YOU CAN'T LICK IT, DON'T DICK IT!"

Sergeant Beckford's gas pain instantly transformed into a roaring laugh as he motioned Danyluk to stand at ease. Almost all members of Alpha Company were bent over in laughter. Many other comments were *thrown* at East, who was now red-faced and sorry he had said anything in the first place.

Sergeant Beckford walked away, but returned suddenly and stood in front of Danyluk. "WAS THERE A FEMALE MOTTO, DANYLUK?"

Once again Moose snapped to attention. "YES, SERGEANT, BUT ONLY EAST CAN REMEMBER IT!" He had now got his own back on East.

The Sergeant moved in front of East who was visibly nervous.

"AND THE FEMALE MOTTO, MR. EAST? COME ON, WHAT DO THE GIRLS SAY?"

East came to attention and spoke softly. "A mufibulus et stufinius, Sergeant!"

"LOUDER, MAN!"

"A MUFIBULUS ET STUFINIUS!"

"WHICH MEANS?"

East filled his lungs before he released, "IF THEY WON'T MUFF IT, DON'T LET 'EM STUFF IT!"

Howls of laughter filled the road. Sergeant Beckford had tears running down his face.

When East stood at ease and stood easy, Beckford slowly shook his head, winked and offered his right hand, which Jack accepted. After they shook hands, Sergeant Beckford walked to the centre front and studied the happy faces of the incomplete company of cadets in front of him.

"NOW IT'S TIME TO BE SERIOUS. NEARLY ALL OF YOU HAVE ATTENDED VERNON BEFORE! THEREFORE, ON BEHALF OF THE COM-MANDING OFFICER, WELCOME BACK! THE FEW OF YOU WHO HAVEN'T BEEN HERE HAVE SOME CATCHING UP TO DO! HOWEVER, YOU'RE IN FINE COMPANY, THEREFORE, YOU SHOULDN'T HAVE TOO MANY PROBLEMS. BEFORE WE..." Sergeant Beckford was rudely cut off by the voice of singer and movie star, Doris Day.

"WHATEVER WILL BE, WILL BE. THE FUTURE'S NOT OURS TO SEE, QUE SERA, SERA. WHEN I WAS JUST, A LITTLE GIRL, I ASKED MY MOTHER..."

The voice was reverberating from Danyluk's duffel bag. All eyes were on Moose who now had his bag open and was flinging clothes out, trying to find his radio. Beckford said nothing, he just casually observed Danyluk's panic and predicament.

After receiving a few direct hits, the radio quit.

Blushing, Danyluk apologized. "Er, sorry, er, Sergeant. I..er..."

"THAT'S QUITE ALL RIGHT, MR. DANYLUK. THAT'S THE FIRST TIME IN MANY YEARS I'VE SEEN YOUR FACE SO RED. I THINK THE LAST TIME I HAD THE OPPORTUNITY TO WITNESS IT WAS WHEN YOU WERE PULLED INTO A SHITTER!"

Everyone broke up, even Danyluk, but not before he gave Cunningham a dirty look.

Sergeant Beckford continued. "BEFORE WE ENTER THE BARRACKS, I HAVE SOME INFORMATION FOR YOU. THE CAMP COMMANDING OFFICER, BRIGADIER KITCHING, HAS CANCELED ALL WEEKEND LEAVE FOR THIS COMPANY. OTHER COMPANIES WILL BE GOING DOWNTOWN TODAY, HOWEVER, YOU PEOPLE WILL BE WORKING."

The sound of sighs and groans came from all directions.

Sergeant Beckford's face turned stern. "I DON'T EXPECT TO HEAR ANY COMPLAINTS OR SOUNDS OF DISAPPOINTMENT! THIS IS ALPHA COMPANY, WE'RE TOUGH, WE CAN TAKE ANYTHING THAT'S DISHED OUT!

"THE CADETS FROM THE PRAIRIE PROVINCES WILL BE HERE TOMORROW MORNING. APPROXIMATELY 63 OF THEM WILL JOIN YOU AND THEY WILL BE EVENLY SPREAD AMONG FOUR PLATOONS.

"NOW, WHEN I FALL YOU OUT, YOU WILL WALK, NOT RUN, INTO THE BARRACKS AND YOU WILL FIND THE BUNK WITH YOUR NAME ON IT. UNDER NO CIRCUMSTANCES WILL YOU CHANGE BUNKS, OR MAKE YOUR BEDS. THE NUMBER WRITTEN UNDER YOUR NAME IS THE PLATOON YOU WILL BE IN. YOU WILL LAY YOUR GEAR ON YOUR BEDS, HAVE A GOOD WASH, COMB YOUR HAIR, AND IN YOUR OWN TIME, HEAD OVER TO THE KITCHEN, WHICH IS RIGHT ...THERE." The Sergeant pointed his pace stick to the location of the nearby kitchen.

"YOU WILL CHANGE INTO YOUR P.T. SHORTS, T-SHIRTS, SOCKS, AND RUNNING SHOES! AT 1400 HOURS, YOU WILL BE FORMED UP IN THREE RANKS ON THE ROAD SOUTH OF THIS BUILDING. THAT ONE...THERE, IN CASE SOME OF YOU AREN'T TOO CERTAIN, OR YOU'VE TAKEN A SEA CADET OR AIR CADET NAVIGATION COURSE!"

The company's laughter was loud, but not for long. Three other Regular Force Sergeants and eight Regular Force Corporals came out of B-33. The first Sergeant was small and his name tag read, SIMPSON. The second Sergeant looked like he had won the Second World War, single-handedly. Everyone knew him 'well.' His name tag read, MACK. The third Sergeant was of Native extraction. He looked mean and lean and his name tag read, PREST.

The eleven sets of eyes scanned the company. Each of them had the knack of making every cadet think he was looking just at him.

Danyluk winced, so did Johnston, who was still holding his can of prophylactic paint.

"Jesus, if we get stuck in *his* platoon..." Danyluk said, referring to Sergeant Mack. "... my arm muscles are never gonna to be the same."

East slapped Moose on the back. "Look at it this way, you could also end up with Simpson. You know how he loves those early morning jaunts."

Danyluk rolled his eyes. The choice of either one was hell, no matter which way it turned out.

"THIS IS SERGEANT SIMPSON, I FEEL HE NEEDS NO INTRODUCTION! AND DIRECTLY FROM THE GLASS HOUSE, THIS IS SERGEANT MACK! SERGEANT PREST HERE IS FROM THE CANADIAN GUARDS!"

As Sergeant Beckford pointed out the names of the Corporals, whispering passed throughout the ranks. Particularly noticeable were the words, "Glass House." Everyone present had heard of that world-famous Canadian military prison.

"I knew it! That guy's an ex-meathead," muttered East. "He may be in the

Royal Canadian Regiment now, but at one time he wore a red cap. Look at the tat-toos on his arms. I betcha he had the prisoners do 'em."

Mack, Simpson and Prest all wore smiles, and this made Wayne suggest to Douglas that they weren't smiles, just signs that some undigested breakfast bacon was creating a little *wind*.

"The only time I ever saw Simpson smile was when Jackson pulled Moose into the shitter. Even then, I wasn't too certain whether it was a held-back-burp, a slight heart attack, or he was trying to get the skin on his face to crack."

Douglas and those within earshot chuckled.

"ALL RIGHT, SETTLE DOWN! YOU PEOPLE WILL HAVE THE HON-OUR OF MEETING THESE KNOWLEDGEABLE GENTLEMEN AFTER LUNCH. RIGHT! ALPHA COMPANY...ATTEN...TION! FALL...OUT!"

Cadets entered building B-33 from the centre front doors. For the next ten minutes, mayhem ensued as they tried to find their bunks.

Cunningham was one of the first to enter, with Rothstein right behind. "CHRIST, THIS JOINT STINKS AND MOOSE HASN'T EVEN OPENED HIS KIT-BAG YET, ISN'T THAT RIGHT, ROTHIE?"

The smell was a combination of stale air, mothballs, Sergeants' Soap, shoe polish, Silvo, Brasso, and old wooden floors which had retained the odor of every foot that had ever walked on it.

Rothstein dropped his gear and pinched his nose. "IT SMELLS LIKE SOME-ONE DIED IN THEIR SLEEP AND THEY JUST LEFT HIM!"

Cunningham grinned and smacked his friend on the back. "BERGIE TOLD ME LAST YEAR THAT WHEN FLIES ENTERED THEIR HUT, THEY DIDN'T HEAD TO THE JON OR THE GARBAGE CANS. INSTEAD, THEY FLEW INSTANTLY TO HIS AND MOOSE'S BUNKS. APPARENTLY ALL THE CADETS IN THE IMMEDIATE VICINITY CHIPPED IN TO BUY FLYPAPER WHICH WAS HUNG FROM THE CEILING ABOVE THEIR BEDS."

In seconds, Jackson had found their area. "HEY GUYS, OVER HERE, WE'RE ALL TOGETHER IN NUMBER ONE PLATOON!"

Slowly the seven Musketeers dribbled in. Jackson was right, they had been positioned in the centre of the northeast wing of the H-hut, on the east side. Danyluk's lower bunk was by the large middle doors. Above him was Cunningham. The next two bunks were for Douglas and Wayne with Wayne up-top. Next to them were East and Rothstein, with Rothstein in the upper bunk, and finally, Jackson and a cadet named Simon from the Irish Fusiliers. Jackson had the upper bunk.

Even though he had to bunk with an Irish cadet, Jackson was ecstatic. "I'M FREE...FREE! JUST THINK, WHEN I GET UP IN THE MIDDLE OF THE NIGHT TO TAKE A LEAK, I WON'T HAVE TO MOVE THE FLYPAPER OUT OF MY WAY."

Moose smiled, but he understood the message. "OH, SCREW YOU, EARL. YOU KNOW AS WELL AS WE DO THAT YOU AND EAST HAD JUST AS MANY FLIES. YOUR BARRACK BOX WAS ALWAYS FULL OF FOOD!"

East walked over to Danyluk. "Oh yeah? At least our flies were only fruitflies. You had the big suckers. Jesus, when they got stuck on that paper, I could hear them all night."

Wayne opened his window. "HEY, WE CAN ALMOST LOOK INTO THE OFFICERS' MESS FROM HERE! ALL THOSE LUSCIOUS NURSING SIS-TERS SIPPING ON ICE-COLD DRINKS."

Douglas unrolled his mattress and dumped all of his kit. He then grabbed his towel, soap, toothpaste, brush, and comb and headed for the centre portion of the building containing the sinks, shower room, toilets, and clothes-drying room. Cadets were entering the area from both wings. Soon, the sinks were jammed with cadets, the showers were occupied, every toilet was flushing and a cadet who hadn't yet learned his lesson had left a full load of washing in the whining washing machine.

After they cleaned themselves up, the seven changed into their P.T. strip and walked over to the cadet kitchen, which was also an old H-hut. Folding-style military tables lined both sides of each of the wings' and the cooking area was in the middle. The menu on the blackboard read: TOMATO SOUP, CORNED BEEF AND CABBAGE, HOT DOGS OR CHICKEN SANDWICHES. Beverages were: MILK, TEA, COFFEE, APPLE JUICE OR WATER.

"I really love this scoff," stated East, with his mouth full. I didn't think I'd ever get used to powdered tomatoes, but they grow on ya."

Wayne was on him like a bee. "It's not the soup you like, it's the saltpetre they put in it. When are you going to learn, Jack? Haven't you ever wondered why you never get a hard-on at Vernon?"

Moose's ears perked up as he stuffed a big piece of cabbage into his mouth. "You wouldn't get me touching the stuff! If a man can't get a hard-on, he may as well just roll up and die. Could you imagine what the world would be like if nobody ever got a boner?"

Jackson laughed. "You don't need a hard-on, Moose. You can slip it to them soft and they'd never know the difference."

East finished swallowing. "SPEAK FOR YOURSELF, BANKS! IT'S NOT THE SALTPETRE THAT STOPS A HARD-ON, IT'S THE SALT TABLETS THEY GIVE YA! YOU'RE THE ONE WHO EATS 'EM LIKE CANDY!"

Although Wayne was having a laugh attack, he wouldn't let up. "BULLLSSH-HIT I DO! I ALWAYS GIVE MINE TO MOOSE! HE'S THE ONE WHO SWEATS LIKE A HORSE! TELL HIM MOOSE!"

Danyluk stopped eating and assumed a solemn look. "SON OF A BITCH! BANKS, YOU ROTTER! NO WONDER I CAN ONLY MANAGE FOURTEEN INCHES! I ALWAYS WONDERED WHAT HAPPENED TO THE OTHER FIVE! I THOUGHT IT WAS THE HEAT UP HERE. I READ A BOOK THAT SAID TOO MUCH SUN CAN RUIN A GUY'S SEX LIFE AND REDUCE A WANG'S SIZE!"

Laughter rattled the table as Danyluk continued eating, keeping a straight face. When it died down and the last grin disappeared, six faces filled with curiosity and doubt glanced at Moose. In the silence, thoughts of total disbelief entered the heads of the other Musketeers. Then like magic, they started nodding to each other, because in Moose's case, anything was possible.

Rothstein changed the subject. "Have you guys noticed something is different this year? I don't know what it is, but there's a change in the military atmosphere."

"Yeah, I've got the same feeling," replied Jackson. "I don't feel as uptight as I have in other years."

The rest agreed and Douglas offered his thoughts on the subject. "Is it possible we've seen the worst, as we know it? This is our fourth year; take a look at the faces of the younger cadets in their first or second year, they look like we used to feel."

"You mean we know the ropes so much that we can catch whatever they throw at us, Doug?" asked East.

"Yeah, I think so. But we can't let our guard down because we all know Sergeant Beckford had a hand in planning this course. You all know, as well as I do, that he insists on improving training. How many times has he told us, 'Don't continually repeat teaching the same things. Always introduce new subjects, that way, you'll constantly create interest.'"

Cunningham sat back on the hind legs of his chair, just barely touching the table to keep himself balanced. "Other than drill, you mean?"

Douglas nodded. "Of course. There's no such thing as perfect drill. We've seen the Queen's Own Rifles on parade. They're near-perfect, but 98 percent is not 100 percent. So, Rothie, I think we know how to handle ourselves in a proper military manner, but I believe the real work is about to begin."

Danyluk's eyes looked preoccupied as he scanned the table for the pepper. "Damn it, I miss Bergie. I'll miss his friendship, his advice and his...his..."

The 'teeterer' tottered his chair forward. "His money?"

"Not his money, Cunningham, you pongo. Christ, is that all you ever think of? I bunked with him for three years in a row. It won't be the same without him. Where the hell's the pepper?"

Wayne handed it to him. "Sure it will, Moose. We were lucky to have him with us during our first year, but *we're* the Bergies now. In three weeks, we'll be training the cadets in Senior Leaders. Remember?...the example we set, they'll set."

Douglas patted Wayne on the shoulder. "Right on, Wayne, that's exactly right. Also, we've got to watch out for some of the bullies that managed to get into Senior Leader Instructors. There aren't too many, but they'll be among us."

"WHO'S COMING WITH ME FOR THIRDS?" called East. "I THINK I'LL HAVE...!"

East didn't get the chance to finish. Rothstein and Jackson pulled him up, handed him his plates, and guided him to the scraping can. Shortly, he found himself marching with the other six, back to B-33.

"ALPHA COMPANY...ATTEN...TION! COMPANY, STAND AT...EASE! STAND EASY! RIGHT...PAY ATTENTION HERE!" Sergeant Beckford paused to look at a cadet with no headdress on. "YOU! WHERE'S YOUR PITH-HELMET?"

"I, ER...IN THE BARRACKS, SERGEANT!"

"WELL, FROM NOW ON, YOU WEAR IT UNTIL YOU'RE TOLD OTH-ERWISE, IS THAT CLEAR?"

"YES, SERGEANT!"

"RIGHT! AS YOU KNOW, ALPHA COMPANY HAS FOUR PLATOONS. THESE ARE THE FIRST PLATOONS IN CAMP...ONE THROUGH FOUR. BRAVO COMPANY HAS PLATOONS NUMBERED FIVE THROUGH EIGHT, AND SO ON WITH CHARLIE COMPANY, ETCETERA. THERE WILL BE 1400 CADETS IN CAMP THIS SUMMER, AND YOU PEOPLE WILL SET THE EXAMPLE FOR ALL OF THEM.

"TOMORROW, THE CADETS WHO WILL FORM THE BALANCE OF OUR COMPANY WILL ARRIVE FROM THE PRAIRIES. AT THAT TIME, I WILL BRIEF ALL OF YOU ON WHAT IS EXPECTED OF YOU, AS WELL AS COURSE CONTENT. MY PLATOON IS NUMBER ONE PLATOON!"

A small cheer rose up from One Platoon.

"OH, YOU WON'T BE CHEERING FOR LONG! SERGEANT SIMPSON

HAS NUMBER TWO PLATOON, SERGEANT MACK HAS NUMBER THREE PLATOON AND SERGEANT PREST IS THE PLATOON SERGEANT OF NUMBER FOUR PLATOON. IS EVERYONE WITH ME SO FAR?"

Danyluk stood to attention, arm extended.

"YES, DANYLUK?"

"SERGEANT, WHO GETS US UP IN THE MORNING?"

Sergeant Beckford smiled and glanced at Sergeant Simpson, before returning his eyes to Danyluk. "YOU DO! THERE SHOULD BE NO REASON WHY YOU CAN'T HANDLE THAT TASK BY YOURSELVES. IS THERE, DANYLUK?"

"No Sergeant, but...what if we sleep in?"

Sergeant Simpson stepped forward. "IF YOU DO THAT, THEN I'LL HAVE YOU! YOU'LL BE MINE!"

Sergeant Mack glared at Danyluk. "IF HE DOES THAT, JUST LET ME HAVE HIM FOR ONE DAY. HE'LL WISH HE'D NEVER LEFT HIS MOTHER'S WOMB!"

Simpson chuckled. "I don't think this one ever did. He spent nine months trying to get out of his mother's, and he's dedicated the rest of his life trying to get back in someone else's."

Simpson's statement got them all laughing. Everyone, that is except Danyluk. He put his arm down and skulked to the stand easy position. He understood their 'message.'

"OUR COMPANY SERGEANT MAJOR THIS YEAR IS WO2 (Warrant Officer 2nd Class) ROSE. SOME OF YOU MET HIM IN YOUR FIRST YEAR. HE'S NOT WITH US NOW BECAUSE HE'S TRAVELING WITH THE PRAIRIE CADETS, BUT HE'LL BE HERE TOMORROW. ALSO, TOMORROW AFTERNOON, OUR COMPANY COMMANDER, MAJOR RATCLIFFE, WILL ADDRESS THE COMPANY AND INTRODUCE YOU TO THE PLATOON COMMANDERS."

East whispered to Jackson. "Rose is the one who said we were all hatched under rocks, remember?"

Earl did. "Do I remember? You bet I do, but I hear he's a good guy."

"RIGHT! TONIGHT'S MOVIE IS, *MISTER ROBERTS*. IT STARTS IN B-3 AT NINETEEN HUNDRED. WHEN I FALL YOU OUT, I WANT ALL OF YOU TO MAKE YOUR BEDS, PUT YOUR CLOTHING AWAY, AND GET YOUR BARRACKS IN SHAPE! ALL REGULAR FORCE STAFF WILL BE IN AND OUT TO ANSWER ANY QUESTIONS YOU MAY HAVE AND TO GIVE YOU A HAND. WHEN YOU GO BACK INTO THE BARRACKS, MAKE CERTAIN YOU READ ORDERS CAREFULLY. ARE THERE ANY OTHER QUESTIONS?"

"SERGEANT, I HAVE A QUESTION!"

Beckford marched over to the cadet. "What is it?"

Johnston stood at attention; his *paint* tin in hand. "Er, how long do I have to carry this thing around with me?"

"What platoon are you in?"

Johnston took a deep breath. "Three Platoon, Sergeant!"

Although Sergeant Beckford smiled, he also grimaced, because he knew what Johnston was in for.

"SERGEANT MACK, YOU'D BETTER SPEAK TO THIS YOUNG FELLOW!"

Sergeant Mack stepped in front of Johnston. "I'LL TELL YOU WHEN, BUT YOU HAD BETTER MAKE CERTAIN YOU SLEEP WITH THAT *THING* TONIGHT! IT'LL BE WITH YOU EVEN WHEN YOU SHOWER, IS THAT CLEAR?"

"YES, SERGEANT!"

Sergeant Mack stepped back and nodded to Sergeant Beckford, who then carried on. "NO FURTHER QUESTIONS? RIGHT! ALPHA COMPANY, ATTEN...TION! FALL...OUT!"

Within minutes of that command, cadets were unpacking, making their beds, and working on their kit. The same thing was happening elsewhere throughout the camp. Once again, Camp Vernon was in action.

A Corporal from the Royal Canadian Postal Corps entered the barracks. "IS THERE A SERGEANT-MAJOR DANYLUK IN HERE?"

Moose was tucking his bottom sheet underneath his mattress. "YES, CORPORAL, THAT'S ME!"

The Corporal handed him a pile of at least ten letters and a parcel. "WE'VE HAD THESE FOR A WEEK! THE POST OFFICE SMELLS LIKE A BLOODY PERFUME PARLOUR." That said, he walked out.

Briskly, Danyluk perused the envelopes. Many had lipstick marks, and one even had large red lettering at the bottom. 'PLEASE, DEAR LORD, LET MY MOOSE KNOW I LOVE AND MISS HIM!'

Cunningham tried to peer over Danyluk's shoulder. "Jesus, I can't believe this. We're only in camp a couple of hours and you clean out the camp post office."

Danyluk paid no attention. As he scrutinized each envelope, he called out a name. "Lovely Doris, delightful Mabel, ho, ho, ho, Sylvia, my turtle dove, and here's one from little Loretta, God what a body she's got..." He stopped quickly. "HEY GUYS, THERE'S A LETTER HERE FROM BERGIE!"

The others quickly gathered around. Bergie had been the seventh Musketeer until he decided to join the Regular Force. Cunningham had taken his place.

All were anxious to hear what Bergie had to say. East was so anxious, he nearly stuck his chicken leg into Danyluk's ear. "Come on, Moose, open it, open it!"

Moose ripped the letter open. "All right, East, don't get your nuts in a knot. It says...

Hello Moose, Doug, Wayne, Rothie, Earl, and Jack. I'm not going to say hello to you, Cunnilingus, until you give me a chance to win back my thirty bucks. Oh, what the hell, Hello Gordie.

Can I say that I miss you guys a lot?...well, I do and at this moment in time I wish I was with ya. If you guys think training in Vernon is tough, you should be here. I thought Depot Training was the absolute. I thought nothing could be worse. Well, believe me, since joining my regiment, the RCEME (Royal Canadian Electrical and Mechanical Engineers), I haven't had a moment to myself. Even when I want to visit the jon, I have to ask for permission. Wow, do we work! I'm with forty other guys and we get up at 0500 every morning. Nobody screams, STAND BY YOUR BEDS! If you're not up, the wrath of the devil himself is upon you. We train all day and finally hit the sack at about midnight. Being on the parade square for four hours a day is a piece of cake...but I can't say that for all the lectures. I did pretty good in math at school, but now I feel like a Goddamned professor. If you guys get the chance to learn how to use a slide-rule properly, do it. What they taught us in school about slide-rules is nothing compared to what they teach us here.

Although most of our instructors are RCEME, guess who our drill instructor is? Would you believe how small the world is? OUR DRILL INSTRUCTOR IS WALSH!"

Danyluk stopped reading. "THAT POOR SON OF A BITCH! HE'S GOT THAT PRICK WALSH! OH, MY GOD...WALSH SHOULD BE WORKING IN A MIRROR FACTORY TESTING MIRRORS TO SEE IF THEY BREAK WHEN HE SMILES. I THINK..."

East tried to grab the letter. "Get on with it...!"

"Okay, okay!" Running his finger down the letter to see where he left off, Danyluk continued reading. "Now let's see...

I can't describe this guy, he's a real asshole. I don't believe he's taken a leadership lecture in his life. He treats everyone like dirt, even his fellow instructors. No one has any respect for him, and he couldn't care less. Seven guys are in detention cells because the inside of their web belts were not as shiny as the outside. The guy hasn't changed a bit since he was our Company Sergeant-Major in Vernon in 1953.

Anyway, Vernon taught me how to survive, so I keep my mouth shut and say nothing. He hasn't recognized me yet...thank God.

You guys are probably just settling in on your first day. How is it...hot? How are the girls...in your case, Moose, all 100 of 'em? Who's sharing a barrack-box with ya this year? Whoever it is, they probably won't put up with what I had to. Here, I've got a barrack-box all to myself. It's Heaven not having left-over food and other people's dirty clothes all over my clean clothes. Just joking, Moose, you were a great bunkmate and we had a good laugh. I never thought you'd get your own back on me for cutting your 'shitter chair.' But you sure did, I guess I taught you real well.

Ed Shanks says to say hello to all of you. We've been kind of lucky because they've kept us together. You know, I still can't get over the fact that a Musketeer would become mint-close friends with someone from the Irish. Just joking. I keep telling Ed that had he stopped frenching Moose's bed, we would have made him a Musketeer. He said he never had a chance to stop because Moose did the same to him."

"You bet I did," said Danyluk. "Do you guys remember the dead fish? Well, I..."

"Moose, just *read* the letter!" East snarled.

"All right, all right! Get that God-damned chicken bone out of my face. Now, where was I...oh, yeah...

Would you guys believe I'm putting muscles on muscles. I haven't got an inch of fat on my body. We work out for an hour in the morning, every morning, seven days a week. What Sergeant Simpson put us through at Vernon is like Kindergarten compared to what we do here. In the afternoon, we've got to go through the obstacle course for another hour. It's hell but I'm getting used to it now.

Oh, I've got some news for you guys. Twelve of us have got an overseas posting already. At first, I thought I was heading for Borden, but I'm off to somewhere near the Suez Canal in two weeks and as luck would have it, Shanks has been posted with me. Just think of it, Moose, Egyptian women. Even you've never tried them, I bet you'd love to be going with us. I'll let you know what they're like.

I've got a few days leave coming and I'll visit you in Vernon next weekend. I don't know who your Platoon Sergeant is, but could you ask him if you could have a couple of hours off. I want to see you guys before I leave, and so does Shanks.

Well, right now, I've got to get back to pressing my TWs (Tropical Worsteds). I don't know what kind of material they used to make these, but when I breathe on them, they wrinkle. I had to write this letter on the ironing board with my back to an open door, because we don't have time to write letters. If we're seen to be not working, the shit hits the fan. Did I make the right decision in joining the Regular Force? I think so, but I miss ya, and would you believe it, I miss good ol' Vernon. Please say hello to Sergeants Beckford and Simpson if they made it back for another summer. All the best and good luck on your course. BERGIE.

P.S. Moose, stay out of Hop Sing's and Wayne, Ed says stop putting silver paper in your epaulettes and impersonating officers. I miss, as Moose would say it, (youse) guys. BERGIE."

There was silence when Moose finished reading the letter and put it back in its torn envelope. They missed Bergie too, especially Moose. It's hard to accept a hole in a team that's fought the *wars* and won. Losing Bergie was like losing an arm or a leg.

Douglas saw the looks on the faces of the other six. "Come on, you guys, let's get to work. He's going to be here in a few days, then we can give him shit again for joining the Regular Force."

Rothstein put his hand on Moose's shoulder. "Moose, did he really use the word, 'youse'?" God, I hate it when the Queen's English is mangled."

Moose acted like he hadn't heard Douglas and Rothstein. Although he didn't say anything, he found it difficult to talk so he reached and turned up his radio and allowed the sounds of, *Don't Be Cruel,* to mingle with the other fanfare in the barracks. After a few moments, however, he split up a cake, pop, and other goodies he'd received from a girl called Alice Prinsett. Then he lay down on his bed to read the other letters he'd received.

He'd met Alice on a bus one day prior to leaving for Vernon. Alice had told him she worked in her father's grocery store, so Moose mentioned the word, 'parcels,' when she wrote down his address.

"You poor boy, is army food really that bad?"

"Alice, you wouldn't believe how bad it is. We survive on food sent from home. I'm going to phone you when I get home. I'll probably be all skin and bone by then."

"SON OF A BITCH, THELMA'S GONE TO SEE THE DOCTOR AGAIN! Oh, it's all right, she's just having a wart removed from her belly-button. DAMN, I WISH SHE WOULDN'T START HER LETTERS LIKE THAT!"

The hut was alive with activity as Jackson made his bed. He could never believe in a million years that he'd be bunking with an Irish Fusilier cadet. It wasn't that Earl had anything against them personally, but he had been 'brainwashed' by the BCR Musketeers. The rivalry between the Irish, Seaforth, and BCR cadets was resolute and there could be no letup. Sure he remembered boxing against the Irish cadets in 1953, but that was three years ago. For some reason over the past few years, cadets from the three regiments who would never associate with each other in Vancouver, were forming friendships in Vernon. He'd seen Douglas buying a pop for a Seaforth cadet named Ashbough, and Wayne actually studying with an Irish cadet named Symington, and of course, every one of them thought the world of Ed Shanks.

"How many years have you been here?" Earl asked Simon.

Simon had made up his bunk and was sitting on their barrack-box, shining his boots. "This is my fourth year. I took IBT (Instructor's Basic Training) the first two years, and last year I took Signals. How about you?"

Earl bounced a quarter on his top blanket. "It's my fourth year also. The group of us guys took IBT in our first year, and followed it up with Signals and Driver Mech. Say, one of your officers is a hell of a good guy. We had him as a Platoon Officer one year. His last name was...Deane. There was another who wasn't too bad, either. Oh, what the hell was his name? I remember, McDonald. Are they still with your regiment?"

Simon nodded. "Yeah, they're well respected. Both of them were Irish cadets, did you know that?"

Earl was studying Simon's capbadge. "No. I guess that's why they're pretty good guys...for Irish, that is. Say, what the hell do you call your hat? It's not a beret, what is it?"

Simon smiled. "It's called a caubeen. Your friend, Moose, keeps referring to it as a carabineer."

Earl picked up the caubeen. "And what do you call this green plumage that fits behind your badge?"

"It's called a hackle. At least Moose has that name correct." Simon then changed the subject. "Did you like Driver Mech?"

"Yeah, it was great. We spent more time taking engines and other machinery apart than driving, but we learned a hell of a lot. I think that..."

They were continuing their conversation when East strolled by. "Jesus, would you look at this. Earl the pearl is actually talking to an Irish cadet like he's known him for years."

The group glanced over, and even Danyluk stopped reading for a fraction of a second. "Simon's a sharp cadet. If you guys can remember, he was their Guard Sergeant-Major last year at the guard competition. The one we won!"

Wayne was loading up his half of the barrack-box. "We didn't win this year though, the Westies took it."

"We beat 'em in drill but our weapons were dirty," said East. "Besides, we've won it every other year. I don't think the Irish have *ever* won it."

Wayne remembered when they lost the guard competition. "The reason the Westies won it was because of Don Rebin...was that his name? Anyway Rebin trained them and if you can remember, he was a damn sharp cadet. He was trained by Beckford, like the rest of us. I betcha Rebin will be after it again next year?"

"That's right and we'd better make certain they don't stand a chance," Douglas replied. "Do you guys also realize we've taken every shooting competition away from the other regiments as well? Ashbough of the Seaforths told me their corps is training hot and heavy to win back some of the shooting trophies. The Irish just want their Wallace-Foley trophy back. We don't have to worry about Rebin on the ranges, because he spends all of his time on the parade square."

When Danyluk finished reading his letters, he jumped up, threw them in his side of the barrack-box and looked around. "Hey, where the hell's my bunkmate...his bed's not made? CUNNINGHAM, WHERE THE HELL ARE

YOU?"

No sooner had he asked, he heard. "ALL BETS DOWN! O.K., YOU, SHORTY...ROLL THE DICE!"

The RCE (Royal Canadian Engineers) cadet held the dice in his right hand and blew on them. He said, "Hold your horses, Zaholuk," as he released them. Unfortunately, luck wasn't on his side. It never could be, because he was playing with Cunningham, who for safety sake, was wearing a phony name tag.

Gordie rubbed his hands together before grabbing the cash. "YES! THAT'S IT, MY LITTLE ENGINEER FRIEND. I'LL JUST TAKE THAT, AND THAT!"

Moments later, six cadets were dragging a brooding Cunningham, toes down, back to his area of the hut. "I'LL BE BACK LATER...GET YOUR MONEY READY!" he yelled over his shoulder.

Unlike other years, the hullabaloo going on in B-33 was restrained. Perhaps it was the fact that most of the occupants were senior cadets in their last year. Oh, there were a few cadets running up and down the aisles and screaming out the windows to someone they knew, but generally the noise was *organized.*

Although this was only their first day, cadets were already working in teams, preparing their kit and their bed space. As usual, the Platoon Corporals in the Regular Force were making their rounds, assisting and generally explaining the proper method of *trying* to survive in a military atmosphere.

"If your bunk is made up, sit on one of the empty bunks, that way you won't ruin **your** *work of art.*"

After an hour or so, Sergeant Beckford entered the barracks with Sergeant Simpson. The other two Sergeants, Mack and Prest, were in the other wing already.

"How's it going guys?" Beckford asked. He had a pile of notebooks, pencils, and pens under one of his arms. "East, do me a favour please and pass one book and one of each of these writing instruments to every cadet on this side of the barracks. Also, I want to you tell them that there's a 3/4 ton truck outside; each cadet is to go and sign for his training manuals."

Douglas liked Beckford immensely. He noted his style and he liked the way the Sergeant had asked East to help out. "We're doing well, Sergeant. How's it going with you?"

The big man walked over to the Musketeers' area. "Good! It's also good to see you guys back."

Moose stood next to the Sergeant. "Bergie's not with us...he joined the Regular Force."

The Sergeant took off his beret and sat down on an empty bunk. "So I've heard. He'll do well. What regiment did he join?"

Moose sat next to the Sergeant. "RCEME, Sergeant. He was also in the RCEME cadets. We just got a letter from him and he's coming up here for a few days. Can we get some time off to see him?"

Sergeant Beckford smiled. "I see no reason why not; let me know when he arrives. Just think, this year when I enter the barracks I'm not going to hear Bergie complaining about not having any space in the barrack-box."

Jackson sat down on the other side of the Sergeant. "That's right, Sergeant. You're going to hear Cunningham complain."

"Cunningham?" The Sergeant automatically felt his back pocket for his wallet. So he's become the seventh Musketeer? Where is he?"

A smiling face appeared from behind a hung blanket that hadn't yet been tucked in. "Here, Sergeant."

"Good to have you with us, Mr. Cunningham. A few of the Regular Force Corporals are looking for you. One in particular says he wants a chance of getting back his two-week's pay."

The smile instantly disappeared from Cunningham's face; money had been mentioned. "WHICH ONE? HE DID? TELL HIM I'M HERE, SERGEANT! WHAT'S HIS FAVOURITE GAME?"

Beckford was still laughing when Sergeant Simpson walked up from his end of the barracks. "DANYLUK, I SAID A SMALL PRAYER LAST NIGHT, ASKING THE GOOD LORD THAT YOU BE PLACED IN MY PLATOON. IT LOOKS LIKE HE'S GIVEN YOU A BREAK."

Danyluk cringed. "Aw, Sarg...I get up in the mornings now. I promise youse won't have to dump my mattress on the floor. Not even once. I'm a changed man. Christ, I nearly got married last year. That's responsibility, ain't it?"

"WHO WAS THE UNLUCKY CANINE?"

Danyluk snickered. "That's not fair, Sergeant. I didn't comment last summer when I saw you leave the Sergeants' Mess with Bigbody Bertha. Jeez, Sarg, if she rolled over on you, she'd break every bone in your body and you'd smother."

Simpson's expression changed as he tried to recall the occasion. "I'll have you know, Danyluk, that Bertha's a very charming young lady."

"She may be charming, Sergeant, but she's all stomach and no tits. She's got to wear ankle socks to keep up the rolls of fat."

Sergeant Simpson glared at Moose. "How do you know that?"

Danyluk's expression turned to one of guilt. "How do I know what?"

"That she's got small breasts?"

Perspiration appeared on Moose's forehead. "How do I know? Well, I er, we've *talked*."

Simpson started biting his lower lip. "I can't believe this...her too? How in the hell do you find the time to share yourself like you do? You're a cadet, you're not supposed to go near the kitchen staff."

Danyluk wiped his forehead with his hand. "I..er, well, I'm organized. It's the Planning and Preparation portion of APUMSHIT!" (the code word for the then, Eight Principles Of Instruction.)

Cunningham broke in. "Sergeant, she was the one Danyluk talked into putting Ex-Lax in Genova's chocolate pudding. Remember the fights...?"

A smile appeared on Simpson's face again. "Ah, yes, the boxing-matches. Anyway, I was only walking her to her car." With that said, Sergeant Simpson walked back to his own end of the barracks, and Danyluk walked outside to pick up his books.

"Damn it, that kid gets around," Simpson mumbled to himself. "How in the hell does he do it? It's a wonder he's not red-raw!"

"How's the guard been the last two years, Sergeant Beckford?"

Beckford glanced at Rothstein. "Excellent, Rothstein. I think it will be even better this year though, because nearly every cadet on this course has participated before."

Danyluk walked back into the building with his manuals. "Sergeant Beckford, who's the Camp RSM this year?"

"RSM Gardiner's back with us."

"Oh, Jesus, he thinks I'm a nudist and a sex maniac."

Beckford stood up. "Well, is he wrong?"

Danyluk thought for a moment before popping out his chest. "No, but because Bergie's not here, I'm going to have to bear the brunt of him alone. Jesus, I'm going to stay out of his way."

Beckford stood up, replaced his beret and placed his drill cane under his left arm. As he walked to the exit, he turned towards Moose. "Danyluk, there's no doubt in my mind that you'll have another run-in with the RSM. Have a good evening, fellas. I'll see you at lights out."

After the Sergeant had left the building, Moose stripped off to have a shower. "SON OF A BITCH, IT'S GARDINER AGAIN!" he yelled as he reached up to the shelf to turn up his radio.

As if Fate were playing a trick, the words, "YOU! STAND WHERE YOU ARE! I CAN ONLY SEE THE LOWER PORTION OF YOUR BODY! IS IT NORMAL FOR YOU TO EXPOSE YOUR CROTCH TO OFFICERS AND CIVILIANS WALKING THE MAIN ROAD OF THE CAMP? YOU ARE SUPPOSED TO CLOSE YOUR WINDOW, MAN! STAND WHERE YOU ARE, I'M COMING IN TO TALK TO YOU!"

Sergeant Beckford's prediction was filled almost instantaneously. RSM Gardiner's voice boomed as he stomped up the stairs, drill cane under his left armpit. He stopped at Danyluk's bunk, facing the naked red-faced cadet.

"OH, MY GOD, IT'S YOU AGAIN! I'M NOT A PSYCHOLOGIST OR A PSYCHIATRIST, BUT YOUNG MAN, YOU NEED HELP! YOUR FIRST DAY IN CAMP AND YOU'VE STARTED ALREADY? YOU'RE AT IT ONCE MORE?"

Danyluk stood rigidly at attention. "Sir, I got undressed to take a shower, sir."

"DOES THIS LOOK LIKE A BLOODY SHOWER ROOM? DO YOU ALWAYS TAKE A SHOWER DRAPING YOUR PRIVATE PARTS OVER THE WINDOW LEDGE? CHRIST, YOU COULD DIG FOR BLOODY WORMS WITH THAT! I ACTUALLY THOUGHT SOMEONE HAD PLACED THE END OF A MOP HANDLE OUT THE WINDOW!"

"Sir, I was trying to turn up my radio, sir."

"I THOUGHT YOU JUST TOLD ME YOU WERE GOING TO TAKE A SHOWER?"

"Well, I er...um..."

"WRAP A TOWEL AROUND YOURSELF, MAN, OR TIE THAT THING IN A KNOT. I DON'T NEED COMPLAINTS FROM THE OFFICERS' MESS, IS THAT CLEAR?"

"Yes, sir."

"I CAN'T HEAR YOU!"

"YES, SIR!"

RSM Gardiner marched out, talking to himself. "Christ, he's back again! I thought he'd be in bloody freak show by now! The officers will think there's an elephant loose in B-33."

Suddenly, the RSM stopped and marched back in. "WHERE'S YOU'RE PARTNER IN CRIME...THE OTHER PART OF THIS SIDESHOW...YOUR ASSISTANT...OH WHAT WAS HIS NAME...PERKY?"

"BERGIE! HE'S JOINED THE REGULAR FORCE, SIR!"

"WHAT BRANCH? PLEASE TELL ME IT'S THE NAVY!"

"THE ARMY, SIR! HE'S IN RCEME, MR. GARDINER!"

Gardiner turned and marched out again, but not before he said, "HE HAS? HE

ACTUALLY PASSED THE 'M' TEST? WHAT THE HELL IS THE CANADIAN ARMY COMING TO?"

The cool water of the showers felt great to the seven Musketeers and one Irish cadet. After the RSM had left, they all felt like getting refreshed because the temperature in the barracks must have been close to 100. Moose was still in a stupor. He had really meant it when he said he'd stay out of Gardiner's way. He faced the wall and looked up at the spraying shower-head. "WHY ME? THERE'S AT LEAST EIGHT HUNDRED OTHER CADETS IN THIS CAMP RIGHT NOW...WHY ME?" he burbled.

Jackson answered, "Because as Bergie once said, 'He knows your name!'"

Wayne, as usual, had shampoo all over his body. "Maybe it's fate? Maybe in another life, you and Gardiner were business partners, or even man and wife?"

East liked that idea. "Yeah, you could have been his hunting dog that kept getting lost."

"IF I'D BEEN HIS HUNTING DOG, I SURE AS HELL WOULD'VE GOTTEN LOST. MAN AND WIFE? CHRIST, CAN YOUSE IMAGINE BEING MARRIED TO HIM IF HE WAS A DAME? SHE'D SAY, 'WE'RE GOING TO SCREW TONIGHT FROM 1900 HOURS UNTIL 1902. FOLLOWING THAT, WE'RE GOING TO HAVE MEAD FROM 1903 UNTIL 1904. YOUSE WILL ONLY SNORE FROM 2005 UNTIL 2008, AND YOUSE WILL CEASE TRYING TO COP A FEEL IN THE MIDDLE OF THE NIGHT, OTHERWISE, I'LL HAVE YA! IS THAT CLEAR, DEAR?'"

Danyluk had them in stitches.

"But who says you'd be the husband? asked Douglas.

The look on Danyluk's face after Douglas' question had Wayne convulsing at the window, trying to catch his breath, and Jack rolling on the floor. The eight had sore stomachs, which only got worse after Rothstein added, "Gardiner would say: "MOOSELLA, MY DARLING, YOU WILL STAND RIGIDLY AT ATTENTION WHILE I UNDRESS YOU. AFTER I HAVE REMOVED YOUR HAIRNET, SHAWL, FROCK, PETTICOAT, AND CANVASS DRAWERS, I WILL GIVE THE ORDER: **ASSUME THE HORIZONTAL POSITION!** YOU WILL BRING YOUR LEFT FOOT UP SIX INCHES OFF THE GROUND AND SLAM IT DOWN ENSURING YOUR LEGS ARE THREE FEET APART. YOU WILL THEN FALL BACKWARDS NINETY DEGREES, ARMS PLACED STIFFLY BY YOUR SIDES, BREASTS OUT AND STOMACH IN. **IS THAT CLEAR, DEAR, MY DEAR?**""

Supper that night was roast beef with mashed potatoes, creamed corn and carrots. the Musketeers all telephoned their girlfriends before the movie, *Mr. Roberts*, started. B-3, the smoke filled hangar, wasn't as packed as usual because the prairie cadets hadn't arrived and many of the other companies had allowed cadets to go into town to familiarize themselves with Vernon.

Following the movie and a pop in the cadet canteen, the Musketeers returned to their barracks. Lights out wasn't far off, and most of them were beat.

Although it was noisy as hell in the barracks, they didn't have to yell at each other. Next day's arrival of the prairie cadets would change that.

"That's the first time I've seen Jimmy Cagney play a role like that," East commented whilst shining his boots and eating a jam sandwich. "Jesus, he's a good actor."

All of them had thoroughly enjoyed the picture. Cunningham's favourite actor was Henry Fonda.

"So's Henry Fonda. Think of the money that guy must be worth? I'd just like to meet him on the set and say, 'Mr. Fonda, sir, how would you like to eliminate your boredom by playing a quick game of poker, with me...no limit?'"

Wayne sat on his pillow and pushed his body down between the sheets. The sides of his bedding were still tucked tightly in. "What would you do with all that money?"

Cunningham lay back, his arms behind his head. "I'd join the best golf club money could buy. Can you imagine me sitting with all the big-wigs in the club's card room? I'd not only take it off 'em on the green, but in the clubhouse, as well. I'd be bloody loaded. No one would call me Cunnilingus then."

"That right, it would be Mr. Cunnilingus," said East.

Wayne had listened with interest, but something else quickly entered his mind. He sat up hastily. "Earl, did you read orders?"

Jackson had opened his window and was leaning out, listening to the music originating from the Officers' Mess.

"Yup, and I know what you're going to ask. No, there isn't any Church Parade tomorrow. We can sleep in until noon if we like. Brunch is served from 0830 until 1300 hours."

Wayne slid down between his covers again. "Can we go into town tomorrow?"

Earl slammed the window shut and got into bed. "Nope! Jesus, Wayne read orders. We're not being allowed into town because they want our kit perfect on Monday morning."

Sergeant Beckford stomped into the barracks. "THOSE OF YOU WHO HAVEN'T HIT THE SACK, STAND BY YOUR BEDS!" He then proceeded with the bed check. Two Regular Force Corporals were with him.

"Corporal, is Sergeant Mack on the other side of the barracks?"

"Yes, Sergeant!"

"DANYLUK, TURN THAT GOD-DAMNED RADIO OFF! DON'T TELL ME YOU LIKE THAT SONG, *DAVEY CROCKETT*?"

East answered for Danyluk. "He does because he refers to himself as, "King of the wild brassiere," Sergeant.

"Screw you, East."

"I TRUST ALL OF YOU HAVE READ ORDERS AND THAT YOUR KIT WILL BE FULLY PREPARED FOR MONDAY MORNING'S INSPECTION? IF YOU HAVEN'T DONE IT, YOU'VE GOT ALL DAY TOMORROW. ANOTHER THING...ALL CADETS WILL BE FORMED UP IN THREE RANKS ON THE ROAD TOMORROW AT 1500 HOURS. THE O.C. (Officer Commanding the Company) WILL ADDRESS YOU THEN! ARE THERE ANY QUESTIONS?"

None were forthcoming, so the Sergeant stomped out, turning out the lights. "GOOD NIGHT, FELLAS, HAVE A GOOD SLEEP!"

As usual, the words, "Good night Sergeant," were yelled, screeched, and sung.

Wayne leaned over the right side of his bunk. "Hey, Doug...should we sleep in tomorrow?"

"We can try, but you know as well as I do, every other year we haven't been able to. What the hell's that crackling noise?"

Wayne's head was still hanging over. "It's East eating potato chips. Good night, Doug."

Douglas replied, "Good night, buddy." Then he cupped his hands around his mouth. "Thanks for sharing them, East."

"Screw you, Danyluk, you'd grab the whole bag."

"What are you talking to me for? I don't even want one."

"Yes you do. You just said, 'Thanks for sharing them, East.'"

"That wasn't me, you snarf!"

"Yes it was, you frump!"

"No, it wasn't!"

"Yes, it was!"

As Douglas rolled on his side, East and Danyluk were still going at it.

CHAPTER III

Sundays are special days in the Okanagan Valley. Unlike the big city where traffic noise drowns out the melodious sounds of church bells - in Vernon, the hills consent to convey the echo for miles and miles around. Vernon in 1956 still wasn't very populated and the small country town image on a Sunday morning was like a scene from a radiant movie. Accompanying the marvelous sound of bells came the faint calls of cattle grazing in the hills, and roosters welcoming another new day.

Inside B-33, however, Elvis Presley sang *Hound Dog*, and the radio was turned up full blast. It was nine o'clock in the morning and the squeal of brakes, the smell of exhaust fumes, the noise of three-ton engines, and tailgates opening with boots hitting the pavement disturbed the serene setting of the Vernon Army Cadet Camp.

The prairie cadets had arrived and were being dropped off at the various huts after they had received their clothing and equipment. After breakfast, they would change into P.T. gear and proceed through the 'sausage machine.'

The action taking place in B-33, quickly spread throughout the camp.

Moose gyrated in the aisle, *playing* a broom and miming Elvis' music. At one point he shook his hips so much, his draped towel almost fell off his usual morning erection.

"WELL, WELL, WELL, THE FARMERS ARE HERE!" some cadet screamed. Others welcomed their 'long lost friends' with similar asseveration.

"YOU PONGO, YOU'VE GROWN A FOOT!"

"HOLY COW, TOM, HAVE YOU STILL GOT YOUR BRACES ON? HOW WAS THE TRAIN RIDE? WHERE THERE ANY DAMES ON THE TRAIN?"

"YOU'LL BE GOING TO THE MEDICAL INSPECTION ROOM AFTER BREAKFAST, DO YOU KNOW ANY CADETS WITH GOUT?"

A cadet from outside yelled, "WHAT'S GOUT?"

"THAT'S WHAT YA GOT WHEN YA GOT A SMALL JOINT!"

"HOW THE HELL DO I KNOW IF SOMEONE'S GOT A SMALL DONG? WHAT DO YOU THINK I AM...A VOYEUR? HEY, MAYBE *I'VE* GOT GOUT?"

The cadet inside screamed back, "WELL, THE DOC'LL TELL YOU IF YOU'VE GOT IT!"

"WOW, THAT'S THE FIRST TIME I'VE EVER HEARD IT CALLED GOUT! I THOUGHT IT WAS JUST CALLED 'S.P.'?"

"WHAT'S S.P.?"

"SHORT PRONG!"

Douglas lay back, listening to all the conversations going on around him. Most of the B.C. cadets were already out of bed, *welcoming* the newcomers. Every year it had been the same; the arrival of the prairie cadets had terminated the opportunity for extra sleep. This was the only day they could sleep in until noon and once again, the surrounding ruckus wouldn't allow it. All other Sundays, they would be up at 0900 at the latest, to attend Church Parade at ten o'clock.

As Douglas put his feet on the floor, Wayne jumped down and whispered,

"Watch Cunningham, just watch the Cunner."

Douglas yawned, rubbed his eyes, and turned to see Cunningham drop a ten dollar bill on the floor. He quickly picked it up again and held it in the air. "HEY, WHICH ONE OF YOU PRAIRIE CADETS DROPPED THIS TEN DOLLAR BILL?"

Almost instantly, the new arrivals took out their wallets or any loose bills they had in their battledress pockets. When they realized the lost bill wasn't theirs, they put their money away again. There wasn't a dishonest soul in the group because not one claimed the bill.

Cunningham tucked his ten-spot inside the waistband of his undershorts. "HEY THAT MEANS I'VE GOT TEN DOLLARS I CAN PLAY STUKE WITH. I'VE LOST ALL MY OTHER MONEY PLAYING THE GAME, BUT THIS GIVES ME A NEW LEASE ON LIFE. ANYONE HERE LIKE TO WIN A LIT-TLE MONEY?"

Like bears to honey, a large group gathered around the *gambler* and a game was going at full speed. Not only did the newcomers not realize they had been set up, but when they had checked their money, it had also been counted by the quickest mind in Vernon, or maybe the world. Even the thicknesses of the various wallets had been *analyzed*.

Douglas stared in utter disbelief. "That's bloody brilliant! Can you imagine what heights he'd reach if he'd put his mind to other things?"

The game didn't take place on Cunningham's bunk because his bed was too close to the centre entrance doors. An area was chosen half-way between the centre doors and the southwest-end door of the building. That way the participants would have lots of time to ditch the cards if NCOs or officers entered.

Cunningham had just jumped out of his bed without making it up. That was Danyluk's job, at least for the first three weeks.

The hot water in the shower felt good but Danyluk only got a bit of it because he had to make both beds.

"SON OF A BITCH...I FEEL LIKE A GOD-DAMNED CHAMBERMAID! AS I WAS FINISHING THE HOSPITAL CORNERS ON CUNNINGHAM'S BED, HE TURNED AND YELLED, 'HEY, YOU'RE GETTING A LITTLE SLACK AREN'T YOU? I LIKE MINE REALLY SQUARED OFF ON THE SIDES, NOT LIKE YOURS! GET WITH IT, MOOSEY!'"

Rothstein was spitting water at the wall. "Well, you will gamble with him, what do you expect? He's the best and you keep taking him on."

Moose was still fuming. "One of the Alberta cadets asked him, 'How do you get that guy to make your bed for you?' Do you know what he told him...do you? He said, 'Yeah, he really admires me because I get him through all of his tests. Put up a few extra bucks and I'll get him to make your bed, as well.'"

Wayne thought it was hilarious and couldn't stop laughing.

"Yeah, you go ahead and laugh, Wayne. I betcha before the end of camp, he'll nail you as well."

East tried to hustle everyone up. "C'mon you guys, there'll be no food left if we don't get a move on."

Jackson threw a towel in East's face. "You've already had breakfast, what are you worried about?"

"That was two hours ago, I'm goin' again."

The cadet kitchen was full when the seven entered. Jackson had brought

Simon with him; even though Simon was an Irish cadet, the two of them had 'hit it off' together. Simon sat at the end of the table, his back to the aisle.

Brunch was *real* eggs with bacon and toast. A second choice was turkey sandwiches with navy bean soup, and the third choice was grilled cheese sandwiches. East and Simon drank milk, but the rest of the Musketeers had started to enjoy tea. They didn't drink it at all a few years back, but Douglas had introduced them to it.

"How come I've never heard of army bean soup?" asked East.

"Because the army don't serve that slop, day after day," replied Moose. "The navy gets it for breakfast, lunch, and dinner."

"Then how come we've got it?"

"Because this is Vernon, you dolt! Anything goes."

"What's on for today?" Wayne asked.

"Well, we're stuck in camp," Jackson replied, "But, we haven't got the whole day off." He took out some notes he'd tucked in the elastic waistband of his P.T. shorts. "I read orders and would you believe right in the middle of the 'Fire Safety' instructions, it says, 'Following the O.C.'s address at 1500 hours, each cadet on the Senior Leaders' Instructors Course will hand in a paper describing the whereabouts of each fire hydrant in camp, including the upper camp. In addition, we've got to note the telephone number of the local fire department and count the number of fire extinguishers in each cadet hut of the lower camp. We have to provide the date each was last checked and the initials of the person who checked it out."

Douglas saluted Jackson. "You really are a pearl, Earl. That's what Sergeant Beckford keeps referring to as 'hidden text.' Nobody reads the fire instructions, at least I don't. That's his way of checking to see if we've learned our lessons of the past."

Danyluk stuffed a big strip of bacon in his mouth. "Jesus that's sneaky. I'll bet we're the only people who know that."

Wayne smiled. "This whole course is going to be that way, I'll betcha. We've got to stay one step ahead of the instructors."

Simon asked. "Do you guys mind if I tell the other Irish cadets on the course?"

The other six exchanged glances, each shrugging. "Nah, go ahead," Earl replied. "But let's keep it at that. I haven't finished yet," he said as he continued to read his notes. "Right smack in the middle of the text on 'Military and Civilian Parking Procedures,' it says we have to note the licence numbers of all the cars parked in the parking areas of the lower camp, and the time we spotted them."

Rothstein's smile stretched from ear to ear. "Wow, talk about one-upmanship! Should we tell the other guys in our platoon, and what about Cunningham, do we drag him out?"

Douglas shook his head. "I think normally we should share the information with the other guys, but not on this first day. They've got to learn to work in teams. Look, we all knew Earl would read orders, but while he was doing that, Rothie was working on Earl's belt. Wayne, you scrubbed Rothie's helmet. I pressed Wayne's clothes while he was shining our boots. The group of us, including Simon, have been working together as a team. All we've got to do now is touch everything up tomorrow."

Danyluk's face lit up with a sneaky smile. "So we leave Cunningham to the wolves?"

Wayne brightened noticeably, indicating he had an idea. "No, we'll give him this day. Moose, write out a separate paper for him with his name on it. Make certain you're next to him on parade and hand it to him at the exact time it's required."

"Son of a bitch, you want me to help him again? Jesus, Wayne, don't you think I do enough for him now?"

Wayne was between Douglas and Danyluk. He put his arm around Danyluk's shoulder. "That's right, old buddy, but before you hand it to him, you get him to agree to cancel the three-week 'work' schedule'...got it?"

Moose caught on quickly. Beaming, he said, "Sergeant-Major Banks, you're a genius! That's exactly what Bergie would do!"

The group laughed as Moose stood and held his mug of tea aloft. "We've got to keep thinking like Bergie. Earl, what would we do without you? UP THE MUSKE-TEERS!" He looked around the table, stopping at Simon. "ALL EIGHT OF US!"

Cadets in the vicinity of the 'noisy table' stopped eating in curiosity when the six stood to join Moose in a toast to themselves. "UP THE MUSKETEERS!"

Simon's proud expression indicated his acceptance into the Musketeers. Although he hadn't met Bergie, he toasted him the loudest.

"TO BERGIE AND EARL!"

"TO BERGIE AND EARL!"

It was blistering in Camp Vernon that afternoon as the seven continued work-ing. They scrubbed, starched, soaped and ironed their clothing for the next day. Other cadets who had attended camp before, but who still hadn't learned their les-son, insisted on using the washing machine and hanging their clothes in the drying room or on the small outside clotheslines in front of the shower room. They would gradually change their ways when they got fed up with the substitution of a 'dirty replacement pair' of undershorts, hung in exactly the same location as their missing *clean* garments.

Although the prairie cadets were gradually getting settled in, the stuke game in B-33 continued hot and heavy throughout the afternoon. It stopped immediately every time Corporals or Sergeants entered the barracks, but resumed just as fast when they left. The smile on Cunningham's face indicated he was doing well; the worried look on the participant's faces attested to what unequivocally would be the final result...being broke while at camp.

"West, you've had nothin' but luck, but it can't stay with ya all the time," a concerned prairie cadet fumed.

Cunningham made a silver dollar appear out of the cadet's left ear. "You're absolutely right. Stick around, maybe it'll rub off on you. Just deal."

The other Musketeers steered clear of the game as they went about their 'busi-ness.' At 1500 hours, when the company was ordered to form three ranks on the road, the prairie cadets had been *cleaned*.

On the way out the door, the bitching continued. "Jesus, I've never lost twenty bucks so quickly in my life!"

"What luck! That guy, West, finds ten dollars and then takes my ten, as well!"

"Can I borrow a fin off of you until I get some money from home? He emptied me out!"

A cadet turned out his pockets and produced one thin dime. "I'd loan it to you if I had it. I've only got a dime left and he even wanted me to throw that into the pot! Mathieson over there even lost his watch and a locket with his girlfriend's pic-ture. West said he can try an' win 'em back when he gets some *dough* from home."

"ALPHA COMPANY, ATTEN...TION! RIGHT...DRESS! EYES FRONT!

STAND AT...EASE! ALPHA COMPANY, ATTEN...TION!"

WO2 Rose's voice was sharp, crisp, and clear, before he turned, faced the Company Commander, and saluted. With his salute returned, he turned to his right and marched to a nearby tree where the other Platoon NCOs and Officers were standing.

Major Ratcliffe's eyes scanned the company. "ALPHA COMPANY, STAND AT...EASE! STAND EASY!"

Rothstein whispered to Wayne, "Interesting, an artillery major. This is the first time we've ever had an artillery O.C."

"I'M CERTAIN THAT SERGEANT BECKFORD WELCOMED YOU TO CAMP VERNON YESTERDAY, HOWEVER, LET ME AGAIN EXTEND THE SAME GREETING!

"I'M NOT GOING TO FALL YOU OUT FORMALLY, WHAT I WANT YOU TO DO IS SIT UNDER THE SHADE OF THE TREE WHERE THE OFFI-CERS AND NCOs ARE STANDING. TAKE OFF YOUR PITH-HELMETS AND RELAX! CARRY ON!"

Moments later, four platoons of cadets were seated, listening with interest.

"MY NAME IS MAJOR RATCLIFFE. I'LL BE COMMANDING THIS COMPANY FOR ITS DURATION AT CAMP. THESE ARE MY OFFICERS. OUR COMPANY'S SECOND IN COMMAND IS CAPTAIN HAMILTON. Gentlemen, just step forward when I mention your name."

Captain Hamilton stepped forward and then returned to his position.

"OUR COMPANY'S ADMINISTRATION OFFICER IS CAPTAIN MILLER, AND OUR PLATOON OFFICERS ARE... LIEUTENANT HARWOOD, ONE PLATOON; LIEUTENANT BENDIXON, TWO PLATOON; LIEUTENANT GRIFFITH, THREE PLATOON; AND LIEUTENANT MCCONNELL WHO WILL BE WITH FOUR PLATOON!"

Stopping his introductions for a moment, the O.C. smiled as he glanced at Lieutenant McConnell. "By the way, Lieutenant, did you ever receive your replace-ment commission scroll?"

McConnell snapped to attention. "Not yet, sir. My office wall is still *nude*."

"Mention that to me later and I'll write *another* letter!"

"Yes, sir."

"OUR COMPANY SERGEANT-MAJOR IS WO2 ROSE, AND OUR FOUR PLATOON SERGEANTS ARE: SERGEANT BECKFORD, ONE PLATOON; SERGEANT SIMPSON, TWO PLATOON; SERGEANT MACK, THREE PLA-TOON, AND SERGEANT PREST IS WITH FOUR PLATOON."

The cadets mumbled to each other as the Sergeants were introduced, particu-larly when Sergeant Mack's name was referred to.

Major Ratcliffe smiled. "YOU'VE OBVIOUSLY MET THESE *GENTLE-MEN!*"

A few remarks were heard but one 'hidden' cadet's voice rose above the oth-ers. "IS SERGEANT MACK RELATED IN ANY WAY TO THE LATE ADOLPH HITLER, SIR?"

Laughter rang out amongst the cadets, officers and NCOs. Even red-faced Sergeant Mack laughed as he quickly perused the group, looking for the culprit.

The O.C. was still smiling when he said, "NOW, NOW, THAT WASN'T CALLED FOR. SERGEANT MACK IS ONE OF THE KINDEST, SWEETEST... AND THE MOST GENTLE OF SENIOR NCOs IN CAMP! THE INFAMOUS

NAME, HITLER, SHOULD NEVER BE MENTIONED ON EARTH. LET IT BE MENTIONED IN HELL, WHERE IT BELONGS. THERE IS CERTAINLY NO SIMILARITY BETWEEN THE TWO BECAUSE SERGEANT MACK'S PARENTS WERE MARRIED."

The laughter travelled all the way to the Lookout, a mile or so south on Highway 97.

"OUR PLATOON CORPORALS ARE...CORPORALS MURPHY AND DUTTON, ONE PLATOON; CORPORALS SPORNITZ AND ETHERINGTON, TWO PLATOON; CORPORALS MCDONALD AND MOLL, THREE PLATOON, AND CORPORALS BROOKS AND REID WHO ARE WITH FOUR PLATOON. OUR COMPANY CLERKS ARE PRIVATES PAZIM AND MAESON."

A buzz of conversation ignited. Now the cadets had met the corporals and the clerks.

"I WANT ALL OF YOU TO OPEN YOUR NOTEBOOKS AND WRITE DOWN THE STATEMENT I AM ABOUT TO RECITE TO YOU. WRITE THIS IN THE MIDDLE OF YOUR FIRST PAGE, AND DURING THIS COURSE, DO NOT WRITE ANYTHING ELSE ON THAT PAGE."

With notebooks opened, all writing instruments were at the ready.

"GIVE A MAN A FISH AND YOU FEED HIM FOR A DAY. TEACH A MAN TO FISH AND YOU FEED HIM FOR A LIFETIME."

The officer paused. "Now, I want you to write down the author's name. He was a Chinese philosopher and his name was Lao-tzu."

Major Ratcliffe proceeded to spell the name. Afterwards, he said, "NOW, AT THE BOTTOM OF THAT PAGE, WRITE, "GIVE HIM THE EQUIPMENT AND..." NOW CIRCLE WHAT I'VE JUST SAID AND DRAW AN ARROW FROM THE CIRCLE AND HAVE IT END JUST IN FRONT OF LAO'S WORD, 'TEACH.'

"YOU SEE, I BELIEVE LAO FORGOT THAT WE CAN TEACH ALL WE WANT, BUT IF THE EQUIPMENT ISN'T AVAILABLE, WE'LL HAVE TO KEEP HANDING OUT FISH ON A DAILY BASIS."

"RIGHT! LET ME GET ON WITH TELLING YOU WHAT THIS COURSE IS ALL ABOUT. IT IS ABOUT LEADERSHIP AND MAN-MANAGEMENT. ALTHOUGH THE TWO GO HAND-IN-HAND, THERE IS A CONSIDERABLE DIFFERENCE. I CAN'T TELL YOU, NOR CAN ANY OF THESE GENTLEMEN TELL YOU, WHAT THE MAKE-UP IS OF A GOOD LEADER. LEADERS COME IN ALL SIZES, ALL PERSONALITIES, AND EACH OF THEIR METHODS ARE DIFFERENT. THE ADHESIVE FACTOR, HOWEVER, IN ALL *PROPER* LEADERS, IS THAT THEY ARE KNOWLEDGEABLE, FIRM, FAIR, AND FRIENDLY AND FOR SOME REASON, WHATEVER THAT MAY BE, THEY GET THEIR PEOPLE TO FOLLOW THEM!

"NOW, DON'T MISUNDERSTAND ME, BECAUSE THERE *ARE* LEADERS WHO ARE BULLIES. HOW THEY DO IT, I DON'T KNOW. BUT THEY CRAWL THROUGH THE CRACKS UNNOTICED AND MAKE IT TO THE SURFACE. UNNOTICED UNTIL THE TRUTH COMES OUT, THAT THEIR FOLLOWERS DO NOT FOLLOW WILLINGLY. THESE ARE THE PEOPLE WHO SAY THE RIGHT THINGS TO THEIR SUPERIORS AT THE RIGHT TIME. AS HUMAN BEINGS, ALL OF US SEE THINGS DIFFERENTLY. THERE ARE THOSE OF US THAT CAN SEE RIGHT THROUGH THE PER-

SON WHO BLUFFS HIS WAY THROUGH...AND THERE ARE THOSE WHO CANNOT.

"DURING THIS COURSE, WE WILL POINT OUT HOW TO DO YOUR BEST IN SPOTTING THE BLUFFERS. UNFORTUNATELY, I MUST TELL YOU, THEY WILL ALWAYS BE WITH US...THAT'S HUMAN NATURE. BUT THEN AGAIN, IN MANY CASES, EVEN THEY CAN BE CHANGED.

"WITH THE ASSISTANCE OF ALL OF THE OFFICERS AND NCOs IN THIS COMPANY, I HAVE DESIGNED A LEADERSHIP COURSE, THAT WILL, I AM CERTAIN, PUT ALL OF YOU PEOPLE ON THE RIGHT TRACK AS FAR AS LEADING IS CONCERNED. LET ME START WITH A TYPICAL CONVERSATION. LET'S CALL THIS A SCENARIO BETWEEN A SERGEANT AND A CORPORAL."

"SERGEANT BLOGGINS, I HAVE A PROBLEM; I WONDER IF YOU COULD HELP ME?"

"I'LL TRY, CORPORAL SMITH, WHAT'S THE TROUBLE?"

"WELL, SERGEANT, WE TALKED ABOUT LEADERSHIP THIS MORNING. WE DISCUSSED HOW LEADERS MOTIVATE, DELEGATE, SOLVE PROBLEMS, MAKE DECISIONS, AND GIVE DIRECTION. I WANT YOU TO KNOW THAT I DO ALL OF THOSE THINGS."

"WONDERFUL, CORPORAL SMITH, SO WHAT'S THE PROBLEM?"

"WELL, SERGEANT, MY PROBLEM IS THAT I CAN'T GET THE MEN IN MY PLATOON TO FOLLOW ME AND I FEEL LIKE AN IDIOT!"

The Major's audience listened incessantly, and there were smiles, because many cadets had been in similar situations at their home cadet corps.

"THE IMPLICATION OF THIS HUMOUROUS, YET NOT SO FUNNY CONVERSATION, IS THAT *IF* ALL OF THE MEMBERS OF CORPORAL SMITH'S PLATOON SHAPED UP AND DID THEIR DUTY AS FOLLOWERS, WHAT A GREAT LEADER HE WOULD BE.

"YOU SEE, CORPORAL SMITH'S STATEMENT CONTAINS A SIMPLE TRUTH. ALTHOUGH HE WAS TAUGHT HOW TO BE A LEADER, LEADERS MUST HAVE FOLLOWERS AND IF HIS PEOPLE DIDN'T FOLLOW, THEN HE MAY BE SOMETHING, BUT...HE'S NOT A LEADER.

"I MENTIONED A MINUTE AGO THAT THERE IS A DIFFERENCE BETWEEN LEADERSHIP AND MAN-MANAGEMENT. WHILE MANAGERS SHOULD HAVE LEADERSHIP ABILITY AND VICE-VERSA, THIS IS, IN REALITY, OFTEN NOT THE CASE. ALL MANAGERS MAY NOT BE LEADERS IN THE DEFINITION THAT THEY CAN GET OTHERS TO FOLLOW THEM. MANAGERS CAN MAKE EXCELLENT PLANS, ORGANIZE AND ALLOCATE RESOURCES, AND IMPLEMENT EFFECTIVE CONTROL SYSTEMS, BUT STILL, THEY COULD LACK THE ABILITY TO INSPIRE OTHERS TO FOLLOW THEM.

"LEADERSHIP IS NOT TELLING PEOPLE WHAT TO DO AND HAVING THE POWERS TO MAKE THEM DO IT. THERE IS A GREAT DIFFERENCE BETWEEN MOVEMENT AND MOTIVATION. THE TRUE LEADER IS ONE WHO HAS THE ABILITY TO *INFLUENCE* OR *INSPIRE* OTHERS TO FOLLOW."

The officer's voice was compelling, and he scanned his audience as he spoke.

"NOW, ALL OF YOU ARE SENIOR CADETS. YOU'RE GOING TO SPEND THREE WEEKS WITH US AND THEN YOU'RE GOING TO BE

ATTACHED TO OTHER CADET COMPANIES. THOSE OF YOU WHO ARE IN THE TOP FIFTY-PERCENT ON THIS COURSE WILL BE POSTED TO THE FIVE SENIOR LEADERS' COMPANIES. THE REMAINDER, IN ADDITION TO SERVING AS *ADMINISTRATIVE ASSISTANTS*, WILL BE POSTED TO THE DRIVER-MECHANICS AND SIGNALS COURSES.

"I WANT ALL OF YOU TO BE POSTED TO THE SENIOR LEADERS' COMPANIES, BUT I KNOW THAT WON'T HAPPEN. IT COULD HAPPEN, BUT IT WON'T. THE REASON IS SIMPLE; SOME OF YOU WILL NOT TRY AS HARD AS OTHERS. THAT IS ALSO HUMAN NATURE. ALL OF YOU ARE DIFFERENT...DO YOU REALIZE THAT?"

The Major stopped speaking and looked around at the silent, shiny faces. East, Rothstein, Jackson, Brice, and Banks glanced at Danyluk. When he spotted their stares, he gave them the finger and a whisper. "Eat your hearts out!"

"DO YOU REALIZE THAT NOT ONE OF YOU IS THE SAME AS THE OTHER. I'M TALKING MENTALLY AND PHYSICALLY. SOME OF YOU MAY BE ON SIMILAR WAVE-LENGTHS, HOWEVER, EACH OF YOU IS DIFFERENT. THANK GOD YOU WERE MADE THAT WAY BECAUSE THAT'S WHAT MAKES THE HUMAN RACE SO UNIQUE...BEING DIFFERENT!

"THIS COURSE IS GOING TO BE INTERESTING, MOTIVATING AND TOUGH! TOUGH TO THE POINT THAT IT WILL ONLY BE SUCH, IF YOU ACCEPT IT THAT WAY! SIMILAR COURSES HAVE BEEN CONDUCTED WITH THE RESERVES AND REGULAR FORCE, AND WE KNOW ALL OF YOU ARE UP TO IT. WHETHER OR NOT YOU CAN INDIVIDUALLY OR COLLECTIVELY ORGANIZE YOURSELVES TO HANDLE THE COURSE MATERIAL WILL BE THE DECIDING PASS/FAIL, FACTOR.

"SOME OF THE MOST COMPLEX MAP READING EXERCISES HAVE BEEN PLANNED. YOU WILL COMPLETE THEM AND USE YOUR EXPERIENCE AS A GUIDE TO DESIGN SIMILAR EXERCISES FOR THE DIFFERENT PLATOONS IN THIS COMPANY AND THE COMPANY YOU WILL BE ATTACHED TO IN THREE WEEKS. IN ADDITION, AFTER SEVEN DAYS, YOU WILL TEACH ALL DRILL AND GIVE ALL OF THE FINAL LECTURES ALLOCATED IN THE COURSE TRAINING PLAN. WE WILL BE ON THE RANGES FOR ONLY TWO DAYS. DURING THOSE TWO DAYS, YOU WILL BE TAUGHT COACHING. WE WILL ALSO BE IN GLENEMMA FOR TWO DAYS. DURING THAT TIME, YOU WILL PLAN MAP READING EXERCISES FOR THE SENIOR LEADER'S COMPANIES TO USE, WHEN THEY ARE THERE. I WANT INNOVATIVE AND DISTINCT EXERCISES PLANNED. WHEN THEY GO IN THE FIELD, YOU'LL BE GOING WITH THEM.

"NOW FOR THE GOOD NEWS. BECAUSE YOU ARE THE SENIOR COMPANY, YOUR DAY WILL START AT 0515 HOURS, WITH BREAKFAST AT 0600. YOU'LL HAVE HALF AN HOUR FOR BREAKFAST AND THAT SHOULDN'T BE A PROBLEM BECAUSE YOU'LL BE FIRST IN THE MESS HALL. THE COMPANY AS A WHOLE WILL COMPLETE P.T. FROM 0516 UNTIL 0530 WITH SERGEANT SIMPSON. YOU WILL BE INSPECTED EACH MORNING AT 0645 AND TRAINING WILL COMMENCE AT 0700 HOURS. TRAINING WILL STOP EACH DAY AT 1900 HOURS. YOU'LL HAVE A FIFTEEN MINUTE BREAK IN THE MORNING AND ONE IN THE AFTERNOON. YOU'LL HAVE ONE HOUR FOR LUNCH AND ONE HOUR

FOR SUPPER. MAKE USE OF THESE BREAKS AND DON'T USE UP ALL OF YOUR MEAL HOURS, EATING."

Although there were looks of utter disbelief, the officer didn't continue. Instead, he took a small piece of white paper out of his pocket.

"SERGEANT-MAJOR ROSE, FALL IN THE COMPANY, PLEASE!"

Rose came to attention. "YES, SIR! RIGHT, FALL BACK INTO YOUR PLATOON POSITIONS ON THE ROAD. QUICKLY NOW, QUICKLY! YOU...GET YOUR FIST OUT OF YOUR PANTS AND GET A MOVE ON!"

No one had his *fist* in his pants, but they all thought someone did.

Once again, the officers, and NCOs did not join their platoons as WO2 Rose formed up the cadets, completed the right dress and formally presented them to the Company Commander, who took over again.

"ALPHA COMPANY, STAND AT...EASE! STAND EASY! All of you have information I require. Those of you who have completed the tasks, form a semi-circle around me and quickly produce your papers...NOW!"

The Company Commander didn't allow time for discussion. Nearly all of the cadets were looking around, wondering what the hell was happening, including Cunningham as Danyluk grabbed him by the arm and hustled him into the small group which formed a semi-circle around the O.C.

Danyluk whispered. "If I give you this, I'm out of my end of the obligation. Take it or leave it?"

Once thing the *gambler* was not, and that was slow to catch on. "Jesus, Moose, I agree, let me have it, quickly!" he muttered as he grabbed the *goods*. Although Cunningham was bewildered, he knew Danyluk had saved his neck.

Out of the whole company, fifteen cadets stood in front of Major Ratcliffe. He accepted their papers and asked them to form up behind him in an extended line.

"I CAN SEE THE EXPRESSIONS ON YOUR FACES! EACH OF YOU, EXCEPT THESE CADETS BEHIND ME, ARE WONDERING WHAT THE HELL'S GOING ON...ISN'T THAT TRUE? WELL, SERGEANT BECKFORD ASKED YOU TO READ ORDERS...ALL ORDERS! WHEN YOU GO BACK INTO THE BUILDING, I WANT YOU TO READ THEM, THEN YOU'LL REALIZE WHY THESE PEOPLE ARE BEING GIVEN THE REST OF THE DAY OFF AND CAN GO INTO TOWN."

Major Ratcliffe turned and shook the hands of the fifteen. "Well done, boys. Leaders aren't born, they're made. So far, you fellows are doing just fine."

After the company was dismissed, eight cadets stayed outside of the hut shaking hands; the rest rushed in to read orders they thought they had already read.

Danyluk rubbed his hands together. "Just think, we can go downtown, and I don't have to worry about your kit," he said to Cunningham.

"The point is, are we all prepared to go downtown?" Wayne asked. "Is everyone's kit ready for tomorrow morning's inspection?"

Their smiles indicated each was prepared. Moose grabbed Cunningham by the throat. "Even yours is done."

Cunningham's face expressed a 'sheepish' look. "Thanks, Moose!"

"Don't thank me, thank Earl. He took the time to read orders properly. Youse know, I've got a feeling that the next three weeks is going to be tougher than tough. If what the Major said is true, we won't even have the time to take a crap. I know we've been organized in the past, but we'd better really get it together this time."

Sergeant Beckford came out of the barracks and joined them. "I'm proud of you guys. Although I nearly had second thoughts, I knew you'd perform those tasks. But I want to ask you a question. Why didn't you share your knowledge with the other guys in the platoon?"

Wayne became the spokesman. "We thought of it, Sergeant Beckford, and you know we'd Normally do just that, but...well...it's the first day and..."

Douglas helped him out. "You tested us, Sergeant, and we tested the other guys."

Beckford smiled and put his hand on Earl's shoulder. "You're the one that read orders, aren't you Jackson?"

Earl cocked his head and returned the smile. "That's one of my jobs, Sergeant, but we all read orders."

A knowing look came to Sergeant Beckford's face as he stood there nodding. "Well, I'm proud of all of you. Have a good time downtown and make the most of it. Unlike other years, you're not going to be seeing too much of it during your first three weeks."

Danyluk came to attention. "Sergeant Beckford, is Major Ratcliffe aware that I require special treatment? My dames will invade the camp if I'm not available."

Beckford had to look away for a moment. Although Sergeants are Gods, even they have a *small* tendency to want to burst out laughing.

"Well, Danyluk, you'll just have to place your women on hold for awhile. Look at it this way, you will have the opportunity of going from grit and muscle to skin and bones in your final three weeks."

"It's gonna be hard on me and my dames, Sarg, but I'll tell 'em it's for Queen and Country!"

"I'm glad your rather exotic way of life has a patriotic side to it, Danyluk. I'd hate to know you if it were otherwise."

Danyluk stuck out his chest and marched knowingly toward the barracks. "Thank you, Sergeant Beckford. Youse is a man who appreciates talent when he sees it. I wish I could say the same for these other imperfect souls."

It was 1630 when eight sharp-looking cadets gave the eyes left to Hop Sing's Laundry as they marched down the hill towards town. Danyluk, as usual, had brought his radio with him and the song, *My Prayer,* with the Platters, filled the dry, hot, sweet-smelling air.

The traffic on Highway 97 was heavy and many cadets were returning to camp, complaining of the walk up the hill and the heat.

"Are you sure the girls had enough time to contact each other?" asked Rothstein.

"They'll be in Polson Park; Debbie said she'd call them right away," replied Wayne. "They're bringing Sheila O'Grady for Simon."

They all glanced at each other, especially Simon. "What...what's wrong? Is she some sort of...is there...is there a problem with her...?"

East gave Simon a nudge and a wink. "You're like the other Irish, aren't you? Don't you like 'em fat, sweaty, and caked in makeup to hide the pimples?"

Simon stopped in his tracks, as did the others. Lost for words, he shrugged, winced and started to turn around as Cunningham grabbed his arm. "Look at it this way; she's got lots of money, it doesn't matter if she drools when she eats."

"Er, thanks, but I'll see you guys in camp."

All hands smacked him on his back as Rothstein came to the rescue. "C'mon, we wouldn't do that to our friends. She's gorgeous. This could be the start of something big!"

As the group started walking down the hill again, Simon still appeared a little distressed, but he knew it couldn't be all that bad when Moose said, "Wadduya mean she drools when she eats? When she's got her teeth in, she never drools. She might spit when she talks, but she never drools."

At the bottom of the hill, the Musketeers turned right into Polson Park. Instantly, the temperature dropped by twenty degrees. The beautiful, tall trees and manicured grass were more inviting to Danyluk than Alma, screaming, "MOOSE, MY LOVE!" as she rushed into his arms. For some reason, the other girls were shy as the smiling couples met, held hands, and tried hard to fix their bashful eyes on each other.

Wayne had his arm around Debbie as she introduced Sheila O'Grady to Simon. Sheila was pretty and her shiny red hair was braided at the back. It was long and exquisite and Simon was lost for words.

Gradually, the couples separated, but they weren't far from each other. Douglas and Diane lay down at their regular spot under the weeping willow tree next to the babbling brook. As usual, he had one arm around her shoulders and his other hand behind his head. His knees were up with one leg crossed over the other, as both stared at the clear blue sky trying to infiltrate the fluttering thin leaves of the weary branches on the giant tree.

"Did you receive my last letter before you left?" Diane asked.

They turned their heads towards each other as he nodded. He was just as shy as she. His faint smile turned into a large grin and they kissed when their eyes met.

"Yes, and as I've always said, you sure have a way with words."

"Well, you know I meant everything I said. I still haven't forgotten the wonderful time we had in Vancouver last March. I really like your mom and I think the two of us hit if off pretty well."

"She thinks you're great. After you left, I kept hearing, 'Douglas, you're going to have to marry that girl; don't ever let her get away.' "

Diane giggled. "And you said...?"

Douglas edged his arm out from under her shoulders and leaned on his elbow, looking into her eyes. "I said, 'Never in a million years would I ever let her get away. I want to spend every single minute of every day with her.'"

Alma and Moose were sitting side-by-side at a picnic table not far from the muffled chatter of Douglas and Diane.

"Did you meet any other girls after I left Vancouver?"

"Alma, you know there's only one dame in the world for me? What do you think I am... Moose, the world's biggest louse? How can you ask me that when you're wearing my mother's ring?"

"Oh, Moose, I'm sorry. But sometimes I wonder. When we were walking around Stanley Park and we passed those two girls, you did yell, 'Look at the ass on the blonde.'"

"Alma, you know I just did that to bug ya. You're the only one for me, you know that? How many times do I have to tell ya that there'll never be another, only you."

Gordie Cunningham and his girl both had to muffle their laughs. They weren't far from Moose and Alma, and although they were wrapped up in their own world, Alma's sincerity attracted their attention.

Maggie looked up for a moment. "What a great couple they are," she said.

"That Moose is such a loyal guy. He really loves her, doesn't he?"

Gordie smiled and nodded as he dealt her a card. "I hope I haven't given ya that Goddamned nine of spades again, I feel guilty about you always having to buy me dinner."

Tickling him, Maggie replied. "I don't mind, I know you're constantly broke. Why do you let those nasty boys take all your money at camp?"

A sad gaze came to Cunningham's eyes. He sighed and took hold of her left hand. "Them's the breaks, I guess. The only person who lets me win at cards is you...and that isn't very often. Say, you've beat me again!"

The serenity of each couple's moments was interrupted by Jack East's voice. "HEY EVERYONE, LOOK AT THE TIME. IF WE'RE GOIN' TO HAVE DIN-NER AND GO BOWLING, WE'D BETTER HIT THE RESTAURANT, NOW! WE'VE GOTTA BE BACK BY EIGHT!" Jack and his girl were up and looking forward to a hearty meal.

Shortly, all of them were heading in the direction of the Silver Grill Cafe. When they entered, they found the place packed with cadets and *Unchained Melody* by Les Baxter blared from the jukebox. Danyluk put a few nickels and dimes in and the next three songs were Elvis's, *Hound Dog, Heartbreak Hotel and Don't Be Cruel.*

"Jeez, that Presley's the cat's meow," commented Moose.

East was already eating. "He should be, your buddy Red Robinson plays a lot of his records."

Alma grabbed Moose by the scruff of his neck. "YOU NEVER TOLD ME YOU KNEW RED ROBINSON!"

Danyluk's head flopped around in a few directions. "You never asked me. I...er..one of these years I'll introduce you to my buddy, Red."

Alma had stars in her eyes. "Wow, thanks Moose. Just think, my Moose knows Red Robinson."

Over the next hour, Alma mentioned it sixteen times. She even told the wait-resses and the cashier. When they moved over to the bowling alley, the manager even asked Danyluk if he could get Red's autograph for his teenage girls.

"Sure, but I've got to meet them first," he whispered. "I sorta look out for my buddy, Red. I don't want him to get writer's cramp."

The manager didn't know it at the time but his agreeing to the introduction was the worst mistake of his life.

When the eight returned from town, B-33 was a madhouse. Like every hut the Musketeers had lived in before, it rocked with activity. Cadets were everywhere, ironing, shining, washing, shaving, showering, screaming, jumping and yes, even though they were senior cadets, they used the fire extinguishers as water cannons.

To the sounds of toilets flushing, orders being read, bedsprings being kicked, radios blaring, the washing machine whining, barrack-boxes and windows being slammed shut, the circuit breakers clicking, and a hundred-and-seventy some-odd conversations taking place, good old B-33 shuddered as the cadets *informed* it that another summer of training had started.

After lights out, when Sergeant Beckford had left the barracks, Moose got up and showed Cunningham the new watch Alma had given him. "I have been ordered that this watch will never be used as a gambling asset. She says if it is, we're both gonna lose our nuts."

Cunningham's eyes widened as he perused the watch. When he saw it was a

Timex, his interest waned.

"Moose, Moose, you know I've turned over a new leaf. I'm not the old Gordie you knew in Vancouver. I'm on a training course now. I've got responsibilities, not only to myself, but the other Musketeers, as well. That watch is your property, not mine, I want nothing to do with it."

Moose thought that was nice. "Gee, O.K., Gord. I'm sorry I sort of insulted ya. You're all right, do ya know that?"

"I'm not the hard-hearted bastard you thought I was. Besides, I've grown out of Timex watches."

"Hey, who told ya it was a Timex. It's a ..."

Cunningham was out of bed like a shot. He grabbed Danyluk's wrist. "Jesus Christ, she gave you a Bulova? Any jewels in there?"

Danyluk waved his arm around. "Sixteen. Nothin's too good for the old Moose. See, I don't have to wind it, either. When I move my hand and wrist, it winds itself."

Jackson sat up in his bunk. "That's too bad, your watch will always be over-wound."

"SCREW YOU, EARL!"

A minute of silence lapsed before Cunningham got back into bed and spoke again. "Hey, Moose, D'ya still like to play craps?"

"Yeah, sure, but I ain't got any money. You know that?"

Cunningham chuckled. "Don't worry about that old buddy, old pal. Let's talk about it in the morning."

As it had done untold times before, twenty minutes after Cunningham's last statement, tired old barracks B-33 permitted the moon to light up the faces and bodies of its sleeping 'soldiers.' Some had kicked off their upper sheet and blankets; others were wrapped in just a sheet, or hidden under all the covers. If the Corporals were in a good mood when they did their final check, they would pick a blanket off the floor and throw it on a sleeping cadet. But good moods were rare.

Throughout the night boys would talk in their sleep to members of their family, their girlfriends, and yes, even to their Sergeants. Sometimes their voices would just trail off, but other times, they were quite adamant.

"I'LL WRITE TO YA, MOM!"

"I'LL BE O.K., GRAN. TAKE YOUR PILLS AS THE DOCT..."

"LOOK AFTER THAT BIKE, OR I'LL HAVE YOUR NUTTTTS!"

"Piston, barrel, butt, body, biiipodddd!"

"Sergeant Mack, you can take thiiiiis paiiint and shhhove it!"

"Whyyy didn't you reeeead the effffin orrders?"

"O.K., alllll moneeee innn the pot. MOOOOOSE, YOU CAN THROW IN YOUR WATCH....NOT THE TIMEXXXX, THE BULL...OVA!"

In a few hours, it would be cool again in B-33 and those who weren't covered up would subconsciously reach for their blankets. If their hands couldn't find them, they would shiver until morning. Yes, old B-33 had experienced it all before. If it could talk, it would tell thousands of stories, however, this night, like all the others, it just creaked as it cooled, and let the sound of the gentle wind entering its windows compete with the snoring.

CHAPTER IV

Sergeant Simpson's voice shook the building as he stomped into the barracks and started turning over mattresses and pulling off blankets. It was 0515 hours, Monday morning, and the sky was just brightening in the east.

"STAND BY YOUR BEDS! C'MON YOU LAZY LOT, I SAID, STAND BY YOUR BEDS! YOU PEOPLE HAVE EXACTLY ONE MINUTE TO FORM THREE RANKS ON THE ROAD! YOU...YOU SEX MANIAC, STOP MAKING LOVE TO YOUR PILLOW AND GET YOUR ASS ON THE ROAD!"

Danyluk and the other Musketeers had never forgotten the *kind and gentle* tone of Sergeant Simpson's voice. Within seconds, Moose was stepping into his P.T. shorts and pulling them up over his usual morning erection. It was an automatic reaction because, like his compatriots, he was still partially asleep as he bounced from leg to leg.

"Jesus, only one minute? We haven't even got time to take a pee? Sergeant, I've gotta piss like a racehorse!"

"YOU DON'T LOOK LIKE A BLOODY RACEHORSE, YOU LOOK LIKE AN ELEPHANT! PULL YOUR PANTS UP, MAN, THE END OF YOUR *TRUNK* IS SHOWING ABOVE THE ELASTIC. GET ON THE ROAD! YOU SHOULD HAVE THOUGHT OF YOUR PREDICAMENT BEFORE YOU WOKE UP!"

Moose ran for the door, bitching to Cunningham who was just behind him. "If I had of thought of that before I got up I would have pissed the bed!"

Cunningham nodded, but he wasn't looking at Danyluk's face. "I don't think you should run with that watch on, you might just damage it!"

Although the air was fresh, it was cold as the shivering cadets of Alpha Company jogged towards the upper camp. The little bit of morning dew kept some of the dust settled, however, when 170 cadets tromp, dust and dirt flies everywhere.

Although Sergeant Simpson was the only Senior NCO present, the Platoon Corporals jogged beside their individual platoons.

"WHO ARE WE?" Sergeant Simpson bellowed.

"Who the fuck cares!" Danyluk murmered as he *smiled* at Cunningham.

"I SAID WHO ARE WE?"

Every voice in the company responded as one. "ALPHA COMPANY!"

Cunningham couldn't get over Moose's expression. "What the hell are you laughing for?"

"Who's laughing? I'm trying to catch my breath and I've got a Goddamned stone in my left runner!"

"WHAT ARE WE?"

"Fucking idiots, that's what we are!" Danyluk mumbled.

"THE BEST!" replied the company.

After jogging around the upper camp and back to B-33, the cadets of Senior Leader's Instructors completed twenty-five pushups and twenty-five sit-ups. When they were fallen out, there was a mad rush to the jon. Danyluk made certain he was at the urinal first. Cadets were piling into the room and all of the cubicles were full.

"THE GOD DAMNED BUGLER ISN'T UP AT THIS UNGODLY HOUR! WHAT THE HELL AM I DOING HERE?"

"Hurry it up, up front!" someone yelled.

Moose turned his head slightly to one side. "Screw you, some of us have big bladders."

The young cadet next to him said, "Cripes, you've got a big bladder, as well? Hey, Charlie, this guy'll never have gout! He's at the end, and we're all pissin' on his wang."

Johnston dragged himself next to Danyluk at the urinal and dropped his prophylactic paint tin on the floor. His arms were so tired he couldn't raise them to assist his aim, so he let his shorts fall to his ankles and nature looked after the rest. Although he was totally beat, he still had a sense of humour.

"After this, if I ever see another tin of paint, I'll draw a picture of Mack bending over and ram it up his ass! Christ, the tip of my wang tells me the water's cold!"

"Yeah, and deep too," Moose replied with a smile, as he took two minutes to tuck it in and then left to add to the unorganized acts of confusion taking place in his wing."

"MOOSE, WAS I SEEING THINGS? YOU WERE AT THE END OF THE URINAL BUT THE TIP OF YOUR WANG WAS DOWN THE DRAIN HOLE." Johnston yelled after him.

"IT'S WELL TRAINED!" was Moose's reply.

With Pat Boone's voice originating from the Kelowna radio station, the song, *Ain't That A Shame*, boomed throughout the east wing of B-33. At times even Pat was drowned out from the noise of over eighty cadets trying to prepare for the day ahead.

The Musketeers were organized, more organized than most. Within minutes, they had showered, brushed their teeth, combed their hair, and made and squared off their beds after aligning them. They had brushed and mopped out their bunk spaces, and lined up their barrack-boxes with exact care. Clean towels were hung, evenly measured, at the end of the bunks, the folds to the right. Wash basins which had been shined the day before were placed in the middle of their blanket dust covers. Running shoes which had been scrubbed minutes earlier would be worn over to the mess hall, along with coveralls. After breakfast, the running shoes would be laced and placed neatly on the shelf behind their bunks. The laces must not be twisted and that's all that was allowed on the shelf. Everything else, except an adroitly hung buttoned-up battledress uniform, would be put away. These uniforms were on hangers behind their bunks in between the windows which were open with precisely the same amount of space at the top and the bottom.

Major Ratcliffe had been right. The only cadets in the kitchen at that time of the morning where the ones from Alpha Company. Reveille hadn't been blown when East held his plate out a little longer to ensure he got more than the normal three pieces of bacon.

The eight Musketeers squeezed in at one table. They were wide awake now, and ready for whatever was to be handed out. While a few other cadets had also learned the lessons of the past years, the majority of guys in the mess hall wore their neatly pressed khaki shirts, pants, hosetops, boots, and puttees. These pants and shirts would become creased from sitting at breakfast. The Musketeers had yet to change, but they allowed themselves enough time, and they would look sharp on parade. Much sharper than the rest.

"I've got a feeling this course is designed to either make us or break us," offered East.

Like everyone else, Moose wolfed his food down quickly. "There should be a limit to what we have to go through. I had to take a piss so bad my tonsils were floating. That Simpson is a sadist."

Douglas was in deep thought. "If we're going to survive, we've got to beat them at their own game. We've been through all this before...well, not exactly, but we've got to stay one step ahead. Gordie, you won an alarm clock from one of those prairie cadets, where is it?"

Cunningham smiled at Moose. "It's in my sixteenth of *our* (he pointed at himself and Moose) barrack-box. Jesus, Moose, I'm supposed to have half the box, can't you put some of your shit down below in your suitcase? (All suitcases and duffel bags were stored below in the hut.) What the hell is that tin pot with the belt attached to it?"

"That's my steel jockstrap. Wayne made it for me."

"What the hell are you going to do with a steel jockstrap?"

"I've got plans, I may even..."

Douglas got them back on track. "Gordie, how about lending me the clock? I'll get us up fifteen minutes before Simpson arrives."

Although East's mouth was full, he could still verbally protest. "Jesus, we don't get any sleep now and you want to get us up even earlier?"

Douglas nodded. "That's right! Our beds will be made *before* Simpson arrives. Just think, Moose, you can take a leak and have the whole urinal to yourself."

Moose grinned and cocked his head. "Perfect, Dougie, I, for one, am with ya! Screw Simpson and his elephant comments."

Earl took a note out of his coveralls pocket. "O.K., listen to this. Come closer," he said, as eight heads moved in toward the centre of the table.

Whispering, Earl read from the small piece of paper. "The colour for the day is purple...the number for the day is twenty-six, and the code word is, Penticton."

Rothstein sat back again, sipping his tea. "What the hell's that all about?"

Earl continued. Sergeant Simpson attached a page to the Daily Routine Orders. No one saw him, not even me, but I knew it wasn't there last night. I just happened to flip up the cover, and there it was."

"The sneaky buggers," Simon offered. Those were the first words he'd said all morning, other than, "Earl, get your feet outa my face!"

Wayne leaned back, briskly stroking his chin. "They want us to read everything there is. That's the only way we're going to pass this course. Good job, Earl. Right... let's get out of here!"

As the group stood up, Wayne recognized East's expression and grabbed him by the arm. "NO YOU CAN'T GO BACK FOR SECONDS!"

They heard reveille being blown as they marched towards B-33.

"ALPHA COMPANY, ATTEN...TION! STANDAT...EASE! ALPHA COMPANY, ATTEN...TION!" Sergeant-Major Rose turned and saluted Major Ratcliffe.

"ALPHA COMPANY HAS 187 CADETS ON PARADE, NO CADETS ON SICK PARADE, AND THEY ARE READY FOR YOUR INSPECTION, SIR!"

The roll had been called earlier by the Platoon Corporals. Also, before the sergeants and officers arrived, the corporals had sized the company by platoons. By the time the Company Commander and his officers arrived, the sergeants were in front of their platoons, with the corporals in the rear. The company was already at the open order when Sergeant-Major Rose took it over.

When the Platoon Officers arrived, they started promenading the full length of the company, ensuring that when they turned, they always turned inwardly, never showing their backs to the cadets. They stopped just prior to the Sergeant-Major handing over the parade. Now they were at ease, evenly spaced out behind the Company Commander, each facing his own platoon's right marker.

"Thank you, Sergeant-Major, fall in, please."

"SIR!" Sergeant-Major Rose saluted again and turned smartly to his right, marched and halted next to the right marker of number one platoon. He turned about, dressed himself off and stiffly stood to attention, pace-stick parallel with his body, the large end of it in the palm of his right hand.

Major Ratcliffe waited for the Sergeant-Major to assume his position before he took one pace forward.

"ALPHA COMPANY, STANDAT...EASE! ALPHA COMPANY, ATTEN...TION! COMPANY, STANDAT...EASE! FALL IN THE OFFICERS!"

Each officer came to attention and saluted, and the Company Commander returned their salutes. When that was completed, they marched to a position in front of the individual right markers of their platoon. As the officers marched forward, each Platoon Sergeant turned and called his platoon to attention. Then he turned smartly to his left and halted in front of the second man in the front rank. The officers then halted in front of the right markers, turned to their right, and returned the salutes of their sergeants. Sergeant Beckford, of course, was in front of One Platoon.

"GOOD MORNING, SIR!"

"GOOD MORNING, SERGEANT BECKFORD; FALL IN, PLEASE!"

Sergeant Beckford saluted again; turned about and marched to the rear of the platoon, halting a pace or so behind the platoon corporals.

Lieutenant Harwood marched to the centre of the platoon, turned and faced his cadets. He then waited for his sergeant to get into position before he stood his platoon at ease, called them to attention again, and then stood them at ease. Following that, he turned smartly about and stood at ease himself. The same procedure took place with all of the other platoons.

The Company Commander continued. "ALPHA COMPANY, ATTEN...TION! ALPHA COMPANY, STANDAT...EASE! I WILL BE ALTERNATING MY INSPECTIONS DAY BY DAY. THIS MORNING, I WILL INSPECT NUMBER ONE PLATOON! THE OTHER PLATOON COMMANDERS MAY CARRY ON WITH THEIR OWN INSPECTION! SERGEANT-MAJOR ROSE, YOU WILL JOIN ME, PLEASE!"

"SIR!"

As the Sergeant did before him, Lieutenant Harwood came to attention, turned about, called his platoon to attention; turned to his left and halted in front of the second cadet in the front rank. The Company Commander halted in front of the right marker. Salutes were exchanged.

"GOOD MORNING, SIR! NUMBER ONE PLATOON READY FOR YOUR INSPECTION, SIR!"

"THANK YOU, LIEUTENANT HARWOOD, PLEASE STAND THE SEC-OND AND REAR RANKS AT EASE!"

Lieutenant Harwood took up a position behind the Company Commander but in front of Sergeant-Major Rose. He then called for his Sergeant.

"SERGEANT BECKFORD, WILL YOU JOIN US, PLEASE, AND STAND THE CENTRE AND REAR RANKS AT EASE!"

Beckford carried on with his task and stood behind Sergeant-Major Rose as the group walked the front rank, backing up slightly so they could start at the right hand marker. The marker's name was Danyluk.

The O.C.'s eyes reviewed Danyluk's scrubbed-clean pith-helmet and slowly moved down over his body to his boots.

"Excellent turnout, Danyluk. The only thing I can see wrong is that someone has issued you a name tag which needs mending. Speak to one of the company clerks at noon and it will be replaced. Well done, my boy!"

"THANK *YOU*, SIR!"

At exactly the same time the Company Commander was inspecting cadet Rothstein, Number Three Platoon's Sergeant Mack was standing in front of cadet Johnston. He gently took the paint tin away from him and winked. "I'm proud of you, Johnston...damn proud of you. Well done!"

An amazed Johnston didn't know what to say. "ER, THANK...THANK YOU, SERGEANT!"

"Exceptional turnout!"

"THANK YOU, SERGEANT!"

In all, the inspection took only ten minutes. Ten long minutes because boot soles and the insides of belts were checked, along with the inside brass.

After the inspection, the best-dressed cadet in each platoon was asked to fall out. They stood side-by-side, facing the company, while Major Ratcliffe and Sergeant-Major Rose made the decision as to who was the overall best-dressed cadet in the company that morning.

After a hand-shaking exercise, a drill cane was handed to Cadet Danyluk and the rest were asked to resume their positions.

"CADET DANYLUK OF ONE PLATOON IS TODAY'S STICKMAN! AS ALL OF YOU CAN SEE, HIS DRESS IS EXCELLENT! THAT'S THE WAY I WANT EACH OF YOU TO LOOK!

"ALTHOUGH I ONLY INSPECTED ONE PLATOON, I WAS VERY IMPRESSED BY THE DRESS, DRILL, AND DEPORTMENT OF THAT PLA-TOON! I BELIEVE WE'VE GOT OFF ON THE RIGHT FOOT. KEEP UP THE GOOD WORK!

"SHORTLY, I WILL INSPECT YOUR BARRACKS. FROM WHAT I SEE HERE, I DON'T THINK THERE WILL BE MUCH OF A PROBLEM INSIDE. MY CONGRATULATIONS!"

The company was standing easy as Major Ratcliffe spoke. "Now, those of you who know today's colour, step forward and form up behind me."

Instantly nine cadets marched forward. The ninth one was Johnston. He mentioned later that he had seen Earl, *making notes* by the bulletin board.

The other cadets were shrugging and mumbling to each other. One even said, "It's those creeps, again. What are we doing wrong?"

Sergeant Simpson shook his head. He didn't think anyone had seen him post the page. Sergeant Beckford just smiled. He knew the combined talent of the Musketeers.

Major Ratcliffe addressed Danyluk. "What's the colour?"

"PURPLE, SIR!"

Then Douglas. "And the number of the day?"
"TWENTY SIX, SIR!"
What's today's code word, East?"
"PENTICTON, SIR!"
The Company Commander smiled and took their names before asking them to fall back in.
"NOW, I'M NOT GOING TO TELL YOU PEOPLE HOW THESE CADETS GOT THIS INFORMATION. YOU CAN ASK THEM IF YOU WANT TO FIND THAT OUT! I WILL SAY THIS, THOUGH...START READING ORDERS! ALL ORDERS! IS THAT CLEAR?"
"YES, SIR!"
"DURING POP BREAK THIS MORNING AND THIS AFTERNOON, THOSE NINE CADETS WILL HAVE A POP ON THE HOUSE!"
After a few more formalities, the cadets of Alpha Company were allowed to pick up their notebooks, pencils, pens, and manuals which they had placed on the ground just outside the building. The Company Commander, the Platoon Officers, and Sergeant-Major Rose entered B-33 to inspect the building as four sized-platoons headed for the parade square. As they marched away with Danyluk in front, other signs of activity were taking place in Camp Vernon. Along with a few heads, a few *fingers* appeared out of other hut windows. One of the Corporals calling the step said, "YOU DON'T SEE THOSE UN-GENTLEMANLY GESTURES ORIGINATING FROM THE 'KIDDY' COMPANIES BECAUSE YOU'RE LOOKING TO YOUR FRONT! RIGHT?"
"RIGHT, CORPORAL!"

Although the Musketeers and most of the other cadets in Alpha Company had experienced drill in temperatures exceeding ninety-five degrees, it was a pleasure to complete drill movements between the hours of 0700 and 0900. Not only did the cadets appreciate the opportunity to show their stuff, and work with professional drill instructors, the air was cool and that ever-refreshing and wonderful early morning Okanagan scent filled every nostril.
Each platoon worked separately on the giant parade square. Sergeants Simpson, Mack, and Prest were excellent drill instructors, however as Wayne whispered out of the corner of his mouth to Douglas, "On a scale of one-to-ten, they only rate five, compared to Sergeant Beckford's expertise."
As usual, Sergeant Beckford started from the first drill movements in CAMT 2-2 (Canadian Army Manual of Training): the attention, stand at ease and stand easy positions. Unlike other times, he made a running comment of the little secrets that make drill instructors unique and effective.
"NEVER GIVE A DRILL COMMAND ON THE MOVE UNLESS YOU'RE MARCHING WITH YOUR TROOPS. WHEN YOU'RE TEACHING DRILL, YOU'RE CONSTANTLY ON THE MOVE, OBSERVING YOUR PEOPLE FROM DIFFERENT ANGLES. HALT, FACE THEM, AND STAND AT ATTENTION WHEN YOU GIVE EACH ORDER. WHEN YOU'RE TEACHING DRILL MOVEMENTS, BREAK THE MOVEMENTS DOWN. DEMONSTRATE THE COMPLETE MOVEMENT...THEN BREAK DOWN THE MOVEMENT IN NUMBERS AND DEMONSTRATE EACH NUMBER. THEN DEMONSTRATE THE FIRST MOVEMENT AND PRACTISE IT UNTIL IT BECOMES PERFECT BEFORE YOU MOVE ON TO THE SECOND MOVEMENT. HAVE THEM

CALL OUT THE TIME CONTINUOUSLY."

Throughout the two-hour session, cadets were called out to teach the actual drill. Sergeant Beckford nurtured each lad individually.

"SCAN THEM...SCAN THEM! LOOK AT EVERYTHING THEY DO! THEY'RE ACTING AS ONE, THEREFORE YOU CAN SEE WHEN SOME-THING IS OUT OF PLACE! MAINTAIN EYE CONTACT, MAN...THEY WON'T LOOK AT YOU, BUT YOU MAKE BLOODY CERTAIN YOU'RE LOOKING AT THEM! CONSTANTLY MOVE WHEN THEY'RE ON THE MOVE! ONLY THEN CAN YOU OBSERVE AND BREAK EVERY BAD HABIT. LET THEM HEAR YOU! BELLOW IT OUT, 'GET YOUR ARMS UP, THAT MAN...PUSH DOWN ON YOUR THUMBS...GET YOUR ARMS UP TO THE MAN'S WAIST IN FRONT OF YOU!'"

Sergeant Beckford was a master of the parade square. He had been taught properly therefore everyone he taught had to do it right. His voice never tired.

"YOU, GET YOUR CHIN UP! THERE'S NO MONEY DOWN THERE BECAUSE I PICKED IT ALL UP BEFORE YOU GOT HERE. DRIVE YOUR ARMS BACK, MAN...DRIVE YOUR ARMS BACK! DON'T BEND THE ARMS...I SAID DON'T BEND THE ARMS! GET YOUR CHEST OUT! YES, YOU...GET YOUR CHEST OUT! YOU...YOU HORRIBLE LITTLE MAN, WHAT THE HELL ARE YOU STICKING YOUR ASS OUT FOR? ARE YOU IN HEAT? MY FEMALE DOG STICKS HER ASS OUT JUST LIKE YOU...BUT ONLY WHEN SHE'S IN HEAT! WHAT THE HELL'S THE MATTER WITH YOU, HAVE YOU GOT A PIECE OF SOAP STUCK UP YOUR ASS FROM THIS MORNING'S SHOWER? DON'T WIPE YOUR ASS WITH YOUR ARMS, BRING THEM STRAIGHT BACK...THAT'S BETTER! DON'T SCRATCH YOUR NOSE, THAT MAN! WHAT WAS THAT? I DON'T CARE IF A KILLER BEE LANDED ON IT!"

Actually no one had spoken to the Sergeant. His comments weren't aimed at anyone in particular. If they were, no one knew who they were aimed at. Every man thought he was talking to him, alone.

"I CAN'T HEAR YOU! CALL OUT THE TIME! YOU...THAT MAN, I'VE HEARD YOU YELL LOUDER IN THE JON WHEN YOUR ASS IS PLUGGED UP. GET IT OUT MAN, GET IT OUT! GET YOUR FEET UP! I SAID GET YOUR BLOODY FEET UP! BEND THE KNEE AND SHOOT THE FOOT FOR-WARD! KEEP YOUR KNEES PARALLEL WITH THE TOE OF YOUR BOOT! LET YOUR FOOT HANG, MAN...DON'T STICK IT UP IN THE AIR! GET YOUR FINGERS TOGETHER...THAT'S BETTER! NO DAYLIGHT BETWEEN THE ARMS...NO DAYLIGHT BETWEEN THE ARMS. WHAM, DRIVE IT DOWN! GET YOUR STOMACH IN... SUCK IT IN...ARE YOU PREG-NANT?...WELL, ARE YOU? CALL IT OUT, MAN...IT'S ONE, TWO THREE, ONE...NOT NINE, TEN ELEVEN, TWELVE! LEFT, RIGHT, LEFT, RIGHT, LEFT, RIGHT...NUMBER ONE PLATOON, HALT! STAND STILL! DON'T MOVE! STAND STILL! STANDAT...EASE! STAND EASY! TAKE OFF YOUR HELMETS AND SHAKE YOUR HEADS!"

While the cadets whispered to each other, Sergeant Beckford would say to all of them, "I like what I see! If I could only have you guys for a few months, we'd make the Queen's Guard look like they were bloody Girl Guides."

Danyluk was sweating. "A few months? Did you hear him, he said a few months? Christ, I feel like I've been at it a few years!"

Rothstein nodded. "You have! One minute with Beckford is like a month with the others."

Danyluk still complained. "Jesus, I've got blisters on my blisters. They're starting to bleed."

Douglas asked, "How in the hell did you get blisters, are your boots too tight?"

"Naah, I was watching the French Foreign Legion on our new television set and since they don't wear socks, I didn't, either."

Douglas winced. "Jesus, Moose, they wear different boots compared to what we wear; you'll be down to the bone if you don't do something about it."

"What'll I do? Don't forget, I'm the stickman, I'm supposed to set an example."

"Just tell Sergeant Beckford you've got a hole in your sock and you'd like to go and change them."

Danyluk came to attention, forearm extended. "SERGEANT BECKFORD!"

"YES, YOU SHARP-LOOKING CADET, WHAT CAN I DO FOR YOU?"

"Er, Sergeant...I've got a hole in one of my socks...would you mind if I went and changed them?"

"WHAT? YOU JUST GOT THEM THE DAY BEFORE YESTERDAY? HAVE YOU BEEN TAKING THEM TO BED WITH YOU, AND WINDING YOUR NEW WATCH?"

Danyluk didn't catch on, but a few of the others did. Laughter filled their portion of the parade square. "ER, NO SERGEANT! I DON'T WEAR ANYTHING TO BED!" He wondered how Beckford knew he had a new watch.

Banks was bent over in laughter. "His thing wouldn't fit into his sock anyway."

"ALL RIGHT! I WAS ACTUALLY WONDERING WHAT WAS WRONG WITH YOU...YOU WERE MARCHING LIKE YOU HAD NO SOCKS ON AT ALL! BE BACK HERE IN FIVE MINUTES!"

Danyluk returned and after two hours of drill, the company marched over to the upper camp for a lecture on map using before the pop truck arrived. The excuse for a *road* was dusty; those who held a cold bottle of Kik Kola to their foreheads didn't realize they had mud all over their faces. The Musketeers and Johnston received their pop first and it was free. During the break, cadets by the dozen came over to ask how they knew the code word, colour, and number. When told, they realized just how astute they would have to become.

"That Sergeant Mack's a pretty good guy," Johnston said, sitting down and motioning that he had one arm longer than the other.

Danyluk tore his eyes away from the comic he was reading. "How soon we forget. You were cursing him a few hours ago."

"I know, but he's got that certain knack about him. It's as if he wants us to know he's only putting on the act."

Douglas agreed. "That's called man-management and it's rubbing off on us, as well. If we can take what they dish out, then they're with us. If we can't, and we act like wimps, then they lay it on heavier, until we figure it out. Let's face it, whatever they ask is reasonable. It may seem tough at the time, but it's still reasonable."

The group concluded that Douglas was right, then Jackson changed the subject to discuss an earlier scenario.

"You shouldn't have let Lieutenant Harwood hear you," Jackson told East.

"I didn't think he could because he was talking when I whispered it to you."

They all chuckled, then Simon slapped East on the back. "I'll say this much

They all chuckled, then Simon slapped East on the back. "I'll say this much for you, Jack, you've got guts. When he asked you to stand up and tell everyone what you said, you told him all right."

Johnston hadn't heard the remark because he'd been in another lecture room receiving the same lesson from *his* Platoon Officer. "What did you say?" he asked.

East affected his proud look with an ear-to-ear grin. "I told him what Sergeant Beckford told us a few years back. 'SIR, MURPHY'S MILITARY LAW NUMBER FOUR SAYS: THE MOST DANGEROUS THING IN THE COMBAT ZONE IS AN OFFICER WITH A MAP!' "

The whole group of them laughed, and then Johnston asked, "What was his reaction?"

East still had an exaggerated crazy grin on his face. "He didn't say anything, he just laughed with the rest of us. I think he knew I was probably right. Don't you guys remember what Sergeant Beckford told us a few years back? Remember, when he was in Wainright? He was sitting under a tree discussing platoon and section tactics with his platoon, when an officer came by in a jeep and told him he was in the wrong position. When he informed the officer he wasn't, the Lieutenant ordered him to move his platoon five-hundred yards to the west. The Sergeant moved the platoon even though he knew they'd be in the target zone when the shelling started."

East's audience was wide-eyed. "What the hell happened?" Rothstein asked.

"Nothin' happened. Beckford got on the 'blower' and informed the Battle Captain to hold fire because he'd been ordered to move his men there. Five minutes later the same officer appeared in his jeep. 'Ah, Sergeant Beckford, you're, ahh, you're in the wrong position again. I want you to move your men 499 yards to the east.'"

"No apology?" asked Johnston.

East nodded. "You got that right. Great leadership, eh?"

Danyluk lit up a Sweet Caporal cigarette and stopped reading his Combat Kelly comic book. "Once in a while ya gotta speak up. I got a blast for saying something similar down at the armouries last month when Lieutenant Steacy was giving us a lecture on man management. He asked how inspiration takes place and I gave him Sergeant Simpson's version of the answer. I said, 'Inspiration is like shit, you have to eat something first!'"

While the rest laughed and shrugged wondering what Danyluk's statement had to do with the original conversation, Moose went back to reading his comic book.

Douglas asked Danyluk how his feet were.

"They're all right now. I filled my socks with that foot powder they gave us. Now I know why rubbers are called French Safes. The Foreign Legion probably puts 'em on their feet."

"You were stupid not wearing socks in the first place," said Wayne.

Moose closed his comic and stuffed it into his notebook. "We've got the only television set on our street and our house was full of visitors when I saw it. Everyone agreed it would be a great idea. It's not like radio; they don't lie on television, you know."

East didn't agree. "Who says they don't? 'You'll wonder where the yeller went, when you brush your teeth with Pepsodent?' They show some dame brushing her teeth, but her teeth ain't yellow, they're white."

Danyluk wouldn't give in. "What do ya want, some broad with yellow teeth or black teeth starin' into the camera? Besides, I don't look at the dames' teeth, I look at their bazookas...and sometimes, their personalities."

As the Musketeers passed Sergeants Simpson and Beckford when they re-entered the building, East and Danyluk were still at it.

"You mean you go out with dames with yellow or black teeth?"

"Why not? Ya can't see 'em in the dark. Jesus, you're fussy...just like the rest of the guys. Beauty is skin deep, you gotta accept the dame for what she is. She may not have great teeth, or her breath might even smell like garlic, but she could have a great body and a super character. All ya gotta do is hold your breath when you French kiss 'em."

"Since when did you start thinking that way? You've always told us your broads have gotta have a million-dollar smile and a billion-dollar body. A guy would have to hold his breath until he's blue, with the dame you're describing."

"Jesus, you're getting personal, East. Why do I always have to explain the facts of life to you? A few years ago you didn't even *believe* in French kissing."

"I still don't because I like to taste my own food. You say I'm getting personal? You were the one who told us some dame's braces nearly ripped your tongue apart. Now *I'm* getting personal?"

"Yeah, you're getting personal! I don't know if it *was* her braces, because she was sucking the cap off a ball-point pen that was in her mouth."

"You mean you gave her the tongue knowing she had the top of a ball-point pen in there?"

"I didn't know it! The doctor found it when he stopped her from choking to death. The thing wedged in her throat because of the wad of bubble gum she was chewing."

"Moose, are you saying you slipped her the tongue knowing she was chewing bubble gum and she had something else in her mouth besides?"

Danyluk used his stick to push East through the door. "That's it! I'm not sharin' any more of my exploits with you."

East stopped in the middle of the doorway. "It's just as well. You remind me of the French politician who was always kissing babies."

"So what's wrong with kissing little babies?"

Prior to East being pushed again, he said, "Before they're born?"

Simpson smiled as the duo walked by. "They say if the men are bitching, everything is going well. These guys never seem to bitch, they just talk about sex."

Beckford agreed. "If Danyluk had his way, his *women* wouldn't have any teeth. He learned his lesson with the one who wore braces. Now he asks them if they've got anything in their mouths. If they hesitate, he's got his finger in there quick. He doesn't take chances anymore."

An amazed look seized Simpson's face. "You've got to be joking? He asks them that and then shoves his finger in their mouths? That's kinky stuff?"

"That's our Danyluk," replied Sergeant Beckford. "At least he's honest. If they haven't got anything in there, they soon will have."

"How the hell do you know these things?" asked Simpson.

"After six weeks with these guys, I know how many hairs they've got on their heads."

Simpson was still shaking his head and mumbling to himself as he entered the building. "Christ, if this kid is like this now, what's he going to be like when he gets older?"

Beckford laughed. "That's exactly what RSM Gardiner asks!"

Lunch tasted absolutely fabulous that afternoon because it had been a long blistering morning. The choices were: hot, open, roast beef sandwiches with gravy. Hot dogs, or corned beef and cabbage. Although time was short, East had all three. He actually had to talk Jackson into going back for corned beef and cabbage for him, because one of the serving ladies asked him if he'd been through before.

"Not me, ma'am, you must be mistaken."

Wayne became the spokesman for a couple of minutes and made good sense. "We've got to finish in half-an-hour and wash yesterday's kit. It'll only take about five minutes to dry and we'll iron it at supper time. Don't forget, we're back on parade at 1300, so make sure we start shining our boots no later than 1250."

All eagerly agreed and when they were formed up in three ranks on the road, eight gleaming pairs of boots looked just as good as those worn by the Sergeants, maybe better.

When training is in session, the bird's-eye view of Camp Vernon compares to ants around an anthill. With companies marching in all directions; individual cadets taking bearings with compasses; baseball, soccer, and pushball games; vehicles ferrying cadets to the beach, etc., the camp is alive with activity.

The same thing was happening in the various lecture huts throughout the encampment, and the four platoons of the Musketeers' company filled four very hot lecture rooms. Even though all of the windows were open, the scorching heat of the midday sun suppressed the enthusiasm felt in the cool of the morning.

The lectures were about leadership and it takes a special kind of instructor to maintain interest when perspiration is seeping from every pore.

Major Ratcliffe's instruction was sufficient to arouse the curiosity of *men* learning the techniques of how to control *men*.

"...SO YOU SEE, IF YOU ARE GOING TO BE THE LEADER, IT IS ESSENTIAL THAT YOU KNOW WHICH WAY YOU ARE GOING. ESTABLISHING THE DIRECTION AND SURVEYING THE TERRAIN THAT IS GOING TO LEAD TO THE ACCOMPLISHMENT OF THE MISSION AND OBJECTIVES ARE PART OF THE PLANNING PROCESS. LET'S LOOK AT THE STEPS OUTLINING THE BASIC PLANNING PROCESS THAT YOU, AS A LEADER, WILL WANT TO FOLLOW IN CLIMBING THE LADDER TO LEADERSHIP SUCCESS."

The major picked up some chalk and wrote on the blackboard.

'1. *Determine what is to be done; the mission and purpose.*'

"East, what does that mean?"

Although East was sweating from the heat in the stuffy room, he enjoyed this topic. All the Musketeers did.

"Er, well...we have to have a goal, and..."

Major Ratcliffe smiled. "Good, very good, but let's call the big goal...the mission, O.K.?"

East nodded. "Well then, we need a series of goals to achieve the mission."

"RIGHT!" The officer walked the width of the room. "Exactly right, East. So now that we think we know our purpose and our mission, we'll do what East has suggested."

'2. *Define the goals to be accomplished in successfully completing the mission.*'

"YOU ALL KNOW WHAT I MEAN." The Major fluctuated his voice to

Time flew for those who were interested. Over the next two periods, they covered the rest of the material.

'*3 Develop specific objectives to be accomplished.*'

'*4 Analyze the environment for threats and opportunities.*'

'*5 Determine your comparative advantage against your competition's.*'

'*6 Consider alternative approaches for achieving the goal.*'

'*7 Develop a strategy for accomplishing the objectives.*'

'*8 Develop an organizational structure and climate that will support the strategy.*'

'*9 Determine short-range plans and programs as part of the overall strategy.*'

'*10 Develop an evaluation and feedback (control) system.*'

'*11 Implement the plan and modify if required.*'

When it was close to quitting time, Ratcliffe summed it all up and left them with more thoughts.

"Remember, many times, the *remedy* for having lost sight of the vision of the enterprise is to increase the efforts and drive the followers forward. This inevitably leads to disaster. That, gentlemen, is why errors are made and people are killed. Your job as a leader is to protect your people. If you don't, another leader will step forward.

"A final point to bear in mind is the importance of contingency plans that can be put into operation should something unexpected go wrong. The leader who is truly on top of things comes to expect the unexpected, to realize that nothing is going to work out exactly according to plan. Remember that!"

With the heat nearly unbearable, and dust and dirt flying, Alpha Company marched back to their quarters. Major Ratcliffe had made a lot of sense and each Musketeer knew the importance of this series of lectures.

"I think I'm going to enjoy this course," Rothstein whispered. "We can really sink our teeth into this stuff!"

Although Danyluk was the stickman, he didn't feel comfortable marching in the front of the company, so he had joined his buddies in the ranks. "But he said things always go wrong. Nothing went wrong when we moved those sleeping Irish pongoes onto the parade square."

Jackson didn't agree. "Our prank wasn't pulled off perfectly, Moose. Our time evaluation was way off. We were going to do it in fifteen minutes, it took us over half-an-hour. What if one of the Corporals had decided to visit the jon and noticed our beds were empty?"

"But that could have happened anyway," retorted Danyluk.

Douglas butted in. "Earl's right in a way, Moose. What he's saying is the more time we took, the more time our beds were empty, thus we left ourselves more open than we should have."

"Well, Bergie was the leader, he should have planned for that!"

Wayne was marching behind Danyluk. He grabbed Moose's stick for a moment, putting him out of step. "Maybe he did plan for it, we'll never know, but he did want to do it in fifteen minutes and it took more time than that."

"YOU, GET INTO STEP!" blared a Corporal.

Moose's expression of *distaste* went unnoticed. He got into step quickly and continued the discussion.

"That happened to me at a house party once. I followed this dame into her bathroom at home. She walked up the stairs and I timed myself. I was exactly five seconds behind her. I knew her mother visited the jon every thirty minutes and

seconds behind her. I knew her mother visited the jon every thirty minutes and she'd used the jon fifteen minutes before. My timing was down perfectly...I had fifteen minutes all to myself. I opened the door a little, put my hand in and turned out the lights...it was now pitch black and..."

"Get to the point," East said.

"I *am* getting to the point. Anyway, I put my hand over her mouth and asked her if she had anything in it. Then..."

Earl was losing the gist. "What? You asked her if she had anything in your hand?"

Danyluk gave East a slow stare. "Not in my hand, you creep...in her mouth! Christ, I knew she had nothing in my hand, what's the matter with you?"

"Get on with it!" East demanded.

"Well, I couldn't see her response so I slipped it in her mouth to make sure and..."

Jackson was still lost and now totally astounded. "You dirty thing. You just slipped your wang in there and...that's immoral as hell!"

Danyluk's frustration was wild. "What in Hades are you talking about, Earl? Get your mind out of the gutter, man...I slipped my finger in her mouth and..."

Jackson howled, he hadn't heard Danyluk's previous conversation with East. "YOU WHAT? YOU SLIPPED YOUR FINGER IN HER MOUTH? I'VE HEARD OF PERVERTS BEFORE, BUT YOU TAKE THE CAKE! JESUS, YOU GET YOUR JOLLIES OUT OF STICKING YOU FINGER IN DAMES' MOUTHS?"

Now Moose was confused and didn't have the energy to explain.

East snarled, "Will you get on with it! What's the matter with you Earl? He was just checking for objects or gum?"

Earl looked at the sky. "God give me strength! You do the same thing? I've read a lotta books on sex but I must have missed the finger in the mouth bit. What is it, the saliva on the finger that turns a person on? You mean feeling gums is better than feeling bazookas? I've never tried it!"

The three platoons in the rear must have wondered what was so funny because now even the Platoon Corporal was out of step because he couldn't control his laughter, or catch his breath as he tried to speak. "I've...forgotten...what he was even doing in the bathroom. DANYLUK WHAT WERE YOU DOING?"

Moose was laughing too. "AS I TRIED TO SAY, I HAD HER ON THE BATHROOM FLOOR WITH MY FINGER IN HER MOUTH AND ALL OF A SUDDEN THE DOOR OPENS, THE LIGHTS GO ON, AND MY GIRLFRIEND WALKS IN."

Earl's eyes crossed. "I thought you said you had your girlfriend on the floor with your finger in her mouth? Now another one walks in?"

"NO, YOU PONGO...NOT ANOTHER GIRLFRIEND, THAT GIRL-FRIEND! I'D MADE A MISTAKE...IT WAS HER MOTHER IN THE JON! I HAD HER MOTHER ON THE FLOOR!"

At that moment, the platoon was crossing the highway. The drivers of passing cars would have thought the cadets in Number One Platoon had all been drinking. Every lad was laughing and smacking his sides. All were out of step, including the Corporal. He couldn't call the step he was bent over in laughter. The expression on Moose's face made it even worse.

"IN THE FIVE SECONDS I TOOK TO FOLLOW HER, MY GIRLFRIEND HAD TURNED INTO HER ROOM. HER MOM HAD BEEN SITTING ON THE

JON AND STOOD UP WHEN I TURNED OUT THE LIGHTS. WHEN MY GIRLFRIEND WALKED IN, SHE SAW ME WITH HER MOTHER AND THE MOTHER'S GIRDLE WAS DOWN AROUND HER ANKLES. I DIDN'T EVEN KNOW THAT!"

The cadets roared as the Corporal let out a laugh that would stampede an elephant.

"MY GIRLFRIEND WAS SHOCKED TO SEE HER MOTHER, GIRDLE AND PANTS DOWN, WITH ME NEXT TO HER WITH MY FINGER IN HER MOUTH. I HAD A HEART ATTACK! MY GIRLFRIEND WAS SPEECHLESS AND HER MOTHER WAS GOING WILD. JESUS, HER MOTHER WAS FURIOUS. SHE GOT UP, PULLED UP HER PANTIES, GRABBED ME BY THE NECK AND ASS, AND TOSSED ME DOWN THE STAIRS! I WENT FLYING! THE NEXT MINUTE, I WAS GRABBED BY THE NECK AND ASS AGAIN AND WAS TOSSED DOWN THE FRONT STAIRS!"

The company was now on the road outside their hut and the Corporal had gained some control over himself. "ALPHA COMPANY, HALT! ALPHA COMPANY WILL ADVANCE, LEFT TURN! COMPANY, FALL...OUT!"

Three platoons rushed into the hut, but not One Platoon. They gathered around Moose to hear his story. Even the Corporals stayed behind. One of them asked, "I'll bet you never heard from the girl again? What about her father, wasn't he mad as well?"

"She never had a father, her parents were divorced. You got that right, Corporal, she never spoke to me again."

"Couldn't you explain it to her?" Rothstein asked.

Moose shook his head. "She wouldn't listen, but all wasn't lost."

The Corporal wedged right in next to Danyluk now. "What do you mean?"

As Danyluk walked into the hut, he said, "Her mother phoned me every five minutes. She was better than her daughter! No braces, either."

As they were washing up, Wayne asked, "What about the house party, did it break up after you were tossed down the stairs?"

"Hell no, but I had to hitchhike home. I was the hero of the day to those guys. Hey, now that I think of it, where's Cunningham? He was there...he was the one who drove me, and..."

Cunningham was standing behind him with a smile a mile wide when Moose grabbed him.

"Cunner, I wondered why you were so quiet? You saw the whole thing and you didn't give me a ride home, you pongo. Why didn'tcha?"

"Moose, you wouldn't want to know!"

Danyluk released his grip. "Yes, I do so want to know."

"Well, after you *left*, I got it on with Audrey. I still see her now and then; her braces are gone."

"You rotten creep. Audrey was one of my favourites." Moose went back to combing his hair. "She's got lots of money, too!"

"I know, that's why I see her. Are you still dating her mother, Sybil?"

"Nahh, I draw the line with older dames. They've got the experience but I need the challenge."

Cunningham started grinding his teeth. He always did that when he was in deep thought. "Good...that's good...that's excellent!"

Moose looked at Cunningham in utter disbelief. "You wouldn't?"

The *gambler* put his arm around Moose's shoulder as they headed towards their bunks and then to the mess hall. "Why not? Someone's got to pay my way through law school!"

On the way to the kitchen, Danyluk saw a small figure standing by the highway. The cadet had his hands in his pockets. He'd move a few pepples with his boots and then lift his head and look north, before staring at the ground again.

"You go ahead without me, I'll be right there," Moose told Cunningham, before walking towards the boy. When he was about ten feet away, he knew the problem.

"Hi, is your name Anderson?" Danyluk asked.

The cadet was still looking at the ground as he slowly shook his bowed head. Danyluk could barely hear his reply. "No, it's...it's...Jamie Archer."

Moose knew the cadet's name wasn't Anderson, but it was a good way of starting the conversation.

"What company are youse in, Archer?"

As the cadet raised his head, Danyluk could see the lad's eyes were red and watery. He quickly wiped them before he replied, "Charlie Company."

"Well, my name's Danyluk, but my friends call me Moose and that means youse can call me Moose. C'mon, let's go sit on those steps over there." He had to nudge the small cadet to get him moving. When they arrived they sat side by side and Danyluk did the talking.

"Is it your first year?"

The cadet didn't reply. He nodded slightly, staring at the steps below.

Danyluk noticed the boy's knees were skinned. "What happened to your knees...did you fall down?"

Once again, the reply was faint. "The big guy in the bunk above me pushed me when I tried to get my badge back and I lost my footing."

"He's got your badge and he pushed you? What sort of a pongo is this creep? Is he a bully...?"

The cadet nodded and then took off his pith-helmet. "I don't know how I ended up in Charlie Company; all my friends are in Bravo Company. Fifteen of us came to camp and I'm the only one in Charlie Company."

Moose had a lump in his throat as he parted the boy's hair with his hand and wiped away a stray tear casually rolling down the lad's cheek.

"What regiment are youse with, Jamie?"

"The King's Own Calgary Regiment."

Danyluk sat up straight and grabbed him by his right arm. "THE K.O.C.R.s? YOU'RE IN THE FAMOUS, KONG'S OWN CHINESE RIFLES? DO YOU MEAN TO TELL ME I'VE FINALLY MET SOMEONE IN ONE OF THE FINEST REGIMENTS IN THE WORLD? CHRIST, IT'S MY LUCKY DAY! MY THIRD DAY AT CAMP AND I MEET ONE OF KONG'S OWN...LEMMEE SHAKE YOUR HAND, SIR!"

They smiled as the cadet lifted his head and Danyluk pumped his hand. "Have you eaten?" asked Moose.

"No...I..."

Moose edged him to his feet. "Were you...er, did you have a homesickness twang when I first saw you? Were you actually homesick? I didn't think you were, but you sorta looked...a little...?"

The cadet put his helmet back on and walked towards the mess hall with

Danyluk. "Yes, er...no...NO, I was just looking at the highway!"

Moose put his arm around the little guy's shoulder. "That's what I thought. I like lookin' at the highway, too. I've ain't never met a KOCR, but I know they don't get homesick. Charlie Company, eh? Well, Cadet Jamie Archer, from the famous KOCRs, let me tell youse about Charlie Company! Oh, by the way, what hut are youse in...and what's this other cadet's name?"

Danyluk took Archer to Alpha Company's side of the mess hall and after introducing him to the Musketeers, the two sat alone at a table. Although Moose knew he only had half-an-hour, he told Cunningham he had to catch up on a few things and Gordie got the message. He would handle Moose's chores.

Over the next thirty minutes, Archer's eyes lit up as Danyluk told him of his exploits when he was in Charlie Company, a few years earlier. More than a few times, Archer burst out laughing, and for that matter, so did Moose.

After supper, Moose walked into Archer's hut with him. About half way down the aisle, he sat down on the cadet's bed and acquainted him with camp life and how he should organize himself to be one step ahead of the rest. The cadet listened with interest and took notes. He was still taking notes when a heavy-set cadet jumped up on the upper bunk and began reading a comic book. He was just as tall as Moose, but a couple of years younger.

Danyluk stood and slowly drew the comic book out of his hands. The cadet sat up quickly, curling up his right fist in protest. "HEY, WHAT THE F...?"

Moose said nothing as he gave the boy a *tap* on the right side of his face. Actually it was a little harder than a tap; it must have been because the lad's cheek bore a white impression from the pressure of Moose's fingers, and then that exact same spot starting turning red. When Moose said, "Come with me!" he didn't argue. Not that the cadet wanted to comply with the *suggestion*; Moose had grabbed him by the front of his shirt was *gently* assisting him down.

The two entered the drying room and Moose closed the door. "You've got my friend's badge, where is it?"

The cadet's nervousness showed. "You're his *friend*? I...I was only...I didn't know. It's in my barrack-box."

"How many more have you got?" Danyluk's icy stare burned through the cadet.

The cadet didn't answer, so he got *another* tap on the other side of his face.

"Six...only six." The boy's eyes started welling up.

Danyluk was now nose-to-nose. "Now youse listen up here, Mister. If I don't knock your teeth out within the next minute, we're going to leave here smiling. If I knock your teeth out, which I'm probably going to do anyway, I'll be the only one smiling...your expression will be one of 'gumming' after you spit out your teeth and a little blood."

Someone tried to enter the drying room but Danyluk slammed the door shut again.

Moose's voice was calm. "Do you know what a bully is?"

"Yes...yesss."

"Are you a bully? WELL, ARE YOU?" Danyluk's nose was almost in the cadet's mouth.

"I...I've been told I...I can be..."

"Well, bullies don't stick around long in this camp. I don't know who trained youse incorrectly, but they also don't exist in cadets." Moose raised his arm and the cadet cowered. "Dddon't, please."

He lowered his hand and then used it to lift up the cadet's chin. Now Moose felt a little remorseful.

"Listen...look at me. I don't like doin' this. I'm going to make a deal with youse. If there are other bullies, I want you to sort them out. Also, I want all of those badges given back within the next two minutes. I want you to look after my little buddy. He's a good kid, as you probably are. The difference between the two of youse is that if he were your size, he wouldn't push his weight around. He'd use it to help people, as you're going to do. Is that clear?"

"Ye...yes."

"Good! Now I know your name and I'm going to watch you for the rest of camp. Did youse hear what I said...I know your name?"

"Yes...I understand."

Moose smiled. "Good, then we can be friends, right?" He gave the cadet a friendly shove. A shy smile appeared. "I'm sorry I took his badge. I..er, I'm sorry."

Danyluk held out his hand and after a fraction of a second, it was accepted. "Hey, we all make mistakes. I'm sorry I smacked ya. I had no right to do it, but one *good* turn deserves another. I didn't like what youse did to Jamie's knees. A physical action requires a physical reaction. Will youse accept my apology?"

The cadet straightened up and smiled again. "Yeah...I guess I needed..."

When the duo returned to Archer's bunk, Moose said. "Well old buddy, I've gotta go now. How about meeting me for lunch tomorrow, O.K., Jamie?"

"Archer beamed. "Really? I'll be there...thanks Moose."

The other cadet said, "Can I come?"

Moose walked away. "Why not? By the way, ya got a minute-and-a-half left to do your duty."

After supper Alpha Company was back on the parade square again. Sergeant Beckford was in fine voice, although he must have had a beer at supper because he belched a few commands to the marching *troops.*

"WATCH YOUR DRESSING! DRESSING BY THE RIGHT! NOW, WATCH THIS TURN...PICK UP YOUR RIGHT FOOT AND DRIVE IT DOWN! NUMBER ONE PLATOON...LEFT...TURN! THAT'S BETTER! YOU...YES YOU, QUIT WIPING YOUR ASS...GET YOUR ARMS STRAIGHT BACK! DON'T LOOK DOWN, DON'T LOOK DOWN...I PICKED UP ALL THE MONEY OFF THIS PARADE SQUARE BEFORE YOU GOT HERE! YOU, YOU HORRIBLE EXCUSE FOR AN ANKLE-BITER, GET YOUR CHINS UP. YES, I SAID CHINS...YOU LOOK LIKE A GOD-DAMNED BLIFFY...TEN POUNDS OF SHIT IN A FIVE POUND BAG! BY THE TIME I'M THROUGH WITH YOU, YOU'LL LOSE THAT TEN POUNDS! LEFT, RIGHT, LEFT, RIGHT...!"

At 1900 that evening, the training day ended. Alpha Company was marched to the south road outside of the building and dismissed. They were told to read orders and work on their kit for the following day. Instantly the Musketeers undressed and headed for the showers, but the shower room was full.

Douglas looked around, "Where's Jack? Ah, there you are; get in there and do your thing!"

While the Musketeers waited at the entrance *chewing the fat,* Jack squeezed in and within minutes' all the others were running out.

"JESUS, WHEN THAT GUY STARTS FARTING, IT'S UNBEARABLE IN THERE!"

"HE SAYS IT'S AN SEAFORTH TRADITION. CHRIST, THOSE GUYS IN THE SEAFORTHS ARE ANIMALS!"

It didn't take long for Jack to empty the shower room. When the Musketeers entered, Danyluk opened the window for five minutes, to *clear the air.*

As usual, Wayne had shampoo all over his body, and held his face under the showerhead. "Jack, what would we do without you?"

"You could let me have thirds more often."

"WHERE ARE YOU?" screamed Wayne, in a deep voice.

Moose caught on. In his timid maiden's voice, he replied, "I'M HIDING!"

"WHERE ARE YOU?" Wayne bellowed again.

"I'M HIDING," replied a timid Moose.

"YOU'RE HIDING? IF I FIND YOU, I'M GOING TO SCREW YOU!"

Moose tried to hide his smile. "YOU WILL? I'M IN THE CLOSET!"

The Vernon 'Shower Room Players' took their bows amidst applause and laughter.

Minutes ago they had all felt beat, but the hot water gave them new energy. Moose got back on the subject of women. "Did you guys see the new dishwasher? She's only about sixteen or seventeen and she's built like a brick shithouse!"

Rothstein knew the situation. "Keep your paws off her, Moose, she's the daughter of the head lady in the kitchen. Her name's Penelope. She was at the dances at the arena last year and she goes out with one of the local punks."

Moose grabbed his crotch. It was an automatic reaction when women were discussed and women were always a point of conversation.

"I knew it! You use your right hand to grab your crotch when we talk about dames, but you use your left hand when we pass Hop Sing's," said Jackson.

"I'm organized," was Moose's reply. "When I know it's a sure thing, I use my right hand. I like to reassure 'Old Guts And Glory!'"

"Who the hell is Old Guts And Glory?" Earl asked.

Danyluk had an insidious smile on his face when he dropped his hands to his sides and faced Earl.

When everyone laughed, Earl knew. "Jeez, I should have known. You call that thing Old Guts And Glory?"

"Ya got a better name?"

"Yeah, how about, Nosey Knob? If it's not standing to attention like a sensory antenna, it's always pushing itself into situations where it's got no business."

Moose grinned. "Bullsssshit! When it comes down to business, Old Guts And Glory wrote the book. It can be tough, or it can be gentle, depending on the situation."

Wayne stood at the open window, laughing. "The only time that thing is gentle is when you're sleeping. Even then your bed looks like a goddamned tent. Last year we piled four mattresses on top of ya and that didn't even work."

"Like I told ya, I was dreaming about lovely, luscious Lucinda...the girl who showed me how to use it when I was thirteen."

"How old was she?"

Moose dried himself off. "Age doesn't count when you're in love. I think she was around...er...what's thirty-six, twenty-four and thirty-five added together?"

As the group of them went back to their bunks, each of them was slapping Moose on the back. Simon asked, "Luscious Luscinda was ninety-five?"

"Hell no, that was her measurements!" Moose replied. "I never really knew

As usual, B-33 was a madhouse. With Fats Domino filling their end of the hut with his song, *Ain't That A Shame*, One Platoon prepared for the following day.

After Sergeant Beckford made his rounds and the lights were out, Cunningham asked Moose why he'd talked to the Sergeant for five minutes.

"That cadet I introduced youse to in the Mess Hall is in Charlie Company, but he should be in Bravo Company with his buddies. HE'S IN THE KONG'S OWN CHINESE RIFLES!"

If Danyluk thought there would be a reaction from somewhere in the darkened hut, he was right.

"SCREW YOU! IT'S THE KING'S OWN CALGARY REGIMENT, WHO-EVER YOU ARE, YOU CREEP!"

Moose smiled and comfortably rolled over onto his side. He went to sleep allowing the conversation to continue at the other end of the hut.

"NO, IT'S NOT...IT'S THE KINK'S ONLY CHIMPANZEE RESERVE!"

"Up yours!"

"And yours, too!"

"I can recognize your voice, you're in the LAMBS EVER READY!"

"It's the LOYAL EDMONTON REGIMENT, YOU DINK!"

"IS THAT LIKE THE SALLY'S LUMPY HORS-D'OEUVRE'S, OR AS WE MEN SAY, HORSES OVARIES?"

"WHO SAID THAT? IT'S THE SASKATCHEWAN LIGHT HORSE, YOU PONGO!"

"Screw you!"

"Same to you!"

"UP THE WINNIPEG RIFLES!"

"Yeah, I agree; up yours, Winnipeg Rifles."

The teasing died down after a few yawns, but throughout the night, cadets talking in their sleep, entertained the walls of creaking H-huts.

"Those Irish Fussyliarrrrs, they're..."

"He was stuck in the Fifteenth-Field, not the Thirrrteeenth Fiiieeeld..."

"I'm a Lord Strath...so up yoooourrs fella!"

"PPCLI means pretty Priscilla counts her lice in her..."

"Dear Mom, sennd monnneee. I got screwed out of mine by ZZZaholuk."

The sleeping 'self-conversations' weren't limited to regimental comments. Amidst the chatter, there was always, *"Piston, barrel, butt, body...oh, what isss it?"*

A moment of silence followed before the word, *"BIPOD!"* was bellowed.

With showers dripping, bed springs squeaking when someone rolled over, the washing machine whining because someone had forgotten to turn it off, Danyluk leading the chorus of snorers, and its walls creaking, old H-hut B-33 sheltered its *soldiers* for the night. They'd done O.K., for their first training day; damned good, indeed.

After bottles of Kik Kola...heat or no heat...its back to the aiming rests.

"GET 'EM UP, UP, UP!"

A slight pause after unloading. Why? To turn off Danyluk's radio, of course. Shortly, they'll learn the real meaning of the word, 'gout.'

About to be sized. "YOU, YES YOU! DID YOU TWITCH YOUR NOSE?"

Major General Chris Vokes, CB, CBE, DCO, CD, inspects cadets stripping and assembling a Bren gun.
"Can you do it blindfolded?"
"Yes, sir! We even talk about them in our sleep."

"RIGHT, PAY ATTENTION HERE! YOU TWO ON THE END, GET YOUR EYES ON YOUR RIFLES, NOT THE POP TRUCK!"

CADETS ON SATURDAY MORNING PARADE
With the rolling hills of Vernon in the background, cadets 'stand easy' prior to weekly inspection. Each week a noticeable improvement is seen in smartness on parade.
(Author's note: It was cool on the parade square on Saturday mornings, that's why the weekly inspection-parade was held on that day. Then someone suggested to a Commanding Officer that it would be nice if certain officers had the weekend off. The choice of day was changed to Friday nights. Blistering hot Friday nights, and the tradition continues.

A typical cadet Bren gun team. This picture was taken in the morning, before lunch. In the afternoon, this hard-working close-knit crew, played baseball, went swimming, and ended up going to one of the nearby lakes to fish.

FOUR CADETS FROM CALGARY
"Hold it up, son...hold it up!"
"I may need a hand, Sergeant!"
"Oh, all right! But I'm going to mention to Sergeant Simpson to give you more pushups."
"It's O.K., Sergeant, I don't need a hand. I said, I don't need a hand, Sergeant."

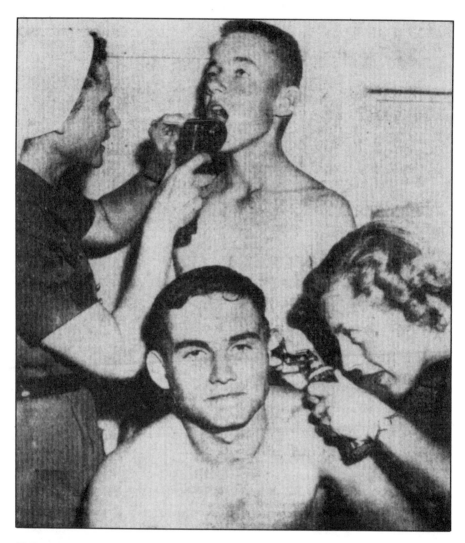

"SAY AHR-R-R!"
Medical inspection time for two of 1200 cadets. These two Nursing Sisters never knew what lay in store for one of their friends.

A SWIM PARADE AT KALAMALKA LAKE
"We'd better smile."
"I ain't smilin' with you, you Frenched my bed last night."
"O.K., pay me back the money you owe me."
"I'll smile, I'll smile."

VERNON CADETS DESIGN THEIR OWN 'C' COMPANY FLAG
"I think we should have stayed with our size 62 cup brassiere flag."
"Nah, this gives us better representation."
"Say, just where the hell is our old brassier flag?"
"Some cadet by the name of Danyluk asked for it. He says he's gonna send it to a girlfriend he knows in school."

CADETS HAVE REAL 'PASSING OUT" PARADE AT CAMP BORDEN, ONTARIO
Combined heat and humidity caused a few cadets to pass out at Camp Borden. Medical-types attended the casualties and they recovered quickly. Does it bring back memories to those of you who attend(ed) Vernon?

REVEILLE
Yes this happy fellow woke up the camp in the mornings. After his second day on the job, no one would speak to him. Even fellow bandsmen turned their backs on him. So, he simply said, "I'll blow reveille fifteen minutes earlier." After he said that, he had more friends than he knew what to do with.

PHYSICAL TRAINING
"Smile! I don't just want to see gas pains." "We're smiling, we're smiling."

THE PICTURE DIDN'T TURN OUT WELL, BUT THE SIGN SURE DID
What went wrong? Ask Trudeau and Hellyer.

WIPE THAT SMILE OFF YOUR FACE
"Did you scratch your private parts on my parade square?"
"No, Sergeant!"
"Yes you did, I saw you!"
"No, Sergeant! I had a wasp on my thumb."
"Show me your thumbs. Where's the wasp?"
"It flew off, Sergeant."
"It did? Get down and give me ten."

PAY PARADE
"Name?"
"Jones, sir!"
"We don't have a Jonesir on our list."
"No Jones, sir."
"Oh, NoJonesir? No, we don't have that name, either. What's your name again?"
"Jones!"
"Why didn't you say so in the first place. There you are, Jones...five dollars.
What's this generation coming to? Half of them don't know their names."

"Excellent, just excellent. Increasing the powdered eggs, saltpetre and salt tablets, must be working."

A REWARD FOR EXCELLENT MARKS
"I got one, I got one!"

CHAPTER V

If he had been at home, Douglas Brice wouldn't have heard his mother's first up-the-stairs holler, trying to wake him up. Like most teenagers, he hated getting up in the morning.

This morning, however, was quite different. He wasn't at home and although the song was faint, he sensed that, *Ling Ting, Tong,* by the Five Keys, was originating from Cunningham's clock radio, laying next to him on his pillow. He had set the timer the night before and the second he heard it, he jumped out of bed like a flash. It was cold in B-33 and he was the only one up. Normally, someone got up and had a shower before Sergeant Simpson arrived, but not this morning.

"Wayne, Wayne, wake up, you pongo and get Jackson, Simon, East and Rothstein up."

Wayne sat up scratching his head as Douglas walked over to get Danyluk and Cunningham out of bed.

"I'm getting up, Sergeant, really I am," Moose uttered after being shaken.

"Moose, get up! I'm not the Sergeant, you creep. If I were, your mattress and blankets would be on the floor. Get your ass out of bed and go have a pee!"

Danyluk tossed his bedding back and put his feet on the floor. He was just about to stand up when Cunningham knocked him in the head attempting to crawl down. He almost ended up perched on Danyluk's shoulders.

"Sorry, Moose! I didn't think you two were up yet! Christ it's cold in here. What I need is a little game of craps to warm things up."

Moose was really still asleep. "Wha...what do you mean, 'You two?'"

Gordie was bright eyed. "Why you and Old Sputs And Gory of course! If you don't wait until that thing goes down, you may never be able to pee."

Danyluk was finally awake. Still naked, he headed for the jon. "It's Old Guts and Glory, not Sputs And Gory, you pongo!"

After a quick wash, the eight got dressed in their P.T. strip and then made their beds. This was the first morning any of them could remember Danyluk not cursing about having to put his P.T. shorts on over his normal morning erection.

Jack East was eating a banana that he'd stored from Mug-up the night before.

"Jesus, Moose, you look like a normal human being this morning. Hey guys, Moose can be ordinary just like the rest of us. I think..."

Jack was going to say something else, but Sergeant Simpson stormed into the barracks. He was actually bellowing before he opened the door and started turning over mattresses.

"STAND BY YOUR BEDS AND FORM THREE RANKS ON THE ROAD! C'MON YOU LAZY PEOPLE, LET GO OF YOUR ROCKS AND PUT ON YOUR SOCKS! DANYLUK, LET GO OF YOUR MEAT AND COVER YOUR FEET!"

Moose sang his reply. "Oh Sergeant...I'm already up! It's me you see here standing by my bed!"

Simpson stopped in his tracks and stared at what he thought was a ghost. "MY

GOD, I CAN'T BELIEVE IT...YOU CAN LOOK NORMAL IN THE MORNING. SOMEONE GET MY SECRETARY ON THE PHONE AND TELL HER THE ELEPHANT IS DEAD!" With that said, he carried on down the aisle and marched over to the other wing. "C'MON YOU LAZY PEOPLE, GET RID OF THE LOAD AND FORM UP ON THE ROAD! YES...THAT MEANS YOU! WHAT DO YOU MEAN, DOES THAT MEAN ME? CERTAINLY IT MEANS YOU! WHO THE HELL DO YOU THINK YOU ARE?"

Everyone knew Simpson was talking to himself. His statements drew a few early morning laughs, and those who were slow, weren't slow for long. The Sergeant made certain of that.

Again B-33 became a beehive of activity. Amidst the yawns, gripes, yearns of, "I'm bursting, please can I take a pee," the cadets of Alpha Company pulled on their P.T. strip and formed three ranks on the road.

When Sergeant Simpson returned to the Musketeer's wing, he called the eight of them aside.

"I'm impressed, fellas, I really am. I'm finding it increasingly difficult to stay one step ahead of you, and really that's exactly the way it should be. In my opinion, you eight epitomize the result of this training, yet you're doing it on only your second day. Well done, boys, but I want you to know I'm going to try to stay one step ahead of *you*."

Danyluk's grin widened. "We expect that, Sergeant, but don't forget, we're not just shapely legs and pretty faces...you're lookin' at brawn and brains."

Simpson stared at Moose for at least ten seconds; their eyes locked on one another. It was almost as if Sergeant Simpson was lost for words and was looking right through him, stalling for time. Moose lifted his chin a little, anticipating a reply, then moved it even higher, but the Sergeant remained silent. Finally Danyluk broke the ice. "Gotcha, didn't I? Ya know 'em when ya see 'em!"

Simpson glanced at Douglas and pointed at Danyluk. "Is he for real?"

Brice stood at attention. "Every inch of him, Sergeant!"

As Simpson marched outside, he said aloud, "GAD, CAN YOU IMAGINE WHAT THIS COUNTRY WOULD BE LIKE IF WE HAD MORE LIKE HIM?"

It was cold as they started jogging towards the upper camp, but Moose still had his chest out. "More like me! You guys heard him, he said, 'This country would be better if there were more people like me.' He's a fine man, that Sergeant Simpson!"

"He didn't say that," replied East. "He said, 'Can you imagine what this country would be like if there were more like you!'"

"Well, that's the same thing, you pongo! Jesus, Jack, get with it! It's the same thing, isn't it, Rothie?"

Rothstein's eyes were nearly closed because he hadn't really awakened yet. "I er, well Moose, oh what's the use - yeah, it's the same thing."

Moose continued jogging with his head moving confidently from side to side. "From now on, it's me and Sergeant Simpson."

East wasn't finished. "You and Sergeant Simpson? What about your dames?"

The word 'dames' got Moose back on track. "Yeah, dames. Just think, if I was home I'd be lying next to utterly gorgeous, beautiful, and wonderfully divine and devoted Daphne. Instead, I'm insulted, I get no sleep, no respect, and I've got dust in my eyes, in my ears, up my nose and up my ass! I know I've said it before, but what the hell am I doing here?"

Douglas was out of breath but he could still laugh and be heard. "Who the hell is devoted Daphne? You're springing a new one on us, Moose! We've never heard of this one...who is she?"

Danyluk was nearly out of breath also. "She's the lovely, lovely creature that delivers our morning paper, The News Herald! Oh Daphne, my love, you're going to miss old Moose when you climb up the tree. I won't be there to help you in my window."

"MOOSE, HOW IN THE HELL DO YOU DO IT?" Cunningham asked, as he tried to get into step. "CHRIST, YOU GO TO BED WITH DEVOTED AND DIVINE DORIS, AND YOU WAKE UP NEXT TO DIVINE, DEVOTED, ETC., ETC., DAPHNE! WHAT VITAMINS ARE YOU TAKING?"

"Hey, who told you I take them things? It comes *au natural* with me. Doris sings me to sleep and Daphne wakes me up. What a breast!"

Rothstein was finally awake. "You mean what *breasts!*"

Danyluk gave Rothstein his offended look. "Hey, I know what I mean. With Daphne it's, 'what a breast.' She's got one bigger than the other."

Sergeant Simpson now got into the act. He had overheard some of the conversation. "Then she's not normal?"

Simpson got the same glance Moose gave Rothstein. "Sergeant, of course she's normal. Just because she's got one breast bigger than the other doesn't mean she's not normal. When I get through with her, they'll both be the same size. I'm even helping her right buttock to grow, and her left..."

Simpson shook his head and picked up his pace. "Please, please, don't tell me any more, I don't think I could take it!"

The hut was impeccable when the occupants of B-33 headed over to the mess hall for breakfast. Along with the outside sector that had been cleaned, raked and the rocks arranged, the partially opened windows were even, bunks, barrack-boxes, and dust covers were aligned, and all beds were tightly made with their sides squared off. Each cadet's buttoned-up battledress hung neatly on hangars behind each set of bunks, and sitting in the middle of each dust cover was a brightly shined wash basin. Even these were lined up and appeared like a recently dressed rank of the guard. There wasn't a speck of dirt or dust anywhere because each bed space had been brushed and mopped out.

Following breakfast, the centre area of the hut would look the same. All sinks would be washed and wiped dry, the drying room and shower room would be cleaned out, and the toilet area mopped and sanitized.

Although B-33 was about three-hundred yards from the fence overlooking the golf course, Douglas and Wayne had judged their time and after changing from their P.T. strip to their summer dress, they marched over to the old parade square to gaze at the nearby hills. The scenery was stunning at any time, however, in the mornings, with the air so fresh and clear, even the glistening dew highlighted this breathtaking scene even more.

Douglas always got lost in thought when he had the opportunity to view this picture-postcard vista. The sun had risen from behind the hills and promptly, lost shadows emphasized the precipices and rolling ground created by eons of winter wind, rain and snow.

The highway running north-south at the base of the hills was bare of traffic and the only sound they could hear other than roosters and cattle, originated from the nearby huts.

Douglas spoke first. "When I'm at home, I actually dream of this spectacle. I hope in the future they don't allow buildings and factories to be built over there."

Doug's persistence in pointing out such beauty had worked on Wayne over the years. Wayne hadn't really appreciated it as much in his first year. Now, he understood.

"I agree, but unfortunately I think this whole valley's going to be transformed because of increasing population and industry. Look at the changes that have taken place in the four years we've been here. The horses have gone in the fields south of us, and if you look closely down there, more buildings are going up. There's a few more houses being built around Kalamalka Lake, as well."

Douglas couldn't tear his eyes away. "I know. I wonder if these people appreciate what they've got. Y'know, reading about Europe in school, I think the Europeans have solved the secret of melding growth in with the surrounding splendor. In Canada for some reason, we don't do that...the search for the almighty dollar does away with common sense. A town planner in West Vancouver pointed that out recently. Instead of beautiful mountains and trees, in twenty years there'll just be more houses and factories. God, does it ever stop?"

Wayne sighed. "Yeah, it could if enough people cared and they were listened to. I betcha real estate companies are even after this camp land."

Wayne's statement annoyed Douglas. He looked at his watch and nudged his friend. In seconds they were marching back to B-33. "That would be a bloody shame. There's loads of land around here that could be used without disturbing the setting. And what about the future, what's going to happen when the children of the grandchildren of the pioneers of Vernon ask about their heritage? We wouldn't have Stanley Park in Vancouver if some wise forefathers hadn't glimpsed destiny. A perfect example is Polson Park. It's big now, but in the future, it'll be like a postage stamp stuck on the sidewalk in the middle of a large metropolis."

When Douglas and Wayne arrived back, Alpha Company was just forming up on the south road. Shortly, the company would be sized and the roll would be called. The procedure was exactly the same as the previous morning, except that the Company Commander inspected Number Two Platoon. Lieutenant Harwood and Sergeant Beckford inspected their own platoon, as did the officers and Sergeants of Three and Four Platoons.

These were senior cadets, therefore very rarely did Sergeant Beckford bellow, "YOU, GET YOUR EYES TO YOUR FRONT!"

Lieutenant Harwood didn't miss much. "You have a mark on your pith-helmet, Simon, what is it?"

Simon knew better than to move an inch of his body. He stood stiffly at attention, not moving his eyes, which stared through the officer in front of him.

"Probably a soap-mark that didn't rinse off, sir!"

"Get it off at noon, all right?"

"Yes, sir!"

The officer moved on to a cadet whose name tag read, 'Young.' "You've done a good job on your brass, Young, however, I see a bit of white material in the upper corner of the buckle. Do you use a brush after you put Brasso on it?"

"Yes, sir!"

"Well, you didn't brush hard enough. Don't let that happen in the future!"

"Right, sir!"

The inspection took ten minutes and after the selection, Douglas was handed the stick. He was made stickman for the day.

"Sir, may I march with my own platoon?"

Sergeant-Major Rose agreed. "Yes, the choice is yours. IF YOU ARE SELECTED STICKMAN, YOU MAY MARCH IN FRONT OF THE COMPANY, OR WITH YOUR PLATOON!"

"Thank you, sir!"

Major Ratcliffe ensured everyone was 'at ease' while he addressed his company.

"I MUST TELL YOU THAT I'M EXCEPTIONALLY PLEASED WITH YOUR TURNOUT AND YOUR QUARTERS. THIS IS MY FIRST YEAR WORKING WITH CADETS AND I'M FORTUNATE THAT I'M COMMANDING SENIOR PEOPLE!

"YESTERDAY, GENERAL KITCHING INFORMED ME THAT HE WATCHED OUR COMPANY MARCHING TO THE UPPER CAMP. ALTHOUGH THE *ROAD* HAS TWO-TO-THREE INCHES OF DUST, HE WAS MOST IMPRESSED WITH YOUR BEARING. YOUR ARMS WERE UP AND YOUR DRESSING WAS PERFECT. HOW YOU MANAGE THAT WHEN YOU CAN'T SEE IN FRONT OF YOU IS BEYOND ME. WELL DONE!

"AS YOU KNOW FROM READING ORDERS, YOU PEOPLE WILL CONDUCT THE PARADE TOMORROW. WE WILL CHANGE SUPERNUMERARIES EVERY THREE DAYS. YOU WILL PICK UP THE BADGES OF RANK FROM YOUR INDIVIDUAL PLATOON SERGEANTS.

"NOW, PLEASE UNDERSTAND...WE'LL BE ON THE SIDELINES, HOWEVER, YOU WILL INSPECT YOUR OWN PLATOONS AND YOU WILL BE CRITICAL WHEN INSPECTING YOUR PEERS AND YOUR QUARTERS. WHEN YOU MOVE ON TO OTHER COMPANIES, YOU'LL UNDERSTAND THE SIGNIFICANCE OF BEING IMPARTIAL. ARE THERE ANY QUESTIONS?"

A cadet in Number Three Platoon snapped to attention, his left forearm parallel with the ground. "SIR, WOULD IT BE POSSIBLE TO EXTEND THE LUNCH PERIOD BY HALF-AN-HOUR AND ADD THAT HALF-HOUR TO THE END OF THE TRAINING DAY?"

No one complained.

"WHY DO YOU WISH THAT?"

"WELL, SIR...WE'RE FIRST IN THE MESS HALL IN THE MORNINGS, BUT AT NOON AND AT SUPPER, WE'RE IN THE LINEUP WITH THE OTHER COMPANIES. WE CAN WASH AND DRY OUR CLOTHES IN THAT EXTRA HALF-HOUR AND IN THE EVENING, WE'LL HAVE MORE TIME TO STUDY. CLOTHES DON'T DRY AS FAST AT NIGHT, SIR!"

Major Ratcliffe glanced at Sergeant-Major Rose, as well as the Platoon officers and Senior NCOs. The expressions on their faces tended to agree. A decision was made.

"GOOD POINT! I CAN SEE NO REASON WHY NOT! WE'LL CHANGE THE TIMINGS AND I'LL INFORM THE TRAINING OFFICE AND THE COMMANDING OFFICER. I FEEL CERTAIN THEY'LL AGREE. THANK YOU! ANYTHING ELSE? NO...? RIGHT! ALPHA COMPANY, ATTEN...TION! STANDAT...EASE! FALL OUT THE OFFICERS!"

Each Platoon Officer came to attention, and marched forward to form a semi-circle in front of Major Ratcliffe. After they halted, the officer on the extreme right, who in this case was always Lieutenant Harwood, took one small step forward and saluted. The other officers saluted at the same time. The Officer Commanding returned their salutes, Harwood stepped back; they turned to their right and marched in single file behind the O.C., and stood at ease. As soon as the officers marched forward, each individual Platoon Sergeant marched to the front of his platoon and stood at ease.

When that was completed, Major Ratcliffe carried on again.

"ALPHA COMPANY, ATTEN...TION! (Even the officers came to attention.) SERGEANT-MAJOR ROSE!"

"SIR!" The Sergeant-Major marched from his position to a position in front of his O.C., and saluted.

Rose's salute was returned. "CARRY ON WITH TRAINING PLEASE, SERGEANT-MAJOR!"

"SIR!" Sergeant-Major Rose saluted and stood facing his present position until the officer returned his salute and marched off with the Lieutenants. The Sergeant-Major then turned around.

"ALPHA COMPANY, STANDAT...EASE! STAND EASY!"

Sergeant-Major Rose now had a few moments to say something, as did the Platoon Sergeants.

The protocol of falling out and dismissing the officers normally took place after training, however in Vernon, after a long hot day, the final dismissal was completed informally by either the Company Sergeant-Major or one of the Platoon Sergeants. Major Ratcliffe's procedure, while unorthodox, allowed the cadets to have more time to themselves following training. (You may notice the officers were never dismissed. While he fell them out, he never dismissed them. Had he dismissed them, their tasks would be over for that day.)

Over the next few days, from early morning until 1930, the cadets of Alpha Company, received review-lectures, lessons, and mutual instruction practise on drill; review-instruction on the rifle as well as bren and sten guns; a complete review on map-reading, including use of the compass and protractor; Military Writing; Range Theory; TEWTs (tactical exercises without troops); Instructional Technique; Interior Economy; Man Management and Leadership, leadership and more leadership. (Author's note: I mention these because of their significance in the overall cadet training process of that era.) The leadership periods included: *ORGANIZATIONAL CONSTRAINTS; GROUP CLIMATES; THE MANAGEMENT OF FRUSTRATION AND CONFLICT; ORGANIZATIONAL DEVELOPMENT, NOT OVERDOSE; COMMUNICATION IN PRACTISE; TYPES AND TRAITS OF FOLLOWERS; RECRUITMENT AND SELECTION OF FOLLOWERS; HOW TO GET MOTIVE/ACTION, RATHER THAN JUST MOVEMENT; RINGING THE BELL-SHAPED CURVE; AND DELEGATION, DECISION-MAKING, AND TEAM BUILDING.*

With very little time to themselves, the cadets of Alpha Company pursued the Course Training Plan contents with great interest and vigor. There were no boring moments because this course was designed to train them as knowledgeable instructors. They were treated maturely and their instructors shared their many secrets with them. Several times, officers and Sergeants stepped in during periods of mutual instruction.

"DON'T BLUFF! NEVER, NEVER BLUFF! YOU MUST KNOW EVERY BIT OF WHAT YOU'RE TEACHING. THERE IS NO ROOM FOR BULL SHIT-TERS, MEN CAN SEE THROUGH THEM INSTANTLY! IF YOU'RE ASKED A QUESTION AND YOU DON'T KNOW THE ANSWER, TELL THEM YOU'LL LOOK IT UP AND INFORM THEM. THEN MAKE DAMN CERTAIN THAT YOU DO JUST THAT! GET THAT KNOWLEDGEABLE AIR ABOUT YOU...BE CONFIDENT, BUT NEVER OVER CONFIDENT! GRAB WHAT'S KNOWN AS 'THE KNACK'...MANY PEOPLE REFER TO IT AS...JUST THAT... *'IT'*! GRAB ON TO *'IT'*! ALWAYS BE ENTHUSIASTIC, NEVER BE DULL REGARDLESS OF HOW YOU FEEL! IF YOU SHOW THEM THAT YOU DON'T WANT TO BE THERE, THEY'LL WONDER WHAT THEY'RE DOING THERE! IF YOU EXHIBIT YOU WANT TO BE THERE, THEY'LL WANT TO BE THERE WITH YOU! REMEMBER, YOUR JOB IS TO BE A LEADER AND TEACH, NOT TO BE A GOD AND TEACH! IF ONE OF YOUR STUDENTS IS MORE KNOWLEDGEABLE THAN YOU, THAT'S WONDER-FUL...THAT'S WHAT YOU WANT...HOWEVER, TREAT HIM TACTFULLY WITH REGARDS TO THE QUESTIONING AND ANSWERING TECH-NIQUES! GENTLEMEN, IF YOU CAN RECOMMEND SOMEONE ELSE TO PASS YOU ON THE WAY UP THE LADDER, THEN YOU'VE CONQUERED THE 'KNACK!' DON'T PUT YOUR CAREER FIRST, YOUR JOB IS TO LOOK AFTER *THEIR* CAREERS, YOU'RE ALL THEY'VE GOT...REMEMBER THAT! IF YOU DO YOUR TASKS PROPERLY, SO WILL THEY! DON'T WORRY ABOUT HOW YOU'RE BEING EVALUATED, THAT'S NOT YOUR CONCERN. ISN'T IT COMMON SENSE?...IF YOU MANAGE TO UNDER-STAND, TEACH AND LEAD WITH THE 'KNACK' YOUR FUTURE WILL BE WELL LOOKED AFTER! AFTER THIS COURSE, YOU MAY STICK YOUR CHEST OUT AND SAY, 'HEY, I'M AN INSTRUCTOR AND A LEADER,' BUT WHEN YOU DO THAT, JUST MAKE SURE THAT YOU KNOW WHAT A LEADER AND AN INSTRUCTOR IS...HE'S ONE THAT HELPS OTHER PEO-PLE. REMEMBER THAT WORD...*HELPS*!"

One question stood out throughout the course and while it wasn't meant as an insult to any entity, it was asked constantly. "IN OFFICER TRAINING, WHAT IS THE DIFFERENCE BETWEEN WEST POINT AND SANDHURST?" (Our method [Canada's method] of training officers in those days was based on the British Sandhurst system. As well, our method of training NCOs was based on the British style of training.)

Each cadet in Alpha Company knew the answer and they were proud to repeat it. "HAZING IN ANY FORM DOES NOT TAKE PLACE AT SANDHURST! AT SANDHURST, PEOPLE ARE MATURELY GUIDED AND TAUGHT TO GUIDE!"

(Author's question: How hazing crept through the cracks and reared its ugly head in Canada's military colleges, I'll never know. Then again, considering the *reasoning* of our near-past and present *military leaders* perhaps it's as obvious as apple pie?)

On Friday, their seventh day at camp, the cadets of Alpha Company were dis-missed at 1630 hours, instead of 1930. This allowed them to wash up and get a just space in the lineup for meals. Tomorrow was Saturday, which meant the first Saturday Morning Inspection, followed by exams, a sheet exchange, and another of the infrequent mail calls. This evening, after supper, they would prepare their kit for the parade, make ready B-33 for inspection, and then they could study.

When the company was dismissed for the night, the Musketeers were in deep conversation. East was giving Danyluk a blast for eating a banana that East had placed on the ground with his notebook during pop break.

"It wasn't me. I don't like bananas, they give me gas."

Jesus, Moose, I know it was you, because you had a piece of banana on the front of your shirt. I had to go through the whole afternoon with nothing to eat. What if I'm called upon to clear out the shower room? My normal routine of taking a deep breath and letting one go would fail. It would only be a sputter."

"Jack, I didn't take it. If it was an apple, I might have, but not a banana! What you saw on my shirt was a piece of Cunningham's apple pie...you know, out of the parcel he won from that cadet?"

East was in one of his stubborn moods and when it came to food being taken from him, he hung in a discussion with the determination Cunningham unleashes when there are only pennies in the pot.

"BULLLLSHHIT, MOOSE! I KNOW...!"

The conversation stopped when Douglas pushed them through the doors into B-33. He had a phone message from the headquarters building in his hand. "BERGIE ARRIVES AT NOON ON SATURDAY!"

Douglas was immediately surrounded by six of the original Musketeers, then Simon was dragged in by Jackson. Each tried to read the message, but Banks grabbed it out of Brice's hand, pushed his glasses up his nose, and read with the authority of a judge reading the jury's verdict.

"DOUG'S RIGHT! THE MESSAGE CAME IN AT 1430 TODAY. IT'S ADDRESSED TO CADET SERGEANT-MAJOR DANYLUK, ALPHA COMPANY. IT READS, 'LANCE CORPORAL ARTHUR BERGUR OF THE ROYAL CANADIAN ELECTRICAL AND MECHANICAL ENGINEERS, WILL ARRIVE AT THE VERNON TRAIN STATION AT NOON ON SATURDAY. HE WILL TAKE A TAXI TO THE CAMP.'"

Moose grabbed the note from Wayne. "HEY, THAT'S ME...CADET SERGEANT-MAJOR DANYLUK." Once again, his chest was out and he displayed his fiendish grin. "Jesus, he's made Lance Corporal already, can youse believe that?"

"He musta done great in Depot Training," said an excited Jackson.

Moose put his arm around Earl's shoulders. "He shoulda done, he had me to teach him. Why, I taught him everything I know!"

Jackson lifted Moose's arm off. "Not everything, thank God, Bergie still dates normal dames, I bet."

The remark didn't faze Danyluk who still stared at the note. "Wow, a Lance Corporal in the RCEME coming to see us!"

"Well, he's one of us, who the hell else is he going to see?" East snarled, the missing banana still on his mind.

Rothstein wedged his way in. "You know, that's the first time I've heard his first name. I didn't know it was Arthur, did any of you guys?"

They looked at one-another and shook their heads. Moose was the only one who knew. "I did, 'cause he asked me to stop calling him Art the fart! What the hell did you pongoes think it was, Bergie Bergur?"

At supper that night, the table conversation was all about Bergie. Bergie cutting Danyluk's 'shitter' chair, Bergie and Danyluk being caught balls-naked by the RSM, Bergie planning the Genova raid at Kin Beach and the fights, Bergie planning the 'night attack' on the two sleeping Irish cadets, Bergie and his various short-cuts for survival.

"We owe him a lot for what he taught us in our first year," said Douglas. "If you think about it, we didn't have a clue until we met him. Our own senior guys didn't tell us anything about this place."

Moose nodded. "AND, he was my bunk-mate, my partner, *his* confidant!"

"What did he ever confess to you?" Jackson asked.

Moose tilted back on his chair. "Many things...things I can't tell you creeps because I was like a priest. I'd say, 'Go on, my son? Oh, there's more? Well tell me that too?'"

A pea flicked from Wayne's knife hit Moose square in the middle of his fore-head. Moose didn't retaliate because he knew it would start another food fight.

"So, you don't believe me, eh, Banks? Suppose I told you that..." Danyluk stopped speaking, his facial expressions indicating his mind was moving like Cunningham's did when there was five-cents remaining in the pot. The conversation had reminded him of something. He got up and started running for the door. "THAT HE FOUND TWENTY-DOLLARS OUTSIDE THE HEADQUARTERS BUILDING ON THE LAST DAY OF CAMP LAST YEAR AND HID IT UNDER THE COMMANDING OFFICER'S STAIRS!"

Immediately, the table was emptied except for East, who continued eating as the rest rushed after Danyluk. Although they ran out of the mess hall, they *marched* in double-quick time to the headquarters building. Within seconds, Danyluk was down on his hands and knees, his arm feeling around underneath the steps. The others gathered about him.

"YOU! YOU PEOPLE! WHAT THE HELL ARE YOU DOING?" The camp RSM's voice was loud. He didn't march over to them, however.

Danyluk took his arm out and stood at attention like the rest of them. "WE'RE TRYING TO RESCUE A BIRD, SIR!"

"OH, THAT'S FINE THEN, CARRY ON! The Musketeers didn't hear the RSM's other mutterings as he marched away. "That'll be the foggy Friday when he rescues a bird. Christ, he's everywhere. Probably got a worm on the end of his thing to entice the poor creature...it's bigger than his arm. The distressed animal will likely die of fright! Should be in a flippin' freak show...no, the audience would panic! And he's going to be a doctor? What the hell is the world coming to?"

When the RSM's back was to them, Danyluk didn't put his arm back under. He just stood there with a smirk on his face and displayed the twenty. "Any further doubts, Mr. Banks?"

Wayne cocked his head. "Moose, my boy, I take it back. You owe me one shot with a pea. What are we going to do with it now?"

Danyluk already knew. "We're going to split it eight ways. That's, that's, er...that's..."

Rothstein was the mathematical genius. "That's two-fifty each."

"Er, exactly Rothie. That's what I was going to say," said Moose.

"But what about Bergie?" Douglas asked.

The group marched back to B-33 and Danyluk answered, "Screw Bergie, he's got more money than the rest of us combined. Jesus, he's on Lance Corporal's pay, you know?"

B-33 was like a circus when the Musketeers, less East, returned to the bar-racks. It was Friday night and that meant cleaning, cleaning, and more cleaning.

"Earl, what's our section's responsibilities?" Douglas asked.

"We've got the shitters, but we don't have to do them until tomorrow morning," Jackson replied. "East is in there now, weighing up the job."

Cunningham laughed. "You mean weighing down the job, don't you? By the way, who did take his banana?"

Jackson's smile was contagious. "No one did. I peeled it and Moose slipped it under East's rear end just as East sat down. Moose had some of it left on his fingers and it came off on his shirt, that's why Jack was suspicious."

None of the others had noticed. Cunningham roared out laughing, "You mean it's all over the ass of his pants?"

Earl and Simon started moving their bunks over to the other wall of the hut. "Well it's hardened now, but take a look when he comes out. Half the guys think he's thrown up from the wrong end. With Jack, anything's possible."

"YOU ROTTEN CREEPS!" were the only words Jack bellowed as he came from the centre area. "MY BUDDIES, AND YA DIDN'T TELL ME I HAD WHITE SHITE ALL OVER MY ASS. SOME CADET JUST SAID, 'HEY, MACK...YOU'D BETTER CHANGE YOUR DIET, IT'S SUPPOSED TO BE BROWN!' CHRIST, NO WONDER THE GIRL SERVING ME AT SUPPER WOULDN'T GIVE ME SECONDS! 'BY THE LOOKS OF YOU YOUNG MAN, YOU SHOULD TAKE SOMETHING TO STOP THE *RUNS* IF THAT'S WHAT THE PROBLEM REALLY IS?' O.K., IF YOU THINK BERGIE ALWAYS GOT HIS OWN BACK, YOU FELLAS JUST WAIT...AND DON'T ASK ME TO CLEAR OUT THE SHOWER ROOM IN THE MORNING!"

The other Musketeers couldn't talk, they were laughing so hard at the sincerity on Jack's face as he took off his pants, held them up and looked at the seat. Another howl rang out when they saw what East couldn't see. The stain had gone through to his undershorts. When he took them off, they were like starch.

"I WONDERED WHY THE SKIN ON MY ASS WAS SO STIFF!" he stated, grabbing his towel and heading for the shower room.

When the laughter died down and East was back to normal, the Musketeers joined the others on their side of the hut, moving all of the bunks from one wall to the other. Barrack-boxes were piled on the bunks and the *cleared* portion of the floor was mopped out and scrubbed. When the black *hardwood* floor was wet, it was really hard to see just how clean it was because it had been scrubbed so often; it was just a mass of dirty, black-coloured slivers. But those dirty-coloured slivers had to look and smell clean even though the change wasn't noticeable. The following day when the hut was inspected, the aroma of Sergeants' Soap and white scrubbing powder would indicate the floor had been properly done.

After one side was scrubbed and dry, all the bunks were gently lifted back, along with the bunks from the unclean side. With the floor of the other side of the wing clear, the scrubbing and mopping process took place all over again.

Cadets wearing coveralls swarmed the place like bees in a hive. Each section of each platoon had individual responsibilities. While the floor was being scrubbed, windows were being cleaned, shelves were being washed, brass light fixtures were shined, the top of the Corporals' cubicle walls were washed, and the *garden* was raked. Additionally, briquettes of coal which in many cases substituted for rocks to form a pathway or spell the name of the company were whitewashed, the outside stairs were scrubbed, railings washed and the fire extinguishers which were handily used to squirt water all over the floor (as well as bodies and faces) were filled and shined.

In approximately two hours, B-33 looked spotless. The inhabitants walked around in either their socks, bare feet, or clean-soled running shoes to ensure the *floor* remained clean.

Some initial work was completed in the centre sink area, the shower room, drying room and toilets, however, because these rooms were heavily used during the evening and in the morning, the main cleanup job would wait until just before breakfast.

By eight o'clock, most of the cadets of Alpha Company were studying for Saturday morning examinations. The Musketeers took their notebooks and manuals over to the Cadet Canteen with them. They were rich because Danyluk had split up the twenty dollars, and two-dollars-and-fifty-cents in 1956 was a large amount of money.

As they sat in the *garden*, Moose put his notebook down, took a big swig of his Kik Kola and reminisced. "Y'know, guys, even though Bergie isn't here, he's still looking after us."

Wayne lowered his book, took off his glasses, and rubbed his eyes. "Wait till we tell him we found his twenty. He won't believe it."

Simon was more interested in studying. "These conventional signs are easy, but they're so bloody small to see on a map. Take a look at this one and tell me what it is. Is that a marsh or a cemetery?"

Rothstein looked over Simon's shoulder. "It's got the letter 'C' in the middle so what do *you* think it is?"

Moose answered before Simon did. "If it's got the letter 'C' in the middle, it's a cow pasture."

Rothstein gave Moose a hesitant glance. "I suppose a pig pen's got a 'P' in the middle, right?"

Moose shook his head. "Nope, that's a parliament building."

Jackson couldn't take it. "Jesus, Moose, a 'P' represents a post office."

Danyluk stuck out his chest. "No, it doesn't, that's a small building with a flag on it."

Wayne got into the act. "Then what's a circle of broken lines with a 'W' in the middle of it, smart ass?"

Danyluk smiled. "On military maps?"

"Yes, on military maps!"

"It's a whorehouse!"

Cunningham stopped studying and laughed aloud. "Trust you to think of that. Y'know, that's not a bad idea, all fighting would come to a sudden stop when the men on both sides noticed the conventional sign was that of a whorehouse. There'd be instant peace."

"You mean instant *piece*," Danyluk said as he showed everyone his map. "Look here, there's a small 'W' right across from this camp. It's right where Hop Sing's is."

East grabbed the map and squinted, looking for the sign. "You put that there, you pongo!" He continued staring at Danyluk's map for a moment. "What the hell are these conventional signs? There's a whole buncha 'NTs' and 'GTs' and 'DWMs' and DTLIs and DTDs and what's this final one, DTSAS?"

Moose snatched his map back. "Never youse mind, you're too young!"

Instantly seven bodies were around him trying to get their hands on his map. "C'mon, please Moose, don't hold anything back on us!" Douglas pleaded.

Moose gave in. "Well, they're my personal and confidential conventional signs. NT means, no tits, GT means, great tits, DWM means, dames with money, DTLI means, dames that love it, DTD means, dames that don't, and DTSAS means, dames that scream and scratch."

Jackson went at Moose again. "DTD? YOU'VE ALWAYS TOLD US WHEN YOU'RE AT THE HELM, ALL GIRLS ARE DTLI? WHAT'S WITH THESE DTDs?"

Moose swallowed a few times and moved his shoulders around. Jackson had caught him off guard. "Well, I...er..."

"SO YOU HAVE BEEN TURNED DOWN? SOME DAMES *DO* SAY NO?"

"HEY, WHO SAYS SO? THE MOOSE IS NEVER TURNED DOWN! THE ONLY TIME I GOT TURNED DOWN WAS WITH MY GRADE TWO TEACHER."

"I BET *HE* WAS MAD!" shot Earl, running for the door.

Moose was up and after him like a bullet, but Earl was still the fastest runner. "I'LL GET YOU FOR THAT ONE, JACKSON!"

Simon closed his book. "You were goin' at it in grade two?"

Moose cocked his head from side to side. "*No*, I wasn't going at it in grade two! I was goin' at it in grade one! This girl who was in grade three was playing soccer with us and her face was getting red. I said, "Can you kneel and take a big breath?" because my dad always said that's what you have to do if you get tired."

"Yeah, go on!"

"Well, she thought I said, 'Can I feel your big breasts?' She smiled, grabbed me and we went behind the school. Jesus, I can remember wanting bigger hands."

"Wanting bigger hands with a kid in grade three?"

Moose thought for a quick moment. "Well, she was also fat, if I can recall."

"So that was the first of your sexual encounters?"

Moose grabbed Simon by the front of his shirt. "Yes that was the start. How old were you?"

All eyes were on Simon now, and he was red.

"Well, I er...about...er..."

Moose released him, put his arm around his shoulder and edged him towards the door. "C'mon virgin, I'm not tellin' you any more stories 'cause you'll probably head for the crappers like Jack does with his National Geographic magazine."

East nearly choked on the cookie he was eating. "SCREW YOU, MOOSE! YOU'RE THE ONE WHO'S ALWAYS GOT MY MAGAZINE!"

On the way back to B-33, once again, Jack was the target of the conversation. It was quiet when they arrived back because most cadets were studying. Moose turned up his radio and filled the shack with the voice of Clyde McPhatter singing, *Treasure Of Love.*

The Musketeers had gone to bed when Sergeant Beckford entered and bellowed, "THOSE WHO ARE NOT IN BED, STAND BY YOUR BEDS!" He stopped at Cunningham's bunk. Gordie had already made his bed Saturday-morning style, and was sleeping on the floor with only one blanket.

"Aren't you going to be a little cold in the middle of the night?"

"I don't think so, Sergeant. Moose tells me he does it once in awhile and it saves time in the morning."

The Sergeant smiled. "But he wraps his foreskin around himself to keep warm. What are you going to do?"

Gordie put on his confident look. "I could do the same, Sergeant!"

An inquisitive look took over Sergeant Beckford's face. "Oh, you mean Danyluk's going to sleep there with you? That's stretching it a little tight, isn't it?"

Cunningham sat up as Sergeant Beckford moved on. "No, I didn't mean...Sergeant, I didn't mean that...I"

Beckford pretended not to hear him, but his *friends* didn't, especially Wayne.

"Any guy that would want to keep warm by wrapping himself in Moose's foreskin has got to be sick, isn't that right, Doug?"

"Jesus, you'd better believe it...real sick! I've heard of getting rained on, but never *veined* on."

With the lights out and Beckford gone, the topic remained unchanged. Even a couple of cadets from across the aisle got in their two-cents worth.

"Hey, Barry, I always told ya those BCR cadets were weird."

"Yeah, especially the *gambler*! If he's not after one type of skin, he's after another!"

Cunningham yelled, "UP YOUR KILT, YOU SEAFORTH PONGOES!"

"See what I mean, Barry?"

"Yeah, we'll have to make certain we've got our legs closed the next time we play stuke."

Danyluk came to Cunningham's aid. "Open or closed, you've got nothing there anyway. All you Seaforths are the same, all mouth and no balls. Hey Gordie, did I tell ya the one about the three doctors?"

"No, ya didn't, Moose! Tell me."

"Well, there were these three doctors, see, and the first one said, 'I like operating on BCR cadets because when you open them up everything is numbered. One goes to one, two to two, three to three, etc. All ya gotta do then, is sow them up and send 'em away.'"

"Then the second one said, 'I like operating on Westie cadets because when you open them up, everything is colour-coded. Blue goes to blue, red to red, green to green, etc. They're really easy to work on.'"

"The third one said, 'Well, I've got ya both beat. I like working on Seaforth cadets because they've only got two moving parts.'"

"'What are those?' the first doctor asked."

"'Their assholes and their mouths and they're both interchangeable.' Goodnight, Gord."

"Goodnight, Moose."

Although it was probably the light breeze, when B-33 creaked, it sounded like a slight chuckle.

CHAPTER VI

"WELL, SINCE MY BABY LEFT ME, I'VE FOUND A NEW PLACE TO..." The sound of Elvis Presley's voice singing *Heartbreak Hotel*, nearly scared Douglas half-to-death. The clock radio had gone off exactly at 0630, the same time as the camp bugler blew reveille. Immediately, Moose also turned on his radio and One Platoon's end of the barracks came alive with song.

Danyluk made a dash to the urinal and then rushed through his wing to form up on the road. "C'mon you creeps, if we're not out there in one minute, Sergeant Simpson will have our asses!"

Douglas didn't quite understand what Moose was doing. "Moose, there's no P.T. this morning, remember, it's Saturday? Sergeant Simpson won't be here until we're ready to get on parade."

Danyluk looked at his watch. "SON OF A BITCH, it's twenty-five to seven, half the day's nearly gone. Just joking, Dougie. C'mon you lazy bums, let go of your wangs and start brushing your fangs!"

Cunningham stretched and got up from the floor. "Damn, I'm stiff. That's the last time you're going to talk me into that, Danyluk."

Moose walked over to him. "Oh, quit complaining, moneybags. Look, your beds already made up...we've still got to do ours."

Only half the inhabitants of B-33 were up when the eight Musketeers headed for the showers. They were fortunate because only a couple of guys had gotten there ahead of them. That meant they didn't have to use East to stink the place out. Actually, other cadets were so used to East, they left the minute he entered, which meant he didn't have to demonstrate his *talent* too often.

Wayne opened the window wide to get rid of the steam. "Is everyone in the platoon clued in as to our little plan?" he asked.

Rothstein had been appointed to explain to the other sections in One Platoon what was expected of them this morning. "It's gone beyond our platoon, Wayne. The other three platoons are going to join in. I've got a feeling that Beckford will notice it right at the start."

Cunningham liked that statement. "I'll give you five-to-one, he doesn't! We've been practising it all week when he's not around and I think we're nearly perfect."

Douglas had to yell to be heard over Danyluk's singing. "DON'T FORGET, WE CAN'T WEAR WATCHES ON PARADE TODAY, AND YOU GUYS WITH GLASSES WILL HAVE TO DO WITHOUT THEM!"

"Blast, I'll be as blind as a bat!" quipped Wayne.

Danyluk stopped singing for a moment to make a statement, then he returned to his song: "SHE WAS ONLY THE FARMER'S DAUGHTER, BUT ALL THE HORSEMEN KNEW HER! Why don't youse use a white cane instead of a rifle?"

Rothstein cringed. "God, I hate that word, 'youse.' Speak the Queen's English, you dolt!"

Simon laughed. "Moose, why don't *you* use your wang instead of a rifle?"

Gargling with a mouthful of hot shower water, East burbled, "Because he's got no upper sling swivel. For that matter, where would he place the bayonet?"

Danyluk was oblivious to it all as he continued his song. "THE LOCAL GEN-TRY ALL KNEW, SHE HAD SOOT UP HER FLUE, BUT THAT DIDN'T STOP THEM AT ALL!"

Following their shower, the Musketeers went for breakfast. East was asked to only have one helping, because as Jackson said, "You're losing control of it, East. You're slowly slipping them out on the parade square, and attracting flies."

After breakfast, the various sections of One Platoon went to work on their individual responsibilities. Rothstein and East tackled the urinal, Danyluk and Jackson cleaned the toilets and wiped the top of the partitions and doors; Douglas and Wayne brushed and mopped the floor; and Simon and Cunningham did the windows, cleaned the washing machine, and shined the light shades and brass light fixtures.

When it was time to get on parade, B-33 shone inside and out. The only thing they were concerned about was a missing light bulb, inside, between the doors at the end of the southeast wing. That problem was solved after Moose visited one of the nearby huts. When it was screwed in to the socket, it was guarded so it wouldn't be stolen again. Shortly, the cadets in the 'donor' hut would be looking for a light bulb. Eventually, after several huts were 'robbed,' a light bulb was missing from the east-side entrance of the Sergeants' Mess.

The parade procedure was different this morning. After the roll call, Alpha Company was sized by company as usual, and marched to the lower camp weapons' stores to pick up rifles and bayonets. After receiving them, the guard was split into two and sized individually. Of the Musketeers, Rothstein, had been appointed Guard Commander, Danyluk and Jackson were Guard Lieutenants, and Cunningham was a Guard Sergeant.

The rifles were immaculate because the cadets who were incarcerated in the guardroom *volunteered* to clean them.

All of the Platoon Sergeants would join them shortly, however, the Platoon Corporals had gone along with the trick the company was about to play.

One of them said, "Are you guys certain you can pull this off?"

"Corporal, just try us and see," assured Danyluk.

The Corporal stood to attention. "GUARD, ATTEN...TION! FORM TWO-DEEP! RIGHT...DRESS! EYES...FRONT! THE GUARD WILL FIX BAYO-NETS! FIX...BAYONETS! ATTEN...TION! YOU PEOPLE ARE PERFECT, KEEP IT UP! GUARD, SLOPE...ARMS! GUARD, ORDER ARMS! STAN-DAT...EASE! STAND EASY!"

"Well, what do you think?" asked Danyluk.

"PERFECT! ABSOLUTELY PERFECT!" replied the Corporal. "RIGHT, LET'S GET ON THE PARADE SQUARE. THE COMPANY SERGEANT-MAJOR AND SERGEANTS WILL MEET US THERE AND COVER ANY LAST POINTS! GUARD COMMANDER, CARRY ON!"

The Cadet Guard Commander, Major Rothstein responded, "Yes, Corporal! GUARD, ATTEN...TION! SLOPE...ARMS! MOVE TO THE RIGHT IN FILE, RIGHT...TURN! BY THE LEFT, QUICK...MARCH! LEFT, RIGHT, LEFT, RIGHT! WATCH YOUR DRESSING! LEFT WHEEL...WATCH YOUR DRESS-ING ON THE WHEELS!"

As two other Platoon Corporals stood in the middle of the highway to stop what little traffic there was, the cadets of Alpha Company smartly marched onto the giant parade square and proceeded to halt on their right marker who was already in position. The right marker procedures had been carried out moments earlier by the Cadet Regimental Sergeant-Major, under the watchful eyes of RSM Gardiner.

"GUARD, MARK TIME! GUARD...HALT! THE GUARD WILL ADVANCE, LEFT...TURN! ORDER...ARMS! STANDAT...EASE! STAND EASY!"

"They look damned good," said Sergeant Mack to Sergeant Simpson. Simpson agreed, but Sergeant Beckford was shaking his head. "Yes, they do, but something is wrong! Are they bringing their arms up shoulder-high or waist-high?"

Mack still had his eyes on his platoon. "Waist high and that halt was bloody perfect. Jesus, Bill you're like a little old lady at times. They are nearly flawless!"

Sergeant Prest and Sergeant-Major Rose agreed wholeheartedly with Sergeant Mack and even the camp RSM had come by and said, "The guard looks exemplary, gentlemen. Keep up the good work."

Bill Beckford started smiling and shaking his head. "Well, I'll be a monkey's..."

Simpson moved closer. "What? What do you see that we don't?"

Beckford let out a deep laugh, smacked his buddy Simpson on the back and motioned the other Senior NCOs to join him as he marched towards the guard. When the NCOs gathered, all faces in Alpha Company were serious. Some cadets were wiping off their boots with small rags and others were dusting off their rifles. Not a smile was visible.

Sergeant Beckford stood six feet in front of them. "GUARD, ATTEN...TION! THE GUARD WILL UNFIX BAYONETS! UNFIX...BAYONETS! ATTEN...TION!"

"EXCELLENT!" bellowed Rose.

Sergeant Beckford slowly turned and stared at the Sergeant-Major. "Yes, sir, they really are excellent, however, if you will take a closer look...GUARD, STANDAT...EASE! STAND EASY!"

The faces of the Company Sergeant-Major and other Sergeants turned a little pink. They now realized that one of the oldest tricks in the book had been pulled off with utmost perfection. The cadets of Alpha Company had been using the wrong hands for each drill movement. Instead of the rifles being on the left shoulders, they were on the right. They had swung their left arms, and bayonets had been placed on the weapons with the right hand. They had completed all drill movements in an opposite order, including foot drill. On the advance, they had pivoted on the ball of the right foot and the heel of the left foot, however, instead of bringing up the right foot and slamming it down, they had brought up their left foot and slammed it back.

Sergeant Beckford's *gas pain* indicated that the jig was up and laughter resounded throughout the company. It was a chain reaction which started each junior and senior NCO alike, laughing.

"WE'VE BEEN PRACTISIN' A WEEK TO PULL THIS OFF!" Moose yelled. "WE WEREN'T GOING TO DO THE PARADE LIKE THIS, WE JUST WANTED TO SEE IF WE COULD PULL IT OFF THIS FAR!"

Beckford still grinned as he spoke. "Well, you certainly did fool some of the gentlemen here, *and* the camp RSM. Adjust your weapons and bayonet frogs. Well done, don't you think so, *gentlemen*?" he said, as he glanced at his fellow NCOs who were all shaking their heads and smiling.

Sergeant-Major Rose marched to the front. "IF YOU PEOPLE CAN DO DRILL LIKE THAT, THERE CAN BE NO EXCUSES FOR SCREW-UPS

DOING IT THE PROPER WAY, CAN THERE?"

"NO, SIR!" was the thunderous and jolly response.

"GOOD SHOW, GUYS! YOU CERTAINLY HAD ME FOOLED! ALSO, I WISH TO CONGRATULATE ALPHA COMPANY NOT HAVING ANYONE ON SICK PARADE TODAY!"

The parade that morning was nearly letter-perfect. Although it was hot, and a few members of other companies passed out, and had to be helped to the sidelines, not one member of Alpha Company swayed as General George Kitching marched through the ranks inspecting them. They had been through it all before, and now they were professionals.

The Cadet Parade Commander accompanying General Kitching was a tall cadet from Driver Mechanics, and his Second In Command was from Number Four Platoon of Alpha Company. The Cadet Battalion RSM was a cadet from Number Three Platoon in Alpha Company. All of these positions changed weekly, as did company appointments.

Following the usual procedure of presenting arms for the general salute, the inspection took its normal course.

General Kitching, as usual, looked immaculate in his uniform. His military bearing was faultless and he expected his cadets to be the same. "You're very well turned out, Brice!"

"Thank you, sir!"

"How many years have you attended Vernon?"

"This is my fourth year, sir!"

"What are your plans for the future?"

"At this point, I'm uncertain, sir!"

"Well, keep up the good work!"

"Thank you, sir!"

The general stopped about eight times while inspecting the two ranks of the guard. Most of the cadets knew that the general's facial expression usually didn't change very much, however, Major Ratcliffe told them afterwards that when the general left the guard to inspect Bravo Company, Kitching's face expressed a feeling of complete satisfaction and pride.

"All of you know that General Kitching follows the principle of leadership by example. The general has seen it all and has done it all. He knows what he wants and he expects his cadets to understand that."

General Kitching well understood the *annoyance* of the hot sun *scorching* the body of each cadet standing on the sweltering parade square. He completed his inspection in approximately thirty-five minutes and returned to the dais.

The Cadet Parade Commander then carried on.

"BATTALION...ATTEN...TION! CLOSE ORDER...MARCH! RIGHT...DRESS!" When the dressing was completed, he then marched forward and saluted the general.

"SIR, THE CADETS OF THE VERNON ARMY CADET CAMP ARE READY FOR THE MARCH PAST, SIR!"

General Kitching returned the salute. "THANK YOU, COLONEL FERNIER, PLEASE CARRY ON!"

Cadet Marcel Fernier was one of fifty cadets from Quebec. Fifty cadets from British Columbia and the prairies were on exchange in cadet camps in Quebec.

"BATTALION, SLOPE...ARMS! MOVE TO THE RIGHT IN COLUMN OF

ROUTE, RIGHT...TURN!"

After the supernumeraries had attained their marching positions, the commander carried on.

"BATTALION, BY THE RIGHT, QUICK...MARCH!"

With the cadet drum and bugle band sharing time with the cadet pipes and drums section, the cadets of the Vernon Army Cadet Camp completed the march past in style, each cadet snapping his head to the right when they passed the dais after the command, "EYES RIGHT!" was given. They all knew they must look the reviewing officer in his eyes. General Kitching, in turn, had the unique knack of looking into each of their eyes, as he stood rigidly in the salute position.

Following the march past, the guard ordered arms again and the battalion was dressed. After that, the Cadet Parade Commander returned to the dais.

"SIR, WOULD YOU LIKE TO SAY A FEW WORDS TO THE CADETS?"

General Kitching returned the commander's salute. "YES, STAND THEM AT EASE, PLEASE AND STAND THEM EASY!"

When the cadet commander had completed the general's request, as was part of *his* trademark, General Kitching said, "PLEASE COME UP HERE AND GATHER AROUND ME!"

The guard individually grounded arms, as did the band with their instruments. It only took a matter of seconds for 1400 cadets to form a semi-circle in front of General George Kitching.

"I'M SORRY I TOOK SO LONG TO INSPECT YOU, BUT THIS IS A VERY BIG PARADE SQUARE AND UNLIKE THE REGIMENTAL SERGEANT-MAJOR, I DON'T HAVE SIZE TWELVE FEET."

Quiet laughter roamed the ranks.

"THIS IS THE FIRST OPPORTUNITY I HAVE HAD TO TALK WITH ALL OF YOU AND I LOOKED FORWARD TO IT.

"YOUR PARADE TODAY WAS EXCELLENT AND I WISH TO CONGRATULATE YOU. THROUGHOUT THE NEXT FIVE WEEKS, YOU WILL OBVIOUSLY CONTINUE TO IMPROVE AND THE VERY FEW MISTAKES YOU MADE TODAY WILL SURELY DISAPPEAR.

"OVER THE PAST SIX DAYS I HAVE SPOKEN WITH MANY OF YOU WHILE YOU WERE TRAINING, AND I AM EXTREMELY PLEASED WITH YOUR BEARING AND DEPORTMENT, NOT JUST HERE IN CAMP, BUT DOWNTOWN AS WELL. YOU ARE A CREDIT TO THE NATION AND I COMPLIMENT YOU ON YOUR DESIRE TO ACHIEVE HIGH MILITARY AND PERSONAL STANDARDS. I HAVE ALSO THANKED YOUR OFFICERS AND NON-COMMISSIONED OFFICERS.

"THIS CAMP EXISTS FOR YOU...NOT FOR MYSELF, OR MY STAFF. IT IS ONE OF TWELVE CAMPS ACROSS THE COUNTRY THAT THE GOVERNMENT HAS DESIGNATED FOR ARMY CADET SUMMER TRAINING. THE SIX WEEKS OF TRAINING YOU RECEIVE HERE WILL ALLOW YOU TO RETURN TO YOUR HOME CORPS AND IMPART THIS KNOWLEDGE TO OTHER CADETS WHO ARE FOLLOWING IN YOUR FOOTSTEPS.

"THE FACT THAT YOU GAVE UP YOUR CIVILIAN SUMMER TO ATTEND VERNON SPEAKS FOR ITSELF. EACH OF YOU WANTS TO LEARN, ADVANCE AND MATURE, THUS BECOMING MORE SELF-CONFIDENT, AND RESPONSIBLE CITIZENS OF THIS GREAT COUNTRY.

"THERE IS A DIFFERENCE BETWEEN SELF-RESPONSIBILITY AND

RESPONSIBILITY TOWARDS YOUR FELLOW MAN. WE TEACH BOTH OF
THOSE ATTRIBUTES HERE AND I WANT YOU TO UNDERSTAND THE
DIFFERENCE. IF WE CANADIANS ARE TO SUCCEED AS A NATION,
THEN WE HAVE TO ACHIEVE IT BY ASSISTING ONE ANOTHER. I WANT
ALL OF YOU TO COMPREHEND THAT FACT. ALTHOUGH THERE IS INDI-
VIDUALISM IN THIS WORLD, THIS PERSONAL TRAIT MUST BE REGU-
LATED BY DEMOCRATIC TEAMWORK.

"IF EACH OF YOU WERE TO PUT A HAND IN A BUCKET OF WATER
AND WHEN YOU TOOK IT OUT, YOU FOUND THERE WAS A HOLE IN
THE WATER WHERE YOUR HAND WAS, THEN YOU PERSONALLY DON'T
HAVE TO WORRY ABOUT TAKING OTHER PEOPLE'S OPINIONS INTO
CONSIDERATION."

More chuckles wafted through the air.

"NOW, TO CHANGE THE SUBJECT, I WANT YOU TO KNOW THAT I
AM COMMITTED TO CONTINUALLY IMPROVING THE LIVING QUAR-
TERS AND FOR THAT MATTER, ALL BUILDINGS IN CAMP VERNON.
THIS NEW PARADE SQUARE IS A FAR CRY FROM THE DUST BOWL IT
USED TO BE. AS I LOOK AROUND, I CAN SEE THAT NOT ONE OF YOU
HAD A NOMADIC SPIDER CRAWL UP YOUR SHORTS THIS MORNING."

Although the laughter of cadets grew louder, many knew what the general was
referring to. Those who had previously paraded where the new parade square now
stood had received the bites of those *nomadic* spiders, as well as other *quasi-mili-
tary* bugs.

After the Advance In Review Order, General Kitching left for the headquarters
building, as did all of the other officers. RSM Gardiner took over.

"I HOPE GENERAL KITCHING'S WORDS DIDN'T MAKE YOU THINK
YOU ARE PERFECT, BECAUSE YOU ARE FAR FROM IT! I COULD FILL A
NOTEBOOK WITH ALL OF THE MISTAKES I SAW TODAY! HOWEVER,
FOR YOUR FIRST WEEK IN CAMP THE PARADE WAS NOT BAD AT ALL.
HOWEVER, THERE IS ALWAYS ROOM FOR IMPROVEMENT!

"WHILE THE PARADE WAS IN PROGRESS, CERTAIN OFFICERS AND
MY STAFF WERE INSPECTING YOUR QUARTERS AND THEY LIKED
WHAT THEY SAW. IN MY *HUMBLE* OPINION, YOUR QUARTERS WERE
BETTER THAN THIS PARADE!

"NEVERTHELESS, THE BEST COMPANY IN CAMP THIS WEEK
IS...WAIT FOR IT...ALPHA COMPANY!"

Grumblings travelled throughout the ranks, in all companies but Alpha.

"I KNOW, I KNOW. MANY OF YOU BELIEVE THAT THE SENIOR
CADETS HAVE AN EDGE. WELL, THAT JUST ISN'T TRUE AT ALL. MY
STAFF'S JOB IS TO ENSURE THAT YOU PROGRESS WELL, AND IF YOU
DON'T, THEN IT'S MY STAFF'S FAULT! NOW, I DON'T WANT ALPHA
COMPANY WINNING EVERY WEEK, IS THAT CLEAR?"

The response from all companies, excluding Alpha, was earsplitting.

"YES, SIR!"

The cadets of the guard shook hands with their left hands, because they had
rifles in their right hands.

"THE WORD PERFECT IS SPELLED, A.L.P.H.A.!" Moose bellowed. "AND
THE WORD BEST IS SPELLED, O.N.E. P.L.A.T.O.O.N.!"

The RSM continued. "AND, ALPHA COMPANY, IT ISN'T NECESSARY

FOR SOME OF YOU TO DISPLAY YOUR FINGERS TO YOUR JUNIORS!

"AS A FINAL POINT, THE CITY OF VERNON HAS INFORMED US THAT THE DANCES START AGAIN TONIGHT AT THE ARENA, AND YES, MIDNIGHT PASSES WILL BE ISSUED TO THOSE OF YOU WHO HAVE EARNED THEM. IF YOU'RE NOT PLANNING ON GOING TO THE DANCE, REMEMBER THERE ARE MOVIES IN B-3 TONIGHT AND TOMORROW NIGHT!"

There was a loud cheer.

"FOLLOWING LUNCH TODAY, HAVE A GOOD RELAXING WEEK-END...YOU'VE EARNED IT!"

After the RSM left, Alpha Company handed in their weapons and was marched back to B-33. A three-ton truck pulled up and each cadet had to hand in his upper sheet and pillowcase. Then each received one clean sheet and a pillow-case.

While they were making their beds, a Corporal marched in with the mail, and both wings of the hut gathered in the Musketeer's end. "MAIL CALL! READ 'EM AND WEEP!"

For the next five minutes, the Corporal threw letters and parcels to eager out-stretched hands. "DANYLUK, DANYLUK, DANYLUK, WARRINGTON, BRICE, DANYLUK, DANYLUK, POTTS, LEVEILLE, BANKS, BROOKS, DANYLUK, DANYLUK, JACKSON, DANYLUK, BRIGADIER GENERAL MOOSE, FIELD MARSHAL MOOSE, MAJOR MOOSE...JESUS, WE'VE GOT SOME OFFICERS' MAIL BY MISTAKE."

"NO, NO, THAT'S ME ALSO, CORPORAL!"

The Corporal looked up from his pile. "THAT'S WHO? WHO THE HELL'S MOOSE?"

Danyluk smiled sheepishly. "My secondary dames just know me as Moose! My real name is Danyluk to my favourites."

The Corporal shook his head. "What names do you know *them* by, NAGS?"

"HEY, NONNA MY DAMES ARE NAGS!"

"JUST HOW MANY BROADS HAVE YOU GOT?"

Moose stuck out his chest. "Well, I've got..."

"GET ON WITH IT!" cried East. "We haven't got all bloody day. He's got more dames than your dog's got fleas. AND MOST OF HIS NAGS HAVE GOT FLEAS!"

Moose got upset. "UP YOUR NOSE, EAST! AT LEAST MINE DON'T HAVE LICE!"

"SENIOR CADET MOOSE, CUNNINGHAM, SIMON, COURT MARTIAL MOOSE...COURT MARTIAL MOOSE? *COURT MARTIAL MOOSE?*"

"She's not too bright, Corporal!"

"Christ, you can say that again."

"SHE'S NOT TOO BRIGHT, CORPORAL!"

"Jesus, let me out of *here*," mumbled the Corporal.

The recipients of the letters didn't have time to read them. After the Corporal marched out talking to himself, Alpha Company formed three ranks on the road and was marched to the lecture rooms in the upper camp.

Sergeant Beckford was waiting for his platoon, along with Lieutenant Harwood. Sergeant Beckford did the talking.

"RIGHT! THIS WRITTEN EXAM COVERING ALL SUBJECTS SHOULD

TAKE YOU ABOUT AN HOUR-AND-A-HALF! IF YOU FINISH BEFORE THEN, JUST PASS YOUR TEST PAPERS TO ME OR LIEUTENANT HARWOOD, BEFORE YOU LEAVE!

"I WANT EVERYTHING OFF YOUR DESKS EXCEPT YOUR PENCILS, PENS, AND PROTRACTORS! WRITE YOUR NAME AND PLATOON NUMBER IN THE UPPER-RIGHT-HAND-CORNER OF THE FIRST PAGE!

"WHEN YOU RECEIVE YOUR TEST, YOU CAN START!"

Both Douglas and Wayne were out in forty minutes. Rothstein caught up with them on the *road* leading to the lower camp. The three had spring in their step because the week was over and a relaxing weekend lay ahead of them.

"How'd you guys think you did?"

"A piece of cake," said Wayne.

Douglas was a little more hesitant. "Good, I guess, but some of those leadership questions were tricky. For example, Illustrative Case 'A'...the case of Cadet Nicholas Allenby and his brother Ken. I considered question one. *'Does Nicholas' behavior have something to do with his stage of development? Since he has changed his demeanor from the positive of the past to its current negative form, might it not change to positive again in the future through maturity?'*"

Wayne indicated he agreed with Douglas, however he didn't consider that question. "Not me. Something has to make it change. I considered question two. *'What part does communication play in this situation?'* The more he communicates with his peers, the more he sees reality.'"

Rothstein had a habit of biting his lower lip when he was uncertain. "I considered question three. *'The motivation factors. What are they? If the kid is motivated, then he could change back!'* No, let me rephrase that, he *would* change back! His brother just wasn't interested. There's no simple solution to this type of situation. I think all the principles and techniques have to be understood and utilized."

Wayne thought the scenario was great. "Jeez, I liked the whole descriptive process of the problem these two cadets were having. Whoever designed the leadership questions was a bloody genius."

Douglas and Rothstein agreed.

Gradually, over an hour-and-a-half, all cadets of Alpha Company were in their quarters doing odd jobs. Before lunch, they would prepare their walking-out dress, which was short pants, shirts, boots, hosetops, puttees, regimental web belts, and berets.

Moose was complaining about one of the questions on the exam when someone came up behind him and put his hands over Moose's eyes.

"GET LOST, CUNNINGHAM YOU CREEP! YOU'RE NOT GETTING YOUR HANDS ON THIS NEW MONEY I GOT IN THE MAIL!" He turned around and nearly fainted.

"BERGIE? SON OF A BITCH...BERGIE!" He wrapped his arms around the smiling soldier in front of him. "HEY, GUYS, BERGIE'S HERE!"

In a fraction of a second, all the Musketeers were gathered around a proudly-grinning Bergie who was dressed in tropical worsteds. He'd grown somewhat, and was lost for words. Not that he could'nt talk, he was receiving so many pats on his back he would have sounded like a Morse code key.

A moment later, Ed Shanks walked into the shack and he was surrounded as well. Every Irish cadet in camp appeared to be there. Instantly, Simon had his arm around his friend's shoulders. The normally proud Irish were even prouder, this day.

All of the Musketeers had lumps in their throats. Their old buddy Bergie looked like a real soldier. He had been right about muscles being put on muscles. He was taller, broader, and both of them had their wings.

"SON OF A BITCH! YOU'VE JUMPED OUT OF A PERFECTLY SAFE AIRPLANE? GOD, I CAN'T GET OVER THIS!"

Bergie just stood their with a giant grin, shaking offered hands coming from all directions. Every cadet in B-33 had heard about the famous Bergie. He was a living legend.

Eventually, the Musketeers stole the soldiers away and surrounded them, sitting on a bunk.

Bergies eyes welled up a bit. "I really missed you guys. I never realized how close we were until you saw me off on that train. I gotta tell ya, that was a rough ride."

Moose had his arm around his best friend. "Bergie, don't you realize we were the same way. Losing you was like losing an arm. When your train went out of sight, I actually ditched the dames and walked all the way home. Gordie offered me a ride and I said no. Jeez, you look great. Hey guys, look at him!"

Douglas pumped Bergie's hand again. "It hasn't been the same without ya. Not one of us said good-bye to each other that night. Everyone walked home in a daze. The last time I saw Moose, he was walking back on the platform somehow thinking there might be a problem with your train and you'd come back." Douglas was trying to smile, but it was hard. He didn't let go of Bergie's hand. "It hasn't been the same without you."

Bergie was embarrassed by the reception. Even though Moose's arm was still around his shoulder and wasn't coming off, he cleared his throat, stood up and changed the subject.

"Are we going to eat? Jack, how come you're not guiding us to the mess hall?"

East quickly shook his head and came back to the real world. The fact that Bergie had arrived had actually taken his mind of food. "Bergie, you, er...you can have my chair, which is your old one. C'mon, pal, welcome home."

On the way to the kitchen, both Bergie and Shanks were smacked on their backs so many times it's a wonder each of their spines wasn't dislocated.

"MOVE ASIDE, YOU PEONS," Danyluk yelled as he ushered the group to the head of the line. "THESE TWO ARE REAL SOLDIERS AND THEY'RE SPECIAL GUESTS OF THE CAMP!"

Surprisingly the cadets did move apart with little or no quarrel, and Bergie took his usual chair at the Musketeer's table. It was tight seating, but they moved their table away from the wall so that both ends could be utilized.

For the next hour, with only interruptions from *passing hands* that gave each of them more smacks on their backs, Bergie and Shanks answered all questions put to them and brought themselves up-to-date on Vernon.

"What made you decide to get your wings?" asked Wayne.

Bergie pointed at Shanks. "*He* made me decide. One day, some officer asked, 'Those of you who would like to take a jump course, step forward.' The next second I felt this arm dragging me forward with him. Since we were in the front rank, we were noticed right then and there, and I couldn't back out."

Rothstein let out a giant laugh. "Was it tough?"

Shanks still had the sneakiest grin on his face when he answered. He knew it had taken Bergie a few days to forgive him. "I think we both found the thirty-foot tower a little more trying than actually jumping from an aircraft. When you're up in the air, you've got no time to think and you lose any sense of height. When the light goes on and someone screams, "STAND UP! HOOK UP!" The next minute you're shuffling towards the exit. I *volunteered* us because we needed the jump pay."

"I nearly shit myself on that first jump," said Bergie, with a tinge of serious-ness in his tone. Although the training gets you ready for it, you're never really too sure."

"What's this thing called a sweat jump?" Jackson asked.

Both Bergie and Shanks were trying to eat between questions. It was Bergie who answered. "I haven't had one yet, but Shanks has." He glanced at Edwin.

"It's hard to describe, but for some reason my sixth jump was really mentally hard on me. My mind insisted this was it, I was going to die. Actually the jump was the same as all of the others, but I was a hell of a lot more hesitant."

Danyluk wasn't even concerned about his food. He placed his arm around Bergie's shoulders again. "So my buddy's goin' overseas? Jesus, I wish I was going with ya!"

A glazed look came into Bergie's eyes as he looked down at the table. "I wish you were all coming with us." He looked up again. "We've met a hell of a lot of ex-cadets lately. Every time we meet other Regular Force groups, we always recognize someone we knew at Vernon. Doug, do you remember Hitchens?"

Douglas thought for a moment before his eyes lit up. "Yeah, the guy I kicked in the nuts during my first year?"

"That's him. He's in the Strathcona's." (Lord Strathcona's Horse [Royal Canadians] - LdSH [RC]) "The son of a bitch went armoured. He was on the train coming west with us, heading to Abbotsford to visit his folks. You wouldn't recog-nize him now; he hasn't got an ounce of fat on him and he's not mouthy anymore."

Douglas smiled and shook his head. "He turned out to be a pretty good guy."

"How are all the dames?" Bergie asked.

There was a moment of silence at the table before Danyluk spoke. "Dames? We've been too busy to even think of dames. Do you remember how we thought IBT was tough? Well, this course is even worse. It's leadership, leadership and more leadership!"

"His right hand will never forgive him," said Cunningham. "By the way, Bergie, how would you like a little game of craps while you're here? You too, Shanks, you know, no limit and...?"

Wayne came to the soldiers' rescue. "Christ, Gordie, give it a rest. Besides he probably hasn't forgiven you for taking his weights at the last game. By the way, Bergie, do you have to wear boots and puttees with TWs? Those weights look great."

"They cost a buck a set at the base store. I've brought each of you guys a set. Yeah, sometimes we can wear low shoes with TWs, but most of the time it's boots and puttees."

One by one, each of the Musketeers expressed thanks for the thrill of getting a new pair of Regular Force weights.

"Oh, and Bergie, we found that twenty," Moose stated. "It was as good as the day you put it under the steps."

Bergie had obviously forgotten it, but now he was reminded. "Trust you to think of that. I..." Bergie didn't finish speaking, he just snapped to attention in the seated position, so did Shanks. Sergeants Beckford and Simpson were standing by the table.

"Not bad," said Sergeant Beckford as he glanced at Simpson. "They train them right in the Regular Force. Just relax guys, it's great to see you."

Both Bergie and Shanks sat easy and stood up to shake the extended hands of both Sergeants. Bergie looked a little shy when he answered, "It's great to see you again, Sergeant Beckford...Sergeant Simpson. So you came back again?"

"Someone has to look after Moose," replied Sergeant Beckford, shaking Shanks' hand. "My congratulations on your earning your wings. How long are you here for?"

"Thank you. We leave on tomorrow afternoon's train, Sergeant."

Simpson picked up his right foot and stomped it down. "Blast! Are you telling me I won't have the chance of ordering you to, STAND BY YOUR BEDS!?"

Simpson had said it with tongue-in-cheek and laughter filled the table.

"I think you know we've been through all that, Sergeant. But I gotta tell ya, at least you were fair. You gave us a minute, not just ten seconds."

Sergeant Beckford smiled and placed his large hand on Bergie's right shoulder. "Well, son, we're very proud of you. You've probably got a lot to catch up on, so we'll mosey along. We'd like to see the two of you before you go back, though, is that all right?"

Bergie and Shanks stood up and shook the Sergeants' hands again. "We'd like that, Sergeant and thanks for looking after Moose for me."

After the Senior NCOs had left, Danyluk put on his *hurt* look. "Look after me? *Look after me?* I should be goin' with ya just to look after you guys. The only person who looks after me is Alma."

Bergie chuckled. "And Gertrude and Hilda and Agness and Penelope and Olive and Betty and Ginny and...!"

They had finished eating, so Moose grabbed his friend to leave the mess hall. "Oh, all right, them, too."

As the group of them left and Jackson let the screen door slam, he turned to Bergie and Shanks. "There's a dance at the arena tonight, have you guys called your girls?"

Shanks nodded. "Yeah, we called them from the train station. Hey, our baggage is in the chapel, is there a spare set of bunks in B-33?"

Danyluk still had his arm around Bergie's shoulders. "You bet there is and we've even got bedding for youse. Even if there wasn't any bunks, I'd sleep on the floor and youse could have my bunk, Bergie."

"Er, thanks Moose, but, er...I think I'd rather sleep on the floor, than use *your* bunk."

"HEY, WHATSAMATTER? ARE YOUSE GETTIN' FUSSY?"

"No, not really. It's just that I know the bunk's occupant. Remember? I've been your bunkmate all these years?"

As they entered B-33, Rothstein said, "Moose, you've got to stop bastardizing the Queen's English!"

"Why?" Bergie replied. "He bastardizes the human race!"

Ten *men* gave Hop Sing's the eyes left that afternoon. Even though Bergie and Shanks weren't on camp staff, the Provost Sergeant gave them the once-over anyway. The eight cadets were immaculate just like the two Regular Force soldiers that joined them on their trek down the hill towards Polson Park.

Bergie marched with Shanks in front of the others who were also in pairs, as Earl handed out the midnight passes.

"You know, I even missed the walks up and down this hill. When Ed and I were on the train, we talked about the things we hated most about camp. But after you're away from the place, you realize it wasn't that bad after all. There's something about Vernon that makes people want to come back and stay. I think I'd like to retire here, heat or no heat. I know you feel that way, Doug, but many of the guys we met back east who served as cadets here spoke exactly the same way. It's as if the camp and the city were one. Jesus, I hope this town never gets so big that the compatibility disappears."

Earl was thinking exactly the same thing. "It isn't just limited to Vernon, Bergie. When East and I hitchhiked to Kelowna last year, we shared that feeling. I know you guys have done the same thing, but we experienced it first hand, as well. We walked up to a house which had a sign saying, 'Sleeping Room To Let' and the woman who came to the door treated us like long-lost sons. "Come in boys, come in," she said. "My, don't you look smart in your uniforms. Bert, come and look at these two boys from the camp." She wanted ten dollars for the room for the night, but when she found out we only had ten dollars between us, she gave it to us for five dollars, and threw in breakfast. Wherever we went, people were asking us about the camp and what we did. It's the Okanagan, Bergie. It's a piece of paradise three-hundred miles away from the big city. Doug's right, it is God's country."

Although he was marching, Douglas took a small bow. "Thank you, Sir Earl, that's what I've been saying for the past three years. When I'm in Vancouver, I think of the wind lashing up the lake at Okanagan Landing. The giant trees swaying and the mist surrounding the cattle up top on the far side. Last year when we *arranged* that weekend pass and all of us slept in the changing room, did you see the size of the moon reflecting on the lake? Every star in the Heavens was out that night and there wasn't a sound."

"You mean there wasn't a sound until the clouds came and the rain started," added Wayne. "I enjoyed sleeping on the beach, but it was crowded as hell in the changing room. The next morning, when that guy and his son came in to change, they must have thought the place was invaded by hobos."

Rothstein remembered. "They fed us breakfast, didn't they? If I'm not mistaken, Jack asked them if there were any more eggs and the guy went to the store to buy some more. Wow, that was great. The whole weekend was great...a feeling of complete freedom. We only had a dollar each, but we ate hot-dogs like kings, drank pop like kings and..."

"And got burned like kings," Cunningham interrupted. "If you guys can recall, even Moose's ass was burnt to a crisp. You didn't like it, did ya Moose, when the medical orderly threw the cream at ya? You thought the nurses were going to smear it all over your ass?"

Moose laughed. "Well, at least I tried, didn't I? There weren't any dames around, so I went bare balls at the end of the pier. I put my trunks on when that fat mouthy broad arrived." Moose imitated her high pitched voice. *'TRUDY, STAY AWAY FROM THE END OF THE PIER UNTIL THAT NAUGHTY BOY PUTS HIS PANTS ON. WHAT IS THIS WORLD COMING TO?'* "

Cunningham remembered more. "You didn't say that when she was feeding you. If I can recall, she even invited you into her tent that night and you went."

"Yeah, only after her husband went into the pub for a beer," Moose retorted. 'How old are you?' she asked me as she turned up the lantern. I took one look at her in her nightdress and said, 'I'm just turning twelve.' *'Twelve, did you say twelve? My, you are a big boy for twelve, aren't you?'*"

Simon wished he had been there. "Quick thinking, eh Moose? I betcha that saved your bacon?"

"It saved more than that! If she had sat on me, I'd be finished."

"Yeah," said East. "Especially if she sat on your face. She'd say what the fat broad said when she sat on Pinocchio's face. 'Tell a lie, please tell a lie.'"

Danyluk laughed with the rest of them and then gave East an annoying glance. "Smart ass. She'd had a few drinks and she did make a grab for me. I moved just in time and her head hit the lantern. She ended up falling on her daughter, Trudy. The daughter wasn't too bad but she was only thirteen."

Douglas thought back to the time. "How come we didn't have the girls with us?"

Bergie broke in. "Because it was a *guy's* weekend. Remember, we took a vote and decided we needed to be alone for one weekend? Except Moose. He wanted Alma there."

Moose nodded. "Yeah, but I was democratic, wasn't I? I went along with youse guys when we voted."

"YOU, GET YOUR ARMS UP!" A passing Provost bellowed out of his jeep.

"Who was *he* talking to?" Bergie asked, looking around. "We've all got our arms up."

"It's that creep, Corporal Adams," replied East. "There's always a bad apple, and believe me, the Provost have got one there. He's rotten to the core and he thinks he's God's gift to the law enforcement society."

Bergie turned around for a moment. "Earl, you're always drawing, why don't you make up a new comic book hero and call him, *'MR. SUPER MILITARY POLICEMAN?'* Just think, he could be faster than a speeding powder puff, more powerful than a potato, and able to leap little cadets with a single..."

"Hey, Bergie," Shanks said. "Why don't you clue these guys into what we did to our equivalent of Corporal Adams? Remember?"

Instantly, Bergie became the old Bergie. He came up with one of those ideas he was famous for. The group of them were near the entrance to Polson Park when he asked them to gather around him. Over muffled chuckles, a plan was arranged to *take care* of Corporal Adams.

As usual, Polson Park was peaceful and beautiful. Many cadets were already in the park, but the only apparent noise was that of the gardeners trimming the hedges and mowing the lawns. The click of sprinklers echoed from every direction.

The girls were sitting under the covered bleachers watching a ladies' softball game, and when they saw the guys, they made a mad rush. Although Bergie and Shanks' girls were shy, they charged into the boys' open arms. Moments later, all the girls were asking the same questions the Musketeers had asked at lunch. There were, however, a few differences.

"You didn't meet anyone while you were training, did you?"

"Who me? Never!" Bergie replied.

"There's only you, sweetheart," Shanks said.

Polson Park was an excellent place for the cadets to 'come down to earth' and relax. Each time the cadets entered, the world seemed new and unruffled. The park allowed all worldly problems to disappear as if time stood still. The routine of the camp and the uncompromising sun ceased at the entrance. It was utopia; a small patch of green serenity in a world of organized confusion. The fact that girls were there was an extra stroke of the Creator's brush.

The girls felt exactly the same way. The boredom that comes with not being able to get a summer job, or their daily responsibility with housework, ended when they relaxed under the giant branches of ageless trees.

Although Polson Park existed all year 'round for the girls, it wasn't the same without their boyfriends. Now it became an enchanting forest that allowed their hearts to flutter and their minds to run free.

Douglas and Diane didn't sit down at their usual place. Instead, holding hands, they roamed the paths, stopping periodically to shyly look into each other's eyes. It was another gorgeous day and because they were together, the world really did stand still.

Diane slipped her hand out of his and placed it around his waist. "I've got some wonderful news."

Douglas had his arm around her shoulders as they walked over the small wooden bridge. "What is it?"

"I've been accepted at UBC. I've finally decided I'm going to take up nursing," she said as she gently kissed him on his left cheek. "And, I've been accepted into a sorority. My grandmother's best friend helped me to get in."

Douglas couldn't control his actions. "YAHHOOOO! THAT'S ABSOLUTELY THE BEST NEWS I'VE EVER HEARD! JESUS, THAT'S FANTASTIC!" He pulled her so close he could feel her heart beating. "THEN, WE'LL BE TOGETHER? DIANE, YOU REALLY KNOW HOW TO MAKE A GUY'S DAY!" he shouted as he lifted her off her feet and swung her around. "GOD, I'M HAPPY FOR YA! HOW DID YOU FIND OUT THIS SOON?"

Tears of joy had filled Diane's eyes. She helped him gently wipe them away. "I guess it's one of the advantages of living outside of Vancouver. I sent everything in at the end of June and I received a response yesterday. I've got to register in September. Pretty quick, eh?"

Douglas kissed her on her forehead. "PRETTY QUICK? What are you, some sort of genius?"

She bashfully looked at the ground. "Well, I think straight 'A's helped?"

"STRAIGHT 'A's? WOW, I'M IN LOVE WITH A INTELLECTUAL!"

Moose and Alma had heard the ruckus and walked over. "What's with you two?"

"MOOSE, ALMA! DIANE'S BEEN ACCEPTED AT UBC!"

Within seconds everyone had gathered around and Diane was the centre of attention. Her face went beet-red and she didn't know what to do with her hands.

Over the next two hours, while the group roamed the town, the University of British Columbia was the main point of conversation. The owner of the Capital Cafe, Mr. Ma, was delighted, too; he actually bought each of them a soda.

"My daughter down there, you rook her up. I send letter that you coming to Vancouver. And you, Bergie, where you go?"

Bergie dropped some money into the jukebox and played *Ebb Tide* and *Don't Be Cruel.* "We'll be in the sunny desert eating figs by an oasis," he replied, pointing at himself and Shanks.

Although Bergie was smiling, a somber gaze sobered the faces of the others and Mr. Ma. After four years of great association, new friends and a lot of fun, time was pulling them apart.

"You come back as instructors and see us?"

Bergie's smile departed. "We hope so, Mr. Ma, we hope so."

Douglas, Wayne, and their girls had supper at Diane's house that afternoon. The table conversation shaped around Diane going to Vancouver and attending UBC. After dinner, the boys did the dishes and put them away, and Diane's parents dropped the four teenagers off at the arena.

"WE'RE GOING TO THE SERGEANTS' MESS, WOULD YOU LIKE US TO PICK YOU UP AFTER THE DANCE FINISHES?" Diane's dad shouted through the car window.

"NO, THAT'S O.K., DAD, DOUG'S GOING TO WALK ME HOME!"

As usual, the arena was packed. It appeared that every cadet in The Vernon Army Cadet Camp had decided to attend the dance, date or no date.

With their berets tucked through their epaulettes, badges to the front, hundreds of boys made the rounds attempting to meet someone who would dance with them. Trying to *participate,* they even toured the floor and tapped the shoulders of dancing couples. In most cases, they were told to take a hike or get lost, but sometimes couples would generously part and the boys would finish a dance with someone else's girl.

It never failed that some girls would only dance with each other, turning down the pleading *soldiers.* Eventually though, throughout the evening, even these girls finally *surrendered* to the *tender wishes* of the outcasts and new relationships were formed.

Tears smoothly rolled down Bergie's girlfriend's cheeks as he held her close to the sound of Dean Martin's, *Memories Are Made Of This.* "Will I see you again?" she asked, not looking into his eyes.

"Look, I'm only going for six months, I'll be back the minute my tour is finished. I'll have some leave coming then and I'll rush up here."

"Please look after yourself while you're away," she said nesting her head on his shoulder.

"Don't worry about me. Any guy who can live three summers with Moose can take on the world. I'll be all right. Just make certain you look after yourself."

As the night wore on, neither of them really heard the music, just being with each other was enough as they slowly moved through the invisible crowd.

In the throng at the far end of the arena, another conversation was taking place. Diane and Douglas were also lost in their own world and really paid no attention to Gogi Grant's, *Wayward Wind,* other than to allow themselves to be wrapped up in the haunting background sounds of the song.

"You know when I'm with you, everything remains the same as it has for the past three years. Douglas, I love you more than life itself. If...if there's a reason why God put us on this earth, then I know what it is."

"So do I," he replied, bending backwards and staring into her eyes. "I think about you every moment of every day. I don't know how you get straight 'A's in school, because I don't...you're on my mind constantly."

When Cunningham and Maggie waltzed by, Gordie was in *deep communication* with Maggie.

"No, you're wrong, Maggie! The ace counts as either eleven or one. For example, if I dealt you two aces, you could either be bust, or have two points, or twelve."

"But what about stuke? Isn't that two aces back-to-back?" she asked.

"Listen, you want to win, don't you?"

"Yes! But it seems I only win when we're not playing strip poker?"

"Then pay attention and listen to me. If I dealt..." Cunningham's voice faded as the couple shuffled away.

"Is he always like that?" Diane asked. She was amused by Maggie's seriousness.

"He's super. The kind of a guy everyone wants on their team. Whenever things come to the nitty-gritty, Gordie's always there. He's like Moose, and the rest of us for that matter. It's one for all and all for one."

Diane's face beamed. "But how does he get things done, he's always gambling? I've never seen or heard him have an intimate conversation with Maggie."

Douglas laughed. "Whoa, don't cut him short there. You heard her, he always wins at strip poker. She'll lose again tonight when he walks her home. Hey, do you like that song?"

When *Ebb Tide* finished, it was followed by, *Unchained Melody, Rock Around The Clock, Hound Dog* and *Don't Be Cruel*. In the heat, shirts which had been neatly pressed a few hours before, draped like dishrags.

Douglas enjoyed walking Diane home and he appreciated marching back to camp without the constant sear of the sun's rays. The night air, while still warm, was freshened by a light breeze and a million stars filled the Heavens.

After he had kissed her good night on the front porch, Diane's dad opened the front door and had asked him in for a Kik Kola. He looked at his watch but it was already eleven-thirty, and he had to be back by midnight. "No, thank you, sir. If I leave now, I'll just make it back in time."

"Good night, son. Take care of yourself. Are you certain you don't want a ride?"

"No, thank you. Good night."

The *hill* was alive with cadets heading back to camp. Someone in Polson Park bellowed out, "ARGO!" but Douglas knew lone cadets weren't in there at night. Groups of cadets taking the back shortcut were probably just fooling around, he thought to himself.

He had decided to walk back on Hop Sing's side of the road and when he passed the hospital, Danyluk spotted him and ran over. He was alone because Bergie and Shanks said they wouldn't be back for awhile.

"Jeez, I've got a problem," said Danyluk, trying to get into step.

Douglas rolled his eyes at the sky. "Don't tell me, let me guess. Alma's pregnant?"

For the first time in a long while, Moose really looked worried. "Not that big a problem, but nearly just as big. Did you see the posters at the arena tonight?"

Douglas thought for a moment, "Yeah, what about them?"

Although Danyluk was supposed to be marching, he kept walking but held his hands up to the sky. "What about them, he asks? What about them? I'll tell you what about them! In three weeks, Red Robinson is coming to town to host a dance at the arena."

Douglas gave Danyluk a frown, as if to ask what the problem was. "Yeah, that's great! I said to Diane, 'Funny isn't it? We've got to travel three-hundred miles away from Vancouver to see Red, because he's so popular in Vancouver.' You should be happy your buddy's coming to Vernon."

Danyluk tried to pick up the step again, rolled his head, grimaced and looked away. "That's the problem, I've never met Red Robinson in my life. Jesus, Doug, use your head, how the hell could I hang around with someone of Red's calibre? Christ, he's the biggest attraction in North America and you think I know him?"

Douglas had already figured it out that Danyluk didn't know Red, but played dumb anyway.

"Listen, Moose, you don't have to play the game with me. I'd just like to see him, but if you don't want to introduce us to Red, well, that's all right."

"DOUG, I DON'T KNOW RED ROBINSON! HOW THE HELL WOULD I EVER MEET RED ROBINSON? I listen to his show, that's all. We all do."

BULL SHIT, MOOSE! THE WHOLE CAMP AND TOWN KNOWS THAT YOU KNOW RED ROBINSON. ARE YOU SAYING YOU LIED TO ALL OF US?"

Moose cleared his throat and actually moved his fingers around inside his unbuttoned collar. "Well, er, no...er, it's just that...er..."

"Well then, when Red comes to Vernon, take two minutes out of your *very valuable time* and introduce us to him. Jesus, Moose, how can you be so selfish? Red comes to town and you don't want your friends to share some of your time with him?"

Danyluk didn't know what to say. He just shook his head. "Well, I'll see what...er, Red might be too busy to even see me?"

"COME OFF IT, MOOSE! YOU AND RED ARE LIKE THIS." Douglas crossed the first two fingers of his right hand. "THAT'S WHAT YOU SAID, ISN'T IT?"

Danyluk regained his composure. "YEAH, THAT'S WHAT I SAID. I..ER..I'LL SEE WHAT I CAN DO!"

All of the Musketeers were back in the barracks when Douglas and Danyluk arrived. Half the cadets were asleep, so the Corporal walking the aisle held his finger across his lips to ask them to quieten down.

Douglas rubbed it in even more, but he kept his voice down. "Hey, you guys, Red Robinson is coming to town and Moose is going to introduce us to him."

East, Jackson and Rothstein ran over like a shot. East was eating a jam sandwich but he could still talk as he slapped Danyluk on the back.

"Are you serious? Wow, Moose, that's great!" East then passed along the news to other nearby cadets.

"Hey guys, when Red Robinson comes to town, Moose is going to let us meet him. He's one of Red's best friends."

Danyluk instantly passed wind and had to run for the jon. He very nearly didn't make it; he was followed by at least fifty people, talking to him over one of the partitions.

Even the Corporal had followed and he was impressed. "Will you get him to play a request for Doris and me?"

A cadet added, "Moose, I know I don't know ya and I don't even know what ya look like, but I'll give ya three pop coupons if ya could introduce me and Betsy to him."

Another said, "Red Robinson read one of my requests on the radio about two months ago, would you tell him it was me who wrote it? My name's Arne Gibbons."

"Will you get me his autograph, Moose? Is that your name, 'Moose'? I'd sure like his autograph! Moose, here's a piece of paper, will you get Red to sign it?" A piece of white paper was pushed in underneath the toilet door.

As Douglas was getting in between his sheets, he heard, "SON OF A BITCH, CAN'T A GUY HAVE A SHIT IN PEACE AROUND HERE? BUG OFF!"

As Moose's *entourage* re-entered their wing without their hero, other comments were offered.

"Let's not bug him, we'll never meet Red. This guy, Moose, what does he look like? I'll speak to him tomorrow!"

"I've always wanted to meet Red, I hope this Moose fella will introduce me."

"Jeez, wait till I tell the guys in Delta and Echo companies."

As cadet Douglas Brice rolled over on his side to go to sleep, East and Jackson were still talking. "You thought Moose was lying, didn't you?"

"Jack, I never said that. I knew he knew him. God, swallow your food before you talk, will ya? You just hit me in the eye with a piece of meat."

"Sorry, that's our old Moose."

Wayne leaned over and whispered. "What the hell brought this on?"

Douglas grinned as he lay on his back again with his hands behind his head. He was now making plans for *old* Moose. "Don't ask, I'll tell you tomorrow."

In 1956 cadets of the Vernon Army Cadet Camp always looked forward to Sunday morning because they were allowed to sleep in a little longer. Although the mess halls opened at 0800 hours for the early risers, they also stayed open until 1300 hours and served brunch until that time.

Church Parades were always held at ten o'clock and it was compulsory for all cadets of the Christian faith to attend. At 0900 hours each Sunday, the camp Duty Officer and Duty Sergeant made the rounds of the huts and instructed the one Corporal on duty in each hut to ensure their people were up. Most of the camp staff had Sundays off unless they were in the field, bivouacking in Glenemma or other areas. This particular Sunday morning, a Corporal from the other side of B-33 was on duty and he was pretty thorough.

"C'MON, YOU PEOPLE, FORM THREE RANKS ON THE ROAD. I'M GOING TO CALL THE ROLL IN TWO MINUTES. YOU MAY WEAR YOUR REGIMENTAL HEADDRESS AND IF YOU DON'T WANT TO WEAR BOOTS AND PUTTEES, YOU MAY WEAR YOUR RUNNING SHOES AND SOCKS WITH MILITARY SHORTS. C'MON, GET YOUR ASSES IN GEAR! IF YOU HAVEN'T EATEN, YOU CAN EAT AFTER THE CHURCH SERVICES!"

Corporal Moll stormed through both sides of the barracks screaming his lungs out. Then he came upon two sleeping *cadets* in a set of bunks.

"YOU TWO, WHAT THE HELL ARE YOU DOING IN BED? WHAT DO YOU THINK THIS IS, SLEEPY HOLLOW?" Instantly, Bergie's mattress was turned over onto the floor with him in it. Moll was just about to attack Shanks' mattress when Douglas returned to get his beret.

"Corporal, those two aren't cadets. They're guests here for the weekend."

The Corporal was unmoved. "Guests? You say they're guests? I COULDN'T GIVE A DAMN IF THEY'VE GOT THE O.C.'s PERMISSION TO SLEEP IN; EVERYONE GOES ON CHURCH PARADE!" The next minute, Shanks was on the floor. "GET WASHED AND DRESSED IN ONE MINUTE!"

Douglas wasn't about to give in either. "CORPORAL, THEY ARE GUESTS OF THE COMMANDING OFFICER! THEY'RE ONLY HERE FOR TWO

DAYS, THEN THEY'RE BEING POSTED OVERSEAS. THEY DON'T HAVE TO ATTEND CHURCH PARADE!"

Corporal Moll mellowed quickly. "You, you mean these two are guests of General Kitching?"

"That's right, Corporal, and when they complain, it'll be up to me and Cunningham to do our duty and inform Major Ratcliffe that I told you they were."

Douglas mentioned Cunningham's name because he knew the Corporal owed Gordie some money.

Moll picked up the mattresses and starting straightening out the beds. "Hey, who's going to complain, right fellas? It's just been a little misunderstanding, that's all. Here, you guys get right back into bed, there that's it. Barry's the name and fairness is the game. Even your buddy Cunningham will tell you that. Why I've lost more money to him than any of the NCOs around here. Now, are you comfortable boys?"

Bergie played it to the hilt. "I'd like another pillow please, Corporal."

"Another pillow? Here, have two of them, my friend." Corporal Moll yanked two pillows off the next set of bunks. "Any guests of General Kitching are guests of mine," he said, as he tucked in their blankets and marched out the door with Douglas following.

"FALL OUT THE NON-DENOMINATIONAL CADETS! COME FORWARD AND YELL OUT YOUR NAME AND RELIGION!"

Rothstein snapped to attention and marched over to the Corporal. "ROTHSTEIN, CORPORAL! I'M JEWISH!"

The Corporal ticked off Rothstein's name and motioned to him that he could go back inside the hut.

"SIMON, CORPORAL! I'M JEWISH!"

Corporal Moll did the same with Simon.

"BHAMJI, MOHAMMED, CORPORAL! I'M MUSLIM!"

"SINGH, PANJIB, CORPORAL! I'M A SIKH!"

"COHEN, CORPORAL! I'M JEWISH!"

One by one the non-Christians went back in the hut.

"DANYLUK, MOHAMMED, CORPORAL! I'M A MIXED BAG, BUT NOT CHRISTIAN!"

"Who?" The Corporal looked up for a second.

"DANYLUK, MOHAMMED, RANJEET, ANGUS, CORPORAL!"

The Corporal now shook his head and stared at the cadet standing in front of him. "With a name like Danyluk, how the hell can you say you're non-denominational? Isn't Danyluk a Ukrainian name?"

Moose stood stiffly at attention, not moving an eye. "It might be, Corporal, but I think it's Scottish. My father's name is Jock and I never ask questions about such matters!"

"You never ask questions about such matters? What kind of a fucking nut do you think I am? I wasn't born yesterday *Angus, Mohammed, Ranjeet Danyluk*, GET BACK IN THE RANKS! Christ, what'll it be next, Jock Ranjeet Anderson?"

Danyluk took a spare stamped set of Joining Instructions out of one of his pants pockets and presented it to the Corporal.

"Here are my papers, Corporal."

Corporal Moll put on his glasses and read the instructions. "Oh, I'm sorry. I, er...beg your pardon, er...Ranjeet, er whatever. It says here your father is Scottish

Ukrainian and your mother is a Sikh, but was raised with a Muslim family that practises Buddhism? Is that right?"

"Yes, but she doesn't attend confessions, Corporal!"

"I should bloody hope not, er, Mohammed, Ranjeet, or whatever your name is. O.K., you can fall out. ARE THERE ANY OTHERS?"

"YES CORPORAL!"

The Corporal looked at his roll book again. "NAME?"

"CUNNINGHAM, MAHATMA, GANDHI, CORPORAL! I'M A NEVA-DIAN!" Cunningham pulled a white piece of paper out of his pocket and was about to hand it in.

"No, no...you keep the paper. Jesus, you too? The gambler? Your father must have served in India, right? Is Nevadian similar to Sikh?"

"Yes, Corporal and my father was Captain of his polo team. I think he also had something to do with inventing the game of..."

Corporal Moll raised his hand to stop the cadet from talking. "That...that's all right. Christ, Sergeant Beckford's got himself a real melting pot hasn't he? O.K., FALL OUT!"

After a truck picked up the Catholics and Corporal Moll marched away towards B-3 with the Protestants, Mohammed Ranjeet Angus Danyluk and Mahatma Gandhi Cunningham rolled on their bunks in stitches.

"How in the hell did you get a set of Joining Instructions like that?" Cunningham asked.

He was so pleased with himself, Moose picked up a broom and presented arms. "I've had three years of that crap, so I filled in all my forms with those names, and I covered nearly every religion. Somehow they made it through the system. How'd you do yours?"

"My what?" asked Cunningham.

"Your Joining Instructions. I saw the paper you were about to show him."

The gambler's smile widened from ear to ear. "I made a last minute decision. It was blank and I gambled he'd never check it out after looking at yours."

Danyluk knighted Cunningham with the end of his broom. "Absolutely brilliant, Mahatma."

"I thought so, Ranjeet!" replied Cunningham.

Bergie and Shanks couldn't get back to sleep after being tossed on the floor.

"A good ploy, guys," uttered Bergie from across the aisle.

"BERGIE MY BOY, YOU'RE AWAKE?"

Bergie sat up. "Moose, you've learned everything I taught you. But one religion other than Christian would have been enough."

"HEY, ONE RELIGION WASN'T ENOUGH LAST YEAR!" Moose said, as he sat on Bergie's bunk. "I was hustled back into the ranks so fast, my head was spinning."

"That's because there's no such place as 'Mormandy.'"

Moose grinned. "Well, how the hell was I supposed to know Mormons don't come from there?"

Both Bergie and Shanks headed for the shower room, but not before Bergie said, "And your father can't be a direct descendent of William of Grapefruit. It's William of Orange, you dink. That's why they didn't believe ya!"

"HEY, AT LEAST I WAS CLOSE, WASN'T I?"

Bergie's voice trailed off, but echoed as he entered the shower room. "No,

William of Grapefruit wasn't a Mormon."

Sergeants Beckford and Simpson joined the Musketeers, Bergie and Shanks for brunch that afternoon. Actually, Sergeant Beckford had asked the RSM if it would be possible for the two lads to have brunch in the Sergeants' Mess, as special guests, but he was turned down. However, although the group had to use two tables, at least the Senior NCOs had the opportunity to say good-bye before the duo left at 1500 hours.

Sergeant Simpson got a kick out of the fact that both boys had been dumped on the floor by Corporal Moll. "I taught that Corporal everything he knows. It's good to see him doing his job properly."

"You can say that again," offered Bergie. "If it wasn't for Doug saying we were guests of General Kitching, we'd have been singing the hymns with everyone else."

Beckford looked at Brice. "Guests of General Kitching?"

Douglas went a little red in the face. "I didn't lie, Sergeant. Everyone who lives here is a guest of General Kitching."

Beckford smiled and carried on eating. "Hmm, good thinking, my boy."

Throughout the hour, the occupants of both tables roared at the fact that Danyluk and Cunningham pulled one over on Moll. Even the Sergeants seemed to laugh when they glanced at each other, however, they were most likely brandishing gas pains.

Following brunch, Sergeants Simpson and Beckford drove Bergie and Shanks to the boys' girlfriends' houses. The Musketeers were going to meet their girls in Polson Park and catch up with the two of them at the railway station.

When everyone met, the train was already at the station platform and the mood was somber. Both Bergie and Shanks' girls had been crying, because their eyes were still red. They had said their good-byes and just stood there with their guys' while the rest gathered around.

"Ed, take care of this guy, will ya?" Moose asked. "If ya don't, ya gotta answer to me."

Shanks laughed. "Quit worrying, I've looked after him thus far, haven't I?"

When "ALLLL BOAAARED!" was bellowed, offered hands came from all directions.

Bergie and Shanks kissed their girls. Then Bergie turned towards Douglas. "Doug, make certain everyone keeps up the traditions."

"I will, Bergie, I will. Look after yourselves, guys. Thanks very much for the weights."

A lot was said, but there never seems to be enough time to say everything when loved ones are leaving. As all hands waved, the train pulled away and picked up speed.

"SEND US SOME FIGS OR DATES!" screamed Danyluk.

"WE'LL DO THAT!" yelled Ed, smiling. "YOU GUYS TAKE GOOD CARE OF YOURSELVES. HAVE YA GOT THAT? WE'LL BE HOME FOR CHRIST-MAS. BY THAT TIME, WE'LL WANT TO FEEL THE RAIN AND SNOW ON OUR FACES! GOOD LUCK ON YOUR COURSE, FELLAS!"

Before the train went out of sight, smiles became lost looks of sadness as Bergie blew a kiss to his girl, followed by the thumbs up sign to everyone.

There was silence for a few moments as the girls got together before couples parted. The boys had to be back in camp for supper, so they arranged to meet at the bottom of the hill at 1630.

It was hot walking up the hill and not much was said. Once again, the Musketeers had lost Bergie and it hit Moose the most. He'd even stood on the platform a little longer waving to his best friend who was on a train that had already vanished. Alma had nudged him away, but he still glanced back.

"What's the movie tonight?" asked East, perspiration oozing from under his beret.

"It's *The Desert Fox,* with James Mason," replied Jackson in a voice that was almost a whisper.

CHAPTER VII

Week two in Camp Vernon was just as hot and the training just as heavy as week one. It didn't matter how much water was sprinkled on the coarse *grassy* areas of camp, green was a colour hard to find. On some days, the temperature passed the hundred-degree mark and the water evaporated as soon as it hit the ground.

From Monday through Wednesday, the cadets of Alpha Company had owned the parade square, morning and night. They had plotted and plodded every inch of Area Ten in the upper camp, taking Map Using; attended endless instructional and mutual instructional periods on Leadership, Technique of Instruction, Military Writing, Range Coaching, Physical Training For Boys, and instruction and mutual instruction on the rifle, sten, and bren guns.

Although the week was only half-over, at 1930 hours on Wednesday evening, the cadets of Alpha Company were tired, weary, and moaning and groaning amongst each other.

When Sergeant Beckford dismissed the company, he noticed it right away. "Well, Simp, they're finally bitching!"

Sergeant Simpson spotted the symptoms as well. "You bet they are, Bill. We must be doing something right. I've never seen so many people happy in their work."

It didn't matter if they had dust all over their boots, hosetops, puttees, pants, and shirts, nearly all of the cadets entering B-33 flopped themselves on their beds.

Wayne was even too tired to lean over the top. He just faced the ceiling and spoke. "Once again I'm going to ask that famous question. Who the hell talked me into coming back this year? I've got dust in my ears, dust in my eyes, dust in my nose, dust in my mouth, and I'm certain my feet are black as the hobs of hell. My eyes are sore, my legs are sore, my arms are sore, my back is sore, Christ, it's a wonder my wang's not sore."

It took a lot of energy to laugh, but Douglas, who looked like he'd spent twenty four hours in a dust storm, managed a chuckle. "Well, that's one part you don't want to get sore."

Cunningham stood up to get undressed. He glanced at Moose lying there with his eyes closed. "Yeah, this poor bastard's probably got a half-a-ton of dirt stuck inside his foreskin. He's been dragging his ass and rubbing his crotch for the last two hours."

A smile appeared on Moose's face. It must have been a smile because some white teeth appeared amidst the caked mud and sweat on his face.

"I was rubbing my crotch thinking of lovely, luscious Luscinda. The memory of her is the only thing that's kept me sane for that past hour-and-a-half."

Gordie stripped off and headed for the shower with a towel wrapped around his waist. "COME ON, YOU GUYS, LET'S GRAB A SHOWER BEFORE THE HOT WATER'S GONE!"

Rothstein joined him. "We don't have to worry, we'll get East to let out a 'rocket.'"

"Oh, yeah? Well, I've got news for you. East has been in the can since we arrived back. We can't count on him tonight."

That did it. After Cunningham's statements, six other Musketeers ripped off their clothes as fast as they could. Without Jack, they had to share the shower room and it would be three to a nozzle. Moose, however, got preferential treatment because *he* knew Red Robinson.

"Are you Moose? Jesus, you must be! We raise horses and your wang could match any of theirs. Here, you can share this shower with me. How's Red?"

Danyluk ignored his *admirer*. "Doug, have youse ever read any of Ernest Hemingway's books?"

Douglas thought for a moment. "Yeah, I read, *Death In The Afternoon.*"

"Was it any good?"

"I thought it was great, why?"

A serious Moose cupped the shower faucet for a moment and then allowed those around him to receive water again. "Because I've decided to buy, *The Bone Always Rises.*"

Howls of laughter filled the shower room. Still chuckling, Douglas replied, "Moose, you're thinking of Hemingway's novel, *The Sun Also Rises.*"

A bewildered expression came over Danyluk's face before the start of a smile appeared. "YOU BASTARD, CUNNINGHAM! YOU LIED TO ME AGAIN! If that's the case, I suppose, *For Whom The Bone Trolls,* is out of the question, as well?"

Once again the shower room erupted in laughter.

"Maybe not," suggested Rothstein. "Perhaps Sigmund Freud wrote some books with those names?"

"Who's Sidney Floyd?" Moose asked Rothstein.

"He's sort of a sexual psychological analyst. He may be still alive, I don't know."

Danyluk rubbed his hands together. "God, if the guy's still alive, I wonder if he needs an assistant?"

The cadets of Alpha Company came back to life after the shower and a bit of relaxation. Within a few hours, the uncommonly subdued barracks was once again like New York's Times Square on New Year's Eve. Its inhabitants were all over the place. Some were ironing, others washing, etc., however Douglas and Wayne were in one of the Corporal's cubicles in the other wing of the building. They had a pen, a writing tablet, an envelope and a stamp with them.

"How are we going to do this, we don't know the address of C.J.O.R. radio?" Wayne asked Douglas.

Wayne plunked down on the Corporal's bunk, while Douglas opened the writing pad and sat down on a chair in front of a small desk.

Douglas thought for a moment. "Well, we'll leave our return address off the envelope and just send it to, *Mr. Red Robinson, Radio Station CJOR, Howe Street, Vancouver, British Columbia.* How does that sound?"

Wayne agreed. "Yeah, that should do it. O.K., now, what do we say?"

"Well, let's try this," Douglas said as he finished writing the address and the date.

Dear Red:
We're two cadets who live in the West End who are super fans of yours. You're the guy who brought radio to life in Vancouver, and when we get home from school,

we tune you in the minute we're in our rooms. Although we've never met you, (we tried a few times, but we were always at the end of the line and couldn't get in) we feel like you're one of our best friends.

It didn't take Douglas and Wayne very long to create a letter which affirmed their loyalty and sincerity to Red, and their ingenuity towards solving Danyluk's problem.

We're in army cadets. We parade at the Beatty Street Drill Hall and we volunteered to attend the Vernon Army Cadet Camp for the summer. This is our fourth summer.

Anyway, Mr. Robinson, sir,..

Wayne didn't like that. "We can't say Mr. Robinson, sir, he's only a year older than us. He says on the radio, everyone should just call him, Red."

Douglas agreed and the letter was rewritten up to that point.

Anyway, Red, we have this friend of ours. His name is Moose Danyluk. He's a really great guy, but sometimes he says things he doesn't mean to say. For example, over a week ago, he told certain people that he knows you and that you're one of his best buddies. Well, there are over fourteen-hundred cadets in camp this year and probably all of them think that you and Moose are like brothers. He even told them you take his advice on what records to play. Can you actually believe that, Red?

There is a large ice skating arena here in Vernon and the other night we went to a dance and saw one of your posters. It says you're coming up here to host a dance in the arena. When Danyluk saw your posters, he nearly had a bird. All the cadets in camp now want Danyluk to introduce them to you. He's really worried and because he's one of our best friends, we're trying to help him out.

We know you are really busy, Red, but well we don't want our friend to get lynched. No, they won't lynch him but they would probably French his bed every night and put dead fish in it, along with a lot of other things that we can't mention.

We also know we shouldn't be asking this, but could you play a record for him at the arena and say, this is a request from my good buddy Moose Danyluk? It would sure save his ~~skin~~, in his case, skins.

Thanks Red, from two fans in Vernon. If you can't do it, we'll understand.

Yours truly,
(Both cadets signed)
Cadet Douglas Brice and Cadet Wayne Banks,
Alpha Company - Senior Leader Instructors' Course,
The Vernon Army Cadet Camp,
Vernon, British Columbia.

The letter was folded, placed in the envelope and the stamp was affixed.

"Jeez, I hope Red replies," said Wayne.

"Don't hold your breath, he's a busy guy. But you know something, I've got a feeling he'll understand Moose's problem. Let's face it, he's a teenager like us and he stated on the radio once that he served in air cadets. I know what air cadets think of us army grunts, but when it comes to the crunch, even the guys in light blue come through. Also, I think Red is down to earth."

Wayne held the letter in his right hand and smacked it against his left. "Well, I don't share your optimism, but here's hoping." With that said, he walked out to mail it.

Banks had to study and clean like everyone else, but the post office was only a minute away, to the right of the headquarters building at the top of the camp's main road.

Mail from the camp was delivered to Vernon's main post office each morning at nine, therefore the letter would be on its way the next day.

When he returned, the two of them shook hands, cocked their heads, winked, and carried on with their chores.

That night as he shined his boots, Red Robinson's *really and truly best friend and buddy* was none-the-wiser.

When the lights were turned out, there was more banter than usual because for the next two days, the company would be on the rifle and sten ranges. Although it would be hot as hell up there, it was a break from the routine of the parade square and the hot, musty lecture huts in the upper camp.

Wayne leaned over. "When I was at the post office I saw a mint mustard-and-light-green, two-toned Chevy drive by on the highway. Jeez, General Motors are makin' mint cars. Last year, when they introduced the wrap-around windshield, they caught all the other car companies by surprise. Have you seen the new Buick and Oldsmobile?"

Douglas kicked the springs of Wayne's bunk with his feet. "Yeah, GM's really got some nice models. I..."

"Speaking of mustard," Rothstein interjected. "Did you guys see the argument East got into at the Dance last Saturday? I thought there was going to be a fight."

East heard him and quickly swallowed the last part of the sandwich he was chewing. "Oh, Rothie...Jesus, there wouldn't have been a fight. The dame had no cleavage. Her boyfriend was just trying to make a big deal out of nothing."

"Bull shit, Jack! You had your hand in there. I heard ya say, 'I'm sorry, my dear, these little things do happen.'"

Jackson sat up. "When did that occur? This is news to me."

Rothstein continued with his story. "Jack was standing eating a hot-dog in front of the first upper row of seats. He was leaning over the dance floor waving his hot-dog to the beat, and some mustard and relish spurted out and fell down some dame's front. The wad was big enough, her bazookas must have been covered with it."

Laughter filled both sides of the aisle, as Rothie continued. "The broad's boyfriend wasn't there so Jack thought she was alone. He rushed down and started taking it out with his hand. That's when her partner turned up and wondered what was going on. 'HEY, WHAT THE HELL DO YOU THINK YOU'RE DOING, PLAYING DOCTOR?' he said."

East got out of bed and stood in the aisle. "Bull shit I did. I didn't use my hand, I had a napkin. What bazookas are you talking about? She was flat. Her chest looked like Moose's, it was concave."

Moose didn't like that. "UP YOUR'S, JACK!"

Jackson couldn't believe it. "Wow, all over her bazookas. Did you get it all out?"

"Well...nearly...the guy pushed me, so I left it up to him."

Cunningham finally got into the act. There were no *suckers* asking for a game, so he had put away the cards and dice.

"I SAW THAT BROAD WHEN SHE WAS DANCING. SHE HAD MUS-TARD, KETCHUP, RELISH, AND ONIONS, ALL OVER THE TOP OF HER HEAD. CHRIST, IT WAS EVERYWHERE! WHEN SHE WAS JIVING, SHE SHOOK HER HEAD AND A BIG BLOB BOUNCED ONTO THE SIDE OF THE NECK OF THE GIRL NEXT TO HER. THAT GIRL STOPPED IN HER TRACKS AND NEARLY HAD A HEART ATTACK. SHE LOOKED AROUND WONDERING WHERE IT CAME FROM. SHE WAS STARING AT THE CEIL-ING AND HOLDING UP HER HANDS AS IF WAS RAINING THE STUFF."

Guffaws rolled from bunk to bunk. Even a grinning Corporal came out of his cubicle. "You guys are animals."

Cunningham wasn't finished and couldn't help laughing as he told his story. "Corporal, you don't know the half of it. When the dame started dancing slow with her boyfriend, he nestled into her neck and got the shit all over his face and couldn't figure out how he got onions in his mouth."

Wayne couldn't take it, he was in stitches. He got out of bed and leaned out the window.

"Jack, where was your girl when this happened?" Simon asked.

Jack had defended himself, so he had gotten back into bed. "She was in the can. I got some of the stuff on her, as well."

"THAT'S OUR JACK!" Douglas yelled, before he rolled over and went to sleep.

Shortly, it would be quiet in B-33, but not before Jack was chastised a little more.

"Jack, why do you have to put a whole bottle of ketchup on your hot-dogs?"

"Earl, do I tell you how to eat? No! So don't tell me!"

"It's a wonder you can even taste the meat!"

"I taste the meat, Earl; don't you worry about me, I taste the meat!"

"I'll bet you don't," quipped Danyluk.

"SCREW YOU, MOOSE! JUST BECAUSE YOU LIKE IT RAW! JESUS, YOU'RE SICK!"

A voice from across the aisle said, "THE BROAD HE GOES OUT WITH DOESN'T HAVE TO WEAR LIPSTICK, SHE'S ALWAYS GOT KETCHUP ALL OVER HER FACE!"

"WHO SAID THAT!? I RECOGNIZE YOUR VOICE, YOU CAN'T TALK, YOU SEAFORTH PONGO! SHEEP SHIT AND HEATHER, THAT'S WHAT YOU GUYS ARE!"

When the Corporal re-entered his cubicle and closed the door, he mumbled, "Animals, these guys are animals!"

"STAND BY YOUR BEDS! COME ON, YOU PEOPLE, QUIT PLAYING WITH YOUR FUTURE WIFE'S EXCUSE FOR A HEADACHE AND START GETTING PREPARED! BECAUSE WE'RE ON THE RANGES, THERE IS NO P.T. TODAY! JACKSON, WHAT'S THE DRESS OF THE DAY?"

Earl stood to attention. "Sergeant, the dress is, K.D. longs, large webbelt, shirt, boots, puttees, no weights, pith-helmet, and we are to make certain we each bring a ground-sheet, mess-tins, and utensils and our water canteen filled with water."

"Not bad! What's today's code word? Try that one on for size!"

Earl wasn't caught by that question either. Seconds earlier, he had walked into the Corporal's cubicle and found the piece of paper. "It's castrate...er, catastrophe, Sergeant!"

Simpson was more than amazed. "How in the hell did you know that?"

Earl stood at attention, smiling. "Because when you entered the building, you went straight into the Corporal's cubicle. You normally never walk in there, *and* you didn't go near the bulletin board."

Quite impressed, the Sergeant didn't know what to say. "That's my boy. Good man, Jackson."

After screaming, "LOVE IT! LOVE IT!" Danyluk said, "You're always full of surprises, Sergeant!"

Simpson grinned. "Cadet Danyluk, a part of my job is to ensure that my subordinates never assume. Did you believe we were going to perform physical training today?"

Danyluk cocked his head and started nodding. "Well, I...er, not really, well..."

"If you want to do some, I'll certainly oblige you." Simpson glanced around their end of the hut. "I'm sure all of these fine fellows would like to join you?"

In a fraction of a second, four pillows were thrown at Danyluk. He got the message. "NO! NO! SERGEANT, PLEASE...CARRY ON! I WAS JUST MAKING A LITTLE MORNING JOKE, THERE."

As the Sergeant marched out, he said, "That's what I like to see...a man happy in his work. Good *stuff*, Danyluk. A little morning joke will have everyone laughing and looking forward to another great and challenging day."

To the sounds of Chuck Berry's, *Maybelline*, Fat's Domino's, *Ain't That A Shame*, Frank Sinatra's, *Love And Marriage*, and *Moments To Remember* by the Four Lads, amongst others, the cadets of the eastern wing of hut B-33 showered, dressed, and cleaned their barracks before heading over to the kitchen for breakfast.

"It's about time we got back on the ranges up here," Moose said, referring to the fact that during the past couple of years, range work had been sparse.

"Well, Driver Mechanics and Signals companies don't do that much shooting," Douglas replied. "What did we have last year...a half-a-day, and the year before that ...the same?"

East was wading through a giant plate of pancakes. "Yup, that was about it. Hey Doug, do you remember the time you won the money off that Corporal?"

Douglas' face lit up. "Do I? But there won't be any of that today, because we're going to be coaching each other. Even if we're coaching someone who is good, we've still got to cover the procedures."

Like most of the BCR cadets, Cunningham was also an excellent shot. "How about two-bits in the hat, winner take all?"

Over the next five minutes, rules were ironed out and each Musketeer put twenty-five cents into a pot which Rothstein held for safekeeping. Shooters would write down their own individual scores on the rifle, bren, and sten guns, and whoever was coaching would initial it. The scores would then be compared at the end of the second day on the ranges.

Danyluk rubbed his hands together. "Two dollars will buy me a couple of rings. One for lovely Ilene and the other for precious Irene."

East stopped shoveling for a moment. "Jesus, Ilene and Irene? Where the hell did these two strange names pop up from?"

Moose put on his dazed and in-love look. "They work in the kitchen at the Officers' Mess. Neither one thinks the other knows me. If I win the pot, I'm going to get them each a different ring. Can you imagine the fun they'll have comparing their rings with one another? Ilene knows me as Moose, and Irene thinks my nickname is Horse."

Cunningham, as usual, tilted on the two back legs of his chair. "Jesus, you're really original, Moose. I can hear them now. 'This guy, Moose, bought me this ring, what do you think?' The other will say, 'Well, isn't that nice, but look at this one. A stud by the name of Horse bought it for me.' If anyone overheard their conversation they'd say, 'Christ, what is this place...an animal farm?' "

Moose closed his eyes and rubbed his chin. "Yeah, I shouldn'ta used Horse, perhaps Herc would have been better?"

Cunningham slammed forward. "Herc? What the, er, where does that come from?"

Danyluk slowly sucked in air and pumped out his *chest.* "Hercules, you creep."

Gordie understood. "Oh, I get it! I understand what you mean. The real Hercules impressed the girls with the strength of his massive arms. You can do the same with your massive knob, right?"

With that said, everyone except Danyluk dragged East away from the table and headed out the door. Banks could barely talk because Moose had gotten to him again. He roared his head off. "I can see it all now. Moose holding up those giant pillars with his knob. HAAA!"

Moose started laughing with Wayne as he slapped him on the back. "At least I'd be *able* to hold them up!"

If the cadets of Alpha Company thought that the dust on the *road* leading to the upper camp was bad, the vehicle path leading to the ranges was worse. Although they were in the backs of a convoy of three-ton trucks, the three to four inches of *road* dust kicked up by the giant tires found each cadet's torso obliging as the Internationals and Dodges *manipulated* the steep winding sunburned hills, west of Highway 97.

Although range officials were already on site, their job would be easy today. They would conduct the range practises, however, all of Alpha Company's staff would be utilized in teaching the fine art of coaching. Most of the cadets were very proficient at shooting, but coaching was another matter altogether. In one week's time, these boys would be coaching the cadets of other companies. When it came down to weapons training, the watchword was 'safety' and there could be no excuse for even the slightest mistake.

When the vehicles stopped behind one another, it was impossible to see ten yards in any direction. The clouds of fine dust hung in the sweltering air, not settling at all.

Sergeant-Major Rose's voice pierced the haze. "MOVE AWAY FROM THE VEHICLES AND FORM UP IN THREE RANKS BETWEEN THE TWO AND THREE-HUNDRED-YARD FIRING POINTS! C'MON, YOU PEOPLE. EVEN THOUGH I CAN'T SEE YOU, I KNOW YOU ARE DAWDLING!"

The scene of cadets leaving the vehicles resembled a First World War movie where soldiers emerged through smoke or gas. Their faces were all dirty brown and the colour of their pith-helmets matched that of the ground.

Wayne started spitting out the dust. "Phfffssst! My mouth is full of this shit; I wonder what the inside of my lungs look like?"

"How'd ya like to do P.T. in this stuff?" Douglas asked.

Danyluk answered instead of Wayne. "Hey, that wouldn't be such a bad idea. Simpson would be counting the pushups, but he wouldn't be able to see us. We could just be lying down and flopping our arms to make a noise."

"Not bad," said Wayne. "Not bad at all, but that would mean that we'd have to run all the way up to this God-forsaken place."

After the company was formed up, the Range Officer asked them to sit down. The ground in between the firing points was dusty and full of rocks and pepples, but at least they could see each other.

Ensuring that the cadets' backs were to the sun, the officer continued. "RIGHT, PAY ATTENTION HERE! WE'LL BE USING FIFTEEN TARGETS THIS MORNING AND WE'LL BE FIRING FROM TWO, THREE AND FOUR-HUNDRED YARDS! WE'LL BE USING THE STEN RANGE SIMULTANE-OUSLY WITH THE RIFLE RANGE AND FOR THE LAST TWO HOURS OF EACH DAY, WE'LL BE FIRING THE BREN FROM TWO AND THREE-HUN-DRED YARDS!

"THE POP TRUCK WILL BE HERE AT 1000 AND 1500 HOURS. ALSO, INSTEAD OF BOX LUNCHES, A HOT MEAL WILL BE SERVED ON BOTH DAYS.

"NOW, YOU ARE THE SENIOR CADETS. YOU'LL BE RETURNING TO YOUR CORPS AND YOU'LL BE EXPECTED TO ASSIST ON RANGE EXER-CISES. MOST OF YOU ARE VERY PROFICIENT, HOWEVER, YOUR COM-PANY STAFF JUST WANT TO COVER THE FINER POINTS IN COACHING.

"BECAUSE OF THE SIZE OF THIS COMPANY, THERE WON'T BE MUCH TIME FOR CHIT CHAT. WE ALSO WANT YOU TO TAKE NOTES WHEN YOU ARE WAITING FOR YOUR RELAY TO FIRE. ARE THERE ANY QUESTIONS, SO FAR? NO? O.K., THEN, I KNOW YOU'RE NOW GOING TO LOVE WHAT I HAVE TO DO."

There were a few groans as the Range Officer took his clipboard out from under his arm and proceeded to read Range Standing Orders and Range Safety Instructions. He droned on for at least half-an-hour, however, this was an SOP (Standing Operating Procedure) and a must. He pointed out the range boundaries, firing point rules, butts rules, ammunition loading rules and procedures, the location of the safety truck, use of stretchers and first-aid kits, etc., telephone procedures, flag procedures, point-men procedures, and covered *everything* with regard to safety on the ranges with respect to various weapons and ammunition.

When he was finished, the Range Officer appointed One Platoon to the firing point at two-hundred yards. Two Platoon was in the butts, Three Platoon was on the sten range, and Four Platoon loaded the ammunition and provided fresh magazines, collected empty magazines, and provided the telephone personnel, the flag-men, the gate-men and point-men.

One Platoon was split up into their normal sections with perhaps a few changes to accommodate the number of firing point positions. While a section was firing, the remaining sections would attend short refresher courses on all range procedures, including holding, aiming, and firing - immediate actions - care and cleaning, and loading and unloading of magazines.

"WHEN CARRYING THE WEAPON, IT WILL BE POINTED DOWN! THE FIRING POINT PROCEDURE HAS CHANGED! WHEN YOU'VE FIN-ISHED FIRING, YOU *WILL NOT* HOLD THE WEAPON AT A THIRTY-

DEGREE ANGLE WITH THE BOLT OPEN! WHEN YOU'VE FINISHED FIR-
ING, ENSURE THE BOLT IS OPEN, THE SIGHTS ARE DOWN AND THE
WEAPON IS ON THE GROUND NEXT TO YOU, MUZZLE POINTING AT
THE BUTTS, BOLT HEAD UP! GENTLEMEN, I WANT YOU TO THINK OF
SAFETY, SAFETY, AND MORE SAFETY! IF YOU HAVE POSITIVE SUGGES-
TIONS OR IDEAS THAT I HAVEN'T COVERED, PLEASE INFORM ME!"

This year, the Musketeers were fortunate again because they were all together
on Relay One. Sergeant Beckford had arranged this, however he spread them out so
that they were in every second position. That way, they could verbally assist, or
keep an eye on other shooters as a method of assisting the coaches and range personnel.

For the past week or so, every cadet in Alpha Company had read and been
tested on the manuals, *Range Procedures and Safety*, and *Rifle Coaching as an Art*.

When the practises commenced, Sergeant Beckford, Major Ratcliffe,
Lieutenant Harwood, the Platoon Corporals and the range staff were one-on-one
with the cadets who were firing. These assistants were in the prone position on the
right-hand-side of the cadets, but were approximately one foot back. It didn't matter if the shooter knew what he was doing, a calm confident voice reminded him to
attain the proper firing position, loading, aiming, and how to breathe properly. In
addition, the Range Officer always preceded his orders with an explanation of what
he wanted to see. This way, the total picture was presented to the cadets.

The same thing was happening in the butts. Lieutenant Bendixon, along with
Sergeant Simpson, Captain Miller, Captain Hamilton, Two Platoon's Corporals, and
additional range staff, were one-on-one with the cadets marking the targets. Even
the company's clerks, Privates Pazim and Maeson, were present, but they spent
most of their time *pushing paper* back and forth between the officers.

Each cadet was quietly guided on how to properly place the target in the holding apparatus, how to efficiently raise and lower the target, how to signal accurately, and how to score. Particular attention was paid to grouping practises. They
would count the rounds as they were fired and if one or two shots were *pulled* and
out of the group, they were noted. When the cadet from the firing point walked up
to the butts to review his particular target, the butts cadet would then remind the
shooter. "SEE THAT HOLE THERE? YOU PULLED YOUR SEVENTH SHOT!
DO YOU REMEMBER WHAT YOU DID WRONG? THAT ONE THERE WAS
YOUR FOURTH SHOT; IT LOOKS TO ME LIKE YOU WINCED!"

All cadets were also shown how to adjust the sights of the rifle...what tools to
use, and so on.

The Range Officer was true to his word. When the pop truck arrived,
shooting ceased and each cadet had the opportunity of quenching his thirst. It
was so hot on the ranges, most cadets went through the water in their canteen
bottles shortly after arriving. These were quickly refilled with ice-water
brought by the pop truck.

When the meal truck arrived, containers filled with lifesaving teenage-stomach
needs were lined in a row. *Volunteers* dished it out into offered mess-tins which
were later swilled out in containers of soapy water, then rinsing water.

The officers and NCOs always ate last.

There was absolutely no shade on the Vernon ranges and no way of escaping
the dust or flies. When Sergeant Beckford heard a loud voice complaining,
"CHRIST, THERE'S A WASP IN MY STEW AND IT'S STILL MOVING!" he

would extend his professional advice freely.

"DON'T TELL EVERYBODY, THEY'LL ALL WANT ONE! IT'S MEAT AND THAT MEANS PROTEIN, MY BOY! EAT IT! YOU WANT TO GROW UP TO BE BIG AND STRONG, LIKE ME, DON'T YOU?"

"BUT SERGEANT, YOU JUST TOOK ONE OUT OF YOUR MESS TIN AND FLICKED IT ON THE GROUND!"

Beckford smiled, "I'M ON A DIET, AND BESIDES, I'M ALLERGIC TO AIR FORCE FOOD! TOO RICH FOR THE BLOOD!"

"It don't mix well with that early morning beer on your corn flakes, eh, Sergeant?"

"DON'T WORRY ABOUT ME...JUST KEEP YOUR MIND ON *YOUR* FOOD, OR YOUR *WOMEN*, DANYLUK!"

Following each day on the ranges, the cadets of Alpha Company cleaned weapons and studied for Saturday morning's examinations.

After supper on Friday afternoon, they prepared their hut for the usual Saturday morning inspection. The barracks always needed more care and attention after range work because of the dirt and dust brought back inside. The dust was so fine, nothing escaped being covered in it.

Danyluk stood outside on the centre stairs of the hut, shaking out his blankets. "Just look at this, I've actually brought back the whole firing point," he said, lost in a cloud of dust that actually moved across the road.

Banks was next to him doing the same thing. "Me and Doug just cleaned out our barrack box, we've got an inch of it in there."

"YOU! YOU THERE! JUST WHAT THE HELL DO YOU THINK YOU'RE DOING?"

The coughing RSM had marched through 'the cloud' which was slowly moving across the road. "ARE YOU TRYING TO RUIN THE OFFICERS' DAY? IS IT YOUR INTENTION TO GET DUST IN ALL OF THEIR *SOFT DRINKS*?"

Both cadets stood at attention as Wayne answered. "NO, SIR! WE'VE RETURNED FROM THE RANGES AND WE'RE JUST SHAKING OUT OUR BLANKETS, SIR!"

"WELL, DO IT ON THE OTHER SIDE OF THE HUT OVER THE SMOKING PIT!"

"YES, SIR!"

"IT LOOKS TO ME LIKE YOU'RE INTENTIONALLY CUTTING OFF THE SUN OVER THE OFFICERS' MESS GARDEN! IS THAT CORRECT?"

"NO, SIR!"

The RSM marched away, hacking. "CARRY ON!" He also mumbled to himself, "Him again, but at least this time he's got his clothes on. Something must be working right!"

As the duo walked through the centre area of the hut to the other side, Danyluk screwed up his face and changed his voice to a whine. *"We sure don't want any of OUR dust to get into the officers' drinks, do we now?"*

Wayne laughed and put on his posh accent. "When the dust flew over their fence, the conversation probably went like this. 'I say, Eggbert old chappie, you've got some of that accursed dust in your mint tulip.'"

"'Bloody hell, Cuthbert, you're absolutely righto old boy. It seems to be coming over the fence from that nasty hut just up the road. Reminds me of *Indja* during the uprisings. I said to my batman, 'Godfrey, where the dickens is all of that loathsome grit coming from?'

"'There's a troop of horses riding by, sir.'"

"'Bloody hell, Godfrey, go and tell them to walk their horses when they pass the Officers' Mess. Let them ride by the Sergeants' Mess or the Mens' Mess, but they should walk them past where the *gentlemen* gather, Godfrey.'"

"'But there's a war going on, sir.'"

"'Not at tea time, Godfrey. Everything stops for tea. Go and tell them that!'"

Danyluk laughed so hard, he had to hold his stomach, as he and Wayne continued shaking their blankets. "You've sure got the accent, Wayne."

Wayne snickered. "I learned it from Doug. He puts it on when he tells the Queen Victoria, story."

Danyluk flapped his blanket. "Queen Victoria, story?"

"Yeah, apparently one evening, Queen Victoria said to her husband, Prince Albert, 'I say, Albert, I wonder what all of the poor people are doing right about this time?'"

"Prince Albert replied. 'They're probably screwing, my dear.'"

"'What? They're screwing? They do that too? Much too good for them, Albert!'"

A voice came up from the smoking pit. "HEY, WE'RE TRYING TO HAVE A SMOKE IN PEACE HERE. TAKE YOUR DUST ELSEWHERE!"

Moose shook his blanket again. "SCREW YOUSE!"

"Oh, sorry, Moose. We didn't recognize ya. How's Red?"

With the floors duly washed and scrubbed, windows washed, light shades and fixtures polished, shelves and all window ledges dusted and washed, the cadets of Alpha Company studied for their upcoming exams. All eight of the Musketeers went over to the Cadet Canteen, where the sounds of *Hound Dog*, filled the immediate area.

After everyone got a pop, Rothstein was surrounded. He slowly took out his notes and perused them, not looking at the anxious faces waiting to hear who won the pot for the highest score.

"Well, it was close, really close," he whispered.

Each cadet nodded, mouth open, waiting for the name.

Rothstein casually looked around the table. "Yep, it was really close."

East couldn't take it. "Come on, Rothie, give us the news."

"All right, all right...it was really close."

Now, Moose got into the act. "FOR CHRIST'S SAKE, WE KNOW ALL THAT! WHO WON THE GOD-DAMNED THING?"

Rothstein gently took the money out of his pocket. "Don't rush me, I could make a mistake and present it to the wrong person. This was a close contest."

Moose sat back smiling. "O.K., O.K.!"

After he stood up, Harvey Rothstein said, "THE WINNER IS..."

The whole group leaned forward.

"THE WINNER IS...WAIT FOR IT! CADET...damn it, where's that other paper?"

"OH, COME ON!" screamed Danyluk.

"THE WINNER IS...IT WAS TIED! THE POT WILL BE SPLIT BETWEEN BRICE AND SIMON!"

"Blast, I thought I had it," said Moose, slapping his knee.

Harvey presented Brice and Simon with $1.00 each, and shook their hands. "On behalf of the committee, which is me, my congratulations on your fine efforts. Moose, you were third, and would you believe it, I was fourth."

"SPEECH! yelled Wayne, watching the two pocket their money.

Douglas laughed. "I couldn't have done it without my trusty shoulder rag." He bowed. "I want to thank my coach and the rest of you guys for not shooting as well as you can."

Simon also bowed. "It's an extreme pleasure taking money from the BCRs, amongst others."

After a few boos and whistles, he sat down and they all started reading their notes again.

"Well, at least we get paid this weekend," said Wayne. "Five whole dollar-roos!"

East took a bite of his chocolate bar. "I've never been so broke in my life. It's going to be nice to have money in my pocket."

Rothstein couldn't believe it. "You're broke? You're always drinking pop and eating chocolate bars...where do you get *that* money from?"

East pointed to Gordie who was quietly reading his notes. "I borrow it from him."

Rothstein winced. "YOU WHAT? WHAT INTEREST IS HE CHARGING YOU?"

East smiled. "Only three percent."

Cunningham stopped reading and looked up over his notebook. "BULL SHIT! IT'S SIX PERCENT! I CHARGE THREE PERCENT FOR GAMBLING MONEY ONLY!"

Jack already knew that but was trying Cunningham on for size. "Oh, O.K., six percent!"

Danyluk didn't like that at all. "Jesus, Gordie, can't you give your buddies a break now and then?"

"HEY, DO I TELL YOU HOW TO LOOK AFTER YOUR DAMES? BUSINESS IS BUSINESS AND PLEASURE IS PLEASURE. MY PLEASURE IS DOING BUSINESS."

"I wonder what Bergie's up to right now?" Douglas asked.

Moose took a long swig of his pop. "He's probably ridin' a camel into the nearest town, lookin' for dames."

"Can he ride a camel?" asked Simon.

A broad smile came to Moose's face. "If he's looking for the ladies, he can. Bergie's like me, anything is possible when the smell of perfumed flesh is at hand."

Jackson said, "They don't wear perfume in the desert. It's so hot there, the only smell would be camel shit and body odor."

"I DIDN'T SAY IT HAD TO BE A SWEET SMELL!" Moose shot back. Many a good time can be had if youse can hold your nose."

The group laughed and recoiled at the same time. That night after the lights were turned out, the conversation continued.

"You mean to tell me you'd get it on with a dame who smells of camel shit and body odor?" Jackson asked Danyluk.

"The smell the nose picks up can be changed with your mind," Danyluk replied. "If you want camel shit and body odor to smell like rosebuds on a spring morning, all you've got to do is imagine it."

A voice from across the aisle entered the conversation. He was talking to his bunkmate. "Did you hear that? Danyluk's now going out with a broad that smells like camel shit and he likes it. I told ya about those BCRs, they're weird."

Even the Corporal got into the act as his voice came out from behind his cubicle. "DANYLUK, HOW THE HELL DO YOU KNOW WHAT THE SMELL OF CAMEL SHIT IS LIKE? THERE'S NO FUCKING CAMELS HERE IN VERNON? JESUS, JUST HOW STRANGE ARE YOU?"

"CORPORAL, I DIDN'T SAY THAT! I SAID THE MIND CAN CHANGE ANY SMELL. I DON'T CARE IF IT'S BEAR SHIT, OR LION SHIT! IF YOU WANT, YOU CAN CHANGE THE SMELL, IT'S POSSIBLE!"

The Corporal came out of his cubicle. "Who the hell is this broad who smells like camel shit?"

Moose sat up. "I don't know. I..."

"YOU DON'T KNOW? YOU ACTUALLY GO OUT WITH A DAME THAT SMELLS LIKE CAMEL SHIT AND BODY ODOR AND YOU DON'T KNOW WHO SHE IS?"

Moose was getting exasperated. "I DIDN'T SAY THAT! I SAID IT'S POSS..."

The Corporal walked back into his cubicle. "CADET DANYLUK, YOU ARE ONE MIXED-UP CREEP!"

A voice from across the aisle, said, "You can say that again, Corporal!"

"UP YOUR NOSE! GOD, YOU SALLY LIGHT HORSES ARE ALL THE SAME! HORSE SHIT AND GOSSIP, HORSE SHIT AND GOSSIP!"

"I'll have you know I'm in the Canadian Scottish Regiment!"

"SAME THING!" said Moose. "BULL SHIT, SHEEP SHIT, HEATHER AND GOSSIP!"

Although Moose couldn't see the cadet, he heard, "You should talk, you certainly know your *shit*! Be it camel or *otherwise!*"

By the time the whispers travelled from bunk to bunk down both sides of the aisle, the story had changed a little. Some cadet came over to Danyluk's bunk.

"Hey, Moose, I've heard you like Camel cigarettes. I'll get you a pack if you introduce me to Red Robinson."

"OH, BUG OFF! I SMOKE SWEET CAPORALS OR MILLBANKS!"

The cadet disappeared. "All right, don't get your nuts tangled. Jeez, some guys just can't be pleased."

After kicking down his covers, Wayne leaned over. "Wow, Doug, do you find it's really hot in here?"

Douglas was lying on top of his covers as most cadets were. "Yeah, I've got a feeling it's going to rain during the night. It's been muggy all day."

"It is going to rain," said Moose. "I heard it on the radio, but I ain't closin' the window because it's too damn hot."

About half-an-hour after the chatter died down, the first few drops could be heard hitting the roof of B-33. Within ten minutes, the hut was bombarded with the sound of pelting rain. The noise of water bouncing off the road outside woke Douglas up, so he closed his window and the windows behind the other Musketeers. At the time, Douglas was so tired, he didn't realize his leg had pulled out the cord of his alarm clock.

"STAND BY YOUR BEDS! C'MON, YOU LAZY PEOPLE, GET YOUR

TENT POLES DOWN AND LET'S GET THIS SHOW ON THE ROAD! "GOTCHA, DIDN'T I BRICE?" Sergeant Simpson yelled, making his normal rounds awakening the shivering *horde* of sleeping cadets.

"SERGEANT, IT'S PISSING DOWN OUT THERE! SURELY TO GOD, YOUSE DON'T WANT US TO GET UP IN THIS WEATHER? CAN'T YOU SUGGEST TO GENERAL KITCHING THAT THE PARADE SHOULD BE CANCELED?"

"DANYLUK, POLE VAULT YOURSELF OUT OF THAT SACK, NOW! YOU CAN DO IT YOUR WAY, OR WE CAN DO IT MY WAY. THE CHOICE IS YOURS!"

Moose stood on the floor with his erection at the 'high port.' He was fortunate that Douglas had closed his window, because the cadets whose windows were open, were soaked. The wind accompaning the rain had found the open windows most inviting.

Danyluk grabbed his towel, dropped it on his third leg, and waddled towards the shower. "C'MON, YOUSE GUYS! GET IN WHILE THE WATER'S HOT!"

It wasn't long before the shower room was jammed full of cold cadets. Those who couldn't fit in stood near the doorway, taking advantage of the steam-clouds that filled the crowded sink area. This created a few problems for the cadets trying to shave at the sinks. Their mirrors kept fogging up, and patches of unshaved chin *fuzz* would be noted later during the inspection.

Wearing their P.T. strip with sweaters and ponchos, the Musketeers joined the lineup for breakfast. The Heavens were wide open and these extra layers of clothing kept them dry. They weren't used to lining up outside the mess hall in the morning because on most days during the week, they were up before the rest of the camp. However, this being Saturday, all companies were *gently* awakened at the same time.

"Jesus, will you just look at this, it's teeming," said Jackson. "Do you think it'll stop before tonight?"

"It's got to stop before tonight," Moose replied. "If it doesn't then we may just have a few problems with Bergie's plan. The creep will wake up if the rain hits his face."

Douglas motioned them to keep their voices down. "The weather shouldn't bother us. There's eight of us, but if we have to add a couple more, then so be it. Jack, did you recce the Nursing Sisters' quarters?"

East moved closer. "Yeah, that's why I barely made bed check last night. I felt like a voyeur, so did Rothie, but he was only holding the ladder. Christ, I had my nose right up to the window; if someone had seen us, we'd be..."

Wayne stopped him from rambling. "O.K., Jack, what did you see?"

Jack continued. "Well, you know the nursing sister that you guys thought had no tits, she's built like a brick..."

"NOT THAT!" Wayne then regained his composure, and lowered his voice again. "Not that! What about the bunks?"

East got back on track. "Oh...yeah, they use single bunks and there are two empty ones, but they're not near the door. They're on each side of the aisle in between two Nursing Sisters."

Moose rubbed his hands together. "BLOODY FANTASTIC! So the thin sister's got big baz...?"

Douglas gave Moose the elbow. "Moose, let's concentrate on the plan, not some woman's anatomy, all right? Gordie, you measured the distance, what is it?"

"Exactly two-hundred-and-seventy-six yards, and that's going around the ditches and staying on the grass. If we used the roads, approximately two-hundred-and-ten yards."

Douglas remained the spokesman as they climbed the stairs and pushed back their poncho head covers as they entered the mess hall. The fine smell of breakfast and the dry warmth didn't deter Brice's train of thought.

"Good, good. Now, Earl, what time does the Junior Ranks Club close?"

Earl's plate was being filled when he tilted his head towards Douglas and whispered, "One-thirty in the morning. I know he'll be there until that time; he's the PMC." (President of the Mess Committee).

Rothstein belly-laughed, then lowered his voice. "That means he'll be as pissed as a nit."

When the eight were seated, the final timings were *arranged*. Wayne's job was to look for loopholes that could cause problems, but he didn't appear worried. "I think we're O.K., *if* the rain stops. If it doesn't, then we'll need a little help, that's all. We've still got the ladder and Rothie said he tested the doorknob and opened the door an inch. That means we're on for tonight!"

Douglas automatically nodded. "And the light from the shower room?"

"We turn it off for exactly two minutes," replied Wayne. "Fifteen minutes before the Provost jeep does its rounds."

Smiles were the order of the day as the diners delved into their powdered eggs. Tonight was the night Corporal Adams, *Super Military Policeman,* would remember for the rest of his life.

"Now, can we talk about the finer things in life?" asked Moose. "Jack, my boy, just how big *are* her glands?"

As Jack leaned forward to talk, seven other upper bodies eagerly joined him, ears in the receiving position.

When fourteen-hundred pairs of feet march on a soaking wet parade square, problems can arise. But on this day, difficulties were few, except for the odd slip and slide. Without the blistering sun in their eyes, fewer people passed out, and although they were soaked through to the skin, the cadets of the Vernon Army Cadet Camp paraded with pomp and pageantry.

As usual, General Kitching took little time going through the ranks. He always knew what he was looking for and if he saw exemplary dress, he stopped and commended the cadet.

The summer clothing the boys wore had been washed so many times, the rain easily eliminated any trace of ironing, starch or no starch, soaped creases, or non-soaped creases.

Following the march past and advance in review order, General Kitching did not ask all ranks to gather around him. He simply thanked the cadets, complimented them on their dress and deportment, and wished them a safe and happy weekend. He kept his speech purposefully short because of the pounding rain.

After the general left the dais, Mr. Gardiner announced that Alpha Company, once again had won the pennant and that he did not want to see it happen a third time.

"ALTHOUGH WE ARE ALL VERY PROUD OF THEM, NEXT WEEK

WILL BE THEIR LAST WEEK IN FORMAL TRAINING AND I WOULD LIKE TO SEE SOME OTHER COMPANY GIVE THEM A RUN FOR THEIR MONEY! ALSO, THERE SEEMS TO BE MUD EVERYWHERE IN MOST OF THE HUTS, BUT NOT IN B-33. WHAT DID YOU DO, ALPHA COMPANY, STAY AWAY FROM BREAKFAST?"

After returning from breakfast, all cadets in B-33 had taken off their running shoes in the entrance way before re-entering the hut. The shoes were then rinsed off in the shower room, covered with white 'IT' polish and placed neatly on the shelves. Also, one towel from each cadet, had been sent out for professional laundering, consequently, the towels on the ends of the bunks were brilliantly clean and white.

"I ASKED, DID YOU STAY AWAY FROM BREAKFAST?"

Even in rain, Alpha's response was ear splitting. "NO, SIR!"

"WELL, YOU ARE TO BE CONGRATULATED! WELL DONE! NOW, BEFORE THIS MICROPHONE SHORTS OUT ON ME, PARADE COMMANDER, CARRY ON!"

After handing in their weapons, Alpha marched back to B-33 and each cadet 're-made' his bed in conventional style.

The sounds of Perez Prado's, *Cherry Pink And Apple Blossom White*, came from Danyluk's radio as the mail Corporal walked in, soaked to the skin. He carried more parcels than usual, but this time, none of them were for the Musketeers.

"THE THINGS I HAVE TO DO TO GET THE MAIL THROUGH!" he quipped, taking off his beret and shaking it in the direction of the eagerly awaiting cadets.

"ROTHSTEIN, EAST, FRANCIOS, FUKUI, HEPPNER, SINGH, CADET COLONEL DANYLUK, CADET CAPTAIN DANYLUK, CADET MAJOR DANYLUK, CADET MAJOR-GENERAL DANYLUK..." He paused. "I must be in...? Is this the barracks with that weird cadet? The nudist who calls himself, Moose-the-Juice-Danyluk, or whatever? The one who knows Red Robinson?"

Many cadets were pointing at Danyluk, who stuck out his chest. "YES, YOU'VE CALLED IT RIGHT, CORPORAL. NOW, ARE THEIR ANY MORE LETTERS FOR ME?"

The Corporal continued staring at Danyluk for a few seconds, then shook his head before he started again. "After seeing you, I have no idea why the girls in the Vernon Post Office want to meet you! BRICE, WATSON, OKEEFE, BANKS, YOUNG, JACKSON, CADET FIELD MARSHALL DANYLUK!"

In all, Danyluk received nine letters and each of the other Musketeers received one.

It was quiet in the hut as cadets lay on their bunks reading letters from their loved ones. Some had lost smiles on their faces, others laughed and even cringed as they read about the antics of their brothers or sisters at home.

"SON OF A BITCH, I'VE GOT A GIFT CERTIFICATE FROM MURRAY GOLDMAN, THE CLOTHIER! CAN YOU BELIEVE THAT? HERE I AM DOING THE QUEEN'S BUSINESS, THREE-HUNDRED-MILES AWAY FROM HOME, AND MY OLD BUDDY, MURRAY, SENDS ME A GIFT CERTIFICATE? IF I BUY A SUIT, I CAN QUALIFY FOR A FREE PORTABLE RADIO."

A cadet in the 43rd Field Artillery, yelled, "OH BULL SHIT! YOU DON'T KNOW HIM, ALSO! YOU'LL BE TELLING US YOU KNOW HOP SING, NEXT! HEY GUYS, DANYLUK SAYS HE KNOWS MURRAY GOLDMAN,

THE CLOTHIER."

Danyluk was lost for words. He knew he already had a problem with not knowing Red Robinson and since he didn't want to get himself in any deeper, he simply ignored the *gunner*.

"Maybe he sent it to you because he knows you're three-hundred-miles away," said Cunningham. "Credit Gal, Evelyn, must have told him you haven't been around. I bet she really gets sick of you putting the make on her every time you go in the store?"

"Hey, she loves it! I wouldn't mind meeting Mrs. Johnson, either. Murray keeps saying, 'And a good evening to you, Mrs. Johnson.' If she's good enough for Murray, she must be some nice dame...and..." Moose paused while he opened up another letter. "Christ, it's an overdue bill from Murray Goldman. Damn that Hilda, she promised me faithfully she'd pay Murray's bills. She was the one who talked me into buying fifteen pairs of beautiful silk gaunch, and now she's not paying the bill. No more up-the-alley knee-tremblers with her." No sooner had he said it, a puzzled look came over his face, and he scratched his head. "No, maybe it was...Ruby?"

Wayne leaned over the side of his bunk. "I bet if Murray new Danyluk was shopping at one of his stores, he'd cancel the account. Goldman's threads are mint!"

Douglas asked, "Do you buy your clothes there also?"

There was a loud thump on the floor as Wayne jumped down. "Sure I do, everyone in Vancouver does. Murray's got the finest clothes in town. Don't you remember I went there with you once? You bought two suits and we got Sammy, Pat, and Manny's autographs?"

Douglas nodded and smiled. "Yeah, his famous salesmen. I remember Murray serving us a coffee, too; he's a real down-to-earth guy. Murray's clothes never seem to wear out and they're always in style. If ya want to be measured perfectly, all ya gotta do is ask for Sammy, Pat, or Manny."

The bedding truck arrived and each cadet waited to exchange one sheet and a pillow case. Douglas noticed something was wrong with Rothstein. The boy's face was pale and he was ill at ease as he stood in the line. Douglas put his arm around his friend's shoulders and spoke sympathetically, in a low voice.

"What's the problem, Rothie? Bad news from home?"

Harvey looked at the ground and sighed. "It doesn't look good with my Mom. The doctor has recommended that she check into the hospital for more tests. That was on Wednesday. She'll be in there now."

Harvey's concern transferred to Douglas' face. "Listen, Rothie, after the exams, why don't you go up to the company office and make a collect call home? It'll be quiet in there and maybe your dad will be able to explain everything to you? I'm sure everything will be all right."

A small confused smile came to Rothstein's lips. "Yeah...thanks, Doug, I...er, I think I'll do that."

Douglas still had his arm around Harvey's shoulders. "C'mon, pal, we've got a few minutes, I'll buy you a pop."

Harvey nodded and the two of them grabbed their berets and headed for the cadet canteen. Four of the other Musketeers noticed them leave, but not one joined them. They understood what Rothstein was going through and it would be better if he wasn't 'crowded.' Once before, in 1953, Douglas and Harvey had fought the *war* and won, and it would be better if the two were left alone to talk.

Danyluk hadn't perceived anything. He was concentrating on the evening raid. His job was to *lift* an extra set of bedding without being caught. With Cunningham distracting the Corporal, it took Moose five minutes and he managed to get two sheets, a pillow, a pillow case, and four blankets.

For some reason, the exams were tougher that morning. The questions didn't want just answers, they required reasons leading up to solutions. The range test in particular was fully concerned with immediate actions, not just dealing with misfires, but with range personnel, firing actions, and positions as well. Also, if the cadets in Alpha hadn't memorized the actual range control commands, firing commands, and Butts procedures and commands, they lost points.

Just before lunch, the company was marched down to B-3 and paid. Each cadet lined up in alphabetical order and when he approached the seated Paymaster and his assistant, he halted, saluted, and remained at attention. A junior officer stood behind the Paymaster along with a Provost Corporal wearing a nine-millimeter pistol. The officer who was standing, returned the salute.

The Paymaster's assistant crossed off the cadet's name after calling it out. In addition, he mentioned the amount of money due.

"BRICE, DOUGLAS! FIVE DOLLARS!"

The Paymaster repeated Brice's name and the amount of money. He then counted and placed five one-dollar bills on the table in front of Douglas.

Douglas signed on the line indicated, scooped up the money, held it in his left hand straight by his side, and saluted with his right. The same junior officer returned his salute.

Brice said, "Thank you, sir," before smartly turning to his left and marching away, swinging his right arm only. When he was outside, he counted the money, put it into one of his pants pockets, and returned to B-33 on his own.

Within fifteen minutes, everyone in the company had been paid.

Rothstein's mood was a little bit more relaxed over lunch. He had called home, and just speaking with his dad had made all the difference in the world. Although each of the Musketeers wanted to know how things were with his mom, no one asked. It would be better if the subject was left alone.

"This rain isn't letting up," stated East. "If it's like this tonight, we're going to have a few difficulties moving that bastard."

"Well, the radio says it's not going to stop," replied Danyluk. "But we've got contingency plans. I've asked those two Canned-Scots, (Canadian Scottish Regiment. CScotR) across the aisle to help us. One of 'em said, 'That means we're going to have to sleep in our shorts.'"

"What does that mean?" asked Wayne.

Danyluk gave Wayne his know-it-all look. "It means those creeps never wear undershorts. They don't wear them under their kilts, they don't wear them to bed and I'll bet they don't wear them during the day. Christ, they must have balls like leather!"

East swallowed quickly, which was out of the ordinary. "Hey, maybe that's the reason Scottish cadets get first pick of the dames? There's no messin' around, everything's always *handy*. I'll betcha that's the way dames like it?"

Moose put his thinking cap on. "Youse know what? I'm going to borrow one of those kilts and see if they work. Why I could increase my supply of women by..."

Cunningham shook his head. "It would never work with you, Moose. Your wang would be hangin' below your kilt. Also what if you got a hard on? With that plow-stick of yours, your sporran would be perpendicular with the floor."

"Listen, Wayne, there's nothing purple about my dicular. Speak for yourself, Ol' Blue Veins."

Simon joined in the laughter. "You know, Moose, if you did wear a kilt, you could train that thing of yours to take your skeandhu out of its case."

"Shit, that's easy. He could train his nuts to do that," Jackson stated.

For the first time that day, the conversation got Rothstein laughing, and throwing in his two-bits worth. "He wouldn't have to wear a skeandhu, he could just slip the end of his knob down his hose-tops. If the Provost asked him what it was, he could say, 'It's my skintool!'"

Bellows of laughter filled the mess hall and in particular, the area surrounding the Musketeers' table. It was Cunningham, of all people, who got their thinking back on track. "O.K., so you guys are *not* going to the dance tonight, you're taking your girls to the movies, right?"

Jackson nodded. "Right, aren't you coming with us?"

A sly smirk appeared on Gordie's face as he rubbed his hands together. "Are you kiddin'? It's payday, I can make a killing tonight! Doug's going to wake us up, so are we all clued in?"

They glanced at each other; each indicated he knew *his job*.

"Good then," Cunningham said, smiling. "If we're all finished, I'm going over to catch a few suckers, er, I mean players." With that said, he slid his chair back, showed everyone the palms of his hands, made a fifty-cent piece appear out of Rothstein's ear, and walked out.

Because of the rain, the Musketeers met their girls at the bowling alley that afternoon. As planned, they would bowl a few games, have dinner at the Capital Cafe and then go and see the two movies which were playing at the Capital Theatre, next door. The movies were *Paleface* and *Friendly Persuasion*.

The grand old theatre was packed with cadets, but once again, as planned, Wayne and Debbie had made certain they were first in line and saved a good portion of the back row. Even though the girls had brought umbrellas, each couple was wet. It was raining harder than ever and the lineup was long, even winding around the corner a half-block to the west.

Wayne and Debbie were left of centre in the back row, with Diane and Douglas on their right. To their right sat Jack's girlfriend and Jack and two very wet, fat, teenage girls, who had bought loads of chocolate bars, ice-cream bars, popcorn and soft drinks. Next to the *large ones* were Moose and Alma, followed by Rothstein, Jackson and Simon, each with *their* girls.

The group wasn't happy they had been split up by the "*two whoppers*," as Banks referred to them, but there was nothing they could do about it. When the girls had first arrived, Wayne tried to tell them that the seats were taken, but the reply was typical.

"PISS OFF! YOU CADETS THINK YOU OWN THE WHOLE TOWN. WELL THESE ARE *OUR* SEATS AND WE'RE GONNA SIT *HERE*!" said the larger of the two, sitting left of Moose. Actually, she wasn't exactly sitting left of Moose, she was so big, half of her body was nearly in Moose's chair. If he moved a fraction of an inch, he rubbed up against her. The same situation existed with the other girl sitting to the right of Jack.

"Jeez, I feel like I'm sitting in a sardine tin," Moose whispered to Alma. He couldn't even put his arm on his left armrest. It was covered with wet clothed flab, and the girl's massive right arm was nearly in his lap. The damp smell from the girls' clothing was nauseating.

Alma tried to ease his concern. "Oh it'll be all right. Maybe she'll wedge over when the movie starts." She had been talking with Rothstein's girl and really hadn't noticed Moose's *real* predicament.

On the other side of the girls, East had the same problem. "If I ever get that fat, just sew up my mouth," he commented.

The *blimps* were oblivious to the problems they were causing. When a boy walked down the centre aisle to the front, one girl leaned towards the other and whispered, "Look, there's Michael, and he's alone. God, what I wouldn't give just to hold his sweaty basketball shirt. I can't stand it, I'm falling in love."

"Why don't you write him a note and I'll deliver it?" murmured the other.

Instantly, the girls stood up, grabbed their goodies and edged to their right heading for the lobby. Danyluk, Alma, and the others had to stand and lean way back because if they didn't, the flabby duo would have gotten stuck in front of them.

"DON'T TAKE OUR SEATS! OUR COATS ARE ON THEM AND WE'LL BE BACK!" Danyluk's *seat-mate* ordered.

Over giggles and with ten minutes to go before the movie started, the *immenser one of the two* wrote a note to Michael.

'My sexy-sexy darling. I'm madly in love with you and I can't stand it any more. I know you winked at me before, but I never winked back because I was shy. My loins are wet and quivering to lie next to you. I want to share all of me with you. Take me, take me. Love & XXXX...Alberta Schwartz.'

While Moose's *partner* crammed past the others again, and sat in her seat next to Moose, her friend headed down the aisle to deliver the note. When she arrived, she was shocked to find another girl had joined Michael, so she put the note into her upper blouse pocket and waddled back to her seat. This time, she faced everyone as she forced herself down the row, her backside bobbing the heads of those in the row in front. As she passed Moose, it was so tight, the note came loose and fell in his lap as he sat down. Moose now thought the note was for him. Smiling confidently, he read the note while the two girls were in deep conversation.

"Did you deliver it?"

"No, I couldn't, Betty Beswick's with him. She's a hussy, that Betty. I bet you she gives him *everything*?"

The *more huge* of the two was now visibly upset. "THE WHOLE SCHOOL KNOWS THAT, WHY...!"

As the lights dimmed, the girl was interrupted by Moose nudging her. His face was lit up with a lusty smirk as he gave her a nod, a wink, closed his eyes and put his lips together making a kissing sound.

The *immense one* turned to her friend but motioned her head in Danyluk's direction. "This beanpole cadet asshole just winked at me."

"Just ignore him, Alberta. He's after your body; they're all the same in that camp. Lecherous bastards! Do you want to change places?"

"No, I can see better here."

After the newsreel and cartoon, Alberta had to go to the bathroom. "Are you coming with me, Eunice?"

"Yes, and we'd better get some more refreshments, the movie's about to start," she replied, searching the floor for a chocolate bar she had placed there.

The other one was in a hurry. "Are you coming?"

"Oh hold on a second, Alberta, you won't pee yourself. I seem to have lost my Mars bar."

How she managed to find the wrapper was a miracle. "I must have eaten it," she said, wedging by everyone again.

East wiped his mouth, let out a slight burp and never took his eyes off the screen. Mars was his favourite kind.

Alberta pushed Danyluk backwards with her buttocks. "GET YOUR HANDS OFF MY ASS!"

All eyes in the immediate area were now on Danyluk who played the role of the perfect innocent. It had to be a mistake because his hands were by his sides.

As Eunice crammed *by* Moose, she smiled, winked, and whispered, "She gets like that; I'm trying to change seats with her."

Moose kept up his innocent facade.

When the two *huge ones* returned, getting to their seats was once again a major exercise. They were loaded down with goodies, and a great deal of Eunice's popcorn fell on the heads of people in the row in front.

Some cadet turned around. "WHAT THE HELL ARE YOU DOING BACK THERE?"

No sooner had he spoken, Alberta wiped his face with her ass as she inched by.

"Does that answer your question?" replied Jackson. "We should charge you for that feel. Feeling with your nose is double."

Twice during *Paleface*, Alberta whispered to Eunice, but while doing so, she didn't realize she was rubbing Moose with her flab. Although Moose had one arm around Alma, he thought Alberta was getting *friendly*, so he *gently slipped* his other hand on what he thought was Alberta's thigh. Actually his hand ended up in Alberta's popcorn bag.

For a fat girl, Alberta moved fast. She yanked her popcorn away so quickly, half of the box's contents ended up over the long-suffering people in the next row down. Moose had butter all over his fingers so he wiped them on her skirt, as she tried to calm down the irate couple in front who were now standing up and complaining.

While Alberta stood and *talked* to the couple in front, she also blasted Moose.

"I SAID, GET YOUR HANDS OFF MY ASS! DO YOU HEAR ME?"

Other complaints were loud. "KEEP IT QUIET BACK THERE!"

"SHHHHHH!"

"LADY, HOW ABOUT SHUTTING UP AND LETTING US WATCH THIS PICTURE?"

"HEY, YOU WITH THE MOUTH LIKE YOUR BODY, PUT A SOCK IN IT!" "WHOEVER KEEPS PUTTING HIS HAND ON *HER* ASS HAS GOT TO BE THE LOSER OF THE CENTURY!"

"CHRIST, WHO'D WANT TO PUT THEIR HAND ON THAT ASS?"

Eunice reached for her pop on the floor. When she couldn't find it, she got out of her seat, inadvertently placing her popcorn on top of it, and got down on her hands and knees. How she managed to force her body onto the floor was a major physical accomplishment. The empty pop cup and straw were at the feet of the girl in front of her, and Eunice assumed it had slid down and the girl had helped herself.

She forced herself onto her feet and slapped the girl's head. YOU'VE GOT A NERVE, DRINKING MY POP! WHY DON'T YOU BUY YOUR OWN, YOU HUSSY!"

Not only did the girl stand up, but so did her boyfriend and the cadet couple in front of Alberta.

"WHO THE HELL ARE YOU TALKING TO? I NEVER TOUCHED YOUR POP!"

Alberta got into the act and stood up. "IF MY FRIEND SAID YOU DRANK HER POP, THEN YOU DRANK HER POP! FORK UP TWO-BITS, YOU SLUT!"

The girl's boyfriend was so upset, he came around to the back row and stopped in front of East. By now the whole audience was in an uproar, trying to get some peace and quiet.

"LISTEN, FATS, WE NEVER TOUCHED YOUR POP! NOW BE QUIET OR WE'LL CALL THE MANAGER!" He went back to his seat.

Things settled down for a minute until Eunice realized her popcorn was missing. She stood up and slammed the guy's head. "O.K., PIMPLE-FACE, WHERE'S MY POPCORN?"

The projectionist heard the riot, stopped the film, and called the manager, who was in front of Jack trying to sort things out.

"Listen, girls, we're going to give you a refund, please come with me."

Eunice wasn't having any of it, and was thoroughly upset with the couple in front. "COME WITH YOU? THIS HUSSY JUST SWIPED MY POP AND HER BOYFRIEND, PIMPLE-FACE HERE, JUST LIFTED MY POPCORN!"

"SHE'S IMAGINING IT ALL! HOW THE HELL COULD WE DO THAT? WE'RE TRYING TO WATCH THE MOVIE IN PEACE!"

"IN PEACE? YOU PROBABLY ATE MY CHOCOLATE BAR, TOO, YOU ASSHOLE!"

"WHO ARE YOU CALLING AN ASSHOLE? YA FAT BITCH! YOU AND TWO-TON-TESSIE HERE SHOULD BE IN A BOOBY-HATCH!"

"WHO ARE YOU CALLING TWO-TON-TESSIE?" screamed Alberta as she stood up to take a swipe at the name caller. She missed and ended up on Danyluk's lap again. "GET YOUR HANDS OFF MY ASS! WE'RE LEAVING ANYWAY! AND AS FOR YOU, MICHAEL, I WOULDN'T LET YOU TOUCH MY BODY!" she screamed at Michael, sitting up front.

The manager said, "My name's not Michael."

"NOT YOU, YOU GOOD-FOR-NOTHING! THAT ASSHOLE IN THE FRONT...THE ONE WITH BETTY BESWICK! COME ON EUNICE, WE'RE LEAVING!"

"Aw, do we have to?"

"WELL, YOU DON'T THINK I'M STAYING HERE, DO YOU? THIS PERVERT'S BEEN RUBBING ME SINCE WE CAME IN HERE!"

Danyluk was trying to explain to Alma and didn't stand as Alberta tried to storm by. Suddenly she tripped, landed on his lap, and attempted to stand up again, assisted of course by Danyluk's left hand.

"SON OF A BITCH, WOMAN!" he yelled rubbing his crotch with his right hand. She had also stomped on his left foot.

"IF YOU TOUCH MY ASS ONE MORE TIME, I'M GOING TO SLAP YOUR FACE SO HARD!"

Eunice couldn't pry past Danyluk either because his watch band had snagged the back of Alberta's skirt, and whether she liked it not, his hand was now on her bottom and he was going with her.

Alberta stopped in front of Alma and tried to turn around, not knowing Danyluk's predicament. "I WON'T TELL YOU AGAIN, YOU SEX MANIAC, GET YOUR HANDS OFF MY ASS!"

The theatre erupted in laughter as Alberta, followed by Danyluk and Eunice, left the row and *fought* through the door.

Many comments were heard throughout. "HEY, IT'S THAT GUY MOOSE! JESUS, LOOK WHO HE'S LATCHED ON TO NOW!"

"HEY, MOOSE! IF SHE SAT ON YOUR LAP, YOUR WANG WOULD BE FLAT!"

Eunice still screamed as she left the auditorium. "YOU ASSHOLES, YOU OWE ME SIXTY CENTS! WE'LL BE WAITING FOR YOU OUTSIDE!"

"YOU JUST DO THAT, YA FAT COW!" replied the furious and nearly frothing fellow in front of Jack.

The movie still didn't start for a few minutes because the *girls* could be heard yelling at Moose in the lobby.

"GET AWAY FROM ME! WHAT THE HELL DO *YOU* WANT? I SAID GET YOUR HAND OFF MY ASS! DON'T GIVE ME THAT WATCH BAND SHIT. TAKE THAT, AND THAT! NOW YOU'VE GONE AND RIPPED MY SKIRT. I'LL BE WAITIN' FOR YOU OUTSIDE, YOU SEX MANIAC. WHAT NOTE? WHAT? MY LOINS WOULDN'T BE WET FOR YOU AT ANYTIME, YOU ANIMAL!"

With the *girls* gone, the balance of *Paleface* and the main attraction, *Friendly Persuasion,* continued in peace..

It was still pouring when the group left the theatre to have milk shakes at the Capital Cafe. The guys laughed at Danyluk's circumstances, while the girls discussed the love and devotion that filled the screen in *Friendly Persuasion.*

Afterward, since Debbie was staying overnight with Diane, Douglas and Wayne went in one direction and the other couples went their own way.

"You'd better come in and dry yourselves off," Diane said to the boys on the front porch of her house.

Both boys smiled because they knew Diane's parents weren't home, but it was eleven-thirty, which meant bed-check would be held in a half-hour.

"We'd like to," replied Douglas who had wound Diane up in his arms. "But it will take us half-an-hour to march back."

Over the next five minutes, each couple said their good-byes in their own romantic, dark secluded spot on the front porch.

"Do you want to borrow my umbrella?" Diane asked as the boys left the protection of the verandah and walked down the stairs.

Wayne yelled back. "WE'D NEVER LIVE IT DOWN IF WE WERE SEEN WITH ONE OF THOSE."

With kisses blown, two soaked-to-the skin *'soldiers'* headed back to Camp Vernon. The walk would seem short, because of their animated discussion about Danyluk and East's earlier antics at the movies, and the important *job* which lay ahead of them this night.

Most cadets in B-33 were still up when Wayne and Douglas arrived. The other Musketeers had returned and the 'ribbing' the group of eight was famous for had already started. Other cadets in the hut had been in the theatre as well as one of the Corporals. They, too, had witnessed the ruckus.

The Corporal who had seen it all stood at the end of Danyluk's bunk. "Let me ask you, why would you possibly want to grab an ass that big?"

Moose's face was innocent of any wrongdoing. "I didn't grab her intentionally, Corporal. I only touched her when she was landing on me, or when I had to *guide* her past me."

"Bull shit, Danyluk! When the girl was giving shit to the people in front of her, you even grabbed her then.

Moose had been in bed, but now he flung the blanket aside and stood face-to-face with the Corporal. "Oh, sure! Here I am sitting next to my girlfriend, and I'm going to rub some other dame's ass? That's suicide, what do you take me for?"
East got involved. "How about the time when you tried to feel her thigh but your hand ended up in her popcorn? You know, the hand you wiped all over her ass a few seconds later?"

Danyluk walked over to East's bunk. "I was trying to get the butter off my fingers. Besides, you can't talk, you ate all night for free. Jesus, you wolfed down two of the other dame's chocolate bars, you drank her pop, and you finished off her popcorn. It's no wonder the broad was furious. You're just lucky she didn't twig on to the fact that it was you, instead of the couple in front."

East grinned. "Ya gotta be quick!"

Danyluk got back into bed. "What were they doing there, anyway? Wayne, you were suppose to save those seats."

Wayne had stripped, dried himself off, and was putting on a dry pair of undershorts. "I tried like hell to stop them, but those dames were tough. The one next to you...oh, what was her name?...Alberta!...she said, 'Listen fuckee, let's go outside and settle this!' There was no way I was going to get in a fist fight with that broad."

"LIGHTS OUT IN FIVE MINUTES!" the Corporal bellowed, heading back to his cubicle. "WELL, IN MY OPINION, DANYLUK, YOU'RE STILL AN ANIMAL!"

Moose shot back, "YOU'RE JUST JEALOUS BECAUSE YOU WEREN'T SITTING NEXT TO HER! WHAT WOULD YOU HAVE DONE IF SHE HAD SENT YOU A NOTE?"

The Corporal stopped and walked back to Danyluk's bunk. "What note are you talking about? Are you saying all chicks are crazy for you? Here's a broad that you don't even know and she's writing you a note? Get with it, Danyluk! Christ, you've got an ego the size of...your...your prick."

Once again, Danyluk jumped out of bed and produced the note which he had hidden underneath his pillow.

"Oh, yeah? Well let me read this to youse. Does this sound like I'm imaginin' all this stuff? And ya gotta smell this thing, too! It's got perfume all over it.

'MY DARLING, I'M MADLY IN LOVE WITH YOUSE AND I CAN'T STAND IT ANY MORE. I KNOW YOUSE WINKED AT ME BEFORE, BUT I NEVER WINKED BACK BECAUSE I WAS SHY. MY LOINS ARE WET AND QUIVERING TO LIE NEXT TO YOUSE. I WANT TO SHARE ALL OF ME WITH YOUSE. TAKE ME, TAKE ME. LOVE AND KISSES, ALBERTA SCHWARTZ.'"

While Moose was reading, most cadets on their end of the wing had gotten out of bed. The note interested them greatly.

Rothstein said, "Wow, she took the Danyluk course in clear diction and quick thinking. Moose, she didn't say, 'youse.'"

"Jesus, I'm gettin' horny just listenin' to ya," another one added. "Let me smell that thing."

The cadet had grabbed Moose by the arm and and wouldn't let go. He got his nose on the note before Moose could push him away.

Another one said, "If her loins got wet, you'd drown lying next to her!"

"All right, all right, I get your point, Danyluk," said the Corporal, as he tried to get a whiff of the note. Moose pulled it back and tucked it into his undershorts. Before he went to sleep, his undershorts would go flying and the note would be tucked back under his pillow.

"So there, Corporal! It's funny though, I don't ever remember winkin' at that dame. I don't think I've ever seen her. On a scale of one to ten, I'd give her a zero. That wouldn't stop me from seein' her, but I'd still give her a zero."

The Corporal grinned. "You must have seen her. Anyway, she wants to share all of herself with you. Did you get that...all of her? Jesus, she's got enough to share with the whole barracks, never mind you alone. Next time, pick 'em a little thinner."

Moose couldn't take that from the Corporal. "ME, PICK 'EM A LITTLE THINNER? WHAT ABOUT YOUSE?"

Douglas walked back from the shower and got into bed. He'd heard Moose's last words and decided to verbally assist him. "YEAH, CORPORAL! DOESN'T ALBERTA SCHWARTZ COMPARE TO THAT BIG ONE YOU'RE ALWAYS TAKING TO THE JUNIOR RANKS CLUB?"

The Corporal came out of his cubicle again. "I wouldn't be seen dead or alive with someone that big."

Jackson wouldn't take that statement. "Come on, Corporal? I suppose that's not you makin' out in that black Volkswagen every night with the fat one that works in the Sergeants' Mess kitchen? The one with flab around her ankles and hairy legs. We see ya!"

"You bet we do," added East, eating an apple. "That broad's so fat, *your* school motto must have been, if you can't chew it, don't screw it!"

The Corporal smiled as he turned off the lights. "You bastards have got eyes in the back of your heads."

Danyluk was still annoyed as he rolled over on his side, mumbling. "The pot calling the kettle black. His broad's even bigger!"

Some cadet across the aisle said. "Hey Moose, can I buy that note off ya?"

Moose laughed. "Get lost, you Westie pansy. Go get your own notes."

"I'm not in the Westies, I'm in the Patricia's."

"Same thing...infantry grunts!"

Gradually, the jesting stopped and B-33 was quiet. Ten minutes later, though, East and Rothstein silently slipped out of their beds, put on their K.D. longs, sweaters, running shoes, berets without badges, and ponchos. They quietly walked through to the other wing and left the building via the southwest door.

Although the cadets had closed all of the windows, old B-33 creaked a little in the wind, and the only other sound was the rain slamming against the roof.

Douglas got silently out of bed when the radio alarm next to his head alerted him. As he made his 'rounds' waking certain people up, the luminous hands on his watch read, 0200 hours.

"We won't take our ponchos, the rain has eased," he whispered.

Very quietly, eight cadets left the building through the same southwest door used by East and Rothstein. Simon carried the spare bedding Moose had 'stolen' the day before off the back of the sheet exchange truck.

Stealthily and about three feet apart, the group made their way around the back of the nearby NCO's building and encircled East in the shadows outside the building's shower room. He had taken off his poncho, but like the rest, he had mud all over his running shoes.

East kept his voice very low. During fieldcraft lectures, they had been taught not to whisper because the sounds of whispers travel much further at night when *normal* noises aren't common.

"They must have closed the Junior Ranks Club early. He came staggering in at 0130. I've been in there, and he's on the bottom floor in the seventh bed left of the entrance. He's snoring his head off!"

Douglas glanced at Wayne who left immediately to liaise with Rothstein outside the Nursing Sisters' quarters, approximately a hundred yards away, behind the headquarters building. He met his accomplice behind the dark east side of the building.

When Wayne approached his compatriot, Rothstein also kept his voice low. "We've got a problem. They're all in there and they're all asleep, but the damn door's locked."

"Did you try the other side?" asked Wayne, his heart pounding.

Rothstein had done his *homework* and pointed towards the end of the building. "Yeah, locked as well, but that window's open. We need the ladder."

Wayne shook his head. He knew this area of the camp was patrolled the most. "Christ, we'll be reducing the odds if we make two trips with the ladder. If you stand on my shoulders, do you think you'll be able to get in?"

Rothstein considered the task and nodded. "Yeah, that might do it."

It was going to be tough for Harvey, but he had taken his running shoes off, so the sounds of his feet sliding on the wall of the building wouldn't make any noise.

Wayne crouched and pressed his palms on the wall, while Harvey got on his shoulders and stood up. As Wayne strained under his friend's weight, Rothstein grasped for the windowsill. When his shoulders were just below the window, he jumped slightly and shimmied sideways to get one foot on the ledge. Within five seconds, he was in. He leaned out and spoke calmly and confidently.

"Meet me at the north door."

Wayne took off his shoes and waited until the door was opened before he crept up the few stairs to enter. The door creaked loudly, which rankled the nerves of both boys. Rothstein applied a little upward pressure, lifting the door and closing it to the point where it wasn't fully shut. The squeaking stopped.

They stood there a few moments waiting for their eyes to become accustomed to the small amount of light entering the sleeping quarters from the washing area. The room reeked of perfume.

With hearts thumping, just as they started to make their move, a toilet flushed. Applying a quick upward pressure to the door, they moved outside again and stood at the top of the steps; hearts now beating wildly. Both boys knew they were very vulnerable if a patrol vehicle or foot sentry were to come by, so they made their way down the stairs and around the east side again.

"Jeez, this is nerve-wracking," said Rothstein, licking his lips to no avail. Both boys were so nervous, their mouths were bone dry. "Also, we're going to leave mud everywhere. It's stuck to our socks."

Wayne did his best to swallow, but managed a small smile. "Let's just hope we can pull it off. We'll clean up the mud after the final move."

Within five minutes, the cadets were back in the hut. East's description helped immensely, so they knew exactly where the single unused bed was. Two minutes later, the curled-up unused mattress was taken off, and the bed was lifted up and placed within three inches of the bed and occupant next to it.. With that done, they left.

The others were waiting patiently. "What the hell is holding them up?" asked Jackson. No sooner had the words left his mouth, he spotted their silhouettes. "Oh, it's all right, here they come now."

Wayne and Rothstein explained why they were behind schedule and received a few pats on their backs.

"Right, let's get to it!" Danyluk murmured.

Carefully, eight of the ten cadets split into two groups of four and entered the NCO's building from a side door and an end door. This kept any noise to a minimum and almost immediately they surrounded the single bed of the *feared* Corporal Adams. Still snoring and lying on his back, his position was perfect for *the move*.

At this point, everything was done with hand signals. Not one word was spoken because they knew the book would be thrown at them if they got caught.

As Simon placed the spare bedding behind the bunk, Danyluk and Cunningham crept in with the ladder and held it parallel with the single bunk bed. As practised, the two CScotRs each took an end to help them. The other six split and stood three-to-a-side of the snoring Corporal. On the silent count of three, his mattress was ever-so-gently slid onto the ladder: bedding, pillow, and most important of all...body. This move had also been practised previously and everything went according to plan.

When that was done, three of the six stayed with the ladder while Wayne and Jackson stayed at the sides and opened up one of the blankets Moose had taken. They held it about a foot above the sleeping Corporal's face. He would definitely not feel the rain.

Douglas picked up all the clothes and the boots the Corporal had worn that day He also picked up a wet mop. The Corporal must have been tired or drunk because his clothing had been left in a pile on the floor beside his bed.

Although the floors creaked, the ten cadets remained in perfect step as they left the building and headed for their final destination. It was darker than usual because of the heavy black clouds, and this assisted the scenario greatly.

Slowly but surely, Corporal Adams was moved across the road, around the headquarters building, and up the few stairs of the Nursing Sisters' quarters. As the rest slipped out of their shoes, Rothstein lifted the door to make certain it didn't creak. Effortlessly, the *dragon* of Camp Vernon was transferred from the ladder onto the spare bed. His mattress was placed about two inches over the side so there would be no gap when the beds were joined. The *beloved* Corporal's face, breath and body were now only inches away from a sleeping Nursing Sister who got into this prank because she just happened to sleep next to the spare bed.

As luck would have it, once transferred, Corporal Adams grunted and automatically rolled onto his left side. In doing so, his right arm went over the sleeping nurse who did not wake up. The Sister and her new bed partner were now face-to-face. It's a wonder the liquor on the sleeping Corporal's breath didn't wake her up.

Some snickering started as Danyluk pumped his groin in and out, but stern signals stopped it in a hurry.

Before the beds were edged the final two inches together, the nurse's 'close side' covers which had been tucked in, were very gently pulled out. Then, as the corporal's covers were peeled off him to his left , the beds were put tight together and he was covered with the nurse's covers and his covers were placed over hers. Now, if either one of them moved, their bare bodies would touch each other.

Douglas placed the Corporal's clothes in a pile on the floor, exactly as the Corporal had left them in his own building.

Now, only a few last things were left to be done and even they were carried out with dispatch. The 'rain' blanket was spread over their covers and was tucked in on the nurse's far side and the Corporal's far side. These two were now tighter than two peas in a pod. After that, Douglas mopped the floor where Rothstein had walked when he first entered.

As Danyluk and Cunningham walked out with the ladder, Jackson and East headed back to the Corporal's quarters with the spare mattress. This mattress now replaced the original, and the extra bedding which Moose had *lifted,* was used to make the Junior NCO's bed as perfectly as he himself would have made it. It now appeared as though he hadn't made it back to his abode after he left the Junior Ranks Club.

The others, with the exception of Wayne, looked down upon the *loving* couple, only inches apart and nearly entwined. The scene made each of them want to howl out laughing, but they dared not. With thumbs up all 'round, the group quietly slipped out of the building, with Douglas mopping up behind them. Wayne crept back into the building wearing the Corporal's dirty boots. He had taken them outside and muddied them up leaving a trail of black footsteps right up to *the* bunk. After that, Wayne crept out on his hands and knees, leaving Rothstein, who was the last to leave. Rothstein gently but firmly pulled the door shut behind him.

When the Corporal's quarters were mopped and the mop returned, the 'night stealers,' in pairs and from five different directions, entered B-33. Not a sound was made because they were now in their bare feet. It only took a few minutes for them to wash off their running shoes before they shook each other's hands and went to bed. The time was 0300 hours and it was raining heavily again.

The sound of Little Richard's voice was loud as *Tutti Frutti,* filled the northeast end of building B-33. It was Sunday morning and most cadets were still asleep, as Danyluk turned up his radio.

"C'MON, YOUSE BUMS! LET GO OF YOUR COCKS AND GRAB YOUR SOCKS!"

Wayne leaned over. "Good morning, Douglas. How are you this fine morning?"

Brice smiled. Hut B-33 was now alive with activity. "What's good about it? We've got to attend Church Parade in an hour."

"Lyons, (an old friend) would say, 'Quite true, old chum, quite true,' but it's stopped raining, *and* East tells us they're serving *real* eggs in the mess hall this morning. Let's grab a shower and get over there before the chicken dies."

Most of the other cadets were up as Wayne and Douglas passed Cunningham. He was surrounded by *suckers* in the entrance-way, and the dice must have been hot because he had a stack of bills in front of him as he threw. "BABY NEEDS A NEW PAIR OF SHOES! YEEAASS, THAT'S IT, MY LITTLE DARLINS!"

"YOU LUCKY PRICK!" Some cadet shouted.

"IT'S NOT LUCK, IT'S SKILL! COME TO POPPA, COME TO POPPA...YEEAASS!" Cunningham said as he threw the dice again and picked up the pot.

The shower room was full when they squeezed in. Both wanted to talk about their early morning jaunt, but not a word was said. Instead, they gabbed about the day ahead of them.

As usual, Wayne's whole body was covered with shampoo. "Do you think Tom will mind making two trips to Kal Beach?" he asked, referring to Diane's dad. The Musketeers hadn't yet had a swim parade, so Tom had volunteered to take them to Kalamalka Beach that afternoon.

Douglas had both hands against the wall as he let the water rinse away the foam. "Nah, he's a great guy. He said whenever he's got the time, he'll take us anywhere, all we have to do is ask."

"Do you think one of these days he might be able to take us up Silver Star Mountain?" asked Wayne. "I'd love to see what this place looks like from the top. It must be a fantastic sight."

Douglas shrugged. "All we have to do is ask. He's still on shift-work but he's says he can plan around it."

"Mint!" replied Wayne, drying himself off.

After they dressed in khaki shorts, shirts, hosetops, boots and puttees, seven of the eight Musketeers headed over to the kitchen. It was East's second trip for breakfast; Cunningham was too wrapped up with his game to eat. He said he'd catch brunch during Church Parade because he didn't have to attend. "With a name like, Mahatma Gandhi, I don't have to attend church, my sons. May peace and divinity smile upon you, my children. Now, bugger off, you're disturbing my game. O.K., GENTS, MONEY IN THE POT!"

The others laughed knowing Danyluk and Cunningham had pulled off the ultimate. Douglas thought to himself, if Bergie were here, he wouldn't believe it. Nobody ever got out of attending Church Parade twice in a row. The NCOs even checked the furnace room looking for *wayward souls*, yet these two were now permanently excused from church.

It was quiet in the mess hall, quiet enough for the group to hear the ever-continuing conversation of the earliest risers of the morning - the kitchen staff.

"OF COURSE, I HEARD THE SCREAMS!" sputtered one of the ladies. "I HAD JUST PARKED MY CAR WHEN I HEARD HER! I ACTUALLY WALKED UP THE ROAD TO FIND OUT WHAT THE TROUBLE WAS! THAT'S WHEN I HEARD THE POLICE SIREN!"

"THE DIRTY BEAST!" said another woman with a Scottish accent. "HE ACTUALLY HAD HER IN HIS ARMS! SHE WAS APPARENTLY ASLEEP BUT SHE HAD HER ARMS AROUND HIM, AS WELL! HE KNEW WHAT HE WAS DOING BECAUSE SHE WAS THE ONLY ONE THAT SLEPT IN THE NUDE!"

A third lady got into the act. "CAN YOU IMAGINE THAT? A MILITARY POLICEMAN TRYING TO RAVISH ONE OF THE PRETTIEST YOUNG NURSING SISTERS IN THE CAMP? I WATCHED HER AS HE WAS TAKEN AWAY;

SHE WAS STILL SHAKING. THE BASTARD WAS ONLY WEARING HIS UNDERSHORTS."

"YOU MEAN HE HAD NOTHING ON?"

"JUST HIS UNDERWEAR. HE'D STRIPPED OFF AND DROPPED HIS CLOTHES ON THE FLOOR. IT'S A WOND..."

The lady serving the *real* eggs, butted in. "ARE YOU CERTAIN SHE WASN'T JUST ACTING BECAUSE HER CAPTAIN WAS THERE? IT SEEMS RATHER FUNNY TO ME THAT SHE DIDN'T WAKE UP?"

"MADGE, IF SHE WAS ACTING, WOULD SHE RUN OUT WITH NO CLOTHES ON? SHE WAS BARE-NAKED ON THE ROAD; SOMEONE HAD TO THROW HER A BLANKET!"

"WHAT WAS HE DOING ALL THIS TIME?"

"WHAT DID HE DO? THE SNEAKY THING ROLLED OVER ON HIS SIDE AND WENT BACK TO SLEEP, ASKING THEM TO KEEP THE NOISE DOWN. THAT'S WHAT HE DID!"

"THE NERVE," said Madge. "WHERE IS HE NOW?"

"IN THE CELLS WHERE HE BELONGS! NOW THAT SEX MANIAC WILL KNOW WHAT IT FEELS LIKE TO BE IN THERE. HE'S ALWAYS PICKING ON THE CADETS WHO ARE BEHIND BARS, NOW IT'S HIS TURN!"

"WHO FOUND THEM?"

"NO ONE FOUND THEM. SHE JUST HAPPENED TO WAKE UP WHEN HE PATTED HER ON THE BUM AND SAID, 'JOSIE, YOU'RE STILL THE BEST!'"

"IS HER NAME JOSIE?"

"NO, IT'S MILDRED!"

"THE DIRTY BEAST!" reiterated the Scottish lady.

Of course, the whole conversation was overheard by the grinning Musketeers. Jackson leaned over to Wayne. "Bergie would be proud of us."

"Jesus, I wonder what's going to happen to Adams?" asked East.

Simon had a worried look on his face. "Yeah, this thing could get serious. She could charge him with rape."

Banks laughed into his hands. "No, they won't. The fact that he called her Josie will indicate he was talking in his sleep. Don't forget, he rolled over after she screamed. They'll figure out he didn't know where he was."

Danyluk's eyes were were like saucers. "Jeez, she had no clothes on, we could have taken a peek. That sister's got a body that won't quit."

"Oh, yeah? And what if she woke up?" asked Jackson. "I'm glad we didn't press our luck."

Rothstein was still trying to listen to the kitchen ladies. "Wow, I'd love to hear the whole story."

Douglas smiled, nudged East, and grabbed their berets. "We will, but right now, we've got to sing some hymns. C'mon, 'guts'!"

The beach at the north end of Kalamalka Lake is one of the finest swimming spots in Canada.

With area temperatures which can climb higher than 35 degrees Celsius, the cool, aqua-green water of Kalamalka Lake can wash away all of life's daily pressures in seconds. Although it was the weekend and the fatigued Musketeers of

Alpha Company had no real pressure on them, the water was rejuvenating and made them feel fresh and alive again.

Because the beach was crowded, the boys shut their ears to the surrounding din and frolicked at the end of the wharf with the girls. They had waited two weeks for this moment and nothing, especially the tone of a megaphone ordering them to get ready to board the trucks, was going to disturb them. They all knew that wouldn't happen because this wasn't an organized swim parade.

Douglas stayed at the diving board raft with Diane. Some of the others were nearby. He had one hand in the water and the other one around Diane's shoulders as they lay on their stomachs, staring into each other's eyes.

"Did you get in trouble with your regiment for coming up here as a cadet this summer?" she asked.

He cleared some of her hair from the front of her eyes and ran his finger down her nose and across her lips. "Not really. They wanted us in Wainright, but they knew they couldn't fight City Hall. What are they going to do, kick five of us out? Not earning the money is a problem, though."

Diane displayed a sympathetic smile. "How much will you lose by not going to Wainright?"

"About four hundred dollars. No, I'm wrong. I'm getting paid a hundred for coming here, make that about three hundred dollars. I'm not concerned about the money, I just want to be here with you. I'll borrow some money to attend UBC."

His girl leaned on her side to face him. "Have you decided what profession you want?"

"No, but I have decided I'm going to take officer training. I could join now, but I don't want to leave you." He turned towards her. "Diane, if I were a few years older, I'd ask you to marry me and we could share our lives together."

Diane kissed him gently. "Is that a proposal, Douglas Brice?"

A earnest grin came to Douglas' face. He loved the way her dimple showed when she frowned. "Hey, maybe it *is*," he replied. "I could set pins for a living and you could get a job as a dishwasher. We could raise a big family and who knows where we could land? We might even end up owning a bowling alley and you could look after the restaurant." He shook his head. "I'm only joking. No, that's not for you, honey. I want you to get your nursing degree and if I can get a couple of years in at UBC before I enter the army, it'll help."

Douglas turned onto his stomach again as Diane walked his back with the tips of her fingers. "I like the part about the big family," she said. "Eight boys and two girls?"

Douglas turned over and sat up quickly. "Christ, that's like having our own platoon. How about two girls and a boy?"

Diane nodded and started tickling him.. "Yeah, that's O.K., I like that better. I could spend more time with you. If we had eight kids...?"

"C'MON YOU GUYS, WERE GOIN' TO EAT!" screamed East, interrupting her. "CUNNINGHAM SAYS HE'S GOING TO BUY!"

Those words were all it took, plus a fraction of a second for eight couples to hit the water and start racing to shore.

Douglas was moving as fast as everyone else. "What brought this on?" he asked Jackson, who was in the lead.

"You know the playing cards Cunningham wrapped in plastic and stuck in the waist of his swimsuit?"

"Yeah, so what happened?"

"Well, he played one game of sudden-death strip poker with Alma. If he won, she took it off, and if he lost, he either took it off or bought food for all of us!"

"YOU MEAN HE ACTUALLY LOST?"

When Jackson replied, he laughed and got water up his nose. "NO, SHE ACTUALLY WON! SHE DOESN'T REALIZE IT YET, BUT SHE DESERVES A MEDAL!"

"YOU CAN SAY THAT AGAIN!"

"I'M NOT GOING TO," Earl sputtered. "I NEARLY DROWNED JUST TRYING TO GET THAT OUT!"

Once on shore, Cunningham tried to change the rules a little. "One hot-dog, fries and a pop!"

Alma grabbed the back of Gordie's bathing suit and started pulling it down. "TWO HOT-DOGS, FRIES, AND A LARGE POP...EACH!"

Cunningham turned quickly, but couldn't shake off Alma's hand. "YOU WIN, YOU WIN! ALMA, GO AND ORDER!"

"THAT'S MY DARLIN'! MY LITTLE GIRL!" Moose bellowed.

"YEAH, AND YOU CAN KEEP HER, TOO! SHE'S STRONGER THAN ALL OF US COMBINED!" Cunningham responded.

When the cadets returned from the beach, it was catch up time. Before supper, they washed and ironed their clothing, shined their boots and brass and had time for a cold shower.

That evening, the movie was *Marty*, with Ernest Borgnine. Afterwards, when it was nearly time for lights out, Gordie told Moose that he reminded him of Marty. Wearing only their underwear, an insulted Moose chased him out the front centre stairs, around the front of the building, back up the northeast stairs of the hut, through their portion of the wing and washing area, down the southwest stairs, around the back of the building, and back up the northeast stairs. When Danyluk finally caught up with him, he was too tired to pound him. But not too tired to stand at attention when the RSM walked up the centre stairs and stood at the foot of his bunk.

"WAS THAT YOU, RUNNING OUTSIDE? DID YOU DO THE ZULU ON THE ROAD AT THE REAR OF THE OFFICERS' MESS?"

Instantly, by good training alone, Moose stopped breathing heavily. "WHERE, SIR? NOT ME, SIR!"

"THEN WHY ARE YOU SWEATING, MAN?"

"PUSHUPS, SIR! MY NIGHTLY 100, SIR!"

Mr. Gardiner stood there for a moment just waiting for Danyluk to breathe heavy. Fortunately, he didn't, so the RSM grunted and marched out mumbling to himself. When he was gone, Danyluk let out two lungfuls of air, flopped on his bunk, and gasped for breath.

Swinging his giant cane, Mr. Gardiner marched towards the Sergeants' Mess, mumbling to himself.

"He probably uses his thing as a goddamned jack. Nightly one-hundred pushups, my ass. I'm going to keep my eye on that man. Christ, does he ever wear any clothes? He'll probably grow up to be like that animal, Corporal Adams."

Chit chat was almost non-existent after the lights were turned out. It would have been drowned out by the Musketeers' snoring, anyway. Especially that of Danyluk and Cunningham.

As the building creaked out a welcome, a full moon came from behind a small cloud and winked at B-33.

CHAPTER VIII

"LEFT, RIGHT, LEFT RIGHT, LEFT RIGHT! YOU! YES, YOU! GET YOUR ARMS UP! GET YOUR CHIN UP, MAN! IT'S CHEST OUT AND STOMACH IN, NOT THE OTHER WAY 'ROUND! DON'T BEND THE ARMS...PUSH DOWN ON YOUR THUMBS! DIG IN YOUR HEELS. DRIVE THOSE ARMS BACK...I SAID, BACK, BACK, BACK! THAT'S BETTER!"

The voice was not Sergeant Beckford's. Instead, it was the voice of Cadet Douglas Brice teaching a drill mutual. Each of the four platoons had been split into four sections of approximately ten cadets each. Twenty-four sections were receiving drill mutuals at various locations on the giant parade square, and each student teaching drill was being assessed by either a Corporal or a Sergeant.

When the pop truck came to the side of the parade square during break, the driver asked, "Is there a Cadet Douglas Brice, here?"

Douglas heard him. "YES, I'M BRICE!"

The driver took an envelope off the front seat of the truck. "I have a special delivery letter for you from Vancouver," he said, handing it to Douglas.

Douglas knew what it was because he saw the letters CJOR in the upper left corner of the envelope. He put it away quickly, and motioned to Wayne to join him. Moose was in a conversation with East and Jackson, so he was none the wiser.

"It's a reply from Red Robinson, isn't it?"

Douglas nodded as he took out the letter, opened it, and started scanning it with his eyes.

"Well, read it to me, too, will ya?" Wayne asked.

A smile came to Douglas' lips. "Hey, Red Robinson's a pretty good guy, just listen to this.

'Dear Doug & Wayne:

I just received your incredible letter about Moose Danyluk. For your information, I spent four years in the Air Cadets, so I can relate to this situation better than most.

As you are aware, I will be coming to Vernon to the arena to put on a Rock N Roll show in a week's time. Because you took time to defend a buddy, I guarantee you I will go out of my way to treat Moose like an old friend. Not only will I play a song or two for Moose, I will invite him up on stage to acknowledge his 'help' with picking my records from time to time. But, for God's sake, don't tell him anything about this. Believe me, I can handle it.

I promise I will not embarrass Moose. As a matter of fact, let's call it my good deed for the day.

Thanks for bringing this situation to my attention. I look forward to meeting you two and Moose and hopefully a few hundred of your army cadet buddies at the dance.

By the way, we expect a big turnout of chicks at the dance. All the dances I have emceed around the province indicate that women dig Rock N Roll. I know you guys dig chicks, so be sure to be there. Keep on Rockin'

"Your Technicolor host on the Pacific Coast." Red Robinson - CJOR Radio.' "

When Douglas finished reading Red's letter, he didn't look up. His grinning mouth was wide open as he just kept staring at the page. Wayne grabbed it and started reading. "My God, Doug, he's going along with us. We've pulled it off!"

Cheshire cat smiles appeared . Douglas still couldn't believe it, as he snatched the letter back again. "Look at this part; it says, *'Not only will I play a song or two for Moose, I will invite him up on stage to acknowledge his 'help' with picking my records from time to time. But, for God's sake, don't tell him anything about this. Believe me, I can handle it.'* CAN YOU BELIEVE THAT? YAHOO!"

Douglas' excitement attracted attention. The other Musketeers were there in a flash.

"Did you get some money from home?" asked Cunningham, pulling his magician act and taking a twenty-five-cent piece out of Wayne's nose and right ear. Douglas quickly put the letter away. "Er, no. Wayne was informed that getting a job with Canadian Pacific Steamships, looks pretty good. I was just congratulating him."

Simon didn't help matters. "Can I have the stamp. I collect stamps."

"It was a postage machine stamp," Wayne replied.

Simon screwed up his face. "Oh, forget it then."

Over the next few minutes, the Musketeers all congratulated Wayne for getting a job. The only person who wasn't smiling was Wayne. He and Douglas wanted to show Red's letter to everyone but Danyluk, but it seemed impossible to separate Moose from the rest of them. They were confident though, that they would eventually pass on the information before the dance night which was six days away.

"Moose is going to shit himself, there's no doubt about that!" said Wayne.

Douglas put his lips to Wayne's right ear. "Wait'll we tell the girls. They'll think it's a blast."

Banks' face indicated he didn't like that idea. "I don't think we should tell them. What if it slips out to Alma? The next minute, Moose will know."

After a short discussion, it was decided that under no circumstances should the girls be told. Not because they couldn't trust them, but just in case a weak moment arose and Alma found out.

They were still chuckling to themselves when Earl came over. "Hey, have you guys heard the news? Sergeant Beckford just told us that when we get attached to the other companies, we'll be issued bush uniforms, *and* Corporal's stripes. If it's too hot, we don't have to wear the jacket, we can just wear khaki shirts with our regimental web belt. "Just think, it will be *Corporal* Jackson!"

Wayne tipped up the bottle and finished the last drop of his Kik Kola. "Corporal Banks has a nice ring to it. Finally, I'm going to be appreciated. I think I'm going to like...!"

He was cut off by the sound of Sergeant Beckford's formal voice. "RIGHT! ALPHA COMPANY, SINCE WE'VE GOT THE WHOLE PARADE SQUARE TO OURSELVES, LET'S GET THESE DRILL MUTUALS OVER WITH!"

For the next hour, all cadets in Alpha Company gave drill mutuals. Then for the last half-hour of the morning, Sergeant Beckford formed them up in an extended line and they completely surrounded the parade square, looking inwards, with about a two-foot space between each of them.

Beckford stood in the middle of the square and swiveled to address them all.

"RIGHT, PAY ATTENTION HERE! BY NOW, EACH OF YOU IS MORE THAN AWARE OF THE LITTLE TRICKS OF THE TRADE. WHEN YOU'RE TEACHING DRILL, YOU MUST ENSURE THAT EVERY PERSON YOU ARE IN CHARGE OF BELIEVES HE OR SHE IS THE LONE RECIPIENT OF YOUR COMMENTS.

"I WANT YOU TO REMEMBER THAT YOU NEVER GIVE DRILL COMMANDS WHEN YOU ARE MOVING, EXCEPT IF YOU ARE MARCHING WITH YOUR TROOPS. WHEN YOU'RE TEACHING DRILL, YOU CAN MARCH AROUND YOUR PEOPLE TO GET A BETTER ANGLE OF SIGHT, HOWEVER, YOU MUST STOP AND FACE THEM WHEN YOU GIVE A COMMAND. IT DOESN'T MATTER IF YOU FACE THEIR FRONT, SIDES, OR BACK, BUT MAKE CERTAIN YOU FACE THEIR FRONT WHEN YOU'RE TEACHING. ALSO, I'M SURE I'VE HAMMERED THIS HOME MANY TIMES...WHEN YOU ARE DEMONSTRATING A DRILL MOVEMENT, STAND YOUR PEOPLE AT EASE AND HAVE THEM STAND EASY WITH THEIR BACKS TO THE SUN. THEN, DEMONSTRATE THE COMPLETE MOVEMENT. WHEN THAT'S DONE, BREAK THE MOVEMENT DOWN AND DEMONSTRATE EACH INDIVIDUAL MOVEMENT SEPARATELY. THEN DEMONSTRATE THE FIRST MOVEMENT CALLING OUT THE TIME, AFTER WHICH, THEY WILL COMPLETE THE FIRST MOVEMENT, CALLING OUT THE TIME.

"FOR EXAMPLE, THIS IS WHAT I WANT TO HEAR. LET'S SUPPOSE YOU ARE TEACHING THE RIGHT TURN AT THE HALT. YOUR PEOPLE ARE AT EASE AND STANDING EASY, NOT TALKING. THIS IS WHAT I WANT TO HEAR.

'RIGHT, PAY ATTENTION HERE! I AM NOW GOING TO TEACH YOU THE RIGHT TURN AT THE HALT. WATCH CLOSELY AS I PIVOT ON THE BALL OF MY LEFT FOOT AND HEEL OF MY RIGHT FOOT; TURN ON A NINETY-DEGREE ANGLE, PICKING UP MY LEFT FOOT SIX INCHES OFF THE GROUND, LEFT TOE POINTING TOWARDS THE GROUND AND PARALLEL WITH THE LEFT KNEE AND SLAMMING DOWN, SO THAT MY FEET ARE IN A THIRTY DEGREE ANGLE.'"

He completed the movement. "'YOU WILL NOTICE THAT MY ARMS REMAINED STIFFLY BY MY SIDES, ALL FINGERS TOUCHING MY PANTS. THERE IS NO DAYLIGHT BETWEEN MY ARMS AND MY BODY. MY EYES REMAINED AT EYE LEVEL AS MY HEAD TURNED WITH MY BODY. MY CHEST IS OUT AND MY STOMACH IN. I DID NOT SCRATCH MY ASS OR PICK MY NOSE! AFTER THE MOVEMENT WAS COMPLETE, I LOCKED MY EYES ONTO AN OBJECT DIRECTLY IN FRONT OF ME!'"

A few chuckles travelled around the square.

"'NOW, I AM GOING TO BREAK THIS COMPLETE MOVEMENT DOWN IN TWO MOVEMENTS. MYSELF ONLY, TURNING TO THE RIGHT BY NUMBERS, RIGHT TURN, ONE! MY BODY HAS MOVED ON A NINETY-DEGREE ANGLE TO MY RIGHT BY PIVOTING ON THE BALL OF MY LEFT FOOT AND THE HEEL OF MY RIGHT FOOT, AND REMAINS IN THAT POSITION. MY LEFT HEEL REMAINS ONE INCH OFF THE GROUND, BODY STRAIGHT, ARMS BY MY SIDES, AND HEAD AND EYES DIRECTLY TO MY NEW FRONT! MYSELF ONLY, RIGHT TURN, TWO! I PICKED MY LEFT FOOT UP SIX INCHES OFF THE GROUND, TOES POINT-

ING DOWN AND PARALLEL WITH MY LEFT KNEE AND SLAMMED IT
DOWN SO THAT MY FEET ARE NOW IN A THIRTY DEGREE ANGLE.

'WE ARE NOW GOING TO PRACTISE THE FIRST MOVEMENT AND
YOU WILL CALL OUT THE TIME...ONE!'"

"SO YOU SEE, PEOPLE, TEACHING DRILL IS LIKE PAINTING BY
NUMBERS! YOU GET YOUR TROOPS TO PRACTISE THE FIRST MOVE-
MENT UNTIL IT'S PERFECT, THEN YOU MOVE ON TO THE SECOND
MOVEMENT AND THEY WILL CALL OUT THE TIME...TWO!. WHEN
YOU'RE HAPPY WITH BOTH, PUT THEM TOGETHER FOR THE COM-
PLETE MOVEMENT AND HAVE THEM CALL OUT THE TIME, WHICH OF
COURSE IS, ONE, TWO-THREE, ONE!

"AS DRILL INSTRUCTORS, YOU ARE REQUIRED TO LOOK FOR
EVERYTHING THAT'S OUT OF PLACE. THERE ARE LAZY SOULS OUT
THERE AND YOUR JOB IS TO GET THEM WORKING AS A TEAM. IF YOU
SEE SOMETHING WRONG, LET THEM HEAR ABOUT IT IN NO UNCER-
TAIN TERMS.

"RIGHT! ALPHA COMPANY, ATTEN...TION! STAND STILL AND LOOK
TO YOUR FRONT! WHAT I SAY, YOU WILL REPEAT IN THE SAME MAN-
NER. IS THAT CLEAR?"

A tumultuous, "YES, SERGEANT!" came at Sergeant Beckford from the
cadets surrounding the periphery of the parade square.

Sergeant Beckford faced one side of the square. "YOU! YES, YOU! GET
YOUR ARMS UP!"

The cadets repeated it with vigor.

"GET YOUR CHIN UP, THAT MAN!"

It was repeated along with the following: "DON'T SCRATCH YOUR ASS!
DID YOU SCRATCH YOUR ASS?! PUSH DOWN ON YOUR THUMBS! PICK
YOUR FEET UP, THAT MAN! GET THAT SMILE OFF YOUR FACE! ALL
FINGERS TOUCH THE PANTS! DRIVE THE ARMS BACK! I SAID, BACK,
BACK, BACK! DON'T WIPE YOUR ASS WITH YOUR ARMS! YOU, GET
YOUR FINGER OUT OF YOUR NOSE! STAND STILL! LEFT, RIGHT, LEFT,
RIGHT! CHIN UP...CHIN UP! GET YOUR SHOULDERS BACK! YOU, YES
YOU! YOU'RE MARCHING LIKE YOU'VE GOT SOMETHING STUCK UP
YOUR ASS...HAVE YOU?! WATCH YOUR DRESSING! DRESSING BY THE
RIGHT! DRESSING BY THE LEFT! RIGHT WHEEL! LEFT WHEEL! HALT!
STAND STILL!"

The cadets weren't moving as they bellowed the commands from the sidelines.
Then Sergeant Beckford injected some humour.

"YOU, GET YOUR HEAD UP AND GET YOUR EYES OFF HIS ASS!
ARE YOU ONE OF THOSE?! WELL, ARE YOU?! WHAT ARE YOU LOOK-
ING AT ME FOR...ARE YOU AFTER ME, AS WELL?! GET YOUR CROTCH
BACK, THAT MAN! YES, YOU! I'M LOOKING AT YOU! THERE'S NO
MONEY DOWN THERE, I PICKED IT UP LONG BEFORE YOU GOT HERE!
DID YOU SCRATCH YOUR CROTCH ON MY PARADE SQUARE?! YOU,
YOU HORRIBLE MAN, YOU LOOK LIKE A BLOODY BALLET DANCER!
YOU'RE TOO CLOSE TO THE MAN ON YOUR LEFT! HAVE YOU TWO
GOT SOMETHING GOING?! AM I HURTING YOU? I SHOULD BE, I'M
STEPPING ON YOUR HAIR! THE INSIDE MAN TURNS SLIGHTLY ON THE
WHEELS, I SAID SLIGHTLY! THAT MAN...YOUR FLY IS UNDONE...WHAT

ARE YOU LOOKING DOWN FOR?!"

When close to two-hundred cadets are shouting out drill 'comments,' it can be quite comical to say the least. Undoubtedly, the residents of Vernon heard Alpha Company that morning.

At lunch time, when the hoarse cadets of Alpha were *dismissed* outside B-33, Sergeant Beckford surprised the company.

"NOW, I HAPPEN TO KNOW THAT ALL OF YOU WANTED TO CON-TINUE DRILL MUTUALS WITH WEAPONS THIS AFTERNOON, BUT WE'VE CHANGED THE TIMETABLE."

Sounds of disappointment erupted from the ranks.

"INSTEAD OF THE PARADE SQUARE, THE COMPANY COMMANDER WITH THE BLESSING OF GENERAL KITCHING, HAS ORDERED..."

He paused and looked at the sweaty faces. "HAS ORDERED..."

All eyes and ears were on Sergeant Beckford. "THAT...YOU HAVE THE AFTERNOON AND THE EVENING OFF!"

More than a few pith-helmets were thrown into the air along with an outburst of jubilation.

"FOR THOSE OF YOU WHO WANT TO GO SWIMMING AT KINSMEN BEACH, TRUCKS WILL BE HERE AT 1430 HOURS. IF YOU WANT TO GO DOWNTOWN, YOU MAY DO SO!"

It wasn't a gas pain on the Sergeant's face; his smile mirrored the expressions of the people to his front.

"ALPHA COMPANY, ATTEN...TION! DIS...MISSED!"

Normally, the company would have turned smartly to its right, paused the necessary count of 'two-three,' and dispersed. This time, however, the silent count of two-three was dispensed with by the boys as they ran for the doors in celebration. It was exactly 12 noon.

Danyluk flopped on his bunk, as did the other Musketeers. "I TAKE IT BACK, I TAKE IT BACK...GENERAL KITCHING'S PARENTS *WERE* MAR-RIED, AND SO WERE MAJOR RATCLIFFE'S."

"You mean you won't mumble the word 'bastards' again?" asked Rothstein.

Douglas had his feet up against Wayne's mattress, giving him 'bumps' that nearly sent him flying. "YEAH, OR CREEPS, OR PONGOES?"

Danyluk had his hands behind his head. "NEVER AGAIN! THAT'S A PROMISE! AS FAR AS I'M CONCERNED, THOSE TWO GENTLEMEN ARE OFFICERS, NOT OCCIFERS. THEY WERE EDUCATED, NOT EDJUMI-CATED!"

As their two Regular Force Platoon Corporals walked through the barracks, Jackson heard one of them say, "He got two weeks confined to camp and he deserves it, the asshole."

"Hey, Corp," said Danyluk. "Are you talking about *our* Corporal Adams?"

Both Corporals sat down on Douglas's bunk. "You know about what happened?"

Moose walked over. "Yeah, we overheard the kitchen ladies. What occurred?"

One of the Corporals rubbed his hands together and smiled like a street merchant in Tangiers. "Well, Mr. Provost is confined to camp for two weeks. He couldn't remember leaving the Junior Ranks Club that night and he thinks some of the other guys in the Provost moved him next to the Nursing Sister. He says he didn't even know where their quarters were. The RSM agreed and defended him, otherwise General Kitching would have thrown the book at him."

"Is he mad?" Wayne asked.

"Naah, he's Miss Milquetoast. I think he'll tone down his attitude for the duration of camp."

"What did the Nursing Sister think of his sentence?" asked Cunningham.

As the Corporals got up to leave, one said, "She actually laughs at it now, but I don't think she's ever going to live it down with the others. They've nicknamed her, Lieutenant Cuddles."

Danyluk rubbed his crotch. "Jeez, I wouldn't mind cuddling up next to that one."

"You'll have a long wait," the Corporal said as he entered his cubicle. "The sisters have had double-locks put on their doors."

Danyluk motioned the group together and whispered, "Would Bergie leave it like this? Do you think he'd do anything else?"

"If I know Bergie..." offered East. "...and I think I do...he'd move the Nursing Sister next to Corporal Adams."

With nods and guffaws, their eyes met. The look of mischief on each of their faces was exciting. Douglas rested his arm on Wayne's shoulder. "You're out of your minds. We'd never get away with it...would we?"

Every cadet in Alpha Company decided to go swimming that afternoon. As usual, they would wear no underwear underneath their P.T. shorts. The dress was a white T-shirt, P.T. shorts, woolen socks, and running shoes. Their swim suits would be wrapped in their towels and they would change down at the beach.

Before the trucks arrived, Rothstein was standing next to Jackson's bunk discussing battle honours with Earl when Wayne passed.

"Jesus, Rothie, you stink to high Heaven, what the hell's the smell?"

Harvey shrugged. "What smell? I can't smell anything?"

Earl pinched his nose, too. "Now that you mention it, Wayne, Rothie - you smell like shit!"

Cunningham was next to East. "If you think Rothie smells like shit, come and get a whiff of East the Beast, here."

Wayne went over and took a whiff of East. "It's the same putrid smell. What the hell are you guys up to?"

Douglas got off his bunk and lifted up Rothstein and East's barrack box lid. He had to take a towel off a bunk to hold over his nose while he moved some clothes around inside the box. Although Rothstein's side was neat, at the bottom of East's side, there was enough rotting food to feed a platoon.

"Rothie, you've been bunking with East so long, you're actually getting accustomed to the stench that's originating from his side."

Rothstein looked at the bottom of East's side. "YOU CREEP, JACK! YOU TOLD ME YOU GOT RID OF ALL THAT FOOD! THAT'S THE REASON YOU CLOSE THE LID IN A HURRY, EH?"

Instantly, Rothstein took out his clothes, placed them on his bunk and dumped the remainder on Jack's bunk. "Christ, look at this. I thought the smell was coming from Danyluk's box."

"UP YOUR ASS, ROTHIE!" was Moose's response.

Since most cadets were outside waiting for the trucks, Danyluk picked up the box with the rotting food and took it to Two Platoon's area of the wing. With assistance from *seven* others, a switch was made quickly. Two cadets in the Royal Canadian Medical Corps had their clothes taken out of their box and neatly arranged exactly the way they were, in their *new box*. Even the combination lock, which had been left open and was probably the factor in making the *switch*, was left precisely as it was...unlocked, on top of the box.

Rothstein and East neatly filled up *their* clean new box, closed the lock and shook hands. "JACK, UNDERSTAND ME...NO MORE FOOD!" Harvey said adamantly.

"Bunk pally of mine, you have my promise!" replied East.

As it turned out, the Medical Corps cadets were not outside, they were in deep conversation in the drying room, taking their clothes off the line. The Musketeers, however, were outside when the duo's *new* box was opened.

One Medical Corps type was doing all the talking.

"So he said, 'Smith, you don't tie a bandage like that...also, never apply a dirty bandage, it's not healthy and...' Phew, who shit themselves? Probably those two Strathcona's across the aisle! Here come the trucks, we'll just dump our clothes in here and press 'em when we get back, alright?"

The other one pinched his nose as he closed the lock. "Yeah, I agree; let's get out of here. It smells like somebody died and decided to stick around out of spite."

Although Alpha Company was loaded with senior cadets, it's amazing how quickly some people forget the antics of years past. For example, Danyluk got wrapped up in a conversation with a couple of Loyal Edmonton Regiment cadets and had to be *assisted* to the front of the line when the trucks were being loaded. He had totally forgotten about the *show parade* which was about to happen. The other Musketeers ensured he had a seat, therefore he could participate without being *on stage*.

As was usual for the ride to Kin Beach, the three-tons headed down the main hill, turning left at the light by Polson Park. The drive to the beach would only take ten minutes, but for some cadets, that would be the longest period of their lives.

Singing started just as the trucks left camp. As the convoy turned left at the bottom of the hill, the Musketeers' truck's choir-group was working on a version of *Old King Cole*, when someone suddenly gave 'the signal.' In a fraction of a second, the cadets who were standing, holding on to the upper frame of the truck had their P.T. shorts whipped down, and then feet from the seated perpetrators were firmly planted in the crotches of the *downed* garments. The fact that the trucks were turning was part of the plan. Trying to cover themselves up, the half-nude cadets let go of the frame, but centrifugal force made them lose their balance. It was impossible for them to fight off the seated culprits' actions.

As vehicle after vehicle turned, the *nudie* shows were the highlight of the Vernon street. Amidst hollers from inside the trucks and hoots and whistles from the viewing public, pandemonium set in as the *moonies* were jostled from one side to the other, or from the tailgate to the cab.

A couple of Canadian Scottish cadets decided to *bare* it out and actually waved to the spectators. Others landed everywhere trying to hide themselves. At one point, Jackson turned his head quickly, trying to avoid the full frontal assault of a speeding crotch, only to lose his complete face in the middle of an accelerating set of a super-bliffy's very, very fat buttocks coming from the other direction. Those in his immediate vicinity actually saw him lose his head completely, and then when it did resurface, he was trying to spit out unseen hair. Whether he got rid of the hair is another question because when he turned his head again, he got an expeditiously advancing naked crotch in his face from which he couldn't escape because of the pushing and pressure from seated cadets on the other side. When *the crotch* was finally dispatched to someone else, Jackson's twisted face was again seen to be spitting out hairs.

If an announcer described the action of trucks full of near-naked, or in some cases, naked cadets, sitting on the laps of their fully clothed comrades, the scene would have attracted news cameras from around the world. Needless to say, Cadet Johnston's young *friend* from the train would certainly have had his mother concerned if her son enclosed pictures of the spectacle in his letter that described his newly acquired knowledge of what masturbation papers were.

Throughout the uproar, the songsters never missed a beat, nor left out any of the words of *Old King Cole*. Except for Jackson. Earl couldn't sing because of the hairs in his mouth.

After the trucks turned, activities became normal, with the exception of a few note-worthy quotes.

"HARLEY, YOU HOMO! I'LL GET YOU FOR THAT, YOU CREEP!"

"JESUS, THAT GIRL WAS ONLY ABOUT THREE FEET FROM THE TRUCK. SHE NEVER SAW MY FACE, SHE'LL JUST REMEMBER ME BY MY APPENDIX SCAR!"

"YOU FRUMP, ROTHSTEIN! THE LADY IN THE CAR BEHIND US TOOK PICTURES WITH HER MOVIE CAMERA. I CAN JUST SEE THE SCENE IN HER LIVING ROOM. BEFORE THEY DISCOVER IT'S AN ASS THEY'RE LOOKIN' AT, SOMEONE WILL SAY, 'THAT'S AN ODD LOOKING FACE!' 'YEAH, WE THOUGHT SO, TOO,' SHE'LL REPLY. 'HIS MOUTH RUNS FROM HIS FOREHEAD DOWN TO HIS CHIN.' AT WHICH, SOME-ONE ELSE WILL SAY, 'THE POOR BASTARD...HIS FACE WAS PROBABLY DEFORMED AT BIRTH!'"

As the trucks neared Kin Beach, anyone within earshot would have heard, *"MY EYES ARE DIM, I CANNOT SEE, I HAVE NOT GOT MY SPECS WITH ME! I HAVE, NOT, GOT, MY SPECS, WITH, ME!"*

After they were unloaded, Alpha Company formed up in three ranks in front of what the Musketeers called, 'Danyluk's Bird Shacks.' After an open order march, all cadets took off their running shoes, socks, and T-shirts and then they were fallen out to change into their swimming suits. When they had changed, they put their P.T. shorts and towels with the remainder of their clothing. This was done so the staff would know if someone was missing when the cadets were told to get dressed.

The Company Sergeant-Major, WO2 Rose, made it quite clear what he wanted to see. "THERE ARE NO LIFE GUARDS ON DUTY, SO YOU WILL USE THE BUDDY SYSTEM. WHEN YOU HEAR A WHISTLE, HOLD UP YOUR BUDDY'S HAND! NOW GET IN THERE AND HAVE SOME FUN!"

As usual, there were only about two or three other people at the beach. When the cadets were fallen out, these tourists or residents must have thought the noise was a volcano erupting. The normally quiet north end of Okanagan Lake was alive and its visitors made the most of the wonderfully refreshing welcome, the lake unselfishly offered.

Within minutes, the couple who operated the small private beverage stand opened up for business and it wasn't long before a lineup had started. Even though the pop truck would arrive around 1500 hours, the cadets of Alpha Company couldn't drink enough, and in East's case, couldn't eat enough.

That afternoon was sheer delight for the company and all company staff. Even Major Ratcliffe and his officers and NCOs participated in splashing fights, but usually lost.

When it was nearly time to leave, most cadets were just lying on the grass. They were smeared in suntan lotion, so five minutes before changing, they rushed into the water for one more cool, invigorating swim.

"IT'S TOO BAD THE GIRLS AREN'T HERE!" Wayne said, tossing a diving Rothstein over his shoulder.

"WE DIDN'T KNOW, DID WE?" replied Danyluk with Simon on his shoulders. They were having a horse fight with East and (spitter) Jackson. "EARL, YOU SHOULD HAVE KEPT YOUR EARS TO THE GROUND. HOW COME YOU DIDN'T KNOW ABOUT THE CHANGE IN THE TIMETABLE?"

"HEY, MOOSE, I CAN ONLY FIND OUT SO MUCH! WHAT DO YOU THINK I AM...SUPER CADET?"

As Moose's *rider* was wrenched off his *horse*, Moose yelled, "YEAH, WE DO!"

When it was time to leave, Danyluk perused *his* changing rooms with a long lost look in his eyes. "I'll never forget the time Gardiner caught me up that tree taking pictures of the old ladies in there. Jesus, he must have thought I was some kind of an evil sex fiend?"

"You made money, didn't ya? I've still got one of those pictures," Wayne replied. "Are you going to do it this year?"

Moose put on his sneaky grin. "Yeah, but I'm going to wait until the Vernon Girl's band is here. I want to catch the base drummer who doesn't wear any panties."

Wayne faced Danyluk and put a hand on each of his shoulders. "For God sakes, why her? When dames are in there, none of them have got panties on. It'll be like smorgasbord!"

Danyluk's face lit up with a devilish smile. "HEY, I'VE NEVER BEEN TO *SMORGASBORG*, BUT YOUSE IS RIGHT! I CAN CATCH THEM ALL!"

"Ya got that right," said East.

"But this time if *he* arrives, we keep Mr. Gardiner, busy...right?"

Banks thought for a moment. "Do I get ten percent?"

Danyluk scratched his head. "YEAH, O.K.! A LITTLE HIGH, BUT O.K.!"

"You bet we'll keep him busy. Real busy!" replied Wayne, rubbing his hands together.

A few hours at Kin Beach can work wonders for weary cadets. The Alpha Company which left camp a few hours earlier, certainly wasn't the company that arrived back. The songs were more spirited and each truck's chorus was louder than ever when they passed the Provost Shack, singing a verse of:

"OH PROVOST, OH PROVOST, SOMETHING WENT WRONG!
WHEN YOUR PARENTS WERE SCREWING AND YOU CAME ALONG!
YOUR DAD TOOK A PISS BREAK AND WENT TO THE BOG! SO YOUR
MOTHER CONCLUDED THE TASK WITH THE DOG!"

As usual, when the Provost Sergeant appeared, the *singing* instantly ceased and all he saw were the squeaky clean faces of a revitalized Alpha Company.

The Company Sergeant Major didn't fall them in when the three-tons stopped outside of B-33, he just bellowed, "YOU'RE NOT ON THE PARADE SQUARE TONIGHT, SO JUST HAVE A GOOD EVENING! IF YOU GO DOWNTOWN, ENSURE YOU'RE BACK BY 2100 HOURS!"

Although they weren't on the square that night, they still had to prepare their kit. The minute the cadets entered the building, it came alive with activity. With a half-hour to go before supper, B-33's inhabitants ironed, washed, polished, showered, wrote letters, turned up their radios, squirted the fire extinguishers, practised drill with the brooms, used their wash basins as drums, snapped their towels at each other, and those in the lower bunks kicked the upper springs, trying to eject their *partners*.

Cunningham, of course, took no part in any of these activities. He was too busy *guiding* a game of poker in Two Platoon's area of the wing. As a matter of fact, not too far from the Medical Corps cadets with the new barrack box. This gave him the opportunity to hear the *cheery* interchange of accusations. The criticism started in the set of bunks next to the medical-types. The two cadets there were with the Loyal Edmonton Regiment.

The lower cadet kicked the upper's springs. "Larry, if I've told you once, I've told you a thousand times, if you need to take a shit, get it over with. If this keeps up, you'll have to sew your ass together before you reach the jon. You're the only person I know that can shit himself, smile, and read a comic at the same time."

His bunkmate jumped down. "What the hell are you talking about? It's not me that stinks, it's one of those Kong's Own Chinese Rifles cadets across the aisle. Either them or those two Lord Strath cadets." (Lord Strathcona's Horse [Royal Canadians] - LdSH [RC].) He pointed at a set of bunks. "HEY, YOU! DON'T YOU THINK YOU'D BETTER MAKE A TRIP BEFORE THE SMELL ALARM GOES OFF?"

The King's Own Calgary Regiment cadet was lying on his bunk reading a letter from home. He didn't hear the comment thrown in his direction, so *Larry*, became louder.

"HEY, KONG'S OWN, OR WHATEVER YA CALL YOURSELVES. IF YOU'RE GONNA TO TAKE A SHIT, USE THE JON, WILL YA? WHAT DID YOU DO, SHIT IN YOUR TOWEL DOWN AT THE BEACH?"

The letter writer put down his pen, stood up, and took a few whiffs. His upper bunk partner took some sniffs as well, and replied: "LEAVE IT TO A LOATHSOME EUNUCH'S RECTUM (referring to the Loyal Edmonton Regiment) TO HAVE HIS NOSE UP HIS ASS! THERE'S NO SMELL OVER HERE, BUDDY, IT'S ALL COMING FROM YOUR DIRECTION!"

Quickly, following their noses, twenty or so cadets walked the immediate area trying to discover the source of the smell. It didn't take long for them to determine that the foul odor was originating from the medical cadets' box, which was open. One of the medical-types must have taken something out hastily and not noticed the stench. Actually, the two *doctors* were oblivious to it all. They were still discussing bandages.

"No, no, no, James, you bend the elbow before you unwind the dressing on it. If the arm is straight, the gauze would come loose."

"But Jonathan, old boy, I'm the one who's becoming a doctor, I should know if..."

He was interrupted by a voice. "HEY, YOU, DOC! YOU WON'T HAVE TOO

MANY PATIENTS IF YOU KEEP SHITTING IN YOUR BARRACK BOX!"

Jonathan stood up. "What *are* you talking about? James, what *is* he talking about? Leave us alone, we're busy!"

Now James got to his feet. "Yes, please leave us alone and take your frightful fragrance with you. Now, Jonathan, as I was saying before we were so rudely inte..."

"LISTEN DOC, THAT FRIGHTFUL FRAGRANCE YOU'RE REFERRING TO IS SHIT, AND IT'S COMING FROM YOUR BARRACK BOX! EVERY-ONE'S EYES ARE WATERING BECAUSE OF IT! NOW, EITHER DUMP IT OUT, OR WE'LL DO IT FOR YOU AND THROW IN A REGIMENTAL SHOWER, TO BOOT!"

James walked to his barrack box. "My good man, if you think that odor is orig-inating from...CHRIST, JONATHAN, WHAT THE HELL HAVE *YOU* PUT IN HERE?"

Jonathan rushed over and hastily took out his clothes. His side of the box was clean.

Jonathan's highbrow attitude changed instantly. "DON'T TRY AND PUT THE BLAME ON ME, YOU POLISHED PRICK! UGH, I CAN'T STAND IT!"

A red-faced James took out his clothes, but had great difficulty removing the ones from the bottom because they were stuck to a gelatinous mess of rotting food. The maggots were an extra attraction.

"YOU BASTARD, JONATHAN, YOU'VE SET ME UP BECAUSE I BEAT YOU ON THE FIRST-AID EXAMINATION AND ACCUSED YOU OF NEVER TAKING A SHOWER! HOW COULD YOU DO THIS TO YOUR BEST FRIEND?"

"I SET *YOU* UP? YOU SAY I SET *YOU* UP? LISTEN YOU CREEP, DON'T TRY YOUR REVERSE PSYCHOLOGY SHIT ON ME! YOU'RE THE ONE WHO WETS THE BED! WHY I WOULDN'T...!"

Jonathan never got the chance to complete his statement. Both he and James were lifted off their feet, fighting, kicking and screaming all the way to the shower room.

Hastily, they were both stripped, *sudsed-up* with Sergeants' Soap, and scrubbed with good old military-style scrub brushes. All of their clothes were tossed in the shower with them and their barrack box was taken over to another hut and *exchanged* for a new, unlocked box. Needless to say, the other hut was empty because everyone was over having supper, and no one noticed the switch.

Although the gooey mess was gone, the stench remained as articles of clothing were removed from the clean box and neatly placed in exactly the same position inside the *old* one.

Undoubtedly, a regimental shower would be coming up for the *new owners* in that hut as well. No one cared where the original box ended up, but it would cer-tainly make the rounds that night.

Throughout the barrack box riot, the Musketeers were joyfully dining, dis-cussing the great afternoon they had had at the beach. When Cunningham came into the mess hall and told them what had happened to the *recipients* of East and Rothstein's barrack box, they became even more jovial.

Danyluk pointed his fork at East. "Jack, we saved your ass today."

East swallowed his mouthful of food quickly, stood up and raised his glass.

"WELL, WE'RE MUSKETEERS, AIN'T WE? IT'S ONE FOR ALL, AND ALL

FOR ONE! UP THE MUSKETEERS!"

The other seven stood up for the toast. "UP THE MUSKETEERS!"

They were even joined by their two Canadian Scottish friends who assisted them with the *night move* of Corporal Adams. "UP YER KILTS!" one toasted. Nine cadets rose and joined him in that toast as well. The words, "UP YER KILTS!" rang out throughout the mess hall.

It had been decided at supper that since all of their kit was done, the group of them would head downtown for the evening. Alma's parents were away for a few days so she offered the use of her basement for a dance. Moose didn't like the idea at first, because he wanted Alma to himself. A dance sounded like a good idea though, so he quickly relented. The two Canadian Scottish Regiment cadets were invited too.

"Just make sure you bring your own chicks," said Wayne. "We know how girls get *attracted* to ya!"

When they entered Alma's big, rambling old house, each Musketeer took off his headdress, webbelt, boots, puttees and hose tops. This left them in shorts, shirts, and heavy socks. As usual, the Canadian Scottish cadets were wearing their kilts. They removed their headdress, shoes, sporrans, spats, and hose tops.

Alma knew how to play the part of the perfect hostess. Her ice-box was loaded with pop and goodies and she had arranged card and patio tables, each with two chairs, in a semi-circle around a make-shift dance floor. All of the lights were turned out and each table had a small, lit candle in the middle. Her record player had a stack of 45s on it and her choice of music was impressive. The basement was large and dark and the glow of the candles produced a romantic setting.

Whispers filled the room as each hand-holding couple looked into each other's eyes and courted. Yes, they were all locked in their own little world - even Cunningham. He had asked for an extra candle so he could show his girl how to shuffle a deck of cards with one hand. As the evening progressed though, he introduced her to black-jack and she had to keep looking for her purse. It didn't matter who she was, when the *master* was teaching, it took money to learn properly.

Although the camp on the hill was only a mile-and-a-half away, it could have been on another planet as far as they were concerned.

Throughout the evening, couples disappeared for awhile and then reappeared holding hands, giggling, and bashfully gazing into each other's eyes. Moose and Alma didn't disappear however. Like her, Moose wore a bartender's apron and helped her continuously, supplying pop, potato chips, sandwiches and cake. When someone called for a waiter, Moose was there. Even when East snapped his fingers, Moose was there with the food, and East's fingers were nearly broken off.

When it was nearly time to leave and they were dancing to *Ebb Tide*, Diane touched on the subject of Red Robinson.

"We'll have to get into the lineup an hour early because people are coming from Kamloops, Kelowna, and Penticton. The whole valley wants to see Red Robinson. Rumors are going around that there won't be room enough, but I think they'll let everyone in. He's a pretty popular guy, isn't he?"

Douglas was dying to tell her about Red's reply, but he daren't.

"He's not just good, he's great! It was Red who changed the whole music scene in British Columbia. Like everyone else in Vancouver, Wayne and I rush home after school to tune him in. He's visited our school for a sock hop and when kids phone him, he actually puts them on the air. He plays pranks on the phone and his antics are hilarious. Everyone's buying Seven-Up because they sponsor his show."

"How old is he?" Diane asked.

"I think he's about the same age as us; maybe younger or a year older, and he's sure got it together. His choice of music is mint!"

"Will Moose introduce you and I to him?"

Douglas chuckled. "I don't think there's any doubt about that. We'd never forgive Moose if he didn't. Speaking of the devil, here he comes now."

Moose turned on the lights and stood on a chair. "O.K., YOUSE GUYS, IT'S THAT TIME...CLOSING TIME, LADIES AND GENTLEMEN, PLEASE!"

A few disgruntled comments were thrown in his direction.

"HEY, I DON'T WANT THIS TO END EITHER, BUT IT'S 2030 HOURS; FOR THE BENEFIT OF YOUSE CANADIAN SCOTTISH, THAT MEANS EIGHT-THIRTY!"

"Up yours, Moose," came a response from a *kilter*. Everyone laughed at his comment.

Since all of the girls were staying overnight at Alma's, good-byes and thanks took five minutes, and another five minutes were taken getting dressed. Getting back to the camp, would require a good twenty minutes

Heading up the hill in pairs, Simon said, "That was one of the best nights I've ever had. Can we do it again?"

"Yeah, but at someone else's house," offered Moose. "I was run off my feet all night. I never got the chance to sneak Alma in the bedroom."

East couldn't take that. "BULL SHIT, MOOSE! EVERY TIME I WAS IN THE KITCHEN YOU WERE AT HER!"

East was marching in front of Danyluk, so Moose kicked Jack's right boot when it was back, making him trip slightly. "I HAD TO STAY IN THE KITCHEN TO KEEP YOU AND YOUR DAME OUT OF THE ICE-BOX. WOULD YOU BELIEVE ALMA MADE SANDWICHES TO FEED FIFTY AND WE ACTUALLY RAN OUT OF THEM! JESUS, JACK, IT'S A WONDER YOUR STOMACH DOESN'T REVOLT! ALSO, YOUR BROAD NEARLY ATE ALL THE CAKES!"

Jack laughed. "She needs nutrition, too."

Moose gave him another *trip*. "YOU CAN SAY THAT AGAIN!"

Jack kept marching but turned around and repeated, "SHE NEEDS NUTRITION TOO."

Rothstein had been quiet most of the night, but his face was full of lipstick. "Where's that CScotR?" he said, looking back. "Oh there you are. I know it was dim in that room and you had your own table, but did you have to sit facing us with your legs open? My girl had her eyes on your crotch all night."

"I know," the kilted one replied with a fiendish grin. "Them's the breaks."

"Next time wear your shorts!"

The other Scot got into the act. "We don't wear our gaunch when we're out with the dames."

"You got that right," replied Jackson. "Did you see this guy when he sat down? His chair caught the back of his kilt and lifted it up. For the next thirty minutes, we had his bare ass facing us. He just left it that way until he got up for a dance."

"We call it air conditioning," the Scot retorted.

All of them were in cheery conversation as they passed the guardroom. This time they weren't *observed* because the door was closed.

When they entered B-33, life went back to normal immediately. In addition to a chorus coming from the shower room, the washing machine was whining, pillow fights were ongoing, all toilets were flushing, barrack box lids were being slammed shut, the fire extinguishers were gushing, cadets were screaming, jumping from bunk to bunk, ironing, starching and soaping was taking place everywhere, cadets with drum sticks were using their wash basins, and upper bunk partners were being kicked up into the air. Building B-33 was normal, but not in one set of bunks. Two very scrubbed-red and clean-looking Medical Corps cadets were trying to solve their differences as they ironed their kit.

"Well, if it wasn't you, Jonathan, who did that to us?"

"I don't know, James, but if I catch the bastards, I'll have their nuts. I'm sorry I called you a bet-wetter."

"Oh, that's all right, Jonathan, I apologize for accusing you of not taking showers."

With a whisper, Jonathan said, "I've got a feeling it was those two Royal Winnipeg Rifles types. Ever since I *borrowed* the large one's pen, he's been giving me dirty looks. We'll have to get our own back, eh what?"

As the two shook hands, James whispered, "We'll wait until they're tired and give 'em the old jock-itch ointment on their balls...what say?"

"Sounds good to me, James, and we'll have to get the rest of these pongoes as well. I've never felt so humiliated in my life getting a regimental shower. If they think they've heard the last of the Royal Canadian Medical Corps, they're dead wrong. Now tell me about those dressings again."

"Well, they have to be kept clean. You see they're originally sterilized by the manufacturer and..."

After the lights were turned out, Douglas lay on top of his bedclothes with his hands behind his head. A big bright full moon lit up Wayne's face as he leaned over.

"Did you stay in the basement all night?"

Douglas nodded. "Yeah, you can say we danced the night away. How about you and Debbie?"

"Well, er, yes, to a point. There was an old fold-out bed in the laundry room."

Douglas grinned. "So you had fun, eh?"

"Wayne dangled a pair of panties. "It could have been better. We had to share it with one of those damned Scots and his girl. He had his kilt up over his head and was bare ass to the breeze. I betcha he's got scratches all over his ass."

"So why should that bother you?"

"It didn't bother me, but I kept having trouble keeping Debbie's attention. We were so cramped, at one point I lifted his hand off Debbie's ass."

Douglas sat up. "You did what?"

"Well Debbie said to me, 'Wayne, just how many hands have you got?' I said, 'Listen, Mac, what the hell are you up to? Isn't one ass enough for you?'"

"What did he say?" Douglas asked.

"He and his girl just giggled and he said, 'Sorry about that, it's so tight on here, I thought it was Francene's ass.' That's the name of his chick."

Douglas couldn't believe it. "Jeez, what nerve!"

"Nerve isn't the word for it. At one point, we were so tightly wrapped together, when Debbie and I turned over, the back of my hand actually *brushed* against his bare ass."

Douglas quickly sat up again. "YOU WHAT? DID HE DO ANYTHING?"

Wayne snickered. "You won't believe it. He said, 'That feels nice, but if you think you're going to get a kiss, you're out of your mind.' All four of us broke up. He's not a bad guy. I'll tell ya, those CScotRs have sure got it made. Good night, Doug."

"You'll have to get yourself a kilt. G'night Wayne."

Before he drifted off to sleep, Douglas tilted his head back and gazed at the giant orange globe in the sky. Even the man in the moon was smiling.

On Tuesday morning, the Musketeers were up and their beds were made when Sergeant Simpson stomped in, started turning over mattresses and bellowed, "STAND BY YOUR BEDS! YOU'VE GOT TWO MINUTES TO FORM THREE RANKS ON THE ROAD! C'MON, MOVE IT! MOVE IT! YOU, YES YOU! RELEASE YOUR FUTURE WIFE'S PLAYTHING AND GET THAT PILLOW OFF YOUR BODY. OKAY YOU PEOPLE, GET YOUR MIND OUT OF THE GUTTERS AND YOUR ASSES ON THE ROAD!"

Although the course finished at noon on Thursday, the balance of that week was three of the toughest days the cadets of Alpha Company ever experienced. In addition to drill mutuals and more drill mutuals, practical and theoretical training increased on all subjects, especially Leadership and Man-Management. Leadership Techniques in particular were laid on hot and heavy. The cadets had to review and learn these.

1. Leadership by objectives and results.
2. Job enrichment.
3. Organizational development, not overdose.
4. How to get the word through the system.
5. Ringing the Bell-Shaped curve.
6. The delegation decision, key to success.
7. Team building. Same club, same ball, same ballpark, same game.
8. It's obvious that the problem, isn't. Problem identification and solving.
9. Effective decision making.
10. The management of time.
11. A job is what you do with your days: A career is what you do with your life.
12. Who am I really. Personal leadership assessment.
13. Creating organization change. How to turn things around.

All day Wednesday, Alpha Company was given a bit of a break as the cadets walked the area known as Glenemma, a military field-training area north of Vernon. The land was leased by the government from the Okanagan Indian Band. There, they received refreshment lectures and exercises on Map Using, Bivouacking, Marching At Night, Section and Platoon Tactics, Survival In The Field, and Field Economy. Two TEWTs (Tactical Exercise Without Troops) were held.

There were some funny moments when the Musketeers passed the famous latrine areas where Danyluk, Jackson and eventually Bergie, went for a *dip.*

For the past three years, Glenemma had been a special place for all of these boys. Other than the camp, it was their second home away from home.

The sunburnt dusty plains of Glenemma are situated between two lush-green mountains. At times, the temperature in the open can soar over a hundred, however, at the northern end, there are large stands of trees that can reduce the heat by at least 20 degrees, beneath their branches. These areas were used for bivouacking the companies of cadets.

Although there are a few lakes within the Glenemma boundary, only Round Lake at the southern end of the plains was used for swimming. Water for drinking and washing utensils and clothes was always trucked in.

Many happy memories raced through the minds of the original Musketeers as they explored the region. Wayne and Douglas even found the cabin they visited in 1953. That year, they had *borrowed* a lantern, and that action alone had started a new friendship between the Natives of the reserve and the seven boys. So far, this year, only Earl had looked up Mr. Brewer, the lantern's owner. Although he didn't have the time to visit him, he telephoned once or twice and passed along everyone's best wishes. Mr. Brewer didn't live in the cabin any longer, it was locked. He had moved closer to the village on the portion of the reserve located on the east side of the western tongue at the north end of Okanagan Lake.

Not too much was said as the Musketeers boarded the trucks to leave Glenemma. If they had their way, they would spend their whole summer here. After all, Glenemma was the place where boys could be boys. Clothes didn't have to be pressed, or even washed, for that matter. They could swim, as Danyluk would say, "Bare balls at the lake," and at night, a billion stars lit up the plains, and a giant friendly moon would go to sleep with them.

Soon, however, the Musketeers would be returning to the area for a week with other companies whose cadets would be just as energetic as they were during their first year.

At 1100 hours on Thursday, Major Ratcliffe taught the company, Leadership Technique Number 14. 'The World's Worst-Kept Secret: How to change every single person you know.'

The large hangar, B-3, was used for this *company* period, and it was cool inside as their Officer Commanding stood on the stage.

"Now, each of you, whether you know it or not, is sending out a not-so-subtle message to everyone else. The message you're sending is, why isn't everything changed to accommodate me? By 'me,' I mean *you*. If it were changed, then you could be happy and comfortable. And if others allowed this to happen to you, you could lead a very relaxed, if not boring life."

Danyluk whispered to Jackson, "Bull shit! The world would be my oyster if everything was changed to accommodate me. We sure as hell wouldn't be bored, eh, Earl?"

Earl was intently listening to the officer and shrugged Moose off as Major Ratcliffe continued.

"But the forgotten fact is, that everyone is sending out the same message, and that message is, '*You* change to meet *my* needs.' Can you imagine that? Every single one of you wants everyone else to change to meet your personal needs.

"Well, I'm going to let you in on what I call, the world's worst-kept secret. How you and you alone, can change every single person you know.

"After I tell you this *secret*, you may say, 'You got that idea from, Christ, Buddha, Mohammed, Aristotle, or Confucius?' Actually I didn't, I got it from Professor Lin Bothwell's book. Maybe Professor Bothwell got it from them, I don't know?"

Smiles and grins accompanied the chuckles from the eager cadets sitting in front of the officer. They were listening to every word that came from his mouth and they wanted to know this worst-kept secret.

Wayne was sitting with the rest of One Platoon in the first few rows of seats, when he held up his hand.

"Yes...Banks?"

"Sir, why call it a secret if all those people knew about it?"

The major smiled. "Good point! That's the question all of us should be asking. If those people used the secret in one form or another, then it really isn't a secret, is it? But you see, it is, because if so few people use this information which they know to be true, then it must be a secret. You'll see what I mean in a minute. You *all* know the rule, but do you follow it?

"First, I want all of you to look at yourselves. The foremost thing you notice about yourself is that you are a very well-rounded individual."

Danyluk held up his hand.

"Yes...Danyluk?"

"Sir, I know some people who aren't well rounded!"

Major Ratcliffe walked down the stairs and over to Danyluk. "I think I know some, too. But maybe their opinion of themselves is that they are well rounded. We're not all the same, though!"

Cunningham whispered to Simon, "He can say that again. Moose isn't the same as everyone else. If we were like him, our brains would be in the wrong head."

The officer remained off the stage, to the front of his audience.

"Now you will learn to change everyone you know. But why would you want to change strangers? What does it mean to know someone? It simply means to have a relationship with someone. What does it mean to have a relationship with someone? It means that your life and that other person's life overlap. Look at the people you're involved with. You're involved with your parents, your girlfriends, your fellow cadets, all your other relatives, your officers, your NCOs, etc., the list is never-ending. You share a bit of yourself with all of them, and they in turn share themselves with you.

"Now for the rule. All of you know the secret so well, you can complete the sentence yourself. 'The way that you change every single person you know is to...?'"

The officer placed his hands in such a manner that he wanted to hear it from everyone. When he raised his hands, most of the cadets answered, "CHANGE YOURSELF!"

Ratcliffe nodded and smiled. He had his audience in the palms of his hands.

"Exactly right. I'm proud of you. Now let's see why this is true. I call it interaction. You share yourself with everyone you want to, and so do those people. Therefore, when you're sending, you're also receiving. Each of you is influenced by the other. If you are not influenced, then you're not mortal. Do you understand what I am saying? A piece of those people rubs off on you, and a piece of you rubs off on them, as well."

Most cadets understood. Those who didn't, asked a nearby friend and then usually started nodding.

"So you see, to be able to change people is to be able to influence them. In an interpersonal sense, there is no such thing as unilateral influence. If we send out the change message, 'I'm O.K., you're just a jerk!' people will tune you out and turn you off. But if you open up to *their* influence, they will open themselves up to *your* influence. If they feel you are closed to them, they will feel closed to you. Simple, isn't it?"

A cadet from the Queen's Own Rifles held up his hand.

"Yes...Stuart?"

"Yes, sir...er, then we should listen and talk to everyone, regardless if he or she is a real dolt?"

Major Ratcliffe's face was serious. "Yes, no one's perfect. Everyone has something to offer. There has to be intercourse."

Up to this point, Moose had been falling asleep. He was now wide awake with his hand in the air.

"Yes, Danyluk."

"Sir, youse might think this is weird, but if we go around screwing every chick that's got a problem...I mean, don't youse think that would be a little unfair?"

The laughter didn't faze Danyluk one bit. He was sincere. "We're supposed to influence them into screwing us? It's not that I wouldn't participate, but ain't it unfair? Also, what about the guys? After we influence them, what do we do then, go out and get some dame to muff 'em? We could run out of broads."

All of Alpha Company, including officers and NCOs, were bent over in laughter. Their Company Commander even found it hard to answer the series of questions, he was laughing so loud. Not Moose, though. His look of pure innocence was real and that made matters even more hilarious. His next statement nearly had everyone on the floor.

"I didn't think I'd like this here theoretical leadership stuff, but Christ, if we get laid every time we influence someone, I'm all for it. Youse can count me in, sir. My dad was in the army but he never mentioned this. This course ain't just mint, it's real George."

It took a good minute for everyone to get back to normal. Actually, they needed a good laugh about that time, but no one thought it would come from a cadet who totally misunderstood his instructor.

Major Ratcliffe threw his chalk into the air and caught it. "No, Danyluk, you're not understanding me correctly. I was talking about verbal intercourse, not the kind you're referring to."

"Damn," was Danyluk's response. "I thought it was too good to be true. Er, sorry, sir."

Alpha's Company Commander waited another minute for other comments and laughter to die down before he continued.

"There is a most common failure in training subordinates and it has to be stopped. If you send a message that says, 'I'm perfect; you're messed up, I'm going to straighten you out,' the other party will usually join a group that has been turned off before and then learn the wrong things through a process of mutual influence within that group.

"The secret of greatness, in terms of personal growth and the influence you can have on others, is the realization that you have something to learn from others - all others. You will notice I said, *all others*."

Douglas held up his hand.

"Yes...Brice?"

"Then sir, if we've got some real trouble-makers on our hands, we must *begin* by accepting them as they are? We *have to* accept them?"

"Yes, you must. When people feel accepted, they feel free to learn, adapt, grow, and change. If they're not accepted, they feel the need to retrench, to defend, to counterattack. If your attitude is one of, 'I'm damn well going to straighten you out,' very little listening or changing will follow."

Someone said, "That's kind of rough, sir. What if the guy has really pulled a dirty one, wouldn't it just be right to hammer him?"

The Major thought for a moment before he answered the question.

"I know what you mean, it is tough. No, physical violence should only be used when it is used against you; at the very last resort, if at all. What is required is that you send that terribly difficult message that says, 'I appreciate you and accept you as a person, and because I appreciate you, I cannot accept what you've done.'"

The O.C., acknowledged another waving hand.

"Sounds kinda mamby-pamby to me, sir. If we start acting like goody-two-shoes people, we won't get *any* respect."

Ratcliffe nodded. He knew he was conversing with teenagers.

"Listen, we're not talking about people who fit into the norm. Your job as a leader is to be able to influence *everyone*. How do you get respect? By demanding it, right?"

The cadet said, "No, I don't think so. If you do that, then you end up bullying them."

"Exactly. You get respect by giving respect. If you try to *take* their respect and hang on to it, you'll lose it. How do you get others to care for you? By caring for them. How do you get others to listen to you? By listening to them. Lao-tzu also said, 'To lead the people, you must walk behind them.' Perhaps he meant that you get others to serve you by serving them. Your people will follow you, only if you follow them. Remember, you can lead from a distance. On this course you've learned many examples of how to lead. The direct approach isn't necessarily always the best approach. Are there any other questions? No, well please let me sum up."

The officer covered all of his points and reiterated, "Whatever message you send out, others will come back in kind. You give indifference; you get indifference. You give hate; you get hate back. You give love; you receive love."

Moose cocked his head and whispered to Jackson, "Now he's on my wave length again."

"Not mine," Earl replied. "I give love, then I get my face smacked."

"It must happen," stated Major Ratcliffe. "This law of human relations is as inexorable as the law of gravity. But don't think it always works perfectly. The law is such that if you send out respect, you will receive respect back. Sometimes it does not necessarily work one-on-one. The other person might respond in a non-reciprocal way. You will find, however, that it usually works well one-on-one. There will be times when you send out a quart of respect and only get a pint back. But what's the alternative? I want you to ponder that. Also, some of you may think this method is somewhat irrational for use in the forces. Well, it may well be that in wartime, but this is peacetime and I would like to think that the Canadian Army is democratic, not autocratic.

"We're all human beings, fellas. If I may quote Sergeant Beckford: 'If you put your hand in a bucket of water and there's a hole in the water when you take it out, then you're perfect, you don't need any help whatsoever.' Did I get that right, Sergeant?"

Sergeant Beckford was at the rear of the company. He smiled. "Thank you. Near enough, sir."

"Remember, to change others, you must change yourself. You influence others by letting them influence you. To change a person, you must accept them as they are. And you get what you give away.

"Now I want to read you a direct quote from Professor Lin Bothwell:

'Your head will tell you no. Your heart will tell you yes. I'm not afraid to state these principles, because they really work. You can find out the truth, either way. If you don't like the approaches outlined here, try influencing others unilaterally; try changing others without accepting them; try demanding and keeping respect, attention, love. The history of the race is replete with the documented failures of these other approaches.'

'If you would change the world, first change the one part of that world you have most control over - yourself. You will start a revolution with eternal repercussions.'"

The room was quiet after the Major finished reading Professor Bothwell's text. The cadets understood the message and were thinking about it.

Slowly, Major Ratcliffe scanned the faces in front of him. "Are there any other questions?"

There was silence. This was their last period of leadership and it had been the best. In three weeks they had learned a tremendous amount of valuable material that would last them for the rest of their lives. Many cadets were gazing proudly at their Senior NCOs and officers. They now knew more than ever what process these gentlemen had been using. At first they thought perhaps some of these methods had been especially designed for training cadets. Not true! They quite obviously knew the Canadian Army used these techniques, *to train 'a team' of individuals. Not robots or yes-men.*

"NOW, HOW MANY OF YOU READ ORDERS THIS MORNING?"

Most cadets held up their hands.

"GOOD, THEN YOU KNOW YOU'VE GOT THIS AFTERNOON OFF TO STUDY FOR YOUR EXAMS TOMORROW MORNING. TOMORROW AFTERNOON, WE WILL LIST THE RESULTS AND INFORM YOU OF WHICH COMPANY AND PLATOON YOU WILL BE POSTED TO. YOU WILL JOIN THAT COMPANY TOMORROW AFTERNOON."

A hand went up. "Sir, er, then we're not the guard for this Saturday morning's inspection?"

A lost smile formed on the Major's lips. "No, Cadet Morris, you've outgrown that now, son. Bravo Company will form the guard for the next three weeks, as well as the Graduation Parade. All of our Sergeants will form a drill cadre and they will now train Bravo Company. The next time we formally form up as a company will be on the final Graduation Parade.

"There's a lot I want to say to you and I feel certain your Platoon Officers and Sergeants wish to do the same. I'll be speaking with you tomorrow morning after your inspection, and tonight I'll be in your barracks talking with individuals. I'm very proud of all of you. To say the least, I'll miss you, and the other companies of Camp Vernon are most fortunate to have you join them. Each of you has worked very hard over these past three weeks. This is my first time working with cadets, and I sincerely hope it isn't my last. My officers and NCOs have certainly dished it out, but you unquestionably ate it up. There were times when I thought you might choke, but you didn't. I might have heard a few coughs, but not one of you gagged."

Although a few smiles appeared, Major Ratcliffe's somber mood was contagious. The cadets in Alpha Company thought the same way because they were now splitting up. Alpha was a team. Oh sure, there were differences, but Alpha was a team. Even the cadets in the Royal Canadian Medical Corps were in accord. They were part of a close-knit crew, but they planned to make their move this very night.

As the company was called to attention when Major Ratcliffe and his officers left, he said, "I'M VERY PROUD OF YOU INDEED! THANK YOU!"

After lunch, the cadets of B-33 felt a little different. The feeling they had was almost as if it was the last day of camp, which of course, it wasn't. In three weeks, they had completed what was normally a six-week course. Now, they were supposedly ready to show their *stuff* to the younger *soldiers* at the camp.

In a way, this wasn't new to the BCR Musketeers because while they had remained in cadets, they had also joined the British Columbia Regiment (DCO) and as such, they were in both the militia and cadets at the same time. When they joined the regiment, the Regimental Sergeant-Major, RSM Pat Patterson, knew the importance of their previous training; therefore he used them to assist and train others in the recruit wing. Training others their own age or older gave Brice, Banks, Danyluk, East, and Cunningham an edge that would come in handy when they encountered the fourteen-year-olds who were waiting for them like elementary and high school kids wait for student teachers.

Building B-33 was peaceful that afternoon. Although the hut was full, the fire-extinguishers stood in their usual places; no one was drumming on wash basins, no cadets were running over the tops of bunks, or in and out of the windows, the shower room wasn't full, the washing machine wasn't whining, barrack box lids were silent, brooms weren't used for rifle drill, circuit breakers weren't popping, and upper bunk inhabitants didn't feel the feet of their partner below. The mood was mature as the squeaky clean, recently showered cadets lay on their bunks studying or writing letters home. When a kitchen girl from the Sergeants' Mess yelled and asked Moose if he'd like to walk her to her car, Moose gracefully declined. "I've got a headache."

Even Cunningham was caught by the tranquillity because when someone asked him to start up a crap game, he said, "Not today, thanks anyway."

At the Medical Inspection Room, however, two very confident cadets were just about to leave after talking to their friend, Medical Orderly Andre Durupt.

"It was very kind of you to give us this salve, Andre. You say we should mix it with the other ointment approximately one-half-hour before use?"

"Yes, James, and be sure each of you wears the surgical gloves I've given you."

Jonathan shook Andre's hand. "It's always nice having friends in high places. We owe you one."

Andre wasn't looking for praise. "It's always a pleasure to assist fellow Medical Corps types, and particularly up-and-coming young doctors. Maybe someday you can give me a free vasectomy. My wife and I should have about ten kids by then and I'll be ready for the snip. Tell me, James, where did you get the finely cut horsehair?"

James grinned. "From those dreadful beasts in the field behind your hospital. Jonathan's been snipping away at it for an hour. We're going to mix it in with the solution. Are you certain when this is dripped onto pubic hair, water won't wash it away?"

"Guaranteed. When your *friends* wake up, their testicles will be a little itchy, but it won't be anything for them to be alarmed about. Their morning showers will trigger the delayed action, but afterwards, the itching will stop. I would say the fun should begin to happen about nine-thirty tomorrow morning. Now, you don't need to use much and make certain you spray the alcohol directly on top of the mixture. That will disperse and dilute it. I would suggest you're *friends* will be here by noon."

Jonathan chuckled. "That early?"

"That is also guaranteed," Andre replied, shaking James's hand. "Have fun, and keep it under your hats."

On the way back to their barracks, Jonathan said, "O.K., now; we both have two small squeeze bottles and two long plastic tubes. You've got the mixture, I've got the alcohol. We're going to have to slip these tubes into the prong-slit in their undershorts at exactly the same time. After I squeeze out some of the mixture, I'll tap you, and you let 'em have it with the alcohol. Right?"

James agreed. "Yes, otherwise we'll have to enter twice. If they wake up, we've got a problem, so let's do it with surgical precision."

"You know, James, old sock, it's going to take us a while to do ten people. Maybe we should just do four or five?"

James stopped in his tracks. "Jonathan, my virtuous companion. Ten illegitimate children gave us that appalling regimental bathing. I contemplate it's exclusively equitable that we compensate them for their exertion, don't you?"

Without smiling, Jonathan replied, "James, my worthy contemporary, you are unconditionally correct. When will they learn not to MESS AROUND with the Royal Canadian Medical Corps?"

The two were laughing their heads off until they passed the headquarters building, whereupon arms were up and chests were out.

When they entered B-33 through the Musketeers' end door, the duo were once again talking about bandages, but Danyluk was having a *conversation* with Rothstein.

"For God's sake, Rothie, it's only an indoor chapel. Simon's Jewish and he's coming. It's the quietest place in the camp to study and nobody uses it. It's just another hut made up to look like a small church."

"Moose, I've never been in a church in my life. I don't think I should go in there."

Moose was face-to-face with Rothstein, so he put both of his arms on Harvey's shoulders. "O.K., how's this for reasoning? When I get married..." Moose stopped talking, cringed and shrugged. "Perish the thought. IF, I get married, youse is coming to my wedding, right?"

Rothstein nodded. "Well, I hope *so*! But please, don't use the word, youse."

"Well, where the hell do youse think I'm gonna get married? In a synagogue? Then again I might if the dame's Jewish. D'ya see what I mean?"

Harvey's face lit up. "Yeah, I guess you're right. I'd have to go in a church if you got married. Count me in, I'll join you guys."

"Finally," said Jackson, who was standing five feet away with the other

Musketeers.

After Harvey and Moose grabbed their berets, manuals, and note-books, the group headed for the cadet canteen, bought cold Kik Kolas and headed for the indoor chapel.

Moose was right. No one was there and although Harvey was a little nervous at first, he soon put his feet up, relaxed, and started reading.

The indoor Catholic chapel shared the same building as the Protestant chapel. Both of them were small, but they picked the Catholic chapel because it was a little bigger. It looked like a small church, with pews for about twenty people. Next to each chapel was a small reading room and these were also always empty.

It was Bergie who tipped the boys off that these rooms were ideal for studying, but they hadn't used them before because Rothstein wouldn't join them. Musketeers are Musketeers, and if one didn't go, none went.

About two hours later when they were shooting questions back and forth to each other, a short, balding, military Catholic priest walked out of the door of his quarters which were behind the altar.

"How's it going, boys?"

All feet came off the pews and the cadets sat erect as Jackson handled the response for the group. "Good, Father, I hope you don't mind us using the chapel for studying?"

As the priest walked by them and out the door, he replied, "Not at all, my boy. It's good to see someone in here on days other than Sundays." Then the priest came back in. "Say, I haven't been seeing you on Sundays, Danyluk? Where have you been?"

Moose cleared his throat. "Er, I've, er...I've changed my religion, Father."

The clergyman looked quite surprised although a small smile appeared. "My goodness, my son, what religion are you now?"

Danyluk's brain worked a mile-a-minute. "I'm an Orthodontist Muslim, now, Father. You know, *Allan*, and all that stuff? It keeps me busy."

The priest was still grinning as he walked out. "I'll bet it does...jaws and teeth are a tricky persuasion."

Amidst the howls, Moose asked, "What's so funny?"

Cunningham took a coin out of Moose's ear. "You meant orthodox. Also, the word is Allah, not Allan. An orthodontist is a kinda dentist. Jeez, Moose, you can be so uncouth."

"HEY, YOU FRUMP, WATCH YOUR TONGUE! I COULD BE A MUSLIM DENTIST, YOU KNOW?"

East got into the act. "Yeah, that would make you 'untooth.'"

Cunningham sat down and started studying again. "The only thing ortho about you is your wang."

"KEEP IT CLEAN, CUNNILINGUS, AT LEAST I DON'T BRUSH MY WANG LIKE YOUSE! BESIDES, IGNORANCE IS STRENGTH!"

Simon turned towards Moose. "Where's the priest going?"

"To the Officers' Mess for a brew, what else?" replied Moose.

Rothstein stopped reading. "Does he smoke as well?"

Moose stood up and stretched. "You bet he does. He also smokes my brand, 'cause I bummed one off him a coupla weeks ago."

"Our rabbi doesn't smoke *or* drink."

Danyluk grinned. "Ah yes, but this poor bastard can't screw."

"Are you going to the dance on Saturday night, Moose?" Wayne asked.

Everyone had been briefed and now all eyes were on Danyluk. "I, er, might. If Alma's sick, I might not. Jesus, what's everyone starin' at me for? I know, I know, youse all wanna meet Red, right? Listen, a hundred-thousand people have asked me to introduce them to Red. Er, I can only do so much."

Simon wasn't having any of that. "What did you say? We're not a hundred-thousand , we're eight. Are you trying to get out of...?"

"NO, NO." Moose cringed, then keeping his head straight, he rolled his eyes to the ceiling. How the hell did I get into this, he asked himself. "I'LL, ER, SEE WHAT I CAN DO."

"YOU'D BETTER!" was the *look* he received from the seven.

Wayne had been sitting next to East. "FOR CHRIST'S SAKE, JACK, YOU'VE GOT CHOCOLATE ALL OVER THE BACK OF YOUR PANTS AND ALL OVER THE PEW. IT LOOKS LIKE YOU'VE SHIT YOURSELF. YOU CAN'T GO INTO THE MESS HALL LOOKING LIKE THAT!"

It was time for supper so Jack rushed back to B-33 to change his pants. As the rest walked up the mess hall stairs, no one told Wayne he had chocolate all over the seat of his pants, too. Actually he wore more chocolate than East...a lot more. Amidst chuckles, they followed him up the stairs. Douglas was going to tell him, but grinned and changed his mind. Although Wayne was his best buddy, it was one of those days.

When East finally got to the table, his face was red as can be. "Christ, I'm embarrassed. I never want to see that lady again." he said, pointing to a woman who was serving.

"What happened?" Earl asked.

Jack was visibly shaken and didn't start eating. "Just look at her face, that should tell you."

Seven necks strained to get a view of the lady. She had a nervous condition that made her twitch, wink, and smile at the same time.

East took a swig of his milk. "You guys know how I hold my tray out a little longer so I can get more, don't you?"

They nodded.

"Well, when I held out my tray to her, I said, 'Just a bit more, please.' She winked and smiled, so I winked, and smiled, but she didn't put any more on. I held my tray out and she twitched, winked and smiled again, so I motioned to the plate and winked and smiled again also."

"Yeah, so what happened?" asked Rothstein.

Jack took another sip of milk. "Well, I thought she understood, so I gave her a few more winks and smiles. She winked and smiled and said, 'YOU HARD-FACED CREATURE, ARE YOU MAKING FUN OF ME?'"

"I thought she was joking so I smiled and winked back again and she complained to the Messing Sergeant, who took my name. Jesus, I never knew she had a condition."

After the laughter, Jackson said, "That reminds me of a joke. Did you hear the one about the guy with a harelip who goes into a bar and says to the bartender, (Earl affects (puts on) a speech impediment) *I think I'll have a scotch and water?'*

"The bartender says, (once again, Earl talks with a speech impediment) 'Yes, sir, one scotch and water coming right up'

"The guy says, (speech impediment) 'Has it been busy tonight?'"

"The bartender replies, (speech impediment) 'No, not too busy.'"

"*Another guy comes into the bar and sits next to the guy with the harelip. 'Give me a rum and coke, please bartender.'*"

"*This time the bartender replies (without) a speech impediment, 'Yes, sir, one rum and coke, coming right up, sir. There you are sir.'*"

"*The guy says, 'Thank you. Say, where's all the dames?'*"

"*The bartender says, (without) a speech impediment, 'It's only Wednesday, they don't usually come in until Thursday or Friday nights.'*"

"*The guy with the harelip is now pissed off and says, (speech impediment) 'Say, bartender, I heard you talk to him, you've been mocking me, haven't you?'*"

"*The bartender leans over, points and whispers, (speech impediment) 'No, I'm not mocking you, I'm mocking him.'*"

Earl sat back with a grin. It took a while, but soon, faces indicated they had caught on and howls filled the mess hall. Other jokes entertained Jack as he calmed down and ate his meal.

When it was time to leave, East left through another door so he wouldn't have to pass the lady with the twitch. He didn't know it then, but the next day, he'd be given one hour of mess hall scrubbing and cleaning.

That evening was totally unlike any other evening in B-33, as the cadets of Alpha Company silently studied for Friday's exams. After Major Ratcliffe and his officers and NCOs left the barracks, the only excitement was when Wayne dumped a basin of water over East. It was a form of 'thanks' for the 'free chocolate.'

Sergeant Beckford allowed the lights to stay on until midnight and this suited everyone just fine, especially the cadets in the Royal Canadian Medical Corps. As they figured it, if the lights stayed on, their *antagonists* would be tired. How right they were.

Last day of the course, or no last day, Sergeant Simpson carried out his normal P.T. exercises on Friday morning. As a small *gift* to the company, he even took them on a sightseeing tour of Area Ten in the upper camp. This added approximately another mile-and-a-half to their regular run.

"COME, ON YOU PEOPLE, GET THE LEAD OUT! YOU, QUIT STICKING YOUR HAND DOWN YOUR CROTCH AND PICK UP THE STEP! THE SAME GOES FOR YOU...GET YOUR GOD-DAMNED HAND OUT OF YOUR PANTS! DANYLUK HAVE YOU BEEN TEACHING THESE *NOVICES* SOME OF YOUR WICKED, WICKED WAYS?"

Breathing heavily, Danyluk replied, "Not me, Sergeant, I'm reformed. I haven't got the energy to play with it and run at the same time. Besides, those two are Alberta creeps."

When the company arrived back and was ready to be fallen out, Sergeant Simpson gave them a small pep talk.

"As you know, you're in K.D. longs today. I want to see you dress like you've never dressed before. You're going to appear super-sharp and...!" The Sergeant noticed something and stopped suddenly.

"YOU, DID YOU SCRATCH YOUR BALLS ON MY PARADE?"

"YES, SERGEANT! came a somewhat nervous reply from another direction.

"I'M NOT TALKING TO YOU, I'M TALKING TO...WHAT? YOU TOO?"

"WHAT'S THE MATTER WITH YOU PEOPLE THIS MORNING? HAVE WE GOT A FEW DOSES OF CRABS?"

The Sergeant marched over to a cadet who was dying to rub his testicles. All of his body movements indicated he would give a million dollars to put his hand down to his crotch and have a good scratch. He couldn't even stand still when Sergeant Simpson called him to attention.

"Where were you last night?"

A wiggling cadet replied, "Ssstudying in ttthe cadet canteen, SSSergeant."

"Well, there are no crabs in...!" Once again the Sergeant stopped because the cadet next to the *wiggler* couldn't wait any longer. He shoved his whole arm down the front of his pants and proceeded to claw himself. His eyes were closed and the look of relief on his face indicated he was in Heaven. The cadet behind him did the same.

The Sergeant pointed at the *scratchers*. "Do you three know each other?"

"Not particularly, Sergeant," replied the wiggler who now couldn't care if the Queen herself was standing in front of him. He shoved both of his hands down his pants and realized pure delight.

Sergeant Simpson backed off quickly. "I WANT YOU THREE TO GO HAVE A SHOWER AND REPORT ON SICK PARADE THIS MORNING. IS THAT CLEAR?"

"YES, SERGEANT!" the trio replied in unison, still scratching. The third one in the second rank had actually dropped his military shorts to his knees and was standing in his undershorts, rubbing away with both hands at his crotch.

The rest of the company was going wild, including Danyluk and especially the Medical-types.

"YOU'D NEVER SEE ME DO THAT ON YOUR PARADE, SERGEANT!"

A gas pain appeared on Simpson's face. "DANYLUK, YOU'D BE SCRATCHING YOUR ANKLE, BEFORE YOU TOOK IT OUT OF YOUR PUT-TEES! ALPHA COMPANY, ATTEN...TION! FALL...OUT!"

As the company poured through the two southern doors of B-33, the wiggler couldn't wait until he was in the shower. He took off his military shorts and his undershorts by the fire extinguisher and gave himself a few squirts. His appreciation of the cool water was instantly obvious and he couldn't have cared less about the comments going on around him.

A Two Platoon cadet said, "Jeez, those Royal Winnipeg Rifles cadets are worse than animals. Did you see the colour of his balls, they were red raw?"

His friend replied, "Those pongoes aren't used to this heat. When it gets above eighty, their balls tip 'em off its time for a shower. Probably haven't had one in three weeks."

Andre Durupt was true to his word. The suffering threesome agonized even more when the hot water of the showers hit their bodies. It was probably the first time in the history of the Vernon Army Cadet Camp that scrub brushes were in demand. Normally, scrub brushes were used in giving regimental showers, however on this particular morning, certain cadets voluntarily used all the available brushes to "scrub the skin off their nuts," as Danyluk put it.

The shower scene was similar to that of visitor's day at a leper colony. Ten *inflicted* cadets were using brushes as they stood alone under the showers of one wall. *Healthy* cadets stayed away and used the showers of the other wall.

Each slow or fast stroke with a brush was absolute ecstasy. The *scrubbers* weren't interested in talking, all they wanted to do was message their crotch. They weren't thinking about each other, either. As far as they were concerned, nothing in the world felt so good.

"Jesus, just look at their faces," stated Danyluk. "They look like they're screwing and ready to pop. Hey, I don't know what they've got, but maybe that's a good option, what do you guys think?"

Moose was shoved and nearly landed with the *lepers*.

Once again Andre was right. After ten minutes in the shower, the itching stopped. It wasn't necessary for the trio to go on sick parade. But the fun wasn't over yet.

After their morning inspection, Alpha was marched over to the lecture huts in the upper camp. Each cadet was immaculately dressed until the company tackled the *road* leading to the other side. The sweat and toil used to make their uniforms perfect became a waste of time when the clouds of dust covered them.

Sergeant-Major Rose was in One Platoon's room. Additional six-foot folding tables had been brought in and two cadets sat at each table.

"These examinations should take you about two to two-and-a-half hours. You will have nothing in front of you except your pencils, pens, erasers, rulers, compasses, and protractors. I want all of you to bring your notebooks and manuals up here to the front."

Three minutes later, Rose glanced at his watch. "Right! Turn your tests over, write your name and platoon number in the top right corner, and carry on!"

Periodically throughout the exams, Rose got up from his desk and walked the aisles, looking at their work. Sometimes he would help a little by saying, "Are you sure that answer's correct?" Usually, the cadet would scratch his head and in a few seconds, see where he went wrong.

The same procedure happened in the other three lecture rooms. Sergeant Simpson was with Two Platoon and about three-quarters-of-an-hour into the tests, a cadet in the front row subconsciously slipped his left hand down his pants and started scratching his testicles. He didn't realize he was doing it because he was writing at the same time.

"YOU, QUIT PLAYING WITH YOURSELF AND GET ON WITH YOUR WORK!"

The embarrassed cadet's hand came out in a hurry, but not for long. Two rows behind, a cadet undid his belt and fly buttons and was rubbing his testicles so hard the cadet next to him couldn't concentrate.

"Listen, you're moving the bench and the table, give it a break will ya!"

"WHO'S WHISPERING? STAND UP, THAT MAN!"

The complainer stood up. "I, er just asked Morris if I could borrow his eraser, Sergeant."

Sergeant Simpson walked towards them. "MORRIS, IS THAT RIGHT? STAND UP, MAN!"

As Morris stood to attention, his pants fell down. "That's right, Sergeant!"

"CHRIST, YOU AGAIN? I THOUGHT I TOLD YOU TO GO ON SICK PARADE?"

"Well, er, I wanted to write my exams, Sergeant!"

"GET YOUR PANTS UP, MAN! WHAT THE HELL IS THIS PLATOON COMING TO?"

The next two hours were the worst time ever in the lives of the *scratchers*. It wasn't three anymore, there were ten of them. They were using their rulers, their hands, and their elbows. The grimaced distress on their faces was accompanied by "oohs," ahhs, and the words, "Fuck, I can't take this itchin' anymore."

At one point, a cadet stood up scratching, dropped his pants and undershorts, and stuck his crotch out the open window next to him. Three others immediately did exactly the same thing.

In a nearby hut, Rothstein glanced out the window and said, "What the...? Two Platoon's having a show and tell. Take a look at this!"

Nearly one-third of Two Platoon was now at their windows as Sergeant-Major Rose leaned out of the next hut and yelled, "SERGEANT SIMPSON, WHAT THE HELL IS GOING ON OVER THERE?"

Simpson glanced at his watch and stopped the examinations. With a smile, he said, "I DON'T KNOW, SIR, BUT I'LL TELL YOU, I WOULDN'T WANT IT!"

Within minutes, ten cadets were being marched to the MIR (Medical Inspection Room) by a Corporal who kept his distance. They didn't have their arms up or their chests out. Instead, they had their arms in (*their pants*) and their heads down, as well. Being in step was not important, either. If General Kitching had marched by, he definitely would not have been saluted in the normal manner.

Laughter filled the mess hall at lunch. Even the remainder of Two Platoon joined in the merriment, but not for long. After lunch, they were marched up to the MIR to join their *comrades-in-itch* in receiving a couple of needles each, and the blue ointment treatment with Vaseline.

Andre played his role perfectly. The two instigators were taken aside and given blue ointment, but they didn't receive the shots. If their testicles had not been coated, they would have been hung from the highest rafters after being discovered normal in the showers.

Two of the ten scratchers were held overnight because, as Earl put it, "Their balls and wangs were like raw meat." For the balance of camp, those two in particular never lived it down. They were known as 'raw' and 'rare.' Every time Danyluk passed one of them, he sang a new renamed version of a popular song, *The Yellow Wang of Texas.* Although he didn't sound like Mitch Miller, Moose got the message across and always received a round of applause.

After lunch, Alpha Company was paid. Normally cadets weren't paid until Saturday, however, since they were being *posted* on Saturday, all of that day's procedures took place on Friday.

Following Pay Parade, they were allowed to exchange both of their sheets and a pillow-case. After that, a chubby militia corporal walked in with their mail.

"DANYLUK, CUSSON, BRIGADIER DANYLUK, BRICE, EAST, MAJOR GENERAL DANYLUK, MATHIESON, GREEN, LIEUTENANT GENERAL DANYLUK, LARKIN, DANYLUK!" The Corporal stopped for a second before he continued. "NOGOOD, er, I mean TOOGOOD, LANE, ROTHSTEIN, EAST, REBIN, HEPPNER, AIRD, GENERAL DANYLUK, CAMERON, NEISH, MURPHY, SIMON, DANYLUK, DANYLUK, DANYLUK..." Christ, I never knew you cadets had ranks as high as general. Danyluk, what do you belong to, a fucking military dating service?"

Moose smiled. "These dames don't need a dating service, they've got me."

The Corporal shook his head. "If they all sent you a buck, you'd be rich!"

"HEY, THEY SEND ME MORE THAN THAT! LET'S GET ON WITH *MY* MAIL!"

The Corporal continued for another fifteen minutes and Moose received another ten letters. In addition, Douglas, Moose, and Jackson each received parcels, which were split amongst the others.

Moose lay down on his bunk and opened the first letter. He chose it because of its perfumed essence.

'Dear Moose:

Oh sweetheart, I miss you so much. The days and nights go by so slowly when I'm not climbing in your bedroom window with the morning newspaper. Oh Moosey, I will always cherish the ring you sent me. You have no idea what it meant to me to receive your mother's ring. When I showed it to my mom, she was wearing one exactly like it. The thought of you sending me your mother's ring had an effect on my mother as well. Her face went beet red and she had to clear her throat and leave my room. I guess our mothers have similar tastes. Actually, I think my mom likes you a lot because she keeps asking me when are you coming home. Look after yourself my darling. I have enclosed the ten dollars you need to send flowers to your sick Aunt Martha. My love and body are yours, always. Cecelia XXXXXXXX'

"DAMN IT!" said Moose as he stuffed Cecelia's letter back in the envelope, opened the next one, and started reading. "I didn't think she'd show it to her mother."

'Moose, you rotten bastard:

Today, my daughter showed me the ring you sent her. If that one was your mother's ring, who the hell owned the one that I'm wearing? I've got you figured out Moose Danyluk. You've been diddling me and my daughter. Well, just you wait until you come home, I'll straighten you and that thing out. But then again, just thinking of that thing makes me quiver. Oh just come home soon Moosie and I'll make you forget about that rotten camp. In your last letter you mentioned the fact that there are no girls there and that you're lonesome. I can fix that up in no time.

I have enclosed the ten dollars you need for the Forgotten Soldier's Fund. Sending you this money nearly makes me broke. I was going to go out and buy some wood alcohol to get the green off my finger. It's building up around your mother's ring. Oh well, I guess I can wait until next payday. Are you certain this ring is gold?

Come home soon, Moose my beloved.

Annie with the fanny you like. XXXXX'

"BLAST, ANNIE'S GETTING WISE, I'M GOING TO HAVE TO CHANGE MY TACTICS!" Moose bellowed as he opened the next letter.

'Moose, you big hunka meat:

I'm so sorry to hear that the weather hasn't been so great. It's been wonderful down here on the coast. As a matter of fact, I'm heading right this moment down to Third Beach in Stanley Park. I'm also wearing that very flimsy bathing suit that you like so much. I know, you're probably mad because I'm wearing it, because as you say, everything hangs out. Well Moose, I've got to have a little action too, you know.

The other day the strangest thing happened. I got a call from Murray Goldman's Credit Gal Evelyn. She says because she hasn't received your payment I should come into the store and see her. I said, what's this got to do with me? She said, I co-signed your credit application. Jesus, Moose, I don't remember doing that? I can only remember the day you asked me for a copy of my signature because you said you wanted to compare it to your mother's. Then you said we were made for each other because your mother and I write the same. Anyway, I paid ten dollars on your silk underwear account. You can pay me when you get home. Oh, for-

get about paying me, just bring that body of yours home and wear some of that fine underwear for me.

I have enclosed ten dollars for the Soldier's Skin Graft Fund. I think it's such a shame that young boys should have to have skin grafts on their private parts. I hope you're not donating any skin? You'd better not. I don't even like the fact that you have to donate a pint of blood each week while you're in camp. Oh well, at least your blood goes to good purposes in the Middle East.

I've got to tell you Moose, I'm having a real problem wearing your mother's gold ring. My finger keeps swelling up and it's turning green. I had to have the ring cut off the other day. When I told the jeweler add some gold to make it bigger, he said, O.K., lady, it's your dough you're wasting. What did he mean by that, Moose? Perhaps he didn't like the design of the ring?

Well, darling, please take care of yourself. You know I'll be waiting for you when you get home.

Love and kisses....Hilda.'

Moose closed the letter and thought for a moment. "Now I remember! It was Ruby who talked me into getting the silk gaunch, but it was Hilda's signature I copied."

Although Moose was only talking to himself, those around him tried to keep track. It was an impossible task.

As Moose was reading another letter, it was Douglas who realized Rothstein was missing. Jack said, "Rothie read his letter and headed out the door."

The letter Harvey received was in plain view sitting on top of his covers. Although he had reservations about reading it, Douglas grabbed the letter, his beret and Harvey's beret and rushed out the door to find him. He had an idea where he might be and on the way, he read the letter.

'Shalom, my dearest Son:

I didn't want to trouble you while you are at camp because I know how hard you are working and what it means to you. There are times, however, when we must be strong and face reality when all acts of the pantomime fail to reverse the dreaded truth we have refused to accept. This morning, your mother underwent an operation and she will be in the hospital for at least another three weeks. To tell you the truth, Son, I don't think she's going to make it. I've had many good discussions with Doctor Blomberg, and as kind and considerate as he is, I think I can read between the lines. As you know, I've hidden this from you as best I could, but it wouldn't be fair for me to continue doing that. Besides, you are old enough to see through my false front, if indeed I was successful. I've heard your cries and I've felt your heartache. You probably knew all along, but I tried to spare you the agony I've been going through.

Harvey, I've always recognized, as you did, that it was your mother who painted the happiness in our world. There may have been times when you thought I never appreciated the wonder of her being, because I was always at the plant. Well, Son, nothing could be further from the truth. I remember those days well. Once Rose told me that if I kept working so hard, you children wouldn't know me. She said you kids would wonder who the stranger was, coming in the door. Although your mother laughed when she said it, she was right.

I know I was never there, Harvey and for that, I apologize. It was tough on the family when we couldn't go away together, or I didn't make the time to play base-

ball with you. What could I do? If I hadn't worked hard, we wouldn't have had any-thing. Then again, if I had made the time, perhaps things would be different. Right now, I wish I'd spent every minute of every day by her side. It's sad we never stop to repair the cracks in the overflowing cup of destiny.

I'm not asking you to come home, Son. That decision is up to you. I just want you to know, that we all love you very much.

Say a prayer for your Mother - Love from us all.
DAD.

There were tears in Douglas' eyes as he put the letter away in his pocket and walked to the east fence overlooking the golf course. Sure enough, a lonely figure sat on the grass at the south end, parallel to the old parade square. He had his knees up with his arms around them, and his head down.

Douglas took a deep breath and sat beside him. "Hi, kiddo. I, er, I hope you don't mind...I read your Dad's letter."

Harvey turned slightly, smiled and wiped his eyes with his hand. Douglas handed him a handkerchief and Harvey wiped his nose and eyes.

"Thanks, Doug. No, that's all right. I'm...going to the office; I've got to go home."

Brice nodded. "I know. Would you like me to go with you?"

Tears flooded down Harvey's cheeks again. His voice was low. "No, thanks anyway. Jeez, I...I can't describe this. My mother's going to..."

Harvey couldn't say anything else, he just broke down. Douglas put his arm around his shoulders. Their heads were touching and his tears were flowing too. "Don't talk, Rothie, I understand."

Rothstein needed someone to talk to, and Douglas had all the time in the world to listen to his friend. After fifteen minutes, Douglas removed his arm and patted him on his back. "C'mon kid, we can't sit here, let's head to the office and get it over with."

Rothstein blew his nose, wiped his eyes and stood up as Douglas handed him his beret.

"I'm going to miss you guys."

Douglas smacked the dirt off his and Harvey's pants. "Not as much as we'll miss you. Keep your chin up, Rothie, miracles happen."

Harvey smiled and shook his friend's outstretched hand. Shortly, they were ushered into Major Ratcliffe's office. A train was leaving in three-quarters of an hour. It was suggested by Sergeant Beckford that Rothstein's military clothing should be left in his barrack box just in case he returned. Sergeant Beckford had said that for two reasons. The first being it would ease Harvey's mind, and second, he just might be back.

The Musketeers had little time to say their good-byes as Rothstein changed into his battledress. His talk with Douglas, Sergeant Beckford, and Major Ratcliffe had cheered him up a little.

"I'll tell all your dames that you're suffering because you ain't gettin' any," he said to Moose.

Danyluk grinned and cocked his arm around Rothstein's head. "Great! That means when I arrive home, I'll get the double treatment. You know, Rothie? Like, double your pleasure, double your fun?"

After handshakes, pats, and a few touches of feather-light fists on his chin, Harvey boarded the jeep outside B-33. Douglas handed him the letter and shook his hand again. "Rothie, I've got a feeling a lot of prayers will be said here tonight."

Amidst smiles and waves, Harvey yelled, "DOUG, MAKE CERTAIN YOU PHONE AND TELL HER I'LL WRITE!"

Douglas put his right thumb up. "I WILL. LOOK AFTER YOURSELF!"

When everyone came back into the barracks, the mood was somber. Harvey wasn't lying on his bed, laughing. Instead, his mattress had been rolled and his bedding was folded. The only thing that reminded them of Harvey Rothstein was their memories and a locked barrack box, the key to which had been left in the company office.

No sooner had Harvey left, Jack rushed in. "Did I miss him? SHIT!"

East had been scrubbing the floors in the kitchen. Although someone had told him of Harvey's plight, the Messing Sergeant wouldn't release him to say farewell.

"He said to say good-bye to you," Douglas said as he headed to the cadet canteen to phone Harvey's girl. "He also said you could have all of his food rations."

East smiled. "What a great buddy. I'll eat 'em, too. That woman with the twitch was actually nice to me today. She said..."

Jack didn't complete his sentence because Sergeants Beckford and Simpson entered the barracks, heading towards the bulletin board. He knew they were going to post the results of the examinations and the list showing which company Alpha's cadets would be attached to.

The Sergeants didn't stick around long. They pinned the papers to the board and left quickly, brandishing shrewd gas pains.

The mad rush was on, lead by Earl. In a few moments, all cadets in the east wing, except the rest of the Musketeers, were gathered in front of the notices, trying to find their names. When Douglas walked back in, he waited with the other six until Earl had finished.

"DOUG, YOU TOPPED THE COURSE BY ONE PERCENT," were Earl's first words. "Simon came second; Wayne, you were third; and the rest of us were spread out amongst the top twelve. Can you imagine that, eight of us are in the top twelve?"

In no time, the rest discovered that Cunningham was fourth; Jackson fifth; Rothstein ninth; East eleventh; and Danyluk was twelfth. Two Canadian Scottish and two Seaforth cadets had filled the sixth, seventh, eighth, and tenth positions in the company.

With handshakes all 'round, they waited eagerly to find out which company they had been posted to. None of them wanted to be clerks for the rest of the summer. Each in his own way was wrenching his memory trying to think if he had done something which could prevent him from being posted to a platoon.

Earl smiled and moved the paper above his head so Moose couldn't grab it. "You're not going to believe this."

"OH, GET ON WITH IT!" Danyluk yelled.

"O.K., don't get your nuts in a knot. We've all been posted to Five and Six Platoons of Bravo Company. We've each got a section of approximately ten cadets."

Building B-33 couldn't contain the excitement as the cadets of Alpha Company expressed approval for their tasks over the next three weeks. While the Musketeers gathered on the front steps of the building, other groups were in the drying room, shower room, on the end porches, and even in the furnace room making plans to produce the best platoon in the other companies.

A few lonely individuals sat on their beds wondering where they had gone wrong. They would be posted as clerks or even storesmen with Driver Mechanics and Signals, however, even they were eventually happy when they realized they'd get more time off than the others.

The only two Royal Canadian Medical Corps cadets in the company were posted to the camp hospital for the balance of summer. They congratulated each other as they shook hands.

"I say, Jonathan, old sock, we won't have to put up with those abominable creatures in Senior Leaders, eh what?"

"James, you patriarchal rascal, you, we're finally bound for acknowledgment and distinction. Say old chappie, did I acquaint you with the new-fashioned dressings Johnson and Johnson are...?"

Many enthusiastic conversations took place in B-33 that afternoon, and at 1500 hours when they were marched to the upper camp to hand in their clothing and receive bush uniforms and rank slip-ons, the excitement grew feverishly.

"Christ, I feel like a new person," Danyluk said, trying on his new bush cap.

"We'll have to get some cardboard so our caps will look perfectly squared off like Sergeant Beckford's," replied East.

"Can we wear these downtown?" asked Simon.

Cunningham took the King of Hearts out of Simon's ear. "Yep, we can say good-bye forever to the cadet summer uniforms. We even wear these on the Graduation Parade. Hey, Earl, are we allowed in the Junior Ranks Club or the Men's Canteen?"

Earl knew the answer. "No! That was made perfectly clear in orders. Don't try and sneak in either, because they'll be watching for us."

Shuffling a deck of cards with one hand, Cunningham was downhearted. "Damn it, just think of the money I'm losing?"

Wayne wrapped his hand around the back of Cunningham's neck. "Look at it this way, Gordie, the cadets in Bravo Company haven't even heard of you. It'll be like Smorgasbord."

Gordie's smile widened as he rasped his voice. "Yeah, new *suckers*, er, I mean, clients. It'll be more than smorgasbord."

Moose had heard and used that word before. "Can I ask youse guys a question?"

"Sure, go ahead, Moose," Douglas replied.

"Where the hell is this place called Smorgasborg? Youse guys all seem to have been there, but until recently I've never heard of the place."

With bellows of laughter, Cunningham answered, "And nor should you."

As they were falling in to march back to the lower camp, Douglas said, "You wouldn't like it there, Moose."

"LIKE IT WHERE? WHAT DO YUZ MEAN I WOULDN'T LIKE IT THERE? I LIKES IT ANYWHERE! EVEN IN THE ALLEY!"

"Not in Smorgasborg, you wouldn't."

"O.K., WHY?"

"'Cause that's where gout came from."

"NO SHIT? REALLY, DOUG?"

"YEP!"

Although he lost his step, Moose turned. "HEY, CUNNILINGUS! YOUSE MAY HAVE YOUR MONEY, BUT I'VE STILL GOT MY ORIGINAL WANG!

AND I DON'T USE THAT PEROXIDE SHIT, EITHER!"

Cunningham glanced at the Corporal next to him. "What the hell was that all about?"

The Corporal just shook his head. "Don't ask me, he's one of yours, thank God."

At 1900 hours that evening, the *newly* dressed cadets of Alpha Company were marched into the hangar called B-3. Major Ratcliffe, his officers and NCOs were on the stage.

"I CAN TELL THAT THE TRAINING YOU'VE RECEIVED HAS BEEN TAKEN TO HEART. WHEN YOU WERE MARCHING DOWN THE ROAD, I THOUGHT A REGULAR FORCE COMPANY WAS VISITING VERNON."

Applause and whistles filled B-3.

"RIGHT, I'M GOING TO MAKE THIS BRIEF. YOU'VE GOT THE BAL-ANCE OF THE WEEKEND OFF, HOWEVER, YOU MUST REPORT TO YOUR NEW POSTING'S OFFICE AT 1900 HOURS ON SUNDAY NIGHT. AT THAT TIME, YOU'LL BE SHOWN YOUR QUARTERS AND YOU CAN THEN MOVE YOUR BEDDING AND BARRACK BOX.

"THIS IS THE FIRST TIME CADETS HAVE BEEN USED IN STAFFING POSITIONS AND I WANT YOU TO KNOW, YOU WILL BE SCRUTINIZED AND THOROUGHLY ASSESSED.

"I'M NOT GOING TO GO INTO DETAILS, BUT ALL OF YOU MUST ADHERE TO FAIR PLAY. REMEMBER WHAT YOU HAVE LEARNED IN THE LEADERSHIP AND MAN-MANAGEMENT PERIODS? YOU ARE NOT GODS! YOU ARE HERE TO TEACH AND TO BRING ALONG THE YOUNGER CADETS. AS SERGEANT BECKFORD WOULD SAY, 'YOU'LL DO IT WITH ALPHA COMPANY FLAIR AND STYLE.' IF THERE ARE COM-PLAINTS, THEY'LL BE INVESTIGATED AND THE OUTCOME WILL BE ONE OF THREE ACTIONS. ONE - YOU WILL REMAIN IN YOUR POSITION. TWO - YOU WILL RECEIVE ANOTHER POSTING, AND THREE - YOU'LL BE SENT HOME.

"AS OF 1900 HOURS ON SUNDAY NIGHT, YOU WILL BECOME THE RESPONSIBILITY OF THE OFFICER COMMANDING YOUR NEW COM-PANY, OR THE OFFICER COMMANDING YOUR TRAINING WING. OUR JOB..." Major Ratcliffe pointed to his officers only, because most NCOs except WO2 Rose, were being posted as well, "OUR JOB, WILL BE TO REVIEW AND COMPILE YOUR ASSESSMENTS AND TO WRITE THE COURSE TRAINING PLAN FOR NEXT YEAR. ARE THERE ANY QUESTIONS?"

A cadet raised his hand. "Sir, if we are to report to our new posting on Sunday night...isn't that a little late to prepare for lectures if we have to give them on Monday?"

"GOOD POINT! WHEN YOU GET BACK TO THE BARRACKS, EACH OF YOU WILL FIND AN ENVELOPE ON YOUR BED DETAILING YOUR DUTIES."

A hand went up. "Sir, will Alpha Company have a company party at the end of camp?"

"MOST DEFINITELY! THAT MEANS YOU'LL BE ATTENDING TWO PARTIES."

"Sir, are we on Saturday Morning's parade, tomorrow?"

"NO, GENERAL KITCHING HAS GIVEN YOU THE DAY OFF. YOU CAN SLEEP IN, BUT DON'T FORGET YOU'VE GOT LESSON PLANS TO PREPARE."

"Sir, if we have complaints, or problems, who...?"

"WHO DO YOU TAKE THEM TO?"

"Yes, sir!"

"YOU'LL USE THE CHAIN OF COMMAND IN YOUR NEW POSTING!"

East's hand went up.

"Sir, where do we eat?"

"YOU MAY EAT WITH YOUR NEW COMPANY, OR REMAIN IN THE SAME MESS HALL YOU'RE USING NOW. THE CHOICE IS YOURS! ARE THERE ANY OTHER QUESTIONS!"

"Yes, sir! What about mail?"

"AH, GOOD QUESTION! ALL MAIL SENT TO ALPHA COMPANY WILL REMAIN AT THE CAMP POST OFFICE. YOU CAN PICK IT UP INDIVIDU- ALLY DURING POST OFFICE HOURS! IS THERE ANYTHING ELSE?"

There were no more hands.

"NO? WELL, WE WISH YOU THE VERY BEST. KEEP YOUR NOSES CLEAN AND LET'S MAKE CERTAIN EVERYONE IN CAMP VERNON IS AWARE OF OUR COMPANY'S PRIDE."

Danyluk raised his hand.

"AH, THERE IS A LAST QUESTION. YES, DANYLUK?"

"SIR, WHAT ABOUT MORNING PHYSICAL TRAINING? ARE YOU SAYING WE WON'T HAVE OUR *FAVOURITE MORNING SERGEANT* WITH US?"

Even on the stage, there was laughter. Except Sergeant Simpson, he had another gas pain.

"I'LL LET YOUR *FAVORITE MORNING SERGEANT* ANSWER THAT. ...SERGEANT SIMPSON?"

Simpson stepped forward to face the cadets. "THANK YOU, SIR. I HAVE BEEN PRAYING MORNING AND NIGHT, AND I'VE EVEN PLEADED WITH MAJOR RATCLIFFE TO LET ME TAKE YOU GUYS OUT EACH MORNING."

Sergeant Simpson had to smile because now he couldn't hear himself think. He waited for the noise to die down.

"BUT HE SAID, NO!"

More fanfare to the rafters.

"SO WE ARRIVED AT A MUTUAL CONCLUSION. YOU PEOPLE WILL BE GIVING THE P.T. IN THE MORNINGS. I CAN FINALLY SLEEP IN."

There was silence as the cadets of Alpha Company glanced at each other. The question had been answered. They now knew they would be up early every morn- ing.

Major Ratcliffe stepped forward again. "THANK YOU SERGEANT SIMP- SON. GOOD LUCK TO YOU ALL AND HAVE A GOOD WEEKEND. I WANT THE TOP TWENTY STUDENTS IN MY OFFICE IN FIFTEEN MINUTES."

Sergeant Beckford whispered into Major Ratcliffe's ear.

"Oh, yes. Thank you, Sergeant Beckford. CADET BRICE, THERE IS A TELEGRAM FOR YOU. IT'S WITH THE ORDERLY OFFICER IN THE HEAD- QUARTERS BUILDING."

Everyone sat at attention as Major Ratcliffe and his officers left the building.

The cadets were then formed up, marched back to B-33, and dismissed.

Wayne joined Douglas to pick up the telegram. "Doug, I wonder who it's from? Maybe it's bad news from Harvey?"

Douglas' face showed some concern. "Let's find out."

After picking it up, they stood outside reading it. It was from Red Robinson.

'DOUG AND WAYNE:

PLEASE TAKE YOUR GROUP TO THE BACK DOOR OF THE ARENA AT EXACTLY 1930. STOP. WHEN YOU ENTER, SILENTLY POINT OUT MOOSE DANYLUK TO THE GUY ON THE DOOR. STOP.

YOUR TECHNICOLOR HOST - RED. STOP.'

Both cadets were nearly bowled over. Receiving a telegram from Red Robinson was like hearing from God himself. They read it again and again on the way back to their quarters.

"YOU PEOPLE! GET IN STEP AND MARCH! YOU'RE WEARING BUSH UNIFORMS NOW, CLEAN UP YOUR ACT!"

The Camp RSM didn't call them over. He didn't need to, his voice could be heard all over camp.

All Musketeers except Danyluk were instantly informed of the cable. It was difficult but the ecstatic expressions on their faces disappeared when Moose was around, so he remained none the wiser.

Ten minutes later, the twenty top cadets of Alpha Company were having coffee and doughnuts in the company office. Although all Alpha students had been congratulated earlier, this was a special, 'well done, fellas' meeting.

Every officer, Junior NCO, Senior NCO, and even the company clerks, Privates Pazim and Maeson were present. Throughout the affair, the clerks sniveled up to Cunningham, trying to find out when they'd have the opportunity of winning their money back...especially Pazim. "Gordie, sweetheart, I've never been so broke in my life. All I've got is a few coins, no *folding-paper* money."

Maeson took a swig of his Kik Kola. "I'm getting fed up drinking this shit. What I want is a cold *clear* beer. Gordie, loan me a deuce, that's the least you can do."

Cunningham kept a straight face. "Not until I hear the magic word."

"PLEASE, WILL YOU LOAN ME A DEUCE?"

That was all it took for Gordie to unwrap two-dollars from a big fat wad of bills.

"There you are, and don't forget I charge weekly interest of twenty percent. You guys are going to have me in the poorhouse if this keeps up."

After the gathering, the Musketeers opened and studied the contents of the envelopes left on each of their beds. Along with timetables and course instructions, each pouch was filled with lesson plans.

Douglas smiled. "Well what d'ya know. On Monday morning, I'm teaching two periods of map using and two periods of holding, aiming, and firing."

Danyluk scratched his head. "Jesus, would you believe this? I've got to instruct four periods of the most boring subjects in the world? Interior Economy and Military Writing. Oh well, I guess the subjects are related."

Jackson looked up for a minute. "How they hell are they related?"

Although Moose was still reading, he casually answered, "I've got to show them how to use the shitter and after that, I'll show them how to use the military letters to wipe their butts."

Moose got a laugh from everyone. They needed a good laugh because it had been that kind of a day.

After mug-up when East walked in with his arms full of sandwiches, Wayne asked, "Surely to God you're not going to eat all those?"

His mouth was full, but a chomping East replied, "You bet I am. Don't forget, I'm eating Rothie's share, as well?"

Cunningham interrupted his poker game. "HEY, JACK! I'LL HAVE ONE OF THOSE. MAKE IT PEANUT BUTTER AND JAM."

Jack sheltered his cache. "GET SERIOUS, CUNNER, YOU TURNED ME DOWN ON THAT TEN-CENT LOAN, REMEMBER?"

"Jacky, Jacky, Jacky. You just didn't have the collateral, that's all. Business is business, my boy. If I loaned you ten cents, I'd have to loan everyone ten cents."

Although his mouth was full, a sneaky grin covered East's face. "I agree, business is business. It'll cost you two-bits for a *half* sandwich.

"GET STUFFED, YOU ROBBER!"

"That's exactly what I intend to do."

After lights out, it became very quiet in the Musketeer's end of the wing. Without Harvey, the team wasn't the same. Each cadet was thinking about him and his sick mom. They said their prayers in their own way, but Danyluk and Jackson mumbled a little louder. They didn't mind if they were heard, Harvey was their friend and they wanted him spared of any emotional pain, and his mom cured.

In the darkness of the hut, only Jackson and Danyluk kneeled and prayed, and Danyluk remained in the kneeling position much longer than Jackson. They were the two Catholics, and this time, Moose embraced his true faith.

About fifteen minutes later, Danyluk came and sat on Douglas' bunk. "Er, Doug, can I ask youse a rather serious question?"

Wayne leaned over to hear the Danyluk muttering to Douglas. He also heard Douglas' reply, "Sure, Moose, what's up?"

"Well, if a dame writes a letter and says she's goin' in the hospital for a stomach lift, but youse knows she's already had one, what would youse think?"

Douglas thought for a moment. "Er, maybe she's put weight on again and has decided to go back for seconds?" He could hear Banks chuckling into his pillow.

"But, er, Doug, she's not fat now. Sure, she's got jugs as big and wonderful as her mother's, but she's not fat. Her mother's goin' in for a tuck as well."

"Well maybe she's just saying that, Moose. Maybe it's a personal problem and she doesn't want to give you the real reason she's going into hospital."

There was silence for fifteen seconds, interrupted only by Wayne's uncontrolled glee.

"Yeah, it's that what worries me," Moose continued. "Er, but what if youse don't remember who she is? SHUT YOUR FACE, AND MIND YOUR OWN BEESWAX, BANKS!"

Douglas sat up. "What do you mean you can't remember her? If you know she's got big bazookas just like her mother, surely you know who she is?"

Moose let out a heavy sigh. "Well, that's also a problem, because I can't remember her mother, either. I've never been to Comox, B.C., at least I don't think I have?"

"Jesus, Moose, let me get this straight. You got a letter from a dame who's going into hospital for a flab-job on her stomach. This is her second trip. She's got wonderful big ones just like her mother, but you can't recall who her and her mother are? In other words, two dames in Comox have both got stomach problems. They are mother and daughter, and they're going into hospital together?"

"Yeah, that's right. It's this last line in the letter which gets me worried."

As he lay back, Douglas said, "Read it to me."

Moose held the letter two inches from his face. *"If it's a little Moose, that's fine, but my Mom, Emma, wants a little Moosella. Love, Jenny. P.S., two more mouths to feed costs bread...send money now."*

Douglas sat up again. "Why didn't you tell me in the first place? you've gone and got mother and daughter pregnant. Moose, you don't need me, you need a padre, maybe even ten of them."

"Shit, Doug, this thing's been buggin' me for days. It don't say they're pregnant, but it seems they are. I ain't been in Comox! BANKS, WILL YOUSE SETTLE DOWN, I GOT SOME SERIOUS STUFF ON MY MIND, REAL SERIOUS STUFF!"

Banks couldn't take it anymore. He was laughing so loud, the Corporal's voice bellowed out of the cubicle. "DANYLUK, TAKE YOUR FUCKING LONELY HEART'S CLUB PROBLEMS TO YOUR PRIEST AND LET ME GET SOME SLEEP! CHRIST, YOU'RE A ONE MAN STUD-FARM. YOU LIVE AND BREATHE DAMES, I CAN'T BELIEVE IT!"

"CORPORAL, I GOT PROBLEMS, YA KNOW?"

"YES, AND I DON'T GIVE A FUCK! HOW IN THE HELL DID I GET IN THIS PLATOON?"

Wayne jumped out of bed laughing and stuck his upper body out the window. "MOOSE, ROTHIE AND I WROTE THAT LETTER!"

"YOU WHAT? SON OF A BITCH! HERE I'VE BEEN GETTIN' GRAY CROTCH HAIR WORRYIN' ABOUT THESE TWO BROADS AND YOUSE AND ROTHIE SET ME UP? O. K., MR. BANKS, THE WAR IS ON. Er, thanks, Doug."

As Danyluk walked back to bed grumbling to himself, Wayne sat on Douglas' bed. "We got him!"

Now Douglas was roaring. "You really had him worried?"

Wayne crawled up to his bunk and leaned over. "Yeah, isn't it great?"

Danyluk yelled. "I'LL PAY YOU BACK, MR. BANKS!"

Another voice was heard before Danyluk had the last word. "YOU'LL PAY ME BACK FIRST!"

"UP YOURS, CUNNILINGUS!"

As every cadet was just dozing off, East said to Jackson, "Hey, Earl, did you see the posters they put out for the movie *High Noon?*"

"No, I don't think so, why?"

Jack finished swallowing something. "Well, the slogan they use reminds me of Danyluk. The slogan says, 'When the hands point up, the excitement starts!' In Danyluk's case, when his wang points up the excitement startles!"

Laughter came from the nearby bunks, and Moose sat up straight. "SCREW YOU, EAST, YOU'RE JUST JEALOUS!"

"Come off it, Moose, why would I be jealous? Small is beautiful! Hey Earl, do you know the slogan for Spam?"

Earl was now asleep, so Simon answered. "Yeah, its, 'If you ain't eatin' Spam, you ain't eatin' ham.' Jack, don't tell me you've got food on your mind again?"

"No, but it reminds me of Moose's personal slogan. 'You won't be my pick, if you ain't chewin' my dick.'"

A voice came over the Corporal's cubicle walls. "JESUS, WILL YOU LEAVE MOOSE ALONE AND LET ME GET SOME SLEEP!"

As Jack started to snore, Moose said, "Hey, Simon, are you still awake?"

"Yeah."

"How do you like Jack's new slogan? 'Speak softly and carry a big sandwich.'"

Jack woke up. "I heard that, Moose. UP YOUR ASS!"

Moose rolled over on his side. "Gotcha!"

Another Friday had ended and it was quiet in the wings of B-33. It wasn't quiet in the drying room, however, because behind the closed door, the faint sound of voices could be heard, particularly Cunningham's.

"Ya bet a deuce and ya throw in a one? I saw ya! C'man, c,man, I wasn't born yesterday, ya know? And cover up that flashlight. Do ya want the Provost to find us? O. K., money in."

CHAPTER IX

Saturday felt like a Sunday for the cadets of Alpha Company, and most of them took advantage of being allowed to sleep in. Eventually though, the band marching by their quarters was so loud, everyone got up. They wanted to see Bravo Company, the new guard, march by.

"Jesus, we've got our work cut out with that company, look at their arms," stated Danyluk.

Cunningham was with Moose at the window. "Not just their arms, look at the way the hold their rifles."

A cadet came over from the other wing. "Er, Moose, will you sign this for me, please?"

Danyluk grabbed the page of a letter which read, *'So you see, Matilda, although I might not meet Red Robinson, I have met his right-hand man, Moose Danyluk and that's close, isn't it? To prove it to you, I got Moose to sign this here letter. You can show his autograph to all your girlfriends.'*

Moose looked up to the ceiling and rolled his eyes. After he shook his head, he said, "Gimmee a pen!"

Danyluk quickly scratched out his signature and without looking at the boy, handed the letter and pen back.

"Gee, thanks, Moose!" The cadet was ecstatic as he headed back to his own wing.

East came over. "It's nice to be famous, isn't it, Moose?"

Moose started making his bed. "Hey, what the hell was I supposed to do...say no? I must have signed about a thousand autographs. They may not mean much now, but when I'm a famous women's private parts doctor, workin' in the sick people's place, they'll be worth real dough."

"Don't you mean, when you're a distinguished gynecologist working in a hospital?"

Moose glared at Simon. "What are you, some sort of a smart ass, same dif, ain't it?"

When all of their beds were made and their bunk spaces were cleaned, the Musketeers met in the shower room. For some reason there was plenty of hot water and with the windows closed, the steam billowed out into the centre sink area.

"What's on today?" Cunningham asked.

As usual, Wayne's whole body was covered with shampoo. "Well, we've got our bush uniforms to get into shape and I don't know about you guys, but I've got four lesson plans to prepare."

"Good idea," said Moose, as he used a special bar of soap to wash under his arms.

Other than during training, this was the only time Jack wasn't eating. With his mouth empty, his voice was actually clear. "Moose, how come you use two bars of soap?"

A sneaky grin appeared on Danyluk's face. "Cause one's perfumed and one ain't. I use the perfumed soap to make my armpits smell like charmpits. Cleanliness is next to Godliness. Youse fellas should try this stuff. Jesus, Cunningham, I passed you the other day and I thought you'd spent the whole week at the Vernon garbage dump."

"SCREW YOU, MOOSE! I AIN'T GOT NO B.O. DID YOU GUYS HEAR THAT? AT LEAST I DON'T SHAVE MY ARMPITS!"

Moose chuckled. "That's because you ain't got nottin' to shave. And I *don't* shave my armpits, look at this."

Cunningham gagged at the open armpit held three inches from his face. "UGH, I CAN'T TAKE IT, SOMEONE PASS ME A GAS MASK, QUICK!"

Smiling and scrubbing, Moose tuned him out. Then he sang his favorite song with the words changed. "YES, DEAR, I HAVE YOUR BANANA, I HAVE YOUR BANANA, TODAY..."

Wayne said, "Moose, you're the only person I know that can guarantee tomorrow, today."

The singing stopped. "What d'yez mean by that?"

"Well, when you do it with a dame, she's gonna learn the results, fast."

"Hey, I use protection. I picked up some rubbers from the MIR."

Cunningham got into the act again. "Those are rubber shower caps, you idiot."

Moose pushed Cunningham away. "Up yours, you virgin. The Corporal...Durupt, told me they're the best on the market. I'll show ya."

Dripping wet, Danyluk left the shower room and headed to his barrack box. He was back in a few seconds with a military prophylactic. "There, smart ass, does this look like a shower cap to youse?"

Jackson grabbed it and stretched it over his head. "Yep, it sure does."

The laughter in the shower room of B-33 could probably be heard at Gracie's Drive In, across from the Provost Shack on the other side of Highway 97.

Before they finished showering, each Musketeer wore 'the cap.' Danyluk was the last to try *it* on and he wore it as he walked back to his bunk, towel hung around his neck, *wang and friends* imitating the movements of a marching Scot's sporran.

"THAT MAN! WHAT THE HELL HAVE YOU GOT ON YOUR HEAD?"

The Camp RSM, Mr. Gardiner, had entered the south end of the wing, but Danyluk was headed north. Danyluk knew the voice only too well. He stopped dead in his tracks the minute he heard it When he finally turned around and stood at attention, the RSM raised his arms to the sky, his big drill cane hitting one the light shades.

"MY GOD, IT'S YOU AGAIN? WHY IS IT EVERY TIME I ENTER THIS BUILDING, YOU'RE IN THE NUDE? DON'T YOU BELIEVE IN CLOTHES, MAN? WHAT'S THAT ON YOUR HEAD?"

Moose's face turned red. "It's, er, it's a rubber, sir."

The RSM closed his eyes and shuddered as he turned and marched out. "I SHOULD NEVER HAVE ASKED? OF COURSE IT IS! IT HAS TO BE? YOU EVEN MANAGED TO STRETCH IT TO GET IT ON YOUR OTHER HEAD! MY GOD...WHAT'S THIS WORLD COM...?"

Gardiner was still mumbling to himself outside the building. "If we had a camp psychiatrist, no one else would be able to make an appointment because he or she would be with *him* all of the time. The pathetic retard."

As a naked Danyluk flung himself on his bunk and started punching his pillow, the guys at his end of the hut were howling.

"Why me? Jeez, I know the Mounties always get their man, but why is this guy always near me at the wrong time?"

Wayne was laughing so hard, he could barely speak. "When it comes to you, maybe every time is the wrong time?"

Moose stood up and stepped into his undershorts. "Banks, you creep, I'm beginning to believe that!"

At seven-twenty that night, as the Musketeers and their girls neared the arena, they couldn't believe the crowd; the lineup was six blocks long. It appeared that every cadet in camp and every teenager in the Okanagan Valley was trying to get in to see Red Robinson.

"Just look at the herd. I'm not gettin' in that line; c'mon Alma, let's go home."

Just moments before, Douglas had clued Diane in, and Diane was quick. "Moose, Alma, we don't have to line up, my uncle's nephew is on the back door. He's going to let us in."

"Come off it, Diane, youse knows I don't like cheatin' - it wouldn't be fair to the others who have been lining up."

"Oh, Moose, what's with you? I've got the feeling that you don't want to see your buddy, Red. That's right, isn't it?"

Moose didn't know what to say. Since the time he left camp, he'd been trying to come up with an excuse to get out of going to the dance, but nothing worked. His friends had an answer for everything he threw at them. They didn't even believe that he had measles, because Wayne had smeared two of the spots.

He was just about to answer Diane, when at least fifty cadets who were in line recognized him. "HEY, THERE'S MOOSE DANYLUK, RED'S BUDDY. HEY, MOOSE...DON'T FORGET TO INTRODUCE US." A cadet turned towards his friends. "HEY, EVERYONE, THAT'S MOOSE DANYLUK, RED ROBINSON'S TOP ADVISOR AND VERY BEST FRIEND!"

Moose took a big breath and let it out as he showed the thumbs up to the group. "I'LL SEE WHAT I CAN DO," he yelled. "RED MIGHT NOT WANT ALL THE ATTENTION, OR HE MIGHT BE TOO BUSY!"

"OH, COME OFF IT, MOOSE. ANYWAY, WE'RE NOT GOING TO LET YOU OUT OF OUR SIGHT!"

The Musketeers and all the girls but Alma were dying to laugh, but they didn't. Old Moose was on the hot seat and they were letting him sizzle.

"Alma, I've got a splitting headache. Let's go have a shake and we'll come back when the line's shorter."

Wayne nudged Debbie and she instantly attacked her purse. "Here, Moose, here's two aspirins. Take them now." She then grabbed Alma by the arm. "C'mon Alma, let's get in there before the crowd starts getting in."

Alma didn't have much of a choice as she was *pulled* towards the back door of the arena, *dragging* Moose with her.

Douglas glanced at his watch. It read exactly nineteen-thirty hours as he banged on the back door. Luckily, no other cadets were there.

He pounded again. When no one answered, that was all Moose needed. "There, you see, that means we've got to get into the..."

The door opened quickly, and as Diane rushed in, she said, "Cousin Peter, how are you? How's the folks?"

Instantly, Moose was dragged in and pushed towards the coat check room. With his back to the guy who opened the door, Red's *friend*, had no idea he was being pointed out.

"That's him there," Douglas said to the fellow who then closed the door and walked over to the stage. Red was standing at the bottom, talking to a few of the local town's council. When his assistant whispered in his ear, Red excused himself for a minute and whispered back. Red's instructions to his assistant were that he should stay with, and stand behind Danyluk so Red could get a good look at Moose. Their *Technicolor Host* then went back to his conversation and the smile on his face indicated he was looking forward to the next hour.

Within twenty minutes, the place was jammed and people were still coming in. Red's *real* assistant did his job properly and followed Moose around enough for Red to get a good look at this Moose person. When Robinson was satisfied, he made a signal to the guy, who immediately left Moose alone.

Moose turned towards Diane. "For a moment there, I thought your uncle's nephew was going to ask me to dance. Christ, the guy never let me out of his sight."

Diane chuckled. "Oh, er, he just wanted to make certain we weren't hassled because we came in the back door. Savvy?"

"Er, yeah, O.K., eh Alma?'

Alma nodded. "Yeah, he seems like a nice guy. Moose, you can introduce me to Red now."

Although Moose was completely surrounded, he managed to find a hole in the crowd. "God, I'm bursting," he replied. "Where's the men's room?"

"Same place where it's always been," replied East. "Are you losing your memory, as well?"

"As well as what?" Moose said as he left.

"As well as getting gray crotch hair," Jack replied, sticking to him like glue.

After Danyluk and East were lost in the crowd, Alma was told about the Red Robinson affair. She instantly burst into a fit, with the rest of them.

She was now as enthusiastic as all the others. "YOU STINKERS!" she screamed. "OH, THIS IS HILARIOUS!"

One of Red's tape machines had been playing background music while people entered the arena. At exactly eight o'clock, when it appeared the queue had finally come to an end, Red Robinson climbed the stairs of the stage. In addition to two assistants, the stage held four large speakers which were hooked up to the arena's main speakers. Actually, the stage was loaded with electronic equipment, stacks upon stacks of 45 rpm records, piles of albums, a desk, three chairs, and a microphone. And now to share the platform with his assistants and equipment was Red Robinson. He grabbed the microphone.

"HI OUT THERE?"

The noise was boisterous. Red was loud, but the excited teenagers were louder. "CAN YA HEAR ME? HI, VERNON!"

That's all it took for Red to get a tumultuous response. "HI, RED!"

Red smiled and walked to the edge of the stage. He was ensnared by a semi-circle of screaming teenage girls twenty rows deep. Some guys were now starting to push in, as well.

"I WANT YOU TO KNOW IT'S GREAT BEING HERE IN GOD'S COUN-TRY. I'VE BROUGHT SOME FABULOUS MUSIC WITH ME, AND I DON'T

THINK YOU'VE EVER HEARD ANYTHING LIKE IT BEFORE! THROUGH-
OUT THE EVENING, I WANT TO GET TO KNOW YOU A LITTLE BETTER,
BUT RIGHT NOW, LET'S JIVE, ROCK N ROLL, AND GET IT ON
WITH...**THIS**...!"

In a fraction of a second, the sounds of Frankie Lymon's, *Why Do Fools Fall
in Love?* filled the arena and swarms of dancing couples were literally tripping over
each other. A good number of girls and guys stayed jumping up and down at the
foot of the stage, so Red shook their hands and signed autographs. For the
teenagers of the Okanagan Valley, this was a night to behold.

Red knew how to control a crowd and that was to keep them busy. Four in a
row followed Frankie Lymon. They were, *Don't Be Cruel, Blue Suede Shoes, Long
Tall Sally and That's Alright Mama.* The music, combined with the noise, the sweat,
the stifling air, the dancing, and the crushing were absolutely fantastic as far as
Red's fans were concerned. They were there to see and hear their idol and if a
bomb had gone off next door, it would have added to their delight.

When the first five records were finished, Red picked up the microphone
again. "O.K., HERE'S YOUR CHANCE TO SNUGGLE UP. ARE YA READY?"

"YEAH!" the crowd roared back, just before Elvis's, *Love Me Tender*, started.
Red followed it up with another four in a row. They were, *My Prayer, Autumn
Leaves, Unchained Melody,* and to Douglas and Diane's joy, *Ebb Tide.*

Danyluk was so snuggled, he could hardly breathe. Even so, he never took
both of his hands off Alma's buttocks.

"You know, Alma, I've got the feeling Red's looking at me. Every time I look
up, he's staring at me. When I try to sneak a look, our eyes meet."

Alma took her head off his shoulder. "Well, he should, shouldn't he? He's one
of your best friends, why wouldn't he look at you? He's probably upset because
you haven't said hello, yet."

Alma didn't see Moose cringe before he answered her. "Er, yes, er, you're
probably right." When she put her head back on his shoulder, he thought to himself,
'What in the hell am I going to do? You and your big mouth, Danyluk. Jesus, how
can I get out of this?'

Over the next hour, Red Robinson played records that had the audience going
wild. This was only the second year of the rock and roll era, and as far as these kids
were concerned, there was only one guy in the world who could introduce it properly and give them the choice they wanted. That was Red Robinson.

At nine o'clock with sweat pouring off everyone, Red asked for the lights to be
turned up as the record, *Green Door*, finished.

"ARE YOU HAVING A GOOD TIME? ...NO?"

Even Red fawned when the audience replied, "YES! MORE, MORE, MORE!"

He smiled. "LADIES AND GENTLEMEN, I'VE JUST LEARNED THAT
ONE OF MY BEST BUDDIES IS UP HERE TRAINING IN VERNON AND
THAT HE'S ACTUALLY WITH US TONIGHT. GOOD FRIENDS ARE
ALWAYS HARD TO FIND, AND I CONSIDER MYSELF FORTUNATE
INDEED TO HAVE THIS GUY AS A CONFIDANT. HE HELPS ME PICK THE
HITS AND I DON'T KNOW WHAT I'D DO IF HE STOPPED OFFERING HIS
KNOWLEDGE OF THE WORLD MUSIC SCENE."

Red had to hold his hand in front of his face when he glanced at the spotlight
attendant. "CAN WE HAVE THE SPOTLIGHT ON MY CHUM OVER HERE.
THAT'S IT, JUST KEEP MOVING IT UNTIL I TELL YOU WHEN TO STOP."

The glare of the light nearly blinded Danyluk, as he strained his neck trying to see Red's friend. Obviously the guy was close because the beam of light was on him and Alma, as well.

"THAT'S IT, STOP! THERE HE IS! LADIES AND GENTLEMEN, PUT YOUR HANDS TOGETHER AND WELCOME THE FRIEND OF FRIENDS. MY BEST FRIEND AND ASSOCIATE, MOOSE DANYLUK."

Moose's jaw opened and remained locked as his eyes crossed and he fell backwards. If Cunningham hadn't been there to stop the fall, Danyluk would have been in the famous *horizontal position.*

The Musketeers and their girls were killing themselves laughing and East nearly choked on his hot-dog when Jackson said, "Just look at him, his lights are on, but nobody's home."

"COME ON UP HERE, MOOSE! C'MON BUDDY, DON'T BE SHY, I WANT TO INTRODUCE YOU TO THIS FABULOUS GATHERING. SOME-ONE GIVE HIM A HAND THERE. THAT'S IT, THAT'S IT; HELP HIM AND ALMA UP THE STAIRS. PERFECT, JUST PERFECT. NOW, CAN WE GET THE PHOTOGRAPHER OVER HERE PLEASE?"

Moose didn't know where he was. The light was blinding him and he had to be literally lifted on the stage. His mouth was still open as Red reached down to grab a limp hand to shake. He then put his arm around Moose's shoulders and an assistant put one of Danyluk's (still) limp arms around Red's shoulders.

Red pretended to whisper into Moose's ear, and with his right hand, he tilted and turned Moose's head so that it looked like Moose was whispering back.

"YES, I KNOW WHAT YOU MEAN, MOOSE. WELL, THERE'S NO PROBLEM THERE. LADIES AND GENTLEMEN, MOOSE TELLS ME THAT A LOT OF CADETS AT THE CAMP HAVE ASKED HIM TO GET MY AUTO-GRAPH FOR THEM. WELL, ANY FRIEND OF MOOSE IS A FRIEND OF MINE. I'VE ACCEPTED MOOSE'S OFFER TO VISIT THE CAMP TOMOR-ROW. I'LL BE HAPPY TO GIVE ANYONE AN AUTOGRAPH. ISN'T THAT RIGHT, MOOSE?"

Moose's mouth was still wide and he still had his infirm arm around Red's shoulders. Red used his right hand to nod Danyluk's head. It all looked real.

"MOOSE, WHAT HAVE YA GOT TO SAY, KIDDO? DO YOU WANT TO REC-OMMEND A RECORD WE SHOULD PLAY?"

Moose tried to talk, but the words just weren't coming out right as Red put his ear in front of Moose's mouth. "Bah, abah, bah, abah..."

"YOU GOT IT! LADIES AND GENTLEMEN, HERE'S, **BE BOP A LULU!** WHAT A CHOICE, MOOSE...WHAT A CHOICE! YA SEE WHAT I MEAN? THIS GUY KNOWS HIS MUSIC."

While everyone was dancing, Red guided Moose to a chair. Alma actually had to close his mouth.

Red held out his hand. "Hi, Alma, it's nice meeting you."

Alma's face lit up with surprise as she shook his offered hand. She was shy and really didn't know what to say. "How...did you...know my name?"

"I told him," a smiling nearby assistant replied. You know I was trailing you guys for nearly thirty minutes."

Red looked at Danyluk. "Is he always as quiet as this? He seems pale, as well?"

Alma started laughing. "I think he'll come around in a few minutes. You have no idea how much of a shock this was to him."

"Oh yes, I do," Red replied. "I think this poor guy probably tried everything to get out of coming here tonight. Am I right, Alma?"

"Red, you're absolutely right! We had to force him to come."

Moose stood up. "Ah, er, ah...er, er, what the fu...?" He shook his head and corrected himself as he smiled bashfully at his Technicolor Host. "Er, sorry, thanks, Red."

Red went over and smacked Moose on the back. "Think nothing of it, Moose old buddy. That's what friends are for. Now, I want you to put these earphones on and I'm going to show you how to cue a record. C'mon, Alma, you can sit next to him."

When the crowd saw Moose with the earphones on, and Red talking with him, they screamed, "MOOSE! MOOSE! MOOSE! MOOSE!" The *man* and his *assistant* were back together again.

The rest of the Musketeers and their girls were having a ball watching 'Good Old Moose' learn how to be a disc-jockey.

Douglas had to yell into Diane's ear to be heard. "RED IS SOMETHING ELSE. HE'S GOING ALL OUT FOR US. JUST LOOK AT MOOSE!"

Although Moose's mouth was open again, he was moving his hands on the dials and cueing records on the turntable. Shortly, the open mouth changed into an ear-to-ear smile. Moose was back to normal. He didn't have a clue what was going on, but he was back to his old self again, *and* he was with his idol. He even gave the thumbs up sign to the cadets below.

In the second half of the dance, Red invited the rest of the Musketeers and their girls onto the stage. Rothie's girl was also there, because Douglas and Diane had picked her up from home on the way to the arena.

"Which two of you are Douglas and Wayne?" Red asked.

They shyly stepped forward. "Er, I'm Doug, and er, this is Wayne. We'd like to thank you for..."

Red saluted them and then put his arm down quickly. "Oops, I forgot, you've got to be wearing headdress to salute, haven't you? You don't have to thank me, Doug, let me thank you. I'm having just as much fun as you guys are."

All the Musketeers laughed as Red introduced himself to each couple and shook their hands. When he found out Rothstein's girlfriend was alone, he said, "Well, we'll have to fix that." The next minute he was down in the crowd dancing with her. The excitement on her flushed face couldn't be described.

The balance of the evening was just as incredible as the first half. In addition to playing all the top tunes on the Vancouver charts, Red played some Glen Miller hits for the benefit of the army cadets in the crowd. After, *Moonlight Serenade*, as well as, The Andrews Sisters big hit, *Boogie Woogie Bugle Boy*, the throng started cheering and whistling.

At the end of the evening when it was time to wrap everything up, Red played six in a row. They were, *Love Is a Many Splendored Thing, Little Things Mean a Lot, Unchained Melody, The Wayward Wind, Memories Are Made of This*, and an obvious request, *Ebb Tide*. But that wasn't all.

"I'VE GOT A REQUEST HERE FOR A FINAL WALTZ! IS EVERYONE READY?"

There were mixed reactions from the crowd. It didn't really matter what Red played, they were with him. Although they hesitated on his choice of beat, Red already knew that, because he wasn't going to play a waltz anyway.

The *final waltz* took the form of, *Honky Tonk, Heartbreak Hotel, Blue Suede Shoes, Don't Be Cruel and Love Me Tender.*

When the lights came on, Red waved and said, 'THANKS VERNON! I'LL NEVER FORGET THIS EVENING AND I HOPE YOU WON'T EITHER. MAKE CERTAIN YOU GET HOME SAFELY! MOOSE HAS INVITED ME TO THE CAMP TOMORROW, AND I AM REALLY LOOKING FORWARD TO IT! GOOD NIGHT, EVERYBODY?"

Good night and thanks were screamed, yelled, bellowed, whistled, hooted and stomped. Even Moose took off his earphones and bowed to the crowd. Then Red took hold of one of Moose's arms and raised it in a manner similar to a referee raising a winning boxer's hand. Danyluk's expression indicated that he felt like a prize fighter.

With good-byes, thanks and tomorrow's arrangements made, the Musketeer couples left the hot arena, entered the cool night air, and headed for Alma's house. All the girls were staying there overnight. After a five minute sojourn, the guys made their way up the hill.

"That had to be the best time in my life," gushed Simon. "Red is just like us...he's one of the guys!"

Moose was quiet as he searched for words and pinched the skin on his right arm. "Am I alive? Is this really me? Was I dreaming? Did I actually spend the whole night on stage assistin' Red Robinson? YOU ROTTEN CREEPS!"

Wayne roared out laughing. "We couldn't tell ya, Moose, it would have ruined the surprise. Red even wanted it kept secret. Can I ask you a question?"

Moose cocked his head but managed to stay in step. "Sure, go ahead."

"What does, "Bah, abah, bah, abah...mean?"

The group's laughter was really loud, including Moose's. "It meant I didn't have a clue what I was doing, what I was saying, who I was with, where I was, or what was going on? SON OF A BITCH, I NEARLY PISSED MY PANTS! IF I'D HAD A WEAK HEART, I'D BE IN THERE," he said, pointing to the Vernon Hospital they were passing.

"NO, IT DOESN'T!" yelled East. "IT MEANS BEE BOP A LULU!"

Danyluk turned around again. "You, you creep. I saw you eyeing Red's sandwich. And you, Cunningham, asking my buddy, Red, 'You probably make good money, how about a quick game of bullshit poker?' I'm happy Red doesn't gamble."

Douglas smacked Moose on the back. "That's our Moose. Now he really is Red's buddy."

"HEY, YEAH! I REALLY AM, AIN'T I? FINALLY, I'VE GOT FRIENDS IN HIGH PLACES!" Danyluk stuck out his chest and said nothing more. He was now the chum of the number one disc-jockey in Canada. Just thinking about it made him lose the step.

When they entered the barracks, Moose was mobbed, not just by cadets, but the company's Corporals who had also waited for him. By the time he hit the sack, his back was sore from all the smacks, and his writing hand was so stiff he couldn't sign any more autographs.

As Jackson came over to Douglas' bunk, exciting chatter took place all over the darkened hut.

"What time is Red arriving tomorrow?"

Wayne answered. "We have to meet him at the Guardroom, ten minutes before noon; he's coming for brunch. Then we're going to give him a tour of the camp."

"Mint," Earl replied, as he went back to his own bunk.

Just before B-33 was enclosed in silence, East said to Danyluk, "I didn't just grab Red's sandwich, he offered it to me."

Moose sat up. "No, he didn't offer it to ya. He said, 'Have you eaten, Jack?' He had to say something, youse was droolin'."

East shrugged. "Well, that's the same thing, ain't it?"

Danyluk put on his whining voice. "*No, it ain't the same thing.* When Red was talkin' to the crowd, he reached for his sandwich and it had disappeared. He actually looked at me. He must have thought I ate it. Jesus, that's embarrassing. And then there was Cunnilingus snapping a ten dollar bill at him all night."

"IT WAS A TWENTY DOLLAR BILL, YOU SNARF! Did you guys hear that? I wouldn't snap a ten dollar bill in front of somebody with dough? I only wish I hadda had a fifty with me."

"DON'T CALL ME A SNARF, YOU FRUMP! YOU'RE THE ONE WHO FARTS IN THE BATHTUB AND BITES THE BUBBLES!"

"YOU ARE A SNARF. I DON'T GO AROUND SMELLING GIRLS BICY-CLE SEATS ON HOT DAYS!"

East finally owned up, a bit. "Well...I might have eaten his sandwich, but I didn't drink his Seven-Up. I drank yours, instead."

"That wasn't mine, you pongo, that was Red's, as well. I heard him say to one of his assistants, 'Hey, where's my drink gone?' When the guy pointed at me, I nearly had a bird. Red said, 'Oh, that's all right then.'"

East put his hands behind his head. "Sorry, Moose."

Danyluk laughed. "Just don't let it happen again. If it does, I simply won't introduce youse to my best buddy again. D'ya hear me?"

"YEAH, YEAH, I HEAR YA!"

Jackson asked Simon, "What's the difference between a male policeman and a female cop?"

"You've got me, what is it?" replied Simon.

Earl chuckled, "Six inches."

It wouldn't be six inches if Moose was a cop," said Wayne.

Earl sat up. "Would ya believe I saw that in a British magazine? Six inches is the difference in height requirements to get on the British Police force. The guy's gotta be a minimum of five-foot-ten, and the dame's gotta be five-foot-four."

As Moose rolled over on his side, he said, "I'd make one hellova good cop, I would."

Wayne decided to enter the conversation. "You can say that again. You'd be the only one with a ten-foot baton. I can just hear the prisoner in the dock complaining, 'Sure Your Honor, I took off, but that cop over there nearly strangled me when he used his lasso.'"

"The judge would say, 'Is that true Constable Danyluk? Where did you learn the fine art of roping?'"

"'Yes, sir. Er, it's my personal technique, Your Judgeship, er, I call it the *wang* procedure and I learned it in my girlfriend's bedroom.'"

"'What? How could you learn roping in your girlfriend's bedroom?'"

"'Oh, sorry, Me Lordship, sire, I thought you said, groping?'"

Before things turned quiet and B-33 creaked, a tired Moose joined the end of the hut in laughter. It had been a long, but grand day.

If buildings could talk, old B-33 would liked to have chaperoned its charges at the dance. But then again, maybe not, because when it came to getting together, the Officers' Mess hut kept turning it down. (Author's note: Don't ask where I dug up that assertion. I was still laughing an hour after I typed it.)

When the Commanding Officer decided to give the cadets of Alpha Company time off, he meant all activities except one. That *one*, was Church Parade. As a result, all cadets of Christian persuasion, excluding Mohammed Danyluk and Mahatma Gandhi Cunningham, were singing hymns in B-3 and the outdoor chapel at exactly 1000 hours.

Ever since his first year in Vernon, when Douglas Brice attended church, he always placed his beret in his pocket, badge down. He also ensured he remembered all the faces of those around him, just in case his badge disappeared again.

This time Wayne made a mistake. He was sitting one away from Douglas' left and he left his beret on the bench when they stood up to sing *All God's Children*. When Douglas glanced around and noticed a hand on Wayne's beret, he quickly put a vise-hold on it and kept singing. The struggling cadet behind couldn't do anything, his hand was locked. The action was carried out so smoothly, the only people who knew what was going on were the two sitting on either side of the *thief*.

After the hymn, Douglas released his grip and slowly turned around. A small, red-faced, guilty-looking cadet from Bravo Company didn't know which way to turn or what to say.

"You see me outside the main doors, following the service," Douglas whispered, releasing his hold.

Although the boy nodded, he was nowhere to be found as the big doors were opened to allow everyone out.

Wayne was furious when he learned about the attempted theft. "Just let me at the son of a bitch. Why didn't you tell me, I would have hammered him, church or no church?"

The sun was blinding when Douglas, Wayne, and East left B-3 and headed across the highway to meet the rest of the Musketeers at Gracie's Drive In. Danyluk had started up a conversation with a teenage girl who was trying to pump up a flat tire on her bike.

"Why don't ya let me walk ya home and I'll fix it for yez?" he asked.

"Because I've been warned about you, and how you *fix* things," she replied. "The girl serving at the wicket is a friend of mine. She tells me you're always hanging around here trying to pick up girls."

Moose stuck his chest out and smiled. "Damn it, I *am* becoming a living legend. Did youse go to the dance last night?"

"Yes."

"Well, take a good look at me. I'm Red Robinson's advisor and confidant. I was on the stage with him all night." He paused for a moment. "That good lookin' record spinner was none other than yours truly."

Instantly the girl turned bashful. "OH, MY GOD, IT IS YOU! WAIT UNTIL I TELL MY FRIENDS AT KAL BEACH. CAN I HAVE YOUR AUTOGRAPH?"

Moose cocked his head and took out his pen. "Certainly, my dear. Here, let me write it on your arm." Even Moose's pronunciation improved. "There you are...*now* can I walk you home?"

The girl started running with her bike. "No, as I said before, the girl behind the counter warned me about you. Besides, if my dad saw me with you, he'd knock your head off."

A sulking Danyluk sipped on his chocolate shake and joined the rest of the guys at a table.

"Why do girls always have dads who want to knock guys' heads off?"

"Nice try, anyway, Moose," Gordie said, shuffling a deck of cards with one hand. "Her father wouldn't have just knocked your head off, he would have killed you."

Moose flexed his right arm. "OH YEAH? WELL JUST CHECK OUT THESE MUSCLES AND SAY THAT AGAIN."

Gordie didn't even look at Moose's *muscle*. "Her old man is RSM Gardiner."

Danyluk nearly choked on his shake. He had to go get a napkin to wipe off his chin.

"CHRIST, WHY DIDN'T YOU TELL ME? WOW, CAN YOU IMAGINE ME FIXING HER TIRE WHEN GARDINER GOT HOME? THAT'S ONE DAME I NEVER WANT TO SEE AGAIN."

"Fixing her tire amongst other things that you thought needed *fixing*," remarked East, finishing off the second of two beef burgers for which Gracie's was famous.

"What time is it?" asked Jackson.

Douglas glanced at his watch. "It's ten to twelve, we'd better be heading over to the Guardroom. Red will be there in a few minutes."

Although the Military Police didn't like cadets hanging around outside their shack, they hesitated when it came to questioning cadets wearing bush uniforms. Even Corporal Adams just kept his remarks to *regularly* dressed cadets.

At five minutes to twelve, Red drove up in a convertible. He was alone, so he must have left his three assistants in the Allison Hotel where they were staying.

Automatically, without reason, the group stood to attention before they relaxed. "Hi Red."

"Hi fellas, I'm sorry I'm a bit late, but I've been driving around town. I took in Kal and Kin beaches, as well. Vernon is really beautiful."

"Are you driving back?" Douglas asked.

"Hop in, guys. No, I'm flying back, but my assistants are driving. Why?"

"Because you should see the view from The Lookout before you leave."

Red didn't seem to mind that the car was crammed full. Douglas and Wayne sat in the front with Red, while in the back, Simon had to sit on East's lap and Cunningham sat on Danyluk's lap. "Keep your hands to yourself," he said.

Moose's face matched the colour of the driver's hair. "COME OFF IT, YOU ASSHOLE!"

"I hope I'm not on it," Gordie replied.

As the car headed up the main road of the camp, turning left at the headquarters building before coming down the other main road to park in the Officers' Mess parking lot, cadets everywhere were waving and thanking Red.

Red waved back and gave them the thumbs up. "Hey, this camp is large," he remarked. "How many cadets are here?"

"About 1400," Danyluk answered. "And the only dames are the ones who work in the kitchens and the Nursing Sisters."

"From what I saw last night, you guys don't seem to be suffering a shortage."

The group of them, including Red, laughed after Simon said, "There's never enough as far as Moose is concerned."

The Musketeers' kitchen was full when Red and the boys entered. This wasn't the norm because on Sundays, the occupants of Camp Vernon were usually downtown checking out the local girls.

Before eating, Red dutifully shook hands and signed autographs as he headed around most of the tables when cadets called him over to answer questions about the music scene and his job at Radio CJOR in Vancouver.

Even the kitchen *women* were impressed. "Ooh, Gert, if I was younger, I'd grab him and we'd never surface for a week. Did you see the way he winked at me?"

"Yes I did, Aggie. When he smiled at me, I nearly fainted. I haven't felt that way since Wilfred came back from overseas."

After he had eaten, Red didn't have much time. He had to return to his hotel for his bags before he was driven to the Kelowna Airport. He did, however, visit the cadet canteen and B-33. While he was in the hut, General Kitching, as well as Alpha's officers and NCOs, asked him if he would like a drink in their messes and a tour of the camp. Unfortunately, he had to decline. As he shook General Kitching's hand, he said, "Thank you for your hospitality, sir. After visiting here, I'm starting to wonder why I was in *air* cadets. This is a fine camp."

Once again, the car was jammed full as Red drove to the Guardroom. It's a wonder his hand was still attached to his wrist as he said good-bye to the Musketeers and the other four hundred or so who turned up. When he saw the Provost's gas pains, he commented, "I don't think I'd like to be in there."

After a few more pats on his back; with thumbs up, he said, "I'll check out the view from The Lookout, Doug. Thanks guys...it's been real George. Don't forget to give me a call when you return to the coast."

In waving seconds, he left as quickly as he arrived. Civilians driving north down the hill must have wondered why so many cadets were blankly staring in that direction.

On the way back to B-33, Moose put his arms around Wayne and Douglas' shoulders. "I'm sorry I called you guys rotten creeps. That's the best time I've had in my life. Thanks for everyth..."

"THAT MAN, THERE! GET YOUR HANDS OFF THOSE PEOPLE AND MARCH!"

As the RSM walked into the Sergeants' Mess, he mumbled to himself. "At least he's got his Goddamned clothes on. If my daughter ever brought someone home like him, I'd strangle the bastard."

Inside the Sergeants' Mess courtyard, he stopped and thought for a moment. 'What am I worrying for? She wouldn't even waste her time *talking* to someone like him.'

That evening when RSM Gardiner was having supper at his rented house on the lake, his eyes popped and his heart skipped when he saw his daughter's 'signed' arm. "WHO THE HECK IS MOOSE DANYLUK?"

"Er, he was just one of Red Robinson's assistants at the dance last night."

Gardiner sighed with relief and smiled. "Oh, that's nice, dear."

At nineteen-hundred hours that night, fifteen smartly turned-out cadets from Alpha Company met in Bravo Company's office. Included in that group were seven Musketeers. The same kind of meeting was taking place in all company and training-cadre offices in Camp Vernon.

The company's office was in the southern end of another H-hut that had been converted to office space. Chairs had been aligned facing a picture of Queen Elizabeth, which hung on the wall behind an old desk, and partitions used to form other offices contained similar furniture and filing cabinets.

"Please be seated. Just relax and take off your berets," Bravo's seated Officer Commanding stated as he counted heads. All of Bravo's officers and NCOs were present, and they were standing beside the OC's desk facing the cadets.

Glancing at his Second In Command, he said, "We appear to be one short? Weren't we supposed to receive sixteen Alpha cadets?"

The 2I/C was just about to reply when a cadet wearing battledress opened the door, stepped in, slammed down his right foot, stood to attention and saluted. "I'M SORRY I'M LATE, SIR! MY NAME IS CADET ROTHSTEIN!"

Smiles of utter disbelief filled the faces of the seven whose heads turned nearly 180 degrees. They wanted to jump up and embrace the cadet with the beaming, impish grin, but now was not the time.

"Ah, yes. Thank you Rothstein, please take a seat." The OC then had to clear his throat to retain the attention of the overwhelmed seven.

"My name is Major Kare, and I command Bravo Company. I'd like to take this opportunity to welcome you to the finest company in camp."

The OC's smile mirrored the smirks on the faces of the cadets in front of him. If he was looking for a reaction, he got one, because now sixteen cadets were clearing *their* throats. They knew which company was the best because that's why they were present.

"All right, all right, I take that back. Welcome to the second best company in camp. However, if you people do your jobs properly, then perhaps I might command the best company in camp. How does that sound?"

The cadets nodded and agreed.

"As you know, this is the first time cadets from the senior company have been attached to train other cadets. Although I was a little apprehensive about the idea at first, I think it's a fine concept. If it proves successful, then the program will continue in the future.

"Now, I know most of you are NCOs in your corps and that you are used to training and dealing with cadets. From what I've been told, you sixteen are the cream of the crop at home, and here at camp, therefore, you shouldn't have any difficulties. I believe that's probably going to be the case, however, this time you're not just training cadets for two hours a week. You're now going to be with them twenty-four hours a day. Sometimes they're going to get on your nerves and perhaps you might get on their nerves, as well. If you've been trained properly, you should be able to handle any situation. Let's face it, these boys are only a year or two younger than you. It is quite possible they won't show you the respect they reveal to these Regular Force gentlemen standing next to me. So let me ask you, what if they don't display regard for you?"

Douglas held up his hand. "Sir, all of us present know full well that we have to earn the respect of the cadets of Bravo Company. The only consideration we require right now is their understanding that we have a job to do. In future years, they'll be in exactly the same position we're in, and we'll make that perfectly clear."

Major Kare smiled and nodded. "Good. Anything else?"

Surprisingly, Danyluk held up his hand. "Sir, we've learned a lot and been through a lot these past three weeks. We understand the meaning behind, 'Do what I do, not, do what I say.'"

Wayne said, "We may not have the man-management experience of your Regular Force Junior NCOs, but we've been taught the same training that allows them to do their job. Well, the theoretical training anyway."

A 72nd Seaforth cadet from Alpha spoke next. "Sir, we're not here to just train Bravo's cadets, we're here to guide them and allow a little bit of us to rub off on them. We know we're good in what we do. How we pass that knowledge along will become the difference between receiving respect or not getting it at all."

After a few other cadets were heard from, the faces of the officers and NCOs revealed proud expressions of understanding. As far as they were concerned, the cadets facing them only lacked experience, and that's what this course was all about.

Throughout the next thirty minutes, Major Kare and the WO2 of Bravo made it perfectly plain what they expected. They laid down the rules and regulations and if an Alpha cadet took it upon himself to bend those orders in any way, he'd be gone.

When the meeting was nearly completed, Major Kare wrapped things up.

"All of my Regular Force Corporals are now going to other cadres. As of this moment, you people are the junior NCOs of our four platoons. The Platoon Sergeants and Officers will still be in the background, but I emphasize, *in the background*. You people will be conducting all instruction and in effect, the cadets of Bravo Company are in your hands. That includes: morning P.T., dress, problems in the barracks, discipline, meal parades, lights out, reveille, swim parades, sick parades, Friday's Mother's Night efforts, Saturday Morning Parades, pay parades, sheet exchanges, and the issuance of Friday night passes. Glenemma comes up a week from now, and you'll be conducting that, as well. Oh, and there is one other thing. Although you all have timetables, etc., I want you to sort out your own 'time off' schedules. Draw these up and ensure the company office has copies. Are there any last questions?"

Simon had a question. "Sir, do we start now?"

Major Kare grinned. "It's now or never. Extra bunks and barrack boxes have been moved into the four cubicles. There will be four of you to a cubicle, if you so desire. When you're not on duty, you'll be sleeping in Alpha's quarters. As of this moment, you're Bravo's NCOs. You will be referred to as Corporal and I'm sure you've all been issued with slip-ons displaying your rank. Tonight, most of Bravo's cadets are downtown or in B-3 watching the movie. Now would be a good time to *move in*. Thank you."

The sixteen cadets stood as the officers and NCOs left the office. As the last Corporal left, seven fiery Musketeers gathered around a grinning Rothstein. In addition to his hand being shaken off, his back would be black and blue that night. Questions came from every direction and Rothstein had difficulty answering them all at once.

"My mom came through the operation with flying colors and told me...! No, she *ordered* me to get back. My dad drove me here."

"Then your mom is going to be fine?"

"I've never seen such a change. They're letting her out of the hospital early. She actually wanted out two days after the operation. She's back to her old self."

"Did your dad stay in Vernon?"

Harvey was just as excited as the others. He wasn't only answering questions, he started shooting them back, as well. "No, he's working tomorrow, he's already gone back. Tell me about Red Robinson. How did it go, Moose?"

Danyluk grabbed his friend by the tie and then released him.

"Rothie, you bastard...! It went great. Now I really am Red's buddy." He paused for a moment. "And if you think you and Banks are going to be let off lightly for that phony letter, you've got another think coming. I owe you two something to remember me by."

Rothstein had forgotten about the letter. Now, he was chuckling his head off with the rest of them. The Harvey Rothstein standing in the middle of them hadn't been like this since last year. He was back to normal and they loved it.

Once again the Musketeers numbered eight, and their alliance was stronger than ever.

"Have you checked in with the Alpha Company office?"

"Yep, and Sergeant Beckford gave me the key to my barrack box."

"Have you told the Headquarters Building that you're back?"

"You bet. A storesman is going to issue me with bush uniforms at 2000 hours. You guys are going to have to help me with the timetables. O.K.?"

"You got it, Rothie."

As they were walking down the stairs after leaving the office, Gordie Cunningham asked, "Say, er, Rothie, er did your dad give you any money to, er...?"

Harvey knew what Cunningham was leading up to. "To gamble?"

Cunningham cleared his throat. "Yeah, that's it, er did he...?".

"He sure did."

"GREAT! HOW MUCH ARE YOU IN FOR? I'LL MATCH...!"

Rothie cut Gordie off. "Put me down for a nickel, the other $9.95 is stayin' in my pocket. Me and my gal have got some catchin' up to do."

"A NICKEL? DID YOU GUYS HEAR THAT? A NICKEL? COME OFF IT, ROTHIE; I RUN A REFINED GAME. THE MINIMUM'S TWO-BITS!"

Rothstein snickered. "Not for me, it ain't. Besides, Moose is the one with all the dough; that's what East told me."

Cunningham's face lit up. "HEY, THAT'S RIGHT. MOOSE, OLD PAL, OLD PARD, OLD KNOB, HOW ABOUT YOU AND I...?"

"IN YOUR EAR, CUNNILINGUS. I'VE GOT TO BEG AND PLEAD FOR MY DOUGH. JEEZ, THAT REMINDS ME, I'M WRITIN' LETTERS TONIGHT; HOW DOES THE VETERAN'S DEFENCE FUND SOUND?"

Wayne said, "I think the VD fund would sound better. A little more appropriate."

Moose put his arm around Wayne's shoulders. "HEY, NEAT! THE VD FUND? YEAH, I LIKE THAT...IT'S GOT A GOOD RING TO IT!" Two seconds later, he took his arm off Wayne's shoulders and gave him a smack on the back of his head.

"WHADUYA THINK, I'M NUTS? YOUSE IS JUST TRYIN' TO PULL A FAST ONE ON ME. IF I SAY VD FUND, EACH OF 'EM WILL KNOW THE DOUGH'S GOIN' IN MY POCKET!"

Laughing and not caring if they were in step, the Musketeers headed to B-33 to pick up their kit and bedding. If someone at that moment had given them a blast, it wouldn't have mattered, because the main thing was, 'Rothie' was back.

Barracks B-33 was a madhouse. Because the occupants were now posted all over camp, they were sorting clothing they would take with them, washing, ironing, shining, and reading instructions. Although the Musketeers were more organized, they, too, had to decide which clothing to take and what to leave behind. Eventually though, they sorted things out and helped Rothstein iron his new uniforms. At 2100, laden with bedding and kit, they headed for Bravo Company's lines. For convenience sake, they wore their coveralls and would change into their bush uniforms later.

When they arrived, B-29 was nearly empty. It was decided earlier that since Brice, Banks, Rothstein, and Jackson were attached to Five Platoon, they would share a cubicle in Five Platoon's end. The other four Musketeers were attached to Six Platoon; therefore they shared the cubicle at the other end of the same wing. The additional eight members of Alpha Company were attached to Seven and Eight Platoons, and were split into fours in the cubicles at each end of the other wing in the barracks.

"This is going to be really tight," Rothstein commented. The cubicles weren't very big and now each held two sets of double bunks. There was, however, room for a small table below the window (which was) between the bunks. Their barrack boxes managed to fit at the end of those bunks. It would be difficult to move around, but the cadets knew they would only be sleeping there. When they had lesson plans to complete, or they had to do their laundry, they would use B-33, or one of the chapels.

After making their beds, they changed into clean bush uniforms. Now immaculately dressed, each checked out the names on the sets of bunks in their wing in order to find out where their individual section cadets were.

Bravo's hut (B-29) was exactly like most of the other barracks in the camp. It was an H-hut consisting of two, large, dormitory-style wings, with a washing room, shower room, and a drying room in the centre between them. A room next to the drying room contained toilets, a urinal, and one washing machine.

Because it was Sunday, B-29 looked like a tornado had hit it. Although beds had been made earlier, some of them had been pulled apart by cadets fooling around. The hut was littered with paper of all kinds, including pages of comic books, furled out toilet rolls, pieces of notebooks, chocolate bar wrappers, and even wrappers from Gracie's beef-burger stand. Kik Kola bottles littered the floor in addition to popsicle and creamsicle sticks and used paper wrappers.

"Danyluk put his hand to his nose. "Jesus, this joint stinks of feet."

As Douglas made his rounds, this hut reminded him of B-21 in his first year. The drying room was full of clothes, indicating Bravo's cadets hadn't yet learned the lesson of protecting their kit. In addition, a review of the cadets' personal wash basins verified that the users weren't particularly fussy if they were shined or not. Dirty running shoes lined the shelves and the colour of them in some ways matched the colour of the towels hung on the aisle-end of the bunks. Battledress uniforms hanging on the walls behind the bunks were not buttoned up and in many cases were not pressed.

Wayne joined Douglas and as they walked the aisle, he said, "We've got our work cut out for us. Can you believe this mess? Wow, it does reek of feet."

Brice shook his head in disbelief. "It reminds me of B-21 a few years back. Now that I think about it, thank God we had Sergeant Beckford."

When the eight of them teamed up with the Alpha cadets in the other wing, their reaction was the same all 'round. A picture didn't have to be drawn for them;

for some reason, Bravo wasn't organized.

One of the two Alpha Seaforth cadets smiled. "These guys are really going to love us. I've just finished looking at the furnace room. That's even a shambles."

"Some of these pith-helmets look like they've never been scrubbed," said Rothstein. "I also doubt whether they know how to iron their laces."

Earl was making notes. "That's nothing. The bulletin board on our side of the barracks has been ripped apart and have you guys seen the shower room?"

East was still chewing as he threw a chicken leg into the overflowing garbage can. "Yeah, there's more dirty underwear and towels in there than Moose's got in his bathroom at home."

"HEY, WATCH YOUR MOUTH! I LOOK AFTER MY SILK GAUNCH. I DON'T LEAVE 'EM IN MY SHITTER, I BEQUEATH 'EM TO MY DAMES." He paused for a moment and grinned. "MOST TIMES I DON'T WEAR UNDER-WEAR, 'CAUSE IT TAKES TOO LONG TO GET THEM OFF WHEN THE ACTION'S HOT."

Simon put his arm on Cunningham's shoulder. "You won't have much time to gamble with these guys, Gordie, they'll have to be organized first."

The 'gambler' didn't like that fact, but he agreed. "I'll just have to survive off Moose."

"SCREW YOU! I AIN'T GONNA GAMBLE UNTIL I FINISH THE 'CANADIAN MOTHERS' LOST SOLDIERS' FUND.' IF LOTSA DOUGH COMES IN, THEN I MIGHT."

"When will that be?"

"In two weeks when I hear from my secondary broads."

"Oh, all right, then."

By approximately 2145, most of Bravo's cadets had returned from the movie, or from downtown. At first they didn't quite know how to accept these young *Corporals* walking the aisle, and after a few seconds, the reality of their existence wore off almost immediately. In their opinion, these 'wet behind the ears' Corporals were cadets just like they were. How was advice from cadets going to improve on pointers from Regular Force Corporals? These guys should just be ignored, then maybe they'd go away.

If Douglas thought B-21 was a madhouse in the old days when it was full, B-29 was something to behold. When all Bravo's cadets had returned, it resembled a busy marketplace. These 'soldiers' were going in all directions at once, yet nothing appeared to be getting accomplished. Cadets were ironing dirty pants and shirts, complaining about lost clothing, jumping over bunks, tables, benches and barrack boxes, running around outside the building, hovering over the smoking pit, spitting out the windows, and generally doing everything except getting ready for bed.

Throughout the disorder, the Musketeers just observed and said nothing. It had been decided earlier that Wayne was to be the *spokesman* for the first two days; therefore at exactly 2200 hours, Wayne stood at the *crossroads* of the aisle.

"STAND BY YOUR BEDS!"

The majority of cadets reacted to his command as if he had spoken to the walls, so he turned off the lights.

The words, "HEY, WHO'S THE 'EFFIN' ASSHOLE?" were heard in various forms.

Wayne turned the lights back on and tried again. "STAND BY YOUR BEDS!"

This time, fifty percent of the cadets stood by their beds. The rest continued to ignore him.

"THIS WING, FORM THREE RANKS ON THE ROAD, NOW! Corporals Brice, Rothstein and Jackson, move them out, NOW!"

With loud complaints and fierce attitudes of defiance, the Musketeers wing of Bravo Company eventually and sloppily, formed into three ranks on the road. Wayne just stood in front of the two platoons and waited until the *noise* died down.

"FIVE AND SIX PLATOONS, ATTEN...TION! STAND STILL!"

Banks glanced at his watch, noted the minute hand and took three places back.

"YOU'RE IN THE POSITION OF ATTENTION! IF I SEE ONE PERSON MOVE OR EVEN BLINK, THE PARADE SQUARE WILL BE BUSY UNTIL MID-NIGHT!"

Five minutes went by until Wayne spoke again.

"STAND STILL! YES, I'M TALKING TO YOU, THAT MAN! YOU, GET YOUR BLOODY EYES TO THE FRONT AND KEEP THEM THERE! STAND STILL!"

Another five minutes ticked away.

"FIVE AND SIX PLATOONS, STANDAT...EASE! ATTEN..TION! Now, I'm going to fall you out. In ten seconds, I'm going to enter the hut and gently ask you to stand by your beds. If I receive the same reaction as I did the first time, we'll be out here again. FIVE AND SIX PLATOONS, FALL, OUT!"

After they turned to their right and paused the normal count of 'two, three,' the mad rush was on, with of course, loud *comments*.

Wayne re-entered the barracks. "FORM THREE RANKS ON THE ROAD!"

Instantly, the rush was on again, with of course, obnoxious utterance.

"FIVE AND SIX PLATOONS, ATTEN...TION! STAND STILL!"

Banks once again glanced at his watch, and this time allowed ten minutes to elapse before he spoke again.

"WHEN I FALL YOU OUT, YOU WILL KEEP YOUR MOUTHS SHUT AND YOU WILL HAVE FIVE SECONDS TO STAND BY YOUR BEDS! IS THAT CLEAR? ALSO, SOME OF YOU ARE NOT WASHING YOUR FEET! I WANT THAT *PROBLEM* STRAIGHTENED OUT!"

"YES, CORPORAL!"

"FIVE AND SIX PLATOONS, FALL, OUT!"

Only the sounds of running feet could be heard. Within five seconds, five and six platoons were standing rigidly by their beds and silence filled the wing as Wayne marched in.

"FIVE AND SIX PLATOONS, STANDAT...EASE! STAND EASY! KEEP YOUR MOUTHS SHUT!"

All eyes were on Corporal Banks as he walked the aisle, stopping at the inter-section.

"WHY ARE THERE CADETS AMONGST YOU WHO INSIST ON RUIN-ING LIFE FOR EVERYONE ELSE; ME INCLUDED?

"I DIDN'T APPRECIATE HAVING TO FORM YOU UP ON THE ROAD, AND I DON'T BELIEVE YOU ENJOYED IT EITHER. WELL, LET ME MAKE IT PERFECTLY CLEAR; THE EIGHT OF US ARE GOING TO BE WATCHING FOR THOSE WHO INSIST ON BEHAVING LIKE CADETS IN CHARLIE COMPANY! IS THIS CHARLIE COMPANY?"

"NO, CORPORAL!"

"YOU'RE DAMNED RIGHT IT ISN'T...AND FIVE AND SIX PLATOONS

ARE THE BEST PLATOONS IN CAMP! WHAT ARE THE BEST PLATOONS?"

Their reaction was as he expected. "FIVE AND SIX PLATOONS, CORPO-RAL!"

"RIGHT, AND DON'T LET ANYONE TELL YOU OTHERWISE! THESE LIGHTS WILL BE GOING OUT IN FIFTEEN MINUTES AND BY THAT TIME, ALL OF YOU WILL HAVE CLEAN FEET AND BE IN YOUR BEDS! IS THAT CLEAR?"

The response was ear-splitting. "YES, CORPORAL!"

"O.K., THEN, GET A MOVE ON!"

There was a flurry of activity and when the lights were finally turned out, everyone was in bed. Wayne now had a problem, it was too quiet in the wing. This was their home and after-lights-out chatter was allowed.

"Does anyone here know what the height of conceit is?" Banks asked.

Not a peep was heard.

"Well, it's a flea floating down the river on his back with a hard-on, yelling, 'open the bridge!'"

A few chuckles were heard, and then some cadet asked, "What's the height of ambition, Corporal?"

Wayne didn't respond, nor did anyone else.

"It's a male mouse crawling up a female elephant's hind leg with the intention of rape."

Laughter rang out and the tension was eased. Wayne received a good response after he said, "GOOD NIGHT, GUYS." A few whispers could also be heard as the Musketeers shut their cubicle doors.

When Douglas, Wayne, Harvey and Earl were in bed, they heard a familiar conversation going on a few bunks down from their cubicle.

"Oh, bull shit. Every time you tell us about your dames, they've all got big gongs. Don't you ever go out with normal dames, like we do? The broad I went out with the other night had boobs like two fried eggs."

"Hey, I don't go out with dames unless they're over thirty-five inches. If you guys settle for less, that's your problem. As for me, I like to play radio, and they've gotta have big ones so I can move the dials."

Wayne chuckled as he leaned over and whispered to Douglas, "Can you believe it, we've got another Danyluk on our hands?"

Brice smiled as he lay with his hands behind his head. "Yeah, and he's in our platoon."

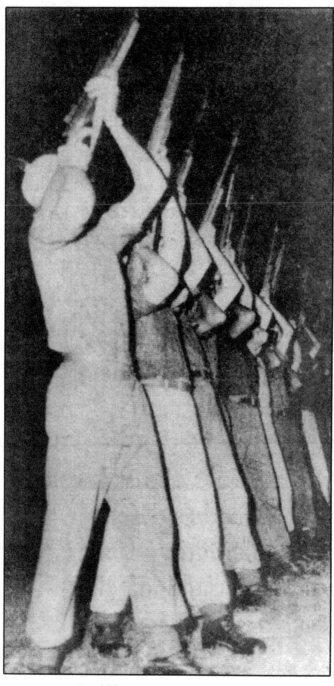

Feu De Joie = Fire Of Joy.

Her Majesty and the Prince Consort visit the cadets of Vernon.
"Excellent, aren't they?"
"Yes, we could certainly use them at Buckingham Palace!"

ALL RIGHT! NOW, FELLAS, YOU'VE USED ENOUGH LIP-BALM TO LAST A LIFE-TIME. LET'S TRY IT AGAIN! TRUMPETS...UP...!"

Signals cadets laying line, and putting up poles. Is it possible one of these innocent faces attached the end of a wire to the urinal in the Sergeants' Mess, with the other end attached to a hand-cranked generator.

Her Majesty and Prince Philip review cadet training.

Wash-up time at Glenemma. Members of the Chief Crowfoot Cadet Corps. (Author's note: Although these youngsters are not members of the Okanagan Indian Band, I think current members of that Band's council, should take note.)

A fire-power display at Glenemma. Cadets were treated to viewing the firing of a 75-millimeter recoilless anti-tank rifle, by members of the 2nd Battalion, Queen's Own Rifles of Canada. Each infantry battalion of the Canadian Army had six of these huge tank busters in its anti-tank platoons. Photo: Charles Steele.

A GROUP OF CADETS IN THE GYMNASTICS DISPLAY AT POLSON PARK
"Is Simpson watching us?"
"Yep! Why?"
"I've gotta scratch my nose."
"Jeez, if ya do that he'll add another mile to our morning run. Cantcha think of somethin' to take your mind, of it?"
"Yeah, all right. Look, mom, no hands."

"AT YOUR TARGET IN FRONT...!"
In many cases, the range was the first introduction to safe, firearms training for the cadets.

A MARCH PAST
The second fellow from the front is in a cold sweat. "Blast, my rifle's slipping, my rifle's slipping, and I know Sergeant Beckford is watching. Why me?"

Cadets R. Rhodes and D.M. Anderson receive congratulations after winning a race during a swim meet at Okanagan Lake.
"Hey, you guys, how'd ya do it?"
"My buddy here, thinks it's the saltpetre in the powdered potatoes."

AH, NAVY LIFE - IT'S GREAT!
Three happy Sea Cadets arriving home from sea cadet camp.
(Author's note: Take a good look at their uniforms. Shortly, Trudeau and Hellyer made Sea Cadets look like green boys and girls from Mars.)

RIFLE EXPERTS
"There you are, my boy...very well done, indeed. How did you get such perfect eyesight?"
"I think it's the powdered tomatoes combined with the saltpetre, sir."

AIR FORCE CADETS WEARING AIR FORCE UNIFORMS, WHICH TRUDEAU AND HELLYER TOOK AWAY.

Training on twin-engine Expeditors, these boys attended one of three air force cadet camps in Western Canada. The objective of this carefully planned air program was to create a camp period that would be enjoyable and educational to all who attended. Exchange programs with other provinces ensured the sharing of common interests, promoted by the air cadet program, and instilled in cadets a broader knowledge, contributing to the development of real Canadian Citizens interested in the welfare of the nation as a whole. (Author's note: I had to show this. Youngsters in light blue, with real aircraft. Wonderful training, that came to a sudden stop.)

A TRAMPOLINE DEMONSTRATION AT POLSON PARK
"How did I get nailed for this? I was supposed to be in the guard."
"Was it you who put the shaving cream in the corporal's hand while he was sleeping?"
"Yep!"
"And then did you tickle his nose with a feather, which then made him scratch his nose?"
"Yep!"
"Need I say more?"

A cadet convoy of Driver Mehcanics Company pause at the Lookout on Highway 97, overlooking Kalamalka Lake. Sometimes two cushions had to be used, as well as wooden blocks on the pedals. Great training that was taken away.

UNDRESSED JEEP
"What's that?"
"It looks like a Kik Kola bottle cap, Sergeant."
"How in the hell did it get in there?"
"Don't know, Sergeant."
"You don't know, eh? Well after this picture is taken, you'll all give me fifty of the best."

DAILY MAINTENANCE IS MOST IMPORTANT
Four cadets polish up their vehicle after a day's instruction, driving over dusty roads in the camp area. Daily maintenance by the boys on their vehicles becomes a matter of pride as the summer progresses.

OH, YOU HAVE NO IDEA HOW THIS FEELS
Only cadets who have attended Vernon, can describe the pure ecstasy of visiting Kalamalka Lake, or Okanagan Lake. Right? Right! Because of short swim suits on hot days, certain rear-ends were white during sporran parades.

THE BEAUTY AND THE BEAST?
No, that's wrong, because Danyluk's not in this picture. Declared to be as smart on parade as any group of regular force soldiers, cadets of the Guard marched through the streets of Kelowna during the annual regatta. Here they meet Miss P.N.E. If Danyluk had been there, he would be sitting next to her, riding in the parade.

PIPERS PRACTICE
Cadet pipers from the Seaforth Highlanders of Canada, and the Canadian Scottish Regiment. Throughout the days and evenings, the sounds of pipes echoed in the nearby hills. Later, these lads would stop traffic with a sporran parade.

INSPECTION OF THE PROVOST
"Now, now, gentlemen. Where's Corporal Adams? There's supposed to be four of you."
"He's gone home, sir."
"I didn't approve that!"
"He went A.W.O.L., sir."

CAMP COMMANDING OFFICER IN 1955-56
Brigadier General George Kitching, CBE, DSO, CD

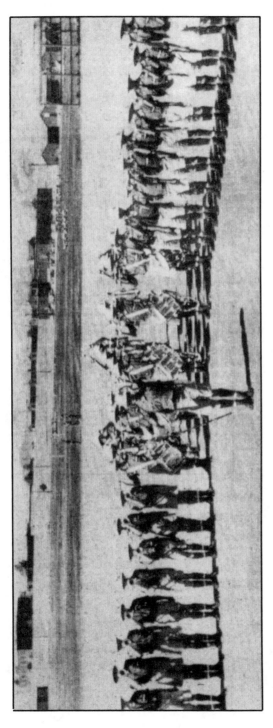

THE CADET BAND IN FORMATION

"There's a bee on my stick."

"A what?"

"There's a bee on my stick and it's walking towards my hand."

"Don't tell anyone else, they'll all want one. Don't move your head, try to blow it off. Blast, it's now on my stick."

"Serves ya right."

"Just how far is this Sugar Lake, anyway?"
"About the same distance as Mable Lake. Just keep ploddin"

"O.K., who knows row, row, row your boat?"
"Oh, come on, Sarge...how about Old King Cole?"
"O.K., let's hear it. 'Old King Cole, was a ...'"

CHAPTER X

The air was fresh and the field of flowers (was) absolutely beautiful, as were the horses Douglas and Diane were riding. Diane was wearing her bikini and her flowing dark-brown hair glistened as the sun's rays continued to explore her already bronzed body.

Douglas decided to stop by a tree he saw a hundred yards to his front. He turned and yelled, "DO YOU WANT TO LIE DOWN FOR A WHILE?"

"She smiled mischievously, "If you want to. Hey, let's shed our clothes and go for a swim in the stream."

As Douglas dismounted, a strange noise penetrated his left ear. The sound wasn't strange for long because in a fraction of a second, he recognized his alarm clock. It was 0530 Monday morning, and instead of being in a gorgeous field with Diane, he was in a cubicle in B-29.

Immediately he awakened his compatriots in the two cubicles and the eight of them headed for the showers. Not one cadet in Bravo Company was up yet.

About a minute or so later, eight yawning Alpha cadets from the other wing joined the Musketeers.

"When the alarm went off this morning, I was having the most wonderful dream. There I was horseback riding in a field of flowers with Diane. She was wearing her bikini and suggested we should shed our clothes and go for a swim in a nearby stream. God, it was real."

"Hey, that was like mine," said Moose. "I had just sneaked into Olga's daughter's bedroom window, only to find out that she was in bed with her mother. I stripped off to get in between them and suddenly both of them held out their arms. I said, 'YOU BET!' got aroused right away and held out *my* arms, then..."

"YEAH, YEAH, GO ON! Y'AV GOT THREE ARMS OUT!" said Jackson. He had stopped soaping to hear the outcome, and had even left his shower to join Moose at the other wall.

"And then Doug gave me a shake and woke me up."

Jackson strolled back to his shared shower and started soaping again. "OH, FOR CHRIST'S SAKE. For a moment there, I thought you were going to say you took both of them on at once?"

"HEY, I'M A ONE-WOMAN GUY. YOUSE WOULDN'T CATCH ME IN BED WITH TWO BROADS...BUT THEN AGAIN, IT'S HAPPENED. I LIKE IT BETTER THOUGH, WHEN IT'S ONE-ON-ONE."

A small lad from Bravo Company entered the shower room. "Hi, Moose."

"IT'S CORPORAL DANYLUK TO YOU!" Moose shot back before he recognized him. Douglas also knew the cadet. It was the boy who was homesick when Moose had met him, and it was the person Douglas had caught trying to steal a badge at Church Parade.

"Jamie Archer, my old buddy. How's it going, Jamie? Are youse happy now that you're in Bravo?"

"YOU BET! I'm still taking your advice...I'm up early, and..." Archer suddenly recognized Douglas. "I er, well I'll see ya later."

After Archer had left, Douglas whispered to Moose about the event in church. "REALLY? WHY THAT LITTLE PONGO! THAT'S WHAT THE BIG GUYS WERE DOING TO HIM WHEN WE FIRST MET. LEAVE HIM TO ME, DOUG."

By 0600, the Musketeers had made their beds and were wearing their P.T. gear. Wayne looked at his watch, stood at the end of the wing for a moment, then started turning over mattresses.

"STAND BY YOUR BEDS! C'MON, LET GO OF YOUR COCKS AND GRAB YOUR SOCKS! I SAID, STAND BY YOUR BEDS!"

When Wayne reached the other end of the hut where his cubicle was, a smile formed on his lips. The 'stud' who had been discussing women's breasts the night before was standing exactly like Moose used to. He slept in the nude and with a morning erection, was bouncing from one foot to the other.

"JJJesus, II've gggotta tttake a pppee," he stammered.

The lad even looked like Moose, but he was slightly short in the 'waterworks' department.

Wayne moved over by Moose. "Corporal Danyluk, this cadet is the spitting image of you a few years ago. Could he be a relative?"

Danyluk shook his head. "NO WAY! ALTHOUGH HE'S BIGGER THAN THE REST OF YA, HE'S GOT SOME CATCHIN' UP TO DO!"

Laughing, Wayne screamed, "YOU'VE GOT ONE MINUTE TO FORM THREE RANKS ON THE ROAD! MOVE NOW! YOU, YES YOU, GET YOUR ASS IN GEAR AND GET YOUR P.T. GEAR ON!"

It took two minutes for them to form up in three ranks.

"PAY ATTENTION HERE! I GAVE YOU ONE MINUTE AND YOU TOOK TWO MINUTES. THAT EXTRA MINUTE GIVES YOU ANOTHER TEN MINUTES OF P.T. THIS MORNING! FIVE AND SIX PLATOONS, ATTEN...TION! MOVE TO THE RIGHT IN GOBS AND BUNCHES, RIGHT TURN! BY THE LEFT, DOUBLE-QUICK, MARCH!"

As they jogged to the upper camp, Douglas and the rest of the Musketeers couldn't believe the similarity of personalities. The 'stud's' name was Williamson and he had been nicknamed, Mule. One of his best friends was a cadet by the name of, Lay, and both of them were in Five Platoon.

"You frump, Mule, you told me these Alpha types were going to go easy on us. I've got dirt up my nose, up my ass, and here we are jogging in the middle of the night."

"What the hell are you complaining for? I'm the one that didn't have time to put any gaunch on. I'll never be able to have kids if my balls have to take this pounding. I wouldn't be surprised if they start swelling up. Jennifer's going to wonder what I've been doing to myself."

Another cadet said, "I told ya, Mule. Go to the MIR and ask for some ball-reduction pills. Did ya go? Probably not!"

"I did go, you idiot. The Orderly, I think his name is, Durupt, just laughed and told me a joke."

Although Lay was breathing heavily, he could still talk. "Well, what was the joke?"

"Well, this here guy with a hoarse throat goes to the doc' and says, 'Doctor, I can't talk, my throat's too sore, what do I do?' "

"'The doc' says, 'Strip off and I'll examine ya.' After the guy strips off, the doc' takes one look and says, 'Christ, no wonder you can't talk, with eighteen inches, your wang's so big, it's tightening up your stomach muscles, contracting your chest muscles, and pulling on your vocal chords. You do have a problem."

"'What do I do?' says the guy with the big knob and the hoarse throat."

"'I'll have to operate,' says the doc'. 'I'll take off nine inches, then your throat will be back to normal. How does that sound?' "

"'Jeez, I don't know?' says the guy. 'My girlfriend may not accept that idea?' "

"'Well, it's up to you,' the doc' replies. 'It'll still leave you with nine inches.'"

"The guy thinks for a minute. 'Oh, all right, I can't go on talking like this; no one can understand me. We've got a deal, let's do it.' "

"After the operation, the guy visits the doc, and in a perfectly clear voice, says, 'Doctor, I want to thank you for saving my voice, but now I've really got a problem. My girlfriend doesn't like the *new* me.' "

"The doctor looks at him, smiles and says, in a *hoarse* voice, 'Too bad! A deal's a deal.'"

Most cadets in Five Platoon roared out laughing. Even the four *Corporals* were in stitches. Mule had told the joke perfectly. Of course, some cadets didn't get it at first, but after a few moments thinking about the doc's hoarse voice, they joined in the merriment.

Outside of B-29, Wayne halted the platoons, stood them at ease and easy.

"NOW, PAY ATTENTION HERE. IN A COUPLE OF YEARS, IF NOT NEXT YEAR, YOU PEOPLE WILL BE DOING WHAT WE'RE ATTEMPTING TO ACCOMPLISH NOW. YOU'LL BE ATTACHED TO A COMPANY, AND YOU'LL BE EXPECTED TO IMPROVE THAT COMPANY'S CONDUCT AND DISCIPLINE. I CALLED YOU GOBS AND BUNCHES THIS MORNING, BECAUSE YOU ARE GOBS AND BUNCHES. THAT TERMINOLOGY IS GOING TO CHANGE."

"WE," he pointed to the seven other Musketeers. "WE'RE NOT NEW TO CAMP VERNON; THIS IS OUR FOURTH YEAR. WE'VE BEEN TAUGHT WELL, AND IT'S OUR JOB TO PASS ALONG WHAT WE'VE LEARNED. FOUR OF US ARE ATTACHED TO EACH PLATOON. WHEN I FALL YOU OUT, GO TO THE BULLETIN BOARD AND FIND OUT WHO YOUR CORPORAL IS.

"THIS HUT IS GOING TO LOOK IMMACULATE THIS MORNING, AS ARE YOU PEOPLE. ALSO, I WANT THAT FOOT SMELL TO DISAPPEAR!

"LISTEN TO YOUR SECTION COMMANDER AND HEED HIS ADVICE. ARE THERE ANY QUESTIONS?"

Mule Williamson came to attention and held out his hand. "Corporal, are we going to have P.T. like this every morning?"

"MOST DAYS, HOWEVER, WE CAN REDUCE THE TIME IF YOU GET ORGANIZED. ANYTHING ELSE?"

There were no other questions.

"RIGHT! FIVE AND SIX PLATOONS, ATTEN...TION! FALL, OUT!"

The time was 0630. Since breakfast was at 0700 hours, the cadets of Bravo Company had half-an-hour to shower, make their beds, clean the area around their bunks, and get dressed. Throughout that half-hour, the eight Musketeers worked feverishly, because they only had a short time to get these cadets dressed properly and get the hut into shape.

As Douglas called a quick meeting around a cadet's bunk, the other section commanders did the same thing.

"Each of you, show me the uniforms you are going to wear today."

When they were produced, Brice nearly vomited. Of the twelve cadets in his section, only two sets of clothing were absent of stains or marks, and even those weren't pressed properly.

"Right! Well, you people are in for a blast this morning, but tomorrow will be like night versus day. Right now, let's grab a quick shower and then get your beds fixed up."

Douglas had a shower with the cadets in his section and afterwards he made certain they each brushed their teeth and combed their hair. Following that, they dressed in their coveralls and made their beds to his specifications. String was used to line up bunks and barrack boxes. Each bunk space was brushed and mopped out. The sets of battledress hanging behind the bunks were neatly buttoned up and the pants were turned up so they didn't hang below the bottoms of the tunics. The towels were filthy, but nothing could be done except hang up the cleanest of each cadet's two towels.

When it was time for breakfast, Douglas joined his section in the mess hall. Afterwards, he dressed while his cadets got dressed and then made certain last minute checks were made. Although the cadets weren't perfect, the wings of the barracks were spotless. That night, sections would be allocated specific tasks in the washing-centre of the hut. Douglas' section had the toilets, washing machine, and the urinal.

At exactly eight o'clock that morning, Bravo Company was sized, formed up on the markers, and left at the open order march.

The cadets of Bravo Company were used to the procedure of officers promenading until the Officer Commanding took over the parade. They had participated in this process since Day One of camp, however, up till this time, they themselves had not carried it out. It had been decided that the cadets of Bravo Company would form the contingent of officers and NCOs and continue with this drill, but it would not take place until Day-Three of Alpha's involvement.

This particular morning, company officers would not be on parade. The parade would be conducted by Corporal Banks and the other Alpha cadets. Bravo Company's Sergeants were there, but they stood aside and assessed the cadets of the senior company.

While Wayne acted as the Officer Commanding, Douglas acted as the Company WO2. The other Alpha cadets took over the roles of the various platoon officers, Sergeants, and Corporals.

The parade went flawlessly because the sixteen Alpha cadets had had it drilled into them daily in front of B-33. They knew the procedure inside and out.

After Douglas handed the parade over to Wayne, the officers were then fallen in. Wayne stood the parade at ease and informed Number Five Platoon that he would inspect them that day, and that each other Platoon Officer would inspect his own platoon.

Douglas joined the Officer Commanding, (Wayne), the Platoon Officer, (Jackson), the Platoon Sergeant, (Rothstein), in the inspection. The rank structure of Six Platoon consisted of Simon as Platoon Officer, Cunningham as the Platoon Sergeant, with East and Danyluk as Platoon Corporals. The other eight Alpha cadets filled the rank structures of Seven and Eight Platoons.

Wayne started with the Right Marker. "What's that on your shirt?"

The cadet glanced down, before looking up again. "It's ketchup, sir."

"Why did you look down? Aren't you always supposed to be looking to your front?"

"Yes, sir."

"Well, in the future, you keep your head and eyes to your front! Is that clear?"

"Yes, sir."

"I thought you wore your coveralls to the kitchen this morning?"

"I did, sir. I also wore this shirt yesterday."

"YESTERDAY? Take a note of this cadet's name."

As Wayne moved on to the next *man*, the Right Marker received the wrath of Jackson, Rothstein, and Douglas.

Although the inspection was to only take fifteen minutes, the turnout was so bad, it lasted half-an-hour. Many comments were made and names taken.

"When did you last shine your boots?"

"Yesterday, sir."

"Did you use shoe polish?"

"I didn't have any, sir."

"Why didn't you buy some?"

The cadet couldn't answer that question. He had obviously spent his money on everything but shoe polish. His name was also taken.

Wayne moved from *man* to *man*. "Did you shave today?"

"No, sir. I haven't shaved since I got here, sir."

"Why not?"

"I don't shave my legs, so why should I shave my face, sir?"

"DON'T BE SMART! What's your name? Where is your name tag?"

"Williamson, and I lost it, sir."

"Do you read orders, Williamson?"

"Er, some of them, sir." Although the cadets were not facing the fierce sun, in many cases, perspiration was running down their faces...Williamson's face in particular.

"Do you think it would be right for you to spend two to three days in the guardroom, simply because you refuse to read all orders?"

The cadet didn't expect that question. He'd heard about the guardroom and that was the last place he wanted to be.

"I, er, wouldn't like that, sir."

"Well, Williamson, you'll read all orders from now on and if I see you with a beard again, we'll let the Provost show you how to shave. Savvy?"

"Yes, sir."

"You're a bliffy, aren't you, Williamson?"

"What's a bliffy, sir?"

"It's ten pounds of shit, stuffed into a five pound bag. Aren't you, Williamson?"

"I, er, yes sir, I am."

Wayne moved on saying, "Then perhaps we'll let the Provost get rid of five of those pounds, also."

In all, only one cadet was spared having his name taken down. Five Platoon was a shambles and the rest were no better. After a short discussion with one of the Sergeants, Wayne received permission to adjust the timetable. For the next three hours until lunch time, they would work on their kit, and they would catch up with missed training in the evening.

Before falling out the officers, Wayne stood the cadets easy and addressed the parade.

"I'VE BEEN HERE FOR THREE WEEKS. PERHAPS DURING THAT TIME, I WAS TOO WRAPPED UP TO NOTICE CADETS OF OTHER COMPANIES, I DON'T KNOW? I DO KNOW THAT I HAVE NEVER WITNESSED SUCH A DESPICABLE TURNOUT IN MY LIFE. YOU PEOPLE HAVE HAD ALL WEEKEND TO WORK ON YOUR KIT, AND YET YOU DIDN'T EVEN CONSIDER IT. ALL OF YOU KNEW YOU WOULD BE THE NEW GUARD, YET YOU CONTINUE TO HIDE WHAT LITTLE COMPANY PRIDE YOU'RE SUPPOSED TO HAVE.

"WELL, GENTLEMEN, AND I USE THE TERM VERY LOOSELY, EFFECTIVE RIGHT THIS MINUTE, FOR THE BALANCE OF CAMP, YOU'RE GOING TO FORGET THINKING OF YOURSELVES, AND START THINKING OF BRAVO COMPANY. YOU'RE GOING TO LIVE, EAT, AND SLEEP BRAVO COMPANY.

"WHEN YOU'RE IN THE JON, THE MAGAZINE WON'T BE NATIONAL GEOGRAPHIC, IT'LL BE BRAVO COMPANY ORDERS! IS THAT CLEAR?"

For the first time in his life, Wayne received the full barrage of a company's response. "YES, SIR!"

After the officers had been fallen out and Douglas had said a few words, Bravo was fallen out and the *lessons* began.

Douglas took his section under a tree, exactly the same way Sergeant Beckford had taken his platoon under a tree in 1953.

"I don't know what's happened with this platoon, and I don't want to know. I do know I can't believe what I witnessed this morning. That's going to change, right now. You're going to work in teams. Your kit will be perfect and ready at all times, as will your barracks, your drill, and your deportment."

Over the next fifteen minutes, Douglas explained what he wanted from them. Then for the next two hours, he demonstrated bed-making, how to scrub towels, clothes, and pith-helmets. He taught them the art of ironing, soaping, starching, boot-polishing; basin, belt and brass shining, the cleaning of running shoes as well as ironing laces. Finally, after their battledress had been ironed, he had every one of them clean out and organize their barrack boxes. Then he got the *platoon's barber* to cut certain cadets' hair.

"How long have you cut hair, Mellish?"

"This is my first year at camp, Corporal. Er, I've just started. I do it to make a few dollars. I bought these clippers with my first pay of five dollars."

"Good, do your clippers pull?"

"A bit, but, er..."

Douglas cut him off. "They pull? Good! It'll teach these guys to visit the camp barber more often. What do you charge?"

"Two-bits, Corporal."

"O.K., after you cut their hair, make note of their names and I'll make certain they pay you on Saturday."

Throughout both wings, all cadets received the same lecture on how to survive at Vernon. At 1130 hours that morning, they wore their coveralls over to the cadet canteen. The same coveralls they would wear at lunch.

After lunch when they were inspected again, like Charlie Company in 1953, Bravo Company shined. Their bodies were scrubbed, the hut was impeccable, their clothing was so stiff it looked new, and their belts, brass, and boots shone like mirrors. Pith-helmets that hours earlier wouldn't have been picked up free at the Vernon garbage dump were scrubbed so clean, they would have been envied by the finest regiments in India. Bravo Company looked like Alpha Company, and Wayne told them so.

"...I'M PROUD OF ALL OF YOU. JUST TAKE A LOOK AT YOURSELVES. THAT'S BRAVO COMPANY PRIDE. IT FEELS GREAT, DOESN'T IT?"

"YES, SIR!"

"THAT'S THE WAY YOU'LL BE FROM NOW ON. YOU WILL ALWAYS HAVE A CLEAN UNIFORM READY. NOW, WHEN YOU MOVE AROUND CAMP, YOU'LL MARCH! YOU'LL GET YOUR ARMS UP, YOUR CHINS UP, YOUR STOMACHS IN, AND YOUR CHESTS OUT! WHERE'S WILLIAMSON?"

A voice in the rear rank of Five Platoon screamed, "HERE, CORPORAL!"

Wayne marched in front of Five Platoon and took a good look at Williamson. "ARE YOU STILL A BLIFFY, WILLIAMSON?"

The cadet's chest was out. "NO, CORPORAL!"

An-ear-to ear grin hit both of their faces at the same time. "YOU BET YOUR LIFE YOU'RE NOT! THERE ARE NO BLIFFIES IN BRAVO COMPANY. RIGHT?"

The company's reply, "RIGHT, CORPORAL!" was so loud, Wayne had to tap his right ear with the palm of his hand. That action got all cadets laughing.

Prior to the Alpha cadets arriving, the cadets of Bravo Company had probably had many discussions amongst themselves about having other cadets attached to their company. They had no idea what to expect and they couldn't have cared less anyway. As far as they were concerned, cadets were cadets. They thought they'd have it easy. This attitude changed quickly. Although they were still a little resentful and perhaps envious, their introduction to these senior cadets was quite different from what they anticipated. It became obvious immediately that the Alpha cadets were not bullies or braggarts. They appeared to care about the people in their charge and they followed the principle of, *do what I do, not, do what I say.* Although they were from another company, these newcomers were now a part of Bravo, and it showed. In a few cases, however, it took time for some people to accept change, especially if a portion of that modification meant peers giving orders and running the program. These *holdouts* would have to be won over. While the cadets of Alpha had received enough theory to do just that, they would now have to delicately put that philosophy into action.

It took a few days for the Musketeers to get to know everyone in their individual sections. Before long though, they recognized the strengths and weaknesses of their charges and took these traits into consideration when they worked with them.

The character of the boys from Bravo Company was no different than any teenager's. Some were more than willing - others were lazy. Certain cadets were brilliant, others were slow learners and had to be shown twice. The company was typical. There were spotless cadets, dirty ones, sly ones, mouthy cadets, shy people, eager and willing to listen cadets, unorganized and ultra-organized boys, individuals who didn't allow peer pressure to change them, fol-lowers that insisted other people lead the way, *shit-disturbers,* and natural born leaders who solved the problems created by others. Many of them had bad habits that had to be broken; others had no sense of routine whatsoever and had to have standards drilled into them.

In short, the Musketeers had a real melting-pot of distinct personalities on their hands and their job was to mold them and get them thinking, not just as individuals, but as team-mates as well.

At the end of Day One, eight very tired Musketeers met at the smoke-pit between huts. Although they did their best with their boot-cloths, their boots were dusty, their uniforms wrinkled, and they were physically and mentally beat. They had taught all of the lectures that day, answered all of the questions, passed along helpful information, handed out mail, solved what seemed to be millions of prob-lems, and put a company to bed in a proper manner. The cadets waking up tomor-row knew the routine and had clean uniforms, etc. They knew about good studying habits and how to judge their time. The cadets of Bravo were just fine, but the *Corporals* from Alpha didn't know what had hit them.

It was Douglas who tried to put his finger on their problem. "We're doing something wrong, here. We've been with these cadets since six o'clock this morn-ing, and here it is, 2245. Just look at us. If I stood up right now and someone blew on me, I'd fall over. I've never been so tired in my life. Not only..."

Moose butted in. "If some dame blew me, I wouldn't stand up either."

The rest were too tired to laugh, they just listened as Brice continued. "Not only is my mind shot, my body aches, and I can't figure that out. For the past three weeks, I've been working my butt off physically but today for some reason, even every hair on my head aches."

Douglas glanced at them. "Well, for the past hour, I've been giving our plight a lot of consideration and I want your input here. We were organized as cadets, but we're sure as hell not organized as NCOs. I don't think eight of us should sleep in the barracks, and I don't think eight of us have to be around all of the time. Gentlemen, we've forgotten..."

Danyluk interjected again. "Doug, you're right, I..." This time, he stopped short when he received a glowering look from Brice, a stare he hadn't witnessed very often. When Douglas was in this mood, no one interrupted him. Douglas hung fairly loose most of the time, but when he was serious, those on the receiving end knew better than to interfere.

Danyluk quickly realized his mistake. "I'm sorry, Doug...er, carry on."

"Moose, my nerves are a little shot, so let me speak and then I want your input, O.K.?"

"Er, O.K., sorry, Doug."

Douglas stood up. "We haven't given our jobs enough thought. Here it is nearly 2300 hours and our kit's not done, nor have we worked on our lesson plans for tomorrow. That means we're going to be up until nearly 0100 hours and I want to tell you, that's not good enough.

"All right, before I sit down, I propose the following. Only two of us will sleep in the barracks. That's one per cubicle. We'll take turns on a weekly basis, and make arrangements for the weekends. The live-ins will be the only ones taking the company for P.T. The six others will arrive just before morning parade, but they'll leave following training. They'll check in once or twice during the evenings, and they'll do the kit for those living in.

"Now, as far as lesson plans are concerned, the two live-ins will split their time with the cadets. That means while one is working with lesson plans, the other is out in the barracks sorting things out, and vice-versa. Also, there'll be no more showering with the cadets. We shouldn't even be talking around here, the walls have ears. When the live-ins get back from P.T., they'll head over to B-33 for a shower and to change clothing, and two of the other six will take over until they return. O.K., I've had my say. What do you think?"

There was silence for a few seconds before Wayne spoke. "You've hit the problem on the nail. If you think about it, Beckford and Simpson took turns, so did the corporals. No wonder they always looked sharp and were well prepared. Jesus, we've been too wrapped up in ourselves trying to do a good job, we've forgotten the basics - organize, coordinate, and delegate."

Rothstein laughed. "We've looked after Bravo but we haven't taken care of our own needs."

"That's what I was going to say, before I was so rudely cut off," Moose added, smiling at Douglas. Danyluk continued, but only after he'd received a tired grin from Douglas. "Let's start right now. Wayne, you're the Big Cheese until Wednesday, so you have to stay. Gordie, deal us all a card. Low card stays with Wayne."

Wayne snickered. "You mean, low card stays with the *Big Cheese.*"

"Moose, how do you know I've got my cards with me?"

"Is the Pope, Italian?"

"Why, does he play cards? Yeah, I've got them. Here, I'll hand you each a card from the deck, and..."

Gordie took the deck out, but Moose grabbed his arm. "Noooo you don't. We'll each pick our own card, thank you."

Gordie grinned but didn't argue. All of a sudden, Rothstein stood up. "Moose, finally, you're not using the word, 'youse'. Did you guys hear him? He said, 'you.'"

Danyluk spread the deck. "Well, I'm serious now. I never use that word when I'm serious. O.K., youse can all pick a card."

After they each chose a card, the selection was complete. East would stay with Wayne and a roster would be made up the following day. Earl asked whether the other eight Alpha Company types on the other side should know of the plan.

"Yep, we'll tell them tomorrow," replied Douglas. "They went right to bed. Lord knows how they're going to teach without lesson plans. Their kit will look the shits also."

Over the next ten minutes, six barrack boxes were quietly moved out. In addition, Wayne and Jack's kit was given to the other six. Although the live-ins had clean bush uniforms for the following day, their other set would be perfectly washed and pressed, and their boots would be shined for them. Before going to bed, the only thing East and Banks had to do was to quietly have a shower and prepare their lesson plans. Before the six left, arrangements were made to remove a set of bunks from each cubicle in the morning.

"Hey, which one of us is going to wake the other up?" asked East.

Wayne took the alarm. "I was going to suggest that you wake me up when your nose catches the kitchen's smell of bacon frying ...but on second thought, I'll take the alarm."

"Smart ass," replied Jack. "I wouldn't head over to the kitchen before I got you up. I'd head over after I got you up."

Bravo Company on Day Two of the Musketeers' appointment was not the same company as it was on Day One. The cadets had learned quickly. After P.T. and their showers, they wore their coveralls over to their mess hall, and only after their hut was perfect did they change into their shirts, short pants, hose-tops, boots and puttees. Their helmets had been washed, their belts and boots shone, their hair was cut, and their bodies were clean. The new-found pride in Bravo was obvious.

The Musketeers' reorganization came off just as well. After Wayne had *gently* suggested to the Bravo cadets to, "STAND BY YOUR BEDS!" and "FORM THREE RANKS ON THE ROAD!" the company completed its P.T. with perfection. Afterwards, while Banks and East showered and changed in B-33, Danyluk and Jackson took over. When the live-ins went back to have breakfast with the company, Moose and Earl joined Brice, Rothstein, Cunningham, and Simon in B-33's kitchen.

It didn't take long for the eight Alpha Company cadets on the other side of B-29 to realize that the Musketeers were operating on a new schedule. As all eight jogged over to the upper camp, they noticed that only Wayne and Jack were present, so they quickly rearranged their itinerary accordingly. When the company returned, six of them left for B-33. Later, two double bunks would be moved out of their two cubicles, as well.

The Bravo Stickman that morning was, of all people, Williamson, the former bliffy. He asked after he had received the stick if he could fall in with his platoon and Wayne agreed.

"THE FACT THAT CADET WILLIAMSON DIDN'T WANT TO MARCH IN FRONT OF THE COMPANY AND CHOSE TO BE WITH HIS PLATOON INDICATES THAT BRAVO PRIDE IS ALIVE AND WELL!

"I WANT TO CONGRATULATE EACH OF YOU THIS MORNING. YOUR BARRACKS IS SPOTLESS, EXCEPT FOR THAT SAME SMELL OF FEET. YOUR DRESS IS MAGNIFICENT, AND COMPARED TO YESTERDAY, YOUR DRILL HAS IMPROVED ONE-HUNDRED PERCENT.

"THERE IS ALWAYS ROOM FOR IMPROVEMENT, HOWEVER, AND I DON'T WANT ANY OF YOU TO THINK YOU CAN REST ON YOUR LAURELS. THIS COMPANY HASN'T EVEN BEGUN TO START WORKING YET. I'VE REVIEWED YOUR PREVIOUS WEEKEND TEST RESULTS AND I'M NOT HAPPY WITH AN AVERAGE OF SIXTY-TWO PERCENT.

"REMEMBER NOW, YOU'RE WORKING IN PAIRS. TEAMWORK PAYS OFF. DON'T SIT AROUND THE MESS HALL AT LUNCH TIME; INSTEAD, GET BACK HERE AND START WORKING ON YOUR KIT FOR THE FOLLOWING DAY. IT TAKES TEN MINUTES TO SCRUB YOUR CLOTHES AND TEN MINUTES FOR THEM TO DRY. YOU CAN IRON THEM IN THE EVENING, AND AFTERWARDS, I WANT YOU TO STUDY. I DON'T CARE IF YOU STUDY IN THE CADET CANTEEN, THE JON, THE CHAPEL, OR WHEREVER, HOWEVER, YOU MUST STUDY. TEST RESULTS HAVE TO IMPROVE, AND BY GOD, THEY WILL!

"LAST NIGHT, I HEARD AN EXPRESSION I HAVEN'T HEARD IN YEARS. SOMEONE CALLED ME A 'BIG CHEESE.'"

Wayne was grinning as howls arose from the ranks.

"I'M GOING TO DESIGNATE AN AREA ON THE BULLETIN BOARD WHICH SHALL BE REFERRED TO AS, 'THE BIG CHEESE CORNER!' I FEEL LONELY BEING THE ONLY BIG CHEESE, SO AFTER SATURDAY MORNING'S EXAMINATIONS, THE TOP TEN CADETS, IF THEIR MARKS ARE ABOVE 80%, WILL BECOME BIG CHEESES, AND THEIR NAMES WILL BE ADDED TO THE BIG CHEESE LIST. BIG CHEESES WILL HAVE THEIR TWICE-DAILY KIK KOLAS PAID FOR THEM FOR THE WEEK THEY'RE ON THE LIST."

Although the rest of the Musketeers, except Douglas, glanced at Wayne as if he should have his head examined, the applause from the company of cadets was earsplitting.

"NOW, FOR THE BALANCE OF THE MORNING, YOU'RE ON THE PARADE SQUARE WITH WHOM I BELIEVE TO BE, ONE OF THE BEST DRILL INSTRUCTORS IN CANADA...HIS NAME IS SERGEANT BECKFORD. GIVE HIM ALL YOU'VE GOT, AND YOU'LL ENJOY EVERY MINUTE OF IT!"

The cadets were standing easy and their faces indicated it would be impossible to enjoy three hours of drill in temperatures hovering around ninety-five degrees.

Wayne was still smiling as he made them a deal. "IF YOU GIVE HIM AND HIS ASSISTANTS ALL OF YOUR COOPERATION AND ATTENTION, I PROMISE YOU, YOU WILL ENJOY IT, AND YOU'LL LEARN MORE ABOUT DRILL THAN YOU EVER DREAMED.

"AFTER LUNCH, I'M GOING TO ASK YOU WHAT YOU THOUGHT OF SERGEANT BECKFORD AND HIS METHODS. IF YOU DIDN'T LIKE IT, YOU CAN TOSS ME IN THE SHOWERS. HOW'S THAT FOR AN UNDERSTANDING?"

Hoots, whistles and sounds of glee joined rubbed hands. These guys remembered standing on the road on Sunday night and they wanted nothing more than to show Banks their *appreciation.*

"TOMORROW, CORPORAL ROTHSTEIN IS GOING TO TAKE MY PLACE AS, 'THE BIG CHEESE!' HIS ASSISTANT BIG CHEESE WILL BE CORPORAL JACKSON. GIVE THEM YOUR BEST. ALSO, FROM THIS MOMENT ON, YOU PEOPLE WILL BE CONDUCTING THE MORNING PARADES. A LIST WILL BE POSTED ON THE BULLETIN BOARD DEPICTING THE DAILY OFFICERS, COMPANY SERGEANT-MAJOR, AND NCOs, ETC."

After the formalities of falling out the officers, Bravo Company was marched to the parade square. The Musketeers now had the morning to themselves. In B-33, *moneybags* Banks took more ribbing after Cunningham started it.

"You might be the Big Cheese, but don't look to me for donations. Are you out of your flippin' mind? Free pops for the Big Cheeses?"

"It's a good idea, ain't it?" Wayne said, gathering his underwear so he could wash it.

"Yeah, it's a great idea, but who the hell's going to pay? Don't look at me. I'm no mark."

East had a grin from ear to ear. He didn't have a clue what Banks had in mind, but he somehow knew the money was going to come out of the *gambler's* pocket. All those years of being set up by the world's greatest card-shark came back to him.

"You can say that again. I've always been the mark, you creep."

Banks gave Douglas a wink. "Should you tell him, or do you want me to?"

Cunningham had a sixth sense. At this moment he knew he was being centered, he just didn't know how they planned on doing it.

Douglas indicated that Banks should break the *good* news. "Well, Gordie, old pal, old buddy, you may not like this, but then again I believe you'll think it's fair."

A look of disgust came over Cunningham's face as he sat down. "Get on with it. But I'm tellin' ya, you're not getting a cent from me."

"Well, Doug and I decided that since you're going to gamble with the cadets of Bravo Company, ten percent of your winnings should go into a fund. That fund will be called the Big Cheese fund."

Cunningham stood up as quickly as he had sat down. "BULLLL SHITTTT! I'VE GOT TO SWEAT BLOOD AND TEARS FOR THAT DOUGH. GET IT OFFA MOOSE'S, HORNY MOTHERS' FUND OR WHATEVER IT'S CALLED!"

Moose put his nose in Cunningham's face. "MY RESERVE IS DRYING UP. THE DAMES ARE GETTING WISE. BESIDES, TEN PERCENT WON'T HURT YOUSE, YOU PONGO!"

"UP YOUR NOSE, MOOSE! YOU'VE GOT LETTERS COMIN' IN BY THE THOUSANDS!"

"YEAH, BUT THE DOUGH'S DRYIN' UP. MY BIRDS ARE NOW ASKING ME FOR MOOLAH! COME ON, CUNNILINGUS, YOU'VE GOT MORE THAN YOUSE NEED. TEN PERCENT AIN'T GONNA BREAK THE BANK!"

"Don't be a cheap screw," said Jack. "Do I complain when you take my dough?"

Gordie smiled, as did all of them. If anyone ever complained, East did.

Cunningham glared at East. "YOU DON'T BLOODY COMPLAIN? THAT'S ALL YOU EVER DO!"

"Please, spare us the profanity," stated Rothstein.

Cunningham ignored him. "CHRIST, JACK, WHEN YOU GET MARRIED, I PITY YOUR WIFE. IF SHE WAS GOING TO WASH YOUR PANTS AND FOUND A NICKEL IN THE POCKETS, YOU'D WONDER WHERE IT WAS! I CAN HEAR IT ALL NOW, 'COUGH IT UP, DEAR, OR YOU'RE CUT OFF TONIGHT! AND I ALSO WANT THAT PENNY I LEFT IN MY SHIRT' "

Jack now threw his chocolate bar wrapper aside and stood up. "Hey you guys, am I like that? Moose, am I like that? Jeez...I..."

Gordie capitulated. He picked up the wrapper and threw it in the nearby garbage can. "OH, ALL RIGHT THEN! BUT ONLY TEN PERCENT. IF IT'S SHORT, THE REST OF YOU WILL HAVE TO DIVVY UP."

Actually, both Douglas and Wayne thought they would get more of an argument out of Gordie. He was obviously in a good mood this morning and he actually beamed a little when everyone shook his hand. Although this sign of benevolence worried them a little, at least he had agreed. Now they would have to keep an eye on him to ensure he passed along the correct percentage.

"For a shit, you're not a bad shit, Gordie. Hey guys, instead of a Big Cheese, let's make Gordie a Big Shit!" were East's final words on the subject, but not Gordie's.

"If anyone takes a big shit around here, it ain't me. Everyone in the company knows who the indisputable Big Shit is, because he's always in the jon! No names, no pack drill, Jack."

"How many guys went on sick parade, this morning?" asked Simon.

Wayne took out his book. "Just one. His name's Archer. This kid's been on sick parade quite a few times. Also, he was the filthiest on parade yesterday."

Both Moose and Douglas' eyes met and Douglas spoke first. "Moose, that's him...that's the one. He's the cadet who tried to steal Wayne's capbadge...the cadet you helped."

A concerned Danyluk nodded. "Maybe I was suckered, I don't know. Leave it with me, I'll talk to him later. He's in my section."

Wayne was upset over that incident. "You do that, Moose, because if you don't, I will. His marks are low, he's lazy, he lies a lot and he's got a tendency to blame all of his shortcomings on other people. Before you ask me how I know all that, I took the time to look at his file."

Tuesday afternoon was another busy one for the Musketeers. After lunch, until 1630, they gave lectures to their sections on the rifle, bren and sten guns. The training area Bravo used was not over in the upper camp, but in the field behind the huts overlooking the golf course.

This was the second day each of the Alpha Company cadets had worked with the cadets in their sections and they were getting to know them better. In turn, the cadets were getting to know their new *Corporals*.

"Are you falling asleep, Archer?"

Archer's eyes were barely open. "No, Corporal Danyluk."

"Well then?"

"Er, well what?" The cadet's response got some snickers from the other nine sitting in a semi-circle with him.

"Archer, I just asked you to name the stripping sequence of the bren gun. What is it? I've covered it four times, you must know it by now?"

"Er, it's, it's, er..." The boy didn't have a clue, so Moose made it easy for him. "O.K., let's try something else. What's the first thing we do when we approach the weapon?"

Archer's eyes lit up. "Er, we prove it?"

Moose smiled. "RIGHT! THAT'S GOOD! THAT'S THE ANSWER I WAS LOOKING FOR! We prove the weapon."

Danyluk now threw out an overhead question which got them all thinking, before he chose a person to answer.

"Now, how do we prove the weapon?" Moose asked, scanning the group and looking them in the eyes. After a few seconds, he picked. "Phillips?"

"We cock it and look in the breech to make certain it's clear, then not pointing the weapon at anyone, or pointing it down at the ground, we take off the magazine, fire it, cock it, and fire it again, leaving the breech open."

Moose held out his arms. "What am I doing here? You people don't need me, you know all the answers. Very good, Phillips, excellent!"

The cadets smiled. They liked Danyluk. He was a good instructor and he treated them as human beings.

"Right, now let's strip it again. O.K., we've proved the weapon and the magazine is off. What's next in the stripping sequence? Burns?"

"The piston group, Corporal."

"Good, that's what I want to hear. What's next...Agostino?"

"The barrel, Corporal."

"Agostino, you are absolutely correct. What's next, Cooper?"

"Er, the...er, butt?"

"This man is an unblemished genius. Cooper you are correct. How did you know that?"

Cooper grinned, as did those around him. "Er, well, er...in the sequence of stripping things...er..."

Danyluk got him on track again. "Don't tell me, I already know. All you had to think of was your girlfriend's butt, right?"

"RIGHT, CORPORAL!" Cooper replied amidst some hand clapping.

"How often do you think of her butt, Cooper? One hour, two hours, three hours a day?"

Another cadet said, "Don't answer him, Cooper, that's a personal question. How utterly crass."

Danyluk glowered at the *advisor*, as Cooper answered.

"Er, one hour, Corporal."

"That's not enough, man. What are you, man or mouse?"

"Man, Corporal!"

"Then you must think of her butt twenty-four hours a day. I do, and for that matter, so does Archer, here. That's why he couldn't answer the first question I gave to him. Isn't that right, Archer?"

Archer stuck out his chest. "RIGHT, CORPORAL! THAT'S ALL US MEN THINK OF!"

Cooper wasn't slow. "Corporal, why would you and Archer want to think of my girl's butt all of the time. Haven't you got your own dames?"

Danyluk loved Cooper's comeback, and had to join his cadets in laughter, which resonated throughout the other nearby sections.

"No, I didn't mean that, Cooper. I meant I think of my own girl's butt, so does Archer. Right, Archer?"

"I've never met your girl, Corporal; but I *was* thinking of Cooper's dame, she's got a butt that won't quit."

Cooper's reaction was instant. "Screw you, Archer! Get your own broad."

Moose threw his hands in the air. "Who said this section was dull? Nobody did. Alright, we've got the piston group out, the barrel, and butt off...what's next?"

A cadet by the name of Laitricharde-Reed held up his hand. The same cadet who offered some *advice* to Cooper. Slightly chubby, with brown wavy hair and a straight nose, the cadet appeared to be exerting himself just by holding up his hand.

"Yes, Reed?"

"It's not Reed, it's Laitricharde-Reed, Corporal. The body is next."

Danyluk gave the cadet a uncanny look. "You are right, it is the body, but, er, we don't use first names in the army, Reed. Your friends obviously call you, Milky Dick, so keep your first name for your girlfriend when you're next to her BODY! Got it?"

Laitricharde-Reed was a very serious cadet. "No, Corporal Danyluk, you're wrong. My first name is Bertram, my middle names are Pierre Archibald, and my last name is, Laitricharde-Reed. My friends call me, Bertie, and, I wouldn't think of getting close to my girlfriend until I'm engaged, or married. Also, while I deplore the word, 'body' - I will accept the word, 'form.'"

Danyluk put his nose in *Bertie's* face. "Well, isn't *that* nice? If your friends call you, Bertie, what do your *enemies* call you?"

"I do not permit myself to acquire them, Corporal. I affiliate only with the finest of my peers, and I utterly discard my permitting fastidious observance to people who have a disinclination towards me. Hence and accordingly I do not have...*any*. Nor does my father, who is..."

Moose backed off two inches. Although he was lost for words, he didn't let the cadet continue. "How old are you?"

"I'll be turning fifteen in September. My parents are taking me out of school and we're traveling to Hawaii. It ought to be rather fun, I should imagine? Actually I find school a nuisance anyway. It doesn't challenge my exceptional aptitude. I have an IQ of..."

Danyluk didn't let him complete his IQ either.

"You may not make it to your fifteenth birthday, Pierre, or Hawaii either, for that matter. And you're going to have your first enemy if you ever call me wrong again. I'm never wrong...often incorrect, but never wrong. Got that, Arch?"

All eyes were on Laitricharde-Reed. Inwardly, so were his own. "Er, yes...er, Corporal Danyluk. I understand."

"Good! Well, we've got the piston group, the barrel, the butt, *Archie's* body, what's the last part we remove from the body? Archer?"

"The panties, Corporal."

"WHAT?"

"Er, the bipod, Corporal."

"PERFECT, ARCHER! THAT'S WHAT I WAS LOOKING FOR! ACTUALLY, YOUSE WAS RIGHT THE FIRST TIME, BUT THIS IS A MILITARY LESSON, NOT SEX EDUCATION. COME TO THINK OF IT, WOULDN'T IT BE BETTER IF THIS WAS SEX INSTRUCTION?"

"YES, CORPORAL!" came a stimulated response.

"I agree. Good job, fellas. Ya got a 'P' and four 'B's.' Remember that! Well I see the pop truck is here. Reed, I want you to watch the weapon while the others get their drinks. Phillips, as soon as you get your Kik Kola, replace Milky, here."

"Yes, Corporal. Say, can I ask you a question, Corporal?"

"You most certainly can, as long as it's easy. I hate hard questions, they give me gas and I start burping out nonsense like Reed."

Phillips laughed, but Laitricharde-Reed didn't. "What's the 'P' and four 'B's'?"

"Phillips, I knew one of you would ask that. Do I have permission to put my hand on your shoulder?"

"Yes, Corporal, you can put your hand on my shoulder."

"Well, I'm not going to. Why the hell do you want me to put my hand on your shoulder? It's 'P' for piston, and 'B' for all of the other parts. Piston, barrel, butt, body, bipod. Get it?"

Phillips felt like a dummy. "Silly question, eh, Corporal?"

"Not at all, my boy. If you don't ask, you'll never learn."

With that said, Danyluk joined the other Musketeers who were off to one side. East handed Moose a pop he had bought for him, but didn't wait for a 'thank you' because he was in a deep discussion with Simon.

"I should know, I'm a bren gun instructor at our cadet corps. You Irish are always working on those damn Bofors guns. I'll betcha, until you got here, you never knew what a bren gun looked like." East stated.

"Jack, we take instruction on the bren gun, too," replied Simon. "I saw it in the book. At least I thought I did. Moose, when a barrel is removed from a bren gun, is it the 'barrel-locking-lever, or the barrel-locking-pin' you lift up? I say it's the barrel-locking-pin, but Jack disagrees."

The other BCR cadets could have answered Simon's question, but they left it up to Moose. It was too hot for these discussions, anyway.

"Simon, my son, it's called the barrel-locking-lever. You're getting it mixed up with the body-locking-pin. You know, that little pin you push through to slide back the butt? If you didn't push it, you wouldn't get the piston group out."

Simon accepted Danyluk's answer. "Jacky, my apologies, I owe you a chocolate bar."

"Just one?" East asked.

"Oh, all right then, two chocolate bars. My God, you BCR cadets are gluttons."

Douglas saw the look of satisfaction on Moose's face. "How'd it go, Moose?" "Good. A great period with a superb instructor. These guys are pretty sharp. They're making notes and paying attention. How about you?"

"Excellent," replied Douglas. I'm starting to understand all of the distinct personalities in my section."

Danyluk tried to remove a hair from between his teeth. "I should go to where they bottle this stuff and meet the broad who lost this," he said, referring to the hair and his Kik Kola. "I've got one poor bugger in my section with a name that could make the book of records. He's called, Bertram Pierre Archibald Laitricharde-Reed. I call him Milky Dick. He's a bit of a pompous prick, but I think he'll come around."

Rothstein didn't like the choice of name. "Milky Dick? How in the hell did you get that name, it's coarse?"

Danyluk finished the last of his Kik Kola, but still had difficulty removing the hair. "Now don't get snobbish like him, Rothie. What's the French word for milk?'

Rothstein thought for a minute. "Lait."

"Very good, Rothie, very good. Now, what's the English nickname for someone called Richard?"

Rothstein nodded. He had caught on. "I get it...Dick."

"Believe me, Rothie, this guy would be called Milky Dick even if he didn't have a name like Bertram, Pierre, Archibald, Laitricharde-Reed. He's one of a kind."

"Then he's a bit like you?"

"Youse could say that, but we're 180 degrees apart. If you do say it, I'm goin' to transfer him to your section."

Rothstein winced. "Little joke there, Moose. Please keep him, I've got enough problems. One of my cadets bites the heads off grasshoppers. He wasn't paying attention so I said to him, "What the hell are you looking over there for?"

"He didn't look at me, he just answered, 'I've got my eyes on...that.'"

"I couldn't see anything, nor could anyone else, but then the guy made a mad grab, put his hand to his mouth, and the next minute he was chewing something."

Rothstein's description nearly turned East off the drumstick he was gnawing on. "That's really sick. Do you mind, Rothie, I'm eatin' ya know?"

Rothstein grimaced. "So what else is new? You bet it's sick, and he reminds me of you when he chews."

Wayne had been quiet up until now. "If ya wanna talk sick things, I've got all of ya beat. A cadet in Danyluk's section has got a foot problem. His name's Mancinelli, and even when I'm fifty feet away from him, I can smell his feet. Haven't you guys noticed there's always the smell of feet in our side of the barracks? Or even both sides for that matter?"

"HEY, THE FACT THAT HE'S IN MY SECTION MEANS WE SHOULD OVERLOOK THE STENCH!" Moose cringed. "But it's really hard to ignore."

East actually couldn't finish his drumstick just thinking of the smell. "Have I noticed it? You bet your life I have. I had my window wide open last night, and I thought the smell was coming back in. Just wait until you two take over tonight," he said pointing at Earl and Rothstein.

"I know *that* guy," said Gordie. "I've already taken fifty-cents offa him. It was kinda rough, but I got used to the smell. When money's involved, I can get used to any smell, but it was really rough." He thought for a moment. "So *that's* the reason only the two of us were playing? I wondered why the other guys weren't joining in."

Wayne still had a disgusting look on his face. "Well, it seems that you and Moose are the only ones who can handle it. This is really serious. The other cadets won't go near him, and personally, I can't blame them. Even though the poor bugger takes his boots off outside, when he walks in, the smell follows him. Apparently there's a medical term for his condition, but I don't know what it is. After supper, I'm takin' him up to see the doctor. I actually feel sorry for this guy."

"We coulda used him during the first three weeks," said Simon. "When East was out of gas, we coulda brought him in to clear out the showers."

Wayne didn't laugh. "Listen, it's worse than that. Before I came here, I actually went into that hut there..." He pointed out a nearby hut. "... and washed out my nostrils. If we had brought him into the showers, he'd be the only one in there." He glanced at Moose. "What's so funny?"

"I went out with a dame like that once. Wow, did she ever smell. What an eerie broad. Her name was Olga and when I kissed her, she had an uncontrolled twitching problem, like that of a corpse. But once I got past the smell, everything was fine. I had it licked."

The faces on the other seven turned sour as they pretended to throw up.

"Although she had lotsa money, I gave her up to one of my friends in the Irish. But she calls me now and then, though."

Simon interrupted his vomiting act. "Up your ass, Moose. Only the Seaforths or the *Canned Scots* take those kind," he said. (He was referring to the CScotRs.)

Moose was still grinning. "Whatever. Anyway, what do you think the doctor can do?"

Banks shrugged. "I haven't got a clue, but something's got to be done. I've taken the cadet aside and spoken with him. Apparently this ailment started when he reached puberty. After he finishes camp, they're going to operate on his stomach. The guy lives here in Vernon. He's a BCD." (British Columbia Dragoons.)

"Why the hell would they operate on his stomach when he's got a foot problem?" asked Jackson.

"Do I look like a doctor?" quipped Wayne.

"No, but you smell like one," Douglas said, as he stood up and slammed Wayne on the back. "Let's go, we've got more lectures to give."

When the afternoon was complete and Bravo Company was about to be dismissed, Wayne said, "WE WERE VERY PROUD OF YOU TODAY. THIS COM-

PANY IS COMING ALONG FINE. RIGHT NOW, I'D SAY IT'S THE BEST COMPANY IN CAMP!

"NOW, DON'T FORGET, WORK IN TEAMS AND GET YOUR KIT READY FOR TOMORROW. KEEP YOUR TOWELS CLEAN, AND MAKE CERTAIN YOU STUDY YOUR NOTES.

"ALL RIGHT! THIS MORNING I MADE A DEAL WITH YOU. I SAID YOU COULD TOSS ME IN THE SHOWERS IF YOU DIDN'T LIKE THE THREE PERIODS OF DRILL. I'M SURE YOU'VE DISCUSSED IT...WHO WANTS TO BE THE SPOKESMAN?"

Williamson, the company's Stickman was next to the right hand marker of Five Platoon. He stood to attention with his arm extended.

"YES, WILLIAMSON?"

"YOU WERE RIGHT CORPORAL BANKS! WE LEARNED A LOT TODAY FROM SERGEANTS BECKFORD AND SIMPSON AND WE ENJOYED IT. WE'VE DECIDED NOT TO THROW YOU IN THE SHOWERS."

A smiling Banks said, "YOU SEE, I KNEW YOU'D LIKE IT! RIGHT! BRAVO COMPANY, ATTEN...TION! DIS...MISSED!"

The company smartly turned to their right; paused for the silent count, and marched forward five paces. They didn't, however, rush into the barracks. Instead, a squirming Banks was lifted up and taken into the showers. Although he shrieked, he didn't mind it a bit because the water helped get rid of the smell of feet.

Five minutes later, a soaking wet Musketeer with a squishing sound emanating from his boots, joined his friends and marched to B-33. Spirits were high in Bravo Company and Wayne had paid the price.

"I think the doctor's right, Corporal. I know it gets the other guys down, but there's nothing I can do about it."

"Well, Mancinelli, if you feel that way, I'll see the OC and request the change. Can you do it today?" replied Wayne. He was returning to B-29 with the cadet with the foot problem. The doctor had *suggested* since the lad resided in Vernon, it would probably be more convenient if he lived at home and visited the camp daily, for training. For Banks, it was the suggestion of a lifetime.

The cadet also understood. He couldn't take the ribbing any longer. "It's best for everyone. I'll go and pack now."

As they neared the entrance to the barracks, Wayne said, "Just fold your blankets and leave them on top of your rolled-up mattress, so Corporal Jackson can hand them in tomorrow. While you're doing that, I'll get your duffel-bag from underneath the hut." All duffel-bags were tagged and stored in alphabetical order down below.

Half-an-hour later, Cadet Mancinelli was picked up by his father and driven home. He would report to camp every morning at 0800 hours, and he would not participate in physical training. The doctor suggested this because he wanted to keep the boy's feet dry and free from sweat.

After the move, Jackson, Rothstein and all cadets on both sides of B-29 breathed in the fresh air with a sigh of relief.

At mug-up that night, all of the Musketeers met and decided that since a week of field training was coming up in Glenemma, they would take the weekend off. A couple of Alpha cadets from the other side of the hut offered to sub for them, if the favour was returned at a later date. The deal was made.

It was stuffy and close in camp that evening. All the cadets, officers and NCOs were listless and perspiring heavily. They hated this kind of weather, but everyone knew it preceded the much-awaited rain which was predicted. Danyluk's radio tipped them off to that.

'Yes, Okanagan, you can expect heavy rain tonight and for the next few days. A storm is on its way up here from the coast and it will be followed by another storm.'

It was so hot, all the Musketeers were just wearing their undershorts as they ironed their bush uniforms, pressed their puttees, and shined their boots for the following day.

Moose walked outside the center doors and glanced at a small thermometer on the wall. It read 102 degrees.

"Hey, fellas, can you believe this? Here it is, 1930 hours and the temperature is still over a hundred. I betcha this is going to be one hell of a storm."

No sooner had he said it, the Camp RSM noticed him. "YOU, YOU HORRIBLE LITTLE MAN! HOW MANY TIMES HAVE I TOLD YOU NOT TO APPEAR OUT THAT DOOR WITHOUT CLOTHES ON?"

"BUT SIR, I'VE GOT CLOTHES ON, SIR!"

"YOU CALL THAT RAG YOU'RE WEARING, *CLOTHES*?"

"THESE ARE SILK, SIR! MURRAY GOLDMAN'S BEST GAUNCH!"

"GET INSIDE!" the RSM bellowed as he marched away, mumbling to himself. "Silk? How the bloody hell can *he* afford silk from Murray Goldman, when I'm wearing polyester from Ernie's Underworld? My God, that man seems to get everything he wants. What's this world coming to?"

At 2030 that night, the Heavens opened up. East looked like a drenched rat when he came in from mug-up with his wet sandwiches. Like the other Musketeers who had visited B-29 to check on their sections, he neglected to take a poncho, so his P.T. gear was sopping wet.

After East got back, Danyluk and the four others rushed into B-33. The first thing they did was dry off their hair, then Moose took off his T-shirt and rung it out, out the window. He then took off his P.T. shorts and his underwear and was going to wring them out as well, but had second thoughts and closed the window, heading for the shower room.

"This is one time the RSM isn't going to catch me."

The hut was half-full that night, because gradually, other Alpha cadets had opted for the same live-in program the Musketeers had adopted. Being soaked to the skin didn't bother Cunningham, though. He stayed in his wet clothes and started a crap game going in the drying room.

The Musketeers enjoyed their new-found freedom. Because they were now on 'unpaid camp staff,' they didn't have to adhere to the regular time of lights out. If they wanted to stay up all night, they could. Not that they did, because most of them were dead beat from instructing all day in the hot sun.

Douglas had finished his kit and lesson plans and was just lying on his bed in a pair of coveralls when Sergeant Beckford walked into the barracks wearing civilian clothes under his military raincoat. He came over and sat on Douglas bunk.

"How's it going?"

Douglas sat up and put his feet on the floor. The other guys, except Cunningham and Danyluk, joined them. "Really good, Sergeant. Jackson and Rothstein are with Bravo Company for the next two days."

Beckford smiled. "I've heard nothing but praise for you fellas. Are you getting the hang of all the mixed personalities?"

Wayne cocked his head. "You bet, Sergeant. This isn't the *swan* we thought it would be. Basically about seventy-five-percent of Bravo's cadets fit the norm. It's that other twenty-five-percent that keeps us on our toes."

The Sergeant appeared to be looking right through Wayne. Memories of these boys kept coming back to him. These fourteen-year-olds of 1953 were mature now. They appreciated other people's feelings and understood the tact that must be used when dealing with individuals that didn't fit in the customary sphere of influence.

Beckford had heard about the boy with the foot-odor problem. At one time, these cadets would have laughed and made fun of him, but not anymore. They understood their role, and tried to help. The military method of bringing them along was working well.

"Where's Danyluk?"

"He's still in the showers, Sergeant." East replied.

No sooner had the Sergeant asked, a smiling, squeaky-clean Danyluk appeared, wearing a towel around his waist.

"Sergeant Beckford, I admire youse guys. If we were like some of these Bravo cadets when we were fourteen, you should have locked us up and thrown the key away."

Beckford nodded and grinned. "Moose, have you got a cadet in your section by the name of...?" He took a piece of paper out of his pocket. "...Laitricharde-Reed?"

Danyluk put on a pair of silk underwear. "*Have* I? Unfortunately...yes, I do."

The Sergeant paused for a moment, chewing his lip. "Do you know who his father is?"

Moose sat next to Douglas. "No, but he must be a bit of a nut to give the kid names like, Bertram, Pierre, Archibald. He was going to talk about his father today, but I cut him off. Why, what's up, Sergeant?"

"Well, his father is none other than Lieutenant-General Robert, Pierre, Marcel Laitricharde-Reed."

Danyluk swallowed. "Never heard of him, what's his claim to fame?"

"What's his claim to fame? He commands our troops in Europe, but right now, he's visiting Vernon. He's staying at a motel downtown and about an hour ago, he telephoned General Kitching and complained about a certain Corporal picking on his son, and calling his son *names*."

There was silence for a few seconds. Moose lost his smile and an expression of complete seriousness came over his face. As the day's activities raced through his mind, he shut the window to drown out the sound of the pelting rain. He remembered the lesson, especially his involvement with *Bertie*.

"I didn't pick on him, Sergeant. I may have made a wisecrack about his name, but the kid is a smart ass. I'm just giving him a bit of torment to break him of his arrogant mannerisms."

"Is he that bad?"

"Well, I wouldn't use that word, but he's...odd. I, er, get the impression that he's been spoiled and he expects special treatment. I really don't quite know how to label him. He's certainly a loner, and to my knowledge, the other cadets in the platoon steer clear of him."

"Did you call him, Milky Dick Reed?"

"I don't know if I called him Milky Dick Reed, but I did give him the title of Milky Dick."

Sergeant Beckford didn't like hearing those words. He shook his head, took a deep breath and let it out. "I thought we taught you better than that. What's the world's worst-kept secret, Danyluk?"

Moose lowered his head and slowly nodded. He remembered Major Ratcliffe's lecture only too well. The Musketeers had discussed that leadership lecture for hours, and now he'd thrown that knowledge aside and reverted to a verbal bully.

"I'm sorry, Sergeant. I made a mistake. What would you like me to do, apologize to him?"

The Sergeant smiled. He knew Danyluk, and from Danyluk's description of the lad, he also knew how hard it would be for Moose to acknowledge his mistake and apologize. Still, this senior cadet was prepared to do it if it was necessary.

"General Kitching didn't inform Major Kare, he told Major Ratcliffe instead. Since Lieutenant Harwood's on leave, it's come down to me, and..."

There was a loud knock on the inside door. When it opened, Archer, the small cadet Danyluk had helped a few weeks back, was standing there. He walked slowly down the aisle, stopping at the Musketeers.

Sergeant Beckford said, "What can we do for you?"

The dripping-wet boy stood at attention. "Er, would it be possible for me to talk to Corporal Danyluk?"

Moose stood up. "We're in a meeting right now, Archer. Can it wait until later?"

Although Archer's arms were stiffly by his sides, he fidgeted with the seams of his soaked, short pants. "Can I wait, Corporal? It's pretty important."

Moose's mind was on Laitricharde-Reed, not on Archer. "Er, sure. If you want, you can wait for me in the drying room, I'll be with you shortly."

Archer took off his pith-helmet and tramped away as the discussion continued.

Sergeant Beckford glanced at the Musketeers present. "Moose, I didn't want to mention this in front of the others, but...well, you're all very close, I don't want *them* to make the same mistake."

"That's fine, Sergeant, we all appreciate it," replied Danyluk. "So what do I do?"

There were a few seconds of silence before Beckford spoke again. "Well, now I have to tell you that General Laitricharde-Reed and his son are in General Kitching's office. General Laitricharde-Reed wants you to apologize to his son in there. You don't have to put on your uniform, just wear your coveralls, boots, and your regimental headdress."

"Will General Kitching be there?"

"No, he's allowing General Laitricharde-Reed to use his office. The best of luck, son. Just remember to use your head in the future."

After Sergeant Beckford left, the others gathered around Danyluk. "Wow, this Bertie, or whatever his name is, is a real prick," offered Wayne.

East was so upset, he re-wrapped the balance of the sandwich he was eating. "His father must be one also if he sticks his nose into such trivial matters."

Douglas reached up to the shelf, brought down Moose's boots, and handed them to him. "Just get the bloody thing over with. Should we go with you?"

Moose slipped into his coveralls, and quickly put on his boots. "No, I made the mistake, I'll handle it."

"Don't forget you've got Archer waiting for you in the drying room?" Simon reminded him.

Danyluk buckled his webbelt around his waist. "That's right, I almost forgot about him," he replied, as he headed in that direction.

When he arrived, he found Archer had joined in Cunningham's current game of stuke and had six one-dollar bills in front of him. "Is this guy one of yours?" asked Cunningham.

Moose knew something was up. "He sure is."

"Well, get him the hell out of here before he cleans me out. He started with two-bits and look at his pile now."

A grinning Archer picked up his money and his pith-helmet and united with Moose. No one was in the shower room so Danyluk motioned they would go in there to talk. "Now, what's this important problem that won't wait?" Moose asked.

Five minutes later, Moose and Archer left the building.

Danyluk didn't enter the front of the headquarters building, instead, he climbed the few stairs leading to the outside door of the Commanding Officer's office, opened the screen door and knocked.

A tall, thin man, immaculately dressed in a starch-pressed sports shirt and pair of slacks, opened the inside door. He was the spitting image of his son.

Danyluk saluted.

"Thank you, Corporal Danyluk, please take off your poncho and come in. You may leave it on the porch."

As he entered, Moose was a little tense, but he didn't show it. The general had been alone in the office. Sergeant Beckford had implied that *Bertie* would be there, as well, but he wasn't.

General Laitricharde-Reed sat on a leather couch which was against the wall between two windows. He motioned that Danyluk should sit on the leather chair in front of General Kitching's desk. The walls of the fair-sized and carpeted office were adorned with pictures of every former Commanding Officer of the camp, as well as photographs of the various Graduation Parades throughout the years. A door leading to the CO's secretary's office was closed.

"I'm Cadet Laitricharde-Reed's father."

Danyluk sat upright in the chair, his arms on his lap with his fingers entwined.

He nodded a small smile that acknowledged the man. "Yes, sir. I've been familiarized with that, and your rank."

Laitricharde-Reed was a soft-spoken man. His gray hairline receded and he didn't have an ounce of fat on him. He had one arm on the arm of the couch and the other in his lap. Danyluk noticed the muscles of the general's upper arms were massive.

"I'm not here officially, Corporal Danyluk. I'm visiting this region with my wife, and as you know, my son is in your platoon. I'm here because he telephoned me this evening and informed me of your comments. He didn't appreciate being referred to as, Milky Dick Reed, and he says your attitude towards him is one of distaste. Is that right?"

Moose looked the general in his eyes. "No, sir. I don't dislike your son, as a matter of fact, I hardly know him. I apologize for calling him those names. It was asinine of me, and I should have known better. I haven't been brought up, or for that matter, *trained*, to treat people in that manner and it won't happen again."

Danyluk's response took the general by surprise. This clean-cut young man sitting in front of him wasn't the image of the ogre, young Laitricharde-Reed had presented him with.

"Thank you. I understand this is your first year as an instructor with cadets?"

"Yes, sir. Although I'm an instructor at my cadet corps, this course allows us to lead and teach cadets for three weeks during the summer. It's a little different than instructing at the home corps level."

"I'm certain it is. A lot of responsibility and trustworthiness goes with your acting rank. You do realize you're accountable for your actions and your position shouldn't be taken lightly?"

"Yes, sir."

"Corporal Danyluk, I understand Bertie is not the easiest person to get along with. He can be arrogant at times, and he's definitely self-centered. My wife and I had him late in life and he's been raised in a rather inflexible environment. My postings have taken my family all over the world, and Bertie's changed schools and friends so often, he hasn't been able to plant any roots. He's never been able to relax because of that, and unfortunately, I haven't got the time to spend with him. I treat him as a soldier, but my wife spoils him. Do you understand what I'm getting at? Also, when we've been on various bases, I know he uses my position as a crutch."

Danyluk relaxed a little. He liked the man in front of him. "Yes, sir, I do. My task was to discover that information, but, I haven't had the time, nor do I have the necessary qualifications to do it properly right now. I will, though.

"Sir, I've been the subject of ribbing many times in my life, and I assumed your son would take it the same way that I did. I now realize, that when this hazing occurred, it was done with tongue in cheek, and was accepted by me as such. I guess I teased Cadet Laitricharde-Reed in too serious a manner. His attitude got me upset and I didn't think before acting. It won't happen again, sir. I can assure you of that."

General Laitricharde-Reed stood up and shook Moose's hand. "I know it won't, Corporal Danyluk. I want you to have a *talk* with my son. You needn't apologize to him, that's not necessary. As a matter of fact, if you have your tongue-in-your cheek, you can refer to him as, Milky Dick. I recognize he's not an angel, that's why he's here. How he managed to get through the first three weeks, I'll never know. He's been on the phone every ten minutes asking to come home. What I want you to do, is to bring him along in a military fashion, peer to peer. I've already given him a blast for complaining to me. He can't make it in life by clinging to my coattails. There is a right way for him to conduct himself, and what better chance is there of his learning, than here, in these surroundings. But use a little tact called, 'IT.' Know what I mean, son? It doesn't pay to label someone without trying to understand them first."

"Yes, sir, I do."

The general held out his right hand. "I'm glad we had this little talk, Corporal Danyluk. I was never a cadet, but I wish I had been. Keep up the good work, and get, *Milky* on the right track."

Moose's grin went from ear-to-ear as he stood and shook the tall man's hand. "Thank you, sir. You have my promise."

The general smiled and nodded. "Good-bye, Corporal Danyluk."

Corporal Danyluk saluted, turned, and walked out. "Thank *you*, sir."

After he pulled his poncho on, Moose didn't march back to B-33, instead, he headed for B-29, the home of Cadet Bertram, Pierre, Archibald, Laitricharde-Reed.

The normally bustling roads of Camp Vernon were nearly empty because of the driving rain. Most cadets were inside their huts with their windows closed.

When he entered the building, Rothstein and Jackson were demonstrating the proper way to polish boots.

"Moose, what brings you over here in this weather? asked Earl.

"I've got some business with a cadet in my section. Laitricharde-Reed."

Earl cringed up his face, walked away from the nearby cadets so he couldn't be heard, and whispered, "Oh, him. Mr. Mouth. He's over there lying on his bunk."

Cadet Laitricharde-Reed was reading a sports-fishing magazine when Danyluk stood next to him.

"Do you like fishing?" Moose asked.

The boy's mediocre look turned into a gaze of excitement as he flung down his book, not worrying about what page he was on. "Do I? I've got four rods and I manufacture my own flies. I really don't get a chance to use them very often, but when I do, look out fishes."

"That's my favorite sport, as well, said Danyluk. I used to hold the record for catching the biggest salmon that swam up the Fraser River. It took me forever to land it. After we weighed it, we let it go."

Bertie immediately sat up and planted his feet on the floor. He loved this subject. "Oh, how terribly wasteful that is. I never let them go. When I catch them, they're caught and they end up in the pan! What did you let it go for?"

"Well, I like catching them for sport, but they're too beautiful to kill. Not too many of them make it to the spawning grounds as it is. I use a yellow copper-beetle as a lure. A friend of mine makes them, and when you've got one of those on the end of your line, you can't miss."

Laitricharde-Reed would have talked fishing all night. "I've never even heard of a yellow copper-beetle. What do they look like?"

"Well, we'll discuss that later," Danyluk replied. "Right now, you and I are going for a walk...grab your beret."

"Do you mind if also take my poncho? It's pouring out there?" the cadet asked.

"Sure, that's fine."

After they left the building, Danyluk led Laitricharde-Reed to the fence overlooking the golf course. The course was empty, but a few die-hards were sloshing about, hoping to finish their game before it became too dark.

A couple of Bell-tents used for lectures weren't far away, so they headed for them and took off their ponchos. Danyluk sat on a table in front of the blackboard, as did Laitricharde-Reed. The sound of the rain hammering the top of the tent was noisy, but the atmosphere was cozy.

"You know why we're here, don't you?" Moose asked. His face was stern as his eyes burned into the cadet.

Laitricharde-Reed fiddled with his fingers, as his eyes roamed the ground. He found it difficult to look at the tall Corporal sitting across from him. "Er, I've got an idea. I, er..."

"So, your father's a general?"

The boy looked up for a fraction of a second before staring at the valley below. "Yes, he commands Canada's troops in Europe. He's here on a holiday."

"I understand that. And as you know, I've just left him. Why did you go to all that trouble?"

"What trouble?"

"The trouble you went through to have me meet your father. It was kind of you, but he's a busy person, and I'm not exactly without things to do, also. So let me ask you again, why the rendezvous?"

Laitricharde-Reed didn't quite know what to say, so he didn't reply. His face started blushing as he returned his gaze to the brown dusty *grass* which formed the tent's floor.

"Your dad and I have just had a really good talk. He tells me you're homesick, and that you don't like it here. Is that right?"

Once again the boy didn't answer, so Danyluk continued. "LOOK ME IN THE EYES!"

Blinking a mile-a-minute, Laitricharde-Reed looked up. Their eyes met for only a fraction of a second.

"You know, when you're with the other cadets you come on pretty strong. What if they saw you like this? Mr. Know-it-all, finally lost for words. Well, let's forget your father for a moment. What's your relationship with a cadet named Archer?"

Danyluk noticed the boy's body jerk. "Have you told your dad that you've got three cadets working their butts off for you and stealing things? Have you told him that you've threatened them with failing the course? Have you told your dad that they do your boots and your uniforms, that they make your bed, that they steal cap-badges for you, and that when they give you money, you don't have to pay them back? Have you told your father that you cheat on your examinations? Have you mentioned that you tried to get one of your fellow cadets to steal a Saturday Morning test-paper from the company office?"

Laitricharde-Reed's eyes started welling up and he started sniffing. "I, er...have you told him?"

Moose took out a handkerchief and handed it to him. "Wipe your eyes and blow you nose, man! I don't want to see any more tears! You're supposed to be a man of the world. You're the general's *son*. How long have you been doing things like this? Probably a long time, eh? In every place you've travelled to with your family, you've used your old-man as leverage so that you could get your own way. Isn't that just fucking dandy?"

"Did, er...does he...?"

"No, he doesn't know! I'm not like you, Laitricharde-Reed. I don't think any-one is like you. You're one of a kind. Jesus Christ, I wonder what this world would be like if every general in the world had a son like you? Think of it, wouldn't this planet be a better place to live if everyone was like you?"

Bertie never took his eyes off the ground.

Moose lowered his voice, his eyes indicating he wasn't in the mood for non-sense. "I'm going to tell you one more time, look me in the eyes."

Slowly, their eyes met. "Suppose the Chief of the Defence Staff had a son, and he treated you like dirt. Would you set up a meeting with your father? Not bloody likely! Suppose he set up a meeting with you and *his* father? Then you'd be on the *receiving* end, wouldn't you? You're used to this sort of thing, you'd probably love that."

"I'm sorry. I should never..."

"Save it! Don't apologize to me. You haven't hurt me, Laitricharde-Reed. The only person you've ever hurt is yourself, and...the people you suck into being your *slaves*. Now, when we've finished this talk, you're going to get your shit together and call another meeting. A meeting without me or your father. A meeting with just four people present. You, and those other three cadets. You're going to apologize to *them*, and you're also going to inform them that your influence would not have affected their standing on this course. DO YOU UNDERSTAND ME?"

"Yes, Corporal."

For the next few minutes, they discussed what life was like living with one of the highest ranking officers in the Royal Canadian Army. It hadn't been easy for *Bertie*. He was an only child and not once had his dad taken him to a movie or (gone) bowling, etc. His father was always busy, all over the world, and his mother found it necessary to join her husband in many of the social involvements which accompanied the *job*. Bertram Laitricharde-Reed was often left in the care of either a man-servant, or a Corporal who was the general's batman. (Prepared his uniforms, etc.)

Last summer, the boy had gone with his father to Washington for what was supposed to be a two-day trip. The general's plans changed on the second day and young Bertram had spent three weeks alone in a hotel suite. Sure, he could use room service and order whatever he wanted, but he'd been lonelier than hell. He couldn't go home, because home was in Europe and his mother was on a tour for the Red Cross. He saw his dad for ten minutes in the morning and was usually asleep when he returned.

Only once during that whole three weeks did he enjoy himself. A couple with two teenage boys had checked into the next suite for two days. The woman kept spotting Bertie sitting in the lobby, and she asked her husband to find out about the boy. He did, and they invited him to see some of the sights of Washington, DC, with them. When they left, he was on his own again. He'd been on his own most of his life.

It was the general's batman who had suggested young Laitricharde-Reed should join the Royal Canadian Army Cadets, and the general, his wife, and Bertram had agreed.

Danyluk listened with concern. The information he had learned in the many leadership periods had taught him there are always two sides to every story. Also, he remembered the worst-kept secret in the world.' Major Ratcliffe had taught them well.

He decided to change the subject. "I understand you're the finest baseball player in the company? Not just baseball, I've been told you excel at all sports, and when teams are picked, the team captains want you."

A puzzled look came across Laitricharde-Reed's face. "I didn't know that?"

"You've been shutting everyone out. There are a lot of people who would like to be friends with you if you'd let them. They'll accept you for what *you* are, not for what your father is. You could make some real chums while you're here. Companions that will stay thick and thin with you for life. Would you believe, Archer actually said he feels sorry for you? You've threatened him but he still likes you."

The cadet's face went blank and he swallowed. "I didn't know that, either."

"Well you know it now. Listen, you've got a good head on your shoulders, you could ace this course if you wanted to. What would your dad think if he was informed his son had topped the Senior Leader's course at camp?"

"Wow, he'd...he'd go wild. I've never done that before...I've never topped anything."

Moose smiled. "But you could have. Listen, I know you've got a tough row to hoe. I know your father casts a big shadow, and that perhaps he expects too much from you? Is it possible he does that because you've never given him anything? Your marks are mediocre at school, and you don't put out more than a fifty-percent effort on anything you do. Do you think he cheated when he was your age?"

Laitricharde-Reed quickly shook his head. "He'd never do that in a million years."

"You're absolutely right, *Bertie*." Both of them smiled.

"And neither should his son. You're your *own* man, you don't have to follow in your father's footsteps, but if you want to, do it by yourself. Prove it to yourself that you have it within you to become the best cadet in your company, or camp, for that matter. If you want it bad enough, nothing in this world can hold you back. But other people can't do it for you, and your dad can't help you. It's up to you."

The cadet had been nodding. "Thanks, Corporal Danyluk."

Moose got off the table and put on his poncho. "I apologize for calling you Milky Dick. I had no right to do that. I guess I didn't like your attitude at the time and in a weak moment, I was childlike. If you come back here next year, and you don't take signals or driver mechanics, you'll be doing what I'm doing now. Anyway, do we have a deal? Can I count on you, counting on yourself?"

"No one has ever taken the time to talk to me this way. You bet, Corporal."

Moose patted Laitricharde-Reed on the back. "That a boy. If you've got any problems, come to me. And if you need any help, that's what I'm here for. Got it?"

"Got it, sir, thanks."

As they walked back to B-29, Danyluk said, "Don't ever call me, *sir*, my parents are married. Now, *Milky*, tell me all youse knows about fishing."

"Well, my grandfather used to fish, and I...Corporal Danyluk, did you say, 'youse knows'?"

"I sure did."

"Isn't that improper English?"

"It sure is. Now, youse was mentioning your grandfather?"

When Moose entered B-33, the Musketeers, except Rothstein and Jackson, were on him like bees to a hive."

"Jesus, what took you so long?" asked East. "We were just about to go to the guardroom looking for you."

Moose sat down and explained Laitricharde-Reed's situation. He didn't explain all of the personal details the boy told him, but he presented the predicament as he saw it.

Douglas was shocked. "And I thought Archer was stealing Wayne's badge. Instead, he was putting it back after Laitricharde-Reed's other *friend* had taken it. Damn, once again, I should never have assumed."

"That's the reason Archer never met you at the main doors of B-3," Moose explained. "He wasn't stealing the badge as you thought, and he wasn't about to tell you who did. He's a good kid, that Archer, I really like him. Also, the reason why he's always had a sloppy uniform and his marks were low was because he was always catering to Laitricharde-Reed."

"Are you certain Laitricharde-Reed's on the right track now?" Cunningham asked. He'd returned from the drying room earlier and the other Musketeers had clued him in.

"I'm absolutely positive of it," stated Moose.

"That Archer's a cunning little pongo," said Gordie. "He's always got a smile on his face and he nearly cleaned me out."

Moose shook his poncho off out the window. "That's why I like him, he reminds me of a young Cunningham. He even arm-wrestles like you."

Douglas kicked at Wayne's springs. After Banks landed, he said, "By God, you're right. He even looks like you, Gordie. Without the killer instinct, of course."

"BULLLL SHHITTT! He's not that handsome. He looks like Moose."

Moose slammed his window shut. "I knew you'd say that. Why in God's green earth does everyone have to look like me...*swave and deboner?*"

Gordie came over and sat next to Moose. "Do you remember when we were in Polson Park, a kid in a pram looked just like you?"

"Er, I think so."

"Do you also remember when we were walking past the hospital in town, two twins were playing ball and they looked just like you?"

Moose put his dumb look on and cocked his head. "Er, they definitely did."

"Do you remember when we were in Gracie's Drive-in, when that car came in and the three kids in the back seat looked like you."

"Could have been my brothers and sister," Moose replied. "I sure do."

"Well then? The whole world looks like you. But there's a reason."

"And what's that, Gordie?"

"You've been out with most of the dames. You've got more illegitimate children out there than, than...than..." Gordie moved his hand in a small circle, looking for someone to help him out.

East came over. "Than Carter's got pills."

"Right, more kids than Carter's got pills. The whole God-damned world is starting to look like Danyluk. Moose, if you keep up this lifestyle, the human race will have to wear numbers on the front of their bodies, because everyone will be getting mixed up. Christ, can you guys imagine a whole battalion of Mooses?"

"You mean with their balls hanging out the legs of their pants?" asked Banks.

"Yeah, and their wangs tucked into their puttees," Gordie responded.

A grinning Moose lay on his bunk. "Hey, youse guys have just hit it on the head. I know what I'll do...I'll..."

Simon hadn't said much until now. "Sell sperm to the sperm-banks? If you did that, no one else would have a chance. The banks would be full."

"Nope! I'll put an ad in The Vancouver Sun. 'TALL AND HANDSOME SOLDIER WITH TIME ON HIS HANDS, WILL MAKE YOUSE THE MOTHER OF THE YEAR. YES, YOUSE CAN HAVE A GUARANTEED LOVELY LOOKIN' CHILD, FOR ONLY FIFTY BUCKS. DON'T TAKE CHANCES HAVIN' YOUR KID LOOKIN LIKE YOUR HUSBAND, OR SOMEONE ELSE IN YOUR FAMILY THAT'S UGLY; DO IT IN STYLE. SEND MONEY, YOUR ADDRESS, AND MEASUREMENTS. NO FAT LADIES, PLEASE, UNLESS YOUSE IS WILLIN' TO PAY A HUNDRED DOLLARS! LET YOUR CHILD LOOK LIKE YOUR GOOD LOOKIN' NEIGHBOUR'S CHILD, YOUR BUS-DRIVER'S CHILD, YOUR POSTMAN, YOUR GROCER, OR YOUR GARAGE-MECHANIC'S CHILD. I CAN DO THAT FOR YOUSE! WHEN IT COMES TO GOOD LOOKIN' KIDS, REACH FOR THE EXPERIENCE OF A LIFETIME! THE MOOSE IS LOOSE!'"

Moose got up and opened his barracks box. "GUYS, I'LL BE RICH! Where the hell is my writin' pad?"

Although they could keep the lights on all night if they wanted to, the occupants of B-33 were tired and the hut was dark by 2230 hours. All of the windows were shut and the sound of the rain pounding against the roof and sides of the building wasn't needed to put them to sleep. The last laugh of the night for the Musketeers was when East said, "Moose, that's the best idea I've heard in years. I'll handle all of the administration. You and I will set up the deal. I'm with ya."

"It won't pay much, Jacky, and your writin' hand will get sore."

"His writin' hand is always sore anyway," said Banks.

Douglas sat up. "Yeah and he doesn't have to write to get it sore."

"Up your noses, you guys, I think it's a good idea. Moose, I'm with ya. I'm really with ya. The idea is fabulous."

'BARRRROOOOM' The crash of thunder shook their building, and a voice from across the aisle said, "East, will you quit farting. We're not in the showers now, you know?"

Danyluk came to Jack's rescue. "That wasn't East, you dummy. It was the RSM sneaking one out. He's probably just left the Sergeants' Mess and is heading towards his car."

'CRRRASSSHHH, BARRROOOM' More thunder and the lightning turned the night's darkness into high noon.

"Jack, if you believe in it so much, will ya take the fat dames off my hands?"

There was silence for a few moments. "What's my cut?"

Moose snickered. "Ten percent, that's all you're worth."

More silence followed before Jack answered. "Stick it in your ear."

"There you are, some appreciation. I thought you were really with me?"

"He's chicken shit," some CScotR cadet added fom across the aisle. I'll take the fat ones for you,Moose."

"How much will you want from me?"

"Ten percent is fine."

"Although I can't see ya, I can recognize your voice. You've got a deal. Say, you're pretty smart for a CScotR, ain't youse?"

"You bet I am. The Seaforths will take the fat broads off my hands for five percent, and I'll pocket the other five."

"UP YOUR ASS!" a 72nd Seaforth cadet yelled. "Jesus you Canned Scots are crass. I'm ashamed you wear kilts."

"Yeah, and I'm ashamed you wear shorts under your kilts. Why, I'll betcha in the wintertime, you antler-heads actually wear long underwear."

When the Musketeers finally went to sleep, the two Scots were still going at it, and all other Scots were now getting involved. Although it was dark in the hut and they couldn't see each other, they yelled insults as only Scots can.

Shortly, no one heard the thunder.

Even when dark, heavy, water-laden clouds cover the Okanagan Valley and a fresh north wind bends and rattles the trees, the beauty of it all is something to behold. At least Douglas and Wayne thought so. Douglas had talked the other Musketeers into taking the east road around by the golf course fence, when they headed towards B-29 for another day's training. The rain that morning hadn't let up, it was pouring as he and Wayne viewed the hills across the valley, that were partly shrouded in mist .

"I must be out of my cottin'-pickin' mind lettin' youse guys talk me into taking this route on a day like this," bitched Moose. Like the others, he was wearing his poncho and had drawn the hood-string so tightly, only a small circle of his face was exposed to the weather. Under their ponchos, they were dressed in bush uniform pants, khaki shirts, sweaters, webbelts, regimental headdress, boots, weights, and puttees.

When they arrived, they were surprised to find that the building was immaculate. The normally trampled mud and grime always collected on the P.T. run was nowhere to be seen. Even the cadets' ponchos were dry. They were also puzzled to find the cadets standing by their beds as Harvey and Earl called the roll for Five and Six Platoons.

"RIGHT! BECAUSE OF THIS ARRANGEMENT, YOU HAVE AN EXTRA FIFTEEN MINUTES BEFORE OUR FIRST PERIOD THIS MORNING. CATCH UP ON ANY LAST THINGS YOU HAVE TO DO. FIVE AND SIX PLATOONS, ATTEN...TION! CARRY ON!" bellowed Rothstein. Then he walked towards the six others.

Simon couldn't believe the state of the hut. "Rothie, how did you do it? This place is spotless."

"I used my head, that's what I did. It was raining so hard, I canceled the outdoor physical training and we had it indoors."

Jack flipped back his poncho's hood. "INDOORS?"

"Yep, indoors! Don't worry, Earl and I joined them. Everyone ran on the spot for ten minutes, and completed thirty sit-ups and forty pushups. Listen, any idiot can get soaked. We accomplished the goal, but we did it in a different manner, that's all."

Douglas grinned. "That's brilliant. Why didn't Simpson think of something like that?"

"Because he's a sadist, that's why," said Danyluk. "Jesus, it would have been great if we were allowed to do it this way. But let me ask youse Rothie, haven't youse taken away a bit of the challenge?"

Rothstein was writing out the sick parade list. "I don't believe so. We also didn't follow the procedure for the normal morning parade. We held the parade indoors. Jack and me inspected Five and Six Platoons, and Spiess and Neish inspected Seven and Eight Platoons, on the other side. All cadets were over on this side of the hut for the P.T., though. Listen, any fool can get wet. You know yourselves, how many times have we worked on our uniforms to get them filthy in two minutes?"

East wasn't sure if he liked the idea. "Well, you can do it your way when it's your turn to run the show," Rothstein replied. "Major Kare, along with his officers and NCOs were here, and it didn't seem to bother them. How often do we get rain? Two, maybe three times during the summer, if that? I figured these kids deserved a break from the bullshit of silly routines."

A few moments later, it was unanimously agreed that Rothstein's methods were sensible.

"Also, I've changed the timetable for this morning. The rain is supposed to ease off this afternoon, so instead of map and compass in Area Ten in this weather, we'll be in the tents for the first three periods. We'll teach this afternoon's periods of Leadership and Technique of Instruction, now."

"You're the boss, boss," said Wayne.

Moose smiled. "Good shrinking, er, I mean thinking, Rothie. Say, how's

Laitricharde-Reed doing?"

Rothstein put his hand on Moose's shoulder. "Moose, I don't know what you did, but you've pulled off a miracle. The guy's a different person. He's part of a team of four and I've never seen four people work so hard in their lives, present company excepted, of course."

"Of course," commented Jackson.

Rothstein's plan went well that morning. Each Musketeer taught Leadership and Technique of Instruction in the tents under the pounding rain. The cadets of Bravo Company appreciated Rothstein's earlier consideration and it showed.

"SO THAT'S WHAT IT TAKES TO PULL OFF THE PERFECT LEC-TURE," Douglas stated to his section. "LET'S FACE IT, YOUR JOB AS INSTRUCTORS IS TO KEEP EVERYONE ATTENTIVE. WE'VE ALL HAD TO SIT AND LISTEN TO BORING TEACHERS. I DON'T THINK THERE'S ANY-THING WORSE THAN THAT. SO, LET'S COVER IT AGAIN. THERE ARE AT LEAST SIX WAYS OF MAKING INSTRUCTION INTERESTING AND GET-TING YOUR POINT ACROSS. WHAT ARE THEY? GIVE ME ONE..." he paused and looked around. Douglas enjoyed using the 'overhead' method of asking questions. If he had used 'direct' questions, the ones who weren't asked wouldn't think.

"Yes, Tong?"

"Use 'comparisons,' Corporal. Compare different situations."

Douglas nodded. "Good, right on. And another...Mellish?"

"Give 'reasons,' Corporal. By using various reasons, it stimulates thought."

"Yes, that's right, Mellish." He changed the subject for a minute. "How's business lately?"

Mellish went a little red in the face. "A lotta these guys think my clippers pull too much."

"Do they? Well, at the price you're charging, they should be prepared to accept a little pull now and then." He got back on track. "What's another one...?"

A cadet madly waved his hand. "Curtis?"

"Use 'examples,' Corporal."

"Perfect. Yes, examples have to be used. And another one...Schmidt?"

"Statistics, Corporal. Using statistics generates thought."

"You bet they do. Very good. Are there any more...? Hawthorne?"

"Testimony, Corporal. Testimonials allow people to remember."

"Exactly. Churchill used that method a lot. Very good. Another one...? Chandler?"

"Restatement, Corporal. If you have a class restate something enough times, the students will not forget it."

Douglas nodded. "Restatement is one of the best methods. Excellent! So you see, there are many methods of creating interest. Let's put them into a code-word so you won't forget them. He stood to one side as he wrote on the blackboard. "We'll call the word, '*CRREST*!' COMPARISONS, REASONS, RESTATEMENT, EXAMPLES, STATISTICS, AND TESTIMONY. WHAT'S THE WORD?"

His section yelled, "CREST!"

"One more time, what is it?"

"CREST!"

"With how many 'R's'?"

"TWO, CORPORAL!"

Douglas ticked off the words he had written on the blackboard. "We've just used the method of *restating*. Are there any questions?" he asked, glancing at his watch.

"No? O.K., it's time to wash up for lunch. Cadet Drinkwater, march the section back to their barracks. Remember now, I want all of you to wear your sweaters under your ponchos this afternoon. We'll be tramping Area Ten in this rain. Thank you."

As his section marched back to B-29, Douglas collected his notes and his lesson plan and waited until the others were finished. Although Rothstein and Jackson headed back to Bravo's barracks, the other five arrived in minutes. As usual, East was in a *deep* conversation with Moose.

"Bullshit, Moose. Sex is not a sense. Hey, Doug, the Moose here says 'sex' should be one of the senses. Instead of five, he wants to make it, six."

East and Danyluk had been teaching one of the Principles of Instruction, 'Use of the Proper Senses.'

"Jack, I don't teach it that way, but I believe it should be. There's touching, smelling, hearing, seeing, licking, and groping."

A laughing Douglas put on his poncho and joined the others back to B-33's kitchen. "Moose, what the hell is groping? The other five make up the way you can have sex, don't they?"

"HEY, SPEAK FOR YOURSELF. NOT THE WAY I DOES IT!"

"Well, describe it," said Wayne.

"WHY SHOULD I? IT'S ONE OF MY SECRETS. WHEN IT COMES DOWN TO THE NITTY-GRITTY, ONLY MY DAMES KNOWS WHAT GROPING MEANS. I'LL GIVE YOUSE A HINT. FIRST, YOUSE GOT TO SEE 'EM, AND SEEING IS BELIEVING, RIGHT?"

"All right, that's one sense. You can see 'em, but does that mean you can have sex without touching?" Simon asked.

Danyluk stuck out his chest. "No, you have to have touch. Christ, you couldn't have it, if you couldn't touch it. Did you hear this creep? He says you can get it on without touching."

"How about hearing?" asked Cunningham as he took a card out of Simon's ear. Moose held out his arms to the black clouds above. "Natch. The broad has to say yes. Well in most cases they do. I know dames that say no, and when I don't pursue it, they give me shit. Then other times when the same ones say no, and I persist, I get shit again."

"Where does smell come in? asked East. "And licking, for that matter? Jesus, Moose, if you have to smell and lick, you're not having sex, you're having dinner."

Moose gave East his special grin. "Same thing, ain't it?"

"YOU ARE GROSS, MOOSE DANYLUK! DID YOU GUYS HEAR THAT? SEX IS THE SAME AS HAVING DINNER? YOU ARE SICK, SICK, SICK!"

All of the Musketeers, except East were roaring their heads off as East pretended to throw up. "I'm not going to be able to eat lunch after listening to that."

Gordie got into step. "Well, that's the five senses, so where does groping come in?"

"I'll give youse another hint. SWEAT! And another one...STICKIN'!"

East stopped everyone. "There you are. I knew you'd finally admit it. Remember the conversation we had at Glenemma, three years ago, when I said we could get stuck like dogs and you said we couldn't? Now you admit it, eh? You said you'd stand at the end of my bed with a bucket of water if I got stuck, remember?"

Danyluk's stomach got sore from laughing. "Jacky, I said 'sticking,' not getting stuck. Listen, I'll give you one more hint. If you sweat, you get sticky, right?"

"WHO SAYS I DO? HOW THE HELL DO YOU KNOW I GET STICKY IF
I SWEAT? HOW DO YOU KNOW I EVEN SWEAT WHEN I GET IT ON? NOT
EVERYONE'S LIKE YOU, YOU KNOW? NOT EVERYONE SWEATS AND
THINKS OF SEX AS LIKE HAVING DINNER! YOU'RE AN ANIMAL,
THAT'S WHAT YOU ARE!"

The group had started moving again but East had turned around and was
marching backwards, waving his arms as he gave Danyluk a piece of his mind.

"YOU, THERE! YES, YOU! WHAT THE HELL DO YOU THINK YOU'RE
DOING? CONDUCTING A GOD-DAMNED ORCHESTRA? GET OVER
HERE!"

As a sheepish East strode towards the wet RSM, five very smart *soldiers* had
their arms up and their chests out as they marched towards B-33, ponchos rustling.

"Finally, he's got someone else other than me," a smirking Danyluk murmured.

Just before they entered B-33, Delta company marched past with *Corporal*
Johnston calling out the step. Nine cadets in the first platoon were carrying paint
tins.

Johnston winked at the Musketeers as he bellowed to the *persons in
possession*, "AND YOU'LL SLEEP WITH THEM TONIGHT, AS WELL!"

The rain eased off somewhat that afternoon, as Bravo Company completed
four orienteering exercises in Area Ten, south of the upper camp.

This type of training prepared the cadets for the upcoming week they would
spend at Glenemma.

Although Area Ten wasn't nearly as big as the large field-training region
thirty-some-odd miles north of camp, it was big enough for cadets to learn how to
relate their maps to the ground, how to measure and march on bearings, and how to
properly complete resections and intersections to locate their precise position on
their maps.

The Musketeers had spent three hours setting up these exercises and they were
proud because very few sections got lost.

The first program called for cadets to locate their position on their maps, by
judging their distance from natural objects, such as green areas, streams, rivers,
lakes, mountains, etc.

Next, they learned how to discover their approximate location by taking bearings on other objects in the distance or near-distance, such as bridges, churches,
schools, hills, mountains, transmission lines, railroad tracks, etc., and figuring out
their position along the *one* line which they drew on their maps.

After they were fairly proficient, they completed resections and intersections.
They would take two bearings, draw two lines, and where those lines met, was their
location. Or, two, or three sections that knew where they were would measure bearings on a lost section that was visible to them. The sections taking bearings were
spread out and transmitted their bearings to the lost section by using Fifty-Eight set
radios. The lost section plotted the two or three bearings coming at them from various locations, and where those lines intersected, was their section's location on the
map.

Last, but not least, various orienteering exercises allowed them to visit different points for which they had written instructions on how to get there. A Musketeer was at each rendezvous, timing them and would give the section other written instructions to *guide* them to other positions. These exercises were timed and accuracy-points were added or deducted from a total that would be calculated later. The winning section would receive the 'NEVER GIVE AN OFFICER A MAP' trophy, which Danyluk had made up. It was a large tomato can with handles screwed into the sides. The container would then be filled with Kik Kola and each cadet in the winning section would take a swig from it.

As luck would have it, Danyluk's section won the aptly-named trophy. When the company was later formed up in three ranks outside B-29, Rothstein called out the names of the cadets in the winning section, and their *Corporal.*

Cadet Laitricharde-Reed had been the leader of the section and all his people knew they wouldn't have even come close if he hadn't been there. This *kid* had a good head on his shoulders and he could reason well. He also delegated a lot, and Archer proved to be more than an able assistant. They were now good friends.

As each member of the winning team took a drink from the *trophy,* Danyluk's chest stuck out a mile.

"I know all of you want to hear from, ME, the world's greatest Corporal, and the *man* partially responsible for this win."

Only Moose's section applauded. The rest of the company offered other boisterous, tongue-in-cheek comments, such as: "IT WAS FIXED!" "NEVER GIVE A CORPORAL A MAP, EITHER!" "WE SAW YA GIVIN' THE LAST CHECKPOINT CORPORAL FIVE DOLLARS!" "BLOODY LUCK, THAT'S ALL IT WAS!"

"ARE YOUSE BUMS SAYIN' WE *RIGGED* THE EXERCISES?"

"YES!" The response was tumultuous.

"WELL, YOU'LL NEVER KNOW, WILL YA? TO BE SERIOUS FOR A SECOND...AT THE START, I SAID, "MAY THE BEST SECTION, WIN!" TODAY, THE BEST SECTION DID TRIUMPH!"

Moose's grin grew as many *other* comments flew in his direction.

Laitricharde-Reed's speech was just as short. "IT WASN'T LUCK, IT WAS INTELLIGENCE AND SKILL, AND ONLY ONE SECTION IN THE COMPANY HAS THOSE QUALITIES!"

Although the rest of the company knew Laitricharde-Reed's group had put on the best show, they jokingly *informed* him of their opinions, as well. He cringed from the outcry.

Before dismissing the company for the day, Rothstein advised the cadets about the next two days on the ranges.

"WE'VE CHANGED THE DRESS! YOU'LL WEAR YOUR PITH-HELMETS, K. D. LONGS, SHIRTS, YOUR SOCKS, AND RUNNING SHOES. MAKE CERTAIN YOU BRING YOUR PONCHOS AND FILL UP YOUR WATER CANTEENS! ALSO, BRING ALONG YOUR SHOE-RAGS. SOME OF YOU MAY WISH TO USE THEM AS PADDING!"

Earl had been kind of quiet most of the day. Quiet in the sense he was looking for the *rotten bastards* who had got to him.

"NOW! THIS MORNING, CORPORAL JACKSON HERE, NOTICED SOMETHING VERY ODD HAD TAKEN PLACE WITH HIS PERSON OVERNIGHT!"

Smiles were everywhere. Cadets were whispering in each other's ears, and chuckling rallied throughout the ranks.

"WHEN PULLING UP HIS P.T. SHORTS, CORPORAL JACKSON NOTICED THE HAIRS ON HIS LEFT LEG HAD BEEN SHAVED OFF!"

The laughter was loud, and the smiles originating from every Musketeer except Corporal Jackson made it get louder.

"WHEN WE WENT TO B-33 TO HAVE OUR MORNING SHOWER, THE GOOD CORPORAL ALSO BECAME COGNIZANT OF THE FACT THAT ANOTHER PORTION OF HIS LOWER BODY HAD ALSO BECOME HAIR-LESS!"

Howls filled the area, as cadets held their stomachs from laughing. Rothstein found it difficult to keep a straight face, for that matter, so did Earl and the rest of the *Corporals*.

"AFTER CORPORAL JACKSON RECOVERED FROM HIS MASSIVE HEART ATTACK...HE..."

Rothstein burst out laughing with everyone else. After a few moments, he regained his composure and continued.

"HE ASKED ME IF THERE WAS A DISEASE GOING AROUND THAT EVENLY TAKES OUT HALF YOUR CROTCH HAIR AND THE HAIR OFF ONLY ONE LEG..."

Banks couldn't take it. He had to turn and stagger away. If the cadets hadn't been in the ranks, they would have been rolling on the ground. The situation was hilarious, as Bravo's exuberance echoed against the nearby huts.

"THAT SORT OF THING WILL NOT HAPPEN AGAIN! IF IT DOES, WE'LL FIND OUT WHO THE GUILTY PARTY IS AND LET THEM HAVE THE PARADE SQUARE TO THEMSELVES ALL NIGHT LONG!

"CORPORAL JACKSON HAS A WEEKEND PASS AND WAS PLANNING ON GOING DOWN TO THE BEACH WITH HIS GIRLFRIEND! HE DOESN'T KNOW WHETHER TO SHAVE HIS OTHER LEG, OR PRETEND THE *BARE* ONE'S BROKEN AND WEAR A CAST. UNDERSTAND ME, IT WON'T HAP-PEN AGAIN!"

Rothstein glanced at Earl. He could only look at him for a second, otherwise he'd have erupted again. "CORPORAL JACKSON, HAVE YOU GOT ANY-THING TO ADD?"

Earl went from the side of the company, to its front. "YES I CERTAINLY HAVE, CORPORAL ROTHSTEIN! LET THE GUILTY CULPRITS BE ON NOTICE, THAT IF I FIND OUT WHO THEY ARE, THEY'LL WISH THEY NEVER LEFT THEIR MOTHERS' WOMBS. THAT'S IF THEY WERE *BORN*. I HAVE A FEELING THOSE PONGOES WERE HATCHED UNDER A ROCK!"

A few moments later, Rothstein took over again. "BRAVO COMPANY, ATTEN...TION! DIS...MISSED!"

After they had turned to their right and marched forward a few paces, a high-spirited and *chatting* Bravo Company entered their quarters. Many cadets had their arms around each others' shoulders and their laughter was contagious.

All the Musketeers had dinner together that night, and Earl couldn't live it down.

Danyluk was the first to offer his opinion. "I know your dame shaves her legs, but if she sees yours, she going to wonder what the hell she's going out with?"

Douglas asked, "Earl, why the hell didn't you wake up?"

A grinning Earl, replied, "I was totally beat. I had to solve problems with the University of Victoria, my mom, and my girlfriend. Afterwards, I resolved fifteen-million problems in the barracks, prepared my lesson plans, and went to bed. I didn't even notice my leg until Rothie mentioned it to me. Christ, I was half asleep doing P.T. I nearly had a bird when I got in the shower. I had to face the wall when some smart ass Westie said, "Hey darlin,' do you pluck your eyebrows too?"

Their table exploded with laughter, but Earl wasn't finished.

"Then a CScotR left the showers for a few seconds and came back in with a bottle of shaving lotion. He said, 'I'll bet you normally wait until the room's empty before you shave. Don't forget you've got another leg to do. Here, put some of this aftershave lotion on your crotch. When your girlfriend's down there she'll think you just got a little mixed up.' The nerve of the asshole. I've got a feeling those Seaforths are right. The CScotR's are crass."

Other cadets sitting nearby, must have wondered what was so funny. All Musketeers were pounding their table as they laughed.

"Listen, guys, do me a big favour and try to discover who set me up. This type of thing doesn't to happen to Musketeers. Bergie would be furious if he found out. Let's repay those rotten creeps."

After a few laughing moments, it was decided that each of them would keep an ear to the ground.

"You know, part of the problem is, we're tellin' 'em all of our secrets," said East. "But they ain't supposed to use 'em on us."

Cunningham agreed. He stopped rolling his dice for a few seconds. "That's right, some Bravo cadets actually call *themselves*, Musketeers. We've taught them far too well!"

Banks slapped Jackson on the back. "Not to worry, Earl, old pal, old pard. We'll find out and get our own back." With that said, they all shook hands and stood up. All but one raised their glasses. Jack's mind was on food.

"Up the Musketeers," toasted Wayne, as he took a chicken leg out of East's hand, and handed him a glass of water. "Er, sorry, er, a simple mistake," stated an embarrassed East.

"UP THE MUSKETEERS!"

After supper, Rothstein and Jackson headed back to B-29 and the others went to B-33 for a shower and a change of clothing. When they had completed their uniforms for the following day, which included Harvey and Earl's clothes, they added up their spare change and went across the highway to Gracie's drive-in. Although dark clouds were still lingering, the rain had stopped and the air was fresh.

Not too many cadets were at the eating place, but quite a few were across the road, marching down the hill towards town. Without the blistering sun, it was a pleasure walking down and even up the hill for that matter.

As usual, Danyluk brought his radio and when they arrived, Kitty Kallen's 1954 hit, *Little Things Mean a Lot*, was playing.

"I'm gonna write Kitty and tell her she's got it all wrong. Big things mean a lot," a serious Moose *informed* the others.

After they pooled their funds and placed the money into East's hand, he went to the wicket for burgers and chocolate shakes. Cunningham found a table and sat with the rest, shuffling a deck of cards. "She's not singing about wangs, you creep. She's singing about the little things lovers do for each other."

"Oh, come off it, Gordie. She's gone and got herself wrapped up with a millionaire with a small prong, and now she's tryin' to convince him everything's fine."

There was a loud discussion at the counter before East rushed over.

"HEY, I'M SHORT HERE!" Both of his side pockets had been turned inside-out and they were hanging out. "WHO DIDN'T PUT THEIR MONEY IN? JESUS, I'M ASHAMED, THE GIRL JUST ACCUSED ME OF CHEATING HER!" Perspiration had formed on the top of his forehead and the girl in the window tapped her pencil while waiting to be paid.

They all looked at each other. Everyone had put their money in.

"SOMEONE AIN'T! bellowed a very concerned East. "YOU PONGO, CUN-NINGHAM, IT'S YOU, I KNOW IT IS. EVERY TIME I GET THE FOOD, I GET THE *TREATMENT*!"

Gordie smiled contentedly. "Jacky, Jacky, calm down my son. You've always had a problem with figures. If someone didn't put all of their money in, please allow me to straighten out the confusion. Here's seventy-five cents, keep the change, my boy."

East quickly counted the combination of pennies, nickels and dimes and rushed back to the wicket. He was already eating when he returned and passed out the other burgers.

"YOU GUYS CAN GO UP AND GET YOUR OWN SHAKES! WHY IS IT, I'M ALWAYS THE ONE WHO GETS THE SHAFT?"

Moose took a bite of his burger and pointed to East. "Ya got to keep the change, didn'tcha? Quit complaining!"

East stood up and threw his wrapper in the garbage bin. "TWO CENTS! THE CREEP GAVE ME TWO CENTS! KEEP THE CHANGE? I'LL KEEP THE CHANGE ALL RIGHT. I'VE GOT A PROBLEM WITH FIGURES? JUST WAIT UNTIL NEXT TIME, CUNNILINGUS! LET ME TELL YOU..."

Cunningham paid no attention to him. It was Wayne who interrupted.

"You've always had a problem with figures, Jack. When the dames are fat, you like 'em. When they're well-rounded, you don't like 'em. That's a problem, ain't it?"

Jack was obviously still upset. "WHO SAYS I LIKE FAT DAMES? I LIKE 'EM WELL ROUNDED! YOU'RE THINKING OF MOOSE, YOU DINK!"

Danyluk put his feet up on the bench and sat back sipping his milkshake. "I takes 'em any way they come. Beggars can't be choosers. There was a time when..."

Moose's jaw dropped and he instantly stopped talking; his eyes were glued to a huge girl at the wicket. She had an immense girlfriend with her and both of them were scrutinizing him.

He slowly turned his head down a little towards the others, and mumbled under his breath. "Oh shit! Not them again."

Smiles filled the faces of the remaining five Musketeers, but not the girls'.

"EUNICE, IT'S THAT ASSHOLE FROM THE THEATRE! screamed Alberta Schwartz, expressing her unrefined *feelings* as vocally as ever. "HE'S THE ONE WHO KEPT PINCHING MY BUM! WHY YOU SON OF A BITCH, I'LL..."

The 'girl' from that famous night out at the movies made a mad dash for Danyluk. With her right arm raised and the palm of her hand in the *smacking* position, she came at Moose with the anger of a crazed bull elephant.

Danyluk never moved so fast in his life as he hopped over one table, then another.

"It's amazing," said Gordie, as he continued playing solitaire, "They either love him, or they hate him. Do you think this is hate?"

Simon's eyes enjoyed the chase. "Naaa, this is definitely love."

"I NEVER INTENTIONALLY FELT YOUR ASS!" bellowed a fleeing Danyluk.

"YOU FELT ALL OF ME, YOU SEX FIEND!" replied three-hundred pounds of charging lard.

"WELL ,YOU SENT ME THE NOTE!" gasped Moose.

"I WOULDN'T SEND YA THE SWEAT OFF MY TITS!" a breathless Alberta replied.

Danyluk jumped over another table. "I WOULDN'T EXCEPT IT, EITHER!"

Douglas couldn't stop laughing. "Did you guys hear that? He's finally drawn the line."

"Wouldn't *you*?" Gordie casually replied, as he stuck out his foot, which sent the *lady* flying onto some nearby grass. Her body was exhausted, but not her voice. "EUNICE BYGDNES, GRAB THAT SEX MONSTER FOR ME!"

"YOU BET I WILL, I'LL GET HIM FOR YOU, ALBERTA!" a *horny* Eunice screamed, the smile on her face indicating she meant it. "HE'S PROBABLY THE SHIT WHO ATE MY CANDY AND DRANK MY POP! I'LL CATCH HIM AND SIT ON HIM FOR YOU!"

A tired Danyluk responded, "WOMAN, I DIDN'T TOUCH ANYTHING OF YOURS! AND I MEAN, ANYTHING!"

"YES, YOU DID, YOU SAVAGE BRUTE! YOU COPPED A FEEL OF MY RIGHT BREAST, *AND* YOU SNAPPED MY BRA STRAP! DID YOU THINK I COULDN'T FEEL IT?"

Although Moose was slowing down, he was still faster than Eunice. At least until he responded.

"I THOUGHT I WAS GRABBING YOUR ANKLE."

"WHY YOU CHEEKY..." Eunice picked up speed. "CORPORAL ADAMS, I'LL HAVE YOUR NUTS FOR THAT!"

Now it was Wayne's turn to burst out laughing. "Did you guys hear that? In the theatre he must have said his name was Corporal Adams."

Although Moose was worn out, he still had a mammoth smile on his face and one comment left, as he ran across the highway.

"AS FOR YOUR BRA STRAP, WHO MAKES YOUR BRASSIERES, JONES TENT AND AWNING?"

With his radio under his arm and Frankie Laine's song, *High Noon*, blaring, a breathless Danyluk ran behind the Provost shack and headed for B-33.

Eunice thought twice about crossing the highway. She was also out of breath and stopped her pursuit.

After a few minutes, both girls walked down the hill, their arms filled with beef burgers and shakes. Although Alberta's mouth was full, her message was clear.

"YOU TELL YOUR FRIEND, CORPORAL ADAMS, I'LL HAVE MORE THAN HIS CONKERS WHEN I'M FINISHED WITH HIM! Isn't that right, Eunice?"

"Alberta, I'm going to tell my old man about him."

With so much *stuff* in her arms, Eunice dropped one of her milk shakes. As it splattered all over the sidewalk, a passing Provost jeep stopped.

"Need a hand, ladies?"

Alberta scowled at the smiling driver. "We've had enough of the military's hands. PISS OFF!"

Although Corporal Adams didn't like her response, he got out of his jeep anyway, and winked at Eunice, "What are you going to do now, fats, lick it up? Here, I'll help you."

All Corporal Adams wanted to do was offer assistance, but as he bent down to pick up the empty container, he didn't realize Eunice had moved closer to take it from him. Without looking, as he passed it up, his hand went up her skirt, milkshake container and all.

"YOU FILTHY BEAST! LEAVE MY GIRLFRIEND ALONE! EUNICE, THEY EVEN TRY TO RAVISH US ON BUSY STREETS!"

The jeep drove off quickly as both girls downed their goodies and made a grab for the speeding driver.

"YOU LECHEROUS PRICK!" screamed an enraged Miss Schwartz.

Bowled over with laughter, the remaining Musketeers each had to have another milkshake to soothe their throats. Gordie slipped East two-dollars and sent him to the wicket. "MAKE MINE STRAWBERRY THIS TIME," he yelled to Jack, before turning his attention to the other three.

"Say, you guys, did you hear Eunice's last name?"

Simon nodded. "Yeah, Alberta yelled something like, Bidg..., er Bigness. That was it, BIGNESS! Cripes, the name goes along with her body."

Gordie agreed, but he knew something else. "It might be pronounced kinda like that, but I bet it's, *Bygdnes*. Which makes her the daughter of..." He moved his right hand around in small circles, trying to draw the information from them.

Douglas whistled. "You don't mean?" Instantly he adopted Gordie's sneaky grin. "Yes, you do...Jesus, she even looks like him."

"Like who?" Wayne asked, his nose in Douglas' face.

"Sergeant Bygdnes, our Messing Sergeant, Douglas replied. "The one who gave Jack the extra duty. He lives in Vernon...that's who it is."

When East returned with the shakes, they told him.

"Haaa, can you imagine what will happen when she goes home and tells him Corporal Adams treated her like that? That she buys her brassieres from Jones Tent and Awning?"

"Hey, where the hell's my change?" Cunningham inquired.

"What change? You only gave me two dollars. There's a delivery charge, you know?"

Cunningham glared arrows at East. "O.K., Jacky! Don't say I didn't ask ya."

East rolled his eyes up and cringed, then he had second thoughts. "Oh, all right. Here," he said, dropping some change into Gordie's outstretched hand.

Wayne's eyes were in another direction as he pointed. "Will you take a look at that?"

Three other heads followed the direction of his arm. Hop sing was closing up and had five girls with him as he locked up his shop.

East's lower jaw dropped and his straw went up his nose as he automatically went to sip his shake. "So that's Hop Sing?"

They were all standing on the sidewalk eagerly staring down the hill. "Get a load of the dames," said Simon. No sooner had he spoke, *Hop Sing* turned around for a fraction of a second.

Douglas put his arm on Wayne's shoulder. "The guy's white, he can't be Hop Sing?"

"I'll betcha he's Hop Sing's bodyguard," said a gawking East.

Gordie didn't agree. "Jack, if he's the bodyguard, then Hop Sing must be dressed up in drag."

The rest of them laughed as Wayne gave them a nudge, "Listen, let's get back and tell Moose we've finally seen Hop Sing, and she's a beaut."

As they crossed the highway, East said, "If Hop Sing is a drag queen, Moose will never be the same. It's the mystique of the joint that's keeping him alive."

The group of them chuckled when Gordie added, "Now we know what the sign means. 'Our *STAFF* will be preased to serve you.' I'll betcha the guy's got a *staff* a mile long, maybe even bigger than Danyluk's?"

By the time they reached their shack, they had agreed unanimously that no one in the world, "has a bigger wang than Moose. No one! Not even Miss Hop Sing!"

Half-an-hour later, a disgruntled Danyluk cupped his fingers on Hop Sing's window, but because it was dark inside, he couldn't see anything.

"Damn!" he mumbled as he put his hands in his pockets, kicked a rock, and strolled back to his hut.

"YOU! YES, YOU! GET YOUR HANDS OUT OF YOUR POCKETS AND MARCH!" a smirking Corporal Adams yelled from his jeep.

Although Moose was now marching, he thought to himself, 'You, you bastard, you've got the second-half coming.' Then at the entrance to his barracks, a demoralized Danyluk muttered, "DAMN?...a drag queen?"

When Moose Danyluk entered the showers with the other Musketeers that evening, he had no idea a telephone was ringing in the Provost shack. The Provost Sergeant, Sergeant Bill Gabriel, had just finished locking the cell doors for the night and caught the phone on its fifth ring.

"Provost..., Sergeant Gabriel?"

"Bill, Larry Bygdnes here."

Gabriel lit up a smoke and put his feet on his desk. "Larry, you old food hoarder you. Did you get us that twenty-pound turkey for the Sergeants' Mess raffle?"

"I'm working on it, Bill. It's not easy, you know? The Messing Officer, Major Figby-Jones, has got eyes in the back of his head. We've got an honest Messing Officer this year, Bill, it's going to take a little time, but I'll get one for you. Listen, I'm not calling you about that. I'm calling about your Corporal Adams. The *women's* man."

"Yeah, I've taken him under my wing a little more. He's been relatively quiet since the Nursing Sister *episode*. What about him?"

"Quiet? I'll say he's been quiet. The son-of-a-bitch has changed his methods. He tried to feel up my daughter in the back row of the theatre."

Gabriel pounded his half-finished cigarette into the ashtray and quickly put his feet on the floor.

"WHAT? Larry, I'm really sorry. When did this happen?"

"A week or so back. I didn't know about it until tonight. My daughter came home crying. She recognized him at Gracie's drive in. He even asked her if she had her brassieres made at Jones Tent and Awning."

Gabriel yelled into the phone. "THAT S.O.B. IS SUPPOSED TO BE OUT

THERE WORKING AND HE'S HANGING AROUND GRACIE'S DRIVE IN?"

"That's not the whole story, Bill. Little Eunice has a delightfully charming friend. A really sweet young lady. Alberta Schwartz, is her name and the wife and I have known her since birth. That same night in the theatre, he never left Alberta alone, either. Had his hands all over her breasts and her buttocks. Your Corporal's sick, Bill, really sick! At first I was going to call the RSM, but, well, maybe the 'old boy network' is better, eh?"

Gabriel fumed, "Yes, that's right, Larry. You just leave it to me. Is there anything else?"

"Yes, one last thing, Bill. Your man steals *little* girls' candy and drinks. When they went to the washroom, he just helped himself. Bit of an asshole, eh?"

"AN ASSHOLE? HE WON'T HAVE AN ASSHOLE BY THE TIME I'M THROUGH WITH HIM! THANKS, LARRY!"

"Thank *you*, Bill."

After he slammed down the phone, Sergeant Gabriel picked up the radio handset. "ONE ALPHA, OVER!"

A squelched voice response came out of the speaker. "ONE ALPHA, SEND YOUR MESSAGE, OVER!"

That night, Sergeant Gabriel broke all the rules of proper voice procedure. "ONE ALPHA, GET YOUR ASS IN HERE, NOW! OUT!"

Two minutes later, Sergeant Gabriel heard the squeal of jeep brakes, then footsteps coming up the stairs.

"What's up, Sarge?" asked a grinning Corporal Adams.

"WHAT'S UP? WHAT'S UP!? YOUR HAND...THAT'S WHAT'S UP! YOU FEEL UP SERGEANT BYGDNES' DAUGHTER AND YOU ASK WHAT'S UP?"

A shocked expression came over the Corporal's face. "Sergeant Bygdnes' daughter? I didn't know...she..., anyway, I was just trying to give her a hand with her milkshake and..."

"I'LL SAY YOU WERE. YOU'VE GOT YOUR HANDS EVERYWHERE. ANYWAY, SAVE IT! IT'S TOO LATE NOW TO DISCUSS IT; YOU SEE ME IN MY OFFICE IN THE MORNING!"

"What a change," Douglas whispered to Wayne, as they observed the cadets of Bravo Company complete their own morning parade. "They've improved a thousand-percent compared to a few days ago."

All of the Musketeers were on the sidelines along with Bravo's officers, and the other *Corporals*, watching the cadets. From the time the members of the company left their barracks, everything had come off perfectly.

Although the sun hadn't been up very long, it was scorching on the backs of the cadets.

"These cadets are taking it seriously," Wayne replied. "They don't give any favours when they inspect themselves, and their drill is nearly as perfect as Alpha's. The heat isn't getting them down, either. Sergeants Beckford and Simpson have done it again."

Cadet Archer was the Commanding Officer that morning. Before he fell out the Cadet Officers, he addressed the company.

"I WASN'T IMPRESSED WITH NUMBER FIVE PLATOON TODAY. THAT'S THE REASON I HAD SERGEANT-MAJOR LAITRICHARDE-REED

TAKE TWELVE NAMES. ALSO, SOME CADET SAID, 'COME OFF IT, ARCHER, QUIT PLAYING THE ROLE OF A PRICK!' I'M NOT PLAYING THE ROLE OF A PRICK, I'M JUST DOING MY JOB. THE SOONER WE *ALL* REALIZE THAT, THE BETTER! I'VE ONLY GOT THIS POSITION FOR A DAY...ONE OF YOU WILL HAVE IT TOMORROW AND IF THAT PERSON WANTS TO BE MISTER NICE GUY, SO BE IT! REMEMBER WHAT CORPORAL CUNNINGHAM SAYS...'NICE GUYS FINISH LAST!'"

Gordie immediately turned red as he became the focus of attention. "I was referring to playing stuke," he whispered.

"HE ALSO SAYS, 'NEVER GIVE A SUCKER AN EVEN BREAK!' SO SUCKERS, IF NICE GUYS FINISH LAST, THEN I'M NOT GOING TO BE A NICE GUY!" Cadet Archer added.

Gordie cringed.

"THE TRUCKS WILL BE HERE SHORTLY TO TAKE US TO THE RANGE. MAKE CERTAIN YOU'VE ALL GOT YOUR PROPER EQUIPMENT. BRAVO COMPANY, ATTEN...TION! FALL OUT THE OFFICERS!"

The cadets acting as officers came to attention and marched forward and halted, forming a semi-circle in front of Archer. The right-hand man stepped forward a half-pace, and all of them saluted. After Archer returned their salute, the right hand man took a half-pace backward, then they turned to their right and marched off the parade.

While this was going on, the cadets acting as Platoon Sergeants came from the rear of the platoons and after halting in front, turned and faced the Commanding Officer.

"SERGEANT-MAJOR!" Archer bellowed.

"SIR!" replied Laitricharde-Reed, as he marched from his position on the extreme right side of the company, to a position two paces in front of Archer, and saluted.

Before he turned to his left and marched away, Archer returned the salute and said, "CARRY ON, PLEASE!"

Laitricharde-Reed waited until the Commanding Officer was out of the boundary of the parade before he turned about and bellowed, "BRAVO COMPANY, STANDAT...EASE! COMPANY ATTEN...TION! FALL OUT!"

The cadets smartly turned to their right and marched forward the usual five paces before they entered their barracks to pick up their gear and notebooks, etc.

Major Kare made his notes before leaving for the company office, so did the other regular force officers of Bravo Company. When the major was about thirty feet away, he returned and marched over to Rothstein.

"Is there a reason why you've got them in running shoes today?"

Rothstein saluted, and the salute was returned. "Yes, sir. From the experience I've had on the ranges, boots are not necessary. These cadets are working hard to preserve their boots and we want them to look great on Saturday morning. We'll win the best company this Saturday, sir, but I'm not certain about next weekend because of Glenemma. That'll be murder on their boots."

The Major smiled. "Very good. Thank you, Corporal Rothstein."

Rothstein saluted before leaving, and Major Kare responded appropriately.

While waiting for the trucks, the Musketeers gathered with the other *Corporals*.

"I think youse guys were puttin' me on last night," stated Danyluk. "Hop

Sing's not a drag queen. Youse probably saw some customer leavin' the shop with some of Hop Sing's dames."

"Moose, why would a customer have the keys?" asked East.

Danyluk scratched his head in deep thought. "Hey, maybe Hop Sing's not Chinese. Maybe he's white? That's it...I'll betcha Hop Sing's white."

Cunningham flipped a coin and it landed on the back of his left hand. He spoke as he sneaked a look at it. "Jesus, Moose, use your head...any one of the two. How could a white guy have a name like Hop Sing?"

Moose had it all figured out. "You've all heard of Hopalong Cassidy. Remember Hoppy, he's white? Hop Sing's real name could be Hopalong Singster, or somethin' like that?"

East nodded. He usually liked Danyluk's ideas. "Hey, yeah. Hop Sing is probably a nickname. Good shrinkin', er, I mean good thinkin', Moose."

The rest of the Musketeers just gave the duo weird looks as East and Moose strolled away to discuss the situation. "Moose, old buddy, did I tell ya that Hoppy's my favorite cowboy and his horse is..."

East's voice faded as they walked away.

Within minutes, a loaded convoy of trucks was winding its way up the dusty range road.

After they unloaded and Rothstein and Jackson were forming up the company, Wayne said to Douglas, "You know, Doug, if there's any place on earth that resembles hell itself, it's this region of the camp. Banks could barely see his buddy because of the churned-up clouds of dust left by the departing three-tons. "Hell couldn't be hotter than this and they probably issue dust-masks down there. I'll betcha our lungs will be half-full when we leave."

Douglas just nodded and shook his head at the same time. He agreed wholeheartedly with Wayne. The only shade on the ranges was in the butts and even then, it was stifling hot. Many times, he'd asked himself how the Range Officer managed to stand it. Everyone in camp knew the Range Officer because he was the one with the burnt-black face. His assistants looked the same. Their faces were also black from spending day upon day on the ranges.

"RIGHT, PAY ATTENTION HERE, BRAVO COMPANY! FOR THE NEXT TWO DAYS, YOU'LL BE FIRING GROUPING PRACTISES FROM ONE HUNDRED YARDS, SNAP AND RAPID PRACTISES FROM TWO HUNDRED YARDS, AND APPLICATION PRACTISES FROM THREE AND FOUR HUNDRED YARDS," the Range Officer bellowed from his megaphone.

"ON THE AFTERNOON OF DAY TWO, YOU'LL ALSO FIRE SINGLE AND AUTOMATIC FIRE FROM THE BREN AND STEN GUNS. THE BREN GUNS WILL BE USED AT THREE-HUNDRED YARDS AND YOU WILL BE FIRING THE STEN GUNS ON THE STEN RANGE. NOW, I WANT YOU TO GATHER AROUND ME AND FIND YOURSELF A COMFORTABLE PIECE OF GROUND TO SIT ON."

Finding a select piece of ground was easy because it was all the same...hard and dusty, as the cadets sat and listened to the never-ending list of Range Standing Orders, etc. Half-an-hour later when he was finished reading, he split the company up.

"WE'RE USING TWELVE FIRING POINTS THIS MORNING. FIVE PLATOON WILL FIRE GROUPING FIRST. SIX PLATOON WILL BE IN THE BUTTS, SEVEN PLATOON WILL LOAD AND DISTRIBUTE THE AMMUNI-

TION, AND EIGHT PLATOON WILL BE SPLIT UP. THOSE OF YOU IN EIGHT PLATOON WILL BECOME TELEPHONE MEN, FLAGMEN, YOU'LL ASSIST THE FIRST-AID PERSONNEL, AND BE APPOINTED AS POINT MEN. ARE THERE ANY QUESTIONS?"

A small cadet in Five Platoon held up his hand. "SIR, DO THESE GUNS HURT WHEN YOU FIRE 'EM?"

The Range Officer smiled. Actually it could have been a gas pain. "FIRST OF ALL, THEY ARE NOT GUNS, THEY ARE RIFLES. SECOND, THEY DO PACK A BIT OF A PUNCH, BUT YOU'LL LEARN HOW TO HANDLE THAT. ARE THERE ANY OTHER QUESTIONS?"

"HAS ANYONE EVER BEEN SHOT?" A cadet asked.

"NO, AND WE DON'T WANT ANYONE SHOT BECAUSE OF THE PAPERWORK AND THE MESS. KEEP YOUR EARS OPEN; PAY ATTENTION TO YOUR INSTRUCTORS AND EVERYTHING WILL BE FINE. REMEMBER THE LECTURES YOU'VE HAD ON THESE WEAPONS! BEAR IN MIND THE HOLDING, AIMING, AND FIRING PROCEDURES, AS WELL AS IMMEDI-ATE ACTIONS!

"RIGHT! CORPORAL ROTHSTEIN, YOU'RE IN CHARGE OF THE BUTTS THIS MORNING, PLEASE TAKE FIVE PLATOON DOWN THERE NOW AND SET EVERYTHING UP! ER..." He looked at his notes. "CORPORAL JACKSON, YOU WILL BE SECOND-IN-COMMAND OF THE BUTTS! THE FOLLOWING CADETS FROM EIGHT PLATOON WILL REPORT TO THE BUTTS WITH CORPORAL ROTHSTEIN." He reviewed his list again. "BURKE AND MCRITCHIE, YOU'LL HANDLE THE PHONES, and...and, and, BROPHY AND LAMMIE, YOU'LL OPERATE THE FLAGS! CORPORAL ROTHSTEIN, WE HAVE TWO ALPHA COMPANY MEDICAL-TYPES ATTACHED TO US FROM THE CAMP HOSPITAL. ONE WILL JOIN YOU IN THE BUTTS, AND THE OTHER WILL REMAIN HERE ON THE FIRING POINT. A COUPLE OF EIGHT PLATOON CADETS WILL ASSIST THEM. NOW, WHERE ARE THOSE MED...?"

Rothstein glanced around. There they were in living glory. The two Alpha cadets from the Royal Canadian Medical Corps. They were standing by the lone vehicle, discussing something about bandages.

"Actually James, I prefer Professor Michael Warrin's method of dressing wounds, it's so uncomplicated and..."

Yes, Jonathan, old boy, you are absolutely correct. At first, I thought about Professor Anthony Grass' proposal and...oh, oh, we're being called. Blast, I've been commanded below to those ghastly *ends* again."

"They refer to them as the butts, old sock. I'll see you subsequently when we'll sip a couple of those invigorating soft drinks. I do hope you will allow me to purchase one for you?"

"Of course, old fellow. Well, T.T.F.N, Jonathan."

"Yes, that will be just splendid. Ta, ta for now, James."

All of the Musketeers except Rothstein and Jackson joined other Alpha Company cadets acting as coaches. For every Bravo cadet, an Alpha cadet or a Regular Force Corporal joined him.

"Have you fired one of these before?" asked Douglas, as he stood next to a *shooter*.

"No," a nervous, dusty-faced cadet replied.

"What's your name?"

"Mawhinney, Corporal."

Douglas spoke slowly and confidently. "O.K., Mawhinney, all we have to do is listen to the Range Officer and concentrate on getting a good score. I think you're going to enjoy this. It would be better if we were using slings, but even if we're not, you'll do well."

"CHANGE THE FLAGS! NUMBER ONE RELAY ASSUME THE HORIZONTAL POSITION!"

The flags were changed at the firing point, and when the order was relayed by telephone, the flags were changed at the butts, as well.

"O.K., here we go, Mawhinney." Brice got down next to the boy, making certain the lad was in the proper firing position: body on an angle, feet about a foot apart. "That's it. You're holding the rifle correctly...very good. Just rest and keep your finger off the trigger. Where's your shoe-rag?"

"In my pocket, Corporal."

"Well, take it out, fold it and place it inside of your shirt over the meat of your shoulder. That's it...good. Now, let's just listen to the Range Officer."

"THIS RELAY, LOAD!"

"Right, pick up the magazine with your right hand and place it on the weapon. Give it a tap to make certain it's properly on...that's good. O.K., now, let's look at ourselves...the rifle is in the centre of your left hand on the fore stock; fingers together. Move your left elbow a little more to your middle, that's it, good. Now, close the bolt, apply the safety catch, and remain in that position; finger off the trigger.

"THIS RELAY, RANGE...TWO HUNDRED!"

"O.K., the Range Officer now wants you to lift up your rear sights and make certain they're as low as they can go. Never flip them up, just lift them up. Good! Now, take of your safety. Finger still off the trigger, that's it."

"TWO ROUNDS, WARMING, INTO THE BANK BEHIND THE BUTTS! IN YOUR OWN TIME...FIRE!"

"Right. Lift up your butt and place it into the meat of your shoulder. That's it, good. Get comfortable...shut your left eye; make certain you get the tip of the foresight-blade dead-centre in the hole of the rear aperture. I want you to put your trigger finger in as far as it can go. Good...wrap your other fingers around the small of the butt...that's fine. Now, when you're ready, squeeze your whole right hand, including your trigger finger. That way, you won't pull your shot."

'BWWAMMM!' The rifle and the boy jerked. Douglas had been looking at the backstop of the butts.

"Not bad, Mawhinney. I saw the ground splatter. How's your shoulder?"

"O.K., Corporal. Jeez, these things kick."

"You'll get used to it. That was excellent. Now, don't move your left elbow; just lower your rifle butt and cock the weapon again. Good. O.K., let's do the same thing over."

After the second round, Douglas made certain the cadet didn't change his position. The boy kept his left elbow in the same position and was allowed to rest his left arm on the ground with the rifle...bolt open. Mawhinney took his right hand off the rifle, which was all right.

"TARGETS UP! THE NEXT FIVE SHOTS WILL NOT BE INDICATED!

THIS RELAY, FIVE ROUNDS GROUPING! AT YOUR TARGET IN FRONT...IN YOUR OWN TIME...FIRE!"

"Now, the name of the game here, Mawhinney, is to make sure we get all our rounds as close together as possible. It really doesn't matter where they are on the target, as long as they are close together. So, I want you to fire every round off exactly the same way. Same squeezing, same breathing, same aim, etc. O.K.?"

"Yes, Corporal."

"Good man!"

With coaching, the cadet brought up the butt; placed it properly, making certain the weapon was not on an angle; cocked it; shut his left eye; took a full breath; let half of it out; aimed and fired. He did the same with the remaining four rounds.

After he'd fired the last round, he kept his left forearm up, brought the butt of his weapon down, opened the bolt and rested, no finger on the trigger.

"THIS RELAY, UNLOAD!"

Under Douglas' guidance, the cadet cocked the rifle, took off the magazine, aimed and fired dry, cocked it twice, aimed and fired dry, remaining in the resting position with the bolt open.

An Alpha cadet went from weapon to weapon looking to ensure each breech was clear. "CLEAR!" he screamed as he passed each weapon.

"O.K., just place your weapon down, bolt head up. That was great, Mawhinney. What are you rubbing your shoulder for?"

The cadet smiled. "I'm just trying to find out if it's still there."

"If what's still there?"

"My shoulder, Corporal."

"RIGHT! CHANGE THE FLAGS! TARGETS DOWN, BUT DO NOT PATCH!"

The Range Officer's instructions were relayed to the butts by telephone.

"THIS RELAY, STAND UP WITH YOUR WEAPONS, MUZZLE POINTED DOWN TOWARDS THE GROUND AND TO YOUR FRONT! KEEP YOUR BOLTS OPEN! WE'RE GOING DOWN TO LOOK AT YOUR TARGETS. REMAIN IN EXTENDED LINE AND STAY EVEN WITH EACH OTHER!"

As the relay walked to the butts, other cadets were picking up the empty magazines and casings, and placing newly loaded magazines at each firing point position at the same time.

Rothstein had allowed all of the butts cadets to take off their shirts if they wished to do so. Although the Range Officer questioned this move, he didn't ask them to put them back on. It was one of the hottest days of the summer and he informed the boys to watch each other for sunburn.

"Cadet Mawhinney, you've gone and shot yourself an eight-inch group. That's not just good, it's bloody great!" said Douglas. "And, they're nearly all in the bull's eye. Good shooting!" He shook the proud cadet's hand.

"Thanks, Corporal. I couldn't have done it without you."

"Sure you could. You can't put me on. You're an old pro at this. RIGHT?"

"RIGHT, CORPORAL!"

The Range Officer and his armourer went from position to position, adjusting sights. Only a slight adjustment had to be made to Cadet Mawhinney's rifle.

Brice got a kick out of listening to Cunningham, who was on the next target with a cadet.

"O.K., Cadet Robert Hansen, I owe you two-bits. You actually did well. Are we on for the same bet on the next practise? Are you going to give me a chance to win my money back?"

"Sure, Corporal Zaholuk. Say, you look a bit like Corporal West, in another platoon?"

"Er, he's a relative."

"Oh."

While the Range Officer was going from rifle to rifle, the Musketeers didn't know that two *distinctively different*, but connected, conversations were taking place elsewhere: at Alberta Schwartz's house, and the guardroom.

Eunice Bygdnes packed her baby-doll pajamas in her suitcase and glanced around the messy bedroom. She had spent the night at her best friend's house.

"Alberta, I told my father about that horny cadet from the theatre. You know, Corporal Adams?"

Alberta was still in bed, eating a piece of the greasy roast beef her mother had cooked the night before. She wiped her fingers on the front of her nightgown. "SHIT! Eunice you didn't?! Oh what did you go and do that for?"

"Well, I didn't like what he did to us. Can you imagine, such nerve...Jones Tent and Awning, indeed?"

Alberta pushed the last of the fatty animal flesh into her mouth, got out of bed and waved her *big* arms to the ceiling. "Eunice, what did you do that for? Dotty Wallace told me on the phone that she saw him at the dance when Red Robinson was here, and he's Red's special assistant. His name isn't Corporal Adams, it's Goose Fannylick, or somethin' like that."

Eunice was flabbergasted. "What? Red's special assistant. Oh, what have I done, Alberta?"

"Eunice dropped her nightgown to the floor. Standing nude in front of the open window, she stuck her head out. "I didn't like the prick, either, but if he knows Red Robinson..." She suddenly stopped speaking when she saw a neighbour's boy staring at her. "I'VE GOT THE PERFECT BODY, HAVEN'T I, TOMMY? WHY DON'T YOU TAKE A PICTURE, YOU ASSHOLE!"

The young male teen belly-laughed before answering. "YOU SURE COULD HAVE IF YOU LOST THREE-HUNDRED POUNDS OF UGLY FAT. HEY, WHY NOT JUST CUT OFF YOUR HEAD?"

"STICK IT UP YOUR ASS!" Alberta yelled, slamming the window shut and pulling the curtains.

"He didn't say that when we were on his front porch one night. Anyway, where was I? Oh yeah, the guy's Red's special assistant." She swooned. "Red's my idol. I'd run the width of the Sahara, just to get near him. Oh, why did you tell your dad?"

Eunice put her shoulders back. "I'd suck Red's socks clean instead of washing them, but, what's done, is done. I can't change it, Alberta. My Dad wants us up in the guardroom in half-an-hour. He's holding the guy there so we can identify him."

In the Provost shack at camp, Corporal Adams had been made to wait in a small cell that wasn't being used. He was dressed immaculately because he knew the Sergeant was furious over something. While he was sitting there, he'd gone over the previous evening with a fine-toothed comb. It was an accident. The Sergeant couldn't blame him for an accident. He'd actually tried to help the girls out.

"CORPORAL ADAMS, GET YOUR ASS IN HERE!" bellowed Sergeant Gabriel.

The Corporal stood up, straightened out his clothing, marched in, and stood at attention. He was surprised to find that Sergeant Bygdnes was also in the room. Only the three of them were there when Adams closed the door behind him.

"SIT DOWN! SERGEANT BYGDNES WISHES TO ADDRESS YOU!"

"Sergeant, I..."

"DID I GIVE YOU PERMISSION TO SPEAK?!" Gabriel bellowed.

Bygdnes took a deep breath. "YOU KNOW MY LITTLE GIRL IS THE SUNSHINE OF MY LIFE? YOU DON'T HAVE ANY CHILDREN, SO YOU WOULDN'T HAVE ANY IDEA! NOW, I'M GOING TO ASK YOU WHAT SERGEANT GABRIEL ASKED YOU. DID YOU, OR DID YOU NOT, PUT YOUR HAND UP MY LITTLE EUNICE'S SKIRT?"

The Corporal took a deep breath. "Yes, I did, but it was entirely by accident, Sergeant. I don't make a habit of doing such things."

"Did you also have your hand on her milkshake?"

Corporal Adams crossed his legs. "Certainly I did! She'd dropped it and I was trying to help out, that's all."

"Corporal Adams, what do you mean she dropped it? She had placed it there so she could go to the bathroom. You just wanted to drink it, didn't you, Corporal?"

"Sergeant, how in the hell could she go to the bathroom, there were too many people around? Also, it was empty. It was all over the ground."

"I suppose her chocolate bar wrapper was empty as well?"

"I didn't know she had a chocolate bar. Her hands were bull of burgers."

"DON'T BULL SHIT ME, ADAMS! SHE COULDN'T GO TO THE BATHROOM WITH HER HANDS FULL OF BURGERS! THEY DON'T EVEN SELL BURGERS THERE! YOU EVEN FINISHED OFF HER POPCORN!"

"That's what I'm telling you, Sergeant. She had no intention of going to the bathroom. Popcorn, what fucking popcorn?"

Sergeant Bygdnes lit up a smoke. "How do you know that? How the hell do you know when my little girl and her cute little friend want to relieve themselves?"

"Well, I er, I'm not that familiar with their habits, but, er, it seemed like an odd place to..."

Sergeant Bygdnes ground his cigarette into the ashtray. "You mean you couldn't care less if they pissed themselves? Were you drinking, man? I'm not talking about going to the bathroom there, I'm talking about walking to the bathroom. They wouldn't piss while they were sitting. But you wouldn't let them do that. Oh, no, you had to let them suffer. You finished off their goodies and then proceeded to maul my little kitten, didn't you? And you couldn't keep your hands off her tiny friend, either."

Adams uncrossed his legs. He was getting upset by all of this.

"THEY WEREN'T SITTING! HOW THE HELL COULD THEY SIT? SERGEANT BYGDNES, I NEVER TOUCHED YOUR DAUGHTER'S FRIEND, AND I RESENT THIS LINE OF QUESTIONING!"

"DON'T YELL AT ME! She couldn't sit down because you had your hand up her skirt. So you resent it, eh? Well, let me tell you something, Mister. I happen to know you tried to feel up her friend, as well. You just couldn't keep your hands off her little ass and breasts. My baby told me all about it, you animal."

Corporal Adams stood up. "GET THOSE BROADS...er, get your daughter and her friend in here, Sergeant. Let me hear them say that to my face."

"Oh, don't you worry about that, Corporal. They're coming here now. And if what they say is true, I'll be asking Sergeant Gabriel here to assign you to kitchen duty for the balance of camp."

Within minutes the two *girls* came up the stairs and sheepishly entered the guardroom.

Sergeant Gabriel got up and walked around to the front of his desk. "Come in here, my dear, and bring your little friend in with you. That's it, come in, Alberta, sweetheart...don't be shy."

Both *bashful little* girls entered the office and paid little or no attention to a scowling Corporal Adams. They just smiled at him. Although they knew him from the street, they were waiting for Moose to be *dragged* in.

Bygdnes shut the door. "O.K., pumpkins. Is this the man who tried to have his evil way with both of you?"

They had been saved, but Alberta nearly blew it. "WHO THE F...., er, er, yes, that's him, Mr. Bygdnes. Isn't that right, Eunice?"

Eunice had to hold her crotch, otherwise she would have wet herself. "Er..." She felt lightheaded and nearly fainted. Her father helped her to a chair.

"Er, yes Daddy dearest, that's him. Could I have a glass of water, please?"

A smile came to Corporal Adams' lips. This had to be a set-up. This wasn't real; it couldn't be happening.

"Better get one for me as well, Sarg. Listen, er...what's your name, er, Eunice? You know it was an accident. And you, er, Alberta, I never touched you."

"GET YOUR OWN WATER, YOU LECHEROUS BASTARD! Oops, sorry, my little kumquats. "That's it, Bill, you've heard the story."

The Provost Sergeant replied, "Yes, I certainly have. Thank you girls, you can leave now."

Sergeant Gabriel watched Corporal Adams stand up with the girls. "NOT YOU, ADAMS!"

"THIS RELAY, TEN ROUNDS APPLICATION! DO NOT SHOOT AT THE INDICATORS! AT YOUR TARGETS IN FRONT, IN YOUR OWN TIME...FIRE!"

Brice patted Mawhinney on the shoulder. "O.K., kiddo, remember, the bull's eye counts for four points, the inner ring for three, the magpie ring for two, and you only get one point for an outer. After each shot, wait for the indication. If you get tired, just rest, but don't move your left elbow."

"Corporal, is that true, what I just heard?"

"What did you hear?" Douglas asked his student.

"I just heard Corporal Zaholuk say to Hansen, 'That's twenty bucks you owe me. Want to go double-or-nothing?'"

Douglas smiled and winced. "I'm certain the good Corporal was just joking."

"Wow, he sure looks serious to me, Corporal Brice. Is he related to Corporal Cunningham?"

Douglas was still grinning as he glanced at Cunningham and Hansen. "I...ah...I think they're second cousins, and I don't think the cadet is going to end up owing him any money. O.K., let's go for a possible. That's forty points. Carry on!"

At the end of the day, Bravo Company was dirty and tired as the cadets cleaned weapons outside the weapons stores. Each cadet had fired grouping, snap, rapid, and application practises. Tomorrow, they would fire more application and spend some time on the bren and sten guns.

When it was time for dismissal, Rothstein looked pleased.

"BRAVO COMPANY, YOU DID A GREAT JOB TODAY. THE MAJORITY OF YOUR SCORES WERE EXCELLENT, AND EVERYTHING RAN LIKE CLOCKWORK. I'M CERTAIN YOU WERE PROUD WHEN THE RANGE OFFICER SAID YOU WERE ONE OF THE BETTER COMPANIES HE'S WORKED WITH!

"CORPORALS EAST AND SIMON TAKE OVER FROM MYSELF AND CORPORAL JACKSON TONIGHT. THERE'LL BE NO MORE SHAVING ANTICS! ALSO, THOSE OF YOU WHO KEPT YOUR SHIRTS OFF TOO LONG, PICK UP SOME GUCK FROM THE MEDICAL INSPECTION ROOM!"

Chuckles were heard throughout the ranks. The cadets hadn't forgotten the shaving episode. For that matter, neither had Earl. In addition to losing the hair on one leg, and half his crotch, he noticed later, the hair had been shaved from his right arm as well.

"YOU'LL ALL BE HAPPY TO HEAR THAT THERE HAS BEEN A CHANGE IN FRIDAY'S TIMETABLE. BECAUSE EVERYTHING RAN SO SMOOTHLY TODAY, IF IT GOES THAT WAY TOMORROW MORNING, SHOOTING WILL CEASE AT NOON. MAJOR KARE HAS MADE ARRANGEMENTS FOR A SWIM PARADE AT KAL BEACH!"

Instantly, there was new life in the cadets. Amidst the roar of approval, pith-helmets, notebooks and shoe-rags were tossed into the air. The boys of Bravo Company appreciated Major Kare's consideration.

"NOW, WHEN YOU GET INTO THE BARRACKS, TAKE THE LOAD OFF YOUR FEET...REVIEW YOUR NOTES, AND TAKE A SHOWER! THE GROUP OF US..." Rothstein pointed to the other Alpha cadets. "...ARE PROUD TO BE WORKING WITH THE BEST COMPANY IN CAMP! BY THE WAY, WHAT *IS* THE BEST COMPANY?"

With ear-to-ear smiles, the words, "BRAVO COMPANY!" came back loud and clear.

"YOU ARE RIGHT! BRAVO COMPANY, ATTEN...TION! DIS...MISSED!"

After the company turned to its right and marched the five paces before disper-sal, a cadet rushed over to Corporal *Zaholuk* and stood at attention.

"Er, Corporal, I think you owe me five dollars."

Cunningham had actually started marching away with Banks and Danyluk. He stopped. "Want to make it double-or-nothing tomorrow?"

"Er, no, thanks, Corporal. I don't know how accurate I am on the bren and sten."

"You mean I don't get another chance?"

"That's right, Corporal. Five dollars, please."

Cunningham cringed. "Here, ya little bas..." Instead of completing the sen-tence, he smiled and handed over a five-dollar bill. "Good shooting, Hansen, you deserve this."

Cadet Hansen grinned and replied, "Thanks, Corp," as he scooped it up and marched away.

Moose couldn't believe it. "Was the kid that good?"

"That good? Do you know what regiment he's with?"

Danyluk shrugged. "Nope, who's he with?"

Cunningham smacked Moose on his back. "Of all the luck, I end up with a cadet from our own cadet corps. He's a BCR and do you know who taught him how to shoot?"

"No, who?"

"HIM!" Cunningham replied, pointing to a nearby grinning cadet by the name of Douglas Brice.

As the group of them marched away, Gordie separated.

"WHERE THE HELL ARE YOUSE GOIN'?" yelled Moose.

"I'M GONNA CALL MY STOCKBROKER AND MY BOOKIE! HOOF HEARTED'S RUNNING AGAIN, AND I'M GONNA BET THE DOUGH I'VE MADE ON CRUISER COPPER! AFTER THAT, I'M GONNA HAVE A SHOWER AND HEAD OVER TO DRIVER MECH! SOME KID BY THE NAME OF NADEAU GOT FIFTY DOLLARS FROM HOME, AND...!" The gambler turned around. "AND...wait for it...A PARCEL!"

"HOW THE HELL DO YOUSE KNOWS THAT?" bellowed Moose.

Gordie didn't turn around this time. "ONE OF MY *PAID* INFORMERS TOLD ME!"

"That guy's got ears everywhere," Moose told Wayne as they marched to B-33. "I wouldn't mind bein' on the payroll."

"What valuable information would you have that he wants?" asked Rothstein.

"Information on dames. I've got info on all the dames in town. Pick a dame, and old Moose knows if she does, or she doesn't."

As they entered B-33, Moose was still discussing his expertise. "That's worth money, ain't it Rothie? He may know the stock market and the horses, but it's me, the Moose, who knows the dames."

"Let's grab a shower," said Douglas. "We're covered from head to toe in dust."

They stripped to their shorts, grabbed their towels, and headed for the showers. The shower room was empty because most guys who weren't with other companies had gone over to eat.

Rothstein slowly turned the hot water to cold. "Cunnilingus doesn't want information on dames, Moose. He wants information on money matters."

But Rothie, I've got dames with moolah. Take Olga Metikov, for example. She's gonna inherit her folks' used clothin' store. What a broad. She's..."

Jackson burst out laughing.

"HEY, IF YOUSE WANTS TO LAUGH AT OLGA, YA GOTTA GO THROUGH ME FIRST!"

Earl was having a *fit*. "I'm not laughing at Olga, Moose. Her name reminded me of a certain person Rothie tried to find this morning. Ain't that right, Rothie?"

Now Rothstein broke out laughing. "Did you have to remind me?"

"Tell us," said Wayne. He already had the feeling that the boys of Bravo had got to one of the *Corporals* again; and he was right.

It took a few seconds for Rothstein to settle down. "Just before you guys entered B-29 this morning, I glanced at my list and only one cadet was goin' on sick parade. I yelled, "MEHOFF, YOU HAD BETTER HEAD OVER THERE NOW!""

"Go on, what happened?" asked Douglas.

"Well, I couldn't find the guy, so I called over all the cadets in the other wing. Now everyone was on our side of the barracks. I yelled, 'MEHOFF, COME AND

SEE ME AND I'LL GIVE YOU A SICK REPORT.' When no one came forward, some cadet said, 'He's slow, Corporal, better use his first name as well.' I looked at my list. His first name was Jack. 'JACK MEHOFF! JACK MEHOFF! WILL SOMEONE PLEASE COME FORWARD! JACK MEHOFF!' I yelled. When the laughter started, I figured it out. Cadets were rolling in the aisle laughing. Those little buggers had got us again. Talk about being embarrassed..."

"Got you?" stated Jackson. "They'd already got me!"

Moose looked at Earl's crotch. Jackson had shaved the other side, and he was bare. He'd also shaved his other leg and arm, as well.

"YOUSE CAN SAY THAT AGAIN!"

Once again, the shower room in B-33 rocked with howls of laughter.

That evening, before the Musketeers headed over to the cadet canteen, they spent an hour in B-29, just talking to cadets and answering questions. They had completed their own kit as well as East and Simon's, before leaving.

The talk in Bravo's hut was mainly about shooting and the day's activities. Shooting scores had been posted, and Cadet Hansen, who was *coached* by Cunningham, had the highest score. Douglas' student, Mawhinney was second, Mellish was third, and a cadet from the Seaforths by the name of MacKenzie was fourth.

East roamed the aisle. "BEFORE YOU RETIRE, I WANT TO SEE YOUR KIT FOR TOMORROW. THAT INCLUDES BOOTS, BELTS, HELMETS, AND WHATEVER!"

A cadet entered the barracks, loaded down with sandwiches from the mess hall. "Here's your grub, Corporal East."

Jack attacked it instantly. "Thank you, Ryeberg. Keep this sort of thing up and you'll grow up to be big and strong, like me."

Ryeberg grinned and walked away. "Nah, thanks anyway, Corporal. I stopped eating peanut butter and jam when I was four. Don't forget, you've got to show me how to get my boots looking like yours."

Although his mouth was full, Jack replied. "All in good time, my boy, all in good time."

Just as he finished eating, another *loaded down* cadet approached him.

"Here's your scoff, Corporal. I asked the kitchen staff, as you said, but Corporal Adams just told me to screw off. He ain't never heard of sardine an' jelly sandwiches."

"Thank you, Turner. Did you say, Corporal Adams? Is he the same one...the Provost Corporal Adams?"

"Yeah, he does his thing in the kitchen now, Corporal."

It was boiling hot in B-33 that night as the Musketeers just lay on top of their blankets. The lights had been turned out and half the cadets who weren't attached to other companies were already asleep.

"HEY, YOUSE GUYS, LET THE AIR GET TO YOUR BALLS ONCE IN A WHILE," said Moose, referring to the fact that just he and the Scottish cadets didn't wear any shorts to bed. "IF YA WANT A HEALTHY WANG AND HEALTHY BALLS, YA GOTTA LET THEM BREATHE!"

"Jesus, Moose, just how healthy do you want 'em? If they get any healthier, you'll have to carry them around in a pack sack."

Moose laughed. "In the words of John Ruskin, 'Quantity is never an accident; it is always the result of intelligent effort.'"

Douglas sat up. "Ya got it wrong, Moose. He said, 'Quality' not quantity."

"Bull shit, Dougie. He got it wrong."

Jackson had nearly been asleep, then he'd heard Moose. "How come everyone's wrong but you, Moose?"

"HEY, I AIN'T SAYIN' I'M ALWAYS RIGHT! BUT USUALLY I AM, YOUSE KNOWS THAT, EARL. Wayne, do you remember when we were in Nanaimo and I was on sentry duty for the first time?"

Wayne started chuckling. He knew the story only too well. "You bet I do. So does everyone else in the regiment."

Moose came over and sat on Douglas' bed. "Was I wrong?"

Wayne leaned over. "No, you weren't wrong, it, er, it was your method, that, er...was different, that's all."

"HEY, I HAD MY ORDERS! AND ORDERS IS ORDERS! I'M NOT ONE FOR DISOBEYING ORDERS! YOUSE KNOWS THAT!"

Now all the Musketeers and the Scottish cadets who were listening, had gathered around Douglas' bunk. "What happened?" asked Rothstein.

Moose told his story. "Well, in the Orders Group, I was ordered, and I mean ordered, not to admit any car into the camp, unless it had a special identification seal."

"Yeah, yeah, go on."

Although it was dark, the others could see Moose grinning. "Well, how the hell did I know the first unmarked car contained the Assistant Chief of the Defence Staff, Lieutenant General Robert Shallow? I said to the driver, 'Turn this vehicle around, youse ain't comin' in here...ya got that?'"

"Shallow sez, 'Don't listen to him, driver, just tell him to lift the barrier and drive on!' Can ya believe that? I wasn't born yesterday, ya know?"

Banks belly-laughed. "Tell 'em what you said."

"I'm now standin' next to the general's window. I said, 'LISTEN YOUSE! YES, YOUSE, THERE! I'M A SENTRY AND I'M ON DUTY! Youse ain't goin' anywhere, turn this heap around, NOW!'"

"'DRIVE ON!' screams Shallow!"

"Now I'm pissed off, so I cock my sten and I tap on the window. Shallow opens it. 'DO YOU KNOW WHO I AM?' he screams."

"I said, 'NO I DON'T KNOW WHO YOUSE IS, AND I'M NEW TO THIS GENERAL, WHO DO I SHOOT FIRST, YOUSE OR THE DRIVER?'"

Wayne remembered so well, he jumped out of bed, and started laughing out the window. Everyone else was in stitches also.

"Did you let 'em through?" asked a Scottish cadet.

"NOT ON YOUR LIFE! Shallow was still screaming his head off as they drove away."

"Did ya get shit for it the next day?" Jackson asked.

Moose cocked his chin. "Nope, 'cause I was right! I didn't know Shallow, and he didn't know me. So you see, Earl, the old Moose is usually right."

When everyone had gone back to bed, a still-smiling Douglas Brice, lay on top of his covers with his hands behind his head and tried to envision the scene Moose had just described. It must have been hilarious, he thought to himself.

Two minutes later, he was still grinning as he rolled on his side and went to sleep. The only sound in B-33 was Danyluk's snoring.

"JUST SHORT BURSTS!" Brice yelled to Cadet Mawhinney who was firing a bren gun for the first time.

The Musketeers had joined East, Simon, and Bravo Company at 0745 hours, and at 0830 hours, they were already on the ranges. East had continued the routine of the morning inspection, and everything had gone exceedingly well.

When the company of earlier shining, scrubbed-clean faces unloaded, their skin wasn't glistening anymore. Instead, the cadets' *kissers* were covered with mud. Even at 0830 it was hot enough for their sweat to act as a magnet for dust.

"IF YOU FIRE LONG BURSTS, YOU WON'T BE ACCURATE AND YOU'LL HAVE TO CHANGE BARRELS OR KEEP CHANGING YOUR GAS REGULATOR!" Brice had to yell because of twelve bren guns firing.

Mawhinney nodded. He had his left hand wrapped around the small of the butt, and his right hand grabbed the pistol grip, right forefinger on the trigger. His legs and feet were together, with the toes of his running shoes implanted onto the ground.

Unlike the previous day, Douglas and his section had been in the butts for the first two hours of shooting. The morning was going like clockwork, but when they appeared on the firing point, the guns were hot.

The bren fired one or two rounds and stopped. "REMEMBER YOUR IMME-DIATE ACTIONS. COCK THE WEAPON, CHECK YOUR MAGAZINE, AND TRY AGAIN!"

Once more, the gun fired and jammed.

"RIGHT! MAGAZINE OFF AND COCK THE WEAPON! O.K., HERE'S A DUMMY ROUND, CRAWL UP THE SIDE, GRAB THE CARRYING HANDLE WITH YOUR RIGHT HAND, LIFT UP THE BARREL LOCKING LEVER WITH YOUR LEFT, AND PUSH THE BARREL FORWARD A BIT! THAT'S GOOD...NOW, WITH YOUR LEFT HAND, TURN THE GAS REGULATOR TO THE NEXT HOLE! GOOD! O.K., BRING THE BARREL BACK IN, LOCK IT AGAIN! GOOD! O.K., MAGAZINE ON, COCK THE WEAPON, AND LET'S CARRY ON!"

With the change made, the gun operated perfectly.

"REMEMBER, JUST SHORT BURSTS! TRY TO MAKE IT TWO OR THREE ROUNDS AT THE MOST!"

They had previously gone through single-round shooting and Mawhinney's score was excellent. Now the weapons were on automatic and the cadets enjoyed this type of firing more than others. Some of them insisted on firing long bursts, however, it didn't take much time to empty the magazines at that rate of fire.

When they were finished with the bren, they moved on to the sten range and fired single and automatic practises in the standing position at twenty-five yards. Mawhinney didn't find the sten to be an accurate weapon; for that matter, neither did the other cadets.

Just before the trucks arrived to take Bravo Company back to camp, the cadets cleaned the brens and stens which would be used by Delta Company that afternoon.

East stood in front of his dirty-faced company on the road outside of B-29. "PAY ATTENTION HERE! THAT WAS A GOOD MORNING. NEEDLESS TO SAY, CORPORAL SIMON AND MYSELF ARE PROUD OF ALL OF YOU. YOUR TOTAL SCORES WILL BE POSTED ON THE BULLETIN BOARD

AFTER SUPPER!

"YOU'VE GOT TWENTY MINUTES BEFORE THE KITCHEN OPENS , SO I WANT YOU TO TAKE A SHOWER!

"NOW REMEMBER, TONIGHT IS MOTHERS' NIGHT! IN ADDITION TO WORKING ON THE BARRACKS, YOU'LL BE SPENDING AN HOUR-AND-A-HALF ON THE PARADE SQUARE WITH SERGEANTS BECKFORD AND SIMPSON! THAT MEANS THAT YOU WON'T HAVE TOO MUCH TIME TO PREPARE YOUR KIT FOR SATURDAY MORNING'S INSPECTION! EAT YOUR LUNCH QUICKLY, AND YOU'LL HAVE ENOUGH TIME TO GET BACK HERE AND WASH YOUR CLOTHING FOR TOMORROW! IN THIS WEATHER, IT'LL DRY IN TEN MINUTES...JUST LEAVE IT IN YOUR BAR-RACK BOXES AND YOU CAN PRESS IT TONIGHT! MUG-UP THIS EVENING HAS BEEN EXTENDED BY FIFTEEN MINUTES!

"NOW, YOU ARE ALL FAMILIAR WITH SWIM PARADE PROCE-DURES. THE TRUCKS WILL BE HERE AT 1330 HOURS! YOU WILL NOT WEAR ANY HEADDRESS. YOU'LL WEAR A T-SHIRT AND P.T. SHORTS! DO NOT WEAR ANY UNDERWEAR UNDER YOUR SHORTS; YOUR SWIM-SUIT IS TO BE ROLLED UP IN YOUR TOWEL. I ALSO DON'T WANT YOU TO WEAR ANY SOCKS, JUST YOUR RUNNING SHOES!"

"ARE THERE ANY QUESTIONS?"

The normal question was asked. "CORPORAL, WHY CAN'T WE WEAR OUR SWIMMING TRUNKS UNDER OUR P.T. SHORTS?"

The routine answer was given. "WHAT DO I LOOK LIKE, A WALKING ENCYCLOPEDIA? DON'T ASK SUCH SILLY QUESTIONS!"

"ANY OTHER QUESTIONS?"

"CORPORAL, CAN WE MAKE ARRANGEMENTS TO MEET OUR DAMES AT THE BEACH?"

East smiled and rubbed his right hand's thumb and forefinger together. "IF YA DON'T, THERE'S SOMETHING WRONG WITH YA! ALSO, TELL THEM TO BRING MOOLAH!

"ANYTHING ELSE? NO? RIGHT! BRAVO COMPANY, ATTEN...TION! FALL...OUT!"

A cloud of range-dust erupted when the cadets turned to their right and marched forward the usual five paces. East and Simon joined their cadets, and, in a matter of minutes, an immaculate B-29 would look like a cyclone had blown through.

As soon as the company disappeared, while the rest of the Musketeers went for a shower in B-33, Jackson headed to the phones. In an undemocratic vote, he had been elected to phone all the girls to ask them if they could be at Kalamalka Beach at 1400 hours.

As usual, Wayne's body was covered with shampoo as he laughed at Danyluk's 'words of wisdom' statement. "An optimist is the Sergeant who goes to the window every morning and says, 'Good morning, God.' The pessimist is the Sergeant who goes to the window and says, Good God, morning!"

"Where'd you hear that?"

Moose opened up the shower room window. "Sergeant Simpson told me that in 1953. He said he gets up in the mornin' and says, 'Good morning, world!' But that I get up and say, 'Good mornin', wang!' "

"He's right," said Wayne. "I've heard you, so has everyone else."

"Bull shit you have!"

Jackson joined them as Douglas backed Wayne up. "Come off it, Moose, how many times have we heard you say, 'O.K., guys, let's take a shower!' "

Moose thought for a moment while he rinsed his body off. "Well, ya gotta be friendly to your body parts. Hey, they look after me, so I look after them."

"But you carry it a little too far," stated Rothstein. "A couple of weeks ago, before you were *Red's buddy*, guys leavin' the shower always mentioned the nut who talked to himself in there. I heard one cadet say, 'Who the hell is, Old Guts and Glory? The other guy said, 'Whoever the hell he is, he doesn't like Sergeants Soap. That fruitcake in there keeps apologizin'. Did ya hear him? 'I'm sorry, Guts, I'll buy youse some Palmolive tonight, O.K.?' Then he said, 'Now quit arguing, the three of ya. Old Moose is gonna get youse looked after.'"

The others broke up and Rothstein still wasn't finished.

"Apparently, after hearing you, one of the cadets said, 'Are you talkin' to me, Mac? That's kinda nice of ya, but, er, who's the broad what's gonna look after me?' You just stared at him blankly and said, 'What are you talkin' about? Why the hell would I wanna do that? Hey youse, ya got any Palmolive, my pals don't like Sergeants' Soap?'"

Simon popped his head in the doorway. "I've picked up your mail. Do you want it now before I go back to B-29?"

Six dripping bodies eagerly joined Simon in the sink-area of the centre section of the hut. Although the envelopes were a bit wet, their contents weren't.

"Doug, you and the Cunner have got parcels, but Corporal Dallas wouldn't give 'em to me. You've got to go and sign for them."

After they had dried themselves off, the Musketeers lay down on their bunks and read the news from home. Douglas felt a little guilty because he hadn't yet written to his mom. There was a ten-dollar bill enclosed with his letter.

'Dear Doug:

You must really be enjoying yourself this year, because I haven't heard a word from you. I was going to telephone to find out if everything is all right, but it must be, otherwise I'm certain you would have been on the phone to me.

I've been working shift work lately, Son. The hours aren't the greatest, but it pays more money. More money to make payments on the new Marconi television set I've bought. Yes, that's right, I've finally bowed to your pressure and purchased one. What a marvelous contraption. You were correct, we should have got one when they first came out. I find that I'm...

Brice kicked Wayne's springs. "My Mom's purchased a television set. It's a Marconi, just like yours."

Wayne stopped reading for a moment and peered over. "Great, now when I come over for supper, we won't have to rush home to my house to watch, *Father Knows Best.*"

When Wayne's head disappeared, Douglas returned to his mom's letter..

...slowing down on the housework, watching it all of the time.

The weather here has been fabulous. I hear it's also very hot and dry in Vernon. Did the two storms we had here come your way? They didn't last long, but the power went out in a lot of areas.

There was an article in the Vancouver Sun about Red Robinson hosting a dance in the Vernon region. Did you get a chance to see him? He mentioned that he had a tour of the camp and he was very impressed with the manners of the cadets. Apparently, he was an air cadet. He seems like a very nice person. I don't listen to that kind of music, but I know you love it.

The other day I had lunch with your Aunt Flo. She's wrapped up in the Bridey Murphy interviews. Have you heard about Bridey Murphy? A woman, I think she lives in the States, has been taken back beyond her birth through hypnosis. Evidently, in another life, her name was Bridey Murphy. She even took newspaper reporters to her grave-site, somewhere in Ireland. Can you believe it? Your Aunt Flo sure does, but I'm not too convinced - yet. Flo says I should be the first one to believe it because I read tea leaves. When I listened on the radio, the woman broke out into a broad Irish accent. One wonders...?

Colonel is fine and has asked me to pass along his love. He misses you throwing his ball to him down at the beach. I've been a little remiss in doing that lately, because I'm always watching television. We went down to the beach today, though. Mickey the cat is fine, as well.

Well, Son, there isn't too much more to report, except to say we all miss and love you. I know you're having a good time, and because you're young, I'm really happy you are. You'll probably be eight-feet-eleven when you return home.

Please look after yourself, Doug. Spend this ten dollars wisely. Say hello to Wayne for me and tell him he can now watch television at our house for a change. Also pass along my love to Diane.

All my love...
Mam XXXX
P.S. I know I complain about the house being too noisy when you're here. Would you believe it's now too quiet? Even the dog and cat have stopped stomping. They seem to tiptoe.

Don't forget it's your birthday shortly. I'm going out tomorrow to buy you a card. Let's consider this ten-dollars a birthday present, all right?

A lost smile came over Douglas' lips as he put his hands behind his head and stared above him at the mattress of Wayne's upper bunk. He shook his head, thinking his mother was one in a million. She worked hard to keep the household up and she never complained. Very rarely did his mother get sick, and she was always interested in his activities.

Danyluk's voice brought him out of his trance. "YAHOO, I'VE HIT THE JACKPOT!"

He'd no sooner said it when Cunningham got up like a flash.

"YOU'VE GOT WHAT? HOW MUCH? COME ON! COME ON! HOW MUCH?"

Jumping up and down, Danyluk held out and kissed two twenty-dollar bills and a ten-dollar bill. "Mabel's old rich uncle gave her fifty dollars for the 'Soldiers With Dysentery Fund!' Guys, I know we're spending the whole weekend at the beach...I'll buy us the grub."

Cunningham grabbed Moose's arm. "But, but what about me?"

"Well, I'll let youse buy some grub too."

A frustrated Cunningham said, "No, no, no...er, can we partake in a little game of...er...?"

Moose's smile lit up the building. "STUKE? I'LL SAY WE CAN! I'LL PUT

TEN BUCKS ASIDE FOR STUKE! YOU'RE THE GREATEST AT GAMBLING; I'M THE GREATEST AT RAISING THE DOUGH!"

Cunningham smacked and rubbed his hands together. "THAT'S OUR OLD MOOSE!"

Rothstein broke up the mutual admiration society. "It's 1315 and don't forget, we've all got to attend the beach this afternoon, whether the girls are there or not."

At once, bush uniforms went flying as the revelers got into their P.T. shorts, etc., and headed for B-29. When they arrived, they found East having further words with Bravo Company.

"THERE'S BEEN A SMALL CHANGE TO THE TIMETABLE THIS WEEKEND! ON SATURDAY, AFTER EXAMS, PAY PARADE AND THE SHEET EXCHANGE, YOU WILL BE ON THE PARADE SQUARE UNTIL 1300 HOURS. THE MESS HALL WILL REMAIN OPEN UNTIL YOU'VE FINISHED DRILL!"

The reaction from the cadets wasn't very enthusiastic.

"HEY, HEY, HEY! GET YOUR CHINS UP! THIS IS BRAVO COMPANY, THE GUARD! DON'T FORGET, YOU'RE AT GLENEMMA ALL NEXT WEEK, THAT MEANS ONLY ONE MORE WEEK UNTIL GRADUATION PARADE! YOU DON'T WANT TO LOOK LIKE THOSE OTHER COMPANIES ON THE PARADE SQUARE, DO YOU?"

"NO, CORPORAL!" the cadets replied.

"WELL, THEN? WHAT'S THE BEST COMPANY?"

"BRAVO COMPANY!"

"AND WHAT'S THE BEST PLATOON?"

It was hard to discern what they bellowed back, because each platoon called out their own number.

"AND WHO'S THE BEST LOOKIN' CORPORAL?" East turned his smiling face towards the Musketeers.

"YOU ARE, CORPORAL!" Most cadets were laughing as they screamed it out.

"PERFECT, JUST PERFECT! YOU'RE COMING ALONG FINE, BRAVO COMPANY, AND THERE'S NOT A LIAR AMONGST YOU!"

More laughter rose throughout the ranks as the trucks pulled up.

"I'M NOW GOING TO FALL YOU OUT. BOARD THE TRUCKS PROPERLY, AND LET'S BE ON OUR WAY! BRAVO COMPANY, ATTEN...TION! FALL...OUT!"

It didn't take long before the three tons were loaded and rolling out of the camp, each truck's chorus singing various army songs. Most Alpha cadets were sitting in the cabs, however, one was assigned to the back of every vehicle, for safety's sake.

Although most cadets in Bravo were new to the *ropes*, quite a few of them made certain they had a seat. These were the smart ones, because when the Dodges and Internationals turned right and passed the high school at the bottom of the hill, the usual 'show parade' with a different twist took place.

Most standing cadets had one or two hands firmly gripping the upper frame of each motor vehicle. When the signal was given, the action was like lightning. At exactly the same time as the *victims* had their shorts pulled down, other sitting cadets grabbed the *exhibitionists'* T-shirts and yanked them up over their heads. This action was executed in a fraction of a second and created mayhem in the backs of the vehicles. Not only couldn't the *exposed* cadets cover their crotches, they were wrapped up in their T-shirts, and they couldn't see.

Bare bodies bounced everywhere to the sounds of whistles originating from the school's summer students sitting on grass next to the road.

The scene in each truck was just as crazed, as laughter shot from the seated cadets whose feet were firmly implanted in the crotches of the P.T. shorts which were down around the ankles of the *offerings*. The instigators also had their heads turned to one side so they wouldn't get a set of buttocks or a crotch in their kissers.

Regardless of how hard the *shows* tried to pull up their pants, it was impossible. To grab hold of their shorts, they had to let go of the frame. When they let of the frame, they got further tangled in their T-shirts.

When the three-tons turned right on the highway leading to Kalamalka Beach, the *presentation* ceased and everything was back to normal. Well, not quite everything, because the cadets had to untangle themselves, and comments resounded all the way to the beach.

"YOU ROTTEN PRICK!"

"MY BUDDY! YOU'D DO THAT TO YOUR BUDDY?"

"WHERE'S MY TOWEL...WHO'S GOT MY TOWEL" YOU, YOU PONGO!"

"WHERE AM I?"

"WHO'S THE HOMO WHO PUSHED HIS ASS IN MY FACE?"

"GET YOUR FEET OUT OF MY MOUTH!"

"LOOK AT MY SHORTS, THEY'RE RIPPED RIGHT UP THE CROTCH! HOW THE HELL AM I SUPPOSED TO MARCH TO THE CHANGING SHACK?"

"OH CHRIST, SOMEONE'S HEAD HIT ME RIGHT IN THE BALLS! NOW MY FUTURE WIFE WILL HAVE TO BE OFFICIALLY INSULATED!"

"IT'S *ARTIFICIALLY INSEMINATED*, YOU DUMMY, AND THEY ONLY DO THAT TO ANIMALS!"

"I DIDN'T SAY MY GIRLFRIEND WAS PERFECT, YA KNOW!"

Another one said, YEAH, SHE'D QUALIFY!"

"OH YEAH? THEN SO WOULD THE COW YOU GO WITH!"

"HEY, MY WANG GOT PUSHED INTO SOMEONE'S EAR. I'M SURE IT WAS AN EAR! THAT WAS KINDA NICE. WHO'S GOT AN EAR THAT FEELS LIKE A DAME'S THING?"

Someone replied, "YOU DON'T EVEN KNOW WHAT A DAME'S THING FEELS LIKE!"

"NOW I DO! YOU BETCHA! HEY, THAT'S THE WAY TO LEARN! WHERE'S THAT EAR? GIMMEE IT ANYTIME!"

After they were unloaded and the trucks left, Major Kare addressed the company in front of countless curious civilians.

"MAKE CERTAIN YOU USE THE BUDDY SYSTEM. WHEN YOU HEAR A WHISTLE, HOLD UP YOUR BUDDY'S HAND! NOW, I WANT YOU TO LEAVE YOUR T-SHIRTS, TOWELS, AND RUNNING SHOES RIGHT WHERE YOU ARE. AFTER YOU HAVE CHANGED, BRING BACK YOUR SHORTS AND PUT THEM WITH THE REST OF YOUR GEAR!" He stopped for a moment, looking at some cadet who was grabbing his crotch with one hand, and his rear-end with the other.

"What's wrong with you? Have you got to go to the bathroom?"

"NO, SIR, MY SHORTS HAVE SPLIT RIGHT UP THE MIDDLE! CORPO-
RAL EAST SAYS, IF I LET GO, I'LL LOOK LIKE A DELTA COMPANY
CADET!"

"Oh. You'd better not let go, then. BRAVO COMPANY, ATTEN...TION!
FALL...OUT!"

The cadets didn't concern themselves with marching five paces after they had
turned to their right. They just ran, charging for the changing shack. When they
returned with their P.T. shorts, the water was the first thing on their minds.

Wayne spotted Debbie and Diane waving. They were sitting on blankets with
the other girls, about fifty yards away.

"WE'LL BE RIGHT THERE AS SOON AS WE CHANGE!" he yelled.

Of all the beaches in the Okanagan Valley, Vernon's Kalamalka Beach, at the
north end of the lake bearing the same name, is really something to behold. It isn't
very large compared to the splendid beaches in Kelowna, or Penticton, the other
two beautiful cities in the valley, but anyone who visits Kalamalka, treasures the
experience.

The water in Kalamalka Lake is pure aqua-green and the sunburnt hills and
tree-covered mountains bordering its east and west confines mirror an angelic
vision of gracefulness and tranquillity when they frolic in the ripples created by
water-skiers, or lone fishermen casually discharging their lines.

Even on a active day, Kalamalka's dazzling expanse cherishes the necessity of
complete freedom it's playmate sunbathers, swimmers, and fishermen acknowledge
and accept in grateful awe.

When the boys emerged from the changing room, their bashfully smiling girls
were waiting for them. Hand-in-hand, they were guided to individual blankets
which held picnic baskets, portable radios, and suntan lotion.

Diane's face was all squished up. "What's happened to Earl's arms and legs?"

"To make a long story, short, he had them shaved while he was sleeping. They
got his crotch, as well."

Diane burst out laughing, but had to smother her feelings when Earl's girl
turned around and said, "*He* tells me this is the new style."

Diane's radio was playing, *Anastasia*, when they found her blanket and
flopped, face down.

"Douglas Brice, do you realize that we've hardly seen each other this summer?" she said, spreading some cool, soothing, scented balm on his back.

He had his arms under his chin and the attention he received felt wonderful. "I
know. It's not that I don't want to be with you every minute, it's, er...well, it's the
responsibility of this course we're taking. We all thought the last three weeks would
be a breeze, instead, it's the other way 'round."

When she finished his back, Diane lay next to him with her left arm over his
upper body. "Are we still spending the weekend at Okanagan Landing?"

He turned his head towards her. "Uh huh, nothing in the world can stop this
weekend, babe. We've made arrangements so that all of us are free, how about the
girls?"

Smiling, she started parting his hair with her fingers. "It's all arranged. Alma's
even gone and bought herself a bikini."

"Why'd she do that? What's wrong with the bathing suit she's got now?"

"It's one-piece, and you know how Moose likes to rob her of a single part?"

They both chuckled. "Doug, is he serious about her?"

Douglas had to think for a moment. He was always straight with Diane and although he knew their conversations weren't passed along to Alma, he knew how much Diane liked the couple.

"Yeah, I think he is. Moose says a lot of things about other girls, but I believe he's joking half the time. He's one of a kind...er, Jesus, that's a difficult question. Are you asking me if Moose and Alma's relationship can be permanent?"

Brice loved Diane's dimple when she grinned or laughed. The expression on her face at this moment really made it stand out. Almost whispering, she replied, "Yes."

He took a deep breath. "Y'know, for some reason I believe she's the only girl he is serious about. If he lived in Vernon, I don't believe he'd ever look at another girl. Not that she'd let him, either. When they first met..."

Douglas couldn't finish his statement because two buckets of what felt like ice-cold water hit both of them. "AGGGGH! JESUS! WHAT THE...?

The two of them were now standing on a soggy blanket. Although the water had miraculously missed the picnic basket and her radio, Diane's clothes were soaked.

"Speak of the devil," Douglas said, watching the backs of Alma and Moose run away.

"THEY GOT US, TOO!" Wayne yelled. "We were gonna warn you, but what the hell...?

As Douglas shook his wet hair, water sprayed in all directions. "THANKS GUYS! O.K., THIS CALLS FOR A PLANNED RETALIATION...ARE YOU WITH US?"

Both Debbie and Wayne were eager and willing.

The two couples didn't walk in the direction of Moose and Alma, instead they slowly headed towards the changing rooms, appearing as if nothing had happened. Then, they strolled along the highway back towards the refreshment stand at the other end where the culprits were lying.

In ten minutes, the guilty parties had forgotten all about their *dirty work*, but not Wayne and Douglas, as they *borrowed* large chunks of ice and a bucket of smaller pieces from the back door of the kiosk. Two minutes later, to the tune of, *Hound Dog*, blaring out of Danyluk's radio, Moose had large pieces of frozen water shoved down the back of his shorts, and Alma got them on her back. This initial *attack* was then followed up by a bucket of ice dumped all over them.

Amidst laughter from everyone in the immediate vicinity, Alma and Moose did an involuntarily Zulu dance for a good thirty seconds, and both sounded as if they were familiar with the language as well. Words such as, "AGHH, OOGH, EEAGH, JESAGHH." Especially, "AGHH WHAT..THE OOOH..FU...GHH? THAT'S, IGGGHCOLD!"

"THAT'LL TEACH YA, YA ROTTEN CREEPS!" bellowed Wayne. His words falling on deaf ears under of the ongoing shuffle.

As the jig continued, the remaining Musketeers and their partners chuckled away, lying on Cunningham's blanket.

Gordie's snickering stopped. "HEY, WE'RE TRYING TO HAVE A SERIOUS GAME, HERE!" he said, pointing to his girl and the money-pot.

East had enjoyed it so much, he didn't mind having to pick the sand off his chocolate bar or his girlfriend's hot-dog, for that matter.

When Moose and Alma finally ran into the water, they were followed by six other couples. The splashing and churning which erupted eventually developed into horse-back fights and the boys picking up girls by their arms and legs and throwing them up into the air.

One couple didn't join in. They were too busy discussing cards. "Maggie, how many times have I told ya, an ace counts as one, or eleven."

"Well, all right, all right, excuuuuuse meeeee. I'm not perfect you know? I thought I was bust. Now what do I do?"

Gordie grinned as he took the pot. "Well, you can't do anything now 'cause I've seen your cards, I have to take your money. Ya got any more in your purse?"

The girl looked through her purse. "Well, let's see. I can't use this, because it's my Mom's birthday next week, and..."

"C'man, c'man! How much have ya got?"

"Hold your horses, Gordon. I can only spare eighty-seven cents."

"PERFECT, THAT'LL DO! I'LL DEAL!"

After the cadets of Bravo Company finished their stint on the parade square that evening, B-29, like every other hut, was prepared for Saturday Morning's Inspection. Competition would be tough this Saturday because Alpha cadets were directing and pitching in throughout the camp.

Danyluk's section of cadets was responsible for the outside windows, Bravo's half of the smoking pit, and the *gardens* encircling the hut. Actually, there were no gardens. Why the term was used was beyond everyone because the *gardens* consisted of two or three strands of dead weeds growing in the middle of two inches of dust.

As Moose utilized one of his *many* artistic talents and formed the word, 'BRAVO' out of coal briquettes, he had no knowledge of a telephone conversation taking place between a *petite young thing* and Corporal Adams. The good Corporal was sitting at his new boss's desk, talking to his *new boss's* daughter.

"Hi there, is this...Eunice?"

"Yeah, what if it is?" a loud, gum-chewing voice replied.

"Well, you probably won't remember me, Eunice, but I'm the guy who stopped his jeep to help you pick up your milkshake. I don't usually make a habit of doing that sort of thing, but I wanted to help out a beautiful girl in distress. If you can recall, I also met you in the Provost shack?"

There was silence for a few seconds, before Corporal Adams shook his head, covered the mouthpiece, spat, and spoke again. "I'm not talking about your girl-friend, Alberta, I'm referring to you." This time he rolled his eyes to the ceiling and grimaced. "You are truly a very attractive young lady."

Eunice's voice became charming. "Do you really think so, er...I can't remember your name?"

"My friends call me...Stud, but my first name's, Rory. When I first saw you, Eunice, I couldn't believe a young woman with so much loveliness existed on the face of the earth." After shaking his head, he covered the mouthpiece and spat again.

She took out her gum and stuck it under her phone table. "Oh, er...thank you, Rory, or would you like me to call you...Stud?"

"You can call me anything you want. I just want to be near you, morning, noon and..." He grimaced again, "...night."

"Oh, so do I, Stud. I always knew I was cute, but your words send my head spinning. Wanna meet tonight, dearest?"

Corporal Adams sat up straight in his chair. "Well, you see, Eunice sweetheart...I can't. After the two of you blamed me for...I should be so lucky, attacking you, I've been confined to camp working in the kitchen."

"Rory, Rory, oh damn, we didn't mean to...what can I do, darling?"

Stud spit on the floor again. "Well, I think I've figured out the problem. Your father obviously was not talking about our meeting on the hill, am I right, Beautiful One?"

Eunice unbuttoned the three top buttons of her blouse and stared at herself in her mirror. "Yes, yes my darling. It was my horrible friend Alberta who *nailed* you for the theatre episode..."

"Theatre?...my love...?"

The *beautiful one* kissed the phone. "Yes, Alberta and I were in the theatre lately and a cadet tried to have his way with us. He said his name was Corporal Adams, that's why you were blamed. Oh, Stud, what did we do...?"

Corporal Adams paused for a moment. "Do you happen to know his name, My Sweet?"

"Yes it's, Fannylick, or somethin' like that. I think it's Goose...no, it's Bruce Fannylick. He was Red Robinson's assistant when Red held the dance. Oh, my wonderful beloved, what have I done to you?"

"Sweetheart, do you know what he looks like?"

"Yes, the bastard's tall, blondish, and a bit thin. Well, really not that skinny. He's about seventeen or eighteen. Besides feeling us up, the asshole stole all our goodies and got us kicked out of the theatre."

That was all Corporal Adams wanted to hear. "Well, my *Little One*, leave it to me." He spat and then had another thought. "Would you be prepared to tell your dad...I mean, er..."

"Oh darling, yes, yes, I'll tell him we made a mistake." She undid two more buttons. "When can we meet?"

"Shortly, my petite baby, shortly. Look after your body for me, will you?" he sneered and wiped his mouth. "I'll call you in a few days, all right? Good-bye, my darling."

Eunice quivered, "I'll count the seconds while I'm splashing my breasts with cold water to make them firm for you. Good-bye, my dashing dearest."

"Er, yeah, do that. Farewell my *turtle-dove*."

After Corporal Adams hung up the phone, he smacked his hand on the desk. "FANNYLICK, EH? USE MY NAME, WILL YOU? I'LL GET YOU, WHO-EVER YOU ARE! THAT'S GUARANTEED!"

The Corporal's voice was so loud, if it hadn't been Mother's Night in B-29, Moose might have heard the *name* that sounded similar to his. But he didn't, he was far too busy washing windows with his section of cadets.

"YOUSE, GET RIDDA THAT SMUDGE! WHEN THE MORNING SUN HITS THESE WINDOWS, ALL THE MARKS SHOW UP!"

The cadet who was up a ladder leaned back to get a better look. When he spotted the smear, elbow grease took care of it immediately.

The activity inside the hut was just as meticulous. The floors had been scrubbed clean, now the touching-up had begun.

"That looks good," Wayne said to a cadet shining the copper urinal pipes. "But who cleaned out the trough?"

"I did, Corporal," a busy voice replied. The same cadet was now shining the chromed flushing handles of the toilets.

"Did you use Bon-Ami, or whatever that powder is?"

Cadet Drab came out from one of the toilets. "No, I didn't think it needed it."

Smiling, Wayne walked up to the sweating boy and put his hand on his shoulder. "Well, think again, Drab."

"But Corporal, whoever inspects the pissers won't be putting their head in there, will they?"

Wayne laughed. "I really don't know, but what if they do? Do you want us to lose points? Say, you're always talking about your friend's motorbike, how clean does he keep it?"

"It's spotless, Corporal. Pete even shines the spokes."

"Good, that's called, pride. What are you going to do when you grow up?"

"I haven't decided, but I like motorbikes. Maybe I'll join the police force."

Wayne smacked Drab on the back. "Would your vehicle be dirty?"

"NO, SIR!"

"Right! So let's get to it and put some powder in that trough. Also, don't call me, sir, my parents were married."

As Corporal Banks walked out, a grinning Cadet Drab attacked the urinal again. "Can ya believe that, some officer actually sticks his head in here?" he said to the pipes polisher.

"I know. An NCO sure as hell wouldn't do it," replied his friend, Laveille.

Wayne popped his head back in. "And you, Laveille...make certain there's no dust on top of the shitter partitions."

"Gotcha, Corp!"

Drab was on his knees. "Excuse me, Corporal Banks. If some officer sticks his head in the pisser, does he stick his head in the shitters, as well?"

"Drab, that's a good point. Maybe you should do the insides of them, too?"

"Jeez, Corporal, er...do I hafta...?"

"No, just make certain they're brushed out. Alright?"

Drab's grin reappeared. "Sounds good to me, Corporal."

Jackson, in the meantime, was in the shower room pointing to a portion of the floor. "WHAT'S THAT?" he asked a cadet who was down on his hands and knees.

"Corporal Jackson, that is soap crud and I've gone over it four times."

Earl smiled and grabbed a scrub brush. "Only four times? Move over and I'll give you a hand."

While Earl scrubbed away in the shower room, Gordie Cunningham was hanging two gleaming-white towels on the end of each set of bunks. The towels had been sent out to the cleaners after each cadet had chipped in fifteen cents.

"The fold is always to the right," he said to his assistant. "Also, the amount of distance at each end has to be the same as in the middle." He stopped explaining and stood on a chair.

"PAY ATTENTION HERE, EVERYONE! THESE TOWELS WILL NOT BE USED! TOMORROW, MAKE CERTAIN THE SPACE IN BETWEEN THEM IS THE SAME AS THE AMOUNT OF SPACE AT EACH END! CARRY ON!"

"How's that, Corporal?" a cadet asked Rothstein, after showing him a recently scrubbed folding table in the middle of the aisle.

"Not good enough! I can still see some traces of Khaki-It. Where's that old toothbrush you were using earlier?"

"I had to sneak it back, the owner wanted to brush his teeth."

Rothstein grimaced and swallowed. "With that? Whose toothbrush was it?"

"Corporal East's. He left it lying on his bed in the cubicle. Should I *borrow* it again?"

"Does he know you used it?"

"No, Corporal. He doesn't know Laveille used it in the shitter, either. Should I go and get it?"

Rothstein cringed. "Er, no, just use a regular scrubbing brush."

"YOU WON'T GET A SHOCK!" screamed Simon. "JUST PUT THE PIPE CLEANER IN A QUARTER-OF-AN-INCH AND GET THE DUST OUT!" he said, guiding a cadet who was getting the dust out of electric wall sockets.

Simon had to yell because the cadet band was playing and marching outside the end of B-29. "THAT'S IT, DON'T PUT IT IN ANY FURTHER IF YOU WANT YOUR HAIR TO REMAIN IN ITS PRESENT STATE!"

After hearing some cadet yell at the end of the hut, all cadets rushed out the door. The pipes and drums section of the band were in their 'sporran parade' state of dress. Twenty white, bare bottoms swayed at the end of the drum and bugle band. The rays of the summer sun had tanned every inch of their bodies, except those portions usually covered by their bathing suits. All the pipers had on were shoes, spats, hose-tops, belts with sporrans, and their headdress. No smiles were *exposed*.

East stood at the doorway sticking his tongue out, trying to look at it. "LET'S GET BACK TO WORK!" he bellowed, wincing and moving his tongue around his teeth, gums, and lips. As he passed Brice, he said, "Ya know, Doug, you were right. That toothpaste they issue at the MIR tastes awful."

Friday had been a long day as the Musketeers minus East and Simon, lay on their beds following lights out. After range work, the beach, and Mother's Night, all of them were beat, but it was stifling in the barracks, making it difficult to sleep.

When Rothstein told the others about East's toothbrush, their whole end of the hut erupted in laughter.

Douglas gave Wayne's bunk a kick. "He actually thought it was the toothpaste."

"With all the crap he's got in his mouth, I'm surprised he noticed the difference," Wayne replied.

At the other end of the hut, two others who had overheard the conversation didn't think it was hilarious at all.

"That's unequivocally appalling, Jonathan old sock. Can you imagine the execrable micro-organisms the impecunious fellow deposited into his system? What regiment are those heathenish villains with?"

"What other, old boy! That somewhat tall, blondish imbecile, who was Red's attaché, keeps intimating that the Canadian Scottish Regiment is utterly the most superlative fraternity on the face of the planet."

"Are you positive he's not a Seaforth or a Calgary Highlander? They're the equivalent, you know. They breed!"

"No, no, James, I know all three establishments wear those despicable rags, or whatever they're labeled, er, kilts, but there is a variance betwixt them. I've heard the Canadian Scottish carry lead in their frontal pouches to massage their genitals while they march. The Seaforths and Calgary Highlanders don't practise such vulgar actions because at birth, they were restrained from possessing similar organs. I've heard gossip that they even squat when they pee."

In seconds, four Seaforth, two Canadian Scottish, and two Calgary Highlander's stood at the bedsides of the *elitist* duo. In subsequent seconds, both medical prodigies were *delicately* being carried to the showers, bedding and all.

"BLOODY HELL, GET YOUR FRIGHTFUL HANDS OF ME, YOU SCOTTISH SHEEP SHIT AND HEATHER DEGENERATES!"

"I SAY, DO YOU HAGGIS-STUFFERS REALIZE YOU'RE WARRING WITH THE SON OF A REGISTERED MALE NURSE?"

"PUT ME DOWN! THIS IS UTTERLY ANNOYING, DO YOU KNOW WHO YOU'RE TRIFLING WITH? I WAS FIRST IN MY FIRST-AID CLASS! JONATHAN, WE WON'T FORGET THIS!"

"GET YOUR HAND OF MY LEGS, YOU DISCOURTEOUS EX-SCANDINAVIAN AND SPANISH SHIPWRECKED BEASTS! RIGHT YOU ARE, JAMES!"

"What the hell's happening down there?" asked Jackson.

"Anything can happen at that end," replied Moose. "Thank God the couth and culture types are all up at this end."

Earl lay down again. "They are? Who are they?"

"Why youse and me of course."

Bravo's barracks and *grounds* looked like a work of art. The sheets of cardboard the cadets obtained from the kitchens allowed each squared-off set of Saturday-Morning-Inspection-style bedding to appear as if it were molded on the rolled-up mattresses.

The cadets of the company were no different. Each of them had had a cold shower before they dressed in their starched and soap-pressed khaki pants and shirts. Their boots, pith-helmets and belts gleamed in the hot morning sun, and every set of properly worn puttees and hose-tops were exactly even along the ranks.

East had used his head that morning. Instead of marching the company to the weapons stores, he had let them go individually. The cadets stayed on the pavement, not going near any *grassed areas*.

Upon receiving their weapons, they were sized into two, two rank guards of honour and fixed their bayonets. After that, they marched onto the parade square under their own rank structure. The boys of Bravo looked as sharp as could be and all of the Alpha cadets were very proud of them, indeed.

This particular morning, the Cadet Battalion Commander was a cadet from Bravo Company. His name was Laitricharde-Reed. Ever since his *talk* with Danyluk, this cadet had shone. He wasn't operating on his father's name now. Instead, *Bertie* was his own man, and proud of himself as he conducted the parade procedures.

"BATTALION, ATTEN...TION! SLOPE...ARMS! BATTALION, GENERAL SALUTE...PRESENT...ARMS!"

On the third weapons movement, as each guard member slammed down his right foot, the band of the Vernon Army Cadet Camp played the general salute and General George Kitching accepted the homage with pride.

"BATTALION SLOPE...ARMS! ORDER...ARMS!" Cadet Laitricharde-Reed marched up to the dais. "GOOD MORNING, SIR! THE CADETS OF THE VERNON ARMY CADET CAMP ARE READY FOR YOUR INSPECTION, SIR!"

"Thank you," the General replied as he returned the cadet's salute. "Please stand them at ease..." General Kitching then paid the cadets a little more respect. "It's extremely hot this morning, so have them stand easy."

The cadets knew that having the privilege of standing easy during a morning inspection didn't mean moving around. They could relax a little more, but movement was limited. Of course, when the General inspected them, each individual company was called to attention.

Starting with the guard, General Kitching briskly made his rounds of the parade. Both the drum and bugle band and the pipes and drums played softly during his inspection.

The general stopped to read a boy's name tag "Where are you from, MacKenzie?" .

MacKenzie's eyes were glued to the buttons on General Kitching's tunic. "VANCOUVER, SIR!"

"And what regiment do you serve with?"

"THE 72ND SEAFORTH HIGHLANDERS OF CANADA, SIR!"

"Ah, yes, a fine regiment with a grand and glorious history."

"THANK YOU, SIR! WE'RE PROUD OF OUR REGIMENT, SIR!"

"So should you be, MacKenzie. You also have a superb armouries, isn't that right?"

"IT IS THAT, SIR!"

"Excellent turnout, MacKenzie. With cadets like you, your regiment is very fortunate."

"THANK YOU, SIR!"

In all, General Kitching stopped about fifty times while inspecting the parade. Because they were allowed to stand easy, very few cadets passed out. A few did, however, and they were moved to the sidelines, where they sat down, drew up their knees, and rested their heads. Of course, they were given advice from two other very professional *soldiers*.

"Just relax and take deep breaths. You'll be all right. You were just a little tense out there, that's all. Do you understand?"

"Yes, Corporal," a cadet experiencing dizzy spells, replied.

The *Corporal* then addressed his friend. "You know, James, old boy, I didn't sleep a wink last night. That's the last time I'm going to sleep on the bottom surface of any room."

"Yes, old chum, I agree. But Jonathan, what else could we do, our bedding was soaked, we had to sleep on the floor?"

"How many of those, 'ladies from hell' live in our barracks, old sock?"

His friend replied, "I think about twenty, but not all of them participated in embarrassing us. Some are attached to other companies."

"Most unfortunate for them, old pip. I have to go along with what Doctor Bowmer once said. He said, 'An ass for an ass, and a crotch for a crotch.'"

"No, I think you've got it all wrong, old fellow. He said, 'An eye for an eye, and a tooth for a...'" James then caught on and laughingly continued, "Oh, yes, old warrior, I see what you mean. God, I pity those poor, illegitimate, misbegotten scalawags when we get through with them."

"Jonathan, we simply have to teach them not to take the Royal Canadian Medical Corps for granted. Oops, here comes another *sickee*. Sit here, my lad and take deep breaths. Now, Jonathan, let me explain a new method of wrapping dressings..."

After inspecting the drum and bugle and pipe bands, General Kitching returned to the dais and allowed Laitricharde-Reed to carry on.

"BATTALION, ATTEN...TION! CLOSE, ORDER...MARCH! BATTALION, RIGHT...DRESS!" After the dressing, he ordered, "EYES...FRONT!" Then he turned and marched to the dais. "SIR, MAY WE CONTINUE WITH THE MARCH PAST, PLEASE?"

The Inspecting Officer returned the salute. "YES, PLEASE CARRY ON!"

Following an commendable march past in which Bravo Company really excelled, General Kitching had them ground arms and asked the parade to gather around him.

"THANK YOU FOR SUCH AN EXCELLENT TURN OUT AND PARADE! I CAN SEE, WITH EACH WEEK, YOU ARE BECOMING MORE AND MORE PROFICIENT WITH YOUR DUTY!

"THIS IS ONLY THE END OF YOUR FOURTH WEEK. I AM EXTREMELY PLEASED WITH THE WAY YOU ARE PROGRESSING, PARTICULARLY WITH YOUR TRAINING, YOUR BARRACKS, AND YOUR PERSONAL DRESS. MR. GARDINER INFORMS ME THAT THE ALPHA COMPANY CADETS HAVE HAD A LOT TO DO WITH THIS, AND I AGREE..." The general glanced over at the Alpha cadets on the sidelines, and nodded to them. "...THAT THEY ARE WORKING HARD AND MY OFFICERS AND NCOs ARE INDEED VERY PROUD OF THEM. THIS KIND OF ON-THE-JOB TRAINING SHOULD HAVE BEEN INTRODUCED A LONG TIME AGO. MY RECOMMENDATION TO OTTAWA WILL BE THAT IT SHOULD MOST DEFINITELY CONTINUE.

"COMPARED TO THE PAST, VERY FEW PEOPLE HAVE BEEN SENT, OR HAVE ASKED TO BE RETURNED HOME THIS SUMMER. THIS INDICATES TO ME THAT INDEED, YOU REALLY DO LIKE IT HERE..." He stopped and smiled as the chuckling died down. "SO WE MUST BE DOING SOMETHING RIGHT!

"PLEASE KEEP UP THE GOOD WORK. WHEN YOU MARCH AROUND CAMP OR DOWNTOWN, REMEMBER WHO YOU ARE AND WHAT YOU ARE! YOU CARRY A PROUD TRADITION ON YOUR SHOULDERS, AND YOU ARE THE FUTURE OF THIS COUNTRY. ONCE AGAIN, WELL DONE!

"IN A FEW MINUTES, THE RSM WILL INFORM YOU WHICH IS THE BEST COMPANY THIS WEEK. FROM WHAT I'VE SEEN TODAY, IT WILL BE A MOST DIFFICULT DECISION."

General Kitching glanced at Laitricharde-Reed, who responded correctly.

"RIGHT! FALL IN YOUR ORIGINAL POSITIONS!"

After the Advance In Review Order was completed and General Kitching had left the dais, Mr. Gardiner addressed the parade.

"WITH ALL DUE RESPECT, GENERAL KITCHING WAS FAR TOO KIND TO YOU TODAY. YES, THE PARADE WAS MOST IMPRESSIVE, HOWEVER, THERE IS ALWAYS ROOM FOR IMPROVEMENT. INSOFAR AS BARRACKS ARE CONCERNED, MY STAFF HAVE INFORMED ME THAT ONE PARTICULAR BARRACKS IS AHEAD OF THE PACK BY A MILE. CONSEQUENTLY, THE BEST COMPANY THIS WEEK, BOTH ON THE PARADE SQUARE AND IN THEIR BARRACKS, IS...WAIT FOR IT...BRAVO COMPANY!" Gardiner played with the ends of his mustache. "CONGRATULA-

TIONS, BRAVO, I'M VERY PROUD OF YOU, INDEED!"

As Bravo's pennant was hoisted up the flagpole, the cheering of Bravo's cadets was nearly as loud as that of the attached *Corporals* standing on the sidelines. To hear the RSM, particularly this RSM, state that he was proud, was an accomplishment that could not be denied.

"IT WAS A *FAIT ACCOMPLI,*" yelled Moose to the other NCOs of Alpha who stood there discussing which was the best platoon. "NUMBER FIVE AND SIX PLATOONS REALLY STOOD OUT ABOVE THE OTHER TWO!"

After a few other comments were thrown in his direction, Moose gave them the D&M finger. "LET'S SEE HOW WELL YOUR PLATOONS PERFORM AT WATERBALL AFTER LUNCH!"

It had been decided that since the sprinklers were having no effect whatsoever in assisting the *grass* to grow, two fire hydrants would be turned on, with one hose attached to each. With two platoons to each hose, and fifty yards apart, they would try to move a volleyball past each other with each hose's ferocious stream.

"YOU BET WE WILL!" replied an Alpha cadet attached to Eight Platoon.

After handing in their weapons, the cadets of Bravo Company attended a mail-call, exchanged a sheet and a pillowcase and got paid. Shortly afterwards, they undertook their Saturday Morning Exams.

A large portion of these exams were written by the Musketeers, and they assisted in marking them. To no one's surprise, the marks of Five and Six Platoons were substantially higher than the other two.

At lunch, a grinning Banks slapped Douglas on the back. "The Beckford system always comes through. Our guys were miles ahead of the other two platoons."

Douglas agreed with reservation. "Yeah, but we're supposed to be working as a company. We'd better have a talk with the other eight Corporals."

"What time are we being picked up?" East asked. Although he and Simon were supposed to be on duty, they made a switch with a couple of Canadian Scottish Alpha cadets. Also since Douglas and Gordie were supposed to be on duty Sunday, they owed the CScotR cadets a day, as well.

"At three o'clock, just after the waterball game," replied Rothstein.

Moose stuck out his chest. "It's going to be great wearing civilian clothes again, eh guys?" He was referring to the fact that each of them had scrounged a pair of jeans. They would wear their own white T-shirts and running shoes.

Gordie put his hand over Danyluk's mouth, and whispered, "Jesus, Moose, not so loud, do want Corporal Adams to hear you?"

The famed Corporal Adams couldn't hear Moose, because he was far too busy on the telephone in his boss's office.

In a company staff-room, a clerk answered the phone. "Alpha Company, Private Pazim here."

"Ah, yes, Private Pazim...Corporal Adams here, have you got your company's nominal roll handy?"

"Yes, what can I do for you?"

"I'm attempting to find a cadet with a name similar to er, Fannylick. His first name is Bruce."

Adams could hear Pazim shuffling paper, "Er I don't think so, er...Corporal Adams, sweetheart."

Adams cleared his throat. "Keep your *sweetheart* smooth-talk for your creditors. What do you mean, you don't think so? Is he listed, or what?"

Now Private Pazim cleared his throat. "Ahem, he may be, or he may not be. I've got all the companies nominal rolls. Er, Corporal, what's in it for me?"

Corporal Adams paused for a moment before speaking. "I'll pretend I didn't hear that, Private Pazim, like I pretended not noticing you sneaking two turkeys into the Sergeants' Mess."

"But Corporal, I was only doing that for Sergeant..."

"Ah, ah, ah, Private Pazim, I don't have to inform you what possession is when it comes to the law, do I? Suppose Major Figby-Jones knew you passed along two turkeys?"

The Corporal heard Pazim shuffling more paper. "We don't have a cadet in Alpha Company by that name, but there is a cadet in the band with a similar name. His name is Cadet Bruce Pannytuck. I've checked the other nominal rolls' he's probably the one you're looking for. What's he done?"

"Does Eaton's tell Woodward's, Private Pazim? By the way, I still haven't decided whether or not I'm going to nail you for those turkeys. Good-bye."

After hanging up, Pazim said. "Rotten son-of-bitch. Only the Provost will take assholes like him."

Corporal Adams smiled sneakily. "So, Cadet Bruce Pannytuck is in the band, is he? Well, well, well! I think I'll just pay him a short visit."

As Corporal Adams entered the band hut, an Alpha Corporal spotted him and stood to attention. Adams was feared, especially in the cells. "Are you looking for someone, Corporal?"

Adams ran his finger along the top railing of a set of bunks, then blew away the supposed dust. "Yes, what does Cadet Bruce Pannytuck look like?"

"Pannytuck? We've got two of them. Bruce...he's tall, thin, and he's got dirty-blonde hair. He's in the showers right now because his father's..."

The Corporal didn't wait to hear anything further. He just walked into the shower room, grabbed the naked and now panic-stricken Pannytuck by the throat, and slammed him against the wall. "So, you low down scum, we meet for the first time, eh?"

Pannytuck couldn't talk and started turning red as he tried to wrestle Adams' arm away from his throat, but to no avail. The Corporal was strong, real strong.

"SO, YOU FEEL UP SOME BROAD IN THE MOVIE THEATRE AND TELL HER YOUR NAME IS CORPORAL ADAMS, EH? WELL, YOU'RE NOT CORPORAL ADAMS, PANNYTUCK, I'M CORPORAL ADAMS AND I'M GOING TO..."

Corporal Adams didn't know what hit him. He knew he'd been quickly turned around, and heard, "OH NO,YOU'RE NOT!" but that was all. Pannytuck's father had come into the shower room, witnessed his son's dilemma, grabbed the Corporal's arm, swung him around, and with one punch to the face, sent him flying into the still-spraying shower. When he came around, Sergeant Bill Gabriel, Sergeant Larry Bygdnes, and Mr. Pannytuck were standing over him. The shower had been turned off, and in addition to a black eye and a broken nose, the *good* Corporal was soaked.

"I WANT YOU TO LAY CHARGES AGAINST THIS BASTARD!" a fuming Pannytuck Sr. bellowed, trying to get at the Corporal again.

Sergeant Gabriel got in between the two, and yanked Adams to his feet. "I can assure you, we will. Now, please take your boys and go camping for the weekend as you planned.

Shortly after Mr. Pannytuck had gathered up his *two* sons and left, Corporal Adams was whisked away in a vehicle displaying a flashing red light.

As the Military Police truck drove towards the guardroom, a hilarious game of waterball was being played in the field outside B-29, and the whole camp was watching.

Two fire hoses, fifty yards apart, had been turned up full-force and ice-cold flowing water was fiercely and freely streaming from massive nozzles. Each hose's spout had to be held by at least three cadets, as they assisted two separate teams of two platoons to drive a single ball into the other's end zone.

Naturally all Alpha Corporals had to participate with the cadets of Bravo in the now four inches of saturated mud covering the area.

Although they were supposed to be playing rugby rules and tossing a lateral ball to their team mates, Moose had grabbed the ball and was running like a bat out of hell towards the other end.

At the halfway point, with a full-force jet of water at his back, he ran into a wall of water aimed at his front and decided he'd better pass the ball to Archer. It never happened, because the intensity of the full frontal force, as well as the advance of an adversary, knocked him on his bottom with the ball. The rear wall of water had forced his shorts down and turned him over, face firmly planted in the mud. The cadets went wild demonstrating their enthusiasm of seeing a Corporal in this state; fifty of them grabbing Danyluk, trying to move him so they could get at the ball.

When the ball popped free, sans Danyluk, it squirted in East's direction on the sidelines. East wasn't playing at that moment. Instead, he was yelling and screaming with a chicken leg in his mouth. When he was hit with both *barrels*, he was lifted up and flung face down into the mire, chicken leg and all.

Danyluk was stomped on many times as he tried to get up and pull up his pants. The problem was, he had more mud inside his pants than on the outside. When he finally got his shorts up to his knees, he was hit from behind again and sent soaring.

The game only lasted half-an-hour, but when it was finished, three accomplishments had been served. First, Camp Vernon had checked out two of their fire hoses. Second, never, since the First World War, had there been a mud-scene similar to this *athletic* event; and third, every single cadet of Bravo Company and their NCOs experienced a jet-rinsing like never before. At the end of the game, everyone was packing fifty pounds of heavy, wet mud, and if they hadn't been rinsed off, it would have taken ten years to get B-29 looking like a regular hut again. After a few cold pops in the cadet canteen, all eight Musketeers were together once more, and the warm water of the showers in B-33 felt great.

Wayne opened the window because Jack had been called upon to *clear* out the room. "We showed 'em who the best platoons were. Those pongoes from Seven and Eight won't want to take *us* on again, I'll betcha!"

Danyluk held his head under the nozzle. "Jesus, I'm sore. I must have been stepped on at least fifty times. East, you sure as hell didn't help, trying to protect your chicken leg. Holding the leg up with one hand and trying to grab the ball with your other."

"It's plural, you mean 'chicken legs,'" said Gordie. "He had one tucked into his waistband, as well. He couldn't catch the ball you threw to him because he was feeling to keep his other leg safe."

"Yeah, two perfectly good chicken legs completely ruined," complained East. "People are starving all over the world, and my meaty chicken legs end up in a foot of mud."

"And you tried to find them afterwards, you twerp."

"Screw you, Cunner," replied East. I was lookin' for Wayne's glasses, wasn't I Wayne?

"Yeah, I think so, Jack."

"You think so, you think so? Do you actually believe I'd rinse them legs off?"

Wayne put his glasses on. "Well, didn't you?"

East shrugged under the water. Well...just one. The other was beyond my standards for comsumption."

"Jeez, it must have been battered to hell," quipped Gordie. "I did see ya suckin' on the bone, though, didn't I?"

"Get screwed, you pongo," replied East.

Douglas was still trying to get the mud out of his ears. "Moose, you must have been kicked in the nuts about a hundred times, and the ball hit you there about fifty times, yet you *survived*. I thought you'd go down for the count, but you didn't even wince. Wayne said to me, 'It's game over for *his* family jewels. They are positively beyond repair. He'll probably have to start up a Soldiers' Busted Testicles Fund!'"

Rothstein agreed. "Your balls must be made of iron, Moose? Four of those CScotRs who kicked you had to be taken to the MIR with broken toes."

The proud Moose didn't answer. He just left the shower room for a minute and came back holding up a weird-looking contraption. "Remember this, youse guys?"

Howls filled the shower room as Moose held up his steel jockstrap.

"I wore this under my gaunch. I knew those creeps were out to get me."

Wayne had made the device. "Moose, you old creep, then it did come in handy after all?"

Danyluk strapped it on again. "Wayne, you invented the greatest friend of mankind. When a guy wears this, he can take on the world and win. My nuts were protected throughout."

When the eight left the shower room, *man's greatest friend* created a small problem for the wearer, because the RSM was visiting the barracks, sipping a coffee and talking with a cadet. Danyluk was walking backwards still discussing his *Scottish triumph*, when he *bumped* into the RSM's back.

It didn't have to be explained to Danyluk who he'd hit. At the last minute he had heard the Sergeant-Major's voice.

"OH, SHIT!" Moose said, covering the side of his head as he quickly walked away.

Now *wearing* half his coffee, a fuming Regimental Sergeant-Major turned. "THAT MAN WITH HIS BACK AND HIS ASS TO ME! YES YOU...TURN AROUND AND GET OVER HERE, NOW!"

Moose halted, turned smartly around and marched towards the Sergeant-Major and halted.

"MY GOD, IT'S YOU AGAIN! SOME ONE UP THERE MUST HAVE IT IN FOR ME! WITH FOURTEEN-HUNDRED CADETS IN THIS CAMP, I HAVE TO BE CONTINUALLY RUNNING INTO YOU. THIS TIME HOWEVER, YOU RAN INTO ME! WHAT THE HELL IS THAT CONTRAPTION YOU'RE WEARING, A GODDAMNED GIRDLE, OR ARE YOU TRYING TO BECOME A BOY SCOUT WITH A NEW METHOD OF CARRYING YOUR FRYING

PAN? WHAT IS IT, MAN?"

Moose stood rigidly at attention. "It's a steel jockstrap, sir."

"OF COURSE IT IS! HOW FOOLISH OF ME! A WHAT? DO YOU MEAN TO TELL ME YOU'VE GOT THOSE ORGANS OF YOURS CRAMMED INTO THAT THING? WHEN DO YOU USUALLY WEAR IT, WHEN YOU'RE SLOW DANCING WITH THE LADIES?"

Moose smiled. "The ladies wouldn't like me to wear this when I'm with them, Sergeant-Major."

Even though he had coffee all over him, a gas pain appeared on Mr. Gardiner's face. "OH YES THEY WOULD, OTHERWISE THEY'D BE FIVE FEET AWAY FROM YOU! GET OUT OF MY SIGHT, YOU ABNORMAL MALFORMED MONSTROSITY!"

A roar of laughter erupted from Moose's end of the barracks. Just watching him turn and march wearing only his *protector* was an exhilarating million-dollar experience.

"AND WHEN YOU TAKE THAT THING OFF, KEEP YOUR PRIVATE PARTS, ALL OF THEM, OFF THE WINDOW LEDGE! IS THAT CLEAR?"

"YES, SERGEANT-MAJOR!"

After the RSM had left the building, half the hut gathered 'round inspecting the steel work of art.

"So that's why MacTavish's toe is broken, is it?" asked a Seaforth cadet.

His question started the group of them wondering where MacTavish was. But they needn't have worried, because the cadet was safe in the Medical Inspection Room. Well, *safe* isn't exactly the word, because earlier...

"I say, Jonathan, old stick. Don't you think we've permitted those appalling Canadian Scottish Cadets to suffer sufficient pain? They've been perched in the waiting chamber for over an hour."

"James, old pip, they've been delivered to us by God himself. Andre and I have commingled up this homogenous mixture which they must take every hour for discomfort. Actually, Andre is examining their feet this very minute as we converse. He assures me that each will have a bottle to take back to the barracks with him."

"Oh, bloody effulgent, Jonathan old knob. So we can guardedly affirm that the Canadian Scottish have been *cured*, now it's time for the Seaforths and the Calgary Highlanders?"

"Yes, James, old friend. You, Andre and I will deliberate on them following the departure of these revolting haggis hacks."

At the same time as the Musketeers picked up their weekend passes and met the girls at the upper road leading to the highway, a confrontation was coming to a close in the guardroom. Corporal Adams, with a black and blue *kisser,* was sitting facing Sergeants Gabriel and Bygdnes.

Sergeant Gabriel was furious. "Well, you picked the wrong cadet. Do you understand that, you simple-minded idiot? The evening of the theatre episode, Cadet Pannytuck was with the band in Kelowna. Where the hell did you learn your investigative techniques...surely not in the same Provost School I attended?"

Corporal Adams poked a finger into his mouth. One of his teeth was loose and he spoke in a very low voice.

"Sergeant, I've explained everything to you. If I got upset, I'm sorry. There's nothing more to tell. Some cadet used my name with your daughter in the theatre. I've been blamed for everything, but I haven't done anything."

Gabriel lit up a smoke. "You're very lucky, Corporal. Larry and I have questioned the girls and they confirm your story. If they hadn't, you'd be in the Glass House right this very minute, and I don't have to tell you how other prisoners treat members of our corps, do I?"

Fear appeared on Corporal Adams' face. He knew, only too well. "No, Sergeant."

"I'm treating this as an honest mistake and I'll explain the situation to Mr. Pannytuck when he returns tomorrow night. Now go and clean yourself up; I'm returning you to Provost duty, AND NEVER AGAIN WILL YOU TOUCH A CADET!" Sergeant Gabriel then glanced at Sergeant Bygdnes. "Larry, is there anything you would like to add?"

"Yes, thank you, Bill. Corporal, my wife and I will be at the Sergeants' Mess dance tonight, and our little baby, Eunice, wants you to drop over and explain everything to her. She really feels sorry for the mix-up."

It was hard to tell if Corporal Adams winced from the pain, or the invitation, as he slowly rose from his chair. Every movement brought on pain, but the thought of having to spend the evening with *little* Eunice was worse. What the hell could he do, he thought to himself? The answer came suddenly - absolutely nothing.

"Thank you, Sergeant Gabriel, and you too, Sergeant Bygdnes."

When eight couples unloaded their gear from the cars at Okanagan Landing, Douglas Brice was once again lost in the beauty of the Okanagan Valley, particularly the north-east arm of Okanagan Lake. It was a gorgeous day and the glistening blue water was as inviting as ever.

Hardly any cars were in the parking lot of the old Sutherland Arms Hotel, and very few people were camping north of it next to the washing shacks used by travellers with trailers and tents. Only two people were on the wharf, and the beach was empty.

After a few good-byes, only two cars remained. Maggie had her mother's car, and Jack East's girlfriend had the other. Her dad was away on business, so her mother had allowed her to take the car for the weekend.

"Give us a hand, Doug," Wayne asked as he picked up a small coal-barbecue stove out of the trunk of Maggie's mother's car. Maggie's vehicle was the only one loaded with equipment so the departing parents wouldn't get wise to the fact that this was an overnight stay.

The activity woke Douglas out of his trance. "I'm sorry," he said, grabbing the contraption by its legs. "I was just thinking how great it is to be back."

Shortly, three tents, two Coleman stoves, one barbecue, and other related equipment and necessities were hauled onto the beach.

Diane had brought one of the three tents, but after a short discussion, she and Douglas decided they didn't need it. The weather was fantastic and both of them wanted to sleep out. Moose and Alma, however, set their tent up instantly and although it must have been scalding inside, both of them quickly disappeared, their tent door zipped and tied.

Not by planning, Cunningham and Maggie were closest to the hotel, with Simon and Sheila ten yards north of them. Next to them were East and Jackson and their girls. They had decided to stay together. Rothstein and his girlfriend were about ten yards north of the foursome, followed by Wayne, Debbie, Douglas, and Diane. Moose and Alma's tent was away from the rest, about twenty yards north of Douglas and Diane.

It was a lazy afternoon. Nothing in the world was organized and that appeared to be what everyone wanted. Seven of the couples had camped out in exactly the same spot the past two years and had learned that if events weren't organized, everything went better.

As Douglas and Diane went to change into their swim suits, Brice noticed everything was the same as it had been before. Even the old changing shack on the south side of the hotel hadn't been repaired. The 'IRLS' and 'OYS' entrance doors were still half-off their hinges and the same peepholes were inside. As he changed, he tried to find his initials from the past three years, and there they were, a little faded, but they stood out among the others.

Douglas was the first out and he walked the few metres to the beach and skimmed a rock. It was quiet, except for the lapping of the lake intermingling with the faint sounds of a country waltz which was emanating from the open pub door of the grand old wooden structure.

The various colours of the peaceful sun-bleached hills on the far side of the lake presented a scene that could only be captured by Carl Larsson, he thought.

He'd studied about the Swedish painter in school, and since then had obtained any reasonably-priced print which was offered. The painter had lived from 1853 until 1919, and when Douglas was fifteen and had first seen a Larsson print in an old pawn shop, he saved his money, bought it and had had it framed. Before framing, he memorized some words which had been printed on the back.

'Carl Larsson, 1853 - 1919 - unstable, sensitive, a splintered personality, self-centered, who loved mankind as a matter of principle, but now and again impulsively hated one or another of its individuals. An idol who peeled off his geniality and turned out a twinkle. In his pathetic nakedness, he stood here, a man, an individual of much goodwill and an artist with a splash of genius, of which the world has allowed so few.'

Diane arrived and slipped her hand into his. "You're in Carl Larsson's world again, aren't you?" Her radiant face and dimple made Douglas smile proudly, openly appreciative of being with such a beautiful girl, in God's country.

"Was it the expression on my face?" he asked, letting go of her hand and putting his arm around her waist.

They both explored the lake and the hills with their eyes. "It's more than that, Douglas. Your whole being participates in swallowing it up. It's as if your life has stopped and is being recharged by your thoughts. Am I right?"

He gently kissed her on her forehead, before returning his gaze to the scene in front.

"One-hundred-percent correct, as usual." he whispered. "Diane, every time I'm here, I don't want to eat, drink, walk, talk or whatever. It's as if I was made to be a part of it. I subconsciously probe to see where I would fit in, but there's no room...it's been completed without me. I understand that now. I'm entrusted to look and touch, but I'm not allowed to join."

Diane guided them to an old log on the beach and they sat down. "But Douglas, perhaps experiencing such a feeling is like joining. Sweetheart, you don't have to search, the fact that you feel this way makes you an honorary member. You're already in there. Not your body, Doug, your *mind* has been graciously and unselfishly allowed in. You've been getting the two mixed up."

Douglas moved his arm up around her shoulders and didn't say anything for at least a minute. "For the first time in my life, I think I now understand. You've explained it perfectly."

"Well I know you like a book. I may not have the sensitivity you most definitely reveal when it comes to nature, but I sense your feelings, and they're wonderful. I'm happy you're not a painter, but at the same time, I wish you were. I'd pay any price to see this through your eyes. But if you were a painter, I couldn't share you."

East's voice broke in. "HEY, YOU GUYS, ARE WE GOIN' SWIMMIN' OR WHAT?" He and his girl had changed and they were sitting at the end of the wharf eating sandwiches she had prepared.

Moose and Alma's tent flap opened and the world could hear their conversation. "ALMA, HE SAID, 'OR WHAT?' I LIKE THE 'OR WHAT' CHOICE!"

"LISTEN, YOU CREEP, HE DIDN'T MEAN 'OR WHAT?' IN THE WAY YOU THINK. HE MEANT, 'OR WHAT?'"

"AW, C'MON, ALMA. LET'S 'OR WHAT?'"

"THE TROUBLE WITH YOU, MOOSE DANYLUK, IS THAT YOU NEVER WANT TO EXPERIENCE THE FINER THINGS IN LIFE. LOOK AT THAT WATER, ISN'T IT JUST GRAND?"

"ALMA, I TOOK FIFTEEN MILLION SHOWERS THIS MORNING, AND NOW YOUSE WANTS ME TO GO SWIMMING? YOU'RE THE ONLY FINER THING IN MY LIFE...LET'S 'OR WHAT'?"

"THANK YOU, MOOSE, BUT 'YOUSE' IS GOIN' SWIMMING! NOW, GO GET CHANGED!"

Soon, everyone gathered at the end of the wharf. Although it was Saturday, there wasn't a speedboat or motorboat on the lake. A few people way on the far side were paddling canoes, but the lake was bare and wondrous as all of the couples lay side by side, smearing suntan lotion on each other.

"I bumped into Eunice Bygdnes in the grocery shop this morning," said Maggie, picking up the cards just dealt by Gordie. "God, I thought *I* had to buy a lot of groceries for this weekend, but she had three more bags than I did. Do you remember her, Moose?"

Moose grabbed a sandwich out of Alma's basket. "Maggie, please don't ruin my day. Of course, I remember her. The realm remembers her. She's got the second-most-foulest mouth in the universe. Her fat friend, er, Alberta qualifies as first."

Maggie laughed as she asked Gordie to, "HIT ME!" before she continued with her story. "Well, Eunice may be fat and all that, but she's finally got herself a boyfriend at camp. GORDIE, I SAW THAT! YOU'RE DEALING FROM THE BOTTOM AGAIN!"

"Who in his right mind would go out with that slob?" asked Rothstein.

"GORDIE, I'M NOT GOING TO PLAY CARDS WITH YOU IF YOU KEEP CHEATING. THAT'S HOW YOU WON THAT STRIP POKER GAME! She says her new boyfriend is Corporal Adams."

Smiling amazed faces met each other, and the boys sat up. Even Gordie took his eyes off the cards for a moment. "CORPORAL ADAMS? THE PROVOST

CORPORAL? JESUS, HE MUST REALLY BE HARD UP!"

"She says she's going to have him all alone at her house tonight. Apparently he's sporting a black eye and a broken nose."

"Is he?" asked Danyluk. "I betcha he got that from Alberta when he ditched her for the *cute* one. Jesus, no wonder they're eatin' at home. Could youse imagin' goin' into a fancy restaurant with that dame?"

"No, tell us what would happen," said Diane.

Moose cringed. "I can't because I'd have to use their language."

"We won't listen to those parts," Diane replied.

"Yeah, we'll shut our ears when you use those words," added Alma.

Moose thought for a moment. He didn't like swearing at the best of times, except for the words, "Son of a bitch!" Those words were his trademark.

"Well, after she'd dumped her wad of wet gum in the waiter's white glove, he'd probably say, 'And what would the madam like?'

'ER, I'LL HAVE THE FUCKIN' ROAST BEEF, AND MAKE IT AN EXTRA LARGE PORTION FELLA, OR I'LL HAVE YOUR NUTS! ALSO, GIMMEE LOTS OF THAT SON-OF-A-BITCHIN GRAVY! WHAT KINDA POTATOES YA GOT?' "

'Well, madam, we've got mashed, fries, au gratin...'

'WHAT THE SHIT DID YOUSE CALL ME? AU WHAT?'

'No madam, that's a type of crisp-fried potato.'

'OH, YEAH! WELL, ALL RIGHT! I'LL TAKE THE AU CRAP! BUT DON'T TRY AND BULL SHIT ME OR I'LL HAVE YOUR ASS! WHAT'S YOUR NAME?'

'My name is Francois, madam.'

'WELL, FRANCO'S MADMAN, I LIKES NIBBLIN' WHEN I'M WITH MY OLD MAN, SO LET'S HAVE SOME SHIT TO GNAW ON, AND GET THE LEAD OUT OF YOUR PANTS! HOP TO IT, FRANCIS!'"

Throughout his impersonation, Moose had them rolling on the wharf, laughing their heads off. Wayne couldn't take it; he held onto his stomach as he fell into the water.

"And I'm not gonna tell ya what that Alberta dame would be like," continued Moose.

Although tears of laughter were tripping her, Diane insisted, "Aw come on, Moose, tell us."

After some coaxing, Moose finally agreed. "Well, if she was at the same table, it would go somethin' like this. 'WHAT DUZ YOUSE WANT?'

'Madam, I am your waiter for the evening.'

'OH, YEAH! WELL, WE AIN'T FINISHED PICKIN' YET. PISS OFF AND WE'LL CALL YA WHEN WE WANT YA! AND KEEP YOUR HANDS OFF MY ASS!'"

"When the food is served, she'd say, 'HEY, YOUSE, FRANKIS. DID YOUSE TOUCH MY TIT WHEN YOUSE DROPPED OFF THE FUCKIN' BEANS?'"

'I beg your pardon, Madam?'

'A HARD-ON, EH? DON'T FUCK WITH ME, FRANKIE! I KNOW YOU'RE WARM FOR MY FORM, BUT BEGGIN' AIN'T GONNA HELP YA! YOUSE FRENCH PRICKS ARE ALL THE SAME! I SAID, KEEP YOUR HANDS OFF MY TITS WHEN YOU'RE SERVIN' THE SHIT! YA GOT THAT, FRANCOIEEE MADMAN, OR WHATEVER THE FUCK YOUR NAME IS?'

'The madam is indeed wrong. I'm going to call the maitre d'hotel.'

'WHY, IS THAT WHERE YOU'RE LIVIN'? LISTEN, SMART ASS, YOU'VE BEEN PINCHIN' AND GRABBIN' A FEEL SINCE I GOT IN THIS JOINT! I'M SAVIN' THIS TENDER PHYSIQUE FOR MY GROOM, SO KEEP YOUR GRUBBY PAWS TO YOURSELF! YA GOT THAT, FUCKEE? EUNICE, HAND ME THAT SPARE FORK, THIS ASSHOLE JUST TOUCHED MINE! CHRIST, THEY EVEN GROPE FOR ME IN THE RESTAURANT, CAN YA BELIEVE THAT? THEY JUST WON'T ALLOW DECENT GIRLS TO REMAIN VIRGINS, WILL THEY?'"

When Moose was finished, he couldn't take it himself. He was still laughing as he joined the rest in the water. His face was red because he never used such language. How he said it in front of the girls, was beyond him.

Rothstein laughed so much, he swallowed some water and started coughing. "Moose, I've never heard profanity like that, and hearing it from you..."

"Rothie, what are ya talkin' about, youse heard them in the theatre? I'd never talk like that to my worst enemy. Can you imagine girls speakin' like that?"

Douglas dunked Wayne's head. "They're not girls. Shave their heads and put 'em in jackboots and you've got a couple of Provost. Adams and Eunice were made for each other."

The remainder of the afternoon went brilliantly. Besides swimming, diving, loafing, and being pushed in from the wharf, some local fellow docked his speedboat and was kind enough to allow them all to go water-skiing. As usual, East was the best male skier; the girls were all equally proficient.

When it became time for the *boater* to leave, he insisted he wouldn't take any money for gas, and just wished the couples all the best.

"COME AND GET IT!" yelled Wayne when it was time to eat. He and East served up steaks, hamburgers, hot-dogs, and potatoes in their skins. East was wearing a chef's hat which his girlfriend had brought, and Moose said that's what he should wear daily at camp. "Then they wouldn't bug ya on the parade square, if ya've got a chicken leg in your hand, instead of a rifle."

As the couples sat and ate leaning against logs, the sun made it's westerly trip and the air cooled a little. Danyluk and Diane's radios started playing 'three in a row,' and to the sounds of Elvis's, *Don't Be Cruel, Hound Dog, and Heartbreak Hotel,* romance was in the air.

When it was dark, they lit a small fire just off the beach and roasted marshmallows.

"It's hard to believe we start our fifth week on Monday," said Simon, passing a roasted marshmallow to Sheila. "For some reason, this summer's gone faster than the others."

His girl took hold of his hand and squeezed it. "It always does when you don't want to leave. Are you coming back next year?"

Simon put his arm around her shoulders and brought her in. He laid his head on hers. "You bet I am. I'm coming back as a Corporal, as long as you're here. Did you have any trouble getting out of the house for the weekend? What did your mom and dad say?"

Sheila giggled as she asked the others. "I think all of us are staying at each other's houses this weekend, aren't we?" All the girls nodded.

"But what if your parents phone to check on you?" he asked.

Maggie took a coin out of Gordie's ear. "Our contingency plans have been well prepared. We simply all decided to move to the next house, that's all. They won't phone eight houses. Besides, I think some of our moms know. Although they don't say anything, they remember their youth. It isn't lying, it's, it's..."

"It's planning and preparation," offered Moose, using one of the 'Eight Principles of Instruction.' "Jesus, I like that code word, 'APUMSHIT.' It can be used in any context. Anyway, I do the same thing at home."

Alma gave him an inquiring look. "Why do you have to?" she asked.

Moose had been caught off guard. That didn't happen very often and he had to think quickly. "Er, well, I er, really don't. But let's say I wanna go fishin' all night, I just say I'm over at Doug or Wayne's place."

"What kind of fishing, Moose?" Alma now had him by the scruff of his neck.

"Fishin' fishing, that's all. I cast a mean line, ya know?"

Earl chuckled. "You can say that again."

"I cast a mean line, ya know." Moose reiterated.

Alma released her grip. "Well, it better be just that. If you're fooling around on me, Moose Danyluk, you won't see the..." This time Alma didn't finish her statement. What she and Moose did at Kal beach, happened to them. Douglas and Diane dumped two buckets of water over them.

Moose and Alma never moved so fast in their lives. Immediately, everyone was dragged into the water for another dip, and for some reason, it was Gordie who decided to start the action by grabbing Maggie's top. Before long, all tops were tossed onto the wharf and a few male swimsuits as well - mainly, Moose's, Jackson's, Simon's, Brice's, Cunningham's, Rothstein's, Banks' and last of all, after a *bitter* fight, East's. It had taken fifteen people to separate him from his garment.

"THIS IS EMBARRASSING!" he bellowed. "I'M NOT LIKE YOU PEOPLE, I'M NOT AN EXHIBITIONIST!"

"YOU ARE NOW!" replied a laughing Danyluk, tossing Alma's bottoms on to the wharf.

"MOOSE, YOU ROTTEN CREEP!" she screamed. Actually, Alma had tried to defend herself, but Danyluk, famous for his 'indescribable, expeditious, biological, rigging,' also had the fastest hands in the west. Before long, other fast hands joined in the caper, and the remaining bikini bottoms were on the wharf.

Even though a trillion stars lit up the nighttime sky, it was pitch black in the water at the end of the pier. When they got out to dive or just to lay on the dock, no one was around to hear the gleeful sounds of happy, splashing teenagers as they allowed the warm water and gentle breeze to explore their bodies, and soothe the baking of the scalding afternoon sun.

At exactly the same time as the Musketeers and their girls were *lounging* at the end of the dock, a similar, but much more involved sort of lounging was taking place in the darkness of Eunice's house.

"Jesus, Eunice, *sweetheart*, get off me, you're smothering me. I can't breathe."

"Oh, shut, up ya big baby; mamma's goin' to give ya everything ya need."

"For Christ's sake, Eunice, you've ripped open my fly. The Goddamned buttons are all over the floor. You've also re-cracked my ribs, Goddamn it!"

"Fuck your ribs. Lemmee atcha!"

"Eunice, there's not enough room for both of us on this bed, also, your high-heels are digging into my shins. Jesus, must you suck in my whole face when you kiss?"

"Shaddap and put your hands on me. Rub me, rub me. Listen fuckee, do you want me to tell my dad, you did the dirty work?"

In the silence of the night, only the immediate neighbours heard Corporal Adams' scream as his shorts were literally ripped up and off in a full frontal attack by the enemy. As far as he knew, his testicles had gone flying with them.

Before Diane turned off her radio, *Unchained Melody* had finished and *Ebb Tide* began as Douglas unfolded his blanket. "I don't have a sleeping bag like you," he said, softly. "They won't issue them, for some reason."

He couldn't see Diane, but she had taken off her towel and was already underneath the smooth lining of her bag. "I've put two of them together," she whispered tenderly. Silently she lifted up the side, "Oh Doug, I..." She stopped for a moment, and orange moon beams lit up her face as he knelt next to her. "...darling...please come in?"

Gradually, with or without towels, the others dispersed to their own little section of the world to *discuss* life, its meaning and fulfillment. Some lay arm in arm and spooned, others sat and talked, or just walked the beach hand in hand. The breeze, the moon and the stars became supporting nighttime players in a scene from an act in *Arabian Nights*, and for sixteen teenagers, the whole universe was theirs.

CHAPTER XI

It takes a lot of trucks to move a company of four platoons to Glenemma, and they were lined up outside of B-29 at exactly 0900 hours on Monday morning.

The Musketeers had been in Bravo's barracks since 0800, helping the cadets pack the proper gear and equipment for a week. Although lists had been posted, some of the boys had crammed everything but the kitchen sink into their large and small webbed packs, and even then, that wasn't enough.

"Where the hell do you think you're going with that?" Wayne asked a cadet, who was in the process of dragging his mattress out the door.

"In the bivouacking lectures, you said any fool can be uncomfortable, Corporal Banks. I just ain't gonna be one of those fools."

"Put it back and roll it up. Christ, we're not staying for a year, you know?"

Eventually when all the mattresses were rolled, the windows shut, and the doors locked, Bravo Company boarded the vehicles for the field training area. The songs started as soon as the trucks started rolling.

The Musketeers were fortunate they were altogether as they sat in the back of a three-ton with the extra NCOs of Alpha Company. The memory of the fabulous weekend was still on their minds, and it showed.

"How'd your weekend go?" a Seaforth *Corporal* asked Danyluk, to no avail. Moose was wrapped up in his thoughts; so were the others.

At 0700 hours on Sunday morning, East had awakened the dead with his call, "HEY, BREAKFAST IS READY! COME AND GET IT! IT LOOKS AND SMELLS GREAT!"

Although the sun was hot and climbing, the lake was a mirror and the air was fresh with scent. The only sounds other than East's voice and the lapping of the water were the lowing of roaming cattle atop the hills across the lake, and a lone rooster somewhere in the immediate vicinity. The livestock appeared as black spots against the rugged, dusty, sunburned land. In the distance, a train whistle called.

Amidst giggles and chuckles, thirteen tired but starry-eyed *exhibitionists* reached for their towels so they could run to the end of the wharf and pick up their bathing suits. Alma and Moose swam the distance, *au naturel*.

A couple of fishing ten-year-old boys with amazed smiles were already on the dock when Moose arrived, climbed out and started searching.

"Ya see, Tommy, that's what ours will look like when we get older."

His buddy wasn't convinced. "No way, Peter, I've got a brother his age and he ain't freakish like that."

Moose laughed inwardly and slipped into his shorts. He then threw Alma's bikini parts into the water and she grabbed them.

While everyone searched and sorted out their swimming suits, East kept yelling, "C'MON, IT'S GETTING COLD AND WE'RE HUNGRY!"

East and his girl had retrieved their clothing earlier, and that bugged Gordie.

"THE LEAST YOU COULD HAVE DONE IS BRING OUR TRUNKS BACK TO THE BEACH, YOU PONGOES!"

Gradually, everyone got dressed and had a morning dip before breakfast. East was right, he'd cooked up a fabulous meal of bacon, eggs, sausages, hash-browns, toast, coffee, tea, and pop.

Conversation was limited, but shy smiles and body language substituted for the lack of spoken words, until East broke the silence.

"Jesus, Gordie, you were playing cards all night long. Don't you ever give 'em a rest once in awhile?"

For a change, it was Gordie's mouth that was full. He swallowed quickly. "How the hell do you know we were playing cards?"

"Cause we could hear you. The whole bloody beach could hear you. Do you have to yell when you say, 'THE POT'S MINE, ALL MINE!' How the hell could you see the cards?"

"Because he asked me to bring a Coleman lantern, that's how," replied Maggie, combing her hair. "And like a fool, I did. You took four-dollars-and-ten-cents off me, you, you..."

"Louse?" offered a smiling Gordie.

"Yes, you louse. I want that money back, I was going to buy a birthday present for my mother."

Diane laughed. "You mean you guys were gambling all night? What time did you stop?"

Rothstein scooped up some scrambled eggs. "Who said they stopped? At four-thirty, I woke up to the sounds of, 'BABY NEEDS A NEW PAIR OF SHOES! C'MON, YOU DICE! THAT'S IT! THAT'S IT!'"

A reluctant Cunningham handed the money back to Maggie. "Well, I wasn't the only one making noise last night, even from where, we were we could hear Moose snoring." He pointed to Moose. "And you guys had a tent. Alma, how did you stand it?"

Moose replied instead, and then got bonked on the head with a rolled-up towel. "It was Alma doin' all the snorin'. Youse guys know I don't snore."

East stuffed two giant pieces of bacon into his mouth. "Also, who went swim-min' at two-thirty in the morning?"

Gordie poured himself another cup of coffee. "Jesus, Jack, what did you do, stay up all night on guard duty, or something?"

Sheila had a shy look about her as she squeezed Simon's hand. "We did. With all the stars and the moon, the lake was like molten silver. It was wonderful."

After breakfast, when the dishes were finished and everyone packed up, they relaxed and swam at the end of the wharf until late afternoon. At four o'clock, two cars were jammed and the boys were dropped off at camp just in time for supper. The drivers didn't release their passengers on the highway in front of the guard-room. Instead, they drove past the British Columbia Dragoons armouries and took the back road leading to the road east of the hangar, B-3.

Diane held out her hand. "Doug, will you phone me the minute you get back from Glenemma?"

Douglas leaned outside the open rear window and kissed her. "I don't know how I'm going to do it, but I'll phone you before I get back."

That night, the Musketeers didn't say too much to each other during supper and the movie. Their many wonderful memories of the magic of Okanagan Lake, kept them preoccupied.

"What was that?" asked Moose, coming out of his trance. The Seaforth cadet had grabbed him by the arm, as the trucks sped towards Glenemma.

"I said, how did your weekend go?"

"Good, really good. What happened at camp?"

The Scottish cadet grinned. "You mean what didn't happen. Just take a look at MacTavish and that should tell you how it went."

Moose glanced at the pale MacTavish sitting next to the cab. It was obvious he didn't know where he was, and the three other Canadian Scottish cadets around him appeared just as sick.

"My God, they look horrible. They've suffered all that just from kicking me in the nuts?"

"All of them have had the constant shits since they came back from the MIR. It must be a reaction to the medicine they received for their toes. MacTavish shit himself twice on parade this morning and I'll betcha he needs a dump right this minute."

"Are they still taking the prescription?" asked Rothstein.

"Yeah, apparently if they don't, infection could set in. They've been warned to take it every four hours."

Moose laughed out loud. "HEY, MACTAVISH! THAT'LL TEACH YOU TO KICK ME IN THE NUTS!"

A gray-faced cadet glanced at Moose for only a fraction of a second before he grimaced again, stood up, tightened his buttocks and held on to the seat of his pants.

The scenic ride to Glenemma was full of song as the exhilarated cadets of Bravo Company belted out...!

'Aye Seaforths Aye, triumphant we're bound; the battle is won on the enemy's ground; Jerry says we're from hell, and he isn't wrong; his blood we have shed to keep Canada strong.

'Aye Seaforths Aye, forge front from your trench, and carry our flag over enemy stench; our guns blaze with glory, our badge glows with fame; each man shares the honour - our regiment's name.'

Other ditties followed, such as, OH PROVOST, OH PROVOST; OLD KING COLE; THE NORTH ATLANTIC SQUADRON; THE QUARTERMASTER'S STORES; LULU; QUEEN FARINA; SHE WENT INTO THE WATER; THE PARA-CHUTIST'S SONG; and THE C SCOT Rs HAVE GOT THE SCARS...!

When Moose sang the latter, he always changed the words. "The C Scot Rs may have the scars, but the Dukes have all the women."

Turning off the highway onto a dusty, climbing, winding, tree-lined road, Wayne started up a chorus of, 'WE COME FROM THE WEST BY THE SEA!'

Soon, even non-BCRs were singing it, except of course, MacTavish and his friends. All four were now standing, and the incessant bouncing made their trip pure agony.

'We come from the west by the sea; and a mighty battalion are we; we will add more fame to our glorious name and the province of old B.C.'

'We're the Duke of Connaught's, and we're damn good shots, and we're out to help the Tommy beat the Hun; and while we're over there, you bet we'll do our share, and we'll stay in the battle, 'till it's won, won, won!

'Every morn, we hear reveille blowing; we are one day closer to the foe; they must fall, but we will always be; the Duke of Connaught's from old B.C.'

When the three-tons broke out into the open and continued north along the western boundary of the flatlands of Glenemma, the *vocalizing* stopped because all their lungs were full of dust. Not just lungs, every part of their bodies. It was impossible to see beyond two feet and the drivers really had to be 'on their toes,' to refrain from hitting the trucks ahead of them.

Finally, they stopped at the near-northern wooded area, and the 'Desert Rats' of Bravo Company unloaded.

The Company's Sergeant-Major could be heard, but not seen. "RIGHT! MOVE AWAY FROM THE VEHICLES AND MAKE CERTAIN YOU'VE GOT ALL YOUR GEAR! FORM UP IN YOUR PLATOONS! QUICKLY NOW, QUICKLY!"

When the vehicles left, more dust hung in persistently hovering clouds.

"NOW, PAY ATTENTION HERE! QUICKLY AND WITHOUT PANIC, I WANT YOU TO BREAK INTO YOUR SECTIONS AND FOLLOW YOUR SEC-TION CORPORALS TO YOUR BIVOUAC AREA. THE TIME IS NOW...TEN-HUNDRED HOURS. FOLLOW THEIR INSTRUCTIONS AND BE WASHED UP FOR LUNCH AT NOON! CARRY ON!"

As the weighted-down Bravo cadets dispersed, fifty yards away, two very clean and *uncontaminated* Royal Canadian Medical Corps cadets sat in a field ambulance under the shade of a large pine tree. They had arrived earlier with the advance party and even their boots remained shiny.

"Jonathan, old sock, just look at those four distressed individuals racing in the direction of the tree line. Why they're actually going the wrong way, old fellow."

His friend chuckled. "I have no pity for them, James, old rod. Moreover, it's quite apparent they do not have any lavatory tissue-paper with them."

"Nevertheless, are we still volunteering to join the other *servers* at lunch today, James, old cock?"

"Jonathan, old stick, it's for a good cause. If we didn't, we wouldn't get the other four Seaforths and Calgary Highlander bastards, would we? Now let me demonstrate Nurse Helen's famous method of wrapping dressings. First, you...!"

Bravo Company had been assigned three large treed areas in the centre of the northern end of the flatlands of Glenemma. Although these tracts of land had been used by cadets many times before, one year's grace erased nearly all signs of earlier usage. Previously marked fouled ground sites still remained, however, and Major Kare's instructions insisted that they would be used again. His directions also made it quite plain that when the cadets made up their hootchies, they would not cut any live trees.

The Musketeers would find Glenemma different this year, because they wouldn't be together in pairs, or in threes. Instead, each Alpha Company *Corporal* would stay with his section of cadets. Still, they weren't that far apart, Douglas thought. Six Platoon, with East, Cunningham, Simon and Danyluk were only about sixty metres away.

Although Bravo's cadets had received lectures in Area Ten on how to make hootchies, etc., each section corporal covered the fine points again before dispatch-ing pairs of *Desert Rats* to start building.

Luckily, Five Platoon was close to the water trailer, or water truck, whichever vehicle was being used. This privilege did not come without responsibility, how-ever, because when the members of the platoon finished making their hootchies, they had to build wash basin stands. Also, during the lectures in camp, a cadet by the name of Glover had suggested that since they were in the *field* for a week, it would be nice to have showers. To comply with his request, Five Platoon scrounged old garbage cans, put holes in the bottom, and hung them from trees. Hoses were then attached to a one-spout garbage can which was kept higher and filled by hand.

As was the same every year, the cadets thought Glenemma was the cat's meow. This was their break from the rigourous standards demanded in Camp. Sure, they had to keep their hootchies maintained, and their areas had to be kept clean, but there would be no spit-polishing, shining, ironing, and the like. Lights out was a thing of the past; after all, who could turn off the moon and stars? They knew that Sergeants could do anything, but drew the line with that action.

"That is absolutely unique," Douglas said, as he praised two cadets who had built a hootchie with a hanging, swinging roof. The roof was attached to ropes and if the weather was good, it could be swung to the side and not used. If it rained, or there was heavy dew, the roof more than covered the cadets' blankets and ground sheets. Also, instead of any sort of frame, they had simply dug a sump (ditch) around the perimeter of their bed space.

"Thank you, Corporal," replied a smiling Cadet Archer. "We thought we'd rather see the stars through the branches of the trees, than stare at the top of a poncho."

Other cadets also liked the idea, and soon, additional winning architectural *domiciles* were erected.

When they were finished their chores, Douglas' section washed their bodies from the waist up and took off their boots, puttees, long pants, and khaki shirts. They changed into clean socks, running shoes, T-shirts, and khaki shorts. Pith-helmets weren't worn in Glenemma, just regimental headdress.

Although it was sweltering within the treed area, it was at least ten degrees hotter outside, and their T-shirts would keep off the bugs and the burning sun.

"Look at the bloody blisters on my hands," Chandler said, holding his hands out so his friends Mellish and Drinkwater could see. The three of them had been assigned earlier to help build the platoon's 'thrones' and urinal ditches. Remembering an experience in 1953, Douglas planned their location and ensured they were built well away from any of the section areas and walking routes which undoubtedly would be travelled by General Kitching or other dignitaries.

"Those shitters will last a lifetime," quipped Mellish, proud of himself for a job well done.

Drinkwater was eager to get *his* words out. "I just got back from takin' a look at Six Platoon's shitters. Corporal Danyluk must think he's at Buckingham Palace. We've just got logs, but they've built twelve seats and they've wrapped burlap around them. They also got top marks from the medical corporals who are making their rounds."

No sooner had Drinkwater finished, two Alpha medical-types entered Five Platoon's area, carrying a folding military stretcher and a first-aid kit. In seconds, they called Brice, Banks, Rothstein, and Jackson to a meeting. James started the conversation.

"I say, where the devil is your platoon's first-aid station?"

"If you'd bothered to look, it's in the centre of our area," replied Wayne.

James ticked off a box on a piece of paper attached to his clipboard. "Show us; we're going to leave this equipment there!"

Upon reviewing the small clearing, both *doctors* grunted approval. "Yes, I'd say this is quite adequate. You have an undeviating vehicle route progressing suitably into it, and it is removed from your lavatories and habitable areas. What do you think, Jonathan?"

Jonathan nodded. "Rather disparaging. I favour voluminous burnished regions, however, it will do. At least it's equidistant, which is one propitious thing. Tell me, chaps, where in Hades are these disgusting, nasty little flies coming from?"

Rothstein grinned. "Have you been visiting Seven Platoon's area?"

"Yes, old fellow, we've just come from there."

"Well, *old chappie*, you've just brought them with you."

Jonathan gave Rothstein a loathsome glance. "Now show us your body-waste facilities."

After a few moments, both *experts* reviewed the 'trenches' and ticked off other boxes on their clipboards.

James inspected the ditches thoroughly. "Yes, utterly sufficient, but barren of epidermis."

Earl couldn't stand these previously described, "two creeps."

"What the hell do you mean, 'barren of epidermis?'"

James cocked his head and arrogantly put his hand on his hip. "My good man, you obviously haven't analyzed the elegant job Six Platoon has accomplished with their amenity benches?"

"Yes, homogeneous quality and thoroughly commodious. They've applied sacking, which permits one's derriere to breathe. They're so well constructed, we've decided to bivouac with them." added Jonathan.

Earl couldn't take them any longer. "Listen, you pongoes, what the hell are you talking about? When I take a dump, I certainly don't consider the fact that my ass can breathe. If anything, I want to get out of there in a hellava hurry, so I won't choke. Now tick that off on your clipboard, and take a hike! That means, bugger off!"

Jonathan's face turned red. "Well, I never...! We have yet to inspect the wash basin platforms."

Earl turned Jonathan around and pushed him with his boot against his rear end.

"They're in THAT direction, and they won't allow your armpits to breathe either. Now, bug off!"

About twenty paces away, James turned towards Jonathan, who was writing something down. "That uncivilized creature. Such nerve? Let's add him to our list, shall we?"

His friend smiled fiendishly, "He's already added, old knob."

When Douglas completed inspecting his section's hootchies, he was pleased. As instructed, the cadets had used waste branches to build A-frame structures. Boughs of evergreens with ponchos wrapped around them were used as mattresses, and all covering ponchos or ground sheets were overlapped to ensure there would be no leakage in case it rained. Some cadets had used string to form tables and even coat racks. Many ingenious ideas had come into play, and Brice liked that. The cadets were thinking and leading, rather than following.

While their cadets rested, and with half-an-hour until lunch time, the four Musketeers of Five Platoon headed over to Six Platoon's area.

"Come to see how the better half lives, have you?" quipped Moose He was carving a toilet roll holder, which would be placed near his *special* throne.

Actually, Six Platoon's layout was good. It was obvious, just by looking at the other areas, which *Corporals* had had the benefit of being trained by Sergeants Beckford and Simpson.

"No, we just thought we'd come and see how you made out with those medical-types," Earl replied. "I gave them the boot!"

Moose put his arm around Earl's shoulders. "Ahh, you shouldn't have done that, Earl. To coin a phrase, old knob, you'll never get Brownie points that way. We put up with their strange mannerisms and they gave us top marks."

East appeared out of nowhere, eating a sandwich. He'd overheard the conversation. "Tell 'em the real reason, Moose. Don't bullshit your compatriots."

A guilty expression appeared on Danyluk's face. "Well, O.K., O.K., I'll tell 'em, but first, where'd you get the 'sarnie'?"

East pushed the last of the sandwich into his mouth. "At the messing tent. I smooth-talked a duty cadet into making it for me. He's also making me a plateful for tonight."

Moose just shook his head. "We treated those creeps like normals because of, Zaholuk here...!" He pointed at Gordie. "Moneybags asked them if they enjoyed a game of stuke now and then, and both of the jumped at the chance. You should have heard them.

'OH, JAMES, HAVE YOU STILL GOT THAT TWENTY-DOLLAR BILL RESERVED IN YOUR STOCKING, OLD STICK?'

'MOST DEFINITELY, OLD STUMP, SHOULD WE PARTAKE IN A GAME OF CHANCE THIS EVENING? ZAHOLUK, YOU APPEAR TO BE AN HONEST FELLOW, DO YOU RUN A STRAIGHT GAME?'"

"Needless to say, when Gordie heard that, his eyes lit up, he came in his pants, and started unwinding the burlap faster. 'The straightest in camp, and if you *doctors* set up your hootchie here, I'll let you use my personal shitter,' he said to them."

Cunningham didn't care for the ribbing. "COME OFF IT, MOOSE, YOU WANT SOME OF THEIR BREAD, AS WELL. I PERSONALLY CAN'T STAND THEM, BUT WHEN IT COMES DOWN TO THE NITTY-GRITTY, MOOLAH IS MOOLAH? RIGHT JACK?"

Jack took a chicken leg out of his pants pocket. "Don't ask *me* that question. If I'd had my way, they'd have walked away bowlegged after receiving a size-eleven boot up each ass. Anyway, we did the next best thing."

"What's that?" Wayne asked.

"Danyluk gave 'em the best spot in the world to build their hootchie. Right next to Mancinelli."

Douglas laughed out loud. "I'd forgotten about him. Isn't he the guy with the smelly feet?"

Moose had his sneaky grin on his face. "That's him. He had a whole clearing to himself and looked a little lonely. After the medics set up their hootchie, I noticed Mancinelli had built his on a slope, so I asked him to move it closer to theirs. His entrance, where his feet will be, is only about three feet from the back of their hootchie, where their heads will be."

The sound of a hand-driven siren interrupted their laughter. "COME AND GET IT!"

When the Musketeers arrived at the mess tent, combination tools and mess-tins in hand, the lineup was long and winding. Twelve cadets had *volunteered* to dish out the food, and they were being assisted by two Alpha Company medical orderlies.

This appeared odd to Douglas, because it wasn't necessary for them to help out.

For some reason, Lord knows what, something clicked in Douglas Brice's mind. He whispered into Wayne's ear and after watching the servers for a moment, Wayne nodded and whispered back. Then he called Earl over.

"Earl, don't eat a hot meal for lunch. Just eat the sandwiches which are already made."

At first, Earl didn't know what to think, but Wayne's head motion, pointing out the two smiling medics, quickly convinced him. "Thanks pal, I think I'll do just that."

Then Douglas called over Cadet Mellish. "Mellish, will you do me a favour, please?"

"Sure, Corporal."

Douglas muttered something into Mellish's ear. The boy smiled. "O.K., Corporal, you can count on me."

With that done, Douglas and Wayne headed over to Seven and Eight Platoon's lines to have a *talk* with MacTavish and his *friends*.

It wasn't hard finding the four. They were allowing their derrieres to 'breathe' over the 'body waste' trenches.

After a fifteen-minute discussion, four seething Scottish cadets were out for blood.

"No, we're going to play the game their way," said Douglas. "Just stop taking the stuff they gave you in the MIR, and let them think you're still sick. We'll know if I'm right in about an hour, when..." He stopped talking for a second. "How many more of you helped throw them in the showers?"

"Four others," MacTavish replied.

"Well, it's a shame to see four others go through what you've been through, but at least we'll know if my hunch is correct. Also, don't say anything to them, we'll clue them in later. That's imperative...O.K.?"

For the first time in three days, smiles appeared on four ashen faces. If the truth be known, four *breathless* and red raw derrieres were probably grinning as well.

"ALL RIGHT, WE'VE COVERED THIS MANY TIMES BUT WE'RE GOING TO COVER IT ONE MORE TIME." Wayne drew a vertical line on the blackboard. All of Five Platoon's cadets sat around in a semi-circle attending his lecture on map using. The tree's green-branch umbrella kept the ferocity of the sun's rays out of the classroom area.

"LET'S SAY THIS IS A NORTH-SOUTH GRID LINE. ANY NORTH-SOUTH GRID LINE, ON ANY MAP. WHAT IS IT?"

"A NORTH-SOUTH GRID LINE!" the cadets replied.

"RIGHT! NOW I'M GOING TO GO APPROXIMATELY TWENTY DEGREES TO THE EAST (right side) AND DRAW ANOTHER LINE ON A SMALL ANGLE!" Wayne drew another line approximately the same size, and it connected with his original line, at the bottom. "FOR SIMPLICITY'S SAKE, LET'S CALL THIS A MAGNETIC, NORTH-SOUTH LINE. NOW, I'M GOING TO GO FURTHER EAST (right side) AND DRAW ANOTHER LINE AT AN ANGLE OF 170 DEGREES FROM THE GRID LINE. WE'LL CALL THIS, ONCE AGAIN FOR SIMPLICITY'S SAKE, THE BEARING LINE. NOT GRID, NOT MAGNETIC, JUST THE BEARING LINE." Wayne then drew a line from the end of the other two, down towards the bottom of the blackboard. This line was almost vertical, but naturally it ended ten degrees east of the grid line.

"O.K., PAY ATTENTION HERE! ALL BEARINGS ARE MEASURED CLOCKWISE FROM A FIXED POINT! DO YOU UNDERSTAND THAT? YOU MUST HAVE A FIXED POINT, THEN YOU MEASURE YOUR BEARING CLOCKWISE?"

All faces stared at him, indicating they understood.

"GOOD! NOW WATCH WHAT I'M GOING TO DO!" Wayne put his chalk halfway up the original gridline and drew a circular line, ending at the bearing line. He then went a little higher, and on the magnetic line drew another circular line ending on the bearing line.

"NOW, TAKE A GOOD LOOK AT THE TWO CIRCULAR LINES I'VE JUST DRAWN. IN YOUR HUMBLE OPINION, WHICH LINE IS THE LONGEST?" When he threw out the 'overhead' question to his class, a large number of hands went up.

"SYMINGTON?"

"The circular line from the grid line to the bearing line, Corporal."

"RIGHT! EXCELLENT. NOW I'VE ALREADY GIVEN YOU THE ANSWER, WHAT IS THE BEARING OF THE BEARING LINE FROM THE *FIXED POINT* OF THE GRID LINE?"

He glanced around. "AITKEN?"

"A hundred-and-seventy degrees, Corporal."

"PERFECT! THAT'S ABSOLUTELY RIGHT!" He looked around again. "WHICH CIRCULAR LINE IS THE SHORTEST? CISECKI?"

"The circular line from the magnetic line to the bearing line, Corporal."

Wayne smiled. "HEY, I SHOULDN'T BE UP HERE, YOU GUYS SHOULD BE! CORRECT, CISECKI, CORRECT! SO, WHAT IS THE BEARING LINE FROM THE FIXED POINT OF THE MAGNETIC LINE? ANDERSON?"

"One hundred-and-fifty degrees, Corporal."

Banks put down his chalk and held his hands to the sky. A GENIUS, THAT'S WHAT YOU ARE...A NATURAL BORN GENIUS! ABSOLUTELY CORRECT! SO YOU SEE, GENTLEMEN, WITHOUT TAKING THE ANNUAL CHANGE INTO CONSIDERATION, YOU NOW KNOW HOW TO CONVERT MAG-NETIC BEARINGS TO GRID, AND GRID BEARINGS TO MAGNETIC. THE SECRET IS THE FIXED POINT! ARE THERE ANY QUESTIONS?"

There were a few questions, but none were of a misunderstanding nature. Wayne answered them, and for the next hour, Five Platoon's cadets worked in teams, converting bearings from a paper-exercise Wayne had devised and handed out.

At the same time as Wayne assisted his cadets, Corporal Rae of the Calgary Highlanders was giving a lecture to Eight Platoon.

"SO, IF WE HAVE A WIND BLOWING FROM THE NORTH AND WE LIGHT A FIRE KNOWING FULL WELL THAT THE ENEMY IS TO OUR SOUTH, IS THAT WISE?" He checked the eager faces. "DEANE?"

"If the enemy all had colds, it really wouldn't matter, Corporal."

All of Eight Platoon's cadets chuckled, for that matter so did Corporal Rae, but only for a moment. The seconds following that moment were a lifetime for the good Corporal because, after letting out a tumultuous, obnoxious fart, he immediately messed his pants and all of his cadets knew it. They were sitting north experiencing a slight southern breeze.

(Author's note: For the benefit of you readers of the air force persuasion, messing his pants simply means he shit himself. You naval types might have difficulty with the word, 'fart.' The Concise Oxford Dictionary describes *fart* as follows: emit wind from anus; fool about or around; emission of wind from anus; contemptible person.)

Amidst howls of laughter, a stiff-legged, red-faced, and humiliated Corporal Rae left the lecture area as best he could. After cleaning up a mess, he, too, joined his friends, all three of them, at the wooden *breathing* apparatus. Needless to say, the status of lectures in Seven and Eight Platoons was, 'Gone With The Wind!'

Douglas, in the meantime, had asked Wayne to release Mellish for a minute, and he questioned the lad.

"How'd it go?"

"Pretty good, Corporal. I kept my eye on them as you asked me to, and they put some sort of a white powder on certain Scottish Corporals' food. Not very much, just a sprinkle. They also whispered to each other when they saw Corporal Jackson eating sandwiches. It was almost as if they wanted him to eat a meal, instead."

"Thanks, Mellish, that's great. What kind of containers did they use to dispense the powder?"

"Er, let me think. They took 'em out of their pockets, and...they were yellow. Yeah, that's it...they were small yellow glass bottles."

"Mellish, I owe ya one. Thanks a lot. Please keep this to yourself, all right?"

"My lips are sealed, Corporal. I wouldn't even tell my wife, if I had one."

Douglas laughed. "You mean you're not married yet?"

"Naa, I'm not gonna consider it until I'm at least fifteen."

After Mellish had gone back to the map using exercises, Douglas Brice went to his hootchie, took off his boots, lay back with his arms behind his head and smiled. "O.K., you Royal Canadian Medical Corps villains, we've gotcha!"

In the meantime, the two first-aiders were resting in their ambulance, awaiting a visit from four Scottish cadets. When they didn't appear, the duo walked over to Seven and Eight Platoons' lines. Surprisingly, lectures were continuing and the four Scottish cadets were actually smiling whilst they were instructing. That is, smiling on the outside. Only they knew of the agony their bowels had been subjected to, and the torment of humiliation they had suffered on the inside.

The wide-eyed duo walked back to their vehicle, totally puzzled. "Jonathan, old rag, what the hell did we do wrong? Are you certain we gave them enough?"

"Absolutely James, old prod, I'm trying to figure it out myself. The only hypothesis I can present, is that it's too hot here, therefore, we must give them more than the regular dosage."

"Jonathan, how much *remedy* do we have left, old stick?"

"Oh, we have sufficient, my good fellow, but I don't believe we should volunteer to serve at supper. It would be too conspicuous. Let's give them twice as much *treatment* at breakfast, that way we'll also get that Jackson asshole."

James chuckled. "Isn't life wonderful, old knob?"

His friend replied. "Ah, yes, especially when we're having fun. Now, my old worn-out flask, let me show you how we can cheat on this Zaholuk deadbeat."

That afternoon, while Seven and Eight Platoons were practising Advance to Contact methods in the lower flatlands of Glenemma, Five and Six Platoons endured a very serious map and compass exercise encircling the total perimeter of the training area.

As usual, the cadets were working in sections and after each leg of performance, the section leader changed. Every cadet had a map board, a map, a prismatic compass, and a protractor. A great amount of walking was involved, along with some very precise map using. Needless to say, the sun didn't allow compromise because Glenemma's temperature went well over the hundred mark. Nevertheless, spirits were up.

"Jesus, what I wouldn't give to just jump in that lake," a tired and sweating Cadet Eldridge muttered to his friend Cadet Ryeberg, as their separated section reviewed Round Lake from a high position on a nearby hill.

"Jump in it?" his companion asked as he took off his beret and wiped his brow. "All I want to do is stand on the shore and drink it dry. Anyway, let's quit dreamin', 'cause we can't. From this position, we've got to measure a bearing to the centre of the lake, draw a line through it on our maps, and connect it to a conventional sign on the other side."

The two boys used their compasses and from their known position on their maps, converted their magnetic bearing to grid, and drew lines. Other cadets not too far away did exactly the same thing.

Both of them were right on. Eldridge took off his glasses and wiped his eyes. "It's that building on the other side of the lake. That's our next checkpoint."

Ryeberg agreed. "Do you think they'd mind us walking through the lake?"

Eldridge grinned as both cadets stood up and started walking. "I hope you've got your 'Jesus sandals' on, the map says it's deep."

As they neared the lake to walk around it, they heard giggling, yelling, and splashing. Squatting behind a bush, they couldn't believe their eyes. Two bare, teenage Native girls were having the time of their lives in the cool blue water.

"Christ, check out the bazookas on the cute one," whispered Ryeberg, his eyes as wide as saucers. "How much time are we ahead of the others?"

Eldridge gave him a coy glance. "You wouldn't? Er, I mean...we could get in shit! We're fifteen minutes ahead of them."

Ryeberg didn't miss a blink, quickly taking off his boots and socks. "Remember what the Corporal said in that leadership lecture? 'Make a decision and carry it through.' Well, I've made a decision and I'm gonna carry it through!'"

"Gotcha," replied an excited Eldridge, tugging at his boots. "My dad never told me it was gonna be like this."

In the split second it took the boys to reach the lake, they were tripping on khaki shorts and underwear trying to take them off. Ryeberg announced their presence.

"YOO HOO, GIRLS! MAKE WAY FOR A BCR AND A SEAFORTH! HE MAY BE HARMLESS, BUT I'M NOT!"

The embarrassed girls immediately ducked under water, but not for long. One grinning bashful *swimmer* popped her head out and said, "Hey you've still got your watch on."

"PICKY, PICKY..." a naked Ryeberg replied, swimming towards them.

Ten minutes later they were out, dressed, and on their way, waving. Not one of the other cadets in the section had seen them. Also, none of the others had made a similar decision because the girls had also left.

"Jeez, they're cute. Ya know, I kinda like the bit about making a decision and carrying it through?" said Ryeberg.

"Yep, those leadership people really know what they're talkin' about. Say, do ya really think they'll meet us later?"

"YOU BET!" said his grinning, rejuvenated friend. They're spending some time in that log cabin at the north end of Glenemma. Now don't forget what we told 'em. I'm Corporal Danyluk, and you're Corporal Cunningham. AIN'T LIFE GREAT IF YA FOLLOW THE RULES?"

"IT COULDN'T BE BETTER!" replied a restored Cadet Eldridge, buckling up his belt.

When training ceased at 1730 hours that afternoon, the sweat-soaked cadets of Bravo Company attacked the water vehicle and *showers* with vigour second to none. Before changing into clean clothes and resting in their hootchies, each of them had the opportunity of buying an ice-cold Kik Kola from the visiting pop truck.

A good amount of training had been completed this day, and Major Kare, as well as his officers and NCOs, were impressed with the professionalism of the Alpha Company cadets.

As the Company O.C. and his staff were discussing course reports, another debate was taking place in Five Platoon's first-aid clearing. All of Alpha's Corporals, sans two medical-types, were sitting in a semi-circle, deliberately keeping their voices low.

MacTavish finally had colour in his cheeks. "Thanks, Doug. We're actually back to normal."

"Yeah, but *we're* not, you creeps," stated Corporal Rae. "Why didn't you warn the eight of us before you allowed those pongoes to *doctor* up our meals?"

"Dave, we couldn't," replied Wayne. "We were only working on Doug's hunch. We know it's a bugger what you went through, but there was nothing we could do."

Rae finally calmed down. "Jesus, that's embarrassing. We've shit ourselves so many times, our platoon's run out of asswipe..." He laughed. "...not to mention the fact that when cadets needed to have a crap, *we...*" he pointed to himself and three of his compatriots, "...were always sittin' there. The same thing must have been happening in the other platoon. One cadet said to me, 'You, again, Corporal? You're supposed to throw up your food, if ya don't want the calories.'"

Laughter was muffled as the meeting progressed. In fifteen minutes, it was finished, but only after an orderly plot had been agreed upon.

That afternoon, all cadets, officers and NCOs welcomed the sound of the food siren, along with the shout, "COME AND GET IT!"

"HEY, CORPORAL ROTHSTEIN, WHAT'S FOR SUPPER?" bellowed Moose. Rothstein and Jackson had decided to assist the *volunteers* serve up supper.

Moose, like all of the other staff members was at the end of the line, waiting for the cadets to go through. The medical-types were at the end also, and as far as they were concerned, everything was normal because now eight Scottish cadets weren't present. Actually, MacTavish and his chums had attended an earlier sitting, and went unnoticed. Part of the plan was to keep the *doctors* thinking MacTavish and his three friends were still taking the *prescription*.

"IT'S VEGETABLE SOUP, BEEF STEW, MASHED POTATOES, CORN ON

THE COB, AND PEAS!" replied Rothstein. "THE SECOND CHOICE IS SLICED CHICKEN, MASHED POTATOES, AND GRAVY. YOU CAN ALSO HAVE SANDWICHES, IF YOU WANT!"

Moose acknowledged his friend with a nod. "GOOD GRUB! "IT'S BETTER HERE THAN IN CAMP!"

When Rothstein and Jackson ate, they moseyed over to Douglas and handed him a small amount of flour mixed with salt, wrapped in waxed paper.

About an hour after dinner, the Alpha Corporals were called to an 'O' group (orders meeting) to discuss the day's activities, to receive further instructions, and to get problems off their chests. Just before it was finished, Douglas made a point of suggesting a swim parade at Round Lake. For some reason, the thought hadn't crossed Major Kare's mind.

"Well, we know the water's clean because other companies have used it before us, but we haven't got any life guards with us."

"Usually, the staff acts as lifeguards, sir. There's an old rowboat on the shore that the Native people allow us to use. Also, cadets must use the buddy system."

Major Kare gave the suggestion some thought. "All right, Corporal Brice, but I want all staff cadets to be alert. You can go in the water, but your job is to keep your eyes open. Also, I want a limit set as to how far cadets can swim out, and I want the boat at that boundary. I think the lads deserve a swim. While you're swimming, my officers and NCOs will plan tomorrow's exercises. Oh, I also forgot to mention...has there been a problem with some staff cadets in Seven and Eight Platoons?"

MacTavish supplied the answer. "Sir, some of us must have caught a little stomach flu, but it seems to be over now."

The officer smiled. "Very good. I'm glad to see you pulled through O.K. Are there any questions? Oh, before I forget, I think we're very fortunate to have two highly qualified first-aid cadets with us. Have you people met Corporals Jonathan Hall and James Watt? Of course you have, they're Alpha cadets, aren't they? Well, they are doing a fine job. At this moment, they're checking the cadets' feet for blisters."

Following the meeting, when the cadets of Bravo Company learned that they were going swimming, cries of jubilation were heard throughout the bivouac areas. Even the *doctors* were happy.

"I say, James, old prong, let's join these dispossessed beasts for a dip, eh what? I'd like you to wash off your feet."

"A good idea, Jonathan, old whacker. Yes, *your* feet as well. But I understand they're going in unclothed. Don't you think that's a little audacious? Also, I'm not too certain if the water isn't a little suspect." He chuckled. "Don't want to drink it and end up like MacTavish and his cohorts, do we?"

Jonathan was taken aback. "Bloody hell, James. Did you say unclothed? You mean to tell me they're going to swim naked, bare, nude, stripped, exposed? My God, old sock, this is the Twentieth Century, just how unrefined are these dolts? The only person who's going to review this perfect body is my future wife, and I'm not certain who that's going to be. I may not even show it to *her*. She may faint from the wonder of it all."

"Yes, I know what you mean, Jonathan, these *people* are animals. Listen, old dong, just by luck I happened to have brought along two pairs of polka dot under garments. Let's wear those, shall we?"

"Bloody true!" his friend replied.

While James and Jonathan talked about their swimming attire, four singing platoons of happy cadets made the trek from their lines to Round Lake. Most of them were just wearing Khaki shorts and running shoes. No underwear, no socks, no shirts, and no headdress. Even towels weren't really necessary, because it was still stifling hot; their bodies would dry in seconds upon leaving the water.

On the shore, Douglas explained the rules. While doing so, the other staff cadets dispersed themselves in the lake, and Jack East and Harvey Rothstein took the boat out to the swimming limit.

Still in three ranks, Douglas told them to leave their clothes on the ground exactly where they were standing. That way, when everyone was out, they would know if someone was missing.

"YOU'VE EARNED THIS...GET IN THERE!"

Brice had his back to the lake and was nearly trampled by the hoard of high-spirited naked bodies rushing by. He hadn't yet undressed, and whether he liked it or not, his section took him in with them. Two minutes later he spread his clothes out to dry on the nearby bushes and went back in.

Normally calm, the water of Round Lake surged like the agitation piranhas create when they attack an animal. Cadets jumped, dived, got tossed, walked on their hands, rode their buddies as horses, raced each other, and generally had the time of their lives. Their voices reverberated through the nearby hills and anyone listening to a recording of them would have been envious of the fun they were having.

"Christ, just get a load of that," Danyluk murmured, upon seeing James and Jonathan walk towards the water's edge in their *costumes*. One wore red polka dots, and the other, green and blue.

"They live in their own little world," Douglas replied. A second later, he had a chat with Cadet Mellish.

Mellish's eager grin opened wider and wider. "Sure thing, Corporal, I think it'll take about twenty of us."

"That's another one I owe you, Mellish. And remember, no one put you up to it?"

"HEY, THIS IS GOING TO BE A PLEASURE, CORPORAL!"

Five minutes later, while James and Jonathan were standing up to their chests discussing Nurse Helen's method of applying dressings, they were grabbed, stripped of their polka dots, and tossed in over their heads. Both could swim pretty well, so that wasn't a problem. At the start, however, when they were being held up to have their shorts removed, they fought and screamed fiercely, but to no avail.

"I say, Jonathan, old sweat, dressings aside, this is just what the doctor ordered. Why we...WHAT THE...WHAT THE BLOODY HELL DO YOU PEOPLE THINK YOU'RE DOING? PUT ME DOWN, YOU'RE TOUCHING A MEMBER OF THE CAMP HOSPITAL STAFF!"

"YES, GET YOUR FILTHY LITTLE PAWS OFF MY GARMENT, YOU PEONS! DO YOU REALIZE I WON THE FIRST PRIZE FOR APPLIED DRESSINGS?"

It was impossible for them to protect themselves because half the cadets in the company were now involved in the action.

"THIS IS DOWNRIGHT... MY GOD, JAMES, THEY'RE RIPPING OFF MY UNDERSHORTS. GET YOUR GRUBBY LITTLE FINGERS OFF MY TESTI-

CLES, YOU FILTHY BEASTS! JUST BUGGER OFF! DO YOU KNOW WHO I AM? I'M CORPORAL HALL OF HER MAJESTY'S ROYAL CANADIAN MEDICAL CORPS!"

"YES, AND I'LL HAVE YOU KNOW, I SERVE WITH HIM. THIS MAY EFFECT MY RESEARCH PAPER ON WART OINTMENT. AGHHH, WHICH ONE OF YOU LITTLE BASTARDS SCRATCHED MY RIGHT BUTTOCK WHEN YOU RIPPED OFF MY SHORTS? MY GOD, JONATHAN, THIS IS UTTERLY DEBASING! YOU! YOU, THERE, REINDEER OR WHATEVER YOUR NAME IS! STOP THEM THIS MINUTE!"

"I THINK HIS NAME IS MUSK OX OR WATER BUFFALO OR SOMETHING LIKE THAT. HE WON'T HELP, IT TAKES HIM AN HOUR JUST TO WASH HIS FORESKIN. MY REGISTERED-NURSE FATHER WILL HEAR OF THIS. HE DEVELOPED THE HALL METHOD OF CUTTING OUT INGROWN TOENAILS! ALSO, MY MOTHER'S A MEMBER OF THE INDEPENDENT ORDER OF THE DAUGHTERS OF THE EMPIRE! JAMES, WHAT WILL MY FUTURE WIFE SAY ON OUR WEDDING NIGHT WHEN SHE FINDS OUT I'VE BEEN STRIPPED BEFORE?"

"WELL, THIS ISN'T EXACTLY THE FIRST TIME, JONATHAN, IT'S THE THIRD BLOODY TIME. I'M STARTING TO FEEL LIKE A DAMN MANNEQUIN!"

Throughout the event, all other staff cadets kept straight faces and looked the other way.

An hour later, when the happy, singing company got dressed and headed back to their lines, two unhappy *mannequins* got out of the water to find their towels had disappeared as well as their shorts.

At nine o'clock when it was getting dark, permission was received for the cadets to light a small fire. They didn't do it for warmth, it was lit more for the sake of providing a medium to day-dream by, or just to get lost in the glow of the flames.

Slowly but surely, cadets eating sandwiches and drinking cocoa sat around the fire singing songs. The same songs that all cadets sing - the same songs they all *should* sing. (Author's note: The same songs certain officers deny that cadets sing.)

At ten o'clock, with yawns and stretches, flashlight beams crossed the barren plains of Glenemma. Some made patterns, others disappeared into the distance as the cadets of Bravo Company went to their hootchies for a well deserved night of rest.

After the cadets had retired, Major Kare came over to Douglas. "I hear the swim parade went very well."

"Yes, sir. It was what they all needed. Thank you, sir."

"Don't thank me, Corporal Brice...thank you. We'll let them do that more often. Say, how do you find those two medical-types? Do they seem normal to you?"

Douglas shrugged. "Normal? Well, er, we haven't given it much thought, sir. Why?"

"Well, when I was driving back from camp this evening, the two of them were walking naked on the upper road. Rather odd to be walking around naked, isn't it?"

Moose wanted to burst out laughing, but he held it back. "Er, they're medical personnel, sir. Apparently, er, one of their fathers is a registered male nurse."

Major Kare didn't quite know what to make of Danyluk's response. "Really?

That's nice, but why do they walk around naked, cupping themselves? Are they afraid of flies touching their private parts?"

It was Rothstein who made everyone burst out howling. "Sir, were they cupping their front with two hands or one?"

"Two hands, Corporal Rothstein."

"Then their rear-ends were uncovered, sir?"

Yes, why?"

"Then they shouldn't have had any problems with flies on their front, sir."

That night, as instructed, Gordie insisted on playing the game in his hootchie, rather than the *doctors'* abode. It wasn't an easy task, but showing them a wad of bills quickly convinced them.

"Besides, I've got more light in my hootchie. I like to see the cards when I'm playing."

Jonathan winked at James. "Oh, all right then, Zaholuk, but we're rather new to this game, you'll have to show us how to play. Is an ace, one or eleven?"

While both grinning cadets motioned to each other, neither one noticed the gas pain on Cunningham's face. When it came down to playing cards for money, Gordie never missed anything - especially sneaky winks.

The card game didn't last very long. In fact it only lasted three-quarters-of-an-hour before two 'cleaned out' medical-types followed their flashlight beams to their area.

"What the hell is the matter with you, James? I told you before, when you had the pot you were to tap my foot twice when you were dealt a face card."

"Jonathan, old shooting stick, I did tap your foot but it didn't seem to make the slightest bit of difference. You've got a nerve talking to me in such a disgusting fashion? It was my twenty, don't you forget that! You now owe me ten dollars!"

"Damn it, Jonathan, we were supposed to take him to the cleaners, not let him put us in the poor house. Bloody hell, we're broke? He really got me upset when he said, 'It's been a business doing pleasure with you two neophytes; come back again.'"

"I just don't understand it, James. That Zaholuk's uncanny; he kept getting twenty one. I wonder if he's ever played that Cunningham cardsharp we've heard about? Now that would be a game to watch?"

"It certainly would be, old handle. Let's get back to dressings...did I tell you the time I..."

While both medics walked back to their lines, Douglas and Wayne met by the ashes of the burnt-out fire, the expressions on their faces indicating the evening was most successful indeed.

"Have you got their stuff?" asked Wayne.

Brice patted his best friend on the back. "I made the switch ideally. Each little yellow container now contains flour and salt." Then he opened up his left palm, revealing some white powder wrapped in waxed paper. "This is the mixture East and Simon will serve to them tomorrow. How about you?"

"A piece of cake," Wayne replied. We should hear the fun anytime now."

Banks didn't know how right he was. Glenemma was really quiet except for the odd cricket calling his mate and a slight breeze feeling the leaves of trees and the coarse *grass*.

The sky was ablaze with stars and shooting stars, but eyes were needed to appreciate them. Shortly, two Alpha cadets would have the scene blocked out for awhile.

"You know, James, old dick, I utterly oppose these outdoor lavatories, the stench is ghastly. It's all so bloody uncivilized, isn't it?"

"Absolutely, old fez, that's why I jumped at the chance to use these burlap-covered seats. Can you imagine what the others are...WHAT WAS THAT?"

"What was what? You're hearing things, old...MY CHRIST, THE LOG'S BREAKING! QUICK, JAMES, GRAB THAT...DON'T GRAB ME YOU IDIOT, GRAB..."

Old fez and old dick never had a chance. Wayne *had* done the *job* perfectly and Jonathan had taken James with him.

"KEEREIST! OH, MY GOD! GET OFF ME, YOU, YOU...AGHGH, I'M COVERED FROM HEAD TO TOE IN HUMAN EXCRETA! OH THE SMELL. I CAN'T SEE! YOU AND YOUR BURLAP-COVERED...GAD, WHERE AM I?"

His friend couldn't speak for a moment, he'd landed face down. After a wipe with his hand, he communicated quite plainly.

"YOU'RE COVERED?" he sputtered. "HELP ME! HELP ME! MY NOSE IS PLUGGED, I CAN'T BREATHE! JAMES, TELL ME I'M DEAD! I'VE GOT TO BE DEAD! I MUST BE IN HELL?"

It took at least two long minutes for the stinking, screaming duo to untangle themselves and crawl out of the *lavatory*. Now the crickets of Glenemma certainly had lots of competition.

Meanwhile down at the beach, four people were having a grand time.

"Hey, Danyluk, any time ya make a decision and carry it through, count me in, will ya? I never thought I'd meet a girl here. Scratch me a little more to the right, please, babe...yeah, that's it."

"I sure will. Do ya remember the other guys at camp sayin' Glenemma was tough? Well, if this is tough, I'll take it anytime. This is like Hawaii. C'mere darlin'! By the way, Cunningham, Ida and I are gonna go to the movies when Glenemma's over. Do you and Melissa wanna come?"

"You bet we do! Just think, we've tried for four weeks to meet dames, and we get to meet 'em here. Ain't life great?"

"You *know* it is. Why, it's almost as great...!" Ryeberg stopped talking and started listening. He thought he'd heard something. "I think I hear some officers coming; we'd better take off. Grab my clothes, will ya please, Ida, my darlin'?"

The bashful girl reached for Ryeberg's clothes. "Sure Danyluk, honey."

As Ryeberg, Eldridge, and the two girls disappeared into the night, two young *officers* entered the lake.

James was most upset. "JUST DON'T TALK TO ME, YOU FOOT-SMELLING ASSHOLE! YOU'RE THE ONE WHO PULLED ME IN! LOOK AT ME...I'VE PROBABLY GOT EVERY DISEASE IN THE BOOK! MY GOD, WHEN I THINK OF IT, I WANT TO THROW UP! I CAN'T GO NEAR THOSE CADETS TOMORROW, I'LL SMELL LIKE SHIT!"

His associate was also incensed. "YOU SMELL LIKE SHIT OR FEET AT THE BEST OF TIMES, YOU INBRED EXCUSE FOR A HUMAN BEING! GAD, EVEN WHEN I EXHALE, I CAN SMELL IT!"

With the girls gone, and the moon lighting their way, Ryeberg and Eldridge took the upper road back to their hootchies.

Ryeberg smiled. "Nah, but from the sound of 'em, they're with Seven and Eight Platoons."

"Jeez, officers are weird, ain't they?"

"Those two are, and they're both right. Their breath does smell like shit. I can smell it from here."

"So can I. Don't they ever think of gargling?"

"Nahh, they're officers, they can do anythin' they want. Why, I'll even betcha they can go for a whole week without changin' their underwear, or havin' a bath or a shower."

"Wow, a whole week? Are you sure?"

"Am I sure? Sure I'm sure! By the smell of those two, they probably haven't brushed their teeth since they arrived in camp!"

"Wow, the lucky bastards."

Douglas Brice opened his eyes and glanced at his watch. It was 0625 and he could hear activity taking place outside around his hootchie. Some cadets were already washed and dressed, talking to their friends about sounds in the night, or just things in general. He placed his hands behind his head and listened. It wasn't their conversation which woke him, it was the air. Since coming to Vernon at the age of fourteen, Douglas cherished the scent of the Okanagan's sweet, fresh morning air. He'd even tried to describe it in letters home, but had found it impossible. The closest he'd come were a few words he'd written to his mother in 1953.

'...therefore I can't describe it. Is it possible God creates it to sit on his porch and read the morning newspaper before he lets his cat in? I'd like to bottle some and send it home, but how can I mix a fragrance so pure as the dew which rides the wind to capture the essence of the trees, the lakes, the flowers, and the sky. Mom, I couldn't even make the bottle which would have to have the fragility of butterfly wings with all the colours of a rainbow.'

Douglas was awakened from his trance by a head popping into his hootchie.

"Good morning, *Corporal* Brice? May I ask what the hell you're still doing in bed? Not that we all wouldn't like to indulge in the same practise, however there's work to be done."

Brice smiled, threw back his blanket, and pulled on his pants. "Wayne, trust you to ruin a beautiful moment. I was trying to think how I could describe the aroma of the morning air."

Banks crawled in and lay next to Douglas. "You wouldn't think it was so wonderful if your hootchie was set up in front of Mancinelli's. I've just come from over there and both *doctors* are accusing the other of having halitosis of the feet. The smell is so bad, I couldn't get that close myself. They still haven't figured out the source. One said, 'Jesus, what is it with you? You didn't reek like this in camp? Here you are telling everyone else to use foot powder, when you could use a hundred tins of it yourself.'"

"The other replied, 'I bathed my feet, you imbecile; but I didn't see you washing between your toes. Oh, no, not you! You're too fucking cheap to use soap in those places. You've heard the time old question, *does a bear shit in the woods?* Well, let me tell you, my foot-smelling friend, if we had fifty pounds of raw hamburger outside our hootchie, a bear wouldn't come near us to take a shit. He'd be too busy throwing up. I got up in the middle of the night just to get away from your

too busy throwing up. I got up in the middle of the night just to get away from your stench, but your boots must have been out there, so I had to come back in.'"

After Wayne departed, Douglas headed for the water vehicle chuckling to himself all the way. The medical-types had brought it on them themselves, he thought. Oh sure, it had all started when East's barrack box was substituted for theirs, but even if that hadn't happened, they always seemed to put their feet in their mouths. He'd met other Royal Canadian Medical Corps cadets before, but normal ones. These two *posh* little boys were each trying to be someone they weren't. They had to be brought down to earth quickly, for their sake.

Breakfast that morning saw a new crew of *volunteer* cadets serving the food along with East and Simon. The victuals vehicle that had arrived just minutes before, was leaving. After unloading new stainless steel containers filled with chow, it was reloaded with the containers brought for the previous night's meal.

Brice joined the other NCOs at the end of the cadet line. "How'd ya sleep?" asked Moose. He was the first of the Corporals and he kept glancing at the held-out mess tins the cadet had in front of him, still caked with food from last night's supper.

"Jesus, did youse wash those after youse last used them?" he asked the cadet.

"No, Corporal. My mom always tells me food tastes better the second day."

"Get over there and wash 'em. Do youse want everybody to think you're in the Irish, or the Nineteenth Alberta Dragoons?"

The cadet turned and smiled. "But Corporal, I am in the Irish."

Moose nodded and cringed. "It figures. Get over there and wash 'em out anyway."

"I had a great night's sleep," replied Douglas. "And you?"

"Not bad, but I'm thinkin' of movin' Mancinelli further away. When the wind blows, I can still smell the toes."

Douglas laughed. "Are you serious? He's already about seventy-five yards away from you."

"I know, and youse can bet your sweet ass I'm serious. Even standin' here, the stink is still in my nostrils."

No sooner had he spoken, a couple of medics joined the end of the line; their droopy eyes indicating they hadn't slept too well.

Moose turned around. "HEY, YOUSE TWO! BEFORE YOU DO ANYTHIN' ELSE THIS MORNIN', I WANT YOU FIX UP THE SHITTER CHAIRS YOUSE RUINED LAST NIGHT! YA GOT THAT?"

A tired but still proud James replied. "My good man, why do you think it was us who destroyed those lavatory benches?"

An adamant smirk appeared on Danyluk's face. "Because, dear fellow, I heard the both of youse screamin'! THAT'S WHY! I also hope youse didn't pollute the lake, because I wanna go swimmin' there today?"

Both doctors turned beet red and returned their attention to other matters.

After everyone was served, East and Simon filled their own plates and joined the other NCOs sitting and leaning against a patch of pine trees. Once again, the medics didn't join the other Alpha cadets and that suited the sixteen of them just fine.

Banks whispered, "How'd it go?"

The smiles on East and Simon's faces indicated an answer wasn't necessary, but Simon responded anyway. "We gave them a little extra, just for convenience sake."

together, even MacTavish and his friends.

"Blast, they've stopped taking their hourly medication. Is it possible they've figured it all out?"

"No, old toe-breath," his friend replied. "They're not that smart. Their feet have probably improved, that's all. We'll give the whole group of them a dose at lunch. Speaking of feet, I want you to see Dr. Smedley the minute you return to camp. You've got one hell of a problem."

"Why Jonathan, you old cheese-cutter you. You know bloody well it's not me. If anyone should see Doctor Smedley, it's you. Jesus, if there was a battle with you in it, the enemy would take off without a shot being fired."

Day Two in Glenemma was one of the hottest days of the summer, therefore Major Kare decided that training would cease at 1300 hours. The cadets would have their lunch then, and afterward, attend a swim parade at Round Lake.

Leadership lectures started at 0830 hours and were to finish at 1030. At that time, Six and Seven Platoons would undergo the map using exercise Five and Six Platoons took on day one, and the 'advance to contact' methods would be taught to Five and Six Platoons.

The cadets of Bravo Company enjoyed attending lectures in Glenemma because, unlike camp, where they had to sit in smoldering old huts, here they could relax under the trees and feel a bit of a breeze.

Jackson tossed the chalk into the air with one hand and caught it with the other, as he finished wrapping up two leadership lectures to Five Platoon.

"SO YOU SEE, TEAMWORK IS THE SECRET TO SUCCESS. YOU, AS LEADERS, HAVE GOT TO UNDERSTAND THAT. AND ALL THE THEORY IN THE WORLD WON'T HELP YOU UNLESS YOU PUT IT INTO ACTION. IT'S A FUNNY THING, THOUGH, ALL GOOD LEADERS WILL TELL YOU THAT THE MORE YOU EXPERIENCE SITUATIONS, THE THEORY YOU LEARNED WILL BECOME MORE AND MORE USELESS. LET ME READ TO YOU A QUOTE FROM AN AMERICAN FOOTBALL COACH.

"HE SAID, *'I'M JUST A PLOW HAND FROM ARKANSAS, BUT I HAVE LEARNED HOW TO HOLD A TEAM TOGETHER. HOW TO LIFT SOME MEN UP, HOW TO CALM DOWN OTHERS, UNTIL FINALLY THEY'VE GOT ONE HEARTBEAT TOGETHER; A TEAM.*

'THERE'S JUST THREE THINGS I'D EVER SAY: IF ANYTHING GOES BAD, I DID IT. IF ANYTHING GOES SEMI-GOOD, THEN WE DID IT. IF ANY-THING GOES REAL GOOD, THEN YOU DID IT. THAT'S ALL IT TAKES TO GET PEOPLE TO WIN FOOTBALL GAMES FOR YOU.'"

"QUITE A STATEMENT ISN'T IT? NOW, I DON'T KNOW IF THAT COACH WAS IN THE ARMY, OR WHATEVER...BUT I DO KNOW THAT EVERY GOOD OFFICER AND NCO DOES THE SAME THING.

"YOU DON'T HAVE TO BE BRILLIANT TO BE A GOOD LEADER. BUT YOU DO HAVE TO UNDERSTAND OTHER PEOPLE - HOW THEY FEEL, WHAT MAKES THEM TICK, AND THE BEST WAY TO INFLUENCE THEM.

"THERE ARE A LOT OF BRILLIANT PEOPLE IN THIS WORLD WHO ARE, AND WILL REMAIN, INEFFECTIVE LEADERS. WHY? BECAUSE THEY ARE SO INTERESTED IN THEMSELVES AND THEIR OWN ACCOM-PLISHMENTS THAT THEY NEVER GET AROUND TO APPRECIATING AND UNDERSTANDING THE FEELINGS OF THE OTHER PEOPLE WHO ARE

SHARING THIS WORLD WITH THEM.

"SOMETIMES, USUALLY LATER IN LIFE, THESE TALENTED, EGO-CENTRIC INDIVIDUALS SUFFER PAINFUL HARDSHIPS. THEY UNDER-STAND, OFTEN FOR THE FIRST TIME, THE KIND OF PROBLEMS LESS-TALENTED OR LESS-FORTUNATE PEOPLE HAVE SUFFERED ALL THEIR LIVES. THEY SUDDENLY DISCOVER A NEW AND IMPORTANT DIMEN-SION: SENSITIVITY TO THE FEELINGS, EMOTIONS, AND EXPERIENCES OF OTHER PEOPLE.

"EFFECTIVE LEADERS DON'T WAIT FOR LIFE TO BRING THEM TO THEIR KNEES BEFORE THEY APPRECIATE THE KIND OF PROBLEMS OTHERS ARE FACING. INSTEAD, THEY CONSTANTLY TRY TO PUT THEMSELVES IN OTHERS' SHOES - TRYING TO IMAGINE HOW THEY WOULD FEEL IN THE SAME CIRCUMSTANCES. THEY ARE CONSTANTLY AWARE OF WHAT MAKES THEM TICK, AND THEY TRY TO BE HELPFUL; AT THE SAME TIME THEY ASK OTHERS TO HELP THEM."

Earl saw the expressions of the cadets' faces. They were taking it all in. They understood what he was telling them.

"ARE THERE ANY QUESTIONS? YES, MELLISH?"

In another copse of trees not far away, Danyluk was wrapping up two periods of leadership for Six Platoon. Although Mancinelli was with them, there wasn't the slightest odor of feet, because Moose had used his head. Mancinelli attended the lecture, sitting on a wooden apple box with his feet in a wash basin of soapy water.

"PRESIDENT EISENHOWER HAD A WONDERFUL QUALITY, AN AIDE ONCE OBSERVED. 'HE COULD LOOK AT PEOPLE WITH A SMILE AND GET THEM TO DO WHAT HE WANTED.'"

"IT'S A WONDERFUL QUALITY TO HAVE. OTHER THINGS BEING EQUAL, A FRIENDLY, LIKABLE SUPERVISOR IS ALWAYS MORE PERSUA-SIVE THAN ONE WHO ISN'T.

"THERE'S NOTHING WRONG WITH A PLEASANT, GOOD-NATURED APPROACH TO PEOPLE AND PROBLEMS...IN FACT, THERE'S NONE BET-TER. THE STRANGE THING IS THAT WE SO OFTEN FORGET TO USE IT!"

Mancinelli put up his hand. "Why, Corporal?"

Moose thought for a minute. "Good question? ONE REASON IS THAT...UNDER THE PRESSURE OF ORDINARY THINGS, WE SOMETIMES TAKE OURSELVES A LITTLE TOO SERIOUSLY. WE GET TO THINKING ABOUT OUR OWN FEELINGS AND PROBLEMS, AND FORGET ABOUT THE OTHER FELLOW'S.

"ANOTHER REASON, PROBABLY A BIT MORE SUBTLE, IS THAT SO MANY PEOPLE THINK THEY HAVE TO BE GRUFF OR GRUMPY IN ORDER TO APPEAR FIRM AND DECISIVE AND TO GET THINGS DONE. THAT SIMPLY ISN'T SO!

"YOU CAN BE JUST AS FIRM AND DECISIVE WITH A SMILE ON YOUR FACE AS YOU CAN WITH A SCOWL. AND JUST AS CONVINCING TOO...ONCE PEOPLE HAVE LEARNED THAT YOU HAVE A HABIT OF MEANING WHAT YOU SAY AND FOLLOWING THROUGH TO MAKE IT STICK. REMEMBER? MAKE A DECISION AND CARRY IT THROUGH!

"IF WE ALL PUT A LIST TOGETHER OF THE BEST TEACHERS WE HAVE IN SCHOOL, OR THE BEST OFFICERS AND NCOs WE'VE WORKED FOR..."

FOR..."

Moose wrote on the blackboard.

"WE WOULD ALL FIND THEM - ONE - THEY WERE APPROACHABLE AND EASY TO TALK TO;

TWO - THEY RARELY BECAME OVEREXCITED OR FLEW OFF THE HANDLE;

THREE - THEY DIDN'T LET A FEW PROBLEMS POISON THEIR WHOLE OUTLOOK;

FOUR - WHEN THEY WERE WITH YOU, THEY ALWAYS TOOK A FRIENDLY, PLEASANT APPROACH;

FIVE - THEY MADE CERTAIN THEY SHOWED CONSIDERATION FOR YOUR FEELINGS AND ALL THOSE WHO WORKED FOR THEM."

Danyluk smiled at them. "Take a look at me. Am I a bastard to work for?"

After he heard a cheerfully resounding, "YES!" he said, "Damn! Why did you answer that question?"

"SO YOU SEE, IT'S NO PLEASURE TO WORK FOR A DISAGREEABLE, GROUCHY BOSS. HIS ATTITUDE IS BOUND TO CREATE FEELINGS OF DISTASTE AND RESENTMENT THAT WILL, SOONER OR LATER, HAVE AN ADVERSE EFFECT ON THE PERFORMANCES OF HIS SUBORDI-NATES.

"WHEN IT COMES TO DEALING WITH PEOPLE, THERE ARE VERY FEW THINGS THAT CAN'T BE DONE WITH A PLEASANT APPROACH AND A SMILE ON YOUR FACE...AND DONE BETTER BECAUSE OF THEM."

A cadet held up his hand. "But Corporal Danyluk. We're not all built the same. Some of us think a lot differently than others. What you're saying is that we all have to be persistent when it comes to treating others properly...aren't you?"

"YOU BET I AM! AND DON'T YOU FORGET IT! REMEMBER, YOU CAN USE ALL THE TACT IN THE WORLD, BUT, YOU HAVE TO BE PER-SISTENT *AND* CONSISTENT IN THE THINGS THAT YOU DO.

"WRITE THIS DOWN. I'M GOING TO GIVE YOU A QUOTE FROM AN EX-PRESIDENT OF THE UNITED STATES, CALLED CALVIN COOLIDGE.

President Coolidge said: *'NOTHING IN THIS WORLD CAN TAKE THE PLACE OF PERSISTENCE. TALENT WILL NOT; NOTHING IS MORE COMMON THAN UNSUCCESSFUL MEN WITH TALENT.*

'GENIUS WILL NOT; UNREWARDED GENIUS IS ALMOST A PROVERB.

'EDUCATION WILL NOT; THE WORLD IS FULL OF EDUCATED DERE-LICTS.

'PERSISTENCE AND DETERMINATION ALONE ARE OMNIPOTENT. THE SLOGAN 'PRESS ON' HAS SOLVED AND ALWAYS WILL SOLVE THE PROB-LEMS OF THE HUMAN RACE.'"

"I HEAR THE POP TRUCK COMING. READ MR. COOLIDGE'S QUOTE! READ IT, REREAD IT, AND THEN READ IT AGAIN! THANK YOU, THAT'S ALL! GO HAVE A POP! IF SOME OF YOU HAVEN'T GOT ANY MONEY, I'LL LOAN IT TO YOU AND YOU CAN PAY ME BACK WHEN YOU GET PAID!"

Moose gave out a few dimes and wrote the names of the borrowers in his 'little black book.'

When the cadets had left, Simon walked over to him. "Moose, that was one of

come you don't butcher and bastardize the Queen's English when you teach? You know, like you usually do when you speak to us?"

Moose erased the blackboard and, with tongue-in-cheek, replied, "Simon, old buddy, old pard, but I'm doin' just that. D'ya remember the joke about the guy with the harelip sitting in the bar? D'ya remember the bartender's response?"

Simon nodded. "Yeah, yeah, I do, go on."

Danyluk put his arm around his friend's shoulder. "Well, then, you should know I'm mockin' the Queen's English, not my tongue."

Sauntering away, both of them broke out laughing.

While Seven and Eight Platoons were strolling over the plains reading their maps, and Five and Six Platoons were practising 'advance to contact' methods, a different style of *advance to contact* was taking place in Vernon.

"Damn it, Eunice, that's the fourth set of fly buttons you've ruined this week."

"Well, if you'd take the Goddamned things off before I have to rip 'em off, it wouldn't happen would it, you big beautiful hunk, you? C'mere, I'm gonna smother you with..."

Although his pants fell down, Corporal Adams fought his way to the standing position and pulled them up again. "Forget it, Eunice. I'm not participating anymore until you give me the name of that cadet."

"I'll tell my father."

"Frankly, sweetheart, I don't give a damn!" (Author's note: Once again, for the benefit of readers of the air force persuasion, Corporal Adams isn't trying to emulate Mr. Gable. Also, you naval types needn't worry either. In HMS Bounty, Captain Bligh did not make that statement to his cabin boy. Then again, he just could have. Vancouver stock promoter Murray Pezim, however, may have said it to one of his wives.)

Eunice spit out a fly button and stood up. "Oh, all right, all right, what do you want to know?"

"I simply want to know his name, that's all."

The stout one thought for a moment. "Mouse? No, no...Moose! Yes, that's it...his name was Moose!"

Corporal Adams wrung his hands together, not worrying that his trousers fell to the floor again. "Ah ha, so he's Native is he?"

"Eunice pouted, sat down and patted the couch next to her. "C'mon and sit next to me, Adams, honey; he might have been, I don't know."

Adams straddled to the couch thinking to himself. 'What I don't have to go through, just to solve a case?'

In the meantime, Danyluk was lying next to a cadet section commander, approximately a hundred yards in front of a concealed enemy.

"O.K., you know they're in there. You're in charge of this section. Your bren group is off to one side providing covering fire, what are you going to do with your rifle section?"

The young section leader went deep in thought. "I don't see any reason to charge, Corporal Danyluk. Why don't I just send out a barrage of rifle-grenades?"

That wasn't the answer Moose wanted. "Er, that's a good idea, but what if don't wipe out all the enemy?"

"Then I'd fire more rifle grenades, Corporal Danyluk."

"Then I'd fire more rifle grenades, Corporal Danyluk."

That still wasn't the answer Moose was looking for. "But what if there were more enemy just to the right."

"I'd get 'em with another barrage of rifle-grenades, Corporal Danyluk."

"All right, all right, but there's more enemy to your left. What would you do then?"

"More rifle-grenades, Corporal Danyluk."

Moose was flabbergasted. "Just a cottin-pickin' minute. Where the hell are you getting all these rifle-grenades from?"

The cadet section leader smiled. "From the same place you're gettin' all the enemy."

"GET YOUR ASS IN GEAR!" bellowed Danyluk.

The cadet didn't push his luck. "BREN GROUP SUPPLY COVERING FIRE, RIFLE SECTION, MOVE...NOW!"

As eight cadets ran firing towards an unseen enemy, two medical cadets were doing almost the same thing.

Jonathan scurried out of the hootchie screaming. "YOU'VE WHAT? WHY YOU FILTHY MANIFESTATION, YOU! YOU'VE GONE AND SHIT YOUR-SELF IN OUR HOOTCHIE? OH MY GOD, I CAN'T ENDURE THE SMELL! WHAT THE HELL IS HAPPENING TO YOU, JAMES? YOU DRAG ME IN THE TRENCH, YOUR FEET STINK TO HIGH-HEAVEN, AND NOW YOU'VE SHIT YOURSELF? I CAN'T TAKE THIS ANYMORE!"

An embarrassed James slowly crawled out. He didn't need any weights at the bottom of his K.D. longs, because they were full.

"I'm sorry Jonathan. I haven't been feeling well since breakfast, and..."

"DON'T STAND THERE AND EXPLAIN. GO AND CLEAN YOURSELF UP, YOU NO GOOD..."

Jonathan shouldn't have gotten himself so excited. After letting out a intense blast of anal-air, he too messed his pants. Standing there with a much confused expression on his face, he now had to admit his mistake to James.

"NOW, YOU SEE WHAT YOU'VE MADE ME DO? IT'S CONTAGIOUS BECAUSE I'VE ALSO SHIT *MYSELF*!"

That last statement really irked James. "WHAT *I* MADE YOU DO, YOU SLIMY CREEP? I'VE CAUGHT THIS FROM YOU, YOU LOW LIFE! YOU'RE ROTTEN FEET HAVE BROUGHT THIS ON! OH GOD, I FEEL HORRIBLE. NEVER IN MY LIFE HAVE I FELT THIS BAD."

As best they could, and still accusing each other, both *medical experts* slowly walked to the *shitters* they had just finished repairing. Of course, they never dreamt that two 'carpenter' cadets, namely Brice and Banks, had also lent a hand fixing them, after the original work was complete, that is.

Sitting on the *thrones*, the 'two oenologies of human waste,' as Danyluk referred to them, tried to rationalize their situation.

"Jonathan, it must be the heat and your feet. I've never done a thing like this in my life...well, not since I was a baby. My God, it's running through me like water."

"James, I keep telling you, the problem isn't with my feet, it's with your bloody feet. I bet when you *were* a baby, not one single person ever said, 'Cootchie Coo,' and wiggled your toes. If they did, they'd have to wear a gas mask because if the smell of your toesies didn't blind them, your diaper would have."

"Oh, quit being so..." There was a loud 'CRAAAACCKK!' "...here we go

AGGGGAIIIIN!"

James was so right because both of them fell and landed face down.

Standing up and running his hand through his *hair*, Jonathan was lost for words. Like his friend, he was covered from head to toe, and it was running out of him at the same time.

As they attempted to crawl out; in another area of Glenemma, merriment was the order of the day at the messing tent.

"No, we didn't leave, we waited behind some trees until they went in," said Wayne, explaining matters to the other Alpha cadets. "We witnessed the whole thing."

"And you say they'd already shit themselves before they went in?" asked Rothstein.

"You bet," a smiling Banks replied. "And now they've got a real problem. We haven't got a water trailer because the other one's enroute...also, the whole company is going to be down at the lake."

Most of them had just finished eating and they were laughing so hard, they had to hold their stomachs. It was tough keeping their food down.

East pushed the last of three pieces of cake into his mouth. His laughter expressed his feelings perfectly. "And they thought *they'd* be here serving lunch."

"I think we can throw the remainder of that powder away," said Douglas. "I wouldn't wish the treatment they've had on my worst enemy."

If MacTavish and Rae had had their way, all the powder would have been used up. "Please, let's give it to them one more time," begged MacTavish. "The whole bloody lot of it."

After a few minutes discussion, it was decided the medics had been through enough.

Moose quickly looked at his watch. "Hey, you guys, it's swim time," he said, getting up and washing out his mess tins and utensils. "Who's scheduled to march the company down to the lake?"

Earl glanced at some notes. "Not us. We supervised it yesterday, so today Bravo's officers are handling it. All the company's NCOs are back at the camp teaching on the parade square. To give us a break, the officers volunteered. We can actually have some fun this time."

With that said, sixteen staff cadets dispersed to their own areas to shed themselves of their underwear, to put on a pair of khaki shorts and to make their own way to Round Lake.

While Earl was getting undressed, a familiar figure peered into his hootchie. "Hello, son?"

"Mr. Brewer, sir?" a surprised Earl replied. Like Earl, Mr. Brewer was Native and had met the boy in 1953 here in Glenemma. A not-too-tall, elderly gentlemen with clear, piercing eyes; the old man had seen the good and bad of the world and could tell amazing stories.

Earl pulled on his shorts. "It's good to see you again, sir. What brings you here?" Actually Earl had kept in contact with his friend and had visited him during the first week in camp.

"I had a little trouble finding you, but Wayne pointed out your wickiup. How's it going?"

Crawling out and shaking his friend's hand, Earl replied, "Fine, sir, and you?"

"Good, my son, very good for an old man. You've grown in three weeks."

Mr. Brewer chuckled. "Danyluk and Cunningham are your friends, aren't they? Didn't you bring them to the village last year to go horseback riding?"

"Yes, sir, I did. Why?"

"Did you know they're goin' around with my granddaughters? And they've even had a midnight swim?"

Earl was astonished. "Well, between you and I sir, I knew about the midnight swim, but I never knew the girls were your granddaughters. They don't even look alike, or Native for that matter."

Brewer smiled. "So you knew about the swim, eh? Well, son, they are my granddaughters and I watch over them pretty good. I want you to tell the boys to go easy. I know they haven't touched the girls, and I just want to make sure they know the rules. Do you understand me?"

Earl swallowed and thought to himself. Touched the girls? Jesus, Danyluk's tent was hopping all night. "Er, yes, sir, I sure do. I'll, er, talk to 'em, sir."

The smile had gone from Mr. Brewer's face. "That's good. Well, I've got to go over to the mill now. Take care of yourself and make sure you visit. Next week's your last week in camp, isn't it?"

Earl still had a dumbfounded look on his face. "Er, yes sir, it is."

Brewer nodded, shook the boy's hand, and said, "Then I'll see you next week." He turned and left as silently as he had arrived.

While Earl pulled on his T-shirt and slipped into his running shoes, he still couldn't believe it. "Alma and Maggie are his granddaughters? Wow, I didn't know that. You bet I'll talk to those two."

Round Lake was a beehive of activity when Earl arrived, stripped off, and entered the refreshingly cool water. He spotted Danyluk with Cunningham on his shoulders, having a *horse* fight with Douglas and Wayne.

"MOOSE, GORDIE, CAN I SEE YOU TWO FOR A MINUTE!"

The duo met him half way. "What's up?" asked Moose.

"You'd better steady yourselves before I tell ya. Mr. Brewer just left and he told me that Alma and Maggie are his granddaughters and he knows about the midnight swim. He doesn't believe you've touched them, and he wants me to make it quite plain that you'd better not even think of it."

"WHAT?" Moose yelled. "ALMA'S MR. BREWER'S GRANDDAUGHTER? I NEVER HAD A CLUE! JESUS, EARL, WHAT DID YOUSE TELL HIM?"

Earl smiled. "I didn't tell him anything. If I told him what I *know*, the both of you would have arrows in your backs right this minute. Either that, or you'd be up to your necks in sand and the bugs would be gettin' atcha."

Gordie was just as surprised. "SHE DIDN'T MENTION IT TO ME! I REALLY DIDN'T KNOW!"

Moose was still in a state of shock. "HE DON'T WANT ME TO TOUCH HER? SOMETIMES I'VE GOTTA FIGHT TO GET AWAY. I DON'T FIGHT VERY HARD, THOUGH. LISTEN EARL, THEY DON'T EVEN LOOK RELATED?"

"Well, they are, and you've had the warning." With that said, Earl swam out to join the others.

Both Gordie and Moose stood scratching their heads, before Moose said, "Mr. Brewer's granddaughter? What a small world, eh, Gordie?"

"Maggie lied to me, Moose. She told me her grandfather lived in Edmonton. Ya can never tell, can ya?"

"Wimmin are sneaky some times, Gordie, my lad."

Seconds later, some cadets in the company started laughing and it was contagious. The whole company of cadets were now laughing their heads off watching Jonathan and James stroll down to the beach on the west side. They weren't very far away and both naked boys were covered in what looked like mud.

Major Kare called Alpha's cadets out of the water. "There they are again. It looks like they've both had a mud bath and they're coming in for a rinse. Are those two for real? And look, one's even squatting to relieve himself. I don't believe this? By God, they're both *squatting* now."

Danyluk squinted and smiled. "Well, sir, did I tell you that one has a father who is a registered male nurse. His mother's also a member of the Independent Order of the Daughters of the Empire."

Major Kare's idea of finishing training early was really a good idea, because that afternoon the temperature shot up to a hundred-and-five. Even though the cadets had the benefit of the shade of the tress, hot wasn't the word, it was boiling. When the pop truck driver passed out the mail, enthusiasm for receiving news from home wasn't as high as it usually was in camp.

"ELDRIDGE, RYEBERG, GENERAL DANYLUK, MAJOR-GENERAL DANYLUK, COURT MARTIAL DANYLUK, BRICE, EAST, MOOSE DANYLUK, MELLISH, HUT CORPORAL DANYLUK, BANKS, ROTHSTEIN, STODDARD, FEDORUK, COMMANDING OFFICER DANYLUK, BROOKS, CANTERRA, KONISHI, C.O. IN CHARGE DANYLUK, AND THE FORGOTTEN SOLDIERS FUND!" The driver stopped for a moment. "THERE'S A LETTER HERE FOR THE ALPHA COMPANY 'V.D., AND CLAP SOCIAL FUND CAPTAIN,' WHO'S THAT?"

"RIGHT HERE! THAT'S ME, ALSO!" screamed Moose.

When the driver passed out the letter, he said, "V. D., and Clap Social Fund? We're getting a little raunchy aren't we?"

"Hey, there's nothin' wrong with volleyball, dominoes, and clapping," replied Moose.

In no time flat, the driver took out a camera and snapped a picture of Danyluk.

"What the hell's that all about?" asked Moose.

The driver got ready to pass out mail again. "Apparently the girls in the Vernon post office want to see what you look like."

Moose's usual sneaky smile arrived. 'The least you could have done is waited until I had combed my hair. Do they want any autographs, as well?"

The *mailman* didn't answer. "JACKSON, HUNKAMOOSE, LOVERMOOSE, MOOSE YOU BASTARD!" Once again the driver had to stop. "Jesus, it's a wonder you're not skin and bone?"

"He is," stated East. "When he's got a boner, it's all foreskin! Get on with it!"

The driver just stared, smiled, shook his head and, continued. "AND PARCELS FOR BRICE, SIMON, CUNNINGHAM, EAST, MEGAMOOSE AND LOUIE-GENRAL MOOSELIPS!" Another glance at Danyluk. "LOUIE-GENRAL?"

"I've taught her a lot, but I never could teach her to spell," quipped Moose, loaded down and heading for his hootchie.

It was silent for only a few moments following the mail call. As each recipient sat with his back against a tree to read the news from home, individual comments flew from all directions. "HEY, WE'VE GOT A NEW CAT!"

"MY DAD'S PAINTED MY ROOM!"

"WOW, MY SISTER'S GOT ENGAGED!"

"MY MOTHER WANTS TO KNOW WHERE I GOT ALL THE NATIONAL GEOGRAPHICS, SHE FOUND STORED IN THE BATHROOM CUPBOARD!"

"MY BROTHER PAUL HAS JOINED THE NAVY, WHAT A CREEP!"

"MY MOM GOT A SPEEDING TICKET!"

"BERTHA'S HAD ANOTHER SET OF TRIPLETS!"

That comment stopped some cadet from reading his *own* letter. "ANOTHER SET? CHRIST, HOW MANY SETS IS THAT?"

"FIVE! PRETTY GOOD, EH? WHAT A GAL!"

"FIVE? WHO THE HELL IS THE LUCKY FATHER?"

"HOW DO I KNOW, BERTHA'S A SHEEP, YOU DUMMY!"

That night, as the cadets of Bravo gathered in the open to sing songs and tell jokes, their request for a fire was denied. The weather was just too hot and Major Kare was concerned about flying sparks. Not having one didn't dampen their ardor, though, because the off-key sounds of *Poor Little Lamb, Bless 'Em All, Over There,* and other songs, echoed in the night.

After the songs, it was joke-telling time and a cadet from Eight Platoon started the ball rolling by telling a joke.

"THIS HERE GUY, CHARLIE, WAS OUT GOLFING SEE, AND NEEDED TO TAKE A LEAK. SO HE WENT BEHIND A BUSH AND CAME RUNNING OUT, SCREAMIN' THAT A RATTLESNAKE HAD BITTEN HIM ON THE END OF HIS WANG."

Someone yelled, "HE MUST HAVE HAD A PRETTY LONG WANG?"

"HEY, I'M TELLIN' THIS JOKE! ANYWAY, SO HIS FRIEND RAN TO A PHONE AND CALLED THE DOCTOR. THE DOCTOR SAID, 'QUICK! CUT A SMALL 'X' ON THE SPOT THAT WAS BITTEN, AND SUCK OUT THE VENOM. DO IT QUICKLY AND YOUR FRIEND WILL BE ALL RIGHT!'"

" 'IS THERE ANYTHING ELSE WE CAN DO, OTHER THAN THAT?' "

"'NO, THAT'S ABOUT IT. IF IT ISN'T DONE, THEN YOUR FRIEND WILL PROBABLY DIE,' SAID THE DOC."

"THE GUY HUNG UP THE PHONE IN A HURRY AND RUSHED BACK."

"'WHAT DID THE DOC SAY?' THE INJURED ONE ASKED, WRITHING IN PAIN."

"CHARLIE," HE REPLIED, "THE DOC SAYS, YOU'RE GONNA DIE!"

The cadet took a bow amidst hoots, whistles, and clapping.

That golfing joke started another from a cadet in Six Platoon.

"THIS HERE GOLFER, SEE, WAS ABOUT TO TEE OFF WHEN HE HEARD A VOICE COME FROM A NEARBY BUSH"

"'PSST! HAVE YOU GOT ANY TOILET PAPER IN YOUR POCKET?'"

"THE GOLFER REPLIED, 'NO!' AND GOT READY TO SWING AGAIN."

"'PSST! SURELY YOU MUST HAVE A KLEENEX IN YOUR POCKET?'"

"'LISTEN, WHOEVER YOU ARE...I DON'T HAVE A KLEENEX, EITHER,' THE GOLFER REPLIED, READY TO SWING AGAIN!"

"'PSST! HEY, OUT THERE! ARE THERE ANY LEAVES AROUND THAT YOU CAN PASS IN HERE?'"

"NOW THE GOLFER WAS GETTING MAD. 'NO, THERE'S NO GOD-DAMNED LEAVES HERE, EITHER. LISTEN, MAC, I'M TRYIN' TO PLAY A

DAMNED LEAVES HERE, EITHER. LISTEN, MAC, I'M TRYIN' TO PLAY A GAME A GOLF HERE, YA KNOW?'"

"THERE WAS A SECOND OF SILENCE AND WHEN THE GUY WAS ABOUT TO HIT THE BALL AGAIN, HE HEARD, 'PSST! HAVE YA GOT CHANGE FOR A FIFTY?'"

Clapping, hoots, and whistles followed, as the cadet took a bow.

Not to be outdone by the other platoons, a cadet from Five Platoon stood up. "DIDJA HERE THE ONE ABOUT THE GUY WHO WAS BORN WITH A WANG AN EIGHTH-OF-AN-INCH LONG? WHEN HE HAD A HARD-ON HE COULD ONLY MUSTER A QUARTER-OF-AN-INCH. ANYWAY, ONE DAY HE READ ABOUT A DOCTOR IN SOUTH AFRICA WHO HAD SOLVED THIS TYPE OF PROBLEM BY GRAFTING ELEPHANT TRUNKS. HE HEADED FOR SOUTH AFRICA, HAD THE OPERATION AND WHEN HE GOT HOME, HE HAD NO PROBLEM FINDING A DAME, SO HE GOT MAR- RIED.

"DURING HIS HONEYMOON FEAST, THE WEIRDEST THING HAP- PENED. HIS ZIPPER CAME DOWN, HIS NEW WANG CAME UP LIKE A PERISCOPE, SNIFFED AT THE FOOD, GRABBED A COUPLE A BUNS AND DISAPPEARED. ONLY HIS NEW WIFE SAW THE ACTION."

"'GOD, HENRY,' SHE SAID. 'CANT YOU CONTROL THAT THING? IT'S EMBARRASSING ME!'"

"'I'M TRYIN' DEAR,' HE REPLIED, HITTING IT WITH THE END OF HIS FORK."

"WHEN SMALL CHICKENS WERE SERVED..."

He was interrupted when someone yelled, "CORNISH GAME HENS, YOU PONGO!"

"HEY, WHO'S THE ONE TELLIN' THIS JOKE! ANYWAY, SMALL CHICKENS WERE SERVED, AND THE SAME THING HAPPENED AGAIN. HIS WANG SNATCHED A COUPLE OF 'EM, SUCKED UP A GLASS OF WINE, STOLE SOME BREAD-STICKS AND BURPED."

"'HENRY,' SHE SAID, 'NOW I REALLY AM EMBARRASSED.'"

"'YOU'RE EMBARRASSED,' HE REPLIED, MOVING AWKWARDLY ON HIS CHAIR. 'DO YOU WANT TO KNOW WHERE IT'S STORING THE STUFF?'"

A bellow of laughter echoed throughout the area, and because it was dark, no one noticed two Medical Corps Corporals laughing along with everyone else. Well, actually they were finally noticed, but only by Moose. He went over and sat next to them.

"Good to see youse guys. They're a pretty good group, ain't they?"

"Yes," replied Jonathan, sheepishly. "We...we didn't really notice their distinct personalities before. Er, I guess they are a pretty nice bunch."

"All cadets are the same," offered Moose. "They're just kids like youse and I. They don't take life too seriously, because it's not that time in their life when they should. Do youse understands what I mean?"

James had been staring at the ground. He looked up. "Yes, I think we under- stand more than ever. After the swim parade...we had a talk. I guess we've been acting like a couple of idiots, haven't we?"

Danyluk smiled and his *second* self showed. "Well, I'm really not the one qualified to tell you whether or not you did or you didn't. I do know that some-

through good comradeship. Remember, we can be individuals, but at the same time, we've got to understand that we're a part of a team. It's sort of like a chain. If there's a weak link, the chain is no good. You've taken leadership, therefore you know what Emerson said? 'It is one of the most beautiful compensations of this life that no man can sincerely try to help another without helping himself.'"

Both boys nodded. They'd heard it before. James stood up. "Er, Moose, can I ask you a question?"

"Sure, shoot?"

"Er, can we, er...become friends with you fellas?"

Danyluk laughed, and reverted to his old *self*. "It ain't gonna be easy?"

"Why? Er, what do we have to do?" asked Jonathan.

"You don't have to do nothin' but keep your feet clean."

Now both medical-types grinned and appeared embarrassed. "We now know it wasn't *our* feet, Moose. Also, we've spent the last half hour washing Mancinelli's feet and disinfecting them. Had we known he had that problem, we might have helped before. But then again, perhaps we wouldn't have. I think we've learned our lesson. We're going to make certain he's looked after."

They were all standing as Moose got in the middle and put his arms around their shoulders. "Jesus, you should each get the Victoria Cross for doing that." Moose put his tongue in his cheek. "Are you also prepared to accept the fact that we exchanged barrack boxes with you? That's why you got the regimental shower."

Both glanced at each other before James opened up. "YOU WHAT? WHY YOU ROTTEN BAS..." He had a smile on his face when he stopped talking, as his friend blurted into the conversation.

"YOU CREEPS!" screamed Jonathan. "That's what started this whole thing."

"Not really," replied a grinning Moose. "You two were loners at your end of the barracks. You just looked after your own bed space and you had to be told to pitch in and help out when it came to platoon duties. Remember?"

"Yeah, we know," Jonathan said quietly. "We've both learned a good lesson. Sorry about our attitude."

"C'mon," said Moose. "I'll introduce ya to the guys."

Most of the Alpha staff were sitting in a circle chewing the fat when Moose brought James and Jonathan over. Just before he sat down, he said, "Anyone who takes care of Mancinelli should become a national hero. I take my hat off to you guys."

When the three joined the circle, Jonathan whispered to James. "I don't know if it was such a good idea moving Mancinelli's hootchie next to Moose's?"

After handshakes, laughs, and smacks on their backs, two *changed* Alpha cadets realized there was a world other than dressings. A world that consisted of making friends, listening with concern to other people's problems, understanding that each was different, yet very similar, and that all parts of a machine have to do their own job in order to keep the other parts working and the total team productive.

It was hot, really hot in Glenemma that night. Hootchies came down quickly, revealing a sky so full of diamonds, one more couldn't be added. Along with such brilliance, a giant old moon smiled with confidence and a very tired Danyluk squirmed in his sleep, subconsciously wondering why his feet smelled.

When Moose shook Brice's feet and said, "Get your ass out of bed, it's five-thirty," Douglas didn't know what was wrong.

"WHAT'S THE MATTER? WHAT...WHAT'S THE PROBLEM?"

Danyluk stood there with just a towel wrapped around his waist. "Nothing's wrong, Dougie my pal, it's just that the water truck has arrived and if youse wants to get a shower, get it now before the others wake up. Wayne's over there now."

As Moose moved on to wake up the other Musketeers, Douglas lay back again. He had been in a wonderful sleep dreaming about being lost on a desert island with Diane. Before Moose had awakened him, Diane had been feeding him pieces of coconut, and he was smiling as she slipped them into his mouth.

"Coconut? I can't stand coconut," he said as he grabbed his towel.

"GGGOOD MMMORNING, CCCORPORAL BBBRICE!" East bellowed, turning blue under one of the showers. Although he was shivering, he still had a piece of wet bacon in his hand, indicating he'd raided the kitchen.

"YYOU CAN HAVE MMY SSHOWER!"

"Good morning, Jack. I don't know if I want it, if it's that cold?"

Jack was out now, quickly drying himself off. "Ah, you'll love it. As Moose says, 'It gets the blood running through your pecker.'"

Wayne had been combing his hair on the other side of the shower-tree. When he heard Jack's statement, he popped his head around. "MOOSE DOESN'T NEED A SHOWER TO GET THE BLOOD RUNNING THROUGH HIS PECKER. IT NEVER STOPS RUNNING THROUGH HIS WANG. NOW THAT I THINK ABOUT IT, HE MUST HAVE ONE HELL OF A STRONG HEART JUST TO KEEP THE BLOOD RUNNING THROUGH THAT FORESKIN OF HIS. GOOD MORNIN', DOUG?"

"GGOOD MMMORNING WWWAYNE! SAY, WWHAT'S THE OCCA-SION? HOW CCOME MOOSE GGOT UP SSO EARLY?"

Wayne appeared with his towel wrapped around his shoulders. "Ya got *me*. He also spent half-an-hour washing his feet. I'll see you guys at breakfast. Right now I've got to check on my section's *cleanliness*."

By the time the siren sounded, along with, "COME AND GET IT!" the lineup was long and winding. Actually, all cadets were up and washed a half hour before breakfast was served. The alluring smell of bacon and eggs must have wafted through their nostrils the minute the food arrived with the water trailer.

While the Musketeers were eating and talking with their friends, a three-quar-ter-ton truck came to a halt in the vehicle parking area. Two Sergeants got out, walked over to Major Kare and his officers, and after a few minutes, headed towards the Alpha cadets.

"IS THERE ANY FOOD LEFT FOR TWO STARVING SERGEANTS?" one of them asked.

Sergeant Beckford didn't have to say it the second time because eighteen sets of hands offered to serve him and Sergeant Simpson.

Moose stuck his chest out. "So, now the truth comes out! Food in the field, *is* better than the Sergeants' Mess, isn't that right, Sergeants?"

Simpson smiled. "Danyluk, the reason we're here is to take you on a morning run. Get your P.T. gear on, quickly."

Moose didn't know what to think. "Er, ah, what...? Are you, er ser....?"

Although both Sergeants smiled, Beckford was a little more solemn. He accepted his breakfast which was served on a cardboard plate.

"No, you're O.K., Danyluk. We're going to let you off the hook this time. But next time, be prepared to do some jogging. I, er, wonder if the eight of you..." He pointed to Brice, Banks, Rothstein, East, Jackson, Cunningham, Simon, and Danyluk. "...could join us for a few minutes after you've eaten?"

Ten minutes later, eight inquisitive cadets sat in the back of the truck as it drove to Round Lake. When it was parked, Sergeant Simpson asked everyone to sit down. Then the two Sergeants sat down with them, and Beckford did the talking. The tone of Beckford's voice was entirely different than what they were used to.

"You know I don't beat around the bush, so what I've got to say, I'll say quickly."

When both Sergeants took their headdress off and appeared fidgety, the boys knew that something was very wrong.

Beckford looked at no one in particular when he cleared his throat and whispered, "At four-thirty this morning, the camp Duty Officer received a telegram from Vancouver. It was from Bergie's dad. Er, yesterday, a jeep Shanks and Bergie were riding in...hit a land mine. Ed Shanks is dead, and Bergie has been badly injured and may not live."

Beckford's normally tough dry eyes, were full. "He's on a hospital ship and we'll know within the next twenty four hours."

Expressions of total disbelief and pain contorted eight faces. Moose's jaw dropped and a complete blank look took over.

Sergeant Simpson also cleared his throat and spoke very low. "If it's any consolation, Ed didn't suffer...he was killed instantly. At this point, we don't know the full extent of Bergie's injuries. Er, we're very sorry, boys."

Moose's eyes started welling up and he turned and listlessly walked away. The others couldn't say anything, they were all in shock. Simon immediately stood up and walked to the water's edge, wiping his eyes.

Sergeant Simpson continued. "There won't be a funeral for Ed for another month. The ship is remaining on duty and then his body will be flown from France."

Nothing else was said. Nothing could be said. Each cadet's mind recalled the happy send-off of Bergie and Ed just weeks before.

"SEND US SOME FIGS OR DATES!" Moose had screamed as their train departed.

"WE'LL DO THAT!" Ed replied. "YOU GUYS TAKE CARE OF YOUR-SELVES! HAVE YOU GOT THAT? WE'LL BE HOME FOR CHRISTMAS! BY THAT TIME, WE'LL WANT TO FEEL THE RAIN AND SNOW ON OUR FACES! GOOD LUCK ON YOUR COURSE, FELLAS!"

"WE'LL BE HOME FOR CHRISTMAS!"
"WE'LL BE HOME FOR CHRISTMAS!"
"WE'LL BE HOME FOR CHRISTMAS!"
"**WE'LL BE HOME FOR CHRISTMAS**!" echoed through Douglas's mind, as he slowly wiped his eyes with his hand and looked at Wayne. "He won't be coming home for Christmas."

Wayne nodded and took off his glasses. "I know. Jeez, I can't...?" His words just trailed off because he had to swallow and couldn't finish his sentence.

Harvey walked over and stood beside Simon. His friend was very close to Shanks because they were both in the Irish cadets together.

Sergeant Beckford's face turned firm again as he replaced his beret and stood up. "STAND UP, FELLAS," he ordered. "YOU TWO, SIMON AND ROTH-STEIN, GET OVER HERE!"

Both boys' eyes were red when they meandered back.

Beckford stood in front of them. "Listen guys. Not one of us can change what's happened. If we could, it would already be done. You all know that!

"Bergie and Shanks joined the Canadian Army, knowing full well that they were becoming soldiers. A soldier's task is to defend his country and its customs with his own life. That's a soldier's job, fellas. Simp and I saw it all in the Second World War and Korea. We could tell you stories that you wouldn't believe. We lost a lot of very close friends and we couldn't let it get us down. Sure, we had a good cry and we may have pounded on the nearest tree and hurt our hands, but that's all we could do.

"Edwin was one hell of a fine kid, and a worthy soldier. He knew the risks because they were instilled in him from the first day he joined the regular force. So did Bergie. Listen, there are lots of things we don't teach you as cadets. One of them is, we don't motivate you to accept death."

Beckford looked them all in their eyes. "Oh yes, you can be taught to interpret death. For Christ's sake, that's what becoming a soldier is all about...death. Soldiers have died for causes for thousands of years, and will, for thousands more years to come. And do you want to know something else? If any one of them knew he was going to die, he wouldn't have joined. No one knows when his time is up. But, by God, if they enjoy doing what they are doing until that time, then they agree to whatever fate has in store. As friends, we must also accept the results of their destiny. Shanks and Bergie would want it that way!"

Beckford ran his hand over Simon's hair. "Listen, son, I know you were very close to Edwin, but right now, I want you to be a soldier. I want you to understand what's expected of you *now*. Do you *know* how to do that?"

Simon looked up and in a low voice, said, "No, Sergeant."

"Well, I want you to say, 'A friend of mine has died for his country. I can't bring him back, but I can protect his dreams, his hopes, and his beliefs. He was a chum of mine and I am grateful for that. Although he's gone, I've got his memory and with every breath in my body, I'll cherish it always!' Have you got that?"

"Yes, Sergeant," replied Simon.

Beckford replaced his beret. "Listen, two weeks ago, the both of you..." he stopped talking and pointed at Rothstein and Simon, "...told me that after you finished high school, you wanted to go to Israel for a year, to work on a kibbutz. Well, this is your last year of high school, are you going?"

Rothstein answered, "We think so, Sergeant. It's just a matter of getting permission from our parents and putting together the necessary money."

"Well, fellas, I admire your conviction and there's no doubt that with such determination you will achieve your goal. But you know as well as I do, that people are dying over there to protect *their* country. Knowing that, are you still prepared to go?"

Both boys nodded and said, "Yes, Sergeant."

Beckford smiled. "Well, if you knew death was a certainty, you might think twice. But you don't, therefore you most likely will go, and, God forbid, you may die. That, is your choice! But if you die, then as a good friend, I have to accept that the decision to go was yours and yours alone. As painful as it may be for me, I have to rationalize that it was your wish to become involved. Do you understand me?"

The boys nodded again and all seven understood a little better now.

One by one, the Sergeant shook their hands. "It's damned tough losing someone close. I don't know how many times I've said it, but only time can ease the pain and mental anguish you're experiencing. Grief cures itself in time. That I can assure you," he said, walking to his vehicle. "In cases like this, we don't know why it happens, and so far, no one has come up with a magic wand that calms the trouble waters of reason. Also, is this grief brought on by a selfish thought that you won't have them around, or because they're just gone? Think about that.

"Simp, you stay here with these guys. I'm going to catch up with Danyluk. I'll be back shortly."

Before he got inside, Sergeant Beckford turned, "Now if you think I'm mean for talking to you this way, and you believe I've got no feelings, then you need your heads examined. I might not have known Bergie and Shanks as well as you people, but I knew them; and as I think the world of you, I thought the same of them. At four o'clock this morning, I went for a walk around the camp, and cried *my* eyes out. Right now I'm thankful that Bergie's still alive."

Sergeant Beckford didn't return to the lake. After he picked up Danyluk, he drove up a country road where the two of them could talk.

In the meantime, Sergeant Simpson discussed the matter with the seven others for two hours before they walked back to the bivouac area. When Beckford returned shortly after lunch, he dropped Danyluk off at his hootchie, picked up Sergeant Simpson, and drove back to Vernon.

That day, eight other Alpha cadets took over and conducted Bravo Company's training. With two staff cadets per platoon, everything went smoothly.

Moose Danyluk walked up the mountain on the west side of Glenemma, Douglas and Wayne walked a few miles to a store to call Diane and Debbie, Rothstein and East stayed in East's hootchie, and Simon and Earl took the boat out on the lake. Gordie Cunningham was going to go with them, but although Moose had an hour's head start, Gordie decided to climb the mountain looking for him.

At dusk when the singing started, six Musketeers were asleep. Gordie and Moose, however, were still up the mountain, sitting ten feet apart on the same piece of ground on which Douglas, in 1953 had said, 'God must use to look out over his domain.'

When they came down the next morning, two sympathetic medical cadets patted them on their backs, gave them breakfast as well as medication for their blisters, cuts and bruises, and advised them to get some sleep.

The remaining Musketeers had joined a large company map and compass exercise that started at 0830 hours that morning and was to finish at 1630. Along with the six, the cadets in Moose and Gordie's section longed for the sleeping duo, but they understood that sleep was probably the best cure for losing two friends and taking on the mountain.

At noon, the company met at the south end of Glenemma and each cadet ate a box lunch which they all carried in their small webbed packs. Lunch never tasted better, for that matter, neither did the water. Usually water from a water trailer tastes horrible. It tastes even worse when drunk from a water canteen bottle, but in such heat, it was like a blessing from Heaven.

"Did Diane say she was going to tell their girls?" Wayne asked, referring to Shanks and Bergie's girlfriends. Both boys were sitting with their sections in the shade off the main highway.

"Yes," a solemn Douglas replied. "But she talked to one of their dads first. Apparently he's a minister. He'll make it a little easier and..."

Apparently he's a minister. He'll make it a little easier and..."

Douglas was interrupted by Rothstein's voice calling for him. "CORPORAL BRICE, CORPORAL BANKS? They heard him ask some cadets, "SAY, DO YOU KNOW WHERE CORPORAL BANKS AND CORPORAL BRICE ARE? THANKS!" he replied, after he was told.

Rothstein was smiling but covered in sweat and out of breath when he found them. "HEY, YOU TWO CREEPS, BERGIE'S GONNA BE ALL RIGHT! HE'S GOT A BROKEN ARM, A BROKEN PELVIS, AND THEY TOOK SOME SHRAPNEL OUT OF HIS LEGS, BUT HE'S GONNA BE FINE!"

The good news messenger threw his beret on the ground and was now flat on his back with his arms out, trying to catch his breath.

"WHO TOLD YOU?" Douglas asked excitedly, leaning over Rothstein.

"MAJOR KARE JUST GOT A MESSAGE FROM CAMP! SOME SHRAP-NEL JUST MISSED BERGIE'S LEFT BALL. APPARENTLY, WHEN HE WOKE UP, HE ASKED IF HE WAS IN ONE PIECE AND IF THERE WAS A COLD BEER AROUND!"

Banks just stood there with a childish grin. "THANK GOD! THANK GOD! THANK GOD! HAVE MOOSE AND GORDIE BEEN TOLD?"

Rothstein sat up and grabbed his beret. He was as happy as hell and it showed. "DID YOU HAVE YOUR EYE ON MY CAPBADGE, CORPORAL BANKS? MAJOR KARE IS TELLING THEM NOW. HE JUST HAPPENED TO SEE ME ON THE HIGHWAY."

A Bravo cadet who knew of the disaster asked, "Does Bergie know Shanks is dead?"

The bearer of good news put on his beret, looked down at the ground, and slowly shook his head. "I don't know, Major Kare didn't tell me."

When Harvey rushed away to tell the others, he yelled, "ANYWAY, YOU PONGOES GET YOUR CHINS UP, ALL FOUR OF THEM...AND GET YOUR CHESTS OUT!"

At four-thirty, when the sweaty worn-out company met at the lake to have a swim, Danyluk and Gordie were already up to their necks. The expression on Moose's face suggested he'd been born again.

As flailing bodies attacked the water, the cadets' peeled off piles of clothing remained in three ranks on the shore.

"DIDYA HEAR THE NEWS?" Moose bellowed to the other Musketeers. Although his hands were cupped around his mouth and he used his best drill voice, it was hard to hear him over the ecstatic sounds of rapture, released by the cadets of Bravo Company.

Six Musketeers sloshed in together. "YOU BET WE DID!" screamed Douglas. "JEEZ, IT MUST BE NICE, YOU TWO HAVIN' THE DAY OFF?"

"HEY YOU GUYS, I TOOK TWO BUCKS OFF HIM!" Gordie shouted.

Moose pushed him away. "YEAH, YOU CREEP, THAT WAS FOR THE, FORGOTTEN SOLDIERS WITH DIARRHEA FUND!"

When the eight of them met, it was like a twenty-year reunion. Hands were grabbed and when Simon jumped on Moose's back, they both fell over.

Under the watchful eyes of Bravo's officers and recently returned regular force NCOs, the cadets of Bravo Company forgot about map reading, and eight Musketeers endeavoured to escape their sorrow in the paradise of Round Lake.

camp are always welcomed after staying four days under the stars. The boys had enjoyed their freedom, the lake, and the naked nighttime universe, but sleeping in a comfortable bunk, meeting their compatriots from other companies, and being able to visit town had been a beckoning thought from Day Two.

On Friday morning, after breakfast, everyone pitched in to clean up the camp. Trenches were filled in and foul-ground signs posted. Hootchie areas were left spotless and any dead branches that had been used to make 'A' frames were taken apart and dispersed, making it nearly impossible to detect that people had camped there.

Like all companies before them, the cadets of Bravo had been taught to take care of Glenemma. The Native people who lease the land to the army, have always had a good relationship with Camp Vernon, and all Camp Commanding Officers have cherished the cooperation always received from members of the Okanagan Indian Band. For well over seventy years, the alliance between the Department of National Defence and the Native people of Vernon has been one of mutual respect.

When the trucks arrived at 1030 hours, Bravo Company and its staff were packed up and ready to roll. Shortly, all polished faces would be caked in mud, as the vehicles' tires threw up clouds of swirling dust to settle on any uncovered sweaty skin.

Songs started as soon as the three-tons came out on the highway.
"There are rats, rats, as big as alley cats,
in the stores, in the stores.
"There are rats, rats, as big as alley cats,
in the Quartermaster's Stores.
"My eyes are dim, I can not see,
I have not got my specks with me.
"I have, not, got, my, specks, with, me!"

"There is gravy, gravy, enough to float the navy,
in the stores, in the stores.
"There is gravy, gravy, enough to float the navy,
in the Quartermaster's Stores.
"My eyes are dim I can not see,
I've got too much, Goddamned beer in me.
"I've got, too, much, Goddamned, beer, in, me!"

"There are Sheiks, Sheiks, enough to last for weeks,
in the stores, in the stores.
"There are Sheiks, Sheiks, enough to last for weeks,
in the Quartermaster's Stores.
"My eyes are dim, I can not see,
I don't give a damn who's in bed with me,
I don't, give a damn, who's in bed, with, me!"
An after-chorus sang:
"As long as she's living,
I don't, give a damn, who's in bed, with, me!"

The guys in East and Jackson's truck learned a new version of the song.
"There are farts, farts, all bottled up on carts,
in the stores, in the stores.

"There are farts, farts, all bottled up on carts,
in the Quartermaster's Stores.
"They were made by Moose and he saves them there,
he takes off a lid when he needs fresh air,
"He takes, off a lid, when he needs, fresh, air."

At the time East was singing the song, he had no idea his name had replaced Moose's, in Moose's truck. For that matter, Jackson had no idea that the name Jackson had been substituted in Gordie's truck.

As the trucks turned into Camp Vernon, one song was saved for last.

"Oh Provost, oh Provost, just please let us pass,
or we'll transfer our dust, right up your ass.
"We've had a week off, and it sure was a hit,
and we sure didn't miss ya, ya big bags of shit!"

CHAPTER XII

Unloading in front of B-29 could be compared to falling down when the bulls are running. Cadets with gear were all over the place, and they had come back with half the dust in Glenemma.

After the company was formed up in three ranks, Major Kare addressed the cadets while they were in the stand easy position.

"I'LL BE TALKING WITH YOU LATER. IN THE MEANTIME, I WANT YOU TO KNOW THAT I'M VERY PROUD OF YOU!

"NOW...YOU'VE GOT THE BALANCE OF THE DAY OFF TO CLEAN YOURSELVES AND YOUR KIT. UNFORTUNATELY YOU HAVEN'T GOT THE NIGHT OFF. IN ADDITION TO MOTHER'S NIGHT, YOU'RE ON THE PARADE SQUARE FROM 1930 UNTIL 2100 HOURS, AND YOU'VE GOT STUDYING TO DO!"

There were a few groans, but Major Kare ignored them.

"CONSIDERING THE LOOK OF YOU NOW, IT WILL BE A MIRACLE IF WE WIN THE PENNANT TOMORROW. BUT THEN AGAIN, WE SHOULD BE ABLE TO, SHOULDN'T WE?"

"YES, SIR!" bellowed the company.

"ONCE AGAIN, GOOD SHOW, FELLAS! LUNCH IS IN A HALF HOUR. GET CLEANED UP AND I'LL SEE YOU LATER."

After the Company Sergeant-Major dismissed the cadets, B-29 came alive again. Some cadets just fell on their bunk springs without rolling down the mattresses. Others quickly stripped, throwing their clothes in each others' faces. In no time, the sinks were full, so were the showers, and the toilets. As the washing machine whined, the lineup at the urinal was long, and rambunctious. The fire extinguishers were aimed accurately; windows were opened; barrack boxes were opened and slammed shut; bunks were bounced and jumped on; brooms were used as rifles and pace sticks; irons were out; circuit breakers blew; shoe polish - starch - Brasso - Silvo - and all cleaning materials were in use; upper bunk occupants were kicked skyward, the water fountain was attacked, and towels were flicked. Home had never been sweeter; and to improve matters, Bravo's regular force Corporals took over until the Alpha cadets could go over to B-33 and clean up.

The Musketeers' hut wasn't a bit like B-29 as eighteen Alpha cadets unpacked and hit the showers. Actually, the hut was empty and that's just the way they liked it.

"I've still got the smell of feet in my nostrils," Moose complained, soaping up his legs.

James and Jonathan laughed as James said, "We didn't really move Mancinelli back to you on purpose. We just had to move him somewhere. The trees were dying around our hootchie and even the bugs were tits up."

Wayne shampooed his body. "Say, where was Mancinelli last night? Moose, did you move him again?"

Moose didn't have to answer, because East *answered* for him. "SO THAT'S IT? YOU ROTTEN BASTARD, DANYLUK! THAT'S WHO WAS IN THAT

STRANGE HOOTCHIE BUILT BEHIND ME? JESUS, I GOT UP AT TWO-THIRTY TO WASH MY FEET! EVEN MY CHICKEN LEG WITHERED! MY THROAT WAS SO DRY THIS MORNING, I COULD ONLY EAT HALF MY BREAKFAST."

Moose couldn't stop laughing. "WHAT ARE YOU COMPLAINING FOR? AT LEAST YOU ATE HALF OF IT!"

"YEAH, BUT I THOUGHT THE EGGS WERE ROTTEN, YOU CREEP! EVEN NOW, EVERYTHING I SMELL STINKS LIKE FEET! I'LL GET YOU, MOOSE!"

Gordie moved over next to Jonathan and James. "Say, guys, who do you work for in the MIR? Er, are you on your own, or do you have to report to someone?"

Gordie had been requested to ask the question by cadets MacTavish and Rae, who were particularly interested in the response.

Jonathan did the talking. "We work for a really great guy. He's a regular force corporal named Andre Durupt. Of all the Orderlies in the hospital, he's the best."

"So he looks after you, does he? Does he also show you how to dispense medication?"

"You bet," replied James. "Andre's our buddy. Say, can I ask *you* a question?"

Gordie soaped up his chest. "Sure, shoot?"

"Is your name Zaholuk, Chandler, or West?"

Grins came over all but two faces when Gordie said, "It's none of them, my name is Cunningham."

The medical-types looked like they'd seen a ghost. It was James who snapped out of it first. "CUNNINGHAM? THE FAMOUS CARD SHARK CUNNING-HAM?"

"None other," replied Gordie, washing his crotch with expensive French soap.

"Hey, er, Gordie," said Moose. "Could I try...?"

Cunningham didn't miss a beat. "Forget it, Moose. Do you actually think I'd use this bar of soap again after you had it on...that?"

Moose shrugged and continued using Sergeants Soap. When Moose ran out of soap, the only person who would ever *loan* him any was Bergie. Even then, Bergie washed off the bar, afterwards.

"CUNNINGHAM? JESUS, JONATHAN, WE'VE BEEN HAD!"

A massive smile came over Gordie's face as he cocked his head. "Yeah, but you tried to get me, didnt'cha? Naughty, naughty."

When East opened the window to let out the steam, he said, "WHEN I FILL UP MY LUNGS, THE WHOLE OKANAGAN VALLEY SMELLS LIKE FEET!"

That odour would be with them for a while, because Moose had wrapped up Mancinelli's boots in a plastic bag and brought them with him. While East was attempting to cleanse his nostrils at the shower room window, he had no idea the aromatic items were in the middle of a folded-up mattress on an unused bunk across from his. At that very moment, an unseen eye-watering, throat wrenching, nostril-clotting haze surrounded East and Rothstein's bunk area. The concealed enemy was indeed, deadly. Although the nauseating stench seemed to cling to anything within ten-thousand metres, East and Rothstein were in the middle of ground zero.

A shower was all they needed to feel *human* again. East was first out because lunch was being served. Rothstein followed him and upon opening their barrack box twice, to smell inside, Harvey arrived at one conclusion.

With his face all cringed up, he said, "Jack, do me a favour, please. Will you, er, put your Glenemma clothes in your duffel bag or whatever you've got. Your clothes reek of feet."

East agreed and piled his dirty clothes into his large pack and proceeded to get dressed. "Ah, it's great to be back, eh Rothie?"

Unfortunately for Jack, because he'd been subjected to Mancinelli's *welcome* all night long, he didn't realize how explosive the *bomb* really was. "Rothie, just think, wonderful grub, clean sheets, clean clothes, beautiful dames, and..."

"Er, Jack...you're going to have to wash your blankets. They're pungent as hell. It's as though Mancinelli was standin' next to ya."

Douglas and Wayne arrived, still drying their hair. Their faces turned from smiles to utter disgust as they neared their bunks.

"JESUS CHRIST," said Wayne, "HAS MANCINELLI BEEN IN HERE? WHOSE BUNK DID HE SIT ON?"

Other Alpha Company cadets walking through the Musketeers area just plugged their noses and looked at the ceiling.

With his eyes, Harvey motioned that the stench was originating from East. In the meantime, the instigator, Moose, was having a fit. He had opened a window and placed a hand over his mouth so the guys couldn't hear him.

Finally it was Douglas who caught on. "ALL RIGHT, MOOSE, WHERE ARE THEY?"

Although Rothstein had to blow his nose and wipe his eyes, East's expression was one of, 'what's the problem?'

A howling Moose reached for his plastic bag, unrolled a mattress, and once again smothered the *greatest weapon on earth.*

I'm sorry, fellas, I brought 'em back to have 'em disinfected and I'm gonna place 'em in a field so they can air out."

"YOU ROTTEN PRICK!" screamed Rothstein. "I THOUGHT MY LIFE WAS COMIN' TO AN END. I'M SORRY, JACK."

Jack wasn't paying attention. "Hey, you guys, grub is on."

MacTavish and Rae were there in a flash. Rae grabbed the bag. "Oh no you're not! These can fit in with our other scheme, eh what?"

Nods and smiles appeared on all faces. Moose took hold of the bag, twisted it and placed an elastic band around its tightly wrung neck. "Yeah, that sounds like a good idea. Let's include these as well. The pongo deserves it."

Of the eighteen Alpha cadets who headed towards the kitchen, only sixteen knew of the plot to 'repay' a certain Medical Orderly by the name of Corporal Andre Durupt.

The Musketeers pleasure of sitting in a mess hall once again, adjacent to their friends, was obvious. They sat at two close tables and ate off clean plates with clean silverware and clean cups.

Earl had read orders and had made notes. "We've got to design twenty questions for tomorrow's tests and at 1500 hours we're to report to Bravo's office to pick up course report inputs." (Comment forms - the Alpha cadets had been assessing the cadets in their sections. These commentaries would form part of the eventual course reports, completed by the Platoon Officers, with a final assessment by the O.C. of the company. While the Alpha cadets had been monitoring Bravo's cadets, the officers and NCOs of Bravo had been assessing the Alpha cadets, and these observations would go to Major Ratcliffe, O.C. of Alpha Company, for his company's course reports.)

"Also, did you guys know that the Alpha cadets who weren't attached to other companies formed the guard for the Kelowna Regatta and the Penticton Peach Festival? They accompanied the band and everything went well," continued Earl.

"The lucky creeps," offered Gordie, practising his one-handed shuffle. "I'd planned on being there so I could clean out the band. Those guys have lots of dough."

Earl wasn't finished. "Who's Lieutenant Steacy?"

All BCR cadets stopped eating and Danyluk turned his face towards Earl, "He's a BCR officer here on staff, why?"

"Well, apparently, you guys..." He pointed at the BCR cadets. "...are having a 'Duke's' picnic, Sunday night at Cosens Bay. The trucks leave B-3 at 1700 hours and Lieutenant Steacy is running the show."

East actually stopped eating for a moment. "Hey, great! There'll be hot dogs and watermelon and hamburgers and..."

Brice, Banks, Cunningham, and Danyluk glanced at each other. A moment later, so did East. That's what had stopped him from talking. He knew what they were all thinking. Three non BCRs would have to be invited.

Jack volunteered a solution. "Well, what are you concerned for? I'll go and see Lieutenant Steacy and ask if Earl, Rothie, and Simon can join us. It's that simple. I'll tell him Musketeers are Musketeers. He'll understand."

Brice nodded to Jack. "Yeah, I think he'll go along with it, he's a good guy."

Moose pointed his fork at Douglas. "What do youse means he's a good guy? He's the Goddamned Tech-Adj., at the regiment. Him and that S.O.B. Cox always seem to catch me when I'm havin' fun at the Nanaimo Indian Hospital."

Banks laughed. "That's because you keep takin' off with one of the tanks, you idiot. When four tanks are in formation, one keeps headin' off towards the open windows of the TB hospital. And guess who's tank that always is?"

"MINE! AND I'LL HAVE YOUSE KNOW EVEN THE CREW COMMANDER CAN'T STOP ME WHEN I'M DRIVIN' THE DAMNED THINGS! THOSE BROADS ARE NICE!"

Gordie looked concerned. "Jesus, Moose, the patients there have got TB. Surely to God you don't want to catch that, do ya?"

"Hey, who kisses 'em? Maybe the officers and NCOs do, but not me. And you can't talk, Gordie. Who's always in there with a deck of cards? Half the broads can't buy anything 'cause you've got their dough. Ya don't worry about TB then, do ya?"

Gordie took a coin out of Moose's ear. "That's different, money's money. TB to me, means Today's Bucks!"

Earl patiently waited for the conversation to die down before he continued.

"Did I tell ya that Bravo's on the parade square all day Sunday and all day Monday? Also the boxing matches are on Sunday night. Would you believe there's only four cadets fighting from Alpha Company? Gordie, they want you to help out in the corners."

"Hey, I've helped out for three years running. This time I'm sayin' no and goin' to the Dukes picnic. I'll tell 'em that."

East suddenly stood up with a chicken leg in his hand. "Hey, what if some of our guys are fighting? They won't be able to go to the Duke's picnic?"

Wayne shook his head in desperation. "You can sit down. No Dukes will be fightin' you creep. Only the Seaforths, Irish and the Westies like bleeding. You know how they always breed?"

"Yeah."

"So, they like to bleed as well."

"Really? Well, bully for them." A relieved Jack sat down again and started chomping.

Jackson kept going through his notes. "Let's see...Bravo's on the parade square all day Monday, we've got that day off, and..."

Moose grabbed the notes to look at them. "WHAT'S THE MATTER WITH YOUSE, EARL? YOUSE SHUDDA MENTIONED THAT RIGHT AT THE START!"

Earl snatched his notes back. "Hey, I'm methodical, not like you. Er, now where was I? Oh, yeah..."

Danyluk interrupted again. "Can the dames come to the Duke's picnic?"

Earl put on his squeaky voice. *"No, the girls can't come to the Duke's picnic!* Let me get on with this, will ya? Tuesday morning is the practise for the swim meet. It's at Kin Beach. Tuesday afternoon, we're in Polson Park practising for the sports meet. Wednesday, we're at Kal Beach for the swim meet, and Thursday, the sports meet is held at Polson Park until 1400 hours. Course reports are signed between 1500 and 1700 on Thursday. The Graduation Parade is held at Polson Park at 2000 hours on Thursday night and we hand in our kit on Friday morning."

"I'm gonna try and keep these bush uniforms," stated Moose.

Simon shook his head. "They'll just nail ya and you end up payin' for 'em."

Earl continued. "There's a company picnic for Alpha on Monday night, and there's a Bravo picnic on Tuesday night. Both are at Kin Beach. Alpha Company gets its pictures taken this afternoon, and Bravo Company gets its pictures taken tomorrow afternoon. Timings are the same, 1430 hours. Finally, gentlemen...and I use the term loosely, at three o'clock this afternoon...that's fifteen hundred hours to you, Moose. You and East are to be interviewed on CJIB radio. A car will be at B-3 at 1445 and it will return you to camp at 1530. While you guys are on the radio, we'll pick up your course report inputs."

Actually, Moose had already heard about the upcoming interview, but he went into mock shock anyway. "What? I'm on the radio with East? Where the hell are our scripts, our director, our make-up person, our wardrobe dame?"

"Our food truck, our lighting man, our hairdressing broad, our..." East was interrupted when MacTavish and Rae squeezed in at the table.

With all heads in the middle, excited chuckles, giggles and guffaws were muffled. The plans for Corporal Durupt were now finalized and Jonathan and James were none the wiser.

Shortly, everyone sat back with confident expressions on their faces. Moose put his arm around MacTavish's shoulders. "Yep, sounds good to me. Serves the pongo right, too."

When a grinning East stood up to get 'thirds,' he was hauled out the door.

"But I'm only making up for the lack of food in Glenemma!" he protested.

"Bull shit, Jack. You were never out of the kitchen tent."

"All right then, I need it to help clear the stench from my nostrils."

"Try again, Jack."

"Would you believe me if I said, food assists my sexual desires?"

"Whuddya mean? You have to fart to get it on?"

"Hey, yeah, yeah, that's it! That's exactly what I have to do!"

"No, we wouldn't...but then again...nah, no we wouldn't."

The balance of Friday saw activities of cleaning, polishing and more cleaning for the cadets of Alpha and Bravo Companies. The wear and tear of Glenemma took its toll on boots, clothing, belts, blankets, and the like. These items had to be restored to their original state, and it took a lot of elbow grease to achieve that goal. Also, although Alpha's barracks didn't count as far as the inspection went, it still had to be up to par, so did the cadets' dress. Bravo Company's quarters and its inhabitants dress was a different matter; they had to be letter perfect.

The Musketeers worked in teams getting their clothing clean. When that was complete, they got together with the other eight Alpha cadets and designed the necessary questions which would form part of Bravo's Saturday morning examinations.

For the first time in two weeks, all Alpha cadets were together again, having their platoon pictures taken with their Corporals, Sergeants, and Officers. Following the photo session, Sergeants Beckford and Simpson walked the barracks to have a talk with *the friends of Bergie and Shanks*. Sergeant Beckford was the spokesman.

"We've received another call from Bergie's mom and dad. Apparently the lad was totally shaken up when he learned of his friend's death; however, he's holding up well. In his phone call to them, he passed along his best wishes to the group of you and says he looks forward to seeing you in Vancouver. He'll be home shortly for rest and recuperation. He also called Edwin's mom and dad, and I think that conversation was good for both parties. Er..."

It was obvious Sergeant Beckford found it difficult to speak. He kept blinking and fidgeting with his pace stick. "Er...Bergie has asked that you all attend Edwin's funeral."

"We'll be there, Sergeant. He needn't worry about that...we'll be there," said Moose, softly.

Beckford and Simpson both nodded. "That's fine, son. Simp and I will be there, as well. Right, er, well, we've got to get on with our course reports; let's go Simp. Oh, before I forget!" The Sergeant glared at Danyluk and East. "We're looking forward to hearing you on the radio today."

"Sergeant, do you want my autograph now, or later?" asked East.

Simpson grinned. "It depends on whether or not camp embarrassment is kept to a minimum."

After the Sergeants had left, Danyluk sloped arms with a broom handle. "Did youse hear that? Whether or not camp embarrassment is kept to a minimum? Don't the guy realize he was talkin' to Moose Danyluk, friend and number one assistant to Red Robinson? The *man* who picks the records for the world's best radio announcer? The guy who advises his buddy and protects the airwaves? Why if it wasn't for me, music could go in an entirely different direction."

"Yeah, straight up," quipped Gordie, practising his art of throwing dice against the wall. "If you really made the picks, we'd be listenin' to that fiddle shit all day. I can hear it now... And here's the number one hit that's the sensation of the nation. *'Mother don't wait for the shrimp boats tonight, Father's comin' home with the crabs.'"*

Moose stuck out his chest. "Bull shit! I'd be a great radio announcer. Maybe even as good as my buddy, Red." Moose used his broom handle as a microphone. "I'd say, 'Hello all youse good lookin' broads out there. Yes, youse...the housewives, the secretaries, the funeral parlour assistants and yes, all youse dames who want to be mothers. It's me, your old Moose, the man with the goose. Here's the number one record, *'Gettin' it steady, means keepin' it ready.'*"

Douglas laughed at Moose so hard, he nearly kicked Wayne off his upper bunk.

While all *attached* cadets of Alpha were working on their various course report input forms, Simon glanced at his watch and turned up Moose's radio. "Gather around fellas, the stars are about to mouth off."

The announcer's voice was crisp and clear. "...and that's the news to three-thirty. Stay tuned for further news on the hour and half-hour. Now it's time for..." (Band music started.) "...news from the hill, a daily public service program of CJIB Radio.

"Today, joining us from the Vernon Army Cadet Camp, are cadets Jack East and Moishe Danyluk." (The music stopped.) "Good afternoon boys, it's good to have you with us."

"It's good that we should be with youse and the name's not Moishe, it's Moose." came a response.

The announcer cleared his throat. "Er, yes, well, thank you, er, Moose. Now, I understand we've just come from Glenemma were we underwent outdoor training...is that correct?"

East's voice came out of the radio. "No! At least I didn't know that."

There was a pause while the announcer cleared his throat again and shuffled some papers. "Er, you say you weren't training in Glenemma? It says here you *were* training in Glenemma."

Moose answered. "We didn't realize that youse was there with us."

"Ha ha, ha. No I didn't mean we were with you. I simply meant that *just the two of you* were training in Glenemma. Am I right?"

"Youse is absolutely wrong."

"What? Well, ahem, I'm sorry about that. I must have been given the improper information. What have you boys been doing this past week?"

"We've been at Glenemma," said East.

There was a pause while more papers were shuffled. "Oh, then the two of you have been in Glenemma?"

"Yes, but it wasn't just the two of us, we were with others."

"Yes, er, that's what I meant. Now, how did you find Glenemma?"

East spoke again. "We didn't!"

More shuffling of papers. "WHAT? I thought you said you were there?"

"Youse is right. We were there. But we didn't have to find it, because we wuz driven there in trucks."

Another pause, then the announcer laughed. "Ha, ha. Oh, I see...a little 'in' joke there. That's funny."

"Glenemma's no joke," said East. "Did you think it was a joke, Moose?"

"No! Who told youse Glenemma was a joke?"

"WHAT? No, boys, I didn't mean that Glenemma was a joke. I thought you were making a little joke. Now, what was the essence of your training."

"Mainly Turner's feet," replied East. He didn't mention Cadet Mancinelli's real name. "I had it the last night, and I think I've still got it. The guy's got a stomach problem."

"GOT WHAT? WHAT DID YOU HAVE?"

"The essence. I couldn't even get rid of it in the showers today. I even had some trouble eating my lunch."

"You mean some cadet got a stomach problem exercising in Glenemma?"

"Who told youse he exercised? If he hadda exercised, it coulda gotten worst."

"Don't you mean, worse?"

"With feet like that, it was, *worst*. It's the worst stink I ever smelled."

Needless to say, all Alpha cadets listening to the program were now rolling in the aisles. General Kitching, however, must have been hopping and all of Vernon must have felt sympathy for the radio announcer, who normally never experienced this sort of *communication problem*.

"LET ME GET THIS STRAIGHT? SOME CADET HAD AN ABDOMEN PROBLEM?"

"No, he wuz a Protestant, at least we think he wuz a Protestant. He coulda been a Catholic, but he sure wasn't a problem, Abdullah. What does youse thinks, Jack?"

"Moose means he ain't Muslim."

A long pause followed. "What persuasion is he?"

"Youse means who could he persuade? No one. No one went near him unless he had his feet in a tub. We had to take away his boots."

"Then he had a foot problem, not a stomach problem?"

"Who sez he had a stomach problem? They gotta operate on his stomach, that's all."

"He hasn't got a stomach problem, but they've got to operate on his stomach?"

"Youse is right. We think his pipes go down to his feet."

"Ah, so he's a Scottish cadet and he plays the pipes, is that it?"

"No, he's a BCD cadet who lives here in Vernon. If he played the pipes, no one would be watching, never mind listenin'. Ain't that right, Moose?"

"Yeah, he's got hellitoes's. Youse knows, he's got hell in his toes? He should learn to play the pipes with his feet."

"Boys, I think you mean halitosis and you're saying someone has bad breath?"

"How did youse knows that? It's impossible to smell his breath."

"So the boy was sick?"

"We didn't see him wear a turban, did we Jack?"

"No."

The announcer got himself together. "Not Sikh, sick! So, he has a problem? Did he cut something?"

"Yeah, cheese and rotten eggs. Youse shudda been there. All the trees and bugs died."

"You mean there was a large conflagration? How did it start?"

East replied. "He took off his boots."

Moose replied. "We didn't have a church service, so there was no conflag...er, congregation."

The announcer appeared tired. "He took off his boots, and there wasn't a church service? What did he do, stomp out the fire with his boots?"

"No, youse is wrong. The fire was in his boots."

The radio personality welcomed a hand signal from his producer. It meant there was only one agonizing minute to go.

"Ahem, well it certainly has been a great pleasure talking with you boys. Where are you from?"

"We already told ya. We've just come from Glenemma. Ain't that right, Moose?"

"Yeah, Glenemma."

No, I mean, er, where do you live when you're not here in Vernon?"

"Me? Prince George."

"I'm close to him. Er, Rupert Prince."

"You mean Prince Rupert, don't you?"

"Whatever. Yeah, that sounds good. Youse been there?"

"And with which regiments are you serving?"

"Youse means food, or pop or sumpin' like that?"

"No, what regiments are you with?"

"Er, I'm with the Seaforths."

"Me? I'm with the Irish."

"Then the both of you wear kilts, don't you?"

"Youse can bet your sweet fanny we do. The broads like 'em. Ya wanna know why?"

"Er, NO THANK YOU! What company are you in?"

"Well, Moose was thinkin' about joinin' IBM but now he's thinkin' about a medical career. I'm lookin' towards Campbell's Soup Company. It's good scoff and when it comes to food..."

"No, no, no, I mean what company are you in at the camp?"

"Oh, Delta Company."

"Er, yeah, that's right, Delta Company."

(Band music started again in the background.) "Well, that's it, ladies and gentlemen. Two fine young men from the hill. Thank you, boys."

"Thank youse, sir."

"It's been your, er, our privilege, sir."

Danyluk and East shook the announcer's hand just after they went off the air. When they were out of the building, the interviewer looked around his control room and screamed to his producer, "O.K., WHO'S THE WISE GUY? MY WHOLE CAREER HAS BEEN RUINED IN TEN MINUTES. WHO'S AFTER MY JOB?"

During the ride back to camp, Moose had his chest out and his tongue in his cheek. "That was fun. The guy asked all the right questions. Jeez, those radio announcers are on the ball, ain't they?"

East grabbed an apple out of his pocket and took a big bite. "Ya gotta be on the ball when you're live on the air."

When the duo arrived back in B-33, they were flooded with requests for autographs. Both boys took a few bows and signed with pleasure.

"You guys sounded nervous," said Simon.

Jack threw his apple core in the garbage can. "Well, we were a little nervous, but I'll betcha that's the best interview of the summer for the guy at the station."

After the autograph session, both Jack and Moose were given course report input forms and they went to work writing their assessment of the Bravo cadets in their sections.

Earl quickly read orders and rushed over. "Hey, although we're on duty tonight and confined to camp, all companies are allowed up till midnight. There's a movie in B-3 that starts at 2145. It's called *Morning Departure*, with John Mills."

Douglas was there in a flash. "John Mills is my favourite actor. What's the movie about?"

Jackson's eagerness to pass on the news was contagious. "It's the story of a British submarine that goes down to the bottom and they can't get it back up..."

Gordie interrupted for a moment. "If Moose hadda been there, they wouldda gotten it back up. Ain't that right, Moose?"

"There's never a problem in gettin' it to stay up, Gordie," Moose replied, before he went back to his course reports again. "If I hadda been there, it wouldn't have gone down in the first place."

Earl continued. "I've got more interesting news for you guys. Although we're still attached to Bravo until the Graduation Parade, we don't have to sleep in their quarters anymore. All regular force Corporals are being returned to companies throughout the camp. They're givin' us guys a break."

"Hey great, we're all back together again," said Rothstein. "Are we goin' to the movie?"

After a quick discussion, it was decided they would all see the movie *Morning Departure*.

Before supper, B-33 was quickly cleaned inside and out The meal hour was also kept short so that B-29 would be ready prior to Bravo's cadets heading to the parade square. The cadets would wear their P.T. strip, pith-helmets, heavy socks, boots, and their webbelts.

B-29 was like a madhouse as bunks were moved over to one side and then back again so that the floor could be scrubbed and re-scrubbed. The Bravo cadets were more than aware their time was limited, therefore, there could be no chewing the fat. They had a lot to do before lights out and it was made quite clear to them that if they wanted to go to the movie, they would have to study from 2100 to 2145 hours. The cadets knew they would be tired after they were finished with rifle drill, but their spirits were up because they were in Bravo Company, the best.

Sixteen Alpha cadets pitched in hard to make B-29 look like a palace again. Dust from Glenemma had settled everywhere, even on the window panes.

While the barracks was being prepared, four regular force Corporals were downtown at the Laundromat washing towels which had picked up every possible Glenemma stain. *Pounds* of bleach, however, did marvels and when the towels were returned, they only had to be ironed by their owners.

The main problem was with boots. It would take more than Sergeant Beckford's method of one million small circles, lots of shoe polish, *gallons* of water and *a heap of elbow grease* to get them glittering again.

That night while watching the movie, all cadets, including the Musketeers, would be shining their boots.

Just before the movie started, two simultaneous telephone conversations took place. Moose talked with Alma, as Ryeberg talked to one of the Native girls he had met at Glenemma.

"I've cried my eyes out over Edwin's death and I've said a prayer every minute for Bergie. Thank God he's all right," said Alma.

"Me, too," replied a very solemn Danyluk. Nothing has ever hit me so hard.

We're so close, it was as if was my own life had ended. I never want to go through that again, Alma. I couldn't go through it again."

"Sweetheart, life is full of ups and downs. Unfortunately, sadness is part of it all. Existence itself imposes the loss of loved ones, darling. It's something that can't be avoided. It's a never-ending cycle and we just have to make the best of it while we go around."

"I know that, Alma, but..." Moose suddenly thought of something and his other personality appeared. "Say, youse didn't mention to me that you're Native?"

Alma paused for a moment. "Are you talking to me?"

"Certainly I'm talkin' to youse. Who else would I be talkin' to?"

"I never mentioned it, because I'm not Native, you dummy."

"Mr. Brewer says you are. He also knows that we spent the night at the beach. You also didn't tell me Maggie was a relative of yours and she's also Native."

"Moose, have you been out in the sun without your helmet again? Who the hell is Mr. Brewer and who says Maggie's Native?"

"Mr. Brewer, you know, your grandfather? He..."

Alma interrupted him. "Mr. Brewer? Isn't he Earl's friend?"

"Yeah, that's him."

"He's not my grandfather you, creep. Also, it's none of his business if we spent the night at the lake."

"But Alma...Earl told me..."

Ryeberg's conversation was entirely different. "Hi babe, it's, er, me...Corporal Moose Danyluk here. How are you?"

"Oh, hello, Corporal Moose. Are we still going to the movies tomorrow night?"

"You bet we are, babe. I really enjoyed our...swim. I keep thinking of the way the moon shone on your skin."

"Me, too. I've never been skinny-dipping with a boy before. My Grandfather says not to do it again."

"You told your grandfather?"

"No, I didn't, Melissa did. I got mad at her for telling him."

"Jeez, I betcha he's out for my hide."

"No, he says he likes you and Cunningham and he's warned you guys to keep your hands to yourself. He's gonna talk to both of you about it."

Ryeberg's heart pumped faster. "He knows me? Jesus, I er, when is he going to talk to...us. Hey, we didn't touch you."

"I know, but he's heard of your reputation. He said it was a miracle that you didn't. Also, he describes your anatomy different than what we saw." She giggled, "Do you know what I mean?"

Ryeberg chuckled. "Well, er...it was dark, er, the water was cold...it shriveled up, er..."

"It did? Oh...O.K. So we'll see you tomorrow night. We're not going to the dance, we're going to the movies, right?"

"Yeah, we'll meet you and Melissa in Polson Park at six o'clock, all right?"

"Great! See ya, Corporal Moose."

Although both conversations were entirely unrelated, neither party knew of the *hilarity* that would take place at Polson Park at six o'clock on Saturday night, when Alma meets Ida.

The large hanger B-3, was jammed with cadets. It seemed everyone in camp

wanted to see, *Morning Departure* with John Mills. The pungent smell of shoe polish, Brasso Silvo, and cigarette smoke hung in the stale air of the hulking old building as on screen, the British Navy attempted to raise one of Her Majesty's
submarines off the ocean floor, to no avail.

When it was over, many cadets sat motionless, still staring at the screen,
totally oblivious to the racket of others leaving. The Musketeers were a part of
that group.

Morning Departure was partly based on a true story and the Captain of the
submarine was one of a few who couldn't make it out because they lacked sufficient breathing devices to get them to the surface. Many got out, but some had to
stay behind. Also, air hoses couldn't be attached to the sub because of very rough
weather above. As the movie ended, the captain was saying a prayer.

Jack was so influenced by the ending, he sat there with an unfinished sandwich
in his hand. "Gee, I really feel sorry for those guys. They never had a chance."

Gordie's mouth was open and his deck of cards had not left his pocket. "Did
you notice that the Captain stayed behind? That's leadership, all right. Wow."

"Why didn't they bring another submarine alongside and transfer air from one
to the other?" asked Harvey, smacking Moose on the back of his head.

"Because no one thought of it, I'll betcha," Danyluk replied. "That certainly
would have saved them. Youse is right, Harvey."

Wayne finally snapped out of his daze. "Christ, it was only a movie. John
Mills is still in Britain, making millions. Whatsamatter with you guys?"

Wayne's comment woke up Earl. "But I'll betcha it was based on a true story.
You know guys, wars are tough. When Sergeant Beckford spoke to us at the beach,
for a moment I thought he was reliving an overseas experience. I could see it in his
eyes. When one of your best buddies dies right next to ya, and ya haven't got time
to think of it, it must be heartbreaking as hell."

Slowly the group of them headed for the door. They were the last ones in B-3
and the movie still played heavily on their minds as they marched to B-29.

"How's this look, Corporal?" Mellish asked Douglas, showing him his polished webbelt.

"Great, have you done your boots and your uniform?"

"Yes, Corporal. Do you think we'll win the pennant tomorrow?"

Douglas slowly inspected Mellish's boots. "If all the cadets in this company
have prepared their kit like you, I don't think there's any doubt whatsoever."

A proud, grinning Mellish marched away.

"Hey, we're missing a towel here," Danyluk announced at the end of a set of
bunks.

"It's being ironed right this minute, Corporal Danyluk." a cadet replied.

"Oh. Make sure it's up there when it's ready."

"Sure thing, Corp."

Wayne sat down on the bunk of a cadet who had turned in. He could smell
shampoo so he knew the lad had just showered. "How'd the drill go tonight,
MacKenzie?"

"Really good, Corporal, but...well, we..."

"What's the problem?"

The cadet sat up and Wayne could see the boy was tired. "We haven't had a
minute to ourselves since coming back. I know we've got tomorrow afternoon and
night off, but we're on the parade square again on Sunday and Monday. They don't

give us a chance to breathe."

A smile broadened Wayne's lips. "You know, that was our major complaint during our first year in camp," said Banks, reflecting on his experience in Charlie Company in 1953. "But for some reason, the more they handed out, the more we took it. I'll bet you a million dollars the guard looked fantastically sharp tonight. Am I right or wrong?"

"You're right, we've never been so good. Sergeants Beckford and Sergeant Simpson said we were better than regular force troops."

"I bet you were. Do you think the guys will be up to it on Sunday and Monday? Or do you think they'll complain and try to get a rest?"

The cadet grinned. "We all got together tonight after we handed in weapons. We're gonna be on the parade square before the Sergeants finish church."

Wayne laughed out loud. Past memories shot by as he gave the cadet a mock punch on his chin. "You know what I like about you?"

The cadet lay back and placed his arms behind his head. "What?"

"Your spirit, your dedication, and your integrity. For most of us..." He pointed at some Alpha cadets. "...it's our last year at camp. We foolishly think we're the end-all and the be-all. That when we leave, the camp will come to a grinding halt. When I talk with people like you, I realize how very wrong we are. Hell, you're gonna be here for three more years and you'll soon be sitting on a bunk like I am tonight. And believe it or not, some cadet's gonna tell you exactly the same thing. That you're overworked, oversexed, er, even underpaid."

The cadet chuckled. "Undersexed too, Corporal. Ralph over there..." The cadet motioned to another cadet who was in bed studying . "...says he thought we'd get it in our first year. He had a whole box of rubbers. Jeez, we leave camp in a week and we're still lookin' for it. He told me tonight we'll probably have to wait until we're sixty-five."

Wayne roared out laughing again and stood up. "Well, that time will fly, you just wait and see. You say he *had* a whole box of rubbers? What did he do with them?"

"Well, he keeps his money in one, and he stores his soap in another. I think everything in his barrack box is wrapped up in rubber. Yeah, even his toothbrush."

The smile on Wayne's face grew wider as he shook his head and glanced at the regimental flashers on the cadet's uniform, hanging up behind the bunk. "I see you're in the Seaforths?"

The boy's face beamed. "You bet! It's the best regiment in the world, Corporal."

"Do you really believe that, MacKenzie?"

"With all my heart, Corporal."

"Good! You make damn certain that nobody ever tells you otherwise. I've got to get over to B-33 now. You may be in the best regiment in the world, but I want you to know something. The best regiment in the world is very fortunate to have guys like you."

He shook the cadet's hand. "Good night, Mac!"

"Good night, Corporal Banks...and...thank you."

A melancholy look came over Wayne's face. "You don't have to thank me, Mac. Let me thank you. Look after this place when *we're* gone, will ya?"

"Don't worry, Corporal, *we will*."

About an hour after the Musketeers went to bed that night, Wayne got up and leaned out of his window. The light on the post outside cast an eerie shadow on the silent road. The whole camp was quiet, except for a cricket somewhere near the old parade square.

In fifteen minutes, four years of Vernon experience ran through his head. It just seemed like yesterday that he had entered B-3 and had to strip for the Nursing Sisters. He smiled and looked at Moose who had just started snoring. Moose had walked to the scales with an erection that could hit a home run, but a tap with a rubber mallet had struck him out.

He thought of Edwin Shanks and Bergie leaving on the train. "WE'LL BE HOME FOR CHRISTMAS!" Ed had yelled.

Before Wayne got back into bed, he'd recalled climbing the poles while on the Signals Course and grinding gears on the Driver Mechanics Course. He'd also spent so many hours on both parade squares, he knew every crevice and every bump.

But now it was coming to an end. The friends, the laughs, the heartrending death of a good chum, and the unyielding spirit of the cadets of Bravo Company. Shortly, he wouldn't be a part of it anymore. He wouldn't be able to look after what few camp traditions had been kept. But MacKenzie would, and he smiled as he thought of the boy's words. "Don't worry, Corporal, *we will*."

As Wayne pulled up his covers and rolled over on his side, he could still hear Cadet MacKenzie's voice. "*We will! We will! We will!*"

Just before sleep came, Wayne mumbled. "MacKenzie, I don't think there's any doubt about that, thank God. And Ed, God bless your soul, we all miss ya. Good night buddy."

Old B-33 creaked in silence as if relieved from the uncompromising rays of the day's burning sun. An hour later, that stillness was broken for a few minutes when MacTavish, Rae, and other Scottish cadets entered the building.

Under the watchful confident face of a smiling moon, they had completed their clandestine *task*.

Danyluk's dream was wonderful. He was on a beach in the South Pacific and Alma was waving a giant fan of feathers over his body to keep him cool. Other girls were feeding him pieces of coconut and cool glasses of wine. The setting was fabulous, but throughout, he couldn't understand why someone was screaming, "STAND BY YOUR BEDS!"

He found out soon enough when he found himself on the floor as Sergeant Simpson hurried down the aisle of B-33.

"C'MON, YOU LAZY LAGGARDS, LET GO OF YOUR THING AND GIVE YOUR BLANKETS A FLING! STAND BY YOUR BEDS! I SAID, STAND BY YOUR BEDS!"

Moose gradually got out from under his mattress and pile of bedding, and threw them on his bunk. He glanced at his watch, which read 0545.

Sergeant Simpson was just returning from the other side of the barracks, as most cadets hopped around on one foot, waiting to visit the jon. "IF YOU'RE NOT STANDING BY YOUR BEDS, IN A SECOND YOU'LL BE LYING BY YOUR BEDS!"

Danyluk stood there with his usual morning erection. "Sergeant, what the hell's goin' on? Don't youse ever sleep?. This is the middle of the night."

"DANYLUK PUT ON YOUR UNDERSHORTS! WHAT DO YOU MEAN

WHAT'S GOING ON? IT'S SATURDAY, THAT'S WHAT'S GOING ON! YOU PEOPLE HAVE HAD IT SO SLACK THESE PAST TWO WEEKS, WE'RE GOING TO GO ON A LITTLE RUN. YOU'VE GOT ONE MINUTE TO FORM THREE RANKS ON THE ROAD! MOVE NOW!"

There was a mad dash to the urinal and toilets. Moose's second *head* refused to go down, and as he ran, he tripped trying to pull up his P.T. shorts.

The lineup at the urinal was never-ending, but in twenty seconds he finally made it.

A cadet standing next to him said, "Hey, it's Moose Danyluk. I'm actually standing next to Moose Danyluk; Red's assistant. Moose, can I get your autograph, I never had a chance to get it before."

Moose looked at the ceiling. "Jesus, here I am havin' a piss and youse wants my autograph. Do I look like I'm in the mood to sign autographs? D'ya think I sign autographs when I'm pissin'?"

Moose, I'm not askin' ya to sign it now. I know if you let go of that thing, it'll drag along the bottom and get sucked down the hole. How about when you're finished? I got a pen here, and..."

"I DON'T SIGN AUTOGRAPHS IN THE SHITTER!"

"Well, why not? Ya signed Peterson's while you were havin' a dump?"

"GET LOST YOU CREEP!"

The cadet ambled out, mumbling to himself. "Once they become celebrities, they forget their friends."

"WHAT FRIENDS? I DON'T EVEN KNOW YA!"

The morning air was fresh as Alpha Company formed up in three ranks on the south road outside B-33.

"IT'S THESE LITTLE SURPRISES THAT KEEP YOU PEOPLE ON YOUR TOES," bellowed Sergeant Simpson. "ALPHA COMPANY, ATTEN...TION! MOVE TO THE RIGHT IN THREES, RIGHT...TURN! DOUBLE-QUICK, MARCH!"

"Can you believe this?" Danyluk said to Jackson as the company kicked up the dust on the road leading to the upper camp.

"No, but I can believe that!" Earl replied, glancing to his left at two single beds, placed side-by-side in the middle of the large parade square. There was no space between them and it looked like one blanket had been stretched over both occupants. As well, barrack boxes had been neatly placed at the end of both beds, along with boots, clothing, and the like.

Even the boisterous laughter of Alpha Company didn't faze the two sleeping Corporals who now had the biggest bedroom in the world.

As Moose burst out laughing, MacTavish who was up front, turned and winked. "Good job, eh?"

When Sergeant Simpson jogged from Six Platoon to Five Platoon, he slowed down as he passed Moose. "I don't know who *they* are, but that's where you'd like to be, isn't it, Danyluk?"

"Christ, Sergeant, we've only got a week left. I was gettin' my balls in shape to go home, now they're gonna look like raw meat again. I shudda worn my steel jockstrap."

Simpson smiled. "Danyluk, your balls probably looked like raw meat when you were born. I can see it all now. When the nurse passed you to your mother, your mom must have said, 'What the hell is that dragging on the floor? Didn't you cut the umbilical cord?' The nurse most likely replied, 'We sure did, Mrs. Danyluk, but those are your new baby boy's balls.'"

The guys around Moose were in stitches, but Rothstein made them hold their stomachs. "Then his mom said, I DON'T MEAN THOSE, I MEAN THAT...THAT OTHER UGLY LOOKING THING? The nurse replied, 'Oh that? That's his fore-skin. Are you Jewish Mrs. Danyluk?'

"'No, why?'"

"'It's just as well. Even a Rabbi would look the other way, or ask for a raise if he didn't get a power saw.'"

"SCREW YOUSE GUYS!" screamed a grinning Moose.

After a run through the upper camp, fifty push-ups and fifty sit-ups, Alpha Company returned to B-33. It was now six o'clock and the air was still relatively cool as Sergeant Simpson addressed the cadets.

"I THINK YOU PEOPLE NEEDED THAT! NOW WHEN I FALL YOU OUT, THIS BARRACKS WILL BECOME SPOTLESS AND THEN YOU'LL CARRY ON WITH YOUR OTHER DUTIES! IS THAT CLEAR?"

"YES, SERGEANT!"

"GOOD! ALPHA COMPANY, FALL...OUT!"

Sergeant Simpson got his wish. When his cadets went over for breakfast, B-33 *was* spotless. After their run, the boys had showered, touched up the barracks, and changed into their coveralls. Their starched and soaped bush uniforms, polished boots, and belts would be put on after they returned.

It was hard to squeeze ten people at the table, but somehow it was managed, as MacTavish and Rae explained their *night move*.

"There's two beds out there," whispered Simon. "We know you got Andre Durupt, but who's the other poor bastard?"

The two Scottish cadets really didn't have to answer; their faces indicated who it was. "It was an afterthought," stated Rae. "When we were *moving* Durupt, we just happened to pass Adams' bunk. That's his shirt up the flagpole."

"Yeah, that's what took us so long," offered MacTavish. "Durupt looked so lonely, we thought he needed a partner."

East stopped pushing the food for a moment. "Did everything go smoothly?"

"It was a piece of cake," replied MacTavish. "We nearly had heart attacks with Durupt because he sat up just after the move. But that was it. He lay down again and the next minute was snoring. Adams was his usual easy self. He must have been loaded because we could smell beer on his breath. Also, when we moved his clothing out on the parade square, we noticed he didn't have any buttons on his fly. Jeez, that guy's loony."

Douglas chuckled. "Wow, when they get up, they're going to be furious as hell."

"It'll take 'em a while to do that," said Rae. "We bound them with mine-tape from shoulders to ankles. They're so tightly tied to each other and their beds, it'll take ten pairs of scissors to free 'em. Ya can't see the tape because they're covered with two blankets. They couldn't get up if their lives depended on it."

"Tell them about the sardines," said MacTavish.

Rae's eyes lit up. "Oh, yeah. One of our guys got a parcel from home with a tin of sardines in it. I opened it and poured the juice all over the top part of their blankets. I also squished a couple up and smeared the bottom part of their pillows."

All faces grimaced with a smile.

"What about the fleas?" asked Gordie.

His question caused quizzical looks on all faces except the Scottish cadets. Apparently Cunningham was the only one to know about the fleas. "Did you get the fleas?"

Moose stuck his head low in the middle of the table and whispered. "What fleas? What are you talking about? Fleas?"

"You bet," Rae replied. "The group of us worked for an hour yesterday, gathering grass fleas. We gave 'em fifty and a few bugs as well. No, to be honest, they got more bugs than fleas. Jeez, they're gonna be itchy, I'll say that much."

"And wild, because they can't scratch, either," stated Wayne.

With smiles all 'round, ten contented cadets sat back in their chairs. Once again, a *job* had been pulled off perfectly.

A cadet rushed in and headed to another table. "HEY, YOU GUYS, THE RSM'S MARCHING TO THE PARADE SQUARE BECAUSE THERE'S TWO BUNKS ON IT. C'MON, LET'S GO SEE THE ACTION."

Casually, sixteen Alpha cadets got up, cleaned off their plates, and made their way to the east side of the highway across from the parade square. They were fortunate because Gardiner had just arrived at the beds and forced his massive drill cane under his left armpit.

"WHAT THE BLOODY HELL ARE YOU PEOPLE DOING? GET OUT OF THOSE BEDS, NOW!"

"DID YOU HEAR ME? I SAID, GET OUT OF THOSE BEDS RIGHT THIS MINUTE! THAT'S AN ORDER!"

"WHAT THE HELL DO YOU MEAN, YOU CAN'T? I SAID, GET UP, YOU LAZY LUMMOXES!"

"WHAT WAS THAT?" Gardiner marched forward five paces and peeled back the blankets. Both bodies were mummified in mine-tape. The RSM turned to a nearby Sergeant.

"GET THE PROVOST UP HERE WITH SOME SCISSORS! THESE LAZY BLOCKHEADS NEED TO BE CUT FREE! SO IT'S YOU AGAIN, IS IT, CORPORAL ADAMS? WHAT DO WE HAVE TO DO TO KEEP YOU IN YOUR OWN QUARTERS?"

"AND WHAT'S YOUR NAME?" he asked the other.

"SPEAK UP, MAN! OH, DURUPT, IS IT? WHICH COMPANY ARE YOU WITH? THE WHAT? THE HOSPITAL? YOU'RE WITH THE HOSPITAL? WHAT THE HELL ARE YOU DOING CAMPING OUT HERE ON MY PARADE SQUARE, WITH **HIM**?"

"WHAT THE HELL DO YOU MEAN YOU DON'T KNOW *HIM*? OF COURSE YOU KNOW HIM, YOU'VE BEEN SLEEPING WITH HIM ALL NIGHT! I WANT YOU TWO IN MY OFFICE AT TEN O'CLOCK SHARP! IS THAT CLEAR?"

There was a soft reply.

"I CAN'T HEAR YOU!"

"YES, SERGEANT-MAJOR!" two reclining *bodies* blared.

"WHAT THE HELL ARE YOU PEOPLE TWITCHING FOR? HAVE YOU GOT SAINT VITUS'S DANCE OR SOMETHING? WHAT WAS THAT? YOU HAVE THE NERVE TO ASK ME THAT!? SCRATCH YOUR OWN PRIVATE PARTS, YOU SWAGGERS!"

The scene was so hilarious, all cadets watching had to muffle their laughs.

When the RSM marched off his parade square, the tightly bound, twitching duo resembled two people trussed in straight-jackets.

As the Alpha cadets marched away, Rae said by the time the two were cut free, they'd need straight-jackets.

Bravo Company gleamed as they drew weapons and attached the bayonet frogs to their webbelts. Each cadet had cleaned and painted his own rifle sling and frog with 'White It' and there wasn't a smudge on any of them. In addition, they had taken their bayonets back to their barracks and these deadly objects shone as if they were freshly chromed.

All Bravo cadets had made their own way to the weapons stores in the lower camp, stepping carefully to ensure boot-dust was kept to a minimum. Just prior to forming up and being sized in two guards, they passed around small rags to wipe their boots. The full drill treatment would be carried out this morning and every cadet was looking forward to it.

The appointed Cadet Guard Sergeant-Major stood to the centre front of the front rank and faced his cadets. "GUARD, ATTEN...TION! GUARD...NUMBER!" Instantly, the cadets of the front rank called out their number from the right, one, two, three, four, etc.

"GUARD, FORM...TWO DEEP!" Only the numbered second rank cadets moved. Odd numbers took one pace forward to their front, even numbers took one pace backwards.

"GUARD, RIGHT...DRESS! All cadets except the right hand marker took one small pace forward, (silent count, one-two) paused another silent count (two-three), and all heads shot to their right, except the front and rear markers. The rear marker judged his distance. While all cadets looked to their right, the left arms of those in the front rank went up shoulder-high to their side, allowing the person on their left to shuffle and maintain a straight rank and a proper distance between them. All bodies touched an arm. The rear rank did not put up their arms. Instead, they made certain they shuffled exactly in place behind the man in front of them, and in a straight line with their marker. (Visibly used the second man to the right of them.)

When the quick shuffling stopped, the Guard Sergeant-Major called, "EYES, FRONT!"

"FORMING TWO FORMATIONS OF GUARDS, TALLEST ON THE RIGHT, SHORTEST ON THE LEFT...IN TWO SINGLE RANKS...SIZE!"

All cadets smartly turned to their right, remained in their ranks but fell in and shuffled in sizing order, the tallest cadets on the right, down to the shortest, on the extreme left of each rank. The cadets were now shoulder to shoulder.

"GUARD...NUMBER!" Only the front rank called out their number. The people in the rear rank made note of it. Each cadet in both ranks now knew where he was going. Odd numbers would form the front ranks, even numbers, the rear ranks, in two formations of the guard.

"REAR RANK LEFT...TURN! EQUIDISTANT TO THE FRONT RANK, BUT LEAVING SIX PACES, QUICK...MARCH!" The rear rank marched and then marked time when they were equal with the front rank, but with a six-pace gap.

"SECOND FORMATION OF THE GUARD...HALT!" WILL ADVANCE, RIGHT...TURN! STAND FAST THE RIGHT HAND MARKERS, ODD NUMBERS ONE PACE FORWARD, EVEN NUMBERS ONE PACE STEP BACK...MARCH! ODD NUMBERS TO THE RIGHT, EVEN NUMBERS TO

THE LEFT, RANKS - RIGHT AND LEFT...TURN! FORMING TWO RANKS OF TWO FORMATIONS OF THE GUARD, QUICK...MARCH!"

When the drill movements were completed, two sized, independent formations of the guard were marking time on two markers who still facing their front. The gap between the formations was maintained.

"GUARD...HALT! THE GUARD WILL ADVANCE, LEFT...TURN! GUARD, RIGHT...DRESS." All cadets, except the extreme right hand marker, took one small pace forward and then carried on with the right dress procedures again.

"GUARD, EYES...FRONT!" All arms came down as heads and eyes shot to their front.

"THE GUARD WILL FIX BAYONETS! FIX!" Right hands holding rifles shot forward, left arms took their bayonets out, to the proper count. Bayonets were now unseen, in left hands slightly left of centre of each cadet's left buttock.

"BAYONETS!" The bayonets were brought around in the shortest possible manner, placed, and clicked on the rifles, to the normal count. All left hands with palms to the right were brought forward equal to the left side of the body then smacked against the bayonets; as well, to the normal count. All heads were slightly cocked towards the bayonets and all eyes were on the bayonets.

"GUARD, ATTEN...TION!" All weapons were brought back to the attention position, toe of the rifles even with the toes of their right boots. Heads and eyes were now to their front, left arms stiffly by their left sides.

Two, two rank formations of the guard now stood at attention. From the way they were sized, each formation had the tallest cadets on their flanks, sizing down to the shortest cadets in the middle of each formation.

At this point, the Guard Sergeant-Major handed over his guard to the Guard Commander, who fell in his officers.

Wayne whispered to Douglas. "These guys have come a long way from the first day we saw them. To tell you the truth, I think they're just as good as Alpha Company."

Douglas murmured out of the corner of his mouth. "Methinks you're right."

While the guard had been forming up, other cadet companies were being sized and formed up in front of their respective huts. The band was already on the square.

"GUARD, STANDAT...EASE! GUARD, STAND...EASY!" Weapons were now held to the centre front of each cadet's body, both hands on each weapon.

"GUARD!" Weapons shot out to the fully extended right arm of each cadet. Their left hands shot to their sides.

"GUARD, ATTEN...TION! SLOPE...ARMS! MOVE TO THE RIGHT IN FILE, RIGHT...TURN! BY THE LEFT, QUICK...MARCH!" Instantly, all left feet shot forward, heels dug in, right arms were brought straight back, elbows locked, as the march proceeded.

(Author's note: I never realized how difficult it was to accurately describe drill movements...particularly with weapons. I've had to do the best I could, considering that if these movements were summarized properly, it would have added another hundred pages to the book.)

When the guard halted on the parade square, it was approximately twenty yards to the centre front of the dais.

Shortly, other companies were marched on, and when General Kitching arrived, the parade took its normal course: the General Salute, followed by an inspection, the march past, the General's comments and the Advance In Review

Order.

It was most obvious General Kitching was proud of his cadets. A very smart soldier himself, he knew the amount of effort the cadets had put in preparing for this parade. After calling them forward and informing them of his feelings, he relaxed a little.

"I'M SORRY I NEVER HAD THE CHANCE TO VISIT BRAVO COMPANY IN GLENEMMA. I DID VISIT ALL OF THE OTHER COMPANIES DURING THEIR FIELD TRAINING, HOWEVER, SINCE THIS IS MY LAST YEAR, MY STAFF AND I WERE WRAPPED UP PLANNING NEXT YEAR'S CAMP.

"FROM WHAT I HEAR, BRAVO, YOU EXCELLED, AS DID THE ALPHA STAFF CADETS WHO ASSISTED YOU WITH YOUR TRAINING. MY CONGRATULATIONS TO BOTH COMPANIES. GOOD WORK, INDEED!

"AS YOU KNOW, THIS IS OUR LAST WEEK IN CAMP. NEXT FRIDAY THE GRADUATION PARADE WILL BE HELD IN POLSON PARK AND ON SATURDAY, I'LL BE SEEING YOU OFF AT THE TRAIN STATION.

"I WANT YOU TO KNOW HOW VERY PROUD I AM OF ALL OF YOU. WE'VE HAD A FINE SUMMER AND I AM EXTREMELY PLEASED WITH THE NEW SENIOR LEADER INSTRUCTOR'S COURSE. MY OFFICERS AND NCOs HAVE INFORMED ME OF HOW WELL THIS COURSE PROGRESSED, AND I AM RECOMMENDING THAT SIMILAR TRAINING CONTINUE.

"ONCE AGAIN, MY CONGRATULATIONS TO YOU ALL. I LOOK FORWARD TO SEEING YOU AT THE SWIM AND SPORTS MEETS, AS WELL AS DURING YOUR REGULAR TRAINING.

"NOW, THIS WEEK I ASKED THE CAMP RSM IF I COULD PRESENT THE PENNANT. HE PROTESTED SLIGHTLY, HOWEVER FOR SOME REASON I WON."

As he passed an envelope to General Kitching, a gas pain appeared on Mr. Gardiner's face. Rather a large one, as he tucked his big drill stick under his left armpit and toyed with the ends of his mustache.

"THANK YOU, MISTER GARDINER." The general reviewed the contents of the envelope and smiled. "WITHOUT A DOUBT, THE BEST COMPANY THIS WEEK, IS..."

Necks were strained.

"ONCE AGAIN...BRAVO COMPANY!"

Bravo's cheer was long and loud.

"I KNOW HOW HARD YOU OTHER COMPANIES WORKED, HOWEVER, BRAVO SEEMS TO HAVE DISCOVERED THE SECRET WHEN IT COMES TO CLEANING QUARTERS. WELL DONE, BRAVO COMPANY!"

When the parade was finished and the guard had handed in their weapons, all of Bravo's cadets shook each others' hands and slapped each others' backs. Major Kare, his Officers and NCOs congratulated them and passed along their compliments.

Although Sergeants Beckford and Simpson were not with Bravo, they had been training them on the parade square and they turned up to congratulate them. In their opinion, Alpha was still the number one company, but Bravo was one hell of a close second.

A quick bedding exchange took place for all companies, followed by a mail call, and a pay parade. After that, the cadets of B-29 were allowed a fifteen minute pop break in the canteen, then they were marched to their tents and lecture huts for Saturday Morning Examinations.

In the cadet canteen, Cadet Eldridge sauntered up to Cadet Ryeberg. "Did you phone Ida?"

"You bet I did. Melissa and her are going to meet us in Polson Park at six o'clock tonight. I told her we're going to take them to the movies, not the dance. I've put us in for midnight passes and since this is the only day we've got off, we'd better make the most of it. Have you still got those rubbers?"

"Er, yeah! Should I bring the 'em?" his friend asked.

Ryeberg stuck out his chest. "Well, er, sure, er...why not? Er, we can never tell if...say, do you know how to put them on?"

"Put what on?"

"The rubbers, you pongo!"

"No, I thought you did?"

"I think there's a secret to it?"

"Secret, what secret?"

Ryeberg looked worried. "Christ, the only thing I've ever done with them is fill 'em up with water. I, er, think you just, er, roll 'em on."

Eldridge scratched his head. "Roll 'em on what?"

"On your wang, you dummy."

Eldridge was still puzzled. "You mean like a marble? You just let 'em roll off your wang?"

"No! Ya stick your wang into them. Got it?"

"Yeah, yeah, I er, think I know what you mean?"

Ryeberg smacked his friend on the back and stuck out his chest. "Good! I've been told, they hold back the load."

"They do? How do they do that?"

"You know? The rubber stops the load!"

"Oh, I see. Say, what's the load?"

"How the hell should I know, I ain't never had one yet. Have you?" asked Ryeberg.

"Have I what? replied his friend.

"You know? Er, have you blown, er, well, you know?"

"Have I blown my nose? Sure, lots of times, haven't you?"

"Not your nose, you idiot! Have you blown your wang?"

"Listen, Ryeberg, how in the hell can I blow my wang? You mean when I'm on a bus and my wang sneezes, I'm supposed to whip it out, get a hankie, and blow it? I don't know about you, but when I've got a cold, my wang don't sneeze. For that matter, it don't even cough. Got it?"

"I didn't mean that, you..." Ryeberg got flustered. "Oh for Pete's sake, bring the rubbers anyway! If anything else, we can always throw some water balloons in the theatre."

While the two *men of the world* were discussing *noses*, Moose was questioning Jackson.

"I think Mr. Brewer's gone senile on us. Alma ain't his granddaughter, neither is Maggie."

"Who told you that?" asked Earl.

"Alma did. Jeez, I felt like an idiot after I asked her. How in the hell did youse get the impression Alma and Maggie were his granddaughters?"

Earl looked bewildered. "Mr. Brewer told me. All right, if they ain't his grand-daughters, how'd he know about the midnight swim?"

A silly expression hit Moose's face. "I don't know. Maybe he's a voyeur, or the girls are illegitimate?"

Jackson appeared apathetic. "Oh, just forget it. I'll talk with him again. Jesus, Moose, you're gettin' everything mixed up these days. You must be makin' too much money with your various funds."

While Earl and Moose were discussing *family members*, a conversation was taking place at Eunice's house.

"YES, I'M BACK IN THE GODDAMNED CADET KITCHEN. SOME SON OF A BITCH MOVED MY BUNK ON THE PARADE SQUARE. I WAS WITH SOME HOMO BY THE NAME OF DURUPT! JESUS, HIS BREATH STUNK LIKE SARDINES! AND HIS FEET! OH, MY GOD, HIS FEET WERE SOME-THING ELSE."

"YOU WERE THAT CLOSE TO HIM?"

"THAT CLOSE? THAT CLOSE? I EVEN GOT HIS FUCKING FLEAS! I'VE GOT BITE MARKS ALL OVER MY BODY! WHAT KIND OF A GOD-DAMNED HOSPITAL ORDERLY IS HE...FULL OF FLEAS?"

"Oh, Corporal Adams, honey. Quit complaining and get those pants off and I'll take a look at your bite marks. I'll kiss 'em better."

"JESUS, EUNICE, IS THAT ALL YOU EVER THINK ABOUT? I'M WALKING AROUND RIGHT NOW WITH NO BLOODY BUTTONS ON MY FLY. THEY'RE ALL OVER YOUR HOUSE. I'LL GET THAT SON OF A BITCH, MOOSE! I'LL BET HE DID THAT TO ME! I'LL GET THE BASTARD, YOU JUST WAIT AND SEE IF I DON'T!"

Eunice took off her blouse. "How do you like my new uplift bra?"

Adams ignored her. "YES, THAT'S WHO IT WAS, I BET! CHRIST, I HAD FLEAS IN MY MOUTH, FLEAS UP MY NOSE AND EARS AND FLEAS UP MY ASS! WE WERE SO TIGHT I COULDN'T EVEN SCRATCH! AND THOSE FEET OF HIS. I CAN'T GET THE SMELL OF FEET AND SARDINES OUT OF MY NOSTRILS."

"Say, you're sorta weird, being so close to someone you don't even know. Sweetheart, I've also bought new crotchless panties. Do ya wanna see 'em?"

"I'VE NEVER HAD THIS HAPPEN TO ME IN MY LIFE. NO CADET BY THE NAME OF MOOSE IS GOING TO MAKE A FOOL OUT OF ME! I'LL GET HIM, YOU JUST WAIT AND SEE! WHY I'VE EVEN GOT A SPIDER BITE ON MY...Eunice what are you doing? Oh, please, not again? I haven't recov-ered from last time, and I've got a spider bite on the end..."

"OH, SCREW YOU! GET THOSE PANTS OFF, OR I'LL RIP 'EM OFF, YOU ASSHOLE! IF YOU CAN SPEND THE NIGHT WITH SOME HOMO, YOU CAN LOOK AFTER *LITTLE* OLD ME! Mommy's gonna give you some candy before I take you to the movies tonight. Phew, did you change your socks today?"

"YES, I CHANGED MY SOCKS! IT'S NOT MY FEET YOU SMELL, IT'S HIS FEET. THE ODOUR IS COMING FROM EVERY PORE IN MY BODY! ALSO, WHO IN THE HELL SEZ WE'RE GOING TO THE MOVIES?"

Eunice ripped off his pants. "I DID YOU ASSHOLE!"

"Oh all right then, maybe it'll cool me down. God Eunice, you're breaking my back."

"I'LL BREAK OFF YOUR PRICK IF YOU DON'T GET IT UP! JESUS, YOU STINK!"

While the cadets of Bravo Company were writing their exams, the eight Musketeers read their letters in B-33. Gordie Cunningham had received one from a brokerage firm he'd never heard of. As he opened it, he couldn't understand why they had sent it. Shortly, he was laughing out loud.

"Hey guys, listen to this:
'To all stockholders.

Dear Mr. Cunningham:

Our records show that you are holding shares in the following companies:

1. American Can Company Ltd.

2. Western Natural Gas Company Ltd.

3. Northern Tissue Co.

4. Western Water Company Ltd.

Owing to uncertain market conditions, at the present time we advise you to sit tight on the American Can, hold your Water, and let your Gas go.

You will be greatly interested to know that the Northern Tissue touched a new bottom today, and thousands have been wiped clean.

Yours very truly,

SQUATT, LEAVITT AND U.R. DUNNFOR, INVESTMENT BROKERS.' "

The look on Gordie's face had them all chuckling. All except East.

"I think my Dad's got shares in American Can," he said, biting on a banana. "No, maybe it's Continental Tin, or Amalgamated Containers. Let me see...he sold his International Plastics to buy...anyway it's one of them. I'll bet..."

Gordie picked up his writing tablet. "I think I know who sent me this. I'm gonna write and ask him to buy me five-thousand shares of Northern Tissue. Let's see what the creep says then."

East's seriousness kept them howling, and Danyluk's letter made it worse.

"Guys, listen to this"

'My darling Moose:

You very wonderful person, you. I never dreamed that you had such a big heart. When it comes to big things, you take the cake.

When I received your letter about the SOLDIERS WITH THREE TESTICLES FUND, I went collecting door-to-door in my neighborhood. I have enclosed a cheque for sixteen dollars and seventy-five cents. I do hope it helps those poor boys who must have one removed.

The funniest thing happened while I was collecting. When I knocked on a door, a girl opened it and gave me the oddest look. She told me three testicles were old hat, that she'd been collecting for the SICK SOLDIERS WITH FIVE TESTICLES FUND.

Moose, she wouldn't give me a name, but she said the boy who's running the charity is in Vernon. Would it be possible for the two funds to merge?

Also, you won't believe how small the world really is. When I started this letter, another girl knocked on my door with a collection tin in her hand which read, SUF-FERING SOLDIERS WITH SIX AND A HALF TESTICLES FUND!

I gave her a dollar and she said if I donated two dollars more, I would stand a chance of winning a prize. It's a testicle key chain, with a real testicle embedded in plastic. She also spoke about some diarrhea fund, but I didn't let her tell me what the prize was on that. Oh, you poor, poor boy. Come home soon with your two testicles intact.

All my love, Margo. XXXX'"

"She sounds like a real nice girl. Where did you meet her?" asked Wayne.

"At a Salvation Army meeting," replied Moose.

Instantly all eyes turned in his direction. "You're not a member of the Salvation Army," said Rothstein. "I think you've got to play an instrument to get in that organization."

Moose smiled. "Oh, I play an instrument all right."

Simon laughed. "I'll bet you do and you read National Geographic music, as well. Wasn't that you playing in the jon the other night?"

"Screw you, Simon! I play the triangle and she plays the tambourine. When we met, it was love at..."

"First bite?" asked Douglas.

"How did you guess?" were Danyluk's last grinning words.

Just before they left to have lunch, East said, "I'VE GOT IT!"

"Got what?" asked Jackson. The rest also looked concerned.

"MY DAD SOLD HIS INTERNATIONAL PLASTICS TO BUY DOCTOR NAG'S DOG FOOD. NO, IT COULD HAVE BEEN WORLDWIDE ZINC. YES, THAT'S IT! I'VE GOT IT! HE BOUGHT WORLDWIDE ZINC, AND ANOTHER FIVE-HUNDRED SHARES OF...!" When East stopped counting on his fingers and looked up, he was alone. "SAY, YOU GUYS, WAIT UP FOR ME! DON'TCHA WANNA KNOW ABOUT DOCTOR NAG'S..."

At 1430 that afternoon, sixteen Alpha cadets were honoured that they were asked to join Bravo Company when platoon pictures were taken. The cadets of that company had insisted that their new *Corporals* be seated alongside them.

After the photo session, Major Kare addressed his company.

"WELL, I WOULD LIKE TO TELL YOU THAT YOU'VE GOT MORE TIME OFF, HOWEVER, YOU HAVEN'T. ALTHOUGH YOU'VE GOT THE BALANCE OF TODAY, THIS COMPANY IS ON THE PARADE SQUARE ALL DAY TOMORROW AND ALL DAY MONDAY."

There were a few groans, but most cadets understood.

"BUT I DID MAKE ARRANGEMENTS FOR YOU TO HAVE SUNDAY AND MONDAY NIGHTS OFF!"

Cheers of appreciation were loud.

"PLEASE KEEP IN MIND THAT OUR COMPANY PICNIC WILL BE HELD AT KIN BEACH ON TUESDAY NIGHT. THE TRUCKS WILL LEAVE HERE AT 1700 HOURS.

"NOW FOR THOSE OF YOU WHO ARE NOT GOING DOWNTOWN, THERE'S A MOVIE IN B-3 TONIGHT. IT'S CALLED, *FROM HERE TO ETER-NITY.* ALSO, DON'T FORGET THERE'S BOXING IN B-3 TOMORROW NIGHT! I DON'T THINK ANY OF YOU ARE ENTERED. THE CADETS ARE FROM ALPHA, CHARLIE, DELTA, ECHO, FOXTROT, GOLF, AND HOTEL COMPANIES.

"ARE THERE ANY QUESTIONS?"

A cadet came to attention, shooting out his arm. "SIR, AFTER WE RETURN OUR KIT ON FRIDAY MORNING, DO WE HAVE THE REST OF THE DAY OFF?"

Major Kare smiled. "YES, BUT ONLY AFTER YOUR BARRACKS ARE CLEANED UP!"

There were no further questions, and after the company was dismissed, the Musketeers headed to B-33 for a shower.

"Are we all on for the dance tonight?" asked Gordie, smearing a brand new bar of ambrosial French soap all over his chest.

Next to him, Moose soaped up with Sergeants' Soap. "God, that smells nice. Listen, dearie, if you keep on usin' that stuff, I might ask you to dance."

The *gambler* laughed. "Screw you, Moose. East told Jackson that when you danced with him you kept stepping on his feet and you never allowed him to lead."

When Jack heard that statement, he dropped his shampoo. "I DID WHAT? I NEVER SAID NO SUCH A THING! WHAT ARE YOU TALKING ABOUT, GORDIE? MOOSE, I'VE NEVER DANCED WITH YOU! EARL, WHAT ARE YOU BULL SHITTING EVERYONE FOR?"

The shower room erupted in laughter. Gordie loved bugging East. Normally he did it by taking Jack's money in restaurants, but he got his digs in at other times, as well.

Moose carried it further. "I never said that, Earl. I said when Jack asked me to dance, he had his hands all over my ass. It wasn't a sexual gesture, he simply wanted the sandwich I had in my back pocket."

"BULL SHIT! WHAT THE..." Jack couldn't complete his words because he started chortling as well. "That'll be the day when I grab Moose's ass. There's nothing there to grab. A whippet's got more meat on his ass than Moose."

More laughter was interrupted by the entrance of Jonathan and James. Both boys had the weekend off from hospital duty.

Jonathan closed the window. "Did you guys hear about Corporal Durupt? This morning he was found in bed on the parade square with that asshole Provost Corporal."

Straight faces were now the order of the day. "Yeah, what happened? Has he got somethin' going with that guy?" replied Moose, reopening the window.

James closed the window. "He doesn't even know the fellow. I'll tell you, he's mad. He said the guy's breath reeked of sardines and his feet stunk to high Heaven. Right now he's up at the stores trying to exchange his mattress because of the smell and the fleas. The Provost Corporal's loaded with fleas."

Before opening the window, Wayne rinsed the shampoo of his body. "If he doesn't know him, why the hell would he sleep with him in the middle of the parade square?"

Jonathan closed the window. "Andre figures some of the guys who sleep around Adams...yeah that's his name, did it so the medical staff would learn just how filthy the guy really is. He's told the doctor and the doc's going to have Adams' side of the hut fumigated, as well as Adams. Andre also says Adams' foot problem is the same as Mancinelli's. That'll call for a second operation."

Moose opened the window and stood in front of it so it couldn't be closed again. "Andre's really pissed off, is he? What a shame that..."

"YOU, THERE! YES, YOU! WHAT THE BLOODY HELL ARE YOU STICKING YOUR ASS OUT THE WINDOW FOR? STAND STILL THAT MAN, I WANT TO SEE WHO YOU ARE!" The Camp RSM's voice was really loud this time.

Moose and the others never moved so fast in their lives. In seconds, Moose had run to his bunk and was underneath the covers.

No sooner had they fled, a tall cadet from the other side walked in and got under a shower. Loud voices from the shower room soon shook the building and silenced the cadet's singing.

"ARE YOU SOME SORT OF A EXHIBITIONIST? WELL, ARE YOU?"

"Sergeant-Major, I had to take off my clothes to take a shower."

"I KNOW THAT...DON'T GET SMART WITH ME, YOUNG MAN! DO YOU ALWAYS STAND IN FRONT OF THE WINDOW WAVING YOUR ASS?"

"I was just putting my towel on the bench, Sergeant-Major."

"NOW I'VE HEARD JUST ABOUT EVERYTHING! YOU HAD YOUR ASS STICKING OUT THE WINDOW, DIDN'T YOU? DIDN'T YOU?"

"Well, er, it's possible, but..."

"ARE YOU A FRIEND OF THAT MANIFESTATION CALLED DANY-LUK?"

"Why yes, I asked for his autograph and..."

"WHY DID YOU WANT HIS AUTOGRAPH?"

"Because he's a star. He's big in the..."

"I *KNOW* THAT! MY GOD, SON! HOW OLD ARE YOU?"

"Sixteen, sir."

"WHEN DID YOU START BEING TURNED ON BY THOSE THINGS?"

"When I was fourteen, sir."

"WHAT THE HELL IS THE WORLD COMING TO? LISTEN TO ME, MAN, THERE'S NOTHING WRONG WITH THE BODY YOU'VE GOT. GO OUT WITH A GIRL...GET IT ON! FIND OUT FOR YOURSELF THAT SIZE ISN'T EVERYTHING. JUST BECAUSE DANYLUK'S HUGE, DOESN'T MEAN THAT YOU HAVE TO IDOLIZE HIM, DOES IT? IT'S NOT GOOD FOR YOUR HEALTH!"

"Er, all right sir. But I've sent his autograph to my girlfriend as well."

"YOU TOLD HER?"

"Yes, sir. She says she wants to meet him."

"I'LL BET SHE DOES! AND YOU DON'T MIND?"

"Not at all, sir. We share everything. She's even asked for his picture."

"WHAT? HE'S GOT PICTURES?"

"He says he has, but he charges for 'em."

"YOU MEAN YOU'RE ACTUALLY GOING TO BUY ONE FOR YOUR GIRLFRIEND? MY GOD MAN, SHE'LL FAINT!"

The cadet relaxed and smiled. "Oh, come on, Sergeant-Major, he ain't that big. Red's bigger."

As the RSM marched out, he was once again talking to himself. "I can't believe it. Now that creep's signing autographs and selling pictures. To make matters worse, the boys are asking for them and sending them to their girlfriends. They *share* these things? God, whoever thought the fifties were going to be like this? And Red's bigger? I don't know who Red is, but I sure pity the poor bastard."

When the RSM had left the building, Moose ran back into the shower room to retrieve his towel. The admiring cadet was now drying himself off.

"Hi Moose! The RSM and I were just talking about you. He knows how big you are in show business. Isn't it great being so popular with the RSM as well as the rest of the world?"

Moose didn't take the time to talk, in case the RSM returned. "WHAT'S THAT? YEAH, REALLY GREAT!"

At five-forty-five that afternoon, the Musketeers' girls met in Polson Park, waiting for their boys. It was wonderfully cool as they sat in the stands watching a group of small local boys play baseball. The fifty or so parents and friends were cheering loudly, and because Alma felt a little sad, she moved away from the main group and seemed lost in a daze.

Actually, Alma had been feeling sort of lost all day, knowing that next Saturday at this time, Moose would be gone. "God, time flies," she mumbled to herself. "It only seems like days since he arrived."

Although Alma appeared to be watching the game, her mind was on Moose, not baseball. She was in a daydream and didn't notice or hear the conversation of the two Native girls that sat behind her. That is until a certain name was mentioned.

"Melissa, Isn't it amazing how we met those cadets. They're so cute and so polite."

"I know, Ida, but grandfather says you'll have to watch yourself with Corporal Moose Danyluk. Apparently he's got the fastest hands in the west."

Alma's eyes opened wide as she slowly turned around and then quickly turned back, pretending to watch the game; her mind going at a mile a minute, as she listened to their statements.

'The fastest hands in the west?'
'Amazing how we met the cadets?'
'Watch yourself with Corporal Moose Danyluk?'

"JUST WHO THE HELL ARE THESE GIRLS?" she asked herself.

Alma didn't have to wait long to find out, because the girls talked openly.

Chuckling shyly, Ida said, "Yes, isn't it a coincidence that grandfather knows Moose? I mentioned that to Corporal Moose on the phone and he was so charming and shy. He even said his 'willie' shriveled up in cold water."

"He told you that? How come?" asked Melissa.

Ida chuckled. 'Because grandfather told me Corporal Moose was hung like a elephant. He sure isn't when he's in cold water."

'OH, YES HE IS!' Alma thought.

Both girls burst out giggling and tried to muffle themselves. In the meantime, Alma wasn't laughing, she was fuming.

Melissa fidgeted with her handbag. "Can I tell you a secret, Ida?"

"Oh, Melissa, you know you can. If anyone does too much talking, it's you."

Melissa giggled again. "Well, I never mentioned this before, but Corporal Gordie touched my right breast. I gave him such a smack, he'll never do that again."

"THE NERVE!" Ida replied, moving a bit closer. "What did it feel like?"

"It was wonderful. His hands are so soft. And I don't know if I should tell you something else?"

"Why? You know I won't tell anyone!"

"Well, er...your Corporal Moose touched my left breast and grabbed my ass."

Alma's ears grew twice their size. She wasn't missing anything.

Ida stood up in a hurry and then sat down again. "WHAT? MY CORPORAL MOOSE GRABBED YOUR ASS?" screamed Ida.

"Ssshhh, not so loud. That was when we first met in the water, remember? I think it was before he decided he wanted you."

"Oh, well that's all right. Do you think we should let them put their arms around us in the movies tonight?"

Melissa started smearing lipstick again. There must have been fifteen coats on her lips. "Yes, but I don't want to go any further. Not too much further anyway. Well, I might let him...God, his hands are smooth. I wonder what's keeping them?"

Alma got up and turned around. "YOU HUSSIES!" she yelled, before leaving the bleachers and walking over to her friends. "MAGGIE, CAN I SEE YOU FOR A MOMENT, PLEASE?"

"What's her problem?" asked Ida.

"She's probably just a jealous bitch because she ain't got a boyfriend," Melissa replied, giving the finger to Alma's back. "NOSY PARKER!"

Maggie walked over to Alma. "What's up?"

"Do you see *those two*?" she said, moving her head and eyes to point them out. When Maggie looked, another finger movement was given.

"Yes, SAME TO YOU?" yelled Maggie. "Alma, what brought this on?"

Over the next few minutes, Alma explained everything, and Maggie's voice got louder as Alma continued.

"WHAT? WHAT? NAKED IN THE *WATER*? YOU'RE JOKING! YOU'RE *NOT* JOKING? OH, MY *GOD*! ARE *YOU* SERIOUS? THEY WHAT? THAT LOUSE! *SHRIVELED* IN THE WATER? HER RIGHT *TIT*? HER REAR *END*? THIS IS WAR! I'LL SMOOTH-HANDS *HIM*! THOSE HARLOTS! HE'LL FIND IT DIFFICULT TO *PICK UP* HIS DECK OF CARDS!"

While Alma and Maggie were *whispering*, they were too wrapped up in their conversation to see Ida and Melissa walk out of the stands to meet Ryeberg and Eldridge. Holding hands, they disappeared around the corner.

When Alma and Maggie returned their attention to the two *hussies*, they noticed they were gone.

"Those sneaky creeps, they've picked them up already. C'mon, Maggie, let's search the restaurants, then we'll check out the theatre."

Alma and Maggie were so mad, they didn't bother telling the rest of the girls where they were going. Five minutes later, the Musketeers arrived.

Diane rushed into Douglas' arms. "Hello, stranger," she said, as he swung her around.

Douglas smiled and kissed her. "Stranger isn't the word. I just got a phone call from my mom asking why I haven't written. I told her there's only so many minutes in a day."

Hand-in-hand, they slowly walked to their special place beside the creek. With no one around, it was quiet and cool as he took off his beret and webbelt and lay down next to her, staring into her eyes.

"Douglas Brice, do you realize you leave next Saturday and other than at the beach, we haven't had any real time together?"

He put his arm around her waist and pulled her in close, very close. "Well, would you believe, I've got the day off tomorrow, not the night. And, I've got all day Monday off. What should we do?"

An enamoured smile came over Diane's face. "I know what I'd like to do, but we could go out to the farm," she said softly. My gran's been after me for weeks to visit them and I can get the car."

Douglas revealed a shy smile before he moved some hair out of her eyes and kissed her. "I know what I'd like to do to," he replied, squeezing her. "That's a super idea. Let's go to the farm. Can Wayne and Debbie come?"

"If they didn't, I'd think something was wrong. Did you know...?"

Diane was interrupted by the sound of Moose's voice.

"HEY, YOUSE GUYS, WHERE THE HELL'S ALMA AND MAGGIE?"

Diane propped herself up on her knees. "THEY WERE WITH US A MINUTE AGO. I THOUGHT THEY WERE WITH THE TWO OF YOU?"

"DO THEY LOOK LIKE THEY'RE WITH US? WE THOUGHT THEY WERE IN THE JON, BUT THEY WOULD HAVE FLUSHED THEMSELVES DOWN BY NOW!"

Gordie whispered something in Moose's ear.

"OH, FOR CHRIST'S SAKE, CUNNILINGUS, NOBODY WANTS TO GAMBLE AT THE MOMENT! GIVE IT A REST AND LET'S GO LOOK FOR THE GIRLS!"

Moose and Gordie sauntered away with Moose calling, "OH, ALMA, MAGGIE, WHERE THE HELL IS YA? WE'RE COMIN' TO GETCHA, YOUSE LUCKY DEVILS!"

"I wonder where they went?" Diane asked, before she regained her previous thought and lay down again. "Did you know Wayne has asked Debbie to come to Vancouver?"

Douglas plucked a piece of grass and started chewing the end of it. "Yeah, he told me. He really doesn't know what he's going to do right now. I hope he doesn't work on the ferries or get a job. If he does, I'll really miss him, we've been closer than brothers for a long time. Is she going?"

Diane peered up at the blue sky breaking through the trees. "I think so. We haven't talked about it too much, because Wayne won't tell her his plans."

"He won't tell me, either. For some reason he just wants to get away. More and more he reminds me of James Dean, the movie actor. The other day he showed me a picture of himself walking down Granville Street. You know, one of those street pictures someone takes? They hand ya a ticket, and in a week the picture's ready?"

"Yes."

"Well, he actually looked like James Dean. The same facial expression, the same stride. He had a cigarette in his mouth and he was wearing an open raincoat. Diane chuckled. He's a great guy, maybe he just wants to see the world. Maybe he'll even go to Hollywood?"

Douglas sat partly up, leaning on his elbow. "Hollywood? You mean to get in the movies?"

"Yeah, wouldn't that be exciting?"

Shaking his head, Douglas said, "No. Not Wayne. Now, Moose would be another matter. The only trouble is there wouldn't be enough starlets for him to conquer."

They both laughed when Diane said, "I can see it all now. '*THE THING AND I,*' starring Deborah Kerr and Moose Danyluk."

"Or how about," '*LOVE IS A MANY SPLENDORED THING,*' starring Stud Danyluk."

Their fun was interrupted by Moose and Gordie arriving.

"Speak of the devil," said Douglas.

"THEY AIN'T IN THE PARK, SO WE'RE ALL HEADIN' OVER TO THE DANCE. ARE YOUSE GUYS COMIN'? THEY'RE PROBABLY OVER THERE

BECAUSE THEY'RE MAD AT US FOR SOMETHIN' WE DID."

"What did you do?" asked Brice.

Moose pushed his lips together for a moment. "YA KNOW, I CAN'T REMEMBER DOIN' ANYTHING! HOW ABOUT YOUSE, GORDIE?"

Cunningham had a quizzical expression on his face as he scratched his head. "MAGGIE MAY HAVE BEEN MAD BECAUSE I BEAT HER AT STRIP POKER, BUT SHE KNOWS I ALWAYS WIN. I CAN'T THINK OF ANYTHIN', EITHER!"

As the Musketeers and six of their girls walked over to the arena, the movie theatre on the main drag was starting. It was packed because it was Saturday night. As chock-full as it was, fate had placed Corporal Adams and his *little* girl in the row in front of two *certain* couples.

Fate must have played another part in the selection of the movies as well. The first picture was *Dracula*, followed by, *Night of the Werewolf.*

After the opening cartoon, Eunice decided to stand up and get some more popcorn while the *Dracula* credits were running.

"WELL, GIVE ME SOME MONEY, ASSHOLE!"

"Pay for it yourself. I've already bought you two bags."

"YOU CHEAP BASTARD! AFTER ALL I'VE DONE FOR YOU!"

Ryeberg couldn't see the screen. "Down in front, please!"

"UP YOUR ASS, SOLDIER BOY! ADAMS, ARE YOU GONNA GIVE ME THE MONEY, OR DO I HAVE TO TAKE IT?"

Adams whispered. "Jesus, Eunice keep it down, I may know someone in here. Take this fiver and bring me back the change."

"UP YOURS! I'LL KEEP THE GODDAMNED CHANGE FOR INTERMISSION!" Eunice then attempted to *fight* her way to the aisle in the dark.

When the feature started, Ryeberg slowly put his arm around Ida. At first she shrugged it off, but persistence prevailed and smiles came over two faces scrutinizing the screen.

In the meantime, Eldridge placed his hand on Melissa's knee and it was thrown off three times. She didn't argue, however, when he put it around her shoulder.

"EXCUSE ME! HEY, I'M TRYIN' TO GET BACK IN HERE! MOVE YOUR GUT BACK, POPS! SAME WITH YOU, LADY!"

Eunice tripped slightly just before she found her seat and half-a-bag of popcorn ended up on Corporal Adams' lap.

"CHRIST!" He lowered his voice again. "I've got no buttons on my fly, and now my crotch is loaded with popcorn."

Eunice stood up again. "WELL, LET ME GET MY HAND IN THERE AND TAKE IT OUT, YOU IDIOT! GOOD FOOD SHOULDN'T GO TO WASTE!"

"Eunice, get your hands out of my fly."

"Down in front, please."

"UP YOUR ASS, SOLDIER BOY! HERE ADAMS, STAND UP AND PUT THIS BAG UNDER YOUR CROTCH! HEY, WHERE'S YOUR SHORTS?"

Half the theatre yelled, "WILL YOU SHUT IT UP BACK THERE!"

"They're at your house. Don't you remember ripping them off me?"

"Down in front, please."

"LISTEN ASSHOLE, WILL YOU SHUT YOUR MOUTH? I'LL SIT DOWN WHEN I GET THE REST OF MY POPCORN OUT OF HIS CROTCH!"

When someone finally fetched the manager, he said, "Oh it's you again is it?. How did you get back in here? Listen, keep it down or I'll move you out like last time. Got it?"

"YEAH, I'VE GOT IT...AND NOW I'M GOING TO EAT IT! GO COUNT YOUR TICKETS!"

After a final warning from the manager, the next thirty minutes were relatively quiet as Eunice ate her popcorn. During that time, Ida and Melissa were so scared by the movie, they allowed the boys to slowly move their arms down their backs to their waists, bringing the girls in closer.

When Eunice finished her popcorn, she decided to move her big arm around Corporal Adams' shoulders. Ryeberg now couldn't see any part of the screen, so he tapped Eunice on her arm.

"Excuse me, could you move your arm, please? I can't see."

"AIN'T THAT JUST TOO BAD! SCREW YOU!"

That was it. Eunice in all her loveliness had got Ryeberg upset. He tapped Eldridge and they excused themselves and headed for the Men's room.

"How many rubbers did you bring?"

His friend felt in both of his front pockets. "Two. I was gonna bring the others but they were full of soap and toothpaste. Did we need 'em as well?"

"No, two's enough. Let's fill them up. That dame in front of me is now gonna get hers."

When the boys walked back through the lobby, they turned sideways as they passed the confectionery counter. The manager and staff didn't notice a thing, especially two large bubbles.

At intermission, Eunice decided she would enter the food line again. She hadn't returned when the second movie started and this suited Ryeberg just fine.

When she emerged into the darkened theatre, she let it be known that she was back.

"LET ME THROUGH! HEY, I'M CARRYIN' STUFF, YA KNOW. MOVE YOUR ASS, POPS! AH, THAT'S BETTER!"

Just as Eunice flipped her seat to sit down, Ryeberg let one of the containers slip down the back of her chair, landing right under her buttocks.

'WHOMP!' the noise was loud. For that matter, so was Eunice when she surged up, spilling her popcorn all over the heads of the people in front of her.

"AGGGHHH! WHAT THE...? HEY, I'M COVERED IN...WHAT IS THIS SHIT, POP OR SOMETHIN'? I'M FUCKIN' DRENCHED, YOU ASSHOLE, WHAT THE HELL DID YOU DO?"

Adams was also on his feet. He, too, had been soaked from the waist down.

"WHAT DID I DO? YA MEAN, WHAT THE HELL DID YOU DO, YOU LOW LIFE? JESUS CHRIST, I'M COVERED IN WATER, I'VE GOT NO SHORTS, MY CROTCH IS SOAKED! I'M SICK AND TIRED OF YOU EUNICE! I DON'T GIVE A DAMN WHO YOUR FATHER IS, I'M..."

As Adams was yelling, Melissa, in all her innocence, said, "Why did you do that, Corporal Moose?"

Adams, his eyes on fire, turned towards Ryeberg. "SO, YOU'RE THAT SON OF A BITCH, ARE YOU? NOW I KNOW WHAT YOU LOOK LIKE! LET ME...AT..."

Adams made a mad grab for Ryeberg who ducked and gave the Corporal the other *container* right in his face. The NCO was now totally sopping as he tried to climb over the seat to get his hands on one of the now-fleeing foursome.

The theatre was in pandemonium as Adams chased Ryeberg down the aisle, screaming obscenities. The other three, knowing they weren't *wanted*, just stood and laughed, watching Eunice chasing Adams, screaming, "THAT'S NOT HIM, FUCKEE! CORPORAL ADAMS, HONEY PIE, WHATAYA DOIN'!"

It took the manager and two assistants to drag the screaming Adams and Eunice out of the theatre.

When it was quiet, the manager apologized, the movie came back on, and four smiling teenagers moved to the back row and started necking. The excitement had thrown the girls off guard, and both had thrust Mr. Brewer's warnings to the wind.

The outrageous scene had been witnessed by Alma and Maggie who were scouring the threatre looking for Moose and Gordie, to no avail. When they heard Adams screaming Moose's name and chasing another cadet, they suddenly realized how very wrong and childish they were to have suspected Danyluk and Cunningham of two-timing them.

Alma grabbed Maggie's arm, hustling her out the door. "Oh, my God, Maggie, what have we done? Those boys must have just been using Moose and Gordie's names. To think that I doubted my darling Moose. What are we going to do?"

Maggie took a coin out of Alma's ear with her right hand and a deck of cards of out her skirt pocket with her left.

"Pick a card and don't tell me what it is," she said, as both girls walked a-mile-a-minute towards the arena.

Alma took one, glanced at it, and held it to her chest.

"The card you selected is either a club, a spade, a diamond, or a heart. Am I right?"

Smiling, Alma answered, "You certainly are!"

Maggie giggled. "Also, it's either an Ace, King, Queen, jack, or it's a number from two to ten. Am I still right?"

Alma feigned an astonished look. "How do you know these things? That's absolutely amazing. Now, how is that going to help us?"

With the confidence of Cunningham, Maggie placed the card back in the deck. "The card you took tells me that we don't have to say anything. We simply had other things to do. Right?"

As both girls laughed and slowed down a little, Alma agreed. "Right!"

The *gambler's* girl lightly took hold of Alma's left forearm. "I've learned a lot from Gordie. That's exactly what he would have done, but it cost me an article of clothing to learn each stage of the trick."

Diane removed her head from Douglas' shoulder and they kissed amidst the sounds of Roger Miller's, *Autumn Leaves*, resonating from the arena's sound system.

Because it was the last dance of the summer, the place was brimming with cadets and local teenagers trying to squeeze in as much fun as five weeks in God's Country could offer.

Douglas held Diane close. "If I join the regular force before you've finished your degree, will you still come with me?" His voice was soft and hesitant, as if he didn't want to ask the question which was nagging him.

Diane let go of him for a second and clasped both of her hands around his neck. With their faces only inches apart, her reply could barely be heard as tears filled her eyes. "Sweetheart...you don't have to ask me that. Ask me if we should soar on the northern lights, live on moonbeams, ride the wind, or float away on the seven seas. I just want to be near you, always. Oh babe, please, don't...don't ever leave me."

Douglas' eyes filled up and with a smile he lifted her off her feet and twirled her around. "I'm sorry," he whispered. "I'll never let you out of my sight."

Although there was hardly any room to move, for Douglas and Diane the dance floor was the universe, alone, graciously glittering and silent, except for the sounds of Gogi Grant, singing *The Wayward Wind.*

On the other side of the universe, it wasn't as quiet.

"ALMA, WHERE THE HELL HAVE YOUSE BEEN? GORDIE AND ME HAVE BEEN LOOKIN' FOR YOUSE TWO ALL NIGHT LONG."

"We had things to do," Alma replied, taking hold of Moose and forcing her way to the floor. "We women are quite unpredictable, you know?"

"YOUSE IS TELLIN' ME! NOW JUST WHERE WERE YOU?"

As Alma and Moose got lost in the throng, Gordie asked the same question.

"WELL, WHAT HAVE YOU BEEN UP TO? I'VE PLAYED TWO GAMES OF SOLITAIRE ON THE UPPER ROW OF SEATS WAITING FOR YA!"

Maggie grabbed him, heading for the floor. "GOOD FOR YOU! WHERE'S THAT MONEY YOU OWE ME?"

"WHAT? WHAT MONEY ARE YOU TALKING ABOUT? I DON'T OWE YOU ANY MONEY?"

"OH, YES YOU DO! YOU FIGURE IT OUT!"

The question of owing money took Cunningham's mind off his immediate problem. He never did ask her again where she was. Maggie had learned well.

When the eight Musketeers arrived back in the barracks that night, most faces were covered in lipstick, and as usual, other members of the hut were forced to listen to the banter.

East didn't care for a certain observation made by Rothstein. "I DID IT ON A DARE! I DON'T GO AROUND LIFTIN' UP KILTS! BESIDES, THE THING *WAS* WEARING SHORTS!"

Rothstein placed his clothes in his half of their barrack box. "Phew, our box is startin' to smell again," he said, as he found a half-eaten sandwich and threw it out the window. East didn't see the action otherwise he would have really been upset.

"YOU SNEAK, JACK! YOU KNEW IT WASN'T A GUY! YOU KNEW SHE WAS A MEMBER OF THE VERNON GIRLS BAND!"

Jack got out of bed. "ROTHIE, NOT AT FIRST, I DIDN'T! SHE WAS DANCIN' WITH SOME SEAFORTH AND I HAD MY BACK TO THEM. MY GIRL SAID, 'I WONDER IF HE'S WEARING SHORTS?' BEFORE I TURNED AROUND AND LIFTED THE KILT, THE SEAFORTH HAD SWUNG HER AROUND SO THAT THE DAME'S BACK WAS FACING ME! I HAD NO IDEA I WAS LIFTIN' THE KILT OF A BROAD!"

Danyluk was sitting on his barrack box taking off his socks. "I'm with *youse,* Jack. They all look the same, don't they?"

"UP YOUR ASS, DANYLUK!" screamed a Seaforth from across the aisle. "You know, you Dukes really amaze me. Ya spend half your time liftin' up girls skirts and smellin' girls' bicycle seats on hot days. Why don't you add a little couth and culture to your lives and join a real regiment? A regiment that would eliminate your sneaky, wicked urges."

Now Moose was into the act. "And which regiment are we talking about?"

"Why, the Seaforths, of course! There's only one...the rest are only pretenders."

"You mean we should give up the benefit of pants and put on those silly skirts?"

Now the Seaforth was out of bed. "C'mon, Moose. You know as well as I do that you've been pleading with me to borrow my kilt. The only reason I don't loan it to you is the fact that I'd have to have it double dry-cleaned when I got it back. Besides, you couldn't wear it because your balls and wang would be draggin' all over the ground."

Moose was lost for words so the Seaforth started chuckling and got back into bed.

"I heard the slap," said Simon, referring to East's deed. "Even though it was loud in there, everyone heard it when she slammed you one in the face."

Jonathan ran over from the other end. "Let me see your face. Yep, you need cold compresses on that. Wow, what did she look like? A logger could only give you a slam like that? James, come and take a look at this."

As James rushed over, East felt the left side of his burning face. "Apparently she was the base drummer. Christ, of all the broads, I pick the one with the biggest arm muscles."

"THE BASE DRUMMER?" bellowed Danyluk. "SHE'S THE ONE I'VE BEEN TRYING TO MEET. SO SHE DOES WEAR PANTIES? THANKS JACK, NOW I CAN TAKE HER OFF MY LIST!"

The medical experts applied cold, soaking-wet toilet paper to Jack's face.

Wayne was at his window again. "Jack wasn't upset because he got hit. He got upset because his hot dog went flying into the crowd. Some girl slipped on it and went skidding on her ass."

"That'll teach ya to dance and eat hot dogs at the same time," said Douglas.

"TWO HOT DOGS!" corrected East. "WHEN SHE HIT ME, I KNOCKED THE DOG OUT OF MY GIRL'S HAND AS WELL!"

The cubicle door squeaked open and a yawning Corporal came out, wiping his eyes. "Let's hit the sack, guys. Some of us are working tomorrow. I guess you've heard about Corporal Adams?"

"No, what happened?" asked Earl. He'd been asleep, but East's voice had woken him up.

"He got kicked out of the theatre tonight, with some fat broad by the name of Eunice. Apparently he was screaming, 'I'LL GET YOU MOOSE, JUST YOU WAIT!'"

Danyluk took off his shorts and got ready to get into bed. "MOOSE? THERE'S ONLY ONE MOOSE AND THAT'S ME? I WASN'T AT THE MOVIES AND IF IT'S THE BROAD I'M THINKIN' ABOUT, I'D BE A HUNDRED MILES AWAY!"

The Corporal stretched. "Well, there must be two of you, because he was yelling your name all the way to the guardroom. He's in there now. Apparently his pants kept falling down because he had no buttons on the front."

Moose stood up. "You mean he's locked up?"

As the Corporal re-entered his cubicle he said, "Yeah, the manager of the theatre called the RCMP. Good night, guys."

"Good night, Corporal," Danyluk said, getting into bed.

For a few minutes it was quiet in B-33, but the silence was broken by a loud, "EEEEYYAAAOOOUUU," as Moose came bounding out of bed, screaming.

"SON OF A BITCH! WHAT THE HELL...?" He backed up so fast he ended up sitting on Douglas' head.

When he was pushed off, he cautiously went back and slowly put his hands under the covers. Seconds later, Moose stood in the aisle holding a live mouse by the tail.

"ALL RIGHT! WHICH ONE OF YOU ASSHOLES PUT THIS GUY IN MY BED? IT WANTED TO NEST IN MY CROTCH!"

Laughter wafted throughout the hut as a naked Moose walked outside to release the mouse.

"YOU! THAT MAN! WHAT THE HELL ARE YOU DOING? GET OVER HERE! OH, IT'S YOU AGAIN, IS IT? AND YOU'RE NUDE AGAIN ARE YOU? WHAT THE HELL ARE YOU DOING? HAVE YOU SET YOUR CAMERA TO TAKE NIGHT PICTURES OF YOUR BODY? MY GOD, SON, WHAT...!" The wrath of the RSM was loud and swift.

Ten minutes later when Danyluk was back in bed snoring, a certain Seaforth cadet across the aisle chuckled and whispered to himself, "Got ya, ya BCR creep."

Another Seaforth cadet came over. "Good work, Jock. Is that the mouse you've been talking about, the one you named Haggis? Are you still feeding him each morning?"

After a few more chuckles, Jock answered, "Yeah, that's him. He's now earning his keep."

As Douglas and Wayne stood in front of the Provost shack waiting for their girls, company after company entered B-3 to attend Church Parade. The looks on the cadets' faces was sour. They didn't appreciate being forced to attend church on the day they could sleep in, or do absolutely nothing.

Over breakfast Douglas had explained to Wayne about Danyluk's mouse event and Wayne couldn't get over the fact that he'd slept through it.

"A live mouse? Who the hell would do that to Moose?"

"Our Seaforth *friend* from across the aisle. I heard his buddy come over and congratulate him."

"Have you mentioned this to Moose?"

A horn beeped as Diane's car turned off the highway onto the entrance road. "No, not yet. I'll tell him at the Duke's picnic tonight. It'll be a riot watching the retribution."

The ride to Diane's grandparents farm was the break both boys needed. Diane had brought some civilian clothes for Douglas and Wayne and they changed into them at the first gas station along the way. For the moment, khaki had completely disappeared from their lives.

"How's Jack East's face this morning?" Debbie asked, tightening her grip on Wayne's hand in the back seat.

"The swelling's gone down," replied Banks. "I'll bet that's the last time he lifts up a kilt."

All four of the car's occupants laughed aloud, before Diane said, "Of all the girls in the band, he had to pick on the toughest. Did you see the look on her face when she turned around and slugged him?"

Wayne stuck his free hand out the window. "No, but I saw the expression on East's face. It was as if the Third World War had started. He didn't give a damn about getting hit, the fact that he and his girl lost their hot dogs meant more."

Jeez, this is nice country," offered Douglas. It's a wonder more people don't live here. Since we started on this road, we haven't seen another car."

Diane pushed her sunglasses farther up her nose. "That's the reason Gran and Gramps bought this place. They just want to be away from it all."

Before the car pulled off the highway into the farm, Douglas had explained Moose's episode with the mouse and both girls thought it was hilarious.

"A live mouse in his crotch? It's a wonder he didn't have a heart attack?" added Debbie.

"Who, the mouse, or Danyluk?" Wayne quipped, chuckling with the three of them.

"Well, well, well! It's about time," Gramps said, standing at the door kissing both girls on their cheeks and shaking the boys' hands. "MOTHER, THEY'RE FINALLY HERE!"

Diane's stout little grandmother came to the door wiping the flour off her hands onto her apron. After kissing the girls and welcoming the boys, she said, "I'll bet you could smell my pies all the way from Vernon. Well, don't just stand there, sit yourselves down and I'll give each of you a big piece of fresh apple pie and a nice glass of ice cold milk."

The setting was perfect for the boys, especially Douglas. He loved the way both grandparents doted on Diane and Debbie and their antics while they were growing up. The small house was spotless and the smell of recently baked pies and cinnamon filled his nostrils. Eating his pie, he thought about their way of life. Both of them were so spry and healthy. Diane's grandmother loved cooking and her husband cherished pottering around and working in the garden. They were remarkable role models, and he thought if ever there were a contest for the best grandparents, they would win hands down.

"How'd you boys get the civilian clothes?" Gramps asked. "I thought you'd have to raid the trunk in the attic when you got here?"

"They're Dad's old clothes," replied Diane. "Fit kinda good, don't they?"

Diane's Gran laughed. "Well, your father didn't always have a paunch. At one time, he was as solid as the rock of Gibraltar. It's only when he moved away from the farm he started getting a little soft in the tummy."

Debbie patted Gramps' stomach. "But what about this?"

"I earned this with old age and good eating," he said, slapping his belly with both hands. "This is an example of great farm cookin' and if I didn't eat it, I'd be put out with old Shep."

"You bet you would," Gran said, gently pinching his cheek. "Now, what are you kids going to do?"

Both girls started doing the dishes. "Not much," Diane said, putting on an apron. "These guys need a rest, so we're just gonna lounge around. Is the boat repaired?"

Gramps lit up his pipe. "Yep, fixed it last week, and I'll give you four fishing rods. Remember now, if you catch Fat Phyliss, throw her back. I've only ever caught her once, but I warn her every time I'm out there, the next time she may not be so lucky."

"Who's Fat Phyliss?" asked Wayne.

Gramps stood up. "You mean you boys have never heard of the world-famous Fat Phyliss?" He smiled and took a photo out of his wallet. "Well, being city slickers, I can understand it. This is a picture of her. Gran shot this on the day Phyliss fell for the bait. She's the fattest old trout on earth."

"And the smartest!" offered Gran.

"I'll say she's the smartest. Phyliss can actually spot a phoney fly or worm a hundred miles away. The only reason I caught her was because I didn't feed 'em that day."

"You feed your fish?" Douglas asked.

"You bet we do and they've all got names, too. Here's a picture of Alice and this one's Henry...oh, and here's Philbert. He's the greediest of the group. We throw 'em all back, they're part of the family."

After showing Douglas, Wayne handed the snapshots back to Gramps. "Well, sir, if we catch any, we'll throw them back."

Fifteen minutes later, the four teenagers were sitting in a rowboat in the middle of the lake trolling their lines. Diane was up front, Douglas was rowing, and Wayne and Debbie were astern.

"That was nice of your Gran to pack a lunch for us," Wayne said, bringing in a little line and letting it out again.

"I love them so much," Diane replied. "When I've got the car, I'm never away from here."

"Did you...?" Douglas skimmed the water with the oars and fell backwards, looking up at Diane with a foolish grin on his face. "Did you ever camp out overnight here?"

Diane assisted him back up. "All the time. The night before you arrived in Vernon, Debbie and I camped out on that far bank over there. We played a game of counting shooting stars, multiplying them by twenty and said that's how far your train had travelled from Vancouver."

A far away look came over Douglas' face. "I was thinking of you, too. Do ya think that's sorta like deja...?" He didn't have time to finish his question because Wayne had a bite and the reel was unwinding fast.

In the excitement, Banks made the mistake of standing up. He was so ecstatic with his catch, he forgot what to do and the next minute fell overboard, fishing rod and all.

Still holding on to the rod, Wayne swam the twenty yards to shore and waded out, still reeling in his catch.

"YOU'VE CAUGHT FAT PHYLISS!" screamed Debbie, laughing her head off.

Dripping wet and trying to reel in Phyliss, Wayne replied, "FUNNY, EH? I'LL PHYLISS YOU AS SOON AS I'VE SORTED THIS OUT!"

Seconds later, Wayne was on his knees holding the fish and gently taking the hook out of its mouth. When the hook was clear, he placed the big trout in the water and it swam away as if nothing had happened.

"HEY, I THINK YOUR GRAMPS WAS BULL SHITTIN' A BIT! SHE'S BEEN CAUGHT LOADS OF TIMES! CHRIST, SHE JUST LAY THERE AS IF TO SAY, 'O.K., MAC, YOU'VE HAD YOUR FUN, NOW LET ME GO.'"

Diane couldn't control her laughter. "THAT WASN'T PHYLISS! YOU CAUGHT PHILBERT! HE PUTS UP A FIGHT IN THE WATER, BUT NOT WHEN HE'S OUT!"

Just looking at Wayne had everyone laughing, including the *catcher*, as he swam out to the boat Douglas had rowed closer to the shore. After a quick grab for Debbie, she was in the water as well.

Paddling after him, she yelled. "YOU CREEP! I'LL GET YOU, WAYNE BANKS!"

Glancing at each other, but not saying a word, both Douglas and Diane jumped in and joined their friends.

"I HOPE YOUR WATCH IS WATERPROOF?" Diane shouted, swimming to the bank.

"IT IS, HOW ABOUT YOURS?"

"YEAH, BUT MY NEW HAIRDO ISN'T!"

When the two newcomers arrived on shore, Wayne swam back to get the boat. Within five minutes, he had it tied to a tree, and took out the lunch basket and the blankets.

Even though they were in the shade, the sun was so hot, their clothes were dry before lunch was set up. Gran had made roast beef sandwiches and packed them with large pieces of apple and rhubarb pie. To quench their thirst, two thermoses of ice-cold milk with four glasses were neatly placed in the basket. For dessert they had chilled pieces of cooked peaches, which were in individual containers.

The setting was so serene as the four ate lunch watching swallows skim the surface of the mirror-like lake, with Alice, Henry, Philbert and Phyliss jumping out periodically to see what was happening.

Wayne and Debbie stood up, grabbed their blanket, and proceeded to walk around the bend.

"And where are you two going?" Diane asked, trying to keep a straight face.

Two grinning, mischievous smiles were answer enough, however, Debbie replied, "Oh, just around the corner. We're going to check on whether or not Fat Phyliss is in her pool."

Shortly, both Douglas and Diane heard their companions swimming, splashing, and yelling as they cajoled in the lake.

Diane got up, casually stretched, and walked the few paces to catch a glimpse. When she covered her mouth to muffle her laughter, Douglas couldn't stand the suspense, so he went over, too. Debbie and Wayne had shed their clothes and were having the *time of their lives*.

Douglas took hold of her hand. "Er, do...er you think...we. Well, we *are* out of sight of Gran and Gramps?"

Diane smiled at the expression on his face, kissed him, and sat down to take off her pumps. "Way out of sight," she replied. "Besides, I know they've done it."

Moments later, two more bare, tanned teenagers with white buttocks ran into the water to join their friends. Horse-fights followed, along with diving, floating, and each girl trying to balance on her boyfriend's shoulders.

Three-quarters of an hour later, four naked bodies stretched out on their own blankets, wrapped in each others' arms. Debbie and Wayne remained around the point.

Diane shyly peered into Douglas' eyes and ran a finger down his forehead to the tip of his nose. "How many times have I said that I love you?"

"At the last count, it was one million and one. How about me?"

"The same, she whispered."

That afternoon, two young couples who were madly in love released their innocent inhibitions, allowed their passions to flame and permitted the warm caress of the sun, the gentle stroke of the breeze, and the sparkling lustre of the lake to join them.

Meanwhile in the lake, Philbert had just returned from a quick jump to check out the surface insect action.

"Did you see any bugs, dear?" asked Phyliss.

"No, but I spotted that son of a bitch who caught me!"

"What's he doing now?"

"He's naked with some broad on the beach, the lucky bastard!"

"Not so loud darling, Junior's *school* is nearby."

(Author's note: Hey, why not? Who says fish can't talk?)

When Diane dropped both boys off in front of the Provost shack, galaxies of stars remained in the four teenagers' eyes. The ride back to camp had been mainly silent with understood, shy smiles.

None of them had wanted the afternoon to end, but Wayne and Douglas had to return to attend the Duke's picnic at Cosens Bay. Also, on the way back, Diane had stopped at a gas station so the cadets could reclaim the colour khaki.

Douglas leaned in the driver's window and kissed Diane. "We've got the day off tomorrow, where should we meet you?"

Diane bashfully replied, "How about Polson Park at two o'clock?"

"Great! Also, if you phone your Gran and Gramps, will you thank them again for us?"

As Diane drove away, her voice said, "I will, sweetheart. I love you."

"ME, TOO!" Brice yelled, nudging his friend who was still in a dream world. "Snap out of it, Wayne. It's back to bully beef and bayonets."

Wayne put his arm around Douglas' shoulders. "You know, Doug. That was the best afternoon I've ever..."

The Provost Sergeant didn't allow him to finish. "YOU TWO! GET YOUR ARMS UP AND MARCH! CAMP ISN'T FINISHED YET!"

"BLESS 'EM ALL...BLESS 'EM ALL...THE LONG AND THE SHORT AND THE TALL! BLESS ALL THE SERGEANTS AND W. O. 2s..."

Three, three-ton trucks, two of which were loaded with singing BCR cadets as well as Jackson, Rothstein, and Simon, wound their way past Kal Beach and turned off on the Cosens Bay road. When they stopped, the beach was empty except for a small motor boat which was just pulling away.

After a safety pep-talk by Lieutenant Steacy, the water was attacked with vigour while some senior cadets and the Lieutenant set up the barbecue stands and started cooking the food.

"We'll be going back to camp now, sir," said one of the drivers. "We're leaving one vehicle here in case there's a problem. What time would you like us to return?"

Lieutenant Steacy returned the Corporal's salute and glanced at his watch. "Thank you, Corporal. Er, 2230 hours should be fine."

Following a final salute, two trucks left the area and the driver of the remaining vehicle lent a hand with the cooking.

This was the first time since coming to camp that all the British Columbia Regiment (DCO) cadets had gotten together. Stories were told and laughter echoed in the nearby hills. Kalamalka Lake offered its all. It was still warm from the day's blazing sun and barely a ripple could be seen in the aqua-green mirror of awe.

"Sir, thanks very much for allowing our three friends to join us," Douglas said to the officer.

"You didn't tell me one of them was with the Irish," Steacy replied, smiling.

"Er, ah...I didn't...think..."

The Lieutenant broke out laughing as he slapped Douglas on the back. "Just joking. I hope he's not the one who paints green shamrocks on our tank and cannons on Armistice Day, New Year's and Saint Patrick's Day?"

"Er, no...it's not him."

"Well then, it's a pleasure for us to have him. What's his name?"

Actually, Simon was already there, lending a hand. "This is him here, sir. His name's Simon."

Steacy turned over some wieners. "So, you're in the Irish, eh, Simon? When are you going to join a *real* regiment?"

Simon grinned. "That's the reason I joined the Irish, sir. I'd already checked out the others."

Once again, Lieutenant Steacy's grin broke into a laugh . "Damn it, you've been trained by Wes Deane."

"Do you know Lieutenant Deane, sir?"

Still smiling, the officer replied, "Yes, we're friends, but don't tell him I told you that."

Later, they lit a small fire and the cadets sat around it singing songs and eating untold hamburgers, hot dogs, and slices of watermelon. Afterwards, they washed it all down with Freshie, milk, cocoa, or Kik Kola.

With songs in full swing, Douglas sat next to Danyluk. "Did anything happen while Wayne and me were away today?"

"Not much, but apparently Corporal Adams was told to get off the parade square when Bravo Company was doin' drill."

"Why? What happened?"

Moose took a big bite of his burger. "I wasn't there, but apparently he kept rushing up to a cadet named Ryeberg, askin' him if his name was, *Moose*. When Beckford called him over, Adams yelled somethin' about gettin' fumigated. He was really pissed off."

"What's Ryeberg have to say about it?"

Moose shrugged. "Nothin.' He says he don't even know Adams, other than the guy tried to grab him in the theatre. He thinks the guy may be a homo."

Douglas placed his tongue in his cheek. "Jeez, Adams is really weird, isn't he? Do ya think he's flipped his lid?"

A laughing Danyluk replied, "He must have, if he thinks Ryeberg is me."

By ten-thirty that night, under a giant full moon, all the equipment had been loaded in the truck, but it wouldn't start. Not only that, the other vehicles hadn't arrived.

Numerous attempts at trying to get the one remaining three-ton going failed and the only conclusion that could be reached was that the battery just didn't have enough power.

The driver appeared a little sheepish. "Sir, I *did* complete a first parade." (Checked everything out before leaving camp.)

At eleven-thirty, with still no sign of the other two trucks, Lieutenant Steacy started the group walking. "We'll phone the camp from Kal Beach."

It took an hour-and-a-half before the cadets were finally picked up and with each truck's choir singing, *"WE'RE THE DUKE OF CONNAUGHT'S, AND WE'RE DAMNED GOOD SHOTS..."* a few middle fingers appeared in the windows of the darkened camp as they returned.

When the Musketeers entered B-33 and undressed, everyone else was asleep. Even Moose's Seaforth *friend* was snoring loudly.

Wayne crawled up to his bunk. "That was beyond a doubt, the best day yet."

Douglas lay with his hands behind his head. "Did you bring back any articles of Debbie's clothing?"

A head popped over the side. "No, I've stopped doing that. She was catching too many colds."

They both snickered and yawned as the same full moon that had guided the group from Cosens Bay to Kal Beach lit up their wing of the hut. Before long, six of the eight joined the other occupants in competing for the title of the world's best snorer.

Twenty minutes later, two of the eight got out of bed, grinning.

"Gordie, warm up that shaving lotion a bit. Don't hold it under the tap too long, otherwise it might explode."

As Gordie headed for the taps, Moose took a safety razor out of his side of the barrack box and sneaked across the aisle to the heavily snoring Seaforth. Looking at the lad's peaceful, sleeping face, Danyluk whispered and sang, "It's pay-back time for you and your friends, you creep."

CHAPTER XIII

Major Ratcliffe meant it when he said he changed the timetable to give the cadets of Alpha Company Monday off. Not only didn't Sergeant Simpson appear, the fanfare created by the band and other companies marching by wasn't loud enough to wake up the majority of the sleeping senior cadets.

Of course, some had headed over to breakfast before the sitting was shut off at eight-thirty, and East was one of them. About half-an-hour after re-entering the hut and making his bed, he slammed a broom handle down on a folding table in the middle of the aisle.

'WHAM! WHAM! WHAM! "C'MON, YOU LAZY BUMS, LET GO OF YOUR JOKE AND GRAB YOUR SOAP! IT'S NINE O'CLOCK! C'MON! C'MON! C'MON!"

Naturally Moose and Gordie were now wide awake, because they wanted to see certain cadets' reactions. Danyluk dropped his towel on his usual morning erection and headed for the showers, while Gordie asked some cadet across the aisle if he wanted to throw dice for a buck a throw.

"SCREW YOU CUNNINGHAM, I'M FAMILIAR WITH THOSE DICE!"

Soon, all the Musketeers were in the showers, except for Gordie. He'd found a sucker at the other end and was raking in the cash.

Although the showers were gushing at full-blast and the noise in the shower room was loud, everyone heard the screams originating from the Musketeers side of the hut.

"AAAGGGGHHHH! AAAIIIEEEEE! OH, MY GOD!"

Moose's chest came out. "Wow, it sounds as if someone's closed a window on his fingers, doesn't it?"

"WHO'S THE ROTTEN, DIRTY BASTARD? STEP FORWARD!"

Moose continued to smear Gordie's marvelous-smelling French soap, which Cunningham hadn't agreed to loan him. "No, it couldn't be that, it must be something else?"

"JESUS, I HAVEN'T GOT A HAIR LEFT ON MY CROTCH, MY LEGS, OR MY ARMS! ALL RIGHT, YOU...YOU...! HEY, READ THAT FOR ME WILL YA?" Obviously, at that point, three of his fellow Seaforths had joined him, because the words, "THEY GOT YOU GUYS, TOO?" followed.

The rest of the Musketeers had caught on and broke out laughing when Rothstein said, "It almost sounds like someone's singed themselves accidentally."

"I WAS SUPPOSED TO GO ON A SPORRAN PARADE TODAY! I CAN'T GO OUT LOOKIN' LIKE THIS! STEP FORWARD, YA SNEAKY PONGOES!" There was a short pause, and then: "WHAT? WHAT ARE YOU SAYIN'? YOU'VE GOT TO BE JOKING?"

Running footsteps were heard just outside the shower room entrance. When Jackson put his head around the corner, he saw three red-faced Seaforth cadets looking in a mirror, rubbing the areas that *used* to house eyebrow hair.

"OUR EYEBROWS, AS WELL? MY GOD, I LOOK LIKE A SHAVED

PEACH! ALL RIGHT, YOU GODDAMNED MISBEGOTTEN CANADIAN
SCOTTISH PONGOES, YOU WANT IT THIS WAY, YOU'VE GOT IT!"

Moose rinsed off and grabbed his towel. "Sounds like the CScotRs got to
them. We'll have to watch those guys."

"How'd they know it was them?" a cadet from the other wing asked.

Moose dropped his wet towel, knowing full well that it would land on his per-
petual erection. When the towel fell to the floor, he said, "Damn, I must be getting
old, it's gone down. Must be the soap." Then he answered the cadet's question.
"Oh, er, I think they discovered the writing."

The dripping wet cadet rushed after Moose. "What writing?"

"I believe the words, 'UP THE CScotRs,' replaced their wang hair."

"You mean they used a ball-point pen?"

"No, a laundry marker. It'll take 'em a week to scrub it off."

As Moose casually applied Gordie's French talcum powder and got dressed,
the screaming continued on the other side of the aisle. Three CScotR cadets were
laughing so hard, they were bent over holding their stomachs.

Finally one of them gained control of himself and said, "At last the Seaforths
all realize which is the better Scottish regiment. They even write it on their
crotches."

That statement really got the other Scots uptight. **"UP YOUR ASSES!
DON'T ANY OF YOU BASTARDS GO TO SLEEP TONIGHT, OR ANY
OTHER NIGHT, BECAUSE IF YOU DO, WE'LL BE THERE!"**

The hullabaloo in the barracks was so loud, it attracted the RSM who just happened to be marching by.

"WHAT THE HELL'S GOING ON IN HERE?"

There was instant silence as Gardiner played with ends of his giant mustache.
"WELL, SOMEONE SPEAK UP! WHAT'S GOING ON?"

One naked, red-faced Seaforth cadet was about to pull up his undershorts as he
turned around. "Er, I just cracked a joke...that's all, Sergeant-Major."

Mister Gardiner couldn't help but notice the 'crotch' writing as he moved
closer to the lad. "WHAT THE...?" His eyes started reading. "UP THE CScotRs?"

The undershorts were pulled up fast, but too late. "Er, yes...er, Sergeant-Major,
I er..."

"WHAT THE HELL IS IT WITH THIS COMPANY? I'VE HEARD OF REG-
IMENTAL PRIDE, BUT THAT'S THE BLOODY LIMIT! I SUPPOSE YOU'RE
TAKING PICTURES OF THAT AND SELLING THEM TO THE GIRLS,
LIKE...WHERE IS HE...ER, DANYLUK?"

Danyluk was fully dressed as he stood up and put his chin in the air. "Here, sir.
Youse will notice I'm clothed today? I've turned over a new tree."

"A NEW *TREE*? THAT'S CERTAINLY A WONDER!" The RSM then
pointed to the 'walking signpost.' "IS THIS ONE OF YOUR STUDENTS?"

A grinning Moose still had his chin up. "No, sir! We BCRs don't mingle with
riffraff peasants, especially if they're Scottish."

Gardiner took his giant drill cane out from under his armpit and started
marching to the exit. "NEVER IN MY LIFE HAVE I WITNESSED SUCH
UTTER INSANITY! SHAVING OFF HIS PUBIC HAIR TO ADVERTISE HIS
REGIMENT? WHAT THE HELL IS THIS WORLD COMING TO? IT'S A
TOTAL DISGRACE!"

As the RSM marched out the door, Danyluk bellowed, "THAT'S WHAT I

TOLD 'EM, SERGEANT MAJOR!"

The RSM was out of sight when he mumbled, "He must have done it with a Goddamned mirror." Shortly the Seaforth cadet started laughing with everyone else.

"I MAY BE LAUGHING NOW, BUT YOU CANADIAN SCOTTISH PONGOES SURE AS HELL WON'T BE WHEN WE'RE FINISHED WITH YA!"

Monday was a fabulous day for the Musketeers. Although they were all a little disheartened when they learned that the few Alpha boxers hadn't won any fights the night before, just being downtown with their girls on a weekday, got rid of that disappointment in a hurry.

"We would have won if I'd been there," Gordie boasted.

Danyluk gave a Cunningham a shove. "But youse wasn't there, so quit complainin'!"

"Hey, quit shoving. Have you forgot who's payin' today?"

Moose wiped imaginary dust off the *gambler's* epaulettes. "Oh, sorry Gordie, youse big pal 'o mine."

With the aid of Gordie Cunningham's *bank*, the group went bowling, ate banana splits, and rented horses in the BX area of Vernon. Because Alpha Company was having its picnic at Kinsmen Beach, they said good-bye to the girls on the steps of the stately court house and headed back to camp at 1700 hours.

It was still hot and the hill was tough, as a perspiring, puffing Gordie complained: "Moose, you could have paid your share today. Christ, you've got every broad in Vancouver sendin' you money for your various funds."

"Gordie, Gordie, Gordie. When are youse gonna learn that I've also got other responsibilities? I gotta send money to my dames that are broke. Amongst other things, it guarantees me a smile and hug when I get home. Now, quit bitchin' and pick up the step."

Gordie slammed his foot down on a half-pace. "Oh, well, er...that means, we can share them and...?"

"NOT ON YOUR LIFE!"

"O.K., THEN! YOU OWE ME TWENTY DOLLARS AND STOP USIN' MY FRENCH SOAP AND TALCUM POWDER...GOT IT? AND LEAVE MY AFTERSHAVE ALONE, WILL YA?"

"WHY SHOULD I, YOU DON'T SHAVE?"

"WHADUYA MEAN I DON'T SHAVE? HEY, JACK, YOU'VE SEEN ME SHAVE, HAVEN'T YA?"

Although East was marching, he could still sneak a bite of his chocolate bar. "NOPE!" Then he had second thoughts. "OH YEAH, I'VE SEEN YOU SHAVE YOUR ARMPITS. DO YOU USE THAT STUFF AS A DEODORANT?"

"SCREW YOU, EAST!"

The thought of owing twenty dollars weighed heavily on Moose. "Er, well perhaps we can arrive at some sort of a sharin' arrangement. Yes, leave it with me, and er, I'll check my list."

B-33 was hopping when the Musketeers returned. The place looked like the aftermath of a political convention. The floor was a mess with unfurled toilet rolls, pop bottles, chocolate bar wrappers, popsicle bags and sticks, milkshake containers, beef burger wrappers, pages of newspapers, crumpled-up notebooks, water basins and the top of shoe polish tins filled with water for shining boots, shoe polish, brushes, toilet plungers, mops, brooms, overflowing garbage-cans, mattress covers, irons, liquid starch, Brasso, Silvo, rags, helmets, wastepaper baskets, buckets, fire extinguishers, mops and their squeezers, soiled writing tablets, Sergeants' Soap, powdered scouring soap, spilled foot powder containers, salt pills, odd socks, towels, running shoes, Webbo, Khaki 'It' and white 'It.'

In addition, radios were blaring, irons kept overpowering the circuit breakers, barrack boxes were out of line and crammed, bunks had been moved, folding tables and benches were being used as ironing boards, the showers were all occupied, the toilets were full with one overflowing, the washing machine whined, all sinks were being used by belt scrubbers, cadets were jumping on and over bunks, running up and down the aisles, out the windows, and up and down the stairs. *In short*, it resembled a live anthill.

It was more than obvious that the cadets of Alpha Company had enjoyed their day off. Although the barracks looked like hell that night, in the morning, it would be spotless.

Most cadets didn't eat supper. Naturally, East was first in the lineup, saving spaces for the rest to have a drink, but with hot-dogs, hamburgers, watermelon, and whatever being served later, the majority of cadets had decided not to overload their stomachs.

At 1900 hours, a happy, smiling company of cadets just dressed in P.T. gear and wearing their swimsuits under the shorts this time, were formed up in three ranks on the road, waiting for the trucks.

"HEY, YOU PEOPLE, QUIT SNAPPING YOUR TOWELS!" screamed a Corporal.

The ride to Kin Beach was an opera of song, especially as the trucks passed the Provost shack. This past week, many Alpha cadets had attended other company picnics at Kin Beach, so they taught everyone a new song.

"OH PROVOST, OH PROVOST, WE'RE LEAVIN' YA NOW,
BUT DON'T WORRY, YOU ASSHOLES, WE'RE MAKIN' A VOW.
IF WE PICK UP A SHEEP AND IT WANTS TO BE BRED,
YOU DON'T HAVE TO DROOL, IT'LL BE IN YOUR BED!"
And an after chorus sang, *"JUST WEAR YOUR WADERS!"*

There wasn't a soul on Kinsmen Beach when the three-tons arrived and the company was formed up in three ranks.

"Where's Sergeants' Beckford and Simpson?" Simon asked Earl, knowing full well if anyone knew, he would.

"They're on the parade square with Bravo Company. They'll be with us tomorrow night when we come here with Bravo."

When the Company Sergeant-Major passed the parade over to Major Ratcliffe, the OC stood everyone at ease, and then had them stand easy.

"I HAVE BEEN INFORMED THAT IT'S CUSTOMARY FOR ALL OFFICERS AND NCOs TO BE DUNKED ON THESE COMPANY PICNICS! SO BE IT! WE'RE PREPARED FOR THAT EVENT, HOWEVER, PLEASE HOLD BACK SUCH ACTION UNTIL WE SET UP THE BARBECUES AND COOK THE FOOD! IS THAT A DEAL?"

The reply was cheery and loud. "YES, SIR!"

As the cadets were responding, another truck arrived.

"WE'RE FORTUNATE TO HAVE THE CAMP SWIM STAFF WITH US

TONIGHT, BUT EVEN SO, I WANT YOU TO USE THE BUDDY SYSTEM WHILE YOU'RE IN THE WATER! LET'S CONTINUE TO BE AWARE OF WATER SAFETY AT ALL TIMES.

"I'M NOT GOING TO FALL YOU OUT FORMALLY. JUST MAKE CERTAIN YOUR SHORTS, T-SHIRTS, RUNNING SHOES, AND TOWELS ARE NEATLY PLACED SO WE CAN TELL IF SOMEONE IS MISSING. ALL RIGHT?"

"YES, SIR!"

"RIGHT! ALPHA COMPANY...CARRY ON AND HAVE FUN!"

With loud exuberation, the cadets' first promise was broken. Immediately, all officers, NCOs, and clerks were carried off and thrown in the water. It wasn't easy and some put up a bit of a fight, but to no avail. They would be wet when they cooked the food.

"HEY, I'VE GOT *PAPER* IN MY POCKETS!" screamed one of the clerks. Private Pazim, kicked and flailed his arms all the way to the water. The cadets carrying him knew he was referring to the fact that he was going to take on Cunningham later that evening. So far, Pazim had experienced nothing but bad luck when he played poker with Gordie, but he always hung in there, trying to win.

His partner, Private Maeson, bellowed, "YOU CREEPS, I'VE GOT TWO BOTTLES OF ICE-COLD, CLEAR *POP* IN MY POCKETS!" Likewise, *his* carriers knew he had a couple of cold beer in his pockets. He was dumped gently.

The north east end of Okanagan Lake gyrated with appreciative, eager, energized teenagers that night. Although a fire wasn't allowed, a circle was formed and all officers and NCOs joined in singing the songs that VACC (Vernon Army Cadet Camp) is famous for. Although they thought it was impossible, the cadets learned many new limericks from their staff, and the laughter could probably be heard at Okanagan Landing, the place where the Musketeers had *spent* the night.

Throughout the evening, each Musketeer often glanced at the old Sutherland Arms Hotel; his expression indicating fond memories of a wonderful *experience* under the stars.

After hamburgers, hot dogs, blueberry pie, watermelon, oranges, apples, cold milk, apple juice, cocoa, and Kik Kola, the songs continued until the trucks arrived at 2230 hours. Just before they loaded, Major Ratcliffe and his staff were thrown in the lake once again. This time, Private Pazim had no paper, because he'd lost it all to Cunningham.

The shack was still the same madhouse when they returned. When one of the Corporals entered, he cringed, closed his eyes, and walked directly to his cubicle, yelling, "I CAN'T BEAR TO LOOK! LIGHTS OUT IN TEN MINUTES!"

In twenty minutes, when the lights *were* turned out and cadets were still scurrying to bed, a CScotR cadet ripped his sheets trying to get in between them.

He directed his comment strictly to the Seaforth just down the aisle. "OH, SO YOU'RE INTO FRENCHING BEDS, ARE YOU? YOU'RE CERTAINLY ASKING FOR IT!"

"I DIDN'T TOUCH YOUR BED," came the reply. "YOU GUYS ARE IN FOR MORE THAN THAT, MISTER!"

Gordie crept over to East who was nearly asleep. "Jack, Jack, what's a canonized eight and nine of clubs put together?"

East rubbed his eyes. "It's Danyluk's wang size in the morning. How the hell should I know, you pongo? Shit, you've just taken all of Pazim's money, are you at it again?"

"I bet that creep's bull shitting me," Gordie said, creeping back to a two-man card game at the end of the hut.

A cadet from the other side tapped Danyluk on his shoulder and pushed something in his face. "Say, Moose, someone was going to steal this off the line in the drying room. I knew it had to be yours so I grabbed it. Can I have your autograph now?" After he asked, he took a few sniffs. "Jesus, you smell like a French whore."

Moose pulled the thing out of his face and sat up. It was a dirty-coloured jockstrap someone had washed and hung up to dry. He spit because the garment had touched his lips.

"HEY, WATCH YOUR MOUTH. I'M WEARIN' A FRENCH AFTER-SHAVE CALLED, '*LE TOUCHES VU DE ASS!*' BESIDES, HOW THE HELL DOES YOUSE KNOW WHAT A FRENCH WHORE SMELLS LIKE. HAVE YA SMELLED ONE?"

"No, but I wanna."

Rothstein had heard Moose and laughed. "It's called, '*A Touch of Class!*'"

"WHATEVER. ANYWAY, THAT'S NOT MINE, YOU IDIOT. US BCRs DON'T WEAR SUCH THINGS. CHECK WITH THOSE SCOTTISH PONGOES ACROSS THE AISLE. NOW BUGGER OFF!"

"But what about your autograph?" the boy asked, pulling the contraption off his head, where Moose had *placed* it.

"What regiment are youse with?"

The cadet's eyes lit up as if God had entered the room. "The best, of course. I'm with the 15th Field Artillery Regiment in Vancouver."

Moose lay back and rolled on his side. "Too bad. I never give autographs to anyone in the 15th Field. Now if youse hadda said, Rocky Mountain Rangers, I mighta considered it."

"Why's that?"

"Because what's the sense of me signing anything, youse guys don't know how to read."

The lad stood up. "And they do?"

Moose chuckled. "Nope, but they pay! Ya got any moolah?"

"UP YOURS, MOOSE!"

"HEY, IT'S SERGEANT-MAJOR DANYLUK TO YOUSE, YA CHEAP PRICK!"

When the night finally came to a close and nearly everyone was asleep, the only eyes open were those of the Scottish cadets. They watched each other like hawks. Eventually though, even their eyes closed. It was a Mexican standoff.

Unfortunately for some of them, it was a lop-sided Mexican standoff. Later, while four Seaforth cadets were snoring, they also had their sideburns shaved off by none other than Cunningham, Danyluk, Rothstein, and Simon. Also because the Scots insisted on not wearing undershorts to bed, the words, '*Princess Mary, RULES!*' were written on their bare derrieres, in laundry marker ink, of course.

"STAND BY YOUR BEDS! C'MON, YOU PEOPLE, LET GO OF YOUR SHAFT AND GET ON WITH YOUR CRAFT! WHAT THE HELL HAS HAP-PENED IN HERE? THIS BUILDING LOOKS LIKE IT'S BEEN INVADED BY A GROUP OF KINDERGARTEN KIDS! QUICKLY NOW, QUICKLY! YOU'VE

GOT ONE MINUTE TO FORM THREE RANKS ON THE ROAD! MOVE IT!
MOVE IT! MOVE IT!"

While Sergeant Simpson ran down the aisle turning over mattresses and
pulling down blankets, most cadets were up, however some still lay on the floor
where they'd been dumped and others just sat dazed, sitting on the edges of the
bunks with blankets wrapped around themselves.

Par for the course, Moose straddled to the jon experiencing great difficulty
pulling his P.T. shorts up over his *customary* morning erection. "JEEZ,
SERGEANT, THIS IS OUR LAST WEEK AND WE'VE ONLY GOT SWIM 'N
SPORTS PRACTISES TODAY, WHY DIDN'T YOUSE GIVE US A BREAK?"

"BECAUSE THIS IS ALPHA COMPANY, THAT'S WHY! NEVER IN MY
LIFE HAVE I SEEN SO MANY WIMPS! YOU'VE GOT THIRTY SECONDS
LEFT!"

It wasn't until after a jog to the upper camp, followed by fifty pushups and
fifty sit-ups that four Seaforth *soldiers* became the centre of attention at the morning shower *pageant*. Also, up to that point, these poor souls hadn't even noticed
that their sideburns had been trimmed past the top part of their ears. Naturally, the
CScotRs didn't have a clue because they hadn't participated in the *deed*, and they
weren't in the showers.

"OF ALL THE ROTTEN, LOW-DOWN, DIRTY...THOSE CREEPS...!"
screamed one of the four who were all turned around, looking down, trying to see
the *work* of the Canadian Scottish *artists*.

**"CAN YOU BELIEVE THIS? WE LOOK LIKE SOMEONE'S PUT A
GODDAMNED BOWL ON OUR HEADS TO CUT OUR HAIR...!
PRINCESS MARY, WHEREVER YOU ARE, YOUR HENCHMEN HAVE
JUST COMPLETED THEIR LAST UNJUST ACT! THIS ISN'T GONNA BE
A BATTLE, WE'RE NOW TALKIN' TOTAL WAR! JESUS, TO THINK WE
JOIN THOSE GUYS IN SPORRAN PARADES! THEY'RE NOT SCOT-
TISH, THEY'RE GODDAMNED ANIMALS!"**

When they left, the laughter in the showers was almost louder than that of the
Canadian Scottish cadets, who now thought one or two of their own had completed
the midnight caper. Not one of them had denied being involved in the action, thus
the Seaforths assumed they were the, **"GUILTY BASTARDS!"**

It was hilarious for all onlookers, watching the Seaforths pull on their underwear trying to cover, 'UP THE CScotRs' on one side of them, and 'Princess Mary
RULES!' on the other. Had Mister Gardiner been there, he'd have been mumbling
to himself all day long.

After breakfast, massive convoys of three-tons moved all companies to Kin
Beach for the swimming competition trials. Signs had been posted all week advising the townsfolk that Kin would be used that morning, therefore very few civilians
were present.

The trucks took the western route to the beach road and there were no 'show
parades.' The cadets standing up, nervously holding onto their shorts with one
hand, and the frame of the trucks with the other, were left alone.

The occupants of one Alpha truck, however, 'mooned' the Provost shack
whilst they passed and the Provost Sergeant took the vehicle's license number.
When the cadets saw him writing, shorts were pulled up quickly, but not quickly
enough.

From nine in the morning, until noon, the cadets of VACC earnestly tried their best to make the various company swimming teams. They knew their company's pride was on the line, and even those lying around kept tomfoolery to a minimum.

Although the Musketeers' girls said they might be there, they didn't show. A great number of other girls did, however, and they cheered their boyfriends on, even yelling excitedly if their beau placed last.

By noon, the swim staff had decided which cadets would represent their companies and the three-tons appeared to return everyone to camp for lunch. All of the Musketeers had qualified for an event and Danyluk was a natural to take the diving awards.

In the mess hall, Moose pointed his potato-laden fork at Jackson. "Did youse see the RSM watchin' me? He was just waitin' for me to bring out my camera and climb the tree above the girls' changin' shack. Shit, did I ever fool him."

Everyone at the table knew Moose had been caught doing it before. East actually stopped eating for a moment. "Why, what did you do?"

A proud Danyluk stuck out his chest. "While Gardiner was observing me, I had Johnston up the tree. He took two rolls of pictures of the cadets' girlfriends while they were changing. I won't be selling pictures of old dames this time. No siree, old Moose now has the real thing."

"Don't forget, we share the dough," Gordie stated, with a full mouth.

Moose patted Gordie on the head. "All right, all right! But I get to use all the 'Touche la vu du'...or whatever the crap's called."

Cunningham winced and nodded.

Douglas started everyone laughing when he reminded them of the handful of thick, gooey mud thrown all over the back of the leader of the swim staff. The mud covered the guy's back and legs, and stuck like glue. Once it was released, the muck 'thrower' disappeared under water.

"It serves the guy right," said Wayne. "He stands there like a starched pimp, all dressed in white, with a white pith-helmet and little whistle. Christ, he was furious. Do we know who threw it?"

East stood up to go back for thirds. "Some cadet in the Westies did it. I heard him boastin' about it later. He got the guy's assistant as well, and still wasn't caught."

"Good stuff," offered Moose. "Jeez, I loved the tantrum the head honcho threw. It was if his life had come to an end. Pompous fool. I laughed when he couldn't blow his whistle. He had to borrow his friend's and took half-an-hour wiping it off beforehand."

Simon had been quiet up till now. "The boss of the sports staff is just the same. It's too bad there's no mud at Polson Park. We could let him have it this afternoon."

Jackson looked at his notes. "Hey, there's a mail call in five minutes." With that said, the table cleared and East had a full fork pulled from his hand as he was lifted up and carried out.

"ANDERSON, FERGUSON, FERNANDEZ, DANYLUK, DANYLUK, DANYLUK, MOOSE DANYLUK, GENERAL DANYLUK, COURT MARTIAL DANYLUK, BRICE, WATT, MCALPINE, JOHNSTON, SYMINGTON, DEAN, OBER-OINTMENT DANYLUK" The Corporal paused. "What the hell is Ober-Ointment?"

Moose's hand was out continuously. "It's a German officer's rank, Corporal."

The Corporal cringed. "What, in the German Medical Corps?"

"Could be? She's German, but a little on the dumb side. Can we get on with the money, er, the mail call, please?"

"ROTHSTEIN, BANKS, MCCARTNEY, STUART, NEISH, JACKSON, BEKKATTLA, THE CHAIRMAN - S.S.W.S.D.D. FUND..." Another pause. "What the hell's, S.S.W.S.D.D?"

Danyluk snatched the letter. "It's my, Silent Soldiers With Serious *Doormat*, Diarrhea, fund. Wanna join? It's ten-bucks."

"Are you the Chairman?"

"You bet!"

"Don't you mean, *dormant*?"

"Hey, sounds good! That's the word I was lookin' for."

"Where's the 'dormant' come in? Does that mean the ailment's comatose or lethargic?"

"Er, yeah, that's close, sumpin like that." Moose took out a pencil and a piece of paper. "What were those words?"

"Forget it! SIMON, EAST, BANKS, AITKEN, CARRINGTON, PATTERSON G.H. AND PATTERSON E.B., SALMON, ARMENEAU, WARRINGTON J., WARRINGTON M., WARRINGTON B., RAE, MACTAVISH...AND PARCELS FOR EAST AND THE CHIEF OF THE S.S.W.N.S.S.D.D. FUND!" The Corporal paused one last time. "Don't tell me. It's the Serious Soldiers With Not So Serious *Doormat* Diarrhea, fund...right?"

"Say, youse is smart, how come you're in the P.P.C.L.I.?"

As the Corporal left, he replied, "I got kicked out of the BCRs for having brains."

At 1330 hours that afternoon, the band led all companies down the hill to Polson Park for the sports trials. The parade was so large, as the band entered Polson, companies were still leaving camp, with the Provost directing traffic around the parade. The dress was similar to the morning's dress: P.T. strip, heavy socks, running shoes, and pith-helmets.

Not all cadets were involved in these trials. Throughout the summer, the sports staff had selected various individuals for the 440, the 100-yard dash, all relays, the high-jump, tug of war, javelin throw, baseball toss, etc.

Fortunately, but really by personal choice, none of the Musketeers were entered this year. Alpha Company had some great sportsmen which meant the eight could spend more time with their girls, who were already in the stands.

Since these were only trials, a cheering section wasn't as essential as it would be on Thursday. The Musketeers knew that loud cheers spurred on the *athletes*.

During the events, each couple disappeared into their own world in the cool paradise of Polson Park. Most cadets had tucked their recently arrived letters into their elastic waistbands and read them while relaxing.

Douglas and Diane found their same spot next to the creek, Wayne and Debbie were on the other side by the small bridge, Danyluk and Alma went to the Capitol Cafe for banana splits, Rothstein, East, Jackson, and Simon sat at picnic tables next to the concession stand and Gordie and Maggie played stuke at a table by the entrance.

The park was packed with 1400 cadets and girlfriends of those who had them, including Ryeberg, Eldridge, Ida, and Melissa.

"Er, Ida...now I don't want you to get mad, but I've got something to tell you."

"Corporal Moose, I couldn't get mad at you."

Ryeberg swallowed. "Well, supposing I told you my name's not Moose Danyluk and his name's not Gordie Cunningham?"

Ida's face turned serious. "Why would you lie to us? There was no reason to lie?"

Eldridge and Melissa kept silent, with Eldridge allowing Ryeberg to do all the talking. "Er, at the time, in case we got caught, or you told on us, er...well, we used other people's names."

Both girls giggled.

Now Ryeberg was grinning. "What are you laughing about? Aren't you mad at us?"

Ida took hold of her *man's* hand. "We'd already figured that out, because our grandfather told us about Moose's measurements and Gordie's card habits."

Now Eldridge looked puzzled. "Moose's measurements?"

"Yeah, if he was Moose Danyluk, then he'd had an operation that lopped off fourteen inches. We put two and two together. If he wasn't Moose, and you didn't have a deck of cards in your hand, you couldn't be Gordie Cunningham. Right, Melissa?"

"Right!"

Ryeberg stood up. "Why you little..." With two cadets chasing them, a tittering Ida and Melissa ran until they were exhausted, which just happened to be in a secluded area.

In an area not so secluded, Corporal Adams and Eunice searched in vain for the real Cadet Moose..., whatever his last name was.

"BUT CORPORAL ADAMS, HONEY CHILD, WE'RE WASTIN' OUR WHOLE AFTERNOON LOOKIN' FOR THIS ASSHOLE WHEN WE COULD BE IN *LITTLE* EUNICE'S BEDROOM PLAYIN' HOUSE."

Adams cringed. That's the last thing he needed. "YOU JUST POINT HIM OUT TO ME. THAT BASTARD'S GOT TO BE HERE SOMEWHERE! WHAT'S HE LOOK LIKE AGAIN?"

Feigning a pout, she replied, "I AIN'T TELLIN' YA UNTIL YOU KISS ME AND GIVE ME A QUICK FEEL!"

An exasperated Corporal Adams didn't know what to say. "EUNICE, I CAN'T DO THAT HERE! WE'RE IN THE MIDDLE OF A...!"

The good Corporal couldn't finish his statement because Eunice hauled him into the bushes. In seconds flat, his pants were *ripped* down. "JESUS, EUNICE..." He lowered his voice. "Jesus, Eunice, I just sewed those buttons on."

"FUCK THE BUTTONS! C'MERE, YOU BIG HANDSOME SON OF A BITCH, YOU!"

That afternoon, Adams and Eunice never did find Danyluk. By the time they emerged from the bushes, cadet companies were marching back up the hill.

"THERE, NOW SEE WHAT YOU'VE MADE ME DO...I'VE MISSED HIM AGAIN!"

Eunice had stars in her eyes and Danyluk was the last thing on her mind. "Daddy says it's all right if I bring you home for supper."

Adams looked at the sky and took a deep breath. "Eunice, I'm not going to your house for supper. I've still got to find this Moose character."

"ALL RIGHT, YOU ASSHOLE, BUT THAT MEANS THAT YOU'RE GONNA STAY WORKIN' IN THE GODDAMNED KITCHEN. MY DADDY WILL TALK TO SERGEANT GABRIEL AND..."

Adams had no choice. "O.K., O.K., Eunice. Let's go to your house for supper.

"YIPPEE!" screamed the *little one* as she flung herself onto his unopened arms. "NOW, GIMMEE A QUICK KISS AND ANOTHER NICE FEEL!"

Five minutes later, when the duo walked to her house, Adams had to hold the front of his pants together and neither one of them knew about the tell-tale grass stains all over her pink tights and his pants and shirt.

After supper that night, WO2 Rose entered the barracks.

"I WANT ALL CANADIAN SCOTTISH CADETS FORMED UP IN THREE RANKS ON THE ROAD IN FIFTEEN MINUTES. YOUR DRESS WILL BE KHAKI SHORTS, SHIRTS, HOSE TOPS, BOOTS, PUTTEES AND PITH-HEL-METS!"

The cadets didn't ask why. When Sergeant-Major Rose gave an order, the word 'why' just didn't exist.

For the next hour-and-a-half, fourteen Canadian Scottish cadets (most were on the other side of the hut) completed every drill movement in the book on the old parade square with the Sergeant-Major.

There were no two-minute breaks so they could shake their heads, or relax a little. When they were finished and marched back to the barracks, Rose kept them at attention and said only a few words.

"THE WORDS, 'PRINCESS MARY RULES!' WILL BE SCRUBBED OFF YOUR ASSES AND AT NO FUTURE TIME WILL THEY BE DISPLAYED TO THE PROVOST SERGEANT. DIS...MISSED!"

As the bitching CScotRs entered B-33, a smiling Seaforth cadet whispered to his buddy. "It worked, Jock. Phase One of the retribution worked."

His friend grinned. "Isn't it great to be alive, Angus. Just wait'll they encounter Phase Two."

That evening, eighteen Alpha cadets joined Bravo Company for their picnic at Kin Beach. Although the medical wonders of the world, Jonathan and James, could have stayed behind discussing dressings, their *learning* experience with Bravo made them want to be there.

Wayne and Douglas had the opportunity of riding in the cab of one of the trucks and it was Wayne who opened up the conversation.

"Have you noticed something about this company?"

Douglas nodded. He'd perceived it the minute he saw them formed up outside B-29. "There's a big difference since we first joined them, isn't there?"

"They're bloody perfect," Wayne replied. "Even in their P.T. strip, their drill is excellent. Not only that, they've been at Polson Park all day and look at their dress. Since they arrived back, they've washed and ironed their shorts and T-shirts. Did you see their running shoes? They're so Goddamned white, they gleam."

Douglas had been nodding throughout. "It's good to see it, Wayne. Those guys will be in Alpha next year when they get attached to *another* Bravo. The tradition has been maintained."

Wayne still couldn't get over it. "Jeez, I feel proud of them. When they got on the trucks, there wasn't a smile or a joke...listen, they're not even singing songs."

Wayne spoke too soon, because the minute the trucks cleared the Provost shack, *Old King Cole* started. He smiled. "That had me worried for a moment. They've probably heard about Rose's treatment of the Canadian Scottish."

Douglas agreed. "Remember Sergeant Beckford's saying: 'Leave nothing to chance.' Well, these guys are doing just that."

When the trucks were unloaded at Kin Beach, four platoons of cadets couldn't keep their eyes off the water. The Bravo Company cadets needed this respite and could hardly wait to jump in. They had worked hard on the parade square, day and night, until they were perfect. Also, although the company would be at the beach all day Wednesday and at Polson Park all day Thursday, they would be back on the square Wednesday night and would form the guard for Thursday's Graduation Parade. Above and beyond, they were proud and it showed.

After Major Kare's pep talk, Kin Beach shook with the boys' frenzied attack on the water. Unlike Alpha Company, these lads didn't throw their staff in the water right away. At this moment, they wanted the lake all to themselves. The staff would be *taken care of* later.

Because there were too many cooks, the Musketeers joined their *old* charges in the crystal-clear revitalizing liquid and renewed friendships that had started after Week Three in camp. Little did they know, they too, would be thrown in after eating.

Later, while everyone ate, the Musketeers went over to Sergeant Beckford and Sergeant Simpson who also needed this well-deserved break.

"Sit ye down," Beckford said, pointing to the ground in front of him. "Danyluk, Sergeant Simpson tells me you're still bitching every morning when it comes to P.T. Is that true?"

Moose had taken off his bathing suit and was sitting in just his P.T. shorts with his legs drawn up. "Well...it's...that's it, it's a tradition. If I didn't bitch, his day would be shot."

Simpson chuckled. "My day's shot now. I'm eating and your trunk is hanging out one leg of your shorts, with your balls out the other. Do you mind?"

Moose quickly put his legs down and pulled a little on his shorts. "Er, sorry about that, Sergeant."

"Has anyone heard from Bergie?" Sergeant Beckford asked. When he saw that they hadn't, he said, "I'll call his family to find out what's happening."

East, who was loaded down with hamburgers, directed his question to both of them. "Are you coming back next year?"

Beckford lay back. He was tired and it showed. Also his voice was a bit hoarse. "I am, how about you, Simp?"

"I think so, Bill." He glanced from left to right at the Musketeers. "What about you fellows? What are you going to do?"

Wayne shook his head. "No, I'll be working."

Simon played with the grass. "I'm coming back, if they take militia Corporals."

East quickly finished one of his burgers. "They take militia Corporals, don't worry. Yeah, I'll be doin' the same thing, but I wanna work in the kitchen."

Danyluk brought his legs up and quickly put them down again. "Doug and I might be here. We have to find out what the regiment wants. We may be in Wainright. If I'm gonna attend university and work in the sick people's place, I'll need all the moolah I can get."

Rothstein shook his head and laughed. "Hospital."

Moose grinned. "Yeah, that's the word I was lookin' for."

The boyish expression on Moose's face got them all howling. Beckford actually sat up. "So you're still thinking about becoming a doctor, are you?"

"You bet. A kindagologist."

Danyluk needed Rothstein's assistance again. "Gynecologist."

"Exactly," replied Moose.

With all of them chuckling, Beckford looked at Jackson. "How about you, Earl?"

"Well, I'm thinking about taking law. It's kind of difficult with my mom being in a wheelchair, but...if we can get a homemaker, I think I'll be able to pull it off. I've also thought..."

Earl never had the chance to finish because the group was surrounded and hauled to the lake with all the other officers and NCOs.

At 2230 hours that night, the Musketeers gathered around Gordie and Moose's bunks, just talking about the good time they had had.

"A stock broker, promoter, with clients who play cards and roll dice?" Rothstein asked Gordie. "Did you actually tell Sergeant Beckford that's what you're going to do?"

Cunningham shuffled one of his many decks. "Right on! Also, in stayin' where the dough is, I'm lookin' at lawn bowling or golf as a hobby. Hey, at least I'm gonna make some money. Are you serious about being a math teacher?"

Rothstein took a card out of the face-down deck offered by Gordie. He glanced at it and held it against his chest. "I wasn't fooling. I am going to teach math."

"Nine of hearts," said Cunningham, opening up the deck so Rothstein could slip the card back in.

Harvey's eyes lit up. "How in the hell do you do that? You're never wrong."

A Corporal yelled, "LIGHTS OUT IN TEN MINUTES!" and Gordie beamed. "In my business ya can't be wrong. Wanna try for a buck?"

"NO THANK YOU, MR. CUNNINGHAM! JESUS, DON'T YOU EVER GIVE UP?"

"In my business ya can't give up, either. How about two-bits?"

"GO SCREW YOURSELF!"

As Rothstein walked away, Moose kissed a ten-dollar bill. "CAN YA BELIEVE THIS? THE VERY FIRST DONATION TO MY 'HUMBLE SOLDIERS WITH ADVANCED GOUT' FUND!"

Danyluk started reading the letter. "Hey, listen to this:

'OH, MOOSE, UNTIL YOU TOLD ME WHAT GOUT WAS, I HAD NO IDEA. WHAT A SHAME THAT SO MANY BOYS ARE INFLICTED WITH THIS CONDITION. I REALLY FEEL GUILTY NOW BECAUSE BEFORE I MET YOU, I DUMPED A GUY WHO HAD GOUT. NOW I'LL HAVE SLEEPLESS NIGHTS WORRYING ABOUT THE POOR INVALID.' "

Sergeant Simpson must have been tired the next morning, because he didn't turn up and the Corporals were in no mood to lead the company in P.T. It was just as well anyway, because how can three Canadian Scottish cadets go jogging with the words, 'CUIDICH 'N RIGH' written in laundry-marker ink on each of their lower legs. After all, their socks would be down to their ankles and it would be seen. Also, how could the same cadets go into the showers with, 'HELP THE KING' written in the same colour ink in perfect English from their belly-button down to where their pubic hair *used* to be. Oh sure, they could turn toward the faucets and maybe it wouldn't be noticed. But if they did that, other people showering would have to 'bare witness' to very large letters written on their buttocks which once again read, 'CUIDICH 'N RIGH'.

Yes, it was a very difficult decision indeed. And once the shock of that was over, how could they justify displaying their hair, which now resembled a medieval English monk's *haircut*, complete with a small bald spot up top at the back. It was certainly a time to remember, because once the screams stopped, comments flew in all directions.

"YOU SEAFORTH CREEPS! WE HAD A SPORRAN PARADE PLANNED FOR TONIGHT! YOU ROTTEN GOONS! WE HAD TO PUT IN AN HOUR-AND-A-HALF ON THE PARADE SQUARE AND NOW THIS HAPPENS? WELL LET ME TELL YOU..."

It really didn't matter what the CScotRs planned, because the Seaforths were now organized. Each one of them stayed up for two hours during the night, waking up the next *man* when it was his shift.

The very tedious *work* had taken the Seaforth cadets a whole night because they had to wait until their *victims* rolled on their sides, or their backs, so they could finish the *job*, but to them, the price was well worth it. Four red-eyed Seaforths jigged in merriment.

"WELCOME TO THE CLUB, YOU PRINCESS MARY SLOBS! NOW *YOU* **KNOW HOW IT FEELS!"** came the reply.

Shortly, with the help of a few of the cadet platoon barbers, the hairstyles of three Princess Mary monks' were tapered, but now they resembled US Marines...with of course, a small bald spot at the back of their scalps.

Scrub brushes in the showers were of little use, but my, they were tried and by the time the company boarded the trucks for Kalamalka Beach, it was doubtful if the trio had any skin left on their bottoms, their lower stomachs, or their legs. At least the Seaforth cadets had shown some mercy. The good friars were left with their eyebrows, as well as the hair on their arms and legs.

The residents of Vernon turned out by the hundreds to watch the VACC swim meet, held near the diving boards and the wharf at Kal Beach. Although it was a bit of an inconvenience, the public didn't mind 1400 cadets joining them. Those cadets who weren't entered in the various competitions could swim with the public in the lifeguard-protected area, east of the wharf.

Nearly every cadet in camp who had a girlfriend met her at the beach, and many mothers and fathers turned up with picnic baskets loaded with goodies. When lunch time rolled around, those who weren't *dining* with friends were handed a box lunch.

Minutes after the trucks arrived, the encounters started and the cheering began. Large coloured ribbons pinned to swimsuits indicated which company the cadets were in, and after each event, a military sound-system announced the results.

The weather at the beach was perfect, hovering around eighty-five degrees, and between meets, cadets could do anything they wished. This suited Gordie Cunningham and Maggie just fine because they played stuke or poker with cadets in the band and other junior companies. For obvious reasons, Gordie used another name that day. The one-man gambling fame of Cunningham, Miller, Rammington-Smythe, Gandhi, Zaholuk, West and Chandler had spread throughout the camp, therefore he introduced himself as Al St. Dennis, from the Queen's Own Rifles. In some instances, it became *dicey*.

"Hey, ain't I played with you before? Ain't you Miller from Delta Company?"

Showing no nervousness whatsoever, Gordie answered, "I wish I was. I played that frump and he cleaned me out."

"The creep cleaned us all out during the first week. We think he cheats."

"Yeah, I got the same impression. Now, let's stop talkin' and start playin'!"

Close by, but out of hearing distance, another card game was in progress.

"Gee, Maggie, I haven't seen you since graduation. When did you start playing cards? Is five dollars enough to get in this game?"

"Oh, hello Barbara. Sure five dollars will get you started. I don't play this game very often, but we should have some fun. Now has everyone got their money ready, I'll deal first. Well, isn't that just luck...I've got twenty-one already."

Nearby, on a blanket laid out by the concession stand, East and his girl were eating hot-dogs and listening to Rosemary Clooney's, *Hey There*, softly wafting from the radio.

"Gee, I like that song. I'm sure gonna miss you when you're gone, Jack."

Their eyes met as Jack licked some mustard off his hot-dog. "Z'mm baghlonna bhiss ypyhou, pthoogh."

"Jack, baby, please don't talk with your mouth full. I said I'm really gonna miss you when you're gone. Here, let me wipe some of that mustard off your chin."

East swallowed. "I'm gonna miss you, too. Who taught ya how to cook like that?"

"My mother. Do you really like my cooking?"

Unfortunately, Jack had taken another bite. "Duouff I phealy wriike phyorr cooghing? Tshorpe I douougg."

"Oh, Jack darling, this is so romantic. Where...WHERE ARE YOU GOING?"

A running East quickly swallowed and turned around. "I'M ENTERED FOR THE BACKSTROKE! SAVE THAT HAFFA HOT-DOG FOR ME, WILL YA!"

Alma and Moose were not far away. They lay reclined listening to the next song broadcast by CJIB, Perry Como's, *Wanted*.

"Moose, did you have to wear that small bathing suit? It looks like a tiny hankie. The bulge is not just flagrant, it's downright embarrassing. Every gal on the beach stares as she goes by."

Danyluk had his sunglasses on and his arms behind his head. A smile appeared on his lips. "Let 'em eat their hearts out, Alma. I'm savin' this for youse only."

Alma wrapped one of her arms around him. "You devil, you. Am I really your only girl? Be honest now."

Danyluk turned his head to face her. His sunglasses hid his eyes. "How can youse ask such a question? I proposed, didn't I?"

"Er, that's right, you did, but, er, you didn't mention the year."

Moose stared at the sky again. "Alma, Alma, Alma. I said I'd marry ya as soon as I finish kindageologist school."

"But Moose, to become one of those might take a lotta months?"

Danyluk heard his name over the loudspeaker. He quickly sat up and took off his sunglasses. "Naah, one year at the most. I can be an advanced student because I kinda know all the stuff already. Will ya wait for me?"

After Alma said, "You know I will," a certain suspicious look came over her face. "Know all the stuff? Who have you been practisin' on?"

Moose stood up and tried to equalize the bulge in his crotch. "Oh, er, you mean, other than you?"

A bashful Alma softly replied, "Yes, darling."

As he walked towards the wharf, he replied. "I READ NATIONAL GEO-GRAPHICS IN THE JON!"

Alma said, "Oh," but she still didn't know what he meant.

Wayne and Douglas lay together with Diane and Debbie. They had put their blankets together, and both couples adored the song, *I Get So Lonely*, with the Four Knights.

When it ended, Diane winked at Wayne and Debbie and placed a small wrapped parcel in Douglas' hand. "Happy Birthday, Doug."

Brice sat up quickly. Once again, he'd forgotten. He knew his birthday was coming up but somehow it had slipped his mind.

With his face beaming, he kissed Diane and Debbie and shook Wayne's offered hand. Wayne also handed him a present. The card read, 'To a great friend, from Wayne and Debbie.'

Douglas placed his arm around Diane's shoulders and drew her in. "What can I say, but thank you." He glowered at Wayne and Debbie. "As for you guys, what kind of a buddy is it who doesn't remind his best friend. Thanks very much, guys."

"Well, c'mon, open 'em up," Debbie said, turning up *Don't Be Cruel*."

Diane's present was a silver ball-point pen with a tiny BCR badge soldered near the top. She knew from the expression on his face what he'd say when he kissed her again. "Wow, er, thank you. Diane, you're not supposed to spend the family inheritance on me, ya know? How'd you get this small crest?"

Laughing, Diane explained that she had written away to Fairbanks Jewelers in Vancouver and Mr. Fairbanks Junior had telephoned her back. He told her he was an officer in the British Columbia Regiment (DCO) and recommended the pen.

Wayne and Debbie's gift was also of a regimental nature. A shop in Vernon was selling old hat badges and by a stoke of luck, Wayne had found an old D.C.O.R. (Duke of Connaught's Own Rifles) badge. They were so rare, he and Douglas had never seen one before.

Douglas thanked them again, shaking Wayne's hand, and kissing Debbie on the cheek. There were no royal bumps for him this time, because the Musketeers were scattered all over the beach. However, around them, other cadets were receiving birthday tosses in blankets.

Brice was lost for words; the thought of the presents meant a lot to him.

"That's the first time I've ever seen..." He stopped because he heard his and Wayne's name being called. They got up and left.

To the sounds of, *Poor People of Paris*, by Les Baxter and his orchestra, Diane and Debbie put on their sun glasses, lay back, and soaked up the sun.

At the Awards Ceremony at the end of the day, Alpha Company won most of the events, with Bravo Company coming in a close second. All the Musketeers received ribbons for various swimming competitions and, as usual, Moose amassed all the diving awards.

When the trucks drove away, hundreds of girls, parents, and friends waved and screamed their good-byes to the departing cadets. Planning ahead, the Musketeers had made arrangements to meet their girls at Polson Park for the sports meet, the following day.

There was a movie in B-3 that night and it started late so that Bravo Company could complete their evening shift on the parade square. At 2100 hours, *The Desert Fox* was shown again. Although most cadets had already seen it, the hangar was full.

Throughout the film when the reels were changed, the usual exciting chatter was missing. Cadets seemed to just sit, silent, not saying much. As in the years before, they knew the camp was coming to a close and that meant the fun, frolic, and camaraderie they had shared for six weeks was coming to an end.

Sure, most of them looked forward to going home, but that's because they knew they had to go. If things were different, the majority would have stayed for another year, or another ten years, for that matter.

Vernon - the camp, the city, and the surrounding countryside - was their home-away-from-home, and deep inside, the boys didn't want to leave. For the senior cadets, this was their last year, which meant they would join the ranks of the summer visitors...previous cadets who came by each summer to say hello and to check and see if the traditions were being maintained. All the visitors had gleams in their eyes, but they were too old to participate anymore. Their attitude was the same as younger brothers who visited the camp with cadets' parents; they longed to be involved.

The words 'Mexican standoff' wouldn't describe the actions of the Scottish cadets that night. Both the Seaforths and the Canadian Scottish cadets never took their eyes off one another. But one good thing did happen. Before the movie, when it was time for an announced Sporran Parade, both groups buried the hatchet and participated regardless of the *feelings* they held for each other.

With pipes and drums beating off at the head of four platoons of marching un-kilted cadets, the largest Scottish assembly ever, strode the roads of the camp and a portion of the main highway before ending up on the giant parade square for fifteen minutes.

Wearing nothing but glengarry or balmoral headdress, sporrans, boots/shoes, spats and hose tops, the Scottish cadets of the western provinces, lead by the Seaforths and the Canadian Scottish, kept up their *distinctive and noble* tradition.
'Bare assed' to the breeze, the lads were proud to present the words, 'PRINCESS MARY RULES, CUIDICH 'N RIGH, and HELP THE KING to an amazed, grinning public and an equally proud, cheering turnout of other non-Scottish occupants of the Vernon Army Cadet Camp.

A sporran parade is a very serious ceremony and throughout the various drill movements, not a smile was seen. Only when the cadets marched back across the highway and were dismissed on the old parade square did they howl and roar with ironical, hilarious, comical intensity.

After a good laugh, and much back-smacking, the marchers didn't return to their barracks half in the buff. Instead, friends had brought their kilts and shirts, and now they got fully dressed.

Later that night, the cadets of B-33 learned that 'Cuidich 'n Righ' meant, 'Help the King.' Apparently in days of old, a King was about to be gored by a large stag, and the cry, 'Help the King' brought clansmen to his rescue. The Seaforth cadets were proud as they explained the meaning to everyone.

Before lights out, other regimental mottoes, slogans and battle cries were discussed. Throughout, though, Scottish eyes met each other. They may have been brothers-in-arms while marching, but there were limits afterwards.

Before everyone was asleep, MacTavish visited a downhearted Danyluk. "Sorry, Moose, but it just wouldn't have worked out."

Apparently a Scot was rushed to the camp hospital and Moose had worn the cadet's headdress, sporran, spats and hose tops, ready to join the parade.

"We don't mind showin' our asses, but your wang was hangin' below the sporran. I'm afraid that's not on."

"I CUDDA SCOTCH-TAPED IT UP!" Moose shot back.

"MOOSE, EVEN IF YOU TIED A KNOT, IT STILL WOULD HAVE HUNG BELOW THE SPORRAN! IF YOU SCOTCH-TAPED IT UP, IT WOULD HAVE HUNG OVER THE TOP OF THE SPORRAN."

"BULL SHIT! SCOTCH TAPE WOULD HAVE WORKED!" bellowed Danyluk.

MacTavish displayed some sympathy, but sporran parades were serious business. "OH SURE, AND SUPPOSE IT CAME LOOSE, NOT TO MENTION YOUR BALLS? WE'RE NOT GODDAMNED EXHIBITIONISTS, YA KNOW!"

"MY BALLS WOULDN'T HAVE HUNG BELOW IT!"

MacTavish patted him on the shoulder. "IT'S HARD TO TELL WITH YOU, MOOSE! ANYWAY, THANKS FOR YOUR INTEREST."

When the lights were turned out, Moose was still mumbling to himself. "...They just don't appreciate good talent."

"STAND BY YOUR BEDS AND FORM THREE RANKS ON THE ROAD!" bellowed Sergeant Simpson as he rushed down the aisle yanking mattresses on the floor, turning them over, dragging out pillows, and pulling down blankets.

"JUST BECAUSE THERE'S ONLY THREE DAYS LEFT DOESN'T MEAN YOU'RE IN A GODDAMNED HOLIDAY CAMP! C'MON, LET GO OF YOUR BLEAKERS AND GRAB YOUR SNEAKERS!"

Keeping up his personal custom, Moose once again complained. "Aw, Sergeant, youse just ruined a beautiful dream. There I was, frolicking with this here gorgeous mermaid. I talked her in to joinin' me on the beach and..."

"A MERMAID? DO YOU WANT SCALES ALL OVER THAT NINTH WONDER OF THE WORLD?"

Danyluk yanked up his shorts and quickly headed for the jon. "IT AIN'T FUSSY, SERGEANT! WHAT'S A FEW SCALES BETWEEN DIFFERENT SPECIES GETTIN' IT ON?"

"DANYLUK, YOU'RE ABSOLUTELY CORRECT. I'VE ALWAYS SAID YOU'D SCREW A ROCK PILE, IF YOU THOUGHT THERE WAS A SNAKE IN IT!"

"SAY, SERGEANT, THAT'S NOT A BAD...!"

"IF YOU'RE GOING TO THE JON, GET MOVING!"

"I'M GONE!"

This morning, Sergeant Simpson kept them jogging around the lower camp. At various times they passed other running companies and the band, marching and weaving in and out of various roads, loudly playing their instruments. Whenever they met, middle finger messages of 'hello' were *fondly* displayed.

After the usual fifty pushups and fifty sit-ups, the company was fallen out to have a shower, prepare their hut, and have breakfast. East could hardly wait.

"Did you smell the bacon and eggs as we passed the mess hall?" he asked Jackson, who was still half asleep and rubbing his eyes. "Them were real eggs, not the powdered ones."

Earl didn't bother replying, but Danyluk did, yanking off his shorts and draping his towel over a monumental erection that had remained throughout the exercise period. "How in the hell do youse knows that?"

"It's a matter of texture. Not only can I taste the difference in fibre, but I can also smell..."

"GO SCREW YOURSELF, EAST!"

During the shower, Jackson said his first words of the morning. "There's a storm on the way from the coast. We'll be getting rain sometime today or tomorrow."

Moose was still in his questionable mood. "Earl, since when did youse become a weatherman? There's not a cloud in the sky. Christ, it's a wonder youse don't mention snow."

Gordie rushed in. "Hey, where the hell's my...? Moose, that's my last bar of beau mo'nde French soap. Give it here, you creep."

Danyluk was finished with it anyway. He passed a half-bar to Cunningham, who snatched it away. "Keep your cottin' pickin' hands from my side of our barrack box, will ya? I've gotta work like hell to pay for this stuff and you help yourself?"

"When I was Bergie's partner, we used to share," replied Moose.

Gordie lathered up. "Yeah, I know how you guys used to share. You'd wear Bergie's underwear and he'd have to go and buy new ones."

Unnoticed by Gordie, Moose was now using a wonderfully-scented French shampoo. "BULL SHIT! BERGIE HELPED HIMSELF MANY TIMES TO MY SILK GAUNCH! ISN'T THAT RIGHT, EAST?"

Jack stepped out of the shower for a second to take a bite out of a stale doughnut which lay on the window ledge. "Yeaghph phtoo phsine whizz phboots."

This upset Moose because he needed an answer. "Swallow your food before you talk, will ya, ya pongo!"

East swallowed. "I said, yeah, to shine his boots."

"BULL SHIT! HE DIDN'T SHINE HIS BOOTS WITH MY UNDERWEAR! WAYNE, DID YOU HEAR THAT? JACK SAID..."

"I heard him. Jack, you're wrong. Bergie shined his brass with Moose's gaunch."

As Cunningham grabbed his shampoo, a puzzled look came over Danyluk's face. "Jeez, I always wondered where those stains were comin' from. That rotten..." Then Moose remembered his buddy was injured. "Well, he can shine his boots or brass with 'em anytime. But don't youse gets any similar ideas, Cunningham."

Gordie smiled. "How do ya think I get my belts so polished. Silk works wonders, ya know. It's great with Khaki It."

As a mumbling Moose left the shower, he said, "Now I know why Alma said I should go for a checkup."

At 1000 hours that morning, with the band leading, the cadets of the Vernon Army Cadet Camp marched to Polson Park.

As company after company made its way down the hill, the RCMP and the Provost were up on the highway south of the camp, directing northern traffic to the west road leading downtown. Travellers would turn onto the highway again, at the light on the intersection close to the entrance of the park.

When the band turned into the park just dressed in P.T. strip, with running shoes, heavy wool socks and their pith-helmets, the last company was marching past the Provost shack on the lower camp road .

Companies were fallen out after entering the cool, shaded, utopia of green. When the last company dispersed, the camp sports staff got the meet under way.

This was cheering time because company pride was on the line. With parents, girlfriends, and relatives sitting in the covered bleachers screaming away, the cadets ran, jumped, relayed, threw, tossed, and pulled themselves through the various events. The cheering never let up for a moment, and although Sergeants Beckford and Simpson had been working with Bravo Company, their loyalty remained with Alpha when it came to the tug of war. With both Sergeants rallying on their squad, no other company came close to winning.

The Musketeers weren't entered in any of the matches, however they were talked into replacing some of Alpha's smaller cadets in the tug of war. With heels dug in and hands clenched, they started by beating Bravo and then took on the rest.

At lunch time, box lunches were handed out and various couples separated and found a spot where they could be nearly alone. Douglas and Diane, of course, went to their usual place. In addition to a nice soft blanket, Diane had packed a picnic basket.

"There's a storm heading here from the coast," she said.

Douglas helped himself to a sandwich. "Jeez, that's weird. Earl mentioned that in the showers this morning . There was nothing said on the radio, so I wonder how he knew?"

Diane poured out two cold glasses of Freshie. "This one isn't just going to pass in a few hours. It stretches way out into the Pacific. Vancouver's been getting rain for a week. Take a look upwards."

Douglas glanced up and saw small dark clouds through the branches of the trees.

After they'd finished eating, Diane rested her head on his chest as she lay on a forty-five degree angle to his body. Both were chewing the ends of pieces of grass, watching the clouds quickly roll in.

"Are your mom and dad coming to the Graduation Parade tonight?" he asked.

"They wouldn't miss it for the world. We're getting here early because I think it's going to pour."

Douglas thought of the past three years. "I don't think it's ever rained on a grad parade. If it does, the field will be a quagmire. I pity Bravo having to go through all their drill movements in that."

Diane moved, lying on her stomach next to him, with her arm around his chest. "What time does your train leave on Saturday?"

"Ten o'clock," he replied. "I wish you were coming with me."

"So do I. But I'll see you in a week. We can go to the PNE (Pacific National Exhibition). Can you imagine, we're actually going to go to school together?"

Brice laughed. "UBC is a big place. We may get lost and never find each other." Then he thought for a moment. "But don't worry, kid, I'll find you. As a certain movie star once said, 'There's wolves in them thar hills.'"

She kissed him. "Well, if any of those thar wolves come near me, I'll kick 'em in the pods and pound them into the ground. What about you with female wolves?"

Douglas tried to hide his grin. "Well, depending on what kind of *fur* they have..."

He never had the chance to finish because Diane started tickling him. "Depending on what kind of fur? Why Douglas Brice, I'll..."

"ALL COMPETITORS TO THE FIELD!" blared.

It only took a moment for them to pack up and head back to the meet.

"If any female wolves come on to me, I'll simply give them Danyluk's phone number. He'll have 'em skinned in seconds."

They were both laughing as Douglas ran towards the tug of war ropes.

Following the last pull, Danyluk ran into the stands and grabbed Alma's arm. "C'mon, we've got an hour left, you can buy me a banana split."

"THERE HE IS!" screamed Eunice, ripping the sleeve of Corporal Adams' shirt in her excitement. "THAT'S HIM THERE!"

"WHERE?" replied the Corporal, holding onto the front of his pants.

Eunice grabbed his hand and nearly pulled him off his feet. "LET'S GO, WE'LL CATCH THE BASTARD!"

By the time the *little* couple arrived at the point where she'd seen Danyluk, he and Alma were long gone. A fruitless search followed.

"DAMN IT, EUNICE, I THINK YOU JUST SAID THAT TO GET ME OVER HERE!"

"DARLIN', I DID SEE THE ASSHOLE, REALLY I DID! THE SON OF A BITCH WAS WITH SOME TALL BROAD WITH A PONY TAIL. LET'S YOU AND I SEARCH OVER BY THOSE BUSHES!"

Adams stopped in his tracks. "Oh, no, you're not. I know what you've got..."

What could Corporal Adams do when he was tossed onto her shoulders? Absolutely nothing, but scream. But he couldn't scream either because she had her other hand over his mouth. No, in his mouth.

At three o'clock that afternoon, the parade was formed up and presentations were made. Alpha Company had won the majority of awards, and the company responded with deafening approval. Bravo Company was second, with Delta Company placing third.

While the cadets were marching out with the band leading, Corporal Adams didn't know what to do. "Jesus, Eunice, those were a new pair of undershorts you just ripped off me. I'm still sore from the last time. Can't you act like a lady?"

"WHAT THE SHIT ARE YOU TALKING ABOUT? MY DADDY SAYS I'M ALWAYS THE PERFECT LITTLE LADY, YOU GREAT BIG HANDSOME BASTARD..."

Although she was yelling, the music of the band drowned her out along with the help of a few claps of thunder..

When the cadets returned to camp, there wasn't time to dilly dally. They had course reports to review and sign, and this evening, they would look the sharpest they'd ever been.

From the minute each company entered its barracks, clothes were scrubbed, dried, soaped, starched, and ironed. Boots gleamed, laces, hose tops, and puttees were pressed, belts and brass shone like mirrors, and because they were to wear their regimental headdress, badges were *gone over* like never before.

All of these items would be put on just before they fell into three ranks for the march down the hill. When supper time came around, cadets wore their coveralls. After supper the showers would be in full operation and each cadet would be squeaky clean when he got dressed. Even all traces of Scottish *writing* would disappear.

At 1500 hours, four folding tables were set up in the drying room. A Platoon Officer sat behind each table with a Platoon Sergeant. One by one, in alphabetical order, cadets were called in to read and sign their course reports.

Being close to the top of the alphabet, Douglas was called in by Sergeant Beckford and asked to sit down. Cadets from the other three platoons were sitting at their respective tables.

Lieutenant Harwood looked up for a minute. "This is your course report, Cadet Brice. I'd like you to read it and sign your name at the bottom. If you have any questions, Sergeant Beckford or myself will be only too happy to answer them."

"Thank you, sir," Douglas replied, taking the four-copy form out of the officer's hand. After he read it, he picked up the nearby pen, signed his name, stood to attention, and faced the officer, who signed it as well.

"A very impressive report, Cadet Brice."

"Thank you, sir."

"Did you enjoy the summer?"

"Yes sir, I really did. For a first of its kind, this course was great."

Beckford smiled. "I got the impression you floated this summer. Er, by floating, I mean, you could have studied for your exams a little more. Am I right?"

Douglas thought for a moment. "You're probably right, Sergeant. This is my fourth year. I...thought someone else should...well..."

"You mean you didn't want to top the course?"

Douglas remained at attention, fidgeting with the sides of his coveralls. "It would have been nice, but...er, I've been through...er..."

"Are you tired of cadets?" asked the officer.

"No, sir, but, well I'm sort of ready to move..."

The officer placed the report to one side. "Ready to move on?"

"Yes, sir."

Sergeant Beckford and Lieutenant Harwood glanced at each other, before the officer spoke. "Well, Cadet Brice...there's no doubt in my mind, whatever you decide to do after you've finished cadets, you'll do it well. Our congratulations on a fine job this summer."

Douglas shook their offered hands. "Thank you, sir. It's been great working with both of you. He winked at Sergeant Beckford, smartly turned around, and marched out.

At the dinner table, Gordie showed the group a massive wad of bills. "The dice were really hot today. Maggie and I really cleaned up. My forty-percent of her end totalled thirty-seven dollars."

Wayne couldn't believe it. "Are you telling us, she gives you forty-percent of her winnings?"

Cunningham leaned back on two legs of his chair. "Natch, I taught her everything she knows. That don't come cheap because I had to pay to learn."

"But she's your girlfriend," said Douglas.

"I know, but business is business. She tried telling me there'd be no necking if she had to pay the percentage, but that didn't bother me."

Now Moose entered the conversation. "Are youse sayin' you'd rather have the moolah than neckin' with her?"

"Yep!"

"Youse has got a screw loose, Cunnilingus. Jesus, she's a nice dame. Why I'd even pay her to..."

Cunningham sat upright. "Hey, watch your mouth. You're talking about the woman I love."

"The woman youse loves? What the hell would youse be like if ya hated her?"

Gordie sipped his tea and smiled. "It's a matter of training. She knows what she means to me, but there are limitations to everything. I told her if we get married, we'll start our kids learnin' a simple stuke game at age two. By the time they're four, I want them to know the works."

"What's the works?" asked Moose.

"I haven't got the time to tell you."

"TELL ME!"

Gordie started thinking. If Moose wanted the works then he was going to get the works.

"Well, by four years of age, they'll know: correct odds, house percentages, playing strategy, detection of cheating methods, betting on the horses, betting on sports, including baseball, football, basketball, hockey, elections, prize fights, golf..." He stopped for a moment. "Yeah, especially golf. I like that game. I also want 'em to have the up on lotteries, sweepstakes, pools, raffles, the numbers game, bingo, race horse Keno, casino side games, carnival and amusement park games, black jack, roulette, slot machines, Cheminde Fer and Baccarat, private craps, bank craps, dice game odds, poker, gin rummy, punch-boards, chain lotteries, pyramid clubs..."

Moose couldn't take it anymore, so he cut him off. "O.K., O.K., youse wins. My God, Cunnilingus, if they know all that by the age of four, there'll be nothin' else left for them to learn?"

Gordie was in one of his moods now. He'd been challenged and Moose wasn't going to get off lightly. "Moose that just goes to show what you know. By the age of six, I want them to know all about private betting. You know, hustlers and cheats propositions? Have you heard of propositions?"

Moose winced. He was sorry he asked the question in the first place. "No, the only time I was propositioned was..."

"I'm not talkin' about that kind of propositioning, you pongo. I want my kids to learn: the fly and sugar, the odd man coin, the spinning coin, the tossing coin, spelling propositions, the lollapalooza hand, put-and-take, the match pile, birthday percentages, auto license plate percentages, percentage propositions with cards, the matching card proposition, deck cutting propositions, two-roll crap propositions, and..."

"Enough, enough!" Moose pushed Gordie's face away from his. "With kids like that, youse'll never have to work for a livin'."

Cunningham relaxed. "That's the general idea. Right now, I've got Maggie reading up on..." He took a piece of paper out of his pocket. I told her I want her to pay particular attention to: cheating at private games, the mechanic's grip, the pick-up stack, the Riffle stack, the old-style overhead shuffle stack, false shuffles, nullifying the cut, false cuts, the prearranged or cold deck, second dealing, peeking, the bottom deal, palming, belly stripper systems, marked cards, how to spot a marked card cheat, how to..."

Cunningham's nose was in Danyluk's face so Moose put his hand over the *gambler's* mouth and backed off. "I apologize. All right, so youse deserves forty-percent of her cut. Christ, I never knew youse learned all that."

"Do you want me to tell you more?" Gordie asked making a coin appear out of Moose's nose.

"NO, AND I PITY YOUR KIDS!"

Cunningham grinned. "Why? I can tell you what they'll know by the time they're twelve. They'll learn..."

Instantly he was alone. Even Jack East had left the table, grabbing an apple on the way out and shaking his head at the amazement of it all.

"HEY, I'M NOT FINISHED," Cunningham yelled.

As the group walked back to B-33, they discussed their course reports with each other.

At 1900 that evening, all cadets were formed up on the old parade square and the road, ready to march to Polson Park. Humidity was the order of the day. The camp RSM ordered every cadet to take his poncho or ground sheet and throw it in the back of his company's equipment-truck. Distant thunder and lightning were getting closer and dark clouds filled the sky. It was apparent that at amy moment the Heavens were going to open up.

"IF IT'S RAINING WHEN THE PARADE FINISHES, YOU WILL DRAW A PONCHO OR GROUND SHEET FROM THE TRUCK. DON'T WORRY IF IT'S YOURS OR NOT, BECAUSE YOU'LL BE HANDING THEM IN TOMORROW!" bellowed RSM Gardiner.

"NOW REMEMBER THIS IS ALPHA COMPANY! ALTHOUGH BRAVO COMPANY, THE GUARD, IS MARCHING AHEAD OF YOU, YOU PEOPLE ARE THE PRIDE OF VACC AND EVERYONE KNOWS THAT! I WANT YOUR CHESTS OUT, YOUR ARMS STIFF AND UP, AND I WANT THE CITIZENS OF THIS CITY TO SAY, "NEVER HAVE I SEEN SUCH DRILL AND SMARTLY TURNED-OUT CADETS! IS THAT CLEAR?"

"YES, SIR!"

"I CAN'T HEAR YOU!"

"YES, SIR!"

Gardiner cringed and smiled. He knew they were up for it.

Bravo Company was sized in two formations of guards. Every belt was *perfectly* in line.

(Author's note: Although my editor said this note would be too disruptive, I had to disagree with her. These days, more than in the past, I pay particular attention to **sized** troops on parade. It's detestable seeing belts up and down throughout the ranks. I don't see it with British troops on parade, nor, very little for that matter, do I see out-of-line belts worn by military college cadets. Perhaps that is one of the reasons our military college's are supplying more and more honour-guards for visiting dignitaries.

Maybe it's time for Peter, Paul and Mary to write a new song for the regular force and militia, entitled, **'Where Have All The Drill Sergeants Gone?'** But then again, we know where they've gone, don't we? They went home after Trudeau and Hellyer started playing silly bloody idiotic games with the military's tried and tested traditions. When I even think of the *actions* of those two, I want to throw up. Sorry about this. Thanks for bearing with me. I'll get on with the story.)

Bravo Company looked exemplary. Throughout the sized ranks, every belt was in line, all short pants, rolled-up sleeves, hose tops and puttees were exactly even, and every gleaming white rifle sling was so taut, it could have been used to launch arrows.

The Cadet Battalion Commander came from Driver Mechanics, and most of the other cadet officers and NCOs were from Driver Mech, Signals, and Bravo Company.

The cadets of Alpha had been asked to decline parade positions, in order that other cadets could receive the much-needed practise required for future years. In years past, all of the Musketeers as well as most cadets in Alpha Company, had been in command positions of some sort. As it was, for this parade, Jackson was the Cadet Company Commander; Rothstein was the Company Sergeant-Major; Douglas was a Platoon Officer; Gordie, a Platoon Sergeant; Banks and Simon were Platoon Corporals; Danyluk, the right marker; and behind him on the extreme right files of One Platoon were East and MacTavish.

"BATTALION, ATTEN...TION!" Fourteen-hundred left legs were lifted six inches off the ground, left toes parallel with the left knee and slammed down. **WHOMP!**

"BATTALION, SLOPE...ARMS!" Although each cadet in Bravo Company carried out three movements completing the slope arms, each individually timed movement was perfect. Bravo Company had learned, *the knack*.

"BATTALION, MOVE TO THE RIGHT IN COLUMN OF ROUTE, RIGHT...TURN!" After the supernumeraries had made their move..."BY THE RIGHT, QUICK...MARCH!" was given.

This time, the pipes and drums of Scottish regiment cadets started off the marching parade. At the bottom of the camp road, the Cadet Battalion Commander turned left along the lower road leading past B-3 and when he reached the highway, he turned right and ordered, "DRESSING AGAIN BY THE RIGHT!"

As the parade marched down the hill, no one lost his step; all heads and arms were up, their dressing was perfect, and each face carried a serious expression. The difference between these cadets now, and the way they were when they had arrived in camp, was like night and day, particularly the cadets of the guard.

At the bottom of the hill, when the parade followed the Cadet Battalion Commander into Polson Park, heavy rain started. The downpour would continue all evening, but it wouldn't dampen the spirits of the cadets.

After the battalion of cadets halted in formation and the right dress was given, the parade carried on normally.

They were now lined up on grass and across a muddy baseball diamond. Although their boots were muddy, the creases had left their clothing, and they were soaked through to the skin, the cadets of VACC kept their chests out and their chins up as General George Kitching inspected them. The General himself was drenched even before he started marching through the ranks.

"Did you enjoy the summer, Kennedy?"

"Yes, sir!"

"Are you prepared to go back to your cadet corps and teach them what you've learned?"

"I certainly am, sir."

"Where are you from?"

"Winnipeg, sir."

"Good turnout, Kennedy!"

"Thank you, sir!"

General Kitching didn't allow the rain to deter him from taking the time to speak to individual cadets. They wanted to speak with the general, just as much as he wanted to talk with them.

"How long have you played the pipes, Rae?"

"Since I was four, sir!"

"Did you enjoy serving with the band this summer?"

"I served with Alpha Company this summer, sir! When I have the chance, I play with the pipes and drums."

"Oh, I see. The general looked the boy up and down. I have three questions to ask you. Is that kilt heavy when it rains?"

"Yes, sir, but we don't mind it, sir!"

Kitching nodded. "Who cut your hair and what...what's that writing on your knees?"

Although it wasn't supposed to happen, a small smile came to Rae's lips as he stood at attention looking to his front. "Are you sure you want to know, sir?"

The smile was contagious. "Er, perhaps not. I see a few Scottish cadets seem to have the remains of writing on their legs. Good turnout Rae!"

"Thank you, sir!"

Sheets of rain fell as General Kitching inspected his cadets. In the stands, parents, friends, and visitors huddled together. The wind was cold and at times, the deluge blew into the bleachers.

When Diane spotted Douglas, she stood and gave him the thumbs up. He saw her, but made only one move. She couldn't see him wink. Other people pointed out their *soldiers* with particular screams of, "THERE HE IS!" "HELLO, SON!" "YOUR FLY'S UNDONE!"

At the back of the stands on the top row, a couple scanned the parade using binoculars. Along with Corporal Adams, Eunice had brought her best friend, Alberta.

"DID YOU SPOT THE SON OF A BITCH, ADAMS, DEARIE?"

"Not yet, Eunice. Try and keep your voice down."

As usual, Alberta was in top form. "WHY THE HELL SHOULD SHE? LISTEN FUCKEE, SHE LIVES IN THIS TOWN! SHE CAN SAY..."

Little Alberta and Eunice didn't notice Sergeant Bygdnes sitting with Sergeant Gabriel, five rows down. Sergeant Bygdnes turned his head around and called, "EUNICE DEAR, WHO'S USING THAT HORRIBLE LANGUAGE UP THERE?"

The *little one* had to think quickly. "IT'S THOSE NAUGHTY TEENAGERS OVER THERE, DADDY!"

Gabriel and Bygdnes eyed two teen couples quietly sitting watching the parade. Two of the youngsters were visiting from England.

Gabriel stood up. "HEY, YOU! YES, YOU!" When he had their attention, he continued.

"KEEP YOUR VOICES DOWN AND WATCH YOUR LANGUAGE, OR I'LL COME UP THERE WITH SOME BARS OF SOAP!"

The pounding rain combined with the band playing made it difficult for the four to hear Gabriel.

"What was that all about, one asked another?"

"SURE THING, POPS!" a lad replied, shrugging to his friends. "I think he said something about the Pope's car. Probably another one of those army types who's been out in the sun without his helmet and he's had a few beers."

In all seriousness, the British boy smiled, nodded, and gave Gabriel the thumbs up. "IF IT'S THE POPE, HE PROBABLY RIDES AROUND IN A LORRY OR A TANK!"

"What did the little bastard say?" Bygdnes asked Gabriel.

Gabriel liked what he heard. He acknowledged the boy's response and returned his eyes to the parade. "He said he doesn't want the soap, he's sorry and thanks."

"I should hope so. A little discipline never hurts, Bill."

After the march past was complete, General Kitching cut his address short and only spoke for about five minutes. After thanking the cadets, he said he was very proud of them, and mentioned their progress at camp; why they should continue the traditions, etc., and wished them the very best of luck.

Although the cadets of Alpha Company did not compete for the Best Cadet in camp this year, to his surprise, but no one else's, Simon was called forward. His marks had been the highest by a fraction, and he was named as the best cadet in Alpha Company.

"He deserves it," Douglas mumbled to Wayne.

"But he's from the Irish Fusiliers," Wayne replied, slightly moving his lips, but looking to his front. "Christ, we'll never live this down. The shamrocks will be painted even bigger now."

"Yeah, but he says his second choice is the BCRs."

Douglas' smile was mirrored by Wayne's lips. "Oh, well that's all right then," Banks replied.

Most of the Musketeers received awards. Douglas won the trophy for the best shot in camp. The Best Cadet award went to Cadet Laitricharde-Reed. For the first time ever, this boy had done something entirely on his own. He would have liked his dad to have been present when he received his trophy but it wasn't necessary. He was his own *man* now, because earlier on in summer training, he'd learned his lesson, and nothing could hold him back.

The Second Best Cadet award went to Cadet Archer. Moose stuck his chest out even further when Archer's name was called. He'd *talked* with both of them.

After half-an-hour of awards with the sound system cracking up because of the deluge, the Camp Regimental Sergeant-Major, Mister Gardiner, addressed the parade. Unlike General Kitching, he didn't feel sorry for the *ducks*.

"WHAT A SUMMER WE'VE HAD. ONCE AGAIN I'VE WITNESSED BUNKS ON THE PARADE SQUARE, BRASSIERES AND SHIRTS UP THE FLAGPOLE, AND NUDISTS EXHIBITING THEIR BODIES AT EVERY CHANCE. THE CANNON WAS PAINTED SEVEN TIMES, MY JEEP WAS STOLEN TWICE, HOP SING RECEIVED A LETTER TO VISIT THE CAMP!" He paused..."ALONG WITH HIS *DAMES*?..."

Laughter erupted in the stands.

"THE COMMANDING OFFICER RECEIVED TELEPHONE CALLS OFFERING MONEY FOR SOME DIARRHEA, OR GOUT FUND. THE MEDICAL OFFICER RUSHED TO UBC TO CHECK UP ON THE ACTUAL MEANING OF THE WORD *GOUT*. LADDERS WERE LEFT OUTSIDE THE NURSING SISTERS QUARTERS, AND THE FEMALE KITCHEN LADIES RECEIVED LOVE NOTES AND OFFERS OF PROPOSAL. YES, MY TELEPHONE WAS HOOKED UP TO THE SILVER GRILL CAFE; TAXIS ARRIVED AT BOTH THE OFFICERS' AND THE SERGEANTS' MESSES ASKING FOR COURT MARTIAL MOOSE - WHOEVER THE HELL HE IS..."

Up in the stands, Adams said, "Did you hear that? The guy's name is Court Martial Moose. Ah ha...so the name is Court M. Moose, is it? I've gotcha, you little son of a bitch."

Needless to say, down on the field, a certain chest was pushed out even farther.

"...WHEN I WAS IN CIVILIAN CLOTHES, A CADET ASKED ME IF I HAD A MEXICAN CREDIT CARD. WHEN I ASKED WHAT IT WAS, HE TOLD ME IT WAS A SIPHON HOSE...HIS GIRLFRIEND'S CAR WAS PARKED NEXT TO THE DRIVER-MECH COMPOUND! THE OKANAGAN INDIAN BAND WANTS US TO STOP THESE MIDNIGHT SWIMS! I NEVER KNEW WE HAD ANY MIDNIGHT SWIMS! THE GOLF COURSE HAS COMPLAINED, ALONG WITH THE LAWN-BOWLING CLUB! THE VERNON GIRLS BAND GOT SICK OF TELEPHONE CALLS ASKING WHICH IS THE ONE WHO DIDN'T WEAR ANY PANTIES. THEY'VE INFORMED US THAT ALL OF THE GIRLS DO."

The laughter rose even higher after that comment.

"OUR MANY STUDS ARE TAKING PICTURES OF CERTAIN PARTS OF THEIR BODY AND CHARGING FOR THEM. GIRLS HAVE VISITED THE CAMP IN THE MIDDLE OF THE NIGHT; PIZZAS HAVE BEEN DELIVERED AT THE SAME TIME, BUT UNFORTUNATELY THE C.O. AND I DON'T EAT THEM. CLEAR-WRAP WAS PLACED OVER THE NURSING SISTERS' TOILETS! AND LAST, BUT NOT LEAST, SOME CHAP FROM SIGNALS ATTACHED A SMALL WIRE TO THE URINAL PIPE IN THE SERGEANTS' MESS. THE OTHER END OF THE WIRE WAS FIXED TO AN ELECTRICAL HAND-WINDING CHARGER. CERTAIN MEMBERS OF THE SERGEANTS' MESS, MYSELF INCLUDED, WERE LEFT WITH NO DOUBT THAT WATER DOES CONDUCT ELECTRICITY. ANY STREAM OF WATER!"

The applause from the stands and cadets was deafening as the RSM played with the ends of his mustache.

"I COULD GO ON AND TELL YOU ABOUT THE CERTAIN HABITS OF SCOTTISH CADETS , BUT IT'S WET AND I'VE RUN OUT OF TIME. AT THIS MOMENT, THE INK ON THEIR BODIES IS PROBABLY RUNNING DOWN THEIR LEGS..."

Alpha's laughing and cheering was most prominent.

"...ANYWAY, I JOIN THE COMMANDING OFFICER IN SAYING THAT I'M INDEED VERY PROUD OF EACH ONE OF YOU AND I HOPE TO SEE YOU RETURN!

"YOU'VE WORKED AND PLAYED HARD, AND THAT'S WHAT IT'S ALL ABOUT. GO BACK TO YOUR UNITS AND PASS ALONG YOUR KNOWLEDGE. ALWAYS KEEP IN MIND THAT THIS IS A CADET **TRAINING** CENTRE. IF I HAVE ANYTHING TO DO WITH IT, OUR PROGRAMS WON'T GET SOFT! IT IS HERE IN VERNON, WHERE THE MILITARY STANDARDS AND TRADITIONS OF THIS WONDERFUL COUNTRY ARE MAINTAINED. HOLD THOSE CHERISHED EMBLEMS AND CUSTOMS CLOSE TO YOUR HEART, BECAUSE EVERY SECOND OF EVERY DAY, THERE ARE MILITARY ARMCHAIR QUARTERBACKS WHO WANT TO RIP THEM APART! DON'T ASK ME WHY...AS A MATTER OF FACT, DON'T EVEN ASK THEM. ALTHOUGH THEY CAME THROUGH THE SAME SYSTEM, THEY'LL NEVER TELL YOU THEY DID IT FOR PERSONAL GAIN ALONE!

"LIKE MAGGOTS AND BUGS, THESE *PEOPLE* WILL ALWAYS CRAWL THROUGH THE CRACKS. NOT ONLY IS IT YOUR JOB TO STOP THEM, YOU MUST NEVER BECOME ONE OF THEM! IN ADDITION TO POSSESS-

ING THE CHARACTERISTICS OF SNAKES, THEY'RE BLOODY *YES MEN*, AND I CAN'T STOMACH *YES MEN*, CAN YOU?"

"NO, SIR!"

"TONIGHT, IN THIS WEATHER, I WITNESSED A FINE PARADE. YOUR DEMONSTRATIONS WERE EXCELLENT AND I WANT TO PARTICULARLY THANK THE GUARD FOR COMPLETING THE BEST *FEU DU JOIE* I'VE EVER SEEN. MY CONGRATULATIONS, BRAVO COMPANY!"

The RSM took a letter out of his pocket.

"THE COMMANDING OFFICER HAS ASKED ME READ A LETTER FROM MR. RED ROBINSON, FROM RADIO CJOR IN VANCOUVER. IT READS:

'TO THE COMMANDING OFFICER, STAFF AND CADETS OF THE VERNON ARMY CADET CAMP.

'WHEN I VISITED THE WONDERFUL CITY OF VERNON, MANY CADETS ASKED ME IF I COULD MAKE IT UP FOR THE GRADUATION PARADE. BELIEVE ME, I TRIED, BUT BEING ON THE AIR, CURTAILS MY TIME.

'I'VE ALWAYS BEEN VERY PROUD OF THE YOUTH OF THIS COUNTRY, BUT TOURING THE CAMP, I HAD A LUMP IN MY THROAT THROUGHOUT. YOU SEE, MY JOB ALLOWS ME TO TALK WITH TEENAGERS ALL OVER THE PROVINCE, BUT NEVER HAVE I MET SUCH FINE, POLITE YOUNG PEOPLE, AS I DID IN VACC. TO TELL YOU THE TRUTH, I WANTED TO JOIN IN AND TRAIN WITH THEM. THAT'S IF YOU'D TAKE AN EX-AIR CADET.

THANK YOU VERY MUCH FOR YOUR HOSPITALITY AND FOR CONFIRMING TO ME THAT WITH OUR YOUNG PEOPLE, THE FUTURE OF CANADA, WILL ALWAYS BE IN GOOD HANDS.

MY SINCERE BEST WISHES,

RED ROBINSON.' "

Mister Gardiner folded Red's letter amidst loud applause, cheers, and whistles.

When the RSM was finished, The Vernon News took pictures of everyone and the parade completed an Advance In Review Order for General Kitching, followed by three cheers.

Before the cadets left to march back up the hill, ponchos and ground sheets were issued. Although the proud, smiling *soldiers* were soaked through, they wouldn't get any wetter.

Shortly, to applause, waves, thrown kisses and screamed-out comments, fourteen-hundred cadets marched out of Polson Park and up the hill. Regardless of the weather, chins and arms were up, chests were out, and pride was expressed on every face. This had been their night and it had been pulled off perfectly.

After the parade was dismissed, East joined others as they rushed into the mess hall for mug-up. When he finally entered the barracks, with sandwiches which were soaked, but eatable, he found everyone was gathered around Simon. For winning the Best Cadet in the Company award, Simon was very humble, *indeed*.

"Thank you, thank you. It just goes to show what I've been telling you black-hats amongst others, all along. He bellowed, "WHAT'S THE BEST REGIMENT?"

"THE IRISH FUSILIERS!" came a deafening response from all Irish cadets in the vicinity.

"AND WHAT'S THE BEST ARMOURIES?"

"GILFORD STREET!"

"AND WHO HAS THE MOST BATTLE HONOURS?'

"THE IRISH!"

After Simon's last statement, auguments ensued for the next hour. He didn't know what he started because all the barrack room lawyers spouted off battles of old. At the end, nothing had changed.

'BARRRROOOOOM! CRAAAAACKKK!'

It was suddenly daylight as lightning lit up the sky. Although no one thought it was possible, the rain was falling even heavier now. Throughout Camp Vernon, all windows and doors were shut as water gushed through the drainage ditches running down the sides of the main roads.

Normally on this night, officers and NCOs appeared to sit on bunks and chew the fat. But not tonight because it would have been the same as standing underneath the showers.

The barracks looked like the aftermath of an British soccer match when Moose took out his pictures and started selling them. Cadet Johnston had done an admiral job.

"STEP UP AND PAY!" yelled Danyluk. "THERE ARE NO REFUNDS AND WE'LL START WITH THE UGLIES AND MOVE UP GRADUALLY! FIFTY CENTS A PHOTO, MY FRIENDS!"

"YOU AIN'T GOT NO FRIENDS!" commented a cadet from the Fort Garry Horse, holding out two quarters.

"Just pay my clerk," Danyluk instructed his paying *customers,* who handed their money to Jackson and walked away with a picture after Earl counted the change.

"HEY, WE SHOULD HAVE A CHANCE TO SEE WHAT WE'RE BUYIN'!'

"BEGGARS CAN'T BE CHOOSERS!" Moose replied. "That's it, that's it, just give my accountant your money. Next!"

Absent mindedly, Moose started flipping through some pictures that weren't of the girls changing room at Kin Beach. By accident, Johnston had included two rolls of pictures of himself with his Chinese girlfriend. The beautiful girl was standing in front of an ice-box in a bikini, and without her bikini top, smiling bashfully throughout. The next group of pictures were of an unclothed Johnston, smiling just as bashfully, on a white bearskin rug. He was holding a teddy bear as he lay on his stomach. Whoever took the pictures must have said *act like a baby.*

Earl had his head over Moose's shoulder. "Jesus, we can't sell those! He'll kill us!"

The next *customer* wanted his picture. "C'MON, C'MON!"

Moose and Earl's eyes met. "How much money have we made on top of our cost?"

Jackson looked in his small cardboard box. "About eighteen dollars."

A sneaky grin hit Moose's face. "Have ya got your scissors?"

"Yeah, I can get 'em."

"Good, just cut off their heads."

Earl slapped Moose on the back. "Brilliant! You're some kinda genius."

"THE NEXT GROUP OF PHOTOS ARE A BUCK APIECE! THESE COME FROM A VERY PRIVATE COLLECTION. I COULD CHARGE MORE, BUT WHAT'S MONEY AMONGST FRIENDS! There you are, sir."

The cadet walked away and came back with a picture of Johnston on the bear skin rug. Johnston's head was missing.

"HEY, I CAN'T TELL IF THIS IS A GUY OR A DAME?"

Moose grabbed the cadet by the front of his shirt. "What do you think we are? Do you think we'd sell pictures of guys?"

"Er, no."

"GOOD! MOVE ON! NEXT!"

When all the pictures were sold, only one other cadet complained. "SAY, FOR THAT KINDA MONEY I SHUDDA GOT ONE WITH BOOBS! THESE ARE LIKE TWO FRIED EGGS!"

East came rushing over. "Who's got fried eggs?" He was *moved* aside.

Danyluk took the picture out of the cadet's hand. It was Johnston on the rug again, but he'd moved his upper body a bit towards the camera.

"HOW MUCH DID YOUSE PAY FOR THAT?"

"A BUCK!"

"EARL, TAKE A LOOK AT THIS. IT'S HER IN ALL HER GLORY!"

Earl snatched the picture away. "Wow! Look at that ass, and the hair on those legs."

Moose took two dollars out of the box. "YOU PAID A BUCK...I'LL BUY IT BACK FOR TWO!"

The cadet grabbed the picture back. "NOT ON YOUR LIFE!" As he walked away, he said, "HEY, YOU GUYS, I'VE GOT..." He turned. "What the hell's her name?"

"Youse has got the lovely, Joan Stone," replied Danyluk.

"HEY, YOU GUYS, I'VE GOT THE LOVELY, JOAN STONE...AND SHE DON'T SHAVE HER LEGS!" In seconds, he was mobbed.

Earl grabbed Danyluk's arm. "Joan Stone?"

When Moose grinned and winked, Jackson roared out laughing.

Fortunately for both of them, Cadet Johnston was on the other side of the barracks, rolling dice with Cunningham. Gordie had won another seven dollars by the time the game came to an end.

A drenched Corporal entered the barracks, took off his raincoat, and shook it as he closed the inner door. "LIGHTS OUT IN TEN MINUTES!"

The cadets of Alpha didn't need ten minutes; it had been a tough day. Shortly, to the sound of the rain pounding on the roof, most cadets, including the Musketeers, were asleep.

An hour later, a Canadian Scottish cadet appeared at a Seaforth's bed. "Can you get your guys to agree to a truce for tonight? We're beat!"

"Sure, if you're on the level."

"We are."

"O.K., then." After both cadets made their rounds and informed their friends there was no more need for the nighttime vigil, more snores filled a creaking B-33. Although the sleepers were noisy, the beat of the rain was louder. Even louder than two creeping cadets who weren't that happy with their pictures. A snoring Moose never heard them open up the unlocked barrack box at the foot his and the *gambler's* bunks.

"STAND BY YOUR BEDS! C'MON, C'MON, LET GO OF YOUR HANDLES AND GRAB YOUR SANDALS. IN ONE MINUTE, THIS COMPANY WILL FORM THREE RANKS ON THE ROAD!"

It was raining so hard, Sergeant Simpson had elected to wear a poncho rather than a raincoat, as he did his *job* moving quickly up and down the aisle before heading over to the other wing of the barracks. When he returned, everyone was up, even Moose, who wasn't bitching.

"No comments today, Mr. Danyluk?"

Danyluk had already put on his P.T. shorts. Now he pulled his T-shirt over his head and started running on the spot before he headed towards the door.

"Not today, Sergeant. I'm always prepared to do P.T. on the last day. Let's get it over with."

In the blinding rain, about halfway back from the upper camp, Danyluk was in the middle of a conversation when all of a sudden his shorts split right up the centre. The only thing holding the two legs of the garment together was the elastic waistband.

With laughter behind him *baring witness* to a, "lily white ass," and roars from those in front, turning to behold, "the fire hose and buckets," swinging away, Moose Danyluk didn't know what to do. The same thing also happened to Cunningham's P.T. shorts, but Gordie was wearing underwear.

Someone had painstakingly undone the stitching on both Moose and Gordie's shorts, only leaving about one stitch every inch. Eventually the jogging pulled those stitches apart. Neither cadet knew how they qualified for such treatment. As far as Gordie was concerned, it could have been a poor loser. In Moose's case, it could have been anything.

With one hand in front and the other hand holding his rear, Danyluk begged Sergeant Simpson to release him from the morning's pushups and sit-ups. Although Simpson expressed some sympathy, "NO BLOODY WAY!" was his response.

By the time the soaking wet, mud covered company entered B-33, Danyluk's ass was caked in two inches of mud, and his dames' *joystick (and friends)* were almost unrecognizable, as well as sore.

In the steaming showers, Moose was furious as he spread his bar of Sergeants' Soap. Gordie had cut off Danyluk's French *entitlement*.

"I'LL GET THE CREEPS THAT DID THIS! JESUS, MY WANG FELT LIKE IT WAS DIGGIN' FOR WORMS!"

Banks had to open the window he was laughing so hard. "HOW IN THE HELL CAN YOU KEEP A HARD-ON WHEN YOUR BUILT-IN SHOVEL'S DIGGIN' IN A FOOT OF MUD?"

"IT AIN'T EASY! JUST GOOD HEALTHY PLANNIN', I GUESS. SAY, ON SECOND THOUGHT, THAT SOFT MUD FELT PRETTY GOOD!"

Anyone up Silver Star Mountain that wet morning, surely would have heard the joyous howls originating from an open shower room window in B-33.

After Breakfast, all cadets changed into their battledress pants, shirts, boots, and puttees. With their camp clothing and equipment folded and piled in ponchos, they waited by their beds until the trucks arrived to take them to the giant hangars in the upper camp. It was raining too hard to form three ranks on the road. Their battledress pants would have gotten soaked and nothing was heavier, or looked worse, than wet battledress.

All vehicles had their tarpaulins on when they pulled up. For the cadets, the ride to the upper camp was reminiscent of their first day after arrival. This time, instead of clouds of dust being kicked up by tires, it was sheets of mud.

"I must have grown," East said. "These pants were a bit too big for me when I got here, he said, referring to his battledress pants.

Rothstein was cramped, sitting in the middle of the floor by the cab. "It's the food, Jack. You've eaten five meals to every one of ours."

"Hey, do I look fat?"

Rothstein snickered. "No, you don't. That's the amazing part of it. If any one of us ate like that, we'd all look like Danyluk's fat friends...oh, what's their names...er, Alberta and Eunice."

"HEY, WATCH YOUR MOUTH! THEY AIN'T MY DAMES. I HAD NOTHIN' TO DO WITH 'EM AND I DON'T WANT TO KNOW 'EM."

Wayne gave Moose a quizzed look. "YOU DON'T WANT TO KNOW 'EM? YOU ALMOST RAPED THEM IN THE THEATRE!"

"BULL SHIT I DID! JUST BECAUSE MY FACE WAS ALWAYS DUG IN TO THAT ALBERTA BROAD'S ASS, DOESN'T MEAN WE HAD SOME-THING GOIN.' SHE WAS IN AND OUT OF HER SEAT EVERY MINUTE. I COULDN'T SIT BACK FAR ENOUGH WHEN SHE WENT BY."

Gordie kept shuffling a deck of cards. "IF YOU'RE NOT SNIFFING BICY-CLE SEATS, YA GET YOUR JOLLIES WITH ASSES IN THE MOVIES, EH, MOOSE?"

"UP YOURS, CUNNILINGUS!"

Instead of waiting outside, when they unloaded, all cadets were moved into the centre portion of the hangar while storesmen checked the return of each article.

"BANKS: TWO TOWELS, WHITE, FOR THE USE OF!" a storesman bel-lowed.

His assistant ticked off the clothing card. "Banks: two towels."

"ONE, ONE-INCH WEBBELT, MARK THREE, FOR THE USE OF!"

"Banks: one, one-inch webbelt."

Other warehouseman were doing exactly the same thing throughout the build-ing. When the cadets left, other three-tons arrived and were unloaded at once.

On the way back to the lower camp there was lots of room in the backs of the vehicles. "What's on for today?" asked Simon.

No one answered right away, because the rain had changed all their plans. Jack took an orange out of one of his pockets. "We could go bowling, but don't forget we've gotta be back in camp before supper. Say, are the girls still joining us for lunch?"

Each Musketeer nodded as Gordie took a coin out of Douglas' crotch. "Yeah, and East tells me we're having Shepherds Pie."

"What do we do when we get back to the barracks?" asked Moose. "We cleaned it up this morning. Why the hell are we confined to barracks until after lunch?"

Earl read his notes. "Jesus, I wish you guys would read the bulletin board once in a while. We're gettin' our platoon and company pictures today, along with the special edition of the Vernon News. Say, Moose, wasn't that Johnston I saw you talking with the hangar. What's he want?"

A guilty look appeared along with a smile and a finger across his lips. Moose whispered, "He wants a picture. He says since he took 'em he should have gotten one, free."

Jackson's face mirrored that of Moose. "TOOK 'EM? HE'S IN 'EM!" Then he lowered his voice so only the Musketeers could hear.

"He's the Goddamned star...what's her name, Joan Stone. Gordie, can you keep him busy gambling tonight? If he sees his picture being passed all over camp as Joan Stone, Johnston will do one of four things."

"What are *they*?" asked Gordie.

Earl's guilty look disappeared, but his grin spread from ear to ear. "One, he'll strangle us. Two, he'll have a heart attack. Three, he'll shit himself, or four, he'll immediately apply for a sex change."

"I think it'll be it'll be a combination of three and four," Cunningham offered casually. "Knowing Johnston, after he shits himself, he'll think of the money angle of becoming Joan Stone, the porno star with hairy legs, a shiny ass, and fried egg bazookas. Sure, I'll keep him busy, if he's got dough."

"Johnston's always got dough," said East; his voice low. "He's the cheapest creep in the cadet corps. Next to Gordie, that is."

"UP YOURS, EAST!"

A cold wind accompanied the rain when the cadets unloaded. When they entered B-33, each was handed company and platoon photos. Five minutes later, the paymaster entered the barracks and paid everyone three-dollars-and-fifty-cents. His trusty Provost guard eventually got tired of telling cadets that the pictures cost seventy-five-cents each.

Shortly, members of Alpha Company went around asking others to sign the backs of their photographs. Many other comments were written along with the signatures.

Every time Johnston came over to the Musketeers side of the barracks, he was escorted back with Gordie's arm around his shoulders. On the third time, he said, "WHAT'S WITH YOU, CUNNINGHAM? GIMMEE A CHANCE TO BREATHE, WILL YA? I JUST WANNA SEE THIS DAME, JOAN STONE, EVERYONE'S TALKIN' ABOUT!"

Moose was drinking a pop East had brought him from the cadet canteen. When he heard Johnston's statement, he uncontrollably coughed, and the front of his shirt was covered. He had to think fast.

"Say, here's some negatives they returned with the pics. They didn't print them and we're all trying to figure out what they are."

Johnston held one up to the light. "CHRIST! DID YOU...? HAVE YOU TAKEN A LOOK AT THESE?"

"Not yet, Tommy, but we're..."

Johnston tried to hide his anxiety. "Ahem...er, let me have them, Moose. I think they belong to a friend of mine. I'll put them in for developing."

Moose handed them over and Johnston disappeared back to his side of the barracks, whistling.

At noon, the cadet mess hall was full of cadets and visitors. All of the Musketeers girls were there, as well as Corporal Adams, who was going from table to table, asking cadets if they knew someone with the first name of, Court. When he arrived at Moose's table, he was told that a cadet by the name of Court M. Moose was in Charlie Company and that Charlie used the other mess hall. In a flash, Adams was gone.

After lunch, Diane said, "Maggie and I have got cars. Should we go bowling?"

Since all parents were home, bowling was agreed upon. When they arrived, the place was nearly empty because of the weather.

With *Ebb Tide* playing ten times, and Elvis Presley, Rosemary Clooney, The Crew Cuts, Bill Haley and the Comets, Doris Day, Kay Starr, and Dean Martin entertaining from the jukebox, each couple bowled, danced, and quietly talked. Many times conversation wasn't necessary as the young lovers stared into each others eyes and let the world roll by.

Polson Park would have been the next place to go, but the rain hadn't let up so they went to see Mr. Mah at the Capital Cafe. As usual, he bought all his regulars a soda and *fixed* the jukebox so it would play without money.

Time flew and before long it was four-thirty. The cadets had to be back at VACC by five, but Diane and Maggie took the long way back, around the north end of Kalamalka Beach, winding up on Highway 97 south of camp.

The drive was quiet and Diane never let go of Douglas's left hand. Debbie was sitting on Wayne's knee next to them in the front seat, with Moose and Earl and their girls in the back. The rest were in Maggie's car which wasn't so quiet because they were squished together and East and his girl couldn't eat their burgers. Rothstein got some of East's burger juice on his pants and nearly had a fit. Cunningham kept drilling Maggie on the rules of how to gamble sensibly at Bank Craps. "JESUS, MAGGIE, WILL YOU TRY TO REMEMBER THAT 'OLD MAN PERCENTAGE' SLOWLY BUT SURELY EATS UP YOUR CHANCES OF WINNING. REMEMBER, YOU'VE GOT TO WIN IN THE FASTEST TIME POSSIBLE."

"OH, ALL RIGHT, BUT I WAS CLOSE, WASN'T I?"

Gordie cringed. "BUT YOU'LL BE GAMBLING WITH MY MONEY!"

"IT'LL BE *OUR* MONEY, GORDIE!"

"SINCE WHEN?"

"YA WANNA WALK, KIDDO?"

"Yeah, er, you're right, Maggie. It'll be *our* money."

After soft good-byes, kisses, hugs, tears, and more hugs, the boys marched in the rain up to B-33. The place was a madhouse and the minute they entered, Johnston yelled, "DANYLUK, YOU ROTTEN PONGO!"

Moose's heart pumped so fast he nearly passed out. But it slowed down quickly when Johnston walked over to him. "WHERE'S THAT PICTURE YOU PROMISED ME?"

In a fraction of a second, Johnston had Gordie's arm around his shoulders and he was being edged back to his own side of the barracks. "ALL RIGHT, GORDIE, ALL RIGHT! JESUS, YOU'RE MONEY-HUNGRY. I'M IN FOR TWO BUCKS! YA KNOW, ONE OF THESE TIMES I MIGHT GET TO SPEND TEN SECONDS ON YOUR SIDE OF THE BARRACKS!"

Throughout supper and for an hour after, cadets trudged all over camp saying good-bye to friends they'd made over the past six weeks. Driver Mech cadets who always gave everyone the finger came over and shook hands. Signals cadets who did the same when they were up the poles, dropped by. All were soaked through, but it didn't matter because this was it...their last night together.

Just before it was time to head over to the final movie of the season, the whole of Bravo Company marched into B-33. For eighteen Alpha cadets, this was a real honour because none of the other companies had done the same for their staff cadets. Then again, maybe it wasn't an honour, because the eighteen cadets were stripped to their shorts and tossed in cold showers. Yes, it was an effort of distinction, because they could have been thrown in wearing their battledress.

"Jonathan, old stick, if I get tossed into the shower one more time, I'm going to be so mad, I'll just spit. I SAY! YOU, YOU HORRIBLE LITTLE BEASTS, GET YOUR SQUALID DIMINUTIVE PAWS AWAY FROM MY PERSON."

Both cadets were being carried to the showers, along with sixteen others.

"Commence accretion of the saliva, James, old knob. Say, did I speak with you in regard to Nurse Helen's reverse knot bandages. ER, YOU, YOU APPALLING EXCUSES FOR EVERYTHING NOT WORTH EXISTING, GET YOUR NASTY LITTLE TENTACLES OFF MY BUTTOCKS."

Actually, the 'famous' duo were smiling and putting on the act because the enthusiasm of Bravo had rubbed off on the *changed* individuals.

General George Kitching and all of his officers and NCOs joined the cadets in B-3 that night. Two movies were shown and Red Robinson would have been proud to be there again. John Wayne starred in, *Island In The Sky* and, *The High And The Mighty*; two air force pictures.

Between reels, all of Alpha's officers and NCOs made the rounds talking with cadets and wishing them the best of luck.

Sergeant Beckford came and sat with the Musketeers. "I know I'm not supposed to be saying this, but...well, I'm going to miss you guys. I don't know if it's going to be the same without the group of you being together."

Moose put his arm around the Sergeant's shoulders, then quickly took it off after Beckford's glance. "Look at it this way, Sergeant. I'm now going to move on to other things. If youse needs a free vagsectomys or a free appendixture operation, youse can call on me."

Rothstein came to the rescue. "He means free vasectomy or appendix operations."

Beckford grinned. "Can't I have both?"

"SURE YOUSE CAN! I'LL NEED THE PRACTISE! YOUSE CAN HAVE 'EM AS MANY TIMES AS YOUSE WANTS 'EM!"

There was a hint of loneliness in the Sergeant's eyes when he shook their hands. "The best of luck fellas. God bless!"

After the movies, all hut windows were closed because of the drumming rain and the strong wind. The streets of camp were quiet, but not the shacks. Cadets got rid of any junk collected over the summer and all barracks were full from top to bottom with garbage.

As usual, bunks were placed together with blankets hung around them, making them tunnels. When they were complete, members of various regiments climbed in and discussed the previous six weeks. The Musketeers were no exception. To the sounds of the *Last Post*, they held their final meeting. Oddly enough, it was Wayne who started it off. He could barely see the others because it was dark.

"So this is it, eh? I've got to make certain I get all of your addresses before the train pulls into Vancouver."

Moose scratched his head. "Oh, come off it Wayne, we'll see you at the armouries, won't we?" When Danyluk didn't use pigeon-English, he was serious.

"No, I've made up my mind. The minute I get back, I'm handing in my kit. I wanna see the world."

East was at the end of the tunnel and although he couldn't be seen, everyone heard him take a big bite out of a juicy apple. "Pheybve I'be jchweoin phheu."

They all chuckled when Simon said, "For Christ's sake, Jack, swallow first."

"MAYBE I'LL JOIN YOU!" East reiterated, this time in English.

"I thought you were coming back here?" asked Douglas.

"I might, I don't know yet. If there's a job in the kitchen, I will."

"I think this has been the best year yet," offered Rothstein. "But you cheap creeps forgot my birthday."

"Douglas slapped his friend on the back. "I almost forgot my own, what are ya talking about?"

The blankets moved and Gordie crawled in. "You guys can baby-sit him from now on. The little pongo ended up takin' five bucks off me."

Jackson couldn't believe it. "But Johnston can't play cards."

"We weren't playin' cards. He got sick of the game. We were playin' mah-jo'ng, a Chinese game he said Hop Sing taught him.

Moose's ears went up. "WHO TAUGHT HIM?"

"Hop Sing."

"WHY THAT ROTTEN LITTLE BUGGER. AFTER ALL I'VE DONE FOR HIM, HE DIDN'T EVEN INTRODUCE ME! I'LL BETCHA THOSE PICTURES WERE TAKEN AT HOP SING'S JOINT! THAT'S IT...HE WASN'T ON A BEARSKIN RUG, IT WAS LAUNDRY! WHY THAT...!"

Moose was interrupted. Rain or no rain, in the distance, the pipes and drums started. Another group of Scottish cadets were holding a sporran parade.

"You know, if I've learned anything," said Earl, "I've learned that we're all the same...it doesn't matter what regiment we come from. The guys from the Seaforths, Canadian Scottish, Fort Garry Horse, Queen's Own Rifles, PPCLI, Lord Strathcona's, the Medical Corps, and whatever, are damned good guys."

"HEY, YOU DIDN'T MENTION THE IRISH!" yelled Simon.

He pushed Earl lightly when he heard the reply, "I know...," followed a few seconds later by, "...and the Irish, Artillery, Engineers, BCRs, BCDs, Winnipeg Rifles, Saskatchewan Light Horse, Kong's Own, the Calgary Highlanders, the Loyal Edmonton Regiment, the Westies, the Rocky Mountain Ram..., er Rangers, and the Nineteenth Alberta Dragoons. Have I missed any? Christ, there's so many regiments represented here, I can't remember them all."

"I think you missed some western, *and* eastern regiments," East said, peeling an orange and slipping the skin in Rothstein's pillowcase.

The sounds of shuffling feet and a head popping into the tunnel disturbed the group. MacTavish had a flashlight and shined it in Moose's face. "Moose, us Scots are gonna hold a sporran parade and we've found a sporran for you. Are you with us? You wear your own headdress, boots, and socks."

Danyluk crawled outside the tunnel and dropped his undershorts like a shot. "YOUSE BET I AM!"

"GOOD, WE'RE MEETING IN THE DRYING ROOM."

In seconds, a naked Moose had put on his boots and beret and was standing in the drying room.

Even with their blankets up, the others could hear Moose say, "YOU ASS-HOLES! OH, ALL RIGHT!"

Soon all blankets came down and the cadets of Alpha Company went out on the road to watch the parade.

To the sounds of two pipers, all the Scottish cadets walked proudly down the aisle and out into the rain where they formed into three ranks. When they started marching, a tall, lanky bare-assed British Columbia Regiment (DCO) cadet took up the rear with a broom handle at the slope arms.

With his chest out and his chin and right arm up, Moose Danyluk had finally fulfilled his lifetime dream of becoming a Scot on a sporran parade. He didn't seem to mind the rope around his waist, holding up the head of a black, dirty wet mop, *partially* covering his crotch.

At 0700 hours on Saturday morning, Sergeant Simpson entered the barracks and stomped down the aisle without bellowing a word. Automatically, cadets tossed off their blankets, jumped out of bed, headed for the jon, or still half asleep, searched for their P.T. shorts, T-shirts, running shoes, and socks.

For some reason, Moose was wide awake. He knew there wasn't going to be any running that morning. Quickly pulling his shorts up over his usual morning erection, he placed his makeshift *sporran* over his head and parted it in the middle like a girl's hairdo. With one hand on his hip, he greeted the Sergeant. "SAY, YOU RUCK RIKE SERGEANT SIMPSON, THE RIKEABLE SERGEANT WHO LUNS WITH US EVELY MORNING. HOP SING AND I HAVE NOTICED YOU LIKE LOWLING IN THE RAUNDRY!" Moose used his other hand to keep parting the front of his face.

As everyone killed themselves laughing, a gas pain hit the Sergeant's face.

"DANYLUK, YOU MAKE A BETTER BROAD THAN A STUD! I'M GOING TO ASK HOP SING IF HE WANTS A PERSONAL CONCUBINE!"

Moose took off the *wig*. "What's a concubine?"

Simpson ignored him and marched out of the building. "O.K., YOU PEOPLE, HIT THE SHOWERS! YOU'LL ALSO BE HAPPY TO KNOW, THE RAIN HAS STOPPED!"

"HEY, SERGEANT, WHAT'S A CONCUBINE?"

With Cunningham in the jon, Moose quickly grabbed the French soap and shampoo and rushed into the showers. Soon, he was joined by all the others.

"THE WHIP!" yelled Banks, using a deep voice.

Moose caught on quickly. His timid maiden's voice followed. "OH, NO! NOT THE WHIP! PLEASE, NOT THE WHIP!"

"THE WHIP, I SAY," Banks bellowed again.

Moose pleaded on hands and knees. "PLEASE, SIR...NOT THE WHIP! ANYTHING BUT THE WHIP!"

Banks smiled sneakily. "ANYTHING?"

Moose tried not to smile. "THE WHIP, THE WHIP, I'LL TAKE THE WHIP!"

For the last time, the Vernon 'Shower Room Players' took their final bows amidst howls of laughter and applause.

Squirting shampoo, Moose asked. "What's a concubine, East?"

Jack threw some cherry pits out the window and placed his half-eaten orange on the window sill. If anyone knew the answer it would be Jack, because he partially knew what gout was.

"There are three meanings. One, it's a female porcupine. Two, it's a large dill pickle or cucumber. Three, it's a Greek cigarette."

Moose squirted more shampoo on his head. "A female porcupine? A cucumber? A Greek cigarette? What the hell's Sergeant Simpson talking about?"

East shrugged. "Maybe he's tryin' to tell you that Hop Sing's dames might wanna be pricked, or somethin' like that."

Moose tipped the bottle of shampoo again and rubbed like hell. "Yeah, that's it. He wants me to service Hop Sing's dames. Good old Sarge."

Ten minutes later, amidst laughter, Cunningham's French shampoo bottle was empty and Danyluk was still rubbing to no avail. In the meantime, Gordie smelled like a French stripper.

Moose flung the bottle aside and tried the soap. Still no suds. "CUNNILUNGUS, YOU ROTTEN CREEP, WHAT THE HELL HAVE I BEEN USING?"

Gordie couldn't control himself. Evidently everyone knew but Moose. Cunningham had visited the joke shop and substituted a non-lathering liquid for the French shampoo, and had bought a bar of similar soap. In seconds, Moose was back to using Sergeants' Soap.

When a few people left the showers, a Canadian Scottish cadet rushed in looking for a certain Seaforth cadet. "AH HA! THERE YOU ARE, YOU NO GOOD..."

"What's the problem?" replied a grinning Angus.

"YOU'RE THE ONE WHO PUT THAT CANNED FART UNDER MY MATTRESS. I'VE BEEN UP ALL NIGHT YELLING AT MY BUNKMATE TO GO TAKE A CRAP!"

"Well, canned farts for the Canned Scots," replied Angus.

Once again the shower room erupted. Apparently a few other people had visited the joke shop. Also, the CScotR never noticed that when he wrapped his towel around himself, there was a large cocoa stain at the back; dead centre, where his rear-end was. All the Canadian Scottish had matching stains, for that matter. *Comments* could be heard everywhere throughout the barracks.

"WHAT DID YOU DO, SHIT YOURSELF?"

"HEY, YA GOTTA QUIT WIPIN' YOUR ASS WITH YOUR TOWEL?"

"IF YOUR TOWEL'S LIKE THAT, I'D HATE TO SEE THE INSIDE OF YOUR KILT!"

"YOU'RE A BLOODY DISGRACE TO THE CLANSMEN!"

"HEY, YA PRINCESS MARY'S CREEP, JOIN THE SEAFORTHS AND KEEP YOUR ASS CLEAN!"

"WHAT DID YOU DO, SPIT IN YOUR TOWEL? YA GOTTA GIVE UP THE SMOKES!"

As the Musketeers left the shower room, two groups of Scots were yelling at each other. Although the Seaforths had had the last laugh, there were threats of revenge on the train.

"I'LL HAVE YOUR ASS, YA CUIDICH N' RIGH, CREEP!"

"YOU'D LIKE THAT, WOULD'NCHA, YA PRINCESS MARY'S, SLOB!"

The words were actually tossed in fun. All Scottish cadets bonded together through thick and thin. Sure, there were times when they *got* each other, but that wasn't as bad as when they took on other regiments. Then all non-highlanders really had to watch out.

At breakfast that morning, Gordie stood on a chair and the kitchen staff came out.

"CAN I HAVE YOUR ATTENTION PLEASE. ON BEHALF OF ALPHA COMPANY, I HAVE BEEN ELECTED TO MAKE TWO PRESENTATIONS. SERGEANT BYGDNES, WILL YOU STEP FORWARD, PLEASE!?"

Bygdnes received a plaque thanking everyone in the kitchen for great food and fantastic service. He thanked the cadets.

"NOW, MY LAST PRESENTATION IS FOR THE KITCHEN LADIES. GERT, WILL YOU COME UP HERE, PLEASE!?"

Gert, weighing at least three-hundred pounds and in her early sixties, waddled forward.

Cunningham stepped off the chair and held up a vegetable tin with the label ripped off. "I WANT YOU TO PUT YOUR HAND IN THERE AND PICK THE UNLUCKY, ER, THE LUCKY RAFFLE WINNERS!"

Eagerly, Gert brought out two tickets and handed them to Gordie, as he stepped back on the chair.

"THANK YOU, GERT! THE LUCKY KITCHEN STAFF MEMBERS ARE...WAIT FOR IT...MADGE AND HILDA! STEP FORWARD, MY DEARS!"

Madge came running out, tossing her apron on the counter, straightening her hair, and rubbing her hands together. Hilda bashfully followed.

"LADIES AND GENTLEMEN, LUCKY MADGE HERE HAS WON...WAIT FOR IT...HAS WON...MOOSE DANYLUK FOR FIFTEEN MINUTES! GIVE HER A BIG HAND! AND HILDA HAS WON HARVEY ROTHSTEIN!"

Moose turned white and slid under the table. After he was *dragged* out, a grateful Madge wrapped her arms around him and planted a wet sticky one on his lips. "OOH, HE'S LOVELY!" she yelled.

Rothstein had tried to crawl out the window, but the screens stopped him. Hilda gave him a squeeze and a kiss.

Both boys took off, but didn't realize other women were guarding the doors. The last the cheering mess hall saw of them was when they ran into the kitchen pursued by Madge and Hilda. The ladies had played their part well and the sound of applause was thunderous.

Ten minutes later a grinning Danyluk and Rothstein entered the barracks. How the secret had been kept from them was a miracle. Moose waved his fist at Cunningham. "I'LL GET YOU, GORDIE, YOU PONGO!"

When Moose and Harvey were surrounded, they told their story about how the *girls* had cornered them next to the cooler. The next minute they were each handed a piece of birthday cake. The top of the cake read, 'Happy Birthday, Rothie, we didn't forget. UP THE MUSKETEERS!'

Over the next few minutes, Gordie explained Douglas' plan to everyone. Rothstein's birthday had been forgotten by himself and his friends, so they had to make up for it. As for Moose, well, Gert "kinda liked him."

"DID MADGE KISS YA?" asked East.

Rothstein blushed. "KISS ISN'T THE WORD!"

When Sergeant Bygdnes entered the barracks carrying a very large cake, paper plates, and plastic forks, the queue was instant. East tried to go back for seconds and was stopped seventeen times.

When nine-twenty rolled around, B-33 was spotless. Sure, the garbage cans were overflowing, but the mattresses were rolled, the floor had been swept and certain windows were shut. The same thing was happening throughout the camp as trucks pulled up in front of all the huts. The only occupants left were the yelling prairie cadets saying good-bye to their buddies. These lads were scheduled to leave the next day.

This year, the Seaforths and the Canadian Scottish had volunteered to 'moon' the Provost. As cadets in half-serge piled out with duffel bags on their shoulders and shook hands with all of Alpha's staff, the Corporals handed pennies to the Scots.

Sergeants Beckford and Simpson stood by a certain, loaded three-ton.

"REMEMBER TO DO YOUR JOGGING, DANYLUK!"

"I WILL, SERGEANT! FROM MY BEDROOM TO THE DAMES'

HOUSES!"

Both Sergeants reached up and shook various hands. "All the best, Brice...Banks, all the best fellas!"

"THANKS, SERGEANT BECKFORD! LOOK AFTER THE TRADITIONS, WILL YA?!"

"WE WILL...YOU DO THE SAME!"

Douglas spoke quietly, "Will we see you at Edwin's funeral?"

Beckford solemnly nodded. "We'll be there, son."

As the trucks pulled away, Moose yelled, "TELL HOP SING I'LL VOLUN-TEER AS A PORCUPINE AND TELL HIS DAMES TO STOP USING CUCUM-BERS! ALSO SERGEANT, SMOKIN' GREEK CIGARETTES AIN'T GOOD FOR YA!"

"What the hell was that all about?" asked Beckford, waving.

Simpson put his hand on his friend's shoulder. As he waved, he grinned and replied, "When it comes from Danyluk's lips, who knows?"

The Provost Sergeant, Bill Gabriel, knew better than to be outdoors as the trucks passed and the singing started. When the pennies started hitting his building, the Scots pushed-up their kilts and revealed twenty-or-so bare bottoms from Alpha alone. Other companies did the same.

A gas pain appeared on the Sergeant's lips. "Damn it! I guess if you can't beat them, you've got to join them. Adams, get up there and moon 'em back! Adams! Adams, where are you?"

It was hot at the railway station. Just as scorching as it had been when the boys had arrived. The train was long and steam escaping from underneath each car filled the platform as vehicles dropped off their *cargo* and went back for other loads.

As usual, the departure was informal. The cadets weren't formed up - they had to stay in groups, but the camp Commanding Officer allowed them to say good-bye to their many friends they'd met during the summer. General Kitching and his immediate staff walked around shaking hands.

All the Musketeers' girls joined hundreds of others waiting for their boys. Although they bashfully grinned, this was a melancholy moment. A moment they'd dreaded since the day of arrival.

Diane flew into Douglas' arms and they kissed as they held each other tightly. An eternity passed before he gently lifted her chin and looked into her welling eyes.

"I'll phone you the minute I arrive, all right?"

Diane didn't answer, she just nodded and played with the top button of his shirt.

"Where's your mom and dad?"

"My Mom's at the farm and my Dad had to work. They both send their love," she whispered.

Sensing full tears, Douglas took her hand and they walked over to Wayne and Debbie.

A few feet away Alma was laying down the law. "LISTEN HERE, MOOSE DANYLUK...YOU MAKE CERTAIN YOU WRITE AND I WANT TO SEE YOU BACK UP HERE SOON. HAVE YOU GOT THAT?"

Moose winced and kissed her. Do youse thinks I wouldn't be here? Naturally I'll be here. There ain't no other dames, Alma. I promise you that...Scouts honour."

"THERE'D BETTER NOT BE ANY!" The next second they were in each other's arms.

"Buy a book on mah jo'ng," Gordie said to Maggie who was making notes. "I want ya to brief me on the phone. In the meantime, I promise ya I'll learn all about Piquet. I've gotta pick up a thirty-two card Piquet pack. Boy, will we make money with that."

From one end of the platform to the other, couples and groups huddled together writing down addresses and phone numbers, passing gifts and parcels to each other, and saying good-bye. At ten o'clock, a uniformed train official glanced at his pocket-watch. "ALL ABBOOOARRED! ALL BOOOOARRRED!"

With their duffel bags on their shoulders and still holding hands, the Musketeers and others joined the lines for their various cars.

Diane kissed Douglas again. "I love you."

He grinned. "You'd better. I couldn't live without you. So I'll see you in ten days?"

"You know you will. Will you meet me?"

Douglas still held her hand as he climbed the stairs. "MEET YOU? I'LL BE CAMPING OVERNIGHT AT THE STATION!"

Diane walked the outside of the car searching for him in the windows. Soon a window opened at the end and he grabbed her offered hand. This time his eyes were a little moist. After a few seconds, the train's whistle blew and the train slowly started moving. "HOW MANY TIMES HAVE I TOLD YA I LOVE YA?" he asked.

She let go of his hand. "FIFTEEN-MILLION, THREE-HUNDRED THOU-SAND, FOUR-HUNDRED-AND-TWENTY-ONE!"

He returned her blown kiss. "MAKE THE LAST TWO FIGURES, TWENTY-TWO !"

In the meantime, as Moose was between cars, yelling to Alma. Suddenly a Jeep screeched to a stop and Corporal Adams came running out with a very fat *lady* holding his hand.

"THERE HE IS! THERE'S THAT SON OF A BITCH!" screamed Eunice.

"WHY YOU...! FINALLY I KNOW WHO YOU ARE, YOU ROTTEN BAS-TARD!" bellowed Adams.

As the train picked up speed, all they saw was Moose's giant smile and his right-hand thumb pointing upwards. Danyluk's words, "HEY, YOUR FLY'S UNDONE!" were swallowed up by a release of steam.

EPILOGUE

On the train ride back to Vancouver, once again, Gordie Cunningham cleaned everyone out. Although he'd been in the camp for six weeks using various names, he *somehow* caught up with the cadets he'd continually missed. Using the name, Albert Hodge, he quickly made up for lost time.

Douglas and Wayne camped out overnight at the train station. Debbie joined Diane for a few days before she returned to Vernon. When UBC started, Douglas and Diane hardly ever left each other's side.

Danyluk, Rothstein and Simon also attended UBC. Mrs. Rothstein's health improved, Wayne took a job on the CPR ferries, East attended cooking school, and Gordie joined the regular force (Royal Canadian Signals) for three years, before he got out and started making millions. Earl Jackson attended UVIC.

Every Musketeer visited Red Robinson at Radio CJOR and thanked him again. Red gave them a tour of the station and presented them each with a 'Theme For Teens' mug. To this very day, Doctor Danyluk treasures it.

When Bergie got home, it was a reunion to end all reunions. He, along with WO2 Rose, Sergeant Beckford, Sergeant Simpson, Sergeant Mack, Sergeant Prest, the Musketeers, the Irish Fusilier Cadet Corps, half of Alpha Company, and all their girls from Vernon, attended Edwin Shanks' funeral.

It was learned later that Corporal Adams went A.W.O.L. (Absent Without Leave) Apparently he couldn't shake Eunice, so he joined the French Foreign Legion. A rumour went around that Alberta caught a steamer and went looking for him. She figured since he'd dumped Eunice, he'd want her *little* form.

As for Johnston, he got his surprise at the Drill Hall in September when a cadet finally showed him a picture of Joan Stone.

"Ain't she somethin' else?" the cadet said, drooling. I sure wish I knew what her face looked like. Also, I'll betcha her boobs have grown since this was taken."

Eagerly clutching and staring at the photograph, Johnston's wide smile faded and he turned white. "DANYLUK, YOU ROTTEN CREEP!"

Danyluk couldn't hear him. He had left cadets and was on a tank in Nanaimo, speaking into his microphone, talking to the tank's crew. "Hey, when we gets to the TB hospital, I want everyone to scream, UP THE MUSKE-TEERS!"

As your writer, that's what I'm about to do. But before that, I want to tell you about the real Moose Danyluk.

Moose is a special kind of person. If he had wanted to, he could have beaten everyone on the exams. Also, he had to force himself to talk the way he did. A true friend, Moose never let anyone down, nor, for that matter, did he let anyone get down.

At that age, somehow he knew a glib personality such as he portrayed, was required to keep things within reason. To this very day, he's exactly the same way.

Danyluk graduated with honours and is a fine doctor. He actually ended up marrying Alma. As you know, the two were made for each other.

The year 1956 was serious, hilarious, special, and sad. It was the turning point in a group of boys' lives, and the fact that Moose was around, made Vernon a whole lot easier, and a lot more fun.

"UP THE MUSKETEERS!"

AUTHOR'S NOTE

When Pierre Trudeau was elected Prime Minister of Canada, I personally believe one of his first actions was to slowly smother the Canadian Forces, in particular the cadet programs the defence organization sponsors. Although the opposition screamed like hell, when they became government, the process continued, with of course, the blessing of the Chief of the Defence staff. For that reason, some of these notes are directed at the Chief of the Defence Staff.

You the reader, may, or may not believe me, but Trudeau's despicable personal commitment to eliminate the fighting spirit of the Canadian Forces, as well as the finest youth training program in the world, has continued for over twenty-five years. That's right, twenty-five years and not once during that time has the CDS (Chief of the Defence Staff) lifted a finger to reorganize the chaos our forces are in, nor place the navy, army and air cadet programs back on track.

Who is to blame for this? Why we the voters are, of course. Trudeau was the start of nearly everything that is wrong in Canada. His arrogant autocratic method of not representing the people's wishes started a landslide of *deaf ear* party politics that would make the founders of confederation turn over in their graves.

I haven't got the time to sit down and write a ten-million page publication on how Trudeau and his successors appointed themselves Kings and Queens of Canada with all the false pomp and pageantry of less than benevolent dictators. Like you, I'm sick and tired of it all, particularly deceitful party politics.

History has judged and will continue to judge Trudeau's *spiteful* and ludicrous actions. When full disclosure reveals the *'pill* of consequences' all of us must eventually take because of his performance, the people of Canada will scream like never before...military matters aside.

But at the same time, we're still in a period in our history when we can right some of those wrongs. I'm certain the political will is there, it only lacks focus. The focus being, that the cadet system, army, navy and air force, was and can be again an incredible youth training program. There is nothing in this country in the way of a national youth instruction program of any description. If we are to believe that the object in Canada is to advance or create a future for the young people, then we had better start *training* young people now! If we don't, we'll find them being *trained* by gangs or by racist organizations of one description or another, or *training* for apprentices in crime.

I cannot sit back and allow the uniformed civil servants of the military to service the pretenders of the Trudeau-*trained* princes and princesses who hovel at the feet of their Monarch.

You know who I'm talking about, don't you? I'm talking about the ever-changing Minister of National Defence and the ever-willing Chief of Defence Staff and his hundred or so (nonentity) generals.

What a delightful combination. A cabinet position that changes as often as the *King* or *Queen* changes their shorts, (I'm assuming it's often) and a paid appointment which carries the *ever-inspiring* prerequisite of saying one word, 'yes,' to the princes and princesses whom he or she works for.

Now, naturally the Minister of National Defence is the CDS's boss, therefore the military *appointee's* loyalty must forever be to that ministry. Blind obedience, rightly or wrongly, if it comes down to it. After all, this isn't a business where proper advice could be the difference between the death or success of the company. This *company* can never go down the *tube* because decent people keep throwing in money, and if they don't throw in enough, the Minister of Finance gets on the phone and borrows more. Sound decisions are not necessary. What is essential is to keep saying 'yes,' keep the job, don't rock the boat, one year prior to retirement speak up, pass it on to a successor, and then collect a fat pension. When the new man or woman takes over, he or she really doesn't have to be briefed. All that is obligatory is to remember the word, 'yes.'

Wait a minute, you say. Isn't the Governor General the CDS's boss? I'm not going to get into that, because in Canada, anything can happen. I'm not even going to get into the fact that the Governor General is indeed the people's watchdog and should take definitive action when the government goes against the people's wishes.

How we, the Canadian public, could allow our so-called *politicians* to place this country in the mess it is now, notwithstanding the condition of our defence department, is beyond me. As the massive damage continues to transpire, we sit around eating popcorn while watching television game shows.

Recently I put the question to a retired Colonel living in Vancouver. "Why do we allow this horrific *mess* to continue?"

His answer was typical. "It's not for us to question the decisions of the Chief of Defence Staff, or his boss. They're in charge and as loyal servants, we follow their wishes."

Blind obedience? You bet! Trudeau really did have the time to eliminate the *sound* thoughts of the average Canadian serviceman. He actually did make robots of the Canadian people.

I'm not complaining about the senselessly ill-written Charter of Rights, Trudeau subjected us to. Nor am I angry about the death penalty that 75% of us wanted but didn't get. I'm not even objecting to the General Services Tax that 87% of us didn't want, or NAFTA, or the national federal debt which totals somewhere around seven-hundred billion. I've been doing what every politician does along with Joe Q. Public, **looking the other way.**

But I am upset about the ever-decaying cadet system, and cadet programs that come under the Department of National Defence. As such, Admiral, (CDS) I'm going to be as stubborn as you are. If you continue to look the other way, I'll be there with thousands of others, who at this moment, are shuffling their feet and readying their pens to make certain you do something about it. Stop the game-playing with the cadet organizations, Admiral. Those who came before you during the past twenty-three years at least had a bit of a conscience (not much though) when it came to cadet funding. Don't treat cadets as you would the regular force and militia. The cadet budget is insignificant when compared to your total spending. Insignificant, but it does so much good for our country. That will be the message sent by the Canadian public to their elected representatives. 'As the sapling, so the maple.'

Right now, at this very minute, socially-minded generals (captains of cocktails and canapés) who have forgotten the true meaning of the words, Armed Forces, are saying 'yes' and thinking up new ways to 'fix' the portion of the wheel that remains unbroken from the Trudeau era, if that's possible. As a result, loyal Canadian servicemen and servicewomen are getting shafted daily from improper training, the lack of proper equipment, genuine educational and meaningful career opportunities, and are forced to play the same stupid game the generals play, without the benefit of big fat pensions.

The youth of this country are in the same boat as far as cadet training is concerned. The finest youth training process in the world has been reduced to a mockery. A training program, which if carried out properly could knock billions of dollars off youth-related crime, has nearly been abolished.

Before Trudeau, army cadets were an integral part of a finely tuned armed forces. They were trained by the regular force, the militia and CSofC (Cadet Services of Canada) instructors who in turn were properly trained. In addition, this cadet organization was also efficiently equipped.

These days, navy cadets join their army and air force counterparts in wearing a shabby rifle-green abortion, called a uniform. Why did DND allow the garage-mechanics clothing corporation to design the present cadet uniform? The current army, navy and air cadet uniform, except for the *cloth* is nearly an exact design of the cadet pattern that DND threw out in 1953. That inferior design was replaced with an Eisenhower jacket of quality serge-type material. It was an impressive-looking uniform our cadets wore with pride. Our sea cadets once wore navy-blue uniforms and they looked and were trained like sailors. In addition, our air cadets wore light blue and they were guided by air force reserves, using *real* aircraft.

The military world as far as Trudeau and Hellyer were concerned consisted of one colour...a shade of rifle-green. Our navy wore green, our air force wore green, our army wore green, and all cadets wore (and are still wearing) green.

If he loved the colour so much, why didn't Trudeau wear green roses, green suits, green shirts, green shorts and green ties as well? Perhaps he should have worn a version of the green work-dress uniform that must have been designed by the bus-driver's association.

That's a good point...has anyone ever seen the CDS wear his green work-dress uniform? After all, in today's created social science society, what's good for the peons should be good for the master of the manor as well.

In addition to their appearance of looking like garage mechanics and being treated like kindergarten children, today's cadets have had trades training cancelled, their equipment has been taken away, their summer camps closed, bonuses may be cancelled, and they can't be properly trained because the system of training loyal officers who really do care, is a total farce.

There is no doubt the forces would dearly love to rid their hands of them altogether, but for some reason the game continues to be played. It's comparable to a duck being shot. The wings are still flapping, but the bird's already dead.

How did it happen? Probably like this. Let me set the scene at the Department of National Defence's 'ivory tower' in Ottawa.

"Get Brigadier Looselap up here!"

Looselap enters and salutes. "You wanted to see me, sir?"

"Ah, yes, Looselap. Some member of parliament has received a complaint that army cadets are taught safe firearms training, signals training and are learning to drive military vehicles. Our sea cadets are being trained by the navy and our air force cadets are actually flying a lot. A little dangerous don't you think?"

"Not at all, sir. More time is spent on safety than on anything else. When young people complete these courses they fully realize the meaning of the word, safety. That's the reason they join...it's great hands-on stuff. At times, our army, navy and air force cadets actually augment regular force training exercises. These young people are receiving fantastic training, sir. Why in Wainright not too long ago, I talked with three air cadets who assisted a regular force pilot in a spotter plane. One cadet navigated while the other two dropped flour bags on so-called *enemy* vehicles."

"Looselap, I don't like receiving letters like this. They're not good for my career. Get rid of all that nonsense. Fix it!"

"Fix what, sir?"

"Why these cadet programs of course! Give them something else, like...more sports...tours...lectures on the new Canadian flag...how parliament works, er, the United Nations as a vehicle for world problems, the importance of party politics, how Canada is Mr. Nice Guy to the world. In short, get rid of the practical aspect."

"Sir, we'll lose them if we do that. Besides, we're talking about cadets...army, navy and air force cadets. They're part of the military establishment. At least that's what I was taught when I took over the job. We've got one of the finest youth training programs in the world. Why, we're a model when it comes to..."

"Are you arguing with me, Looselap?"

"No, sir, I'm just trying..."

"Then get it done. Even the Prime Minister and Mr. Hellyer have initialed this letter. Do you know what that means? I know what it means! It means get rid of the military aspect...is that clear?"

"Yes, sir!"

"Good! Looselap, you're learning. I'm going to make certain that regular force and reserve assistance to cadets is cut back - that means money, personnel and equipment. Damn it, I bet the bosses of the Boy Scouts or Boy's Brigade do not receive letters like this."

"Sir, we're talking about cadets, not Boy Scouts, or members of the Boy's Brigade."

"I thought you were learning, Looselap? Now change those Goddamned programs."

"Sir if you eliminate all that, you'll ruin the system. You were in cadets; I've heard that you thoroughly enjoyed it."

"Looselap, kids are different these days. They don't want to be treated with respect. Certainly I enjoyed it...that's why I'm here, however that was a different era. Anyway, why the hell am I discussing this with you? I've got enough on my plate just trying to assist the Chief of Defence Staff implement unification, integration and cocktail parties. If I accomplish that I might just get a promotion or when I retire even a senior civil posting. Damn the torpedoes, Looselap. Quit being so bloody loyal...think of your career, man."

"I would like to think of our traditions, sir. Hundreds of thousands of young people are involved. They love it. It also keeps them off the streets, and leadership is the..."

"WHAT? You're too sentimental Looselap! We're Canadians, we don't have traditions. Let's have the graduates of social science courses guide and instill the needs of youth. Yes, that's it...we'll keep it looking military, but we'll do it with civilian flair. You know, that's not such a bad idea...I might also suggest that to the

CDS as far as the regular force and the militia are concerned. It's just a game, Looselap...try to stay one step ahead of the next fellow. Give the politicians what they want!"

"But, sir..."

"That's all!"

Looselap salutes and leaves. After he's gone, a hand reaches for the telephone. "Get me Major-General Alwaysagree Lippsealled."

A timid voice answers. "General Lippsealled."

"Alwaysagree, I haven't got time to beat around the bush! I want you to post Looselap. Give him a posting where he'll be dealing with civilian authorities. A job with little or no military significance. Post Brigadier Yessmann in his place."

"Yes, sir!"

"Oh, and Alwaysagree, have Yessmann come and see me. Amongst other things, I want the present method of training officers dealing with cadets changed completely. I want the regular force and the militia out of it. Less emphasis on the military...you know what I mean? I don't want cadets driving trucks or tanks, or receiving safe firearms training. I don't want them in the engine rooms and other areas of ships, and I certainly don't want our air cadets flying with the regular air force, or the reserves. We might keep a couple of cadets doing little things, but er, I want it really toned down. Make them think their involved, but, well...you know what I mean, don't you?"

"Yes, sir!"

"We're living in a fantastic age, Alwaysagree. I'm actually going to help Mr. Hellyer get rid of the terms navy, army and air force. From now on, they'll be called, sea, land and air branches. Jesus, I could just piss myself, I like it so much."

"Yes, sir!"

"Alwaysagree, are you and the little lady coming over for dinner and a game of bridge tonight?"

"Yes, sir!"

"Good...I'm going to show you your part in carrying out unification and integration. Hellova man, that Mr. Hellyer! I love his idea about putting navy, army and air force cadets in green uniforms. Particularly navy and air cadets. It'll get rid of at least fifty-percent of them. Alwaysagree, I'll see you at eight!"

"Yes, sir!"

***

Now, in my first novel, '**Stand By Your Beds!**' I touched upon the present method of training officers that have the responsibility of training cadets. These officers are called CIL or Cadet Instructor's List officers and quite possibly this terminology was initiated by Brigadier Yessmann. Yessmann did his job as ordered as far as army cadet training was concerned. He made certain that the then present army officer system, CSofC or Cadet Services of Canada was abolished and replaced by the present *order* - CIL. He also drastically reduced the amount of regular force and reserve assistance to Royal Canadian Army, Royal Canadian Sea, and Royal Canadian Air Cadets.

It took six weeks of full-time tough training to become a Second Lieutenant in the CSofC and months of additional training to attain promotion. The present day excuses such as, "I haven't got the time," were unheard of.

This training was conducted by officers and senior and junior non-commissioned officers of the regular force. If people didn't have the time to obtain their qualifications, they *DID NOT* work with cadets. To be brief, Yessmann got rid of CSofC and replaced it with the present system.

The current method varies from province to province across Canada. Some provinces hold courses that exist only on weekends (usually a day and a half) and candidates receive their commission scroll after about three or four weekends. Other provinces hold five, eight, or ten day courses and none of these courses, to my knowledge are conducted by the regular force. Perhaps they may even throw in a four-day Captain or Lieutenant qualifying course. I've even heard that some courses don't have written exams...just verbal questions, answers, and discussion.

I'm going to point out again that the candidates attending these courses are loyal, obedient and in most cases have the best interest of cadets at heart. They want proper training, however, the present method has existed for over twenty years and *NOT ONCE* during this time, have the 'know-it-all's and be-it-all's' in Ottawa realized that the system does not work. That, is evident by the strength of individual cadet corps across the country. Oh, I'm not saying kids aren't joining...they join by the scores all right, but the retention factor is unbelievably low. Let me rephrase the fact that Ottawa doesn't realize the problem. *Individuals* in Ottawa do understand the issue but couldn't care less, nor will they take the time to correct it.

A recent discussion I had with a member of the Army Cadet League made everything quite plain to me. That organization has knocked on doors, pulled out hair through frustration and written letters by the ton, trying to obtain additional equipment (old or otherwise) *and* regular force assistance, particularly at the cadet camp level. They have tried to change the CIL CTS (Course Training Standards), but they are told that training is not their responsibility so leave it alone. Isn't that just great? And what about the officers who *are* conducting summer camp training? They know the problems, but their hands are tied so tightly, they can't take the tape off their mouths.

Well, I want to make a couple of recommendation to the present Chief of the Defence Staff. I would like you to take six of your generals - navy, army and air force, who at one time served in cadets, and have them rewrite the Navy, Army and Air Force Cadet CTS specs and following that, the Cadet Course Training Standards for local training. Please don't do as you and your predecessors have in the past; allowed *certain* CIL officers to do the job, with the assistance of Director of Cadets, Six, Seven, Eight, Nine, Ten to-a-thousand, etc. Most of these officers came through the CIL system. Lord love 'em, they don't know any better. Let's get these standards back on track.

Then, after that is done, take the same group of generals and have them rewrite the specs for Course Training Standards for Cadet Instructor's List (God, I hate that term) Officers, and a new CTS. As well, there has to be an OR (Other Ranks) structure within the CIL, or whatever you rename it.

I know eight generals, one of which is a Lieutenant General, and another, a Brigadier General, that would put army cadet training in it's rightful place, instantly. Also, there are navy and air force general officers who would dearly love to see proper naval and air cadet training start again.

I reiterate, this task calls for those who have been through the system in the past; prior to Trudeau and Hellyer. They must start from scratch and not have their hands tied. And of course, please do not inform them that they *must* work within the parameters of present day Course Training Standards, QR&Os Cadets, it's sub-manuals, and cadet related CFAOs. The cadet references, unfortunately were written by officers who weren't qualified and who also had their hands tied behind their backs.

Whoever wrote the specifications for the present day Cadet CTSs probably were never let out of their houses as children. Nurtured to the brink, when they had children of their own, they must have become monks. No, that's not possible because they would believe even chanting is dangerous. It can cause a sore throat.

After that, Chief of Defence Staff, please have the generals rewrite the specs on cadet summer camp training, and then produce a proper CTS for cadet summer camps. You know, include things such as elemental trades training with equipment and proper uniforms, and trained regular force instructors.

Now, if you can't spare these officers, I happen to know a retired Colonel who lives in Victoria. Although I have no idea whether the Colonel would even consider the request, he would most definitely get the job done. What have you got to lose? Just pick up the phone and ask.

Now, after making that statement, I know the Director of Cadets is going to be upset. After all, he should have been fighting for this all along. Oh, yes, *fighting*. So will a good portion of his paid squad of untrained CIL appointees. (I would point out that I'm not implying all CIL officers are untrained. Many are better trained than their regular force and militia *whipping* masters.) Even the Colonel I'm recommending might be upset. Perhaps he's enjoying his recent retirement. Also, since the Colonel is a professional soldier I feel certain he doesn't bear the contempt I have for those in the Ivory Tower. Though, perhaps he should.

My apologies Colonel. I know I have no right to endorse you, but if you took it on, millions of Canadians would breathe easier.

Now, Chief of Defence Staff, the specifications for having a regular force/reserve army, navy and air force also have to be rewritten. And, where are you going to get the money? Why your present budget of course. Any businessman could take the money you already receive and put the Canadian Forces, including the cadet system rightfully back where they belong. All he or she has to do is cut back on the general staff and their support down the line. **Mister Chief of Defence Staff, you've got too many Chiefs and not enough Indians.** If you rewrite the specs for having armed forces, **at this time in world history**, to your surprise, you will find that the whole general and senior officer staffing system is geared for a major world conflict such as the Second World War, if not more so. One must be prepared! **However,** we have three times as many as necessary to achieve that status. We've got enough general officers to run the United States Army, never mind ours. Get rid of the deadweight, Admiral. Rid yourself of at least eighty generals, hundreds of Colonels, hundreds of Lieutenant Colonels and their supporting staff, and you'll be able to hire more Indians and give them proper equipment.

Look at the benefits. You, along with the present-day Minister of Defence would be called into the Prime Minister's office along with the Minister of Employment and have accolades heaped upon you. The Prime Minister might even throw another beloved cocktail party when she or he announces that 100,000 Canadians have been taken off unemployment insurance and effectively enrolled in the armed forces without increasing the defence budget. The new soldiers, sailors and airmen/airwomen, etc., would be delighted at the opportunity because now they would have effective leadership, adequate equipment and training. Finally, our navy, army and air force would gain the added, long missed respect in the eyes of other nations of the world.

Oh, many other matters have to be taken care of as well. Postings have to be extended to five years, instead of every three years. Administration has to be streamlined, thereby reducing the number of civilian and military clerks by sixty-five percent. We must stop modifying equipment to meet Canadian standards. Let's face it, Admiral, by continually changing modern equipment that is readily available worldwide, it just places a great portion of your funds in some of our politicians' *friends* pockets. John Diefenbaker and his successors got rid of most Canadian military industries, why do you still try to design so-called Canadian equipment. The helicopters are a perfect example. Other copies exist that would do the job at a quarter of the cost.

Yes, an impartial businessman could save you more money than you'd know what to do with. At the same time, your forces would be up to strength, properly trained and equipped, and Canada could once again regain its rightful role in North American and world defence affairs.

If it's done, you'll thank me. But I'm not holding my breath.

It takes guts and integrity to reverse this present day abortion, but so far during all these years, I've yet to see anyone step forward, roll up his or her sleeves and get the job done. It's going to be damned hard to eliminate the *Yessmann* tumor because it's been allowed to grow and kill cadet training without the slightest scratch of a scalpel. And don't forget, the Yessmann *tumor* is smothering regular force and militia training as well.

The armed forces of Canada have been undermanned and under-equipped for as long as I can remember. In addition, the emphasis on proper man-management and leadership training in Canada's armed forces has been curtailed drastically.

Right now, the CDS has thrown this book on his desk. "WHO THE HELL DOES THIS CROSS THINK HE IS?" Also, there are those amongst you at the *ivory tower* smiling and hiding your eyes behind those rose-coloured glasses, saying, "Cross, quit patting yourself on the back. The admiral wouldn't read such rubbish."

Well, at least I have *your* attention, and as far as the admiral is concerned, he *knows* I'm right. I'm certainly not one of the thousands of 'yes men' who surround him. The man needs *proper* advice. I'm not saying I'm a hundred-percent correct, however take off your glasses, smell the roses, see and feel the real world, and give the guy the hand he needs. The man has a problem, because he came through the Trudeau *system*. Let him see the proper *light*.

Over the years the various CDSs have been approached by a few well-meaning individuals complaining about the route army cadet training is taking, but the facts offered fall upon deaf ears. The reason? Well, try this on for size. Army cadet training is not important anymore. It's certainly not as important as mess dinners, cocktail parties, and tours with the minister. The CDS has enough on his plate wondering what his 100 some-odd generals and their supporting personnel are getting up to.

So you see, the CDS just hasn't got the time. Don't bother approaching one of his generals either. They're too busy (going around in circles with an endless array of paperwork) worrying about how they can get their next promotion.

Sometimes I say to myself, "Why me?" Why don't I just get on with writing novels about a once-great youth scheme in the *real* days? Well, I can't do that anymore. Like everyone else, I sat around for the same twenty some-odd years waiting for someone else to straighten out the ailing system we call 'creeping military bureaucracy.'

Yes, I am mad as hell and I'm not going to take it anymore. Do I expect the system to change someday? It has to, but only when a great leader comes along. By the way, where have all the leaders gone? Another question is, where is the silent majority? For the love of God, when are they going to speak out?

***

Let's change the subject for a moment. Now the politicians are deciding whether homosexuals should be allowed in the armed forces.

"Oh, now you're opening up a can of worms," my editor told me.

I am? What can of worms am I opening up? I stated in the Introduction of **'Stand By Your Beds!'** that I'm not against homosexuals...or I should say that I'm not against all homosexuals. Homosexuals are not all the same. They are human beings just like everyone else, which means they have their 'bad apples' as well.

While certain small groups of homosexuals are screaming to get into the armed forces openly, other people are screaming that they shouldn't be allowed in.

Let's look at the word 'homosexual.' The Concise Oxford dictionary describes it as follows: '(person) who is sexually attracted by persons of his or her own sex.'

Now, have you got that? It **does not** state, '(person) who *may be* sexually attracted by persons of his or her own sex.' It's cut and dried. **A homosexual *IS* sexually attracted to persons of his or her own sex.**

There are those who say, "God forbid! If our *politicians* allow the shower-rooms, personal living quarters, clubs and offices of the armed forces to be used as the meeting places for *individuals* of the same sex who are sexually attracted to one another, ladies and gentlemen, we will have the biggest nightmare in history. Armies of military lawyers, homosexual or otherwise will have to be hired to hide the facts from the public."

Homosexuals argue that isn't the case at all. That they have always been in the system and there haven't been too many problems. The fact that they should be allowed to come out of the closet is a human rights thing.

Proponents ask, "Why will the Department of National Defence have to hide the facts to give these people a break? After all, it's a perfectly normal lifestyle, isn't it?"

Adversaries answer, "No it isn't a normal lifestyle and although everyone will know what's happening, the truth will never be allowed to leak out. After all, what would people think if 'Jonesey' wrote home and informed his father that he enjoyed the homosexuality of the armed forces so much, he was looking forward to, and giving serious consideration to, becoming a willing partner in anal sex."

Yes, the discussion on whether or not to allow homosexuals in the forces goes on hot and heavy. The pressure is on the politicians and they in turn are putting the 'arm' on the *professionals* who are supposed to be running the armed forces.

Now you and I know that probably thousands of homosexuals have served this country on the battlefield with honor. They are still serving today and are presumably damned fine soldiers, sailors and airmen. But their sexual orientation is kept to themselves. It has never been legal in the forces for them to state their minds when it came down to discussing or choosing a sex partner of the same sex.

I certainly have my opinion whether or not homosexuals should be allowed to openly join the forces, but my beliefs do not count. In addition, I would suggest that the majority of Canadians have their opinions and they don't seem to count either.

At this moment in Ottawa, scores of general officers are running around in circles wondering what to do about this dilemma. At least I think they are. They may be attending cocktail parties, I don't really know. But if they are concerned, I suggest they pull the tons and tons of files they have at their disposal. Files that relate to *problems* of the past. These files should then be delivered to the Prime Minister's office as well as the ever-changing Minister of National Defence's office.

Today I asked a friend of mine whom I believe to be homosexual and who is thinking of joining the forces, if he agrees it should be open. I taped our conversation and it went as follows.

"When are you joining?" I asked.

"Next week."

"Let me ask you a question. Do you believe homosexuals should be allowed into the Canadian Armed Forces?"

"Definitely. I think you know I'm gay; I can do any job heterosexuals can do."

"Are you going to tell them that you're gay?"

"No."

"Why not?"

"Because I'm not one of those."

"One of what?"

"I'm not one of those who stand up on soap boxes. I keep my private life to myself. I don't go into gay clubs and I can't stand the bleeding hearts who try to convince society that the gay way of life is just as normal as...apple pie."

"You mean you don't think it is?"

"I don't know if it is, or not, but I'm not going to get into that. Listen, I'm proud of the armed forces of this country, that's why I want to join. But rules are rules. It's no different than a traffic signal...if the light is red, you stop. If homosexuality is openly approved in the forces, there'll be no red lights, just amber ones, and in time, even the amber will turn to green only. Do you know what happens when you've got two green lights at an intersection?"

"You sound like you've fought your conscience on this one?"

"A little. Maybe I'm the oddball. No, I don't think I am. I believe the present recruiting method is fine. It allows me in. If it's changed, then you've got a Corporal and a Sergeant both wearing uniforms and holding hands. Great image of an armed force, eh?"

"Do you believe that would happen?"

"Do I believe that would happen? Sure I do. That would just be the start of a complete change in the representation of the forces. Certain people want it their way, or no way. They don't believe in rules...they make the rules and everybody *bends* to let them have their way."

"Was that a little play on words?"

(laughter) "No."

"So you believe image, or representation is important?"

"Don't you? The world revolves around image. Open homosexuality in the armed forces would change the image overnight. I could tell you about the problems, but I'm not going to."

"Were you in cadets?"

"Yes, in Alberta, but I didn't attend Vernon. Look, I don't even like discussing this. The people who are demanding open homosexuality in the forces are the minority. They would like you to believe they are the majority, but that just isn't the case at all. The present system is fine. If, for some reason it changes, look out."

"Can I ask you one more question?"

"One more."

"If you get into the forces under the present method and shortly all gays are allowed to come out of the closet in the forces, would it change your bearing and attitude in regards to certain actions?"

"No. As I've already told you, only the minority are making waves. They're the ones who don't believe rules should exist. Believe it or not, the majority of us would be proud to serve our country and protect the present image. Homosexuals are just as human as everyone else. We're not all the same, you know?"

After the interview, we talked for ten more minutes before he headed for the recruiting centre. It wouldn't be fair for me to print his comments on what would happen if the forces present policy is changed.

I keep asking myself what would happen if the current system is changed. Oh sure, there would be homosexuals who don't screw around at this moment in time. *At this moment in time.* But what if they were in a position of seniority of rank, and homosexuality in the forces was legalized? Is it entirely possible that perhaps circumstances would be a little different then? Maybe a lot different?

I have a question to ask. Why this sudden decision to come out of the closet in the military? If these people are already serving, fine, let them keep on serving and they can live their way of life outside of the system. But I'm bothered by the fact that they want to *come out of the closet.* What could be the ulterior motive for this? Is it possible they want to institutionalize their way of life? Institutionalize their method of sexual relationship within Canada's fighting forces? My God, even the more intelligent homosexuals would inform you of the horrific results if that happens.

Right at this minute, certain homosexuals or ultra-liberal thinking people are screaming that I'm making **homophobic** statements. This seems to be the popular word lately. Homophobic? Anyone who questions the homosexual way of life is homophobic? Poppycock! I'm not homophobic. I'm just trying to be reasonable to both sides. I'm not questioning the gay way of life, because I have no right to do that. I can, however question it when it is openly forced on non-homosexuals.

I can only say that the people who are screaming about me being unreasonably prejudicial, are on the wrong footing. They don't have a leg to stand on, because the history of homosexuality in institutes has led continuously and inexorably to events which happened in a certain institution in Newfoundland and nearly every other province. Just read the newspapers when you want to become aware of homosexual institutionalization.

Now Admiral, I know, and you know that the rights of the individual (homosexual or heterosexual) must be protected. In guarding those rights, however, the people making decisions must make *logical* decisions based on a *balanced* assessment of the question, without *prejudice.* But if *certain people* will not accept sensible and competent neutral opinion leading to a decision without labeling it as prejudice or homophobic, how is this process possible? These people nullify any reasonable consideration of the question. As a result, anything ridiculous can be put forth for deliberation and approval is guaranteed, regardless of the circumstances which must follow.

A lot of people are saying, "Many of them would just do their job and keep their desires to themselves."

Others respond, "That may be right, but consider the question, how? If a human being is attracted to an other human being, he or she would naturally make the move to get close to that person. Do we need that problem?"

Canada is slowly but surely losing its traditional base, without any approval whatsoever from its citizenry. Manipulation of the process of guaranteeing proper, democratic formulas for conducting day to day life in Canada has been secretly taking place for years. It's almost at the point where our elected officials can do whatever they want. "Ya can't rock the Charter of Rights boat. Damn the people, they just don't know any better. Let them eat cake and they won't bother us."

I don't remember the Canadian people approving the Charter of Rights. Sure, I remember Liberal Party politicians drafting, approving, and ramming it down our throats. But I also remember the people of this country saying, "We don't want the Goddamned thing in its present form. The only reason it's being drafted is to take our minds of the massive deficit." Another Trudeau smokescreen.

It's not up to me to umpire the gay *minority's* demands, but let's see what the politicians do with the approval of their *military chiefs*. Ladies and gentlemen (heterosexual or homosexual) of the silent majority, it's all a part of the big picture. I'm not the one judging this, the CDS is. At least I think he is. I'm watching this decision very closely though. Finally someone has got to shit or get off the pot. If the CDS bows to political or judicial pressure on this one, then his decision will determine the fate of little 'Jonesey.' **That**, is certain!

Basically, between you and me, the decision has probably already been made. If it hasn't, it will be made by the courts, and 'yessed' by the *politicians* and CDS.

For Christ's sake, it's the people of this country that are supposed to be allowed to make the laws. They elect representatives to administer that will. Their representative does not have the right to misrepresent the wishes of his or her constituents, regardless of their personal opinion. And when it comes to matters of the military, the military brass are paid for making proper assessments of the situation and speaking up. Since Trudeau and Hellyer, the military brass in this country have been doing everything but that.

***

Some of you that read my first book, **'Stand By Your Beds!'** will say, "Oh for Christ's sake, he's rambling on again?" Er, yes I am, but not for long. I promise not to make a two-hour speech as a British General did recently. He was complaining about British politicians having absolutely no understanding of the importance of the regimental family when it is applied as the main integral part of a loyal and disciplined army.

At the end of his speech, he said to his rather large audience, "You all know I'll be retiring soon and I don't suppose I'll be giving any more sermons like this. You see, I want *you* to do that. I want *you* to carry the torch and I want *you* to want those following you to carry it as well. Right now I'm just urinating into the wind...a strong wind coming from every direction that has crept upon us so gently that we never bothered to build a barrier. You will notice I said *us*. Perhaps I'm a little late saying this but I want *you* and your successors to build that barrier. Only then will Britain's beloved armed forces be protected. Please rise and join me in a toast."

"Its traditions!"

"ITS TRADITIONS!" the group reiterated.

"Its honor!"

"ITS HONOR!"

"Its glory!"

"ITS GLORY!"

"THE REGIMENT!"

"THE REGIMENT!"

The general remained standing as everyone sat, then he raised his glass again. "MAY GOD BLESS THOSE WHO PRESERVED OUR FAMILY AND THOSE WHO WILL CONTINUE TO DO SO!"

As I write this, Canadian soldiers are changing their regimental capbadges like kids exchange sports cards. Mr. Trudeau and Mr. Hellyer decided that since hard faced politicians can cross the *floor* feeling quite proud that their salaries and pensions will be well protected, soldiers should be no different. After all, why should soldiers honor the traditions of the regimental family when politicians for their own sake don't have to worry about such trivial matters...particularly the traditions of the country.

The British General was only complaining about the fact that some British regiments were being combined to form one regiment. Often, the new regiment kept the names of the two combined regiments. In Canada, our *knowledgeable* leaders, with the assistance of the *military hierarchy* just rebadge members of regiments at will, or totally eliminate regiments altogether. In doing so, what they're are saying is that traditions are a waste of time in the first place.

Can you believe that? After all, the dead can't complain about the pain and suffering of the men and women who earned their regiment its battle honours, can they?

Also, in eliminating the regimental family, isn't that like saying the Smith family can move into the Jones' house and vice-versa, however, each member of the Smith family must celebrate the birthdays, anniversaries, etc., of the Jones' family and the Jones family should do likewise? Yet that's what this country does with its armed forces.

Maybe it was wise for our leaders to eliminate our regular force Scottish regiments. Can you imagine what would happen these days if a member of the Royal Canadian Regiment was rebadged and had to wear a kilt and had a bowl of oatmeal and meat placed in front of him at the regimental dinner before being asked to stand up and toast the traditions of *his regiment?* His first concern would be to wonder why his crotch was cold, then after he realized he had no shorts on, he might have a little difficulty pronouncing the names of some Scottish battles of old.

Never mind that his nose couldn't handle the smell of haggis...minced heart, lungs, and liver of a sheep, boiled in maw with suet and oatmeal He would be totally lost. All in the name of what I like to call injected ignorant political interference by our elected leaders, made military policy by our *politically minded bureaucratic generals.*

Oh, I could go on, but what's the use. That's exactly what's happening. It's been happening with every regiment in Canada. Certain past and present political masters must really hate the British and French systems of tradition within the regimental family. Also, they must have had something against Scottish and Irish regiments to get rid of them as they did. What a shame.

The current press states that racial hate policies exist in the Canadian Forces. I don't agree, however, the Chinese, blacks and other immigrants who got integrated and adapted into the Scottish, Irish and French related regiments became the genesis of our multi-cultural country. The divisiveness of the racist policies instituted by Trudeau that largely didn't exist beforehand, has ghettoized people in this country.

From what happened, politicians knew nothing at all about the importance of the binding strength each member of a regiment unleashes when the family is threatened. That's how battles are won. For that matter, now that I look back, neither did, nor does the military hierarchy whom I like to call uniformed civil servants. Every general officer past and present (except for some admirals and a few *other professionals*) from Trudeau's time onward should have tattoos on their foreheads, saying, "UNIFICATION AND INTEGRATION AND PROUD OF IT!"

As a point of information, you the reader and I know that the majority of general officers were against unification and integration, but didn't have the guts to speak up...they still don't. On the back of their necks, other tattoos should read, "REGIMENTAL FAMILY? DON'T MAKE ME LAUGH!"

Have I made my position clear yet? No? Well, sit back in your chair and imagine you and everyone in your family changing your surnames every three years. Wow, can you think of the family cohesiveness you would have? Never mind the surnames, change the given names as well...and the birthdays...and the anniversaries...and deaths.

***

Amongst other matters, these notes illustrate my total disapproval of today's *strategy* of guiding teenagers. Once more, procedures put in place long ago by Trudeau and Hellyer, must be corrected.

I hope those who read my first novel, **'Stand By Your Beds!'** fully understood the message I attempted to convey. That by some miracle, politicians in the 50s and 60s were sidelined by *other matters*, and as a result, logic was allowed to take its rightful place in the training of youth associated with Canada's military.

Did this happen by accident? Probably, but we also must consider that at that time, the universities in this country weren't spewing out thousands upon thousands of *graduates* in the social *sciences,* as they have done for the past two decades.

With not as many *qualified* people around to *correct* attitudes that didn't need correcting in the first place, teenagers associated or not associated with the military were allowed to be trained with common sense techniques. Without fanfare and unreal and untested theoretical mumbo-jumbo, teenagers were encouraged to touch and feel the rationale of the real world. They weren't treated as two-year-olds, they were trained how to realistically look after themselves in life and how to fairly treat their fellow man.

I would like to think that the military process of accomplishing this was slightly superior to other methods practised then, and I believe the action of teaching the rudiments of proper behavior, having a proper attitude and developing character was *renowned* in comparison to today's constant bombardment of abstract psychological nonsense.

Young cadets were taught *appropriate* quality-building techniques that fitted their personality and only when they were ready did they get the opportunity of the hands-on training which allowed them to teach leadership to their peers as an example of, "If I can do it, so can you!"

This made them more prepared to handle responsibility and before long made them and their equals better citizens.

All that has changed today and many, including our *politicians* and *military hierarchy* would say it's for the better. I don't believe so.

Sure, nowadays when I talk with teenagers, I find it difficult to see much of a difference from those of yesteryear. However, I don't have much of an opportunity to talk with many. I do however, well understand the problems our society is having with a good portion of them. In most cases they come from good families where the mother and father have decided to allow the *learned* sexual intellectual social workers to help the school teachers in raising them. Let's face it, if the strap and the paddle did return, or if a bit of military-style discipline was used to smarten up teenage trouble-makers, it's a sure bet that we wouldn't need so many social workers and counsellors.

My comments aren't aimed at every teenager, just those who haven't had the opportunity to understand what is expected of them and what they can personally achieve if they aim for the top by trying a little harder.

I actually do believe in the principles of fair, friendly, and firm discipline. I believe that youngsters must be taught to understand what is expected of them. Now, if this means the return of fair discipline and that each juvenile must have compulsory sports or cadet training, then so be it. But not the coddling methods used by the hordes of ultra-liberal thinking social-science graduates whom we have allowed to re-write the book...God no.

These people actually believe that for some untold reason, they practise an exact art when offering their advice in the molding of youngsters. They have convinced themselves, now they insist on persuading *politicians*, the *military hierarchy* and a good percentage of the public, that the professors are right and that theory alone, if preached and followed enough will eventually overcome common sense.

I don't know about you, but I cringe when I have to meet or talk with these *people*. I can't get away fast enough. You see, I talk with them, but they don't talk with me, they talk at me, and for that matter, at you. The verbal gibberish leaving their mouths is so positive, it's as if they attended and were overwhelmed at the secret meetings held by Trudeau and Hellyer. Yet *we* allow these *graduates* to write the book on the *proper* way to bring up children and how to deal with them. The ones I have met have been divorced two or three times and they haven't got a clue how to run their personal lives never mind your children's lives. Also, the streets are full of their *own* children who couldn't take it anymore. Even these kids for the sake of wanting a hot cup of soup, or a place to stay, must have their minds invaded again by daily visits from clones from the Ministry of Social Services. You know the ministry I'm talking about...it's the ministry that never stops hiring. Let's face it, it can't stop hiring; what would all the social science graduates do?

So we now know that our country has civilian and military problems and we understand what makes up a good portion of those enigmas. It's caused by too many Joseph Goebbel graduates, screaming their lungs out and living off the public purse. These *graduates* continue their gobedlygook rhetoric, swaying *politicians*, the *military hierarchy*, and the public that their way of treating youth is correct and as a result, so many kids get mixed up that we have to keep on hiring. Hiring, not to solve the problem...that can never be done because somewhere along the way, logic was thrown to the wind. We hire them for the sake of hiring them. What a bloody mess we've gotten ourselves into. It now takes about four years or more to learn how to talk to, and guide today's youth. That is utter rubbish. In my opinion, most of what is taught is pure theory with no evidence of rationalism behind it at all. The crap these *people* are being taught at the universities and community colleges is unbelievable.

Oh, I'm certain *that* statement will touch a nerve (if it's possible) in *those* who have nothing but nerve, however if these *people* had been given the chance to learn the real leadership and man-management facts, as cadets did in the old days, then even their most ardent believers in conceptual-brainwashing *eventually* would come to realize that there are superior realistic alternative methods to be used when training youth.

Yes, I'm talking about proper cadet training. However, without trying to sound like a broken record, shortly after the forces integrated and unified (ugh, I even hate typing those words) Royal Canadian Army Cadet Training changed as well...unfortunately for the worse. And since no one stood up for any other damage the forces allowed themselves to be talked into, army cadet training has been on the downslide ever since. This almost appears like a nationally planned effort to stop teaching kids about the real world and it well may be. However, with the dedication of Douglas Verdun's CADETS organization, as well as The Army Cadet League of Canada, and its provincial affiliates, I believe eventually that someone will apply enough pressure to straighten the mess up and again allow the youth of this great country (great, not because of politicians, or uniformed military civil servants) to learn the teachings of the past.

Proper army cadet training can permeate character, instill the meaning of dignity and teach young Canadians the responsibility they must exhibit daily if they are going to achieve their rightful place and be proudly accountable in helping to regain and preserve the true purpose of what it means to be Canadian in the original context of confederation.

If Canada is going to remain in the peace-keeping role that Lester Pearson started, then the people involved have got to be properly trained, right back to the fundamentals. That also includes the cadets of this country. The present Chief of the Defence Staff has a wonderful opportunity to rid the military of atrocious past errors in judgment. It's housecleaning time.

If the political and financial mess this country is in, is an example to our *military leaders* of the knowledge and expertise of our *political masters*, then certain facts that came out at the Nuremberg Trials are true. That blind obedience is a fact of life. Thus being the case, Canada, God help it, it's going to need all the help it can get.

***

Before I close, I want to mention that I received a scathing letter from a female admirer of Pierre Trudeau.

Reading her letter reminded me of the ignorance of some school teachers I was once introduced to.

In 1983, a friend of mine decided to obtain his teaching degree. During the latter stages of his education, he taught at a high school in the upper-crust area of Vancouver. His subjects were math and economics and he asked me if I would like to be a guest speaker to his grade eleven and twelve classes. I agreed and brought along a friend of mine who was a Chartered Accountant.

During my discussion with a grade twelve class, I asked if any of them knew what the national debt was. All hands went up and as I got them answering, the average response was approximately thirty billion dollars.

When I informed the class they were all wrong, that the national debt was well over two-hundred billion, (at that time) the actual teacher who was assessing my friend, stood up with a very concerned look on his face.

"Mr. Cross, it was good of you to come here, but er, please try to be correct in your statements. My students know, it's approximately thirty-billion."

The teacher had a picture of Pierre Trudeau on the wall above his desk.

"I am correct," I replied. "I believe you're getting mixed up with the annual deficit. The national debt is an accumulation of those deficits."

Out of a class of thirty students, two students agreed.

During lunch, the teacher asked me to join him for a coffee in the teachers lunchroom, where we proceeded to *discuss* the matter once again.

To make a long story, short. Of the eighteen teachers in the lunchroom, only four of them knew the difference between the annual deficit and the national debt. My friends *assessing* teacher, didn't have a clue that Trudeau had taken the national debt well over two hundred billion. Today, I believe the federal debt is close to, or just over seven hundred billion dollars. I'm not going to bother talking about provincial debt. Someday, when our *beloved* politicians grab 50% out of every Canadian's bank account to straighten out the mess Trudeau started, we'll discuss it then. In the meantime, let's keep watching game shows and eating popcorn.

Who the hell is teaching in our universities these days. I thought the sexual intellectuals (effing know-it-alls) were limited mainly to *politicians* and *military-uniformed civil servants*.

***

As I mentioned earlier, I haven't the time to write a gigantic book about the problems which exist in Canada. At this particular time in my life, my main concern is the way young people in cadets are being ignored.

Politicians and military civil servants seem to be furthering their careers at the expense of youth in this country. The military bureaucrats seem dedicated to absorbing as much of the defence budget as possible, without considering the needs of the end result in proper equipment and training for other than themselves.

We have a new Prime Minister in Canada who now has the opportunity to initiate proper cadet training that will have a direct and positive bearing on the reduction of the escalating youth-crime problem. I hope the Prime Minister has the guts for such a tide-turning initiative.

Considering what I have said throughout, is it possible the reason we do not have capital punishment, because certain politicians and civil servants might themselves be strung up for capital crimes against Canada; such as treason, etc.?

As for homosexuality in the armed forces, all one needs to do is review the past and current headlines of events, cover-ups and the like in *other* Canadian institutions.

***

At this time, there is talk of cadet-camp closures, and the elimination of the cadet summer-camp bonus. Let me say this. Prime Minister, Defence Minister, and Chief of Defence Staff, (whoever you are) if such things happen, there will be a human cry in this country of such magnitude, the ground under your feet will rumble and crack wide open. Whether or not you're at a cocktail party, won't matter. You will drop and your final resting place will not be as hot as those who send you there.

There is a pervasive moral problem in Canada, in that it would appear some politicians and civil servants (including the judiciary, the military, etc.) are prepared to go to any lengths to **be seen** to be administering their portfolios, to the point that some of them are prepared to falsify or withhold information and or evidence of incongruous decisions that would make the average citizen scream (bloody blue murder). The result of such cunning is an eloquent display that covers up their own incompetence and culpability.

As Danyluk would say, "Kinda makes ya wonder, don't it?"

Oh well, some day the tide will turn.

My case rests...for now. Cordell Cross - 7 July 1993.

CHRONOLOGICAL HISTORY OF THE VERNON ARMY CADET CAMP FROM 1898 TO 1987
THIS INFORMATION WAS PROVIDED BY THE VERNON ARMY CADET CAMP

1898   When the population of Vernon was 800 citizens, the Vernon Mounted Rifles was authorized, but never formed.

1908   'C' Squadron, the Canadian Mounted Rifles was authorized. Enrollees totalled 88, and they also formed a band.

1909   A twelve-day Summer Camp was held at Kinsmen Beach. Sixty men participated, with their mounts.

1910   A twelve-day Summer Camp was held at the, then, local Exhibition Grounds. This site proved more suitable for the stabling of horses.

1911   The Canadian Mounted Rifles was increased to Regimental size. With its Headquarters and a squadron in Vernon, other squadrons were *housed* in Lumby, Armstrong and Kelowna.

1911   The Canadian Mounted Rifles, along with Vancouver's 18th Field Ambulance, the 104th New Westminster Regiment, and Armstrong's Independent Infantry Company - participated in a twelve-day District Camp at the Kamloops Exhibition Grounds. This site proved unsuitable for the exercise.

1912   In Vernon, The Canadian Mounted Rifles was redesignated the 30th Regiment, BC Horse. Kamloops was *home* to the 31st Regiment, BC Horse.

1912   For the first time, the District's Summer Camp was held on Mission Hill.

1912   Construction of the Vernon Armory was authorized.

1912   On 01 September, 1912 - Number 368, The 30th British Columbia Horse Cadets was formed. It consisted of 40 cadets (boys) from fourteen to eighteen years of age.

1913   The Vernon Armoury was constructed.

1914   The District Summer Camp held on Mission Hill, consisted of: 30th BC Horse, 31st BC Horse, Seaforth Highlanders of Canada, Rocky Mountain Rangers, The Duke of Connaught's Own Rifles, and a few companies of the Corps of Guides.

1914   The 30th BC Horse, provided a Headquarters and two squadrons to the Second Canadian Mounted Rifles that was formed and training in Victoria. It also provided reinforcements for mounted units throughout the First World War. An addition task included guarding the Vernon Civilian Internment Camp for Germans and Austrians until the end of the war.

1915   A permanent tented camp was established on Mission Hill. Thirty-five-hundred men were trained; their task, reinforcements for overseas units.

1916   With a ceiling of 7000 men, training continued until the end of the war.

1919   From 1919 until 1939, the area reverted to a District Summer Camp for militia training.

19?   The 30th BC Horse was renamed, The British Columbia Mounted Rifles.

19?   The BC Mounted Rifles, renamed, The British Columbia Dragoons.

1939   From 1939 to 1940, an Infantry Basic Training Camp was established, and permanent buildings erected.

1941   The facility was increased to include a Small Arms School.

1942   Increased again to include a Battle Drill School, and trained 24,000 men.

1944   Increased again to train an Infantry Brigade.

1945   Accommodation for the Infantry Brigade was used to form a battalion for service in the pacific.

1946   From 1946 until 1948, many buildings were sold to help relieve the housing shortage.

1949   Reverted to a Summer Camp for the purpose of training militia and cadets.

1950   Cadet Summer Camp quota increased to include Alberta cadets from Western Command, less Junior Cadets who were trained for two weeks at Prairie Command Camp at Clear Lake, Manitoba. Some Saskatchewan, Manitoba and Quebec cadets were present.

1960   Cadet Summer Camp quota increased to include Prairie Command Cadets from Manitoba and Saskatchewan, less Junior Cadets of the prairie provinces who continued to be trained for two weeks at Clear Lake, Manitoba. A quota of Quebec cadets were also present.

1968   Cadet Summer Camp quota increased to include Junior Cadets from Alberta, upon the **closing of the Clear Lake Cadet Camp.**

1970   **Vernon Army Cadet Camp closed after 1970 intake**. Permanent establishment reduced to caretaker establishment.

1971   **Vernon Army Cadet Camp reactivated.** Cadet Summer Camp quota increased to include Junior Cadets from Manitoba and Saskatchewan, **upon the closing of Shilo Cadet Camp.**

1974   Permanent camp establishment approved for CE Production Centre, Supply Section and Maintenance Section, to administer militia units in the interior of BC.

1987   Vernon Camp can accommodate and feed 1000 cadets plus, and staff during summer. During the winter months, it can accommodate and feed 150 all ranks in heated buildings. Fourteen-hundred-and-fifty cadets were billeted in 1987.

Camp area consists of 1000 acres, of which 150 acres are leased to the City of Vernon for spray irrigation. Ten acres are used by the high level weather station. Sports-playing fields are shared with the city, including maintenance by the Vernon Parks & Recreation department. The militia as well as the regular force utilize the training facilities of the camp.

ARTICLE FROM THE VERNON DAILY NEWS - AUGUST 16, 1979

Nineteen seventy-nine marks the 100th anniversary of the Royal Canadian Army Cadet Corps. Cadets trace their origin back to 1861 when the first 'Drill Association,' The Rifle Company of Trinity College, was formed in Ontario. The College training was more related to officers' training, but later that year, The Rifle Company of Bishop's College was formed which included a component of cadets. Our present Cadet Corps actually traces its source to Bishop's College.

During the years 1861 to 1865, six more associations were formed, but little interest was shown until 1879, when 74 new associations were formed with the designation 'Cadet Corps' replacing 'Drill Associations.'

In 1909, Lord Strathcona, Canadian high Commissioner to England, became interested in the cadet movement. He inaugurated the 'Lord Strathcona Trust Fund' and donated a sum of $500,000.00 to be administered for the welfare of the cadet movement. This trust fund, which is still in existence, remains a memorial to Lord Strathcona and his faith in the youth of Canada.

Primarily, because of this new support, the cadet movement thrived across Canada. By the year 1912, Canada had 64,000 cadets in service, and by 1946, 115,600.

Today there are some 413 Cadet Corps spread across Canada as follows: Newfoundland 29; Prince Edward Island 3; Nova Scotia 24; New Brunswick 15; Quebec 110; Ontario 102; Manitoba 17; Saskatchewan 26; Alberta 30; British Columbia 46; Yukon Territories 8; North West Territories 8.

Girls became active in the cadet movement in 1975, and now represent one-third of the enrollment.

The cadet motto is 'Acer Acerpori' - 'As the maple, so the sapling.' The aim of the cadet movement is the same: to make better and healthier citizens of our Canadian Youth.

Vernon's first Cadet Corps was formed in 1912. It consisted of 40 boys and was affiliated with the 30th British Columbia Horse Regiment, the present British Columbia Dragoons. It was designated No. 368 - The 30th British Columbia Horse Cadets and was commanded by Major M. V. Allen (Commanding Officer 30th British Columbia Horse) who was assisted by Mr. C. Gooday.

The first Cadet Camp held in Vernon after the Second World War was opened in the summer of 1949, and trained 1,120 cadets. The first year, the camp was commanded by LCol E. W. Cormack, OBE, ED. This strength increases some years and drops.

Vernon Army Cadet Camp in 1979 will have cadets and staff from all ten provinces, including the Yukon Territories, Northwest Territories, and the United States of America. Although the camp is basically an Army Cadet Camp, Sea and Air cadets will also be included. It is expected that approximately 1,800 cadets will undergo training at the camp this year, with almost one-third of them female. Similar training will also be conducted at other camps across Canada.

The 1979 Camp is commanded by Colonel J. P. Beer, MBE, CD., who is in his fourth year of command.

(Author's note: The camp continues today. It is full during the summer and is used year 'round. A wonderful training establishment.)

A VIEW TO THE FUTURE

An interview in Ottawa, with a retired officer, currently a youth counsellor.

"What do you think of the future of the cadet movement?"

"Currently the movement is a political hot-potato of sorts. No politician really has the courage to address the cadet system in any positive fashion, because he or she is in a Catch 22 position with the left of the political spectrum, who have really no idea what cadets are all about; don't care to learn anything what cadets are all about, and attack anybody politically who would make positive moves to allow the system to move forward. They would prefer to fight youth crime in the street, rather than to allow young people of this country to obtain training and leadership and other qualities that help them to avoid being involved in criminal and gang activities. On the other hand, the ultra-conservatives in this country have totally unrealistic expectations of young people, and expect them to achieve perfect citizenry status without investing anything at all, in terms of effort or funding. Insofar as training is concerned, it would appear that certain people in this country are terrified of having young people know anything, or learn anything that is practical, useful, or in any way relative to real life."

"That's very scary and a far cry from the past. Is there a future?"

"In the past, parents and educators and even those in government had a much more practical view of what the world is all about. Today, people expect to be able to dial up the answer on some computer or some telephone answering machine or phone up some social science service for an instant solution to whatever requirements their children have. They dump them in front of the television; they leave them at the mall; they put them in daycare; they do everything they possibly can to avoid teaching their children. The future looks very bleak unless parents and the rest of society begin to take a more responsible position in regard to youth. If they don't, there is no future for youth."

"So you think the politicians like the way it is?"

"Anything that adds to the confusion, however small, allows politicians to get away with their personal little agendas. If they had their way, they'd get rid of the cadet system altogether. After all, they would be able to increase their bureaucracy five or ten times to fight social problems, as opposed to the cost of curing some of the problems with programs such as cadets."

"Do you see any positive progress in the near-future."

"Well currently, adjustments have been made. A number of years ago, the age limit went from fourteen to thirteen and recently, now to twelve. As a result of lowering the age limit, the level of training has come down to accommodate the younger less physically able cadets. In recent months, the system has seen a mild increase in cadets, mostly the new recruits are teenage girls. There seems to be a bit of a problem, however, with teenage boys. As one lad said recently, 'My mother gives me hell at home; my teacher, she's always on my back; I'm getting out because the girls are driving me crazy.'"

"The system knows that this is a problem and it is aware of it. On one hand, teenage boys grow violent when they're ordered around by females of the same age group. At the corps level, the majority of newcomers will not cooperate with girls in a supervisory capacity, and absolutely refuse for the most part to be involved with the girls. We are aware of this, and are attempting to address the problem. On the other hand, the girls absolutely love the system. They enjoy the responsibility and authority that they can achieve in cadets."

"So you're saying recruiting would improve by keeping the sexes segregated within the cadet organization?"

"No, not really, although it has been proven categorically that boys of this particular age do many hundreds of percent better in their level of achievement, when it's boys only. The mandate of the movement as understood is to integrate boys and girls in the same levels, in the same general age group sort of thing. It is also well known, that young girls feel very threatened in a coeducational system at this particular age, and do much better in an all-girl setting. But again, the system is charged to integrate the sexes."

"In previous times, when cadet corps were segregated, there were many more cadets in both the male and the female corps. That was changed. Was it changed for the better?"

"Obviously not. In the past, both the boys and the girls achieved a much higher level of proficiency in all aspects of cadet training. And there was a much broader, more comprehensive curriculum. However, the mandate is to achieve the same levels of proficiencies in an integrated system. It has been found to date to be virtually impossible to achieve those levels, so in the interim, the expected levels of proficiency have been reduced. It is unfortunate that both the boys and the girls are being short-changed in that regard."

"Do you expect that the level of proficiency will rise?"

"One would hope so, however, the sexual integration aspect is treated as unnatural by both the boys and the girls. As was mentioned before, the girls feel threatened by the boys in competition, and the boys feel victimized and humiliated to a large degree, by the girls. We're trying to change that."

"Has there been any thought given to going back to segregated training?"

"Numerous surveys have illustrated that in educational environments up to senior college level, that those institutions that have remained segregated have the highest level of successful graduates. Those surveys, by the way, are from all over Western Europe and North America. Some institutes that were integrated in recent years have found that their standards and their successes have been reduced. Some are now in the process of offering segregated environments. That I believe would be the logical course, however, the mandate is otherwise."

"I know that girls have always been included in the system, and I believe the organization is much better off with the present fully integrated assemblage, however there are a few drawbacks, what do you think they are?"

"Integration of the sexes of all age groups. Boys and girls from twelve to...fifteen should be trained by members of their own sex. This is very important and in many ways it will be difficult to incorporate. However, if this is done, the retention factor will improve dramatically. At a certain age, there doesn't appear to be a problem with them training together, but there definitely is at the younger age level. Look, at twelve, thirteen and fourteen, boys and girls like to 'hang out' with members of their own sex. Think back to when you were that age, did your close-knit group consist of members of both sexes? Common sense has to dictate here. When boys start to discover girls, and vice-versa, then it doesn't matter."

"With the problems that exist, is there any reasonable expectation that recruitment will begin to improve?"

"If it was possible to reinstitute Trades Training, a Trades Training by the way, that is relative to real life, there would be some hope that interest in cadets would improve. There is no suggestion, however, that integrated, or segregated, Trades Training would be any different for boys than it is for girls. The opportunities would have to be equal for both."

"Why was Trades Training cancelled in the first place?"

"The cancellation of Trades Training, and by the way, safety courses in other areas, such as shooting and highway safety, were also cancelled by the *then* Prime Minister and Minister of Defence, for no other reason than political pressure brought to bear on them by socialist, political activists. These activist groups by the way, have been responsible for a very large number of social problems in this country. Many of them are controlled by larger international politically active associations. These alliances have a very large influence on Canadian government policy to this day. It will be very difficult to reinstitute Trades Training of any consequence because these politically active groups find their most willing recruits in arenas where there are no programs of leadership, man management or trades. That's why you see so many kids who would like to belong to something or be involved in something, ending up in youth gangs, as skinheads, or God help us, as outright nazis. As long as we offer nothing, we receive nothing, so every effort must be made to reinstate Trades Training, proper leadership, and even introduction of an Other Ranks structure within the cadet movement. This, I am sure, would make the cadet system much more appealing to youth. The cadet fraternity and even other organizations would be well advised to challenge youth and be prepared to meet the challenge. I believe they would be pleasantly surprised."

CADET CAMP COMMANDING OFFICERS

1949 - LCol E. W. Cormack, OBE, ED
1950 - LCol J. F. Villiers
1951 - 1952 - LCol D.F.B. Kinloch
1953 - LCol L.J.L. St. Laurent
1954 - Brigadier W.J. Megill, succeeded by LCol J.C. Cave
1955 - 1956 - Brigadier George Kitching, CBE, DSO, CD
1957 - Brigadier J.W. Bishop
1958 - LCol J.H. Mooney
1959 - 1960 - Brigadier J.W. Bishop - LCol W.G.A. Lambe
1961 - Brigadier J. W. Bishop
1962 - Brigadier E.D. Danby
1963 - LCol J. M. Reynolds
1964 - LCol J. A. Cook
1965 - LCol W.H.V. Matthews
1966 - LCol J.S. Edmundson
1967 - LCol R.F. Bruce
1968 - 1975 - LCol C.V. Lilley, MC, OMM, CD
1976 - LCol C.V. Lilley, MC, OMM, CD, succeeded by Col J.F. Beer, MBE, CD
1977 - 1979 - Col J.F. Beer, MBE, CD
1980 - 1981 - LCol D.D. Snow, CD
1982 - 1983 - LCol D. Ardelian, CD
1984 - 1985 - LCol B.M. Munro, CD
1986 - 1988 - LCol R.E. Clark, MMM, CD
1989 - 1992 - LCol M. E. Neil, CD
1993 - LCol M. LaCroix, CD

Author's note: My thanks to the current Camp Commanding Officer, Lieutenant Colonel Marc LaCroix and his staff, for providing this information.

A MESSAGE TO ALL CADETS AND STAFF WHO HAVE ATTENDED THE VERNON ARMY CADET CAMP.

CORDELL CROSS HAS ACCEPTED THE OFFER TO ORGANIZE THE FIRST EVER REUNION OF THE VERNON ARMY CADET CAMP - TO BE HELD IN VERNON 22 - 24 JULY 1994.

PLEASE DIG OUT YOUR OLD LIST OF COMRADES AND CONTACT THEM RIGHT AWAY.
CADETS AND STAFF FROM 1949 TO 1993, WE WANT YOU TO STAND BY YOUR BEDS AND FORM THREE RANKS ON THE ROAD!

FOR FURTHER INFORMATION, WRITE TO:
THE VERNON ARMY CADET CAMP REUNION - 1994
P.O. BOX 88560, 13753 72ND AVE
SURREY, B.C.
V3W 0X1
VOICE MAILBOX (604) 268-9977
YOU CAN TELEPHONE AND LEAVE A MESSAGE, BUT WE'D PREFER YOU TO WRITE.
WE'LL ADVISE YOU ABOUT THE COST AND THE ACTIVITIES

THOUSANDS AND THOUSANDS OF US WILL BE THERE WITH OUR SPOUSES AND KIDS! THIS WILL BE THE OCCASION TO END ALL OCCASIONS! EARLY BOOKING IS ADVISED DUE TO LIMITED ACCOMMODATION IN VERNON. DON'T BE SURPRISED IF WE ALSO USE KELOWNA, PENTICTON, AND KAMLOOPS.
SPECIAL TRAVEL RATES HAVE BEEN ARRANGED ACROSS THE COUNTRY.
SPECIAL HOTEL, MOTEL RATES HAVE BEEN ARRANGED.
SORRY, WE HAVE NOT ARRANGED FOR POWDERED EGGS, POWDERED TOMATOES, POWDERED POTATOES, SALTPETRE, OR SALT TABLETS.

AS SERGEANT BILL BECKFORD, HIS PREDECESSORS AND SUCCESSORS WOULD SAY: GUYS AND GALS, GET YOUR CHINS UP, YOUR ARMS UP AND GET BACK TO VERNON!

SPECIAL GUESTS WILL BE THERE FROM ALL OVER THE WORLD.
YOU MAY EVEN FIND YOUR INITIALS YOU CARVED IN THAT TREE.
SOUVENIRS, ENTERTAINMENT, MEALS, AND THE CAMP YOU LOVE!

NO, MOOSE DANYLUK, YOU CAN'T SLEEP IN YOUR OLD BED!

SPONSORED BY THE ARMY CADET LEAGUE OF CANADA
BRITISH COLUMBIA BRANCH

IT'S TIME TO COME BACK TO YOUR SECOND HOME!

IT IS RUMORED THAT CAMP VERNON MAY CLOSE, SO THIS MAY BE YOUR LAST CHANCE TO VISIT.

BY THE HUNDREDS OF THOUSANDS, PICK UP YOUR PHONES AND YOUR PENS AND KEEP THIS CAMP OPEN.

WHAT IN GOD'S GREEN EARTH IS GOING ON? – CORDELL CROSS

Vernon, B.C., July 22-23-24, 1994

CADET AND STAFF NOMINAL ROLLS OF VACC

I thank Ron Candy of the Vernon Museum, and his regular and volunteer staff for providing what nominal rolls exist. This list of names appeared throughout the years in the Vernon Daily News. The last three years were provided by VACC.

I apologize for the gaps, however the Department of National Defence in Ottawa, refused to provide a complete listing. Additionally, most of the pictures come from the Vernon Daily News. It would appear that Ottawa does not keep pictures of the past. (Cordell Cross)

VACC - 1955

Following is a list of cadets in camp at Vernon:

SENIOR LEADERS' WING: A Company, No. 1 Platoon—Cdts. David Abbey, Cranbrook; Lloyd Atwell, Nelson; Frank Daniels, West Summerland; C. Bdr. Michael Driscoll, Rossland; Cdt. Glenn Elder, Rossland; C. L-Cpl. Gregory Farrell, Midnapore, Alta.; Cdts. Martin Fransen, Revelstoke; Russell Gowanlock, Revelstoke; C. L-Cpl. Bryan Holder, Chilliwack; C. Cpl. James Lines, North Burnaby; Cadets Crawford McLennan, North Burnaby; James Neumeyer, Vancouver; C. Cpls. Peter Nicholls, Cloverdale; Harvey Nielson, Nelson; Cdt. Richard Rahn, Enderby; C. L-Cpl. William Ray, Vancouver; C. WO 2 Eric Rindal, Vancouver; Cdts. Peter Robert, Victoria; Donald Robins, Vancouver; C. Cpl. Ronald Samol, Enderby; C. Bdr. Thomas Scott, Trail; Cdt. Robert Shilton, Cumberland; C. Bdr. Gordon Simpson, Trail; C. L-Cpl. Charles Smith, Victoria; Cdt. John Smith, Armstrong; C. Bdr. Victor Smith; Cdt. Harvey Stark, Chilliwack; Cdts. Donald and David Stewart, Vancouver; C. L-Cpl. Robert Stowell, West Vancouver; Cdt. Allan Symington, West Vancouver; C. L-Cpl. Gary Taylor, North Burnaby.

C. WO 2 Jeffery Taylor, North Burnaby; C. L-Cpl. Robert Timms, North Vancouver; Cdt. William Towe, Port Alberni; C. L-Bdr. Donald Traub, Vancouver; C. L-Cpl. James Turgeon, Kitimat; Cdt. Arthur Turnbull, West Summerland; C. L-Cpl. Ralph Turner, Victoria; Cdts. Robert Unruh, New Westminster; Morris Wagstaffe, Port Alberni; C. Sgt. Donald Watt, Vancouver; C. WO 1 George Watts, Vancouver; C. L-Cpl. Robert Webb, Haney; Cdt. Robert Webster, Vancouver; C. L-Bdr. Herbert Wells, Vancouver; Cdts. Arthur Wheildon, Mission; James White, Chilliwack; C. L-Cpl. Michael White, Vancouver; Cdts. Trevor White, Vancouver; Garnet Wiles, Vancouver; C. L-Cpl. Edward Windsor, New Westminster; C. Bdr. Terrance Woodhouse, Rossland, C. Sgt. Peter Sorensen, Edmonton.

No. 2 Platoon—Cdt. Roy Abrahamsen, Nelson; C. L-Cpl. Terrance Baker, Williams Lake; C. Cpl. Patrick Baltimore, Cdt. Daniel Barth, Calgary; C. S-Sgt. Michael Bennett, Nelson; Cdts. George Black, Calgary; James Cameron, Quesnel; C. L-Cpl. Ian Cole, Hespero, Alta.; C. Cpl. Kenneth Dalman, Blairmore, Alta.; Cdts. David Evans, Midnapore, Alta.; Conrad Frandsen, Salmon Arm; Melvin Flathen, Lethbridge; C. S-Sgt. Robert Furiak, Trail; Cdts. Richard Gentles, Calgary; Donald George, Cranbrook; C. L-Bdr. Simon Goldade, Redcliffe, Alta.; Cdts. Melvin Gorveatt, Millarville, Alta.; James Hall, Quesnel; Robert Harrylock, Calgary; C. Cpl. John Hooper, Cranbrook; Cdts. Michael Horswill, Nelson; James Ida, New Denver; William Jacobs, Cranbrook; Michael Johnson, Rossland; Frank Keane, Rossland; Ernest Killman, Salmon Arm; C. Sgt. Thomas Knight, Coleman, Alta.

C. Bdr. Thomas Koybashi, New Denver; Cdts. Raymond Kumano, New Denver; Abraham McCoy, Cranbrook; Cdts. Allan McIntosh, Williams Lake; Donald McLaren, Lethbridge; John MacLean, Williams Lake; C. Cpl. William McMahon, Calgary; C. L-Bdr. Gary Milne, Oasis; Cdts. Howard Mission, Cranbrook; Richard Martin, Mallaig, Alta.; Edwin Nash, Penticton; C. Cpl. Gerald O'Brien, Calgary; Cdts. James O'Dell, Williams Lake; Richard Patjas, Hespero, Alta.; C. L-Cpl. Jack Pearson, Bashaw, Alta.; Cdts. Norman Picco, Rossland; Larry Potter, Millarville, Alta.; Murray Porter, Redcliffe, Alta.; Stanley Robinson, Williams Lake; C. Cpl. Ernest Smallenberg, Williams Lake; C. Sgts. Lyle Thomson, Leslieville, Alta.; Ronald Treat, Salmon Arm; Cdts. John Widmark, Salmon Arm; Curtis Wheaton, Millarville, Alta.; C. WO 2 Michael Wolfhard, Nelson, and Cdt. Robert Zak, Coleman, Alta.

No. 3 Platoon—Cdts. George Anderson, Vancouver; James Britt, Vancouver; Charles Braithwaite, Lacombe, Alta.; Thomas Buechier, Medicine Hat; John Calcutt, Quesnel; Gary Christie, Vernon; Darrell Dean, Vancouver; John Daimond, Quesnel; Herbert Drew, Vernon; George Duncan, Vancouver; Marvin Dyck, Quesnel; Gregory Freeman, Vernon; C. L-Bdr. Gilbert Gibson, Eckville, Alta.; Cdts. David Graham, Vancouver; Fred Holland, Quesnel; Shoji Inouye, Vernon; Patrick Johnston, Vancouver; Kenneth Kearns, Vernon; Michael Kimmie, Quesnel; Albert Kitchen, Penticton; Peter Koroko, Vernon; Lloyd Lazard, Penticton; C. Sgt. Little Chief, Cluny, Alta.; Cdts. Steven Luchak, Vernon; James McDonald, Vancouver; C. Cpl. Lorne Mackie, Vancouver; Cdts. William Malcolm, Vancouver; Wayne Matthews, Canoe; C. Cpl. Clifford Mawson, Vancouver; C. L-Cpl. Gerald McCulley, Medicine Hat; C. S-Sgts. Harmon Mah, Bashaw, Alta.; Howard Maki, Eckville, Alta.

Cdts. David Mowat, Vancouver; Keith Penneway, Vancouver; C. Sgt. Ronald Peterson, Strathmore, Alta.; C. L-Cpl. Denis Pouttu, Vancouver; Cdt. Gordon Price, Vancouver; C. L-Cpl. Philip Pugliese, Kelowna; Cdt. Clifford Rorick, Vernon; C. L-Bdr. Robert Rounds, Eckville, Alta.; C. S-Sgt. Norman Running Rabbit, Cluny, Alta.; Cdts. Ted Salter, Rodger Schmidt, John Stewart and Russell Synch, all of Vancouver; Trevor Turner, Kelowna; Ernest Van Dresser, Vernon; Leo Verlaan, Vancouver; C. Cpl. Gary Wicks, Strathmore, Alta.; Cdts. David Williams, Vancouver; Edward Wolf Child, Gleichen, Alta.; and William and Harry Wynnchuck, Vernon.

B. Company: No. 4 Platoon—Cdt. J. G. Agopsowiez, C. Cpl. W. N. Alexander and C. L-Cpl. L. W. Ashbaugh, all of Vancouver; Cdt. S. H. R. Allen, Cultus Lake; W. S. Altwasser, Vancouver; C. Cpls. G. L. Ashdown, Kamloops; J. H. Aitken, Vancouver; C. Lt. W. M. Blake, Kamloops; Cdt. E. J. Beard, Murrayville; C. L-Cpl. R. R. Baker, Vancouver; C. WO 2 M. L. Boklage, Armstrong; Cdts. G. L. Boyko, Port Alberni; J. E. Bossons, West Holme; C. L-Cpl. W. G. Beckett, Mission; Cdts. D. S. Black, Vancouver; W. D. Bennett, Alert Bay; C. Sgt. G. R. Bosence, Victoria; C. L-Cpl. L. G. Banni; Cdts. R. A. Banni, D. D. Brager, B. Douglas and R. J. Dannyluck, all of Vancouver; C. L-Cpl. W. B. Donald, Victoria; Cdts.

482

T. Dudoward, Alert Bay; T. D. Donaghue, New Westminster.

M. A. Dussedult, Mission; C. L-Cpl. D. P. Eliasson; Cdt. K. Eakin, New Westminster; C. L-Cpls. R. W. Emrick, Kamloops; R. J. Eldred, Victoria; Cdts. J. R. East, Vancouver; D. S. Erskine, Victoria; D. H. Evans, Vancouver; L. G. Fischer, Medicine Hat; C. L-Cpl. R. J. Flieger, Kamloops; Cdts. T. P. Ingham, Vancouver; J. P. Johnston, West Vancouver; G. F. Jones, Victoria; P. Joseph, Alert Bay; T. D. Janicki, Chilliwack; A. W. Kindt, New Westminster; T. P. King, Alert Bay; M. Kenworthy, Vancouver; F. T. Kaul, Cumberland; R. Kraushan, Vancouver; B. M. Logan, Vancouver; R. M. McGimpsey and A. H. O'Connor, both of Redcliffe, Alta.; C. Cpl. R. Scarlett, Medicine Hat; Cdt. R. Scullard, Cdts. W. E. Young, Gleichen, Alta., and D. G. Anderson, Strathmore, Alta.

No. 5 Platoon—Cdts. E. Barbondy, Abbotsford; C. R. Broomfield, M. Buckley and T. Campbell, all of Vancouver; C. Cpl. J. R. Card, Armstrong; C. L-Cpls. M. G. Clegg, Cloverdale; D. W. Croden, Redcliffe, Alta.; Cdt. A. F. Coupal, Ladner; C. Sgt. G. H. Crighton, Victoria; C. Cpl. M. Crowley, Alberni; C. L-Cpls. D. R. Ferguson, Bretwood Bay, VI; A. M. Forbes, Lanford; C. Bdr. R. M. Fowler,/ Vancouver; C. L-Cpls. D. Fraser, Abbotsford; L. Freisen, Ladner; Cdt. F. D. Gallant, Vancouver; C. L-Cpl. W. J. Knowles, Victoria; Cdts. D. Kraushaar, Lulu Island; E. Ladner, Vancouver; C. Sgt. W. R. Lam, Vancouver; Cdt. W. Lange, Chilliwack; C. L-Cpls. R. W. Leggott, Vancouver; R. K. Leveille, North Burnaby; Cdt. F. Lewis, Cultus Lake; C. L-Cpl. T. Light, Chilliwack.

Cdt. D. A. Linworth, Victoria; C. Sgt. Long, Haney; Cdts. T. G. Mackie, New Westminster; W. Malins, Vancouver; E. J. Martin, Redcliffe, Alta.; T. Mayne, Matsqui; F. H. Meisted, Vancouver; C. L-Cpl. R. D. Miller, Burnaby; Cdts. Jackson Moore, I. D. Morland and D. Morley, all of Vancouver; C. L-Cpl. R. E. Motteram, Victoria; Cdts. A. Mottle, W. G. Munroe and R. B. Murphy, all of Vancouver; R. Norris, New Westminster; D. A. Pasmore, Vancouver; C. L-Cpl. H. R. Patterson, North Burnaby; C. WO 2 G. Pearson, North Burnaby; C. L-Cpl. M. J. Pdesta, Redcliffe, Alta.; C. Cpl. L. A. Querin, Vancouver; C. Sgt. J. H. W. Rathwell, Redcliffe, Alta.; Cdt. F. L. Stuart, Vancouver; C. Cpl. J. G. Schuster, C. Sgt. E. F. Turner, C. Cpl. K. J. Simaluk and Cdt. J. M. Walker, all of Redcliffe, Alta.

No. 6 Platoon—C. Cpl. Bob Lyon and Cdts. Steven McPherson, Murray Colbourne, Ralph Lemire and Bernard Loughran, all of Vancouver; Cdts. Neil Ratcliffe, Armstrong; Garry MacPherson, New Westminster; C. L-Cpls. Douglas MacDonald, Port Alberni; Melvin Pearson, Sydney; C. S-Sgt. Brian McKay, C. Cpl. Robert Bull Bear, Cdt. Bert Mayfield, C. WO 2 Carl Many Guns, Cdts. Julius Many Bears and David Melting Tallow and C. Cpl. David Bull Bear, all from Gleichen, Alta.; C. Sgt. Howard McLeod, Medicine Hat; C. L-Cpl. Brian Richards, Courtenay; Cdts. Raymond Galeazzi, Cumberland; Brian Hyndman, Port Ellis; Ross McKinley, Armstrong; C. L-Cpl. Robert Hill, Mission; Cdt. Larry Sinch, Van-

couver; C. L-Cpl. John McLeod, Vancouver; C. Cdts. Fred Hall, Vancouver; Michael Huntley, Ladner.

C. L-Cpl. Douglas Hennessy, Ladner; C. L-Bdr. Donald Chaplin, Victoria; Cdt. Dale Hayes, Duncan; C. Cpl. Alec Crabbe, Chemainus; C. Bdr. Terry Lyttle, Victoria; C. L-Bdr. Michael Pearce, Victoria; Cdts. Edward Hall and Robert Gordon, Victoria; Robert Siddon, Abbotsford; Bill Read, Ladner; C. Cpl. Gordon Rowley, Abbotsford; Cdts. Robert Pokorny, Vancouver; Arthur Premack, New Westminster; C. Cpl. George Czetwertynski, Qualicum Beach; Cdt. Clive Cross and C. L-Bdr. Mike Currier, Victoria; C. WO 2 William Smith, Cdts. George Pasmore, John Gregory and Terrence and Theo Sawasy, all of Vancouver; Roger Shaw, Victoria; C. Cpl. Bruce Harwood, Chemainus; Cdt. John Ross, Vancouver; C. L-Cpl. Larry Hall, Victoria; Cdt. Chris Simpkins, Vancouver, and C. Sgt. Robin Cuthbert, Victoria.

C Company: No. 7 Platoon—All Alberta boys except where indicated: Cdt. Gordon Adams and C. Bdr. Gerry Beauregard, Rocky Mountain House; Cdt. Michael Behm, Vilna; C. Cpls. Raymond Belanger and Robert Bolton, both of Edson; C. S-Sgt. N. R. Burroughs, Sunnybrook; Cdt. Jim Davenport, Red Deer; C. WO 2 Garry Day, Edmonton; Cdt. Paul Dechaine and C. Cpl. Donald Deetjen, both of Mallaig; C. S-Sgt. Donald Dreever, Edmonton; Cdt. Ron Duda, Grande Prairie; Cdt. Edward Duggan, Calgary; C. Cpl. Ed Hody, Vegreville; C. L-Cpl. Mack Irons, Rocky Mountain House; C. L-Cpl. John Jager, Calgary.

Cdt. Ernest Jansen, Albert Park; C. Cpl. Fred Johnston, Calgary; C. Cpl. John Johnstone, Edmonton; Cdt. Peter Joyce, Edmonton; Cdt. K. L. Kerrik, Fawcett; C. Sgt. Gerry Kesslor, Calgary; C. Sgt. Alfred Kingston, Fort McLeod; C. Sgt. Ernie Lansdown, Innisfail; C. WO 2 Donald Markowsky, Spear River; C. Cpl. John Moti, Hillcrest; Cdt. James Morris, Lacombe; C. Sgt. John Neilson, Westlock; C. L-Cpl. Myroslaw Nimitz, Lacombe; C. L-Cpl. Jim Novosad, Edmonton; Cdt. Percy Nyrose, Lethbridge; C. Cpl. Jim Stanton, Vegreville; C. Cpl. Frank Stenger, Warburg; C. Cpl. Bruce Stetchman, Edmonton; Cdt. Reno Stocko, Calgary; Cdt. Roy Stuart, Millarville; Cdt. Lawrence Sutherland, Fawcett; Cdt. Allan Swain, Mannville; Cdt. John Thomas, Rocky Mountain House; C. Cpl. William Thompson, Mannville.

No. 8 Platoon — C. L-Cpl. David Bauer, Lethbridge; C. Sgt. Jack Blair, Fort St. John; Cdt. Larry Boggis, Edmonton; C. Sgt. Edgard Bourassa, Fort MacLeod; C. Cpl. Dan Bowes, Fort St. John; Cdt. George Bull, Midnapore; C. Cpl. Stephan Butcher, Lesterville, Alta.; C. Cpl. Sam Duckworth, Edmonton; C. Ltd. Woodrow Good Striker, Cardston, Alta.; C. L-Cpl. Dan Healy, Cardston; Cdt. Ken Hoppus, Lacombe, Alta.; C. L-Cpl. Ted Horton, Yellowknife, NWT; C. Cpl. Fred Labouchane, Fort St. John; Cdt. Claude Langlois, St. Paul, Alta.; C. Cpl. Tex Lansdown, Innisfail; Cdt. John Lieskovsky, Hillcrest, Alta.; C. Bdr. George Lllivam, Eckville, Alta.

C. Cpl. Morris Little Bear, Cardston; C. Sgt. Ross Little Child, Hobema, Alta.; C. Cpl. Ken Lockhart, Innisfail;

C. Sgt. L. Lyon, Edson, Alta.; Cdt. Gerry Osetsky, Coronation, Alta.; C. Cpl. Philip Palechuk, Homena; Cdt. Mike Parkyn, Calgary; Cdt. Percy Parsons, Rocky Mountain House; C. L-Cpl. Hughie Pawlick, Grande Prairie; Cdt. Lewis Perrault, Delburne, Alta.; Cdt. Francis Petersen, Blairmore, Alta.; C. L-Cpl. Benny Purnell, Red Deer; C. L-Cpl. John Saunders, Mercoal, Alta.; C. Cpl. John Shavchook, Vegreville; C. Sgt. Bert Shearer, Coronation; Cdt. Morris Shevolut, Waskatenac, Alta.; Cdt. Oley Shynora, Radway; C. Sgt. Oliver Soop, Cardston; Cdt. Larry Spias, Mallaig, Alta.; C. S-Sgt. Ches Spornitz, Edgerton, Alta.; Cdt. Billy Wallace, Innisfail; C. WO 2 Chuck Watt, Fawcett, Alta.

No. 9 Platoon—Cdt. Gordon Barager, Thorsby, Alta.; Cdt. Charles Butterfield, Coronation; Cdt. Ronnie Caine, Rocky Mountain House; Cdt. John Casey, Westlock; C. L-Cpl. Carl Christianson, Sedgewick, Alta.; C. Lt. Vincent Ciochetti, Edmonton; C. Cpl. Glenn, Cruikshank, Alta.; C. Cpl. Gerald Cuthbertson, Lethbridge; C. Sgt. Henry Epp, Calgary; C. Sgt. Robert Ferguson, Lethbridge; C. L-Cpl. Lawrence Fisher, Stettler, Alta.; Cdt. Ronald Forrester, Bowness, Alta.; C. WO 2 Kenneth and C. Bdr. Arthur Fuller, Delburne; Cdt. Richard Garrett, Rocky Mountain House; L-Cpl. George Goldmann, Sedgewick; C. Cpl. Philip Gower, Calgary; C. L-Cpl. Ronnie Griffiths, Calgary; C. Cpl. Ken Haffner, Warburg, Alta.; C. Sgt. John Hamilton, Fort MacLeod, Alta.; C. Sgt. Dennis Hawthorne, McLennan, Alta.; C. L-Bdr. Emile Hebert, St. Paul, Alta.; C. Sgt. Allan. Holburg, Beaver Lodge, Alta. Cdt. Thomas Leaske, Westlock; C. WO 2 Robert MacDonald, Calgary; Cdt. Jock McDonnell, Yellowknife; C. Cpl. Gord MacDougal, Lethbridge; C. L-Cpl. Gordon McLeod, Mercoal, Alta.; C. Sgt. Garry Maisey, Chinook, Alta.; C. Cpl. Lawrence Panther Bone, Carson; C. Cpl. Theodore Poole, Beaver Lodge; C. Cpl. Reginald Rice, Calgary; C. Sgt. Elmer Richardt, Fort MacLeod; C. Cpl. Dennis Robinson, Edmonton; C. Sgt. Tiny Robinson, Edmonton; C. Lt. Norman Ross, Fort St. John; Cdt. Camille Russell, Cardston; C. Lt. Oliver Russell, Cardston; C. Cpl. Lester Tail Feathers, Cardston; C. WO 2 Lewis Walker, Alliance, Alta.; Cdt. Matthew Ward, Lacombe; C. Cpl. Douglas Weisel, McLennan; C. S-Sgt. Fracis Whiteman, Edmonton; Cdt. Robert Whitford, Velna, Alta.; C. WO 2 Lawrence Wildcat, Hobema; C. Capt. Norman Wilkinson, Edmonton; Cdt. Brian Williams, Edgerton; C. Cpl. William Wilson, Vancouver; Cdt. Dennis Wright, Mannville, and C. Capt. Robert Youk, Calgary.

Rifle Coaches—C. Cpl. Eric Arlidge, Edmonton; C. S-Sgt. Richard Belland, New Westminster; C. Capt. Tom Clarke, Beaverlodge; C. S-Sgt. Gerry Couture, Rossland; C. Sgt. Roy Fox, Victoria; C. Lt. Jim Fisher, Edgerton; C. Sgt. Bob Harper, Alberni; C. Cpl. Mike Harrish, Thorsby; C. Cpl. Dennis Hunt, Vancouver; C. WO 2 Arnie Jacobson, Rocky Mtn. House; C. Sgt. Rudy Komik, Sedgewick; C. Lt. Mickey Lee, Vernon; C. WO 1 Ken Lidgren, Lethbridge; C. Cpl. H. N. McRae, New Westminster; Cdt. George Miller, Penticton; Cdt. David Nelson, North Burnaby; C. Sgt.

Bert Odgaard, Edmonton; C. Cpl. Bill Palmer, Enderby; C. Cpl. Bruce Roberts, Victoria; Cdt. Harry Scaife, Vancouver; C. Sgt. Jim Sewell, Calgary; C. Cpl. Morley Smith, Vancouver; C. Sgt. Ronald Soley, Lacombe; Cdt. Bill Bercher, Mission; and C. Capt. Stuart Weeks.

DRIVER-MECHANIC WING: A Company, No. 1 Platoon—C. WO 2 James Burnett, Vancouver; C. WO 2 Arthur Aiello, Vancouver; C. Sgt. Gilbert Atkins, New Westminster; C. L-Cpl. Donald Apps, Cumberland; C. Bdr. Brian Acres, Nelson; C. L-Cpl. Edward Brooke, New Westminster; Cdt. Victor Barton, Vedder Crossing; Cdt. Leeland Bockus, Vernon; C. Sgt. Bruce Browne, Vernon; Cdt. Peter Baldassi, Trail; C. L-Bdrs. Geoffrey and Philip Clark, Vancouver; C. L-Cpl. Carson Carter, Salmon Arm; C. L-Cpl. Cusson, Vancouver; Cdt. Irvine Claughton, Armstrong; C. Sgt. Robert Connaughton, Mission; C. Cpl. Dennis Chobotar, Vernon; and C. Bdr. David Dale, Vancouver.

No. 2 Platoon—Cdt. Frederick Essery, Victoria; Cdt. David Flowers, Victoria; Cdt. Albert Hoffman, Salmon Arm; Cdt. Mervyn Fry, Rossland; Cdt. Peter Fitz-Gerald, Oasis; Cdt. Grant Garner, Royal Oak, V.I.; C. L-Cpl. Gordon Greer, Vedder Crossing; C. Sgt. Fred Dighton, New Westminster; C. S-M. Raymond Jang, Vancouver; C. L-Cpl. William Durring; C. Cpl. Dale Flack, New Westminster; C. Cpl. Gary Ericson, New Westminster; C. L-Bdr. Stanley Gran, Vancouver; Cdt. Patrick Francois, Vancouver; Cdt. Thomas Ray, Vancouver; Cdt. Raymond Glover, Vancouver; C. Sgt. Raymond Desjardins, Mission; Cdt. Egan Frech, Kamloops; C. Sgt. Ralph McKay, Haney.

No. 3 Platoon—Cdt. John Jacobson, Victoria; C. Cpl. Charles Kidd, Nelson; C. Cpl. Terry King, Revelstoke; Cdt. Theodore Kolmatycki, Vernon; C. L-Cpl. Richard Lofgren, North Burnaby; C. Bdr. Laurie MacDonald, New Denver; C. Cpl. Michael MacMillan, Vancouver; C. Bdr. Robert McIver, Vancouver; Cdt. Ernest McLean, Sea Island; Cdt. John McLellan, Victoria; Cdt. Valentino Milan, Rossland; Cdt. Terry Moore, Kamloops; C. Sgt. William O'Connell, Lulu Island; C. Bdr. David Parker, Vancouver; Cdt. James Pasmore, Vancouver; C. Sgt. James Price, Vancouver; C. WO 2 Richard Moore, Errington; and C. Sgt. Donald McLeay, Errington.

No. 4 Platoon—C. Sgt. Herbert Pare, Vancouver; Cdt. John Quayle, Victoria; C. Cpl. Paul Quesnel, South Burnaby; C. Sgt. Donald Reibin, New Westminster; Cdt. Ian Richmond, South Burnaby; Cdt. Robert Richmond, Vancouver; C. Sgt. Stephen Sands, Duncan; C. Cpl. Barry Simms, Vancouver; C. Sgt. Russel Siwak, New Westminster; C. Cpl. Ray Soules, Revelstoke; C. WO 2 Stanley Stolhard, Victoria; Cdt. Robert Sturgeon, Nelson; Cdt. Tennant Thomson, Vancouver; Cdt. Lawrence Toffolo, Trail; C. L-Cpl. William Wells. Vancouver; Cdt. Frank Wernick, Grindrod; Cdt. Ken Wilson, Penticton; Cdt. Gary Whitcomb, Victoria; C. L-Cpl. Ronald Wood, Vancouver; and Cdt. Lawrence Woods, Enderby.

B Company, No. 5 Platoon—C. L-Cpl. Dale Anderson, Edmonton; Cdt. Robert Archer, Edgerton; C. L-Bdr. Donald Beach, Edgerton; C. Bdr. Bernard Belland, St. Paul; Cdt. Stuart Blacklock, Quesnel; Cdt. Julian Brenda, Edmonton; C. WO 2 Allenson Brown, Hillcrest; Cdt. Garry Brown, Edmonton; C. L-Cpl. James Cervo, Blairmore; C. S-Sgt. John Chesney, Edmonton; C. Sgt. Barrie Cook, Stettler; Cdt. Richard Cooper, Sedgewick; Cdt. Graham Crawford, Mannville; C. Lt. Frederick Currie, Turner Valley; C. Sgt. Raymond Cutknive, Hobema; C. Cpl. Donald Disney, Turner Valley; Cdt. James Dornan, Thorsby; and Cdt. Ronald Helwig, Bassano.

No. 6 Platoon—Cdt. Dougall Bailey, Vancouver; C. Cpl. Donald Cromarty, Quesnel; C. Cpl. James Dyck, Quesnel; C. Sgt. Ronald Ekstrom, Lethbridge; C. Sgt. Emery Field, Lethbridge; C. Sgt. John Folkard, Edmonton; C. Cpl. Donald Foster, Edson; C. Cpl. William Gibson, Alliance; Cdt. Bob Gillespie, Vernon; C. Cpl. Philip Gordon-Cooper, Calgary; Cdt. Albert Guilbault, Mallaig; C. Cpl. Gerald Harrington, Spirit River; C. Sgt. Terry Hilborn, Quesnel; Cdt. Jack Hogan, Fawcett; C. Cpl. Dennis Hunkin, Beaverlodge; C. Cpl. Taras Iwasiw, Coleman; C. Sgt. Ronald Jarron, Edmonton; C. Cpl. Trevor Jones, Edmonton; C. Sgt. Lawrence Joyce, Edmonton; Cdt. Ray Kelly, Edmonton; C. Cpl. Terry Mullen, Armstrong; and Cdt. Howard Woods, Westbank.

No. 7 Platoon—Cdt. Edward Kurley, Warburg; Cdt. Howard Leeson, Edmonton; Cdt. Joe Leonard, Yellowknife; C. S-Sgt. Bruce Lloyd, McLennan; C. S-Sgt. Ted McConnell, Calgary; C. Sgt. Robert McIntyre, Frank; C. WO 2 Alphonse Massine, Redcliffe; C. Cpl. Michael Mazur, Mercoal; Cdt. Thomas Metronec, Mannville; Cdt. Peter Myrehaug, Sedgewick; Cdt. Donald Nelson, Edgerton; C. Cpl. Melvin Ness, Bashaw; Cdt. George Ohrn, Warburg; Cdt. Bernard Oullet, Edmonton; C. Sgt. Peter Poburan, Vilna; and Cdt. Lindsay Potter, Lethbridge.

No. 8 Platoon—Cdt. Robert Robertson, Calgary; Cdt. Gary Rombough, Sedgewick; Cdt. Reginald Saunders, Edmonton; C. WO 2 Thomas Shields, Grande Prairie; C. Bdr. Gerald Sjare, Eckville; C. Cpl. Robert Smith, Calgary; C. L-Cpl. Donald Stanker, Bassano; Cdt. William Stutchbury, Westlock; C. L-Cpl. Walter Thurber, Hobema; C. Sgt. Ivan Walker, Mercoal; Cdt. Oliver Wasnea, Waskatenau; Cdt. Lloyd Weisenburger, Delburne; C. L-Cpl. James Wilson, Vegreville; Cdt. Delbert Woody, Coronation; C. Capt. Ian McKenzie, Strathmore; C. WO 2 Terry Patrick, Lacombe; and C. WO 2 J. J. Taylor, Vancouver.

VACC - 1956

BRITISH COLUMBIA

SENIOR LEADERS

C/Sgt Alexander W N, Vancouver; Cadet Anderson G K, Vancouver; Cadet Anderson G, Vancouver; Cadet Anderson D M, Victoria; Cadet Aronold A W, Vancouver; C/Sgt Ashbaugh L W, Vancouver; Cadet Atelivich M, Vancouver.

Cadet Baillie A W, Vancouver; Cadet Baillie B D, Summerland; Cadet Baillie J L, Vancouver; Cadet Banman S M, Vancouver; Cadet Barker C N, Prince Rupert; L/Bdr Barker R J, Victoria; Cadet Barnes R D, New Westminster; Cadet Barwell R G, Chilliwack; C/Sgt

Bates J, Esquimalt; Cdt/Bdr Beattie J R, N. Vancouver; Cadet Beaton P, Burnaby; Wll Bell S C ,Vancouver; Cadet Bennett R W, Newton; C/L/Cpl Bigwood R A, Victoria; Cadet Biles H A, Victoria; L/Bdr Black G, Vancouver; S/Sgt Black J R D, Vancouver; Cadet Black S, Vancouver; Cadet Blondell R, N. Burnaby; L/Cpl Bond J A, Vancouver; Cadet Bond M, Vancouver; Cadet Bonoevich J K, Vancouver; C/L/Cpl Boquis A B, Port Alberni; C/L/Bdr Bougie E C, Vancouver; Cadet Brown R, Vancouver;Cpl Broomfield C, New Westminster; C/L/Cpl Buckle H, Victoria; Cadet Buffie K, S. Burnaby; L/Cpl Burgess W J, Vancouver; Cadet Burgess D N, Vancouver; Cadet Burnett R B, Kitimat; C/L/Cpl Burrows N, N. Vancouver; Cadet Butula E M, Burnaby; Cadet Byers L J, Vedder Crossing; C/Cpl Byrnand A P, Enderby.

L/Cpl Campbell J S, Vancouver; L/Cpl Campbell T T, Vancouver; L/Bdr Campbell W R, Vancouver; L/Bdr Cave R D, Vancouver; L/Cpl Cawthorne C W, N. Burnaby; Cadet Cayer L H, Port Alberni; Cadet Chaplin J E, Victoria; Cadet Charlie W, Kamloops; Cadet Christy M H, Terrace; Cadet Clark B, Vancouver; Cadet Clark H S, Vancouver; D/C/Maj Clark G S, Vancouver; L/Cpl Clark J P T, Vancouver; T/Sgt Clark P H, Vancouver; Cadet Clarke W A, N. Vancouver; L/Cpl Cole W J, Vancouver; Cadet Colter L L, Armstrong; Cadet Conarroe D F W, Courtenay; C/Sgt Connelly A, Revelstoke; Cadet Cook S E, Vancouver; C/Sgt Copley G H, Victoria; C/L/Cpl Corrin D M, Vancouver; Cpl Coulter W, Cumberland; Cadet Coward J, Victoria; C/L/Cpl Coyle J H, Victoria; L/Bdr Creed W M, Victoria; Cadet Crotteau M E, Quesnel; C/Csm Crowley M, Alberni; C/L/Cpl Crowley W, Alberni; Cadet Cruise H W, N. Vancouver; C/L/Cpl Cumming B R, N. Vancouver; Cadet Cunningham G C, Vancouver; Cpl Cunnington J, Armstrong; C/L/Cpl Currier J T, Victoria; Cadet Cuzner R F, Victoria.

Cadet Davis A F L, Vancouver; Cadet Davidson H L, Vancouver; D/Maj Dean D M, Vancouver; Cadet Devison R W, Prince Rupert; C/Cpl Denike K J, Burnaby; Cadet Dick D, N. Vancouver; Cadet Dickson R D, Armstrong; C/Cpl Donesley R W G, Vernon; C/L/Cpl Drab B G, Vancouver; Cadet Duff R L, S. Burnaby; Cadet Dupray J W, N. Burnaby.

C/Cpl Eastick D C, Victoria; C/Sgt Elgstrand G D, Vancouver; Cadet Ellis J B, S. Burnaby; C/Cpl Ellis R D, Abbotsford; C/L/Cpl Ellis W A, N. Burnaby; Cadet Evanoff F, Nelson.

Cadet Farkvam K T E, Terrace; Cadet Pearn J W, Mission City; Cadet Fedyk L P, Vancouver; Cadet Ferguson A R, N. Burnaby; Cadet Fielding G E, Prince Rupert; Cadet Fischer K W, Oasis; Cadet Fleury B L, Vancouver; Cadet Forder W G, Rossland; C/L/Cpl Fotherby R H, Vancouver; Cadet Fortin L P, Victoria; L/Cpl Freeman G D, Vernon; Cadet Fricker E W, Kitimat; Cadet Fricker G H, Kitimat; Cadet Fry A, Rossland.

Cadet Gagnon D, N. Burnaby; L/Cpl Gemmell D, Vancouver; Cadet Germscheid T, Salmon Arm; C/L/Cpl Gillespy D C, Victoria; L/Cpl Girling G H, New Westminster; Cadet Gislason C W, Vancouver; Cadet Godfrey H L, New Westminster; Cadet Gottschau W P, Vancouver; C/Sgt Gran S L, Vancouver; Cadet Grazier J, Vernon.

L/Cpl Hamilton B J, N. Vancouver;

Cadet Hanna F S, Lytton; C/L/Cpl Hans H O L, Vancouver;Cadet Hardin A H, Kitimat;Cadet Harding J, N. Vancouver; Cpl Harris V, Vancouver; C/Cpl Harrison D H, S. Burnaby; Cadet Harrison R F, S. Burnaby; Cadet Healy L F, Quesnel; Cadet Hebert R, Vancouver; Cadet Henry R, Lytton; C/Sgt Heppell M E, Victoria; Cadet Hill R A, Armstrong; S/Sgt Holmberg A R, Victoria; Cpl Hopkins T W, Westbank; Cadet Holmes D W, Summerland; Cadet Huisman J, Vancouver; Cadet Humphreys A A, N. Vancouver; C/Cpl Hyndman D L, Cloverdale.

Cadet Ihaksi B, N. Burnaby; C/Cpl Imrie D A, Ladner; Cadet Isaac T B N, Lytton; Cadet Israel J, N. Vancouver; Cadet Israel R J, Dewdney; C/Cpl Itani B, Westbank; C/Csm Itani T, Westbank.

Cadet James G, Lytton; Cadet Jessiman A, Duncan; Cadet Joadison R H, Vancouver; Cadet Johnson D L, Victoria; C/Sgt Johnston J P, Vancouver; Cadet Johnston L E, Salmon Arm; Cadet Johnston P G C, Sidney; C/Cpl Jones H F, N. Vancouver; C/Cpl Jorgensen G D, Salmon Arm; Cadet Jorgenson J, N. Burnaby; Cadet Jourdenais E, Haney; Cadet Jumbo T, Lytton.

C/Sgt Kamann K, Vancouver; Cadet Kattler M J, Vancouver; Cpl Kearns K, Vernon; Cadet Kenny J, Mission City; C/Bdr King J P, N. Vancouver; C/L/Cpl Kish F W, Vancouver; Cadet Kitcher D, Penticton; Cadet Kore E, Vancouver; Cadet Koski W, Vernon; C/L/Bdr Kostinuk J W, Vancouver; Cadet Kraushaar D, Vancouver; C/L/Cpl Kraushaar R, Vancouver; C/L/Cpl Kruper M R, N. Burnaby; Cadet Kurucz R J, Vancouver.

WO2 Lamey B J, Vancouver; C/Sgt Ladner E B, Vancouver; C/Cpl L'Ami D W, N. Surrey; Cadet Lamy M, Vernon; L/Cpl Langill H, Vancouver; L/Bdr Larsen C A, Vancouver; C/Bdr Larsen E F, Vancouver;Cadet Lee S W, Paldi; Cadet Lemire A J, Vancouver; C/L/Cpl Levens E W, Williams Lake; C/Lt Lines J E, Revelstoke; C/Sgt Loegren R, N. Burnaby; Cadet Lovell L R, N. Burnaby; S/Sgt Lyon R J P, Vancouver.

Cadet Macaulay D, Oanoc; Cadet Macdonald J R, Vancouver; C/Cpl Mackay D, Haney; Cadet Macdonald M, Vancouver; C/Sgt MacDougall A M, Hammond; Cadet Madu B W, Cloverdale; Cadet Martel J E, Vancouver; C/L/Cpl Martin G P, Victoria; Cadet Mayert E J J, Revelstoke; C/Bdr McCoy A, Cranbrook; Cadet McCoy D, Vancouver; Cadet McDougall L J, Vancouver; Cadet McGregor K G, Beaver Falls; Cadet McInnes R I, Trail; C/L/Cpl McIntyre A K, New Westminster; Cadet McIntyre D B, New Westminster; Cadet McKenzie D C, Vancouver; Cadet McClure D J G, Kelowna; Cadet McKenzie R, Aldergrove; C/Sgt McLennan C, New Westminster; C/Cpl McLeod J D, Vancouver; Cadet McMillan C J, Vancouver; C/L/Bdr McRae F, Vancouver; Cadet McTavish J D C, Victoria; C/Cpl Metcalfe E, Vancouver; Cadet Miller G D, Vancouver; Cadet Miller R, New Westminster; C/Sgt Miller R, N. Burnaby; Cadet Milsted L R, Vancouver; C/L/Cpl Mobley B, Kamloops; C/L/Cpl Moore R J W, Williams Lake; Cadet Moore T, New Westminster; Cadet Morris D, Vancouver; Cadet Morris L, N. Burnaby; Cadet Morris R, N. Burnaby; Cadet Mosdell L, N. Vancouver; C/L/Cpl Murphy J G, Vancouver; Cadet Murray I D, Ladner.

Cadet Nelson A F, Vancouver; C/Sgt Neumeyer J, Vancouver; Cadet Newham D H, Abbotsford; L/Cpl Newham J D, Abbotsford; L/Bdr Nielson H L, Nelson; Cadet Noltes V J, Terrace.

L/Cpl Otting K E, Armstrong; L/Cpl Ousey R H J, Vancouver.

Cadet Paddington B W, Vancouver; Cadet Parent A J, Vancouver; Cadet Patmore B, Vancouver; L/Bdr Patterson G A, Vancouver; Sgt Patterson I W, Victoria; Cadet Paul K L, Vancouver; Cadet Paul N, Kamloops; Cadet Pauley T W, Chilliwack; Cadet Pearson N A, N. Burnaby; Cadet Peebles D J; Vancouver; Cadet Petterson V L, Vancouver; Cadet Penneway K L, Vancouver; C/Cpl Phillips G L, Vancouver; Cadet Phillips L L, Vancouver; Cadet Phillips W W, New Westminster; L/Bdr Pickerell G L, Vancouver; L/Cpl Pike R G, Victoria; Cadet Piva R G, Trail; Cadet Pierce F J, Vancouver; Cadet Pleasance K N, Victoria; Cadet Poisson A D, New Westminster; Cpl Price G, Vancouver; Cadet Prior R F, Vancouver; L/Cpl Pruden A F, Vancouver.

L/Bdr Quayle G J, Victoria.

L/Cpl Ramshaw D R, Cumberland; L/Cpl Read D L G, Alberni; C/Sgt Reibin D P, New Westminster; Cadet Restall B E L, Victoria; Cadet Rhodes K, Port Alberni; Cadet Rice-Jones J R, Salmon Arm; L/Cpl Rogers G, Vancouver; Cadet Riopelle P L, Salmon Arm; Cadet Ross G R, Vancouver; C/Bdr Rothery S K, Vancouver; L/Cpl Roughsedge P T, S. Burnaby; Cadet Roy J A, Vernon; C/L/Cpl Ruddell J, Kamloops.

Cadet Sauerberg G, Ladner; Cpl Stephenson J H, Port Alberni; C/Cpl Schmidt W E, Vancouver; Cadet Sojmeoder D W, Rossland; L/Cpl Sheridan T P, Vancouver; L/Cpl Sheridan W, Vancouver; C/L/Cpl Siddon B R, Victoria; Cadet Sidgwick J H, Duncan; Cadet Silva-White K M, Victoria; Cpl Simpkins C L, Vancouver; C/Sgt Singh L K, Vancouver; Cadet Slavinski G C, Cloverdale; C/L/Cpl Smith C B, Victoria; L/Cpl Smith L K, N. Vancouver; L/Bdr Smith R W, Vancouver; Cadet Soglo W L, Vancouver; Cadet Staddard L, Burnaby; Cadet Staten T M, Revelstoke; Cadet Stewart D F, New Westminster; Cpl Stewart W B, Burnaby; Cadet Stonehouse G, Vancouver; WO2 Stothard S L, Victoria; Cadet Supeene C, N. Burnaby; L/Cpl Sutcliffe G H, Vancouver; L/Cpl Symington A T M, Vancouver.

Cadet Taylor F J L, Kitimat; Cadet Taylor R N, Cloverdale; C/L/Cpl Thirlwell J G, Vancouver; Cpl Thomson G R, Haney; Cadet Thorn C B, Vancouver; Cadet Timms R L, N. Vancouver; Cadet Timoffee R, Mission City; Cadet Toma R, Vernon; Cadet Tonick J, New Westminster; L/Cpl Towse K, Vancouver; C/Sgt Traub D W, Vancouver; Cadet Thomson D S, Victoria; Cadet Trutch E, Edmonton, Alta.; C/Cpl Tucker B W, Victoria; Cadet Tucker D G, Victoria; C/Sgt Turgeon J, Vancouver; Cadet Turner R E, Victoria; C/L/Cpl Turner R L, Victoria.

L/Bdr Ure J K, Vancouver; Cadet Urquhart A, Salmon Arm; C/L/Cpl Ursel K, Alberni.

Cadet Vanness L, Rossland; Cadet Van Satvoord A M, Vancouver.

Cadet Waite G P, Vancouver; Cadet Walker D, Burnaby; L/Bdr Walker E R, Victoria; L/Cpl Walker R, N. Burnaby; D/M Walls T, Vancouver; Cadet Waterson R A, Vancouver; Cadet Watson W K, N. Burnaby; Cadet Webber A J, Terrace; Cadet Webber J W, Vancouver; Cadet Welsh D A, Vancouver; Cpl Whale T W E, Salmon Arm; Cadet

White D C, N. Burnaby; Cadet White
I H, Vancouver; L/Cpl White T D,
Vancouver; Cpl Whitehead J. Ham-
mond; Cadet Whitehead R, Victoria;
C/Sgt Wilson T D, Oliver; Cadet Win-
ters D R, Vancouver; C/Sgt Woods H
O, Westbank; C/L/Cpl Woodward G R,
Victoria.
Cadet Yampolsky D, Sea Island; L/
Cpl Young R E, Prince Rupert.

D & M WING
C/Sgt Abbey D K, Cranbrook; Cpl
Agoposowicz J, Vancouver; Cadet Alt-
wasser W S, Vancouver; C/Sgt Boyoko
G L, Port Alberni; C/S/Sgt Christle
G J, Vernon; Cpl Clegg M G, Clover-
dale; C/Sgt Crabbe A G, Chemainus;
C/Cpl Cross C, Victoria; C/Sgt Har-
wood R B, Chemainus; C/Cpl Dyck M
D, Quesnel; Cadet Evans D H, Van-
couver; C/Cpl Garner G W, Victoria;
Cadet Glover R E, Vancouver; C/L/Cpl
Godin P, New Westminster; C/Sgt
Goodman M J, Vancouver; L/Cpl Gra-
ham D J, Vancouver; C/L/Cpl Greg-
ory J M, Vancouver; Cadet Hayes D A,
Vernon; Cadet Henley K F, Brentwood;
C/L/Cpl Inoye S, Vernon; C/L/Cpl
Jacobson J E, Victoria; Cadet Jones
G, Vancouver; Cadet Koronko P, Ver-
non; Cadet Lange W, Chilliwack; C/L/
Cpl Luchak S, Vernon.
C/Lt McDowell T J, Vernon; Cadet
Mackie T G, New Westminster; Cpl
Malins D L, Vancouver; C/Sgt Marri-
ott J, Cloverdale; Cadet Matthews W,
Canoe; C/WO2 Munroe J, Abbotsford;
C/L/Cpl Murphy R B, Vancouver; L/
Cpl McBryer R J, Vancouver; C/Sgt
Mackay R, Haney; C/L/Cpl McLean F
R, Vancouver; S/Sgt Nicholls P C,
Cloverdale; C/Cpl Pearce M D, Vic-
toria; C/Sgt Pouttu D T, Vancouver;
L/Cpl Ratcliffe N A, Armstrong; Cpl
Schmidt R G, Vancouver; C/Bdr
Stearns D N, Rossland; C/L/Cpl Stow-
ell R G, Vancouver; C/Sgt Stewart D
P, New Westminster; C/L/Cpl Thomas
D D, Royal Oak; L/Cpl Verlaan L J,
Vancouver; C/Sgt Watt D E, Vancouv-
er; C/Sgt Wells H G, N. Burnaby; Cpl
Wynnychuk W, New Westminster.

JUNIOR LEADERS
Cadet Alfalter R, Nelson; Cadet Ab-
rahamson R, Nelson; C/Gnr Anderson
T, Cranbrook; Cadet Andrews J J, Cor-
dova; Cadet Beddows D, Chemainus;
Cadet Berry E, Vernon; C/L/Cpl Bish-
op R H, Williams Lake; Cadet Bourgo
D, Vernon; Cadet Boutwell D G, Kel-
owna; Cadet Calver T, Salmon Arm;
Cadet Colter G J, Armstrong; Cadet
Clarke H, Vernon; Cadet Conarroe D
D, Courox; Cadet Currier W C, Vic-
toria; Cadet Davies H, Westbank; Cad-
et Dayton D R D, Kamloops; Cadet
Dempster H R, Terrace; Cadet Denniel
L H, Kitimat; C/L/Cpl Edwards H,
Kamloops; Cadet Evans F R, Kelowna;
Cadet Fielding G E, Prince Rupert;
Cadet Findlay A N, Terrace; Cadet
Fitger D, Kamloops; Cadet Fleck J F,
Kelowna; C/L/Cpl Forest W C, Royal
Oak; Cadet Gili J, Rossland; Cadet
Goodings D C, Chemainus; Cadet Grif-
fin N E, Victoria; Cadet Grieve T,
Rossland; Cadet Hall R W, Kitimat;
Cadet Halverson F A, Enderby; Cadet
Healy C J, Quesnel; Cadet Hickman D
W, Kitimat; Cadet Hunt T, Victoria;
Cadet Johnson K R, Alberni; Cadet
Johnson D R, Oasis; Cadet Lane A P,
Rossland; Cadet Larson F, Revelstoke;
Cadet Lewis E J, Victoria.
Cadet Marshall R C, Port Alberni;
L/Cpl McKinley N, Armstrong; Cadet
Melatini R M, Trail; Cadet Moore G,

Penticton; Cadet Moth L R, Duncan;
Cadet Nelson R, Enderby; Cadet Nim-
mo R J, Saanichton; Cadet Patrick R
W N, Prince Rupert; Cadet Patterson
R C, Cowichan; Cadet Pearson K G,
Sidney; Cadet Perritt C J, W. Sum-
merland; Cadet Philips K, Cranbrook;
Cadet Phillips L H, Lytton; Cadet
Phillips M, Lytton; Cadet Quast L A,
Prince Rupert; Cadet Reynolds S J,
Terrace; Cadet Roberts D, Cranbrook;
Cadet Robinson F G, Prince Rupert;
Cadet Rudell D T, Kamloops; Cadet
Ryan W M, Victoria; Cadet Sather G,
Rossland; Cadet Shehyn D, Revelstoke;
Cadet Shoolingin D, Duncan; Cadet
Simmister M J, Oasis; Cadet Smith R,
Vernon; Cadet Stallard P, Penticton;
Cadet Taylor K L, Kamloops; Cadet
Tempest R, Duncan; Cadet Van Allin
L D, Quesnel; Cadet Van Dressler J,
Vernon; Cadet Walloren D F, Fruit-
vale; Cadet Walton D G, Summerland;
Cadet Wilkins P O, Quesnel; Cadet Wit-
teveen F, Cobble Hill; Cadet Wilson
J A, Prince Rupers; Cadet Zemek R J,
Chemainus.

ALBERTA

JUNIOR LEADERS WING
Cadet Aberdeen E, Cardston; Cadet
Allan E G, Alliance; Cadet Allinott R
D, Edmonton; Cadet Armstrong L H,
Edson; Cadet Armstrong T H, Calgary.
Cadet Bainbridge W, Medicine Hat;
Cadet Barber G C, Cheadle; Cadet Bed-
ford D W, Edgerton; Cadet Bell J R,
Montney, B.C.; L/Cpl Boe E K, Beaver-
lodge; Cadet Bosch H, Killam; Cadet
Botnen D R, Edson; Cadet Braithwaite
T G, Lacombe; Cadet Berry P F, Leth-
bridge; Cadet Briard P, Grande Prairie;
Cadet Brown R C, Stettler; Cadet Buf-
fald V, Hobbins; Cadet Burns R J,
Calgary.
Cadet Carruthers C E, Winfield; Cad-
et Carruthers L G, Winfield; Cadet
Carter J, Yellowknife; Cadet Chalifoux
F J, McLennan; Cadet Christensen E,
Mannville; Cadet Christie R M, Edson;
Cadet Clarke R, Sedgewick; Cadet Cle-
ments R G, Calgary; Cadet Connelly
M J, Calgary; Cadet Connolly D C, Cal-
gary; Cadet Coutts W S, Calgary; Cad-
et Cut Knife C, Hobbema; Cadet Cut
Knife E, Hobbema.
Cadet Davidson H W, Black Diamond;
Cadet DeMarce J A, Turner Valley;
Cadet Denesiuk J, Waskatenau; Cadet
Dillon R, Medicine Hat; Cadet Dubrule
E, St. Paul; Cadet Duffy S E, Edmon-
ton; Cadet Dunn B M, Yellowknife;
Cadet Drolet R D, St. Paul.
Cadet Ferguson K O, Cardston; Cad-
et Flynn G, Calgary; Cadet Frederick-
sen A C, Winfield; Cadet Frizzell D L,
Red Deer.
C/L/Bdr Galbraith N J, Edmonton;
L/Cpl Gilbertson D B, Buck Lake; Cad-
et Glenn R J, Spirit River; Cadet
Greenwood K, Edmonton; Cadet Gor-
don A D, Lacombe; Cadet Graham L C,
Pincher Creek; Cadet Guest W R,
Westlock.
Cadet Haines C D, Calgary; Cadet
Hamilton D A, Yellowknife; Cadet Han-
na J N, Winfield; Cadet Heaver G R,
McLennan; Cadet Hendrigan D D A,
Winfield; Cadet Henes C D, Pincher
Creek; Cadet Hilton S M, Strathmore;
Cadet Hoffman R H, Florsby; Cadet
Holloway F D, Brocket; Cadet Hull W
J, Spirit River; L/Cpl Hume R K, Bea-
verlodge; Cadet Hutchison R, Lacombe.
Cadet Jensen J, Fawcett; Cadet Johns
W R, Montney, B.C.; Cadet Kirkland
A, McLennan; Cadet Krause D K, Ed-
gerton; Cadet Krewenchuk H D,

Grande Prairie; Cadet Knowlton W, Brochet; Cadet Kozak V, Waskatenau; Cadet Kusick H R, Wasel.

Cadet Laidlaw F W, Pincher Creek; Cadet Laidler T P, Mannville; Cadet Lazarowich I D, Edmonton; Cadet Leavens D J G, Edmonton; Cadet Lightning A, Hobbema; Cadet Living H C, Edmonton; Cadet Lortie B, Edmonton; C/Bdr Lott J F, Edmonton; Cadet Lunn D F, Lacombe.

Cadet MacCallum W E, Calgary; Cpl MacKay D E, Mercoal; Cadet McAmmond U, Warburg; Cadet McIntosh L G, Vegreville; Cadet McLaughlin M L, Strathmore; Cadet Maurstad J H, Namaka; Cadet Marx A F, Calgary; Cadet Meilleur W L, Calgary; Cadet Mylre R D, Red Deer.

Cadet Newcombe J W, Clyde; Cadet Niemi J G, Canmore; Cadet Nobel H L, Calgary; Cadet O'Driscoll R R, St. Paul; Cadet Olsen G E, Calgary; L/Cpl Olson B M, Beaverlodge; Cadet Osborne T A, Fort St. John.

Cadet Paquette T L, Forest Lawn; Cadet Paulet R O, Calgary; Cadet Pickering R E, Spirit River; Cadet Pyne B P, Calgary; Cadet Ray D F, Edmonton; Cadet Resler D R, Bashaw; Cadet Rest A F, Millarville; Cadet Roberts A, Westlock; Cadet Rosko M J, Vegreville; Cadet Rothenburger S, Vegreville; Cadet Rukavina C V, Edson; Cadet Russell S, Cardston; Cadet Rutzer A N, Calgary.

C/L/Cpl Sather D, Wanham; Cadet Schleindl M, Edmonton; Cadet Schornagel M R, Bassano; Cadet Schultz E J, Bashaw; Cadet Seaman R A, Calgary; Cadet Shave V L, Thorsby; Cadet Siki A, Yellowknife; Cadet Shortneck J, Hobbema; Cadet Simonds B M, Mercoal; Cadet Sinclair-Smith S F, Okotoks; L/Cpl Smeltzer H I, Buck Lake; Cadet Smith G, Brocket; Cadet Spragge W, Westlock; Cadet Stenton W C, Banff; Cadet Stillwell R T, Black Diamond; Cadet Stuart R H, Black Diamond; Cadet Stunzi F R, Calgary.

Cadet Tourond D M, Black Diamond; Cadet Tronnes J D, Lacombe; Cadet Turcotte L, Edmonton; Cadet Tutty C M, Breton; Cadet Vedres L G, Lethbridge; Cadet Voloshin J, Killam; Cadet Walton W, Calgary; Cadet Wanchaluk D, Edmonton; Cadet Westergaard F E W, Fort St. John, B.C.; Cadet Whiting K F, Banff; Cadet Wuetherich N E, Alliance; Cadet Wyse K M, Lacombe; Cadet Ziefle T H, Pincher Creek; Cadet Zimmerman F E, Vulcan.

Cadet Doherty A, Mannville; Cadet Fuller L F, Delburne; Cadet George A L, Delburne; Cadet Powell R C, Delburne.

SENIOR LEADERS WING

C/Cpl Adams L E, Edson; Cadet Archibald R, Red Deer; C/Lt Arlidge E R V C, Edmonton; Cadet Ausmus W G, Edmonton; L/Cpl Bacon G E, Westlock; Cadet Bartoletti R, Coleman; Cadet Bell J A, Calgary; Cadet Big Head P, Cardston; L/Cpl Bjur T I, Winfield; C/Cpl Black Water A, Blood Reserve; C/WO2 Blair J B, Fort St. John; Cadet Bohnet W, Medicine Hat; Cadet Boman W F, Hobbema; Cadet Boos D P, Edmonton; Cadet Bottineau H A, St. Albert; Cadet Boyowicz D R, St. Albert; Cadet Boyowicz J W, St. Albert; Cadet Brabant W J, Calgary; Cadet Brown A R, Rocky Mtn. House; C/Bdr Brown G R, Edmonton; Cadet Broyles L W, Edmonton; C/L/Cpl Bryant F G, Bowness; Cadet Burzminski D H, Waskatenau.

C/Lt Casey J E, Weslock; L/Cpl Catterall D, Edmonton; Cadet Cayotte P, Hobbema; Cadet Chapman G J, Edson; L/Bdr Chausse D H, Edmonton; Cadet Christensen N, Lethbridge; C/Sgt Claney R M, Edmonton; Cadet Creighton A, Cardston; Cadet Crow M, Cardston; C/L/Bdr Crow Eagle H, Brocket; Cadet Cruikshank G E, Edmonton; Cadet Cumming N E, Canmore; Cadet Curran R M, Eckville; Cadet Cameron V J, Redcliff; C/Cpl Caston D M, Edson; Cadet Clark V J M, Thorsby; Cadet Clarke J G, Vulcan; Cadet Clough S R, Alliance.

Cadet Dalke M, Sunnybrook; C/Cpl Damant J W, Lacombe; Cadet Davidson A G, Edmonton; Cadet Dehod N P, Vilna; Cadet Dorosz M A, Calgary; Cadet Diepold W R, Edmonton; Cadet Drolet H P, St. Paul; Cadet Dubois P E, Cluny; Cadet Dubuc H L, Delburne; C/Sgt Dudder J B, Calgary; C/Bdr Duncan R, Calgary; Cadet Dunlop M A, Thorsby; Cadet Dunn D D, Winfield; Cadet Evens G, Mont.

Cadet Failler L, Coleman; Cpl Faulkner B, Edmonton; C/L/Cpl Finch A E, Stettler; WO2 Fisher D, Edgerton; C/Sgt Fleck D W, Edmonton; Cadet Fletcher K W G, Fawcett; Cadet Flynn E, Edmonton; Cadet Flynn J, Crescent; Cadet Flug K, Redcliff; Cadet Ford W J, Calgary; Cadet Fox R H, Montgomery; C/Cpl Fudger B, Calgary; C/WO2 Fuller K L, Delburne; C/Cpl Gant I C, Eckville; Cadet Geddes D W, Alliance; C/WO2 Gentles R G, Calgary; Cadet Gibson F J, Calgary; Cadet Gilbert C F, Edmonton; C/L/Bdr Gilkes D G, Calgary; Cadet Girling J D, Calgary; Cadet Green M T M, Calgary; Cadet Greenwood M K, Mannville.

Cadet Haggarty K W, Cluny; C/L/Bdr Hamilton R T, Edmonton; C/Sgt Hanna R A, Fort MacLeod; Cpl Hansen E, Belloy; Cadet Harvey L, Bellevue; C/Sgt Hawthorne D, McLennan; Cpl Heacock I K, Edmonton; Cadet Healy C, Gleichen; Cadet Healy L, Cardston; Cadet Heron W J, Red Deer; Cadet Herron L B, Bowness; C/Bdr Hetherington L A, Calgary; Cadet Hill J A, Edmonton; Cadet Hill N G, Edmonton; Cadet Hodson F E, Edmonton; Cadet Holmgren D H, Eckville; Cadet Hunkin M, Halcourt; Cadet Hunter R D, Red Deer; C/Cpl Hutchison W, Lacombe; C/Sgt Jackshaw J L, Bashaw; Cadet Jacobson G W, Rocky Mtn. House; C/Cpl Jegou R P, Innisfail; Cadet Jenson D A, Innisfail; Cadet Jewitt R L, Beaverlodge; Cadet Johnson J S, Edmonton; S/Sgt Jones G A, Clyde; Cadet Jones W, Lacombe; WO2 Joyce J P, Edmonton.

Cadet Kasha F J, Eckville; Cadet Kelly M E, Calgary; C/WO2 Kessler G, Calgary; Cadet Kilpatrick P H, Edmonton; C/L/Cpl Kitchen L A, Edmonton; Cadet Koziak V J, Hobbema; C/Lt Kramer J F, Calgary; C/Cpl Krewenchuk S R, Grande Prairie; Cadet Ladouceur N R, Breton; Cadet Lane L R, Calgary; Cadet Langer L E, Mercoal; C/Lt Lansdown E S, Innisfail; Cadet Larsen A R, Lacombe; C/Sgt Langlois C, St. Paul; Cadet Lavoy D A, Redcliff; Cpl Leake T J, Westlock; Cadet Llewellyn W G, Innisfail; C/Sgt Lloyd B W, McLennan; C/Sgt Lockhart K D, Innisfail; C/WO2 Lyon A R, Edson.

Cadet Marco B C, Lacombe; Cadet McCord G D, Eckville; Cadet McGinnis R, Innisfail; Cadet Maes L R L J, Calgary; C/S/Sgt Magilton W J, Lacombe; Cadet Martin B, Strathmore; Cadet Mathews C R, Medicine Hat; Cadet Muzurenko L F, Radway; C/Bdr Meeres E R, Red Deer; Cadet Mericle

488

D A H, Calgary; Cadet Metfle K, Sunnybrook; Cadet Miller H W, Montgomery; C/L/Cpl Mitton B R, Calgary; Cadet Moisan H J A, St. Paul; Cadet Moore W S, Fort St. John, B.C.; Cadet Morrison R T C, Calgary; Cadet Mottus A R, Eckville; Cadet Moulding R F, Calgary; Cadet Mullan D M, Hobbema; Cadet Myrehaug P, Sedgewick; Cadet MacDonald K, Bellevue; Cadet McCartney R, Breton; Cadet McCord R A, Eckville; Cadet McGuire W, Gleichen; Cadet McIndoe D B, Calgary; C/WO2 McMahon W E, Calgary.

Cpl Nelson D K, Edgerton; C/Capt Nicholson D V, Edmonton; C/Sgt Nunn J R, Edmonton; C/Cpl Nurcombe J G, Innisfail; Cadet Oborne W M, Eckville; C/S/Sgt O'Brien G T, Calgary; Sgt Olson D A, Beaverlodge; C/Cpl Osberg G, Bellov; C/Cpl Palechek P R, Hobbema; C/Bdr Palamarek T, Waskatewau; Cadet Palmer F, Calgary; Cadet Parkin G E, Brocket; C/Cpl Parsons L R, Rocky Mtn. House; Cadet Patten D, Sedgewick; Cadet Patterson E, Red Deer; Cadet Paul C, Calgary; C/L/Bdr Peraske D A, Edmonton; Cadet Pollock E W, Edson; C/L/Bdr Pollock W M, Red Deer; C/Cpl Price D J, Mercoal; Cadet Pomerleau J E, Westlock; C/Sgt Pool T R, Beaverlodge.

C/Sgt Rathwell J H, Redcliff; Cadet Red Crow H, Cardston; C/L/Cpl Redhead R E, Fort St. John, B.C.; Cadet Reid H G, Edmonton; Cadet Robideau A, Grande Prairie; C/L/Bdr Robson C J, Calgary; C/L/Cpl Rogers D B, Calgary; Cadet Rogers D, Delburne; Cadet Romboug B H, Sedgewick; L/Cpl Rombough L, Sedgewick; Cadet Ropchan A A, Edmonton; Cadet Russell A, Calgary.

C/Cpl Sailer G, Medicine Hat; C/Cpl Sakalluk R H, Vegreville; Cpl Saunders R B, Edmonton; Cadet Saxby D J, Vulcan; Cadet Schepanovich B, Edson; C/Sgt Sewell C J, Calgary; C/L/Cpl Schulze R A, Stetler; C/Sgt Sewell C J, Calgary; Cadet Shaw T J W J, Calgary; Cadet Shields W, Edmonton; Cadet Shevolup M E, Waskatenau; Cadet Shupe D W, Gleichen; Cadet Sibbet G E, Lethbridge; L/Cpl Sivertsen K R, Edmonton; C/L/Cpl Smith M A, Vegreville; C/S/Sgt Shvkora O, Radway; Cadet Soltesz D J, Westlock; WO2 Sorensen P J, Edmonton; Cadet Squarek J, Bellevak; Cadet Stauffer K R, Turner Valley; Cadet Stewart A W, Lethbridge; Cadet Stewart J H, Lethbridge; C/L/Cpl Stewart J W, Beaverlodge; Cadet Strader W L, Black Diamond; Cpl Stutchbury W G, Westlock.

Cadet Tail Feathers P R, Cardston; C/Sgt Tannas K W, St. Paul; C/L/Bdr Taylor R, Calgary; Cadet Tew A L, Gladner Park; Cadet Thomson M, Innisfail; Cadet Townsend R W, Edmonton; Cadet Trask G, Canmore; Cadet Trout J E, Bashaw; Cadet Ursel G H, Calgary; Cadet Vaselenak G M, Lethbridge.

Cadet Wagner A J, Innisfail; Cadet Wall R B, Fawcett; Cadet Wallace R E, Innisfail; C/Lt Walsh D F, Calgary; Cadet Wanchulak D, Edmonton; C/Cpl Webber M H, Edmonton; Cadet Weiss A, Medicine Hat; C/Sgt Wills F J, Edmonton; C/L/Cpl Wells W, Cardston; Cadet Wernicke K, Edmonton; L/Cpl Whitford R, Vilna; Cadet Wickens G J, Rocky Mtn. House; Cadet Wiesner L, Yeaford; Cadet Wilcox T L C, Edmonton; Cadet Williams M L, Bucks; C/Cpl Williamson F A, Yellowknife; C/Sgt Wilson J E, Vegreville; Cadet Wilson L R, Vegreville; L/Cpl Wilson K M, Sedgewick; Cadet Wilson W J, Waskatenau; Cadet Wilson W T, Lacombe;

Cadet Wintermute R, McLennan; C/Bdr Withers D W, Red Deer; Cadet Wolf Leg A, Gleichen; L/Cpl Zacharuk L E, Vilna; Cadet Zaharko R J, Sunnybrook; C/L/Cpl Zbryskie R J, Strathmore; Cadet Dubois P E, Cluny.

D & M WING

C/Cpl Ambrose P T, Fort St. John, B.C.; C/Sgt Babiak B, Mercoal; Cadet Bebsib R H, Vulcan; Cadet Brown M L, Beaverlodge; S/Sgt Coombe H M, Edmonton; C/Sgt Cox H E, Beaverlodge; Cadet Crane Bear G, Cluny; C/Sgt Cruikshank G G, Edmonton; C/Cpl Cunningham W E H, Calgary; C/L/Bdr Cadman A E, Vancouver; C/Lt Dacyshyn A, Radway; C/L/Bdr Davenport F J W, Red Deer; C/Cpl Duda R W, Grande Prairie; C/Sgt English J A, Delburne; C/L/Cpl Fisher G L, Stettler; Cadet Flack D N, Mannville; Cadet Flathen M J, Lethbridge; C/Sgt Gorveatt M J C, Turner Valley; Cadet Gibson F J, Calgary; Cadet Gilmour D M, Calgary; C/L/Bdr Griffiths R K, Calgary; L/Cpl Guest G W, Westlock; C/Cpl Hambling R J, Calgary; Cadet Hall J O, Edmonton; C/Rfn Harrylock R A, Calgary; Cadet Heaton D L, Lacombe; Cadet Hooper D S, Sedgewick; C/L/Cpl Hopp A L, Lacombe; Cadet Hopper J, Edmonton; Cadet Ironmonger B, Hillcrest; C/Bdr Johnston C F, Calgary; C/Sgt Kingston V S, Fort MacLeod.

Cadet Laughy R H, Wanham; Cadet Little Bear G, Cardston; C/Lt Little Bear M, Cardston; Cadet Loewen D, Edmonton; C/WO2 Maisey K B, Okotoks; L/Bdr Madsen J, Edmonton; Cadet Martin E J, Redcliff; Cadet Miller W G, Alliance; C/Sgt Mungall B A, McLennan; C/Cpl MacDougal G, Lethbridge; C/Sgt McCulley G, Medicine Hat; Cadet McLaren D R, Lethbridge; C/Cpl McLeod G E, Mercoal; C/Cpl Novosad J G, Edmonton; Cadet O'Driscoll R R, St. Paul.

Cadet Pardely E R, Vegreville; Cadet Patsula T, Edmonton; Cadet Pickering E R J, Spirit River; Cadet Ramsay R F, Edgerton; L/Cpl Ray D T, Edmonton; C/Sgt Rovensky P E, Coronation; C/Lt Scarlett R, Medicine Hat; Cadet Sharkey J E, Mulhurst; Cadet Shave G H, Breton; C/Cpl Taylor L C, Stavely; C/WO2 Thornton R W, Cardston; Cadet Traptow S W, Bashaw; Cpl Wild E R, Hobbema; Cadet Wilson L K, Edson; C/Cpl Woody D D, Coronation; C/Cpl Zak R J, Coleman.

INFANTRY SIGNALLER

C/Sgt Barager G A, Thorsby; C/Cpl Behm M, Vilna; Cadet Blize H, Warburg; C/Sgt Coast E R, Mercoal; L/Cpl Colbourne F J, Westlock; L/Cpl Davis D N, Sedgewick; Cadet Dean W R C, Edmonton; C/Sgt Ditchburn L R, Innisfail; L/Cpl Ferguson B R, Clyde; Cadet Fishbourne T J, Edmonton; Cadet Forister R C, Olds; Cadet Gascoyne W, Sedgewick; L/Cpl Hawthorne L, McLennan; C/L/Cpl Hoppus K A, Lacombe; Cadet Hyder M L, Clyde; Cadet Ingham W S, Griesbactt; C/L/Cpl Iwasiw T J, Coleman; Cadet Johnson R W, Edson.

C/Sgt Kingston A J, Fort MacLeod; Cadet Koehil G, Sedgewick; Cadet Krause G, Calgary; Cadet Leavens D J G, Edmonton; Cadet Logan B, Edmonton; C/Sgt Odorico M, Fort St. John, B.C.; Cadet MacKenzie T, Edmonton; Cadet MacLaughlin L A W, Edmonton; Cadet Papp L J, Delburne; C/Lt Panther Bone L, Cardston; C/Bdr Parkyn M, Calgary; Cadet Perrault L

G, Delburne; C/L/Cpl Prokopchuk A, Fort St. John, B.C.; Cadet Sauve D J, St. Paul; C/Sgt Shields T, Grande Prairie; C/L/Cpl Sokoloski D M, Vegreville; Cadet Sprang R J. Flatbush; C/Cpl Sugden E A, Calgary; Cadet Walker K R, Alliance; C/Cpl West B L, Edmonton; C/Cpl Williams B K, Edgerton; L/Cpl Wilkins G E, Westlock; C/Cpl Jackshaw C C, Bashaw; Cadet Zotek P B, Vilna.

Here're Names Of The Staff

Officers of the Instructional and Administrative Staff of Camp this year were:

Brig Kitching G, Maj Murdoch E St J, Maj Sharpe J G, Maj Trimble H A, Maj Jamieson V C, Capt Arnold A E, Capt Avery A D, Capt Beecher B H, Capt Crawford B B, Capt DeRochie G R, Capt Doherty H A, Capt Douthwaite P L C, Capt Dressler R, Capt Finnigan N O, Capt Gornall R J, Capt Harcus T E, Capt Harlos R E, Capt Henderson O R, Capt Jamieson G T, Capt Langley D M, Capt Marles J D, Capt Murphy R H, Capt MacMillan H R, Capt McKellar R C, Capt McLean K J, Capt Neelin R G, Capt Oram F H C, Capt Preston R C, Capt Roberts L W, Capt Robertson D M, Capt Saunders D A, Capt Seiferling C, Capt Thomas E W, Capt Watton M G, Capt Woodley W R, Lt Arkwright V H, Lt Boldt P A, Lt Campbell J D, Lt Clarke R W, Lt Cranston J A, Lt David J A, Lt Dick K A, Lt Dahlquist H F, Lt Duvarney H F, Lt Duyvewaardt E E, Lt Fisher R C, Lt Foy F C, Lt Gregorash J C, Lt Hawkins R C S, Lt Hobbs G W, Lt Holt G A, Lt Hook J W, Lt Jones W H, Lt LeBlond C M, Lt MacInnis J O, Lt McCallum F L, Lt McDermid J M, Lt McGilp J G, Lt McNeill W B, Lt Minnis J W, Lt Moysa W. Lt (NS) Pelletier M, Lt Pickersgill W F, Lt Robinson D G, Lt Rogers G D, Lt Rogers S T, Lt Roper L A, Lt Thornton R H, Lt Walton D T, Lt (NS) Warren E M, Lt Wilde J H, Lt Wray H, Lt Yuzwa P F G.

2/Lt Auvigne L R, 2/Lt Bernard L, 2/Lt Desjardins M E, 2/Lt Fortier R, 2/Lt Glock H A, 2/Lt Lander A B, Mr (Lt) Hughes G E, Mr (Lt) Inkster J D, Mr (Lt) Phare S, Mr (Lt) Quesnell E A, Mr (2/Lt) Bolton J B, Mr (2/Lt) Brisco G E, Lt Mancinelli E, Capt Majakey J, Lt Johnson S, 2/Lt Dubb W R.

VACC - 1957

The following cadets attended camp during the summer:

BRITISH COLUMBIA

D & M WING

C/Cpl Anderson D M, Victoria; Cdt Anderson G K, Vancouver; C/Sgt Arkwright B P, Port Alberni; Cdt Beattie J R, North Vancouver; C/L Cpl Bennett R, North Surrey; C/L Bdr Black G S, Vancouver; Bdr Bond M, Vancouver; C/L Cpl Britt J E, Vancouver; C/Sgt Buckle H, Victoria; C/WO2 Campbell T T, N. Burnaby; Cdt Charlie W, Enderby.

C/Cpl Christie G J, Vernon; Cdt Duncan G A, Vancouver; Cdt Fleury B L, Vancouver; C/Sgt Frandsen C, Salmon Arm; C/Sgt Goodman M J, N. Burnaby; C/Sgt Hamilton B J, N. Vancouver; Cdt Hanna F S, Lytton; Cdt Hol H J, Richmond; C/Sgt Holder B C, Chilliwack; C/Sgt Hyndman B L, Cloverdale; Cdt Israel J, N. Vancouver; C/WO1 Jakubec GJM, Burnaby; C/L Cpl Johnston L, Salmon Arm; C/WO2 Johnston J P, W. Vancouver. C/Sgt Johnston P G C, Sidney; C/L Bdr Kurucz R J, Vancouver; Cdt Lofgren R A, Vancouver; C/Cpl Mabu W B, Cloverdale; C/S Sgt Moore T J E, New Westminster; Cdt Morris L F C, N. Burnaby; C/L Bdr MacAulay D, Vancouver; C/Sgt MacKay D L, Haney; C/L/Cpl Petterson B L, Vancouver; C/S/Sgt Phillips G L, Richmond; C/Cpl Rhodes K, Port Alberni. C/Cpl Rice Jones J R, Salmon Arm; C/S gt Robinson G M, W. Vancouver; C/WO 2 Singh L K, Vancouver; C/Cpl Slavinski G C, Cloverdale; C/Cpl Stoddard J L, Burnaby; C/Cpl Symington A T M, W. Vancouver; C/Sgt Timms R L, N. Vancouver; C/Sgt Urquhart J, Salmon Arm; Cdt Van Santvoord A M, Vancouver; C/Cpl Waite G P, Victoria; C/L Cpl Waterson R A, Vancouver; C/Lt Whale W E, Salmon Arm.

INFANTRY SIGNALLER

Cdt Bennett A J, Armstrong; C/Cpl Fearn J W, Mission; C/WO 2 Lines J E, Revelstoke; C/Cpl Mayert E J J, Revelstoke; Cdt McMillin J C, Vancouver; C/L Cpl Roy J A, Coldstream; Cdt Smith R G, Vernon; C/Sgt Whitehead J C, Hammond; Cdt Freeman G D, Vernon.

SENIOR LEADER

Cdt Abflater R F, Nelson; C/Cpl All exander D S, Vancouver; Cdt Allen D P, Nechako PO; Cdt Annis C G, Vedder Crossing; C/L Cpl Armenceau W D, Vancouver; Cdt Avery D A, Vancouver; C/Cpl Back D, Haney; Cdt Barclay P B, Victoria; Cdt Barnes D W, Victoria; Cdt Baxter L, N. Vancouver; Cdt Beddows D, Chemainus; Cdt Bedford W C, Haney. Cdt Bell D R, Richmond; Cdt Bennett D W, Armstrong; Cdt Benson R G, New Westminster; C/Sgt Beswick R W, Vancouver; Cdt Biles H A, Victoria; Cdt Bishop C W F, Vancouver; Cdt Boletta J R, Vancouver; C/Sgt Bolton D W, Lytton; Cdt Bond P W, Nelson; Cdt Boonstra H, Matsqui; Cdt Boonstra W, Matsqui; Cdt Boote D K, Vancouver; C/Cpl Boquist A B, Port Alberni. C/Cpl Bosmans J, New Westminster; Cdt Braun A, Vancouver; Cdt Brewer R, Lumby; Cdt Britt G R, Vancouver; C/L/Cpl Brodie L E, Vancouver; Cdt Brown D C, Vancouver; Cdt Bruce S, W. Summerland; C/Cpl Burgess D K, Vancouver; Cdt Calver T R, Salmon Arm; C/Cpl Cayer L H, Port Alberni; Cdt Chisholm J A, Rossland; Cdt Clark A D, Courtenay; Cdt Clark A G, Vancouver; C/L Cpl Clarke B, N. Burnaby. Cdt Clarke H L, Vernon; Cdt Collins J P, Victoria; C/Sgt Conway D, N. Vancouver; Cdt Copp T J, Vancouver; Cdt Cornett J R, N. Burnaby; C/L Cpl Coward J A, Sidney; Cdt Cox D T, Vancouver; Cdt Coxe P N, Armstrong.

C/Cpl Craig G B, Whonnock; Cdt Cunnington J A, Armstrong; C/Cpl

Curl R G, West Saanich Rd; C/Bdr Le Meulenaere M, New Denver; Cdt De Mitri P A, Vancouver; Cdt Desmarais N G, Vancouver; Cdt Dewhurst R E, N. Vancouver; Cdt Dickey G R, Vancouver; Cdt Dixon D E, New Westminster.

Cdt Doty K E, N. Vancouver; Cdt Edginton R, Vancouver; C/CSM Edl G F, Abbotsford; C/S Sgt Elrick D A, Esquimalt; C/Sgt Elrick R G, Esquimalt; C/L Cpl Erickson O C R, Port Kells; C/Cpl Evans E R, Kelowna; C/Cpl Fleck J F, Kelowna; Cdt Fleming J R, N. Vancouver; Cdt Finnigan B W, New Westminster; C/L Cpl Firth D B, N. Vancouver; C/L Cpl Fitz-Gerald P J, N. Vancouver; Cdt Ford R J, N. Vancouver; C/Cpl Forrest W G, N. Vancouver; Cdt Fortin L P, Victoria.

Cdt Foster E D, Vancouver; C/Sgt Fraser H P, N. Vancouver; Cdt Friesan R D, Nelson; Cdt Friesen J F, Vancouver; C/Cpl Frost W C, Royal Oak; Cdt Gagnon G V P, N. Burnaby; Cdt Gebbie N W, N. Vancouver; C/Sgt Glover L M, Abbotsford; Cdt Goodings D C, Chemainus; Cdt Grant W H, S. Burnaby; Cdt Green D C, Alberni; C/Cpl Griffin N E, Victoria; C/Sgt Halabourda R G, Vancouver; C/WO 2 Hallam T D, Victoria; C/Cpl Hall R W, Kitimat.

C/L Cpl Ham W D, Vancouver; Cdt Hannah G W, Brentwood Bay; Cdt Harkies W, Merritt; C/L Cpl Haskins A H, Courtenay; Cdt Haswell R M, New Westminster; C/Cpl Healy J C, Quesnel; C/L Cpl Hennessy R N, Ladner; Cdt Henry S, Lytton; C/L Cpl Hickamn W D, Nechako PO, Kitimat.

Cdt Hicks R H, Canoe; Cdt Hitchens B F, Victoria; C/L Cpl Hodson B R, Vancouver; C/Cpl Hopkins G F, Westbank; Cdt Hunter G W, Vancouver; Cdt Henson K, Canoe; C/Sgt Jorgensen G D, Salmon Arm; Cdt Johanson A, S. Burnaby; C/L Bdr Jones B L, N. Vancouver; C/Cpl Johnson D L, Victoria; Cdt Kapchinsky R L, Port Alberni; Cdt Kelly L J, Vancouver; Cdt Kingzett P J W, Quesnel.

Cdt Knutsvik D L, Kitimat; C/Cpl Ksik T J, Mission; Cdt Kyle J H, Burnaby; Cdt Kyler C M, New Westminster; Cdt Laliberte R W, New Westminster; C/L Cpl Lamy G N, Vancouver; Cdt Lane A B, Rossland; Cdt Lapp G E, Chemainus; C/Sgt Lawrence J B, Victoria; Cdt Leclerc L J, New Westminster; Cdt Lee R, N. Vancouver; Cdt Lemasurier G D, Vancouver; Cdt Leroux A F, Whonnock.

Cdt Louis N, Vancouver; Cdt Lumb J N, Vancouver; C/L Cpl McClure W E, Port Alberni; Cdt McConnell G E, S. Burnaby; Cdt McCrory W P, New Denver; Cdt McDougall J L, Vancouver; Cdt McDowell T, Vedder Crossing; C/L Cpl McIntyre O J, New Westminster; Cdt McKenzie K J, Ladner; C/WO 2 McKinley N, Armstrong; Cdt MacKinnon D L, Victoria; Cl/L Cpl McLennan L H, New Westminster.

Cdt McNeil W, Vancouver; Cdt McRae H, New Westminster; Cdt McRae J H, Ladner; C/L Cpl McRae W A, North Surrey; Cdt Madison P R, Cloverdale; C/L Cpl Marr D R, N. Vancouver; C/L Cpl Marshall C G, Vancouver; Cdt Mason B. W, Nelson; C/Cpl Mate M J, N. Burnaby; Cdt Matheson C E, Quesnel; Cdt Miller G D, Vancouver; Cdt Moore G, Penticton.

Cdt Moore J K, Vancouver; C/L Bdr Mori K, New Denver; Cdt Morris W D, Victoria; C/Sgt Moseley P D, Victoria;

Cdt Moth L R, Burnaby; Cdt Mowatt D J, N. Burnaby; Cdt Neil M E, Rossland; Cdt Nelson A, Vancouver; Cdt Nelson D C, Vancouver; Cdt Nelson R J A, Vancouver; Cdt Nelson R J O, N. Burnaby; Cdt Netzer E, Alberni; C/Cpl Newham K R, Abbotsford; C/L Cpl Nickle J, Sardis; Cdt Nomm M, N. Vancouver; Cdt O'Connor D, Vancouver; C/Cpl Oliver D T, S. Burnaby.

Cdt Olney G J, Vancouver; C/L Cpl Oswald D L, Vancouver; C/Sgt Ouellette B R, Victoria; Cdt Paine M A, Victoria; Cdt Paterson L, Vancouver; Cdt Patrick P J, Vancouver; C/L Cpl Patterson G H, Vancouver; Cdt Pearson G D, Sidney; Cdt Pelkey T B, N. Surrey; Cdt Phillips R M, Lytton; Cdt Piper W A, White Rock; C/Cpl Ponting C J, Aldergrove; Cdt Pope N E, Armstrong; Cdt Preston W L, Vancouver.

Cdt Price W, Alberni; Cdt Ralph D W, Victoria; C/L Cpl Ramage N F, Sardis; C/Cpl Read L G, Alberni; Cdt Robb R J, Vancouver; C/Sgt Rothwell K A, Victoria; Cdt Roulston R B, N. Vancouver; Cdt Roy R A, Vancouver; C/Bdr Ryan F A, Vancouver; Cdt Ryan W M, Victoria; Cdt Rye B E, Quesnel; C/L Cpl Salmon G M, Vancouver; Cdt Shaw G B, Lillooet; Cdt Sheridan J C, Burnaby; Cdt Shoolingtin D D, Duncan; C/Cpl Shussell J J, Kelowna; Cdt Slack J, Cloverdale.

C/Sgt Sloan M H, Victoria; Cdt Slavinski E B, Cloverdale; Cdt Spelchan J G, Armstrong; Cdt Spetch F W, Mt. Currie; Cdt Stallard J P, Penticton; C/Sgt Steadman D J, Victoria; C/L Cpl Stewart D R, Vancouver; Cdt Stewart G A, Port Alberni; Cdt Stewart J, Vancouver; Cdt Stewart W G, Nelson; Cdt Strand W W, Vancouver; Cdt Street E D, Burnaby; Cdt Strong L R, Vancouver; Cdt Takenaka N, New Denver.

C/L Cpl Tarasoff D W, Cobble Hill; C/L Cpl Taylor D N, Ladner; Cdt Taylor J D, Sidney; C/Cpl Tempest E, Duncan; Cdt Terry S J, Lillooet; Cdt Thomson R J, Vancouver; Cdt Towers J E, Comox VD; C/L Cpl Towse K G, Vancouver; Cdt Turner L M, Merville; Cdt Turner R E, Victoria; Cdt Van Dresar J, Vernon; Cdt Verier R, New Westminster; Cdt Walch R A, Victoria; Cdt Walden J W, Vancouver; C/Sgt Walker R E, Victoria; Cdt Walton T H, Vancouver; Cdt Webber L J, Salmon Arm; Cdt Weiss J L, Vancouver.

Cdt Write W M, Vancouver; Cdt Whittaker B A, Vancouver; Cdt Wilkins B, Kitimat; C/Cpl Williams H R H, Courtenay; C/Cpl Wilson J A, Pr. Rupert; C/Cpl Withrow J D, Vancouver; Cdt Wood D G, Saanichton; C/L Cpl Yano V T, Paldi; Cdt Zagersky E, W. Vancouver; Cdt Zemek R J, Chemainus.

SENIOR LEADER INSTRUCTORS

C/L Cpl Burgess D N, Vancouver; C/Sgt Burgess W J, Burnaby; C/L Cpl Byers L J, Vedder Crossing; C/Sgt Clegg M G, Cloverdale; C/WO 2 Cumming B R, N. Vancouver; C/Sgt Davis A F, Vancouver; C/Sgt Dean D M, Vancouver; C/WO 1 Fowler R M, Vancouver; Cdt Gillan R D, Vancouver; C/Sgt Hardin A H, Kitimat; C/Sgt King J P, N. Vancouver; C/Cpl Koronko P, Vernon.

Cdt L'Ami D W, Surrey; C/Sgt Lee S W, Paldi; C/WO2 Lyon R J, Vancouver; C/WO2 Mosdell D L, N. Vancouver; C/Sgt Murphy J, Vancouver; C/Sgt Schmidt W E, Vancouver; C/Bdr Thorn C, Surrey; C/Sgt Trapnel R H, Victoria; C/Sgt Walker D A, Burnaby.

BAND

Cdt Adams W H, N. Vancouver; Cdt Ballard J R, Port Alberni; Cdt Bolton L A, Pr. Rupert; Cdt Brown R, Vancouver; Cdt Calder R, Pr. Rupert; Cdt Cuzner R F, Victoria; Cdt Dawson R E, Victoria; C/Sgt Dick D R, N. Vancouver; C/Sgt Gislason C W, Vancouver; Cdt Goswell J, Pr. Rupert; Cdt Green H S, Pr. Rupert; Cdt Guno R, Pr. Rupert; Cdt Hannah R S, Victoria.

Cdt Isaac G A, Lytton; C/Cpl Isaac T B, Lytton; Cdt Kember P A, N. Vancouver; C/L Cpl Kennedy L W, Alberni; Cdt Lowe R T, N. Vancouver; Cdt McIntosh T R, Port Alberni; C/Cpl McKay J, Greenville; Cdt McLean D W, N. Vancouver; Cdt Machelle G C, Lytton; C/D/Maj Martin W A, Pr. Rupert; Cdt Marvin H B, Pr. Rupert; C/Sgt Nelson A E, Vancouver; Cdt Newell L, N. Vancouver; Cdt Oakley J K, N. Vancouver; C/Sgt Patterson G A, Vancouver; C/L Cpl Scodane A, Pr. Rupert; Cdt Scodane P, Pr. Rupert; C/L Cpl Tweedy R C, N. Vancouver; Cdt. White C L, N. Vancouver.

ALBERTA

D & M WING

C/Cpl Benson R H, Vilna; Cdt Bohnet W T, Medicine Hat; C/Sgt Brabant W J; C/Lt Chapman G J, Edson; C/Sgt Davidson G A, Edmonton; C/Cpl Failler L P, Coleman; Cdt Finch A E, Stettler; Cdt Geddes D W, Alliance; C/Lt Good Striker W M, Cardston; C/A Cpl Jacobson G W, Rocky Mtn. House; PO MC Cdt Kilpatrick G W, Edmonton; C/L Bdr Lane L R; C/L Cpl Martin B J, Strathmore; C/Cpl Novosad J G, Edmonton; C/Cpl Nurcombe J, Innisfail; C/Sgt Reid H G; C/Cpl Rogers D B, Calgary; C/S Sgt Schepanovich B, Edson; C/Cpl Strader W L, Black Diamond; Cdt Tail Feathers, Cardston. C/WO2 Wall R B, Fawcett; C/Sgt Vaselenak G M, N. Lethbridge; C/L Cpl Zacharuk L E, Edmonton; C/Cpl Zaharko R J, Sunnybrook; C/Sgt Zbryski R J, Strathmore.

INFANTRY SIGS

Cdt Ahlstrom R J, Edmonton; C/L Cpt Bedford D W, Edgerton; C/Lt Behm M, Vilna; C/Cpl Bell J A, Calgary; Cdt Berry T, Cranbrook; Cdt Blue J A, Edmonton; Cdt Brauti D, Criesbach; Cdt Church A R, Rocky Mtn. House; C/WO2 Clarke J G, Vulcan; C/S Sgt Cumming N E, Canmore; C/Sgt Duffy S E, Edmonton; C/Cpl Dunlop M A, Thorsby; C/Cpl Fudger B W, Calgary; Cdt Gascoyne S F, Sedgewick; C/Cpl Hyder M L, Clyde.

Cdt MacKinnon R, Edmonton; Cdt MacLeod E T, Edson; C/S Sgt Meeres E R, Red Deer; Cdt Palmer F G, Calgary; Cdt Pappes K J, Edmonton; Cdt Paul C B, Calgary; Cdt Peters R D, Cdt Rosko M J, Vegreville; C/Sgt Shupe D W, Bleichen; C/Lt Shykora O, Radway; C/L Cpl Soltys R W, Calgary; C/Sgt Sprang R J, Flatbush; C/S Sgt Squarek J E, Belleview; Cdt Stroud B, Edmonton; Cdt Tweedy L D, Sedgewick; Cdt Wallace R E, Innisfail; C/WO2 Walsh D F; Cdt Ward W G, Edmonton; C/A Sgt Wickens J G, Rocky Mtn. House; C/Cpl Wilcox T L, Edmonton; Cdt Wild R E, Gleichen; C/L Cpl Womacks G E, Edmonton.

SENIOR LEADERS

Cdt Albert J, Edmonton; C/L Cpl Anderson G T, Calgary; Cdt Allen J A, Edson; Cdt Amyotte A A, Mallaig; Cdt Anderson R E, Cranbrook; C/Bdr Anderson T O, Cranbrook; C/Cpl Armstrong L H, Edson; Cdt Armstrong P, Edmonton; Cdt Arneson J R, Stettler; Cdt Baksa C B, Calgary; Cdt Ballantyne R B, Edmonton Cdt Barnes R, McLennan; C/Cpl Batter J E, Beaver Lodge; Cdt Beauregard E, Edmonton.

Cdt Bell A, St. Paul; C/Sgt Berry P F, Lethbridge; Cdt Birston V, Montgomery; C/L Cpl Bleskan G J, Banff; C/Cpl Blize L H, Warburg; C/L Cpl Bobier R L, Bellot; C/Cpl Boe E K, Beaver Lodge; C/L Cpl Bosch H, Killam; C/Cpl Botnen D R, Edson; Cdt Boychuk S, Radway; Cdt Bray B E, Medicine Hat; Cdt Briscoe N R, Jasper Place; Cdt Brown F W, Edmonton.

Cdt Brown R, Westlock; C/L Cpl Brown R C, Stettler; C/Cpl Buffalo V F, Hobbema; Cdt Buffalo V S, Hobbema; C/Sgt Burns R J, Calgary; Cdt Carriere C L, Calgary; C/Cpl Christenson E H, Manville; Cdt Christenson J L, Sedgewick; Cdt Christie R M, Edson; Cdt Clarke R A, Sedgewick; C/Cpl Clements R G, Calgary; C/S Sgt Coast E R, Mercoal; Cdt Collard V A, Redcliff; C/Sgt Connolly D C, Calargy; Cdt Conrad E K, Griesbach; Cdt Cooper M B, Calgary.

Cdt Craig C D, Nanton; C/L Cpl Cutknife H, Hobbema; Cdt Davis H G, Red Deer; C/L Cpl Day W, Westlock; C/Cpl Dean W R C, Edmonton; C/Sgt Dechaine P A, Mallaig; Cdt Deib R W, Seba Beach; Cdt Demarce E J T, Royalties; C/Cpl Demarce J A, Turner Valley; Cdt Dillon R; Cdt Donaldson M E, Cranbrook; C/Cpl Dornan F, Thorsby; Cdt Doucette L L, Calgary; Cdt Dove R C, Calgary; Cdt Dowdeswell C C, Calgary; Cdt Drabble L G, Calgary; Cdt Eastman J S, Calgary.

Cdt Eriksen A, Calgary; Cdt Fix L M, Stettler; C/Cpl Fliczuk J G, Vegreville; C/Sgt Flug B G, Redcliff; Cdt Foley T, Vegreville; Cdt Folk J W, Edson; Cdt Forai J E, Canmore; Cdt Foster K L, Midnapore; Cdt Frigon R, Edmonton; Cdt Frizzel D L, Red Deer; Cdt Fujiwara Y F, Cayley; Cdt Galbraith J W, Edmonton; C/Bdr Georgeson G J, Banff; Cdt Gervais D E, Calgary; Cdt Goddens W W, Medicine Hat; C/L Cpl Gilmour D M, Downess. C/L Cpl Glenn R J, Spirit River; Cdt Glettig M, Edmonton; Cdt Goble K B, Edmonton; C/Bdr Goodall P R, Calgary; Cdt Good Eagle J, Cluny; C/Cpl Good Eagle L, Cluny; Cdt Greenslade R L, Edmonton; C/L Cpl Guest W, Westlock; C/Bdr Gunn A A, Calgary; C/A Cpl Hagen D E, Red Deer; Cdt Haines C D, Calgary; Cdt Halun N, Radway; C/S Sgt Hambling R J, Calgary; Cdt Hamby E H, Calgary.

Cdt Hamilton D A, Yellowknife, NWT; Cdt Hamula P L, Thorsby; C/L Cpl Hanna J, Winfield; Cdt Hansen K, Breton; Cdt Hawthorne D, Edmonton; C/Cpl Hawthorne L N; Cdt Healy R, Cardston; Cdt Heavener J R, Creston, B.C.; C/L Cpl Henderson K S, Calgary; C/Cpl Hoffman R R, Thorsby; C/Bdr Holloway F P, Brocket; Cdt Holmes R H, Edmonton; Cdt Horie P J, Cranbrook, B.C.; Cdt Houle V A, Jarvie; C/L Cpl Hull W J, Spirit River; C/L Cpl Hutchison R, Lacombe; Cdt Jacobi A O, Seba Beach; Cdt Jamieson D J, Edmonton.

C/Cpl Jensen J, Fawcett; C/Sgt Johnson R W, Edson; Cdt Jordan J W,

Bellevue; Cdt Kepke K E, Edmonton; C/L Cpl Kilgour P, East Pine, B.C.; Cdt Kinsella R W, Edmonton; Cdt Kirby R A, Bowness; C/L Cpl Kirkland G A, McLennan;.Cdt Klassen R H, Calgary; Cdt Knight R G, McLennan; C/Bdr Knowlton W M, Peigan Indian; C/L Cpl Kolpak L K, Lethbridge; Cdt Konschuh J R, Stettler; Cdt Kozoriz J, Edmonton; Cdt Krikken E J, Calgary; Cdt Ladwig F P, Red Deer; C/Cpl Laidler T P, Mannville.

C/L Cpl Manning F R, Lethbridge; C/Cpl Martin R, Lethbridge; C/WO 2 Martin R H, Maillag; C/Sgt Martin W A, Maillag; Cdt Maskell W A, Edmonton; Cdt Maurstad J H, Namaka; Cdt Mayer L, Calgary; Cdt Megli H L, Coleman;Cdt Meilleur W L M, Calgary; Cdt Michaud H J, Maillag; Cdt Milbraith A R, Edmonton; Cdt Mills L, Cardston; Cdt Mills R, Cardston; Cdt Millward H F B, Wainwright; C/Cpl Moisan H, St Paul.

Cdt Nason G E, Red Deer; Cdt Navratil J P; Clyde; C/L Cpl Nichol C N, Beaverlodge; Cdt Nichol J H, Edgerton; Cdt Nielsen B D P, Hose Creek; Cdt Nitz J F, Griesbach; Cdt Noble H L, Calgary; Cdt Odegard W M, Alliance; C/Cpl Oginski R, Edmonton; C/Cpl Olsen G E, Calgary; C/Cpl Olsen M, Beaverlodge; C/L Cpl Osborne T A, Fort St John.

Cdt Palmer R F, Griesbach; Cdt Palmer W E, High River; Cdt Parbely E, Vegreville; Cdt Parker C T R, Calgary; C/L Cpl Parker K H, Montney, BC; Cdt Parker O C, Westlock; Cdt Parkin K D, Pincher Creek; C/Sgt Paulet R O, Calgary; Cdt Pearson J P, Bashaw; C/Cpl Peterson D L, Mercoal; Cdt Philpotts J, Edmonton; Cdt Pitzel R, Bereily; C/L Cpl Polachuk L J, Mercoal; Cdt Pope R C, Edmonton; C/L Cpl Powell R C, Delburne; Cdt Pretty Youngman R P, Cluny; Cdt Puhalsky K, Edmonton; C/Cpl Pyne B P, Calgary.

Cdt Radford J. G, Breton; Cdt Ratcliffe R W, Cranbrook, BC; Cdt Renz G L, Creston. BC; Cdt Repetowski G, Grande Prairie or Teepee Creek; Cdt Rezewski L, Vilna; L/Cpl Roberts J A, Westlock; C/Bdr Roberts D W. Cranbrook, BC; Cdt Romano C, Creston, BC; C/Cpl Ross R D, Yellowknife, NWT; Cdt Rothenberger S G, Vegreville; C/L Cpl Rukavina C V, Edson; Cdt Russell S, Cardston.

C/Cpl Schafer W E F, Innisfail; C/L Bdr Schleindl H M, Edmonton; Cdt Schultz J F, Bashaw; C/L Bdr Schwartz D A, Red Deer; Cdt Scout F, Cardston; C/Cpl Seaman R A, Calgary; Cdt Seaman R D, Calgary; C/Cpl Shave V, Thorsby; Cdt Shields A J, Banff; C/L Cpl Siki A, Yellowknife, NWT; Cdt Simmons C W, Edmonton; C/Cpl Sinclair-Smith F S, Midnapore; Cdt Sinkevich W P, Belloy; Cdt Sivertsen R H,

Edmonton; Cdt Slimmon A K, Medicine Hat; C/Cpl Smeltzer H I, Buck Lake; C/Sgt Smith T W, Calgary; Cdt Smith T W, Calgary; Cdt Spurgeon V W, Edson; C/L Cpl Standing at the Door C S, Cluny; Cdt Stockard R L, Lacombe; Cdt Strong D R, Edmonton; C/Cpl Stuckert H W, Banff; C/Cpl Sugden E A, Calgary; Cdt Swampy J C, Hobbema.

C/Cpl Thillman E, Valemount, BC; Cdt Thomas D F, Black Diamond; C/Cpl Tourond D M, Black Diamond; C/Cpl Townsend R W, Edmonton; Cdt Trieber J S, Redcliff; C/L Cpl Tronnes J D, Lacombe; C/L Cpl Tutty C M, Breton; Cdt Vanoni J L, Edmonton; C/Cpl Vedres L G, Lethbridge; Cdt Vrskovy S, Coleman.

C/Bdr Wadsworth L, Cardston; Cdt Walsworth P, Cardston; Cdt Walmsley T A, Flatbush; C/Cpl Walton W L, Calgary; Cdt Wells E, Yoeford; Cdt Wells R, Cardston; Cdt Wessolleck D, Cardston; Cdt Willis H C, Edmonton; C/L Cpl Wilson D C, Calgary; C/L Cpl Wilson L R, Vegreville; Cdt Witwicki G, Radway; Cdt White G E, Calgary; Cdt Wyse K M, Lacombe; Cdt Yagos R S, Hose Creek; C/Bdr Zieffle T H, Pincher Creek; C/Sgt Zotek P B, Vilna.

SENIOR LEADER INSTRUCTORS

C/WO2 Belanger R J, Edgerton; C/S Sgt Boman W F, Hobberman; C/Sgt Boos D, Edmonton; C/Lt Bull Bear D, Gleichen; C/Lt Caston D M, Edson; C/Sgt Duncan R T B, Calgary; C/S Sgt French T B, Nanton; C/WO2 Gorveatt M J C, Millarville; C/WO2 Harrylock R A, Calgary; C/Lt Hunkin D M, Halcourt; C/Sgt Jegou R P, Innisfail; C/CSM Johnson J S, Edmonton; C/WO2 Jones G A, Clyde; C/Sgt Langer L E, Mercoal; C/WO2 Lockhart K D, Innisfail; C/Cpl Mitton R B, Calgary; C/L Cpl Morrison R T C, Calgary; C/S Sgt Ropchan A A, Edmonton; C/Lt Saxby D J, Vulcan; C/Cpl Stewart A W, Lethbridge; Cdt Sven P F, High River; C/Lt Thornton R W, Cardston; C/Cpl Weisner L A.

BAND

Cdt Blank D G, Edmonton; Cdt Bluett J R, Jasper Place; Cdt Brost G R, Westlock; Cdt Clement W E, Edmonton; Cdt Depagie P A, Edmonton; Cdt Favell F J, Edmonton; Cdt Fleck D A, Edmonton; Cdt Gibson A, Westlock; C/Cpl Kovacs M W, Edmonton; Cdt Kroll A F, Westlock; Cdt Lewis P J, Westlock; Cdt Lux R W, Edmonton; C/L Cpl Mohorich R D, Edmonton; Cdt Moore B W, Beverly; Cdt Saver V, Clyde; Cdt Sayers C P, Edmonton; Cdt Steer B, Edmonton; Cdt Thompson R, Westlock; Cdt Zebis B G, Edmonton.

VACC - 1958

BRITISH COLUMBIA
CADET LEADER COURSE

Abra H J, New Westminster; Abrahamson W V, South Burnaby; Airth B P L, Hammond; Akins W L, Abbotsford; Anderson W D, Richmond; Andrieshyn R K, Vancouver; Annis D W, Quesnel; Appleton K D, Vancouver; Armstrong K W, North Vancouver; Armstrong R G, Quesnel; Ashcroft D L, North Vancouver; August R, Kamloops; Augustine S, Vancouver.

Baines A W, Prince George; Balanow

493

W, North Surrey; Ball N J, New Westminster; Bathurst K R, Vancouver; Bayne A R B, Prince George; Beach N, Prince George; Beale J R, Richmond; Beale K A, North Surrey; Beardmore R J, Port Alberni; Beaton C A. Vancouver; Beck G J G, Vancouver; Bellamy D E, Prince George; Benedict G P, Penticton; Birchmore K W, Vancouver; Bird D I, Victoria; Bleckley J S, Burnaby; Boden J C, Vancouver; Bohnen J, Vernon; Bossons A F, Westholme; Boutwell D G, Kelowna; Bowie J R, Armstrong; Bradley S, Royal Oak; Braybrook D A, South Burnaby; Bride T D, Vancouver; Brint A J, Quesnel; Brown F, Lytton; Brown J A, Victoria; Brown P F, North Vancouver; Brown S W, Trail; Burton N W, Vancouver; Butler A B, Armstrong.

Campbell D N, North Vancouver; Campbell E A, Salmon Arm; Campbell G J, Vancouver; Cant C N, Kitimat; Cant R J, Vancouver; Carrington R B, Vancouver; Cavanagh S T, New Westminster; Chadderton N, Cloverdale; Chambers G P, Rossland; Charlie R, Lytton; Chartrand G V, Clearwater; Chesworth D, North Burnaby; Cizik M, Haney; Clark R R, Vedder Crossing; Clayton J R, Victoria; Clement G R, Brentwood Bay; Coburn G, Port Alberni; Condle D W, Vancouver; Conway B, Penticton; Cooper E H, Vancouver; Copp W R, Vancouver; Cummings R, Nelson; Cuthill T, Penticton.

Dahl J E, Salmon Arm; Dalgarno J, Vancouver; Darragh D B A, Vancouver; Davies A F, Alberni; DeBock E; DeBoer R R, Vancouver; Degenstein J, South Burnaby; Demeter E M, Armstrong; Dentrey G, South Haney; Dockray H F, Quesnel; Donnelly R, Clearwater; Doyle D V M, Vancouver; Drake J D, Vancouver; Drummond R Mc, Vernon.

Eckardt D O, Victoria; Eliasen J A, North Surrey; Fairbanks W D; Fairbridge R P, North Burnaby; Fallow W R, Vernon; Findlater R M, Vancouver; Fisher R W, West Vancouver; Fitzer D L, Kamloops; Flintoff M L, Cloverdale; Fong L D, Vancouver; Forbes R J, North Vancouver; Ford W, North Vancouver; Forster R W, Vancouver; Foster D C, Vancouver; Fraser M J, Vancouver; Fulthorp D G, Trail.

Gall R A, Brentwood Bay; Gibbons M S, Victoria; Gibson D I, North Burnaby; Gilette L, North Surrey; Golder H D, Vedder Crossing; Grant P D, West Vancouver; Grimes D F, Victoria; Gross D L, Deroche; Guilbeault C, Vancouver; Gunn D R, Vernon.

Halls J Mc, Victoria; Hamling L W, Courtney; Hampton G, North Vancouver; Harbord D V B, Duncan; Harrigan R W, New Westminster; Harris P, Courtenay; Harrison R J, Trail; Head R C, North Surrey; Helgason G, Mission City; Henderson G D, North Vancouver; Henry F, Lytton; Henry S, Lytton; Hewat M L, Enderby; Hickey G A, Port Alberni; Hudson D M, Lake Errock; Hudson G Mac, Lake Errock; Hugman T B, Vancouver; Hull S H, Duncan.

Ireland L C, Vancouver; Isaac F, Lytton; Isaac G, Lytton; Jensen L R, Hammond; Johnston K R, Clearwater; Johnstone B E, New Westminster; Jones D, Crescent Valley; Jones T, Penticton; Joss W D, Mission City; Keenan R W, Cumberland; Keizer J, Vancouver; Killman C B, Enderby; King E R, Salmon Arm; Klingspohn U, Kitimat; Knowles D W, North Burnaby.

Lake D J, West Vancouver; Landa B

J, Vancouver; Langlois A E, Montrose; Lansdell G R, Vancouver; Lemmers R P, North Vancouver; Lilley V R, Victoria; Lin D, Vancouver; Linden M; Lund P J, Port Alberni; Lynch W J, Haney; Lystar J K, Chemainus.

MacAulay D, Vancouver; MacDonald A W, Bouchie Lake; MacDonald P B, Port Alberni; MacKinnon J G, Richmond; McCall D H, Kelowna; McClafferty D, Vancouver; McCrea G R, North Surrey; McCrory M J, New Denver; McKay E, Prince George; McKelvay D, Vancouver; McLean B M, New Westminster; McLean F P, South Westminster; McPherson D S, Victoria; Macri M, North Vancouver; Magee L S, Sidney; Major R W, Kitimat; Mansell A E, Hammond; Martin D E, Vancouver; Mattice A J, Whonnock; Millar W K, Kelowna; Miller P N, Vancouver; Miller W R, New Westminster; Mills W E, Vancouver; Mitchell E D, Kitimat; Mizener A G E, Burnaby; Monteski T A, Victoria; Mori D, New Denver; Morrison J, Vancouver; Moses F J, Kamloops; Mugford R E, Vancouver; Muir J A, Ladner; Mulcaster F, Victoria; Munroe L, Victoria; Murton R E, Montrose; Myers K B, Victoria.

Narcisse L, Kamloops; Neal G F, Vancouver; Nolan A T, Prince George; Nordmark W, Port Alberni; Norman S E, North Vancouver; Oda A, New Denver; Olsen F E, South Burnaby; Orpwood L D, New Westminster; Otting W G, Armstrong.

Parker J R, Clearwater; Pawson D E, Vancouver; Pearce P C, Prince Rupert; Pearson R J, Vancouver; Pegg J R, Vancouver; Pelletier J D, Vancouver; Peloquin L A, New Westminster; Peters P H, Kamloops; Petersen J L, Westbank; Phillips M, Lytton; Pinter J, Penticton; Pitt D W, Rossland; Poelzer D A, Vancouver; Preston B D, Vancouver; Price A L, New Westminster; Proudlove L, Vancouver; Pye C, Clearwater; Pye T, Clearwater; Quast D E, Prince Rupert.

Rafferty H, Vancouver; Randall W D, Victoria; Ratcliffe C A, Armstrong; Renaud J R, Vancouver; Renstrom J M, Vancouver; Rice W E, Vancouver; Robbins W J, North Burnaby; Roberts D M, Kelowna; Robertson G D, Kitimat; Robertson J D, Kitimat; Robertson K W, Port Alberni; Robinson G J E, Millardville; Robinson W, Merritt; Rockett R F, Victoria; Rooney D L, New Westminster; Roy J A, Vernon; Rudolph A W, Prince Rupert; Rudyk G C, Vancouver; Russell A A, Mission City; Russell J E, Vancouver; Ryan R A, Vancouver.

Saare J R, Rossland; Sam K, Lytton; Sanger W N, Victoria; Schmidt B C, Vancouver; Scorgie N M, Rossland; Senko J, Vancouver; Seton R N, Cloverdale; Shaw R S, Vedder Crossing; Sherdahl G, Vancouver; Shorrock P L, Vancouver; Silverton I F, North Vancouver; Simoni R R, Vancouver; Simpson L E R, Vancouver; Sinclair G W, Victoria; Skinner J G, Victoria; Skinner K E, Vancouver; Slater R M, North Vancouver; Smith C D; Smith D, Richmond; Smith L E, Clearwater; Southen K R, Vancouver; Spaven B W, Victoria; Spraggs L D, Armstrong; Stacey R, Penticton; St Denis M A, Vancouver; Stearns H A, Rossland; Sullivan R W, North Vancouver; Syverson A T, Vancouver; Szentmiklossy F M G, Vancouver.

Takahara R K, New Denver; Takenaka J, New Denver; Tames G W, Nelson; Temple W D, South Burnaby; Thomson D A, Vancouver; Tiernan L A, Salmon

Arm; Tomlin S, Penticton; Tomma W A, Kamloops; Treat L; Trinder R W, Haney; Tucker N L, Chemainus; Turgeon E R, Victoria; Turner K E, Victoria; Van Boeyen D J, Vancouver; Van Boeyen D W, Vancouver.

Waite D A, Richmond; Walker E J, North Vancouver; Watson K D, Abbotsford; Weaver R G, Nelson; Webber V J, Cloverdale; Weening H, Alberni; Whale K, Salmon Arm; White D, North Burnaby; Whittaker S A, Vancouver; Wilkinson M M, Quesnel; Williams J R, North Burnaby; Williamson J H, Cumberland; Wilnechenko L; Wilson K E, Vedder Crossing; Wilson M J, Courtenay; Wood W S, Penticton; Woodward R H, Alberni; York P G R, North Burnaby; Young T W; Young W T, Abbotsford; Younge G A, Duncan; Zomar M K, Abbotsford; Zomar R A, Abbotsford.

CADET LEADER INSTRUCTOR COURSE

Abbott R J, Vedder Crossing; Abfalter R F, Nelson; Armeneau W D, Vancouver; Back D, Haney; Barnes D W, Victoria; Barnes R D, Burnaby; Benson R G, New Westminster; Beswick R W, Vancouver; Biles H A, Victoria; Birch N A, Vancouver; Bishop C W F, Vancouver; Burgess D K L, Vancouver.

DeFaye T F, Esquimault; Elrick R G, Elrick D A, Victoria; Fitz-Gerald P J, North Vancouver; Glover L M, Abbotsford; Griffin N E, Victoria; Hallam T D, Hannah G W, Brentwood Bay; Hennessy R N, Ladner; Hickman W D, Kitimat; King C F, Trail; Gingzett P J W, Quesnel; Kyle J H, New Westminster; Lee R, North Vancouver.

McClure W E, Port Alberni; McIntosh T, Port Alberni; Madison P R, Cloverdale; Marshall C G, Vancouver; Neil M E, Rossland; Netzer E, Alberni; Patterson G H, Vancouver; Pope N, Armstrong; Preston W L, Vancouver; Roy R A, Vancouver; Ryan F A, Vancouver; Tarasoff D W L, Cobble Hill; Thorne C B, North Surrey; Walker D, **New Westminster.**

DRIVER MECHANICAL
TRANSPORT COURSE

Alexander D S, Vancouver; Allen D P, Kitimat; Bedford W C, Haney; Bond P W, Nelson; Bosmans J, New Westminster; Collins J P, Victoria; Britt G R, Vancouver; Calver T R, Salmon Arm; Cayer L H, Port Alberni; Clarke L H, Vernon; Copp T J, Vancouver; Duncan G A, Vancouver; Edie G, Abbotsford.

Fairbanks W D, Victoria; Finnigan B W, New Westminster; Firth D B, North Vancouver; Fleck J F, Kelowna; Fraser H P, North Vancouver; Goodings D C, Chemainus; Halabourda R G, Vancouver; Healy J C, Quesnel; Henry R, Lytton; Hopkins G F, Westbank; Johnson D L, Victoria; Lamy G J N, Vancouver; Louie N, Vancouver.

McDowell T, Vedder Crossing; McRae H, North Surrey; Mason B W, Nelson; Oliver D T, South Burnaby; Paine M A, Victoria; Piper W A, White Rock; Ralph D W, Victoria; Russell R J, Victoria; Salmon G M, Vancouver; Street E D, Burnaby; Strong L R, Vancouver; Takenanka M, New Denver; Taylor J P, Sidney; Walch R A, Vancouver; Walton T F, Vancouver; Webster F W, Victoria; Wilson J A, Prince Rupert.

INFANTRY SIGNALLER COURSE

Baxter L A, North Vancouver; Bell D R, Richmond; Berry S A, Victoria; Bond M, Vancouver; Britt J E, Vancouv-

er; Brodie L E, Vancouver; Brown C D, Vancouver; Bruce S, West Summerland; Cornett J R, Vancouver; Dewhurst R E, North Vancouver; Grant W, Mission City; Hodson B R, Vancouver; Hyndman B L, Port Kells; Johnston L E, Salmon Arm; Kapchinsky R L, Port Alberni; Kember P A, North Vancouver.

Laliberte R W, Aldergrove; Leroux F, Whonnock; Lowrence J B, Victoria; McCrory W P, New Denver; McIntyre O J, Maillarduelle; McKenzie K D, Ladner; McRae J H, Ladner; Nee F, Victoria; Nelson A, Vancouver; Pearson G D, Sidney; Phillips W W, New Westminster; Preston T, Burnaby; Rainsford C D F, Victoria; Riopelle P L, Salmon Arm; Steadman D J, Victoria; Stewart W G, Nelson; Snyder D W, Victoria; Turner R E, Victoria; Yano V T, Paldo.

BAND

Adams W H, North Vancouver; Bennallack A N C, Victoria; Beyer P G, Port Alberni; Brown R, Vancouver; Collins R J, New Westminster; Easterbrook A, Vancouver; Godin R J, New Westminster; Green H, Lytton; Hannah R S, Port Alberni; Hotell D; McKay J, Lytton; McLean D W, North Vancouver; Martin W, Lytton; Nass A R, Port Alberni; Nye W E, Ladner; Oakley J K, North Vancouver; Pearson A S, Port Alberni; Penman D W, Vancouver; Polkinghorne J M, Victoria; Robinson D, Lytton; Scodane A, Lytton; Scodane P, Lytton; Tweedy C, North Vancouver; Withrow J, Vancouver.

BANFF

Clegg M G, Cloverdale; Dean D M, Vancouver; Lee W S, Paldi; MacAulay D, Vancouver; Mosdell D L, North Vancouver; Thomas D L, Royal Oak.

RIFLE COACH

Barclay P B, Victoria; Beattie J R, North Vancouver; Billingsley R J, Haney; Bolton W C, Lytton; Debock E, Mission; Henry R, Lytton; Jones B, North Vancouver; Kyler C M, New Westminster; Lamy G N.

ALBERTA
NORTHERN ALBERTA AREA

Kaban G D, Edmonton; Bottineau H, Edmonton; Corah E, Edmonton; Dianocky D W, Edmonton; Durocher L, Edmonton; Ferguson P, Edmonton; Fox J, Edmonton; Munro F, Edmonton; Green D, Edmonton; Lucas W H, Edmonton; MacNeill R, Edmonton; McLaughlin J L, Edmonton; McLellan B, Edmonton; McLellan J, Edmonton; Milbraith R, Edmonton; Campbell L, Edmonton; Milbraith A, Edmonton; Ryan W, Edmonton; Niemann K, Edmonton; McGee T V, Edmonton.

Langer L E, Mercoal; Anderson R B, Edson; Basaraba L G, Edson; Bello D A, Edson; Cole M J, Edson; Lee D, Edson; McLeod T, Edson; McNiven G G, Edson; Madison J E, Edson; Nadurak V J, Edson; Pollock J E, Edson; Schepanovich P, Edson; Tanton R J, Edson; Titley W D, Edson; Williamson R L, Edson; Suter D A, Edson; Armstrong H L, Edson; Allen J A, Edson; Schepanovich B, Edson.

Jeffcoat S, McGillivray B; Shadbolt J H, Belanger R J, Edgerton.

Christensen D, James R, Langford D, Tweedy L, Rombough L, Magee R A, Christenson J, Sedgewick.

Depaige P, Fleck D, Gruber R, Lastwika D, Liebert L, Lux R, Manning G, Olinyk G, Van Stienberg J, Woodley N,

Schroll J, Dean W R C, Jamieson J D, Pappes K, Scott R J, Clement W E, Strong D, Mohorich R D, Armstrong P, Faulkner B, Glettig M, Barr G, Bluett J, Christensen E C, Elaschuk J R, Hawthorne D, McRitchie D J, Mason B, Payne K N, Richardson J L, Robinson R T, Sabourin D A, Tell R W, Edmonton.

Hall R A, Pattison T C D, Pither J, Tandrup G, Vanalstyne R G, Van Hemert J, Briscoe N, Lauman F H, Novosad T G, Living C H, Edmonton.

Anderson E, Ferguson D, Pickering E R, Pickering R E, White R L, Glenn R J, Hull W J, Spirit River; Dame W G, Whitford R W, Vilna; Durocher D K, Ness P E, Fort St. John, B.C.; Boisebert J J, Huzil T, Ruznak R, Sakaluk T, Shapka R W, Simpson R, Smiley R K, Pruss R, Krewenchuk H D, Barber E, Krewenchuk R S, Pardley E R, Vegreville.

Bell R, Dubrule C, Moissan R, St Jean E, McLean J, St. Paul; Brown B, Schulz V, McLean R D, Geddes W D, Oregard W M, MacKay C G, Miller W G, Alliance.

Dixon D A, Hume R K, McKay K A, Batter E D, Nichol C, Olson B M, Boe E K, Beaverlodge; McArthur A D, Nolin S J, Reynolds E J, Rigler D A, Grande Prairie; Girard R, Ouellette O, Guibault A G, Mallaig; Bohnet S R, Brenenstuhl W J, Chichak A, Elvin J A, Hoople D E, Lorenz G S, Nagy A J A, Schroder A J, Tomkinson D J, Hill C T, Evansburg.

Basarab D M, Dupius P J, Horn L K, Kirkland G A, McLennan; Buffalo V, Crate F, Cutknife H, Littlechild M, Swampy J, Buffalo F, Cutknife R, Boman W F, Hobbema; Kristensen K A, Latawiec R, Marshall W E, Stockman R, Walmsley T A, Wall R B, Fawcett.

Alenius G L, Alton G E, Feldman D A, Metke H, Monds E, Mudry E M, Fowlik G, Zaharko R J, Thorsby; Bentz T R J, Craik B, Goble G, Guenette D P, Hewitt R J, Richards D C, Symonds D H, Tate M, Edmonton.

Taylor H, Timms T, Palmer F R, Simmons C W, Budd W D, Conrad E K, Greenslade R L, Newberry K G, Townsend R W, Maskell W A, Saunders R J, Ahlstrom R J, Brauti D P, Brown R W, Gale W P, Hawes T, Kautz D J, Kautz G A, MacKinnon R, Mroch J, Sheldon R J, Stroud B L, Yeomans D R, Edmonton; Dunn J A, Krysta R N, Larsen R H, Lindberg K A, Wickstrom R V, Hansen K A, Smeltzer H, Winfield.

Cherniwchan W J, Fedoruk G, Galloway J C, Gorgichuk E, Gorgichuk M, Harasym J J, Harasym W, Spak H, Linklater A, Two Hills; Algot G J, Berg B, Kiziak O V, Kisiak R, Lychak O S, McConnell J G, Derwent.

SOUTHERN ALBERTA AREA

Aven K P, Bauman M, Huckle G D, Rathwell H D, Seed J T, Welfords I H, Redcliff; Degeer W F, Gusek R A, Jacobson K A, Magilton H E, Marco B C, McLean R J, Larsen A R, Tronnes J D, Lacombe; Fisher E W T, Coronation.

McGinnis R, McNeight R J, McWhinnie R J, Pixley N G, Smith D S, Swerdfeger M J, Wallace R E, Jegou, R P, Innisfail; Ginther M, Vulcan; Keeler D W, Maurstad J H, Strathmore; Doe H, Dorosz D E, Joridson N A, Klughart A J, Lloyd G W, Lynes D N, McDonald J E L, Melcher A, Ostler C J, Ostler R D, Ratz E A, Rolheiser D G, Romhild K T, Watson D J, Dorosz M A M, McCumber M B, Noble H L, Clements R G, Calgary.

Graham W A, Menard K C, Pollock W M, Red Deer; Canadine D L, McLeod C, Scott M R, Somers D F, Finch A E, Fix L M, Arneson R, Brown R C, Konschuh J R, Stettler; Egilson J, Heavener D F P, Heric N P, Larsen G S, Pelletier R J, McLennan J L, Heavener J R, Creston.

Alpine A P, Alpine H F M, Jacobsen D G, Johnson W A, Morris A G, MacKinnon D A, Park R, Ratcliffe T S, Weitzel D L, Williams G P K, Horie P J. Ratcliffe R W, Roberts D W, Cranbrook; Baker H A, Burden R J, Dennis M A, Fortinski V, Gillrie B L, Juett D A, Kirkland W M, McAmmond D R, Mellott B L, Nichols J S, Orr E L, Pfiefer D B, Ricks C A, Dillon R P, Goodall P R, Gunn A A, Lane L R, Ferguson H J, Meilleur W L, Calgary.

Darrah M D, English L P, Smith R J, Powell R C, Delburne; Barnaby J W, Bodell G D, Chapman E R, Martin G E, Tuttle F A, Manning R F, Vedres L G, Berry P F, Martin D R, Lethbridge.

Hirsche R W, Kingston R E, Metz T R, Osborne W F J, Viens P M, Ft. MacLeod; Barnes E W, Barnes G G, Beaupre G W, Bertelsen H H, Bertram J D, Greene W, Ledingham M R, Thompson L S, Vaughan K, Medicine Hat; Mooney W P, Saunders D E, Cumming N E, Georgeson G J, Stuckert H N, Banff.

Champion N E, Hancy R J, Matheson B J, Rest A E, Sinclair-Smith F S, Tourond D M, Turner Valley; Big Throat R, Day Rider H, Mills F, Thornton R W, Cardston; Mofford G J, Livingston C E, Parmentier R L, Stuart D E, Weber R W, Rocky Mountain House; Matthews S R, Neratko R R, Vasek J M, Youngberg G D, Squarek J, Vrskovy S, Jordan J W, Megli H L, Hillcrest; Allison J C, Loree D F, Nanton.

Burtis G W, De Vos L, Diett W J, Henry M R, Lebrechthausen T, McDougall R D, Scott J E, Wright J R, Gervais D E F, Paul C B, Seaman R A, Seaman R D, Fudger B W F, Smith T W, Calgary; Many Fires C, Prairie Chicken F, Crane Bear G, Good Eagle J, Cluny; Allison W I, Beatty M S, Bird L M, Campbell J D, Carothers J N, Forbes K J, Goodwin R T, Hartwell P C, Hildebrand R W, Johnstone H E, Looker C R, Moore J A, Parker J S W, Paulet O, Romanowski S, Schlosser R D, Smith, M A, Trottier H J, Violini L R P, Wolford R I, Brabant W J, Doucette L W, Paulet R O, Sven P F, Calgary.

Abram J, Bastien T E, One Owl A, Wezel D, Knowlton W M, Zieffle T H, Brocket; Spotted Bull J, Tail Feathers G, Weasel Fat C, Yellow Horse P, Tail Feathers P, Cardston.

VACC - 1959

Cadets in camp during the 1959 training year:

Abercrombie D R, Vancouver; Abrams J R, Pincher Creek, Alta; Akers W G, Saanichton; Akins J S, Victoria; Aldridge K, Sedgwick, Alta; Alexander B T, Calgary; Alexander M W, N Vancouver; Alexander Mac, Vancouver; Allan H D, Innisfail, Alta; Anderson D, Spirit River, Alta; Anderson J H A, Vancouver; Anderson L D, Salmon Arm.; Anderson N D, Spirit River, Alta; Anderson R S, Strathmore, Alta; Anderson R H J, Pt Alberni; Andrews J J, Victoria; Andrews M A, Kamloops.

Andrieshyn R K, Vancouver; Annis D W, Quesnel; Anslow C A, Victoria; Armstrong R G, Bouchie Lake; Anton son D B, Victoria; Appleby J S, W Vancouver; Archer J F, Beaverlodge, Alta; Armstrong D J, Lacombe, Alta; Aronson D C, Duncan; Auclair V M L, Strathcona, Alta; Auvigne E R, Delburne, Alta; Babiak A R, Bulford, Alta; Bach J T, Vancouver; Bachmann W E, Greisbach, Alta; Bacon R W, Ft St John; Baker G J, N Vancouver; Baker T D, N Vancouver; Baillie J H, Vancouver; Balanow W, N Surrey; Baldwin R W, Prince Rupert.

Ballard W, Montrose; Banys V L, New Westminster; Barnaby, G W, N Lethbridge, Alta; Barnes, G D, Armstrong; Barnes, G G, Medicine Hat, Alta; Bastien B, Brocket, Alta; Bates F G, Cumberland; Bathurst K A, Vancouver; Bat ter J E, Beaverlodge, Alta; Baxter D J R, Victoria Beagle L S, New Westminster; Beale J R, Richmond; Beardmore R J, Port Alberni; Beasley R H, Vancouver; Becker K P, Penticton; Beggs M J, Chemainus; Bell G R, Vancouver; Bell R H, Montney; Bellamy D E, Prince George.

Bellamy H B, Calgary; Benn R S, Wildwood, Alta; Berg B C, Derwent, Alta; Bergum I, Sedgewick, Alta; Berry D E, Vancouver; Bertelsen H H, SW Medicine Hat; Beswick R W, Vancouver; Beynon J R, Evansburg, Alta; Biggar J I, Richmond; Biles H A, Victoria; Billingsley R J, Haney; Biollo F C, W Summerland; Bird D M, Penticton; Bird D I, Victoria; Bird P A, Matsque; Black D K, Calgary; Blacklaw M B, Quesnel; Blaeser G L, Vernon; Blaeser J N, Vernon Blanchard B R, New Westminster;

Bligh M D, N Vancouver; Blumke W, Vancouver; Bobinski R J; Boden J C, Vancouver; Bockhodt D F, Vancouver; Bolton L A, Lytton; Bond R E, Nelson; Bonsteel R E, Calgary; Bower J P, Vancouver; Braithwaite F W, Vernon; Brashko N, Edmonton; Brekkaas C T, Fort St. John; Brennan R G, N Burnaby; Brett R G; Bride T D, Vancouver; Brint A J, Quesnel; Brinton H A, Vulcan, Alta; Brinton R H, Vulcan, Alta; Briscoe G B, Red Deer, Alta; Briscoe N R, Edmonton.

Brown A D, Rocky Mt. House, Alta; Brown G D, Lethbridge, Alta; Brown P, N Vancouver; Brown R, Richmond; Brown R, Richmond; Brown R S, Vancouver; Browning P, Vancouver; Bruce R S, W Summerland; Buckler R A, Victoria; Buffalo C, Hobbema, Alta; Burchill R S, Victoria; Burn A, Cloverdale; Burns J, N Burnaby; Burton N W, Vancouver; Buss R D A, Vancouver; Butler A C, Armstrong; Butler S J, Armstrong; Byers B H, Chilliwack; Byrd E M, Innisfall, Alta; Caldwell S J, Victoria.

Calliou M R, Grande Prairie, Alta; Cambrey R J, Victoria; Campbell E A, Salmon Arm; Campbell J D, Montgomery, Alta; Canadine D L, Stettler, Alta; Carpenter J W, Victoria; Carter R L S, Salmon Arm; Carver E G, Victoria; Caton H S; Chamberlain A W, Vancouver; Charlwood H A, New Denver; Chesworth D A, North Burnaby; Cizik M, Haney; Clarke L H, Vernon; Clayton M W, Salmon Arm; Clements J E, Montrse; Clemett D R, Brentwood; Clinton L N, Griesbach, Alta; Colley B O, Vernon; Collins W K, Lethbridge.

Condie D W M, Vancouver; Cook W E, Nelson; Cooper P J, Victoria; Cooper R J, W Summerland; Corbett D A, Kamloops; Cornett J R, Vancouver; Cortner P N, Ladner; Coss P R, ViVctoria; Coyle J H, White Rock; Crabbe C L, Port Alberni; Crabbe F R, Chemainus; Craik B G, Edmonton; Cullen F P, N Surrey; Currie D B, N Vancouver; Cursons D F, Cloverdale; Cuthill T J, Penticton; Cyr R J, New Westminster; Dahl J E, Salmon Arm; Daleger H T, DeWinton, Alta; Dalke R, Thorsby, Alta.

Danesik T J, Vegreville, Alta; Danroth G K, Prince George; Darrah E G, Delbourne, Alta; Davis W, Cardston, Alta; Davies A F, Alberni; Lean R G, Victoria; DeBoer R R, Vancouver; DeBruyn J E, Port Alberni; Degeer W F, Lacombe, Alta; Dehnke A W, Winfield; Delorme R A, Vancouver; Derosier G L, W Summerland; Devos A A, Calgary; Diduck G E, Edmonton; Dobie D R, Port Alberni; Dockray H J, Quesnel; Downey R J McK, N Burnaby; Doyle D V M, Vancouver; Demeter M E, Armstrong; Dixon D A, Beaverlodge, Alta.

Donstan G, Lytton; Dunford W R, Clearwater; Dunkley D J, Armstrong; Dunham G W, Chilliwack; Dunn A J, Winfield, Alta; Drake J D, Vancouver; Dwyer R L, New Denver; Dwyer W G, Pincher Creek, Alta; Earl A N, Vulcan, Alta; Eckardt D O, Royal Oak; Edgar C S, Kamloops; Eisenhuth M, N Lethbridge; Elliott J W, Vancouver; Ellison J C, Bellevue, Alta; Elrick R G, Richbond; Emslie N C, Salmon Arm; Eriksen I D Montgomery, Alta; Etter M D, Royal Oak; Evanoff J, Nelson; Fahl E A, Calgary.

Falkenberg C E, Alberni; Fedoration D, Edmonton; Fedoruk W, Two Hills, Alta; Felaber E O, Hinton, Alta; Fenton A N, Westbank; Ferguson K H, Spirit River, Alta; Ferris T C McR, W Vancouver; Field G G, Lethbridge; First Rider E. Cardston, Alta; Fisk R G, Alberni; Fitger D L, Kamloops; Fitger H E, Kamloops; Fitzmaurice W H, Vancouver; Flynn T, Calgary; Foesier P J, Turner Valley, Alta; Forbes R, Vancouver; Forster R, Sedgewick, Alta; Fleet R A. Cloverdale; Fotos J C, Prince George; Fraser G R, Edmonton.

Frost M A, Abbotsford; Fuller A B, Delbourne, Alta; Gagnon W A, Vancouver; Gallagher D R, N Burnaby; Garrison T L D, Redcliff. Alta; Gellert K L, Prince George; George S J, N Vancouver; Gerlat E, Macleod, Alta; Ginther M, Vulcan. Alta; Giroux C B, Strathmore, Alta; Gitzel G W, Hinton, Alta; Gladstone J L, Cardston, Alta; Glauser W V, Vancouver; Glebe H R, Honey; Glendinning T W, Strathmore. Alta; Godin R J, New Westminster; Golder F L, Chilliwack; Goodings D B, Chemainus; Goodings D C, Chemainus; Goodland E. Edmonton; Goodstriker A, Cardston, Alta; Goulet L J, Fort St John; Graham L J, Vancouver; Grant P D, W Vancouver; Gray M J, Kitimat; Greaves R G, Entwistle, Alta; Greig R J, Bowden, Alta; Grimes D F, Victoria; Groenhuysen D B, Silverton; Grubb, D McL, Vancouver; Grubb R E, Victoria; Gruber R, Edmonton; Hacker T W H, Lethbridge; Haggard G L B, Cranbrook.

Hamilton M R, Calgary; Haney R J, Millarville, Alta; Hanna R, Haney; Halls J McB. Victoria; Harper R J, N Vancouver; Harrington G R H, Spirit River, Alta; Harris T E, Cranbrook; Harrison R J, Trail; Harvey D W A Abbotsford; Havig M A. Edmonton; Hayhurst R J, Vernon; Healy D M, Cardston, Alta; Healy L, Cardston, Alta;

Hebert R A, Port Alberni; Heiliger C A, Calgary; Henderson G, N Vancouver; Henry R, Lytton; Herbert J R Victoria; Herron S E, Calgary; Hickey G A, Port Alberni; Hill D E G, Fruitvale; Hill E S, Wildewood, Alta; Hill R M, Penticton; Hodge P J F, W Vancouver; Hodgson E J, Aldergrove; Hoglund A E, Vernon; Holland R R, Kelowna; Holloway K G, New Westminster; Honeyman J S, Trail; Honsberger B C, Vancouver; Holt D M, Birch Island; Horn G H, Coleman, Alta; Hotell D M, Prince George; House G W, Vancouver; Huckle G D, Redcliffe, Alta.

Hueckel R G, Brentwood Bay; Hull S H, Duncan; Hulberg A O, Rocky Mt House, Alta; Hume W R, Banff, Alta; Hunter G W, Vancouver; Hunter W J N Vancouver; Huzil J T, Vegreville Alta; Hvlands D E, Vancouver; Ireland L L, Vancouver; Isaac T B, Lytton; Jackson W S, Rocky Mt House, Alta; Jacobson A W, Entwistle, Alta; Jacobson D A C, Vancouver; Jarvis R A, S Burnaby; Jean H G, Port Alberni; Jeffcoat S, Edgerton, Alta; Jensen P, Vancouver; Jervis W G, Silverton; Jenner T J, Hinton, Alta; Jevne W L, Entwistle Alta; Johnson A L, Vedder Crossing; Johnston J W, New Westminster; Johnson K R, Port Alberni; Johnson R E Rocky Mt House, Alta; Johnson W A Cranbrook; Johnston L B, Derwent Alta; Jones K A, Evansburg, Alta; Jones T F, Penticton; Karpchuk M O, Derwent, Alta; Karpes B C, Vancouver Keenan G R, Cumberland; Keenan I W, Cumberland; Kelly G P, Lethbridge Kennaugh M J, Victoria; King E R, Salmon Arm; Kingston R E, Fort Macleod Alta.

Kingzett P J W, Quesnel; Knowles F W, N Burnaby; Knudson K R, Port Alberni; Kurnliw W J, Vilna, Alta Kyler C M, New Westminster; Lamport K B, Victoria; Lang R M, Nelson; Langlois A E, Montrose; Larsen A G, Creston; Lebeck R K, Quesnel; LeBlond C B, Vernon; Lebrechthausen T V, Calgary; Ledingham R McD, Medicine Hat; Lee D, Marlboro, Alta; Leib E S, Haney; LeMasurier P J, Vancouver; Leonard J C, Victoria; Leroux I T, Whonnock; Leroux F A, Whonnock; Leslie R I, Calgary; Lewis D M, Griesbach, Alta; Lidstone B D, Victoria; Liebert L, Edmonton; Lilley R V, Vancouver; Lindberg K D, Breton, Alta; Linden M J, Port Alberni; Littlechild W Hobbema, Alta; Lloyd H B, Rocky Mt House, Alta; Lochhead W McG, New Westminster; Louth O, Turner Valley, Alta; Lowdell W B W, New Westminster; Lowe G T, Penticton; Lucas C R Vancouver; MacDonald A W, Quesnel; MacDonald D A, Vancouver.

MacPherson R D, Vancouver; McCagherty G W, Buck Lake, Alta; McCall D H, Kelowna; McAllister L W B Victoria; McCaskill T W, Vancouver; McCardell D J, Ladner; McClafferty D, Vancouver; McClelland J D, Banff, Alta; McDonald A J, Forest Lawn, Alta; McDonaugh J R, New Denver; McDougall R D, Calgary; McDowell K T, Vedder Crossing; McGimpsey K L, Redcliff, Alta; McHardy P D, Vancouver; McGinness C W, Redcliff, Alta; McGowan W E, Vancouver; McIntosh T R, Port Alberni; McKay K A, Beaverlodge, Alta; McKay R J, New Westminster; McKay T L, Edmonton; McKelvay D Vancouver; McKenzie J D A K, Ladner; McGillis A J, Hinton, Alta; McKnight J, Port Alberni; McLaughlin J L, Edmonton; McLaughlin W R, Ft St John; McLean B M, New Westminster; McMullan B L, Edson, Alta; McNeill O C J, Calgary; McNeight R J, Innisfail Alta; McRae H, N Surrey; McCrory M J, New Denver; McWhinnie R J, Innisfail, Alta; Mack R P, Montgomery, Alta; Macri M A, N Vancouver.

Madison D R A, White Rock; Madsen D R, Prince George; Magee R, Sedgewick, Alta; Magowan W T, Macleod, Alta; Major R W, Kitimat; Mansell A E, Hammond; Marcellais, K A L A, Prince George; Markowsky L, Edmonton; Marlow W W, Edson, Alta; Marsh D, Ladner; Marsh F W, Victoria; Marsh V P, Vancouver; Martel C F, Edmonton; Martin W, Lytton; Maskulak E M, Prince Rupert; Mason S, Vancouver; Matheson B J, Turner Valley, Alta; Mayer C A, Delborne, Alta; Mazurin F M, Edson, Alta; Megli T M, Coleman, Alta; Melnick J F, Haney; Middlemiss C R, Griesbach, Alta; Mikitka W P, Vilna, Alta; Milan G A, Vedder Crossing; Miller G M, Vancouver; Minifie L G, Revelstoke; Miranda L, N Vancouver; Mitchell K K, Edmonton; Mohammed G, Port Alberni; Moilliet E C, Clearwater; Moir L T, Hinton, Alta; Molley J R, Port Alberni; Monroe B W, Vancouver; Monteski T A, Victoria; Mooney W P, Banff, Alta.

Moore H, Lytton; Moore J A, Calgary; Moore L G, Burnaby; Moore P G, Hinton; Morgan G M, Prince George; Mori D, New Denver; Morton E C, Vegreville, Alta; Moses R, Vancouver; Mozell W J, Cranbrook; Mugford R E, Vancouver; Muir J A, Ladner; Mullen J, Edmonton; Munro F H, Vancouver; Munro L E, Vancouver; Murphy S, Innisfail, Alta; Murray D K, Calgary; Murray D E, Wainwright, Alta; Murray M S, Penticton; Murton R E, Montrose; Red Deer, Alta; Myers K B, Victoria; Musgrave W J, Victoria; Myers D A, Myers S, Vancouver; Nadurak V J, Edson, Alta; Nash D W, Armstrong; Nelson G E, N Vancouver; Nelson K J, Victria; Nichol D L, Beaverlodge, Alta; Nielsen T, N Vancouver; Neish J R, Vancouver; Newman G P M, N Vancouver; Nist J P, Rocky Mt House, Alta; Nolan A T, Prince George; Nordmark W J, Port Alberni; Norfolk S E R Clearwater.

Norgard G V, Macleod, Alta; Norman S E, N Vancouver; Nichols S J, Forest Lawn, Alta; Nute G T, Victoria; Oda A, New Denver; Okesn A R, Haney; Olinek E E, Vancouver; O'Mara T J, Victoria; Olsen E M, Quesnel; Olsen F E, Burnaby; Osborne W A, Ft. St. John; Osgood J E, Redcliff, Alta; Overland R L, Calgary; Page J N, Calgary; Palmer F G, Calgary; Panter C, Vulcan, Alta; Parker J R, Clearwater; Parker R W, Montgomery, Alta; Parkinson T B, Port Alberni; Parsons D J, Vilna, Alta; Pash G W, Victoria; Patrash W R, Vancouver; Paul C B, Calgary; Pawson D E, Vancouver; Payment D L A, Burnaby; Payne R H, Edmonton; Pearce P B, Port Alberni; Pearce T N, Victoria; Pearson A S, Port Alberni; Pearson G D, Sidney; Pearson R J, Vancouver; Pedersen L D, Goodfare, Alta; Peet G C, Edson, Alta; Penner R A, Montgomery, Alta; Perrin G L, Lacombe, Alta.

Peterson E A, Lethbridge; Peterson R A, Trail; Petter M E, Victoria; Pettipiece J W, Hastings; Phillips B J, Victoria; Phillips D R, Calmar, Alta; Phil-

lips M H, Calmar, Alta; Pickening D.
Prince George; Picketts D F H, Red
Deer, Alta; Pion E G, Vancouver; Pipe-
stem G, Hobbema, Alta; Podlubny B S,
Derwent, Alta; Polley I R, Edmonton;
Pollock J E, Edson, Alta; Porter M R,
Prince George; Porter R B, Vancouver;
Poulsen H, Westbank; Powell A, Del-
borne, Alta; Powers H E, Edmonton;
Preston C T, Burnaby; Price A L, New
Westminster; Pring A J, Victoria;
Pringle K R G, Victoria; Prins R, Van-
couver; Pruss R P, Vegreville, Alta;
Pura S, Edmonton; Quayle R, New
Westminster; Quast D E, Prince Rup-
ert; Radley K J, Coleman, Alta; Rains-
ford C D F, Victoria; Rajotte R V,
Wainwright, Alta; Randall W D, Vic-
toria; Ransom R E, Vancouver; Rat-
cliffe R W, Cranbrook; Ratcliffe T S,
Cranbrook; Raymond F, St. Albert,
Alta.

Rayner M H, Esquimalt; Renaud J,
Vancouver; Reimer M S, Port Alberni;
Renstrom J M, Vancouver; Rest A E,
Millarville, Alta; Reynolds F, Calgary.
Richard J J, Sardis; Richardson R, Cal-
gary; Richman B A, Royal Oak; Rich-
ter R L, Forest Lawn, Alta; Rigler D
A, Grande Prairie, Alta; Ringrose J H.
Nelson; Riske P H; Robbins W J S.
North Burnaby; Roberts D W, Cran-
brook; Roberts D M, Kelowna; Robin-
son J W, N Vancouver; Rockett R F.
Victoria; Rockwood S A, Salmon Arm;
Roy B D, Grande Prairie, Alta; Rudolph
A W, Prince Rupert; Ruelle A C J.
N Surrey; Rumberg M, Vancouver; Rus-
nak R D, Vegreville, Alta; Russell B
L, Bowness, Alta; Russell J E, Vancou-
ver; Russell R J, Victoria; Ryan J R.
N Burnaby; Ryan W F, Edmonton; Rye
D E, Cumberland; Sakaluk T E, Vegre-
ville, Alta; Saunders A C, Pincher
Creek, Alta; Sauve R H F, Calmar, Alta;
Scarff D M, Westview; Scheer D F, Mac-
leod, Alta; Schlosser D R, Montgomery,
Alta.

Scott D W, Lacombe, Alta; Scott H
L, Lacombe, Alta; Scott J E, Calgary;
Scott M B, Stettler, Alta; Scott R, Jas-
per Place, Alta; Seaman R D, Calgary;
Seaman R A, Calgary; Seed J T, Red-
cliff, Alta; Sehn V, Medicine Hat, Alta;
Senko J C, Vancouver; Eeton R N,
Cloverdale; Shadbolt J H, Edgerton.
Alta; Shade G E, Vancouver; Shannon
M M, Prince George; Shapka R W, Veg-
reville, Alta; Sharpe R W, Prince
George; Shaw D R, Calgary; Shickele
J G, Penticton; Shoemaker D B, Haney;
Shroll J, Edmonton; Shrubsole J E.
Montrose; Silvester H C C, Victoria;
Simpson J P, Whonnock; Simpson R.
Vegreville, Alta; Smith C D, Vancou-
ver; Smith C E, N Surrey; Smith G,
Sedgewick, Alta; Smith D H, Victoria;
Smith L W, Forest Lawn, Alta; Spar-
row R J, Haney; Smith R W, Nelson;
Soosav R, Hobbema, Alta; Sorobey N
T, Vilna, Alta; Spaven A R, Victoria;
Spaven B W, Victoria.

Stanfield W R, Spirit River, Alta;
Stancer C C, Calgary; Stangier J C.
Strathmore, Alta; Stanko P J, Egerton.
Alta; Standish J B, N Kamloops; Steele
G H, Courtenay; Steeves J L, Rocky Mt
House, Alta; Stephen D J, New West-
minster; Stephen M C, Victoria; Sve-
venson M, Revelstoke; Stewart J, Van-
couver; Stewart W G, Nelson; Still S
D, Lethbridge; Stinson H R, Vancouver;
Stobie I, N Vancouver; Straumford D
L, N Vancouver; Sturgeon J, Richmond;
Sutherland T, N Vancouver; Swerdfe-
ger M J, Innisfail, Alta; Sykes G E, N

Vancouver; Symons W, Vancouver;
Syverson T A, Vancouver; Trinder R
W, Haney; Takahara R, New Denver;
Takenaka J, New Denver; Tanton R J,
Edson, Alta; Tavlor H, Edmonton, Alta;
Thomas B R; Thomas D O, Roval Oak;
Thomas R M, Calmar, Alta; Thompson
A W, N Surrey; Thomson G R, Cres-
ton; Thompson K A, Cecil Lake; Thorpe
F, Calgary; Tiernan L A, Salmon Arm;
Titley D W, Edmonton.

Tizzard P C I, Bownerr, Alta; Toner
G B, Vegreville, Alta; Tootoosis F,
Hobbema, Alta; Topham N B, Gries-
bach, Alta; Trainor D T, Vancouver;
Treat L B, Salmon Arm; Turgeon E R
E, Victoria; Ullock M A, Victoria; Un-
garo G, Prince George; Ursel D, Cal-
gary; Van Boeyen D W, Vancouver;
Van Boeyen D J, Vancouver; Van Hem-
ert J, Edmonton; Vaughan K D, Medi-
cine Hat; Veevers J C, Vancouver;
Verge M R, Vancouver; Verheul L, Ed-
monton; Viens J B, Macleod, Alta;
Voigt B W, Entwistle, Alta; Wade R D,
Evansburg; Wagner A T, Goodfare,
Alta; Walsh J, Sedgewick, Alta; Walters
B C, Calgary; Washburn N, Edmonton;
Wainwright G A, Vernon; Waiker W L,
Vancouver; Walker A G G, Westbank;
Walker W R C, S Ft George; Walley R,
Vancouver; Walsh R E, Vancouver; War-
man R R, Kelowna; Way F T, Vavenby;
Webb A J, Abbotsford; Weber D K,
Salmon Arm; Weber R W, Rocky Mt
House, Alta.

Webber V J, Cloverdale; Webster F
W, Victoria; Weetering A J, Medicine
Hat; Welford I H, Redcliff, Alta; West-
fall R G, Penticton; Westlund K C,
Thorsby, Alta; Whapham A O, Van-
couver; Whale W E, Salmon Arm;
White C S, N Burnaby; White D C, N
Burnaby; Wiens V N, Abbotsford;
Wicht C, Victoria; Wilkins J J, Van-
couver; Wilkinson D B, Vancouver;
Williamson W L, Port Alberni; Wills L
C, N Burnaby; Wilnechenko L S, Sal-
mon Arm; Wilson C J, Siroar; Wilson
M J, Courtenay; Wiltse E F, Penticton;
Windrem D O, Victoria; Wood W S,
Penticton; Woods B S, Vancouver;
Woodward B, Salmon Arm; Woodward
R H, Alberni; Worthington D L, N
Vancouver; Worthington E D, S Ft
George; Wyant R H, Salmon Arm;
Yacey R, Myrnam, Alta; Yeomans R D,
Griesbach, Alta; York E J, N Burnaby;
York R P, N Burnaby; Young W T;
Younger G D, Hillcrest, Alta; Zackod-
nik L D, Creston; Zieffle T H, Pincher
Creek, Alta; Zomar M J, Abbotsford;
Zorin D S, Revelstoke.

VACC - 1960

Cadets in Camp this year were:

NOMINAL ROLL OF B.C. CADETS
ABBOTSFORD—Webb, Allen James;
Young, William Thomas; Barber, Fred
A.; Cummings, Fred L.; Kish, Larry;
Harvey, Jim C.; Jackson, Allen Anthony;
Laverty, Charles Michael; Lundin, Rich-
ard Allan; Meier, Robert James; Saxbee,
Lowell John; Thiessen, Lenard Theo-
dore; Wiens, Allen Gordon; Yake, Mer-
vyn Ward; Nagy, Dal Richard; Riske,
John Peter; Roest, Edward.

ALDER FLATS — Capaniuk, Garry
Peter.

BEGREVILLE—Reid, Michael.

BIRCH ISLAND—Holt, Dean Munroe;
Scott, John Wilfred.

CANOE—Fuller, P.

CECIL LAKE—Framst, Kenneth Albert.

CHEMAINUS—Crabbe, Francis Robert; Goodings, Brian Donald; Beggs, Michael Joseph; Mast, Gerd.

CLEARBROOK—Janzen, Jon David.

CLEARWATER—Pye, Geoffrey Maurice; Whitford, Carson Lernford.

CLOVERDALE—Burn, Allen; Anuik, Elmer Frederick; Payne, Richard Frederick; Miller, Richard Gerald.

CUMBERLAND—Dixon, John; Platt, Douglas W.; Ball, John Thomas; Keenan, Gordon Ronald.

COURTENAY—Annand, David A.; Williams, Moelwynn; Steele, Herbert Grant.

CRANBROOK—Mozell, William John; Harris, Terrance Elliott; Beday, Edward Roland; Bennett, Wayne William; Jacobson, Dale Edward; Mooy, Wesley Ronald; Sang, William Hugh; Haggard, Gordon Lawrence Bruce; White, James Larry.

CRESCENT BEACH—Gaze, Alvin Edgar.

CRESTON—Mannarin, Joseph James; Reed, Jerry William.

DIRDAR—Wilson, Clive James.

ESQUIMALT—McLean, Daniel John.

ENDERBY—Murphy, Stanley.

FRUITVALE — Hill, David Edward George; Bertuzzi, Luigi; Boehmer, Lorne Louses; Borno, Patrick John; Plummer, Roy Edward; Seal, Kenneth Arnold; Skulnec, Harold; Vlahovic, Ivan Donald; Erwst, William Ronald.

FORT GEORGE — Walker, Wendell Robert.

HAMMOND—Stephenson, David.

HANEY — Bayduza, Micke; Threlfal, Peter; Bruce, Kenneth Charles.

HORSESHOE BAY — Butler, Eric George; Gibbs, Walter Alan.

KAMLOOPS—Edgar, Charles Stephen; Grandall, Dwight Henry; Demkiw, Alexander (Sandy); Fitger, Howard Eugene; Latremouille, Gary Dennis; Terry, Kenneth Ray.

KELOWNA — Moore, Allan Douglas; Stringer, David McNair; McCall, Douglas Harold; Warman, Richard Roy; Brown, Gary Michael; Davidson, James; Evans, Donald Victor; Gundrum, Wayne Grant; Kasabuchi, Terry.

KITIMAT—Bush, John Howard; Anderson, Robert John; Erickson, Paul Wilhelm; Gray, Michael; Gurrie, Geoffry; Gvorgy, Steve; Smith, Howard; Mazur, Richard.

KINGSGATE—Scott, Thomas Frederick.

LANGLEY—Dick, Garry P.; Harrison, Steven Ward; Nichols, Erp; Pelletier, George; Perry, David William; Rauser, David John; Bateman, David John.

LADNER—Curtiss, Ronald Frederick; Sawatski, Kenneth Walter.

MATSQUI—Bird, Phillip Allen; Grist, Larry; Lundstrom, George Andrew.

MERRITT—Dunnigan, Richard; Post, Hans; Middleton, Larry George.

MINTO—Hunter, Robert A.

NELSON—Cook, Wayne Ernest; Ringrose, Wayne Joseph Henry; Bentley, Danny Dainia; Preston, Robert Howie; Truscott, Donald Lewis; Bond, Roger; Miller, Ronald; Crawford, Bryian Breau.

NEW DENVER — Mori, Harold; D'Wyer, Dennis Lawrence; Demeulewaere, David Leroy; Enockson, Ross Edward; Hashimoto, Sakaye.

PARKSVILLE—Moore, Roger.

PENTICTON — Beardmore, Neil Martin; Bird, Dennis Michael; Westfall, Robert Gerald; Conley, Richard Bruce; Eastman, Barry William; Quick, David Albert; Semeniuk, David; Bent, Barry; Hart, C. A.; Lowe, R.; Stewart, K. S.; Symonds, W. R.; Tannant, C. L.; Hill, Rickey Walter; Corson, Brian Donald; Foster, Gary James; Wiltse, Earl.

PORT ALBERNI—DeBruyn, Erik; Fisk, Roger Goodwin; McKnight, James Robert; Mohammed, George; Emde, Laurn Edward; Laplante, Marcel Raymond; Lorenzo, Ray Douglas; McIntosh, Terrance Ray; Parkinson, Warren David; Vis, Cornelius Petrus; Rooney, Dennis Patrick; Dobie, Daniel Robert; Woodward, Robert Henry; Falkenburg, Eric Charles; Jean, Harvie George; Bowen, Melroy; Falkenberg, William John; Fridfinnson, Walter Stanley; Jensen, Harry Ernest; Johnson, Bernard Harold; Jones, Alvin John; Kainz, Armand Max; Keetch, Michael Hazen; Macdonald, Clifford Patrick; McCurdy, Robert; Morrison, William Keith; Richmond, Gary Richard; Rogers, Kenneth Wayne; Sutherland, John; Theriault, Ray Ernest; Walker, Wayne Warren; Walter, Douglas Harvey; White, Jim Wilfred; Johnson, Kenneth Rae; Reimer, Mike Stanley; Williamson, Wesley Lewis.

PRINCE GEORGE — Danroth, Gary Keith; Hotell, Dake Munro; Morgan, George Marvin; Isackson, Maurice Robert; Nolan, Paul Lloyd; Fotos, John Christopher; Bootham, John Craig; Cunningham, William Francis; Hendricks, Jerry Lewis; Holst, Robert Harold; Hotwell, Alan Robert; McNeil, Kenneth Roy; Mack, John Alfred; Madsen, Ronald Andrew; Prodeahl, Robert James; Cunningham, Gordon Richard; McKay, Kenneth Maxwell; Robb, Brian Garwood; Bellamy, Denis Earl.

PRINCE RUPERT—Maskulak, Eugene Metru; Quast, Donald Emil; Girardet, Paul Marcel; Harris, Christopher Herbert; Martinson, Robert Andrew; Pierce, Douglas James; Sawan, George; Syrette, John Mervin; White, Melvin.

QUESNEL—Craig, Edward James; Hansen, Conrad Odein; Hartley, William Dale; Jackson, George Lewis; Johnson, Timothy Robert; Lothrop, Donald Ernest; Robinson, Stewart Scott; Ynger, Richard Elwood; Webb, Michael Howard.

REVELSTOKE—Minifie, Larry Garth; Alexander, John Carter; McLaren, James.

ROYAL OAK — Malovec, Stephen Charles; Gillespie, Neil Kenneth.

RUSKIN—Goddard, Harold James.

SALMON ARM—Rockwood, Solomon Alfred; Gorrgian, C. O.; Pigeon, G. D.; Woodward, B. M.; Turleski, Ronald Larry; Ross, D. A.

SILVERTON—Senning, William Lionel; Jervis, Wayne Gilbert; Lepsoe, Robert Anthony.

SOUTH BURNABY — Baker, Wayne Thomas.

FORT ST. JOHN—McLaughlin, William Robert; Hellum, Dale; Bacon, Ronald Wayne; Osborne, John Edward.

SUMMERLAND—Derosier, Garry Lewis; Bentley, M. J.; Villene, R.

SURREY — Cullen, Paul Frederick; Brown, Allan George; Cole, John Henderson; Ellingsen, Erling Seth; Elliot, Paul Alec; Healr, Delmer Lawrence; Hollo, Peter Paul; Milne, Ronald James; Morton, Montgomery Leigh; Van Horn, Arthur Neil; Balanow, William; Hollo, George; Alexander, William Macdonald; Fitzpatrick, Richard Leroy; Boyer, Ray-

500

mond; Tomkulak, Lorne; Darmold, Bruce.

TRAIL—Honeyman, John Scott; Peterson, Russell Allan; Crichton, Colin Andrew; Crichton, George Wesley; McCabe, Garry; Whitle, William.

VANCOUVER—Bennett, Ray Clifford; Carter, John Thomas; Goes, Hans Johanes; GoGarten, Wolfgang; MacMillan, Roderick Bruce; McKitchie, Allan; Tully, Robert Stewart; Walker, Wayne Lynn; Wills, Barry Thomas; Wills, Lloyd Charles; York, Irvin James; York, Paul George; Chesworth, Dennis Arthur; Fitzmaurice, William Henry; Mortimer, James Edmond.

Benson, John Frederick; Brintnell, William Ross; Bussy, Edwin William; Cook, Peter; Deans, William; Larson, Robert Michael; Olafson, Brian Keith; Olsen, Armey Joseph; Reid, Russel George; Rockwell, James Alfred; Rogizinski, Benny Henry; Rogizinski, Theodore Julien; Senyk, Steven; Stone, Clifford Arthur; Stone, Steve; Wheeldon, Ronald Michael; Bourne, Ronald William.

Abercrombie, Douglas Ralph; Appleby, John Springett; Back, James Terrance; Bell, Gordon Rae; Bower, John Pierson; Brett, Richard George; Buss, Robert Daniel; Cassap, John Gordon; Currie, Donald Bruce; Downey, Richard John McKenzie; Harper, John Stuart; McCaskill, Trevor; MacPherson, Rollo Drummond; Mason, Sydney; Myers, Sheridan Stewart; Neish, James Robert; Olsen, Frederick Einar; Patrash, Walter Richard; Payment, Denis Lewis Arthur; Pion, Edmund Gerald; Porter, Robert Brian; Prins, Ronald; Stinson, Harold Roger; Trainor, David Thomas; Veevers, James Charles; Walley, Rick; Worthington, David Leonard.

Ashton, Frank Rans; Baines, Robert William; Dwillies, Peter Adolph; Edgett, William Max; Farrell, John Alfred; Heinz, Stanley Wallace; Hughes, Gale Milton; Johnson, Jack Larry; Jordan, Wayne Robert; Shaw, Robert William; Watts, Alexander John.

Hanson, Eric Lorenz Ernest; Hill, Robert Raymond; Lucas, Charles Roy; McKerron, Robert Craig; MacLennon, Donald Ian; Robinson, Jeffrey Walter; Shade, George Edward; Straumford, Donald Lawrence; Withrow, Campbel.

Bathurst, Kenneth Richard; Cornett, James Raymond; McKilvay, Donald; Mugford, Robert Everett; Nielsen, Tom Pilegard; Pawson, David Ernest; Rumberg, Matthew; Sykes, Jeffrey Edward; Symonds, William Howard; Preston, Thomas; Ryan, John Robert; Sturgeon, Howard James.

Baillargeon, Dennis Roy; Barr, Bryan Kenneth; Bligh, Michael David; Bruneau, Jerry Joseph; Burger, William John; Campbell, Peter Bradley; Carr, Gary Ashley; Fitzmaurice, Patrick Alfred; Fraser, Larry Frederick; Gabbott, Simon Anthony; Gibberd, John Davidson; Jones, John Barrett; Logan, Robert Alexander; McGill, Nyle; Newell, Dennis Michael; Nicoll, Alexander Gordon; Page, Garth; Silverton, Garry Clyde; Skibinski, Raymond.

Baker, Charles Raymond; Coridor, Norman Douglas; Donohue, John Essler; Eggleston, Edward; Fairful, Donald James; Greavette, Dave Leo; Hutton, Robert Edmond; Hutton, William John; Langis, Terrance; Magee, James William; Marsden, Michael Edward; Mortimer, James Ronald; Mostert, Dick; Peters, Michael Albert; Pircina, Richard Allan;

Sauve, Daniel Wayne; Slobod, Harry Allen; Soderman, William Albert; Stock, Walter Justin; Sugden, Walyer Charles; Sullican, Harry Brenton; White, Gregory; Wyllie, Grant Thomas; Yee, Raymond Broklyn; Davis, Laurie Alfred.

Bird, David Frank; Burden, Robert Wayne; Cameron, John Stewart; Cameron, Walter John; Carswell, Michael Kent; Drake, James Francis; Dunn, Barry Wayne; Eakins, Peter David; Fish, Gordon Alfred; Fisher, Ronald Earl; Glenn, Colin Michael; Gish, Glen Peter; Johnston, Garry; Johnston, McGeachy Samuel; Klassen, Kenneth Frank; Leckie, Alan Dawson; Logan, Charles Peter; Lugrin, Ronald Charles Richard; McBoyle, Howard Leslie; McCrimmon, Craig; MacLean, James Forsythe; MacPherson, Archibald Henderson; Mitchell, David James; Naylor, Paul Edward; Pion, Joseph Eddie Armand; Poirier, Phillippe Alfred; Sedwick, Kirk James; Sorell, Victor Alec; Spivey, Herbert Albert; Wallace, Kenneth William; Webber, Rodney Donald; Weeks, Ronald Patrick.

Russell, Jack; Thwaites, Gordon; Wood, Edward James; Johnstone, James William; White, Colin Stanley; Brown, Matt Frederick; Drake, J. D.; Forbes, Reginald James; Marshall, Charles Grant; Nelson, Gilbert Edgar; Van, Bryan Daryl James.

VAVENBY—Hunsbedt, Stanley Darrell; Way, Frederick Temple.

VERNON—Braithwaite, Frederick William; Hoglund, Andrew Eric; Jacobson, David Mark; LeBlond, Campbell Barrie; Hayhurst, Douglas John; Bell, Thomas Austin Roe; Benham, Laurel Fraser; Dombrowski, Donald Stanley; Green, Gerald Scott; Hermanson, Garry Leroy; Leek, Brian Francis; Meszynski, Joseph; Moore, Patrick Michael; Schippfel, Paul Curt; Schippfel, Phil Joseph; Dase, Kenneth Eric.

WINFIELD—Dehnke, Waybe Andrew.

VICTORIA—Brayton, Thomas Archibald; Buckler, Ronald Albert; Cooper, Peter John; Grubb, David McClintock; Herbert, John Robert; Leonard, John Charles; Musgrave, William John; Nute, Gary Thomas; Phillips, Barry John; Pring, Arnold James; Richman, Brian Albert; Smith, Harry Deryk; Windrem, Dale Armond; Carpenter, William John; Evans, Terrence Kenneth; Gibson, Robert Allen; O'Mara, Bryan Thomas; Pringle, Gibson David; Tapper, Gerry William.

Alexander, Richard John; Archer, John Douglas; Barr, Lenard Robert; Burton, Frank Ronald; Camsall, Roy Earl; Davidson, John Robert; Fairhurst, Paul Richard; Eames, Harry Albert; Herriott, Michael Kelly; Hollings, William Arthur; Haskin, William George; Lawrence, Joseph William; Letourneau, Robert Joseph; McGowan, Gordon James; McGregor, James Robert; Norby, Loyis Clifford; Normandeau, Daniel Joseph; Parlby, Fred Maxwell; Stables, Kenneth William; Twyman, David Franklin.

Allman, Martin Peter; Auringer, Derrick Raymond; Cochrane, Howard David Leonard; Craddock, Dennis Wayne; Duddy, Colin John; Eden, William Edward; Emerick, Stanley Charles; Freeman, Edwin James; Hagen, Harry James; Harris, Robert William F.; Holmes, Brian Harold; Hunt, Charles Richard; Koczkur, Peter Anthony; McMurdo, Charles Hamilton; Miller, John Earl; Mills, Barry Lloyd G.; Powell, Dennis

Gordon; Semenchuk, Peter Robert W.; Smith, Edward Lawrence; Smith Harold James; Smith, John Walter; Tapley, Raymond Wayne; Whatley, Michael Richard.

Carver, Frederick George; Lamport, Kenneth Bruce; Munro, Lawrence Edward; Myers, Keith Burton; Randall, William David; Cutworth, Glen Stanley; Edginton, Steven Bruce; Etheridge, Nicholas Hagger; Hawkesworth, Richard Brian; Hudson, Roy Peter; King, Ralph John; Mein, Stewart Adam George; Spaven, Robert Allan; Akins, John Stanley.

WELLS—Birk, James Joseph; Cyca, Robert James; Roberts, Roy Roland; Robertson, Donald Alexander; Thatcher, Leonard George; Wales, David Kent; Zipser, Henry Peter.

WEST BENCH—Murray, Michael.

WHONNOCK—Polak, Wolfgang.

WYNDEL—Huscroft, G. M.; Huscroft, George Morris.

NOMINAL ROLL OF ALBERTA CADETS

ALBERT PARK—Langlois, Richard; Thornhill, John William.

BACKLAKE—McCagherty, Gary William.

BEAVERLODGE—McKay, Kenneth Allan; Jervis, Daniel Harold; Jewitt, John; Archer, John Fred; Ray, Larry Carter; Young, William Bruce; Stroker, Kenneth George.

BLACK DIAMOND — Gratton, David Joseph; Klok, Feike Jacob Jan.

BLAIRMORE—Bealie, Fredrick Joseph; Raymond, Brian W. J.; Chabillon, Delbert Everest.

BOWNESS — Teets, Arthur; Denby, Harry Joseph; Russell, Barry Lynn; Tizzard, Peter.

BRETO LAKE — Farnell, Frederick Leslie.

BRETON—Wylie, Robert Alexander.

BUCK LAKE — Fullerton, Lawrence Wyman.

CALGARY—Skarupa, Michael R.; Bellamy, Herbert Bruce; Bonsteel, Ronald Elvin; Stancer, Charles; Bird, Lesslie Maurice; Cox, Clive Lewis; Derksen, Melvin Harold; Thornhill, Edward Stanley; Doe, Leo Nelson; Hill, Darryl; Yard, Peter Gordon; Page, John Nicholas; Thompson, Leonard Andrew; Hansen, Frank Erik; Reynolds, Dave Ralph.

Calkins, William Ernest; Carr, Barry James; Christmas, David; Dennison, James Arthur; Fergusson, MacNaughton; Foster, David; Hobal, John; Jensen, Dennis Michael; Macrae, Wayne Donald; Makin, Douglas John; O'Brien, James George; Patten, Norman Kenneth; Petersen, Kenneth Wayne; Protasiwich, Carl Michael; Van Berkel, Andrew; Bacon, John Edward; Seaman, Robert Dempster; Mitchell, Clayton Benjamin.

CALMAR — Sauve, Randolph Hugo Frank; Thomas, Ryan Michael.

CANMORE—Nelson, Aryland Albert.

CARDSTON—Davies, Chester; Firstrider, Randolph.

CLANDONALD — Good, Allan Alexander.

COLEMAN—Jumarchie, William Steven; Samuel, Steven Richard; Crippen, Ronald Brian; Radley, Kenneth James; Horn, George Harry.

CORONATION — Pidhirney, D. J.; Wakefield, A. B.; Woody, D. H.

DERWENT—Sadowski, John; McConnell, Brian William; Hicks, Robert Blain; Rooskowski, Ronald Victor.

EDMONTON—Allinson, Jack; Arnault, Gary Alexander; Bratvold, James; Mullen, Jackie Joseph John; Washburn, Norman Arthur; Delaney, Victor David; Depagie, Paul Adrin; Donhov, Roger

Alan; Gale, William Peter; Lucas, Robert James; McPherson, Donald Scott; Cannal, Allan J.; Copeman, G. T.; Diduck, Larry John; Powers, Harold Ernest; Pura, Stephen Richard; Shroll, Juergen; Mesjarlis, Leonard Joseph; Duignan, Lawrence James; King, Douglas Richard; Nixon, Thomas; Stern, Allen Edward; Gerling, Harold Joseph; Hanna, Robert; Harter, William; Lewis, Richard John Alan; Jourdain, David Stanley; Kemsley, Graham; McKinlay, Norman; Ayers, Terrance; Kelly, William; Maciuk, Dwayne; Scott, Raymond; McAllister, Lorne William.

EDSON — Rouillard, Donald Albert; Langston, Richard.

ENTWHISTLE—Hoople, Allan William.

EVANSBURG — Wade, Ronald Daryl; Jones, Kenneth Alan; Beynon, Terrance Robert.

FOREST LAWN—De Vos, Atie Adrianius; Eby, Gordon Allen; Richter, Raymond Leroy.

GAINFORD—Hyatt, Laurel.

GOODFARE — Wagner, Allen Ted; Reid, Garry Wayne; Wagner, James Patrick.

HILLCREST — Youngberg, Gordon Denis.

HINTON—McGillis, Allan Jay; Cholik, Thomas Brian; Culbertson, David.

HOBBEMA—Wofle, Gerald; Littlechild, Wilton.

HYTHE—Semenchuk, Ronnie.

INNISFAIL—Bennett, Dallas Garry; Gibbon, Donald Ross; Kerslake, Kenneth Timothy; Langevin, Delano Joseph; Seifried, Wallace August; Wallace, Clifford Allan.

LACOMBE — Scott, Darald Wallace; Marco, Robert Dale; Scott, Howard Terry.

LETHBRIDGE — Barnaby, Gerald Wayne; Hacker, Thomas William; Chapman, Edward Robert; Brown, Michael James King; Cook, Kennith Aaron; Johansen, Ole Christian Blangstrup; Jorgensen, Dennis Robert; Miller, Harley Ray; Roy, William Rene; Plante, G. D.; Peterson, Edward Albert.

LOUSANA — Hudec, Norman Ferdinand; Stenberg, Donald Ian.

FORT MACLEOD—Gerlat, Evald; Norgard, Geoffery Victor; Chilton, Authur Fredrick; Segboer, Murry Lloyd; Hirsche, Roger Willis.

MACLEOD—Magowan, Wesley Thomas.

MEDICINE HAT—Hintz, Manfred Segmand; Knight, Wayne Harvey.

MONTGOMERY—Penner, Robert Allen; Nickel, John Richard.

NORBUCK—Hoath, Joseph Merit.

PENHOLD—Jacquard, Dick.

REDCLIFF—Cameron, Clifford Alan; Campbell, Francis Alexander; Hildebrand, Russel George; Smith, Laurence James; Welford, Iain Hamilton; McGimpsey, Kennith Lloyd.

RED DEER—Briscoe, Bruce Graham; Anderson, Allan J.; Wagar, Lyle; Yule, Gordon.

REDWATER—Thebeau, Allan Robert.

ROCKY MT. HOUSE—Steeves, Jesse Leroy; Mulligan, Dennis Richard.

ROSETOWN—George, Dennis Richard.

SARCEE—Flynn, Thomas; Menu, John Paul.

SEBA BEACH — Seath, Robert Terrance.

SEDGEWICK — Beariso, Cal Calvin; Stephens, Gerald James; Stephens, Harold Lennard.

SPIRIT RIVER—Fildes, Geoffrey David; Stephen, D.; Harrington, Grant Russell; Stanfield, William Ray.

STRATHMORE—Glendinning, Thomas Walter; Vermunt, R. P.

THORSAY—Shave, Richard Theodore.

THORSBY—Westlund, Kenneth Cyril; Zilkiewski, Richard Thomas; Hallan, Fraser David.

TURNER VALLEY—Louth, Orville Elliott; Iuchia, Robert Peter; Owen, Thomas John Frank; Stuart, William Earl.

VEGREVILLE — Ferguson, Lawrence F.; Goshko, Glen Gorrie; Pruss, Rodney Peter.

VERMILION—Brower, Wallace Russel; Seddon, Herbert John; Armstrong, Allan Henry; Scarfe, Howard Alfred; Hathaway, Allan George.

VILNA—Parsons, David James; Shamchuk, Peter N.; Kuryliw, William James; Mikitka, Walter Paul.

VULCAN—Panter, Christopher; Horne, Canson Steward; Brinton, Ronald Harvey.

WAINWRIGHT — Baier, Stanley Gilbert; Fisher, William C.; Bobinski, Roman Joseph; Murray, Donald Edwin; Rajotte, Raymond Victor; Hunt, Gary James.

WARBURG—Mosicki, David William.

WESTLOCK — Bamandail, Gene Lee; Engler, R. P.

WILDWOOD—Roberts, Gordon; Hill, Edward Stephen.

WINFIELD—Dunn, James.

EDMONTON—Morehouse, Paul; Munroe, Ralph; Patsula, Daniel; Paul, Stanley Robert; Sinclair, Randy John; Zander, Michael.

NOMINAL ROLL OF SASKATCHEWAN CADETS

BATTLEFORD—Albert, Elmer; Hoover, Roland Ward; Allen, Patrick Alexander; Erler, Raymond Henry; Fletcher, Bryant Ronald; Koch, Orval Francis; Sack, Ronald James; Jarvis, Colin John; Long, Edward Leslie.

BIG RIVER—Beebe, Roger; Brownfield, Richard J.; Gilbert, John Richard; Kaese, Gregory; Kemp, Robert James; Klyne, Frank; Leach, Orville; Swanson, Norman; Wall, Joseph W.; Webb, Ray W.; Yurach, George F.

BIRCH HILLS—Mae, Robert.

BLAINE LAKE—Dutchak, Barry.

BROADVIEW—Alexson, Ray D.

CARLYLE—McArthur, E.

CARROT RIVER — Baumgarten, Eugene Louis; Holmes, David Leslie; Campbell, Larry Alexander; Joinson, Kenneth Albert; Lecain, Donald Edmond; Wilm, Richard Emil; Gulka, William Alexander; Veith, Clayton Allen.

CRAVEN—Carrier, Allen.

CREIGHTON—McDonald, Fergus Andrew; St. Pierre, Charles Henry; Waroway, Paul Joseph; Watson, Samuel Lewis; Aune, Gary Clifford; Barrow, Robert Ronald; Blake, Robert George; Thompson, James Arthur.

CUTKNIFE—Tootoosis, G. M.

DEER RIDGE—Daniels, Lawrence.

DENARE BEACH—Angell, Gerald William.

DERRIDGE—Badger, Jacob.

DINSMORE—David, Joseph Glen; Ellis, Keith Gordon; White, Donald Wayne; Heacock, Dale Frank; Kerslake, David Theodore.

DUCK LAKE—Cameron, Oliver Alexander; Debray, Donald; Ermine, Lennard; Mercereau, Claude Elie; Perillat, Paul; Petit, Gerald; Pilon, Edward; Sutherland, George Stanley; Busby, Delbert Norman; Horvath, Robert Edward.

EATONIA—Cooke, Brian Lyle.

EDENWOLD—Anaquod, Larry; Dubois, Wayne.

FAIRY GLEN—O'Byrne, Robert Carl; Yaremy, James Harry Michael.

FORT-AL-CORN — Burns, Salem A.; Whitehead, J.

FOSSTON—Zaporosky, Zenon Michael; Kryzanowski, Michael Anthony; Larson, Marwin Leroy.

GOLDEN PRAIRIE—Gieser, Gary Robert; Widmer, Robert Henry.

GOODEVE — Bellegarde, Joseph Edward; Bellegarde, Theodore.

GRENFELL—Bunnie, Sam.

HUMBOLDT—Bobinski, Bruce Hugo; Byj, Peter; Klitch, Gerald; Chutskoff, Sidney; Martin, Michael John; Stephen, Robert Douglas; Weinberger, Franklin Joseph; Morose, Raymond Fredrick; Vanderlinde, Ronald Harry; Hankey, Leander Frederick; Suek, Robert Edward; McMurchy, Ian Archie.

INVERMAY—Dusyk, Lester Lawrence; Dusyk, Marvin; Perret, Roger Wayne; Lee, Wayne; Melynchuk, Kenneth Wayne.

KERROBERT—Janzen, Clifford Fredrick; Allen, Walter; Henning, Frederick David; Lavinger, William; Peacock, Eric Edward; Robson, Frederick Rae; Schwab, Donald John.

KAMSACK—Badger, Charles.

KINISTINO—Turner, Arthur Norman.

LEASK — Duquette, Roland; Ledux, Gordon; Ledoux, Philip Narcissus; Johnstone, Patrick; Arcand, Walter.

LENVALE—Penkala, George John.

LUSELAND — Banks, Ronnie; Busby, Wayne; Jahner, Gregory; Jahner, Ronnie.

MARCELIN — Greyeyes, David; Labrosse, Roger; Mercereau, Claude Paul; Sanche, Albert Ernest; Lafond, William; Desjardins, Clifford Dennis; Tremblay, Edward Peter; Willick, Rolland Robert.

MARGO—Rudyk, William.

MELFORT—Froc, Antivan Vincent Albert; Love, Lloyd Archie; Wittig, Harvey Lorne.

MELVILLE—Kok, Fester; Hacala, Anthony Verne; Black, Frank Hutchition; Gaveronski, Lorne Lawrence; Goebel, Clifford Louis; Sundin, L. G.

MOOSE JAW—Bell, Robert George; Holland, John Wayne; Neufeld, Lawrence Edward; Perry, Kenneth Burl; Smith, Garth Thomas William; Walter, Michael Anthony; Wiebe, John; Wright, Norman James; Snell, Garry Everett; Spencer, Leslie Blair.

MORSE—Dozois, Leo Alfred Francis.

PAYTON—Favel, E. Hubert; Frank, Aloysius; Pete, A. J.

PRINCE ALBERT — Paziuk, Bernard Roger; Zwack, Douglas; Demerais, Arthur John; Amos, Charles Vincent; Carlson, Verti Boris; Charette, Robert George; Cooke, Donald Greg; Eskes, Kenneth Ronald; Kereluk, James; Morin, John Pierce; Wen, Vincent Howard; Wiese, Wayne Arthur; Picklyk, Gerald Zennon; Hummerstone, Eric; Morgan, Garry Bruce; Thompson, Ronald John.

PUNNICHY—Bird, Ivan; Blind, Jack; Blind, J.; Key, William; Morris, H. G.; Morris, Wayne Harvey; Morrison, Clarence; Neckoway, Robert; Pratt, Morley David; Pratt, Robert; Ouskun, Enock; Spence, J. G.; Walker, H.

REGINA — Clowes, Sandy; Anderson, Joseph Michael Dennis; Chretien, Joseph John Albert; Cocks, Dennis Adrian; Anderson, Brian; McLaughlin, James; Carrigan, Dennis Lloyd; Larson, Gary Bernard; Mario, Kenneth Wayne; Rothwell,

Samuel Joseph; Whiteoak, Larry Jack; Hugel, John Michael; Jones, Brian; Kish, Melvin Larry; Mruk, Leo Patrick Alexander; Ridgeway, Douglas Morley; Seiferling, Gabriel Jack; Tasche, Andrew Christopher; Vertes, Charles; Thomson, Larry Wayne; Manz, Raymond John; Cline, Elton Raymond; Anderson, Robert John; Foster, Patrick Martin; Johnson, William Ernest; Perry, Michael Gordon; Dunbar, Marvin; Flaman, Jerome; Gordon, James; Hagley, Larry; Horning, Ted; Huber, James.

ROCKFORD—Saganace, John James.

ROSETOWN — Raven, Marvin Keith; Thrascher, Robert Glen; Alexander, Gerald Robert; Cheyne, Douglas Wayne; Fowell, Fraser Albert; Holler, Robert Frederick; Machan, Gordon Francis; Marfell, Terry Lewis.

ROSE VALLEY—Florness, Arnold Gordon; Irwin, Kenneth Frank; Wilson, Morley David; Anderson, Robert Elgin; Florness, Daryl; Batula, Gerald Mitchel; Batula, William Lyle; Davis, Gerald William.

SASKATOON—Dmytrowich, Ron Larry; Docking, Robert Thomas; Gifford, Edward Blake; Halcro, Gordon Lawrence Bruce; Hoffly, Norman; Mahoney, Michael Dennis; Miller, Rae Phillip; Schofield, William Cyril; Szunyik, Joseph James; Crawford, Robert Laurel; Moore, Harold Wayne; Dlugos, John Joseph; Horley, Lyle L.; Kurenda, Ronald; McCamon, Gary; Moskol, Robert; Mullen, Gary; Peters, Edwin; Williams, Ronald H.; Wilson, Gerald; Eaton, James William; Horley, Lowie E.; Wolfe, David.

SPEERS — Boorman, Robert William; Bomok, Michael William.

SPRUCE HOME—Ermine, Nicholas.

STURGIS—Rose, Clifford Ernest; Pruden, Wilfred; Varemchuk, Ronald Roy; Babiuk, John Len; Holmberg, Gary; Jolson, Garry Wayne.

SWIFT CURRENT—Cameron, William Kenneth; Banman, Robert John; Cameron, Robert Isaac; Sartison, Ronald Fred.

TURTLEFORD — Eischen, Joseph Frank; Edwards, William Ross; Phillips, Thomas Edwain; Rallison, Alfred Robert; Rascher, David John.

VICTOIRE—Dreauer, Paul.

WADENA — Peterson, Gordon Beauford; Stroshein, Gerald Lewis; Bowman, Barry Dale; Hill, Garth Carl; Muir, Roy Kenneth; Wolff, James Donald; Zimrose, Joseph Melvin.

WEYBURN—Lawson, James Murray; Gregorash, John Bruce; Hill, William John; Leask, Robert Joseph; Millen, John Earl; Tabish, Edward Vincent; Thompson, Garry Raymond; Neiszner, Vernon Jacob.

WOOD MOUNTAIN—Goodtrack, Francis.

YORKTON—Palka, Mario Joseph; Skilnick, Lorne Byrne; Ward, Gary Joseph; Wytrykush, Michael Mervin; Erigidear, Bernard James; Mandziuk, Gary; Wantuck, Mervy Edward.

NOMINAL ROLL OF MANITOBA CADETS

BEAUSEJOUR—Holyk, G.; Kilbre, Kenneth; Meuchon, T. P.; Wittmeir, Douglas; Keeper, Lorne; Kellett, Harry; Relf, Charles; Steffes, Cliff; Riley, Jack; Schiller, Gerald.

BETHANY—Boyd, Garry.

BRANDON—Balkwill, Rodney James; Carruthers, Alexander Roy; Dodd, Glen; Stark, Thomas Gordon; Woodward, Richard Jack; McCaig, Blain Allen; Wisemen, Russell Douglas; Sawle, George Leonard;

Ostash, Nicholas.

CHARLESWOOD—Henry, Barry; Winters, Gerald; Winters, John; Huggard, Richard H.; Taylor, William.

CHURCHILL—Wright, Terry; Oelsner, R. Godfrey; Demeulles, Arthur; Ashford, Ernest John; Bingham, Harold.

CRANE RIVER—Moar, Collin.

DAUPHIN—Torrie, Robert Malcolm; Bloomfield, Thomas Edward; Becker, Kenneth; Gosman, Richard; Kerr, Orrin; Nickolson, Keith; Nykiforuk, William; Shick, Dennis.

FLIN FLON—Harkiss, Henry Stewart; Law, Robert John; Rumbal, Thomas Edward.

GILLAM—Kitchikisik, Joseph; Kitchikisik, Zaccheus.

GLENFIELDS—Belton, Jeffrey Robert.

KELWOOD — Weatherill, Douglas Arnold; Krenz, Wayne; Thompson, Lorne Master.

KILDONAN—Jones, Hugh David.

KIRKFIELD—Bilous, Maurice.

McCREARY—McKenzie, Russell; Marcicke, Larry.

WINNIPEG and ST. BONIFACE—Lang, Gerhart; Gloux, Joseph John Paul; Guilbault, Albert George Joseph; Hebert, Gillies; Kahler, Brian; Kusyk, John Hawthorn; Lamoureux, Edward Wayne; Leach, Christopher Paul; Matthews, Douglas; Moroz, William; Nicolson, Cameron; Papp, Joseph; Raineault, Gilbert; Reitmeier, Ronald; Ridd, David; Ringeisen, Werner; Rinne, Fred; Smith, Eric Ernest; Tait, Robert; Tardiff, Andre; Tremblay, Roland; Willerton, David; Collins, Donald; Fanzega, Roy; Foster, Gerald; Lauder, Andrew.

MIDDLECHURCH — Andrews, Gerald Allison; Fulsher, Joseph Brian.

MINNEDOSA — Buck, Douglas; Delmage, Keith; MacDuff, Thomas; Musselwhite, David.

PINE FALLS — Ryan, Dennis; Will, Duncan; Fraser, Robert A.; Gold, Dave J.

PORTAGE LA PRAIRIE—Ripmeester, John.

RIDING MOUNTAIN — Carter, Terrance James.

ROSEAU RIVER—Pierre, Victor.

SELKIRK—Russnak, Thomas.

SHILO—Clinton, Laverne Neil; Stinson, Peter Robin; Burns, Terry Wayne; Dalgheish, Allan; Gagne, Joseph Edward Robert; MacGregor, Cary Alan France; Moulaison, Max John; Morton, Ronald.

ST. JAMES—Jones, Lindel Hugh.

STONE MOUNT—Hepner, Robert.

THALBERG—Parke, Geoffrey.

TRANSCONA — Lamoureux, James; Stein, Robert; Marciniw, Mike.

VIRDEN—Krumins, Aivars; Nield, Robert Bruce; Workman, Robert Alfred.

WINNIPEG and ST. BONIFACE (Cont.) —Burrell, Mathew Osmond; Cairns, Murray Leslie; Davis, James Milton; Cook. Robert James; Covey, James; Golden, Kenneth; Herltein, Orvalie; Rubiletz, Victor William; Anderson, Donald; Dixon, Brian; Gingras, Paul; Kearney, David; Nairne, William; Powney, James; Robinson, Donald; Sharpe, Donald; Slobik, Wilfred; Wiebelskircher, Roger; Anderson, Robert John; Coble, David James; Hebert, Denis Leon Joseph; O'Brien, Kevin James; Rog, Bernard Raymond; Toifl, Edward; Votto, Roger; Van de Vyvere, Bert William; Dudek, Brian; Altvater, Fred; Black, James Fredrick; Gallagher, Patrick; Guziak, Norman; Hluchaniuk, Walter; Martin, Lorne Andrew; Scott, Robert Wayne; Seaman, Garry; Shaley, Robert; Stengrim, Marwin Julian; Cook, Dennis J.; Fedak, Vy;

Finnigan, B.; Gossfield, Alec; Heese, Wolfgang; Howe, Ron; Isaacs, Leroy; Jeffrey, G.; Laronde, Larry; Learmonth, Lloyd P.; Lesage, Larry; McKnight, W. E.; Miller, Glen; Muller, Burkhardt; Pesclive, Joe; Picklyk, Robert; Topley, Roy; Wiebe, D. B.; Belanger, Andre; Boorman, Robert William; Bourgeois, Richard; Cornborough, Larry James; Cyr, Paul Joseph; Davis, William Henry; Michaelis, Kenneth; Thickson, Bruce. WINNIPEGOSIS—Denny, Sidney Glen.

VACC - 1961

The following cadets attended camp in 1961:

Adams, D. W.; Adams, P. J.; Ahern, D. J.; Ahlstrom, L. E.; Ainsley, J. T.; Aitchison, A. K.; Akins, R. N.; Akkerman, Klaas; Alexander, G. R.; Alexander, R. J.; Alexson, R. D.; Allan, R. G.; Allen, D. W.; Allen, Walter; Allsupp, B. R.; Anderson, A. L.; Anderson, B. E.; Anderson, D. J.; Anderson, D. V.; Anderson, J. C.; Anderson, L. H.; Anderson, L. K.; Anderson, L. S.; Anderson, R. S.; Anderson, R. S.; Anderson, R. O.; Anderson, T. J.; Anderson, V. B.; Annand, D. A.; Antoniak, R. L.; Antonson, T. E.; Appleby, R. S.; Arbuthnott, P. J.; Armells, F. R.; Armstrong, D. W.; Armstrong, G. H.; Armstrong, W. P.; Arnal, G. G.; Arrance, D. C.; Arychuk, G. N.; Asher, Robert; Ashton, F. I. R.; Austin, M. J.

Babbs, B. J.; Babbs, R. L.; Bach, R. J.; Backen, M. G.; Bacon, J. E.; Bain, R. D.; Baker, A. R.; Baker, R. H.; Baker, W. T.; Ball, R. E.; Balfour, L. A.; Balkwill, R. J.; Ball, K. A.; Banman, R. J.; Bannister, James; Barnhart, D. B.; Barr, B. K.; Barratt, D. A. N.; Barsalou, G. L.; Baskett, David; Bateman, I. M.; Bates, L. J.; Bator, H. R. J.; Batten, J. E.; Bauer, J. L.; Baugh, W. J.; Bayuk, Martin; Bazant, W. F.; Beckett, P. M.; Beday, R. E.; Beebe, R. C.; Begagne, Claude; Beilner, J. F.; Belanger, E. M.; Bellegarde, E. B.; Bengkston, G. K.; Bennett, G. J.; Bennett, L. V.; Bennett, R. C.; Bent, B. J.; Berry, L. L.; Bettin, R. J.; Bialecki, M. S.; Biggins, M. E.; Bingham, H. G.; Bird, William; Birk, J. J.; Bjarnason, D. A.; Bjornson, Ingemar; Black, D. A.; Black, F. H.; Bielle, N. L.; Blind, T. S.; Blogg, G. A.; Bodry, L. T.; Boisselle, M. F.

Borzel, G. R.; Bosch, A. J.; Botte, Joseph; Bottomley, D. E.; Bourleois, R. A.; Bourne, G. R.; Boyd, D. G.; Boyd, R. G.; Boyer, R. J.; Boylan, G. W.; Brandt, B. E.; Brigadier, B. J.; Brine, J. R.; Britten, P. C.; Brock, R. M.; Brose, G. W.; Brost, A. L.; Brown, L. J.; Brown, R. J.; Brown, W. G. L.; Brownlee, A. R.; Bruce, N. J.; Bruce, J. T.; Bruce, K. C.; Brunham, A. P.; Brydon, J. S.; Buchanan, K. H.; Buchanan, K. R.; Bugaresti, R. M.; Bulger, C. E.; Bull, Ross; Burbee, B. C.; Burbee, K. D.; Burn, Allen; Burnell, D. H.; Burns, J. E.; Burns, T. W.; Burt, D. W.; Burton, F. R.; Bush, J. H.; Bushby, F. G.; Bussey, E. W.; Buzan, G. W.; Bye, M. S.; Byers, P. L.

Caesar, R. T.; Cairns, M. L.; Callaghan, W. D.; Cameron, C. A.; Campbell, R. N.; Campbell, D. R.; Campbell, F. A.; Campbell, J. G.; Campbell, P. B.; Campbell, R. C.; Canabee, Boniface; Capelle, John; Carlson, R. A.; Carpenter, J. W.; Carr, G. A.; Carreck, D. H.; Carreck, N. A.;

Carritt, J. D.; Carruthers, A. R.; Carruthers, G. E.; Carter, B. J.; Carter, J. T.; Carter, T. J.; Case, D. L.; Cassidy, T. C.; Caton, I. H.; Chadsey, G. B.; Chambers, Michael; Charlwood, L. W.; Cherenko, A. F.; Chinn, R. J.; Chisholm, J. H.; Chomos, B. J.; Chopty, Lawrence; Chow, Jim; Cianflone, John; Cimmer, Louis; Cluca, G. M.; Clark, J. D.; Clarke, P. H.; Clayton, J. A.; Cochrane, L. L.; Cocks, P. W.; Cody, J. V.; Comeault, Claude; Common, K. J.; Conley, R. B.; Connal, A. J.; Connaughton, R. E.; Cook, C. P.; Cook, Jimmy; Cook, L. J.; Cook, P. A.; Cooper, E. W.; Coughlin, R. L.; Coventry, F. D.; Cowie, K. G.; Cox, J. N.; Craig, L. J.; Crawford, C. J.; Cresswell, C. A.; Croaker, L. E.; Croy, C. R.; Csano, Arpad; Culbertson, D. A.; Cummings, F. L.; Cunningham, T. J.; Currie, S. E.

Dahl, J. G.; Daniels, D. W.; Danyluk, R. C.; Davidson, J. A.; Davidson, R. W.; Davidson, W. M.; Davies, G.; Dawson, S. T.; Deans, William; Degenstien, E. R.; DeGroot, George; Deguire, P. T.; Dehnke, W. A.; Delbert, R. H.; Deitsch, L. E.; Demeulenarere, D. L.; Demchuk, C. E.; Demerais, L. H.; Demkiw, S. A.; Denby, H.; Denniel, E. L.; Dennison, D. K.; DePagie, P. A.; Derksen, M. H.; Derosier, G. L.; Descalchuk, G. A.; Deschutter, J. J.; Desjardins, C. D.; Desjarlais, G. W.; Despatis, R. A.; D'Etcheverrey, J. A.; Devlin, William; Dias, Alan; Dicer, J. M.; Dick, G. P.; Dinsmore, J. B.; Dissel, W. T.; Dixon, B. L.; Dixon, W. R.; Dmytruk, A. J.; Dobson, P. H.; Dodd, Glen; Dolff, G. E.; Douglas, G. A.; Douglas, J. A.; Downie, R. P.; Dozorec, Henry; Dreaver, G. A.; Drinkwater, R. G.; Dube, G. P.; Dublowski, J. R.; Duddy, C. J.; Duke, L. J.; Duncan, F. A.; Dunlop, R. A.; Durelow, P. D.; Durnin, E. N.; Durward, W. J.; Dusyk, Marvin; Dutchak, Barry; Dyck, J. D.

Eakins, P. D.; Eames, H. E.; Eamor, H. R. J.; Earle, A. C.; Eastman, Barry; Eddy, Allan; Edgar, James; Edginton, Stephen; Edwards, W. R.; Eggleston, D. A.; Eggleston, E. A.; Elder, J. C.; Eleason, L. H.; Elendiuk, T. W. M.; Elliott, Allan; Elliott, Robert; Ellis, S. G.; Emerick, Stan; Engel, K. H.; Ennis, R. F.; Enokson, Ross; Ewasluk, Richard; Evans, R. W.; Evans, Terrence; Everett, W. D.; Ewen, N. R.

Falkenberg, W. J.; Farnel, F. L.; Fedik, Walter; Fentiman, H. B. G.; Ferg, C. R.; Ferguson, A. R.; Feuillatre, C. J.; Field, L. E.; Fish, Gordon; Fisher, B. G.; Fitsch, J. B.; Flaman, August; Flatman, Ron; Fleming, T. E.; Flett, Joseph; Flower, Russell; Flug, R. J.; Flynn, Patrick; Folstrom, E. K.; Fontaine, P. L.; Forbes, G. J.; Fortinski, Chester; Foster, David; Fournier, Pierre; Francois, Harvey; Freeman, J. W.; French, W. E.; Fridfinnson, Ralph; Fridfinnson, Walter; Fritchie, W. L.; Frost, Michael; Fuldrook, James; Fullerton, L. W.; Fulljames, Michael.

Gallacher, G. J.; Gardner, D. K.; Gardner, Larry; Garner, W. A.; Geertsema, Jacob; Geiger, N. R.; George, A. G.; Gerlat, Evald; Gerling, H. J.; Glasson, R. L.; Gibb, W. G.; Gibberd, J. D.; Gilbert, Gary; Gilbert, John R.; Gillespie, Nell; Gillis, R. J.; Gislason, R. D.; Glover, W. F.; Goebel, C. J.; Goebel, C. L.; Godber, R. A.; Goes, J. J. W.; Goggnelig, Gregory; Goluk, John; Goodtrack, Francis; Goodwin, K. L.; Gorrigan, Charles; Goss, B. J.;

Graham, Earl; Graham, E. L.; Graham, G. G.; Granger, G. T.; Grant, David; Gresvette, David; Green, Brian; Green, B. J.; Green, R. R.; Gregorash, J. B.; Greyeyes, A. S.; Greyeyes, F. J.; Grosse, C. R.; Grubb, D. McC.; Guetre, R. J.; Guilbeault, P. R.; Gundrum, W.; Gunn, R. J.

Haase, D. L.; Hackett, P. S.; Hagen, James; Halcrow, K. C.; Hall, Hugh; Hall, R. J.; Halmie, L. J.; Halter, Melville; Hamilton, W. R.; Handley, W. E.; Handyside, K. G.; Hankey, L. F.; Hansen, D. R.; Hansen, F. E.; Hansen, Thomas; Hanson, E. L.; Harder, Tyrone; Hardowa, R. D.; Hardy, B. A.; Hargrave, Tony; Harris, Christopher; Harris, D. H.; Harris, W. N.; Hart, Paul; Hart, Thomas; Harvey, D. A.; Haskin, W. G.; Haughton, T.; Hawkesnorth, N. R.; Hawthorne, Edward; Hay, J. G.; Heagle, G. R.; Healey, Barry; Hedley, Terrance; Helben, B. S.; Heinz, S. W.; Hellum, D. N.; Hendricks, Gerald; Henry, Arthur; Henry, V. L.; Henthorne, Eric; Herle, Michael; Herrington, R. M.; Hewlett, W. B.; Hicke, James; Hidleaugh, R. J.; Hiebert, Jake; Hill, Donald; Hill, Glen; Hills, Jeffrey; Hiltz, K. D.; Hjelmeland, B. J.; Haley, L. S.; Hodal, J. D.; Hodges, A. E.; Hoffman, J. A.; Hollo, Peter; Holloway, M. W.; Holmberg, Brian; Hopkin, R. T.; Hopkins, H. J.; Hotell, A. R.; Howie, R. G.; Huard, R. C.; Hudson, Russell; Hugel, J. M.; Hughes, Leonard; Humphrey, R. L.; Humphries, Glen; Hunt, W. A.; Hunter, R. A.; Huscroft, G. M.

Ignatius, A. P.; Inglis, G. M.; Ingram, D. R.; Ireland, T. P.; Irving, Michael; Irwin, K. F.; Isackson, M. R.; Isbister, V. L.

Jabbott, Simon; Jackson, K. E.; Jacobs, Robert; Jacobsen, Garry; Jahner, G. V.; Jamison, E. B.; Jarvis, P. L. L.; Jarvis, W. E.; Jaschke, L. W.; Jean, R. C.; Jean, Herve; Jeffrey, Gerald; Jeffreys, E. R.; Jensen, Harry; Johnson, Fred; Johnson, G. B.; Johnson, Graham; Johnson, Hubert; Johnson, K. M.; Johnson, P. J.; Johnston, Dennis; Johnston, James; Johnston, J. F.; Jone, C. S.; Jones, John; Jones, N. G.; Jordan, W. R.

Kainz, A. M.; Karst, D. A.; Kaye, D. J.; Keetch, M. H.; Kelly, A. R.; Kelly, B. R.; Kelly, William; Kennard, R. D.; Kennedy, Dennis; Kennedy, D. A.; Kennedy, Ivan; Kennelly, Wayne; Kent, D. E.; Keogan, P. H.; Kerdit, R. M.; Kerr, P. R.; Kerton, E. G.; Ketsa, S. M.; King, R. J. F.; Kingdon, B. W.; Kison, D. G.; Kittle, C. R.; Klepachek, K. J. J.; Kline, John; Klitch, G. J. G.; Klyne, Franlin; Kock, O. F.; Kok, Fester; Kopp, B. A.; Kostiuk, R. C.; Kozak, B. F.; Kozak, P. J.; Kraft, Ralph; Krivoshein, R. W.; Krueger, V. K.; Kuffler, L. E.; Kuhn, N. W.; Kulyk, Alexander; Kurylo, D. M.; Kynel, B. A.

Laatsch, L. H.; Lacheur, W. R.; Lafond, William; Lahaie, J. M.; Laird, W. K.; Langis, T. V.; Langston, Larry; Langton, J. W.; Lanigan, J. J.; LaRose, L. J.; Lauritsen, Eric; Laverty, C. M.; Lawn, Robert; Lawrence, J. W.; Lawson, R. J.; Layton, R. D.; Leach, C. P.; Leach, O. C.; Leask, Gordon; Leask, J. G.; Lebrun, John; Ledoux, Gordon; Leduc, R. H. A.; Lee, D. W.; Leeming, J. R.; Legood, J. E.; Leitch, D. R.; Leonard, A. W.; Leonard, M. R.; Lepsoe, R. A.; Letourneau, D. R.; Levers, J. K.; Levesque, A. J.; Lindgren, D. L.; Lindsay, S. F.; Lindstein,

N. E.; Lissack, K. G.; Lock, D. J.; Logan, D. E.; Logan, T. W.; Long, R. A.; Lorenzo, R D.; Loughins, H. A.; Loverin, J. D.; Lowe, E. C.; Lowe, R. A.; Lowrey, J. A.; Luchak, William; Lugrin, R. C. R.; Lundrin, R. A.; Lundrigan, I. R.; Lunn, H. P.; Luterbach, R. J.

MacDonald, C. P.; MacDonald, D. C.; MacDonald, W. M.; MacGregor, G. A. F.; MacGregor, J. R.; MacIntyre, A. J.; MacIntosh, G.; MacIntosh, J. F.; MacKenzie, B. R.; MacKenzie, G. S.; MacKenzie, K. G.; MacLean, D. J.; MacLean, J. F.; MacLennan, J. J.; MacLeod, Archie; MacLeod, R. J.; MacPherson, R. D.; MacRae, D. W.; McArthur, R. J.; McCabe, G. P.; McCaffrey, J. W.; McCall, Raymond; McCarthy, J. R.; McCulloch, R. J.; McDonald, R. D.; McFarlane, E. R.; McFarlane, G. M.; McGaffin, W. D.; McGladrie, R. A.; McGoran, P. C.; McIntyre, H. A.; McKay, G. R.; McKay, R. W.; McKee, D. J.; McKellar, T. W.; McKnight, J. R.; McKnight, W. E.; McLean, J. C.; McLean, J. R.; McLean, K. M.; McLennan, L. J.; McLennan, R. J.; McLeod, G. A.; McLeod, Oliver; McMahon, R. J.; McMynn, J. G.; McNaughton, N. R.; McNeal, R. G.; McNeil, R. K.; McRae, R. E. G.; Macaig, B. A.; Mackie, W. R.; Maddigan, M. J.; Magee, J. W.; Mager, Allen; Magnussen, R. R.; Magowan, R. A.; Malanchuk, R. W.; Malbranck, R. G.; Malden, J. J.; Mandryk, D. R.; Mangnall, N. K.; Manlon, G. W.; Manz, R. J.; Marcicki, L. D.; Marr, L. E.; Marshall, F. W.; Martin, P. A.; Martin, T. L.; Mast, Gerd; Masterton, D. C.; Measor, D. C.; Meier, R. J.; Melnichuk, K. E.; Melnychuk, K. W.; Mennie, S. G.; Menu, J. P.; Mercereau, R. E.; Mergle, K. A.; Merritt, H. G.; Metke, D. H.; Michaluk, Marshall; Mike, C. L.; Millen, J. E.; Miller, D. J.; Miller, G. R.; Miller, J. A.; Miller, L. G.; Miller, R. G.; Miller, R. D.; Miller, Roland; Miller, W. E.; Millham, C. M.; Millwater, D. A.; Minnis, J. T.; Mitchell, G. I.; Moffat, A. W.; Mohammad, Donald; Mongeon, L. I.; Mooy, W. R.; Moraes, R. E.; Maran, B. P.; Mofen, K. J.; Morgan, E. F.; Morgan, G. B.; Mori, Harold; Morin, Ernest; Morino, J. M.; Morrison, G. D.; Morrison, M. D.; Mosicki, D. J.; Mossey, J. E.; Mostert, Dirk; Mostoway, E. W.; Moulton, W. R.; Mulrooney, J. M.; Munch, R. R.; Munich, George; Murphy, Larry; Murray, R. J. A.; Murray, R. L.

Nairne, W. G.; Naylor, P. E.; Neish, J. R.; Nelson, L. E.; Nelson, Leonard; Nelson, M. R.; Nelson, R. E.; Nesbitt, D. J.; Neufeld, E. E.; Newell, D. M.; Newnes, R. G.; Nichol, J. R.; Nickel, J. R.; Nickerson, B. W.; Nicol, R. P.; Nicolson, J. I.; Norby, L. C.; Norfolk, S. E. R.

O'Byrne, L. K.; Odegard, G. A.; Odermatt, R. J.; Olafson, C. H.; Olafson, J. W.; Olesky, R. D.; Oliver, V. R.; Oliver, W. G.; Olson, K. W.; Ono, Allan; Ouellette, G. W.; Ouellette, Walter; Owen, T. J.; Oxenham, C. A.

Pachal, K. J.; Pachkowski, G. J.; Pacowski, E. P.; Page, J. C.; Page, J. N.; Papps, J. R.; Parisian, B. W.; Paterson, D. W.; Patrick, P. J.; Paulsen, A. J.; Paulin, J. C. C.; Paulson, H. J.; Payne, R. F.; Payne, W. P.; Pearson, B. F.; Peet, G. C.; Peet, R. C.; Pederson, R. K.; Perniale, T. N. B.; Perry, R. T.; Pesclivetch, J. J.; Peters, M. A.; Petersen, D. W.; Pettifor, D. A.; Pfefferle, M. N.; Phillips, Frank; Phillips, R. L.; Picklyk, G. Z.;

506

Pittaway, M. M.; Pirie, R. J.; Plock, J. J.; Podollan, T. N.; Poirier, P. A.; Pollard, B. McK.; Pollock, Kent; Pomeroy, R. D.; Pool, G. R.; Popejoy, B. E.; Potocniak, A. F.; Powell, Thomas; Powers, J. E.; Pratt, M. D.; Pratt, R. K.; Price, A. L.; Price, A. W.; Price, C. R.; Price, Clement; Price, Patrick; Pring, A. J.; Prosner, T. N.; Pura, Stephen; Purdy, R. B.; Pyne, G. M.

Quaal, K. S.; Quesnel, A. E.; Quick, D. A.; Rachwalski, J. W.; Randalls, R. S.; Rascher, D. J.; Rathgeber, R. R.; Raven, A. J.; Ray, L. C.; Razzo, W. T.; Redman, Dean; Reed, Howard; Reid, D. A.; Reid, G. W.; Reid, M. M.; Reid, T. F.; Reitmeier, R. W.; Rekve, G. E.; Remple, R. A.; Remple, R. W.; Rest, G. L.; Reynolds, D. R.; Reznik, R. J.; Rhode, R. P.; Rice, D. J.; Richardson, P. A.; Rickey, Ronald; Ridd, D. M.; Riel, D. J.; Rikley, R. J.; Ring, V. E.; Riske, Peter; Rivers, F. E.; Roberts, B. C.; Roberts, D. W.; Nagy, Steven; Nahannee, G. L.; Nahanee, R. J.; Roberts, G. W.; Robertson, J. D.; Robertson, I. D.; Robertson, W. E.; Robichaud, R. M.; Robinson, C. R.; Robinson, J. W.; Robson, Rae; Rockwell, J. A.; Rogers, D. I.; Rogers, M. J.; Rosner, A. G.; Ross, E. A.; Ross, N. A.; Ross, T. A.; Rothwell, S. J.; Rouillard, D. R.; Rourke, William; Rowlinson, Terrance; Royle, D. J.; Rozon, L. P.; Russell, R. J.; Ryan, D. M.; Ryan, R. D.

Sabatini, Bruce; Sagan, T. J.; Sagmace, J. J.; Sall, A. C.; Sartison, H. G.; Sartison, R. F.; Saxtaunik, K. J.; Sauve, R. H. F.; Sauviat, H. J.; Sawatsky, K. W.; Sawle, G. L. T.; Schaffer, L. E.; Scapansky, A. G.; Schlosser, J. W.; Schmid, T. H.; Schmidt, I. J.; Schmidt, M. W.; Schneider, A. H.; Scott, J. W.; Scott, R. G.; Scott, T. F.; Seaman, G. R.; Seay, B. T.; Sego, R. A.; Seiferling, G. J.; Sells, E. D.; Senger, T. W.; Seto, A. W.; Sewell, A. G.; Shanko, B. A.; Sharman, M. P.; Sharp, R. S.; Sharpe, M. A.; Shaw, J. W.; Shaw, Russell; Sheppard, R. M.; Sherb, T. L.; Sherman, L. M.; Shineton, B. J.; Shokal, Peter; Shook, G. N.; Shuter, J. R.; Sieradzan, Marian; Silverton, G. C.; Silvey, M. J.; Simpson, D. G.; Simpson, I. G.; Sinclair, Randall; Sinnock, C. G.; Sippola, G. G.; Skibinski, R. N.; Skinner, T. C.; Skinner, W. R.; Skolos, Wayne.

Sloan, R. J.; Smalley, L. I.; Smit, Casey; Smith, A. R.; Smith, David; Smith, D. I.; Smith, G. I.; Smith, Howard; Smith, L. P.; Smith, L. W.; Smith, R. R.; Smith, W. M. E.; Smook, L. K.; Soderlund, J. B.; Soderman, W. A.; Sorbin, R. G.; South, J. J.; Sowerby, N. T.; Spearey, W. J.; Spence, David; Spence, S. E.; Spracklin, E. T.; Spraggs, W. H.; Stables, K. W.; Stack, R. J.; Stackhouse, I. R.; Standish, F. P.; Stangtar, J. C.; Stanoffski, R. I. J.; State, B. I.; Stark, A. P.; Starr, A. J.; Steele, J. R.; Steele, I. A.; Stein, R. E.; Steinke, R. C.; Stephenson, D. B.; Stephenson, D. G.; Stephenson, M. E.; Stewart, D. W.; St. Hilaire, A. M.; Stier, G. J.; Stimson, H. D.; Stokes, R. B.; Stone, C. A.; Stone, S. J.; Straight, R. D.; Stregger, R. C.; Stringer, D. McN.; Stroshein, J. A.; Stupnikoff, H. M.; Suek, R. E.; Sullivan, J. J.; Surowy, S. J.; Sutherland, Antolne; Sutherland, Sidney; Swakum, C. A.; Swan, H. T.; Sweet, Thomas; Szova, Michael.

Tack, L. J.; Tait, D. G.; Tait, R. G.; Tannant, Carson; Taylor, H. A.; Taylor, J. C.; Taylor, Mike; Taylor, Robert; Taylor, W. A.; Taylor, W. S.; Tebbutt, G. R.; Teets, A. W.; Tepper, G. W.; Terleaky, R. B.; Terrick, N. F.; Tessman, S. C.; Tessman, T. W.; Tetz, R. D.; Therlault, R. E.; Thom, I. N.; Thomas, B. W.; Thomas, R. M.; Thompson, G. R.; Thornhill, E. S.; Thrasher, R. G.; Tingley, K. W. G.; Tinnish, G. A.; Tipton, J. W.; Tizzard, P. I. C.; Tochor, A. J.; Tomkulak, A. G.; Tomyn, G. E.; Treflak, P. J.; Tuck, C. D.; Tulloch, D. B.; Turcotte, A. J.; Turner D. J.; Tutt, P. C.; Tuttle, H. F. S.

Urac, J. C.; Urquhart, D. P.; Van der Hoek, William; Van der Loos, J. W.; Van Klaveren, A. C.; Van Schaik, John; Van Weele, M. C.; Vere, B. A.; Vermunt, R. P.; Vickers, B. G.; Viens, J. B.; Vincent, A. P.; Vinnell, B. S.; Vis, C. P.

Wade, R. K.; Wagner, W. R.; Wagstaff, Wayne; Wainwright, Benjamin; Wakefield, A. B.; Walker, D. L. B.; Walker, W. W.; Walker, W. L.; Walker, W. R. C.; Wallace, C. A.; Wallace, K. W.; Wallace, R. A.; Walley, Rick; Walter, D. H.; Ward, K. T.; Wardlaw, H. G.; Washburn, N. A.; Waskewitch, J. C.; Watkins, L. E.; Watson, A. H.; Watson, B. M.; Watson, N. R.; Watt, T. V.; Watts, A. J.; Watts, L. P.; Weaver, D. H.; Weaver, R. G.; Webb, R. C.; Webber, K. L.; Weber, P. E.; Weels, J. R.; Weekend, C. J.; Wegener, Herman; Welch, T. S.; Wendel, B. W.; Westlund, K. C.; Weston, G. M.; Wetherill, D. A.; Wethersett, M. C.; Whale, A. N.; Whatley, M. R.; Wheeldon, R. M. D.; White, G. D.; White, J. W.; White, W. L.; Whitford, C. I. R.; Whiting, R. W.; Whitley, W. G.; Whitman, R. G.; Whitmore, A. D.; Whyte, G. S.; Widerski, Stanley; Wiebe, G. D.; Wiebe, H. D.; Wiebe, R. H.; Wiebelskircher, R. E.; Wiekenkamp, P. J.; Wiens, A. G.; Wilkinson, D. C.; Wilkinson, R. A.; Will, D. W.; Willard, R. A.; Williams, L. O.; Williams, R. A.; Williamson, A. R.; Williamson, W. I.; Wills, B. T.; Wilm, R. E.; Wilson, C. J.; Windles, K. N.; Winter, D. G.; Winters, G. L.; Wipf, D. G.; Wittmeier, D. R.; Wolfe, G. H.; Wolff, J. D.; Wolfe, Peter; Wollen, I. D.; Womacks, M. E.; Wood, D. K.; Wood, P. M.; Woodward, R. J.; Woods, D. H.; Workman, R. A.; Wormald, B. H.; Wright, F. J.; Wyngaards, W. J.

Yackdowski, G. M.; Yard, P. G.; Yauste, D. C.; Yee, James; Yonkers, T. F.; Young, T. M.; Youngberg, E. A.; Youngberg, J. M.

Zabinski, Brian; Zeck, G. W.; Ziegler, Leo; Zimmer, Rudolph; Zimmerman, R. D.; Zimrose, M. J.; Zomar, D. F.

VACC - 1962

Adams, John Henry; Adams, Patrick Joseph; Aitken, John Robert; Aird, Grant; Akerman, Klaas; Alexander, Richard; Allan, Keith William; Alpen, Peter; Anctil, Gary Ernest; Anderson, Thomas Neil; Anderson, Donald Vernon; Anderson, John Richard; Anderson, Lionel Donald; Anderson, Richard Glen; Anderson, Richard Joachim; Anderson, Victor Brian; Anderson, William; Andre, Glen Herman; Andruniak, Leonard; Annand, Donald; Appleby, Robert Sydney; Appleton, Peter; Arbuthnott, Patrick Joseph; Archibald, Bruce; Armstrong, George Howard; Ashcroft, Melvin Leonard;

Ashdohunk, Bernard; Asher, Ronald; Ashmere, Thomas; Ashton, Albert Edward; Astle, Wayne Edward; Atchison, Colin Grant; Arneson, Marvin; Arrence, Darrell Clifford; Austin, William Edward.

Back, Richard; Badger, Aleck; Bakko, Olaf James; Baldwin, George Ross; Baldwin, Lorie Kenneth; Balkwill, Rodney James; Balton, Roger; Bannister, James; Barker, Harold Wayne; Barnes, Leonard; Barratt, Douglas; Bartel, Garry Leroy; Bartlett, Glen Daniel; Basaraba, Michael David; Bascott, Vern Edwin; Batter, John Brian; Batula, Gerald Mitchell; Bauer, John Larson; Bayuk, Martin; Bazley, Victor Eugene; Beckett, Peter; Bedford, Richard Jory; Bedu, Ronald George; Behn, Heiko; Beirness, Averd James; Belanger, Emilien Joseph; Bellamy, Warren Louis; Belleck, Robert; Bellegarde, Eldon Benedict; Bemben, Robert Michael; Benay, Brian; Bender, Randy; Bennett, Jack; Bennett, Lee; Berkaski, Harry George.

Berreth, Robert; Berry, Gordon; Bertnick, David James; Best, Richard John; Bester, Val; Bettin, Rudy James; Betty, Arthur Gilbert; Bialecki, Stanley; Bickford, Lorne; Bigelow, Edward Albert; Beglow, Jerry; Billeck, Paul Wayne; Binette, George; Birakowski, Eugene; Bird, William Gregory; Bishop, Ronald; Balir, Joseph; Blais, Marshall Norman; Blanchette, Joseph Denis; Blandford, Robert Michael; Blelle, Vallantyne; Bocking, Anthony; Bodden, Michael Stewart; Bodry, Lamont Thomas; Boisselle, Paul; Borzel, Jerald Richard; Boudreau, Richard; Bourbonnais, John Desmond; Boyle, Clarence James; Braithwaite, Irvin Martin; Brandt, Barton; Branstetter, Michael; Brass, Warren Wilfred; Brattland, Al Joseph; Breckenridge, James Nobel; Breslin, Dennis.

Brill, Wayne; Brooks, Ronald; Brose, Garry William; Brose, Michael Henry; Brown, James; Brown, Rickey; Brown, Terry; Browning, Glen Arthur; Browning, William John; Bruce, David Robert; Bruce, John; Bruce, Kenneth; Brunham, Albert Paul; Brunner, Terence Arnold; Bryan, Richard Fredrick; Bryden, John Stuart; Brydie, Lyall Douglas; Bucci, Lewis Cecil; Buck Bruce Alexander; Buchanan, Melvin; Behler, Charles; Bundy, Roger; Burbee, Kerry; Burkholder, William John; Burns, Terry; Burrows, Brian; Burt, Richard; Bush, John Howard; Bushby, Frank George; Byman, Brian Curtis; Byrnes, David Michael; Byrnes, Robert John

Calder, Denis; Cameron, Colin; Campbell, George Liskum; Campbell, Ronald James; Campbell, Thomas Fredrick William; Cantley, Robert Davis; Carreck, Douglas Harry; Carriere, Ronald Joseph; Carritt, John; Carruthers, David Glen; Carson, Raymond; Carter, Jim Barry; Carter, William; Case, Ron-

old, Cassin, Larry; Ceriko, Lloyd; Chabeniuk, Steve; Chadsey, Gary Brian; Chamber, Michael; Charlton, Douglas Glen; Charney, Lloyd; Chiasson, Lyle; Child, Garry; Childs, Gerald Arthur; Cherbo, Robin Peter; Cherewick, Wayne Keith; Chretin, Henry; Christianson, Donald George; Churchill, Roland; Chutskoff, Dale Nicholas; Clues, Gordon Matthew; Clairmont, Guy Allen Steve; Clark, Alan Ingrey; Clark, John; Clark, Leslie Ian; Clarke, Gordon; Clarke, William George; Clarkson, Lionel Warren

Clayton, Greg; Clayton, Jim; Clearsky, George; Clemmer, Bruce Troy; Cobb, Gerald Wayne; Code, Kenneth; Collard, John Louis; Comeault, Claude; Como, Robin; Conkline, Paul Orval; Connaughton, Robert; Conners, Larry; Connolly, David Albert; Conrod, Robert; Cook, Jerome; Cooke, Leslie Joseph; Cookman, Clifford; Cooper, William George; Corbett, Dennis Roy; Cotten, Dennis Leroy; Cotter, Wayne Stanley; Coulbourn, Wayne; Coulter, Robert; Coventry, Robert Terry; Crabbe, Brian Thomas; Cresswell, Michael William Walter; Crete, Laurence Allen; Croaker, Lambert Edgar; Cromley, Dennis Darel; Cropley, Gary Nelson; Crosbie, Ronald Eskrin; Csano, Steve; Cullen, Norman; Cumberland, William Collins; Curry, Terence; Curtis, Richard William; Cutforth, Gary.

Dabb, Peter William; Dagenais, Dennis Philip; Dale, John Oliver; Dale, Ronald John Oliver; Dalgarno, Brian; Dalgleish, Barry Gordon; Damual, Gerald; Dandenault, Robert; Danylchuk, Wayne; D'Arcy, Donald Norris; Dash, Edward Ernest; Davidson, Richard; Davies, Gordon; Davies, Lee; Davies, Brian Ralph; Davis, Robert; Davis, Ronald; Declereq, Ronald Maurice; Degen, Kent Phillip; Degenhardt, John; Deitsch, Laurence Earl; Dejung, Ted Adrius; Delorme, Harold James; Demchuk, Clarence Erwin; Demkiw, Bill; Dermott, Terry; Derouin, Patrick John; Descalchuk, George Allan; Desjardine, Clifford Denis; Desparias, Joseph; D'etcheverrey, John; Dias, Alan; Dick, Fred Allan; Dickson, Lawrence William; Dickson, William Wallace; Diehl, Milton David.

Dimrzio, Frank; Dipalo, Richard John; Dissell, William Thayer; Dixon, David Edison; Dixon, Jim; Dolff, Gerald Edwin; Dolinski, Donald John; Dombrosky, Brian; Donald, Charles Clouston; Donald, Richard; Donoghue, Michael; Douglas, Gary Allen; Douglas, James Allan; Downie, Roderick Paul; Dozorec, James Wesley; Dreaver, Glen Allen; Dreger, Theodore; Drinkwater, Robert; Druskin, Allen; Dube, Glen Patrick; Dubilowski, Jerry; Duff, Frank; Duke, Llewellyn; Dukelow, Patrick; Dallum, Craig; Dunbar, Robert; Duncan, Frederick Arthur; Duncan, Ken; Dunham, James Robert; Dunn,

Peter Malcolm; Dunham, Richard; Durnin, Steven James; 'Durston, Thomas; Dutchak, Anthony John; Dvorak, Roland.

Eames, Howard; Eames, Harry; Eamor, Harvey Raymond James; Earle, Austin; Easton, Robert Donald; Easton, Donald Norman; Eaton, Edward Byron; Edginton, Steven Bruce John; Edlund, David Wayne; Eggleston, Donald Allen; Egli, Charles; Ell, Gary Edwin; Elliott, James Edward; Elliott, Robert; Ellis, Steven Grant; Ellner, David Charles Bruce; Emmerson, Robert Harry; Engbrecht, Peter; Ennis, Robert Francis, Ennis, Frederick Neal; Ens, Larry Wade; Erath, Alfred; Eriskson, Paul; Erlendson, Raymond; Erwin, Earl Sidney; Erwin, Kenneth Frank; Ethier, Ron Mervin; Ethier, Ray Edward; Evans, John Ashworth; Evans, William; Everett, Donald; Ewen, Beverly Wayne; Ezard, Ken David.

Farr, Murray Raymond; Fee, Donald Neill; Fell, Terry; Fenske, Robert James; Ferguson, Robert Bruce; Ferguson, Frances Alan; Fergusson, Allastair Robert; Fidenato, Larry William; Field, Larry Eugene; Fish, Gordon Alfred; Fisher, William George; Fitch, John Brian; Flanigan, John Alexander; Flatman, Ronald; Flexhaug, Leonard Alan; Flower, Russell Arthur; Forbes, Gary James; Forbes, Brian Robert; Forbes, Gordon Leslie; Ford, Douglas Robert; Fortin, Richard Joseph; Fortinski, Chester; Foster, Garry Richard; Foster, John Douglas; Foster, Graham Kenneth; Francis, Robert David; Franklin, Michael William; Franz, Henry; Franc, Robert Adam; Fraser, John Michael; Frerichs, Kenneth Leonard; Fridfinnson, Ralph; Friesen, Victor Burt; Fuller, Gary Edward; Fulljames, Michael Leslie; Fyvie, Robert David.

Gabbott, Simon Anthoney; Gabriel, Thomas William Charles; Gaffney, Wayne; Gallie, Robert Stewart; Gamracy, Raymond Walter; Garner, John Brian; Garsid, Mathew Ronald; Geiger, Norman Roy; Gendron, Lewis Gareh; Gendron, Angus George; Gentile, Gary Joseph; George, Alan Gilbert; George, Ronald Henry; Gerlat, Helmuth; Gerling, Dennis Leo; Gibberd, Wilfred Louis; Giffen, Glen Orville; Gillett, Dennis George; Gilbert, Donald Raymond; Glazier, Ronald; Glover, William; Gnetles, Robert John; Godber, Richard Alan; Goddard, Harold; Goebel, Clarence Jacob; Goebel, Clifford Louis; Goebel, Dennis; Gold, David John; Goluk, John; Gordon, Arthur John; Gouthreau, Edgar Brian; Grahm, Earl Henry.

Granger, Gerald Thomas; Grant, Dale; Grant, Gary; Grant, David William; Gray, Russell Edward; Gray, Kenneth Alan; Green, Don; Green, Thomas Edward; Greenbank, Wilford Allen; Greenlee, Trevor Harold; Gregory, Brian Earnest;

Greig, John William; Grosse, Clifford Roy; Gullbeaul, Peter Donald; Gunther, Robert; Guwick, Ronald William.

Hackman, Russell; Hading, Ronald Mern; Hadland, Raymond; Hadley, Douglas Roy; Hagarty, John Richard; Hahn, Dale Allan; Haight, Derek; Halwrosky, Walter; Halbauer, John Joseph; Hale, Barry Charles; Hall, Darell Mervin; Hall, David; Hall, James Balfour; Hall, Ralph Leslie; Hanchyk, Richard Michael; Hancock, James; Hannam, Norman Leslie; Hanowski, Lorne Joseph; Hansen, Brian; Hansen, Dennis Paul; Hansen, Ralph David; Hansen, Robert Ellwood; Hanson, Larry Elmer; Hamilton, Gordon Burns; Harach, Mervin; Harding, Robert; Harman, Stuart Powell; Harris, Christopher Herbert; Harris, David Keith; Harrison, William Ross; Harrow, Collins; Haskin, William George; Haugen, Harold Wayne; Hazelton, Brian Michael; Hazer, Wayne Cole; Hay, James; Heemeryck, George Maxwell; Heideme, James; Helfenstein, Rodney Glen; Henderson, David Keith; Henderson, Marcel Morris; Hemke, Tex Arthur; Hemphill, David Armold; Hetherington, Robert Edwin.

Heric, Michael Wayne; Herman, Lawrence Alexander; Hessie, Robert George; Herron, John Bradin; Hicke, James Bernard; Hickman, David Alexander; Hicks, William Delbert; Hiemer, Louis Henry; Hill, Donald Thomas; Hill, Glen Elwood; Hills, Garry Lynn; Hiltz, Dale Lawrence; Hobal, John Duncan; Hodge, William Frank; Hodgson, Bob; Holberton, David George; Holling, Glen Walter; Holleman, Samuel David; Holloway, Morris William; Holm, Brian Anton; Holmstead, Ted Edward; Holst, Henry Johan; Honoroski, Fred Victor; Hood, Kenneth David; Hoosha, John Robert; Hoover, James William; Hope, Robert Stuart; Horte, Rodrick James; Horton, Kevin Barry; Houseman, Melvin Ralph; Howie, Robert George; Howarth, Garry Leon; Howarth, Glen Edward; Hoyland, Mike John; Hruska, Dennis Alexander; Hughes, Curtis Laverne; Hughes, Robert Ian; Huizinga, Lothar; Hunt, Albert Keith; Hunt, Donald William; Hunt, Eugene Curtis; Hunt, Wayne Arthur; Human, William Fletcher; Humphrey, Richard Boyd; Husll, Ludwig; Hurad, Roy Clifford; Hurst, Terry Howard; Huxley, Sidney; Huzll, James Kenneth; Huggard, Richard Halpenny.

Ingham, Robert Roy; Ingls, John William; Inglis, Gregory Manchester; Inkster, John Noris; Innes, Craig; Ironside, Michael Walter.

Jaakkoalo, Ilkka John; Jacklo, James; Jackson, Garry Frederick; Jackson, George Michael; Jackson, Leslie Gerald; Jalbert, John Leslie; James, Patrick; Jarrott, Richard Lee; Jean, Leonard; Jean, Romi; Jeffrey, Jack; Jefferies, Christopher,

509

Jenkins, Edward George; Jenneson, Denis Ronald; Jette, Edward Garry Brent; Jiebert, Jake; Joanette, Louis Napoleon; Joe, William; Johansen, Torben Erhardt; Johnson, Brian Wayne; Johnson, Calvin Gordon; Johnson, Duayne Allan; Johnson, George; Johnson, John Laverne; Johnson, Leon; Johnson, Michael John; Johnson, Thomas John; Johnston Arthur David; Johnston, Raymond Archie; Jones, Bernard William; Jones, Bruce David; Jones, Christopher Stan; Jones, Gregory Melvin; Jones, James Martin; Jones, John Eaton; Jones, Martin Lawrence; Jones, Ronald Leslie; Jorgenson, Steven.

Kaleka, Ronald Robert; Kaliciak, Zbignie; Kapak, Peter; Karst, David Albert; Kathrens, Douglas Stanley; Keeling, Wayne Douglas; Kelly, Bruce Reed; Kelly, Francis Richard; Kelly, John Thomas; Kemble, Alan Roy; Kennedy, Darwin John; Kennedy, Dennis Hugh; Kennedy, Donald Arthur; Kent, David Edward; Kerdil, Ronald Mervin; Kerslako, Edward James; Kest, Brian Richard; Kettle, Harry James; Kilmartin, Arthur; King, Edward David; Kinlock, Peter; Kinnee, Daniel; Kisko, Lloyd; Kison, Daniel Uinter; Klein, Roy Bernard; Klotz, Philip William; Klugh, Michael Archie; Koldingas, Leon John Charles; Komock, Michael Joseph; Kotyk, Jack; Kozak, Garry Wayne; Kozuska, Harvey; Krushlucki, Wayne; Kube, Allan Bernard; Kublak, Peter Paul; Kuffler, Larry Edward; Kulyk, Joe; Kundert, David Keith; Kutchel, Robert Alexander; Kwiatek, Peter; Kwiatek, Stanley Joseph; Kyle, Thomas Scott.

Laboucne, Victor Ross; Lafond, William Andrew; Lafournie, Ron Keith; Lahale, John; Laird, Terry; Land, Charles Chester; Land, Robert William; Land, Roger; Landers, Gareth; Lang, Richard Joseph; Lang, Wilfred Alfred; Langell, Gerald; Langton, James William; Laing, Stuart Sinclair; Laplant, Marcel; Laroche, Alfred; Laroque, Lawrence Joseph; Larson, Flemming Miller; Larson, Alex Melvin; Lathrope, Charles L.; Lawes, David Randall; Lawrence, Joseph Wm.; Lawrence, Paul William; Layton, Brian John; Leask, Harold George; Lebrun, James Edward; LeBrun, John; Lecuin, Brian Herbert; Leckie, William Wallace; Leclerc, Aurel Robert; Leefe, Wayne Harvey; Leguee, Roderick; Leeming, James Ray; Leiske, Dale; Leitch, David Robert; Lenoski, Gerry

Lepsoe, Robert Anthony; Leonard, Patrick Joseph; Lettington, Reginald Bruno; Lewin, Lloyd George; Lewis, Jack; Liddell, William James; Limborgh, Donald Van; Lintick, Emerson Stanley; Little, John Harvy; Littlechief, Douglas; Locke, Errol Mathew; Logue, Edwin; Loney, Norv; Long, Richard Alfred; Low, Douglas; Lowe, Edward Colsey Ted; Lowe, Fredrick Arthur; Lowe, John Henry; Lowen, Victor William; Low-

rie, Paul Joseph; Lowry, David; Lucas, Andy Malcolm; Lucas, Roger Gordon; Luchia, Barry Alvin; Luciano, Bruni; Lugrin, Ronald Charles Richard; Lund, Danny Arthur; Lundrigan, Ian Richard; Lusk, Eric Richard; Luxmore, William Bill; Lyc, Joseph Wm. Kirby.

Mackal, Lesley James; Mackey, Allen; Mackie, Wayne Richard; Magee, James William; Magunssen, Richard Ronald; Main, Kenneth Ian; Mainland, Arnold Maxwell; Malek, Jim Leonard; Magnall, Norman Keith; Manion, Gerald William; Marcellus, Raymond Milo; Marr, Harvey Donald; Marshall, Floyd Warren; Marshall, Joseph Wayne; Martin, Barry Walker; Mason, Douglas Lorne; Mason, William Allan; Mast, Paul Alexander; Marchuk, Terry; Matlock, Millson James; Matteotti, Ralph; Maubert, Gerald Douglas; Maxwell, Barry Dwayne; Meyer, Lorne William; Merchant, William Brian; Meade, Louie David; Meehan, Patrick John; Mellett, Wm. Carlan; Mercer, Robert John; Mercereau, Claude; Mercredi, Girard; Megle, Kenneth Andrew; Merke, David Lial; Merrick, Frank Raymond; Merritt, Garry Herbert; Mortal, Chester John; Michelko, Robert Peter; Middlemiss, William.

Miller, Geoffrey George; Miller, Thomas Victor; Milldhall, James; Miller, Jerry Allen; Milne, Robt. Bruce; Minnis, John Terrance; Mitchell, Jay Anthony; Mock, Richard; Moen, Donald; Mohammed, Donald; Montgomery, James Hugh; Moore, David John; Moore, Glen Brian; Moore, Robert Gordon; Moraes, Robert Edward; Moran, Michael; Moreau, Gerald Maurice; Morgan, Eamonn Francis; Morin, Gerald Lawrence; Morris, David Jay; Morris, James Charles; Morrison, Dennis; Mosch, Peter; Mosicki, Donald Stanley; Mossey, John Edward; Mostert, Dirk; Morton, Ronald Bruce; Motuz, William Morris; Mow, George Wesley; Moxham, Gerald; Moysa, Russell Wm.; Mruk, Albert Joseph; Mugford, Phillip Wilfred; Muirhead, David George; Mulrooney, John Murray; Munday, Albert; Munro, David; Munson, James West; Murdhock, John Randolph; Murray, Kenneth; Murray, William Edmund; Myers, Ronald; Magutre, John Robert.

Mcarthur, Collin; Mcbride, John Patrick; McBurney, Robert Philip; McCabe, Garry Patrick; McCaffrey, James Wayne; McCallum, Garry James; McCann, Lesley; McCarry, James Denis; McCaul, Keith Garfield; McClellan, Donald Everett; McComas, Terrence; McConachie, Wayne Robert; McConnell, John Paul; Mccoouy, Lawrence; McCutcheon, John William; McCutcheon, Niel St. Julian; McDonald, John Hugh; McDonald, Stewart Larry; McDougall, Cal; McEwen, Douglas John Wayne; McGregor, James; McGillvray, James George; McGundy, Raymond; McInenly, Richard Ak-

510

ford; McInnis, Donald Hugh; McIntee, Michael Peter; McIntosh, David George; McIntosh, Raymond; McKinlay, Raonald Rose; McKnight William Edward; McLean, Bruce Allan; McLean, Daniel Harold; McLean, Daniel John; McLean, Kenneth Earl; McLennan, Robbie James; McLeod, Bruce; McLeod, Philip William; McLeod, Roderick; McNamara, Brent Leo; McNeil, Roy Kenneth; McNight, James Ira; McPhee, Patrick David; McQueen, Glen Heber.

MacArthur, Gary; MacDonald, Roger Keith; MacDonald, Michael Lloyd; MacGregor, Kenneth; MacInnis, Peter James Michael; MacIntosh, John Floyd; MacIntyre, Arthur Joseph; MacIntyre, Frank; MacKenzie, Gordon Shirley; MacKie, John Albert; MacLean, Alex Leslie; MacLeod, William Alexander.

Nadeau, Maurice; Nadler, James Peter; Nahanee, Gilbert Lorne; Nahanee, Robert James; Nakoneshny, Leonard Joseph; Narraway, Wentworth James; Nazarko, Myron Peter; Neigel, Ronald Wayne; Neigum, Robert Peter; Nell, Ronald Wayne; Neilson, David Norman; Neish, Donald; Nelson, Clifford; Nelson, Maynard Ralph; Nelson, Ross Elner; Nesbitt, Daniel James; Nevison, Robert Joseph; Newnes, Robert Gerald; Nichol Larry Gordon; Nicholson, Frank; Nicolson, John Ivor; Niedersteiner, Edward Karl; Nield, Raymond George; Nield, Robert William; Noga, Richard Michael; Nordstrom, Alvin; Norgart, Edward Louis, Norsworthy, Bruce Edward; Norton, Joseph John.

Oakford, Edward Harold; O'Brian, Reginald William; O'Dell, Elmer Samuel; Oklek, Ronald Frank; Olson, Ronald Raymond; Omeosoo, Raymond Clifford; Orchard, Terrance George; Osborne, Edwin L.; Osland, David Thomas; Overton, Lonn; Ovenham, Charles Arthur.

Page, John Charles; Pageot, Jim Richard; Paradis, Jim Gerald; Parisin, Denace Lloyd; Park, Donald John; Parker, Terry Ronald; Parslow, Richard; Paul, Albert Henry; Paul, Cecil Leslie; Paul, Richard William; Paulin, John; Paulson, Howard John; Pavey, David Roger; Pearce, Albert Lewis; Pennell, Robert Wayne; Penny, Cliff Thomas; Percy, Graham Raymond; Perley, William Bela; Perry, Author Glen; Perry, Georfie Jerried; Perry, Malcolm John; Pete, Dave Lloyd; Peters, Brian James; Peters, Kenneth Wallace; Peterson, Brian Leo; Petersen, Harry Peter; Peterson, Gary James; Petryk, Raymond; Pfeifle, Edward; Phillips, Andrew; Phillips, William James.

Pickering, Pat; Piesse, Doug; Pinch, Dave; Pion, Robert Laurant; Plested, Roger Roy; Plomp, Wayne Fredrick; Pointer, Bryan; Pollard, Nelson Reverne; Popejoy, Barry Edward; Popik, Water Dennis; Portingale, William Scott; Posgay, Ed George; Potter, Dale Henry Arthur;

Potter, Edward Gordon; Potts, Kenneth Edward; Poulsen, Dan; Pound, William Charles; Powell, Michael; Powell, Thomas; Powers, Don Ellen; Prevost, Glayton Henry; Price, Albert William; Price, Chris Robin; Price, Clement Ivan; Price, Ugene Wilford; Prichard, William; Prince, Lawrence; Pritchard, Bill; Pura, Steven; Purvis, Robert; Pyke, David Allen; Pillsworth, Joseph.

Quast, Robert Fredrick; Quinn, Michael George.

Racette, John Harry; Rachwalski, John William; Rae, Gerald; Rae, William; Rafferty, Kent Ward; Rafford, Melvin Gordon; Rathgeber, Ronald Richard; Rathwell, Dennis; Ratson, David Gordon; Rawlings, William Lionel Richard; Ray, Charles; Reader, Gerald Wayne; Renwick, Glen Stanley; Reimer, James Arthur; Rempel, Gary William; Rennie, Gary Douglas; Rennie, Wayne Michael; Rest, George Lawrence; Resvick, Berry Nelson; Rice, David James; Richardson, Robert; Richardson, Cleo Henry; Richardson, David Jesse; Rimmer, John; Ring, Victor Edward; Rivers, Frank Edward; Robb, John William; Robb, Brian Garwood; Roberson, John Author.

Roberts, Terrance; Roberts, Thomas Llewellyn; Robertson, Daniel; Robertson, William Edward; Robertson, Ian Donald; Robins, Graham; Robins, Charles Ray; Robinson, Calvin Ray; Robinson, Wayne Even; Robinson, Danial; Robinson, Ernest; Robson, Ray Fredick; Rockwell, Robert William; Roden, David; Rogers, Richard; Rome, Gerald Beverly; Rope, Warren Grant; Rose, Stanley Donald; Rose, Rodrick Haig; Rosmus, Roy Francis Joseph; Rosoman, Raymond Alexander; Ross, Wayne Hunter; Robson, Richard Ivan; Rowe, John Michael; Rowe, Les Howard; Royal, Donald Albert; Rozon, Leondard Patrick; Russell, Richard Albery; Ryan, Roger Denance.

Sabatin, Bruce; Saigant, David George; Salmon, Peter; Salmuel, John Thomas; Samways, Richard Wayne; Sanders, George; Sawicki, Adam John; Sawry, Harry; Scharbaca, Gary Ross; Scharikow, Michael; Schlichter, Bart High; Schlitter, Elvin Hubert; Schmidt, John Antony; Schmidt, Meinrad William; Schmidt, Robert; Schoh, Robert Allen; Schuffenhauer, David; Schuler, Dennis John; Schultz, Kenneth; Schweigert, Lawrence Alfred; Schyrblak, Clarence Alex; Scott, Arthur Jerome; Scott, Gary Wallace; Sculthorpe, John Henry Alexander; Seay, Brian; Sego, Robert Alan; Sehn, Glen Edward; Sells, Edward Swight; Senft, Randall George; Sewell, Albert; Sexsmith, John Llewe; Sharpe, Mike Allen; Shave, Larry Norman; Shayler, Avery Harry; Shoane, Colin Roger; Shelley, Bryan Henry; Shepanik, Ian Richard; Shook, Gary Norman;

511

Shortneck, Henry Floyd.

Shuttleworth, Don Stewert; Sievewright, Wayne Wilford; Simmonds, Clifford James; Simpson, Doug John; Simnock, Carl Gordon Vanner; Siwicki, Samuel Harold; Skilnick, Frank Gerald; Skoda, Ed Frank; Skorletowski, Eugene; Slugel, Richard; Smart, James; Smith, David Ian; Smith, Dennie Richard; Smith, Douglas; Smith, Gordon Neil; Smith, Harold George; Smith, Howard; Smith, Joe; Smith, Kenneth; Smith, Kenneth Del; Smith, Michael; Smith, Ralph Edward; Smith, Raymond George; Smith, Richard; Smith, Richard Kirk; Smith, Stewart Barry; Smith, Thomas Charles; Smith, Wayne; Smithe, Harry; Smythe, Ernest Charles; Sobkowicz, Wayne; Soderlund, Jerry Bernard; Soganic, Richard James; Sorhus, Collin Norman; Spearey, William James; Spears, Jim; Spless, Jerreld Walter; Spink, Ray Harvey; Spivey, Douglas Norman.

Sponholz, Dennis Earl; Spraggs, Terry Douglas; Sproat, Terry Allan; Stackhouse, Lorne Roy; Standel, Robert Thomas; Standish, Fred; Stanishewsky, Joseph Peter; Stark, Gerald Faye; Startup, Donald; Steele, Hugh Edward; Steele, Jack; Steeves, John James; Steigel, Rodney Daniel; Stein, Gordon; Stekelenburg, Allstair Ben; Stephens, John; Stephenson, Robert; Sterdel, Dennace William; Steward, William Pactric; Steward, William Stanley Gordon; Stewart, David William; Stgerman, Larry; Stickley, Allan David; Stillwell, Campbell McLeod; Stokes, Darryl; Stokes, Ronald Barry; Storey, David Franklin; Straight, Rod Donald; Strylecki, Frank Michael; Stuart, Robert David; Sturdy, John McDonald; Suckling, Bill Arthur; Sullivan, John; Sulz, David Henry; Surowy, Joseph Stanley; Sutherland, Charles; Swanson, Bernard James; Szalanski, Viewslaw; Szale, Frank Edward; Szova, Mike.

Tage, Edward Albert; Tail, Donald Gordon; Talkington, Wilf William; Tames, Larry Lawrence; Taylor, Daniel Arthur; Taylor, Jack Edward; Taylor, Jay Kent; Taylor, John Charles; Taylor, Ray James; Tebbutt, Gordon Ross; Templeman, John; Tepper, Jerry; Terhorst, Thomas Henry; Tesch, Mervin Clarence; Tetz, Robert Dale; Textor, Frederick Ernest; Thew, Douglas James; Thompson, Donald Gordon; Thompson, Richard Douglas; Thompson, Stephen Russell; Thomson, Denis Joseph; Tingley, Kenneth William Gordon; Tizzard, Gordon Charles; Tomkins, Eric Alexander; Toms, Herbie; Tomyn, James Michael; Tordiffe, Archibald Albert; Towle, James Gordon; Tramblay, Raymond Bruneral; Treflak, Peter John; Treseng, Roy Peter; Tribe, Daniel; Troman, John Robert; Truscot, Dennis Raymond; Truscott, Raymond Orvill; Tucker, Richard Bert; Tulloch, Donald Bryan; Turnell, Gordon

Harry; Turnell, Roger William; Turner, Peter; Tuttle, Fred.

Upper, Walter Edward Higgins; Urae, John.

Vance, Howard Percy; Van Doorst, John; Van Herwaarden, Bart; Van Weele, Mathys Cornelus; Vermette, Gerald Donald; Vermette, Roy; Vickers, Arthur Ed; Vickers, Brian; Vilene, Edward James.

Wade, Thomas Leslie; Wagar, Ivan; Wagner, Brian; Wagner, Wayne Edward; Walker, James Brian; Walker, Randy; Wallace Ernest; Walrough, Gary; Walters, Peter John; Watch, Charles; Wark, Terance Dwayne; Watt, Brian Mansfield; Wayspear, Wayne Irving; Webb, Ray; Webb, Roy Charles; Webber, Steven; Wecels, Ferdinand; Weber, James; Weckend, Allan Anthony; Wegner, Herman; Welch, Terrance Stanley; Weninger, Allan Joseph; Werenkl, Kenneth; Werezek, Stanley Morris; Weys, Chris; Whale, Allan Norman; Whitford, Randolph; Whiting, Bob; Whiting, Gary Morris; Whiting, Ron; Whitmore, Allen; Whitney, John Daniel; Whittaker, Randolph; Whyte, William James; Widdifield, Kenneth; Wiebe, Herb Peter; Wiekenkamp, Peter John; Wiggins, Bob; Wilkinson, Robert; Willerton, Phillip; Williams, David; Williams, Tim James; Williamson, Eric George; Wills, Davie; Wilm, Larry Edward; Wilson, Glen; Wilton, Frazer Douglas; Windley, Kenneth Norman; Winser, Ron Frank; Winters, Terry; Wipf, Gerald Dennis; Wiseman, Michael Paul; Witherly William Paul; Witts, John; Wolfe, George; Wolfer, Leo; Wolodk, Ben Boris; Wong, Vernon; Workman, Robert; Worobo, Trevor John; Woytiuk, Danny Walters; Wright, Fredrick James; Wuori, James; Wyles, Laurie Phillip; Wylie, David Roy; Wytrykush, Lorne.

Yackabowski, Gerald; Yausie, Darryl Clayton; Yaworsky, William; Yee, James; Youngberg, Arthur Edward; Yworski, Anthony.

Zado, Craig; Zarft, Erick; Zator, Ralph Edward; Zebinski, Brian; Zebinski, Neil; Zimrose, Melvin Joseph; Zeiklewski, Richard.

VACC - 1963

Adams, David William; Adams, Wayne Robert; Agnew, Keith; Aitken, John Robert; Allain, Ernie; Allain, Michael; Allan, Keith; Allan, Robert; Alphen, Peter David; Anderson, Donald Anton; Anderson, Gordon Edward; Anderson, James Francis; Anderson, Lionel Donald; Anderson, Lloyd Keith; Anderson, Lyle Gordon; Anderson Richard Glen; Anderson, Richard; Anderson, Warren; Anderson, William Oscar; Andrews, John Charles; Anstett, Larry; Arcand, Edward Joseph; Archibald, Kelly Edward; Argue, Michael David; Armstrong, Weldon; Arneson, Marvin Almer; Arnold, Herman; Arnold, Brian Robert;

Arnold, Brian Patrick; Arnott, Harvey Donald; Asapase, Allen; Ashmore, Thomas; Ashby, Robert James; Asher, Ronald Robert; Ashton, Albert Edward; Aunger, Bruce William; Austin, William; Aveyard, Garfield Edward.

Baceda, Layne Hobert; Bacon, Stephen William; Baker, Lorrie Stephan; Baker, William Donald; Bailey, Garry Grant; Bamford, Danny Edward; Bannick, Donald; Bannister, Kenneth Wallace; Bardsley, Robert; Baril, Denis; Barker, Harold Wayne; Barlett, Clifford James; Barran, Mervin Harry; Barrie, Grant Malcomb; Bartell, Garry Leroy Baumle, Allan Joseph; Baron, Roger Dale; Barrey, David Wilfred; Bayduza, Mike Metro; Bayliss, Peter; Baynham, Joseph Michael; Bazin, Douglas Phillip; Bearchief, Melvin; Bearchief, Roy; Beart, Ernest Joseph; Bechard, Phillip Joseph; Beckman, Kenneth; Bedard, John Louis; Bedu, Ronald.

Begley, Michael James; Begr, Ray; Behn, Heiko; Beirness, Averd; Bell, Christopher; Bemben, Rovert Michael; Benedict, George Wallace; Bennet, William Sutton; Bennie, Jack Frank; Bergseth, Elinar; Bernardin, Douglas Wayne; Bergeron, Ernest Arthur; Berry, Gordon; Berry, Lewis Leonald; Berube, John; Bessey, Robert Charles; Betti, Rudy James; Bialecki, Jerry John; Biccum, Gerald Edward; Biccum, Terrance Albert; Biggin, John Charles; Bilawey, John Wilfred; Bird, John; Biller, John; Binette, George Gerry; Blackmore, Eldon George; Blackwood, Stephen Dale; Blair, Dennis Albert; Blais, David; Blais, Marshall Norman; Blanchette, Dennis Joseph; Blazenko, Kenneth John.

Bledsoe, John Kent; Bloomfield, Arthur Stanley; Blunden, Donald Edward; Bob, Dempsey James; Bodnarchuk, Raymond Norman; Bogstie, Douglas Raymond; Boland, Bruce Sinclair; Bolin, Alexander Charles; Borland, Richard William; Borrow, Leonard Arthur; Bosse, Terrance Edmund; Boucher, Joseph Aurel; Boutwell, James Robert; Boudreau, Richard; Bowen, Bradley; Bowman, James Snowden; Boyd, Daniel Howard; Boyd, Richard John; Brady, Gordon Francis; Braithwaite, Ervin; Braithwaite, Irvin Martin; Bramhill, Terry Richard; Bray, John Henry Gresham; Braybrook, Paul William; Brill, Wayne; Brookbank, Richard; Brooks, Ronald Allan; Broome, Michael Allan; Brose, Garry; Brose, Michael Henry; Broughton, David Harry; Brown, Bryson John; Brown, James Sidney; Brown, Jeffery Hamilton; Brown, Keith.

Brown, Larry; Brown, Richard Allan; Brown, Robert Kenneth; Brown, Shaun; Brown, Stan; Brown, Terrance Phillip; Bruce, Richard Wilson; Brydon, John Stewart; Brzoza, Stanley John; Bucci, Cecil; Buchanan, Glen; Buchanan, Melvin Jeoffery; Buhler, Charles Lawrence; Butta, Martin; Bulloch, Lorne Thomas; Bundy, Roger Graham; Burbee, Benjamin Clifford; Burbee, Donald James; Burchak, Michael George; Burchill, Leonard Aurther; Burley, Douglas; Burnell, Dennis Harvey; Burr, Dennis; Burry, David Garfield;

Burton, Joseph; Busby, Barry James; Butlin, Keith Barry; Bronevitch, John; Byman, Brian Curtis; Byrnes, David; Bysterveld, Randall James.

Callas, William Edward; Cambell, Allan Roy; Cameron, Colin; Cameron, James Daniel; Cameron, Terance Lee; Cameron, William; Caponero, Anthony Lawrence; Cantley, Robert Davis; Card, William Douglas; Cardinal, Joseph; Careford, Garry Allan; Carlick, Robert Teddy; Carr, Stanley Roger; Carriere, Ronald Joseph; Carritt, John Douglas; Carritt, Lawrence Melton; Carter, Terrance James; Carter, William Stanley L.; Case, Thomas Martin; Cayer, Danny Edmond; Ceasar, Lloyd John; Chabeniuk, Steve; Chadsey, Garry Brian; Chalmers, Edmond; Chambers, Allan; Chambers, Kenneth; Chambers, Michael Lesley; Chapman, John Trevor; Charles, Tex Louis; Charlie, Peter; Charlton, Delem Douglas; Chartrand, Marcel Gerald; Chaworth-Musters, Robert David; Chen, Dale; Cherbo, Robin; Cherewick, Wayne Keith.

Chretien, Henry Joseph; Chretien, Raymond Joseph; Childs, Gerald Art; Chisamore, Alexander Brien; Christianson, Chester Calvin; Christie, Robert Bruce; Churchill, Charles; Circolo, John Robert; Clark, John; Clark Leonard; Clark Robert; Clark, William; Claxton, Edward; Clayton, James Allen; Code, Kenneth; Cole, Frederick Lloyd; Collins, Greggory; Collins, Robert James; Colquhoun, Stewart John; Combs, Terry Lee; Condie, Gavin Burns; Connatty, Lyle Orrin; Connell, Patrick; Connery, Fredrick; Connor, Charles; Conquergood, Dale Allan; Cook, Greggory; Cookman, Clifford; Cooley, Lloyd; Copping, Kenneth Allan; Corbitt, Kenneth Gordon; Corivor, Paul Denis; Corrigan, James; Corry, Daniel.

Cory, Milton Gordon; Coulic, Ronald Paul; Coulter, William Vernon Terrance; Cousineau, Michael Shaun; Coventry, Robert Terry; Cowpar, Larry Douglas; Coyle, Phillip Terrence; Crabbe, Brian Thomas; Craig, Michael Jeremy; Craig, Lewis Edmund; Cripps, Trevor Kellington; Croaker, Lambert Edgar; Croaker, Wayne Ernest; Crozier, Wayne Kenneth; Crucq, David Stewart; Crump, Edward John; Csano, Archer Steve; Curry, James Harvey; Cust, Melton Joseph; Cyr, Peter Antoney; Dahl, Joseph Gerald; Dale, John Oliver; Dale, Ronald John Oliver; Dalgarno, Brian Roy; Dalziel, Lynn Robert William; Dammann, Dwight Oriville; Dandenault, Donald Arthur; Daniels, Dennis; D'Arcy, Donald Norris; D'Arcy, Thomas George; Dashwood-Jones, Martin; Davidson, Alfred Daniel Wesley; Davidson, Richard Norman; Davies, Brian.

Davies, Daniel Lawrence; Davis, Gordon James; Davies, James Lea; Davies, Ronald; Davis, Vernon Douglas; Day, Daniel; Day, Ellery; Dean, Douglas James; Deback, Brian Jacob; Debock, Fredrick Allan; Degenstien, Kenneth Wayne; Degroot, Henry; Delcourt, David; Delmore, James; Demchuk, Clarence Irwin; Demerais, Charlie; Demkiw, John Peter; Demkiw, William Stephen; Dentrey, Edward Garry; Derson, George; Descalchuk, George Allan;

Detcheverrey, John Andre; Devenney, Jack; Dewing, Richard Arvin; Diakow, Eugene Ivan; Dick, Fredrick Allan; Dickson, William Wallace; Dimarzio, Frank; Dinsdale, Brian Charles; Dionne, George; Dirks, William; Dombrosky, Brian Edmund; MacDonald, Donald; Donohue, John Patrick; Dopson, Brian Leslie.

Dornan, Patrick David; Doucette, Gordon, Clarence; Douglas, John; Drewniak, Joseph; Druce, Gary; Drunken Chief, Roy; Druskin, Allan; Druskin, Ross; Drybrough, Gordon Stephen; Drysdale, Douglas John; Dunbar, Robert Stanton; Dunham, James Robert; DuMontier, Carl Edward; Dunn Peter Malcolm; Durnin, Steve James; Dutchak, Anthony John; Dykes, Douglas; Eadie, Wilfred; Eames, Howard; Eamor, Harvey Raymond James; Earle, Austin Clifford; Early, Ronald; Edginton, Stephen; Edlund, David Wayne; Edmondson, William Robert; Edwards, Charles Larry; Edwards, Lorne; Eggen, Karl Daniel; Eggleston, Donald Alan; Egli; Charles Henry; Eisler, Edward William; Eleason, Larry; Eldridge, Robert Gordon; Elgi, Charles Henry.

Ell, Derrick Edwin; Ellerman, Garry Dennis; Elliot, John Raymond; Elliott, Robert William; Embury, Ralph; Emkelt, Albert; Engbrecht, Peter; Ennis, Frederick Neil; Ens, Larry Wade; Epp, James; Friendson, Raymond Allan; Ethler, Raymond Edward; Evans, Glenn; Evans, John; Evans, Peter; Evans, Robert; Evanson, Donald; Ewen, Beverly Wayne; Ewen, Donald Allan; Ewen, Norman Ross; Fafard, Ernest; Fairhurst, James; Farrow, Auburn; Favell, Allan; Fawcett, Patrick; Fedoruk, Greggory; Fedoruk, Kenneth William; Fenske, Robert; Ferguson, Dale; Ferguson, Francis; Ferguson, Robert Bruce; Fernetts, Terrance; Fevang, Kevin; Fiddler, Frank.

Fisher, David; Fitness, Ian Douglas; Fitzpatrick, John; Flamand, Francis; Flasch, Allan; Fleck, Kenneth Bruce; Flexhaug, Leonard; Fliuk, Clifford William; Flower, Ronald; Flug, Lesley; Fode, James; Fontaine, Jack; Forbes, Brian; Forbes, Garry; Forbes, Wayne Ronald; Ford, Robert; Forgues, Paul; Forth, James; Foster, David; Foster, Dean; Foster, Ronald; Forstner, Wolfegang; Fougere, Eric; Fowler, Kenneth; Fox, Clifford; France, Kenneth; Franke, Dale; Fraser, Berry; Fraser, James; Fraser, John; Fraser, Robert; Fraser, Donald; French, Peter; Frerichs, Kenneth.

Friesen, Victor; Friskie, Glen; Furman, Bobby; Gabriel, Thomas; Gale, Terrance Laverne; Gamble, Raymond; Gamracy, David; Gamracy, Ronald; Gangne, Terrance; Gandy, Lionel; Gariepy, Francis; Garner, John; Garnett, George William; Gaura, Wayne; Gay, Keith; Gemmel, Donald; Gendron; Lewis; Genest, Randy; Gentles, Robert John; George, Ronald; Gerbrandt, Marvin; Gervais, Richard Joseph; Gibberd, John; Gibbon, George; Gibeau, Joseph; Gibeault, Leonore; Gibeault, Ronald; Gibson, Kenneth; Gibson, Robert James; Gilchrist, Cameron; Gilchrist, Kenneth; Gilfillan, Robert;

Gillespie, Allan; Gillett, Dennis George.

Ginther, William John; Glazier, Ronald; Glenn, George Robert; Glenn, James; Godfrey, James; Gomuwka, James; Gorden, Alan; Gordon, Arthur; Goulet, Robert; Gove, Thomas James; Gracie, David; Grady, Glen; Graham, Brian; Graham, David; Graham, Kevin; Graham, Norman; Granger, Edward; Grant, Bryan; Grant, Wayne; Gratton, Robert; Gray, Nick; Green, Stephen Douglas; Greenbank, Wilfred; Greenlee, Trevor; Greenslade, Jerry; Greenslade, Terry; Gregory, Brian Ernest; Gretorash, David; Grill, Donald; Gross Garry Michael; Gruben, Stephen; Guise, Leneord; Gunderson, Gordon; Gunn, Ronald James; Gustafson, Dennis.

Havington, William; Hadley, Douglas Roy; Hadley, Ronald; Haggerty, John Richard; Hains, Phillip; Hall, Dennis; Hall, Derek; Hall, James; Hall, John; Hall, Patrick; Hall, Ralph; Hall, Robert; Hall, Ronad Herbert; Hambugh, William David; Hamilton, Gordon; Hanbury, Douglas Bruce; Hancock, Harold James; Hansen, Alan; Hansen, Frank; Hansen, James; Hanson, Larry; Hansen, Robert; Harasymchuk, Robert; Hargrave, Anthony; Harlton, Larry; Harper, Edward; Harris, David Heath; Harris, Gordon; Harrison, David; Harter, Rudolph; Hartnell, Gary Earl; Hansel, Klaus; Hay, Ian Patrick.

Hazelton, Bryan; Hazelton, Ronald; Hozelwood, David Andrew; Hazen, John; Heidema, James; Helfenstein, Rodney Glen; Helme, Robert; Hemke, Tex Arthur; Hemus, Harold; Henderson, Gordon Ross; Henke, Wayne Allan; Henry, William Allan; Herman, Lawrence Alexander; Herman, Melvin; Heroux, Philip Emile; Herring, Donald; Hessie, Robert; Hetherington, Russell; Hickey, Joseph; Hicks, William; Hill, Fred; Hill, Glen; Hill, Terrance; Hirsche, James; Hobson, James; Hodge, William; Hodgson, Richard; Hodgson, Robert; Hoffman, Darnell Lyle; Holberton, David; Holling, Glen; Holm, Per; Holmes, Edward; Holst, Henry Hohan.

Hood, David; Hood, Kenneth; Hoople, Kenneth; Hoose, David; Hope, Robert; Hopkins, Greggory; Horte, Roderick; Horton, Kevin; Horwood, John; Houston, James John T.; Howard, David Lorne; Howarth, Glen Edward; Howes, Gary; Howie, James; Hubbel, John; Huber, Tyler James; Hudson, Peter; Huffels, Theodorus; Hughes, Larry; Hughes, Lorne; Huizinga, Lothar; Hull, James; Hull, John; Human, William; Hummel, Keith; Huminsky, Allan; Humphrey, Richard; Hunt, Albert; Hunt, Donald William; Huston, Wayne; Hutchinson, Thomas; Huxley, Keith; Huzil, James; Hyde, Ronald.

Inkster, David; Inskip, Bruce Fred; Jackson, Robert; Jacobson, Calvin Walter; Jalbert, John; James, Harry; Jans, Danny; Jenkins, David; Jennings, Robert; Jette, Brent; Joanette, Louie; Johansen, Torben; Johner, Michael; Johnson, Dwight Andrew; Johnson, Floyd; Johnson, John; Johnson, Michael John; Johnson, Wayne; Johnston, Arthur;

Johnston, Grant; Johnston, Richard; Johnston, William; Johnston, William George; Jones, Bruce; Jones, George; Jones, Gregory; Jones, James; Jones, John; Jones, Newton; Jones, Ronald; Jorgenson, Ole; Jorgenson, Roy; Joy, Richard; Junck, Montgomery John.

Kaliciak, Jan; Kane, Patrick Edward; Kary, Stephen; Kay, Russel Neil; Kaufman, Kenneth Richard; Kawa, Peter John; Keast, Brian Richard; Keast, Ronald; Keehborn, Larry John; Keeler, Richard; Keenan, Eddy Denny; Kelly, Arnold Glen; Kendall, Marvin Wayne; Kendel, Adolf Werner; Kennedy, Clayton Edward; Kennedy, Robert Ernest; Kersley, Mundi John; Kilgore, Rodney Wayne; Killen, Robert James; King, Ronald John; Kinloch, Peter Charles; Kirk, Harry; Kistner, Albert William; Kistner, Gordon Allan; Kitchemonia, Denzil; Kitson, Melvin Arthur; Kitto, Bruce Norman; Klyne, Richard; Knight, Mervyn Arthur; Knipple, James Bruce; Knoke, Joseph; Knoll, Len Henry; Knox, John.

Kobe, Alan Walter; Kobialka, John Stanley; Kobialka, Richard Joseph; Koldingnes, Leon John Charles; Koldingnes, Wayne Ronald; Kolomijchuk, Taras; Kotyk, Jack Lawrence; Kristensen, George; Krokis, Leo; Krutzky, Frank; Krowchenko, David Lewis; Krywolt, Joseph Michael; Kubiak, Peter Paul; Kuchanrsky, William Peter; Kucheran, Maxwell Robert; Kuchmak, Orest Adrian; Kulaway, Mervin Peter; Kundert, David Keith; Kuruluik, Arthur Joseph; Kushnyrick, Dennis Arthur; Kutcher, Robert Alexander; Lacheur, James Douglas; Laboucane, Dennis Alexander; Lafournie, Ronald Keith; Lafrance, Raymond Gerald; Laird, Frederick; Land, Roger Leslie; Lang, Richard Joseph; Lang, Wilfred Alfred; Lange, Roger; Langevin, Jerome Joseph; Langpap, Harold Cyril; Laroche, Alfred; Larose, Lyle Daniel.

Larson, Flemming Miller; Larson, Byron Kirk Glen; Larson, Wayne Douglas; Laser, Leo Henry; Lauer, Kevin Paul; Lavallee, David Noel; Lavallee, Donald Harvey; Lawes, David; Lawrence, Donald; Lawrence, William Paul; Lawson, Clarence; Lear, David Melvin; LeBlond, Glen Bernard; LeBrun, James Edward; LeCein, Brian; Leckie, Wayne Wallace Brian; LeClercq, Dennis Roger; LeFeevre. Eugene Paul; Lehay, Richard William Edward; Leight, Terry Lynn; Lemley, Neil Russel; Lepsoe, Derek John; Leroux, Emile; Leslie, Lawrence Raymond; Letters, Donald William; Lettingeon, Reginald Bernard; Levers, James Kenneth; Lewin, Leonard Earl; Lewin, Lloyd George; Liebich, Emlyn; Linklater, William Thomas; Little Moustache, Nelbert; Litz, James Edward; Logue, Edwin William.

Lootz, John; Lopata, Vincent John; Lopatriello, Robert McRae B; Lorch, Fredrick Daniel; Loucks, Thomas Edwin; Lovett, Gerald Phillip; Lubinlecki, Kevin James; Luchia, Barry Alvin; Luchia, Kenneth John; Lundberg, Carl; Lundrigan, Ian Richard; Lusk, Erick Richard; Lyman, Ross Maurice; Lynn, Glenn James; Mac-

Arthur, Colin; McArthur, David Harmon; McArthur, Richard John G.; McBeth, Ross Edwin; McCallen, Robert; McCallum, Douglas Wade; McCann, Thomas Lorne; McCaul, Keith Garfield; McCooey, Michael Lawrence; McConnell, Wayne Francis; McCormack, Daryl; MacCorquodale, Graham; McCutcheon, John William; McDonald, Donald Joseph; McDonald, Donald William; MacDonald, Douglas; MacDonald, Douglas Wayne; McDonald, Gary Gray; McDonald, Gerald Campbell; MacDonald, John.

McDonald, John Hugh; MacDonald, Kenneth Harvey; MacDonald, Kenneth Robert Bruce; McDonald, Larry Allan; MacDonald, Michael Lloyd; MacDonald, Murray James; MacDonald, Randolph Stowe; MacDonald, Roger Keith; McDowall, Neil Alexander; McEwen, Douglas John Wayne; McGonigal, Kevin Patrick; McGonigle, Raymond Verne; McGonigle, Ronald Wesley; McInenly, Richard; McInnes, Donald; McIntee, Michael Peter; McIntosh, David George; McIntosh, Ronald David; MacIntyre, Arthur Joseph; McIsaac, Peter Neil; McKellar, Robert John; McKenna, Ronald Edward; McKenzie, James Donovan Lloyd; MacKenzie, Richard Arthur; MacKenzie, Robert Murray; McKerracher, Robert Allen; McKie, Brian Robert; McKinnon, John William; McKnight, James Ira; McKnight, Lloyd Ernest; McLaren, George; McLellan, Dennis Alvin; McLennan, Robbie James Edward; McLeod, Alan Duncan.

McLeod, Allen; McLeod, Oliver Elmer; McLeod, Raymond; McLeod, Roderick Alexander; McLeod, Roy Stewart; MacLeod, William Alexander; McMahon, Hugh William; McMahon, Larry; MacMeeking, Archie; McNaughton, Jackie; McNaughton, Noel Robson; McPake, Gordon Thomas; McPhee, Patrick David; McPherson, Douglas Bert; McQueen, Glen Heber; McVeety, Dennis James; Maber, Glen Robert; Mackie, Leslie James; Madsen, Perry; Magaton, Richard George; Maguire, Casey; Mainland, Arnold; Mallalieu, Norman Lindsay; Mann, Berry; Mann, Brian Neil; Mannion, James Edward; Manson, Daniel Bruce; Manske, Werner; Mantel, Olaf; Many Guns, Garry; Marcelus, Ray; Mark, James Ray; Mark, Kenneth Clarence; Marocchi, Norman.

Marsh, Dale Larry; Marshall, Joseph; Marr, Donald Harvey; Martai, Chester John; Martin, Colin Henry; Martin, Stanley; Martin, Wayne Thomas John; Mason, Douglas Lorne; Masters, Douglas John; Matheson, James Bruce; Matlock, Bruce Robert; Matlock, Ronald Harry; Matsalla, Alfonse; Maxwell, Barry Dwain; Mayan, Gregory Maxwell; Meehan, Michael Peter; Meehan, Patrick John; Meier, Leonard Frank; Meier, Richard Greg; Melhus, Alan Fredrick; Melynchuk, Mervin George; Mercer, Robert John; Mercredi, Carcy Joseph; Mercredi, Gerard; Michell, Gordon; Middlemiss, William; Mike, Joseph; Millen, Murray Ross; Millar, Geoffrey; Millard, Morris David; Miller, Kelly John; Miller, Wayne John; Moger, Lyle

Weston; Mohammed, Donald.

Mooney, Douglas Charles; Mooney, Kenneth James; Moore, Martin Joseph; Moran, Terrance David; Moren, Donald; Morris, Dan Stephen; Morton, Stewart Kenneth; Mosch, Peter; Moser, Robert Allen; Mosicki, Kenneth Michael; Mott, William; Mottershead, Arthur Ian; Mowat, Alexander Robert; Mugford, Philip Wilfrid; Mulrooney, Robert Joe; Munbay, Albert; Munday, Edward; Munson, James West; Murray, William Edmond; Musselwhite, Brian Thomas; Murray, Richard George; Mutlow, Gordon; Myer, Wayne Brian; Myers, Ronald; Nadeau, Maurice Lea; Nagler, Murray Ralph; Nahanee, Robert; Nanikasun, Thomas; Narraway, Wentworth Edwin James; Nash, Brian; Nazar, Jim Jack; Nazarko, Myron Peter; Neish, John McFee; Nelson, Nels Steward.

Neville, David John; Newbury, Terry Marcel; Newcombe, Edward Duval; Newnes, Robert Gerald; Nichol, Lawrence Gordon; Nicholson, Mervin Stephen; Nicol, Philip Grant; Nicholson, John Ivor; Neidersteiner, Edward Karl; Nixon, Kenneth Myron; Nours, Curtis; Novistky, Robert Larry; Nuell, Dean Alexander; Nugis, Patrick; Oakes, Terrance Kenneth; O'Brien, Albert James Patrick; Ockey, Gerald Leroy; O'Flaherty, John Reid; Oige, Garry Allan; Oklek, Daniel; Oklek, Ronald Frank; Oliva, Dwight Douglas; Olson, Donald; Olson, Ronald Raymond; Osland, David Thomas; Omand, Franklin George; O'Reilly, Brian Gray; Orlando, Daniel; Ostory, John Chester; Ott, Lloyd Roy; Oulette, Ronald Vincent; Ovans, Bruce Robin; Ovanden, Ronald Charles; Ozeroff, Gregory Fredrick.

Page, Brian David; Pageot, James Richard; Paquette, Craig Daniel; Papsdorf, Eric John; Parisian, Dennis Lloyd; Parker, Ronald Terrance; Parrott, James David; Pasqia, Stanley Donald; Pattern, William Edward; Patterson, Ernest Bruce; Paul, John William; Paul, William Harvey; Paulin, John Charles Carson; Pearson, Warren Harry; Pelltier, Emil Robert; Pennel, Robert Wayne; Penney, Clifford Thomas; Perth, Norman Steve; Perrault, Barry Ian; Perry, Norman George; Peters, John Richard; Peterson, Robert Glen; Peyton, Clive Stanley Waynne; Peyton, John Charles; Phillips, Llewelyn Taylor; Phillips, William James; Pickett, Terrance Leroy; Pidhirney, James Henry Alfred; Pinel, John Dower Marks; Pion, Robert Laurent; Plante, Frank; Plested, Roger Roy; Plomp, Wayne Frederick; Pocock, John Charles.

Pollard, Nelson Laverne; Popik, Douglas Gerald; Porter, Robert Richard; Portingale, William; Potts, Kenneth Edward; Pound, Ronald Edward; Pound, William Charles; Powell, George William; Powell, Michael; Powell, Thomas; Powers, Donald Allan; Poynter, Bryan Albert; Pressacco, Gerald Lloyd; Pridie, Roger Frank; Procunier, Frank Patrick; Pugliese, Richard Arthur; Purdy, Douglas; Purdy, Lyle Calvin; Pyper, Donald Keith; Quelle, Glen Murray; Query, Vaughan Ed-

ward; Quinn, Michael George; Quirico, Mark Leonard; Rabbit-Carrier, Kenneth; Radford, Gordon Dexter; Raeside, John C.; Faffard, Melvin Gordon; Rathweli, Dennis James; Rawlings, William Lionel R.; Ray, Daryl Brent; Rayner, George Allan; Read, Ronald George; Reader, Gerald Wayne; Reading, Robert James.

Readman, Lorne Henry; Reaney, Stanley Allan; Red Gun, Melvin; Reddon, John Robert; Reeves, Robert Charles; Reid, Alexander Robert; Reid, James Douglas; Reimer, Kelly Douglas; Reil, John Allan; Reiter, James; Renny, Victor Frederick; Renwick, Glen Stanley; Reynolds, Raymond George; Rice, David James; Richard, Roger Walter; Richards, Douglas; Richardson, Wilfred Lawson; Richter, Charley Harry; Rickey, Ronald; Riguidel, Larry Glen; Rimmer, John Raymond; Ringer, Russell James; Risk, Colin McLean; Ritson-Bennett, Roland George; Rivers, Brian Michael; Rivers, Frank Edward; Rivet, Roger; Roach, Albert Earl; Robb, John William; Roberts, Brian Charles; Roberts, Gerald Charles; Roberts, John James; Roberts, Terry; Robertson, Dennis Gordon.

Robertson, Edward John; Robertson, Garry Alan; Robertson, Ian Donald; Robertson, William Edward; Robins, Charles Rae; Robinson, Harvey W.; Robinson, Kelvin Ray; Rockburn, Gordon Thomas; Rockwell, David James; Rochon, Joseph Marcel D.; Romanda, Dennis William; Roncin, Edwin; Rook, Dennis Warren; Rose, Gerrick Glen; Rose, Rodrick Hage; Rose, Stanley Donald; Rosenau, Lyle Edward; Ross, Andrew John; Roth, John; Rowland, Donald George; Rowland, Michael Graham; Royce, Brian George A.; Royce, Rodney Lee; Russell, Richard Albert; Rutherford, John Allan; Rutter, Edward John; Ryan, Rodger Dennis; St. Laurent, George Ernest; St. Lawrence, Gordon Gerald; Ste. Marie, Daniel Michael; Sadler, Wilfred William; Sadoway, Ronald Nicholas; Saley, Douglas Norman; Salmon, Douglas Morley.

Samuel, Gerald Benjamin; Sanders, George Brian; Sando, Gerald Glen; Sapizak, Jerry Andres; Sauve, Dennis Eric; Sawatsky, Kenneth Walter; Sawyer, Donald Arthur; Sawyer, James Michael; Sayers, Frederick Blanchard; Schaeffer, Clifford Clarance; Schaffel, Frank William; Schapansky, Allen Glen; Schappert, James Adam; Scheuerman, Melvin Douglas; Schiebelbein, Gerald Peter; Schlosser, Harry Anthony; Schmidt, Dale Rubin; Schneider, Joseph Franz; Schoemeyer, William Casper; Schoening, William Richard; Schroeder, Ronald William; Schuh, Robert Allen; Schmann, Wayne Robert; Schultz, Kenneth Allan; Scott, Wayland Royce; Sculthorpe, John Henry Alexander; Sebulsky, Norbert Cornelius; Sellinger, Gregory Joseph; Semeniuk, Don Wayne; Senft, James Robert; Senft, Randal George; Senior, Clive Bruce; Senuk, Edward; Sexsmith, John Llewelyn.

Shalansky, R i c h a r d Frederick; Shale, Keith; Shannon, Ronald Wayne; Sharkey, Kenneth Lyle; Shape, Russel David; Shaw, Kenneth James; Shayler, H a r r y Avery; Sheane, Colin Roger; Shelton, David Burce; Shepanik, Ian Richard; Shinkewski, Lawrence; Shpikula, William Fred; Shuter, Gilbert Evans; Sidney, Gary George; Sielzie, Stanley James; Sievewright, Wayne Wilfred; Signarowski, Larry Joseph; Sikora, James; Simmons, Thomas George; Simpson, Brian Ray; Simpson, Ernest James; Simpson, Leon Gordon; Sinclair, Edgar Robert; Sinnock, Carl Gordon; Siwicki, Samuel Harold; Skafte, Emil Paul; Skantz, Anders Edward; Skilnick, Frank Gerald; Skipper, Alfred William; Sklapsky, Vernon Blaner; Sluggett, Richard Charles; Sly, Arthur Hohn; Slywka, Ronald Michael; Smiley, George Leon.

Smith, Bruce Foster; Smith, Daryl James; Smith, David Ian; Smith, Dennis; Smith, Donald; Smith, Douglas Leslie; Smith, Garry Lloyd; Smith, Gary Robert; Smith, Gordon Neil; Smith, Harold George; Smith, Hugh Richardson; Smith, James William; Smith, Joel; Smith, Michael; Smith, Peter; Smith, Raymond George; Smith, Roderick William; Smith, Ronald Daryl; Smith, Scot Thomas; Smith, Stewart Berry; Smith, Theodore Albert; Smith, Wayne Alexander; Snowdon, Robert Kellaway; Sobkowicz, Terry; Soganic, Richard James; Somerville, A l e x a n d e r Thomas; Sommerville, William Stephen; Sozova, Michael; Spencer, James Douglas; Spenst, Gerald Henry; Spielman, Dennis; Spivey, Douglas Norman; Sponholz, Dennis Earl; Sproat, Terry Allan.

Staliknecht, Garry Wilfred; Stanishewsky, Joseph Peter; Steeves, John James; Stenerud, Stein Erik; Sterling, Ronald Stanley; Stevens, Douglas Allan; Stewart, Allan George; Stewart, Gordon; Stewart, William Patrick; Stickelmier, Wayne Edward; Stickley, Allan David; Stinchcombe, Robert Michael; Stilwell, Terry David; Stinchcombe, Roger John; Stobart, Anthony Joseph; Stones, David Mallory; Storey, David Franklin; Stotts, Robert Riley; Strikes With A Gun, James A; Stroms, Allan Eric; Stuart, Albert Wayne; Stuart, Robert Taylor; Stupar, Dennis Warren; Sturdy, John MacDonald; Sturgeon, Douglas Gerald; Stutt, William Joseph H.; Sulz, David Douglas; Suddards, Brian Robert; Sullivan, John Joseph; Sutherland, Terry Wayne; Swakum, Cyril Antoine; Swan, John Getty; Swift, Donald Keith.

Tait, Danny George; Taje, Edward Albert; Tamboline, Joseph Edward; Tawse, Graham Alexander; Taylor, Brian Lawson; Taylor, Dale Elle; Taylor, Daniel Arthur; Taylor, John Charles; Taylor, Raymond James; Taylor, Reginald Douglas; Tennant, Leonard George; Tennessy, Timothy Patrick; Terhorst, Thomas Henry; Terpstra, Simon; Tetarenko, Stewart Fredrick; Tetz, Robert; Textor, Fredrick Ernest; Three-Sons, Henry; Thomas, Alvin Dale; Thomas, Archie Patrick; Thomas, Arthur Daniel;

Thompson, Eric Henry; Thompson, Denneth Nicholas; Thompson, Leonard Ross; Thompson, Lorne Andres; Thompson, Stephen Russell; Thomson, Richard Douglas; Thorburn, Kenneth William; Thurston, George Frederick; Tiernan, Neil Edward; Tizzard, Gordon Garry Grant; Todd, Bruce Charles; Todoschuk, Dennis Mitchell; Tokanek, Ben; Tomkins, Eric Alexander.

Tomlenovich, R o b e r t Francis; Tomplins, Thomas Dale Norman; Topp, Bruce Ernest; Tordiffe, Edward Robert; Tottenham, Dennis Gordon; Towie, James Gordon; Trefiak, Dennis William; Tremblay, Dwight James; Trenter, Michael Sidney Sam; Tretiak, Jerry; Troman, John Robert; Truscott, Dennis Raymond; Truscott, Raymond Orville; Turnell, Gordon Harry; Turner, David Henry; Turner, John Holmes; Tyerman, Berry; Tyerman, Lloyd David; Ulmer, Elroy Phillip; Underwood, Victor Gregory; Undger, Dale James; Ure, Richard Allan; Urry, Badur William; Vachon, Lea Alexander; Valley, David Brian; Van Aggelen, William Edward Paul; Van Balkom, David Edwin; Vance, Howard Percy; Vance, Reginald; Vandermolen, P e t e r; Vandervlugt, Eduard; Vanderwoude, William; Vanloon, Gerry Kelvin; Vermitte, Gerald Donald.

Vermette, Richard Donald; Vermilyea, Michael Bruce; Vincent, James; Volk, Jarome Gabriel; Varos, Michael Donald; Wade, Gary Loran; Wahie, Norman Alan; Walinsky, George Gunther; Walinsky, Garhard Richard; Walker, Arthur Edward; Walker, Donald Allan; Walker, James Brian; Walker, Randy Earl; Walker, William Thomas; Walters, Hendrik Robert; Walters, Harold George; Walters, Peter Johns; Wallace, Ernest Lynn; Wardlow, Robert Boyd; Warobo Trevor John; Warren Bryan Stewart; Washburn David; Watch, Arthur Charles; Watt, Brian Mansfield; Watt, Ronald James; Watson, Lloyd Harry; Watson, Thomas; Waygood, Geoffery; Weaver, Ronald Simon; Webb, Robert Russell; Weber, Ricky; Webster, David Bruce; Weeks, Raymond; Weisbrodt, Daniel George E.; Weninger, Allan Joseph.

Wenzel, Norbert; Westbury, Raymond Arthur; Wetherill, Douglas; Weyes, Christopher; Wicks, Charles Alfred; Wiekenkamp, Peter John; Wiest, Garry Ralph; Whaley, Gordon Robert; Wheatley, David Albert; Wheeler, Dennis Franklin; Wheeler, Ronald; White, Douglas; White, Douglas Robert; White, Gary William; White, Reginald Robert; Whitford, Lyle Thomas; Whitford, Robert Harry; Whiting, Garry Maurice; Whittington, Bruce Richard; Whyte, Donald; Whyte, James Wayne; Whyte, Thomas; Wigmore, Jerry Brant; Wilkie, Clarence John; Wilkinson, Robert Lorne; Willems, Lester Joseph; Willerton, Larry Victor; Williams, Alan Frederick; Williams, David; Willis, Brian; Willis, Gary Frank; Wills, David Vincent; Williams, Peter; Williams, Richard Neil.

Wilson, Dennis Francis; Wilson, Garry Grant; Wilson, James Stephen; Wilson, Kenneth Dwight; Wilson, Robert David; Wilson, Roy Thomas; Wilson, Stewart; Wilson, Timothy Vincent; Wiseman, Michael Paul; Wittmeier, Douglas Roy; Witwicki, Thomas Allan; Witzaney, Alexander James; Wolfe, Gerald Brian; Wolfe, Ronald Stewart; Wong, Vernon; Wood, Ernest; Wood, Gerald William; Woodcock, Anthony Edward; Woodrow, John; Woodrow, John David; Woodward, Richard Jack; Wosinski, Kenneth Arthur; Woytas, Myron John; Wymer, Gordon Ricky; Wymer, Robert Edmond; Wytrykush, Arthur Emtro; Wytrykush, L a w r e n c e; Yakimchuk, Burnard John; Yanchus, Terrance; Yates, David Dennis; Yawney, Rudolph Steve; Yaworski, Alvin; Yaworski, Gerald Anthony; Yearley, William Francis.

York, David; Young, Alfred Roy; Young, Lloyd; Young, John David; Yuzicapi, William Brice; Yuzwa, Robert Paul; Zado, Craig Peter; Zado, Dennis Gordon; Zarowny, Brian; Zarrillo, Rocco; Zator, Ralph Edward; Zibinski, Neil; Zurakowski, Donald Lawrence.

VACC - 1964

Allan, Wayne Laverne; Falkland, B.C.; Ashe, Hugh Donald; Tantallon, Sask.; Barilla, John Wesley, Morinville, Alta.; Barry, Timothy Dale; Carrot River, Sask.; Berthelette, Donald James; Pine Falls, Man.; Binns, William Vernon; Yarbo, Sask.; Bird, Barry James; Penticton, B.C.; Bluetchen, Larry Thomas; Stoney Plain, Alta.; Blystone, Don Ralph; West Summerland, B.C.; Bodnaryk, Terrance; Esterhazy, Sask.; Bruce, Norman William; Merritt, B.C.; Butzelaar, Joseph; Saskatoon; Buxton, Christopher Edmond; Inuvik, N.W.T.; Campbell, Ken; Vancouver; Cameron, Harry; Qualicum Beach, B.C.; Charbonneau, Leon; Battleford, Sask.; Clavering, Ronald Arthur; Ladysmith, B.C.; Cockwill, Robert Glen; Carrot River; Cole, Thomas George; Port Coquitlam, B.C.; Collinge, Bert; Evansburg, Alta.; Connacher, Stuart Glen; Merritt; Cottick, William Raymond; Winnipeg; Cullen, Martin Burke; Fort St. John, B.C.; Currie, Lyle McCurdy; Vermillion, Alta.; Danwich, Barry; Drivers Bay, Man.; Dillion, Frank James; Inuvik; Dodds, Kenneth; Kelowna, B.C.; Dunn, Richard Martin; Winfield, Alta.; Elliott, Alan; Hythe, Alta.; Emery, Ray Victor; Richmond, B.C.; Ewanchniuk, William; Edson, Alta.; Fimrite, Douglas; Valhalla Centre, Alta.; Fisette, Brian Albert; St. James, Man.; Fisher, Alfred John; Battleford; Folk, Lawrence Carl; Edson; Fontaine, Donald; Blindfolds, Man.; Forsyth, Ian Joseph; Esterhazy.

Gafka, Colin Paul; Vegreville, Alta.; Gauthier, David Louie; Esterhazy; George, James, Tantallons; Giese, Horst; Kelowna; Girou, Denis; Riviere Qui-Barr, Alta.; Gnyp, Eric; Alder Flats, Alta.; Gould, Herbert Frank; Vermillion; Green, John Hardy; Victoria; Greenbank, Ian;

Langford Park, Alta.; Griffin, William James; Breton, Alta.; Hamar, Ronald George; Entwhistle, Alta.; Hannam, Wilfred Frank; Big River, Sask.; Harcourt, James; Beaverlodge, Alta.; Hardy, Peter William; Victoria; Henderson, Brian; Vegreville; Herbert, Ronald Maurice; Vermillion; Houston, Rodney Morley; O'Keefe Centre, B.C.; Hutchinson, Raymond Gail; Fort St. John; Jackson, Richard Eric; Fort St. John; Jardine, Campbell; Entwhistle; Jeffery, William George; Vancouver; Johnston, Brian George; Victoria; Kailek, Robert; Ranger Station, N.W.T.; Kaiser, Robert; Vermillion; Kellett, William Boyd; Richmond; Kitman, John Louis; Edson; Kootney, Donald; Morinville; Kunkel, Wayne Arthur; Esterhazy; Ladouceur, Donald William; Qualicum Beach; Larson, Ronald Anthony; Edson; Lemire, Claude Yves; Great Falls, Man.; Lerose, Larry Tomas; Battleford.

McDonald, James Ian Wilson; Winnipeg; McNaughton, Jackie; Edson; McNeil, Denis; Brox, Sask.; Martin, Philip; Inuvik; Martynuik, Marvin; Vegreville; Meachen, James David; Carrot River; Melville, Andrew; Brock, Sask.; Merchison, Larry Harvey; Port Coquitlam; Millikin, Stanley; Big River, Sask.; Mitchell, David Thomas; Kelowna; Morissett, Roland Edmond; Powerview, Man.; Mosley, Gordon Richard; Richmond; Mosley, Robert Francis; Richmond; Newbold, Danny James; Penticton; Norberg, G o r d o n; Tuktoyaktuk, N.W.T.; O'Grady, Michael Edward; Richmond; Perlstrom, Charles William; Penticton; Peters, John; Coppermine, N.W.T.; Poulis, Brian Alexander; Fort St. John; Powley, Kenneth Ralph; Quesal, Robert; Esterhazy; Roberts, Timothy Sean Henry; Victoria; Rogers, Lief Alexander; Mulhurst Beach, B.C.; Sager, David William; Inuvik; Sakaluk, James; Bagerville, Alta; Saul, Kenneth Wayne; Fort St. John; Scott, Earl Robert; Port Coquitlam; Semler, Melvin Lawrence; Inuvik; Seve, Gerald William; Edson; Shawn, Barry; Calmar, Alta.; Sinclair, Timothy Brent; Port Coquitlam; Sloan, Ronald Leslie; Penticton; Smalley, Wayne Douglas; Vancouver; Styles, Ian David; Port Coquitlam; Sydney, Charles; Inuvik.

Tait, James Edward; Qualicum; Theriault, Glen Edward; Burnaby, B.C.; Thompson, John Robert; Merritt; Thomson, Raymond Douglas; Birch Pine Fall, Man.; Tiesson, Kenneth Wayne; Merritt; Tilston, John David; Vancouver; Toner, Bernard Joseph; Vegreville; Tumm, Robert; Fort St. John; Tycholaz, Ronald Richard; Merritt; Walker, Ronald Arthur; Brandon, Man.; Weidle, Joseph; Warwick, Alta.; Whitelock, Loarn Joseph; Callwood, Man.; Whitonyk, Terry Nickolas; Derwent, Alta.; Wilkie, Clarence John; Battleford; Wilson, William Charles; Penticton; Wilson, William Louis; Biger, Sask.; Wiltse, Denis Reginald; Penticton; Wrigglesworth, John Sidney; Vancouver; Zawadiuk, Carl Paul; Edmonton.

Abbott, Fred Lewis; Edmonton; Allen, Rodney; Kerrobert, Sask.; Anaquod, Eugene; Fort Qu'Appelle,

Sask.; Anaquod, Glen; Regina; Anderson, Howard Peter; Hinton, Alta.; Aitken, Richard Alexander; Nelson, B.C.; Appleton, Ronald; Edmonton; Baron, Tom; Hafford, Sask.; Barker, David John; Haney, B.C.; Bartlette, Pierre F.; St. Boniface, Man.; Batenchek, Philip Raymond; Winnipeg; Beckett, John Robert; Winnipeg; Beaumont, Robert; Winnipeg; Bellerose, Alvin; Edmonton; Binder, Richard, Inuvik, N.W.T.; Binder, Ronald Nelson; Inuvik; Blackwood, Daniel Caldwell; Williams Lake, B.C.; Booth, David Charles; Sardis, B.C.; Boreen, Hedley; Edmonton; Brodziak, Garry; Hazel Dell, Sask.; Brooks, Larry Williams; Edmonton; Budd, William Keith; Winnipeg; Burzinski, Kristian; Hinton; Campbell, Thomas John; Winnipeg; Carrier, Colin; Craven, Sask.; Chemko, Richard Wayne; Vernon, B.C.; Christie, Douglas Vernon; New Westminster; Christophersen, Arrnie; Edmonton; Coleman, Daniel Joseph; Brandon, Man.; Coleman, Michael Jerome Augustin; Brandon; Cormack, John Allen; Winnipeg; Coutes, Lorry John; Winnipeg; Craig, Christopher; Hinton; Crerar, Robert John; Armstrong, B.C.; K'Anelio, Frank Antonio; Nelson.

Dales, James Allen; Edmonton; Deen, John James; Invermere, Sask.; Demers, Raymond Joseph; Edmonton; Dobie, William Craig; Vernon; Dodds, Earl Robert; Salmon Arm, B.C.; Doherty, William Flyod; Hinton; Doonanco, Raymond; Chilliwack, B.C.; Doucette, Philip; Comox, B.C.; Elliott, Garth Alan; Callvington, Sask.; Everett, Leonard Francis; Vedder Crossing, B.C.; Ewasiuk, Bruce Earle; Montrose, B.C.; Ferguson, Ernest Kenneth; Haney; Ferguson, Richard Gordon; Edmonton; Folk, Vernon Albert Regina; Fraser, Kevin; Winnipeg; Gagne, Dennis Benjamin; Vimy, Alta.; Ganton, Bruce Norman, Edmonton; Garbutt, Ronald Norman; Vernon; Garneau, Raymond Joseph; Legal, Alta.; Gelasco, Paul; Edmonton; Godchiode, Fred; Edmonton; Gorak, Victor John; Chilliwack; Gramiak, Eugene Orest; Hafford, Sask.; Guenther, Gerry Owen; Winnipeg; Harrison, Richard Wayne; Enderby, B.C.; Holman, Theodore; Regina; Hudec, Albert Joseph; Westlock, Alta.; Huhn, Conrad; Humbleton, Sask.; Inkster, Donald Robert; Vernon; Jacoa, Ivano; Nelson.

Kaidennek, Trevor Welsy; Edmonton; Kaszczuk, Stephen; Regina; Kemp, Dale Thomas; Edmonton; Kienholz, Melvin Gary; Nelson; Kindrachuk, Robert Walter; Redberry, Sask.; Kizmann, William; Matsqui, B.C.; Klym, Robert Mathew, Enderby; Koe, Frederick; Inuvik; Korn; Peter; Edmonton; Krachkowski, Ross; Kelvington, Sask.; Kruper, Paul Robert; Edmonton; Lavorato, Gary; Rossland, B.C.; LaBranche, Leslie Raymond; Edmonton; Lambert, Roger Joseph; Haney; Lebsack, Steven Robert; Vulcan, Alta.; Littlejohn, Robert Drew; Winnipeg; Lowry, Garth Cameron; Winnipeg; Luchta, Homan Harry; Hefford, Sask.; Lupul, Brian Peter; Weyburn, Sask.; Leullier, Robert Paul; Winnipeg; McGhie, John David; Edmonton;

McGown, William; Edmonton; McKain, James; Edmonton; Macala, Philip Walter; Invermay, Sask.; Mack, Bervin Lyle; Nut Mountain, Sask.; Madson, Roland; Winnipeg; Makutra, Larry Michael; Edmonton; Martin, Richard; Mayerthorpe, Alta.; Martin, Ronald Kenneth; Edmonton; Maron, James; Edmonton.

McCullough, William Wilfred George; Regina; McGregor, John; Regina; Miller, Robert Colin; Edmonton; Moate, Dennis Wayne; Winnipeg; Mornd, Roger; Winnipeg; Morrell, Marvin Lorne; Vernon; Morrison, Neil Cameron; Edmonton; Mottershead, Arthur Ian; Edmonton; Mowat, Donald; Winnipeg; Murdoch, Michael Blair; Kerrobert, Sask.; Murray, Benjamin; Sardis, B.C.; Myroniuk, Raymond; Edmonton; Neff, Dieter Eric; N. Surrey, B.C.; Nimetz, Terrence Wallace; Regina; Nolan, Wayne Angus; Salmon Arm; Ouellette, Norman Joseph; Legal; Palin, David Allen; Edmonton; Palmer, Albert; Invermay; Partridge, Gary Wayne; Sardis; Paugh, Denis; Trail, B.C.; Pepper, William Leonard; Armstrong; Pitchao, Donald; Kelvington; Polachek, David John; Kelvington; Prain, David; Courtenay, B.C.; Query, Elliott William; Edmonton; Rempel, John; Nelson; Russell, Harvey George; Winnipeg; Ryan, Gregory Austin; Seba Beach, Alta.; Ryder, Keith Robert; Sangudo, Alta.; Rydzik, Henry Eugene Joseph; Vernon.

Sallows, William; Edmonton; Saunders, Charles; Winnipeg; Sakakibara, Wayne David; Vernon; Schimanowski, Ribert Reil; Humbolt, Sask.; Scott, James Howard; Rossland; Seidler, John Walter; Regina; Shiskin, Clifford Dale; Salmon Arm; Smith, Fletcher; Winnipeg; Steer, Kenneth; Edmonton; Stockl, Gordon; Edmonton; Stuckel, Douglas Walter; Langley, B.C.; Szumilak, Donald; Winnipeg; Treat, Charles Harold; Salmon Arm; Truss, Robert Scott; Sedgewick, Alta.; Van De Wallee, Leon Leslie; Venderbos, Gerry; Winnipeg; Vzina, Leonard James; Winnipeg; Walstrea, John; Strathmore, Alta.; Wear, Kenneth John; Harris, Sask.; Weaver, Richard; Nelson; White, John; Edmonton; Wills, Edward William; Vedder Crossing; Wirth, Werner Paul; Hinton; Woods, Norman Barry; Courtenay.

Aldie, Timothy Charles; Edmonton; Allen, James; Edmonton; Archer, James; Melville, Sask.; Ayotte, Ronald; Edmonton; Barnett, Thomas; Winnipeg; Bates, Reginald; Edmonton; Bellec, Raymond; Richmond, B.C.; Berens, Joseph Lloyd; Fort Smith, N.W.T.; Boisvert, Prosper; Sherwood Park, Alta.; Boughton, Roanlad Andrew; Victoria; Brawn, Michael Edward Jeffery; Victoria; Bruno, Marvin; Winterburn, Alta.; Campbell, Charles; Cloverdale, B.C.; Cardy, Anthony Michael; HQ Wescom.; Caron, Edward Emile; Prince Albert, Sask.; Castelsky, Joachim William; Port Alberni, B.C.; Cisecki, John Peter; Vancouver; Chalifoux, Dennis; Edmonton; Chartrand, Henry; Edmonton; Chelus, John; Winnipeg; Church, Charles Richard; Blain Lake, Sask.; Coffey, Dwight Gregory; Kelowna, B.C.; Colcleugh, John; Vancouver; Copeland, George Frank; Kindersley, Sask.; Coyne, Kevin; Fort Smith; Bandenault, Edward James; North Kamloops, B.C.; Demmy, Robert John; Whitehorse, Y.T.; Desjardins, Gabriel; Marcelin, Sask.; Desjardins, Lionel Wayne; Marcelin; Duncan, Donald Roy; Flin Flon, Man.; Desmonie, Gerald; Lorlie Lake, Sask.; Dhillon, Herhort Paul; Victoria; Dowler, George Frederick; Victoria; Dunn, George James; Winnipeg; Durocher, Francis; Edmonton; Durocher, William Donald; Edmonton; Earl, Terry; Fort Smith; Engbrecht, Hans; Victoria; Erlendson, Roy Douglas; Victoria; Exner, Denis; Melville.

Ferguson, Joseph Duncan; Fort Smith; Foster, Dennis; Edmonton; Franke, Allen Donald; Hafford, Sask.; French, Joseph Allen; Moose Jaw, Sask.; Giesbrecht, Gordon; Hay River, N.W.T.; Grace, Joseph; Vancouver; Graham, Daniel; Whitehorse; Grande, Anthony; Winnipeg; Graves, Vernon Robert; North Kamloops; Gray, Sidney; Vancouver; Green, Stuart; Victoria; Hall, Robert Gary; St. James, Man.; Hamelin, Gerald B e n j a m i n; Winnipeg; Hamilton, Roderick Gordon; Victoria; Hammon, Kenneth Walter; Moose Jaw; Hanchakove, William Stephen; Winnipeg; Harding, Donald Wayne; Winnipeg; Hawkes, John; Moose Jaw; Head, Clifford Roy; Kinistino, Sask.; Holt, Richard Gottfreid L.; Winnipeg; Hood, Richard Francis; Victoria; Hunt, Ross Dennis; Victoria; Hunter, Robert Murray; Edmonton; Hutchinson, Bertrum; Fort Smith; Hutchings, Donald Steven; Victoria; Jeffry, Jack; Winnipeg; Jones, Lyle Roberts; Mervin, Sask.; Jorde, Glen; North Kamloops; Kennedy, Alexander Keith; Victoria; Kinnaird, James Alexander; Edmonton; Laderoute, Ronald John; Winnipeg; Lafond, Harry James; Marcelin, Sask.; Lavallee, Philip Louis; Winnipeg; Lawrence, Robert Tony; Melville; Lemmon, Duncan Rodney; Calgary; Leonard, Daniel Robin; Victoria; Lewis, Edward Michael; Bausejour, Man.; Lubbers, Jerry; Edmonton; Luniw, Philip William; Vancouver.

McDonald, Bernard Gregory John; Vancouver; McLaren, Brian Gerald; Melville; McPherson, Richard; Hay River; Maw, Jeffery Wayne; Winnipeg; Mark, Brian James; Flin Flon; Martin, David John; Victoria; Mar tin, Terrence; Fort Smith; Michaud, Wayne; Victoria; Miller, Delvin James; Moose Jaw; Miller, Roy Charles; Victoria; Mykes, Kenneth Leslie Joseph; Winnipeg; Nakano, Roy Hiroshi; Moose Jaw; Niehaus, Gary; Edmonton; O'Connor, Daryl Arthur; Churchill, Man.; Olsen, Kjell, Victoria; Pears, Ronald; Edmonton; Peterson, William George; Kindersley; Pongratz, Alex James; Melville; Quovadis, Peter Fred Henry; Vancouver; Ralph, James Melvin; Winnipeg; Robson, Murray Allan; Kamloops; Robson, William John; Richmond; Rudick, Michael John; Fort St. John; St. Avery, Gerald Stewart; Winnipeg; Sam, Richard; Victoria; Scott, David Peter; Kamloops.

Seginowich, Rennie Wayne; Victoria; Sheppard, Gregory Ralph; Edmonton; Sherff, Larry Duane; Edmonton; Shilproth, Berry Wayne; Crayton, Sask.; Sibbeston, Robert; Hay River; Small, Gordon Andrew; Edmonton; Smith, Paul Clifford; Victoria; Smith, Donald Russell; Moose Jaw; Smith, Richard; Spirit River, Alta.; Smyth, Thomas; Edmonton; Stephens, Dennis; Fort St. John; Stone, Ronald Guy; Portage La Prairie, Man.; Szajowski, Larry Leo; Beausejour; Taylor, Ian; Victoria; Taylor, Ray George; Whitehorse; Tencarre, Sydney; Spirit River; Thom, Brian Jordan; Langley; Thomas, Angus; Hay River; Turner, Daryl Ross; Vancouver; Turvey, Donald Wayne; Edmonton; Vachon, Jeffrey Wm. Paul; Whitehorse; Vollema, Gerlof; Edmonton; Wallace, Jerry Donald; Milestone, Sask.; Wallach, Roger Soney; North Burnaaby; Weishaupt, Peter Brian; Melville; Weselake, Anthony Wm. John Pat; Beausejour; Weston, Gordon Ernest; Fort Smith; Williams, Dennis Frederick; Winnipeg; W i l l i a m s, Frederick George; Flin Flon; Wiznuk, John Nickelson; Winnipeg; White, Daniel Neil; Edmonton; Wolfe, Kenneth William; Hobbema, Alta.; Worsell, Jack; Whitehorse; Young, Kenneth Michael; Vancouver; Zest, Norman Brian; Winnipeg.

Allanback, Robert Roy; Redcliff, Alta.; Armstrong, Robert; Virden, Man.; Aris, Brian Walter; Hillcrest, Alta.; Barry, David Wayne; Lacombe, Alta.; Barton, Carl; Prince Rupert, B.C.; Belore, Robert James; Burnaby, B.C.; Binkley, Ronald Lloyd; Camp Shilo, Man.; Bird, Robert James, Vancouver, B.C.; Bobbie, Denis Michael; Winnipeg, Man.; Bouman, Frans John; Redcliffe; Braybrook, Robert Wayne; Winnipeg; Brogan, Jerry; Winnipeg; Brooks, Frank Douglas; Rosthern, Sask.; Brooks, Ross Irving; Rosthern; Bruce, James Angus; North Surrey, B.C.; Bruce, Robert James Sheridan; North Surrey; Carmichael, Kevin Reid; Vancouver; Carpenter, Steve James; Vancouver; Carter, Harold William; Winnipeg; Carter, Larry Wayne; Calgary; Cerreck, Steven; Duncan, B.C.; Ciona, Steven Michael; Blain Lake, Sask.; Chodyka, George; Coleman, Alta.; Church, Helge; Rocky Mountain House, Alta.; Clark, Gerald Charles; Duncan; Colquhoun, Robert Dale; Virden, Man.; Davidson, Kenneth Peter; Camp Shilo; Descalchuk, Edmon; Rose Valley, Sask.; Detta, Robert Grant; Silverton, B.C.; Dickau, Dale Vernon; Rocky Mtn. House; Kinney, Wallace; Prince Albert, Sask.; Dornan, Paul Leslie; Oyama, B.C.; Druce, Gary Frederick; Victoria; Drunken Chief, Wallace; Cluny, Alta.; Dyer, Raymond Alexander; Portage La Prairie, Man.; Evans, David; Camp Shilo.

Fehr, John; Prince Albert; Fletcher, Randy Glen; New Westminster; Forbes, Robert; Red Deer, Alta.; Fowler, Daniel; Baellview, Alta.; Fox, Alfred; Gleichen, Alta.; Garner, Melvin; Virden; Germain, James; Red Deer; Godwin, William George; Delburne, Alta.; Hambly, William; Regina; Hampson, Clyde; Calgary;

Haney, John; Winnipeg; Hardy, Steven; Hommen, Alta.; Hayes, Ronald; Prince Albert; Hill, William; Winnipeg; Howie, James Keith; Vancouver; Hovdedo, Rudy Richard; Prince Albert; Huckley, David; Prince Albert; Jenks, Jerry Wallace; New Denver, B.C.; Johannson, Allan David; Vancouver; Johnston, Keith C h a r l e s; Vancouver; Kachanoski, Kenneth Wayne; Port Alberni; Keeler, Gerald Michael; Sylvan Lake, Alta.; Kellier, Robert Allan; Calgary; Kinder, Walter John; Millarville, Alta.; Kinley, Larry Alvin; Lacombe, Alta.; Kirk, Jeffrey; Winnipeg; Knoll, Brian Richard; Port Alberni; Knowles, Patrick Anthony; Vancouver; Knowles, Thomas Edward; Vancouver; Klughart Gordon Edgar; Prince Alberta; Kuffler, Robert George; Delburne, Alta.; Landry, Gerard Paul; Vancouver; Lang, Gordon David Brian; New Denver; Leasak, Robert Alexander; Turner Valley, Alta.; Levers, Gerald Richard; Vancouver; Little, Kevin; Winnipeg; Longman, T e r r e n c e James; Rosthern; Lyons, Larry Oral; Okotoks, Alta.; MacDougall, Darcy Wayne; Redcliff, Alta.; MacKenzie, Ian Elliott; Revelstoke, B.C.; McDonad; Kenneth Gordon Sam; Winnipeg; McDonaugh, John Frank; New Denver.

McFee, Ernest; Stonewall, Man.; McDonell, Leslie Duncan; Vancouver; MacDonald, Alastair John; Calgary; Martin, Robert G.; Winnipeg; Mast, Glen Ollie; Chemainus, B.C.; McKinney, William Even; New Westminster; McLean, Robert William; North Surrey; Mengler, Werner; Silverton; Mitchell, Mathew Gordon; Winnipeg; Middlemiss, Gary James; Duncan; Misson, Garry Amour Joseph; Coleman; Moffat, Alexander; Portage La Prairie; Mugleston, James Lewis; Rolston, Alta.; Oberston, Earle John; Ponoka, Alta.; Osgood, Patrick Lavelle; Redcliff; Palmer, Douglas Clifford; Winnipeg; Parro, James; Camp Shilo; Pelland, David Albert; Port Alberni; Peterson, David Carl; Chemainus; Pielak, Dennis; Calgary; Pikor, Anton; Rose Valley, Sask.; Phillips, Andrew; Duncan; Pratt, John Roger; Lacombe.

Reed, Robert John; Rose Valley; Reid, William; Winnipeg; Roberts, Allan; Camp Shilo; Robertson, Richard William Cryle; Vancouver; Rust, Grant Stuart; Burnaby; Sawyer, Robert; Winnipeg; Shapcotte, Himothy Frank; Vancouver; Skibinski, Ronald Neil; Vancouver; Sinclair, Edgar Robert; Winnipeg; Stanhope, Terrence Albert; Duncan; Stephenson, William Murray; Calgary; Stewart, Timothy Neil; Vancouver; Taite, Wayne Timothy; Portage La Prairie; Tennant, Michael; Lacombe; Thomasen, Walley Role; New Westminster; Thompson, George; Black Diamond, Alta.; Turner, Andrew; Camp Shilo; Van Ingen, Frederick; Alberni; Wamusley, Norman William; Regina; Watt, Robert Alexander Frazer; Revelstoke; Wayman, William; Hillcrest, Alta.; Weaslehead, Gerald; Cluny; Welford, Michael John; Red-

cliff; Wells, Robert Gordon; Camp Shilo; Wicer, Robert Roy; Prince Albert; Wong, Larry Jerry; Prince Rupert; Woodley, George Arthur; Duncan; Wunderlick, Robert Roy; Millardville, B.C.; Wytrykuse, William Nicholas; Yorkton, Sask.

Adams, Clifford Bruce; Saskatoon, Sask.; Anderson, Broderick Gurney; Winnipeg, Man.; Appleton, Richard William, North Surrey, B.C.; Arlt, Douglas Leslie; Creston, B.C.; Baird, James Edward; Saskatoon; Baker, Robert Irving; Calgary, Alta.; Baron, Robert Michael; Revelstoke, B.C.; Baynton, Edward Charles; Creston; Beatch, Gregory Richard; Walbert, Sask.; Beatty, Kenneth Joseph; Vulcan, Alta.; Beday, John Paul; Cranbrook, B.C.; Blake, Harry; Winnipeg; Bolton, Randy Dallas; Creston; Boyle, Brent, North Surrey, B.C.; Brigden, Robert William; Calgary; Brose, Ronald; Saskatoon; Brow, Michael; Transcona, Man.; Bruyere, Edward; Fort Alexander, Man.; Cade, Michael George; Vancouver; Campbell, Duncan; Saskatoon; Campbell, Tom; Calgary; Carrier, Joseph Edward; Winnipeg; Cashman, Philip; Calgary; Christionson, Lorne; Creston; Colwell, Bruce; Swift Current, Sask.; Cook, John Blaine; Saskatoon; Copping, Kenneth; Transcona; Couling, William Harvey; Dauphin, Man.; Croft, Gordon Wallace; South Burnaby; Cross, Lorne Robert; Vancouver; Curtis, Richard Albert; Saanich, B.C.; Davis, Dale Roland; Revelstoke; Davis, Kenneth John; North Surrey; Daynes, Ronald Edward; Kimberley, B.C.; DeKort, William; Vancouver; Dool, Lloyd Andrew; White Rock, B.C.; Downing, Gerald Arthur; Squamish, B.C.; Duncan, Maurice; Victoria; Dunfield, Ernest Donald; Dauphin; Dwernichuk, Larry James; Sturgis, Sask.; Evans, Leslie James; Saskatoon; Evanson, Donald Paul; Calgary; Fjoser, Wayne Howard; Ladner, B.C.; Friese, Harvey; Swift Current; Fry, Gary; Swift Current.

Gadd, Keith; St. Robert, Sask.; Garrison, Keith Grant; Red Deer, Alta.; Gloeckler, Ken; Swift Current; Griffin, Bruce; Winnipeg; Griffigh, Earl; Creston; Hall, Derrick Allan; Cloverdale, B.C.; Harrington, Russell Wayne; North Surrey; Harry, Douglas; Winnipeg; Herrod, Donald; Saskatoon; Holloway, Patrick; Revelstoke; Howse, Melton; Calgary; Huckley, Keith; Calgary; Johnston, Daniel; Saskatoon; Kaake, Ronny; Calgary; Kareera, Rick Gregory; Calgary; Kaufman, Kenneth Richard; Winnipeg; Kawa, Peter John; Winnipeg; Kearney, Gerald Thomas; Vancouver; Kelly, Duncan Alexander; Saanich; Kemble, Gary Edward; Red Deer; Kerslake, Patrick Claire; Innisfail, Alta.; Knorr, David Russell; St. Walburg, Sask.; Lebounty, Michael James; Victoria; Lamoureux, John Lucien Joseph; Vancouver; Larsen, Brian Richard; Cranbrook; Levecqe, David Lawrence; Dauphin; Litz, Donald Franklin; Saskatoon; MacDonald, R. B.; Winnipeg; McDonald, Larry John; Victoria; McIlwain, Daryl Frederick; Night Road, B.C.; McKay, Leanard; Norway House, Northern Man.; McLaren, Kenneth Gordon; Revelstoke; McIver, Colin Alexander; Stonewall; McNeil, William Wallace;

Cranbrook; McQueen, Bruce Dwight; Vancouver; McVie, William Stanley; Victoria; Maines, Lawrence Aubrey; Calgary; Mann, Garth Robin; North Surrey; March, Leslie Patrick; Creston; Martin, Barry David; Red Deer; Melting Tallow, Flloyd Frances; MacLeod, Alta.; Mohr, Ray Allan; Saskatoon; Moses, William Frederick; MacLeod; Morrison, Arthur; Winnipeg; Morrison, Lyle William; Cloverdale, B.C.; Murphy, William Christopher; Coronation, Alta; Myette, Thomas Larry; North Surrey.

Nazarko, Taras Walter; Calgary; Nelson, Thomas; Victoria; Nicholson, Kenneth Andrew; Ladner; Olsen, Larry Roach; North Surrey; Olson, Lorne Burdette; Innisfail, Alta.; Oxtoby, Stanley Lyle; Innisfail; Peterson, Albert Norman; Innisfail; Pitman, Kenneth; Winnipeg; Premack, George Edward; North Surrey; Pocha, Melvin Lloyd; Cranbrook; Porter, Graeme Michael; Victoria; Postma, Robert; Calgary; Pyne, Michael Patrick; Saskatoon; Ray, Darwyl Adrian; Cranbrook; Ribecco, Michael; Calgary; Rieberger, Michael John; Innisfail; Riguidel, Lenie; Winnipeg; Robertson, Lee Henry; Sturgis; Rogers, Fred Samuel; Ladner; Ryder, Neil; Kendal, Sask.; Sauve, Stanley Joseph; Strathmore, Alta.; Schaffel, Donald John; Saskatoon; Schatz, John; Saskatoon; Scott, David Wayne; Calgary; Stannard, Douglas William; Coronation; Stones, David Mallory; St. Boniface, Man.; Sunley, Edmond; Saskatoon; Sunley, Richard; Saskatoon; Sutherland, Brian Douglas; Calgary.

Teare, Gaylon Andrew; Strathmore; Turner, Gordon; Cranbrook; Walker, Alan; Calgary; Wasilewski, Andrew; Winnipeg; Watt, Philip Alan; Victoria; Webb, Gary; Cranbrook Wieier; David Michael; Richmond; Wild, Moris Alan; Saskatoon; Wilkinson, David; Strathmore; Wilson, Alphius Joseph; Norway House; Winstanley, Tom Edward; Cranbrook; White, John Gordon; Vancouver; Wynes, Frank Henry; Dauphin; Yatts, Henry Arthur; Cranbrook; Young, Donald Gordon; White Rock; Zacker, Robert Lyle Michael; Revelstoke; Zakreski, Larry Arnold; Saskatoon.

Adams, William Cassidy; Lytton, B.C.; Allen, Daniel Erwin Bennett; Churchill, Man.; Aney, Robert James; Yorkton, Sask.; Baldwin, Brent Marcel; Yorkton; Bargery, James Peter; Nakusp, B.C.; Bartlett, Raymond Glen; Nakusp; Beauregard, Timothy Joseph; Venada, B.C.; Bell, Donald Bennett; Medicine Hat, Alta.; Benson, Kenneth; Picture Butte, Alta.; Berikoff, Philip Roy; Prince George, B.C.; Bird, Peter Malcolm; Portage La Prairie, Man.; Blue, Byron George; Squamish, B.C.; Borylo, Orest Ted; Invermere, B.C.; Boyle, Russell; Invermere; Briza, Jack; North Vancouver, B.C.; Brockmuir, Wolf William; Radium Junction, B.C.; Broda, David; Yorkton; Brooks, Denis; Lethbridge, Alta.; Brown, Edward Alexander; Vancouver; Brown, Harold; Lethbridge; Cameron, Thomas Gordon; Calgary; Campbell, Gordon Doug; Bracknell, B.C.; Campbell, Kenneth Wayne; Brandon, Man.; Carlson, Douglas;

Calgary; Caron, Peter Joseph; Port Coquitlam, B.C.; Chappin, Walter Allen; Prince George; Chmialawski, George James; Fernie, B.C.; Clerence, Victor; Gleichen, Alta.; Cook, Garry Alan; Vancouver; Corney, Denis Wayne; Brandon, Man.; Crivea, Leonard Robert; Vananda, Texada Island. B.C.; Culbertson, Ian Barry; Brandon; Dalmquist, Larry Gordon; Wadena, Sask.; Daradich, Philip Randall; Wadena; Daucet, Leonard Allan; Squamish; Davis, Brian Claycus; Squamish; Denhoff, Gerry Wallace; Calgary; Drenka, Jay Arthur; Squamish; Dumontier, Carl Henry Edmond; Picture Butte; Duncan. Roger David; Nakusp.

Edwards, William Henry; Bowness, Alta.; Erickson, Harold Viggo; Squamish; Esopeko, Daniel William; Yorkton; Finlayson, William Archibald; North Vancouver; Foyston, Donald Earl; Invermere; Fress, Jerry; Picture Butte; Gallant, Ken; Calgary; Garaghty, Tom Martin; Calgary; Godsalve, Terrance Lee; Lethbridge; Gower, William Henry; Medicine Hat; Granger, John Frederick; Vancouver; Hauck, Brian Keith; Calgary; Hawkins, Scott William; Yorkton; Holtkamp, Johannes Maria; Yorkton; Horne. Murray D.; Fort Churchill, Man.; Hrabar, George Stephen; Edmonton; Jacquest, Peter Donald; Calgary; Jardine, Donald John; Squamich; Johnson, Michael R.; Weyburn, Sask.; Just, Albert William Francis; Yorkton; Kennedy, Donald Keith; Squamish; Klein, Alvin Alfred; Swift Current; Koldingas, Donald Keith; Swift Current; Langlos, Bernard Lloyd; Churchill; Legg, Stephen Thomas; Calgary; Levitt, John Frederick; Nakusp; Lyons, Donald Mervin; Calgary; MacPhee, Frederick John; Calgary; McIsaac, Edward John McDonald; Vancouver; McKenna, Dale Francis; Lethbridge; McPherson, Allen James; Calgary; Marzocco, Sammy; Britannia Beach, B.C.; Michell, Robert; Lytton; Minchin. Nigel Peter; Squamish; Misisco, Nicholas Carmen; Fernie; Muir, James Ernest; Langley; Murdoch, Ian Campbell; Calgary; Murray, David William; Weyburn; Murray, Donald Scott; Gleichen.

Nelson, Arnold John; Pincher Creek, Alta.; Nylen, Daniel Frederick; Brandon; Obuck, Anthony William; Yorkton; Ochitwa, David Allan; Yorkton; Olson, Galen Reo Mames; Britannia Beach; Pali, Frank; Vancouver; Pallister, Denis Carl; Portage La Prairie; Pidgeon, James William; Fernie; Phillips; Douglas Ross; Calgary; Pitchford, Brian Douglas; Yorkton; Powell, Gerald Arthur; Fernie; Price, Allan James; Calgary; Quebec, Peter Donald; Swift Current; Rathgaber, Brian Wayne; Calgary; Redmond, John Donald; Vernon; Robinson, Russell Thomas; Pincher Creek; Ross, Rodney William; Calgary; Ross, Russell Andrew; Calgary; Rossetti, Garry Ray; Lethbridge; St. Marie, Darcy Jerome; Blubber Bay, B.C.; Savage, William Gordon; Nakusp; Schandor, Miles Rex; North Lethbridge; Schuh, Richard Wayne; Medicine Hat; Seabrook, Joseph Calvin; Medicine Hat; Sexsmith, Terrence Lee; Prince George; Simmie, Roger Newby; Van-

522

couver; Stair, Clair Bradley; Bowness.

Sinclair, Robert Stanley; Nakusp; Singleton, Robert Gordon; Fernie; Smyth, Steven Maxwell; Calgary; Spencer, Stanford Allan; Calgary; Stringer, Michael Edward; Prince George; Stroshein, Robert William; Wadena; Sturgess, Robert Charles; Medicine Hat; Suhr, Hans Otto; Prince George; Sullivan, J a c k Daniel; Blubber Bay; Thompson, John Douglas; Calgary; Thompson, Joseph Gordon; Weyburn; Troman, James Patrick; Lethbridge; Visser, Gamarv Adrian; Pincher Creek; Walker, Donald John; Lethbridge; Welyuchow, William John; Calgary; Webb, William John; Calgary; Weirs, Jan Miles; Invermere; Wilis, Ronald Wm. Michael; Lethbridge; Williams, Ames Herald; Calgary; Wyatt, Clark Reginald; Calgary; Yacyshen, Gerry Fred; Norquay, Sask.; Yaney, Lawrence; Yorkton; Yanosik, Daniel Lloyd; North Lethbridge; Zepp, John Edward; Yorkton.

Anderson, Lyle Gordon; Creston, B.C.; Argue, Michael David; Fort Churchill, Man.; Bacon, Stephen Willian; Calgary, Alta.; Baker, William Donald; Whitehorse, Y.T.; Barnes, Richard; Vancouver, B.C.; Bamford, Daniel; Edmonton, Alta.; Bayliss, Peter Scott; Calgary; Bembem, Robert Michael; Winnipeg, Man.; Bilawey, John; Vegreville, Alta.; Bledsoe, John Kent; Port Alberni, B.C.; Bloomfield, Arthur Stan; Winnipeg; Brill, Wayne Eric; Vernon, B.C.; Bronevitch, Edward James; Transcona, Man.; Brown, Hamilton Jeff; Calgary; Buchanan, William Burton; Winnipeg; Bulloch, Lorne Thomas; Haney, B.C.; Burns, Terry Wayne; Edmonton; Cameron, James Daniel; V i c t o r i a, B.C.; Chaworth-Musters, Robert David; Cobble Hill, B.C.; Clarke, William George; Beaverlodge, Alta.; Claxton, Edward William; Edmonton; Copeland, Alan John; McCreary, Man.; Corbeil, James William; Port Alberni, B.C.; Coulthard, Gordon Francis; Dauphin, Man.; Craig, Michael Jeremy; Hinton, Alta.; Crucq, David Stewart; Dauphin; Davidson, Daniel Wesley; Vancouver; Dawson, Michael John; Edmonton; Dersch, George; Vancouver; Diakow, Eugene Ivan; Winnipeg; Dirks, William Roy; Penticton, B.C.; Dombrosky, Brian Evan; Edmonton; Dornan, Patrick David; Vernon; Druskin, Allan; Vancouver; Embury, Ralph Martin; Camp Shilo, Man.; Evans, Peter Marines; Edmonton; Evans, Robert George; Edmonton; Evans, William Wentworth; Saskatoon; Fedoruk, Kenneth; Vegreville; Fisher, Frederick Mark; Vancouver; Fontaine, Jack; Winfield, Alta.; Foster, Ronald Stewart; Kerrobert, Sask.; Fraser, Ronald Frederick; Teslin, Yukon Territory.

Gabriel, Thomas William; Vernon; Gibson, Kenneth Richard; Victoria; Graham, David Patrick; Vancouver; Graham, Norman Leigh; Victoria; Gray, Nick James; Winnipeg; Green, Stephen Douglas; Port Alberni; Genest, Randal Calixy; Harris, Sask.; Gruben, William Steven; Moose Jaw, Sask.; Crucq, Allen; Dauphin; Hall, Ronald Hubert Chas.; Kingsgate, B.C.; Hazelton, Ronald Louis; Fort

Langley, B.C.; Hemke Tex Arthur; Silver Heights, Alta.; Holm, Per Zissack; Alberni; Holst, Henry John; Prince George; Howie, James Clark; Calgary; Huffels, Theodorus Franciscus; Vancouver; Hughes, Lorne Gregory; Port Clements, B.C.; Hull, James Lawrence; Duncan, B.C.; Hull, John Raymond; Duncan; Huston, Harold Robert; Dauphin; Jackson, Edward; Fort Garry, Man.; Janas, Danny Dwayne; Calgary; Johner, Michael Winnipeg; Johnson, Dwight Andres; Carrot River, Alta.; Johnson, John Thomas; North Surrey, B.C.; Johnston, Raymond Glen; New Westminster, B.C.; Jones, George Robert; Port Alberni; Jones, Ronald Leslie; Woronick, B..C

Keas, James Gordon; Dauphin; Keast, Ronald; North Vancouver; Keehborn, Larry John; Prince Albert, Sask.; Kendel, Adolph Werner; Kendel, Sask.; Kennedy, Robert Ernest; Moose Jaw; Knoke, Joseph Berner; Prince Albert; Koldingnes, Dwaine; Swift Current; Kolomijchuk, Taras; Calgary; Kuchmak, Orest; Radway, Alta.; Kupresak, Anthony; Winnipeg; Laing, William; Edmonton; Lemley, Russell Neil; Bowness, Alta.; Liddell, William James; North Vancouver; Linklater, William Thomas; St. James, Man.; Linsay, Gary; McCreary, Man.; Lyman, Ross Maurice; Fort St. John, B.C.; MacDonald, Randal Stow; Edmonton; McGovern, Arthur; Winnipeg; McKenna, Ronald Edward; Hardieville, Alta.; McLeod, Raymond James; Pine Falls, Man.; Maber, Glen Robert; Nelson, B.C.; Martin, Colin Henry; Vancouver; Meehan, Michael; Langley; Meier, Leonard Frank; Moose Jaw; Mofford, William John George; Rocky Mountain House, Alta.; Moore, Martin Joseph; Ladner; Murdoch, John Randolph; Kerrobert, Sask.; Mymko, Percey; Dauphin.

Oxtoby, John Chester; Innisfail, Alta.; Parrott, James David; Winnipeg; Payton, John; Winnipeg; Peacock, William John; Kerrobert; Perrault, Barry Ian; Calgary; Porter, Robert Richard; Whitehorse, Y.T.; Porter, Dale Henry; Virden, Man.; Pound, Ronald Edward; Hammond, B.C.; Pound, William Charles; North Vancouver; Pridie, Roger Frank; Hay River, N.W.T.; Proncunier, Rank Patrick; Vancouver; Purdy, Douglas Edward; Calgary; Read, Herbert Willian; Winnipeg; Read, Ronald; Winnipeg; Reil, John Allan; Edson, Alta.; Reiter; Edmonton; Richard, Roger Walter; Winnipeg; Risk, Colin McClean; Bowness, Alta.; Rochon, Dennis Joseph; Winnipeg; Rook, Dennis Warran; Wadena, Sask.; Ross, Andrew John; Victoria.

Sadowey, Ronald Nicholas; Edmonton; Schroder, Ronald William; Evansburg, Alta.;Senfe, James Robert; Calgary; Simpkins, Kenneth Harold; Winnipeg; Sly, Arthur John; Range Tp., RCSA; Smith, Donald Brian; Vancouver; Sterling, Ronald Standish; Prince Albert; Summerville, Alexander Thomas; Cumberland, B.C.; Tait, Danny George; Portage La Prairie; Tamboine, Joseph Edward; Comox, B.C.; Tetarenko, Stuart Frederick; St. Albert, Alta.; Thompkins, Thomas Dale; Calgary;

Thompson, Carl William; New Westminster; Thorburn, Kenneth William; Ladner; Watson, Lloyd Barry, Delburne, Alta.; Weisbrode, Danny George Edward; Regina; Wigmore, Gerry Brent; Regina; Wilson, Roy Thomas; Sedgewick, Alta.; Wheeler, Ronawade William; Beausejour, Man.; White, Frederick; Vancouver; Wood, Gerry; Fruitvale, B.C.; Woodcock, Tony Edward; Revelstoke, B.C.; Wolfe, Gerald Brian; Red Deer; Wosinski, Kenneth; Edmonton; Woytas, Myran; Esterhazy, Sask.; Vallel, David Brian; Moose Jaw; Vermilyea, Michael Bruce; Burnaby; Yates, David; Fallis, Alta.

Bear Chief, Melvin Derrick; Gleichen, Alta.; Bedard, John Louis; Gillies Bay, B.C.; Bennett, William; Hinton, Alta.; Buick, Russell; Winnipeg, Man.; Carr, Stanley Rogers; Innisfail, Alta.; Campbell, Paul Treford; North Vancouver, B.C.; Chalmers, Gary Edmond; Vancouver; Chapman, John Trevor; Sedgewick, Alta.; Christie, Robert Bruce; Calgary, Alta.; Clark, Benjamin Stephen; Lytton, B.C.; Connon, Charles Edmond; Innisfail; Croaker, Wayne Ernest; Cloverdale, B.C.; Devenney, Jack Edward; Cold Lake, Alta.; Dickson, William; Fort St. John, B.C.; Elliott, John Raymond; Saanich, B.C.; Forgues, Paul John; Edmonton, Alta.; France, Kenneth Gordon; Victoria, B.C.; Gorrian, James Llewelyn; Falkland, B.C.; Habington, William Steven; St. James, Man.; Hickey, Joseph Eugene; Edmonton; Hill, Terry Cecil; Camp Shilo, Man.; Holmes, Edward James; Ladner, B.C.; Howard, David Lorne; Falkland; Hadley, Ronald Thomas; Evansburg, Alta.; Humnisky, Brian Allen; Winnipeg; Inkster, David George; Battleford, Sask.; Keast, Brian Richard; North Vancouver; Kirley, Patrick; Edmonton; Kristeensen, George; Vancouver; Larson, Bryan; Fosston, Sask.; Larose, Lyle Daniel; North Battleford; Lehay, Richard Wm. Edward; Warburg, Alta.; Leicht, Terrence Lynn; Innisfail; Luchie, Barry Alvin; Turner Valley, Alta.; Luchia, Kenneth John; Turner Valley.

McDonald, Gary Gray; Beaver Lodge, Alta.; McGonigal, Raymond Verne; Turner Valley; McGonigle, Ronald Wesley; Turner Valley; McIntosh, Ronald; Edson, Alta.; McKenzie, Richard Arthur; Calgary; McKnight, Lloyd Ernest; Fort St. John, B.C.; MacLeod, William Alexander; Pine Falls, Man.; Mantel, Olaf; Edmonton; Matheson, James Bruce; Portage La Prairie, Mark, Kenneth Wilburn; Winnipeg; Matlock, Harry Wesley; Calmar, Alta.; Mercredi, Darcy; Hay River, N.W.T.; Melhus, Allan Frederick; Port Alberni; Mills, Robert James; Winnipeg; Murray, Richard; Flin Flon, Man.; Paquette, Daniel; Hay River; Query, Vaughan; Edmonton; Robb, John William; Penticton, B.C.; Robins, Charles; Baldonnel, B.C.; Riduidel, Larry Glen; Winnipeg; Sauve, Dennis; Calmar; Sayers, Frederick Blanchard; North Battleford; Schmidt, Dalo; Warburg, Alta.; Smith, Bruce Foster; Edmonton; Smythe, Ernest Charles; Comox, B.C.; Soganic, Richard James; Cumberland, B.C.; Southerland, Terry Wayne; Calgary; Stallknecht, Gary Wilfred; Thorsby, Alta.; Stupar, Dennis Warren; Edson, Alta.; Tiernan, Neil Edward; Salmon Arm, B.C.; Trefiak, Dennis William; Hay River; Turnell, Gordon Harry; Vancouver; Walker, Thomas William; Brandon, Man.; Webb, Robert Russell; Spirit River, Alta.; Webber, Marke David; Fort St. John; Westburry, R. A.; Brandon; Wilkinson, Robert Lorn; New Westminster; Williams, Peter; Vancouver; Wolfe, Ronald; Grande Prairie, Alta.; Yearley, William Francis; Vancouver.

Baldwin, Laurie Kenneth; Lacombe, Alta.; Barry, David Wilfred; Edmonton, Alta.; Bazin, Douglas Philip; Edmonton; Bergeron, Ernest; Burnaby, B.C.; Bird, John Sterling; Vancouver, B.C.; Borrow, Leonard A.; Fruitvale, B.C.; Brown, Robert Kenneth; Vancouver; Brown, Stanley; Moose Jaw, Sask.; Butlin, Barry Keith; Lethbridge, Alta.; Cardinal, Joseph; Morinville, Alta.; Carritt, Lawrence Milton; Red Deer, Alta.; Case, Thomas; Portage La Prairie, Man.; Cherbo, Robin Peter; Sirdar, B.C.; Degenstien, Kenneth Wayne; Calgary; DeGroot, Henri; Edmonton; Delore, James John Richard; Winnipeg; Dionne, George; Edmonton; Druce, Gary Frederick; Victoria, B.C.; Edmandson, William Robert; Camp Shilo, Man.; Eggen, Karl Eggen; Gillies Bay, B.C.; Elliott, John Raymond; Evans, Glenn Haydn; Vancouver; Fisher, David; Prince Rupert, B.C.; Flug, Norman Leslie; Fougere; Edmonton; Garnett, George William; Vermillion, Alta.; Gentles, Robert John; Calgary; Gilchrist, Kenneth James; Wadena, Sask.; Gratton, Robert James; Black Diamond, Alta.; Greenslade, Jerry Edmund; Vancouver; Greenslade, Terry Lawton; Vancouver; Hadley, Ronald Thomas; Evansburg, Alta.; Holmes, Tedder; Ladner, B.C.; Hopkins, Gregory; Cranbrook, B.C.; Inskip, Bruce Frederick; Falkland, B.C.; Johnson, Wayne Jeffery; Winfield, Alta.; Johnston, Grant; Vancouver; Johnston, Terrance; Penticton, B.C.; Junck, Montgomery; Morinville, Alta.; Kane, Patrick Edward; Humboldt, Sask.; Kawa, Peter John; Winnipeg; Kinloch, Peter; Vernon, B.C.; Kitto, Bruce; Kelowna, B.C.; Knipple, James Bruce; Rosthern, Sask.; Krowchenko, David Louis; Wainwright, Alta.

Lacheur, James; Vancouver; Lopata, Vincent John; Winnipeg; McArthur, David Harmon; Calgary; McQueen, Glen Heber; Winnipeg; Mark, James Rae; Winnipeg; Marocchi, Norman; Port Alberni, B.C.; Mooney, Douglas; Portage La Prairie; Mowat, Alexander Robert; Winnipeg; Nicholson, Mervin; Moose Jaw; Oets, Martin; Nelson, B.C.; Oige, Gary Alan; Winnipeg; Oklek, Daniel Dennis; Edmonton; Oklek, Ronald Frank; Edmonton; Perih, Norman Sevan; Dauphin, Man.; Pocock; Jack; Haney, B.C.; Reeves, Robert Charles; Edmonton; Richards, Douglas Stewart; Rusthern, Sask.; Rutherford, John Allen; Victoria.

Shuter, Gilbert Evens; Merritt, B.C.; Sicheuerman, Melvin Douglas;

524

Turner Valley, Alta.; Smith, James Darrell; Pine Falls, Man.; Stemarie, Danniel; Blubber Bay, B.C.; Stevens, Douglas Allen; Stewart, Gordon; St. James, Man.; Stinchcombe, Roger John; Vancouver; Suddards, Brian Robert; Edmonton; Turnell, Gordon Harrold; Vancouver; Vincent, James Alfred; Calgary; Varos, Michael Donald; Marcelin, Sask.; Walker, Arthur E.; Balcarres, Sask.; Weaver, Ronald Simon; Nelson; Wesley, Edwin Dave; Winnipeg; Whitford, Robert Harrold; Fort MacLeod, Alta.; Whittington, Bruce Richard; Kelwood, Man.; Wilson, Dennis Francis; Lumby, B.C.; Yearley, William Francis; Vancouver; Yuzicapi, William Brice; Lorlie, Sask.; Zebinski, Neil Graham; Winnipeg; Ferguson, Kenneth Henry; Spirit River, Alta.; Batula, Gerald Mitchell; Rose Valley, Sask.

CADET BAND

Arden, Studee; Victoria, B.C.; Burry, David Garfield; Vancouver, B.C.; Carpenter, David James; Victoria; Clark, Ronald Denis; Fort St. John, B.C.; Clarke, Gary Ashworth; Victoria; Cliff, Stephen Brady; Victoria; Colling, Eric Gary; Port Alberni, B.C.; Cyr, Peter Anthony; New Westminster, B.C.; Diehl, Milton David; Medicine Hat, Alta.; Boland, Bruce Sinclair; Victoria; Bucci, Brian Frederick; Edmonton, Alta.; Burden, Richard; Edmonton; Egan, Derick Charles; Calgary, Alta.; Fawcett, Patrick Ray; Vernon, B.C.; Flett, James; Riviere Qui Bar, Alta.; Funk, Michael Jacob; Lumby, B.C.; Gandy, Lionel Douglas; Victoria; Guest, Randell Michael; Victoria; Gray, Robert James; Port Alberni; Hansen, Alan Robert; North Surrey, B.C.; Heidema, James Malcolm; New Westminster; Hoose, David Roy; Redcliff, Alta.; Hunt, Peter; North Surrey.

Knight, Mervin Arthur; Victoria; MacDonald, Joseph; Edmonton; McTaggart, William Ralph; Victoria; Milard, Morris; North Vancouver; Ockey, Gerald Leroy; Fort St. John; Olson, Jeffery; North Vancouver; Peters, Edward; New Westminster; Plante, Frank; Hay River, N.W.T.; Pontis, Barry; Trail, B.C.; Rabbitt, David John; South Burnaby, B.C.; Renney, Victor Frederick; Vancouver; Royce, Brian George; Edmonton; Shinn, James William; Calgary; Stewart, David Warren; Dorval, Que.; Sutherland, Glen Gary; Calgary; Thompson, Brian Langtree; North Vancouver; Tottenham, Denis Gordon; Vancouver; Turner, William Roy; Coquitlam, B.C.; Van Aggelen, William Edward; Victoria; Vandervlugt, Edward; Edmonton; Van Riksoort, Robert; North Vancouver; Wade, Garrey Loran; Port Alberni; Wallgren, John Raymond; Fruitvale, B.C.; Whitehead, Paul Robert; Victoria; Wong, Hugh; Richmond, B.C.

VACC - 1965

'B' COMPANY

Allan, B. W., Victoria; Allan, G. R., Saanichton; Anderson, R., Lethbridge; Arcand, A. J., Langley; Argall, D., Victoria; Argue, J. E., Camp Shilo; Ashby, L., Prince Albert; Atherton, D. V., Fernie; Aucoin, J., Vancouver; Aymont, W. D., Winnipeg; Bailey, D., Esquimalt; Bak, J., Beausejour, Man.; Barrell, K., Calgary; Bauer, R., Saskatoon; Bawden, A. N., Victoria; Bell, D. W., Cumberland; Bell, D., Winnipeg; Bemister, G. G., Victoria; Benthien, S. J.; Calgary; Bergin, R., Victoria; Berglund, G. A., Carrot River, Sask.; Berschley, B., Winnipeg; Best, G., Saskatoon; Bethel, R. C., Calgary; Bigelow, G., Gleichen, Alta.; Bird, B. E., Vancouver; Blazosek, P., Forest Lawn, Alta.; Bloomfield, H., Fort Garry, Man.; Bocquet, F., Cumberland; Bolger, D., Saskatoon; Bowes, P., Winnipeg; Bowles, G. J. J., Victoria; Bragg, W. H., Lousana, Alta.; Braybrook, R. A., Churchill; Breault, N., Esquimalt; Brittain, J. C., North Surrey; Brown, J., Calgary; Brulotte, R. K., Fernie; Burden, J. D., Medicine Hat; Burkholder, R. O., Victoria; Burnett, P. R., Calgary; Cabelguen, C. M., Fernie; Cameron, D. K., Saskatoon; Campbell, R., Calgary; Carlson, R. A., Sturgis, Sask.; Chayko, D. S., Vancouver; Chomiak, D. A., Lethbridge; Clack, C., Victoria; Clayton, S. T., Victoria; Clermont, E. G., Victoria; Clermont, E. J., Lousana, Alta.; Coates, G. R., Nakusp; Colesnik, D., Kindersley, Sask.; Cook, D. W., Calgary; Courchene, K., Pine Falls, Man.; Cunliffe, R. F., Fernie; Daradich, H. R., Wadena, Sask.; Davidson, R. A., North Vancouver; Davies, R. D., HQ Coy; Dawson, K. J., Winnipeg; Deck, J. A.; Cranbrook; Delguercio, P., Gleichen; Desjarlais, R. W., Calgary; Deroche, G. T., Cranbrook; Dickson, J. G., Redcliffe, Alta.; Dmetrichuk, G., Gleichen; Donahue, D. K., Beausejour; Downing, G. A., Squamish; Driedger, J., Saskatoon; Dufour, D. F., Weyburn, Sask.

Edwards, A. F., Creston; Edwards, L. J., Enderby; Elliott, W., Victoria; Embury, R. C., Lethbridge; Engler, W. G., Medicine Hat; Epp, J. A., Carrot River; Feldman, N. A., Calgary; Fenske, R. D., Battleford; Finlay, G. D., Comox; Fitzgerald, B. W., Victoria; Forsyth, J. R., Vancouver; Gabriel, P. J., Penticton; Gail, S. J., Hillcrest, Alta.; Gallagher, M. P., Calgary; Gardippie, D. F., Saskatoon; Gertzen, D. E., Medicine Hat; Gerun, R., Cranbrook; Gervais, P. J., Battleford; Giacomuzzi, R. K., Blairmore, Alta.; Gillespie, W. E., Beausejour; Gillette, G. C., Victoria; Girourard, D. W., Winnipeg; Giroux, D. M., Weyburn; Golby, R. F., North Surrey; Grange, K. R., Fernie; Griffin, L. R., Squamish; Griffith, P., Victoria; Hall, N. H., St. Vital, Man.; Hanrahan, M. T., Coleman, Alta.; Harder, G. E., Eston, Sask.; Hauck, D. W., Calgary; Hayes, R. R., Victoria; Heinrichs, M. P., Beausejour; Hendricks, R. H., Calgary; Henn, H. J., Saskatoon; Herasemluk, H. H., Lethbridge, Herrod, I. W., Saskatoon; Hill, R. H., Winnipeg; Hinder,

525

R. N., Vancouver; Hinzman, G. E., Medicine Hat; Holberton, G. L., Lethbridge; Holland, G. R., Victoria; Holowinski, G. R., Beausejour; Houle, R., Marius, Man.; Houston, J. G., Victoria; Hovdebo, R. G., Prince Albert; Hruden, J. H., Winnipeg; Jack, D. H., Calgary; Jackman, J. R., Calgary; Jackson, D. V., Calgary; Johnson, R. S., Victoria; Jones, D. M., Calgary; Jones, E. R., Nakusp; Jefferson, H. O., Vancouver; Keating, G. W., Saskatoon; Kennedy, M. J., North Vancouver; Kerr, N. L. Lousana; Kiselczuk, D. S., Blairmore; Klaus, H. B., Esterhazy, Sask.; Kniert, R. F., Fernie; Kowatch, K. K., Calgary; Kunz, A. D., Kindersley. Lachuk, R. W., North Surrey; Lamb, T. E., Victoria; Lamb, W. J., Banff; Larsen, D. W., Beausejour; Leathwood, E. C., South Slocan, B.C.; Lee, B. D., Lousana; Leischner, L. T., Calgary; Lester, L. E., Saskatoon; Leversuch, C. R., Calgary; Logan, K., North Vancouver; Long, S. W., Victoria; Lowrie, M. A., Lethbridge; Lyons, N. N., Okotoks, Alta.; McConnell, D. A., Lethbridge; McDonald, P. C., Winnipeg; McDonough, R. W., Victoria; McGerrigle, R. D., Stenen, Sask.; McGowan, V. N., St. Walburg, Sask.; McKay, R. B., Fernie; MacLean, G. A., St. Paul, Minn., U.S.A.; McLean, T., Cumberland; MacLeod, R. A., Victoria; McPherson, R. R., Calgary; Mackie, R. W., Saskatoon; Marshall, R. C., Fort Churchill; Materi, G. L., Kindersley; Maxson, C. R., Kelowna; Maxwell, H., North Vancouver; Meissner, G. M., Prince Albert; Menow, J. H., Norway House, Man.; Middlebrook, P. J., Slaterville, B.C.; Mills, H. G., North Vancouver; Mimnagh, G., Victoria; Mitchelmore, K. L., Carrot River; Moate, L. G., North Battleford; Molnar, J. F., Nakusp; Moore, M. S., Kelowna; Moore, S. A., Weyburn; Moore, S. A., Victoria; Moran, D. A., Victoria; Murray, B. A., Weyburn; Murray. D. A., Gleichen; Murray, J. I., Victoria; Nelson, C., Letellier, Man.; Nemeth, S. D., Weyburn; Nesbitt, O. W., Whiterock; Nielson, C. F., Calgary; Noble, G. J., Victoria; Norquay, A. G., Winnipeg; Norris, J. F., East Kildonan, Man.; Ohlhauser, W., Medicine Hat; Olson, B. D., Creston; Olson, G. H., Medicine Hat; Orton, E. G., Winnipeg; Osgood, D. G., Medicine Hat; Ottman, Y. A., Wadena; Palmer, L. G., Roseberry, B.C.; Panchyshyn, D. L., Carrot River; Pastula, D. S., Beausejour; Patrick, R., Creston; Paynter, J. P., Norway House; Peachey, R., North Vancouver; Peterson, L. R., Creston; Peyton, A. E., Victoria; Piepgrass, L. D., Canyon, B.C.; Pitman, G., Winnipeg; Pleasants, L. J., North Surrey; Plonka, A. S., Fernie; Podesta, G. R., RTU; Porth, L. W., Victoria Beach, Man.; Post, G. W., Winnipeg; Price, M. P., Weyburn; Price, C. R., Lethbridge; Prud'homme, T. E., Lousana; Pugh, A. D., Rose Valley, Sask; Qually, B. J., Lethbridge. Ras, A. B., Transcona, Winnipeg; Ras, R., Transcona; Restall, C. R., Victoria; Ribecco, V., Calgary; Richman, M. G., Victoria; Robertson. C., Lethbridge; Rogers, B. M., North Surrey; Ross, W. A., Stenen; Rossetti, L. H., Calgary; Rossetti, R. R., Lethbridge; Runions, A. W., Fernie; Rydzycowski, J. J., Winnipeg; St. Pierre, R., Calgary; Sailer, B. A.,

Medicine Hat; Salter, M. W., Courtney; Sam, R. L., Brewster, Wash., U.S.A.; Schenck, S. G., Victoria; Schultz, G. C., Victoria; Seefried, D. R., Calgary; Shields, G. R., Vancouver; Shepard, D. G., Saskatoon; Shewchun, D. W., Notre Dame, Man.; Shorten, W. J., Calgary; Shule, R. D., Saskatoon; Shuster, M. J., Beausejour; Simes, T. A., Stenen; Sinclair, E. R., Nakusp; Smith E. C., Redcliffe; Smith, J. C., Cumberland; Smythe, C. P., Calgary; Smyth, G. B., Calgary; Soganic, M. K., Cumberland; Sopher, S. J., Calgary; Stelck, R. A., Victoria; Staeaczak, P. L., Fosston, Sask.; Steeves, V. D., Calgary; Stevens, D. C., Winnipeg; Swatsky, E. W., Churchill; Tanner, S. W., Cranbrook; Taylor, K. B., Victoria; Taylor, R. M., Prince Albert; Thody, R. A., Victoria; Thomas, B. J., Winnipeg; Thomas, G. P., Battleford; Thornley, T. A., Victoria; Toth, J. F., Lethbridge; Tuck, G. K., Broadview, Alta.; Tweten, R. J., Regina; Van Clieaf, R. F., Medicine Hat; Wallace, L. G., Calgary; Walters, W. J., Winnipeg; Wasylien, N., Coleman, Alta.; Waters, J. A., Duncan; Weir, L. W., Kindersley; Weir, W. J., Kindersley; Westley, C. F., Coleman; Wheeldon, D. F., Vancouver; Wilcox, R. G., Haney; Wilkie, E. G., Battleford; Willis, G. K., Redcliffe; Williams, E. G., Victoria; Wizowich, D. A., Cranbrook; Wood, J. E., Falkland Beach, Man.; Wood, J. L., St. Theresa Point, Man.; Woodley, J. W., Duncan.

'A' COMPANY — B.C. AREA

Abramson, E. J., Revelstoke; Anderson, D. B., Nelson; Anderson, M. C., Kamloops; Basile, E. G., Kamloops; Bordeleau, T. P., Port Alberni; Bower, D. H., Vancouver; Carlson, D. R., Surrey; Clifford, S. M., Nelson; Collins, R. W., Vancouver; Corrier, R. J. Powell River; Cote, P. L., Nelson; Crowther, S. J., Texada Island. B.C.; Dean, R. A., Westsyde; Dubois, L. C., Nanton, Alta.; Duguay, L. W., Qualicum Beach; Elliot, R. C., Penticton; Finlayson, W. A., North Vancouver; Fletcher, J. G., Vancouver; Gabriel, J. C., Vancouver; Gabriel, J. P., Vancouver; Gombos, W., Vancouver; Hawthorne, G. G., New Westminster; Hay, D. L., Revelstoke; Hodgess, D. S., Qualicum Beach; Hohn, P. F., Keleden; Hossack, J. E., Vancouver; Johnson, W. G., Alberni; Johnston, J. B., Vancouver; Jones, D. L., Ladner; Jones, K. A., Vancouver; Joseph, S. C., Alberni; Kenball, J. W., Nelson; Koch, R., Nelson; LoPatriello, N. J., Vancouver. McArthur, M. G., Penticton; MacDonald, G. S., Vancouver; McGregor, S. A., Nelson; McLean, D. M., Vernon; Massicotte, R. L., Prince George; Maxwell, D. W., Burnaby; Mikolajow, A. R., Powell River; New, S. R., Penticton; Nunn, J. A., Campbell River; Panas, D., Prince George; Parker, C. A., Richmond; Parsons, M. A., Texada Island; Pattenaude, L. R., New Westminster; Pearse, L. M., Kamloops; Peel, G. E., Vancouver; Perdue. D. W., Ladner; Phillips, R. L., N. Surrey; Pollitt, K. J., Penticton; Power. B. M., Port Alberni; Premack, D. P., North Surrey; Price, R. T., Port Alberni; Putnam, K. W., Burnaby; Quick, T. G., Richmond; Rathbun.

E. C., Penticton; Rogers, G. B., Ladner; Roth, R., Silverton; Sandre, F., Nelson; Sather, A. O., Penticton; Schindelka, R. R., North Surrey; Shaw, R. J., Vancouver; Short, J. R., Texada Island, Small, W., Prince George; Smiley, J. O., Salmon Arm; Smith, D. G., Kamloops; Smith, G. G., Vancouver; Smith, S. J., Vancouver; Sproul, J. W., Golden; Stabler, J. C., S. Burnaby; Stocks, J. M., Penticton; Taylor, J. P., Port Alberni; Valentine, R. L., Powell River; Vass, J. D., Penticton; Wallin, R. C., Vancouver; Watson, T., Port Moody; Williamson, E. E., Kamloops; Williamson, R. W., Vancouver; Wilson, E. P., Vancouver; Woodrow, J., Vancouver.

ALBERTA AREA

Bablitz, C. W., Edmonton; Bachinsky, L., Sherwood Park; Bailey, D. H., Sedgewick; Barnes, D., Edmonton; Batter, B., Beaverlodge; Beaulieu, H. M., Fort Smith, N.W.T.; Bellerose, E. L., Edmonton; Beavans, R. A., Edmonton; Bline, A. D., Warburg; Bocker, K., Edmonton; Brilia, D., Morinville; Briscoe, K., Edmonton; Brodersen, E. F., Winfield; Buckley, P., Edmonton; Burns, D. J., Stoney Plain; Buysen, W., Sherwood Park; Carstairs, B., Warburg; Carstairs, R., Warburg; Chalifoux, D., Edmonton; Chartrand, D., Edmonton; Clifford, R., Beaverlodge; Connolly, E. T., Thorsby; Corsbie, J. P., Edmonton; Coyle, B., Lethbridge; Crichton, B., Winterburn; Diggins, L. E., Edmonton; Dixon, B. C., Vermilion; Dmetruk, J. A., Edmonton; Dmetruk, M., Edmonton; Durant, A. J., Alder Flats; Durocher, L. H., Edmonton; Epler, A. L., Edmonton; Epp, D. H., Fort St. John, B.C.; Evans, L. J., Edmonton; Faulds, R. G., Edmonton; Febian, F., Hay River, N.W.T.; Ford, R. G., Edmonton; Forsyth, R. C., Morinville; Fortyn, P. A., Edmonton; Fobb, H. J., Sherwood Park; Gagne, D. M., Edmonton; Gilbey, D. J., Edmonton; Girard, J. P., Edmonton; Greenlay, D. W., Edmonton; Gullion, D., Edmonton; Gylander, G. A., Entwistle; Hall, G. F., Edmonton; Halushka, S. W., Breton; Harrison, T., Edmonton; Haukins, P. J., Sherwood Park; Hewins, G. E., Fort St. John, B.C.; Hutchison, R. P., Stoney Plain; Ingledew, R. E., Beaverlodge; Inman, D. E., Vermilion; Inman, D. L., Vermilion; Jardine, C. L., Evansburg.

Jensen, S. P., Breton; Johnson, K. D., Edson; Krauskopf, P. R., Morinville; Kuehn, G. H., Vermilion; Kuzyk, G. A., Thorsby; McDonald, C. R., Morinville; McGeough, J. P., Sherwood Park; McNaughton, D. C., Winfield; Manners, T. G., Fort Smith, N.W.T.; Matulic, J., Calgary; Muller, H. B., Edmonton; Murray, R. J., Edmonton; Nasedkin, D. W., Beaverlodge; Ness, D. J., Sherwood Park; Oliver, B. W., Edmonton; Oliver, G. R., Entwistle; Olsenberg, D. G., Beaverlodge; Olstead, J. E., Edmonton; Parton, G. L., Edmonton; Pye, R. G., Alder Flats; Reid, S. W., Edmonton; Rivet, L. J., Fort St. John, B.C.; Robertson, B. S., Sedgewick; Robertson, D., Fort St. John, B.C.; Rondeau, F. K., Morinville; Sauerborn, U., Mayerthorpe; Sauve, G. W., Thorsby; Searle, W. J., Edmonton; Signort, D. J., Calgary; Siwiski, D. M., Seza Beach; Smith, R. S., Sedgewick; St. Germaine, G. J.,

Edmonton; Swancoat, E. G., Sedgewick; Terpstar, K., Beach Corner P.O.; Velt, R. C., Sherwood Park; Volk, J. E., Sherwood Park; Walker, F. R., Beaverlodge; Webber, J. D., Sherwood Park; Westcott, G. C., Edmonton; Westlund, D. J., Thorsby; Whitaker, K. J., Edmonton; Wiley, D. G., Morinville; Williams, A. M., Edmonton; Wong, F., Beaverlodge; Zajancauakas, N. J., Lethbridge; Zoe, I., Fort Smith, N.W.T.

SASKATCHEWAN AREA

Albert, J. Gallivan; Allefeld, G. K., Brighsand; Balzer, R. J., Saskatoon; Bear, R., Gallivan; Bessette, G. A., Moose Jaw; Boychuk, W. S., Yorkton; Carnegie, E. C., Harris; Cherneske, G., Invermay; Christensen, J., Saskatoon; Clarke, D. B., Moose Jaw; Doan, K. A., Mervin; Frerichs, W. G., Rosetown; Genest, G. R., Harris; Graham, D. N., Saskatoon; Gryba, C. M., Invermay; Hawkes, J. F., Moose Jaw; Herde, B. D., Melville; Huzina, W. J., Melville; Johnson, L. R., Moose Jaw; Kilgour, S. W., Buchanan; Knight, J. C., Invermay; Kutcher, M. W., Moose Jaw; Labelle, R. R., Yorkton; Lepp, D. J., Harris; McMechan, D. L., Rosetown; McWillie, B. C., Saskatoon; Maczek, L. A., Melville; Mault, G. P., Saskatoon; Mealing, L. K., Moose Jaw; Nagy, T. E., Yorkton; Oryschak, W. J., Melville; Puhl, L. W., Saskatoon; Reed, R. E., St. Walburg; Reinson, W. D., Melville; Riehl, R. A., Creighton; Roberts, J. P., Moose Jaw; Robson, G. C., Invermay; Robson J. R., Moose Jaw; Stasiuk, M. I., Edmonton, Alta.; Sully, F. A., Vancouver, B.C.; Turchak, B. M., Melville; Van Buskirk, W. B., Moose Jaw; Whitby, N. D., Yorkton; Whitford, W. J., North Bellford; Wozniak, R. F., Melville; Zinkhan, R. S., Rosetown.

MANITOBA AREA

Akerley, D., Camp Shilo; Anderson, W. J., Portage La Prairie; Andrew, D., Calwood; Barker, B. O., Portage La Prairie; Berthelette, R., Pine Falls; Booth, M. W. A., Camp Shilo; Brauner, F. B., Flin Flon; Brown, K., Pine Falls; Brown, R., Pine Falls; Carefoot, L., Virden; Cunningham, W., Winnipeg; Danwich, K. A., Tranverse Bay; Dixon, D. G., Camp Shilo; Edmonson, J. T., Camp Shilo; Giles, G. T., McCreary; Greentree, D. G., McCreary; Halliday, J. W., Flin Flon; Halpin, R. R., Pine Falls; Hancock, W. E., Portage La Prairie; Hansen, R. D. E., Camp Shilo; Hogarth, L. W., Flin Flon; Jones, G. R., Winnipeg; Keats, R. F., Dauphin; Korpan, A. J., Dauphin; Lelonde, B. J., Brandon; Macdonald, F. L., Virden; Mark, B. J., Flin Flon; Martel, L. E., Flin Flon; Melcosky, I. E., Brandon; Mitschke, D. G., Creighton, Sask.; Patterson, C. R., Pine Falls; Peltz, D. A., Neepawa; Penny, M. G., Virden; Posmituck, D. M., McCreary; Sherrick, W. D., Shilo; Walker, A. G., Brandon; Walter, K. C., Brandon; Watson, W. R., Portage; Whiteford, R. W., Virden; Wright, L. S., Scarths; Zahayko, L. P., Creighton; Zollen, D. F., Flin Flon.

'C' COMPANY

Adamson, N., Whitehorse; Ainsley, R. J., Calgary; Airhart, H. D., Edmonton; Allary, E., Brighsand, Sask.; Aschim, N. R., Humbolt; Auvigne, G. D., Calgary; Bakaluk,

G. S., Winnipeg; Baker, L. D., Elko, B.C.; Barley, W. D., Winnipeg; Bergstrom, A. B., Fruitvale. B.C.; Beringer, N., Lacombe; Bernard, S. C., Surrey; Bigler, G. A.; Rose Valley, Sask.; Blackstone, R. W., Prince Rupert; Bodnarchuk, T., Winnipeg; Bonner, H. J., New Westminster; Bose, C., Merritt; Bowen, R., Red Deer; Brooks, A. G., Rosthern, Sask.; Brown, D. H., Regina; Bruce, M. B., New Westminster; Buckley, R. R., Edmonton; Burke, R., Victoria; Cadotte, R. L. R., Winnipeg; Carby, C., Calgary; Carruthers, J. T., Edmonton; Caslake, V., Regina; Cerniuk, R., Kelvington, Sask.; Chaboyer, W. F., Stonewall, Man.; Chaster, G., Merritt; Christie, R. W. F., Vedder Crossing, B.C.; Closter, G. H., Vancouver; Cockram, J. B., New Westminster; Comack, D. H., Winnipeg; Cooke, R. V., Edmonton; Cooper, R. H., St. Vital, Man.; Coroy, M., Marcelin, Sask.; Cosgrove, R., Ft. Macleod; Coxall, B. A., St. Vital; Crabtree, E. C., Calgary; Crate, D. W., Winterburn, Alta.; Crawford, B. W., Edmonton; Cronin, M., Texada Island, B.C.; Cunningham, D. W., Sherwood Park, Alta.; Cutts, R. J., Fernie; Darkes, J. H., Inuvik, N.W.T.; Davidson, A. E., Lacombe; Davis, J. J., Camp Chilliwack; Davis, R. A., Edmonton; Delorme, D. J., Stonewall; Denney, C. D., Winnipeg; Desjarlais, J. J., Lestock, Sask.; Dewing, T. A., Kinistinow, Sask.; Dibben, A. E., Vermilion; Dickson, D. J., Winnipeg; Dobson, D. A. T., Melfort, Sask.; Douglas, M. J., Winnipeg; Douglas, R. J., Langley; Draginda, J. T., Squamish; Dummerauf, H. J., Vermilion; Duvall, D. H., Hay River, N.W.T.; Dyer, L. E., South Burnaby; Dyck, R. L., Hinton; Dzikowiki, W., Merritt.

Fast, P. W., Merritt; Ferguson, N. L., Spirit River, B.C.; Fitch, R. L., Merritt; Fletcher, A. E., Picture Butte; Folk, V., Regina; Folkerson, A. J., Rosthern; Forsgren, G. M., Merritt; Gaschnitz, G. J., Merritt; George, C. M., Tantallon, Sask.; Gibbon, B. W., Innisfail; Gillard, G. E., Enderby; Girolami, G. H., Calgary; Glover, C. A., Abbotsford; Godwin, I. G., Tantallon; Goodman, D. S., Swift Current; Goresky, P. N., Stonewall; Greenway, W. M., Swift Current; Grier, G .W., Vancouver; Griffin, W. C., Winnipeg; Guise, W. J., Hythe, Alta.; Hald, F., Blairmore, Man.; Hamilton, W., Hay River; Hanson, P. R., Namaka, Alta.; Harrison, K. D., Edmonton; Hartung, R. E., Stonewall; Hatch, R. L., Inuvik; Hawick, B. J., Penhold; Henderson, J. C., Vegreville; Hendy, D. B., Abbotsford; Heppell, C. Y., Vedder Crossing; Hewitt, B. W., Edmonton; Hickling, G. A., Melville; Hill, W. J., Winnipeg; Hills, I. G., Red Deer; Hiltgen, M. F., Vancouver; Hinds, M. J., Winnipeg; Hodgson, C. E., Winnipeg; Hodgson, D. J., Edmonton; Hosack, G. E., Edmonton; Huestis, G. L., Ft. Macleod; Hunchak, C. J., Blaine Lake, Sask.; Hussey, C. M., Winnipeg; Irwin, R. G., Calgary; Inskip, G. H., Falkland; Jackson, T. W., Mount Currie, B.C.; Jaeb, G. A., Humboldt; Janman, W. B., Winnipeg; Janzen, R. D., Strathmore; Jeffery, R. K., Vermilion; Jodoin, P. E., Calgary; John, R., Shalath, B.C.; Johnson, K. G., River Camp, Man.; Jones, R. P., Calgary; Jung, N., Prince Rupert; Kakow-

chyk, R. W., Winnipeg; Keller, D. M., St. Charles, Man.; Kenney, N. L., Winnipeg; Kerslake, C. P., Innisfail; Kidd, M. W., Edmonton; Kidd, T. V., Edmonton; Kilby, A. R. A., Vancouver; Klemn, J. R., Calgary; Komarnicki, W. S .J., Sylvan Lake, Alta.; Korenowski, E. M., Edmonton; Krahenbil, G. A., Regina.

Lacheur, S. A., South Burnaby; Lagimodiere, A. M., Marcelin, Sask.; Lameman, E., Onion Lake, Sask.; Leask, D. G., Prince Albert; Leclair, W. V., Camp Chilliwack; Lee, B. R., Armstrong; Leniuk, D. S., Rose Valley; Lerat, L. H., Bradford, Sask.; Lesiuk, R., Winnipeg; Littlechild, A. M., Hobbema, Alta.; Lloyd, A. W., Winnipeg; Louie, M. C., Mount Currie Reservation, B.C.; Luck, B. P., Calgary; Lumsden, G. L., Edmonton; Lutz, J., Watson Lake, N.W.T.; Lynch, W. M., Regina; Kane, G. A., Winnipeg; McArthur, J. W., Arcola, Sask.; MacDonald, D. A., Winnipeg; McDonald, G. D., Esterhazy, Sask.; MacDonald, N. L., Edmonton; McFee, S. E., Stonewall, Man.; McGillveray, D. F., Vancouver; McGowan, E. B., Winnipeg; MacGregor, C. D., Edmonton; McKay, P. H., Matsqui; MacKenzie, D. B., Armstrong, B.C.; McKenzie, W. D., Winnipeg; MacLeod, B. K., St. James, Man.; McPhee, S. R., Fruitvale; Maher, M. F., Rossland; Maitland, D. F., Prince Rupert; Makarow, A. T., Rose Valley; Marcinew, B. D., Vermilion; Marx, B .E., Sherwood Park; Matiets, L. P., Vancouver; Maynard, K. H., Humbolt; Melia, R. A., Winnipeg; Mernickle, H. G., Rosedale, B.C.; Merrison, R. W., Regina; Mitchell, R., Lilloet; Moreau, R. E., Marcelin; Morrison, S. A., Winnipeg; Muirhead. B. N., Rosedale; Musqua, A. J., Kamsack; Narcisse, R. W., Lilloet; Nelson, D. A., Inuvik; Ness, W. M., Edmonton; Nobiss, L. T., Winnipeg; Nolin, D. B., Winnipeg; Novak, L. A., Hay River; Oakford, D. E., Hythe, Alta.; Ogloza, J. J., Winnipeg; Ovayuak, P., Inuvik Stringerball, Alta.; Palmer, L. G., Chilliwack; Pasch, B. D., Victoria; Peters, R. J., Swift Current; Peterson, A. N., Innisfail; Petiot, G. S., Fort McLeod, B.C.; Phillippe, R. V., Vancouver; Phillips, R. L., Edmonton; Pirrie, B. J., Winnipeg; Pitts, R. J., Vedder Crossing; Poitras, D. P., Coquitlam; Polachek. K. W. F., Kalvington; Power, T. L., Prince Albert; Pramza, J. J., Yarbo, Sask.; Quock, G. D., Whitehorse; Rainbow, B. C., Picture Butte; Reese, D. F., Winnipeg; Reghelini, B. A., Vermilion; Rickey, R. W., Winnipeg; Roberts, G., Winnipeg; Roe, A. P., Edmonton; Roe, L. D., Edmonton; Romaniuk, R. L., New Westminster; Roth, B. F., Vermilion; Rowland, D. F., Vedder Crossing; Roy, M. D., Vancouver; Rust, K. A., South Burnaby.

Sali, P. S., Regina; Sargent, B.C., South Burnaby; Schwab, R. A., Prince Rupert; Scott, E. D., Broderheim, Alta.; Scullion, L. J., Camp Chilliwack; Shotbolt, G. A., Winnipeg; Simonse, K., Edmonton; Skidmore, R. D., Innisfail; Smith, R. G., Innisfail; Smyth, C. F., Vancouver; Stewart, L. W., Falkland; Stoner, R. G., Spirit River, Alta.; Sundstrom, R. G., Fruitvale; Sutherland, R. M., Winnipeg; Sweet, G. F., Edmonton; Swidrowich, R. A., Vancouver; Sylvester. R. E., Armstrong; Takasaki,

528

L., Picture Butte; Tamura, T., Picture Butte; Taylor, F. G., Hinton; Teerhuis, M. W., Winnipeg; Tessman, C. W., Fernie; Thom, L. D., Langley; Thompson, C. G., Edmonton; Towle, T. D., Lacombe; Trotter, R. K., North Surrey; Turner, R. W., Port Coquitlam; Turner, T. N., New Westminster; Ullestad, K. B., Yarbo; Vanin, P., Hills, B.C.; Vannice, R. A., J., Prince Rupert; Vermette, J. L., Winnipeg; Vernon, P. A., South Burnaby; Virkutis, A. C., Winnipeg; Walker, C. W., Red Deer; Wallwin, B. J., Merritt; Ward, R. J., White Horse, Alta.; Weinberger, L. M., Humboldt; Weiss, L. G., Hay River; Widdows, D. W. F., Vancouver; Wiebbe, C. G., Swift Current; Wikstrom, G. S., Kinistin, Sask.; Williams, W. R., Edmonton; Willingshofer, D. G., North Surrey; Wills, D. E., Vancouver; Willson, J. C., Red Deer; Wilson, W. L., Big River, Sask.; Wirth, R. M., Hinton; Wolki, C., Inuvik; Wunderlick, P. J., New Westminster; Yaceyko, R. R., Derwent, Alta.; Young, D. K., Spirit River; Yuzicapi, R., Fort Qu'Appelle, Sask.; Zaharko, R., Derwent.

Anderson, K., Swift Current; Campbell, C. M., Burnaby; Fontaine, R. B., Swift Current; Heppler, B. J., Molville, Sask.; Hushagen, J. M., Lacombe; McFee, B. E., Stonewall; Sibbeston, R. E., Hay River; Swan, R. J., Edmonton.

'J' COMPANY

Arlt, D. L., Creston; Baird, J. E., Saskatoon; Bartsch, D. B., Vancouver; Berens, L. J., Fort Smith, N.W.T.; Bird, P. M., Portage La Prairie; Bombay, R. J., Vimy, Alta.; Boyle, R. E., Invermere, B.C.; Bray, F. C., Lacombe; Braybrook, R. A., Churchill; Broda, D. J., Yorkton; Brooks, F. D., Rosthern, Sask.; Brooks, R. I., Rosthern; Bruno, M. M., Winterburn, Alta.; Colquhoun, R. D., Virden; Copeland, A. J., McCreary, Man.; Davidson, G. W., Lacombe; Day, A. L., Richmond; Daynes, R. E., Kimberley; Dodds, E. R., Salmon Arm; Dodds, K. M., Kelowna; Doherty, E. R., Hinton; Dornan, P. L., Vernon Military Camp; Dumontier, C. H., Picture Butte; Dunn, R. M., Pendryl, Alta.; Dyck, R. L., Hinton; Elmquist, L. G., Wadena, Sask.; Ewashkiw, J. A., Derwent; Fedorus, R. J., Hay River; Feller, G. I., Hillcrest Mines, Alta.; Fress, G., Picture Butte; Garrison, K. G., Red Deer; Gauthier, D. L., Esterhazy; Germain, J. A., Red Deer; Greig, J. W., Victoria; Harder, N., Vancouver; Hauck, B. K., Calgary; Helfenstein, C. L., Thorsby, Alta.; Henderson, B. G., Vegreville; Howie, K., Vancouver; Kesegic, W., Calgary; King, R. J., Lacombe; King, R. S., Lacombe.

Ladouceur, D. W., Qualicum; Larose, L. D., Battleford; Leicht, T. L., Innisfail; Loutit, E. J., Hay River; Luchka, R. H., Hafford, Sask.; Luini, H. L., Hillcrest Mines; McGrath, P. M., Burnaby; McHugh, D. S., Calgary; McKenna, D. F., Lethbridge; McRann, J. W., Spirit River; Marcoux, M. K., Hinton; Mastine, G. N., Camp Shilo; Nicholson, N. A., Calgary; Ockey, J. L., Fort St. John; Pinchbeck, R. C., Vancouver; Pitchko, D. N., Kelvinton, Sask.; Powley, K. R., Qualicum; Pumm, R. T., Aenno Field; Qua Vadis, P. F., Van-

couver; Rathgaber, B. W., Calgary; Reed, R. J., Rose Valley; Roberts, A., Brandon; Sayers, F. L., Battleford; Schoening, R. H., Vernon Army Camp; Schuh, R. W., Medicine Hat; Semmler, M. L., Inuvik; Sibbeston, R. J., Hay River; Simpkins, K. H., Winnipeg; Sunley, R. H., Saskatoon; Thomson, J. D., Calgary; Torman, J. P., Lethbridge; Turner, R. J., Calgary; Toruk, M. P., Chemainus; Walters, K. R., Warburg, Alta.; Wayman, B. W., Hillcrest, Alta.; Weir, J. M., Invermere; Westaway, A. H., New Denver; White, D. F., Vancouver; Wong, L. H., Prince Rupert; Yarmuch, L. M., Derwent; Zacker, A. L., Revelstoke.

'G' COMPANY — B.C. AREA

Barnes, M. J., Chilliwack; Bellec, R., Richmond; Berikoff, P. R., Prince George; Bird, R. J., Vancouver; Bruce, N. W., Merritt; Chen, D., Prince Rupert; Campbell, P., Powell River; Carmichael, K. R., Vancouver; Clarke, G., Victoria; Connacher, S. G., Merritt; Cook, G. A., North Vancouver; Crerar, R. J., Armstrong; D'Amelio, F. A., Nelson; Davis, D. R., Revelstoke; Fletcher, R. G., New Westminster; Fjoser, W. H., Ladner; Garbutt, R. N., Vernon; Giese, H., Kelowna; Gray, S. L., Vancouver; Green, J. H., Victoria; Grinsted, R. E., Ladner; Holloway, P. J., Revelstoke; Jardine, D. J., Squamish; Johannson, A. D., North Burnaby; Klym, R. M., Enderby; Kellett, W. B., Richmond; Knowles, T. E., Vancouver; Landry, G. P., Vancouver; Levers, G. R., Vancouver; McDonald, L. J., Victoria; Porter, G. M., Victoria; Redmond, J. D., Richmond; Roberts, T. S. H., Victoria; Robertson, W. R., Vancouver; Rogers, F. S., Ladner; Rust, G. S., South Burnaby; Sam, R. P., Victoria; Savage, W. G., Nakusp; Skibinski, R. N., Vancouver; Simmie, R., San Lornzo, California; Sinclair, R., Nakusp; Smalley, W. D., Vancouver; Stuckell, D. W., Langley; Tait, J. E., Vancouver; Thom, B. J., Langley; Thomasen, W. R., New Westminster; Turner, D. R., Vancouver; Valentine, R. D., Powell River; Wieler, D. M., Richmond; Wills, E. W., Vancouver; Wong, V., Prince Rupert.

ALBERTA AREA

Allenback, R. R., Burnaby, B.C.; Beatty, K. J., Vulcan; Bennett, W. S., Hinton; Boisbert, P., Sherwood Park; Brigden, R. W. D., Calgary; Butlin, B. K., Lethbridge; Carr, S. R., Innisfail; Buxton, C., Whitehorse; Carter, L. W., Calgary; Cashman, P. L., Calgary; Chartrand, H., Edmonton; Currie, L. M., Vermilion; Demmy, R. J., Edmonton; Denhoff, J. W., Calgary; Dillon, F. J., Inuvik; Earl, T. Fort Smith; Edwards, W. H., Calgary; Evanson, D. P., Calgary; Garnett, G. W., Vermilion; Gerachty, T. M., Calgary; Graham, J. D., Whitehorse; Griffin, W. J., Breton; Hampson, W. C., Calgary; Herbert, R. M., Vermilion; Hickey, J. E., Edmonton; Huxley, K., Calgary; Jardine, C. A., Evansburg; Kaake, R., Calgary; Kailek, R., Reindeer Station, N.W.T.; Kaiser, R. J., Vermilion; Kemble, G. E., Red Deer; Kinder, W. J., Millerville; Kinley, L. A., Lacombe; Lehay, R. W. E., Warburg; Lyons, L. O., Okotoks; Mackenzie, R. A., Calgary; Mantel, O., Edmonton; Matlock, H. R., Calmar; Melting-Tallow, F. F., Fort Macleod; Murdoch, I. C., Calgary; Osgood, P. L., Medicine Hat; Phillips, D. R., Calgary; Postma, R., Calgary; Price, A. J., Calgary; Query, E. W., Edmonton; Reeves, R. C., Edmonton; Sager, D. W., Inuvik; Schandor, M. R., Lethbridge; Smyth, S. M., Calgary; Stockl, G. A., Edmonton; Sutherland, B. D., Calgary; Taylor, R. G., Whitehorse; Tencarre, S. L., Spirit River; Tennant, M. W., Lacombe; Vollema, G., Edmonton; Welford, M. J., Redcliffe; Wintonyk, T. N., Derwent.

SASKATCHEWAN AREA
Baron, J. T., Hafford; Baetch, G. R., Walburg; Bellegrade, D. J., Goodeve; Bodnaryk, T., Esterhazy; Brownfield, B., Big River; Ghenard, G., Vanderhoof, B.C.; Cook, J. B., Saskatoon; Copeland, G. F., Kindersley; Dean, J. J., Invermay; Dinney, W. J., Prince Albert; Evans, L. J., Saskatoon; Franke, A. D., Margo; Franke, D. P., Margo; Gadd, K. D., St. Walburg; Gilchrist, K. J., Wadena; Hannam, W. F., Big River; Hovdebo, R. R., Prince Albert; Kaese, M. W., Big River; Kindrachuk, R. W., Hafford; Krazcuic, S., Regina; Kunkel, W. A., Esterhazy; Lawrence, R. A., Melville; Millikin, S. M., Big River; Nakano, R. K., Moose Jaw; Nimetz, T. W., Regina; Olson, D. O., Sturgis; Peterson, W. G., Kindersley; Quesnel, R. D., Esterhazy; Randall, A. M., Big River; Robertson, L. H., Sturgis; Rope, C. G., Sintaluta; Schimanowsky, R. L., Humboldt; Shinkewski, L. L., Invermay.

MANITOBA AREA
Brow, M. J., Transcona; Campbell, T. C., Winnipeg; Culbertson, I., Brandon; Dunn, G. J., Winnipeg; Evans, D. A., Fort Churchill; Grande, A., Winnipeg; Horne, M. D., Fort Churchill; Humnisky, B. A., Winnipeg; Huston, H. R., Red Deer; Levesque, D. L., Dauphin; Littlejohn, R. D., Winnipeg; Lloyd, D. C., Winnipeg; McIver, C. A., Stonewall; Mills, R. J., Winnipeg; Moate, D. W., Winnipeg; Morissett, R., Pine Falls; Pullens, I. C., Camp Shilo; Schiltroth, B. W., Craithton; Smith, D. J., Pine Falls; Smith, J. W., Winnipeg; Stowell, R. C., Vancouver; Turner, A. C., Camp Shilo; Wasilewski, A., Winnipeg; Wilson, A. J., Cross Lake.

BAND AND HQ COMPANY
B.C. AREA
Westlake, K. R., South Burnaby; Clubb, T. A., Squamish; Erickson, H. V., Squamish; O'Neill, D. B., Squamish; Duckworth, D., Vananda; Olson, J. M., Vancouver; Robinson, C. S., Vancouver; Tambre, T. E., Vancouver; Carpenter, D. J., Victoria; Hill, D. S., Victoria; Lehman, W. A., Victoria; McAleer, R. J., Victoria; Olsen, K., Victoria; Scurrah, M. H., Victoria; Sluggett, L. F., Victoria; Sluggett, R. A., Victoria; Smith, P. C., Victoria; Whitehead, P. R., Victoria; Johnson, R. S., North Surrey; Killeen, M. J., Nelson; Salter, T. E. D., Richmond, Ont.; Cardinell, K. P., Victoria.

B.C. AREA
Wolfe, D. J., Burnaby; Ned, W. L., Douglas Lake; Aitken, D. E., Duncan; Aitken, J. G., Duncan; Burge, D. T. Duncan; Carreck, J. A., Duncan; Carreck, S. V., Duncan; Crabbe, E. R., Duncan; Saul, K. W., Fort St.

John; Brown, J., Kamloops; Anderson, D. J., Lytton; George, M., Lytton; Donaldson, C. R., Nanaimo; Donaldson, R. R., Nanaimo; Bruce, R. J., New Westminster; Coyle, D. G., New Westminster; Healy, J. P., North Surrey; Marsh, I., North Surrey; Schwartz, E. J., North Surrey; Gunn-Fowlie, J. A., Port Alberni; Pelland, D. A., Port Alberni; Perry, I. A., Port Alberni; Richens, F. W., Port Alberni; Stevens, L. S., Port Alberni; Whittaker, J. H., Port Alberni; Gallagher, D. W., Powell River; Hobbs, R. A., Powell River.

ALBERTA AREA
Aschacher, T. P., Blairmore; Bellerose, A. L., Edmonton; Bezler, K. A., Redcliffe; Cornett, J. E., Coleman; Degenstien, S. J., Calgary; Gallant, K. G., Calgary; Gnyp, E. J., Alder Flats; Habdas, W. T., Blairmore; Kennedy, A. W., Calgary; Lechelt, R. D., Mayerthorpe; McKain, S. J., Edmonton; Martin, R. G., Calgary; Pielak, D. D. C., Calgary; Ross, B. A., Thorsby; Simon, M. G., Calgary; VanDerVlugt, E., Edmonton.

SASKATCHEWAN AREA
Gardippi, P. L., Duck Lake; McCarthy, B. D., Weyburn.

MANITOBA AREA
Brogan, T. J., Winnipeg; Bruderer, W. A., Ft. Churchill.

VACC - 1966

Aason, D. B., Port Alberni; Abbott, I. E., Lintlaw, Sask.; Abramson, E. J., Revelstoke; Adams, D., Edmonton; Adams, G. W., Vancouver; Ainey, J., Victoria; Ainsley, R. J., Calgary; Akerley, D. B.,; Alberts, A., Regina; Albrecht, C. M., Calgary; Allan G. E., Saanichton; Allen, G. R., Red Deer; Anderson, J. F., Leduc; Anderson, M. C., North Kamloops; Anderson, R. J., Winnipeg; Andrew, S. A., Esterhazy; Andrews, B., Edmonton; Antsett, R. M., Vancouver; Archer, K. L., Dauphin; Argue, J. E., Winnipeg; Arlt, D. L.; Armstrong, J. W., Petaigan, Sask.; Arthur, J., Portage La Prairie; Aseltine, N. C., Merritt; Ashe, W. B., Portage La Prairie; Aucoin, J. M., Vancouver; Auvigne, T. R. B., Calgary; Aymont, D. W. Winnipeg.

Babic, J. W., Calgary; Bablitz, C. W., Edmonton; Bablitz, H. A., Edmonton; Bachinsky, L., Sherwood Park, Alta.; Bahr, R. A. A., Calgary; Balagan, R. D., Vegreville; Balanecki, D. K., Edmonton; Ball, J. D., Victoria; Balzer, L. K., Saskatoon; Barber, G. S., Victoria; Barber, H. W., Powell River; Barbonoff, D. R., Regina; Barembruch, R. W., Surrey; Barker, B. O., Portage La Prairie; Barnes, M. J., Vedder Crossing; Barstad, G. A., Gleichen; Barich, D. G., Radium Hot Springs; Bateman, W. K., Calgary; Batenchuk, M. L., Winnipeg; Bauer, L. V., Winnipeg; Bauer, R. G., Saskatoon; Bawden, A. N., Victoria; Beach, E. E., Edmonton; Bear, E. T., Greighton, Sask.; Beaudoin, F. R., Sunning Gale, Man.; Beaulieu, H. E., Ft. Smith, N.W.T.; Becker, B. C., Winfield, Alta.;

Beckett, D. J., Winnipeg; Belcourt, B., Marlboro, Alta.; Belkin, L. N., Calgary; Bennett, R. J., Powell River; Benson, P. J., Humboldt; Benthien, S. J., Calgary; Bergin, R., Victoria; Bergstrom, A. B., Fruitvale; Bernard, S. C., Cloverdale; Berridge, M. C. E., Winnipeg; Berthelette, R. L., Pine Falls, Man.; Best, R. G., Vancouver; Bethel, R. L., Saskatoon; Bevan, T. D., Edson; Bigelow, G. A. J., Gleichen; Bittle, A. V. A., Camp Shilo; Black, G. W., Winnipeg; Blaker, R. W., Vancouver; Blishen. R. E., Vancouver; Blize, A. D., Breton, Alta.; Bloomfield, H. R., Winnipeg; Bluetchen, L. T., Stoney Plain; Bocquet, F., Cumberland; Bodenchuk, D. A., Edson; Bodnarchk, T., Winnipeg; Boisvert, R., Sherwood Park; Boiteau, D. L. J., McCreary, Man.; Borley, R. B., Marville, Alta.; Botrakoff, M., Salmon Arm; Boulding, B., Saskatoon; Bourasse, D. J., Lebret, Sask.; Bourgealt, L. J., Weyburn.

Bourgeois, N. J., Winnipeg; Bouten, R., New Denver; Bowcock, L. T., Fernie; Bowie, F. A., Edmonton; Boyda, R., Headingly, Man.; Bradley, H. E., Big River, Sask.; Bradley, R. W., Chemainus; Brandon, A. W., Edmonton; Braybrook, R. L., Yarbo, Sask.; Braybrook, R. W., Winnipeg; Bready, R. C., Vananda, B.C.; Breer, R. K., Saskatoon; Brereton, W. D., Winnipeg; Briscoe, W. G., Fort St. John; Brown, G. F., Fort St. John; Brown, I. P., Edmonton; Brown, J. D., Fruitvale; Brown, J. D., Dauphin; Brown, J. R., Winnipeg; Brown, K. A., Pine Falls, Man.; Brown, M. J., Lethbridge; Brown, R. F., Pine Falls; Brown, R. G., Pine Falls; Brown, R. R., Virden, Man.; Browning, C. H., Edmonton; Brownlee, J. C., Vegreville; Bruce, M. B., New Westminster; Bryce, D. J., North Surrey; Buchanan, K. D., Kindersley; Buck, R. T., Calgary; Buckley, P., Edmonton; Buikema, F., Turney Valley; Bull, A. L., Invermay, Sask.; Bulloch, L. T.; Bulloch, M. R., Haney; Bundy, K. L., Vancouver; Burge, D. T., Vancouver; Burge, D. T., Duncan; Burke, R. D., Regina; Burnell, D. R., Winnipeg; Burnett, P. R., Calgary; Burns, L. J., Duck Lake, Sask.; Burr, G., Bruno, Sask.; Burrage, J. D., Haney; Bush, W. G., Chilliwack; Buysen, J. A. A., Sherwood Park; Buysen, W. C., Sherwood Park.

Cadotte, R. L. R., Winnipeg; Cairns, R. K., New Westminster; Cairns, R. T., New Westminster; Cameron, H. D., Qualicum Beach; Cameron, K. W., Winnipeg; Campbell, B. J., Powell River; Campbell, C. M., New Westminster; Campbell, P. T., North Vancouver; Campbell, R. W., Calgary; Cant, S. F., Vancouver; Canvel, R. W., Coquitlam; Carefoot, L. M., Virden; Carlson, C. A., Calgary; Carnegie, E. C., Rutland; Carstairs, B. J., Thorsby, Alta.; Cashman, P. C., Calgary; Cattee, H. J., Penticton; Cawley, C. M., Delisle; Chapman, M. F., Sedgewick; Charles, A. L., Edmonton; Chaykowski, I. M., Wadena, Sask.; Chemerika, D. D., Winnipeg; Chipeur, D. V., Swift Current.

Charney, E. M., Wadena; Chow, R. L., Moose Jaw; Christie, R. W., Ved-

der Crossing; Clarke, R. J., Moose Jaw; Clark, W. J., Edmonton; Cleough, Chemainus; Coates, G. R., Nakusp; Coates, J., Victoria; Cobledick, D. L., Edmonton; Cochrane, L. F., Winnipeg; Cocks, B. J., Calgary; Cole, D. E., Bellevue, Alta.; Collins, J. G., Burnaby; Collison, A. F., Winfield; Condon, J. A., Victoria; Conley, D. C., Winnipeg; Conacher, A. K., Merritt; Connon, R. N., Innisfail; Cook, D. W., Calgary; Cook, G. A., North Vancouver; Corsbie, J. P., Edmonton; Cosgrove, R. C., Ft. McLeod; Courchene, F. V., Pine Falls; Couttes, R. B., Regina; Cowan, S. J., Kelowna; Cox, C. O., Blemore, Alta.; Coxall, B. A., Winnipeg; Crabbe, E. R., Chemainus; Craig, R. A., Morinville; Crofford, R. B., Kindersley; Croft, G. W., Burnaby; Cronin, K. F., Red Deer; Cronin, P. M., Red Deer; Cronk, T. E., Victoria; Crouch, R. R. A., Chilliwack; Crozier, J. W., Dauphin; Crozier, A. S. A., Dauphin; Cunningham, W. R., Kelwood, Man.; Czarneck, E., Edmonton.

Daniels, B. R., Cranbrook; Daniels. L. G., Deer Ridge, Sask.; Dary, E.S., Winnipeg; Dawn, D. W., North Surrey; Davidson, R. A., North Van. couver; Davis, B. G., Victoria; Davis, D. E., Toronto; Davis, G. E., Shilo; Davis, G. W., Flin Flon; Davis, J. J., Toronto; Davyduck, L. G., Winnipeg; Day, R. L., Regina; Daymond, D. W., Edmonton; Deck, R. G., Cranbrook; Decock, S. A., Winnipeg; Decoteau, R. P., Calgary; Degenstien, S. J., Calgary; Demchuk, D. J. D., Saskatoon; Dempster, R., Vancouver; Dermody, D. J., Milestone, Sask.; Deroche, G. T., Cranbrook; Deroche, J. M., Regina; Dick, A. F., Lytton; Dickson, J. R., Medicine Hat; Dixon, D. J., Shilo; Dodds, E. H., Salmon Arm; Dodds, M., Vancouver; Doan, W. S., Mervin, Sask.; Donnelly, B. J., Turner Valley; Doucette, R. A., Port Alberni; Douglas, B. K., New Westminster; Douglas, R. J., Langley; Dryden, J. K., North Surrey; Dubois, D. R., Edenwold, Sask.; Dobush, L., Winnipeg; Dueck, D. A., Winnipeg; Duhamel, L. E. R., Abbotsford; Duquette, E., Vancouver; Dunbar, K. B., Port Alberni; Duncan, R. D., Winnipeg; Dunn, D. G., Winnipeg; Dunstan, J. R., Lytton; Durand, D. J., Edmonton; Durant, C. L., Alder Flats, Alta.; Deroche, J., Regina; Des Jarlais, R. M., Sask.; Duval, D. M., Prince Albert; Dwight, L. W., Winnipeg; Dwolinsky, W. M., Port Alberni; Dyck, G. B., Rosetown.

Earl, M. D., Victoria; Economy, T. M., Vancouver; Edci, F., Ft. Good Hope, N.W.T.; Eddington, W. J., Vancouver; Edwards, C. M., Red Deer; Edwards, J. D., Prince Albert; Egberts, M. P., Powell River; Elliott, D. C., Verdin; Elliott, M. W., Spirit River; Elliott, R. C., Shilo; Ellis, T. N., Salmon Arm; Emms, L., Winnipeg; England, L. N., Calgary; Ens, L. W., Saskatoon; Epler, A. L., Edmonton; Epp, G. D., Prince Albert; Evans, D. W., Vancouver; Evans, L. J., Edmonton.

Fabro, D. B., Coleman, Alta.; Fane, F. W. J., Vegreville; Faulds, R., Edmonton; Fayant, W. P., Lebert,

Sask.; Fedorko, R. T., Winnipeg; Fedoruk, D. G., Vegreville; Feldman, N. A., Calgary; Fernets, B. M., Saskatoon; Fischer, J. W., Chilliwack; Fisher, W. T., Black Diamond; Flaman, J. L., Regina; Flaman, T. F., Regina; Fletcher, C., Lethbridge; Fletcher, R. G., New Westminster; Fleet, L. F., Nelson House, Man.; Focht, B. S., Regina; Fontaine, R. B., Swift Current; Forsyth, D. A., Virden; Forsyth, J., Sunnybrooke, Alta.; Foss, H. J., Sherwood Park; Fawkes; Fox, T. M., Vancouver; Frank, A. A., Regina; Fraser, D. B., Burnaby; Frater, W. T., Invermere; Frame, A. M., Vancouver.

Gabriel, J. C., Vancouver; Gaede, J. E., Calgary; Gagne, D. M., Edmonton; Gaidosh, W. M., Winnipeg; Gale, R. J., Fernie; Gallagher, D. W., Powell River; Gallagher, T., Sherwood Park; Gallerneault, T. F., Prince Albert; Ganderson, M. L., Stoney Plain; Gareau, E. R., Fernie; Garon, B. P. J., New Westminster; Gass, C. I., Beaver Lodge; Gauthier, B. R., Winnipeg; Gawryluk, P., Fernie; Gelasco, G. A., Edmonton; George, D. F., Winnipeg; George, P., Winnipeg; Geraghty, P. J., Calgary; Germain, J. A., Red Deer; Gibberson, D. R., Haney; Gibson, G. W., Gleichen; Gibson, J. P., Portage La Prairie; Giesbrecht, P. D., Winnipeg; Gilbert, S. J., Moose Jaw; Gilchrist, D. D., Saskatoon; Gilewich, R. S. J., Winnipeg; Girouard, D. W., Winnipeg; Glass, S. R., Richmond; Glenn, J. B., Mayerthorpe; Gladue, A. J. Man.; Glover, C. A., Okotoks; George, C. M., Tantallon, Sask.

Goeree, H. D., Edmonton; Goffinet, R. E., New Denver; Golden, E. L., Calgary; Goodchild, T. S., Edmonton; Goodman, D. S., Swift Current; Goodwin, C. J., Victoria; Goore, S. A., Wadena; Gordon, P. H., Courtenay; Gordon, R. J., Rossland; Gorak, J. V., Chilliwack; Gertzen, R. A., Medicine Hat; Gough, R. G. J., Edmonton; Grace, M. J., Burnaby; Graham, D. W. G., Dauphin; Grande, A., Winnipeg; Grant, R. J., Victoria; Grant, C. E., Brandon; Grant, D. M., Lethbridge; Grant, S. H., Winnipeg; Gray, G. T., Edmonton; Green, D. C., Blubber Bay; Greengrass, D. W., Burnaby; Greenway, W. M., Swift Current; Gregory, B. J., Powell River; Griffin, H. E., Breton, Alta.; Groome, D., Sherwood Park; Guldie, H. P., Saskatoon; Gunn, N. J. P., Lyntlay, Sask.; Guyon, C., Edmonton; Haarsma, D. J., Winnipeg; Hackl, N. D., Humboldt; Hagley, N. D., Regina.

Hall, J. A., Nakusp; Hamill, C. J., Winnipeg; Hamilton, A. J. W., Regina; Hankins, C. B., Sutherland, B.C.; Hanson, R. I. W., Shilo; Harrison, T. W., Victoria; Hartemberger, W. G., Sask.; Hartung, M., Winnipeg; Hauck, D. W., Calgary; Hayter, J. W., Vancouver; Hegan, M. G., Melville; Helfenstein, C. L., Thorsby, Alta.; Hemminger, W. A., Brandon; Heppler, J. B., Melville; Herde, B. D.; Melville; Herman, T. T., Hafford, Sask.; Herrington, D. L., Melville; Heusts, G. L., Ft. Macleod; Highway, D. M., Brochet, Man.; Hilgers, R. M., Bruno, Sask.; Hill, D. H., Rossland; Hill, R., Merritt; Hill, W. J., Manitoba.

Hillier, M. R., Edmonton; Hirsch, J. L., Redcliffe, Alta.; Hoar, D. F., Shilo; Hodgson, C. E., Winnipeg; Hohn, P., Kaleden; Holberton, G. L., Lethbridge; Hollman, D. F., Red Deer; Holloway, P. J., Revelstoke; Holmes, G. G., Flin Flon; Holmstrom, H. A. H., Wadena; Hopkins, C. R. C., Cranbrook; Hordbin, M. C., Brandon; Houston, L. S., Okanagan Centre; Houwig, J., Edmonton; Houdebo, R. R., Prince Albert; Howard, D. A., Edmonton; Howerton, M. J., Edmonton; Howie, J. C., Calgary; Hughes, R., Sherwood Park; Humphrey, D. L. Fernie; Hunter, B. A., Edson; Hunter, B. A., Vancouver; Hutchison, R., Stoney Plain; Huxley, B., Calgary; Holmes, A. M., Ladner.

Ireland, G. K., New Westminster; Jack, D. H., Calgary; Jackman, J. R., Calgary; Jackson, P. A., Delburne, Alta.; Jackson, P. A., Penticton; Jardine, C. O., Evinsburgh, Alta.; Jardine, C. L, Evansburg, Alta.; James, E., Gleichen; Jarves, R D., Innis, Alta.; Jealous, G. R., Cranbrook; Jenkins, C. R., Ft. Mcleod; Jensen, F., Vancouver; Jensen, S. P., Breton, Alta.; Jerome, R. H. C., Red Deer; Jackson, J., Surrey; Jahn, W. A., Coleman; John, C. R., Victoria; Johnson, J. A., Paswegin, Sask.; Johnson, J. B., Vancouver; Johnson, J. S., North Battleford; Johnson, L. R., Moose Jaw; Johnson, R. L., Beaver Lodge; Johnson, R. T., Victoria; Johnson, R. W., Victoria; Johnson, W. R., Calgary; Jones, D. D., Saskatoon; Jones, G. N., Black Diamond; Josephson, R. J., Vancouver; Joyner, D., Haney; Just, A. T. L., Yorkton; Johnson, M. D., Moose Jaw.

Kaiser, R. J., Vermillion; Kakowchyk, R. W., Winnipeg; Kalenchuck, C. A., Sturgis, Sask.; Kawahara, G. T., Nakusp; Keating, I. D., Winnipeg; Keats, R. F., Dauphin; Kehn, C. T., Medicine Hat; Kellett, R. A., Vancouver; Kelly, J. R., Virden; Kelly, R. R., Victoria; Kendall, D. F., Skidegate, B.C.; Kendall, D. J., Swanson, Sask.; Kennedy, L. G., Kamloops; Kennedy, M. J., Vancouver; Kerr, W., Winnipeg; Kesegic, W., Alta.; Kilgour, C. G., Victoria; Kimball, D. C., Bedgerton, Alta.; Kinley, L. A., Lacombe; Kinnear, J. G., Vancouver; Kitella, J. A. S., Saskatoon; Kitson, W. H., North Kamloops; Kitteringham, D. B., Creighton; Klaus, H. B., Wadena; Korpan, A. J., Dauphin; Kowatch, D. G., Edmonton; Kozar, G. A., Flin Flon; Krawetz, W. R., Port Alberni; Kucey, J. D., Wadena; Kuhn, E. H., Bruno; Kunkel, L. D., Esterhazy; Kostyk, M. W., Winnipeg; Kyle, G. J., Edmonton; LaFlamme, L., Edmonton.

Laduranteay, A. L., Alta.; Lagertstrom, R. J., Burnaby; Lambert, R. J., Haney; Lanchick, M. W., Vancouver; Lane, D. A., Calgary; Laporte, G. A., Winnipeg; Larkin, W. F.; Larose, L. T., Battleford; Larson, B. L., Fositon, Sask.; Laruin, W. F., Edmonton; Laursen, B. Virden; Lavallie, D. J., Prince Albert; LaValley, L. J., Regina; Lavineway, D. R.,

Man.; Lavoie, J. L., Edmonton; Law, R., Nakusp; Lazurko, L. N., Willowbrook, Sask.; Leask, D. G., Prince Albert; Leclair, W. V., Vedder Crossing; Leitch, J. N., Penticton; Leicht, J. D., Innisvail; Lekman, W., B.C.; Lemon, B. W. A., Milestone, Sask.; Lesiuk, G. J., Sherwood Park; Lesiuk, R., Winnipeg; Lesley, J. J., Vancouver; Leslie, J. J., Vancouver; Lester, L. E., Saskatoon; Leveille, R. M., Breton; Levesque, P., B.C.; Lewis, P. M., Mayerthorpe; Lievers, P. J. Ft. McLeod; Lilley, L., Portage La Prairie; Lillow, G. T., Kamloops; Linderbeck, L. W. T., Langley; Lingenfelter, A. L., Vancouver; Lingenfelter, S. M., Vancouver; Lister, R. B., Vancouver; Livingstone, B. L., Winnipeg; Loeder, H., Edmonton; Loewen, G. E., Abbotsford; Logan, K. T., North Vancouver; Loutitt, R. D., Yorkton; Love, B. K., Inuvik, N.W.T.; Lowe, A. D., Vancouver; Lowrie, M. A., Lethbridge; Lueke, E. A., Bruno; Lusk, K. E. J., Haney.

McAleer, R. J., Victoria; McAra, M. N., Esquimalt; McBride, W. R., Sedgewick, Alta.; McCooey, T. J. D., Victoria; McCreadie, W. E., Edmonton; McDonald, C. R., Morinville; McDonald, D. M., Haford, Sask.; McDugall, P. A., Victoria; McGerrigle, R. D., Stenen, Sask.; McIntosh, F. M., Nakusp; McIntyre, G. E., Burnaby; McIntyre, M. S. T., Shilo; McIntyre, W. D., Burnaby; McKay, G. T. Redcliffe; McKay, R. B., Fernie; McKay, T. J., Prince Albert; McKimmie, S. S., Mayerthorpe; McLeod, I. R., Victoria; McMillan, J. D., Edmonton; McNulty, G. E., New Westminster; MacPhee, F. J., Rusylvia, Alta.; McPherson, M. J., Kindersley; McTaggart, K. J., Revelstoke; McTeer, J. K., Trail; MacAdam, R. B., Winnipeg; MacArtney, M. T., Ladner; MacDee, I. J., Edmonton; MacDonald, R. A., Chemainus; Machek, P. J., Victoria; Mackie, J. T., North Surrey; Mackie, R. W., Saskatoon; Mackwood, P. A., Innisfail.

MacMillan, R. A., Vermilion; Madigin, W. R., Edmonton; Magatan, B. G., Nelson; Maihiot, R. A., Calgary; Makarow, A. T., Rose Valley; Malcolm, D. H., Winnipeg; Millison, A., Langley; Manylux, D. F., Vermilion; Marcinew, B. D., Vermilion; Marjoram, R. A., Speers, Sask.; Markstrom, L. R., Revelstoke; Marshall, W. A., Red Deer; Martenberger, W. G., Regina; Martin, D. F., Calgary; Martin, J. D., Beaverlodge; Martin, J. E., Rosetown; Martin, R. S., Nelson; Mason, M., B.C.; Mason, M. S., Victoria; Maters, C. I., Duncan; Mathews, R. D., Saskatoon; Matiets, L. P., New Westminster; Mattson, G. M., Mayerthorpe; Maxwell, D. W., Penticton; Maxwell, H. G., North Vancouver; Maxwell, T. R., Abbotsford; May, M. C., Weyburn; Mayo, C. W., Vancouver; Mazur, M. C., Winnipeg; Meachan, K. G., Carrot River; Meir, J. J., Edmonton; Meilike, G. F., Burnaby; Meise, K. B., Prince George; Melia, R. A., Winnipeg; Melton, A. C., Calgary; Meyer, L. W., Vancouver; Mike, E., Duck Lake, Sask.; Miller, J. F., Vancouver; Mills, C. W., Vancouver; Mitton,

R. K., Calgary; Mohs, G. W., Merritt; Moore, M. S., Kelowna; Moren, B. D., Vermilion; Moreno, J. M., Vancouver; Morrison, D. N., Medicine Hat; Morrison, R. P., Pincher Creek; Morrison, S. A., Winnipeg; Morrow, K. W., Esterhazy; Morsette, R. L., Fernie; Mosser, R. B., Prince George; Mottershead, D. E., Comox; Mowat, D. J., Winnipeg; Moxam, D. J., Vancouver; Mozotsky, H. R.; Moxham, R. B., Fort St. John; Mullen, R. B., North Saskatoon; Mulrooney, D. K., Red Deer; Murphy, G. B., Melville; Murphy, G. R., Prince George; Murphy, J. P., Red Deer; Murphy, P. R., Port Moody; Murray, N. S., Calgary; Murray, R. S., Edmonton.

Nagy, G. B., Regina; Nagey, T. L., Regina; Nantes, M. N., Victoria; Neal, E. K., Victoria; Neff, K. W., North Surrey; Neigum, R. V., Kelowna; Neill, P. C., Melville; Nelson, A. D., Alta.; Nelson, D. B., Inuvik; Ness, W. M., Edmonton; Nichol, D. E., Beaverlodge; Nicholson, B. A., Winnipeg; Nicolson, R. A., Winnipeg; Nicholson, N. A., Calgary; Nimetz, R. D., Regina; Nolan, C. R., Vulcan; Novak, L. A., Hay River, N.W.T.; O'Connell, A. L., Beaverlodge; Odynsky, M. J., Kamloops; Oige, B. G., Winnipeg; Oliver, D. E., Entwistle; Olsen, W., Victoria; Olson, D .C., Big River, Sask.; O'Rourke, P. M., Fernie; Osborne, W. J., Hinton; Osgood, J. A., Medicine Hat; Ostash, P. P., Brandon; Ottermann, L. A., Wadena.

Palin, B. M. S., Edmonton; Palmer, J. R., Chilliwack; Panas, D., Prince George; Papineau, R. W., Edmonton; Park, G. S., Calgary; Paterson, D. J., Port Alberni; Payette, J. R., Portage La Prairie; Payne, D. E., Lousana, Alta.; Peachey, R., Vancouver; Pearcy, D. E., Virden; Pearson, K. C., Vulcan; Pelland, D. A., Port Alberni; Pennie, B. K., Vancouver; Pennycok, L. M., Carrot River; Perkins, A. R., Fernie; Perry, I. L., Port Alberni; Peterson, D. E., Kindersley; Peterson, L. R., Victoria; Phillippe, R. V., Vancouver; Phillips, D. A., Edmonton; Phillips, D. R., Calgary; Phillips, W. J., Winnipeg; Pickering, J. D., Winnipeg; Pierrie, B. J., Winnipeg; Pitras, L. S.; Plimmer, W., Calgary; Pleasants, L. J., B.C.; Pocock, R. G., Haney; Podwinski, G. R., Vancouver; Poitras, L. S., Winnipeg; Polachek, K. W. F., Kelvington; Polischuk, D. W., Breton; Pollitt, R. J., Penticton; Pollock, D. W., Pincher Creek; Poole, M. S., Victoria; Pope, G .B., Fort St. John; Popp, K. B., Flin Flon; Power, B. M., Port Alberni; Power, T. L., Prince Albert; Price, C. R., Lethbridge; Prince, G., Winnipeg; Putsey, D. F., Vancouver; Pyke, W. G., Winnipeg; Qually, J. B., Lethbridge; Querin, J. D., Powell River; Quick, T., Richmond.

Ras, B. A., Transcona; Ras, R., Transcona; Rathgeber, D. B., Melville; Reed, R. G., Shilo; Reghelini, R. A., Vermilion; Reid, R. I., Creston; Reid, T. A., Glidden, Sask.; Reilly, T. O., Clony, Alta.; Reimer, L. H., Burnaby; Renneberg, A. F., Bruno; Resch, G. F., Medicine Hat;

Richard, M. D., Lebret, Sask.; Riopel, P. C., Edmonton; Ripley, R. W., Ft. McLeod; Ripley, R. W., Winnipeg; Rixon, T. J., Calgary; Roberts, E. F. H., Edmonton; Robertson, C., Lethbridge; Robertson, K. B., Vancouver; Robinson, C. S., North Vancouver; Robinson, M. C., Hay River; Robson, F. L., Burnaby; Rogers, B. J., Vancouver; Rogers, G. B., Ladner; Rogers, T. T., Vermilion; Rogozinsky, K. J. M., Rosetown; Rondeau, F. K., Morinville; Ror, R. D., Weyburn; Rose, P. E., Victoria; Ross, C. H., Calgary; Ross, D. J., Winnipeg; Ross, R. C., Victoria; Ross, R. E., Saskatoon; Rossetti, L. H., Calgary; Rossetti, R. R., Lethbridge; Rozylo, H. A., Vancouver; Ruben, G. T., Edmonton; Rust, K. A., Burnaby.

Salter, N. S., Courtenay; Sass, K. S., Kelowna; Sauerborn, U., Mayerthorpe; Saul, K. W., Fort St. John; Savard, S. M. P., Calgary; Sawatzky, D. R., Shilo; Sawatzky, E., Medingly, Man.; Sawicz, K., Winnipeg; Scanian, J. A., Calgary; Schilroth, L. R., Creighton; Schmaltz, I. P., Redcliffe; Schneider, B. P., Battleford; Schneider, C., Flin Flon; Schneider, D. L., Regina; Schultz, C. H. A., Red Deer; Schultz, G. S., Edson; Schwab, K., Langley; Schwap, G. L., Langley; Scott, C. K., New Westminster; Scurrah, M. H., Victoria; Seitz, M. A., Regina; Seginowich, W. M., Victoria; Senft, R. J., Calgary; Senko, J. M., Humboldt; Shandro, B. W., Vegreville; Shaw, D. B., Vancouver; Shaw, R. J., Vancouver; Sheskey, W., Edmonton; Shields, G. R., Vancouver; Shiloff, F. M., Brandon; Shiloff, G. A., Brandon; Shineton, R. E., McCreary, Man.; Short, J. R., Wananda, B.C.; Short, R. N., Prince Albert; Shuter, S. J., Lower Nicole, B.C.; Simes, T. A., Stenen, Sask.; Simes, W. L., Quill Lake, Sask.; Simmons, K. E., Wadena; Simmons, A. J., Burnaby.

Sitter, K. F., Calgary; Skibinski, B. B., Vancouver; Skinner, J. M., Abbotsford; Skuce, B. L. S., Lyntlay, Sask.; Sly, R. N., Camp Shilo; Smart, G. D., New Westminster; Smith, D. G., Red Deer; Smith, D. J., North Surrey; Smith, G. P., Brandon; Smith, J. C., Cumberland; Smith, J. H., Nakusp; Smith, J. W., Red Deer; Smith, M. G., Edmonton; Smith, P. G., Vancouver; Smith, P. J., Waidam, Sask.; Smith, R. I., Winnipeg; Smith, W. A., Fernie; Smyth, G. B., Calgary; Snow, G. A., Salmon Arm; Snowdon, J. D., Ft. McLeod; Soenen, O. L., Edmonton; Sommerville, P. R., Sturgis, Sask.; Sopher, J. S., Calgary; Souliers, J. L., Sherwood Park; Spicer, C. J., Calgary; Stadnyk, J. I., Virden; Stamm, R. V., Vancouver; Starling, W. L., Inuvik; Steele, S. O., Salmon Arm; Stenhouse, J., Gleicher, Suais, B. W., Burnaby; Suecroft, T. I., Thorsby, Alta.; Summerfelt, I. L., Edmonton; Sunderland, N. L. T., Calgary; Sundstrom, R. G., Trail; Stephens, D., Fort St. John; Stepski, R. E., Prince George; Stern, N. M. D., Swift Current; Stewart, L. J., Virden; Stonechild, A. B., Regina; Stroshein, R. W. Wadena;

Stuby, R. G. F., Fort St. John; Swan, C., Winnipeg; Swan, N. F., Calgary; Swan, R. J., Toronto; Swanson, E. G., Creston; Swift, B. L., Vancouver.

Tawpisin, W., Leasuk, Sask.; Taylor, A. R., Winnipeg; Taylor, F. J., Winnipeg; Taylor, J. P., Port Alberni; Taylor, R. M., Prince Albert; Terpastra, K., Beach Corner, Alta.; Tessman, C. W., Fernie; Thom, L. B., Langley; Thomas, G. P., Battleford; Thomas, L. E., Traueres Bay, Man.; Thompson, C. C., Black Diamond, Alta.; Thompson, R. E., Kamloops; Thompson, D. J., Sask.; Thomson, G., Winnipeg; Thomson, L. M., Vancouver; Thoresen, F. C., Calgary; Thorp, D .J., Saskatoon; Thue, G. D., Dauphin; Tiessen, D. J., Merritt; Todd, B. F., Lethbridge; Torjusson, G., Merritt; Tourond, G. P., Turner Valley; Touround, M. S., Pincher Creek; Towle, T. D., Lacombe; Tracey, G., Sherwood Park; Trayling, D. M., Burnaby; Truthwaite, K. D., Winnipeg; Traydal, D. C., Sexsmith; Tuck, C. J. K., Hillcrest, Alta.; Tucker, A. D., Prince Rupert; Turner, G. S., Weyburn; Tutte, K. R., Burnaby; Tymchuk, B. I., Edmonton.

Umoak, F., Tuktoiaktuk, N.W.T.; Usher, K. J., New Westminster; Vallee, J. E., Port Alberni; Van Der Molen, R. G., Port Alberni; Van Heriwefhe, D. A., Lacombe; Vanim, P., New Denver; Van Rikkort, A., North Vancouver; Vass, J. D., Penticton; Veilleaux, D. A., Pine Falls; Velt, R. R., Sherwood Park; Verbenkov, N., Vancouver; Vernon, P. A., Burnaby; Vollman, C. A., Gleichen.

Waddell, P. R., Port Alberni; Waditaka, A. M., Prince Albert; Waffle, W., Wainwright; Wainman, R., Inuvik; Waites, C. T., Vancouver; Waiker, C. A., Brandon; Walker, J. H., Pine Falls; Wallace, W. V., Sedgewick; Wallin, R. C., Burnaby; Walmsley, R. C., Esquimalt; Walton, C. S., Vancouver; Ward, W. J., McCreary; Warman, T. G., Saskatoon; Warriner, D. T. G., Big River, Sask.; Warwick, D. W., North Battleford; Wasilewski, A., Winnipeg; Wasylyshyn, L. J., Ft. Smith, N.W.T.; Watson, P. A., Pine Falls; Watters, C. I. A., B.C.; Weir, R. M., Cumberland; Weiss, S., N. Surrey; Weiszner, N., Winnipeg; Weitzel, G. H., Battleford; Wellings, J. W., Vancouver; Weselak, G. G. T., Esterhazy; Wesley, J. C., Camp Shilo; Westaway, A. H., New Denver; Weston, G. E., Ft. Smith; Wheaton, H. V. G., Winnipeg; Wheelhouse, B. R., Vernon; Whitby, B. T., Yorkton; White, A., Pincher Creek; White, R. A., Rosetown; Whitley, G. A., Winnipeg; Whittaker, J. H., Port Alberni; Wiebe, C. G., Saskatoon.

Wildeman, T. W., Edmonton; Willet, S. N., Edmonton; Willetes, B. L., Creighton, Man.; Williams, C. S., Stonewall, Man.; Williams, W. R., Edmonton; Willingshofer, D. G., North Surrey; Willson, J. C., Red Deer; Wilson, D. B., Calgary; Wilson, E. P., Vancouver; Wilson, J. G., Vancouver; Wilson, S. S., Lethbridge; Wilson, W. C., Edson; Wilson, W. L., Big River; Wilson, W. M., Duncan; Winstanley, M. J., New Westminster;

Winzoski, A. J., Beausejour, Man.; Witherly, C. R., Sherwood Park; Wolkie, C., Inuvik; Wolkie, P., Inuvik; Wong, F., Beaver Lodge; Wong, L., Prince Aupert; Wood, J. E., Winnipeg; Woodley, R. J., Saskatoon; Woods, B. N., Vancouver.

Waren, B .E., Edmonton; Worem, B. E.; Wozniak, M. L., Melville; Wozniak, R. F., Melville; Wright, D. A., North Kamloops; Wright, P. W., Port Alberni; Yates, B. R., Fallis, Alta.; Yockey, O. B., Saskatoon; Young, B. D,, Calgary; Zacher, G. G., Regina; Zastre, F. H. E., Winnipeg; Zazelenchuk, R. J., Saskatoon; Zest. D. F., Winnipeg; Zroback, F. F., Vancouver; Zubeck, T. J., Vernon; Zwicker, R. M., Crows Nest Pass.

VACC - 1967

PT COY

Bulloch. M., Haney; Burr, G. M., Bruno, Sask.; Christiaens, H., Kindersley, Sask.; Clubb, T., N. Vancouver; Davis, G. W., Flin Flon, Man.; Diehl, R. H., Blaine Lake, Sask.; Eschuk, J. L., Winnipeg; Fox, G. R., Edmonton; Gallagher, T., Sherwood Park, Alta.. Gough, R., Sherwood Park; Haegeman, K., Winnipeg; Haggerty, C. S., Shilo, Man.; Hill, K., Winnipeg; Lane, G., Shilo; McDougall, WW., Winnipeg; McMillan, K. J., Melfort, Sask.; Mason, R., Matsen, Ont.; Miller, F., Vancouver; Mulrooney, D., Red Deer, Alta.; Porter, P. R., Carman, Man.; Pyle, P., Shilo; Randall, B., Big River, Sask.; Rayner, K., Marathon, Ont.; Sawicz, J. P., Winnipeg; Schultz, M. K., Winnipeg; Sharkey, V. K., Edmonton; Souliere, M., Sherwood Park; Swift, B., Vancouver; Van Rikxoort, T., N. Vancouver; Wright, P., Port Alberni.

HQ COY (BAND)

Austin, H., Calgary; Baird, D. A., Calgary; Bedea, P., Calgary; Blishen, A., Haney; Blishen, R. E., Haney; Block, L. G., Nelson; Boivin, A. R., Burnaby; Bruyere, E., Edmonton; Cairns, R., New Westminster; Cameron, M., New Westminster; Campbell, C., Burnaby; Carreck, J., Duncan; Carroll, J., New Westminster; Cavaliar, L. R., Edmonton; Chaykowski, A., Rockland, B.C.; Chipman, R., Port Alberni; Clark, A. J., N. Vancouver; Clarke, K., Victoria; Cleough, J. H., Chemainus; Crawford, R. J., Victoria; Cronin, K. F., Red Deer, Alta.; Cruthers, A. L., Burnaby; Davis, R. D., Victoria; Delroy, G., Edmonton; Dillon, F., Inuvik, NWT; Donaldson, D. E., Nanaimo; Field, C. J., Vancouver; Fuller, C. D., Victoria; Gabdois, J. G., Coquitlam; Gadbois, L. D., Coquitlam; Granger, P. D., Vancouver; Hancharuk, T., Edmonton; Hanlan, K. N., Burnaby; Holley, M., Vancouver; Hughes, G. A., Calgary; Hutchings, M., Victoria.

Jack, G. D., Calgary; Keuflar, T. M., Sherwood Park; Lang, G. K., Calgary; Lesiuk, G., Sherwood Park; MacDonald, B. M., Edmonton; MacDonald, D., N. Burnaby; McBride, R., Burnaby; McDougall, P., Victoria; McGrath, D., Calgary; McNualty, J.,

New Westminster; McNulty, G. E., New Westminster; Marocchi, D. R., Port Alberni; Marshall, D., Calgary; Martin, J., Vancouver; Melin, D. J., Thorsby, Alta.; Mercer, D. F., New Westminster; Metcallefe, V., New Westminster; Miller, R., Victoria; Mundorf, K., Edmonton; Netherton, S., Victoria; Nimko, R. J., Edmonton; Nutt, T., Vancouver; O'Krainetz, G., New Denver; Pakin, B., Edmonton; Paul, J., Edmonton; Paulo, A., Victoria; Perry, I. L., Port Alberni; Pflug, D., North Surrey; Poynter, L. J., Burnaby; Power, B. M., Port Alberni; Power, P., Port Alberni.

Radford, J. T., New Westminster; Riley, P., New Westminster; Rixon, P., Calgary; Ross, K. W., New Westminster; Scott, M., Saunders, B.C.; Shelvey, B. M., Calgary; Smith, G., Edmonton; Smith, S. J., Edmonton; Smith, W., Port Alberni; Spratt, E. T., Trail; Tippett, R. R., Calgary; Treleaven, D. B., Port Alberni; Tutte, K. M., Burnaby; Usher, K., New Westminster; Vallee, R., Port Alberni; Vandermeer, R. W., Burnaby; Wall, L., North Surrey; Warburton, P., New Westminster; Ward, D. B., Victoria; Weber, B., Edmonton; Weikum, M., Port Alberni; Welsh, G., Kelowna; Westlake, K., Burnaby; Weston, B., North Surrey; Williams, D., North Surrey; Williams, M. R., Calgary; Wilson, B., Duncan; Wilson, D., Duncan; Wooffindin, N., Vedder Crossing, B.C.; Wuychuk, M., Edmonton; Wylie, L. R. J., Fort McMurray, Alta.; Zawartka, A., Warburg, Alta.

A COY

Ackerman, E., Kinnaird; Adams, J., Haney; Adams, M., North Surrey; Aldred, J. D., Nanaimo; Allan, K. N., Victoria; Anderson, P., Cawston, B.C.; Andress, M. R., Burnaby; Ashcroft, D., Richmond, B.C.; Atchison, K., N. Vancouver; Auer, R., Vancouver; Austin, .R., New Hazelton, B.C.; Avis, C., Coquitlam; Balent, A., Vancouver; Baron, A., Haney; Baxter, W. A., Kitimat; Beaddy, W., Richmond; Beam, J., Cranbrook; Bell, R., Agassiz, B.C.; Benson, L. E. Williams Lake, B.C.; Bergstrom, A. B., Fruitvale, B.C.; Blackman, D., Abbotsford, B.C.; Bomford, F., Cobble Hill, B.C.; Bouchard, G., Alberni; Boulier, G., Burnaby; Bowe, N. Burnaby; Bragg, J. D., N. Vancouver; Braun, S. D., Abbotsford; Brett, D., Vancouver; Broad, D. G., Merritt; Browne, J., Sidney; Buchanan, T., Nanaimo; Buchar, W., Smithers; Bukta, R., Abbotsford; Burdett, R. J., Nanaimo; Burrows, L., Vancouver; Busby, T., Kaleden; Buscumb, R., Creston, B.C.; Burton, D., Alberni; Butt, M., Coquitlam.

Cavanaugh, R., N. Vancouver; Chadwick, B., Cassidy, B.C.; Clark, M. J., N. Burnaby; Clarke, W., Port Coquitlam; Clarke, W., Burnaby; Coan, P., Vancouver; Coleman, S. J., Penticton; Colwill, D., Chilliwack; Conconi, R. L., Victoria; Connacher, R. M., Merritt; Connor, R. M., Aldergrove, B.C.; Conway, S. R., N. Vancouver; Coomer. S. R., N. Burnaby; Coombes, L., Vancouver; Crobin, J., Nanaimo; Cornell, M., N. Surrey; Cox, D., Vernon; Cox, R. N., N. Vancouver; Deigard, D. C., Burnaby; Deleenheer. R., Williams Lake; Dem-

535

chuk, R. A., Cranbrook; Dent, J., Alberni; Dettwiller, D. R., N. Wellington, B.C.; Distan, B., Port Coquitlam; Dixon. D., Victoria; Doucette, B., Victoria; Dyson, W., Victoria; Elson, J.. Coquitlam; Escude, V., Victoria; Etherington, R., Vancouver; Farrell, L.; Wellington; Fidler, R.. Duncan; Forrer, R. C., Port Coquitlam; Franssen, G., Vernon; Fredette, R., Telkwa, B.C.; Friend, E., Victoria; Funk, B., Vancouver; Gallagher, N., Kitimat, B.C.; Galpin, R. J., Vancouver; Gass, F., Port Coquitlam; Gaw, D. L., Saanichton; Godber, R. E., N. Vancouver; Grant, K. A., Burnaby; Green, L. W., Victoria; Greengrass, D. W., N. Burnaby; Grieve, M., Kelowna; Glazier, D., Clear Brook, B.C.; Gledhill, R., Mission City; Goly, A. E., Toronto, Ont.; Gorby, J. S., Vancouver; Gorak, Z., Chilliwack; Gordon, D., Courtenay; Gotro, P. E., Vancouver; Haigh, B., Alberni; Hall, E., Abbotsford; Hames, B., Chilliwack; Hankey, D., N. Surrey; Hansen, M., Kitsuksis, B.C.; Hare, R. B., Victoria; Harris, B. R., Vancouver; Harris, R., Chemainus; Heeps, G. C., Vancouver; Hein, W., Chilliwack; Herriott, R., Chilliwack; Herrington, R., Sidney; Holliday D., Victoria; Horrobin, M., Vancouver; Jameson, J., Duncan; Jenkins, L. G., Penticton; Johannson, T. J., Burnaby; Johnson, D., N. Surrey; Jones, T. A., Revelstoke; Joseph, M., New Hazelton.

Kabesh, L., New Westminster; Keil, W., Victoria; Kidd, G., Victoria; Kraus, W. E., Merritt; Kruysifix, P., Victoria; Kvammen, M., Burnaby; Lamothe, F., Coquitlam; Lawley, J., N. Vancouver; Lewicky, G., Burnaby; Leonard, W., Victoria; Logan, D., Cumberland; Lopthien, W. T., Vancouver; Lowney, P. H., White Rock; Low, R. R., Vancouver.

MacGregor, L., Prince George; MacDonald, T., Haney; MacDonald, N. G., Cranbrook; MacLean, D., Vernon; MacDonald, S., Pt. Alberni; McConnell, J., Vancouver; McCulloch, D. B., Haney; McDougall, M., Victoria; McLean, T., Victoria; McMmanus, J., Burnaby; McMmanus, M., Burnaby; McNaughton, D. C. N. Surrey; Magee, D. M., N. Vancouver; Mallach, N., Rutland; Mantel, C., Vancouver; Mason, R., North Vancouver; Mauro, S., N. Vancouver; Merriman, W., New Westminster; Miles, M. B., Victoria; Mills, R., Vancouver; Mills, W., Victoria; Mitchell, D., Comox; Mingay, W., Merritt; Molnar, R., Burnaby; Moore, D. C., Victoria; Moore, W. C., Coquitlam; Morris, J., Sardis; Morrison, D., Richmond; Morrison, R. G., Vancouver; Munsterman, D., Revelstoke; Myers, R., Cultus Lake.

Neal, R., Nanaimo; Nemrava, J., Castlegar; Nielsen, R., Kitimat; Norris, P., Ioco; Nyman, J., New Denver; Oelker, H., Victoria; Olinek, D., Vancouver; Olson, P. J., Alberni; Oisson, J. R., Penticton; Ouellette, L., Vancouver; Paul, R., Hudson Hope; Peeters, J., Victoria; Peterson, M., Victoria; Pfiefer, A. R., Vancouver; Pick, G., Victoria; Pool, F., Summerland; Poulier, G., Burnaby; Powell, D., Williams Lake; Poznackuck, D., Vancouver; Press, G., Vancouver; Price, C., Chilliwack;

Proctor, W., Nelson; Quanstrom, P., Smithers;

Raffelsieper, D., N. Vancouver; Rainer, J., Victoria; Raitt, C., Penticton; Rausch, W. G., Merritt; Renwick, J., Burnaby; Roberge, P., Victoria; Robinson, C., Terrace; Rogers, M., N. Vancouver; Rogers, R. P., N. Vancouver; Rosmus, K. C., N. Vancouver; Rowat, B. E., Vancouver; Ruff, A., Victoria.

Sache, D., Rosedale; Sanderson, C., Quesnel; Scheffer, L., Victoria; Scherger, D., Vancouver; Schifferns, R., New Westminster; Schmidt, J., Kelowna; Scott, C., Victoria; Senum, R., N. Surrey; Shanks, P. A., Oliver; Shaw, R. M., Vancouver; Shirritt, R., Kamloops; Sjoman, P., Terrace Bay; Smith, V., Victoria; Soderberg, C., Oliver; Sorko, G., N. Vancouver; Stewart, J., Penticton; Stainbrook, R., Salmon Arm; Steenvoorden, F., Castlegar; St. Marie, D., Revelstoke; Stobbart, D., Port Alberni.

Tames, L., Nelson; Tanasichuk, A. Richmond; Taylor, T., Haney; Tellier, M., Victoria; Thibeault, R., Revelstoke; Thomas, R. P., Langley; Thompson, W. B., Burns Lake; Timmermans, P., Kitimat; Toms, G., Port Alberni; Walker, J., Quesnel; Watson, E. Summerland; Westad, L. E. Langley; Westerlund, R., Kamloops; White, R., Vancouver; Whitmore, N. P., Vancouver; Whittington, R. A., Port Alberni; Wood, K. J., Haney; Worden, R., Vancouver; Worth, W., Gordon Head; Wozney, D., Vancouver; Wright, R., North Kamloops; Young B., Smithers; Zado, K. W., Vancouver; Zadoroznyj, G., Vernon; Manarey, D., Penticton.

B COY

Achtemichuk, G., Edmonton; Adair, D., Breton, Alta; Aldred, R., Calgary; Balfour, D. L., Ft. St. John; Bambrick, W. J., Red Deer, Alta; Baptiste, R., Hobema, Alta; Beart, A. J., Westlock, Alta; Bedford, T., Calgary; Belanger, E. D., Edgerton, Alta.; Belseck, R. J., Fort St. John; Bennett, R. I., Hinton, Alta.; Boisvert, P. G., Sherwood Park, Alta.; Borshowa, D., Rycroft, Alta.; Buttazzoni, A., Lethbridge; Campbell, B. E., Lousana, Alta.; Cartwright, D., Lacombe, Alta.; Castor, G., Edmonton; Cerney, W. J., Frank, Alta.; Connon, G. A., Innisfail, Alta.; Cronin, R. G., Red Deer; Croteau, K. E., Blairmore, Alta.; Crowell, H., Edmonton; Dade, R. J., Stettler, Alta.; De Meulenare, P., Edmonton; Desharnais, R., Frank; Devenney, T., Edmonton; Dougan, K., Edmonton; Dilts, M. C., Edmonton; Dunlop, B. W., Breton; Dunne, P., Stony Plain, Alta.; Forbes, R. S., Vermillion, Alta.; Foster, T. P., Alder Flat, Alta.; Gaudet, J. J., McMurray, Alta.; Gilbertson, J., Mayerthorpe, Alta.; Gillis, R., Calgary; Gower, J. T., Westlock; Motsch, G., Edmonton; Gylander, G. R., Entwistle, Alta. Harris, R. S., Fort McMurray, Alta.; Hinton, C. R., Fort Smith, Alta.; Hills, S. C., Red Deer; Holton, S. R., Gleichen, Alta.; Hughes, K. F., Sherwood Park; Jerome, F., Inuvik, NWT; Jobb, L., Edmonton; Kay, E., Calgary; Knutson, Fort St. John; Krusel, L. R., Calgary; Kublar, D., Edmonton; Kulikowski, M. J., Edmonton; Kuzmicz, A., Calgary;

536

Laine, R. E., Calgary; Kaglik, Inuvik, NWT; Lafournie, E., Lethbridge; Lamb, B., Calgary; Landry, D., Vimy, Alta.; Larkin, R. J., Edmonton; Logan, D. G., Westlock; Luck, L.. Calgary; Lyons, D., Lousana; Maghagak, A., Cambridge Bay, NWT; Maier. F.. Redcliff, Alta.; McCallion, R., Edmonton; McLaren, Edmonton; Mansell, B., Hay River. NWT; Marcoff, P. M., Edson, Alta.; Marushy, D. M., Greencourt, Alta.; Mayham, C., Hay River; Nichol, R. D., Beaverlodge, Alta.; Nicolls, D., Alder Flats; Orich. B., Lethbridge; Osborne, N., Edmonton.

Phillips, T., Edmonton; Piecharka, L., Innisrail; Roberts, B., Edmonton; Robertson, B., Chetwynd, B.C.; Romsess, R., Lethbridge; Sargent, G., Vegreville; Schwartz, B., Eastpine, B.C.; Senner, D., Spirit River, Alta.; Skrypnck, Edson; Speakman, L., Alder Flats; Staples, R., Sherwood Park; Stoner, C., Spirit River; Tipman, K. J., Edson; Tomazewski, A. S., Sunnybrook, Alta.; Tomaszewski, E. T., Sunnybrook; Tremblay, Redcliff; Truss, R. G., Sedgewick, Alta.; Twerdoff, R. G., Killam, Alta.

Vandenbrink, M., Edmonton; Walker, M. J., Beaverlodge; Ward, J., Edmonton; Warner, E., Red Deer; Weber, J. A., Fort St. John; Williams J., Vermillion, Alta.; Wingay, W., Merritt; Woods, H., Gleichen; Yaceyko, M., Derwent, Alta; Yarmuch, D. T., Derwent; Ziemann, R.. Edmonton; La Roche, J. A., Edmonton; Tuch, G., Hillcreast, Alta.; Baer, A. M., Whitehorse.

C COY

Amanuik, T., Regina; Andres, W., Moose Jaw; Arcand, M., Leask, Sask.; Armbruster, R., Melville, Sask.; Atton, P. N., Saskatoon; Backman, T., Melville; Bakoway, J. S., Saskatoon; Ballendine, H. W., North Battleford, Sask.; Binns, B. R., Yarbo, Sask.; Brecht, W., Humboldt, Sask.; Brewster, L., Prince Albert, Sask.; Bunnah, C. R., Lac Vert, Sask.; Burnett, J., Battleford, Sask.; Bye, D. A., Naicam, Sask.; Campbell, L. J., Swift Current, Sask..; Carleton, M. D., Neville, Sask.; Christians, H., Kindersley, Sask.; Clark, R. A., Swift Current; Clelland, T. W., Weyburn, Sask.; Cockburn, K. J., Turtleford, Sask.; Davidson, E., Melfort, Sask.; Dean, R. L., Invermay, Sask.; Dickson, G. A., Moose Jaw; Dubois, W. D., Moscow, Sask.; Durnin, M. P., Regina; Fisher, P., Madena, Sask.; Fraser, P. C., Regina; Gosselin, R., Moose Jaw; Gryba, P. L., Invermay; Head, K., Saskatoon; Hill, G., Swift Current; Hoegi, W. E., Rose Valley, Sask.; Ingram, L. R., Spruce Lake, Sask.; Inkster, R. A., Battleford; Hagen, W., Invermay.

Jestin, G. A., Naicam; Johansson, D. E., Saskatoon; Johnson, K. L., Regina; Johnston, B. E., Kerrobert, Sask.; Klimosko, B., Humboldt; Kopeck, B., Regina; Kunkel, P. Esterhazy, Sask.; Lamb, J., Prince Albert; Larose, L. M., Battleford; Lawrence, J. M., Turtleford; Lenton, K. R., Regina; Levitt, R. C., Saskatoon; Lilly, J., Esterhazy; Livingstone, D. E., Rosetown, Sask.; Lix, B. R., Weyburn, Sask.; McMillan, K. J., Melfort; McDonald R. A., Carrot River, Sask.;

McLaughlin, B., Regina; McLean, G. C., Melville; McLean, S. W., Big River, Sask.; McDonald, N., Kerrobert, Sask.; McWillie, D. J., Saskatoon; Melander, R. A., Moose Jaw; Melton, L., Regina; Mercereau, R., Marcelin, Sask.; Michaud, D., St. Walburg, Sask.; Moberg, E. G., Yorkton, Sask.; Molnar, T. A., Yorkton; Morgan, C., Saskatoon; Moroz, A., Wadena, Sask.; Murphy B. W., Prince Albert; Murphy, J., Carrot River; Nagy, K. W., Yorkton; Nagy, L. J., Yorkton; Neill, W., Melville; Nycholat, E. H., Fosston, Sask.; Pawelko, M. B., Esterhazy, Sask.; Penner, D. J., Saskatoon; Peterson, C., North Battleford; Phillips, L. A., Moose Jaw; Proll, D. A., Lac Vert.

Reid, D., Melville; Riseing, E. C., North Battleford; Rose, W. R., Sturgiss, Sask.; Sali, K. E., Regina; Seibel, A. J., Regina; Seidel, D., Kindersley; Shary, S., Wadena; Shirley, J., Kelvingston, Sask.; Shule, T. J., Saskatoon; Simpson. G. R., Weyburn; Skafte, S. B., Speers, Sask.; Smith, R. E., Saskatoon; Stein, F., Big River; Szmorog, J., Regina; Trenchard, D.. Melville; Trotchie, R., Saskatoon; Tsakires, N., Regina; Ursel, D. F., Glenella. Man.; Walker, B. R., Moose Jaw; Walker, R. E., Prince Albert; Wiser. L., Turtleford; Wiwcharuk, L. G., Usherville, Sask.; Zeigler, J.. Battleford; La Fond, L. B., Marcelin, Sask.

D COY

Andrew, A. N., Kelwood, Man.; Arnott, A. E., Winnipeg; Bain, R. G., Winnipeg; Ball, G., St. James. Man.; Beaudry, R., Winnipeg; Benedet, D., Fort William; Bourgeois, P., Power View, Man.; Bourret, J., Fort Arthur; Bozzo, R., Port Arthur; Burke, A., Fort William; Cambell, B. W., Winnipeg; Cameron, B., Winnipeg; Camphaug, C., Fort Churchill, Man.; Cason, J. H., Gilbert Plains, Man.; Cote, R., Dauphin, Man.; Crookes, R., Atikokan, Ont.; D'Andrea, L., Fort William; Davis, R., Virden, Man.; Dayholos, W. F., Glenella, Man.; Dowhy, J., Fort William; Downie, P., St. Bonniface, Man.; Dueck, D. W., Altona, Man.; Dufault, A. P., Dauphin.

Favreau, T. M., Kenora, Ont.; Fostey, R. A., Emerson, Man.; Fraser, C., Winnipeg; Gardner, F., Emerson; Giest, J., Flin Flon, Man.; Gionet, R., Marathon, Ont.; Graham, D., Atikokan; Graham, J., Marathon; Grisdale, L. J., Scanterbury, Man.; Grisdale, R., Fort Alexander, Man.; Grouette, P., Dinorwic, Ont.; Grover, L.. Port Arthur; Guimond, A., Ft. Alexandra, Man.; Guimond, N., Ft. Alexandra; James, B., Ft. Alexandra; Jameson, R., Winnipeg; Johnston, M., Emerson; Hotas, B. L., Fort Churchill; Haggerty, C. S., Shilo, Man.; Harrison, D., Winnipeg; Hiller, R., Schreiber, Ont.; Hogarth, D. F., Flin Flon; Kirkby, T., Fort William; Korpan, C., Dauphin; Kullman, D., West Kildonan, Man.; Learmonth, K. D., Winnipeg; Lejeune, D., Dryden, Ont.; Lilley, C. E., Portage La Prairie, Man.; McCormack, B., Winnipeg; McEwen, R. D., Virden; McGregor, D., Flin Flon; McKinstry, D. W.. Port Arthur; McKie, J. J., Fort William; McParland, N. P., Schreiber, Ont.; Maki, T., Atikokan; Martei, R. A., Altona, Man.; Martin, J. W., Schreiber; Martin, I. J., Schreiber; Miller, D. C., Pine Falls, Man.; Miller, E. G., Winnipeg; Mitchell, W. W., Fort Garry, Man.; Moshonsky, R. P., Fort William; Murphy, T. J., Kenora, Ont.

Nelson, L., Altona; Pirie, P. E., Keewatin, Ont.; Robb, G. A., Dauphin; Robinson, L. E., Dryden, Ont.; Robinson, R. A., Fort Garry; Ross, N. G., Marathon; Rychkrand, W. C., Winnipeg; Salamondra, W. D., Creighton, Man.; Sawchyn, J. F., Pine Falls; Schwark, W. R., Emerson; Serkin, H. F., Winnipeg; Shaffer, W. S., Shilo; Stinson, M. G., Virden; Styan, J. W., Winnipeg; Temple, X., Portage La Prairie; Turbide, R., Dryden; Urbanski, W. C., Balmertown, Ont.; Watson, S., Pine Falls; Webster, A., Virden; Westerby, R., Atitkokan; Williams, H. J. Flin Flon; Wilson, D. K., Kelwood, Man.; White, J., Atikokan; Wissian, A., Port Arthur; Wylie, W. A., Portage La Prairie; Zubrecki, D., Red Lake, Ont.

E COY

Anderson, L. D., Winnipeg; Anderson, R. T., White Rock, B.C.; Antonation, J. W., Brandon; Armstrong, J. G., Calgary; Baker, M. A., Victoria; Berrow, G. B., Powell River; Bevans, C. A., Lillooet; Bighetty, P. E., Puketawagan, Man.; Billing, R. H., North Surrey; Bomhoff, H., Winnipeg; Botting, R. W., Winnipeg; Bourgeois, R. M., Transcona, Man.; Brown, C. D., Calgary; Burtniak, D., Stony Mountain, Man.; Byron, P. J., Burnaby; Campbell, J. A., Black Diamond, Alta.; Carriere, K. G., Cumberland House, Sask.; Chretien, J. C., New Westminster; Coccola, A. J., Powell River; Cook, E. N., Cumberland House, Sask.; Cook, P. E., Cumberland House; Coombes, P. J., Hudson Bay, Sask.; Craig, B. G., Naicom; Crawford, R. G., North Surrey; Davidson, D. D., New Westminster; England, G. R., Winnipeg; England, L. N., Winnipeg; England, R. K., Winnipeg; Erickson, S. E., White Rock; Essex, A. J., White Rock; Fosseneuve, M. G., Cumberland House; Fouquette, A. P., New Westminster; Gee, R D., Invermere, B.C.; Goertzen, L. P., North Surrey; Gillespie, M. A., Calgary; Glaseman, L. O., Brandon; Greene, L. C., Calgary.

Hancock, R. J., Calgary; Hart, H. S., Norway House, Man.; Hayward, R. R., White Rock; Hussey, A. R., Winnipeg; James. R. M., Calgary; James. T. M., Lillooet; Jones, E. D., Fort Macleod; Krasniuk, B. M., East Kildonan; Kucherka, G., Port Arthur; Lane, D. J., Medicine Hat; Lawrence, C E., Calgary; Lawrence, D. F., Brandon; Leslie, R. D., Brandon; MacLeod, M. J., Calgary; McLaren, G. D., Calgary; Mahe, S. L., Calgary; Makowski, S. L., Calgary; Maynard, D., Victoria; Meise, F. F., Prince George; Michel, P. J., Winnipeg; Moulaison, D. W., White Rock; Neall, R. A., North Surrey; Nickerson, W. P., Calgary; Nilsen, S. K., North Surrey; Normand, D. P., Calgary.

Olson, J. N. Vancouver, Pollock,

G. A., Pincher Creek, Alta.; Prior, W. M., White Rock; Pyun, S., Brandon; Rasmussen, D. G., Calgary; Rasmussen, D. G., Calgary; Richard, J. R., North Surrey; Richardson, J. A., Fort Macleod; Roe, K. R., Calgary; Robinson, E. C., White Rock; Roger, W. C., Ladner; Sandall, R. C., White Rock; Scott, G. W., Victoria; Stangler, D. W., Medicine Hat; Stelmach, R A., Transcona, Man.; Stewart, D J, North Surrey; Streerup, B. H., Calgary; Sutherland, G. C., Calgary; Sutherland, M. R., White Rock; Sutherland, R. K., White Rock; Panas, R. D., Prince George; U'ren, W. P., North Surrey; Vanclieaf, T. B., Medicine Hat; Vicic, S. R, Fernie; Watkins, W A., Medicine Hat; Webber, H. J., Victoria; Webster, T. K., Fernie; Wigman, R. H., White Rock; Wilkinson, D. A., Dryden; Williams, C. E., Ladner; Lozinske, L. E., Hudson Bay, Sask.; Attig, R. L., North Surrey.

F COY

Abbott, R., Atikokan; Appleby, R., Vancouver; Banbar, J. J., Calgary; Berg, E. P., Rosthern, Sask.; Bernat, R., Moose Jaw; Blaquiele, E. J., Redcliff; Boen, L. J., Melfort; Brown, R., Edmonton; Buchenauer, Kelowna; Buikeme, F., Black Diamond; Campbell, S., Sherwood Park; Carlsen, G., Victoria; Chambers, D., Turtleford; Clark, B. D., Waterways, Alta.; Clark, S. A., Shilo; Man.; Clease, G. E., Beaverlodge, Alta.; Coates, G. R., Nakusp; Coates, L., Kindersley; Collin, G. M., Edson; Compain, L. E., Winnipeg; Conly, T. M., Weyburn, Sask.; Crown, D. M., Fort William; Cuppen, J. C., Fort Macleod; Dart, D. M., Beaverlodge; Deane, L. J., Winnipeg; Deslauriers, P. J., New Westminster; Dueck, R. B., Abbotsford; Edwards, P. L., N. Vancouver; Evans, D. R., Revelstoke; Ewashkiw, R. D., Derwent; French, R., N. Burnaby.

Galpin, J. M., Entwistle, Alta.; Garneau, E. R., Fernie; Garner, G. E., Haney; Gifford, T. A., Haney; Goodhew, D. A., Saskatoon; Graham, R. D., Victoria; Green, L. K., Winnipeg; Guenther, G. P., Dryden, Ont.; Guest, L., Rossington, Alta.; Hahn, J., White Rock; Halstead, D. J., North Surrey; Hansford, W. D., Burnaby; Haniliak, G., Cambridge Bay, NWT; Hannah, P. J., Prince Albert; Hanson, A. D., North Surrey; Herbert, V., Atikokan; Hickey, W. A., Vedder Crossing, B.C.; Hilgers, R. M., Bruno, Sask.; Hinton, T. W., Fort Smith, NWT; Hobbs, R., Emerson; Hodgson, J. L., McKenzie Island, Ont.; Houghton, V. R., Winnipeg; Jackson, I. R., Abbotsford; Jeffery, G. A., Calgary; Johnson, A. G., Edmonton; Johnson K. B., Winfield, Alta.; Kacan, C. W., Balmertown; Kempf, T. M., Vancouver; Kennedy, R. T., Port Moody; Kish, K., Regina; Kunkel, L., Lapointe, L. W., Saskatoon; Lerohl, A. W., Mayerthorpe, Alta.; Lopata, S. S., Winnipeg; Love, D. W., Calgary.

MacKinnon, D. A., Port Arthur; McArthur, D. F., Fort Churchill; McCallum, R. L., Rosetown; McCartney, R. A., Fort St. John; McClay, K. T., Vancouver; McCutcheon, B. D., Fruitvale, B.C.; McDonald, T. A.,

538

Calgary; Madsen, D. S., Rutland; Manyluk, D. F., Vermilion; Mason, M. S., Victoria; Mazyn, A. H., Hafford, Sask.; Menzies, R. M., Vancouver; Misura, R., Coleman, Alta. Moorey, D., Schreiber; Naylor, B., Calgary; Nokony, D., Kerrobert, Sask.; Normoyle, K., Vancouver; Oliver, J., Wadena, Sask.; Pattenaude, M. New Westminster; Peddie, P. D., Lethbridge; Penny, D., Virden, Man.; Perry, N., Innisfail; Reilly, G.A., Calgary; Resch, R. J., Medicine Hat; Royle, P. J., Victoria; Rudrum, J. W., Fruitvale.

Sampson, R. D., Edmonton; Sanche, A., Marcelin, Sask; Sanderson, L. A., Stony Plain; Sanna, J., Balmertown; Sarnecki, D. D., Calmar, Alta.; Sexton, D. A., Winnipeg; Shemko, R., Pincher Creek; Smith, K. A., Vancouver; Smith, R., Nakusp; Sombrutski, B., Dryden; Spiess, R., Vancouver; Sproat, H., Milestone, Sask.; Stewardson, J. W., Lebret, Sask.; Strom, D., Cumberland House, Sask.; Strachan, J. H., Cumberland, B.C..; Stutt, O., Edmonton; Sutton, H. J., Calgary; Swanson, E. E., Creston; Tait, R. R., Hudson Bay, Sask.; Tolonen, R., Lacombe, Alta.; Tootoosis, M., Hobbema, Alta.; Weir, R. M., Cumberland; Wénarchuk, E. U., Flin Flon; Wojcik, A. L., Kelvington, Sask.; Wolkie, P., Tuktoyaktuk, N.W.T.,; Wood R. A., North Surrey; Wright, P. E., Richmond, B.C.

G COY

Adams, D. J., Edmonton; Alberts, A., Regina; Anderson, K., Coquitlam; Armstrong, B. C., Abbotsford; Ashdohunk, J., Sintaluta, Sask.; Bablitz, H. A., Edmonton; Bakke, K., Atikokan; Bahr, R., Calgary; Bergeron, E., Winnipeg; Bethel, R., Regina; Bodenchuk, D. A., Edson; Boisvert, R., Sherwood Park; Boiteau, D., McCreary, Man.; Boasch, G., Port Arthur; Bourgeois, J., Transcona; Briscoe, W. G., Fort St. John; Chasson, J., Marathon; Chipeur, D. V., Red Deer; Connacher, A., Merritt; Cook, D. W., Calgary; Crawford, R. D., Camp Shilo; Croffard, R., Kindersley; Crouch, R. A., Victoria; Cunnington, R. N., Winnipeg; Derbowka, J., Wroxton, Sask.; Dermody, D. J., Milestone, Sask.; Doan, W. S., Mervin, Sask.; Dueck, D., Winnipeg; Duncan, R. D., Winnipeg; Eddington, W., Vancouver; Fedorko, R., Winnipeg; Ferrie, M., Invermay; Fletcher. C., Lethbridge; Freeborn, L., Marathon; Gaidosh, W., Winnipeg; Gass, C. I., Beaverlodge; George, P., Winnipeg; Gibson, G. W., Gleichen; Gilbert, L., Moose Jaw; Gordon, P., Courtenay; Grant, D., Lethbridge.

Halliday, J. W., Flin Flon; Hambley, S., Victoria; Hansen, R. I., Regina; Hastings, D. G., Dryden; Hayter, J., North Vancouver; Hendy, D. B., Abbotsford; Hegan, T. D., Melville; Hills, I. G. Red Deer; Holmes, A., Ladner; Holomego, M., Port Arthur; Hughes, R., Sherwood Park; Hunter, A. D., Edson; Jealous, G. R., Cranbrook; Johnson, J. A., Paswegin, Sask.; Johnson, M. D., Moose Jaw; Jones, D., Saskatoon; Josephson, R., Vancouver; Kalenchuk, C., Hyas, Sask.; Kelly, Virden; Kimball, D., Edgerton; Kinnear, J.

G., Vancouver; Kitson, B., North Kamloops; Kitteringham, D. B., Creighton; Kostiuk, D. J., Saskatoon; Laduranteay, A., Edmonton; Laflamme, L., Edmonton; Laursen, B., Virden; Lemon, B. W., Milestone; Leniuk, D., Rose Valley; Leveille, R. M., Breton, Alta.; Loeder, H., Edmonton; Loutitt, R., Yorkton; Lusk, K. E., Haney; Machek, P., Victoria; McLeod, R. A., Pine Falls, Man.; Mellon, Calgary; MacPhee, F. J., Rusylvia, Alta.; Malyk, G., Dryden; Meachem, K., Carrot River; Meilicke, G., Burnaby; McAra, M. N., Victoria; McBride, W., Sedgewick; McNeill, J., Kenora; Milligan, J., Big River, Sask.; Mitton, R., Calgary; Mulrooney, D., Red Deer; Murphy, G. R., Kitimat; Neill, P., Melville; Nicholson, B., North Surrey; Nicolson, R. A., Winnipeg; Niemi, K. O., Port Arthur; Nimitz, R., Regina; Norton, B. N., Winnipeg; Novokowsky, B. J., Saskatoon; Paterson, D., Port Alberni; Payne, D., Lousana; Pearson, B. K., Minnedosa, Man.; Pickering, J. D., Winnipeg; Purves, C., Port Arthur.

Rioux, D. C., Camp Shilo; Ror, R., Weyburn; Reinson, W. D., Melville; Rossetti, L., Calgary; Rothenburger, R. W., Port Arthur; Rushton, M. W., Kenora; Ryder, F., Lebret, Sask.; Sass, K., Kelowna; Saul, K. W., Fort St. John; Sawatzky, D. R., Shilo; Schultz, G., Edson; Schneider, D., Regina; Scoullar, H. S., Prince George; Siegfried, D. R., Port Arthur; Shiloff, F., Brandon; Simmons, K., Wadena, Sask.; Smith, D. J., North Surrey; Smith M. G., Edmonton; Snelgrove, W. S., Winnipeg; Stamm, R., Vancouver; Stengel, H., North Surrey; Stephens, D., Fort St. Johr; Stuby, R. G., Fort St. John; Stern, N. M., Swift Current; Swan, M., Calgary.

Tippe, M., Swift Current; Trayling, D. M., Burnaby; Warriner, D., Big River, Sask.; Waters, C. I., Duncan; Watson, P. A., Pine Falls, Man.; Weiss, S. J., North Surrey; Weiszner, N., Winnipeg; Westerby, R. B., Atikokan, Ont.; White, G., Atikokan; Williams, C. S., Stonewall, Man.; Wilson, D., Calgary; Wozniak, M., Melville, Sask.; Wright, D., Swift Current; Young, B., Calgary; Zastre, F. E., Winnipeg; Zest, Winnipeg.

J COY

Andruniak, F., Minnedosa, Man.; Balzer, L. K., Saskatoon; Beaudoin, F. R., Trail; Braybrook, R. L., Yarbo, Sask.; Brown, R. F., Pine Falls; Bryar, L. J., Marathon, Ont.; Cant, S. F., Vancouver; Cunningham, W. R., Manitoba; Duhamal, D. H., Atikokan; Giberson, D., Haney; Groome, D., Sherwood Park; Herrington, D. L., Melville; Jackson, P. A., Penticton; Jahn, A. W., Coleman; Kunkel, L. D., Esterhazy, Sask.; Lindquist, R. S., Dryden, Ont.; MacKenzie, W., Vancouver; Mailhiot, R. A., Calgary; Markstrom, L. R., Revelstoke; Mohs, G., Merritt; O'Rourke, P. M., Fernie; Pleasants, L. J., North Surrey; Popp, K., Flin Flon; Reid, R. I., Crescent, B.C.; Robertson, G. C., Calgary; Ross, P. J., Marathon; Shineton, R. E., McCreary, Man.; Stadnyk, S., Virden, Man.; Summerville, P., Sturgis, Sask.; Ward, W. J., McCreary.

539

Berridge, M. E., Winnipeg; Bigelow, C. A., Gleichen, Alta.; Bittle, A. K., Shilo; Bourgeault, L. J., Weyburn; Bradlie, H. F., Big River; Brown, J. D., Fruitvale; Buysen, J. A., Sherwood Park; Buysen, W. C., Sherwood Park; Chaykowski, S. M., Wadena, Sask.; Chorney, E. M., Wadena; Collisson, A. F., Winfield, Alta.; Connon, R. N., Innisfail, Alta.; Decoteau, R. P., Calgary; Fane, F. W. J., Vegreville, Alta.; Gerow, W. G., Big River, Sask.; Glass, S., Richmond; Greentree, D. G., McCreary; Hald, F., Red Lake, Ont.; Hankins, C. B., Summerland, B.C.; Johnson, R. W., Victoria; Larson, B. L., Fosston, Sask.; Leicht, J. D., Innisfail, Alta.; Lesko, W. F., Shady Lake, Sask.; Lister, R. B., Vancouver; MacDonald, R. A., Brookdale, Man.; MacDonald, R. A., Chemainus; McGregor, A., Nelson; McKimmie, G. S., Mayerthorpe, Alta.; McTaggart, K. J., Revelstoke; Maxwell, H. G., N. Vancouver; Moffat, A. M., Regina; Mosser, R. B., Prince George; Moxham, R. B., Fort St. John, B.C.; Pennie, B. K., N. Vancouver; Premack, M. P., North Surrey; Poitras, L. S., Winnipeg; Rose. P. E., Victoria; Schneider, C., Flin Flon; Scott, R. F., Chilliwack; Shandro, B. W., Vegreville; Thomson, K. W., Moose Jaw; Treadway, T., Kenora; Walker, J. H., Pine Falls, Man.; Witherly, C. R., Sherwood Park; Zwicker, R. N., Hillcrest, Alta.

VACC - 1968

Aamundsen, C., Weyburn; Abbott, Wm., Edgerton, Alta. Acheson, C., Innisfail, Alta.; Achtimichuk, G., Edmonton, Adams, J., Mayerthorpe, Alta. Aitken, G., Chilliwack, Akerlay, B., Shilo, Man.; Aleck R. T., Vancouver, Allen, R., Haney, Allingham, M. M., Winnipeg, Ambock, H., Calmar, Alta. Anakaer, G. M., Regina, Anderson, J., Vancouver, Anderson, D., Winnipeg, Anderson D. New Westminster; Anderson, J. R., Fort William, Ont., Anderson, L., Atikokan, Anderson, R., Winnipeg, Andrew, J. D., Winnipeg; Andrews, G., White Rock; Angell, Coquitlam; Ansell, K., Haney, Anthony, R. D., Kelvingston; Antonius, T., Winnipeg; Arcand, E. W., North Battleford; Archibald, B. Vedder Crossing, B.C.; Appleton, G., North Surrey, B.C.; Archibald, W. Chilliwack; Armstrong, R., Abbotsford, Attig, F., North Surrey; Attley, D., Churchill; Aucalair, E., Coquitlam; B.C.

Bablitz, R., Edmonton; Backman, W. A., Brandon; Bagg, A., Calgary; Ball, L., Langley; Balmer, E., Churchill; Banadyga, L. M., Kelvington, Sask.; Barber, D., Victoria; Barcelo, D., Victoria; Barnard, L. F., Atikokan, Ont.; Barnowsky, D. G., Hafford, Sask.; Barettee, D., Chetwyn; Barteski, K. B., Engermay; Bastke, K., Port Coquitlam; Baugh, R. A., Red Deer; Beasant, M. A., Kenora; Beckett, R. E., Vermillion; Bedea, P., Calgary; Bedry, R., Blairmore; Begoray, J., Edson; Belanger, R., Calgary; Belseck, R., Ft. St. John; Bemis, H. W., Swift Current; Bennett, D., Calgary; Bennett, R., Hinton; Berezon, D., Westlock; Bertstrom, A., Fruitvale; Berrow, G.,

Powell River; Bessette, M., Vancouver; Bierman, H., Chemanus; Bigler, M. L., Rosevalley, Sask.; Billing V., North Surrey; Bilous, D., Ruskin; Binks, B. W., Victoria; Bird, A. T., Portage LaPrairie, Man.; Bird, G., North Vancouver; Black, L. D., Weyburn, Sask.; Blackall, J. N., Vancouver; Blair, B., Sherwood Park, Alta.; Blewett, T., White Rock; Bodenchuk, W. J., Edson;; Bogart, M., Edmonton; Boiteau, L. D., McCreary, Man.; Boivin, G. M., New Westminster; Boles, S., North Surrey; Bonnell, M. L., Vancouver; Boon, F. R., Red Deer; Bordeleau, D. A., Delta, B.C.; Bos, H., North Surrey; Bosch, D., Sherwood Park, Alta.; Boulding, K. P., Saskatoon; Boyd, D., Strathmore, Alta.; Bradshaw, A. E., Winnipeg; Brassard, R., Abbotsford, B.C.; Bridges, J., Burnaby; Brin, A., Kamloops; Brochu, R., Hammond; Brown, A., Texada Island, B.C.; Brown. B., Vancouver; Brown, J., Vancouver; Bryce, L., North Surrey; Buchanan, R., Kindersley; Bugg, W., Melville, Sask.; Burchill, K., North Vancouver; Burnett, P. J., Battleford; Buscumb, R., Creston; Burnett, G., Calgary.

Callioux, J. A., Hinton; Cameron, E., Duck Lake City, Sask.; Cameron, M, New Westminster; Campaigne, L., Calgary; Campbell, K., Fruitvale; Cancelliere, D., Revelstoke; Carnegie, I. B., Edmonton; Caron, S., Ladner; Carr, D., Evansburg; Carriere, C. M., Cumberland House; Carruthers, K., Kinistino; Carter, D., Campbell River; Cartwright, R. J., Lacombe; Cheran, E., Innisfail; Chinn, K., Edmonton; Chipman, M., Nakusp; Chipman, R., Port Alberni; Churchwell, G. D., Prince Albert; Cisar, J. L., Pincher Creek, Alta.; Clare, R., Narathon, Ont.; Clark, A. J., North Vancouver; Clark, G. D., Hinton; Clark M., North Burnaby; Clark. S. G., Brandon; Clark, S., Swift Current; Clark, S., Shilo; Clayton, M. R., La Prairie; Cleland, S., Invermere; Clements, G., White Rock; Colwell, R. A., Swift Current, Connacher, R. M., Merritt; Connelly, M., North Surrey; Couch. G. L., Dauphin, Man.; Cousins, A., Chilliwack; Craddock, R., Edson; Crofford, C., Moose Jaw; Cuthbert, A. F., Portage La Praire; Cyr, M., Pine Falls; Cameron, K. W., Boniface Man.

Dade, R. J., Stettler; Daintrey, D. J., Saskatoon; Dale, D. J., Moose Jaw; Dance, P., Vancouver; Davidson, M., Port Alberni; Davies, C., Vancouver; Dean, D., Pine Falls; Dean R., Invermay, Sask.; Deegan, T., Vancouver; Demchuk, R., Cranbrook; Dennis, M. E., Calgary; Desaulnier, D. J., Dryden, Ont.; Des Roches, B., White Rock; Detta, J., Silverton; Deveau, G. D., Haney; Devito, J., Terrace, B.C.; Dey, L. A., Swift Current, Sask. Diamond, D. A., Victoria; Dober, W., Edmonton; Dobo, P. S., Vancouver; Dolen, P., Ft. St. John; Donald, R. J., Humbolt; Donnelly, H., Abbottsford; Draffin, R. J., Winnipeg; Duclos, D., Pine Falls, Man., Duff, M. W., Prince Albert; Dunlop, R. D., Brenton, Alta; Durston, G. K., Brandon; Dwolinsky, G. A., Port Alberni; Dufault, A., Dauphin; Dunford, B. E., Calgary; Dunlop, B., Brenton, Alta.; Dunn, P., North Vancouver; Durrer, A., Haney; Eagles, E., Merritt; Eaton, K. J., Victoria; Edmunds, G. B., Edmonton;

Edwards, P. L., North Vancouver; Elmer, F. P., Calgary; Eisler, A. J., Regina; Ellefson, M. W., Burnaby; Elmes, S. J., Vancouver; Elton, L. T., Saskatoon; Lesley, A., Edmonton; Engerdahl, W. B., Haney; Erb, D. P., Weyburn; Essex, J. T., White Rock; Evoy, D. M., Edmonton; Farmer, K. L., Dryden, Ont.; Fenwick, D. R., Flin Flon; Ferguson, J. D., North Surrey; Ferguson, T. J., Port Alberni Finlay, R. D., Yorkton, Sask.; Finnerty, G. J., Vancouver; Fisher, S. M., Black Diamond; Flemminks, F., Calgary; Fleury, E. J., Fort William; Flood, D. B., Vedder Crossing, B.C.; Forseth, R. C., Weyburn; Forsythe, D. S., Vancouver; Fosseneuve, M., Cumberland House, Sask.; Fosseneuve, P. G., Cumberland House; Foster, B., Winnipeg; Foster, D. K., Calgary; Fouchier, E., Madsen; Fradsham, B., Drayton; Freilinger, R. J., Saskatoon; Frost, A. E., Port Arthur; Fuller, C. D., Victoria; Fuller, D. J., Invermere; Fuller, L. J., Saskatoon; Fuller, T., Sarcee, Calgary.

Gagnon, W. E., Moose Jaw; Gale, K., Fernie; Gale, L., Vancouver; Gallagher, P. A., Powell River; Gallant, M. G., Marathon; Garbutt, G. W., Vernon; Gardosch, G., Winnipeg; Gelette, G., Creston; Genaille, V. M., Aleza Lake; Genest, K. R., Moose Jaw; George, A. K., Oyama; Gerolamy, G. J., Emerson; Getty, T., Winnipeg; Gilderdale, G. W., Merritt; Gillispie, M., Calgary; Glaseman, D. L., Brandon; Glebe, A. F., Ruskin; Godlien, L., Invermere; Gorak, Z. B., Chilliwack; Gorjeu, M. A., Vananda; Gorog, J., Winnipeg; Grant, M., Cranbrook; Gransley, R. J., Port Arthur; Graves, W. A., Antigonish, Nova Scotia; Gray, L. M., Vancouver; Grazier, W. J., Ladner; Green, L. K., Winnipeg; Green, T. D., Salmon Arm; Greene, L., Calgary; Griffiths, D. H., Burnaby; Greyba, P., Invermay; Guimond, A. R., Pine Falls, Man.; Guimond, N. J., Pine Falls; Gustafson, K. R., Burnaby; Guttormson, L. A., Naicam, Sask.

Hahn, J., White Rock; Hahn, H., White Rock; Hall, L., Abbotsford; Hallikainen, A. L., Saskatoon; Halverson, R. A., Calgary; Halverson, T. E., Calgary; Halyk, L. D., Melville; Hambley, J., Victoria; Hancock, R. J., Calgary; Hanel, L. J., Saskatoon; Hansen, P. J., Waterways; Hanson, D. C., Vancouver; Harder, D. F., Eston, Sask.; Harmer, J. B., Fort St John; Harper, P. B., North Surrey; Harris B. R., Vancouver; Harris, D. G., Calgary; Harrison, G. L., Haney; Harrison, L. R., Haney; Harrison, R. V., Salmon Arm; Hart, P. B. K., Calgary; Hartmann, R. J., Edmonton; Hawkins, J. T., Sherwood Park; Hayward, R. R., White Rock; Hendley, H. E., Vedder Crossing; Henessy, B. L. M., Shilo; Henriksen, D. G., Cranbrook; Henry, M. R., Haney; Heron, J. R., Stony Plain, Alta.; Hetherington, C., Vancouver; Heitanen, T. L., Port Arthur; Hill, D., Breton, Alta; Hill, G., White Rock; Hills, S. C., Red Deer; Hinton, L. C., Pine Point, N.W.T.; Hitchings, J. E., Hinton; Hoff, H. E., Prince George; Hugaboam G. L., Nakusp; Holgate, B. L., Salmon Arm; Holmberg, Sturgess; Holmes, Victoria; Honig, W. F., Weyburn; Horkey, J. A. J., Shilo; Horvat, S., Port Alberni; Hoskyda, D. A., Vancouver; Howard, B. D., Kelwood; Howeihe, F., Sedgewick;

Humphrey, W., Abbotsford; Hutchings, M., Victoria; Hufsmith, D. A., Vancouver; Huston, R. W., Merritt; Houwing, J., Edmonton; Inkster, R. A., Battleford; Irwin, J., Regina. Jackson, A. M., Victoria; Jackson, H. R., Haney; Jackson, I., Abbotsford; Jakubowski, D., Fort William; Jang, D. A., Vancouver; Jensen, A., Saskatoon; Johnson, D., Edmonton; Johnson, R., North Vancouver; Johnson, W., Prince Albert; Johnston, B., Great Falls; Jones, D. W., Nakusp; Jones, J. R., Chilliwack; Jordon, R., Calgary. Kancan, C. W., Balmertown, Ont.; Keddie, R., Portage La Prairie; Kelly, M., Marathon; Kennedy, J., Port Arthur; Kennedy, R. J., Fort MacLeod; Kerr, B., Millet, Alta.; Kerr, P. V., Winnipeg; Kidd, G., Victoria; Kingston, G. H., Chilliwack; Kirby, G., Victoria; Klyne, R., Erinferry; Kirby, K. N., Vancouver; Kleefeld, W., Regina; Klein, D., Calgary; Knipstrom, B., Burnaby; Knutson, R., Ft. St. John; Koczwarski, R., White Rock; Kohlman, D., Humble, Sask.; Kohnen, F., Redcliff, Alta.; Koronko, B. A., Vernon; Kozar, A., Flin Flon; Kulyk, G., Wedgin, Sask.

Labach, K. A., Big River, Sask.; Lacey, R., Churchill; Lafournie, E. T., Lethbridge; Lamb, B., Calgary; Lampert, R., Revelstoke; Landry, V., Vimmy, Alta.; Lane, R., White Rock; Lane, R., Calgary; Langenberg, T., Lethbridge; Lapierre, D. J. P., Coquitlam; Laprette, W., Vermilion; La-Rose, L., Battleford; Lauinger, C., Crowbutt, Sask.; Lavalley, E., Regina; Law, W. C., Black Diamond; Lawrence, D. E., Brandon; Legrand, R., Calgary; Leight, H., Innisfail; Lenton, K., Regina; Lepore, L., Vancouver; Leray, L., Prince Albert; Lerminiausx, L., Edmonton; Lerohl, M. L., Mayerthorpe, Alta.; Leslie, J., Vancouver; Letain, D., Edmonton; Light, G., Port Arthur; Logan, D., Westlock, Alta.; Loeser, C. W., Vancouver, Lopata, S. S., Winnipeg; Love, D. W., Calgary; Loyer, M., Frank, Alta.; Loyer, P., Frank; Luchuk, D., Winnipeg; Lukowski, J., Drayton; Lynn, D. W., Victoria.

MacDonald, C. R., Turtleford, Sask. MacDonald, T. O., Haney; MacDonald, T. E., Haney; Macfarlane, C. J., Turtleford; Machek, P., Victoria; MacKinnon, D. A., Port Arthur; MacLean, R. J., Victoria; MacLeod, J. C., Vancouver, MacLeod, R. M., Coquitlam; Madsen, A. H., North Battleford; Mahaits, G. C., Coquitlam; Mahoney, M., Comox; Malach, R. L., Yorkton; Malcolm, P. T., Winnipeg; Malysh, J. P., Vernon; Marand, D. P., Winnipeg; Marshall, P. D., Regina; Marriott, W. H., Vancouver; Marocchi, D. R., Port Alberni; Martens, G. W., Winnipeg; Martin, C. S., Chetwynd; Mason, J., Vancouver; Mealings, R. M., Vancouver; Melnick, W. G., Edmonton; Melnychuk, G. M., Sturgis, Sask.; Menzul, R. D., Vancouver; Melo, F. J., Pincher Creek, Alta.; Mercereau, R. C., Macelin, Sask.; Meyer, K. W., Sherwood Park; Michayluk, M. E., Hafford, Sask.; Micheltrink, T., Calgary; Miko, Sedgewick, Alta.; Miller, A. J., Lethbridge; Mitchell, D. L., Comox; Mitchell, R. C., Kenora, Mitton, M. D., Calgary; Modeland, Antikokan, Ont.; Mohns, B. J., Vancouver; Molloy, J., Regina; Moore, F., Merritt; Moore, R. L., Westlock; Moose, R. J.,

Cumberland House; Monk, M., Vancouver; Moran, O., Mayerthorpe; Moran, G. J., Melville; Morgan, D. R., Saskatoon; Morin, G. M., Cumberland House; Morrell, W. T., Vancouver; Morrison, C. S., Winnipeg; Morrison, R. A., Prince George; Moroz, A. W., Wadena, Sask.; Moulton, P. J., Chilliwack; Mutsch, G. A., Edmonton; Moyes, R. D., Victoria; Moxam, G. R., Vancouver; Modell, G. Fernie; Murdock, W. G., Fish River; Murray, R. G., Weyburn; Myers, R. R., Sardis; Myles, G., Sherwood Park; McAleer, D. R., Victoria; McAskill, D. J., Victoria; McCutcheon, D. G., Fruitvale, B.C.; McClelland, J. D., Vancouver; McFarlane, D. W., Kelwood, Manitoba; McGill, R., Fort Smith, N.W.T.; McIlveen, R. S., Victoria; McInnes, P. J., Calgary; McIntyre, R. B., Port Alberni; McKenna, G. H., Lethbridge; McKenna, G. P., Edmonton; McLaughlin, B. D., Regina; McManus, J., Burnaby; McNeill, Virden; McPherson, D. J., Portage La Prairie; McWillie, D. J., Saskatoon.

Nabess, G. D., Cumberland; Nagy, M. N., Regina; Nault, J. G. E., Kenora; Nault, M. A., St. George, Man.; Naylor, G., Calgary; Naylor, F. R., Burnaby; Needham, R., Vancouver; Nelson, G. L., Verdin, Man.; Nelson, K. R., Edmonton; Neumann, E., Langley; Neumann, H., Langley; Nicholson, A. G., Turner Valley; Nicholls, D. P., Alder Flats, Alta.; Nightgale, M., Cranbrook; Noel, G., White Rock; Nolan, J. A., Calgary; Normand, D. P., Calgary; Nuell, J. W., Calgary.

Oleary, B. P., Richmond; Olekson, L., New Denver, B.C.; Olinek, G. C., Langley; Oliver, J. L. A., Wadena, Sask.; O'Neill, H. J., New Westminster; O'Neill, R., Vancouver; Orlowski, R. M., Invermay, Sask; O'Rourke, D. J., Fernie; Overland, J. G., Calgary.

Paine, D., Victoria; Palate, T. J., Calgary; Palmer, R., Port Alberni; Panas, R., Prince George; Panter, P., Victoria; Parenteau, G., Duck Lake; Parker, C., Keewatin; Parsons, T. J., Saskatoon; Patriquin, R. R., Vancouver; Paulin, D. W., Haney; Peake, J. B., Regina; Peck, B. D., Victoria; Pennington, W., North Vancouver, Peterson, J. J., Prince George; Petroski, D. T., Regina; Pettigrew, G. E., Calgary; Pettigrew, L. A., Calgary; Petty, W. T., Vancouver, Pfeil, D. A., Humbolt; Phanauf, W., Vermillion; Phillips, R. F., Calgary; Philpott, R. K., Victoria; Piche, L. B., Coquitlam; Pickerling, R. N., Winnipeg; Piller, L., Melville, Sask; Podger, R. A. D., Vancouver; Pogson, W. C., Calgary; Polby, B., Balmertown, Ont.; Pon, A., Edmonton; Porter, M., Prince George; Potts, G., Creston; Powell, W. B. B., Haney, B.C.; Powick, R. C., Nakusp; Poyser, G. L., Sedgewick; Poznachuk, R. J., Vancouver, Presseau, J. D., Cultus Lake; Presnce, C. W., New Westminster; Prosser, R., Revelstoke; Prysunka, D. N., Vegreville; Pullen, K., Edmonton; Pumphrey, W., Kelowna; Pyper, R., Winnipeg.

Quick, D. T., Richmond; Quilty, M. B. W., Vancouver.

Racette, M. A., Melfort, Sask.; Randle, W. L., Vancouver, Rasaussen, D., Calgary; Rattray, S. T., Red Deer; Rayner, R. G., Marathon; Reid,

G., Vancouver; Redisky, J. D., McKenzie Island, Ont.; Reed, R. G., Shilo; Reid, A. J., Calgary; Reid, W., Ladner; Reilly, D. J., Calgary; Reilly, M. A., Calgary; Reilly, S. J., Chilliwack; Reis, R. R., Port Alberni; Reite, W. E., North Surrey; Remanda, B., Wynndel, B.C.; Renaud, L., Marcelin; Renyard, B. L., Revelstoke; Reynolds, C. M., Vancouver; Rhodes, K. R., Burnaby; Ribecco, F., Calgary; Richdale, W. L. T., Vancouver; Richards, G. B., Winnipeg; Riguedell, J., Revelstoke; Riguedell, R. A., Revelstoke, B.C. Riley, T. M., New Westminster; Riopel, P. A., Edmonton; Ripley, A., Atikokan, Ont.; Riseing, E. C., North Battleford; Rivet, R. F., Ft. St. John; Rixon, T. J., Winnipeg; Roberts, R. E., North Surrey; Roberts, R., Montrose; Robertson, E. I., Port Alberni; Robertson, R., Trail; Robinson, K., Ladner; Robinson, R. S., Calgary; Robinson, T. L., St. Boniface; Roe, K., Calgary; Rogers, R. G., New Westminster; Romses, R. R., Lethbridge; Rose, D., Redcliff; Rose, D. G., Edmonton; Rosin, R. B., Winnipeg; Ross, J., Port Alberni; Roushton, G. A., Port Alberni; Roussy, P. F., Cloverdale; Rumberger, D. W., Naicam, Sask.; Rumberger, R. R., Naicam, Sask.; Runge, A. R., Bruno, Sask.; Rolheiser, L., Kerrobert, Sask.

Salamondra, W. D., Creighton; Sargent, G. R., Vegreville; Saunders, D., Texada Island, B.C.; Saunders, J., Vancouver; Saunders, R. W., Vancouver; Sauviat, J. E., Vancouver; Savard, D., New Denver; Sawyer, T. S., Westlock; Schaefer, A. T., Fort Alberni; Schafer, L. G., Innisfail; Schauerte, V. J., Alder Flats, Alta.; Schlosser, M., Winnipeg; Schneider, W. G., North Surrey; Schultz, K. A., Edmonton; Schwark, V. R., Emerson; Scott, D. C., Coquitlam; Scott, G. W., Victoria; Seatter, R. B., Calgary; Sedesky, F. C., Kenora; Sedman, B. A., Langley; Selent, J., Edmonton; Senko, T. J., Haney; Sexton, D. A., Winnipeg; Shaflik, C. F., Burnaby, B.C.; Sharp, D. S., Mayerthorpe; Shary, S. P., Wadena; Shaw, R. M., Vancouver, Shemko, R. W., Pincher Creek; Shepanik, E. C., Bruno, Sask.; Shirley, G. S., Weyburn, Sask.; Sibald, R. R., Regina, Sask.; Skoda, D. R., Vancouver; Smith, B. J., Port Alberni; Smith, C. L., Haney; Smith, D. B., Turtleford; Smith. G., Fort William, Ont.; Smith, J. J., Naicam, Sask.; Smith L. M., North Surrey; Smith, M., Edmonton; Smith, O. G., Winnipeg; Smith, R. D., Nakusp; Smith, V. F., Victoria; Smith W. R., Melville; Sombrutski, Dryden; Somerset, W. L., Cranbrook; Sowiak, E. P., Brandon; Spalding, C. N., St. Vital, Man.; Spatuk, M. J., Blairmore; Speakman, J., Olive Flats, Alta.; Spencer, R. J. Calgary; Springer, M. J., Weyburn; Sproat, H. A., Milestone, Sask.; Stacey, R. W., North Surrey; Stadnyk, L. V., Crayton; Stainbrook, R. J., Vernon; Stalmen, D. K. Burnaby; Stamm, R. R. Vancouver; Staven, M. J., Vancouver; Stevens, K. P. Regina; Stevens, R., Vancouver; Stewart, J. M., Fort William; Stewart, J. W., Edmonton; Stobbart, D. B., Ladner; Stobbart, R. B., Ladner; Stock, R. D., Calgary; Stoddart, T. A., Regina; Stogre, R. J., Vancouver; Stokes, G., Powell River; Stoner, A. E., Yarrow; Straarup, B. H., Calgary; Strachan, J. H., Courtenay; Strass,

J. B., Regina; Styan, J. W. G., Transcona, Man.; Suddaby, J. J., Winnipeg; Sutherland, G., Calgary; Swidsinsky, C., Saskatoon; Syroid, D. S., Weyburn.

Tatunak, B., Baker Lake, N.W.T.; Taylor, G. R., Kinisino, Sask.; Taylor, J., Coquitlam; Taylor, J. R., Calgary; Taylor, R. J., Lethbridge; Temple, D. C., Melville; Thoebald, M. R., Winnipeg; Thomas, C. G., St. James; Thompson, R., North Surrey; Thon, K. B., Calgary; Thon, R. E., Calgary Thul, G. P. A., Regina; Todd, H. A., Regina; Todosychuk, R, Vancouver; Turlock, R. P., Victoria.

Ulmer, M. E., Vancouver; Ulmer, M. L., Vancouver; Unger, D. B., McCreary, Man.; Upton, G. V., Calgary; Urbanoski, R. N., Dauphin; Urbanski. J. R., Winnipeg; Urbanski, W. C.; Balmertown, Ont.; Ursel, R. A., Glenella, Man.

Valliere, J., Trail; VanBreda, C., Lethbridge; Van Moll, C. R., Vegreville; Veevers, S. W., Vancouver; Velichka, R. T., Invermay, Sask.; Vezina, A. B., Vancouver; Vicic, S. R., Fernie; Vickers, S. G., North Vancouver; Gogels, R. W., Winnipeg.

Wade, F. R., Virden; Walker, R. E., Prince Albert; Wallace, B. L., Ft. St. John; Wallin, M. D. J., Burnaby; Wannop, P. A., Kelowna; Warburton, P. N., New Westminster; Warren, D. L., Burnaby; Watson, J. K., Richmond; Watt, R. G., Vancouver; Webber, W., Cortney; Weigand, D., Victoria; Weisgarber, R. M., Regina; Welsh, W. E., Calgary; Weninger, H. F., Langley; Wenman, S., langley; Werry, P. E., Calgary; Westerby, D. J., Atikokan, Ont.; White, F., Pincher Creek; Whitmore, M. P., Vancouver; Wiekens, K., Nelson; Wickham, D. J., Hammond; Wigman, R., White Rock; Wike, B. H., North Surrey; Wilkins, F. K., Vancouver; Wilkowski, B., Silverton; Willetts, W. M., Creighton; Willis, R. D., Humboldt; Willmer, D. J., Derwent, Alta; Wilson, B., Calgary; Willson, D. J., Duncan; Wilson, P. D., Edgerton, Alta; Williamson, G. P., Port Coquitlam; Winter, D. P. E., Shilo; Winters, P. J., Nelson; Wojcik, L. A. Kelvington; Wolbaum, A. J., Regina Sask; Wolfe, W. H., White Rock, B.C. Woloski, B., Vancouver; Wong, G., Victoria; Woo, W., Vancouver; Wood, R. N., North Surrey; Woytiuk, B. S., Hafford, Sask.; Wright, P. M., North Surrey; Wright, R. R., Swift Current; Wutzke, E., Redcliff; Wylie, Portage La Prairie.

Aitken, G. J., Sardis; Alden, W., Richmond; Allaire, J. A., St. Boniface; Allan, R.T., Victoria; Allain, M., Revelstoke; Ammatto, G. C., Blairmore; Andersen, D. R., Coquitlam; Anderson, J. F., Flin Flon; Anderson, J. K., Fort William; Andrews, R. A., New Westminster; Antoniuk, K. J., Port Arthur; Arcand, R. J., East Kildonan; Archer, K. W., Fort Churchill; Artindale, F. W., Fort St. John; Ashick, G. R., Port Arthur; Avery, I. G., Vancouver.

Bablitz, R. J., Edmonton; Baker, G. F., Creston; Baker, R. O. L., Creston; Baker, R H., Edmonton; Barber, D. A., Victoria; Barritt, R. H., Edmonton; Barrowclough, R. N., North Surrey; Barteski, K. B., Saskatoon; Bauer, B. C., Kelowna; Baumgartner, D. A., Regina; Beattie, J. A., Lethbridge; Bedard, C. G., Coquitlam; Belanger, R. V., Calgary; Bell, B. A.,

Fort McMurray; Bell, C. E., Sherwood Park, Alta.; Bell, P. A., North Surrey; Bender, R. N., Moose Jaw; Bennett, D. P., Calgary; Bennington, K. A., White Rock; Berezon, D. H., Westlock; Bergstrom, A. E., Fruitvale; Berkenkamp, B. B., Lacombe; Berry, K. M., Port Arthur; Bethune, M. P. J., Vancouver; Beveland, J. T., Vancouver; Biagioni, L. N., Trail; Bilurs, W., Penticton; Bilyk, G. S., Westlock, Birch, C. W., New Westminster; Bird, G., North Vancouver; Bird, J., Duck Lake; Bird, T. A., Fort Smith; Black, L. G., New Westminster; Blaikie, D. G., Transcona; Boast, P. B., Calgary; Bogdan, R., Lethbridge; Boese, B. D., Emmerson; Boivin, G. M., New Westminster; Bone, C. B., Nakusp; Bonnell, M. L., C.F.S. Baldy Hushes, B.C.; Booth, D. R., Saskatoon; Borm, P. R., Westlock; Bosch, D. J., Sherwood Park; Bourgeois, M. P., Elm Creek; Boulet, R. F., Regina; Brassard, R. M. - see SER 80; Bray, J. G., Mayerthorpe; Brenner, K. J., New Denver; Bridges, D. G., Burnaby; Brillenger, B. J., Victoria; Brochu, R. C., Hammond; Brooks, R. C. D., Regina; Broughton, J. E., New Denver; Brownlow, K. W., Revelstoke; Bryce, L. R., North Surrey; Buckmaster, B. G.; East Kildenan; Bugg, W. K., Melville; Burlack, K. W., North Surrey; Burtniak, D., G., Stony Mountain; Bushie, R., Winnipeg; Burridge, R. P., Port Arthur; Butler, R. M., Calgary; Buxton, R. F., Edmonton; Byrne, G. K., Vancouver; Brassard, R. M.,Abbottsford.

Callaway, D. B., Victoria; Cameron, M. A., New Westminster; Campbell, K. A., Fort McLeod; Campbell, K. G., Fruitvale; Campbell, T. R., Vancouver; Cameron, G C., St. Boniface; Capper, B. A., Calgary; Carriere, D. D., Vancouver; Carry, L. M., Cranbrook; Cartier, J. R., Cumberland; Cataford, S. G., Nakusp; Cathcart, C. K., New Denver; Cavangah, J. M., Edmonton; Chaney, A. V., Swift Current; Chapman, D. B., Innisfail; Charbonneau, D. P., Battleford; Chipman, R. A., Port Alberni; Christianson, P. L., Naicam; Chwyl, B. H., Fort St. John; Cisar, J. L., Pincher Creek; Clark, L. D., Weyburn; Clifford, L. H., Prince George; Coghill, R. W., Edmonton; Coghlin, K. R., Moose Jaw; Connelly, M. L., North Surrey; Conpad, P. K., Winnipeg; Cook, G. M., Cumberland; Cook, B. C., Portage La Prairie; Copeland, B. R., McCreary; Cormier, M. A. J., Regina; Coss, T. V. Chetwynd; Cote, A. L., Winnipeg; Couch, G. L., Dauphin; Coughlin, G. A., Swift Current; Croaker, C. A., Aldergrove; Crofford, C. G., Moose Jaw; Cross, J. W., Brandon; Cross, W. L., Hudson Bay; Crouch, H. J., Victoria; Crouch, W. A., Victoria; Cruickshank, R. F., Kelowna; Cunningham, D. R. Vancouver; Custance, R. V., Hammond; Dagg, A. W., Calgary; Dale, D. J., Moose Jaw; Dart, R. P. Beaverlodge; Davidge, P. J., Port Alice; Davies, C. J., Vancouver; Davies, G., Kamloops; Davis, R. W., Naicam; Dean, D. W., Pine Falls; Dean, K. A., Invermay; Decae, R. E., Calgary; Decker, J. W. H., Yellowknife; Decker, R. J. F., Yellowknife; Degenstien, D. R. J., Calgary; Deleeuw, D. C., Calgary; Demkiw, E. W., Hudson Bay; Dennis, L. E., Lake Cowichan; Dentrey, J. W., Port Kells; Desaulniers, D. N., Dryden; Desaulniers, D. J., Dryden; Descalshuk, K. K., Hendon; Deslaurier, M. E., Kamloops; Dey, L. A., Swift Current; Dickie, F. D., Surrey; Donnelly, J. S., Abbotsford; Donnelly, J. M., Lethbridge; Dowhy, L. W,. Fort William; Draffin, R. J., Winnipeg; Drakulic, M., East Kildenan; Drewniak, M., Kindersley; Duff, W. R., Calgary, Dumser, R., Fort William; Dunbar W. C., Calgary; Dunn, R. A., Fort McLeod; Dusseault, R., Vimy, Alta.; Dustin, E. R., Atikokan; Dupont, D. R., Ladner; Dyck, L. D., Yorkton; Dyck, R. E., Calgary.

Eagleson, H., Edmonton, Alta.; Edmonds, G. B., Edmonton, Alta.; Elms, S. J., Vancouver, B.C.; Elson, B. E., Calgary, Alta.; Ellik, A. T., Kamloops, B.C.; Emard, D., Lethbridge, Alta.; Emmott, R. H., Fort Macleod, Alta.; Empson, D., Chetwynd, B.C.; English, D. D., Calgary, Alta.; Erb, D. P., Prince Albert, Sask.; Essex, V. M., North Surrey, B.C.; Essex, A. J., White Rock, B.C.; Essex, G. T., White Rock, B.C; Evans, L. J., Edmonton, Alta.

Falconer, D. R., Calgary, Alta.; Farkas, E. J., Surrey, B.C.; Fearey, J. T., Calgary, Alta.; Fearon, D. J., Victoria, B.C.; Fenwick, D. R., Flin Flon, Man.; Ferilinger, R. J., Saskatoon, Sask.; Fifield, J. A., Lethbridge, Alta.; Finlayson, M. G., Invermere, B.C.; Finnerty, G. J., Vancouver, B.C.; Fisher, H. E., Wainwright, Alta.; Fisher, P. A., Wadena, Sask.; Fitzgerald, M. J., North Surrey, B.C.; Fitzgerald, M. B., Ft. St. John, B.C.; Flagel, W. J., Regina, Sask.; Flett, B. E., Cumberland House, Sask.; Foreman, J. D., Calgary, Alta.; Forsyth, K. R., Calgary, Alta.; Forseth, R. B., Weyburn, Sask.; Fosseneuve, P. G., Cumberland House, Sask.; Franklin, G. R., Prince George, B.C.; Fraser, D. P., North Surrey, B.C.; Fraser, D. J., Winnipeg, Man.; Fraser, G., Saskatoon, Sask.; Freberg, J. A., Revelstoke, B.C.; Freisen, D. A., Humbolt, Sask.; Fuller, D. J., Invermere, B.C.; Funk, R. R., Fort McMurray, Alta.; Funston, R. F., Prince Albert, Sask.

Gagnon, W. E., Moose Jaw, Sask.; Galambos, S. N., Calgary, Alta.; Galloway, D. I., Courtney, B. C.; Garbutt, G. W., Vernon, B.C.; Gascoyne, North Surrey, B.C.; Gauthier, A., Powerview, Man.; Genaille, V. M., Giscome, B.C.; Genest, K. R., Moose Jaw, Sask.; Gentes, O. P., Red Lake, Ont.; George, D. A., Brandon, Man.; Gilhooly, D. G., Fort William, Ont.; Gladue, L. A., Calgary, Alta.; Glasman, D. L., Brandon, Man.; Golley, W. G., Revelstoke, B.C.; Goody, J. M., Vedder Crossing, B.C.; Goosens, T., Cranbrook, B.C.; Gordon, R. G., Victoria, B.C.; Gordon, T.H., Kamloops, B.C.; Goresky, G. W., Stonewall, Man.; Grant S. D., Clive, Alta.; Griffin, H. A., Albion, B.C.; Gregory, R. K. C., Coquitlam, B.C.; Gregory, R. E., Powell River, B.C.; Green, T. D., Salmon Arm, B.C.; Greer, J. L., Regina, Sask.; Gresty, F. T., Saskatoon, Sask.; Griffiths, K. D., Merritt, B.C.; Gurr, A. L., Lethbridge, Alta.

Hachey, C. J., Summerland, B.C.; Haddock, K. C., Calgary, Alta.; Hagen, W. A., Invermay, Sask.; Hahn, P. C., Hilton, Alta.; Halbert, B. A., Winnipeg, Man.; Halbert, D. R., Winnipeg, Man.; Halusiak, J. A., Victoria, B.C.; Hancock, D. W., Ocean Park, B.C.; Hannah, G. A., St. Boniface, Man.; Hanoski, S. A., Re-

gina, Sask.; Hanson, D. W., Namaka, Alta.; Harrison, L. R., Haney, B.C.; Hatton, K. L., Edmonton, Alta.; Hawkes, R. W., Moose Jaw, Sask.; Hayashi, N., Silverton, B.C.; Hayes, A. P., Calgary, Alta.; Hayward, R. R., White Rock, B.C.; Heatherington, G. E., Moose Jaw, Sask.; Heitman, D. F., Red Deer, Alta.; Hellmich, P. H., Vancouver, B.C.; Hellmich, P. R., Vancouver, B.C.; Henrickson, D. G., Cranbrook, B.C.; Henry, M. R., Haney, B.C.; Hess, J., Winnipeg, Man.; Hill, R. R., Regina, Sask.; Hinkelman, T. L., Burnaby, B.C.; Hird, D. B., Coquitlam, B.C.; Hobbs, D. B., Swift Current, Sask.; Hogg, C. D., Lethbridge, Alta.; Hogarth, J. W., Winnipeg, Man.; Holbeche, N. L., Surrey, B.C.; Holmes, D. F., Victoria, B.C.; Holmes, G. J., Coquitlam, B.C.; Holmes, P. G., Victoria, B.C.; Horkey, W. J. P., Shilo, Man.; Hornung, R. L. C., Swift Current, Sask.; Horvat, J., Port Alberni, B.C.; Horvat, S., Port Alberni, B.C.; Hossack, J. A., Winnipeg, Man.; Houle, V. D., Marius, Man.; Houwing, D. M., Edmonton, Alta.; Howard, E. J., Edmonton, Alta.; Hoyer, K. H., Hollywood, Cal.; Hrechka, R. A., Prince, George, B.C.; Huber, A. O., Regina, Sask.; Hudson, K. W., Fort Macleod, Alta.; Hudy, D., Melville, Sask.; Hufsmith, D. A., Vancouver, B.C.; Hulagrocki, J., Kenora, Ont.; Hulme, P. A., Vancouver, B.C.; Humphrey, R. J., Bowden, Alta.; Hunt, D. T., Vancouver, B.C.; Huseby, K. C., Lacombe, Alta.; Inster, C. W., Calgary.

Jackson, W. C., Edson, Alta.; Jackson, A. M., Victoria, B.C.; Jang, D. A., Vancouver, B.C.; Jimmie, S. P., Nelson, B.C.; Jones, M. C., Fort Macleod, Alta.; Jordan, J. R., Victoria, B.C.

Kane, D. J., Humboldt, Sask.; Kanngiesser, C. R., Lacombe, Alta.; Kashar, A. G., Dauphin, Man.; Kasper, W. M., Dryden, Ont.; Keough, Battleford, Sask.; Kerr, D. R. H., Dauphin, Man.; Kerr, P. V., Winnipeg, Man.; Kinch, M. G., Black Diamond, Alta.; King, B. S., Calgary, Alta.; King, K. F., Moose Jaw, Sask.; Kirby, G., Victoria, B.C.; Kirkwood, A. P., Victoria, B.C.; Klassen, S. B., Armstrong, B.C.; Klyne, R., Erinferry, Sask.; Knight, P. A., Port Arthur, Ont.; Koberstein, K. E., Hinton, Alta.; Kohlman, D. A., Humboldt, Sask.; Kohlmeyer, P. G., Flin Flon, Man.; Kohorst, W. C., Creston, B.C.; Konhechny, D. J., Regina, Sask,; Konjolka, L. P., Hinton, Alta.; Koronko, B. A., Vernon, B.C.; Kool, D. W., Cromer, Man.; Kraqchuk, R. J., North Vancouver, B.C.; Krisciunas, A. A., Fort William, Ont.; Kriz, F. J., Regina, Sask.; Kriz, M. M., Regina, Sask.; Krusel, K. C., Calgary, Alta.; Krysa, B. D., Edmonton, Alta.; Kucherka, G. E., Port Arthur, Ont.; Kulyk, T. J., Wadena, Sask.

Lafond, G., Prince, Albert, Sask.; Lafontaine, V. M., Yorkton, Sask.; Landers, D. M., Salmon Arm, B.C.; Langlais, D. A., Dryden, Ont.; Lane, R. P., White Rock, B.C.; Lanski, K. T., Hafford, Sask.; Lapointe, D. A., Stonewall, Man.; Larocque, H. J., Vancouver, B.C.; Laroche, W., Edmonton, Alta.; Larocque, C. W. J., Yorkton, Sask.; Larsen, R. J., Surrey, B.C.; Lavalley, C. S., Regina, Sask.; Lauson, G., Powell River, B.C.; Lavoie, L., Prince Albert, Sask.; Lawrence, W. J., Vernon, B.C.; Lawson,

G. P., Thompson, Man.; Leask, J. J., Turner Valley, Alta.; Lebedoff, C., Ashcroft, B.C.; Leclerc, R. P., Edmonton, Alta.; Leicht, K. G., Innisfail, Alta.; Lerminiaux, L. D., Edmonton, Alta.; Letain, D. F., Edmonton, Alta.; Levitt, D. G., Calgary, Alta.; Lietz, R. G., Regina, Sask.; Lievers, M J., Fort Macleod, Alta.; Ligertwood, W. J., Edmonton, Alta.; Linaker, T. W., Edmonton, Alta.; Linden, R. A., Port Alberni, B.C.; Linden, W. H., Port Alberni, B.C.; Little, R. J., Spalding, Sask.; Littlewol, W. J., Kamsack, Sask.; Long, M. W., St. Vital, Man.; Loughery, J. R., Fernie, B. C.; Loyer, M. E., Frank, Alta.; Lubkiwsk, T. A., Carman, Man.; Lucking, C. F., Carmen, Man.; Lukasiewich R. J., Edmonton, Alta.; Ludkvist, J. E., N. Surrey, B.C.; Lynn, D. W., Victoria, B.C.; Lyons, R. C., Calgary, Alta.

Macala, A. A., Invermay, Sask.; MacDonald, P. J., Shilo, Man.; MacFarlane, C. J., Turtleford, Sask.; MacFarlane, R. B., Turtleford, Sask.; Machek, P. V., Victoria, B.C.; MacKenzie, R. A., New Denver, B.C.; Mackie, L. J., Prince Albert, Sask.; MacKinnon, S. E., Port Arthur, Ont.; MacNeil, L. W., Inuvik, N.W.T.; MacF'herson, I. S., Winnipeg, Man.; Maddigan, D. M., Regina, Sask.; Madill, D. H., Regina, Sask.; Mahoney, M. M., Comox, B.C.; Mahoney, P. B., Comox, B.C.; Mansky, W., Transcona, Man.; Mantyka, D. S., Prince Albert, Sask.; Malach, R. L., Yorkton, Sask.; Malysh, G. P., Vernon, B.C.; Marand, D. P., Winnipeg, Man.; Marcotte, L. H. O., Edmonton, Alta.; Marion, D. E., Thorsby, Alta.; Markstron, K. H., Revelstoke, B.C.; Marocchi, D. R., Port Alberni, B.C.; Marocchi, R. W., Port Alberni, B.C.; Mafriott, W. H., Vancouver, B.C.; Martens, K. L., Dryden, Ont.; Martens, G. W., Winnipeg, Man.; Martin, D. G., Edmonton, Alta.; Martz, R. D.; Calgary, Alta.; Masterson, E., Merritt, B.C.; Matheson, K. I., Lethbridge, Alta.; Mathieson, M., Haney, B.C.; Mathews, D. J., White Rock, B.C.; Mayer, H. W., Edmonton, Alta.; Mayne, E. N., Fruitvale, B.C.; McCallum, G. A., Victoria, B.C.; McCarthy, W. P., Calgary, Alta.; McCreight, J. L., Regina, Sask.; McCue., W. C., Victoria, B.C.; McCutcheon, B. D. G., Fruitvale, B.C.; McDonagh, R. D., Edmonton, Alta.; McEwen, S. D., Winnipeg, Man.; McFarland, D. W., Kelwood, Man.; McGill, R. M., Yellowknife, N.W.T.; McGowan, K. G., Red Lake, Ont.; McInnes, R. D., Nakusp, B.C.; McIntyre, R. B., Port Alberni, B.C.; McIntosh, R. J., Grande Prairie, Alta.; McKay, R. N., Calgary, Alta.; McKenna, E. B., Fort Mcleod, Alta.; McKenna, G. H., Lethbridge, Alta.; McKinnon, D. A., Shilo, Man.; McLean, D. L., Milestone, Sask.; McLean, W. C., Crayton, Sask., McNeill, D. F., Virden, Man.; McPherson, D. J., Portage La Prairie, Man.; McQuair, F. A., Nakusp, B.C.; McRae, T. F., Winnipeg, Man.; Mealings, R. M., Vancouver, B.C.; Meihm, G. H., Transcona, Man.; Mellings, E. R., Duncan, B.C.; Melo, F. J., Pincher Creek, Alta.; Melstrom, W. D., Calgary, Alta.; Middlemiss, C. A., Duncan, B.C.; Milbery, B. K., Winnipeg, Man.; Mitchell, R. B., Richmond, B.C.; Modeland, W. B., Atikokan, Ont.; Moffat, E. G., Regina, Sask.; Moore, F. W., Port

Moody, B.C.; Moore, J., Kelowna, B.C.; Morgan, B. A., Vermilion, Alta.; Morden, R. M., McCready, Man.; Morrison, J. C., Coquitlam, B.C.; Morton, M. M., Hatzic, B.C.; Moulton, P. D., Sardis, B.C.; Mozell, G. M., Fernie, B.C.; Muir, R. G., Fort Churchill, Man.; Mundy, P. L., Calmar, Alta.; Munro, J. A., Cumberland, B.C.; Munro, J. E., Greendale, B.C.; Murray, D. L., Edmonton, Alta.; Myers, J. N., Victoria, B.C.; Myers, W. S., Vancouver, B.C.

Nachuk, H. W., Kenora, Ontario; Nagel, H. H., Vancouver, B.C.; Nahnybida, W. P., Kelwood, Man.; Nault, G. R., Kenora, Ont.; Nault, M. A., St. George, Man.; Nault, R. G., Kenora, Ont.; Naylor, F. R., Burnaby, B.C.; Needham, R. F., Vancouver, B.C.; Neufeld, T., Kerrobert, Sask.; Neuman, I., Langley, B.C.; Newton, G. W., Winnipeg, Man.; Nieradka, T., Camp Shilo, Man.; Nightingale, M., Cranbrook, B.C.; Nikiforuk, E., Prince Albert, Sask.; Nixon, J. R., Victoria, B.C.; Noesgarrd, J., Saskatoon, Sask.; Nolin, D., St. George, Man.; Nordine, E. E., Winnipeg, Man.; Norman, M., Nakusp, B.C.; Northam, M. L., Vancouver, B.C.; Nuell, J. W., Calgary, Alta.; Nuessler, C. M., Coquitlam, B.C.

O'Hara, M., Winnipeg, Man.; O'Leary, B. P., Richmond, B.C.; Olescow, L., New Denver, B.C.; Olecsow, M. J., New Denver, B.C.; Oliver, E. D., Vancouver, B.C.; Olver, G., Saskatoon, Sask.; Orr, D., Calgary, Alta.; O'Neill, M. T., West Vancouver, B.C.; Ottman, W. D., Cranbrook, B.C.; Oulton, W., Breton, Alta.

Palate, J. J., Calgary, Alta.; Palichuk, A. J., Edmonton, Alta.; Park, F. J. K., Transcona, Man.; Parkinson, S. R., Abbotsford, B.C.; Peepeetch, D. W., Regina, Sask.; Pelzer, R. N., Regina, Sask.; Pennington, W., North Vancouver, B.C.; Perdok, W., Thompson, Man.; Peshke, C. D., Winnipeg, Man.; Peterson, J., Prince George, B.C.; Peterson, R., Fernie, B.C.; Phillips, J. E., Winnipeg, Man.; Phillips, R. F., Calgary, Alta.; Phillips, W., Winnipeg, Man.; Philpott, R. K., Victoria, B.C.; Piche, D., Port Coquitlam, B.C.; Philon, P., Duck Lake, Sask.; Plishka, L. P. J., St. James, Man.; Podgorenko, C., Victoria, B.C.; Pogson, W. P., Calgary, Alta.; Poley, B. R., Balmer Town, Ont.; Pope, P., Calgary, Alta.; Popik, R., Thorsby, Alta.; Porter, W. R., West Vancouver, B.C.; Powell, W. D., Hammond, B.C.; Powers, R. D., Revelstoke, B.C.; Proctor, P. E., Cultus Lake, B.C.; Pruneau, T. J., Thorsby, Alta.; Pumphrey, W. E., Kelowna, B.C.; Puranen, D. M., Transcona, Man.; Puryk, D., Invermay, Sask.; Pyde, D., East Kildonan, Man.

Quick, D. T., Richmond, B.C.; Quilty, B. W., Vancouver, B.C.

Raikes, J. G., Vernon, B.C.; Ralston, D. C., Milestone, Sask.; Rathgeber, L. J., Melville, Sask.; Rathgeber, L. L., Melville, Sask.; Reaume, R., Vedder Crossing, B.C.; Reed, G., North Vancouver, B.C.; Reid, G. G., Thunderbay, Ont.; Reid, J. L., Saskatoon, Sask.; Reiger, L. E., Rutland, B.C.; Reite, W. E., North Surrey, B.C.; Relling, G. R., Antwistle, Alta.; Remanda, B. A., Creston, B.C.; Rennie, T., Red Deer, Alta.; Revitt, B. D., Prince, Albert, Sask.; Reynolds, C. M., Vancouver, B.C.;

Rhodes, R. A., Richmond, B.C.; Richards, G. B., Winnipeg, Man.; Richardson, S. M., Richmond, B.C.; Riguedell, J. C., Revelstoke, B.C.; Riopel, P. A., Edmonton, Alta.; Rivers, K. G., Melville, Sask.; Riviere, H. H., Blairmore, Alta.; Roberts, A. G., Calgary, Alta.; Robertson, E. I., Port Alberni, B.C.; Robertson, L. S., Vancouver, B.C.; Robertson, R. R., Trail, B.C.; Robertson, T. A., Moose Jaw, Sask.; Robertson, W. L., Trail, B.C.; Robinson, B. G., North Surrey, B.C.; Robinson, K. E., Ladner, B.C.; Robson, R. L., Delta, B.C.; Rodger, W. R., Richmond, B.C.; Roehrig, P., Anikokan, Ont.; Rogers, G., New Westminster, B.C.; Roh, R. L., Moose Jaw, Sask.; Rook, C. G., Wadena, Sask.; Rose, E. G., Sturgeous, Sask.; Rose, D. G., Edmonton, Alta.; Rose, K. J., Victoria, B.C.; Rosin, K.B., Winnipeg, Man.; Roussy, P. P., Burnaby, B.C.; Roux, R. M., Hinton, Alta.; Rowe, R., Vedder Crossing, B.C.; Rutko, G. W., Invermay. Sask.

Sanna, S., Baltown, Ont.; Sawchuk, I. W., Edmonton, Alta.; Sawyer, T. S., Westlock, Alta.; Schaefer, A., Port Alberni, B.C.; Schaffer, D. L., Regina, Sask.; Schlamp, R. G., Winnipeg, Man.; Schlyter, R. K., North Surrey, B.C.; Schmidt, R., Calgary, Alta.; Schneider, W. G., North Surrey, B.C.; Schuett, M. P., Moose Jaw, Sask.; Schulte, A., Sherwood Park, Alta.; Schulz, D. E., Naicam, Sask.; Scott, J. D., Richmond, B.C.; Seager, C. D., Calgary, Alta.; Seaman, D. W., Portage La Prairie, Man.; Seatter, R. B., Calgary, Alta.; Selleck, N. C., Blue Ridge, Alta.; Sewell, D. R. G., Winnipeg, Man.; Seymour, W. T., Qualicum Beach, B.C.; Shaflik, O. F., Burnaby, B.C.; Sharpe, M. R., Esquimalt, B.C.; Sharples, A. S., Calgary, Alta.; Shemko, R. M., Pincher Creek, Alta.; Shepard, M., Tappen, B.C.; Sheppard, T. J., Summerland; Sheppard, K. D., Surrey; Shermak, D., Calgary; Shewchuk - see Ser; Sigurnjak, R. W., Campbell River; Silano, A. A., Revelstoke; Sill, S. R., Vancouver; Simpson, G. B., Strathmore; Sinclair, R. G., Calgary; Sites, S. D., Seattle; Skitch, A. D., Calgary; Skoda, D. R., Vancouver; Smart, B. R., Chilliwack; Smillie, J. P., Victoria; Smith, G. W., Edmonton; Smith, L. M., North Surrey; Smith, R., Calgary; Smith, R. G., Thompson; Smith, R. D.; Malford, Smith, T. J.; North Surrey; Smyth, S. E., Yellowknife; Snidal, K., Verdun; Solberg, R. L., Milestone, Sask.; Somerset, W. N., Cranbrook; Spilchen, G. D., Edmonton; Spreacher, B. R., Malvill, Sask.; Stacey, R. W., North Surrey; Stainbrook, M. J., Vernon; Stamm, P. R., Vancouver; Stan, A. W., White Rock; Starling, D. K., Victoria; Stephen, F. A., Winnipeg; Stevens, D. E.; Nelson; Stevenson L. W., Edmonton; Stidston, T., Victoria; Stoddart, T. A., Vital, Man.; Strachan, J. H. G., Courtney; Stroshein, T., Wadena; Stuart, K. R., Woodnorth; Suddaby, J. J., Winnipeg; Suerink, J. A., Calgary; Sugden, R., Calgary; Suhr, M. D., Golden; Sutherland, M., Red Deer; Sutherland, R., Marceline, Sask.; Syrett, S. E. C., Argyle; Syroid, D. S., Weyburn; Szabo, J. A., Merritt; Shewchuk, M. J., Ft. William, Ont.

Tabak, A. G., Thompson; Tait, J. C., Burnaby; Taylor, G. R., Kinistino; Taylor, W. K., Armstrong; Tennant, L. D., Calgary; Theobalt, M. R., Winnipeg; Thickett, D. R., Victoria; Thompson, J. W., Black Diamond; Tobin, K. E., Saskatoon; Todd, C. D., Calgary, Tomkiewicz, Madsen; Toth, D. A., North Surrey; Toth, R. W. J., North Surrey; Tremblay, R. G., Winnipeg; Truszynski, T. P., Winnipeg; Turlock, R. T., Victoria; Turlock, R. P., Victoria; Turner, K. J., Swift Current; Turvey, R. W., Surrey.

Urbanski, R. K., Winnipeg; Uri, R., New Westminster; Usher, T., New Westminster.

Van Breda, C., Lethbridge; Vanderbrink, T., Edmonton; Van Eerden, H. L., Calgary; Vanier, D. R., Calgary; Valenthe, J., Port Arthur; Vinge, L. R., Creston.

Wadey, G., Edson, Alta.; Walker, H. J., Penticton; Wallace, B. L., Ft. St. John, B.C.; Wallace, D. C., Ft. St John; Walmsley, I. G., Victoria; Walterhouse, B., Creston; Ward, D. C., McRea, Man.; Ward, G. D. R., Hythe, Alta.; Ward, G. E., Wadena Sask.; Wasney, A. M., Edmonton; Waterhouse, B. G., Calgary; Watkins, W. L., Hudson Bay; Watson, M. R., Victoria; Watt R. G., North Vancouver; Welsh, W. R., Calgary; Welton, B. M., Saskatoon; Welton, C. E., Edmonton; Weninger, H. F. A., Langley; Wenstrom, B G., Atikokan; Westaway, J. A., New Denver, B.C.; Whale, J. H., Salmon Arm; Wheeler, C. L., Vedder Crossing; White, E. A., Pincher Creek; White R. W., New Denver; Whyte, G. T., Robert, Sask.; Wickman, D. D., Haney; Wiegers, L., Saskatoon; Wilcox, T. L., Hinton; Wilkins, J. D., Ladner; Wilkinson, F. K., North Surrey, B.C.; Willetts, G., Creighton, Saskatchewan, Williams, D. B., Edmonton; Willson; R. R., Lacombe; Wilson, A D., Edmonton; Wilson, D. J., Duncan; Wilson J. A., Winnipeg; Wojcik, R.S.M.; Stonewall; Woleaum, A. J., Regina; Wolfe, L. W. J., Cranbrook; Wong, G., Victoria; Woo W., North Surrey; Wooding, G., Vancouver; Woollven, L. B., Colwood; Wright, D. G., North Surrey; Wright, R. R., Swift Current; Wuhlar, J. M., Saskatoon.

Yao, P., Vancouver; Yarama, T. J., Kelowna; Yaworek, S. J., Pine Falls, Yee, J., Black Diamond; York, B. M., Trail; Young, R. R., North Vancouver; Young, R. D., Victoria.

Zazula, H. G., Invermay, Sask.

ANNEX "A"

Ashroft, F F., Surrey. Ball, J. A., Powell River; Benson, P. J., New Westminster; Berg, A M., Cultus Lake; Best H. F., North Surrey; Bjerke, R. L., N. Surrey; Brause, M. W., White Rock; Brewer, R. M., Vedder Crossing, B.C.; Brochurd, Hammond; Buss, L. W., Langley.

Campbell, R., North Surrey; Campbell, S. C., North Surrey; Carraro, B. J., Vancouver; Cass, Q. K., North Delta, B.C.; Catt, L. J., North Surrey; Clements, C., North Surrey; Collisson, K. R., Cultus Lake; Cooper, G. T., Vancouver; Decoste, A. V., Vedder Crossing; Dodgshon, D. J., Coquitlam; Druskin, D., Vancouver; Ellis, D. A., Burnaby; Ellis, P. J., Burnaby; Evans, R. K., Haney.

Faulk, A. P., Surrey; Frame, J. A., Surrey; Freeze, J. D., Abbotsford; Freeze M S., Abbotsford; Gaffney, R. G., Langley; Gilbert, E. R., Cresent Beach; Glover, R. G., Mission;

546

Goodhope, D. R., Cultus Lake; Grover, B. J., Powell Rover.
Harland, L. A., Surrey; Hart, S. G., Delta; Helmer, F. A., RR 3, Sardis; Higgins, J. N., White Rock; Hill, H. G., Powell River; Hillier, G. N., Port Coquitlam; Holbeche, D. W., New Westminster; Holbeche, N. R., North Surrey; Holmes, J. A., Burnaby; Holwill, D. B., Burnaby; Hossfield, D. A., North Surrey; Hyslop, J. C. G., Coquitlam.
Jeffreys, P. C., South Burnaby; ones, T. L., Coquitlam; Kennedy, B. J., Port Moody, Kindlan, D. R., Haney; Klassen, R. J., Abbostford; Kopach, M. P., North Surrey; Kowalchuk, Y. R., North Surrey; Kraft, E. D., Hammond; Krueger, M. P., Delta; Lauzon, J. J., Powell River; Leclearc, N. V., Surrey; Leggett, H. L., Hammond; Lis, J. R., Delta; Lowney, W. D., Haney; Luterbach, J. G., Burnaby; Malo, A. E., Coquitlam; McDonald, D. P., Surrey; McFadyen, B. J., White Rock; McKay, R. G., North Surrey; McKinney, S. R., New Westminster; McMath, G. W., Whalley; Minhinnick, R. G., Vancouver; Moxam, J. F., Hammond; Nazaroff, P. G., Coquitlam; Nicholl, G. W., White Rock; Nicholson, T. C., Thompson; Nilsen, S., North Surrey; O'Krane, E., North Delta; Panas, L., Prince Geo.; Paquette, G. J., Powell River; Peters, K., Cultus Lake; Peters, R. S., New Westminster; Peterson, C. J., Burnaby.
Reeves, A. T., South Surrey; Reid, A. W., Delta; Reid, H., Delta; Remack, J. M., Surrey; Roden, G. J., South Surrey; Ross, C. H., Port Coquitlam; Ross, W. J., North Surrey; Royle, T. H., Victoria; Rushton, B. I., Sardis; Ryan, B. G., Mayerthorpe, Alta.
Sharbinin, K. A., New Westminster; Smith F. W., Cultus Lake; Souter, R. J., Chilliwack; Stanton, M. W., Port Coquitlam; Steele, B. D., North Surrey; Stein, A., Abbotsford; St. Pierre, R. J., Coquitlam; Strachan, K. R., White Rock; Suek, R. J., Langley.
Thompson, G. E., Surrey; Vanbrakel, J. O., Coquitlam; Veldhuizen, B. M., White Rock; Warburton, A., New Westminster; Warlimont, J. E., North Surrey; White, P. D., North Surrey; Wickham, G. A., South Haney; Wood, B. D., Burnaby; Young D. M., Port Coquitlam; Zaporozan, K. A., Coquitlam; Hulme, P. A., Vancouver; Presseau, R. E., Cultus Lake; Munro, D. W., Sardis.

VACC - 1970

A COMPANY

B. Adolph, Burnaby; E. R. Allen, Haney; K. G. Andersen, White Rock; E. A. Bakke, Vancouver; N. Baron, White Rock; G. Beniusis, Surrey; A. R. Bennett, Vancouver; R. Bootsveld, North Vancouver; B. M. Borsholt, North Vancouver; D. R. Bout, Haney; D. J. Bowman, White Rock; R. D. Bramley, Burnaby; K. J. Briar, White Rock; S. P. G. Bryant, White Rock; R. B. Bryson, Vancouver.

V. Cade, Vedder Crossing; S. Campbell, North Vancouver; D. A. Carr, Ladner; R. Carruthers,

Coquitlam; P. C. Cavanagh, Vancouver; R. J. Chicoine, Vedder Crossing; S. Clemens, Surrey; B. C. Clegg, Vancouver; G. G. Conrad, Vancouver; L. Crosby, Burnaby; J. A. Dekker, Surrey; R. S. Denier, Burnaby; H. Dollenkamp, White Rock.

R. Evans, North Surrey; D. Fawcett, Vancouver; L. Fenske, Coquitlam; W. Forrest, Powell River; A. Frisch, Hammond; W. A. Furness, Vedder Crossing; D. Gaulder, Richmond; D. Gibson, White Rock; B. Godfrey, Surrey; R. Godlien, North Surrey; P. Gorbatuk, Powell River; S. Graner, Sardis.

C. Hancock, White Rock; G. Haggstrom, Vancouver; C. Hawes, Vedder Crossing, W. A. J. Henter, Delta; S. Hohm, Vancouver; W. R. Horner, Surrey; B.C. Howard, North Vancouver; R. J. Huggan, Vancouver; R. J. Kolodinski, Coquitlam; R. Kolstad, North Delta; M.P. Kopach, North Surrey; A. P. Koper, Burnaby; D. Kraft, Vedder Crossing.

S. A. T. Lechkobit, Delta; K. A. Lee, Vancouver; T. M. Loehndorf, North Surrey; K. A. Lopthien, Vancouver; D. Loranger, North Delta; R. MacKay, Surrey; R. McBryan, Haney; L. McDonald, Vancouver; N. McGreish, Delta; McIntyre, Vancouver; McKintosh, Vancouver; D. McLean, Haney; S. McNeil, Richmond.

B. Martin, Burnaby; M. Martin, Surrey; R. Martian, White Rock; M. Mason, Port Coquitlam; A. Matthews, Vancouver; L. Michaelsen, Surrey; P. Molloy, Vancouver; T. Molloy, Vancouver.

W. F. Nickerson, Ladner; G. Nicoll, Surrey; K. R. Nixon, White Rock; E. O'Krane, North Surrey; P. O'Riordan, White Rock; R. P. Page, Delta; R. Paquette, Power River; K. Philley, Coquitlam; P. Quigley, Haney; R. Reid, Coquitlam; C. Rice, Richmond; M. A. Roberge, Coquitlam; P. A. Robson, Delta; D. E. Rodgers, Delta; D. G. Roenspiess, Vedder Crossing; G. R. Ryan, Vancouver.

M. R. Sanders, White Rock; B. G. Scott, Richmond; G. J. Shannon, North Surrey; D. W. Shepherd, Surrey; N. F. Smith, Crescent; T. N. Southern, Powell River; R. H. Stackhouse, North Vancouver; M. E. Staple, Maple Ridge; D. R. Stevenson, Surrey; K. E. Thomas, Vancouver; M. Timoshyk, Powell River; D. Townsend, Surrey; H. Tubbs, Surrey; G. E. Tyers, Delta.

L. Veldhuizen, White Rock; G. Walters, Vancouver; R. Warner, Ladner; J. Wiens, Powell River; R. Wiens, Powell River; A. Wilkes, Chilliwack; R. Wills, Surrey; R. Wirtz, North Delta; D. Wood, Surrey; M. Worgan, White Rock; J. Wright, Vancouver.

B COMPANY

B. D. Allen, Royston; M. T. Allain, Merritt; J. A. Balkwill, Victoria; J. A. Ball, Powell River; G. J. Balmer, Grande Prairie, Alta.; D. G. Bauche, N. Yorkton, Sask.; A. P. Beauregard, Regina, Sask.; D. A Belding, Coquitlam; R. W. Bercier, Regina, Sask.; C. L. Berthelette, Pine Falls, Man.; N. H. Bessette, Edmonton, Alta.; B. T. Bjorklund, Thunder Bay, Ont.; D. Doersma, Calgary, Alta;, Boone, Kamloops; R. J. Britton, Duck Lake, Sask.; K. P. Boechler, Saskatoon, Sask.; L. V. Boisvert, Sherwood Park, Alta.; R. B. Brass, Davis, Sask.; E. W. Brown, Saskatoon, Sask.; N. J. Bull, Invermay, Sask.; N. I. Burchnall, Lacombe, Alta.; M. Byrne, Yellowknife, NWT.

D. J. Campbell, Esquimalt; R. C. Campbell, Coquitlam; G. Cherry, Saskatoon, Sask.; D. Chong, Vernon; A. G. Clifford, Dryden, Ont.; D. W. Coble, Saskatoon, Sask.; J. Connors, Victoria; R. J. Corrigan, Prince Albert, Sask.; D. E. Cowan, Vancouver 10; H. E. Craig, Winnipeg, Man.; J. R. Davidson, Regina, Sask.; Davis, Vernon; J. Desjarlais, Regina, Sask.; R. S. Dorion, Cumberland House, Sask.

S. Eastman, Vancouver; A Elliott, Edmonton, Alta.; A. T. Ellik, Kamloops; H. B. Fedge, Wellington, Nanaimo; H. W. Fedoruk, Vegreville, Alta.; W. K. Fitzpatrick, Winnipeg, Man.; H. Fleury, Elmwood, Man.; B. A. Flanigan, Dauphin, Man.; D. Forbis, Calgary, Alta.; D. Franklin, Prince George; R. J. Ruta, Invermere.

G. S. Gardiner, Virden, Man.; D. Gardiner, Virden, Man.; O. P. Gentes, Red Lake, Ont.; E. R. Gilbert, Crescent Beach; C. B. A. Gilewich, Winnipeg, Man.; D. E. Gillard, Edmonton, Alta.; T. R. Goodeham, Cranbrook; K. D. Gowerluk, Atikokan, Ont.; G. Gray, Winnipeg, Man.; D. A. Gregg, Fort McMurray, Alta.; H. A. Griffin, Albion; M. R. Guenette, Edmonton, Alta.; G. R. Guy, Mileston, Sask.; M. Hahn, Hinton, Alta.; B. C. Harrop, NW Calgary, Alta.; S. Hart, Ladner; J. Haugland, Drydon, Ont.; K. M. G. Hazard, CFB Shilo, Man.; A. E. Higgins, Vedder Crossing; J. N. Higgins, White Rock; S. P. Higgins, Brandon, Man.; D. Holwill, Burnaby; D. Hoon, Victoria.

B. W. B. Janzen, Abbotsford; G. R. Guy, Mileston, Sask.; M. Hahn, Hinton, Alta.; B. C. Harrop, NW Calgary, Alta.; S. Hart, Ladner; J. Haugland, Dryden, Ont.; K. M. G. Hazard, CFB Shilo, Man.; A E. Higgins, Vedder Crossing; J. N. Jiggins, White Roack; S. P. Higgins, Brandon, Man.; D. Holwill, Burnaby; D. Hoon, Victoria.

B. W. B. Janzen, Abbotsford; H. H. Jarche, Revelstoke; W. A. Jeffery, Rosetown, Sask.; R. P. Knorr, St. Walberg, Sask.; J. L. Lawrence, Edson, Alta.; R. M. Lawless, Fort St. John; K. L. Lavoie, Regina, Sask.; R. A. Lee, West Vancouver; M. A. Lefurgey, Edmonton, Alta.; A. Lestrat, St. Front, Sask.; R. L. Lynch, Edmonton, Alta.

L. Maciaszek, South Junction, Man.; E. A. Masterson, Mayerthorpe, Alta.; W. A. Maurer, Edmonton, Alta.; R. K. McEwen, Stonewall, Man.; D. G. McAllister, Vernon; K. W. McKenna, Fort MacLeod, Alta.; A. S. McKinnon, Pincher Creek, Alta.; R. A. McKenzie, McCreary, Man.; D. E. McNabb, Warrenton, Man.; R. J. McNabb, Warrenton, Man.; D. Moore, N Vancouver.

G. Neel, Dauphin, Man.; T. G. Oliver, Edmonton, Alta.; B. Okrainetz, Invermay, Sask.; V. W. Olson, Creston; L. H. O'Neill, SW Calgary 3, Alta.; B. P. Onyschtschuk, Port Alberni; K. E. Orr, Burton; Oryniak, Thunder Bay, Ont.; G. E. Palmer, New Denver; N. V. Pavlenko, Lethbridge, Alta.; W. T. Philp, Swift Current, Sask.; R. R. Poirier, Kenora, Ont.; D. Porter, Prince Albert, Sask.; D. J. Poucher, Victoria; D. R. Rennie, Red Deer, Alta.; J. Rigby, Atikokan, Ont.; R. M. Robinson, Dauphin, Man.; C. N. J. Rodgers, Calgary, Alta.; R. E. Ruud, South Junction, Man.

E. A. J. St. Onge, Churchill, Man.; J. H. Seniuk, East Kildonan, Man.; D. A. Seltenrich, Salmon Arm; R. D. Shortland, Thompson, Man.; H. G. Simmons, Winnipeg, Man.; E. G. Smith, Creighton, Sask.; I. M. Smith, Victoria; R. Snell, Portage La Prairie, Man.; C. Souter, Creighton, Sask.; S. G. Stant, Nanaimo; P. E. Stevenson, Vancouver; A. L. Sulz, Warburg, Alta.

M. R. Thomas, Cumberlandhouse, Sask.; S. Thompson, Black Diamond, Alta.; C. R. Todd, Thunder Bay, Ont.; D. G. Tutin, Whitehorse, Yukon; J. M. Vanlier, Vancouver; J. W. Vanlier, Vancouver; J. W. Warren, Victoria; G. Watt, Brandon, Man.; C. Way, Calgary, Alta.; G. A Wickham, Maple Ridge; R. Wikman, Melville, Sask.; D. W. Wilson, Abbotsford; L. Wolsynuk, Vancouver; R. A. Wood, Kelowna; R. N. Wright, Humboldt, R. A. Yates, Victoria.

C COMPANY

A. Alex, Merritt; G. Allen, Nanaimo; C. Anderson, Alderwood, Wash, USA; A. Atkinson, Winnipeg, Man.; E. T. Bashaw, White Rock; G. A. Beasley, Vancouver; L. Beaudoin, Comox; C. Beaupre, Virginiatown, Ont.; I. Belanger, Mattawa, Ont.; B. C. Bell, Hammond; R. C. Bitz, Vancouver; L. Blewett, Coquitlam; M. J. Boyd, Anderson Park, Ont.; R. M. Brewer, Vedder Crossing; R. D. Brochu, Pitt Meadows; J. E. Broughton, New Denver; B. R. Brown, Vancouver;

548

H. L. Brown, North Delta; C. D. Brulotte, Brittain; E. P. Buckingham, Nanaimo; G. G. Buckingham, Kamloops; D. P. Butt, Vancouver.

J. R. Carraro, Vancouver; M. Carr, Sudbury, Ont.; Q. K. Cass, North Delta; R. L. Castle, Mission; P. E. Cherry, Kirkland Lake, Ont.; P. J. Clegg, Fernie; C. R. Clemmens, Surrey; D. G. Cooper, Vancouver; K. A. Cornish, Haney; B. Cottrell, Coquitlam; P. W. Cozens, Victoria; T. C. Craig, Maple Ridge; K. P. Crawford, Victoria; S. C. Cuzner, Sydney Mines, NS.

J. E. Dagenais, Port Coquitlam; D. R. Davies, Kirkland Lake, Ont.; J. R. Dawson, Merritt; T. M. Deluce, Sioux St. Marie, Ont.; P. J. Demerais, Vancouver; J. A. Dickson, Burnaby; B. J. Dodds, Salmon Arm; G. S. Douglas, Vancouver; D. Druskin, Vancouver; M. D. Dubois, Vancouver.

M. J. Ego, Sardis; W. E. Elliott, Prince George; R. K. Evans, Haney; R. Farrell, Wellington; R. A. Farwell, Vancouver; J. E. Fenton, Westbank; G. W. Fitze, Abbotsford; R. J. Fleming, Sudbury, Ont.; W. A. Floyd, Kirkland Lake, Ont.; R. W. Folland, Salmon Arm; G. J. Forbes, Kirkland Lake, Ont.; W. C. Frolic, Surrey; G. A. Furgason, Kelowna; R. R. Furniss, Sardis.

F. Gaal, Vancouver; M. H. Gadbois, Revelstoke; G. C. Gauthier, Mattawa, Ont.; R. Gerbrecht, Kelowna; W. Glintz, Beansville, Ont.; L. A. Glover, Mission; R. Glover, Mission; A. Gneo, Revelstoke; R. Godmaire, Kearns, Ont.; B. J. Grant, Victoria; D. Gravel, Haileybury, Ont. D. Hearne, Haileybury, Ont.; D. Hebert, Sioux St. Marie, Ont.; H. Heyming, Kelowna; D. Hird, Coquitlam; B. Holmes, Victoria; L. M. Hunt, Vancouver; W. Hutchison, Comox; J. Hyslop, Coquitlam; D. E. Janke, Haney; P. C. Jefereys, South Burnaby; R. Jenkins, Kirkland Lake, Ont.; R. John, Nanaimo; K. Johnson, Hamilton, Ont.; J. Jordan, Victoria; J. E. Gadreault, Kirkland Lake, Ont.

B. J. Kennedy, Port Moody; T. H. Ker, Vancouver; J. H. Knol, White Rock; D. J. Kosovic, Vancouver; B. C. Kyle, Winnipeg, Man.; P. K. Lamb, Kamloops; M. J. Landers, Kirkland Lake, Ont.; G. A. Lange, Courtenay; M. V. Larochelle, North Bay, Ont.; D. Leclair, Kirkland Lake, Ont.; R. Lee, Kirkland Lake, Ont.; M. W. Legertwood, Vancouver; G. W. Long, Salmon Arm; J. K. Lowen, Kelowna; D. W. Lowney, Haney; A. D. Lumley, Vancouver.

D. D. McCafferty, Hamilton, Ont.; McCracken, Vedder Crossing; J. M. McElroy, Vedder Crossing; R. McInnes, Nakusp; A. McKerral, Burnaby; R. J. McPartlin, Vancouver; A. Maio, Maillardville; S.

Mancinnelli, Port Coquitlam; B. Marshall, Nanaimo; R. Martin, Salmon Arm; B. Meers, Yarrow; I. S. Mitchell, Victoria; R. J. Moffat, Victoria; F. Monestime, Mattawa, Ont.; B. S. Montgomery, North Bay, Ont.; R. G. Morrison, CFB Borden, Ont.; M. F. Mykytey, Hamilton, Ont.

P. Nazoroff, Kamloops; S. Nemeth, Port Alberni; P. J. Nicholas, Richmond; D. Nikoloyuk, Prince George; S. K. Nilsen, Surrey; L. J. O'Brien, Mississauga, Ont.; M. Oleksow, New Denver; D. G. Olson, St. Vital, Man.; R. E. Orfankos, Sudbury, Ont.; B. Owens, Victoria; R. T. Parkinson, Armstrong; F. Pelkey, North Surrey; M. Peterson, Mattawa, Ont.; J. Pilszek, Sudbury, Ont.; J. P. Proulx, Yak.

B. L. Rallison, Cranbrook; L. Reynolds, Clarkson, Ont.; E. M. Robson, Delta; S. J. Roche, Victoria; R. J. Rolfe, Vernon; C. J. Rouse, Port Moody; C. S. Schneider, Vernon; W. M. Royle, Victoria; H. S. St. Denis, Mississauga, Ont.; R. R. St. Pierre, Coquitlam; K. R. Salter, Kamloops; D. H. Scott, Maple Ridge; D. E. Simoni, Hamilton, Ont.; A. R. Serre, Ottawa, Ont.; B. S. Smith, Port Credit, Ont.; R. A. Smith, Victoria; B. D. Soles, Silvery Beach; H. Speidel, Revelstoke; S. S. Springer, Victoria; C. S. Starr, Richmond; K. R. Strachan, White Rock; J. D. Sturtridge, Sudbury, Ont.; H. W. Sveinson, Vernon; N. A. Sveinson, Vancouver; L. L. Stystad, Coullee Dam Wash. USA; J. A. Szabo, Merritt.

J. J. Tardiff, Kearns, Ont.; D. A. Thompson, Victoria; G. H. Trottier, Prince Rupert; R. S. Turner, Victoria; M. D. Vienneau, CFB Borden, Ont.; D. S. Warren, Victoria; R. J. Weatherly, Prince George; G. Wenzlaff, Vernon; D. V. Wilkinson, Vancouver; G. Windley, Nanaimo; D. A. Wright, Fernie; G. R. Wright, Surrey; P. M. Wright, North Surrey; B. C. Young, Kirkland Lake, Ont.

D COMPANY

R. W. J. Adanyk, Weyburn, Sask; D. C. Akerley, Shilo, Man.; T. M. Allooloo, Baffin Island, N.W.T.; L. S. Atchison, Weyburn, Sask.; L. J. Aubin, Pincher Creek, Alta.; C. Aultman, Port Credit, Ont.; R. H. Baker, Edmonton, Alta.; R. Bannister, Yellowknife, N.W.T.; M. C. Barker, Edmonton, Alta.; L. P. Bauder, Edmonton, L. B. Beasley, Edmonton, Alta.; C. C. Bekar, Yellowknife, N.W.T.; J. A. Bell, Deep River, Ont.; J. R. Berthelette, Jr., Pine Falls, Man.; R. J. Biodeau, Atikokan, Ont.; C. Blackrabbit, Cardston, Alta. G. A. Blondeau, Moose Jaw, Sask.; J. Bozzo, Thunder Bay, Ont.; R. W. Brown, Deep River, Ont.; J. K. Burridge, Thunder Bay, Ont.; D. A. Burroughs, Downsview, Ont.; E. E. Burton, Kelwood, Man.; C. P. Byer, Dryden, Ont.

B. Cairns, Kenora, Ont.; J. P. Carter, Thompson, Man.; C. J. Cassidy, Wood North, Man.; C. G. Cassidy, Wood North, Man.; S. L. Chell, Fort McLeod, Alta.; L. L. Chitouras, Ottawa, Ont.; J. W. Clark, Longbranch, Ont.; J. F. Collett, Aliston, Ont.; D. W. Connick, Wadena, Sask.; E. A. Cornez, Calgary, Alta.; G. M. Coyston, Fort Churchill, Man.; W. C. Creary, Toronto, Ont.; G. N. Cyre, Red Deer, Alta.; J. Czeiffusz, Sardis.

C. E. Davidson, Oshawa, Ont.; R. N. Delorme, New Westminster; J. Dresen, Merritt; P. J. Desrosiers, Pine Falls, Man.; S. J. Dickson, Moose Jaw, Sask.; T. A. Dickson, Weyburn, Sask.; W. P. Dolan, Peterborough, Ont.; A. J. Dubois, Portage LaPrairie, Man.; C. E. Dufault, Dauphin, Man.; R. T. Dusome, Medland, Ont.; D. L. Duval, Midland, Ont.; S. Ellis, Campbellford, Ont.; D. W. Ewanchook, Moose Jaw, Sask.

T. R. A. Ferrier, Toronto, Ont.; J. N. Fisher, Calgary, Alta.; E. R. Fincaryk, Madsen, Ont.; J. V. Fillmore, South Junction, Man.; S. M. M. Flaherty, Calgary, Alta.; B. T. Flynn, Kanata, Ont.; M. L. Forget, Penetanguishene, Ont.; D. W. Frith, Vancouver; P. B. Funk, Merritt; M. B. Gandier, Meaford, Ont.; R. Glenn, Camp Bellford, Ont.; M. G. Godfrey, Meaford, Ont.; I. D. Gray, Calgary, Alta.; D. H. Green, Bowmanville, Ont.; B. A. Grinstead, Merritt; D. D. Gurr, Lethbridge, Alta.

J. K. Haars, Edmonton, Alta.; T. L. Hamelin, Midland, Ont.; G. A. Harochaw, St. Vital, Man.; M. W. Hayes, Streetsville, Ont.; L. D. Henry, Brandon, Man.; R. G. Hershfeldt, Winnipeg, Man.; W. E. J. Hogan, Calgary, Alta.; R. G. Hopgood, Peterborough, Ont.; G. H. Hossack, Winnipeg, Man.; D. E. Huber, Clinton, Alta.; C. J. Humphrey, Shilo, Man.; H. C. Hunter, Streetsville, Ont.; J. R. Hunt, Edmonton, Alta.

A. A. Jansen, Dryden, Ont.; M. W. Johnson, Shilo, Man.; P. R. Johnson, Ajax, Ont.; R. T. Johnson, Thompson, Man.; B. M. Johnston, Thunder Bay, Ont.; J. G. Jones, Aurora, Ont.; G. N. Kapteyn, Edmonton, Alta.; J. T. Kerr, Edmonton, Alta.; T. R. King, Toronto, Ont.; W. Koleszar, Vancouver; R. J. Krisciunas, Thunder Bay, Ont.; J. D. Kulyk, Wadeena, Sask.

M. B. Labrie, Cornwall, Ont.; A. H. Langmuir, Thompson, Man.; J. LaRose, Coquitlam; S. R. Lawrance, Durham, Ont.; S. M. Leahan, Owen Sound, Ont.; K. M. Learmouth, Winnipeg, Man.; R. M. Lekivetz, Victoria, Alta.; L. M. Lengyel, Lethbridge, Alta.; F. Lerra, Toronto, Ont.; J. E. Levitt, Calgary, Alta.; R. P. Literovich, Kenora, Ont.; M. R. Long, Winnipeg, Man.; M. W. MacDonald,

Pentaguishene, Ont.; M. W. J. MacInnes, Weyburn, Sask' W. McDougall, Merritt; P. D. McGreggor, Renfrew, Ont.; R. B. McMillan, Portage LaPrairie, Man.; A. J. McRae, Balmertown, Ont.

C. M. Madl, Carson, Alta.; B. G. Manns, Creighton, Sask.; C. J. Manson, Keewatin, Ont.; D. E. G. Martel, Scarborough, Ont.; W. R. Medak, Innisfail, Alta.; D. R. Melia, Winnipeg, Man.; R. W. Melynchuk, Sturgess, Sask.; P. W. Miller, Thunder Bay, Ont.; M. S. Mulholland, Atikokan, Ont.; M. C. Mintz, Whitehorse, Yukon.

J. A. Noble, Esquimalt; T. W. Nollert, Aurora, Ont.; L. D. Nordine, Winnipeg, Man.; D. E. Novynka, Edmonton, Alta.; H. O'Brien, Ottawa, Ont.; J. D. Oshanski, Winnipeg, Man.; L. E. Pacey, Peterborough, Ont.; R. Patry, Ottawa, Ont.; H. W. Perkins, Edson, Alta.; P. Phillips, Vancouver; C. D. S. Pitcher, Petawawa, Ont.; R. W. Pondy, Winnipeg, Man.; M. J. W. Quinn, Mississauga, Ont.; R. P. Radl, Thunder Bay, Ont.; R. R. Rheault, Redlake, Ont.; E. W. S. Rice, Transcona, Man.; G. S. Roe, Calgary, Alta.; J. C. Rogers, Okotoks, Alta.; G. M. Rowland, Shilo, Man.; M. P. Ross, Winnipeg, Man.

A. R. St. Jacques, Ottawa, Ont.; P. St. Jacques, Ottawa, Ont.; R. F. Salisbury, Petawawa, Ont.; J. F. Sandeski, Weyburn, Sask.; S. A. Savage, Mississauga, Ont.; D. A. Sherb, Brandon, Man.; L. D. Smith, Winnipeg, Man.; J. T. Smyth, Merritt; L. W. Sparling, Belville, Ont.; N. K. Stener, Creighton, Sask.; H. E. Steven, Campbellford, Ont.; J. R. Stoley, Calgary, Alta.; D. A. Strilcuck, Edmonton, Alta.; D. R. Struthers, Cornwall, Ont.; F. R. Sutton, Thunder Bay, Ont.

L. D. Taylor, Weyburn; J. R. Thistle, North York, Ont.; R. K. Lake, Sask.; J. Harty, Regina, Sask.; E. E. Harwardt, Grand Centre, Alta.; J. E. Haw, Lindsay, Ont.; S. Heapy, Fort MacMurray, Alta.; W. Hedin, Dahlton, Sask.; J. Hill, North Battleford, Sask.; R. Hoffman, Calgary, Alta.; R. B. Hudson, Kelowna; R. L. S. Huskilson, Cobourg, Ont.; G. T. Innes, Pilot Butte, Sask.; D. P. Issel, Melville, Sask.; K. L. Jans, Bowden, Alta.; R. A. Jensen, Fort. St. John; D. D. Jeske, Regina, Sask.; D. A. Johnson, Prince Albert, Sask.; K. Kellins, Saskatoon, Sask.; D. A. Kerr, Millet, Alta.; P. L. Kinch, Black Diamond, Alta.; A. Korstanje, Ancaster, Ont.; . W. Kozakevich, Melville, Sask.; D. L. Lafranchise, Edmonton, Alta.; S. L. Laframboise, Regina, Sask.; B. J. Lanz, Regina, Sask.; J. C. Lawrence, Swift Current, Sask.; B. Lawson, Hamilton, Ont.; T. Lee, Kingston, Ont.; H. P. Lepinski, Regina, Sask.;

N. G. Lindsay, Swift Current, Sask.; I. Lipincki, Fort St. John; D. Litke, Hearst, Ont.; R. Lucarelli, Ottawa, Ont.; C. Marshall, Fort Smith NWT; S. Martens, Fort McMurray, Alta.; G. Matt, Regina, Sask.; G. W. Mayberry, Portland, Ore.; M. Maclean, Cobourg, Ont.; J. R. MacLeod, Burlington, Ont.; R. MacMullin, Cobourg, Ont.; K. E. McConnell, Lacombe, Alta.; B. McCoy, Calgary, Alta.; B. G. McIntosh, Clinton, Alta.; R. D. McIntosh, Grande Prairie, Alta.; B. McLean, Edmonton, Alta.; H. McLeod, Saskatoon, Sask.; M. M. McRay, Red Deer, Alta.; W. J. Mercer, Hamilton, Ont.; J. Moore, Dundas, Ont.; T. Moore, Dundas, Ont.; T. M. Mykytiw, Kelowna; R. Nordick, Naicum, Sask.; L. Norris, Chetwyn; C. Northrup, Edmonton, Alta.; J. C. Norwegian, Fort Simpson, N.W.T.; M. Nusca, Toronto, Ont.; F. Nuttall, Hamilton, Ont.; K. O'Donahue, Edmonton, Alta.; L. J. O'Sullivan, Cobourg, Ont.; L. Otte, Regina, Sask.; D. Overholt, Regina, Sask.; B. A. Patton, Lindsay, Ont.; C. Payeur, Hearst, Ont.; D. Peskor, Calgary, Alta.; D. Plamondon, St. Front, Sask.; M. Plamondon, St. Francis, Sask.; B. J. Porter, Prince Albert, Sask.; C. R. Powell, Grande Prairie, Alta.; L. E. Profeit, Whitehorse, Yukon; R. Pruneau, Thorsby, Alta.; J. Purych, Edmonton, Alta.

R. J. Quick, Fort McLeod, Alta.; P. Racine, Ottawa, Ont.; K. L. Ramsey, Saskatoon, Sask.; L. Ranch, Royal Park Store, Alta.; K. M. Reznick, Ottawa, Ont.; M. J. Rosell, Black Diamond, Alta.; S. H. Rosevear, Hearst, Ont.; L. L. Rutherford, St. Catherines, Ont.; H. J. Sanders, Clinton, Alta.; B. R. Sanders, Port Moody; D. E. Schjefte, Saskatoon, Sask.; R. E. Schmidt, Calgary, Alta.; R. E. Schulte, Sherwood Park, Alta.; B. J. Schweitzer, Calgary, Alta.; F. B. Setter, Calgary, Alta.; S. Shepperd, Isley, Alta.; D. Sibbeston, Fort Simpson, N.W.T.; D. Skinner, Hamilton, Ont.; G. W. Slominski, Edmonton, Alta.; G. A. Sparvier, Mileston, Sask.; D. P. Stashko, Grande Prairie, Alta.; C. Stearns, Ancaster, Ont.; S. M. Stephens, Fort St. John; D. M. Stewart, Saskatoon, Sask; D. A. St. Germain, Vanier, Ont.; A. E. Reeve, Swift Current, Alta.

R. W. Tassey, Edmonton, Alta.; B. A. Thibeau, Calgary, Alta.; E. Thompson, Edson, Alta.; J. Toth, Swift Current, Sask.; D. G. Turner, Calgary, Alta.; C. H. Twigg, Carson, Alta.; G. D. Vallet, Whitehorse, Yukon; H. Van Oyen, Calgary, Alta.

D. Ward, Edmonton, Alta.; S. Walsh, Hamilton, Ont.; D. H. Watt, Thorsby, Alta.; G. Webb, Edmonton, Alta.; D. Weimer, Regina, Sask.; J. Wilkinson, Kingston, Ont.; R. Williams, Swift Current, Sask.; P. Wooldridge, Ancaster, Ont.; A. D. Wright, Orleans, Ont.; R. Zaharia, Saskatoon, Sask.; D. J. Ziegler, Regina, Sask.; D. J. Zimmerman, Lacombe, Alta.

G COMPANY

K. W. Affleck, Winnipeg, Man.; A. C. Arp, Naicam, Sask.; B. F. Bella, Melville, Sask.; K. N. Berry, Thunder Bay, Ont.; W. Billups, Penticton; G.S. Bilyk, Westlock, Alta.; D. R. Booth, Saskatoon, Sask.; K. W. Brownlow, Revelstoke; D. Carriere, Vancouver; J. R. Cartier, Cumberland; S. G. Cataford, Nakusp; A. B. Chaney, Swift Current, Sask.; K. R. Coghlin, Moose Jaw, Sask.; B. C. Cook, Portage LaPrairie, Man.; W. A. Crouch, Victoria; D. Cruichank, Kelowna; R. P. Dart, Beaverlodge, Alta.; G. Davies, Kamloops; K. A. Dean, Invermay, Sask.; C. J. Devigne, Kenora, Ont.; J. Donnelly, Lethbridge, Alta.; C. R. Eason, Regina, Sask.

A. P. Faulk, White Rock; J. T. Fearey, Calgary, Alta.; M. J. Fitzgerald, Surrey; V. Flegel, Regina, Sask.; R. R. Funk, Fort McMurray, Alta.; W. G. Golley, Revelstoke; K. D. Griffiths, Merritt.

K. Harkema, Fruitville; L. A. Harland, Surrey; R. W. Hawkes, Moose Jaw, Sask.; R. R. Hill, Regina, Sask.; C. D. Hobbs, Lethbridge, Alta.; R. C. Hornung, Calgary, Alta.; D. M. Houwing, Edmonton, Alta.; K. Hoyer, Hollywood, Calif.; K. C. Huseby, Lacombe, Alta.; R. Jones, Haney; D. J. Kane, Humble, Sask.; W. M. Kasper, Dryden, Ont.; G. Kenery, Saskatoon, Sask.; D. R. Kerr, Dauphin, Man.; W. E. Killeen, Vancouver; A. P. Kirkwood, Nanaimo.

J. J. Leask, Turner Valley, Alta.; D. W. Lemon, Milestone, Sask.; D. W. Levers, Vancouver; T. W. Lineker, Edmonton, Alta.; R. J. Lukasiewich, Edmonton, Alta.; D. H. Madill, Regina, Sask.; K. I. Matheson, Lethbridge, Alta.; R. A. MacKenzie, New Denver; S. D. McEwan, Winnipeg, Man.; R. B. McGuire, Balmoral, Man.; E. B. McKenna, Fort Macleod, Alta.; D. F. McNeill, Verden, Man.; J. C. Meihm, Winnipeg, Man.; R. Morden, McCreary, Man.; J. C. Morrison, Coquitlam; T. P. Murphy, North Surrey.

T. J. Nieradka, Shilo, Man.; C. V. Norris, Vancouver; C. M. Nuessler, Coquitlam; E. D. Oliver, Vancouver; W. T. Oulton, Breton, Alta.; L. B. Panas, Prince George; W. Perdok, Thompson, Man.; W. Pennington, Coquitlam; R. N. Popik, Thorsby, Alta.; J. M. Premack, Surrey; D. T. Quick, Richmond; R. N. Reaume, Vedder Crossing; T. J. Rennie, Red Deer, Alta.; B. D. Revitt, Prince Albert, Sask.; Robertson, Moose Jaw, Sask.; P. Roehrig, Atikokan, Ont.;

C. H. Ross, Port Coquitlam; R. M. Roux, Clinton, Alta.; B. G. Ryan, Mayerthorpe, Alta.

S. Sanna, Balmer Town, Ont.; I W. Sawchuk, Edmonton, Alta.; D. M. Schmidt, Regina, Sask.; A. T. Schulte, Sherwood Park, Alta.; C. D. Seager, Calgary, Alta. R. M. Shemko, Pincher Creek, Alta.; F. P. Smillie, Vernon; S. E. Smyth, Yellowknife, N.W.T.; R. L. Solberg, Milestone, Sask.; J. W. Thompson, Black Diamond, Alta.; T. D. Usher, New Westminster; R. Vigoren, Saskatoon, Sask.; D. C. Wallace, Fort St. John; B. W. Walterhouse, Creston; P. E. Werry, Edmonton, Alta.; A. D. Wilson, Edmonton, Alta.; T. J. Yarama, Kelowna; S. J. Yaworek, Pine Falls, Man.

COMMUNICATIONS AND SAFE DRIVING

G. F. Baker, Creston; G. P. Bilyk, Westlock, Alta.; P. R. Borm, Westlock, Alta.; R. F. Boulet, Regina, Sask.; R. J. Brochu, Hammond; O. C. Bunnah, Lac Vert, Sask.; B. A. Capper, Calgary, Alta.; D. C. Deleeuw, Calgary; M. A. Dusyk, Invermay, Sask.; D. R. Falconer, Calgary, Alta.; G. R. Finlayson, Invermere; G. E. Hetherington, Moose Jaw, Sask.; J. J. Hulagrocki, Kenora, Ont.; W. C. Jackson, Edson, Alta.; J. F. Keough, Battleford, Sask.; M. M. Kriz, Regina, Sask.; R. P. Leclerc, Edmonton, Alta.; M. W. Long, Camp Vernon.

J. A. McCreight, Regina, Sask.; D. R. McDonagh, Edmonton, Alta.; D. C. McLaren, Winnipeg, Man.; P. D. Moulton, Sardis; W. P. Nahnybida, Kelwood, Man.; D. L. Orr, Calgary, Alta.; G. Perreault, Edmonton, Alta.; F. K. Pineau, Shilo, Man.; W. R. Porter, West Vancouver; D. G. Pyper, Winnipeg, Man.; D. C. Ralston, Mileston, Sask.; N. C. Selleck, Blueridge, Alta.; T. J. Sheppard, Summerland; C. E. Welston, Edmonton, Alta.; J. A. Wilson, Winnipeg, Man.; J. Yee, Black Diamond, Alta.; M. M. Zucchiatta, Atikokan, Ont.

BAND COMPANY

L. D. Allen, Calgary, Alta.; S. H. Atkinson, Victoria; R. C. Balkwill, Victoria; R. G. Barrow, Calgary, Alta.; A. Bittner, Calgary, Alta.; J. T. Blewett, White Rock; P. B. Boast, Calgary, Alta.; D. G. Bonner, Coquitlam; B. R. Bowles, Victoria; M. Brause, Surrey; K. R. Brewster, Burnaby; R. B. Broatch, White Rock; J. E. N. Borody, Surrey; D. W. Brooks, Fort McMurray, Alta.; A. D. Bruce, Coquitlam; J. D. Bryson, Nelson; R. J. Butchart, North Vancouver; G. K. Byrne, Vancouver:

R. L. Campbell, Vancouver; M. Cerny, Edmonton, Alta.; B. Chappell, Burnaby; R. Chipman,

Port Alberni; D. Corenan, Calgary, Alta.; B. D. Couillard, Calgary, Alta.; H. J. Crouch, Victoria; W. Dagg, Clagary, Alta.; R. D. Dankoski, New Denver; W. G. Davies, Vancouver; T. M. Davis, Edmonton, Alta.; D. Dickie, Surrey.

R. P. Ebbs-Canavan, Victoria; G. J. Edwards, Surrey; P. J. Ellis, Burnaby; K. R. Erickson, Port Alberni; V. Essex, White Rock; E. Finnigan, North Surrey; R. G. Gordon, Victoria; D. R. Grant, Cranbrook; N. Hall, Vancouver; W. Hallam, Victoria; D. L. Head, Edmonton; S. Horvats, Port Alberni; R. Hunn, Calgary, Alta.

D. W. Jackson, North Surrey; R. S. Kerr, Victoria; H. I. Langille, Prince George; R. A. Linden, Port Alberni; W. H. Linden, Port Alberni; A. D. Lyon, Edmonton; P. V. Machek, Victoria; M. A. Mancinelli, Port Coquitlam; R. W. Marocchi, Port Alberni; P. W. Martin, Calgary, Alta.; A. Matsushita, New Denver; D. J. McCarron, New Westminster; M. A. McKenna, Edmonton; K. A. McMillan, Cranbrook; W. D. McMullan, Calgary, Alta.

K. Melnick, Edmonton, Alta.; M. S. Miller, Ocean Park; M. Mori, New Denver; B. P. Murphy, Calgary, Alta.; K. E. Murray, Calgary, Alta.; B. S. Myers, Vancouver; G. D. Naylor, Calgary, Alta.; M. Norman, Nakusp; A. H. North, Victoria.

L. Piche, Port Coquitlam; J. Pistootnik, Vancouver; C. Podgorenko, Victoria; I. S. Prew, Calgary, Alta.; W. A. Prytula, Kelowna; B. Purton, South Burnaby; R. A. Rebantad, Coquitlam; R. E. Reinke, Clinton, Alta.; R. D. Renaud, Edmonton, Alta.; M. W. Revell, Surrey; B. J. Roberts, Edmonton, Alta.; R. L. Robson, Delta; P. P. Roussy, Surrey; T. T. Royle, Victoria.

J. J. Scarfe, Vancouver; C. E. Scott, White Rock; K. A. Sharbinin, New Westminster; A. Sharples, Calgary, Alta.; S. Sharples, Calgary, Alta.; K. V. Shaw, Cranbrook; A. E. Smith, Edmonton, Alta.; F. J. Suerink, Calgary, Alta.; J. Suerink, Calgary, Alta.; A. Tailleur, Edmonton, Alta.; D. Thickett, Victoria; N. Tully, Port Moody; G. Vizzutti, Calgary; R. White, New Denver; L. Woollven, Victoria.

VACC - 1971

A-1 COMPANY

L. A. Adamick' Weyburn; W. T. Apperley, Regina; R. K. Austin, Regina; P. R. Bailey, Thunder Bay; B.P. Balon, Regina; R. E. Barrett, Thunder Bay; R. E. Bathgate, Weyburn; B. W. Bellamy, Weyburn; R. G. Boyce, Regina; B. B. Breit, Vernon; B. W. Burridge, Thunder Bay; C. A. Butz, Regina.

R. A. Cain, Atikokan, Ont.; M. A. Carlson, Thunder Bay; L. D. Chassie, Keewatin, Ont.; M. F. Clark, Weyburn; L. A. Clarke, CFB Shilo, Man.; C. N. Cryderman, Thunder Bay.

B. E. Day, Balmertown, Ont.; R. T. DeNeeve, Madsen, Ont.; J. Denis, Moose Jaw; R. B. Doak, Shilo, Man.; G. R. Doran, Kenora; K. W. Doski, Thunder Bay; R. W. Downtown, Mortlach, Sask.; B. G. Dunbar, Thunder Bay; K. T. Durand, Atikokan, Ont.; R. K. Dyck, Swift Current.

C. P. Eason, Regina; J. D. Evans-Smith, Thunder Bay; S. P. Ewanchook, Moose Jaw.

W. A. Fenby, Regina; J. W. Frank, Regina; A. R. Fraser, Kenora.

H. P. G. Gambee, Thunder Bay; R. A. Girouard, Atikokan; R. A. Goeres, Weyburn; B. K. Guy, Milestone, Sask.; J. A. Halasz, Atikokan; P. C. Halasz, Atikokan; C. L. Harle, Regina; D. L. Harle, Regina; D. A. J. Harris, Thunder Bay; P. A. Hill, Regina; W. Hoogsteen, Thunder Bay; B. A. Hrycna, Swift Current; P. A. Hulina, Thunder Bay.

S. C. Janzen, Moose Jaw; R. L. Jeske, Regina; D. P. Jones, Shilo.

R. G. Kennedy, CFB Moose Jaw; B. A. Knight, Swift Current; R. J. Koroscil, Atikokan; C. J. P. Kot, Moose Jaw; J. J. Kotz, Dryden, Ont.; B. C. Krentz, Regina; R. A. Kuzminski, Thunder Bay.

R. P. LaJeunesse, Kenora; S. G. Landon, Dryden; R. L. Lemon, Milestone; E. F. Loranger, Kenora.

P. I. McIntosh, Regina; D. H. G. McKillop, Thunder Bay; D. McLeod, The Pas, Man.; D. W. McNair, Shilo; R. P. McNally, Thunder Bay.

W. J. Maki, Thunder Bay; E. W. Makowsky, Kenora; B. A. Mantai, Regina; A. S. Matt, Regina; A. J. Meghot, Thunder Bay; D. P. Messer, Weyburn; J. H. W. Mitchell, Madsen, Ont.; B. R. Murray, Weyburn; B. W. Murray, Weyburn.

S. D. Nagel, Regina; T. P. Nielsen, Thunder Bay; W. E. J. Nowak, Thunder Bay; P. L. Oblander, Regina; M. J. Oliver, CFB Shilo.

S. W. Parker, Keewatin; M. L. Pegoraro, Thunder Bay; L. L. Pickard, Balmer Town, Ont.; D. B. Pointer, CFB Shilo.

C. J. Reaney, McTaggart, Sask.; G. D. Reid, Balmertown, Ont,; R. J. Renwick, Milestone; R. D. Richardson, Moose Jaw; B. P. Riess, Regina; G. N. Riffel, Regina; E. L. Roulston, South Kenora; D. L. Rourke, Regina.

R. M. Saindon, Dryden; A. J. Salamanchuk, Regina; G. W. Sambray, Thunder Bay; G. J. Sanderson, Regina; R. Sanna, Balmertown; A. J. Santo, Regina; L. D. Schlecht, Dryden; D. G. Shupe,

Dryden; R. B. Slater, Regina; B. C Spaulding, Thunder Bay; D. F. Stulberg, Regina.

P. W. Thalhofer, Madsen, Ont.; P. M. White, Shilo; R. J. White, Balmertown; J. E. Wilcox, Regina; T. H. Williams, Swift Current; S. T. Wilson, Swift Current; K. W. Winters, Thunder Bay; W. R. Wittal, Regina; J. A. Wolfe, Dryden.

S. J. Zabloski, Kenora; T. A. Zirrie, Weyburn.

A-2 COMPANY

K. Anderson, Edmonton; D. L. Balon, Alta.; C. K. Bekar, Yellowknife; R. J. Blanchette, Vimy, Alta.; L. H. Bradford, Lacombe; W. J. Braga, Edmonton; A. J. Brazeau, Grande Prairie; D. K. Budziniski, Edmonton; T. C. Burns, Edmonton; R. J. Burnstick, Westlock, B.C.; R. M. Busby, Edmonton.

D. M. Caplette, Edmonton; M. W. Chwok, Edmonton; R. J. Corkery, Sherwood Park, Alta.

D. P. Daigle, Edmonton; R. D. Davis, Edmonton; I. S. Denny, Edmonton; C. W. Dexter, Yellowknife; P. Drader, Lacombe; K. D. Drader, Lacombe; D. N. Dumais, Edmonton; A. J. Dyer, Fort Smith, NWT.; G. R. Dyke, Inuvik.

R. A. Fraser, Edmonton; R. Frei, Dapp, Alta.; V. H. Gauthier, Yellowknife; D. R. Gibson, Grande Prairie; J. D. Giles, Edmonton; B. L. Graham, Ft. McMurray.

K. D. Hambley, Ft. McMurray; P. P. Hansen, Edmonton; J. T. Heath, Inuvik, NWT; B. A. Hedquist, Edmonton; W. R. Henne, Yellowknife; D. M. Hidson, Edmonton; P. W. Hintz, Edmonton; G. C. Hlewka, Edmonton; D. E. Hoffman, Edmonton; S. H. Horn, Edmonton.

R. A. Johnson, Edmonton; S. A. Johnstone, Westlock, Alta.; D. J. Kanuka, Edmonton; R. R. Kay, Westlock; T. W. Kennedy, Saint Albert, Alta.; J. Kok, Edmonton; K. R. Kolot, North Habay, Alta.; F. A. Kramer, Edmonton.

R. G. Larose, Edmonton; R. Lavoie, Edmonton; R. M. Leskie, Edmonton; M. P. Lewicki, Edmonton; J. E. Lockwood, Dapp, Alta.; B. W. Luk, Yellowknife; M. W. Lyon, Fort McMurray.

A. Macpherson, Edmonton; J. T. Macrae, Inuvik; P. S. McConnell, Edmonton; J. J. McDonald, Inuvik; R. B. McDonald, Sherwood Park; T. M. McGinnis, Whitehorse; W. D. K. McGuire, Edmonton; K. M. McKay, Sherwood Park; K. J. Madore, Lacombe; E. P. Mah, Edmonton; D. P. Marceau, Sherwood Park; K. K. Mayer, Edmonton; G. A. Mintz, Whitehorse; C. P. Mittemeyer, Lacombe; B. B. Mottershead, Edmonton.

G. M. O'Brien, Westlock; H. Oosterveld, Edmonton; D. A. Ouellett, Whitehorse.

553

B. Y. Palmer, Grande Prairie; L. G. H. Paquette, Edmonton; D. H. Parker, Victoria; T. R. Paziuk, Edmonton; D. F. Phillips, Fort Smith; B. A. Piro, Yellowknife; R. L. Pombert, Sherwood Park; A. S. Pratt, Dapp, Alta.; G. Preisler, Edmonton.

J. M. Racich, Edmonton; D. A. Read, Edmonton; B. C. Rempel, Fort MacMurray; G. K. Robson, Inuvik; R. N. Russel, Edmonton; M. S. Sapieha, Edmonton; T. M. Sherback, Edmonton; G. R. Smith, Edmonton; S. J. Smith, Sherwood Park; R. K. Stinn, Sherwood Park; S. T. Studney, Yellowknife.

R. J. Vallee, Edmonton; D. M. Van Buskirk, Edmonton.

R. S. Watt, Whitehorse; C. V. Webb, Fort McMurray; K. J. Werstiuk, Fort McMurray; R. M. Wesolowski, Edmonton; R. B. Witty, Yellowknife; L. T. Wren, Whitehorse; J. D. Wright, Yellowknife; D. K. Zarski, Edmonton.

A-3 COMPANY

D. Ames, Victoria; N. Atamanchuk, Surrey.

R. Ball, Port Alberni; B. Beaton, Surrey; L. Binning, Surrey; W. Boutet, Courtenay; C. Bouvette, Port Alberni; B. Bucholz, Port Coquitlam.

E. J. Cadorette, Victoria; D. C. Calvert, Surrey; M. Carr, Chilliwack; C. E. Castle, Surrey; C. G. Catherine, Victoria; B. T. Chanasyk, Surrey; W. R. Chanasyk, Surrey; W. F. Collisson, Cultus Lake; C. A. Cook, Surrey; R. L. Corey, Port Alberni.

D. W. Dash, Victoria; J. T. Dobson, Chilliwack; S. J. Doucette, Victoria; B. J. Edgar, Nanaimo; E. E. Emms, Cumberland; M. A. Erickson, Port Alberni; S. R. Evjenth, Surrey.

D. R. Ford, Vancouver; D. B. Ford, Victoria.

G. E. Gay, White Rock; G. R. Getz, Nanaimo; L. J. Gieni, Port Alberni; J. M. Graham, Chilliwack.

D. M. Haley, Lazo, B.C.; A. P. Hallihan, Victoria; D. A. Hambley, Victoria; T. E. Hanson, Port Coquitlam; J. H. P. Harkin, Victoria; J. J. Harris, Port Coquitlam; F. B. Haws, Vedder Crossing; D. K. Hetland, Port Moody; M. T. Holmes, Burnaby; T. H. Holmes, Sardis; L. A. Homeniuk, Edmonton; J. P. Hyldtoff, Cloverdale.

K. D. Joesbury, Surrey; D. S. Johnson, Port Alberni; W. F. Johnson, Port Coquitlam; S. R. Jordison, Victoria.

G. J. Karlson, Surrey; D. M. Klein, Surrey; A. K. Kulhawy, Surrey; J. P. Kulhawy, Surrey.

G. R. Lacioix, Victoria; J. E. Leach, Surrey; J. A. Leach, Surrey; L. A. London, Surrey.

R. E. MacIntyre, Chilliwack; R. D. McFarlane, Victoria; R. A. McGivern, Surrey; B. W. McLaghlin, Surrey; N. R. McNeill, Sardis; R. E. F. Major, Courtenay; M. M. Mason, Port Coquitlam; A. Mastrovalerio, Surrey; B. R. Mawson, Victoria; K. L. Miller, Comox; B. M. Moore, White Rock; C. M. Moore, Victoria; L. J. Morberg, Victoria; B. A. Murray, Edmonton.

J. F. Newbury, Maple Ridge; R. G Newman, Chilliwack; L. E. Nohl, Surrey; D. F. J. O'Krane, Surrey; B. F. Olynick, White Rock; P. W. Omyschtschuk, Port Alberni; D. G. Orrey, Qualicum Beach; C. G. Owen, Victoria.

M. J. Payette, Nanaimo; B. Pedden, Victoria; T. Plante, Victoria; W. A. Popyk, Surrey; D. J. Prince, Surrey; J. N. Raine, Victoria; M. A. Rusk, Edmonton.

B. R. Sanders, Port Moody; W. L. Schweitzer, Surrey; N. M. Scott, Coquitlam; B. Seppa, Victoria; M E. Stapie, Maple Ridge; G. D. Stark, North Surrey; G. F. Switalski, Surrey.

R. J. Turlock, Victoria; J. A. Turner, Victoria; R. C. Urquhart, Haney; K. E. Vankoughnett, Vedder Crossing; A. R. Vivian, Courtenay.

B. J. Waters, White Rock; D. L. Werbowski, Surrey; A. B. A. Westling, Victoria; N. Wincup, Surrey.

B COMPANY

V. Apperley, Regina; M. A. Bajowsky, Revelstoke; J. R. Beaulieu, Fort Smith; A. R. Bear, Brandon; T. Bennett, Calgary; G. G. Berube, Black Diamond, Alta.; D. M. Blackstrop, Calgary.

K. A. Blanchard, Drydon, Ont.; E. Bonnetrouge, Fort Simpson, N.W.T.; B. D. Boyd, West Vancouver; M W. Bremner, North Vancouver; H. J. Brink, Calgary; S. L. Broddy, Calmar, Alta.; C. D. Brullotte, Burton.

R. Carter, Nanaimo; L. Cashman, Calgary; B. W. Chapman, Moose Jaw; R. Church, Dryden; B. Chwyl, Fort St. John; T. V. Clark, Fort Churchill; R. Cockney, Inuvik; K. Collisson, Cultus Lake; R. Colluney, Calgary; P. Coltura, Hinton; A. Cormans, Nanaimo; J. P. Cox, Vernon; R. Cummings, Courtenay.

G. W. Dale, Vancouver; W. Derepenthgny, Yorkton; D. Dolinski, Kamloops; S. Doubleday, Calgary; A. V. Edwards, Vancouver; L. Einersson, Winnipeg; L. Epler, Edmonton; P. A. Evans, Fort Churchill; R. K. Evans, Maple Ridge.

G. A. Ferguson, Kelowna; R. M. Ferguson, Port Alberni; P. R. Fiorin, Victoria; A. J. Fisher, Dauphin; S. A. Fligel, Regina; R. G. Ford, Punnichy, Sask.; N. H. Fortier, Edmonton; R. M. Frew, Coquitlam.

F. C. Gattinger, Regina; D. V. Glessing, Humbolt; B. Grinsted,

Merritt; D. N. Grinsted, Merritt; R. A. Gunderson, Prince George.

M. Hagen, Port Alberni; R. W. Haines, Mayerthorpe; A. W. Halladay, Lacvert, Sask.; A. L. Halliday, Vancouver; D. R. Hambley, Victoria, R. H. Hayward, Portage la Prairie; W. F. Hengster, Punnichy; R. Hills, Creston; A. Hoogsteen, Thunder Bay; G. L. Hossack, Winnipeg; G. A. Howard, Victoria; L. R. Howat, Regina.

R. J. Irwin, Sherwood Park; J. H. Kalen, Edmonton; K. A. Kalinin, Winnipeg; T. J. Kaufman, Lacombe; K. A. C. Kendall, Salmon Arm; R. G. Kessler, Balmoral, Man.; R. D. Kolstad, North Delta; E. J. Koski, Revelstoke; L. J. Kobach, Black Diamond; W. M. Kulachkowski, Saskatoon.

K. J. Larson, Winnipeg; W. D. Lavoie, Prince Albert; J. H. Lorimer, Thunder Bay; R. S. Lowe, Shilo, Man.

J. N. MacLean, Vedder Crossing; A. J. McCoshan, Winnipeg; R. J. McEathron, Black Diamond, Alta.; M. McKay, David, Sask.; K. A. McMillan, Cranbrook; D. E. McNabb, Warrenton, Man.; A. H. McPherson, Wadena, Sask.; D. G. Mach, Grand Prairie; G. R. Maclean, Melville; B. W. Magee, Calgary; K. Mailey, Calgary; K. G. Markuse, Winnipeg; C. M. Meknychuk, Edmonton; J. E. Miller, Red Lake, Ont.; A. D. Morrison, Turtleford, Sask.; J. R. Morrison, Battleford.

M. J. Nevert, Saskatoon; W. F. Nickerson, Ladner; B. J. Oman, Swift Current; P. O'Riordan, White Rock; P. Owslanyk, Winnipeg.

R. P. Page, Ladner; P. Palmer, New Denver; E. L. Peters, North Vancouver; A. J. Plamondon, Fruitvale; A. F. Proctor, Westlock; R. Prud'homme, Swift Current.

T. Raven, Morris, Man.; L. R. Richards, Winnipeg; D. J. Ritchie, Sturgis, Sask.; R. E. Roberts, St. George, Man.; D. V. Robleski, Brandon; G. D. Ryan, Vancouver.

R. M. Salewski, Surrey; N. N. Sawka, Winnipeg; J. R. Schramm, Summerland; R. Seltenrich, Salmon Arm; P. Shewchuk, Rama, Sask.; D. J. Sluchinski, Alder Flats, Alta.

C. Snardski, Thunder Bay; R. J. Souter, Sardis; G. N. Springer, Kamsack; M. J. Stephen, Surrey; G. St. Germain, Prince Albert.

G. L. Tessier, St. Jean Baptists, Man.; B. Therens, Moose Jaw; E. Thomas, Regina; W. R. Thompkins, Abbotsford; D. A. Toth, Surrey; S. Vinet, Thunder Bay.

B. C. Ward, Edmonton; R. Warner, Delta; D. Watson, Edmonton; L. Wedow, Woodnorth, Man.; P. White, Atikokan, Ont.; J. Wiens, Powell River; A. Wilkes, Vedder Crossing; R. Williams, Innuvik; M. Worgan, White Rock; D. Wringley, Calgary; H. Zalinko, Regina; R. Zurkan, Thunder Bay.

C COMPANY

R. G. Amm, Vancouver; C. B. Anderson, Alderwood Manner, Wash.; D. R. Andrews, Victoria; W. J. Baehler, Kelowna; G. V. Barker, Burnaby; G. Beniussis, White Rock; E. M. Bennett, Prince George.

M. A. Berlingerette, Prince George; F. E. Bone, Nakusp; S. W. Bruce, Coquitlam; G. L. Bruch, Victoria; R. P. Bryant, Victoria; R. B. Bryson, Vancouver; L. L. Burgemaster, Vernon; J. A. Burley, Victoria;

K. Campbell, Kelowna; R. C. Campbell, Vancouver; S. Campbell, North Vancouver; T. Campen, Wellington, B.C.; V. Caron, Prince George; R. F. Carruthers, Coquitlam; S. Casselman, North Vancouver; L. Catchpole, Victoria; J. Catterall, Rutland; J. A. Chambers, Vancouver.

N. Cinderich, Vancouver; P. Clegg, Vancouver; D. Cloke, Nanaimo; W. Cochran, Kamloops; B. Sonsidine, Victoria; R. Corredo, Port Moody; F. Coyl, Burnaby; J. Cross, Kamloops.

D. W. Delmore, New Westminster; L. Duperron, Prince George; A. Durante, Kamloops; L. A. Dzuis, North Vancouver; J. A. Earl, North Vancouver; L. W. Elliot, Victoria; D. J. Errington, Coquitlam.

R. Fehling, Vernon; L. N. Fenshe, Coquitlam; G. W. Forbes, Port Alberni; R. M. Frolek, Kamloops; D. Gavin, Kamloops; D. J. Gingell, Oyama; R. D. Glacer, Vancouver; C. Graw, Hythe, Alta.; B. A. Grimm, Cranbrook; P. A. Grouette, Vancouver; O. R. Gruenhelt, Victoria.

S. B. Hamilton, Coquitlam; J. C. Hancock, White Rock; P. Harkena, Fruitvale; S. W. Harris, Victoria; H. G. Hill, Powell River; J. R. Holmgren, Prince George; B. D. Hope, Merritt; E. A. Howard, Victoria; P. C. Huber, Quilchena.

D. C. Irwin, Fruitvale; T. M. Jefferies, Winnipeg; R. J. Karlodinski, Coquitlam; R. M. Kerr, Victoria; J. G. Kwasnica, Vedder Crossing; S. J. Lamb, Kamloops; R. E. Larson, Revelstoke; L. M. Leedholm, New Denver.

J. K. MacBride, Vedder Crossing; S. J. MacDonald, Victoria; W. J. McIntyre, Vancouver; V. A. Martin, Prince George; L. A. R. Michaelson, White Rock; M. A. Mitchell, Merritt; D. Moore, North Vancouver; W. A. Morran, Victoria.

R. C. Nelmes, Port Coquitlam; R. E. Newhook, Victoria; R. G. Neumann, Langley; G. R. Nicholl, Surrey; S. C. Nielson, Victoria; K. W. Niesson, Abbotsford; B. P. Onyschtschuk, Port Alberni; J. W. Pans, Chilliwack; D. Pettitt, Rutland; B. Palson, North Burnaby; D. Peacock, Victoria; R. Prokop, Vancouver.

J. Ramsey, Lower Nicoln; R. Rebantad, Coquitlam; K. D. Relkey,

Prince George; L. Reimer, Port Alberni; R. S. Rempel, North Surrey; F. Rilling, North Vancouver; M. A. Roberge, Coquitlam; A. T. Roberts, Vancouver; S. Robinson, Kamloops; P. Robson, Delta.

A. R. J. Shaw, Kelowna; M. A. Shaw, North Vancouver; J. P. L. Smeltzer, Surrey; W. Smoker, Yarrow; I. S. Stanishewski, Vernon; N. A. Swift, West Vancouver.

W. Taillfer, White Rock; J. Thorsteinsoni, Port Coquitlam; D. W. Turner, Cranbrook; D. Tychynski, Vancouver; B. Vanderveer, Kamloops; D. Vike, South Burnaby; C. Wales, Summerland; G. Walters, Vancouver; K. Warriner, Salmon Arm; R. Wywka, Delta; B. Yahemeh, Burnaby; G. Yarama, Salmon Arm.

D COMPANY

D. Akselson, Vernon; R. R. Allen, Winnipeg; G. H. Bateman, Winnipeg; D. G. Bitternose, Punnichy; D. J. Bremner, Fort Gary, Man.; J. M. Brunner, Saskatoon; D. P. Burke, Saskatoon; J. B. Burke, Saskatoon; J. A. Burley, Victoria.

M. Callbeck, Prince Albert; G. Carbert, Cochenour, Ont.; G. Carrier, Regina; D. Chartrand, Winnipeg; V. Chassie, Kenora; L. Cherniawsky, Sturgis; A. Collette, St. Jean Baptiste; R. Collins, Saskatoon.

M. Davies, Verden, Man.; W. Davison, Winnipeg; A. Desaulniers, Dryden, Ont.; V. Devlin, Thompson, Man.; B. Dirk, Saskatoon; A. B. Donnelly, Pine Falls; A. Dunsmore, Winnipeg; K. Eastman, Winnipeg; A. Eskelson, Swift Current.

H. J. Gabbert, Thompson, Man.; G. B. Geddes, Punnichy, Sask.; R. B. Gibson, Moose Jaw; G. A. Good, Regina; G. H. Graham, Regina; K. L. Gray, Morris; B. J. Gregoire, St. Jean, Man.

D. E. Hall, Virden, Man.; J. D. Hamre, Moose Jaw; D. E. Hanke, Saskatoon; D. O. Hanke, Saskatoon; R. M. Hanley, Moose Jaw; L. E. Hannah, Winnipeg; D. B. Harty, Regina; M. Hazell, Shilo; W. C. Henton, Kelwood, Man.; K. A. Hiebert, Winnipeg; G. A. Hodgson, Thompson; D. L. Horsnall, Moose Jaw; J. M. Hussey, Winnipeg.

A. L. Issac, Broadview, Sask.; J. P. Jaszcyszak, Dryden, Ont.; K. A. Johnston, Armstrong; L. A. Kirk, Melville; S. J. Knourek, Melville; D. A. Kryzanowski, Wadena, Sask.

G. P. Lacey, Churchill; R. K. Ladouceur, Victoria; K. T. Larson, Regina; R. R. Leclerc, Keewatin; D. R. Leisch, Winnipeg; W. H. Lietz, Regina; M. H. Lindsay, McCreary, Man.

D. K. McLeod, McCreary,; J. A. Madsen, North Battleford; C. M. Matthews, Dauphin, Man.; A. P. Matwyczuk, Winnipeg; J. S.

Michaluk, Wadena, Sask.; G. A. Michon, Regina; A. E. Moate, Winnipeg; E. P. Neault, Regina; L. J. Neudorf, Saskatoon; G. D. Nieckar, Rama, Sask.

D. F. Oliver, Victoria; G. Pedden, Transcona, Man.; J. L. Pfeiffer, Winnipeg; E. M. Pickard, Balmetown; K. P. Porayko, Winnipeg; M. R. Porayko, Winnipeg; S. Pratt, Saskatoon; L. D. Primeau, Prince Albert.

P. J. Quigley, Maple Ridge; D. D. H. Quinn, Dolphin, Man.; D. P. Rabbitskin, Regina; R. Rae, Saskatoon; W. C. Rahn, Armstrong; R. V. Rice, Creighton, Sask.; T. A. Ridgway, Saskatoon; K. J. Ritchot, Morris, Man.; E. R. Robertson, Moose Jaw.

G. G. Schneider, Flin Flon; D. H. Schultz, Swift Current; M. C. Scott, Humboldt, Sask.; B. W. Selander, Swift Current; A. Shaw, Morris, Man.; B. M. Shaw, Melville, Sask.; A. K. Sheen, Victoria; W. R. Simpson, Keewatin, Ont.; R. T. Stalliard, Creighton; W. H. Statz, Winnipeg; J. P. Stefanuk, Saskatoon; R. H. Stevenson, Prince Albert; G. J. St. Goddard, Dolphin; T. J. Stokotelny, Dauphin; B.C. Sutherland, Moose Jaw; D. M. Swidzinsky, Saskatoon.

J. B. Tardiff, Pine Falls; M. Tomkiewicz, Madsen; C. M. Tutte, Vernon; D. Tuttosi, Punnichy; D. Valentino, Thompson, Man.; T. Walsh, Fort Churchill; D. West, Punnichy; R. Wilson, Thunder Bay; J. Wilt, Shilo; W. Winichuk, Belleville.

DVR COMM

E. T. Bashwa, White Rock; L. D. Bauder, Edmonton; N. H. Bessette, Edmonton; R. J. Bryans, Wynndel; E. Cornez, Calgary; G. Davis, Vernon; P. Ellis, Burnaby; G. Enright, Vedder Crossing.

G. D. Foster, Battleford; D. E. Gillard, Edmonton; R. G. Gordon, Victoria; K. D. Griffiths, Merritt; K. C. Harkema, Fruitvale; E. E. Harwardt, Edson; G. M. Kinghorn, Great Falls, Man.

A. H. Langmuir, Thompson, Man.; R. A. Lee, West Vancouver; I. Lipinski, Fort St. John; J. K. Lowen, Kelowna; M. MacInnis, Weybourne; J. McIntosh, Grande Prairie; R. W. Marocchi, Port Alberni; A. E. Martens, Winnipeg.

M. R. Norman, Lac La Hache; C. M. Nuessler, Coquitlam; L. C. Otte, Regina; D. J. Plamondon, St. Front, Sask.

D. P. Rouleau, Vancouver; J. H. Seniuk, Winnipeg; I. M. Smith, Victoria; E. D. J. St. Onge, Fort Churchill.

R. Tassey, Edmonton; C. Thomasson, Winnipeg; H. Vanoyen, Calgary; G. Webb, Edmonton; L. Wiens, Winnipeg; D. A. Wright, Fernie; D. Ziegler, Regina.

E COMPANY

W. L. Agnew, Fort McMurray, Alta.; R. B. Alpaugh, Fort St. John; A. R. Armstrong, Calgary; J. L. Ayrey, Brenton, Alta.; N. S. Balkham, Fort McLeod, Alta.; K. D. Barnes, Red Deer; W. S. Bates, Calgary; R. M. Berg, Calgary.

D. J. Balkwill, Weyburn, Sask.; M. J. Blanchette, Vimey, Alta.; K. Blankenau, Edmonton; N. A. Boisvert, Sherwood Park, Alta.; H. E. Bojda, Red Deer; D. M. Bosch, Sherwood Park; B. J. Brister, Calgary; A. L. Burak, Surrey; B. G. Buttazzoni, Lethbridge.

C, Cadick, Calgary; R. Cantley, Calgary; J. A. Chambers, Vancouver; D. Christensen, Fort St. John; R. Czarnecki, Edmonton; M. Dijker, Calgary; A. Duggan, Edmonton; E. Edwards, Black Diamond, Alta.; K. Fisher, Black Diamond, R. Fitzowich, Calmar, Alta.; R. D. Flynn, Edmonton.

P. C. Gancer, Calgary; K. G. Gemmell, Fort McLeod; K. F. Gerwien, Mayerthorpe, Alta.; R. E. Graham, Edmonton; J. Green, Fort McMurray; E. P. Guenette, Edmonton; D. O. Gunn, Sherwood Park.

R. G. Hamer, Calgary; R. M. Hanson, Grande Prairie; G. R. Harsulla, Vegreville; K. B. Hawkinson, Mayerthorpe; B. Henderson, Calgary; A. C. Hidson, Edmonton; B. Hoffman, Calgary; R. Hunn, Calgary; R. Huseby, Black Falls, Alta.; R. J. Huseby, Black Falls; W. Hutchinson, Nicosia, Cyprus.

B. Imeson, Calgary; C. G. Janzer, Medicine Hat; J. C. Jardine, Black Diamond; K. D. Kelm, Lacombe; K. K. King, Edmonton; R. A. Kirkness, Fort St. John; S. J. Kirtio, Edmonton; B. A. Klimchuk, Red Deer; D. E. Kuefler, Sherwood Park.

J. E. Lawrence, Calgary; B. W. Lindsay, Calgary; W. J. Luke, Yellowknife; R. J. MacLean, Alderflats, Alta.; B. I. MacNeil, Inuvik, N.W.T.; P. J. McElroy, Edmonton; K. L. McGregor, Calgary; D. B. McKinnon, Pincher Creek; C. G. McKnight, Mayerthorpe; D. I. Magson, Pincher Creek; J. C. Mailloux, Edmonton; L. Meyer, Edmonton.

C. J. Nash, Calgary; J. Y. Nicholson, Turner Valley; B. A. Nord, Calgary; S. D. Omilusik, Calgary; P. E. Orr, Calgary.

P. W. Parsonage, Edmonton; A. E. Pasemko, Westlock; F. E. Payne, Edmonton; J. R. Pearson, Fort McMurray; G. H. Peeters, Pincher Creek; C. W. Perry, Calgary; D. K. Peters, Calgary; D. L. Peters, Calgary; Poch, D. A. Pincher Creek.

R. Quick, Fort MacLeod; R. W. Reid, Okotoks, Alta.; W. D. Reitsma, Edmonton; L. J. Ripley, Calgary; T. C. Robinson, Red Cliff, Alta.; R. D. Rogers, Edmonton; D.

M. Rollings, Red Deer; L. J. Rous, Calgary; R. P. Sager, Edmonton; D. K. Sandeski, Weyburn, Sask.; G. A. Sandford, Calgary; R. Schouten, Fort McMurray; M. L. Seibold, Edmonton; J. J. Sheen, Sherwood Park; G. P. Siegfried, Red Deer; A. O. Smiley, Lavy, Alta.; P. R. Smith, Edmonton; D. C. Sorensen, Braton, Alta.; D. A. Sorge, Pincher Creek; L. D. Strymecki, Edmonton; M. A. Sutherland, Edmonton; W. P. Szuta, Weyburn.

S. Tarleton, Calgary; K. Toombs, Lethbridge; K. Tutin, Whitehorse; B. Twigg, Cardston; C. Twigg, Cardston; A. Washie, Fort Rae, N.W.T.; J. Westbury, Calgary; N. Westling, Breton, Alta.; K. White, Pincher Creek; P. Wilkinson, Isley, Alta.; G. Williams, Mayerthorpe; R. Worth, Redcliffe; K. Young, Calgary.

G COMPANY

M. D. Adams, Mayerthorpe; L. J. Aubin, Pincher Creek; J. A. Balkwill, Victoria; J. A. Ball, Powell River; K. R. Bannister, Yellowknife; D. L. Beaudoin, Vawn, Sask.; L. Beaudoin, Comox; F. L. Beek, North Battleford; A. R. Bennett, Vancouver; R. W. Bercier, Regina; C. L. Berthelette, Pine Falls, Man.; L. M. Blewett, Coquitlam.

D. Boersma, Calgary; L. V. Boisvert, Sherwood Park; J. Bozzo, Thunder Bay; W. D. Brandburyk, Port Coquitlam; R. B. Brass, Davis, Sask.; H. L. Brown, Delta; M. J. Byrne, Yellowknife.

R. J. Cairns, Kenora; W. S. Carrell, Goodfare, Alta.; K. R. Casselman, Shilo; C. J. Cassidy, Woodworth, Man.; I. H. Chamney, Innisfail; S. L. Chell, Fort McLeod.

D. G. Chong, Vernon; P. C. Clegg, Vancouver; L. H. Clifford, Prince George; R. J. Corrigal, Prince Albert; B. D. Cottrell, Coquitlam; G. M. Coyston, Churchill.

B. J. Dodds, Salmon Arm; G. S. Douglas, North Vancouver; C. E. Dufault, Dauphin; R. K. Duncan, Westbank; T. Dunlop, Sherwood Park.

D. W. Ewanchook, Moose Jaw; H. W. Fedoruk, Vegreville; G. D. W. Fitze, Abbotsford; W. K. Fitzpatrick, Winnipeg.

H. R. Gagne, Vancouver; O. P. Gentes, Red Lake, Ont.; E. R. Gilbert, Crescent Beach; W. K. Gordon, Victoria; G. E. Gray; Winnipeg; I. D. Gray, Calgary.

S. G. Hart, Delta; L J. Haldahl, Fruitvale; B. D. Holmes; Victoria; G. H. Hossack, Winnipeg; R. B. Hudson, Kelowna; W. K. Hutchison, Comox.

H. H. Jarche, Revelstoke; R. T. Johnson, Thompson; G. N. Kapteyn, Edmonton; B. J. Kennedy, Port Moody; J. Kinney, Abbotsford.

R. W. Larson, Melville; M. A.

LeFurey, Edmonton; R. M. Lekivetz, Victoria; G. Lemon, Milestone, Sask.

B. J. McCoy, Calgary; D. W. McCracken, Chilliwack; J. M. McElroy, Edmonton; R. D. McInnes, Nakusp; A. S. McKinnon, Pincher Creek; H. W. McLeod, Saskatoon; J. R. McNab, Warrenton, Man.; F. J. Martens, Winnipeg; W. A. Maurer, Edmonton; D. W. Munro, Yarrow; B. P. Murphy, Calgary.

C. S. Northrup, Edmonton; J. C. Norwegian, Fort Simpson; V. W. Olson, Creston; C. J. Peterson, Revelstoke; W. T. Philp, Swift Current; R. R. Poirier, Kenora; D. J. Poucher, Victoria; W. A. Prytula, Kelowna; K. Pyper, East Kildonan; J. Purych, Edomoton.

D. R. Rennie, Red Deer; C. J. Rodgers, Calgary; G. N. Roe, Calgary; R. A. Rolfe, Vernon; D. G. Schmidt, Regina; R. D. Shortland, Thompson; R. J. Smith, Victoria; B. F. Snell, Regina; M. Standrick, Edmonton; M. S. Stephens, Fort St. John; P. E. Stevenson, Vancouver; D. A. Strilchuk, Edmonton; H. W. B. Sweinson, Vernon.

E. V. Thompson, Edson; S. W. Thompson, Black Diamond, Alta.; M. A. Tosoff, Prince George; R. W. Toth, Surrey; D. G. Turner, Calgary; D. G. Tutin, Whitehorse.

G. D. R. Ward, Grand Prairie; L. A. Watkins, Surrey; C. R. Way, Edmonton; R. Wikman, Melville.

BAND COMPANY

B. N. Adolph, Burnaby; T. F. Aldoff, Prince George; D. J. Anderson, Saskatoon; N. H. Arnold; Calgary; K. D. Arthur, Calgary.

R. A. Billington, Mayerthorpe; D. G. Bonner, Coquitlam; W. J. Brass, Surrey; S. E. Bremner, Winnipeg; C. D. Broddy, Calmar; K. R. Brewster, Burnaby; S. F. Brown, Surrey; F. W. Brygadyr, Victoria; B. A. Buchanan, Thompson; G. K. Byrne, Vancouver.

M. Capek, Mintoarmie, Man.; B. A. Cassidy, Nanoose Bay; D. Chapman, Winnipeg; B. Chappell, South Burnaby; E. E. Clark, Victoria; A. Coates, Edmonton; D. Coble, Saskatoon; D. Cooper, Victoria; D. Coreman, Calgary; B. Cottrell, Coquitlam.

R. Davis, Edmonton; R. Dellorme, Winnipeg; L. M. A. Desharnais, Calgary; R. DiGuistini, Vancouver; K. Donaldson, Minto, Man; P. Dumonceau, Surrey; A. Edwards, Fernie; V. Essex, Surrey; L. Evans, Surrey.

W. H. Filliatrault, Prince George; J. Findlay, Edmonton; E. J. Finnigan, Surrey; P. J. Fodey, Regina; P. L. Fraser, Saskatoon; D. H. Frederiksen, Vancouver.

F. Gaal, Vancouver; M. D. Gair, Calgary; M. A. Garofano, Burnaby; D. J. Gibson, White Rock; J. L.

Giesbrecht, New Westminster; R. N. Giesbrecht, Transcona, Man.; G. R. Girvin, Cranbrook; D. J. Grant, Victoria; T. R. Grant, Cranbrook.

J. D. Halicki, Surrey; N. M. Hall, Vancouver; N. C. Hawkins, Winnipeg; J. G. Huber, Saskatoon; R. G. Hoffman, Calgary; A. Hussein, Calgary; D. W. Jackson, Surrey; R. J. Jones, Shilo; J. T. Kerr, Edmonton; G. A. Langan, Calgary; H. I. Langille, Quesnel; L. D. Larsen, Regina; R. G. Lawson, Transcoe; T. R. Linfitt, Burnaby.

A. J. MacDonald, Edmonton; W. E. McKinley, Winnipeg; G. C. McKinnon, Prince George; R. P. McLennan, Cobble Hill, B.C.; D. B. McLeod, Edmonton; G. A. Mace, White Rock; D. A. Madill, Regina; W. H. Madland, Prince George; M. A. Mancinelli, Port Coquitlam; P. L. Meredith, Regina; Mr. D. Miller, Winnipeg; A. J. Moffit, Victoria; W. S. Myers, Vancouver.

M. A. Nanka, Burnaby; R. C. Nassi, Delta; J. H. Parnell, Calgary; P. T. Pendl, Port Moody; H. Pete, New Denver; T. Piosseck, Surrey; J. Pistotnik, Vancouver; J. R. Polano, Regina; B. M. Pressey, Winnipeg.

M. W. Rainbird, Calgary; D. R. Roach, Surrey; R. A. Roach, Surrey; K. R. Rose, Shilo; C. J. Rouse, Port Moody.

C. D. Schultz, Calgary; A. S. Sharples, Vancouver; S. J. Sharples, Vancouver; G. G. Shaw, Argyle, Man.; W. L. Sheilds, Victoria; D. J. Smith, Winnipeg.

B. Tawse, Calgary; R. Thachak, Kamloops, P. Thickett, Victoria; M. Thomas, Prince George; D. R. Thomas, Port Alberni; N. Tully, Port Moody; R. Vetter, Saskatoon; R. Vince, Winnipeg; A. E. Vodicka, Calgary.

R. W. Wadsworth, Regina; D. Wagorn, Port Moody; R. Walter, Coquitlam; R. Warrell, Shilo; D. Watt, Saskatoon; L. B. Welsh, Winnipeg; B. J. Winter, Regina; P. Wisminity, Saskatoon; M. Woodsford, White Rock; C. Woollven, Victoria; C. R. Worden, Regina.

VACC - 1973

B COY

F. J. Adams, Winnipeg; W. H. Aldred, Grand Prairie; B. C. Bakuska, Portage LaPrairie; M. A. Beare, Shilo; K. R. Bex, Brandon; T. J. Billson, Winnipeg; N. H. Bonekamp, Pine Falls; P. R. Boulby, Edson; D. A. Bremner, Warren; G. J. Bridgman; Thunder Bay; M. M. Browning, Fort Simpson; J. J. Bulback, Portage LaPrairie; W. M. Burden, Dauphin.

D. J. Carsted, Winnipeg; R. J. A. Chagnon, Powerview; C. A. Caouette, Edmonton; C. H. Caya, Winnipeg; S. B. Cohen, Mayerthorpe; C. C. Crosby, Grand Prairie; L. Dangman, Winnipeg; D. G. Darr, Brandon; D. E. Davidson,

Dauphin; K. B. Davies; Virden; R. C. Davis, Shilo; A. H. Dodd, Winnipeg; R. W. Dubois, Portage LaPrairie; P. E. Dupuis, St. Jean Baptiste; A. A. Duriez, Edmonton. O. Erdell, Edmonton; J. R. Fisher, Dauphin; B. A. Freeman, Virden; M. G. Gibson, White Court; D. R. Godard, St. Jean Baptiste; G. Hall, Whitecourt; J. Hillier, Winnipeg; R. W. Hoban, Pine Falls; T. J. Hrabarichuck, Winnipeg; C. J. Hulsemann, Winnipeg; A. H. James, Edson; P. B. Jandewerth, St. Albert; B. L. Jensen, Leduc; S. J. Jurko, Madsen.

P. Kasper, Drydon; A. Kelm, Winnipeg; F. K. Kennedy, Edmonton; J. Kerr, Winnipeg; I. Kesteris, Thompson; L. B. Kidd, Mayerthorpe; M. B. Kirch, Mayerthorpe; M. V. Hohlmeyer, Flin Flon; S. Kozak, N. Kenora; N. A. Langevin, Edmonton; J. Larocque, Winnipeg; K. W. Lastiwka, Edmonton; I. A. Leverington, Stonewall; J. K. Linton; Edmonton; R. Loesch, Winnipeg; R. Loy, Edmonton; D. W. McArthur, Vermette; K. P. McCartney, Edmonton; B. J. McDonald, Thunderbay; K. F. McKenna, Edmonton; A. R. McLennan, Winnipeg; G. D. McNamara, Winnipeg; D. R. MacKenzie, Winnipeg; R. A. MacKenzie, Kenora; F. E. Martin, Edmonton; T. Masi, Red Lake; D. A. Meyer, Edmonton; D. H. Morgan, Thunderbay; R. Mulders, Fort Churchill.

P. M. Nash, Winnipeg; B. D. Neatby, Winnipeg; C. Nichols, Edmonton; B. L. Norris, Kenora; B. Norwegian, Simpson; D. F. Olmsted, Edmonton; D. J. Paiement, Edmonton; G. R. Pain, Inuvik; B. Parisien, Winnipeg; G. G. Pelletier, McCreary; P. A. Peterselamio, Inuvik; D. L. Picken, Grand Prairie; J. H. Pollard, Ddyden; F. J. Pollock, Winnipeg; T. J. Popp, Whitehorse.

D. G. Reitsma, Edmonton; D. G. Renaud, Edmonton; B. R. Rhinhart, Yellowknife; P. F. Robert, Pine Falls; R. C. Robinson, Rivers: D. G. Russell, Basso.

M. J. Sameluk, Thunderbay; F. M. Schlamp, Winnipeg; N. A. Schubert, Edmonton; D. A. Scott, Brandon; J. A. Shepherd, Whitecourt; L. J. Shupe, Dryden; T. D. Silvaggio, Marquette; H. K. Silvester, Winnipeg; H. W. Smith, Creighton; G. E. Sommer, Whitecourt; J. R. Stein, Thunderbay; S. Stevenson, Hay River; R. B. Stinson, Virden; F. T. Taylor, Winnipeg; B. D. Third, Morris; H. A. Therrtault, Thunderbay; M. I. Trick, Stonewall; N. L. Way, Brandon; F. R. Worth, Winnipeg; M. W. Wozniak, Elsa; M. P. Wren, Whitehorse; R. H. Zorn, Winnipeg;

A-3 COY

G. Airton, Comox, B.C.; L. M. Angers, Hope; D. P. Barker, Burnaby; P. L. Bolger, Victoria; S. D. Borza, Powell River; K. R. Bourassa, Powell River; J. R. Bucher, Hope; B. D. Butt, Victoria. E. M. Bragg, Victoria; A. A. Brown, Richmond; D. J. Brown,

Vananda; A. E. Brygadyr, Victoria'; P. C. Burrell, Vancouver. C. J. Carlson, Sidney, B.C.; T. G. Carson, Hope; D. Castle, Courtenay; B. S. Catherine, Victoria; N. P. Costantino, Vancouver; R. J. Cracknell, Victoria; B. T. Custance, Victoria.

G. R. Davies, Port Coquitlam, B.C.; S. C. Duckworth, Texada Island; H. E. Dunn, Ladner; R. E. Ennis, Port Coquitlam; K. D. Ewart, Victoria; R. D. Fortier, Port Coquitlam.

L. H. Gaetz, Port Alberni, B.C.; D. M. Gagnon, Vancouver; G. A. Garvey, Powell River; L. F. Gaudet, Powell River; B. R. Gosick, Sardis; J. W. Gribble, Powell River; R. R. Gribble, Powell River.

P. A. Henderson, Victoria, B.C.; R. C. Herbert, Victoria; B. A. Humphrey, Port Coquitlam; D. S. Hutchinson, Victoria; J. J. Janz, Hope; G. E. Johnson, Powell River; D. J. LeBrun, Victoria.

G. A. MacCallum, Victoria, B.C.; W. McCausland, Port Coquitlam; T. H. McClymont, Victoria; P. J. McCutcheon, Hope; T. D. McDowell, Victoria; G. W. McLean, Victoria. S. C. Macklin, Victoria, B.C.; A. R. Martin, Victoria; B. J. Matthews, Vanada; B. Matthews, Texada Island; R. J. Matthews, Powell River; R. D. Mitchell, Victoria; A. A. Montgomery, Courtenay; K. S. Moretti, Victoria; B. L. Murphy, Port Coquitlam; M. A. Murphy, Burnaby.

G. E. Nelson, Nanaimo, B.C.; L. E. Nicholson, Hope; I. J. Nordal, white Rock; O. B. Peterson, Victoria; W. R. Philpot, Surrey; G. M. Pool, Victoria; W. R. Pullen, Nanaimo.

G. D. Ratchford, Victoria, B.C.; R. G. Riemer, Ladysmith; M. L. Reit, Powell River; W. R. Robinson, Chilliwack.

R. G. Sasqui, Victoria, B.C.; A. M. Seaton, Powell River; W. A. Small, Powell River; R. E. Smith, Nanaimo; D. D. Stephewns, Powell River; G. C. Stevenson, Vancouver; M. E. Stones, Richmond; C. Stradsin, Victoria.

K. K. Taber, Port Coquitlam, B.C.; R. V. Thurlow, Nanaimo; J. W. Vanderwal, Victoria; G. A. Vadeboncoeur, Courtenay, B.C.; J. B. Veale, Richmond; S. J. Vlake, Vancouver.

D. H. Walsh, Nanaimo, B.C.; R. C. Webster, Courtenay; I. W. White, Victoria; I. P. Whitehead, Victoria; C. R. Williams, Delta; H. R. Zohner, Powell River; L. E. Nicholson, Hope; L. S. Lu, Vancouver.

D COY

M. D. Assiniboine, Regina, Sask.; M. L. Bakusko, Estevan; J. R. Beaulieu, Saskatoon; R. F. Bear, Davis; J. L. Binns, Regina; R. D. Boehen, Regina; R. G. Bonneville, Regina; R. J. Bonneville, Regina; C. R. Bottel ill' Moose Jaw.

W. A. Callbeck, Prince Albert, Sask.; J. P. Carteri, Regina; R. Carteri, Regina; T. A. Carteri, Regina; K. L. Catling, Moose Jaw; P. Chicoine, Prince Albert; B. Chudiak, Kelowna; D. E. Colbow, Moose Jaw.

L. Daniels, Kelowna, B.C.; S. R. Deitsch, Rosetown, Sask.; B. J. Dekker, Melville; R. M. Deschambeault, Prince Albert; P. W. Diewold, Regina; V. A. Dickray, Regina; A. W. Downton, Mort Lach; G. S. Dutton, Estevan.

A. B. Elson, Estevan; R. M. Fauchoux, Prince Albert; R. R. Feberuik, Sturgis; T. D. Fincaryk, Sturgis; B. L. Flemming, Saskatoon; M. J. Fortowsky, Estevan; B. M. Furgason, Weyburn.

J. Gate, Moose Jaw, Sask.; B. J. Gaudet, Prince Albert; L. Geiger, Regina; A. J. Genereux, Regina; C. D. Gerritse, Wadena; B. Gladue, Battlvford; J. J. Gobesek, Regina; J. Grane, Regina; L. Greenwold, Port Coquitlam; D. E. Gress, Estevan; S. P. Griffin, Moose Jaw.

A..Hamann, Weyburn, Sask.; M. Hanoski, Regina; R. Hanoski, Regina; L. Hartenberger, Weyburn; D. Harwood, Regina; S. Hayes, Kelowna, B.C.; D. Haywood, North Battleford, Sask.; S. Hegan, Melville; R. Heine, Kindersley; A. A. Heintz, Estevan; M. Hendricks, Saskatoon; C. Hill, Rosetown; D. Hodgson, Moose Jaw; W. Holmvs, Regina; D. Hubick, Quinton; J. Hutchinson, Regina.

M. Jensen, Kelowna, B.C.; R. Julet, Regina, Sask.; J. Uilback, Yorkton; S. Koaub, Kelowna, B.C.; S. Krahenbill, Regina, Sask.; D. Kulyk, Wadena.

R. Lachance, Kindersley, Sask.; J. Lavers, Yorkton; K. Leach, Regina; L. Leblanc, Estevan; R. Lesann..Saskatoon.

C. S. McAfee, Quinson, Sask.; J. H. McLeod, Prince Albert; L. A. McDonald, Qindersley; T. D. McEachen, Regina; D. B. McQueen, Moose Jaw; K. O. MacInnis, Weyburn; D. T. Mack, Estevan; D. Martin, Estevan; P. J. Mauvieux, Prince Albert; J. K. Meyers, Saskatoon; R. J. Michon, Regina.

W. R. Nagy, Regina, Sask.; R. D. Newsham, Mortlach; R. A. Nichol, Regina; M. Noga, Rutland.

C. S. Olafson, North Battleford, Sask.; R. O. Olson, Regina; J. E. Paduck, Prince Albert; M. E. Papineau, Moose Jaw; R. W. Patterson, Swift Current; Cdt. Petkall, Calgary, Alta.; L. P. Piguia, Naicam; M. H. Powaschuk, Swift Current; K. J. Prytula, Yorkton.

R. L. Reindl, Saskatoon, Sask.; S. Quinton, Regina; T. N. Romanyshyn, Yorqton.

S. Saunders, Kelowna, B.C.; D. A. Sandeski, Weyburn, Sask.; M. R. Schiffner, Moose Jaw; R. M. Scott, Saskatoon; D..W. Swufert, Prince Albert; D. R. Dimpson, Swift Current; G. R. Stilboin, Duff; J. J. Story, Vanscoy; R. W. sukovieff, Quinton.

D. Terrs, Grand Coulee, Sask.; D. R. Tunnicliffe, Saskatoon; W. E. Uhryn, Saskatoon.

K. V. Van Drunen, Regina, Sask.; M. Vigoren, Kelowna, B.C.; M. M. Vieber, Lampman; J. W. Weigers, Prince Albert; D. J. Willette, Estevan; R. W. Williams, Weyburn; R. P. Witwicki, Kelowna, B.C.; G. V. Woodburn, Regina; R. O. Wilson, Regina.

K. Arnolus, Fort St. John; R. L. Arsenault, Taylor; G. J. Ayotte, St. Jean Baptiste; R. L. Ayotte, St. Jean Baptiste, R. M. Ayotte, St. Jean Baptiste, M. G. Baril, St. Jean Baptiste; D. Beauchesne, Edmonton; R. E. Bellemare, St. Jean Baptiste; G. M. Bereheltte, Parview; E. Berwick, Clyde; C. M. Blize, Fort St. John; R. W. Bodnarchek, Ft. MacMurray; B. L. Carrien, Thunderbay; D. W. Carriere, Winnipeg; G. R. Cloutier, Westlock; D. W. Coates, Morris; L. M. Cochrane, Fort MacMurray; R. W. Cochrane, Fort MacMurray; J. M. Collette, St. Jean Baptiste; R. W. Cooper, Ft. St. John; J. R. Dial, Bentley; G. A. Cyr, Power View; V. Davis, Shilo; K. L. Dorschied, Claremont; N. L. Duval, St. Jean Baptiste; R. D. Fedchuk, Grand Prairie; J. J. Fitzpatrick, Fort McMurray; M. A. Fillion, St. Jean Baptiste; D. G. Fountain, Fort MacMurray; K. M. Fraser, Kenora; K. Fraser, Kenora; D. W. Gillies, Lacombe; B. J. Goertzen, Black Falls; R. D. Goulet, Dryden; R. D. Goulet, Dryden; L. A. Green, Black Falls; C. H. Gustaw, Dryden; D. L. Hansen, Fort St. John; S. J. Hayduk, Sherwood Park. L. J. Hendricks, Fort St. John; J. P. Hertz, Kenora; D. J. Hines, Black Falls; D. W. Hlady, Thunderbay; R. M. Houde, Kenora; R. A. Huseby, Black Falls; R. D. Hyndman, LaCombe; P. A. Jaszczyszak, Dryden; Z. Joseph, Ft. St. John; D. E. Kellar, Dryden; D. J. Kelly, Fort MacMurray; D. L. Kopichanski, Red Lake; W. L. Kopichanski, Red Lake.

H. R. Landry, Dryden; G. K. Lehelloco, Pine Falls; R. J. Lindenberger, Fort McMurray; W. T. MacDonald, Dryden; R. A. Mackenzie, Thunder Bay; M. G. Magee, Kenora; G. S. Marion, St. Jean Baptiste; D. M. Matthew, Sioux Narrow; D. C. Meeres, LaCombe; M. M. Nault, Kenora; B. D. Nieradka, Brandon; D. L. Osmond, Powerview; T. D. Ostashek, Fort St. John; P. R. O'Sullivan, Grande Prairie; K. R. Paish, Grande Prairie; M. C. Pardell, Grand Prairie; D. W. Patapoff, Eckville; Q. A. Podulaky, Ft. St. John; D. B. Pollock, St. Jean; R. J. Potter, Dryden; J. Rigg, Sherwood Park; V. B. Rogowsky, Balnmertown.

B. G. Sauer, Blackfalls; T. B. Saunders, Black Falls; G. J. Schafer, Ft. St. John; E. J. Shears, Ft. St. John; J. D. Sheen, Sherwood Park; A. P. Shupe, Dryden; E. W. Sinclair, Kenora; R. D. Slavik, St. John; R. T. Suhkbir, Morris; P. C. Sutton, Ft. St. John; R. A. Thompson, Dryden; F. R. Thalhofer, Madsen; M. A. Vermett, Morrison; B. R. White, Dryden; J. P. Whitford, Pine Falls; D. E. Willson, Lacombe; B. A. Winter, Pine Falls; D. K. Wlodarek, Kenora; G. T. Forrest, Ft. St. John.

D. M. Piche, Hixon; K. K. Pinksen, Kelowna; R. S. Pook, Surrey; D. W. Potts, Burnaby; W. N. Pullan, Merritt.

D. A. Riguedell, Vernon, B.C.; K.

L. Robinson, Gabriola; E. C. Roachfort, Delta; C. J. Rollins, Parksville; R. G. Roy, VeddsCrossing.

C. T. Sadler, Cloverdale, B.C.; R. R. Salvati, Nanaimo; E. D. Sandback, Prince George; G. J. Sannachan, Merritt; C. J. Shaw, Surrey; T. L. Smale, Delta; L. H. Stoneman, Merritt; T. J. Straga, Oyama; D. A. Strong, Delta; M. R. Strong, Delta; B. S. Swedburg, Merritt.

D. A. Taylor, Vedder Crossing, B.C.; G. Thomas, Ladner; R. A. Thompson, Salmon Arm; R. G. Thorburn, Nanaimo; W. J. Tillyer, Burnaby; J. A. Toivola, Coquitlam; R. Tottenham, Revelstoke; K. K. Turunen, Vancouver.

D. S. Watson, Revelstoke, B.C.; D. A. Wilde, Surrey; R. L. Wilkinson, Victoria; B. W. Willford, Revelstoke; J. K. Wolfram, Prince George; K. L. Wolden, Vernon.

C. W. Young, Winfield; S. Zacker, Revelstoke; M. J. Zadworney, Nanaimo; N. E. Howk, Prince George.

"A-2 COY"

S. L. Affleck, St. Vital; B. C. Allison, Winnipeg; R. P. Babb, Winnipeg; M. P. Babcock, Winnipeg; M. G. Barrie, Winnipeg; G. E. Beaudin, Winnipeg; G. M. Beaudoin, Winnipeg; N. M. Boulet, Winnipeg, R. E. Boulet, Winnipeg; D. L. Boushie, Winnipeg, K. K. Bristow, Winnipeg; K. A. Campbell, Winnipeg; A. C. Cecotka, Winnipeg; J. H. Cecotka, Winnipeg; B. B. Chartier, Winnipeg; R. M. Chartrand, Winnipeg; H. J. Chrest, St. James; K. A. Cielen, Old Kildonan; J. P. Clark, Winnipeg; G. W. Copp, Winnipeg; V. Cote, Kamsak; R. B. Cowan, Melville; H. A. Cunningham, Winnipeg; G. W. Dawkins, Winnipeg; F. D. Delwo, Sturgis; J. D. Desnomie, Loralee; G. T. Desroches, Sturgis; D. J. Diakow, Yorkton; T. P. Dielschneider, Melville; B. J. Dischneider, Yorkton; T. F. Dreher, Yorkton; B. J. Drotar, Gordon Road.

R. Eyre, Wadena; B. R. Gambler, Fort Quapelle; B. M. Gambler, Fort Quapelle; T. D. Gilkes, Winnipeg; D. J. Halpenny, Winnipeg; G. A. Inkster, Melville; D. P. Jones, Red Lake; A. L. Kalnicki, Rama; B. K. Kerr, Winnipeg; E. E. Kluk, Yorkton; J. Kosmac, Winnipeg; L. A. Larocque, Yorkton; H. E. Larson, Sturgis; J. G. Littlewolf, Kamsak; K. G. Lonechild; Carlyle; C. G. Longman, Punnichy; T. N. Lucas, Winnipeg; C. M. McGunical, Wadena; D. W. Martens; Winnipeg; J. D. Martens, Winnipeg; M. F. Masyoluk, Winnipeg; M. R. Meehan, Wadena; W. L. Mosionier, Winnipeg; G. C. Mathuik, Yorkton; J. B. Mazer, Yorkton; M. M. Okrainetz, Invermay; D. J. Palaniuk, Sturgis; P. K. Parisien, Winnipeg; L. Parker, Melville; L. R. Saunderson, Winnipeg; R. J. Schuchert, Winnipeg; R. P. Seales, Winnipeg; C. A. Silvaggio, Marquette, Manitoba; L. R. Silvaggio, Marquette; D. E. Zawislak, Winnipeg; J. D. Smith, Invermay; I. G. Spence, Winnipeg; D. S. Szustygesto, Winnipeg; J. P. Taylor, St. James; C. A. Town,

Vermette; N. H. Waldbauer, Melville; K. G. Walker, Sturgis; B. E. Wright, Winnipeg; H. Wysmulek, Winnipeg; B. W. Yachyshen, Melville; L. W. Yachyshen, Rama; P. H. Yamada, Winnipeg.

C COY

A. J. Ahearn, Surrey, B.C.; M. J. Allan, Sardis; D. Ames, Victoria; C. W. Anderson, Nanoose Bay; R. Angelini, Burnaby; B. Ansdell, Vancouver; D. Ash, Coquitlam.

J. P. Ballard, Coquitlam, B.C.; M. F. Barker, Burnaby; S. Beaton, Port Coquitlam; I. Begg, Port Coquitlam; T. D. Behm, Prince George; D. A. Bennett, Prince George; D. Berney, Vedder Crossing; J. A. Bond, Burnaby; W. Broadfoot, Merritt; N. A. Brook, Richmond; J. Brulotte, Burton; J. D. Byers, Victoria.

J. E. Caton, Gabrial, B.C.; B. D. Conyers, Nanaimo; G. Cooke, Surrey; K. K. Coolen, Vancouver; F. Cooper, Nakusp; B. Court, Victoria; F. Curwood, Port Alberni; D. C. Cutrell, Sardis.

A. T. Daniels, Vernon; J. P. Daniels, Vernon; D. A. Denluck, Prince George; A. B. De Simone, Merritt; T. A. Desmarais, Port Coquitlam; S. C. Desmarais, Port Coquitlam.

R. A. Evans, Haney; D. A. Fege, N. Surrey; D. G. Flynn, Richmond; B. R. Flynn, Richmond; L. M. Folland, Revelstoke.

M. W. Gair, Calgary, Alta.; A. S. George, Port Coquitlam, B.C.; J. B. Gibson, Victoria; R. J. Gauthier, Vancouver; G. Graf, Haney; R. E. Graham, Surrey; T. T. Griffiths, Merritt; L. M. Gustason, Haney; V. A. Gustason, Haney.

D. H. Hale, Richmond; J. Heck, Burnaby; T. R. Houghton, Vancouver; B. W. Huston, Merritt; H. G. Jarche, Revelstoke; R. R. Kierner, Surrey; P. A. Kitto, Haney.

G. K. Lavine, Maple Ridge; D. A. Laramee, Haney; K. D. Laramee, Haney; G. K. Lavigne, Maple Ridge; G. R. Lee, Vancouver; R. M. Lewis, Prince George; R. Lloyd, Yarrow.

J. L. McCarville, Prince George, B.C.; G. A. McCluskie, Richmond; D. J. McDougal, Richmond; D. J. McKay, Victoria; S. McRitchie, Vancouver; R. G. Marasa, Coquitlam; S. L. Marshall, Burnaby; D. Meldrum, Hammon; W. E. Mills, Surrey; R. R. Morkman, Gabriel Island; C. T. Moss, Victoria; W. I. Munro, Richmond.

E. J. Nielsen, Summerland; G. P. Noga, Burnaby; A. J. Norquay, Prince George; S. P. Nunn, Sardis; R. F. Orr, Burton.

A-1 COY

D. F. Achtzener, Regina, Sask.; J. H. Atkins, Calgary, Alta.; R. G. Bauer, Regina; M. Beauregard, Calgary, Alberta; T. H. Berg, Weyburn, Sask.; B. K. Birdsell, Estevan; B. K. Blanchard, Calgary, Alta.; B. J. Brink, Calgary; R. A. Briscoe, Calgary.

561

R. I. Carriere, Vstevan, Sask.; K. R. Chase, Calgary, Alta.; P. L. Chynoweth, Calgary; X. J. Cusveller, Calgary; T. Csizmazie, Yukon4 S. Dibbs, Yukon; R. Dimmer, Calgary, Alta; B. K. Donais, Estevan, Sask.; G. Drebit, address unavaitable.

R. M. Ebcrle, Regina, Sask.; R. G. Eberly, Regina; D. G. Eckel, Regina; E. D. English, Calgary; S. J. Esaw, Regina, Sask.; L. A. Fazeras, Calgary, Alta.; D. Fisher, Calgary; K. Fizer, Calgary; G. F. Fraser, Stoughton, Sask.; J. J. Fuller, Calgary.

P. A. Gerritsen, Calgary, Alta.; R. J. Ginther, Calgary; M. J. Goeres, Weyburn, Sask.; S. Conez, Penticton, B.C.; P. P. Gress, Estevan, Sask.

D. M. Hall. Calgary, Alta.; D. Hall, Calgary; D. Hall, Creelman, Sask.; B. Harde, Estevan; C. Harrison, Estevan; R. Hoffman, Calgary, Alta; P. Home, Calgary; W. J. Hamilton, address unavailable.

R. Janzen, Calgary, Alta.; M. Jones, Calgary; C. Kanngiesser' Calgary; G. C. Karoly, Calgary; J. Kennedy, Calgary, J. Kime, Milestone, Sask.; J. Kolenz, Roche Percee; M. Kraus, Estevan; R. Kulhawy, Calgary; Cdt. Kuntz, Estevan.

R. L. Lowey, address unavailab e; R. M. McCrystal, Milestone, Sask.; R. D. McLean, Estevan; D. C. McNab, Estevan; M. F. MacInnes, Weyburn; R. Manegre, Calgary; R. W. Marshall, Calgary; V. Marshall, address unavailable; F. J. Mazzei, Calgary; H. B. Mueller, Calgary; M. L. Murray, Calgary.

S. C. Neis, Calgary, Alta.; D. Paulson, Calgary; T. L. Payne, Calgary; J. R. Ray..Creelman; R. D. Rederburg, Benson; E. G. Rennie, Calgary, Alta.; S. F. Rockwell, Calgary; M. W. Ross, Milestone, Sask.; T. D. Rothery, Calgary, Alta.

B. E. Salamanchuk, Regina, Sask.; E. D. Sinclair, Lampman; B. A. Smith, Calgary, Alta.; M. D. Sproat, Milestone, Sask.; M. K. Styre, Estevan; D. M. Thivierge, Calgary, Alta.; G. E. Trever, Calgary; R. W. Turnball, Calgary. M. D. Wadsworth, Calgary, Alta.; D. A. Watt, Calgary; C. G. Willette, Estevan, Sask.; B. E. Williams, Calgary, Alta; B. E. Williams, Calgary; R. D. Williams, Weyburn; L. J. Wock, Estevan; R. Vanderzee, Calgary, Alta.

"A-2 Coy"

A. J. AuClair, Coquitlam; K. M. Berg, Surrey; R. R. Billings, Fort MacMurray, Alta.; H. L. Brass, Davis, Sask.; C. Brown, Surrey, B.C.

D. R. Cannon, North Vancouver, B.C.; B. T. Carlson, Surrey; J. C. Cathers, Coquitlam; J. C. Clegg, Vancouver; N. E. Deitz, Kindersley, Sask.; C. A. DesAulniers, Coquitlam, B.C.; K. C. Donnelly, North Vancouver.

D. L. Erickson, Delta, B.C.; C. M. Fisher, Richmond; G. Fraser, West Vancouver; D. T. Garside, Bur-

Vancouver; D. T. Garside, Burnaby; D. F. Gildroy, Coquitlam; B. Graf, Maple Ridge; A. M. Gurney, Vancouver.

D. A. Hebert, Ladner, B.C.; B. W. Hendricks, North Vancouver; K. J. Hinds, Surrey; W. M. Hofstra, Saskatoon, Sask.; M. K. Ilaender, Maple Ridge, B.C.

A. D. Johnson, Burnaby, B.C.; T. A. Killam, New Westminster; G. T. King, Burnaby 2,; R. S. Kisun, Cassiar; G. L. LaCasse, Port Coquitlam; T. R. Larson, Kindersley, Sask.; G. G. LeBlanc, Prince Albert; T. G. Lynch, Surrey, B.C.

R. G. McRae, Burnaby, B.C.; D. P. McGuire, Surrey; B. H. McIntosh, North Vancouver; B. H. McLeod, Prince Albert, Sask.; D. M. McPhadyen, Delta, B.C.; B. J. Maedel, New Westminster; J. B. Mahon, Delta, J. D. Matheson, Mt. Lehman; R. W. Matyas, Coquitlam; D. T. Miller, Prince Albert, Sask.; R. L. Montour, Prince Albert; M. T. Morgan, Coquitlam, B.C.; C. G. Mullins, West Vancouver.

L. B. Nedelec, Vawn, Sask.; K. J. Nelson, Vancouver, B.C.; B. R. Nicholson, Delta; R. W. Ogurian, Vancouver; H. K. Ostermann, Richmond.

M. D. Parish, West Vancouver, B.C.: G. A. Parsons, Burnaby, R. S. Patti, Surrey, W. G. Penman, Abbotsford; E. B. Philip, North Vancouver; R. A. Plant, Delta; M. A. Pottage, Richmond; R. R. Prevost, Clearbrook; O. Pudans, New Westminster.

R. W. Rockhill, West Vancouver; G. J. Rouse, Port Coquitlam; K. M. Sawatzky, Kindersley, Sask.; R. W. Scarff, Surrey, B.C.; D. A. Simmons, Surrey; B. M. Smithers, Burnaby; G. P. Stefanuk, Saskatoon, Sask.; G. P. Stiglik, Surrey, B.C.

B. E. Toth, Surrey, B.C.; S. R. Usher, New Westminster; N. A. Vanzanten, Mount Lehman.

M. A. Waenink, Surrey, B.C.; R. A. Walter, West Vancouver; S. W. Ward, Vancouver; D. M. Whiting, West Vancouver; S. J. Williams, Vancouver; D. K. Wolf, Saskatoon, Sask.; R. I. Wulf, Mount Lehman, B.C.

A-3 COY

R. W. Adams, Edmonton, Alta.; P. J. Bassie, Edmonton; K. Belcourt, Edmonton; M. W. Benson, Edmonton; W. K. Bokovay, Edmonton; B. A. Bolen, Edmonton; L. C. Boucher, Rosetown, Sask.; D. G. Boyer, Prince Albert; K. H. Bretzer, Edmonton; K. G. Burnett, Edmonton; P. J. Bury, Edmonton.

B. A. Calsen, W. Kindersly, Sask.; J. M. Charlebois, Edmonton; D. G. Cherry, Edmonton; D. W. Claughton, Edmonton; A. Cleall, Edmonton; L. D. Constantinoff, W. Saskatoon, Sask.; T. H. Cowan, Rosetown.

P. C. Dansdreau, W. Prince Albert, Sask.; R. T. Dlin, Edmonton, Alta.; T. J. Dukes, Rosetown, Sask.; D. K. Elliot, Edmonton, Alta.; G. J. Fedoruk, Edmonton; J. E. Flach, Rosetown, Sask.; D. J. Fleming,

Rosetown; A. D. Forrest, Zealandia; D. J. Franklin, E. Prince Albert.

B. G. Geddes, Kindersely, Sask.; D. J. Gow, Edmonton, Alta.; K. H. Heine, W. Kindersley, Sask.; A. A. Ingram, Spruce Lake; K. G. Jackson, Saskatoon; T. L. Jones, Saskatoon.

D. B. Kilpatrick, Battleford, Sask.; G. A. Langlois, Prince Albert; C. L. LeBrecque, Rosetown; R. J. Lacey, Prince Albert; G. S. Lloyd, Prince Albert.

T. M. McConaghy, Edmonton, Alta.; G. B. McKinnon, Edmonton; M. D. Makulowich, N. Saskatoon, Sask.; M. D. Male, Edmonton, Alta.; B. W. Marks, Edmonton; K. P. Marshall, S. Saskatoon, Sask.; B. D. Martell, W. Prince Albert; C. R. Mercer, Edmonton, Alta.; A. A., Meunier, Edmonton; W. J. Monaghan, Edmonton; E. J. Morgan, Battleford.

D. P. Ogenchuk, Rosetown, Sask.; P. A. Paeiement, Edmonton, Alta.; T. A. Ponto, Saskatoon, Sask.; M. R. Povin, Edmonton, Alta.; J. P. Pylypow, Edmonton.

G. G. Richards, Edmonton, Alta.; T. E. Rogerson, Kindersley, Sask.; K. A. Roy, Edmonton, Alta.; M. M. Ruszkowski, Prince Albert, Sask.; G. W. Sansom, Saskatoon; P. C. Sauer, Edmonton, Alta.; P. L. Schmidt, Edmonton; P. L. Schmidt, Edmonton; P. W. Sevigny, Edmonton; B. A. Shapka, Edmonton; G. R. Siska, Edmonton; B. W. Sorenson, Edmonton.

D. A. Tailluer, Edmonton, Alta.; B. A. Taylor, Prince Albert, Sask.; M. B. Toma, Edmonton, Alta.; L. E. Vallevand, Edmonton; R. S. Walker, Edmonton; A. M. Walton, Rosetown, Sask.; T. A. Weckworth, Prince Albert; W. J. Willis, Edmonton.

W COY

W. D. Anderson, Red Deer, Alta.; G. E. Armitage, Edmonton; M. D. Barker, Black Diamond; S. J. Bayley, Calgary; B. M. BELIERIVE, Slave Lake; R. S. Besse, Edmonton; D. E. Bickell, Calgary; K. A: Bissonnette, Sherwood Park; A. H. Bizio, Medicine Hat; H. Bjerrisgaard, Redcliff.

R. D. Bobeau, Calgary, Alta.; C. D. Bokovay, Edmonton; G. A. Bowbell, Edmonton; R. A. Bowes, Medicine Hat; D. M. Brennan, Edmonton; L. J. Brisebois, Slave Lake; W. S. Budd, Sherwood Park.

T. M. Carry, Calgary, Alta.; T. D. Chynoweth, Calgary; T. R. Cotten, Recliffe; R. S. Davies, Turner Valley; W. H. Davies, Strathmore; J. F. Dobson, Calgary; R. H. Dolomont, Calgary; P. J. Dusseault, Vimy.

B. M. Federuk, Vegerville, Alta.; B. Felkar, Canyon Creek; P. M. Frankow, Edmonton; L. A. Genest, Lethbridge; R. A. George, Calgary; M. L. Gibson, Slave Lake; M. B. Gilbertson, Grande Prairie; D. A. Gilmore, Lethbridge; B. L. Graham, Fort McMurray; M. D. Greger, Calgary.

K. Hand, Lacombe, Alta.; D. Hartwick, Drayton Valley; B.

Hauszka, Bretton; D. Henderson, Calgary; B. Hohmann, Edmonton; C. Hollen, Fort St. John, B.C.; F. Jagt, Strathmore, Alta.; K. Jockims, Lethbridge; A. Jodoin, Calgary.

R. C. Kenny, Vermillion, Alta.; P. Killaly, Thorsby; W. Kisko, Calgary; A. Knapman, Calgary.

J. Langridge, Calgary, Alta.; D. LaPointe, Calgary; B. Larsen, St. Albert; D. Lawrence, Black Diamond; P. Lea, Calgary; M. G. Levac, Fort St. John, B.C.; D. Lind, Red Deer, Alta.; M. Luclow, Fort St. John, B.C.

R'.cDonald, Thorsby, Alta.; W. T. McWilliams, Calgary; J. W. McGuire, Calgary; F. MacDonald, Fort McMurray; R. J. MacDonald, Lacombe; P. R. Major, Medicine Hat; P. M. Malin, Blackfalls; B. L. Marks, Breton; R. E. Martin, Westlock; B. L. MacKeiberg Calgary; B. J. Metzger, Red Deer, G. A. Mitchell, Calgary; B. K. Modenhauer, Breton; E. F. Monk, Calgary; D. R. Motiuk, Edmonton.

T. X. Odermatt, Calgary, Alta.; J. G. Ogston, Medicine Hat; N. Ogurian, Edmonton; D. W. Ostaschek, Fort St. John.

D. Paquette, Edmonton, Alta.; K. B. Pendlebury, Calgary; J. V. Perrot, Calgary; F. P. Phillips, Fort Smith; D. M. Pitts, Edmonton; G. A. Poirier, Calgary; K. C. Pon, Calgary; G. Porisky, Edmonton; G. W. Potts, Fort St. John; E. C. Prefontaine, Innisfall; D. W. Priaulx, Calgary; T. E. Putt, Calgary.

K. H. Ratpgeber, Yeofyd; M. Rinas, Edmonton; J. Robicheau, Red deer; R. L. Robinson, Recliffe.

B. R. Sauer, Lethbridge; B. T. Schauerte, Alderflas; D. J. Scott, Edmonton; A. D. Skeith, Lethbridge; A. P. Sommer, Calgary; I. C. Sommerville, Fort McMurray; F. A. Soreghy, Calgary; J. F. Stenhouse, Calgary; G. R. Storey, Edmonton; G. C. Stukart, Calgary; W. Sutherland, Edmonton; D. G. Swaboda, Calgary; B. A. Szautner, Calgary.

B. R. Torn, Turner Valley, Alta.; R. P. Twin, Slave Lake; J. D. Urschel, Edmonton; K. D. Watson, Red Deer; C. Wolff, Fort McMurray; G. D. Workun, Calmar; J. Vanginkel, Millett; A. P. Zingeler, Calgary; A. P. Johnson, Prince Alberta.

A-1 COY

D. L. Andersen, Busby, Alta.; J. W. Banman, Innisfail; A. G. Barlow, Vermillion; G. R. Barlow, Vermillion; K. B. Bayrack, Warburg; W. G. Bayrack, Warburg; M. C. Bergeson, White Court; I. R. Berry, Kinuso.

B. W. Callioux, Hinton, Alta.; S. C. Campbell, Vermillion; R. A. Chibi, Regina, Sask.; J. D. Crooks, Strathmore, Alta.; R. J. Cross, Lac+vert, Sask.; K. M. Doll, Innisfail.

D. H. Flatla, Strathmore; S. W. Frankcombe, Pincher Creek; D. L. Fuhr, Regina, Sask.; W. J. Gabriel, Regina; W. J. Gardipee, Edson, Alta.; C. M. Gibson, Slave Lake; K. G. Gordon, Red Deer; G. J. Grippen, Red Deer; R. I. Guttormson, Naicam, Sask.; M. P. Hall,

Whitecourt, Alta.; W. E. Harstad, Breton; L. J. Heighinton, Breton; G. W. Hilsbeck, Innisfail; J. D. Hitchings, Hinton; S. C. Hunt, Red Deer; D. C. Izso, Regina, Sask.; B. S. James, Slave Lake, Alta.; H. D. Jestin, Naicam, Sask.; S. B. Jones, Edson, Alta.

D. J. Kreutz, Slave Lake, Alta.; G. B. Lavalley, Regina, Sask.; R. S. Leitch, Slave Lake, Alta.; K. J. Letcher, Hinton; G. L. Levesque, Vermillion; N. L. Lewis, Red Deer; D. F. Lindsay, Hinton.

C. A. Mah, Edson, Alta.; D. R. Masterson, Mayerthorpe; R. G. Morin, Naicam, Sask.; L.'D. Morris, Regina; R. W. Munro, Edson, Alta.;

P. A. Novak, Whitecourt, Alta.; R. W. Parlby, Slave Lake; R. A. Petters, Pincher Creek· V. R. Rathwell, Alderflats.

R. Schimanke, Busby, Alta.; D. A. Schumann, Strathmore; R. K. Seely, Alderflats; D. W. Simon, Alderflats; C. J. Smith, Naicam, Sask.; W. K. Soldan, Red Deer, Alta.; D. W. Stadnyk, Regina,; G. P. Stark, Innisfail, Alta.; C. V. Stuart, Regina, Sask.

M. B. Trodden, Pincher Creek, Alta.; D. J. Trudzik, Rochford Bridge; R. C. Underhill, Edson; L. Valcky, Strathmore; R. J. Visser, Pincher Creek.

B. R. Waldie, Mayerthorpe, Alta.; B. D. Walker, Red Deer; A. S. Weiss, Warburg; A. P. Welsh, Regina, Sask.; b. t. williams, Vermillion, Alta.; M. K. Willier, Hinton,; C. R. Wilson, Edson; T. M. Wynnyk, Warburg; J. K. Zachary, Slave Lake.

A-3 COY

R. Abrahamson, Recliffe, Alta.; A. W. Adshead, Burton, B.C.; B. D. Baxter, Kelowna; K. D. Becktold, Wynndel; B. E. Bengston, Lumby; R. D. Bjarnason, Canyon; F. A. Bjarnason, Canyon,; G. S. Blank, Prince George.

H. Bob, Prince George, B.C.; P. Boscoe, Prince George; T. E. Boulding, Kelowna; M. A. Braden, Prince George; T. E. Boulding, Kelowna; M. a. Braden, Prince George; T. A. Brummet, Kelowna; P. W. Bryans, Wynndel; D. F. Buttazzoni, Lethbridge, Alta.

D. D. Chauncey, Wynndel, B.C.; J. J. Chernise, Revelstoke; G. W. Cherno, Nakusp; W. J. Church, Clinton; G. Cooper, Cranbrook; R. B. Cote, Sparwood; P. A. Cyganik, Ralston, Alta.

D. K. Desgagne, Westwood, B.C.; D. A. Duchesne, Kamloops; P. A. Eftodie, Prince George; D. W. Elvbrum, Trail; D. Gemmell, Victoria; D. A. Golinski, Rutland; D. P. Graham, Trail.

R. Hack, Merritt, B.C.; E. B. Harris, Lac La Hache; G. Herriman, Turner Valley, Alta.; S. Hogg, Calgary; A. A. House, Aparwood, B.C.; B. F. House, Sparwood; V. Hull, Rutland; T. Hurrell, Lethbridge, Alta.

R. Irwin, Fruitvale, B.C.; D. W. Johnson, Prince George; S. Johnston, Erickson; D. B. Kellow, Creston; M. A. Kennedy, Kelowna; C. Kerluke, Wadena, Sask.; R. R. Kleis, Medicine Hat, Alta.; N. A.

Kulchyski, Kamloops, B.C.

R. A. LxFrance, Creston, B.C.; L. W. Levitt, Calgary, Alta.; B. H. Littau, Rutland; L. Lowey, Revelstoke; R. B. McSorley, Rutland, A. E. MacKenzie, Salmon Arm.

S. M. Martins, Medicine Hat, Alta.; V. G. Mayne, Fruitville; R. D. Miller, Fruitvale; G. R. Millgan, Kamloops; N. Mitchell, Merritt; K. D. Moody, Creston; M. L. Moore, Sparwood; K. A. Moore, Lumby; R. P. Norales, Sparwood; J. A. Morassut, Genelle; S. A. Morris, Kelowna; M. H. Moritz, Medicine Hat, Alta.; C. J. Muller, Prince George, B.C.

K. E. Nelson, Calgary, Alta.; J. P. Oerlemans, Medicine Hat; E. Ohmenzetter, Summerland, B.C.; C. Olychuk, Kelowna; W. Parks, Abbotsford; R. M. Pederson, Creston; R. D. Percpluk, Calgary, Alta.; D. R. Popp, Kelowna; E. B. Potts, Lethbridge, Alta.; E. B. Prest, Summerland, B.C.

D. H. Ransom, Prince George, B.C.; R. A. Teitmeier, New Denver; C. S. Roberts, Kamloops; W. D. Robinson, Prince George.

R. A. Samesh, Lumby, B.C. G. B. Scheepbouwer, Salmon Arm; S. J. Shane, Creston; E N. Smith, Westbank; D. Stephvnson, Lethbridge, Alta.; R. B. Storie, Prince George, B.P.; L. A. Stuart, Nakusp; B. R. Studer, Kamloops.

K. D. Tate, Merritt, B.C.; G. O. Thompson, Fruitvale; D. E. Ungaro, Kelowna; J. Vanliet, Rutland; D. R. Viscount, Westhank; R. W. Walker, Merritt; S. A. Walton, Prince George; K. C. Weimer, Calgary, Alta.; R. A. Willford, Revelstoke.

A-2 COMPANY

R. A. Anderson, Dauphin, Man; A. Apetagon, E. Apetagon, R. Apetagon, Norway House, Man; R. F. Augustowich, Churchill, Man; K. L. Bartee, Turner Valley, Alta.; P. D. Basquier, Portage La Prairie; M. R. Bellefeuille, Valmarie, Sask; K. M. S. Berdahl, Calgary, Alta.; D. A. Bouvier, Churchill, Man.; R. J. Blatz, Calgary; R. B. Brecht, Creighton, Sask.; B. E. Bulback, Portage La Prairie.

J. E. Callan, Weyburn, Sask.; E. Clyne, Norway House; B. C. Conine, North Lethbridge, Alta.; S. P. Czaga, North Lethbridge; D. Davis, Flin Flon, Man.; D. Doan, M. C. Doan, McCreary, Man.; M. M. D. Doucette, McCreary; D. W. Driver, Swift Current, Sask.; L. Ducharne, Norway House; J. Duncan, Norway House; W. J. Edettawakabow, Norway House; S. A. Elson, Estevan, Sask.; R. W. Fedyk, Bienfait, Sask.; G. E. Fergusan, Estevan; G. B. Fidler, Fort Churchill; B. A. Folster, Norway House.

C. H. Garrett, Swift Current; M. Gaudreau, Valmarie; C. A. Gotterfried, Creelman; D. W. Grams, S. Weyburn; E. J. Griffin, Heward, Sask.; L. Henry, Regina; L. Hodgson, Moose Jaw; K. Horrocks, Flin Flon; F. Houlse, McCree, Man. Jamieson, Moose Jaw; K. Klassen, Brandon; D. Lane, Fort

McLeod, Alta.; F. Limacher, Regina; D. Lund, Estevan; K. G. McDonald, Weyburn; R. S. McKay, Norway House; V. R. McKinnon, Creelman; R. N. McPherson, Lampman, Sask.; H. R. MacDonald, Lethbridge; D. Morrice, Swift Current; W. J. Muniniawatun, Norway House; I. Muskego, Norway House; M. Muswajon, Norway House.

D. Nelson, Virden, Man.; D. Nelson, Regina; T. Neuman, Mc-Creary; D. Oliphant, Winnipeg; M. J. Paradis, Moose Jaw; G. J. Pawlivsky, South Lethbridge; T. G. Pnney, Lethbridge; D. Powaschuk, Swift Current.

B. K. Rainvelle, Flin Flon; G. B. Ramsey, Brandon, Man.; R. J. Ramsey, Brandon; R. J. Ripplinger, Regina; J. K. Roberts, Modse Jaw; D. S. G. Rogers, Estevan; R. W. Roulette, Portage La Prairie; C. W. Russell, Virden.

S. W. Saboraki, W. Dauphin; S. Sahd, Brandon; A. A. Smith, Dauphin; D. K. Steeden, Portage La Prairie; T. J. Straub, Turner Valley; J. D. Stuart, N.W. Swift Current; T. G. Tait, Portage La Prairie; F. Tarr, Brandon; J. P. Torchak, McCreary; N. D. Urban, Medicine Hat; R. T. Van Ryn, North Lethbridge; J. V. Wqlker, Brandon; K. Weisgerber, Regina; C. J. Wermie, Portage La Prairie; G. Willetts, Creighton; D. J. Wilson, McCreary; K. Wilson, Brandon; L. Wingerter, Lethbridge; K. P. Wock, Estevan.

VACC - 1974

A COY

W.G. Albers, Lacombe; J.C. Andronick, Brandon; A. W. Avery, Vermilion, Alta; T. E. W. Ayotte; Ft. St. John; L. J. Bakuska, Portage La Prairie; D. L. Baudry, St. Agathe, Man.

R. D. Bilodeau, St. Agathe, Man.; D. V. Black, Slave Lake, Alta; M. A. Blize, Ft. St. John; B. J. Bowman, Vancouver; W. K. Brown, Winnipeg; E. F. Bossert, Alder Flats, Alta.

G. W. Bourget, Fort St. John; B. D. Busby, Winnipeg; G. W. Campbell, Vermilion, Alta; R. J. Candline, Winnipeg; D. L. Chartier, Aubigny, Man; R. D. Coates, Morris, Man.

J. G. Cloverdale, Lacombe; A. David, Fort McMurry; E. E. Davis, Shilo, Man; T. J. Davis, Winnipeg; J. Denton, Mewton Siding, Man; K. Derksen, Morris.

J. P. Duncan, Lacombe; R. C. Dupuis, St. Jean Baptiste, Man.; C. D. Flinkman, Slave Lake; C. W. Forrest, Fort St. John; G. A. Fortier, Ft. McMurray; D. J. Foster, Ft. St. John.

T. E. Foy, Vermilion, Alta.; B. D. Gellings, Vermillion; G. M. Gregoire, Ft. St. John; D. B. Gusek, Ft. McMurray; G. W. Hambley, Ft. McMurray; G. J. Hampson, Alder Flats, Alta.

C. E. Hansen, Lacombe; W. D. Hardy, Portage LaPrairie; P. M. Hargas, Warburg, Alta.; D. E. Hayduk, Sherwood Park, Alta.; M. W. Hensel, Ft. St. John; T. A. Herndon, Westlock, Alta.

P. Herrewynen, Sherwood Park, Alta.; B. Hrabarchuk, Winnipeg; R. G. Huseby, Blackfalds, Alta.; J. A. Jones, Lacombe; K.D. Kearns, Westlock, Alta; S. S. H. Kilfoyle, St. Agathe, Man.

D. A. Klassen, Ft. St. John; D. W. Klassen, Ft. St. John; D. G. Kugyelka, Breton; A. L. Lappenbush, Mayerthorpe, Alta.; A. E. Leitch, Slave Lake; I. H. Lewis, Vermillion.

R. S. Loesch, Winnipeg; R. C. Marks, Brenton; B. G. Millard, Portage La Prairie; D. Morrissey, Ft. McMurray; R. D. Newmann, Winnipeg; R. R. Novak, Ft. St. John.

J. H. Owsianyk, Winnipeg; M. R. Pollock, St. Jean, Man.; D. Redsky, Shoal Lake, Ont.; A. W. Reglin, Mayerthorpe, Alta.; D. J. Ritchot, Aubigny, Man.; B. W. Robinson, Breton.

P. B. G. Rossiter, Portage la Prairie; M. M. Shukster, Sherwood Park, Alta.; J. J. Simpson, Fort MacMurray; S. R. Simpson, Winnipeg; E. A. Smith, Winnipeg; T. F. Sprado, Widewater, Alta.

D. M. Statz, Winnipeg; D. A. Stewart, Fort St. John; B. G. St. Hilaire, Aubigny, Man.; D. L. Swanson, Brandon; E. V. Sweet; Breton; J. J. Taylor, St. James.

D. Vacheresse, Fort McMurray; R. Vandale, Fort St. John; R. R. Vulliez, Winnipeg; D. Wasylenko, Winnipeg; E. Wilkerson, Ft. St. John; K. J. Wilson, Dryden.

K. R. Wilson, Hull; K. E. Young, Fort St. John; J. Zawartka, Warburg, Alta; M. Zorn, Winnipeg.

D. Anderson, Winnipeg; F. R. Anderson, Thompson; J. C. Anderson, Laurier House, Man.; A. Aschenbrenner, Innisfail; R.L. Bailey, Calgary; B. W. Baraniuk, Calgary.

J. P. Barker, Turner Valley; C. Bjerrisgaard, Redcliffe, Alta.; M. D. Bower, Pincher Creek; A. Bradburn, Norway House, Man.; R. B. Brown, Calgary; W. S. Burk, Redcliffe, Alta.

A. W. Churchill, Winnipeg; R. A. Cleveland, Thompson; K. Cole, Calgary; D. G. Collingridge, Winnipeg; D. Critchfield, Peace River; A. N. Cunningham, Turner Valley.

J. D. Davis, Winnipeg; C. Dell, Bomber Town, Ont.; K. S. Demond, Shilo, Man.; S. C. DePass, Turner Valley; D. A. Doubinin, Lethbridge; P. J. Dudzinski, Calgary.

R. Eriksen, Calgary; B. C. Evans, Calgary; W. R. Fletcher, Calgary; S. J. Fowler, Red Deer; R. E. Franchewski, Winnipeg; K. G. Furber, Winnipeg.

W. J. Furber, Winnipeg; F. H.

Greig, Calgary; S. O. Hrycyk, Lethbridge; R. W. Inverarity, Dewinton; R. J. Jarratt, Red Deer; L. P. Jensen, Stonewall.

D. G. Jowett, Winnipeg; R. I. Jowett, Winnipeg; F. M. Jungwirth, Red Lake, Ont.; R. G. Keam, Norway House, Man.; L. P. Keith, Stonewall; W. A. Kuz, Redcliffe.

W. J. Kuz, Redcliffe; D. M. Latoski, Balmer Town, Ont.; R. A. Leverington, Stonewall; L. W. Levitt, Calgary; G. T. Lightfoot, St. James, Man.; R. E. Liukaitis, Calgary.

K. L. Lovett, Calgary; D. E. Martin, Innisfail; R. S. McAmmond, Winnipeg; N. A. McKinnon, Pincher Creek; M. G. Morin, Calgary; C. A. Mowat, Norway House, Man.

R. Muskego, Norway House, Man.; T. H. Muswagon, Laurier House, Man.; D. L. Netrefa, Red Deer; B. D. Perpelitz, Red Deer; L. J. Piche, Turner Valley; B. J. Pierce, Calgary.

I. K. Poker, Norway House; G. M. Pon, Calgary; M. E. J. Pull, Stonewall; B. Redhead, Norway House; R. Rigaux, Pincher Creek; C. Ripley, Innisfail.

S. C. Robidoux, Shilo, Man.; E. Ross, Laurier House; M. K. Scribe, Norway House; R. L. Sedgwick, Lethbridge; B. K. Senft, Medicine Hat; D. K. Sharpe, Calgary.

C. D. P. Simmons, Winnipeg; W. N. Skwarchuk, Thompson; M. V. Stinn, Calgary; S. R. Sumner, Thompson; R. J. Szott, Lethbridge; B. A. G. Thibeau, Winnipeg.

A. R. Thomas, Winnipeg; K. R. Thorkman, Pincher Creek; H. W. Tilleman, Redcliffe; S. W. Triska, Lethbridge; J.M. Van Oosten, Calgary; K. M. Wadden, Calgary.

B. R. Wareing, Stonewall; C. R. Willard, Calgary; H. A. Wilson, Norway House; A. F. Yeats, Calgary; M. S. Zingeler, Calgary.

E. J. Altenburg, Dauphin; D. B. Anderson, Calgary; D. E. Arbuckle; Kaewatin, Ont.; R. L. Armstrong, Kelowna; P. Aschenbrenner, Innisfail; W. T. Atkinson, Trascona, Man.

J. S. Beaton, Portage La Prairie; G. J. Belanger, Winnipeg; M. J. Belanger, Kelowna; J. J. Biagi, Sherwood Park; J. A. Bonekamp, Manitoba; J. C. Boulding, Kelowna.

G. A. Braid, Calgary; C. A. Breakey, Edmonton; A. P. Buchanan, Calgary; D. L. Burden, Dauphin; J. C. Caus, Kenora; J. K. Cmolik, Kelowna.

K. B. Cooper, Rutland; R. B. D'Amour, Calgary; J. D. DeVuyst, Fort St. John; J. W. Drinkall, Calgary; W. J. Dumonceaux, Calgary; T. F. Fitzpatrick, Edmonton.

T. R. Fletcher, McCreary, Man.; A. J. Ford, Kelowna; D. E. N. C.

Ford, Calgary; R. D. Fowler, Calgary; D. Foy, Winnipeg; P. S. Fraser, Lacombe.

T. T. Fraser, Kenora; A. W. Ganter, Lacombe; R. G. Gerbrecht, Kelowna; D. J. Grant, Edson; B. C. E. Hall, Kenora; S. F. Henessey, Verdon, Man.

B. K. Hilstob, Kelowna; K. Hirt, Trascona, Man.; T. Hirt, Winnipeg; A. C. Hollstedt, Thunderbay; R. T. Hurbert, Calgary; G. R. Hourie, Portage la Prairie.

D. Husband, Innisfail; D. L. Jefferies, Kelowna; N. L. Joy, Edson; R. W. Joy, Edson; S. R. Kanngiesser, Calgary; G. A. Kaikanis, Calgary.

T. D. Kellsey, Cromer, Man.; P. W. Kelso, Thunderbay; R. W. Kemp, Calgary; K. R. Kohuch, Fort St. John; L. E. Larson, Villeneve, Ont.; B. W. Latkowski, Calgary.

W. A. Ledger, Thunderbay; T. R. Legge, Edson; K. M. Leguilloux, Kelowna; G. Louis, Thunderbay; A. D. Madge, Edmonton; B. A. Marklund, Edmonton.

R. L. Matthew, Calgary; R. W. McDonald, Calgary; F. S. McKenzie, Kelowna; H. G. Metail, Kenora; R. C. Missel, Calgary; L. B. Mulligan, Edmonton.

H. D. Murdick, Dryden; C. D. Nielsen, Hinton, Alta.; M.D.G. Nielsen, Edmonton; R. C. Parker, Sherwood Park, Alta.; R. G. Patton, Kelowna; S. M. Patton, Calgary.

D. B. Penner, Calgary; D. A. Petersen, Great Falls, Man.; R. R. Peterson, Sherwood Park, Alta.; E. B. Piercy, Edson; K. D. Poirier, Calgary; K. D. Polack, Kelowna.

K. A. Postnicks, Great Falls; N. M. Preece, Peers, Alta.; J. M. Race, Great Falls; G. R. Richardson, Great Falls; A. N. Roemer, Calgary; D. W. Schulz, Hinton, Alta.

D. R. Simard, Sherwood Park, Alta.; K. R. Sinclair, Kenora; V. C. Smith, Kelowna; L. W. Therriault, Thunderbay; T. R. Thiessen, Kelowna; G. W. Van Dermeulen, Calgary.

P. A. Vogel, Dryden; M. S. Waygood, St. Albert, Alta.; M. B. Wayne, Edmonton, R. J. Yarema, Dauphin; J. K. Zacharuk, Fort St. John; K. J. Zawitkoski, Edmonton.

B COY

A. H. Anfield, Clinton; A. E. Bodnar, Clinton; D. B. Boneaell, Merritt; K. Booth, Regina; S. M. Buckley, Clinton; R. L. Bugera, Lewis Creek.

R. T. Cataford, Nakusp; J. P. Chendra, Kamloops; F. N. Cosman, Clinton; J. J. Cox, Salmon Arm; R. T. Cunningham, Revelstoke; D. A. DeVuyst, Kamloops.

D. J. Doyle, McLure; K. B.

Fisher, Barriere; W. N. Gaillard, Milestone, Sask.; L. Guraluyck, Regina; A. Hastey, Prince George; D. R. Hoffman, Vernon. R. E. Hume, Merritt; D. C. Jelinski, Regina; E. J. Karczewski, Salmon Arm; R. W. Kohout, Nakusp; D. F. Kosar, Crelman, Sask.; D. A. Krivak, Salmon Arm.

L. B. Laufer, Salmon Arm; R. B. Layman, Wayburn; V. A. Legler, Merritt; M. S. Leopold, Revelstoke; G. I. Little, Penticton; B. R. Mathewson, Kamloops.

J. B. Mazer, Yorkton; S. J. McAstrocker, Revelstoke; R. J. McCrystal, Milestone, Sask.; S. A. McGillivray, Kamloops; J. H. McNicol, Prince George; T. L. Morsette, Prince George.

M. E. Neff, Prince George; D. E. Nesbitt, Barriere; L. A. Nesbitt, Barriere; P. J. E. Neve, Regina; J. A. Novak, Regina; T. J. O'Brien, Revelstoke.

R. J. Pasemko, Salmon Arm; B. H. Pickns, Assiniboi; P. F. Posnick, Nakusp; K. W. Prybylski, Yorkton; E. S. Siwy, Weyburn; M. J. Stadnyk, Regina.

B. R. Strom, Vancouver; C. C. R. Thomas, Milestone, Sask.; P. C. Thomas, Vancouver; M. L. Trembley, Weyburn; B. K. Ulrick, Milestone, Sask.; D. W. Ward, Regina.

G. H. Warriner, Salmon Arm; D. B. Wasstrom, Lac La Hache, B.C.: D. B. Watt, Yorkton; C. D. White, New Denver; J. E. Wilson, Weyburn; R. L. Wilson, Barriere; W. R. Zotzan, Colfax, Sask.

D. W. Barton, Abbotsford; W. L. Battaglis, Whitehorse; S. G. Beirnes, Surrey; R. G. Bell, Whitehorse; B. P. Berestrom, Surrey; P. D. Bird, Burnaby.

G. B. Blackstock, Gallivan, Sask.; R. M. Bovisert, Moose Jaw; R. D. Boudreau, Vancouver; S. W. Braddick, West Vancouver; D. W. Carey, Whitehorse; J. L. Csuk, Surrey.

D. M. Dmytriw, Moose Jaw; D. K. Downton, Mortlach, Sask.; G. C. Downton, Mortlach, Sask.; B. J. Duke, Richmond; G. C. Duncalfe, Abbotsford; K. P. Duncalfe, Abbotsford.

R. B. Duncan, Estevan; D. J. Dunlop, Vancouver; R. M. Eberle, Regina; R. G. Eberle, Regina; J. R. Fehr, Abbotsford, E. J. Fernandes, Vancouver.

B. P. Flegel, Richmond, M. L. Harris, Estevan; M. E. Heier, Estevan; A. E. H. Holgate, Whitehorse; D. H. Howie, Whitehorse; R. B. Jamieson, Bushel Park, Sask.

G. R. Jensen, Surrey; F. F. Kellerman, Surrey; C. B. Kerr, Swift Current; R. G. Kiss, Clearbrook; R. W. Leek, Richmond; M. A. Lopez, Richmond.

S. D. Maclean, West Vancouver; D. M. McClennan, Vancouver; D. J. Martin, Estevan; D. B. J.

Martin, Estevan; D. B. Marshall, Burnaby; R. I. McDonald, Swift Current.

F. B. McKenna, Abbotsford; W. A. McQueen, Burnaby; B. M. C. McSween, North Vancouver; N. Midttun, Surrey; G. F. Olheiser, Estevan.

R. J. Page, North Vancouver; G. R. Pearson; North Vancouver; J. R. W. Poustie, North Vancouver; M. G. Praxl, Aldergrove; K. E. Reed, Vancouver; B. S. Schill, Richmond.

D. G. Seymour, Vancouver; S. P. Smith, Mortlach, Sask.; D. J. T. Storlie, Lampman, Sask.; P. G. Wateland, North Vancouver; D. B. Williams, Delta; L. L. Worley, Surrey; K. A. Wright, Clearbrook; N. A. Campbell, Whitehorse.

B. Adams, Melville; D. G. Adams, Powell River; D. Adams, Prince Albert; C. Akackuch, White Bear Reserve, Sask.; M. Ames, Port Albernie; P. Bailey, Victoria; S. I. Baird, Victoria; M. Bender, Surrey; K. Benz, Victoria; M. Berger, Vancouver; N. J. Best, Burnaby; C. I. Bethel, Delta.

S. A. Bognar, Surrey; J. R. Boots, Victoria; L. Bratushesky, Punnichy, Sask.; Beamish, Fernie; P. Brule, Victoria; R. A. Caine, Langley.

B. R. Chahley, Surrey; D. D. Chalmers, Victoria; I. Cook, Victoria; B. D. Corey, Port Alberni; E. D. Crowe, Regina; V. S. Dean, Surrey.

F. Desnomie, Lorlie, Sask.; S. A. Douglas, Nanaimo; J. S. Fisher, Regina; J. G. French, North Delta; T. R. Fyfe, Qualicum Beach; A. R. Gilhooly, Victoria.

G. W. Goodpipe, Ft. Capell, Sask.; Graham-Marr, Victoria; P. J. Iannone, Cloverdale; S. R. Jones, North Delta; C. A. Kelly, North Delta; M. Kormansek, Victoria.

R. F. Kowalchok, Melville; R. G. Krein, Prince Albert; D. R. Lacasse, B.C.; C. F. Laronde, Sturgis, Sask.; A. G. LeBlanc, Powell River; F. LeDoux, Melville.

F. R. Lekivetz, Victoria; M. J. Leslie, Victoria; R. B. MacDonald, Comox; G. C. Machiskinic, Rose Valley, Sask.; R. Mainwaring, Victoria; B. Martin, Victoria.

M. McClinton, Whiterock; J. F. McCartan, Nanaimo; R. M. McCluskey, Cobble Hill; H. R. McFarland, Terrace; J. D. McGuire, New Westminster; N. H. McLeod, Prince Albert.

L. P. Meredith, Prince Albert; B. G. Mitchell, Victoria; W. S. Morrison, Surrey; T. G. Morris, Victoria; S. A. Moylan, Delta; B. R. Murphy, Whiterock.

J. D. Murray, Vanada, Texada Island; C. Normandeau, Delta; N. Obey, Fort Quapelle, Sask.; D. F. Parker, Vananda; B. D. Pattie, Surrey; E. T. Petersen, Prince Albert.

S. L. Phinney, Surrey; F. Quewezance, Kamsack, Sask.; P. M. Quewezance, Kamsack, Sask.; I. R. Ratchford, Victoria; T. P. Roffel, Surrey; W. A. Shaw, Surrey.

B. Sims, Vancouver; D. W. Smith, Surrey; P. A. Smith, Victoria; R. M. Stewart, Coquitlam; J. K. Stiglic, Surrey; P. D. Tassie, Victoria.

M. D. Taylor, Esquimalt; P. W. T. Waycott, Delta; L. Waun, Coquitlam; E. S. Wiegers, Prince Albert; G. D. Williams, Victoria; R. Zakrzewski, Vancouver; C. L. Zohner, Powell River.

C COY

C. D. Adams, Salmon Arm; L. A. Angers, Hope; D. C. Barker, Burnaby; M. L. Bates, Clinton; K. Benz, Victoria; K. Berg, Surrey; F. A. Bjarnason, Canyon; R. D. Bjarnason, Canyon; P. L. Bolger, Victoria; R. Boniface, Rutland; P. R. Boscoe, Prince George; P. W. Bryans, Wynndel.

A. T. Buck, Port Coquitlam; D. R. Cannel, Delta; M. A. Carriere, Vancouver; R. S. Casagrande, Surrey; J. C. Cathers, Coquitlam; B. S. Cathrine, Victoria.

J. Clegg, Vancouver; L. R. Corvino, Vancouver; M. Daehn, Salmon Arm; P. A. Dander, Vancouver; J. M. Davidson, Vancouver; V. S. Dean, Surrey.

A. Den Dulk, Chase; D. K. Desgagne, Prince George; D. W. Doherty, Kamloops; T. W. Douglas, Port Moody; H. Dunn, Ladner; R. Gandy, Vancouver.

D. E. Gemmell, Victoria; K. Gingell, Oyama; N. L. Gordon, Richmond; B. Graf, Haney; W. N. Graham, 100 Mile House; M. Grasser, Merritt.

R. Hammond, McLure; B. L. Hajesz, Barriere; G. R. Hall, Victoria; E. B. Harris, Lac Lahache; L. W. Harris, Lac Lahache; A. K. Henton, Salmon Arm.

B. G. Hole, Richmond; N. E. Howk, Prince George; D. D. S. Hutchinson, Victoria; M. K. Ilaender, Maple Ridge; A. Jensen, Salmon Arm; E. C. Jensen, Salmon Arm.

D. W. Johnson, Prince George; R. M. Kazakoff, Salmon Arm; S. Kazakoff, Kamloops; R. B. Kildare, Vancouver; T. A. Killam, New Westminster; B. Knight, Vernon.

G. J. Kozma, Vancouver; G. L. Lacasse, Port Coquitlam; P. S. Lea, Richmond; L. S. Lee, Vancouver; R. Gelling, Richmond; D. E. MacDonald, Victoria.

A. E. MacKenzie, Salmon Arm; R. B. MacLennan, Vancouver; J. M. Madsen, Vancouver; G. L. Manley, 70 Mile House; A. Martin, Victoria; R. W. Matyas, Coquitlam.

C. C. McCarthy, Kamloops; M. McClinton, Whiterock; D. P.

McGuire, Surrey; J. M. McIntosh, Victoria; F. W. McKenzie, Burnaby; G. A. McKenzie, Port Alberni.

K. McKenzie, Prince George; N. McMurtrie, Victoria; R. G. McRae, Burnaby, R. M. Meredith, Abbotsford; W. Milosevic, Vancouver; K. Moore, Lumby.

K. S. Moretti, Victoria; D. L. Morrison, Richmond; L. Moss, Victoria; B. R. Murphy, Whiterock; D. D. Nickel, Vancouver; W. L. Nyack, New Westminster.

R. W. Ogurian, Vancouver; W. Parks, Abbottsford; G. A. Parsons, Burnaby; R. S. Pattie, Surrey; R. J. Payne, North Vancouver; W. G. Penman, Abbotsford.

E. M. Pereira, Vancouver; L. J. B. Pereira, Vancouver; G. D. Phoenix, Kamloops; R. A. Plant, Delta; G. M. Pool, Victoria; M. C. Prieur, Tappan.

G. W. Prytula, Kelowna; O. Pudans, New Westminster; R. C. Pybus, Vancouver; T. W. Radford,

C COY (Cont.)

Louis Creek; S. C. Roberts, Kamloops; W. Robinson, Prince George.

T. P. Roffel, Surrey; G. Rogers, Merritt; E. A. Roggeveen, Salmon Arm; G. Rouse, Port Coquitlam; S. Sanders, Chase; R. Sanesh, Lumby.

W. Schalm, Salmon Arm; B. W. Scharf, Victoria; G. B. Scheepbouwer, Salmon Arm; L. H. Scott, Merritt; J. Seidel, Victoria; G. N. Sideen, Port Alberni; D. A. Simmons, Surrey; B. Sims, Vancouver; S. Smith, Vancouver; B. Smithers, Burnaby; P. S. Strasdine, Richmond; B. R. Struck, Prince George.

W. J. Tremblay, Prince George; R. C. Turner, Burnaby; D. Ullian, Merritt; R. S. Usher, New Westminster; J. Vanderwal, Victoria; D. J. Van Oosten, Maple Ridge; T. J. Vanwieringen, Vancouver; D. R. Viscount, Kamloops; S. J. Vlake, Vancouver; M. A. Waenink, Surrey; S. A. Walton, Prince George; K. J. White, Victoria.

G. W. Wild, Richmond; C. R. Williams, Delta, K. B. Young, Richmond; R. Zakrzewski, Vancouver; E. I. M. Bragg, Victoria.

D COY

C. R. Anderson, Portage la Prairie; A. G. Andrews, Portage la Prairie; A. G. Apetagon, Norway House, Man.; G. E. Beaudin, Winnipeg; M. Bender, Surrey; G. R. Benjamin, Dryden.

D. J. Brown, Vananda, B.C.; L. K. Boon, Surrey; K. R. Bourassa, Powell River; R. F. Bousfield, Dryden; B. A. Bumphrey, Port Coquitlam; K. A. Campbell, Winnipeg; D. S. Canfield,

568

Kelowna; L. A. Carmichael, North Vancouver; D. U. Castle, Courtney; R. Chan, Victoria

B. D. Chartier, Winnipeg; K. A. Cielen, Winnipeg; K. R. Closen, Thompson; E. Clyne, Norway House, Man.

J. M. Collette, St. Jean Batiste, Man.; S. G. Companion, Powell River; K. D. Connolly, N. Vancouver; L. S. Cook, Courtney; R. P. Crouch, Victoria.

G. A. Cumming, Comox; D. G. Darr, Brandon; G. R. Davies, Port Coquitlam; R. V. Davis, Shilo, Man.; R. J. DeLorme, Winnipeg; B. Dweitt, Courtney; S. C. Duckworth, Vananda, B.C.

J. Egri, Penticton; L. Egri, Penticton; R. E. Ennis, Port Coquitlam; W. J. Ettawacappo, Norway House, Man.; W. Forster, Surrey; G. B. Fraser, West Vancouver; K. M. Fraser, Kenora.

R. French, Kelowna; M. C. Farnsworth, Port Coquitlam; G. L. Garvey, Powell River; L.F. Guadent, Powell River; K.D. Gauthier, Winnipeg; J.W. Gribble, Powell River; R. R. Gribble, Powell River.

M. L. Gunnlaugson, Rutland; L. D. Hamilton, Nanaimo; K. L. Hanson, Coquitlam; G. A. Hardonk, Nanaimo; R. M. Hardonk, Nanaimo; D. W. Hlady, Thunderbay; W. G. Huffman, Dryden.

K. C. Jackson, Kelowna; F.A. Jaggard, Thunder Bay; M. J. Johnston, Ft. Churchill; S. J. M. Jurko, Madsen, Ont.; G. L. Keith, Stonewall, Man.

D. E. Kellar, Dryden; A. M. Kennedy, Kelowna; J. E. Kirschman, Comox; Kirschman, Comox; K. J. Klassen, Brandon; R. J. LaFontaine, Thompson.

H. R. Landry, Dryden; R. E. Ledger, Thunderbay; R. A. MacKenzie, Thunderbay; M. G. MacLean, West Vancouver; M. G. Magee, Kenora; D. Martens, Winnipeg; J. D. Martens, Winnipeg.

B.J. Mattnews, Powell River; J.F. McCartan, Nanaimo; J.J. McDermott, Port Coquitlam; T.D. McDowell, Victoria; H.B. McIntosh, North Vancouver; A.A. Montgomery, Courtney.

R. T. W. McKinley, Delta; C. G. Mullins, West Vancouver; P. C. Olson, North Vancouver; S. O'Malley, North Vancouver; L. N. Ouderkirk, Surrey; S. Packiewicz, Victoria; J. Page, North Vancouver.

K. T. Patrick, Vancouver; W. M. Pearson, Nanaimo; E. L. Peikys, Dryden; J. Pfleger, Thunder Bay, B. Philip, North Vancouver; D. B. Pollock, St. Jean Baptist, Man.; S. W. Poole, Winnipeg.

D. R. Popp, Kelowna; R. J. Potter, Dryden; W. Poustie, North Vancouver; M. J. Prendergast, Lazo, B.C.; N. P. Price, Victoria; B.S. Ramsden, Brandon; B.G. Ramsey, Brandon.

R. Ramsey, Brandon; M. J. Revell, Surrey; D. A. Riehl, Creighton, Sask.; P. B. G. Rossiter, Portage La Prairie; R.W. Roulette, Portage La Prairie; S.W. Saboraki, Dauphin; C.D.T. Sadler, Cloverdale.

K. Scott, Nanaimo; R. P. Steales, Winnipeg; B. M. Seefried, Cloverdale; A. Shupe, Dryden; E. W. Sinclair, Kenora; J. C. A. Sinclair, Fort Churchill; W. A. Small, Powell River.

A. A. Smith, Dauphin; R. K. Stead, Victoria; R. C. Steere, Surrey; R. W. Steward, North Vancouver; L. C. Sthilaire, Aubigny, Man.; D. L. Swanson, Brandon.

M. D. Taylor, Esquimalt; M. A. Thompson, Victoria; F. R. Thalhofer, Campbell; C. A. Town, Vermette, Man.; W. F. Treloar, Powell River; D. J. Tremblay, Thunder Bay; K. J. Trick, Stonewall, Man.

R. A. B. Walter, West Vancouver; R. B. Wareing, St. Frances Xavier, Man.; R. R. Wasilka, Brandon; M. W. Waters, Vancouver; C. J. Wermie, Regina; D. Whiting, West Vancouver; A. G. Wiles, Surrey.

D. R. Wilkinson, Surrey; H. Wysmulek, Winnipeg; H. R. Zohner, Powell; K. R. Zurch, Nanaimo; J. P. Turchak, McCreary, Man.

E COY

J. E. Abbott, Sherwood Park, Alta.; R. W. Adams, Edmonton; D. S. Anderson, Edmonton; K. Arnoldus, Fort St. John; R. L. Arsenault, Taylor; B. L. Aulenback, P.M.Q. Griesbach.

D. A. Aulenback, Edmonton; M. P. Babcock, Winnipeg; A. G. Barlow, Vermilion, Alta.; P. J. Bassie, Edmonton; K. Belcourt, Edmonton.

J. B. Bell, Fort St. John; M. W. Benson, Edmonton; L. Bilanchuk, Fort McCleod; K. Bokovay, Edmonton; W. A. Bolen, Edmonton; L. C. Boucher, Grand Prairie.

G. W. Bourget, Fort St. John; K. H. Bretzer, Edmonton; R. L. Brogden, Cutknife, Sask.; T. M. Brown, Black Diamond; K. G. Burnett, Edmonton; N. A. Butler, Grand Prairie.

J. A. Cardinal, Edmonton; J. M. Charlebois, Edmonton; P. M. Chynoweth, Calgary; A. Cleall, Edmonton; R. D. Clifton, Winnipeg; L. D. Constantinoff, Saskatoon.

R. D. W. Cooper, Fort St. John; T. W. Courchene, Winnipeg; A. H. Daye, Edmonton; G. C. Dekock, Winnipeg; G. E. Drebit, Calgary; T. J. Dukes, Rosetown, Sask.

D. D. English, Calgary; R. H. Eriksen, Calgary; G. Elliott, Calgary; G. J. Fedoruk, Edmonton; D. J. Fleming, Rosetown; G. T. Forrest, Fort St. John.

D. N. Fullerton, Elrose, Sask.; M. Gair, Calgary; K. E. Gordon, Red Deer; C. M. Gibson, Slave Lake, Alta.; R. J. Ginther, Calgary; B.J. Goertzen, Blackfalds, Alta.

W. R. Gow, Edmonton; M. E. Grover, Lacombe; D. M. Hall, Calgary; D. J. Hall, Calgary; D. J. Halpenny, Winnipeg; D. L. Hansen, Fort St. John.

S. J. Hayduk, Sherwood Park; C. E. Heigh, Vermilion, Alta.; B. Heinz, Redcliffe; R. A. Hill, Edmonton; W. Hofstra, Saskatoon; R. S. Homeniuk, Edmonton.

J. A. Hopkinson, Lethbridge; B. R. Hunt, Hayriver, NWT; R.A. Huseby, Blackfalds; K. Jackson, Saskatoon; B. S. James, Slave Lake; Z. A. Joseph, Fort St. John.

B. A. Kauppila, Edmonton; J. R. Kenney, Calgary; R. Kulhawy, Calgary; K. K. Kuz, Redcliffe; K. J. LaFluer, Grand Prairie; K. J. Langlotz, Winnipeg.

A. J. Lemey, Edmonton; G. J. Levesque, Vermillion; D. F. Lindsay, Hinton; G. H. Little, Edmonton; A. Mast, Leduc; B. W. Marks, Edmonton.

R. W. Marshall, Calgary; H. R. MacDonald, Lethbridge; M. D. Male, Edmonton; D. C. McGee, Saskatoon; R. J. McNeil, Edmonton; B. K. Meckelberg, Calgary.

C. R. Mercer, Edmonton; R. W. Munro, Edson; S. Napoleon, Winnipeg; P. A. Novak, Fort St. John; D.P. Ogenchuk, Rosetown, Sask.; T. D. Ostashek, Fort St. John.

P. A. Paiement, Edmonton; M. C. Pardell, Grand Prairie; G. Pawlivsky, Lethbridge; R. A. Peters, Pincher Creek; T. A. Ponto, Saskatoon; G. Prengel, Winnipeg.

D. A. Prybylski, Yorkton; S. B. Radloff, Sherwood Park; G. G. Richards, Edmonton; M. R. Ridsdale, Grand Prairie; S. J. Ross, Sherwood Park; T. D. Rothery, Calgary.

A. M. Roxburgh, Calgary; R. T. Ryder, Calgary; S. B. Ryder, Calgary; G. W. Sansom, Saskatoon; K. M. Sawatzky, Kindersley; R. D. Slavik, Fort St. John.

P. D. Sauer, Edmonton; E. J. Shears, Fort St. John; J. D. Sheen, Sherwood Park; G. R. Siska, Edmonton; D. M. Slater, Winnipeg; B. W. Sorenson, Edmonton.

E. Spetter, Edmonton; T. E. Stennes, Edmonton; D. B. Stephenson, Lethbridge; R. W. Teel, Medicine Hat; C. J. Thomson, Winnipeg; D. M. Townsend, Hay River, NWT.

M. B. Trodden, Pincher Creek; B.S. Vermeulen, Rosetown; C.A. Wahlstrom, Edmonton; R. S. Walker, Edmonton; R. Walker, Sherwood Park; B. R. Waldie, Mayerthorpe; A.M. Walton, Rosetown; K. Weiner, Calgary; W.

E. White, Edmonton; M. F. Wilke, Edmonton; E. Wilkerson, Fort St. John; P. H. Williams, Hay River, NWT; C. R. Wilson, Hinton.

F COY

M. J. Anson, Winnipeg; D. K. Bauslaugh, Ganges; D. A. Beauchesne, Calgary; D. P. Beauchesne, Calgary; W. G. Benwell, Wadena, Sask.; T. H. Berg, Weyburn.

B. M. Biollo, Revelstoke; H. L. Brass, Davis, Sask.; B. J. Brink, Calgary; K. J. Bristow, St. Norbert, Man.; J. A. Bryson, Regina; S. A. Bunn, Calgary.

R. M. Chartrand, Winnipeg; H. J. Chrest, Winnipeg; R. M. Christianson, Calgary; D. L. Cochrane, Fort McMurray; L. M. Cochrane, Fort McMurray; R. Cochrane, Fort McMurray.

G. W. Copp, Naramata; R. B. Cowan, Melville; R. D. Currence, Calgary; G. W. Dawkins, Winnipeg; J. D. Desmonie, Lorlie, Sask.; M. J. Devenney, Winnipeg.

S. Dibbs, Whitehorse; M. R. Dimmer, Calgary; D. W. Driver, Swift Current; R. A. Dyke, Inuvik; J. A. Eddy, Revelstoke; D. F. Elliott, Estevan.

R. Elson, Thorsby, Alta.; D. W. Elverum, Trail; K. L. Fagan, Calgary; J. J. Fitzpatrick, Fort McMurray; B. G. Geddes, Kindersley; R. Gerritse, Wadena, Sask.

P. A. Gerritsen, Calgary; R. J. Gibson, Rockhaven, Sask.; R. J. Gilchrest, Trail; R. S. Gordon, Inuvik; W. S. Greenland, Inuvik; K. J. Griffiths, Winnipeg.

K. G. Haan, Calgary; B. G. Harde, Estevan; L. J. Heighington, Breton; K. Heine, Kindersley; K. R. Hogarth, Swift Current; Q. Holtby, Valmarie, Sask.

A. A. House, Sparwood; P. T. Hunter, Moose Jaw; S. B. Ife, Revelstoke; G. A. Inkster, Melville; D. G. Jackson, Regina; C. A. Jamieson, CFB Moose Jaw.

D. P. Jones, Winnipeg; M. A. Jones, Winnipeg; I. M. Jurgins, Humboldt, Sask.; C. G. Kanngiesser, Calgary; T. K. Kariga, Calgary; G. Karoly, Calgary.

P. A. Karkanis, Calgary; K. N. Kaytor, Regina; D. J. Kelly, Ft. McMurray; R. H. Kelly, Saskatoon; K. R. Kilb, Revelstoke; D. B. Kilpatrick, Battleford, Sask.

J. M. Kolenz, Estevan; E. Kryzanowski, Wadena; I. Kryzanowski, Inuvik; E. I. Kulyk, Wadena; B. Kuntz, Estevan; M. R. Kusch, Calgary.

K. A. Lacey, Calgary; A. G. LeBlanc, Powell River; C. J. Letkeman, Swift Current; R. J. Lindenberger, Fort McMurray; J. G. Littlewolf, Kamsak, Sask.; T. Livingstone, Regina.

A. S. Lloy, Victoria; C. G. Longman, Punnichy, Sask.; P. J. Lopinski, Humboldt; R. L. Lowey, Revelstoke; J. M. Lowther, Trail; B. J. Lynch, Fruitvale.

R. C. MacDonald, Winnipeg; M. F. MacInnis, Weyburn; M. D. Makulowch, Saskatoon; J. M. Mallory, Cranbrook; P. G. Maltais, Swift Current; R. Manegre, Calgary.

V. G. Mayne, Fruitvale; B. H. McLeod, Prince Albert; I. A. McKay, Swift Current; H. McLaren, Moose Jaw; D. C. McNab, Regina; J. F. Melton, Regina.

R. L. Montour, Prince Albert; D. M. Molnar, Cranbrook; D. J. Mosionier, Winnipeg; G. A. Muir, Trail; A. F. Muraski, Calgary; G. B. Myhr, Swift Current.

J. Natowcappo, Kylemore, Sask.; J. O. Olson, Weyburn; S. A. O'Day, Trail; E. Paquette, Winnipeg; D. F. Parker, Vanada; L. Parker, Melville.

A. Pavlovic, Swift Current; T. L. Payne, Calgary; K. Platz, Cranbrook; D. J. Powaschuk, Swift Current; D. Quewezance, Regina; J. K. Roberts, Moose Jaw.

R. J. Schuchert, Winnipeg; P. Shaw, Inuvik; J. Simpson, Fort McMurray; D. J. Smith, Ft. McMurray; K. L. Stark, Regina; A. P. Sprung, Saskatoon.

J. P. Taylor, Winnipeg; D. M. Thivierge, Calgary; R. G. Thompson, Calgary; D. W. Tuttosi, Punnichy; D. Vacheresse, Ft. McMurray; M. G. Vassos, Melville.

N. Waldbauer, Melville; A. S. Weiss, Warburg; D. G. Wheler, Battleford; C. G. Willette, Medicine Hat; R. A. Willford, Revelstoke; K. R. Williams, Regina.

A. M. Woloshyn, Kuroki, Sask.; J. E. Wood, Regina; B. E. Wright, Winnipeg; T. M. Wynnuk, Warburg, Alta.

H COY

D. J. Adams, Powell River; D. D. Ames, Victoria; I. S. Armar, North Van; M. L. Auld, Cranbrook; D. J. Bantle, St. Albert; J. R. Beaulieu, Saskatoon.

T. D. Behm, Prince George; R. S. Besse, Edmonton; A. A. Bienvenue, Abbotsford; J. M. Bikadi, Powell River; G. J. Billson, Winnipeg; G. M. Blain, Courteney.

C. D. Bokovay, Edmonton; L. K. Bolen, Powell River; K. Bond, Powell River; T. K. Boock, Creston; C. R. Botterill, Moose Jaw; D. A. Bremner, Warren,

G. J. Bridgman, Thunderbay; D. J. Cain, Victoria; B. Cambrey, Victoria; J. Caney, Surrey; C. H. Caya, Winnipeg.

J. J. Charlton, Mount Lehman; L. A. Cheater, Winnipeg; E. T. Clark, Vancouver; R. L. Clear,

Victoria; S. B. Cohen, Mayerthorpe, Alta.; F. D. Cooper, Nakusp.

J. Cudmore, White Rock; W. H. Davies, Strathmore; B. Dekker, Melville; D. A. Denluck, Prince George; J. F. Dobson, Calgary; K. B. Dodd, Vancouver.

P. J. Dusseault, Vimy, Alta.; G. S. Dutton, Estevan; D. J. Faryna, North Vancouver; D. A. Fege, Surrey; B. S. Fitzsimmons, Edmonton; P. M. Frankow, Edmonton.

J. J. Gate, Moose Jaw; L. A. Genest, Lethbridge; R. A. George, Calgary; J. B. Gibson, Victoria; R. G. Gilmour, Vancouver; G. B. Graf, Haney.

T. T. Griffiths, Merrit; J. Gobersek, Regina; P. C. Gorsalitz, Humboldt; J. Hack, Burnaby; H. Hahn, Surrey; D. H. Hale, Richmond.

S. R. Haley, Port Coquitlam; L. Hartenberger, Weyburn; B. H. Hendricks, North Vancouver; E. C. Howk, Prince George; T. J. Hrabarchuk, Winnipeg; A. H. James, Edson.

H. G. Jarche, Revelstoke; D. K. Kennet, Surrey; I. M. Kesteris, Eider Bay, Man.; B. K. Killam, New Westminster; A. O. Knapman, Calgary; K. W. Knipstrom, Burnaby.

D. A. Laramee, Maple Ridge; K. D. Laramee, Maple Ridge; B. E. Larsen, St. Albert; J. L. Laursen, Victoria; K. L. Leach, Regina; B. R. Leftrook, Hendrix Lake.

K. L. Lenko, White Rock; I. A. Leverington, Stonewall; R. M. Lewis, Prince George; C. Livingstone, Vancouver; R. W. Loesch, Winnipeg; R. Lund, Regina.

S. Lusk, Delta; D. R. MacDougall, Edmonton; K. O. MacInnis, Weyburn; J. G. Malloy, Port Alberni; R. G. Marasa, Coquitlam; B. K. Marshall, Delta.

A. Masi, Red Lake, Ont.; D. W. McCarthur, Vemette, Man.; K. McCartney, Edmonton; B. L. McClinton, Surrey; R. D. McMillan, Dryden.

R. E. Meredith, Abbotsford; J. K. Meyers, Saskatoon; R. R. Monkman, Gabriola Island; R. G. Mooney, Riverdale Whitehorse; M. J. Motloch, Fernie; W. I. Munro, Richmond.

W. P. Murray, Edmonton; B. D. Neatby, Winnipeg; D. B. Neufeld, Saskatoon; G. Noga, Burnaby; A. J. Norquay, Prince George; S. P. Nunn, Sardis.

J. M. G. Ogston, Medicine Hat; N. Ogurian, Edmonton; D. F. Olmsted, Edmonton; D. J. Paiement, Edmonton, L. J. Pangman, St. Norbert, (Winnipeg); A. Paquette, North Vancouver.

D. A. Paquette, Edmonton; G. W. Parker, Delta; G. D. Pearson, Powell River; J. Perrot, Calgary;

B. C. Petkau, Calgary; K. S. Pon, Calgary.

T. J. Popp, Whitehorse; E. C. Prefontaine, Innisfail; D. W. Priaul, Calgary; R. Rattink, Port Alberni; R. B. Rhinhart, Yellowknife; D. Rick, Delta.

J. A. Robin, Surrey; G. A. Rogers, Estevan; C. J. Rollins, Parksville; G. M. Ross, Laslo; D. J. Scott, Edmonton; C. J. Shaw, Surrey.

D. R. Shields, Victoria; P. C. Shields, Victoria; A. P. Sommer, Calgary; J. F. Stanhouse, Calgary; W.˙F. Sutherland, Edmonton; D. N. Swan, Abbotsford.

F. W. Taylor, Winnipeg; H. A. Therriaulet, Thunder Bay; J. A. Toivola, Coquitlam; M. W. Tottenham, Revelstoke; N. Vanderlinden, Fort St. John; D. G. Watson, Revelstoke.

W. G. Watson, Cranbrook; W. F. Wawrychuk, Vedder Crossing; D. A. Wilde, Surrey; R. L. Wilkinson, Victoria; R. O. Wilson, Regina; M. P. Wren, Whitehorse.

A. P. Zingeler, Calgary; R. H. Zorn, Winnipeg; A. S. George, Coquitlam.

BAND

R. Bodnarchuk, Fort McMurray, Alta.; M. Bos, Burnaby; P. Bos, Burnaby; M. Braden, Prince George; B.D. Butt, Victoria; J. H. Cecotka, Winnipeg.

D. Conners, Lethbride; R. M. Cooman, Edmonton; M. Coutts, Winnipeg; W. R. Coventry, Fort McMurray; S. T. Crawford, Surrey; B.D. Fischer, Victoria.

G. L. Fleury, Winnipeg; B. Fraser, Winnipeg; W. H. J. Gabriel, Regina; A. Gilchrist, Richmond; D. J. Gow, Edmonton; K. W. Haines, Winnipeg.

P. A. Henderson, Victoria; B. H. Hendricks, North Vancouver; P. Hendrickson, Winnipeg; R. L. Jobagy, Val Marie, Sask.; M. LaGace, Winnipeg; G. A. MacCallum, Victoria.

D. G. MacDonald, Victoria; E. E. R. Magnusson, Regina; D. W. Mattatall, North Vancouver; T. H. McClymont, Victoria; D.W. McLeod, Hinton; L. Menduk, Fernie.

R. Mitchell, Victoria; G. Meyer, Edmonton; L. D. Morris, Regina; M. J. Monk, Duncan; S. L. Pennock, Edmonton; K. M. Piche, Turner Valley, Alta.

D. D. Pickering, Prince George; B. M. Popowich, Winnipeg; B. W. Ragan, Port Alberni; G. D. Rathcford, Victoria; B. R. Reid, Surrey; A. L. Rosenfeldt, Edmonton; S. A. Salaga, Victoria.

P. L. Schmidt, Edmonton; C. C. Schooner, Terrace; D. W. Secuur, Regina; P. W. Sevighy, Edmonton; B. R. Slate, Edmonton; R. Smith, Campbell River; W. R. Taylor, Surrey.

B. A. Taylor, Hinton; M. Vaal-Henke, Terrace; A. Van de Graaf,

Winnipeg; S. G. Van Tassel, Winnipeg; G. Villebrun, Victoria; S. W. Ward, Vancouver; D. M. Whitham, Winnipeg.

DVR COMM

M. W. Bartel, West Vancouver; D. M. Bignell, Trail; K. W. Blakely, Winnipeg; J. D. Bryans, Wynndel, B.C.; T. Cotten, Red Cliff, Alta.; R. C. Davis, Shiloh, Man.

R. W. Derry, Calgary; N. Dimick, Giliam, Man.; W. K. Dobra, Lethbridge; R. L. Donk, Winnipeg; H. R. Edwards, Fernie; D. G. Flynn, Richmond.

R. Gouger, Hinton; C. R. Hollen, Fort St. John; R. S. Howe, Whitehorse; M. M. Hunsche, Red Deer; F. K. Kennedy, Edmonton; W. F. Kuptana, Cape Peary, N.W.T.

F. R. MacDonald, Ft. McMurray; P. R. Major, Medicine Hat; R. B. McSorley, Kelowna; M. J. Millard, North Vancouver; W. J. Monaghan, Edmonton.

E. J. Nielsen, Summerland, M. Noga, Kelowna; W. Puruim, Victoria; D. G. Reitsma, Edmonton; D. G. Renaud, Edmonton; B. K. Richards, Edmonton.

T. E. Rogerson, Kindersley, Sask.; D. G. Shupe, Dryden; L. J. Shupe, Dryden; T. Uhryn, Saskatoon; R. T. Van Ryn, Lethbridge.

OFFICER TRAINING COMPANY NOMINAL ROLL

2 Lt. P. R. Fisher, Ft. McMurray; Lt. B. G. Forbes, 100 Mile House; Lt. G. D. Foster, Battleford; O Cdt. L. P. Goldstein, Winnipeg; Lt. C. E. Goodman, Victoria; O. Cdt. K. S. Healey, Winnipeg; 2 Lt. M. A. Henderson, Ladner.

Lt. M. M. W. Long, Edmonton; Lt. M. R. Long, Prince Albert; 2 Lt. B. R. Mitchell, Sfeelman; 2 Lt. A. W. Ruttan, Revelstoke; A. Capt. W. A. Shattuck, Hudson Bay, Sask.; 2 Lt. L. F. Vaness, Fernie; Lt. K. J. Ritchot, Manitoba.

VACC - 1975

A COY

H. G. Anderson, Port Coquitlam; V. G. Asmunt, Thunderbay; J. W. Barr, Nanaimo; G. E. Bater, Aldergrove; S. A. Bearf, Shilo; K. Bennet, Edmonton; A. E. Benson, Sherwood Park; L. P. Bienvenu, Abbotsford; A. L. Britney, Sardis; L. Buchkovski, Regina; M. Butler, Regina; P. Butts, N. Delta.

M. R. Carleton, Shilo; B. Cassels, Estevan, Sask.; L. J. Catlin, Dryden, Ont.; S. Chafe, Vancouver; T. Clark, Shilo; L. Collette, St. Jean Baptist, Man.; B. Connolly, North Vancouver; W. Connolly, Edmonton; W. Cornell,

Mayerthorpe; A. Corvino, Vancouver; R. W. Crawford, Pt. Coquitlam.

F. J. Daley, Edmonton; C. Demmon, Agassiz, B.C.; G. Dick, Edson, Alta.; S. R. Dixon, Pitt Meadows, B.C.; B. L. Dogniez, Regina; J. H. Dwsianyk, Winnipeg; B. W. Dyment, Fort McMurray; D. G. Ethel, Vedder Crossing, B.C.; J. J. Ethier, Edmonton; L. J. Ethier, Edmonton; S. G. Exner, Pitt Meadows.

B. E. Fawcett, Winnipeg; D. R. Flaman, Regina; D. Gassner, Kindersley, Sask.; D. C. Gay, Nanaimo; B. R. Gefreiter, Stonewall, Man.; J. A. Genoway, Rama, Sask.; K. D. Gosselin, Haney, B.C.; D. E. Green, Nanaimo; M. P. Hale, Sherwood Park; M. G. Harps, Edson; E. A. Hilchey, Regina; D. H. Hildebrand, Abbotsford; P. B. Hoddinott, Maple Ridge, B.C.

A. D. Jean, Vedder Crossing, B.C.; R. E. Jehle, Edomonton; E. K. Jimmy, Thunderchild, Sask.; J. M. Johnston, Thunder Bay; L. Jones, North Battleford; D. E. Keays, Edmonton; D. G. Kidd, Mayerthorpe; R. J. C. King, Estevan; B. M. Klengenberg, Inuivik, N.W.T.; T. M. Lacher, Swift Current; S. G. LaPlume, Edmonton; K. W. Leslie, Chilliwack; O. M. Levesque, Vermillion, Alta.; A. Lilley, Maple Ridge; R. W. Linklater, Thunder Bay; J. B. Lukin, Fort McMurray; M. A. Lutgen, Edmonton.

S. G. Macala, Invermay, Sask.; H. J. Madden, Edmonton; B. D. Mann, Shilo; S. J. Markewich, Thunder Bay; B. H. Martins, Winnipeg; D. Meetoos, Thunderchild; W. B. McGarvey, Delta; K. S. McKee, Fort McMurray; R. B. McMillan, Regina; G. A. Meredith, Abbotsford; W. F. Mika, Nanaimo; D. J. Mitchell, Estevan; M. Moffat, Edmonton; T. D. Nash, Fort McMurray; M. J. Nijman, Estevan.

R. G. Omness, Kindersley; S. G. Otway, Sherwood Park; T. V. Palmer, Nanaimo; R. A. Parker, Winnipeg; J. A. Parlby, Slave Lake, Alta.; K. J. Parsons, Delta; M. L. Porisky, Edmonton; D. A. Racine, Brandon; D. G. Racine, Brandon; K. J. Rainer, Slave Lake; R. R. Ray, Regina; B. W. Reimer, Winnipeg; R. H. Robinson, Breton, Alta.; D. C. Rodger, Sardis, B.C.; F. W. Ross, Nanaimo; R. J. Rusch, Wadena, Sask.

R. B. Sattler, Sherwood Park; W. W. Schmidt, Westlock, Alta.; P. Schnerch, Winnipeg; T. M. Schwab, Regina; G. P. Secuur, Regina; T. D. Shand, Brandon; F. J. Shupenia, Edmonton; C. D. Simmons, Winnipeg; P. K. Silvertsen, Swift Current; M. Sklepic, Sherwood Park; J. Stefanato, Thunder Bay; G. Stewart, North Vancouver; P. S. Stevenson, Swift Current; P. Sutherland, Winnipeg.

J. R. Tait, Estevan; W. Thompson, Chilliwack; A. Thorburn, Nanaimo; S. A. Tompkins, Edmonton; G. Turner, North Battleford; P. G. Wakeland, Ladner; T. Ward, Swift Current; S. C. Weston, Robb, Alta.; D. A. White, Thunder Bay; M. D. Williams, Swift Current; W. A. Wilmot, Swift Current; D. J. Winthrop, Kelwood, Man.; D. Wong, Edmonton; R. A. Zukowski, Edmonton; G. T. Lafont, Calgary; D. G. Collingridge, Winnipeg; D. D. Wiril, Regina.

A COY — SECOND INTAKE

D. M. Allison, Port Moody; J. D. Barron, Fort Churchill; B. Bayda, Saskatoon; C. K. Beaver, Thompson, Man.; G.G. Belanger, Winnipeg; R. A. Belanger, Winnipeg; C. G. Bernhardt, Winnipeg; T. Boe, Vancouver; B. D. Bourque, Naican, Sask.; J. L. Brindley, Ottawa; D. Brown, Winnipeg; D. Brown, Surrey; D. Burgis, Vancouver.

J. Cade, Coquitlam; G. C. Cassidy, Vancouver; B. Chiasson, Prince George; G. M. Christensen, Bella Coola, B.C.; D. Christink, Melva, Sask.; S. M. Ciampelletti, Vancouver; K. J. Clark, Saskatoon; K. Closen, Thompson; R. Constantine, Winnipeg; M. E. Copley, Grandilse, B.C.; S. R. Craig, Port Moody; K. W. Cudmore, White Rock; T. P. Daly, Winnipeg; I. K. Douglas, Maple Creek, Sask.; R. C. Dunkley, Saskatoon.

M. Ediger, Saskatoon; J. J. Elliott, Coquitlam; D. A. Figures, Matsqville, B.C.; M. Flett, Churchill; D. J. Foy, Winnipeg; R. E. Franchewski, Winnipeg; P. Gallant, Vancouver; C. S. Gaylard, Ladner; R. Gebhardt, Melville; P. D. Gray, Winnipeg; T. E. Grist, Graisle, B.C.; W. J. Grist, Graisle.

G. S. Hagerman, Regina; A. J. Hawkins, Winnipeg; A. J. Hayden, Haggensberg, B.C.; D. Henson, Winnipeg; P. J. Hiebert, Coquitlam; K. Huston, Merritt, B.C.; P. R. Hyska, Surrey; K. R. Jamieson, Bushell Park, Sask.; J. Johnston, Revelstoke, B.C.

T. P. Kitchen, Vancouver; J.H. Knudsen, Bella Coola; A. B. Kubisewsky, Kenora, Ont.; M. Kushner, Winnipeg; P. C. Lachapelle, 100 Mile House, B.C.; S. T. Logan, Delta; R. B. Lucas, Thompson; R. V. McCrystal, Milestone, Sask.; J. McGrath, Saskatoon; J. McKenzie, Burnaby; A. Malyk, Winnipeg; D. W. Martin, New Westminster; R. M. Melatini, Graisle; J. Mondor, Winnipeg; A. E. Monias, Norway House, Man.; R. Mooiman, Vancouver; B. S. Morrison, Vancouver; R. A. Murphy, Burnaby.

Y. M. Nair, Vancouver; G. A. Nixey, Saskatoon; R. D. Patterson, Prince George; D. Peterson, Cassiar, B.C.; R. H.

Philipps, Delta; B. Pierce, Coquitlam; R. Pudsey, Langley; K. J. Pull, Stonewall, Man.; D. I. Qualle, Pitt Meadows, B.C.; D. C. Queskekappo, Norway House; R. Rees, Vancouver; A. A. Reid, Vancouver; C. A. Rheaume, Vancouver; K. Rheaume, Vancouver; G. Ross, Milestone.

A. Schabang, Saskatoon; L. K. Shorter, Port Moody; J. A. Sim, Burnaby; T. G. Sinclair, Kenora; M. A. Skadsheim, Winnipeg; D. G. Skinner, Portage la Prairie; T. Slawinski, Saskatoon; R. Sommerfeld, Clinton, B.C.; L. D. Souter, Naicam, Sask.; K. Stanvick, Granisle; D. F. Storoschuk, Cassiar; J. A. Strangeway, Coquitlam; M. A. Taylorson, Vancouver; A. R. Tilk, Saskatoon; G. W. Treleaven, Milestone.

L. Valpy, Revelstoke; A. Vandal, Winnipeg; D. W. Vandal, Winnipeg; R. J. Vandrunick, Coquitlam; R. Vander Vliet, Prince George; D. A. Whitlock, Maple Creek; A. Wilson, Bella Coola; K. J. Wilson, Great Falls, Man.; S. P. Wood, Clinton; L. P. Yanish, Melville; S. A. Yasinsky, New Westminster; T. D. Young, Bella Coola.

B COY

B. Abbott, Camrose, Alta.; L. D. Abbott, Camrose; J. J. Arsenault, Tailer, B.C.; L. R. Ayrey, Breton, Alta.; K. C. Barteski, Invermere, Sask.; I. A. Benedet, Thunder Bay; R. L. Birdsell, Estevan, Sask.; L. M. Brown, Sidney, B.C.; N. Brown, Sidney; J. Carson, Vananda, B.C.; M. L. Corbeil, Victoria; D. Corey, Port Alberni; C. A. Cote, Comox, B.C.; B. L. Crawford, Nanaimo; C. D. Crawford, Port Coquitlam; F. J. Cruikshank, Delta; K. M. Cumpstone, Duncan.

M. A. Davis, Victoria; S. M Dorman, Victoria; L. L. Doucet Steveston, B.C.; J. Dubois, Victoria; A. L. Easton, Chilliwack; A. T. Fiorin, Victoria; G. M. French, Thunder Bay; E. M. Gardner, Powell River; V. D. Genoway, Rama, Sask.; B. Gibson, Victoria; D. J. Green, Sidney; B. Graham, Lazo, B.C.; M. E. Gribble, Powell River; D. R. Griffin, Courtenay; B. D. Harman, Surrey; R. Horansky, Victoria; C. E. Houston, Sidney.

J. R. Irwin, Duncan; R. M. James, Edson, Alta.; G. P. Jarvis, Thunder Bay; D. D. Johnson, Victoria; V. R. Johnston, Courtenay; R. C. Jensen, Richmond; K. E. Kephart, Sherwood Park; H. L. Klein, Sherwood Park; D. A. Lamont, Surrey; D. K. Landolt, Langley; C. J. Leachman, Victoria; T. M. Lehman, Sidney; E. M. Lepage, Saskatoon; G. I. Little, Penticton; R. V. Lloyd, Fort St. John; T. G. Lube, Mile 101, B.C.

M. McDonald, Richmond; R. M. McMullen, Fort St. John; P. L. C.

McNaughton, Richmond; R. G. MacLean, Edmonton; S. O. Masterson, Mayerthorpe, Alta.; S. L. Meunier, Powell River; D. M. Michalko, Saskatoon; J. Miller, Richmond; J. B. Montgomery, Richmond; R. C. Montgomery, Courtenay; J. W. Moore, Victoria; K. M. Mosionier, Winnipeg; M. R. Mulhall, Fort McMurray; H. P. Mulholland, Laslo, B.C.; D. L. Munch, Victoria; T. I. Myttenar, Surrey.

D. M. Naven, Courtenay; L. Nieckar, Rama; T. M. Noakes, Surrey; T. A. Olson, Richmond; C. C. Orr, Richmond; W. Ostashek, Fort St. John; R. Packiewicz, Victoria; M. Perepalkin, Surrey; C. D. Perry, Grande Prairie; C. L. Picken, Grande Prairie; L. C. Pickup, Lazo, B.C.; L. M. Plank, Chilliwack; C. L. Polk, Surrey; R. K. Ponsford, Victoria.

D. J. Radford, Thunder Bay; R. G. Randall, Victoria; E. J. Rich, Richmond; I. K. Ripley, Sidney; L. M. Rosko, Sidney; M. L. Rosko, Sidney; R. A. Royendyk, Port Alberni; K. D. Salmon, Lazo; D. Sanders, Port Alberni; D. B. Shaw, Nanaimo; M. G. Shaw, Victoria; G. M. Shewchuck, Rama; P. L. Skelton, Nanaimo; L. Smille, Victoria; B. K. Smith, Victoria; K. L. Smith, Powell River; R. A. Stepharnoff, Victoria.

S. Trombley, Fort St. John; S. Vardy, Victoria; C. Wagner, Richmond; P. H. Walton, Winnipeg; C. G. Warren, Powell River; C. A. Watterworth, Victoria; L. Wallace, Abbotsford; L. M. Wauthier, Victoria; L. J. White, Richmond; E. L. Whyte, Victoria; R. Wightman, Richmond; M. A. Wilkerson, Fort St. John; L. A. Williams, Victoria; C. Wolfater, Redcliffe, Alta.; B. R. Wollen, Fort St. John; C. York, Courtenay; L. S. Zinkan, Courtenay.

B COY—SECOND INTAKE

A. E. Allen, Vancouver; C. P. A. Antoine, Fort Simpson, N.W.T.; D. M. Armstrong, Deroche, B.C.; C. L. Arsenault, Whitehorse, Yukon; E. Barfoot, Vancouver; S. Barroby, Maple Creek, Sask.; E. Blackwell, Whitehorse; C. M. Blanchette, Britannia Beach, B.C.; S. T. Born, Calgary; C. Bradford, Chilliwack; B. V. Brooks, Calgary; S. Brown, Thunder Bay; D. Brynildsen, Bella Coola, B.C.; G. E. Burnett, Lethbridge.

H. S. Camerson, Delta, B.C.; B. R. Cayenne, Medicine Hat; M. D. Christianson Calgary; C. L. Conant, Whitehorse; C. A. Copeland, Delta; R. J. Derry, Calgary; S. M. Dietrich, Maple Creek; M. Dornian, Whitehorse; A. Duperon, Mission, B.C.; Y. B. Durie, Burnaby; B.C. Fuller, Calgary; M. D. Fuller, Calgary; A. S. Gastel, Calgary; M. Gebka, Saskatoon; J. Gentlemen, Whitehorse; K. H. Gibson,

Calgary; D. E. Graham, 100 Mile House, B.C.; T. Grassick, Coquitlam; J. Gyorgy, Calgary; M. G. Gyuricza, Lethbridge.

C. A. Hande, Wadena, Sask.; R. I. Hardisty, Fort Simpson, N.W.T.; G. W. Heywood, Calgary; S. M. Hill, Regina; K. A. Holden, Fort Churchill, Man.; L. J. Hoffer, Maple Creek; D. A. Houghton, Calgary; G. Hudson, Calgary; C. Huston, Merritt, B.C.; H. Huston, Merritt; S. Hutchinson, Coquitlam; C. Hynes, Calgary; G. S. Iskiw, Calgary; S. Jarvis, Burnaby; L. S. Jervis, Delta; K. D. Johnston, Fort Churchill; F. E. Johnson, Whitehorse; M. E. Jurovich, Whitehorse.

I. S. Kara, Calgary; L. Kampel, Calgary; C. Kristjanson, Wadena; • E. J. Latour, Calgary; B. Law, Black Diamond, Alta.; C. A. Leithwood, Revelstoke; D. M. Lekivetz, Regina; M. A. Lewis, Whitehorse; C. L. Lewis, Prince George; B. M. McDowell, Chilliwack; K. McFarlane, Sardis, B.C.; B. Marchesi,_ Calgary; G. Moeser, Thunder Bay; B. H. Morrisey, Calgary; L. L. Murray, Whitehorse.

M. M. Newell, Calgary; C. Nickel, Vancouver; D. M. Niessen, Delta; A. M. Norquay, Prince George; L. G. O'Neill, Fort Churchill; H. Osborne, Calgary; V. Pawlivsky, Lethbridge; D. M. Peterson, Maple Creek; B. W. Petkau, Calgary; R. A. Potvin, Lethbridge; K. S. Reid, Vancouver; C. A. Rode, Red Deer; A. Schabang, Saskatoon; B. R. Scramstad, Whitehorse; G. Seefried, Calgary; A. J. Squires, Wadena; S. R. Summers, Calgary.

T. Taylor, Vancouver; B. Tenta, Surrey; L. F. Tenta, Surrey; S. Thiedemann, Calgary; J. F. Toews, Calgary; G. T. Vance, Calgary; J. L. Vandrunen, Calgary; B. L. Walker, Merritt; B. Weich, Port Coquitlam; M. G. White, Sardis; S. Y. Wilcox, Vancouver; F. E. Williamson, Calgary; M. Williamson, Calgary; B. A. Wilson, Prince Albert; B. A. Wood, Delta; J. C. Zingeler, Calgary; D. J. Ife, Revelstoke.

B COY—THIRD INTAKE

L. M. Allen, Victoria; I. Andersen, Vernon; K. L. Appel, Barriere, B.C.; K . A. Armstrong, Williams Lake, B.C.; L. Armstrong, Virden, Man.; V. S. Baynes, Kenora, Ont.; C. Blair, Trail, B.C.; H. M. Boyce, Port Alberni, B.C.; P. Cadick, Calgary; A. B. Clark, Regina; C. Cook, Spalding, Sask.; L. G. Constantine, Winnipeg; M. D. Cowden, Sparwood, B.C.; C. A. Christiansen, Calgary; R. E. Cruzelle, Terrace, B.C.; L. P. Cunningham, Penticton, B.C.; M. L. Curtis, Barriere.

• R. E. Daniels, Kitimat, B.C.; S. Dejong, Fort MacMurray, Alta.; M. M. Derbyshire, Edmonton; M.

R. Dodge, Williams Lake; C. Dunnill, Calgary; B. L. Edwards, Fernie, B.C.; S. K. Evaskow, Brandon; B. Gaudet, Comox, B.C.; A. George, Fernie; B. Giese, Prince George; D. C. Glover, Campbell River, B.C.; D. Glover, Campbell River, W. Gorgerat, Brandon; D. Grudeski, Kelwood, Man.; S. A. Grudeski, Kelwood.

P. J. M. Harps, Edson, Alta.; C. C. Hauk, Prince George; A. Hennessey, Virden; D. M. Henton, Kalwood; R. L. Hill, Winnipeg; L. A. Holland, Fernie; C. M. Hoogenberg, Summerland, B.C.; T. H. Hopman, Sparwood; A. F. Horton, Vernon; D. House, Sparwood; L. Howarth, Princeton; L. M. Hutchinson, Regina; K. L. Johansen, Brandon; C. L. Kelly, Campbell River; L. A. Kelly, Salmo, B.C.

E. S. Lafferty, Uranium City, Sask.; M. A. Lafontaine, Victoria; D. J. Levesque, Prince George; L. A. Little, Penticton; V. A. Livingstone, Vancouver; E. McNaughton, Campbell River; H. D. MacTavish, Thompson, Man.; B. L. McLeod, Kenora, Ont.; F. Magee, Kenora; J. I. Major; Longbow Lake, Ont.; J. A. Major, Kendra; J. D. Major, Kenora; C. Meckelberg, Calgary; C. L. Mercer, Comox; B. L. Milne, Williams Lake; T. M. Morcombe, Penticton; S. M. Moss, Fernie; S. Murphy, Vancouver; C. A. Newham, Sparwood; J. Ormandy, Uranium, Sask.; C. A. Ouwehand, Kitimat.

S. J. Parker, Hazelton, B.C.; K. A. Petty, Calgary; W. D. Perpelitz, Sturgis, Sask.; C. Perras, Regina; H. Pierre, Smithers, B.C.; J. G. Pocock, Trail; B. L. Priaulx, Calgary; D. Rembowski, Edmonton; S. A. Reynolds, Vancouver; M. F. Richardson, Kelowna; D. B. M. Risk, Medicine Hat; C. H. Rose, North Kenora, Ont.; S. Roth, Medicine Hat; D. J. Roulette, Portage La Prairie, Man.; G. Sampson, Penticton; M. Sankey, Penticton; M. T. Seiferling, Regina; S. E. Shields, Vernon; N. M. Simison, Campbell River; M. A. Sommerville, Sturgis, Sask.

B. D. Tober, Uranium City; L. Tyler, Fernie; S. Valliere, Calgary; P. G. Verbruggen, Brandon; S. E. Veysey, Terrace; V. V. Vockeroth, Medicine Hat; C. J. Warden, Calgary; K. Wasyliw, Campbell River; M. D. Waterstreet, Salmo; L. A. Whitnack, Summerland; M. M. Williams, Smithers; L. D. Wilson, Sherwood Park; G. Wirth, Regina; C. H. Wright, Vernon; E. L. A. Wood, Calgary; L. I. Young, Penticton; S. H. Zorn, Winnipeg.

C COY

G. Alvey, Vancouver; B. Ashley, Port Moody, B.C.; A. J. Auchterlonie, Sydney, B.C.; T. E. W. Ayotte, Fort St. John, B.C.; A

S. Balsom, Lavington, B.C.; M. Barefoot, Vancouver; C. S. Bat taglia, Whitehorse, Yukon; P. Beardy, Victoria; P. J. Belado, Whitehorse; N. D. Bennett, Victoria; K. E. Benz, Victoria; N. J. Best, Burnaby; M. S. Bhamji, Vancouver; P. D. Bird, Vancouver; G. W. Bourget, Fort St. John; J. E. Boyles, Vancouver; B. A. Brekke, Hagensburg, B.C.; T. C. Broadfoot, Merritt, B.C.; C. R. Brown, Vancouver; G. G. Brynelson, Chilliwack; S. Burgis, Vancouver.

R. A. Caine, Sardis, B.C.; A. S. Chaplin, North Vancouver; S. J. Christian, Victoria; M. C. Colman, Port Moody, B.C.; B. D. Corey, Port Alberni, B.C.; J. D. Devuyst, Fort St. John; D. G. Dickie, Coquitlam; S. A. Douglas, Nanaimo; K. P. Drybrough, Nanaimo; G. D. Dubyna, Richmond; E. R. Dumane, Fort St. John; D. J. Dunlop, Vancouver; P. A. Edge, Richmond; D. Egan, Hagensborg; R. B. Estrada, Salmon Arm, B.C.; M. Feldstein, Vancouver; E. J. Fernandes, Vancouver; C. W. Forrest, Fort St. John; D. B. Frew, Haney.

G. D. Gargus, Fort St. John; I. R. Gordon, Coquitlam; C. E. Gosselin, Salmon Arm; D. Gosselin, Vedder Crossing, B.C.; G. M. Gregoire, Fort. St. John; F. Grimm, Salmon Arm; V. S. Hammer, Hagensborg; M. S. Hatton, Maple Ridge, B.C.; M. J. Heron, Victoria; B. P. Hiebert, Richmond; D. Hoffman, Vernon; A. E. H. Holgate, Whitehorse; C. Holloway, North Vancouver; P. M. Jean, Vedder Crossing; B. C. Jensen, Richmond; S. R. Jones; North Delta.

E. J. Karczewski, Salmon Arm; D. J. Kellett, Richmond; T. D. Komick, Vancouver; P. Kozalides, Courtenay; D. A. Krivak, Salmon Arm; J. A. Kusnir, North Vancouver; L. G. Laufer, Salmon Arm; R. S. Lee, Vancouver; T. D. Little; Vernon; B. D. Lloyd, Vancouver; A. S. Lochan, Vancouver; G. E. Loewen, Merritt; M. J. Logan, Delta; B. W, Lowe, Delta.

R. J. MacDonald, North Vancouver; C. S. MacLeod, North Vancouver; R. J. McLeod, Salmon Arm; R. Mainwaring, Victoria; E. W. Magnuson Whitehorse; A. A. Malczynski, Vancouver; D. J. Marks, Vedder Crossing; D. B. Marshall, Burnaby; B. Martin, Victoria; S. E. Mathiasen, Salmoon Arm; E. B. Mecham, Bella Coola; N. Midttun, Surrey; R. T. Milne, New Westminster; A. A. Montgomery, Courtenay; W. Morrison, Surrey; K. Munro, Chilliwack; M. A. Murphy, Burnaby.

R. R. Novak, Fort St. John; T. J. O'Brien, Revelstoke; R. Opp, Victoria; M. Orr, Richmond; R. J. Page, North Vancouver; R. J. Pasemko, Salmon Arm; B. D.

Pattie, Surrey; G. R. Pearson, North Vancouver; K. Piche, Surrey; D. Pigeault, Vancouver; B. Pilchak, Vancouver; D. S. Pirooz, Richmond; R. W. Poustie, North Vancouver; C. R. Priebe, Chilliwack; J. R. Pyke, Langley.

K. E. Reed, Delta; G. W. Richmond, Surrey; W. P. Rodger, Sardis; A. R. Roughley, Vancouver; G. Ruttan, Revelstoke; H. Schaper-Kotter, Richmond; W. A. Shaw, Surrey; G. E. Sherwood, Salmon Arm; N. A. Simpson, Richmond; D. Smith, Surrey; P. Smith, Victoria; J. K. Stiglic, Surrey; C. L. Strasdin, Victoria; W. R. Svisdahl, Fort St. John; S. E. Thorsteinson, Port Coquitlam; C. Trepanier, Bella Coola; P. Valentine, Maple Ridge; R. E. Vandale, Fort St. John; D. S. Virkutis, Vancouver.

G. H. Warriner, Salmon Arm; L. Waun, Coquitlam; M. Wawrychuk, Chilliwack; D. W. Weir, Vancouver; D. A. Whieldon, Vancouver; R. J. Whiting, North Vancouver; R. D. Wilkinson, Sardis; C. Willard, Chase; D. Williams, Delta; F. Wolski, Victoria; R. W. Woods, Chilliwack; A. Wray, Coquitlam; T. Yuen, Vancouver; R. Zapp, Courtenay.

BAND

D. C. Anderson, Winnipeg, Man.; C. M. Blanshard, Port Moody; B. B. (F) Breit, Regina, Sask.; M. P. Bos, Burnaby; P. C. Bos, Burnaby; K. A. Campbell, Winnipeg, Man.

D. J. Carew, North Delta; K. A. Caterer, Portage La Prairie, Man., B. B. Chobotar, Coquitlam; T. P. Clarke, Edmonton, Alta.; K. G. Dobbson, Edmonton, Alta.; J. W. Drinkall, Calgary, Alta.

B. C. Fraser, Winnipeg, Man.; L. D. (F) Galbraith, Regina, Sask.; P. A. (F) Gallant, Port Moody; A. C. Gardner, Victoria; D. J. Giovannangeli, North Vancouver; J. I. (F) Glendale, Victoria.

S. A. (F) Grubb, Regina, Sask.; S. (F) Haggart, Sidney; G. R. Hall, Victoria; E. H. Harding, Vancouver; M. B. Hawke, Prince George; S. R. Head, Victoria.

C. M. (F) Horner, Fort St. John; G. R. Hourie, Portage La Prairie, Man.; S. T. Howe, Bella Coola; J. G. Huffman, Coquitlam; P. M. (F) Joerissen, Camp Vernon; N. L. Joy, Edmonton, Alta.

W. A. Joy, Edmonton, Alta.; M. L. Kalmokoff, N. Vancouver; C. M. Kane, Victoria; G. C. Karoly, Calgary, Alta.; D. R. Lacasse, North Delta; K. L. Lovett, Calgary, Alta.; G. A. Maccallum, Victoria; D. J. MacDonell, Terrace; L. J. Mackie, Victoria; R. B. MacLennan, Vancouver; E. R. Magnusson, Regina, Sask.; J. Martins, Calgary, Alta.; S. W. Mathews, Calgary, Alta.; H. R. McFarland, Victoria; K. C. (F) McKenzie Calgary, Alta.; N. A. McKinnon, Pincher Creek, Alta.;

B. McMillan, Regina, Sask.; W. A. McQueen, Burnaby.

D. - L. G. McWilliams, Vancouver; A. D. Miller, Richmond; T. M. (F) Montague, Port Coquitlam; P. D. Morrow, Edmonton, Alta.; B. A. Muller, Burnaby; D. L. Myhru, Edmonton, Alta.

D (F) Nangle, North Vnancouver; J. P. Neault, Regina, Sask.; J. L. (F) Neave, Victoria; C. A. (F) Nichols, Surrey;- L. L. (F) O'Connor, Surrey; G. W. Olson, Coquitlam.

W. C. Pallot, Surrey; A. B. Pallot, Surrey; N. E. (F) Pearce, Delta; T. M. (F) Phillips, Calgary, Alta.; R. A. Pomoty, Regina, Sask.; G. D. Ratchford, Victoria.

I. R. Ratchford, Victoria; C. J. (F) Rayment, Surrey; B. R. Reid, Surrey; D. Z. Remenda, Norquay, Sask.; E. P. Remenda, Norquay,

G COY

W. P. Aird, Coquitlam; D. M. Alwood, Prince George; G. A. Assar, Richmond; A. M. Bangs, Mattawa, Ontario; D. L. Barkley, Edmonton, Alta.,; P. M. Barnes, Steveston.

T. L. Barron, Port Moody; V. L. Bellefeuille, Sue Saint Marie, Ont.; E. S. Berner, Richmond; C. L. Bjornsson, Chilliwack; S. L. Bowles, Ottawa, Ont.; E. J. Blyth, Powell River.

C. E. Braun, Kitchener, Ont.; S. A. Brekke, Hagensborg; T. S. Brewer, London, Ont.; B. B. Broad, Victoria; A. M. Brunelle, Mattice, Ont.

J. M. Burrell, New Hamburg; Ont.; B. J. Brynelson, Chilliwack; C. L. Chatham, Port Moody; M. E. Crawford, B.C.; P. S. Cronley, Nakusp; G. N. Cyr, Axilda, Ont.; M. A. Demerchant, Kitchener, Ont.

D. L. Dennery, Barriere; S. E. Devaney, Strathroy, Ont.; D. M. Duke, Kirkland, Ont.; S. E. Ennis, Port Coquitlam; S. L. Entwistle, Ottawa, Ont.; M. Fast, 100 Mile House.

C. L. Fitzpatrick, Kimberly; D. E. Fletcher, Trail; C. M. Gaudet, Powell River; D. E. Gauthier, Creston; S. D. Gordon, Ottawa, Ont.; D. Gravelle, Mattawa, Ont.

S. J. Gravelle, Mattawa, Ontario; S. S. Greyeyes, Regina, Sask.; R. Haenisch, Vancouver; P. M. Haley; Courtenay; B.L. Hall, Victoria; D. S. Haraldsen, Richmond.

G. M. Harvey, Vernon; S. J. Hazell, Ste. Marie, Ont.; C. L. High, London, Ont.; B. E. Johnson, Ottawa, Ont.; L. Jones, Richmond; E. Johnson, Powell River.

A. L. Kellestine, Parkhill, Ont.; J. Kennedy, Powell River; K. Koban, Trail; B. Kopas, Hagensborg; C. E. Landry, Vanier, Ont.; H. A. Layland, London, Ont.

K. A. Layland, London, Ont.; F. J. Legras, Strathroy, Ont.; P. Leithwood, Revelstoke; D. J. Lloy,

London Ont.; J. M. McBride, Surrey; T. McCarthy, Kamloops.

D. I. McDonald, Ottawa, Ont.; M. McDowell, Richmond; B. J. McNaughton, Strathroy, Ont.; M. Maley, Vancouver; T. H. Marshall, Delta; J. Merlin, London, Ont.

L. R. Michaud, Mattawa, Ont.; T. J. Millership, Delta; D. L. Morrison, Surrey; K. Moss, Fernie; D. Mousseau, Cranbrook; T. Mousseau, Cranbrook.

S. Mulholland, Comox; P. P. Nickel, Vancouver; W. L. Nickel, Vancouver; M. B. Norbury, Summerland;· M. C. Normand, Mattawa, Ont.; H. M. North, Ottawa, Ont.

G. J. O'Sullivan, Port Coquitlam; C. L. Parker, Ottawa, Ont.; H. S. Parker, Ottawa, Ont.; M. O. Pasanen, Port Coquitlam; M. E. Paynter, Ottawa, Ont; P. C. Peardon, Ladner.

H. R. Pellerin, Mattawa, Ont.; J. R. Poirier, Sue Ste. Marie, Ont.; L. M. Poulin, Azilda, Ont.; D. J. Ramsay, London, Ont.; D. J. Ramsay, London, Ont.; L. D. Ransom, Prince George.

J. Revell, Surrey; S. M. Rigg, Richmond; M. C. Rockburn, Mattawa, Ont.; C. P. Ross, Saulte St. Marie, Ont.; M. F. Ross, Revelstoke; P. A. Ruttan, Revelstoke.

A. J. Rylatt, Sue Saint Marie, Ont.; C. A. Rylatt, Sue Saint Marie, Ont.; L. P. Sanders, Port Moody; M. L. Sanders, North Burnaby; J. Schieffert, Prince George; C. E. Schroeder, Petawawa, Ont.

C. J. Sidle, Toronto, Ont.; L. C. Steadman, Kitchner, Ont.; A. Steeves, Trail; L. Steeves, Trail; T. L. Stride, Sault St. Marie, Ont.; D. Sutherland, Penticton.

T. Schultz, Surrey; C. P. Ross, Saulte St. Marie, Ont.; S. M. Thibert, Langley; S. Topley, Kamloops; M. B. Trithardt, Port Coquitlam; C. T. Tuomela, Saulte Saint Marie, Ont.

C. L. Wagner, Richmond; C. A. Walsh, Ottawa, Ont.; B. D. White, New Denver; H. G. Wilson, New Denver; K. G. Wilkinson, Ottawa, Ont.; D. A. Wolfe, North Delta; S. C. Zohar, Azilda, Ontario.

E BOY

B. P. Allaby, 100 Mile House; N. Anderson, Calgary, Alta.; P. J. Anderson, Edmonton, Alta.; R. L. Armstrong, Kelowna; K. R. Aulenback, Edmonton, Alta.; H. Bradbury, Calgary; Alta.

D. V. Black, Slave Lake, Alta.; D. P. Behm, Prince George; L. A. Beek, Prince George; B. W. Baraniuk, Calgary, Alta.; R. L. Bailey, Calgary, Alta.; G. A. Braid, Calgary, Alta.

D. P. Brezter, Edmonton, Alta.; R. Bruce, Calgary, Alta.; P. E. Brule, Victoria; A. P. Buchanon, Calgary, Alta.; P. J. Bury, Edmonton, Alta.; S. A. Cameron,

Edmonton, Alta.
J. P. Cerny, Edmonton, Altya.; D. D. Chalmers, Victoria, B.C.; A. Chan, Edmonton, Alta.; J. P. Chandra, Kamloops; R. M. Cinnamon, Slave Lake, Alta.; D. A. Clarke, Prince George.

G. F. Clyburn, Uranium City, Sask.; J. K. Cmolik, Kelowna; K. R. Cole, Calgary, Alta.; T. D. Connolly, Edmonton, Alta.; I. Cook, Victoria; D. E. Cyre, Edmonton, Alta.

R. B. D'Amour, Calgary, Alta.; G. M. Daniels, Calgary, Alta.; J. A. Daniels, Calgary, Alta.; P. J. Dudzinski, Calgary, Alta.; T. D. Eagle, Calgary, Alta.; R. A. Enders, Fort McMurray, Alta.

R. J. Eriksen, Midnapore, Alta.; R. L. Fedoruk, Uranium City, Sask.; A. P. Fern, Edmonton, Alta.; S. M. Fisher, Edmonton, Alta.; T. C. F. Fitzpatrick, Edmonton, Alta.; W. R. Fletcher, Calgary, Alta.

D. J. Flurer, Uranium City, Sask.; G. J. Fortier, Edmonton, Alta.; D. Fountain, Ft. McMurray, Alta.; D. R. Fowler, Calgary, Alta.; R. F. Fraser, Louis Creek, B.C.; K. J. Gallant, Edmonton, Alta.

R. S. Gingras, Fort McMurray, Alta.; D. L. Goss, Black Diamond, Alta.; K. F. Gourlay, Edmonton, Alta.; C. J. Gowen, Calgary, Alta.; R. M. Greenwood, Calgary, Alta.; G. W. Hambley, Fort McMurray, Alta.

E. B. Harris, Lac La Hache,; D. E. Hayduk, Sherwood Park, Alta.; D. E. Hendrickson, 100 Mile House; R. Hoagenberg, Salmon Arm; R. T. Hubert, Calgary, Alta.; D. M. Hutchison, Prince George.

N. G. Jopnston, Westlock, Alta.; I. Jones, Edmonton, Alta.; R. Joy, Edmonton, Alta.; C. W. Julillette, Kelowna; F. Kennedy, Sangudo, Alta.; S. R. Kiel, Uranium City, Sask.

R. Kohnert, Barriere; J. L. Kovacs, Fort McMurray, Alta.; T. Kozub, Kelowna; P. Kulchyski, Vananda; M. Lacey, Calgary, Alta.; D. Lachance, Edmonton, Alta.

A. L. Lapenbush, Maythrope, Alta.; W. Lastiwka, Edmonton, Alta.; D. Lavery, Penticton; J. Lawton, Edmonton, Alta.; F. Lekivetz, Victoria; T. Lewis, Prince George.

R. E. Liukaitis, Calgary, Alta.; B. Lowrie, Edmonton, Alta.; D. MacDonald, Prince George; F. Mackenzie, Kelowna; J. McNicol, Prince George; A. Madge, Edmonton, Alta.

P. Male, Edmonton, Alta.; A. Maller, Kelowna; G. Manley, Prince George; B. A. Narklund, Edmonton, Alta.; R. J. Matthews, Powell River; R. Missel, Calgary, Alta.

M. A. Morrissey, Victoria; T. Morrissey, Fort McMurray, Alta.;

R. Morrison, Sherwood Park, Alta.; M. E. Neff, Prince George; D. E. Nesbitt, Barrier; T. K. Noga, Kelowna.

C. D. Nielsen, Hinton, Alta.; R. M.. Padlesky, Edmonton, Alta.; R. H. Paterson, Victoria; L. E. Perry, McLure,; G. B. Peterson, Metchosin, Victoria; C. R. Phillips, Chilliwack.

B. Pierce, Calgary, Alta.; K. D. Poirier, Calgary, Alta.; K. D. Polack, Kelowna; R. E. Pottry, Victoria; J. J. Pumphrey, Edmonton, Alta.; J. D. Rathwell, Calgary, Alta.

K. L. Rathwell, Calgary, Alta.; K. G. Raven, Prince George; B. L. Reed, Prince George; M. J. Rembowski, Edmonton, Alta.; P. J. Rennich, Edmonton, Altya.; G. S. Rennie, Victoria.

A. N. Roemer, Calgary, Alta.; T. J. Rudolph, Edmonton, Alta.; A. Runnells, Edmonton, Alta.; B. Schill, Kelowna; J. A. Segriff, Calgary, Alta.; M. M. Shukster, Edmonton, Alta.

D. R. Simard, Sherwood Park, Alta.; V. Smith, Kelowna; C. Stevens, Penticton; V. Stockmann, Prince George; P. R. Thompson, Black Diamond, Alta.; P. W. Toupin, Edmonton, Alta.

C. C. Waldman, Calgary, Alta.; M. A. Wankiewicz, Edmonton, Alta.; T. S. Watson, Clinton; M. B. Wayne, Edmonton, Alta..

F COY

K. J. Abraham, Vernette, Man.; J. T. Ajtay, Creston; B. J. Andres, Port Coquitlam; R. D. Bodnaryk, Thompson, Man.; M. A. Borm, Westlock, Alta.; K. K. Boundy, Brandon, Man.

C. D. Brown, Thunderbay, Ont.; G. R. Brownell, Creston; L. B. Brulotte, Fernie; G. W. Campbell, Vermilion, Alta.; A. C. Colvin, Regina, Sask.; C. W. Cowden, Sparwood.

J. R. Crabb, Fernie; L. P. Davis, Edmonton, Alta.; J. L. Dick, Edson, Alta.; D. K. Dodgson, Cranbrook; S. L. Dozorec, Edson, Alta.; D. W. Driedger, Sparwood.

J. A. Dudley, Calgary, Alta.; K. P. Duncalfe, Abbotsford; W.P. Englesby, Cranbrook; K. G. Ethier, Prince Albert, Sask.; B. C. Evans, Calgary, Alta.; R. S. Evans, Mt. Lehman.

G. G. Ewart, Abbotsford; C. G. Flynn, New Denver; S. J. Fowler, Red Deer, Alta.; D. P. Franklin, Regina, Sask.; P. J. Frigon, Whitehorse, Yukon; D. L. Friesen, Whitehorse, Yukon.

D. A. Furlong, Saskatoon, Sask.; L. G. Gabriel, Regina, Sask.; M. Gallacher, Thompson, Man.; D. R. Galtress, Sparwood; M. D. Gardner, Hinton, Alta.; M. Gerritsen, Calgary, Alta.

J. D. Gibson, Thompson, Man.; G. Gorgerat, Brandon, Man.; K. L. Gosselin, Regina, Sask.; S. Gosselin, Regina, Sask.; D. J. Grant, Edson, Alta.; S. A. Gratton, Sturgis, Sask.

C. G. Grubb, Regina, Sask.; B. J. Guthrie, Saskatoon, Sask.; R. I. Haines, Mayerthorpe, Alta.; J. F. Hammett, Estevan, Sask.; S. L. Hart, Regina, Sask.; D. B. Hayes, Fort McMurray, Alta..

D. W. Heatherington, Sparwood; E. R. Hendriks, Regina, Sask.; P. W. Hicks, Vermilion, Alta.; D. L. Horeth, Medicine Hat, Alta.; B. J. House, Sparwood; R. G. Huseby, Black Falls, Alta.

T. D. R. Ife, Cranbrook; K. F. Isberg, Port Coquitlam; L. L. Jeffrey, Prince Albert, Sask.; S. B. Jones, Edson, Alta.; C. Kenny, Medicine Hat, Alta.; L. Kidd, Mayerthorpe, Alta.

R. Kiss, Lumby; P. Knudston, Spalding, Sask.; D. G. Kugyelka, Brenton, Alta.; A. R. Legge, Edson, Alta.; L. M. Lennie, Calgary, Alta.; B. L. Lewis, Uranium City, Sask.

S. Lorenz, Hinton, Alta.; M. McArthur, Vermette, Man.; M. M. McCoy, Calgary, Alta.; R. McDonald, Regina, Sask.; F. McKenna, Abbotsford; S. McKenna, Abbotsford.

L. McMillan, Thompson, Man.; M. McNab, Punnichy, Sask.; C. A. Malito, Westlock, Alta.; E. Marcy, Calgary, Alta.; C. Melton, Regina, Sask.; K. R. Molnar, Cranbrook.

F. Monks, Uranium City, Sask.; M. Morrisseau, Thompson, Man.; B. Morrison, Grande Prairie, Alta.; B. Murphy, Port Coquitlam; D. L. Nordick, Naicam, Sask.; W. G. Oliver, Sparwood.

D. L. Opfergelt, Naicam, Sask.; D. L. Parisian, Winnipeg, Man.; D. Parisian, Winnipeg, Man.; L. Parnham, Uranium City, Sask.;; C. M. Pelletier, Regina, Sask.; R. J. Peters, Lethbridge, Alta.

C. J. Petrie, Fort St. John; J. J. Plamondon, Whitehorse, Yukon; M. Pon, Calgary, Alta.; S. G. Potterton, Calgary, Alta.; S. G. Proctor, Westlock, Alta.; D. M. Reeve, Cranbrook.

M. L. Robotham, Port Coquitlam; B. Robinson, Brenton, Alta.; T. Rose, Winnipeg, Man.; J. J. Roulette, Portage La Prairie, Man.; R. E. Rouleau, Cranbrook; M. C. Rutschmann, Sparwood.

M. A. Sembalerus, Saskatoon, Sask.; B. R. Skeith, Lethbridge, Alta.; R. K. Smart, Battleford, Sask.; C. M. Sturko, Vimy, Alta.; F. R. Tambour, Regina, Sask.; V. M. Tambour, Regina, Sask.

J. L. Thompson, Whitehorse, Y.T.; S. Town, Vermette, Man.; M. Tuttosi, Punnichy, Sask.; N. Walji, Calgary, Alta.; T. Watson, Cranbrook; K. E. Wensley, Thompson, Man.

S. White, Red Deer, Alta.; M. D. Williams, Red Deer, Alta.; M. A. Wolbaum, Regina, Sask.; K. Wright, Clearbrook.

D COY

C. J. Andronick, Brandon, Man.; D. E. Arbuckle, Keewatin, Ont.; A. Asapace, Regina; R. L. Ashcroft,

Maplecreek, Sask.; S. L. Ashcroft, Maplecreek; W. T. Ball, Winnipeg; B. W. Barlow, Saskatoon; P. M. Bauer, Saskatoon; P. K. Beeds, Saskatoon; G. J. Belanger, Winnipeg; K.A. Boath, Transicona, Man.; t B. A. Boutin, Humboldt, Sask.; H. L. Brass, Davis, Sask.; J. L. Briggs, Maplecreek; W. S. Burk, Redcliff, Alta.; B. D. Busby, Winnipeg; C. J. Callaghan, Prince Albert, Sask.; D. L. Carlson, Sturgess, Sask.; J. H. Cathcart, Regina; D. C. Chambers, Turtleford, Sask.; R. E. Closson, Clair, Sask.; D. G. Collingridge, Winnipeg; R. D. Cotes, Morris, Man.

J. D. Davis, Winnipeg; T. Davis, Winnipeg; D. W. Demerais, Prince Albert; K. P. Derksen, Morris, Man.; R. E. Donaldson, Winnipeg; B. Dubbin, Saskatoon; A. A. Duhault, Winnipeg; B. Dutton, Estevan, Sask.; N. Ebert, Humboldt; K. Eliasson, Morris; W. Ettawacappo, Norway House, Man.; T. Federiuk, Sturgess, Sask.; T. Fraser, Kenora; D. Frehlick, Estevan; D. Gabriel, Regina; D. Gagnon, Kenora; M. Gaudry, Hudson Bay, Sask.; G. Goodpipe, Fort Queppelle, Sask.;. R. K. Groves, Dryden, Ont.; W. Gruhlke, Kindersley, Sask.; L. Guralvick, Regina; G. Gustafson, Saskatoon.

J. R. Halischuk, Saskatoon; D. D. Hamilton, Thunderbay; M. E. Heier, Estevan; S. F. Hennessey, Virden, Man.; C. M. Herbert, Melville, Sask.; M. Hilsendeger, Red Cliff; T. Hirt, Winnipeg; J. Hofstra, Saskatoon; S. Hrycyk, Lethbridge; C. D. Hurd, Regina; T. J. Irvine, Saskatoon; L. R. Jamieson, Winnipeg; R. B. Jamieson, Moose Jaw; T. Janik, Winnipeg; M. Jarvis, Thunder Bay; L. P. Jensen, Stonewall, Man.; R. K. Jestin, Moosejaw; E. W. Johnson, Winnipeg.

T. Kanigan, Wadena, Sask.; M. B. Kersten, Regina; S. H. Kilfoyle, Ste-Agathe, Man.; J. B. King, Winnipeg; R. M. Kischook, McCreary, Man.; A. D. Kitchemonia, Kamsack, Sask.; S. A. Klements, Regina; G. T. Kopchuk, Virden; D. M. Kubisewsky, Kenora; T. J. Kutai, Maple Creek; J. C. Lafontaine, Regina; D. J. Lahn, Winnipeg; F. D. Ledoux, Melville; R. A. Leverington, Stonewall; G. T. Lightfoot, Winnipeg; D. T. Lines, Ft. Smith, N.W.T.; R. S. Loesch, Winnipeg; P. S. Luciow, Fort St. John, B.C.

C. MacArthur, Maple Creek; D. H. MacArthur, Maple Creek; D. R. Macri, Ft. Churchill, Man.; K. J. Martinook, Melville; V. L. Meetoos, Turtleford, Sask.; L. Meredith, Prince Albert; H. Metail, Kenora; B. A. Meyers, Saskatoon; B. Millard, Saskatoon; R. S. Miller; Midale, Sask.; R. Minion, Saskatoon; R. Muskego, Norway House, Man.; T. H. Muswagon, Norway House; D. T.

Myran, Portage La Prairie; J. A. Novak, Regina.

D. P. Pilling, Turtleford; S. J. Pilling, Turtleford; K. A. Postnicks, Great Falls, Man.; F. A. Powder, Fort Smith; M. J. Radwinski, Battleford; M. G. Rayburn, Calgary; P. Revoy, Saskatoon; C. C. Richardson, Portage la Prairie; G. R. Richardson, Great Falls; R. Riffel, Winnipeg; B. D. Robertson, Winnipeg.

M. J. Scebenski, Preecville, Sask.; D. E. Schiffner, Moose Jaw; K. N. Shupe, Dryden, Ont.; S. R. Simpson, St. Boniface; K. R. Sinclair, Kenora; J. P. Sivertsen, Swift Current; B. D. Skilliter, Hudson Bay; B. M. Skulmoski, Winnipeg; W. N. Skwarchuk, Thompson; R. C. Small, Melville; D. M. Statz, St. James; H. G. Stein, Melville; D. C. Stevenson, Saskatoon; D. B. Stittle, Hudson Bay; D. L. Swanson, Brandon.

T. A. Tannahill, Battleford; D. S. Thomas, Winnipeg; H. W. Tilleman,'Redcliffe; A. R. Walls, Winnipeg; R. D. Williams, Regina; D. D. Wirll, Regina; J. E. Wood, Regina; D. J. Wright, Inuvik, N.W.T.; S. F. Zuck, Regina.

H COY

M. Barker, Burnaby; M. L. Bates, B.C.; W. L. Battaglia, Whitehorse, Yukon; D. A. Beauchesne, Calgary, Alta.; D. P. Beauchesne, Calgary, Alta.; D. B. Bellefleur, Whitehorse, Yukon.

M. J. Bender, Surrey; A. A. Bienvenu, Abbotsford; L. Bilanchuk, Ft. Macleod, Alta.; W. K. Bokovay, Edmonton, Alta.; L. K. Boon, Surrey; K. R. Bourassa, Powell River.

W. R. Broadfoot, Merritt; P. W. Bryan's, Wynnael; B. A. Bumphrey, Port Coquitlam; N. A. Campbell, Whitehorse, Yukon; W. A. Carper, Delta; W. H. Carr, Calgary, Alta.

R. S. Casagrande, Surrey; D. Castle, Courtenay; J. M. Charlebois, Chilliwack; J. Clegg, Vancouver; R. Cline, Terrace; K. D. Connolly, North Vancouver.

F. D. Cooper, Nakusp; R. D. Cooper, Fort St. John; L. Corvino, Vancouver; G. A. Cumming, Comox; M. Daehn, Salmon Arm; G. Davies, Port Coquitlam.

A. H. Daye, Edmonton, Alta.; A. C. Den Dulk, Chase; T. J. Dukes, Rose Town, Sask.; H. E. Dunn, Richmond; D. W. Elverum, Trail; R. E. Ennis, Coquitlam;.

L. Erickson, Red Deer, Alta.; R. H. Eriksen, Midnapore, Alta.; C. Gibson, Slave Lake, Alta.; M. W. Gair, Calgary, Alta.; A. C. Gilchrist, Richmond; K. E. Gordon, Red Deer, Alta.

N. L. Gordon, Richmond; W. N. Graham, 100 Mile House; D. Gow, Edmonton, Alta.; M. E. Grover, Lacombe, Alta.; W. L. Hajesz, Barrier; L. Hamilton, Nanaimo;

S. J. Hayduk, Sherwood Park, Alta.

A. Henton, Salmon Arm; D. W. Hlady, Thunderbay, Ont.; R. G. Hodgson, Forest Grove; B. G. Hole, Richmond; A. C. Hollstedt, Thunderbay, Ont.; D. H. Howie, Whitehorse Yukon.

R. A. Huseby, Blackfalls, Alta.; D. D. Hutchinson, Victoria; C. Illes, Calgary, Alta.; K. J. Jacobs, Northwest Territories; I. H. Jakeman, Regina, Sask.

K. R. Johansen, Revelstoke; M. J. Johnston, Fort Churchill, Man.; D. W. Johnson, Prince George; R. M. Kazakoff, Salmon Arm; T. A. Killam, New Westminster; D. B. Kilpatrick, West Battleford, Sask.

K. J. Langlotz, Winnipeg, Man.; R. J. Lindenberger, Fort Mc-Murray, Alta.; T. S. Livingstone, Regina, Sask.; M. A. Lopez, Richmond; R. L. Lund, Regina, Sask.; E. M. Macaulay, Delta.

G. M. Mallory, Cranbrook; J. D. Martens, Winnipeg, Man.; A. R. Martin, Victoria; F. W. McKenzie, Burnaby; R. T. McKinley, Delta; H. E. McLaren, Moose Jaw, Sask.;

N. A. McMurtrie, Victoria; L. M. Menduk, Fernie; R. M. Meredith, Abbotsford; D. C. Mcnab, Regina, Sask.; K. S. Morette, Victoria; L. D. Morris, Regina, Sask.; R. W. Munro, Edson, Alta.; W. R. Murphy, Surrey; P. A. Novak, Fort St. John; L. E. Parker, Melville, Sask.; R. S. Pattie, Surrey; T. J. Phelan, Sturgis, Sask.

G. D. Phoenix, Pritchard; G. W. Porisky, Edmonton, Alta.; W. V. Poustie, North Vancouver; M. C. Prieur, Tappan; G. B. Ramsey, Brandon, Man.; D. H. Ransom, Prince George; T. W. Radford, Louis Creek.

T. P. Roffel, Surrey; E. A. Roggeveen, Salmon Arm; A. M. Roxburgh, Calgary, Alta.; E. Sabo, Winnipeg, Man.; K. M. Sawatzky, Kindersley, Sask.

B. W. Scharf, Victoria; L. H. Scott, Merrit; R. P. Seales, Winnipeg, Man.; B. K. Senft, Medicine Hat, Alta.; P. Shaw, Inuvik, Northwest Terr.; G. Sideen, Port Alberni.

J. J. Simpson, Ft. McMurray, Alta.; E. W. Sinclair, Kenora, Ont.; S. Smith, Vancouver; A. F. Soreghy, Calgary, Alta.; B. W. Sorenson, Edmonton, Alta.; R. C. Steere, Surrey.

P. S. Strasdine, Richmond; J. P. Taylor, Winnipeg, Man.; T. J. Temple, Powell River; C. J. Thompson, Winnipeg, Man.; R. G. Thompson, Calgary, Alta.; W. J. Tremblay, Prince George.

J. P. Turchak, McCreary, Man.; D. Tuttosi, Punnichy, Sask.; J. Vanderwall, Victoria; R. Walker, Edmonton, Alta.; A. Walton, Rose Town, Sask.; S. Walton, Prince George.

A. Weiss, Breton, Alta.; D. White, Edmonton, Alta.; I. P. Whitehead, Victoria; D. R.

Wilkinson, Surrey; R. Willford, Revelstoke; K. B. Young, Richmond; R. I. Zakrzewski, Vancouver.

DRIVER COMMUNICATION
S. Barnes, Steveston; H. E. Bashaw, White Rock; J.B. Bell, Fort St. John; E. Bradburn, Norway House, Man.; E. M. Bragg, Victoria; C. L. Evans, Summerland; R. L. Fisher, Silton, Sask.; J. W. Gabriel, Regina; L. J. Goulet, Sparwood; G. B. Graf, Haney; R. LaFlamme, Sparwood; K. P. McCartney, Winnipeg; S. Mears, Richmond; J. Page, North Vancouver.

K. R. Paish, Grande Prairie; R. W. Parlby, Slave Lake, Alta.; I. Parmar, North Vancouver; R. L. Robinson, Redcliffe, Alta.; M. A. Ross, Calgary; S. B. S. Ryder, Calgary; T. Ryder, Calgary; R. O. L. Sedgwick, Lethbridge; R. Spuls, Pt. Coquitlam; A. R. Thibert, Langley; C. R. Warren, Richmond; C. R. Williams, Delta; G. K. Wilson, New Denver; R. H. Zorn, Winnipeg.

CADET INSTRUCTORS
Lt. D. I. Gillespie, Calgary, Alta.
Lt. R. W. Hall, Ft. Smith, N.W.T.
O-CDT (w) S. L. Hosking, Sask.
Capt. J. D. McDonald, Calgary, Alta.
O-CDT I. M. Munroe, Victoria, B.C.
Lt. M. J. Parry, Medicine Hat, Alta.
2-Lt. M. J. Smith, Yellowknife, N.W.T.
Lt. M. F. Thurgood, Vancouver, B.C.

VACC - 1976

A COMPANY
Michael E. Ans, Hay River, NWT.; Terry L. M. Balfour, Vernon; Mark S. Bate, Kamloops; Boris Benkovich, N. Vancouver; Kim A. B. Blake, Burnaby; Zdravko V. Blaskovic, Maple Ridge, B.C.; Bruce A. Boehler, Kelowna; Dale M. Bone, O.K. Falls, B.C.; Ron Browett, Port Coquitlam; Pat N. Bruce, Nelson.
David W. Burns, Trail; Brad B. D. Butler, Cranbrook; Dean L. Cairns, Millbay; Steven John Campbell, Surrey; Jeff B. Cathcart, Crofton; Brian B. W. Charlebois, Chilliwack; Bruce Chrysler, Hay River, NWT; Terry Richard Constantinescu, Penticton; Ted William Conway, Trail; Reid R. A. C. Cooke, Kamloops.
Allan Len Crawford, Surrey; Avin A. Datt, Kamloops; Jim R. Day, Delta; Lindsay J. Depatie, Sparwood, B.C.; Kelly W. Donison, Regina; Kelvin R. Downton, Mortloch, Sask.; Chesley Herold

Easton, Chilliwack; Robert Elliott, Coquitlam; Duane Kevin Elverum, Trail; Gregor Matthews Ensir, Trail.
Dale Joseph Foy, Winnipeg; Randy Gerald Gilkinson, Kelowna; Stuart Gordon, Tsawwassen, B.C.; Gilles Goulet, Sparwood; Jeff David Guenther, Cranbrook; Arthur Hamilton, Chilliwack; Thomas Lawrence Hamilton, Vedder Crossing, B.C.; James Walter Hartel, Thompson, Man.; William Gordon Hawkins, Lister, B.C.
Glen Robert Hayden, Regina; Leslie Joseph Heidt, Regina; Michael Todd Heidt, Regina; Tim Michael Herbert, Mortlock, Sask.; Michael Hibert, Coquitlam; Junior Hicks, Thompson; Chris Homuth, Veddar Crossing, B.C.; Richard Kenneth Honour, Kelwood, Man.; Ron Victor Huntingford, Coquitlam; Derek Charles Glen Hutchinson, Vancouver.
Dale Douglas Jardine, Regina; Bob Gerald, Jenkins, Kamloops; David Jensen, Portage LaPrairie, Man.; David Heath Jones, Kelowna; Greg Stuart Key, Chilliwack; Stanley C. Kruta, Surrey; Douglas D. L. Lamalice, Hay River, NWT; Cyril Gregory Lecuyer, Rossland, B.C.; David M. Llewellyn, S. Delta, B.C.; Tim Hazen MacCartney, Kamloops.
Scott Robert MacDonald, Winnipeg; William Francis MacDonald, Winnipeg; Ian Charles McIntosh, Winnipeg; David McKay, Oliver; Robbie Madden McKellar, Abbotsford; Martin Matthew Makulowich, Kamloops; Don McMillan, Kamloops; Michael Dennis Martel, Port Moody; Dale Mastel, Regina; Lloyd William Merriman, White Rock.
Brian James Morris, Regina; John Edward Mousseau, Cranbrook; Allan Onyschak, McCreary, Man.; Dennis Parisian, Winnipeg; Alan Pearce, Richmond; Vincent S. Penner, Surrey; Raymond Gilbert Perreault, White Rock; Kelly Gerald Poulin, Nelson; Rodney Edward Pratt, Chilliwack; Grant Prosko, Invermay, Sask.
Arthur Henry Rasmuson, Shilo, Man.; Kent Roy Reid, Chilliwack; Reginald Donald Reid, Salmo, B.C.; Gilbert Hendrick Rubens, Coquitlam; Sherwin Israel Rudelsheim, N. Vancouver; Ignacio Sandiego, Winnipeg; Mike James Savage, Delta; David Roopnarine Sawh, Winnipeg; Brad Bernard Schaeffer, Regina; Bruce Christopher Schaeffer, Regina.
James Karl Schiebler, Surrey; Tim Mark Schwab, Regina; Brian Selfridge, Coquitlam; Darryl Glen Sentes, Regina; Ricky Sentses, Regina; Robby Sidhu, Kamloops; Dave Edward Simpson, Langley; Ken Allan Smith, Regina; Kelly James Spearing, Portage LaPrairie, Man.; Peter Raymond St. Arnault, White Rock; .

Duan Robert Stevens, Burnaby.; Drew Stewart, Peachland; Randy Robert Stewart, Peachland; Daniel Stewart Stubbs, Kelowna; Cordell Stanley Thiessen, N. Delta; Gordon Wayne Thomson, Hay River, NWT; Blake Robby Toth, Maple Ridge; Keith Charles Trainor, Kamloops; Rob John Trueman, Surrey; Arnie Tuttosi, Regina; Daryl James Vegso, Kamloops; Andrew Mack Watson, Osoyoos; Wayne Irving Watson, Cranbrook; Robert Michael Welke, Kelowna; Elmer George Wiebe, Creston; William John Wiersma, Duncan; Franz Ludwig Wiesmann, Vernon; .

Harold Edward Wilde,· Surrey; Wilton, Boyd, Sparwood, B.C.; George Williwam Wray, Kamloops; Gerald Wray, Kamloops; Mario Michael Zuck, Regina.

A COMPANY

Micheal L. Armitage, Stewart, B.C.; Mark W. Asmunt, Thunder Bay, Ont.; Norman W. Barclay, Edmonton; Peter V. Bear, Creighton, Sask.; Mark A. Beek, Prince George; Stewart W. Bell, Richmond; James D. Biggs, Inuvik, N.W.T.; Mark R. Blanchard, Nanaimo; Robert R. Bonham, North Castlegar, B.C.; Raymond B. Bousfield, Dryden, Ont.

Kenneth G. Bradford, Chilliwack; Daniel R. Brown, Burnaby; Ly. K. Brownson, Fort McMurray, Alta.; Robert W. Burns, Vancouver; David L. Boisclair, Oliver; Terry D. Burns, Victoria; Dean Cameron, Victoria; Stuart L. Chadsy, Delta, B.C.; David Chapman, N. Vancouver; Grant J. Chapman, Port Moody.

Dennis R. Charest, Hinton, Alta.; Robert M. ·Christy, Winnipeg; Sheldon D. Clare, Prince George; Brian Clarke, Winnipeg; Doug Close, Port Coquitlam; James G. Collinson, Winnipeg; Danny S. Constable, Prince George; Dwayne Cromarty, Victoria; Brun Dahlquist, Port Alberni; Mark Dankwerih, Harrison Mills, B.C.

Timothy Dearborn, Dominion City, Man.; Joe Devison, Victoria; Gordon C. Diment, Brandon, Man.; Kenneth Dobbyn, Burnaby; James Dunphy, Winterburn, Alta.; Karl Duske, Castlegar; Clifford Ellis, Winnipeg; Dennis Evans, Victoria; Todd R. Fence, Burnaby; Charles E. Fletcher, Winnipeg.

Thomas B. Frank, Inuvik, N.W.T.; Kevin W. Gagel, Port Moody; ·Dwain W. Gaucher, Prince George; Omer B. Gaudet, Fort McMurray; Bernard C. Giesbrecht, Vancouver; Glen G.Goudie, Stewart, B.C.; John G. Goudreau, Prince George; Cameron W. Griffith, Coquitlam; Gordon W. Gunn, Greenridge, Man.; Dean Harper, Burnaby.

David A. Harvey, Sidney; Phillip J. Harvie, Fort McMurray; Russell C. E. Haug, Vancouver; Stephen P. Hedlik, Victoria; Robert A. Henderson, Coquitlam; Robert D. Henry, Dominion City, Man.; Daniel C. J. Heron, Victoria; Thomas J. Hill, Victoria; Jonathon B. Holgate, Prince George; Dennis R. Holmes, Letellier, Man.

James M. Hooper, Edmonton; Kevin J. Hooper,· Vancouver; Stewart W. James, Edson, Alta.; Charles A. Johnson, Lacombe; Jonas U. Jonsson, Vancouver; Derek W. Joyce, Edmonton; William J. Jupp, Burnaby; Andre K. Kiraly, Vancouver; James T. Kirkpatrick, Stewart, B.C.; Paul D. Knox, Victoria.

Sunil Krishnan, Coquitlam; Andy M. Laderoute, Brandon, Man.; Jesse B. LaLonoe, Edmonton; Carl Ledwon, Victoria; Scott A. Lewis, Vancouver; James D. Lochan, Vancouver; Athelstan L. Loosmore, Hagensbord, B.C.; Murray D. MacKay, Hagensbord; William McGinty, Vancouver; William J. McLean, Agassiz, B.C.;

Shawn D. McNicholl, Nanaimo; Ron M. Maisonneuve, Clinton; Mike R. Mansell, Winnipeg; Dean W. Marshall, Victoria; John D. Marshall, Port Moody; William S. Martin, Vancouver; Arnold J. Molag, Victoria; Bradley P. Mulcahy, Yellowknife, N.W.T.; Greg W. Mulcahy, Yellowknife, N.W.T.; David P. Murphy, Port Coquitlam.

Zoltan Nagy-Gyorgy, Vancouver; Garnet R. Naylor, Creighton, Sask.; Patrick J. Neal, Brandon; Robert R. Newton, Clinton, B.C.; Dale Norris, Inuvik, N.W.T.; Terry A. Overdiek, Port Moody; Henry P. Panek, Vancouver; Jay L. Petersen, Coquitlam; Ronald D. Pickrell, Edmonton; Don A. Pitcairn, Delta, B.C.

Timmy Placken, Thunder Bay; Robert K. Poirier, Port Alberni; Allen D. Powers, Burnaby; Jaye A. Powers, Thunder Bay; Jody L. Powers, Thunder Bay; Robert A. Richard, Burnaby; Lauren A. Rivey, Winnipeg; Gordon L. J. Rugg, Burnaby; Shawn N. Santone,. Vancouver; Robert David Sekula, Vancouver.

Daniel S. Shanoha, Winnipeg; Larry A. Smith, Vancouver; Stephen C. ′F. Smith, Port Coquitlam; Micheal S. Sommers, Nanaimo; Avelino S. Souto, Oliver; David A. Sweeney, Victoria; Chris A. Travis, Victoria; Jan K. Urbanik, Victoria; Neil D. Van-Der-Hoeven, Vancouver; Jim A. Vanderwal, Victoria.

Erling Walton, Oliver; Royden C. Ward, Nanaimo;. John G. Warrington, W. Vancouver; William Waterman, Prince George; Christopher Watson, Coquitlam; Richard - Weber, Victoria; Terrance A. White,

Thunder Bay; James E. Willians, Sherwood Park; Deryl Wood, Port Moody; John B. P. Zitnik, Vancouver.

A COMPANY

John Dale Aksidan, Prince George; Ron Richard Allen, Salmon Arm; Gary Wayne Anderson, Prince George; Richard Perry Arnaud, Winnipeg; Emil Kjeld Arndt, Naicam, Sask.; Brian Martin Bangay, Edmonton; Allan Wayne Bedford, Calgary; Joseph Edward Bikadi, Powell River; Shane Joseph Bouchard, Uranium City, Sask.

Shawn Joseph Bouchard, Uranium City; Brian Eric Bjorklund, Richmond; Marcello Garbognin, Calgary; Eric Carted, Winnipeg; Rene John Andrew Chenier, Calgary; Robert Cho, Edmonton; David Daniel Clark, Inuvik; Tim Gordon Claughton, Kelowna; Douglas Randy Coles, Richmond; Darryl Charles Ashley Cooke, Ft. McMurray.

Robert Alexander Copeland, Ocean Falls; Grant Alan Cotten, Courtenay; Lance Warren Davis, Prince George; Robert Henry Dechaine, Powell River; Fred Robert Derkach, Saskatoon; Scott James Derkach, Saskatoon; Andrew Dick, Edson; Gregory Dobranski, Golden Prairie, Sask.; Bradley Scott Duncan, Richmond; Kelly Stahl Edwards, Fernie.

Ronnie Glen Eldridge, Inuvik; Daniel Joseph Ethier, Edmonton; Tim Samuel Federiuk, Sturgis, Sask.; Kenneth John Fee, Richmond; Timothy Feher, Vancouver; David John Fink, Yellowknife; Robin Ernest Fisher, Edmonton; Robert Thomas Fleming, Edmonton; Bruce Patrick Francis, Fort McPherson, NWT.; John William Francis, Fort McPherson.

William Fraser, Estavan; Clifford Frencis, Fort McPherson; Robert Joseph Gach, Sidney; Darcy Gordon Goodall, Royston, B.C.; William Edward Guest, Edmonton; Darrell Fraizzer Haggard, Fort St. John; David Alexander Hamilton, Richmond; William Hamilton, Calgary; Steven Hansome, Ocean Falls; Gerald Fredrich Harnden, Courtenay.

Wayne Bernard Harrad, Fernie; Patrick Mcdonald Haynes, Powell River; Bob Hewitt, Edmonton; Micheal Hill, Sparwood; Howard Wayne Hodges, Richmond; Randal Wright Hovey, Winnipeg; Curtis Edward Jetty, Salmon Arm; John Richard Jones, Sidney Victoria, B.C.; Keith Leyburn Jones, Inuvik; Kim Cecil Jorgensen, Estavan.

Robert Paul Kaiser, Richmond; Glen Arron Knudtson, Spalding, Sask.; Robert Michael Klemp, Delta; Glen Stanley Kulchyski, Vanada, B.C.; Bruce Joseph Labelle, Nanaimo; Ricky John

Lester, Inuvik; John Douglas Little, Edmonton; Richard Harry Luck, Richmond; Bruce William Hugh McGown, Ocean Falls; Chris Terrance Matechuk, Maple Creek, Sask.

David Scott Matthews, Powell River; Frank Laverne Matwick, Ocean Falls; Bruce Anthony Milligan, Fernie; Ray Mike Montgomery, Courtenay; Miles Evans Nelson, Edmonton; Daniel Corry Newall, Nanoose Bay, B.C.; Paul James Newton, Richmond; Mervin Lee Oakes, Nakusp; Eldon Ross Okanee, Turtleford, Sask.; Joel Leslie Parker, Calgary.

Douglas John Pascal, Fort McPherson; Kevin Gary Peacock, Fernie; Derek William Petersen, Yorkton, Sask.; Ricky Wayne Picken, Grand Prairie; Kevin Douglas Pistak, Salmon Arm; John Neil Radesic, Thompson; Alain Rivard, Texada and B.C.; Micheal Gene Rivard, Texada Island, B.C.; Douglas James Rose, Richmond; Douglas Andrew Ruttan, Revelstoke.

David Lawrence Sargent, Winnipeg; Peter James Scales, Salmon Arm; Joseph Clifford Schmuland, Winnipeg; Robert Leon Earl Sherwood, Vernon; Chamkaur Sidhu, Sparwood; Ricky Andrew Singh, Ocean Falls; Lyle Henry Smith, Edson; Jeffery Anthony Spruyt, Cumberland; Richard Alan Stewart, Fort McPherson; Brian Alfred Storlie, Lampman, Sask.

Gerald Patrick Thompson, Sherwood Park; Richard Dale Thunderchild, Turtleford; Gerald Wilbert Tomchuk, Fort McMurray; Robert Dunlop Trusdale, Trail; Jim Andrew Turner, Winnipeg; Ralph Reginal Edward Turner, Inuvik; Vance Taylor Turner, Uranium City; Kenneth Martyn Tyler, Fernie; Gavin Alexander Van Kuppeveld, Sherwood Park; Hans Jacob Vester, Courtenay.

Paul Harrison Volk, Richmond; Charles Browne Von, Calgary; Michael Brian Walker, Sherwood Park; Chris Mark Warren, Ocean Falls; Vincent Leonard Wassing, Kelowna; Andre Conroy Weisheidt, Prince George; Steven Whiteley, Langley; Patrick Joseph Williamson, Fort McMurray.

B COMPANY

Roberta Margaret Acheson, Edmonton; Cecilia Sahara Ackroyd, Stewart, B.C.; Sharon Celestine Ackroyd, Stewart; Carolyn Marie Allen, Nanaimo; Kelly Dawn Ander, Surrey; Marie Debbie Babcock, Edmonton; Diane Marie France Beauchesne, Powell River; Louise Marie-Claude Beauchesne, Powell River; Lori Margaret Betteridge, Lazo, B.C.; Lydia Anne Blackman, Lantzville, B.C.

Elaine Janet Blyth, Powell River; Annette Bodell, Richmond; Elizabeth Bodell, Richmond; Joan

Marie Bowes, Medicine Hat; Rhonda May Brow, Texada Island, B.C.; Gwen Jean Bruder, Pincher Creek, Alta.; Laurie Irene Burkell, Campbell River; Melody Renee Cadieux, Yellowknife; Dorothy Sandra Carmichael, Yellowknife; Martha Shirley Charlie, Port McPherson, NWT.

Donna Carol Clark, Inuvik; Carolyn Patricia Collins, Tappen; Elizabeth Leon Cooper, Nakuksp; Corina Marie Crosby, Port Albernie; Alexandra Valerie De-Graaff, Edmonton; Dacy Rae Dostaler, St. Albert, Alta.; Lorna Ruth Drescher, N. Delta; Lisa Ann Duder, Comox; Debbie Denise Fosset, Courtenay; Margaret Teresa Gebka, Saskatoon.

Gina Gibson, Ocean Falls; Kristine Marie Graham, Campbell River; Donna Mary Herie, Powell River; Diana Lynn Hicks; Lazo; Patricia Helen Higgins, Richmond; Carol Ruth Hinse, Slave Lake, Alta.; Silvia Francis Jensen, Richmond; Patty Anne Kelly, Fernie; Leanne Bernadette Kohout, Nakusp; Angela Mary Kreuse, Chilliwack.

Janice Marie Krivsky, Nakkusp; Deidre Laurren Lacarte, Nanaimo; Hilda Charmaine Leader, McLure, B.C.; Shawna Lee Leblanc, Pincher Creek; Suzan Louise Lecompte, Sardis; Debbie Margaret Lewis, Fernie; Verna Elaine Lorenz, Ladner; Carolina Lizama, Richmond; Colette Marie Maclean, Edmonton; Judy Ann McCafferey, Inuvik.

Lori Charolette McNaughton, Richmond; Sherryl Ann Maglione, Slave Lake; Julie Patricia Matcalfe, Ocean Falls; Colleen Anne Matsen, Edmonton; Michele Marie Menard, Inuvik; Heather Maureen Meek, Edson; Carol Ann Miller, Sardis; Nola Lenore Nahirnick, Lake Cowichan, B.C.; Karen Patricia Neave, Port Alberni; Sharon Elizabeth Paulson, Stewart.

Margarida Isabel Pereira, Powell River; Beverly Ann Plantye, Edson; Kathy Ann Pluhowy, Chilliwack; Danielle Louise Primeau, Yellowknife; Sandra Margaret Pruden, Prince George; Kathy Dianne Ramsay, Prince George; Jackie Laurie Rothweiler, Chilliwack; Kerry Dawn Salmon, Lazo; Nesta Maria Semmler, Yellowknife; Cynthia Gayle Simpson, Richmond.

Jacqueline Kim Smith, Yellowknife; Anita Rose Taylor, Courtnay; Lillian Ruth Vaneltsi, Fort McPherson, NWT.; Lily Valerie Warriner, Edson; Karen Lenore White, Tuttleford, Sask.; Debbie Ann Williams, Delta; Joanne Margaret Williams, Whitehorse; Eileen Anne Wilson, New Denver, B.C.

B COMPANY

Roxanne (F) Acheson, Edmonton; Charlene M. (F) Andrew, Victoria; Rose M. (F) Armstrong, Virden, Man.; David M. Baratcher, Edmonton; Scott E. Barker, Rosetown, Sask.; Andrea M. (F) Bashaw, White Rock; Robert C. Bassie, Edmonton; Tommas R. Bezzeg, Calgary; Bradley D. Bluett, Kamloops; Audrey L. C. Bourque, Naicam, Sask.

Shawn C. Brady, Edmonton; Michele (F) Bragg, Victoria; Brian Brass, Prince Albert, Sask.; Sabine (F) Braune, Victoria; Kevin Brown, Kamloops; Edward R. Carlick, Whitehorse, Yukon; Stanley B. Cochrane, Yellowknife, N.W.T.; Brian T. Cook, Kindersley, Sask.; Debbie D. J. (F) Cousin, North Brandon, Man.; Greg P. Currie, Edmonton.

David P. Csizmazia, Whitehorse, Yukon; Geraldine L. (F) Dawson, Edmonton; Dale H. A. Demerais; Saskatoon; Ronald C. Devuyst, Ft. St. John, B.C.; Peter Doyle, Swift Current; Maryke E. Driesen, Lacombe, Alta.; Mark Elliott, Edmonton; J. David Fox, Ft. St. John; Beverly J. Frerichs, (F), Spalding, Sask.; Norman G. Friesen, Lacombe.

Mark C. Gassner, Kinderlsey, Sask.; Shannon M. (F) George, Edmonton; Joanne N. (F) Goulet, Dryden, Ont.; Andrea (F) Grieve, Prince George; Cheryl A. (F) Grover, Lacombe, Alta.; Ken R. Gruhlke, Kindersley; Suzanne L. (F) Guernier, Summerland; Allen P. Haines, Mayerthorpe, Alta.; Colin David Haines, Mayerthorpe; Starla J. (F) Hedin, Archerwill, Sask.

Peter Hensel, Cecil Lake, B.C.; Theresa C. (F) Hilchey, Regina; Douglas Horst, Vermilion, Alta.; Adrian Hunt, Grande Prairie, Alta.; Laura L. (F) Hyndman, Penticton; Joan (F) James, Calgary; Doug Jmaeff, Prince Albert; William Joerissen, Regina; Brian K. Kilby, Edmonton; Chris L. (F) Kindrat, Ft. St. John.

David E. King, Lancaster Park, Alta.; Kenneth Kokott, Swift Current; Anthony Kolody, Regina; Rebecca L. (F) Kuilboer, Edson, Alta.; Myles D. Lachane, Kraten, Sask.; Leeann C. (F) Lafreniere, Ft. St. John; Darcy Lambe, Edmonton; Ron Lang, Swift Current; Paul E. Lemay, Swift Current; Gloria A. (F) Lepine, Ft. St. John.

Wilfred J. Lepine, Ft. St. John; Darlene S. (F) Levesque, Prince George; Robert B. Leyk, Yellowknife, NWT.; Leslie N. Lundy, Prince Albert; Debbie C. (F) Lyson, Vancouver; Terry (F) Mackenzie, Thunder Bay, Ont.; Gail C. (F). MaCabe, Oliver; Colleen A. (F) McCallum, Mildstone, Sask.; Donna (F) McCallum, Mildstone, Sask.; Russell J. McNeil, Vermilion, Alta.

Scott G. Masterson, Mayerthorpe, Alta.; Lenore E. (F) Mitchell, Kamloops; Sammy Moghrabi, Edmonton; Joanne (F)

Moren, Ft. St. John, B.C.; Roberta M. (F) Morin, Dryden, Ont.; Vernon S. Nilsson, Grovedale, Alta.; Lucinda (F) Pelletier, Regina; Margaret E. (F) Pottinger, Victoria; Robert C. Read, Melville, Sask.; Marcel S. Reghelini, Vermilion, Alta.

Darrel E. Reilly, Regina; Richard J. Reilly, Regina; Peter M. Ries, Swift Current; Lynn D. (F) Rimmer, Port Coquitlam; Bruce G. Robinson, Westlock, Alta.; John D. Rocher, Yellowknife, NWT.; Larry P. Rocher, Yellowknife, NWT.; Kathy F. (F) Rogers, Surrey; Tricia J. (F) Saltel, Brandon, Man.; April D. (F) Sanders, Port Moody.

Carlin D. T. Schenk, Grande Prairie; Raymond D. Schlein, Kelowna; Lynne N. (F) Shaw, Surrey; Karen D. (F) Sherwood, Kamloops; Darrin S. Shewchuk, Ramask, Sask.; Curtis P. Shimko, Vermilion; Margarette K. (F) Simpson, Dominion City, Man.; Dolores V. (F) Sinclair, Richmond; Lee-Ann R. (F) Snydal, Lettellier, Man.; Terry L. Stashko, Grande Prairie.

Dannie E. Stilborn, Hudson Bay, Sask.; Donny J. Stilborn, Hudson Bay; Perry M. Styan, Yellowknife, NWT; Ron G. Swaren, Lacombe; David H. Taylor, Regina; Roxanne T. (F) Taylor, Victoria; Cathy (F) Thomas, Port Alberni; Ernie G. Tomashewsky, Edmonton; Murrell D. Trudzik, Mayerthorpe; Jackie (F) Unrau, Maple Ridge.

Rod J. Vandale, Ft. St. John; Patricia K. (F) Voiels, Richmond; Janice M. (F) Waldie, Mayerthorpe; Ken B. Warawa, Vermilion; Danny L. Watson, Lacombe; Paul W. Watt, Regina; John D. L. White, Calgary; Teddi (F) Wilcox, Maple Ridge; Diane R. (F) Worswick, Port Moody; Jacqueline (F) Wright, Brandon; Twyla-K. (F) Yasinchuk, Ft. St. John.

B COMPANY

Brian Robert Abraham, Vernon; Bernadine (F) Akachuk, Carlyle, Sask.; Glen Allen, Revelstoke; Jacqueline Ann (F) Anderson, Winnipeg; Wendy Lynn (F) Andrews, New Dayton, Alta.; Bonnie Lynn (F) Arkell, Powell River; Brenda (F) Beaulieu, Fort Smith, N.W.T.; Peter William Beggair, Fort Smith; Carol Anne (F) Bennett, Langley; Joanne-Sheila (F) Bennett, McCreary, Man.; Delphine (F) Bitternose, Punnachy, Sask.; Kristina Jean (F) Blair, Trail; Joanne Ruth (F) Blind, Punnichy, Sask.; Marguerite Louise Marie (F) Boiteau, McCreary; Lorne William Bonertz, Pincher Creek; Linda (F) Bowcott, Chilliwack; Mona Kathleen (F) Bryans, Wynndel, B.C.; Lucille (F) Carlson, Stewart, B.C.; Geraldine

Theresa (F) Coleman, Fort Smith, N.W.T.; Edward Reginald Connolly, Calgary.

Ken Blair Cowden, Sparwood, B.C.; Gordon Matthew Crawford, Lethbridge; Patricia Ann (F) Cyr, Punnichy; Cindy (F) Dacko, Vernon; David Eugene Davies, Turner Valley, Alta.; Marianne (F) Dickson, Weyburn,; Darcy Norman Drews, Revelstoke; Chantal Marie (F) Docoeurjoly, Vancouver; Cheryl Lynn (F) Durack, Wadena, Sask.; Christina Theresa H. (F) Ewart, Abbotsford.

Lori C. (F) Ferris, Norquay, Sask.; Janine A. (F) Forgie, South Kelowna; Karen Wynne (F) Franzman, Kelowna; Tim David Frizzell, Calgary; Scott Kennedy Gaw, Calgary; Mike Goepen, Calgary; Larry Allan Gorda, Lethbridge; Nina Gay (F) Griffith, Norquay, Sask.; Garth Allen Gustavson, Medicine Hat.; Tom Lyle Hamilton, Lethbridge.

Fred Michael Lanley, Calgary; Wendy Lou (F) Harrison, Stewart, B.C.; Robert William Hemingson, Fort Smith, N.W.T.; Susan (F) Hendrickson, Kelowna; Robert Clarence Herter, Medicine Hat; Richard Jensen, Calgary; Jim Karpuik, New Dayton; Mark Ryan Kaupp, New Dayton; Maurice LeBlanc, Pincher Creek; Terry Rae (F) Little, Weyburn, Sask.

Lee A. (F) MacDonell, Terrace; Gordon David MacIntyre, Redcliff, Alta.; Noel Anthony McConachie, Calgary; Kevin Anthony McLellan, Medicine Hat; Gail Cecilia Ann (F) McNabb, Punnichy; Theo Majnaric, Calgary; Liette Marie Nichole (F) Martel, Port Moody; Brigitte Yvonne (F) Martin, Calgary; Richard Warren May, Warner, Alta.; Dawn Marie (F) Messer, Weyburn.

Keith Wayne Morfitt, Fort Smith; Kevin Morfitt, Fort Smith; Jack Morin, Calgary; Jane Marie (F) Nickerson, Calgary; Debbie Ann (F) Padley, Calgary; Kathy Ann (F) Paulson, Wadena, Sask.; Geoffrey Allen Phillips, Calgary; Debbie (F) Pierce, Coquitlam; Roxanne R. (F) Pratt, Chilliwack; Adeline Vivian (F) Quewezance, Peirgord, Sask.

Linda (F) Quinton, Stewart; Gerri Edna (F) Richardson, Nelson; Gregory Scott Reid, Calgary; Cameron Riley, Calgary; Theresa, Doreen (F) Rose, Winnipeg; Debbie June (F) Roulette, Portage La Prairie, Man.; Dan Elvin Schmidt, Calgary; Ron Mathew Sherback, Calgary; Dean Wesley Sinclair, Lethbridge; Teena May (F) Skadsheim, Winnipeg.

Angel Rose (F) Synnuck, Nelson; Robert Edmond Taylor, Calgary; Denise Elizabeth (F) Thompson, Black Diamond, Alta.; Marie Linda (F) Tirs, Fort Smith, Xeoepo, N.W.T.; Jim Alan Tuttle, Calgary; Ron George, Visser,

Pincher Creek; Carla Rosemarie (F) Walton, Oliver; Garry Randall Ward, Lethbridge; Marena Gaye (F) White, Sardis, B.C.; Darrell Wayne Wilks, Calgary.

Nora Lynn (F) Wood, Norquay, Sask.; Betty Ann (F) Kew, Weyburn, Sask.;

C COMPANY

John G. Anderson, Merrit; Tony Barr, Nanaimo; Larry R. Bearman, Richmond; Brian Bennison, Revelstoke; Thor I. Boe, Vancouver; Don W. Broadfoot, Merritt; Andrew R. Brownlow, Croftan, B.C.; Joseph M. Brunelle, Prince George; Douglas J. Burgis, Vancouver; Jamie Cade, Coquitlam.

Kevin W. Cadmore, White Rock; David R. Canfield, Richmond; Jim R. Carson, Vananda, B.C.; Bernard J. Chiasson, Prince George; Gavin M. Christensen, Bella Coola, B.C.; Bob A. Chubey, Vancouver; Dale T. Corey, Port Alberni; Jim J. Cox, Salmon Arm; Steve R. Craig, Port Moody; Ralf Darbyshire, Salmon Arm.

John L. Davies, Enderby; Roger J. Demeda, Vancouver; Chris W. Drummid, Vancouver; Brian D. Edwards, Gabriel Isl., B.C.; Jim A. Elliott, Coquitlam; Tom A. Estradat, Salmon Arm; Don H. Fossett, Courtenay; Ernest W. Friesen, Westbank; Derril E. Green, Nanaimo; Doug R. Griffin, Courtenay.

Christopher Hagan, Vancouver; Bruce Hardardt, Penticton; Mike E. Hatch, Prince George; Gill Herie, Powell River; Paul J. Hibert, Coquitlam; David Higgins, Richmond; Rorie Holton, Vernon; Walter Horton, Vancouver; Doug Hunter, Richmond; Ken Huston, Merritt.

Pat R. Hyska, Surrey; Richard Ife, Revelstoke; Edward Ingleey Courteney; David Jackson, Williams Lake; Richard C. Jensen, Richmond; Andy Jorgensen, Salmon Arm; Brent A. Kenney, Prince George; Mitchell King, Bella Coola; Steve Krivak, Salmon Arm; David A. Laidlaw, Prince George.

Dale A. Lamont, Surrey; Mike S. Leopold, Nanaimo; Gordon I. Little, Penticton; Hecter M. Lizama, Richmond; Brian D. Lloyd, Vancouver; Simon T. Logan, Delta; Allen A. Luc, Vancouver; Keith A. MacDonald, Coquitlam; Craig W. MacKennon, Burnaby; Murray D. McDonald, Richmond; Keith R. McLean, Richmond; John S. McKenzie, Burnaby; Bruce G. Mander, S. Burnaby; Micheal A. Martell, Vernon; Gary R. Mayert, Penticton; Darrin E. Meroniuk, Prince George; James Meroniuk, Prince George; Donald A. Mikkelson, Bella Coola; Ron W. Mitchell, Surrey; Robert C. Montgomery, Courtenay.

Richard C. Mooiman, Van-

couver; Harold P. Mulholland, Lazo, B.C.; Keith Murphy, Vernon; Yogendra Nair, Vancouver; Scott A. Nymann, Nanaimo; Robert H. Nystrom, Burnaby; Andrew J. A. Oosterman, Ellie McLeod; Tim W. Palmer, Vancouver; Tom V. Palmer, Nanaimo; Jan D. Patterson, Prince George.

Rick D. Patterson, Prince George; Douglas C. Pearse, Richmond; Edward V. Pearse, Richmond; Peter J. Pessione, Vancouver; Brian E. Pilchak, Burnaby; Norman R. Powell, Richmond; Conrad J. Prudhomme, Vancouver; Mike A. Prytula, Kelowna; Ron W. Pudsey, Langley; Craig A. Rheaume, Vancouver.

Keith R. Rheaume, Vancouver; Edmond J. Rich, Richmond; Barry Robinson, Vancouver; Frankie W. Ross, Nanaimo; Garry V. Sakowski, Coquitlam; Kenneth W. Sato, Brookside Park, B.C.; Jeffrey D. Sawatzky, Serento, B.C.; Steven L. Sawatsky, Vancouver; Robert K. Selles, Richmond; Glen E. Sherwood, Salmon Arm.

Ron J. Sommerfold, Clinton; James A. Strangeway, Coquitlam; William I. Thompson, Chilliwack; Blair W. Thorburn, Nanaimo; Chris G. Tikaram, Richmond; Micheal T. Unrau, Vernon; Karim H. Virji, Vancouver; Ted E. G. Volk, Coquitlam; Ken S. Waddington, Port Alberni; Mike G. Warrington, W. Vancouver.

Melvin A. Wilkerson, Winfield; Allan D. Wilson, Bella Coola; Ralph E. Wittenberg, Delta; Cameron D. Wooden, Vernon; Randy S. Woods, Armstrong, Bruce Zelter, Vancouver; Gary B. Zinger, Kelowna.

D COMPANY

Wes Glen Ambeau, Powell River; Luigi Alfonso Ammaturo, Cranbrook; Herbert Carl Anderson, Port Coquitlam; James Brent Anderson, Cranbrook; George Edward Andrew, Victoria; Robert Keith Backman, Chilliwack; Ronald William Barclay, Victoria; James Scott Beaton, Portage LaPrairie, Man.; Clyde Kenneth Beaver, Thompson, Man.; Chester Gordon Bennett, McCreary, Man.

David Terrance Berg, Kamloops; Craig Gordon Bernhardt, Winnipeg; Leo Paul Bienvenv, Abbotsford; Lyall Clifford Bloor, Cranbrook; Timothy Norman Paul Bolan, Sardis; Dean Martin Bryans, Wynndel, B.C.; Greg Paul Burnett, N. Vancouver; Richard James Cann, Nakusp; Calvin Dale Cahoon, McLure, B.C.; Robert Charles Cahoon, Louis Creek, B.C.

Gary William Campbell, Nakusp; Derek Alan Cleem, Dominion City, Man.; Paul Trent Cline, Barriere, B.C.; Jeff Alan

586

Close, Port Coquitlam; Barry William Coles, Silverton, B.C.; Brett Donald Connolly, N. Vancouver; Paul Blake Conway, Montrose, B.C.; John Trever Coulter, Vancouver; William Arthur Craig, N. Vancouver.

Kevin Paul Derksen, Morris, Man.; Frank William Dixon, Coquitlam; Ronnie Edward Donaldson, Winnipeg; Kenneth Pitch Duncalfe, Abbotsford; David James Baird Dunlop, Vancouver; William Joseph Dwyer, Victoria; Keith Dyer, N. Vancouver; John Evers, Victoria; Sheldon George Exner, Pitt Meadows, B.C.; Steven Darrel Fanshaw, Sparwood, B.C.

Robert Allan Faulds, Nelson; Brian Edward Fawcett, Winnipeg; James Rodeny Fehr, Abbotsford; Leland Collin Ferguson, Port Washington, B.C.; Barry Arthur French, Grand Rapids, Man.; Alcide Roger Joseph Gauthier, Powerview, Man.; Robert Geub, North Delta, B.C.; Kevin David Gosselin, Maple Ridge; Yvon Goulet, Sparwood; Ward Trent Haacke, Kamloops.

Andrew Julian Hawkins, Winnipeg; Phillip George Hayes, Winnipeg; Raymond Horansky, Victoria; Gerald Raymond Hourie, Portage La Prairie, Man.; Brian Darrel Hrabarchuk, Winnipeg; Thomas Raymond Hudson, Kamloops; Robert Jack, Vancouver; Kenny Lee Jacobson, Creighton, Sask.; Ilka Tafio Kivi, Coquitlam; Steven Alan Knight, Port Coquitlam.

Alan Bert Kubisewsky, Kenora, Ont.; Darren Cecil Lacroix, Portage La Prairie; Mike John Lamont, Port Coquitlam; Shawn Orvalle Langton, Vancouver; William Alexander Ledger, Thunder Bay; Chester Thomas Roy Ledoux, McCreary, Man.; Derren Russel Lench, Sidney, B.C.; Andrew Sylvester Lewis, Winnipeg; Michael Anthony Lewis, Winnipeg; Art Lawrence Lilley, Haney.

Glenn Kirwood MacLeod, N. Vancouver; Michael John McDonald, N. Vancouver; Robert Daniel McQuigge, Fernie; Paul Joseph Malo, Pine Falls, Man.; Anthony Edward Malyk, Winnipeg; Danny Emile Menard, Sparwood; Greg Alan Meredith, Abbotsford; David William Leonard Mitchell, Thunder Bay; Donivan Michael Morris, New Denver, B.C.; Lawrence Eric Murphy, Winnipeg.

John Harry Owsianyk, Winnipeg; Paul Joseph Pelissier, Winnipeg; Todd Edward Penner, Winnipeg; Rainer Herb Philipps, Delta, B.C.; Allen Graham Philvrook, N. Vancouver; Raymond Peter Preyma, Winnipeg; Kenneth John Pull, Stonewall, Man.; Darrell Glen

Racine, Brandon; Douglas Allan Racine, Brandon; James Edward Rathbone, Barriere.

William Richard Rees, Vancouver; Philip Melvin Regnier, Fernie; Calvin Stanley Richmond, Port Coquitlam; Donald Scott Rodger, Sardis; Peter David Saltel, Brandon; Kenneth Brian Sanders, Burnaby; William Arthur Saylor, Winnipeg; Kenneth Brian Scheer, Trail; Danniel Trent Shanoha, Winnipeg; Vincent Hughes Sharpe, Brandon.

Larry Slot, Richmond; Jack Anthony Stefanato, Kapuskasing, Ont.; Russell Calvin Steinback, Port Coquitlam; William Lloyd Stewart, Louis Creek, B.C.; Gerard William Stolk, Fernie; Kelly Roy Summer, Thompson, Man.; Peter Alan Sutherland, Winnipeg; Martin Alan Trimble, Cranbrook; Mark Darick Urbaniak, Victoria; Alvin Collin Vandal, Winnipeg.

Dennis Luke William Vandal, Winnipeg; Stephen Dale Walton, Winnipeg; Leonard John Wiebe, Creston; Richard Edward Williams, Powell River; Stuart Gordon Williams, Burton, B.C.; William John Wiseman, Barriere; Mario Zorn, Winnipeg.

E COMPANY

Clifford R. Allen, Turner Valley, Alta.; Steven J. Bacha, Edmonton; William R. J. Banks, Calgary; Allan E. Benson, Sherwood Park, Alta.; Jody J. Blize, Fort St. John, B.C.; Gene L. Bowdish, Fort McMurry, Alta.; Brett R. Brown, Calgary; Brian G. Brown, Calgary; Mark Browne, Victoria; Brad R. Bruce, Calgary.

Gary E. Burnett, Lethbridge; Lloyd D. Butler, Grande Prairie; Dennis J. Cena, Edmonton; Kevin L. Chenard, Ocean Falls; Michel R. Charest, Edmonton; Brad Christensen, Yellowknife, NWT.; Gerald A. Clarke, Hinton, Alta.; James A. Clarke, Hinton; Allan R. Colton, Ocean Falls; Wayne Connolly, Edmonton.

Robert T. Coombs, Edmonton; Gary A. Couch, Calgary; Frank Daley, Edmonton; Darren P. Darbyson, Edmonton; Ron J. Diamond, Calgary; Gary Dick, Edson, Alta.; Dudley M. Driscoll, Medicine Hat; Eugene A. Duggan, Edmonton; W. Murray Ediger, Saskatoon; Dave R. Elder, Edmonton.

Terry J. Elkow, Black Diamond, Alta.; John J. Ethier, Edmonton; Lucien J. Ethier, Edmonton; Terry Fiorin, Victoria; Robert J. Fraser, Calgary; Scott L. Fraser, Edmonton; Daniel J. Frioult, Edmonton; Kevin S. Furman, Edmonton; Allan S. Gastel, Calgary; Larry B. Gervais, Calgary.

Mike E. Gribble, Victoria; Kevin Grimes, Calgary; Randy Grimes,

Calgary; Errol Gunst, Calgary; Julius J. Hajdu, Calgary; Stephen D. Hall, Victoria; James W. Hammond, Victoria; Terry Heinz, Redcliff, Alta.; Mark Hewitt, Edmonton; Dave Hirter, Edmonton.

Brian Horn, Calgary; Alan Huggett, Victoria; John A. Huhn, Humbolt, Sask.; Michael Jennings, Yellowknife, NWT.; Derrick D. Johnson, Victoria; Dana Jordan, Calgary; Tom Keeley, Calgary; Edward King, Fort MacLeod, Alta.; Timmy Krawchuk, Edmonton; Nolan W. Lamb, Calgary.

Alan D. Lang, Medicine Hat; Mark K. Layden, Edmonton; David W. Lee, Warner, Alta.; Patrick M. Little, Edmonton; Keith C. Lukan, Humboldt, Sask.; William H. McClelland, Hinton; Jim P. McGrath, Saskatoon; Donald W. McInnes, Edmonton; Richard K. McManus, Yellowknife, NWT.; William G. Madge, Edmonton.

James G. Madore, Lacombe; Barry M. Maizga, Saskatoon; Douglas J. Marquardt, Edmonton; Charles A. Martin, Edmonton; John Mazzei, Victoria; Daryl G. Middleton, Fort St. John; Ken J. Mulloy, Ocean Falls; Thomas D. Nash, Fort McMurray; Blair J. Neeve, Calgary; Martin J. Nickerson, Calgary.

Darcy C. Nilsson, Grovedale, Alta.; George A. Nixey, Saskatoon; James R. Northwood, Calgary; Bill W. Orr, Lethbridge; Wesly A. Ostashek, Fort St. John; John A. Page, Hay River, NWT.; Edward T. Paul, Turner Valley; Tony A. Pergar, Calgary; Shawn D. Peterson, Edmonton; Blaine W. Petkau, Calgary.

Brent P. Pettigrew, Calgary; Michael R. Pettigrew, Calgary; Ronald G. Randall, Victoria; Jan Repa, Calgary; Colin Rootes, Fort McMurray; Douglas N.A. Scott, Victoria; John M. Scott, Calgary; Randy C. Seefried, Calgary; Clayton S. Sepke, Redcliff; Myles E. Sinclair, Robb, Alta.

Ted J. Slawinski, Saskatoon; Barry K. Smith, Victoria; Dwayne A. Smith, Victoria; Dwayne A. Smith, Edmonton; James A. Smyth, Edson, Alta.; Greg R. Spalding, Saskatoon; David J. Stevenson, Edmonton; Steven R. Theidemann, Calgary; Roger A. Tremblay, Calgary; Nick J. Tymchyskyn, Ocean Falls; Gordon T. Vance, Calgary.

Lawrence M. Wauthier, Victoria; Harry H. W. Werner, Medicine Hat,; Scott C. Weston, Robb, Alta.; Julian P. Williams Calgary; Kevin Al Williams, Regina; Martin, Douglas F. Wykeham, Edmonton; Clifford J. Zubot, Humboldt, Sask.

F COMPANY

Ralph D. Allan, Crelman, Sask.; Garry E. Bate, Whitehorse, Yukon; Silvia R. (F) Beaulieu, Grand Prairie, Alta.; Robyn L. Birdsell, Estavan; Delbert M. Blackburn, 'Creelman, Sask.; Coleen C. (F) Bolan, Slave Lake, Alta.; Vivian I. (F) Bourgeault, Saskatoon; Jan. C. (F) Brown, Moose Jaw; Melvin Cale, Danholm; Robert Campbell, Whitehorse.

Bruce Cassels, Estevan; Leigh-Ann (F) Cassels, Estevan; Calvin C. Church, Red Deer; Bruce Clarke, Uranium City, Sask.; Dwain G. Colby, Edmonton; Cheryl (F) Conant, Whitehorse; Sharon (F) Cook, Spalding, Sask.; Gloria (F) Cowles, Fort St. John, B.C.; Richard M. Cross, Hudson Bay, Sask.; Daryl W. Demerais, Prince Albert, Sask.

Malcolm N. Despins, Vimy, Alta.; Micheal D. Dornian, Whitehorse; Ian K. Douglas, Maple Creek; Devis D. (F) Durack, Waenade, Sask.; Mark D. Ernewein, Edmonton; Don J. Fichtner, Regina; Wade H. Fitzgerald, Battleford; Larry H. Flamand, Hudson Bay; Cody J. Friesen, Slave Lake; David B. Gabriel, Regina.

Paul Ganter, Lacombe; Richard L. Gebhardt, Melville; Sylvie F. (F) Gelinas, Saskatoon; Brenda M. (F) Gubrud, Estevan; Sharon P. (F) Guy, Mile-Stone, Sask.; Bill J. Hayes, Cresent, Sask.; Susan M. (F) Hill, Regina; Allan R. Holland, Creighton, Sask.; Loni M. (F) Hutchinson, Regina; Kenneth R. Jamieson, Bushel Park, Sask.

Julie A. (F) Jensen, Salmon Arm; Wivi L. (F) Jensen, Salmon Arm; Edgar K. Jimmy, Saskatoon; Brad C. Jmaeff, Prince Albert; Valerie D. (F) Johanson, Salmon Arm; Jamie C. Jorgensen, Estevan; Milo E. Jurovich, Whitehorse; Parnell D. Knudtson, Spalding, Sask.; Diane C. (F) LaFontaine, Regina; Lynn M. (F) LaFontaine, Regina; Lynn E. (F) LaFreniere, Fort St. John; Lois L. (F) Lee, Warner, Alta.; Linda M. (F) Lepine, Fort St. John; Mark A. Lewis, Whitehorse; Cam E. Lyle, Whitehorse; David G. MacDonald, North Battleford, Sask.; James S. McDonald, Rosetown, Sask.; Dewayne C. McIntyre, Moose Jaw; Dianne B. (F) McLelland, Fort St. John; Norma L. (F) McLeod, Salmon Arm.

Stanely G. Macala, Invermay, Sask.; Hal P. Marcellin, Westlock, Alta.; Lester G. Meetoos, Turtleford, Sask.; Tony T. Meier, Regina; Darlene M. (F) Michalko, Saskatoon; Randy M. Miller, Midale, Sask.; Dennis J. Mitchell, Estevan; Marilyn M. (F) Mitchell, Westlock; Sandra B. (F) Morris, Regina; James J. Mourits, Lacombe.

Laura L. (F) Murray, Whitehorse; Peter J. E. Neve, Regina; Mark J. Nieckar, Rama, Sask.; Jim A. Novak, Regina; Michael S. O'Neill, Moose Jaw; Clement D. Oscienny, Goodeve, Sask.; Mary G. (F) Pasemko, Salmon Arm; Laura A. (F) Paslowski, Rama, Sask.; Orville D. Pede, Yorkton, Sask.; John W. Pelletier, Regina.

Cathy D. (F) Perry, Grand Prairie; Cheryl L. (F) Picken, Grand Prairie; Judy A. (F) Picken, Grande Prairie; Martin R. Polson, Lacombe; Randy A. Pomoty, Regina; Keray J. Rainer, Slave Lake; Barbara A. (F) Rainer, Slave Lake; Richard R. Ray, Regina; Heather B. (F) Redman, Salmon Arm; Wayne W. Renwfck, Whitehorse.

Joey C. Robinson, Slave Lake; Barbara A. (F) Romanycia, Moose Jaw; Marlene A. (F) Romanycia, Moose Jaw; Darrell S. Rousay, Saskatoon; Riley J. Rusch, Wadena, Sask.; Clarence A. Saunders, Lacombe; Marie E. (F) Sandeski, Wayburn; Wayne W. Schmidt, West Lock, Alta.; Grace M. (F) Shewchuk, Ramma, Sask.; Martin A. Skadsheim, Winnipeg.

Ostap Skrypnyk, Edmonton; Grant A. Sorochan, Moose Jaw; David A. Stachowich, Melville; Donald J. T. Storlie, Lampman, Sask.; William R. Svisdahl, Fort St. John; Dean S. Swanberg, Fort St. John; Wayne P. Toker, Regina; Gary E. Turner, N. Battleford; Ronald F. Tuttosi, Punnich, Sask.; Christopher Way-Nee, Edmonton.

Valerie L. (F) White, Charlie Lake, B.C.; Geraldine M. (F) Wirth, Regina; Jane L. (F) Williams, Edmonton; Rhys D. Williams, Regina; Barry E. Worm, Regina; Jay M. Yakabowich, Yorkton; O'Niel A. Zuck, Regina.

G COMPANY

Wendy (F) Aird, Coquitlam; Inga (F) Andersen, Vernon; Sandra (F) Anderson, Cranbrook; Sherri (F) Anderson, Kelowna; Rhonda (F) Andrew, Victoria; Kathy A. (F) Armstrong, Vernon; Lucia F. (F) Bakker, Sherwood Park, Alta.; Pam M. (F) Barnes, Richmond; Carla S. (F) Blair, Trail; Chris M. (F) Block, Edmonton.

Gabriele R. (F) Boehnke, Kelowna; Coreen M. (F) Bohn, Calgary; Debra L. (F) Bowler, Portage La Prairie, Man.; Lynne M. (F) Brown, Sidney; Susan L. (F) Brown, Thunderbay, Ont.; Vicki D. (F) Brown, Moncton, New Brunswick; Angela L. (F) Burke, Edmonton; Bridgette A. (F) Chalmers, Maple Ridge, B.C.; Debrah A. (F) Charlebois, Chilliwack; Crystal A. (F) Chenard, Ocean Falls.

Brenda L. C. (F) Chenier, Calgary; Cheryl A. (F) Christianson, Calgary; Sherry L.

(F) Clark, Victoria; Linda G. (F) Constantine, Winnipeg; Mireille G. (F) Couture, Williams Lake; Mary D. (F) Cowden, Sparwood, B.C.; Michelle L. (F) Curtis, Barriere; Michelle L. (F) Curtis, Barriere; Jennifer P. (F) Daly, Winnipeg; Brenda L. (F) Davies, Turner Valley; Donna M. (F) Davies, Strathmore.

Caroline E. (F) Dawson, Edmonton; Janet S. (F) Dennahardt, Brandon; Michele M. (F) Derbyshire, Edmonton; Theresa M. (F) Desjarlais, Winnipeg; Susan M. (F) Dorman, Victoria; Cheryl K. (F) Doyle, Calgary; Patricia D. (F) Dunsmore, Winnipeg; Yvonne B. (F) Durie, Burnaby; Alma L. (F) Easton, Chilliwack.

Julie E. (F) Empey, Edmonton; Marg M. (F) Empey, Edmonton; Susan K. (F) Evaskow, Brandon; Wendy Y. (F) Evaskow, Edmonton; Angie (F) Fast, 100 Mile House; Patricia A. (F) Gallant, Port Moody; Anita M. (F) George, Fernie; Yolanda A. (F) Gibson, Ocean Falls; Brenda T. (F) Giese, Prince George; Cheryl L. (F) Goodman, Redcliff.

Carol L. (F) Grabowiecki, Carlowrie, Man.; Vera L. (F) Harper, Letellier, Man.; Patricia J. M. (F) Harps, Edson, Alta.; Marrion El (F) Harron, Winnipeg; Joanne W. G. (F) Heesakkers, Richmond; Airdre J. (F) Hennessey, Virden, Man.; Elaine (F) Hill, Sparwood; Maria (F) Ho, Richmond; June M. (F) Holgate, Prince George; Lynn A. (F) Holland, West Fernie.

Patricia A. (F) Holmberg, Sardis; Philippa M. (F) Houlgate, Calgary; Heather J. (F) Huston, Merritt; Kathy K. (F) Huston, Merritt; Susan M. (F) Jeler, Richmond; Debbie L. (F) Jensen, Calgary; Karen L. (F) Johansen, Brandon; Karen D. (F) Johnston, Kelowna; Vicki (F) Keery, Richmond; Joanne J. (F) Kenyon, Abbotsford.

Kathleen E. (F) Kephart, Sherwood Park, Alta.; Corveen D. (F) Layton, Prince George; Claudette L. (F) Lewis, Prince George; Diane J. (F) Levesque, Prince George; Florence M. (F) Lorenz, Ladner; Rose M. (F) Lumbis, Haney; Renee G. (F) MacLean, Edmonton; Linda L. (F) Matwick, Ocean Falls; Janet F. (F) McGregor, Edmonton; Janet F. (F) McInnes, Edmonton.

Peni-Lee K. (F) McNaughton, Richmond; Ann M. (F) McPhee, Edmonton; Karen M. (F) Mitchell, Winnipeg; Geraldine B. (F) Moeser, Thunder Bay.; Shirly M. (F) Moss, Fernie; Alexandria L. (F) Mulholland, Lazo, B.C.; Tam y E. (F) Myttenar, Surrey; Anna M. (F) Noruay, Prince George; Jennifer O. J. (F) Oakes, Courtenay; Judy (F) Ormandy, Uranium City, Sask.

Christine C. (F) Orr, Richmond; Kanta D. (F) Pillai, Vancouver;

Marlene J. (F) Pottinger, Brandon; Pamela L. (F) Pottinger, Brandon; Joann L. (F) Powers, Thunder Bay; Elizabeth A. (F) Reid, Vancouver; Kathryn S. (F) Reid, Surrey; Denise M. (F) Risk; Medicine Hat; Sharon A. (F) Roth, Medicine Hat; Leslie N. (F) Sankey, Quesnel.'

Lanis L. (F) Shannon, Erickson; Nancy L. (F) Shaw, Chilliwack; Theresa E. (F) Shaw, Nanaimo; Pamela L. (F) Skelton, Nanaimo; Judee L. (F) Spruce, Edmonton; Lynn-Marie (F) Taylor, Vancouver; Sherry M. (F) Thibert, Langley; Patricia A. (F) Tikaram, Richmond; Cindy A. (F) Wagner, Richmond; Elizabeth A. (F) Wagstaff, Cranbrook.

Sandra L. (F) Webb, New Westminister; Carol A. (F) Weibe, Burnaby; Janice E. (F) Weisbrod, Delta; Debbie A. (F) Wolfe, Delta; Elizabeth L. (F) Wood, Calgary; Jennifer C. (F) Zingeler, Calgary.

H COMPANY

Greg C. Alvey, Vancouver; Paul J. Anderson, Edmonton; Chris J. Andronick, Brandon; Andrew J. Auchterloni, Sidney; Kevin R. Aulenback, Edmonton; Tex W. Ayotte, Fort St. John; Wayne T. Ball, Winnipeg; Micheal Barfoot, Vancouver; Peter G. Beardy, Victoria; Doug P. Behm, Prince George. ·

Kenneth Benz, Victoria; Mohammed S. Bhamji, Vancouver; Gary W. Bourget, Fort St. John; Susan A. (F) Brekke, Bella Coola; Daniel P. Bretzer, Edmonton; Paul E. J. Brule, Victoria; Sinclair E. Burgis, Vancouver; Bruce D. Busby, Winnipeg; Guy W. Campbell, Vermilion; Norman A. Campbell, Whitehorse.

Dave D. Chalmers, Victoria; John P. Chandra, Kamloops; Dave A. Clarke, Prince George; James K. Cmolik, Kelowna; Robert D. Coates, Morris, Man.; George D. Collingridge, Winnipeg; Marc C. Colman, Port Moody; Tim D. Connolly, Edmonton; William T. Cornell, Mayerthorte, Alta.; Charles W. Cowden, Sparwood.

Mary E. Crawford, Surrey; Dale E. Cyre, Edmonton; Terry J. Davis, Winnipeg; Barry C. Dubbin, Saskatoon; Gerald D. Dubyna, Richmond; Adrienne A. Duhault, Winnipeg; Edward R. Dumaine, Fort St. John; Greg C. Duncalfe, Abbotsford; Neil B. Ebert, Humble, Sask.; Phillip A. Edge, Richmond.

Kippen S. Eliasson, Winnipeg; Ronald J. Eriksen, Calgary; Robert B. Estrada, Salmon Arm; Brent C. Evans, Calgary; George G. Ewart, Abbotsford; Monika (F) Fast, 100 Mile House; Emil J. Fernandes, Vancouver; Shane M. Fisher, Edmonton; Curtis W. Forrest, Fort St. John; Doug I. Frank, Inuvik.

Dwayne D. Frehlick, Estavan;

Robert T. Fyfe, Qualicum Beach, B.C.; Gordon D. Gargus, Fort St. John; Carl E. Glinsbockel, Vernon; Mike E. Grasser, Sparwood; Cynthia G. Grubb, Regina; Wayne R. Gruhlke, East Kindersley, Sask.; Ruth (F) Haenisch, Vancouver; Pauline M. (F) Haley, Lazo, B.C.; Jacqueline F. (F) Hammett, Estevan.

Ryan M. Hardonk, Nanaimo; Earl B. Harris, Lac La Hache, B.C.; Giselle M. (F) Harvey, Vernon; Marvin B. Hawke, Prince George; Don E. Hayduk, Sherwood Park; Danny W. Heatherington, Sparwood; Mike J. Heron, Victoria; Michael A. Hilsendeger, Red Cliff, Alta.; Donald R. Hoffman, Vernon; Richard A. Hoogenberg, Summerland.

Diane (F) Horeth, Medicine Hat; Sandy O. Hrycyk, Lethbridge; Rodney G. Huseby, Black Falls, Alta.; Laverne R. Jamieson, Winnipeg; Robert B. Jamieson, Bushell Park, Sask.; Mark G. Jarvis, Thunder Bay, Ont.; Elaine (F) Johnson, Powell River; Ian W. Joners, Edmonton; Chris M. Kane, Victoria; Ed J. Karczewski, Salmon Arm.

Darryl Kellett, Richmond; Jeanne (F) Kennedy, Powell River; Carol (F) Kenny, Medicine Hat; Cameron B. Kerr, Swift Current; Steven H. Kilfoyle, Treherne, Man.; Ted Komick, Vancouver; Gregory T. Kopchuk, Virden, Man.; Peter A. Kulchyski, Vanada, B.C.; John A. Kusnir, Vancouver; Liard G. Lauder, Salmon Arm.

John W. Lawton, Edmonton; Ron S. Lee, Vancouver; Frank R. Lekivetz, Victoria; Tom D. Little, Vernon; Adrianne S. (F) Lochan, Vancouver; Rodney S. Loesch, Winnipeg; Matthew J. Logan, Delta; Bryan J. Lowrie, Edmonton; Derek B. MacDonald, Prince George.

Craig S. MacLeod, Vancouver; Tammy L. (F) McCarthy, Kamloops; Margaret M. (F) McCoy, Calgary; Robert I. McDonald, Swift Current; Michele T. (F) McDowall, Richmond; Frank B. McKenna, Kelowna; Shaun M. McKenna, Kelowna; Roderick J. McLeod, Salmon Arm; Jim H. McNicol, Prince George; Alfred D. Madge, Edmonton.

Alex A. Malczynski, Vancouver; Brett Marklund, Edmonton; Brian Martin, Victoria; Ken J. Martinook, Melville, Sask.; Bernard H. Martins, Winnipeg; David B. Marshall, Burnaby; Susan O. (F) Masterson, Mayerthorpe; Vernon L. Meetoos, Turtleford; Norman Midttun, Surrey; Frances A. (F) Monks, Uranium City, Sask.

Anthony A. Montgomery, Courtenay; Bernadette L. (F) Moriarty, Surrey; Derek L. Munch, Victoria; Berry L. Murphy, Port Coquitlam; Ian A. Newton, Clinton; Pamela P. (F)

Nickel, Vancouver; Wendy L. (F) Nickel, Vancouver; Richard R. Novak, Fort St. John; Les A. Olson, Yorkton; Mike W. Orr, Richmond.

Glennis J. (F) O'Sulivan, Port Coquitlam; Deborah L. (F) Parisian, Winnipeg; Raymond J. Pasemko, Salmon Arm; Grant Richard Pearson, Vancouver; Cecile A. M. (F) Perras, Regina; Kevin M. Piche, Surrey; Anne B. T. (F) Pilling, Regina; Floyd A. Powder, Fort Smith; Gain M. Pon, Calgary; Mike L. Porisky, Edmonton.

Michael J. Prendergast, Winnipeg; Ken G. Raven, Prince George; Peter J. Rennich, Edmonton; Janice (F) Revell, Surrey; Glen W. Richmond, Surrey; Rod S. Robertson, Vancouver; Cliff B. Robinson, Rosetown; Anthony R. Roughley, Vancouver; Jennifer J. (F) Roulette, Portage LaPrairie; Gordon A. Ruttan, Vernon.

Johannes (F) Schaper-Kotter, Richmond; David W. Secuur, Regina; Michelle T. (F) Seiferling, Regina; Michael R. Seifert, Strathmore; Michael M. Shukster, Sherwood Park; Kenneth N. Shupe, Dryden, Ont.; Neil A. Simpson, Richmond; Dennis M. Statz, Winnipeg; Darrin C. Stevenson, Saskatoon; Douglas L. Swanson, Brandon.

Florence R. (F) Tambour, Regina; Verda (F) Tambour, Regina; Peter F. Thompson, Black Diamond; Bonnie (F) Tober, Edmonton; Steven A. Tompkins, Edmonton; Phillip W. Toupin, Edmonton; Shelley (F) Town, Vermette, Man.; Hurshel C. Utinowatum, Fort St. John, B.C.; Bruce D. Vanderberg, Winterburn, Alta.; Peter G. Wakeland, Delta.

Chris C. Waldman, Calgary; Nazir G. M. Walji, Calgary; Allen R. Walls, Winnipeg; Mark A. Wankiewicz, Edmonton; Glen H. Warriner, Salmon Arm; Lee D. Waun, Port Coquitlam; Mark B. Wayne, Edmonton; Mario Weber, Victoria; David W. Weir, Vancouver; Darren Williams, Delta; Russell S. Woodroffe, Edmonton; Ron W. Wuetz, Prince George; Charles L. Zohner, Powell River; Gary Robert Hall, Esquimalt; Robert F. Riffel, Winnipeg.

STAFF NOMINAL ROLL

Maj. Jeffrey H. Aitken, ADV TRG; Lt. Percy R. Allaby, DVR COMM.; Cpl. Malcolm J. Allan, E.; A-Sgt. (W) Jean S. Appleton, Band; Lt. (W) Kathryn E. Ashby, H; MWO Leonard R. Aylesworth, OT; Cl (W) Gayle E Bain, Sports; Lt. (W) Helen J. Bakker, G; Capt. Lyle A. Balfour, TRG HQ; WO Patrick Balfour, NPF;

Lt. John P. Ballard, H; Pte. Michael F. Barker, GD; Pte (W) Susan L. Barnes, ADV TRG; Maj. Clyde A. Bates, Pay; A-Cpl. (W) Penelope Beardsley, B; Pte. Derrill A. Beauchesne, F; A-Cpl.

Chris J. Becker, C; Col. John P. Beer, HQ; Capt. (W) Shirley N. Begin, Hosp; Maj. George H. Bell TRG HQ;

M-Cpl. William Bendell, ADV TRG; A-Cpl. James M. Bender, D; Cpl. Alan Bennett, ADV TRG; WO. Robert W. Bethel, TRG HQ; A. Cpl. Arthur Bienvenu, E; Pte (W), Cecile Boisvert, B; A. Sgt. Willard K. Bokovay, D; Pte. (W) Catherine L. Bolan, Hosp; Lt. Alexander C. Bolin, E.; OCDT Edward Bonnier, Ot.

A. Sgt. Lee K. Boon, E; Capt. Charles I. Boyd, ADV TRG; Pte. Edward M. Bragg, FP & GD; WO Alexander Braslins, Dent.; OCDT Brad B. Breit, OT: A CPL. (W) Bonnie B. Breit, Band; Maj. Bradley Breit, B; A Cpl. William R. Broadfoot, ADV TRG; Pte. Donald J. Brown, Hosp.; Pte. Shaun L. Brown, ADV TRG.

Pte. Rod S. Browne, Hosp.; Cl (W) Colleen P. Bryan, Swim.; Pte. James G. Brynelson, Sup.; Lt. Edward S. Buchanan, C; Maj. Thomas R. Buchenauer, C; Sgt. Gary Burner, TN; Lt. James R. Caldwell, H; A Sgt. Bradley K. Cambrey, ADV TRG; OCDT, Phillip A. Camire, OT; Capt. (W) Valerie G. Campbell, B;

Capt. Leonard Cantin, R C Padre; Capt. James Cantwell, C; Lt. (W) Cindy V. Carlson, Sports; A Cpl. Lawrence H. Carlson, B; Lt. (W) Doreen G. Carnegie, NPF; Capt. (W) Enid M. Carpenter, G; Ci Murray W. Carpenter, Swim; Pte Peter C. Carter, GD; Pte Kelvin L. Catling, Sports; A Cpl. Victor Cattoni, E.

A Sgt James M. Charlebois, A; Cl (Capt. RTD) William T. Chilton, BIQ; Capt. Leonard Christie, Band; A Sgt. Michael B. Chudiak, E; WO Fraser G. Clarke, A; A Cpl. Stephen G. Companion, H; A Cpl. (W) Brenda L. Conrad G; A Cpl. Robert D. Cooper, D; A Cpl. Larry R. Corvino, D; Capt. Douglas Coughlin, E;

Ci Colin K. Coutts, First Aid; WO Kenneth R. Coutts, HQ; A Cpl. Terry E. Cowles, E; Sgt. Kenneth R. Cox, Maint.; OCDT (W) Diane R. Craigen, BIQ; A Cpl. (W) Charlotte E. Cruickshank, G; Cl Larry J. Davidson, ADV TRG; Pte. Glen R. Davies, D; A Sgt. Ward H. Davies, A; CWO Charles D. Davis, Foods Svr.

Maj. Duncan I. Davis, A; A Sgt. (W) Laurie P. Davis, G; Mcpl. Dennis M. Davydiuk, Maint.; Ci Daniel G. Degirolamo, ADV TRG; Sgt. Donald L. Derosier, CE; Cpl. Robert Derry, C; A Cpl. Derek AF Desrosiers, H; A Cpl. John Dick, A; A Sgt. Micheal R. Dimmer, Band; Pte. Stephen L. Dozorec, G., D.

Ci Peter Dranchuk, Sports; A Cpl. James Drinkall, H; Lt. Robert C. Duncombe, E; WO George A. Dunn, Band; Cpl. Charley Edwards, Sup.; Pte. Harold R. Edwards, ADV TRG; A Cpl. William

PO Englesby, A ; A Cpl. Lesslie P. Erickson, D ; Lt. David J. Errington, H. ; Ci (Capt. RTD) William B. Fairbairn, DVR COMM. ;

Capt. John R.D. Falconer, HQ ; (CDR RTD) Gordon Faraday, P. Chap. ; WO Edward J. Farkas, D ; Capt. Peter W. Padre ; Capt. Robert G. Faulds, H ; Lt. Dennis A. Fege, A ; WO Oswald H. Finzel A ; A Cpl. (W) Katharina I. Fischer, HQ ; A Cpl. Daniel R. Flynn, GD ; A Cpl. (W) Natale Foglia, H.

Ci Robert J. Folk, Sports ; Maj. Roy A. Forbes, HQ ; Ci (W) Edith M. Fowler, First Aid ; A Cpl. (W) Dorothy Franklin, G ; A Cpl. (W) Debra L. Friesen, F ; A Cpl. (W) Patricia Frigon, F ; A Cpl. (W) Linda L. Gabriel, G ; A Cpl. Colin M. Gibson, H ; Capt. (W) June F. Gibson, First Aid ; A Sgt. Arthur Gilchrist, D.

Sgt. Robert G. Gilmour, H ; A Cpl. Frank M. Goldie, E ; Pte. Neil Gordon, Sup. ; Cpl. Barnabas H. Gotudco, MP ; Ci. Gerry Goudge, Swim ; Lt. (W) Mary E. Graham, BIQ ; A Cpl. Wayne N. Graham, ADV TRG ; WO Bernard A. Grant, HQ ; A Cpl. Grant David J. D ; Cpl. (W) Teresa M. Greenwood, TN ; Ci (W) Louise A. Grinstead, Band.

Ci (W) Lorraine M. Gross, TN ; A Cpl. Michael E. Grover, E ; A Cpl. (W) Rachel I. Haines, G ; 2 Lt. David H.E. Hale, BIQ ; Wo Wayne H. Halstead, ADV TRG ; Ci (CAPT RTD) Clarence L. Hamilton, Hosp. ; CWO John R. Hammond TN ; WO Kenneth O. Hanson, TRG HQ ; WO John Harder, Sup.

Capt. Edwin F. Harmsworth, TRG HQ ; Pte. Glenn G. Harries, Sports ; WO Rolf J. Hartmann, H ; Maj. Frederick J. T. Harvey, HQ ; A Cpl. (W) Carol J. Hayes, H ; Ci (CAPT RTD) Alvin M. Hayward, NPF ; A Cpl. Daniel F. Henderson, C ; Lt. (W) Marjorie A. Henderson, NPF ; Lt. Donald B. Henry D ; Ci Arne Hetherington, ADV TRG ; OCDT (W) Rene Hibbert, BIQ ; WO David L. Hickling, DVR COMM ; Cpl. Glen K. Hickman, MP ; Capt. Kevin B. Higgins, ADV TRG ; Capt. William D. W. Hill, Sup. ; OCDT (W) Bobby-June F. Hislop, BIQ ; A Cpl. David W. Hlady, C ; Capt. Mark A. D. Hlady, F ; Lt. Kenneth M. Hoffmann, B ; A Cpl. Bruce Hole H ; Lt. Rodney J. Holowaty, C.

Lt. (W) Barbara A. Holyk ADV TRG ; A Cpl. Gordon Howe, PIO ; A Cpl. David H. Howie, B ; Ci (W) Barbara Howse, Swim ; Capt. Alexander B. Hrycyna, TRG HQ ; Sgt. Keith A. Hughes, Maint. ; OCDT Kenneth G. Hunter, BIQ ; Ci Lloyd Hunter, Post.

A. Cpl. Philip T. Hunter, H ; A. Cpl. David D. Hutchinson, H ; Lt. John F. Isaac, F ; A. Sgt. Clifford Jamieson, C ; WO Allan O. Jeffrey, Foods Svr. ; Cpl. Erik K. Jensen, D ; A. Cpl. Kenneth W. Jestin, F ; Maj. Andy T. Joerissen, G ; Maj. Henry J. Joerissen, Band ; A. Cpl.

Kirk R. Johansen, H ; Pte. Donald W. Johnson, GD.

CWO Marvin C. Johnston, HQ ; Pte. Michael J. Johnston, A ; Sgt. Paul N. Johston, C ; A. Cpl. George C. Karoly, Band ; Lt. Allan J. Kassian, D ; Ci (LCOL RTD) Robert A. D. Kelly NPF ; Ci Kenneth A. Kendall ADVTRG ; Ci (W) Nan P. Kendy, Swim ; Pte. Alexander M. Kennedy, GD ; Ci Donald E. Kenyon, ADV TRG ; A Cp. (W) Linda L. Kidd, B ;

Lt. W. Dwight Kilpatrick, H ; Maj. Paul C. King, F ; Cpl. (W) Karen L. Klassen, Hos. ; A Sgt. Kenneth W. Knipstrom, D ; Cpl. Peter J. Koronko, TN ; A Sgt. William D. Kozlowski, DVR COMM ; Pte. Dennis G. Lacroix, Sup. ; Ci Charles W. P. Lambe, ADV TRG ; A Sgt. James Laursen, A.

Maj. Henry P. Lauzon, TRG HQ ; Cpl. (W) Jocelyn A. L. Lawrence, G ; A Cpl. Perry Lea, C ; Ci (CAPT. RTD) Campbell LeBlond, PIO ; Ci (W) Janis L. LeBlond, Swim ; Pte. Guy G. Legare, ADV TRG ; Lt. (W) Mary B. Leibel, G ; Ci Wayne W. Liebel, Sports ; Capt. Robert M. Lekivetz, TRG HQ ; WO Robert G. Letts, Med.

A SGT. Rick M. Lewis, C ; A Cpl. Andrew J. Liggett, MP ; L Col. Charles V. Lilley, HQ ; A Cpl. Glen Lingel, E ; Ci (W) Kathryn Little, Swim ; A Cpl. Rick Liukaitis, C ; Sgt. James A. Livingston ADV TRG ; A Cpl. James Donald Loewen, MP ; A Cpl. Michael Lopez, H ; A Sgt. (W) Janet L. Lucas, B.

A Cpl. Robert Lund, C ; WO George M. Luscombe, Maint. ; MWO James G. Lynden, GD ; Capt. Derrick S. Lyons, BIQ ; Maj. James R. C. MacBain, AIR ; Pte. Gordon A. MacCallum, Band ; Ci (W) Elizabeth J. MacKenzie, Swim ; Maj. Donald K. MacQuarrie, HQ ; A Cpl (W) Margaret McArthur, B ; Ci Thomas E. McBennett, DVR COMM.

Cpl. (W) Beverly J. McCabe, HQ ; Pte, Charles McCarthy, H ; Lt. (W) Janet McCarthy, B ; A Sgt. (W) Sandra L. McCarthy, B ; MWO John H. McDonnell, G ; Lt. Hugh A. McIntyre, Band. ; Cpl. Philip A. McKerry, MP ; Ci (W) Susan M. McLennan, Sports ; OCDT Roderick J. McLeod, BIQ ; Ci Raymond R. McMullen, ADV TRG.

A Cpl. Warren A. McQueen, F ; A Cpl. Ronnald G. McRae, TN ; Cpl. Wayne Madland, PAM L ; Pte (W) Terry Madore, Hos. ; Ci Gordon H. Mann, Sports ; Sgt. (W) Diane M. Manning, TN ; Lt. Raymond G. Marasa, A ; A Sgt. Steven L. Marshall, C ; Sgt. Ernest A. Martell, Sup. ; CWO Thomas M. Mason, NPF.

Pte. Stephen G. Mears, ADV TRG ; Sgt. Dennis R. Miller, F ; Lt. (W) Pam A. Miller, G ; Lt. David L. Mitchell, F ; A Cpl. Donald K.

Mitchell, A; A Cpl. Gary R. Mitchell, H; 2Lt. Michael Mitchell, BIQ; A Cpl. Michael J. Monk, Band; Lt. Sharples K. Moore, BIQ; Cpl. Kenneth K. Moretti, C.

Pte. Lindsay Morris, E; Maj. Peter D. Morris, RC CHAP.; A Cpl. (W) Roberta Morris, F; A Cpl. Robert A. Morrow, B; Cl Noel P. Mulloy, Sports; Cl Laurence H. Munro, Band; Cl (W) Deborah C. Murray, Swim; Lt. William J. Nangle, Band; Cpl (W) Michele F. Neale, HQ; A Sgt. Gary P. Noga, F.

A Cpl. Michael J. Noga, H; A Sgt. Garry L. Nohr, MP; A Cpl. Peter A. Novak, A; A Cpl. Steven P. Nunn, F; Sgt. Frank O. E. Oertel, Band; A Cpl. Donald W. Ostashek D; Pte. Terry D. Ostashek, E; OCDT (W) Jean M. Palmer, BIQ; Pte. Rick W. H. Parlby, ADV TRG; Lt. Arthur B. Pearce, C.

Pte. Steven Pennock, Sports; Cl Henry W. Perkins, ADV TRG; Lt. Kenneth H. Pettit, ADV TRG; Capt. Matthew John Phillips, Sports; Lt. D'Arcy D. Pickering, A; Lt. (W) Pearl E. Piechotta, B; Maj. Theodore C. Piete, PIO; Pte. (W) Patricia R. Plante, Hosp.; A Cpl. (W) Eliane J. Poburan, MP; Lt. Kenneth S. Pon, E.

Pte. Michael H. Poole, ADV TRG; A Cpl. Brian Popwich, Band; MWO John W. Poucher, TRG HQ; Capt. Peter M. F. Preston, Band; Maj. Alex W. Prytula, Sports; Cl William A. Prytula, Sports; Cl James N. Quinn, Swim; A Cpl. Gary D. Ratchford, Band; MCPL. Donald G. Redecopp, Pay; Pte. David M. Reeve, Fire.

A Cpl. Evan P. Remenda, Band; Sgt. Rettenbacher, TRG HQ; OCDT (W) Margaret R. Rheaume, BIQ; OCDT Roger J. G. Rheaume, BIQ; Sgt. Michael A. Roberge, H; Cl (CAPT RTD) Donald I. T. Roe, HQ; A Cpl. Ted Roffel, A; Maj. Robert G. Rogers, TN; Maj. Russell E. Roney, H; A Cpl. Terrence D. Rothery, F.

Capt. Albert W. Ruttan, A; A Cpl. (W) Patricia A. Ruttan, B; A Cpl. Steven Ryder, C; 2Lt Anna M. Sakowski, BIQ; Capt. Ronald V. Samol, Swim; A Sgt. (W) Melanie L. Sanders, G; A Cpl. Kevin M. Sawatzky, D; Cpl. Alexander H. Schaafsma, Maint.; Capt. Norman W. Schick, D; A Cpl. Brent Schultz, A.

Sgt. Ralph E. Schultz, MP; A Sgt. (W) Toni Schulz, F; Cl Reginald M. Scott, DVR COMM; A Cpl. Ronald Seales, C; A Cpl. (W) Laura L. Semenchuk G; Cl John Semochuk, NPF; Capt. Michael R. Sharpe, ADV TRG; Cpl. Maurice T. Shevalier, Hosp.; OCDT R. P. Shore, BIQ; LCDR Alfred Soucek, MO.

Capt. Rick Spier, DVR COMM; A Cpl. Richard Spuls, Band; Sgt. Walter H. Statz; F; Cl Douglas N. Staveley, Sports; A Sgt. Rodney C. Steere, E; A Cpl. Frederick S.

Stewart, MIR; Cl Ross Stinson, DVR COMM; Capt. (W) Marjorie E. Studer, NPF; OCDT Douglas F. Sturges, BIQ; Lt. Dale Sumislouski, D.

Capt. (W) Vera E. Teslyk, Hos.; A Cpl. (W) Dorothy A. Thach, G; Pte. Donnald M. Thivierge, FP & GD; Sgt. Carl V. Thomas, MP; A Sgt. (W) Jennie-Lynn Thompson, G; A Cpl (W) Joy E. Thompson; B; Pte (W) Ann M. Tibbel, MP; Maj. Norman L. Topham, HQ; Capt. Gordon J. D. Townend, ADV TRG; A Sgt. Wayne J. Tremblay, B;

Cpl. Roy Turner, Maint.; Maj. Reginald J. Tweten D; A Sgt. (W) Penelope L. J. Umpherville, H; A Sgt. Richard S. Usher, H; Capt. Leonard F. Vaness, ADV TRG; A Cpl. Christopher Q. Verchere, F; OCDT (W) Elizabeth F. Waite, BIQ; Lt. Russell Waite, Band; Pte. (W) Patricia A. Walker, HQ; Sgt. Donald G. Waller, E; Maj. James E. Waterton, HQ.

A Cpl. Andrew S. Weiss, A; Pte. (W) Elizabeth M. Welsh, G; Cl Gerd K. Wenzlaff, Sports; MWO Arthur J. Wiebe, Pay.; A Cpl. Daryl F. Wilkinson, C; A Cpl. Randall A. Willford, D; Cl Thomas P. Williamson, Sports; Pte. Graham K. Wilson, ADV TRG; A Cpl. (W) Heather G. Wilson, H; Capt. Robert A. Wilson, ADV TRG; Maj. William J. Woodard, E; Capt. Gunter J. Wriedt, BIQ; A Cpl. Kevin Young, H; A Sgt. Allan P. Zingeler, H.

BAND

Anthony G. Ackland, Comox, B.C.; Richard T. Andersen, Calgary; Rosemary Arnouse, Williams Lake; Clark F. Atkinson, Victoria; Kelly J. Backman, Terrace, B.C.; Ervin E. Beisiegel, Victoria; Cameron I. Biggs, Vancouver; Joseph L. Bokor, Coquitlam; Dwight A. Bristow, Winnipeg; Geoffrey T. Brown, Vancouver.

Robert W. Browne, Nanaimo; Derek G. Burnett, Burnaby; Cory B. Callaghan, Victoria; Alex J. Chisholm, Calgary; William B. Chobotar, Coquitlam; Stephen J. Christian, Victoria; David W. R. Clark, Langley; Kelly L. Clark, Coaldale, Alta.; Roland G. Desmarais, Calgary; Joseph P. Dubois, Victoria.

Rodney G. Elgert, North Delta, B.C.; Stephen P. Farmar, Delta, B.C.; Kelly J. Fitzpatrick, Winnipeg; Wally R. Fletcher, Calgary; Robert D. Friesen, Lacombe, Alta.; Phillip P. Gagnon, Terrace, B.C.; Gwen A. Gallant, Calgary; Allan C. Gardner, Victoria; Alison M. Gebetsroither, Prince George; Mary E. Gerritsen, Calgary.

Peter H. Giesbrecht, Surrey; Joan I. Glendale, Victoria; William M. Greig, Victoria; John W. Gribble, Victoria; Sharon A. Grubb, Regina; Sabrina A., Haggart, Sidney, B.C.; Donald D.

Hamilton, Thunder Bay, Ont.;
Jerry A. Harte, Burnaby; Steven
R. Head, Victoria; Robin C. S.
Hicks, Campbell River.

Norman D. D. Holt, Oliver;
Connie M. Horner, St. John, B.C.;
Lyle S. Hurd, Winnipeg; William
J. E. Jarvis, Campbell River; Joel
M. Johnston, Thunder Bay, Ont.;
Jean M. S. Johnston, Nanaimo;
Wayne A. Joy, Edson, Alta.; Kevin
J. Kirk, Terrace; Kevin M.
Kowbel, Campbell River; Murray
D. Lagace, Winnipeg.

Richard G. Lambert, Borden,
Ont.; Lydia A. Lunan, Rocky
Mountain House, Alta.; Rodney J.
Lyle, Victoria; Roberta E. Mac-
Donald, Regina; Shawn H.
McKinley, Winnipeg; Karen A. M.
MacLean, Calgary; Robert B.
MacLennan, Vancouver; George
R. Marchildon, Port Alberni;
Lloyd J. Martens, Calgary; Dean
R. Martin, Calgary.

Karen Y. Martyn, Courtenay,
B.C.; Michael A. Morrissey,
Victoria; William G. Mountain,
Delta.; Steven J. Muloin, Calgary;
Joseph P. Neault, Regina; Cheryl
A. Nichols, Surrey; Kelly M.
Nichols, Surrey; Grant W. Olsen,
Port Coquitlam, B.C.; Richard H.
Packiewicz, Victoria.; Steve R.
Packiewicz, Victoria.

Sylvia J. Parker, Hazelton,
B.C.; Stewart P. Peddemors,
Surrey; Glen L. Peters, Kelowna;
Janet K. Peterson, Duncan;
Richard H. A. Pfefferkorn, Port
Moody, B.C.; Tiare M. Phillips,
Sardis, B.C.; Ian R. Ratchford,
Victoria; Kevin D. Richards, Port
Moody, B.C.; James B. Richard-
son, Coquitlam; Paul W. Roberts,
Victoria.

Frank W. Rus, Regina; Lorna
M. Saunders, North Vancouver;
Bernice L. Seiferling, Regina;
Mike D. Service, Sydney; Ray R.
Simpson, Victoria; Carl L.
Siwallace, Bella Coola, B.C.;
Wayne Smith, Winnipeg; Lorance
P. Smyth, Delta; Ronald A.
Stepharnoff, Victoria; John M.
Szauer, Williams Lake.

Steve J. Taylor, Victoria;
Brenda M. Tenta, Surrey; Lorna
F. Tenta, Surrey; Rhonda L.
Thibeau, Campbell River;
Joanne L. Tuininga, Campbell
River; Daniel W. Veelbehr,
Hagnsborg, B.C.; Kim M. Wad-
dell, Nanaimo; Kari-Anne Wad-
den, Calgary; William H. Warner,
Terrace; Martin A. Wedam, Port
Alberni.

Mark S. West, New West-
minster; Brian D. Wilson,
Smithers; Darlys L. Wilson,
Sherwood Park; Norman J.
Wygand, Coquitlam; Glen J.
Winship, Coquitlam; Colleen A.
White, Victoria; Martin E. Zim-
mer, Calgary.

VACC - 1991

Adair, P.; Adamkewicz, R.; Adams, J.; Aitken, C.;
Allan, C.; Allan, L.; Amundson, C.; Anderson, M.;
Baehl de Lescure, M.; Barnes, B.; Bayley, L.;
Belmont, S.; Binet, J.; Boldt, A.; Boley, H.;
Bortnick, N.; Botterill, D.; Boucher, L.; Boucher,
M.; Bouten, T.; Bowman, R.; Boyko, F.;
Brassington, P.; Brennan, C.; Briand, D.; Brown,
Charlie.; Brown, Clinton.; Bruneau, D.; Burrows,
P.; Byrne, R.; Bzdel, A.; Campbell, C., Carstairs,
T.; Chan, D.; Chan, R.; Chase, R.; Christensen, K.;
Clack, A.; Clark, M.; Clarke, J.; Clifford, T.;
Cloutier, D.; Coady, M.; Cole, R.; Cone, K.;
Conlin, C.; Connors, J.; Cooper, T.; Croze, P.;
Crummey, S.; Cunningham, J.; Damphousse, G.;
Danner, Y.; Davies, P.; Dennis, K.; Dobmeier, S.;
Duazo, T.; Dubuc, C.; Duffill, R.; Duiker, D.;
Dyck, L.; Dyck, S.; Eilers, G.; Elliott, K.;
Embleton, M.; Emde, W.; Emmons, T.;
Engelbretson, J.; Fisher, J.; Fisher, K.; Fisher, M.;
Forry, D.; Fortin, P.; Francis, M.; Friesen, S.;
Firtsch, M.; Gagne, I.; Gallant, A.; Gee, D.; Gillis,
G.; Glena, R.; Goetz, D.; Goodman, J.; Graham,
D.; Gravel, D.; Grenier, L.; Haberstock, B.;
Hansen, R.; Harden, D.; Hardy, R.; Harland, A.;
Harrow, N.; Hart, N.; Haslam, N.; Haughian, R.;
Hawkins, L.; Hayes, L.; Head, D.; Heary, P.;
Heimbechner, A.; Heinrich, D. Henderson, R.;
Henderson, T.; Hickman, B.; Hildebrandt, L.;
Hobbs, C.; Homeniuk, E.; Humphrey, B.;
Hurtubise, M.; Hykaway, C.; Ingram, L.; Inniss,
Y.; Jobin, R.; John, C.; Johnson, H.; Johnson, L.;
Johnston, D.; Kerr, J.; Kidd, D.; Kimber, K.;
Kindrachuk, T.; Kleen, D.; Knaap, K.; Knudsen,
M.; Kovaltsenko, K.; Kranenburg, L.; Krause, R.;
Krauss, L.; Krieger, C.; Kurulok, D.; Lacey, R.;
Larochelle, D.; Larsen, A.; Lavallee, N.; Lemay,
R.; Liggett, J.; Liggett, P.; Lindsay, K.; Littlemore,
K.; Luj, J.; Macaskill, N.; MacDonald, J.;
MacDonald, R.; MacKenzie, Randal; MacKenzie,
Richard; MacPherson, C.; Mahan, S.; Malecki, T.;
Mann, C.; March, M.; Markin, G.; Marshall, B.;
Masny, M.; Materi, B.; Maynard, W.; McBain,
W.; McCall, I.; McDermid, J.; McInnes, M.;
McKenna, S.; McLeod, M.; Meehan, J.; Melo, A.;
Merkel, J.; Meyer, K.; Meyer, M.; Meyer, S.;
Miller, T.; Mills, J.; Miranda, T.; Morrison, T.;
Morrow, D.; Morton R.; Mulligan, S.; Murray, W.;
Neal, M.; Neil, M.; Nelson, M.; Noakes, T.;
Novak, M.; Noewn, C.; Olsen, F.; Paino, J.; Palud,
M.; Pangalia, D.; Parr, G.; Parr, J.; Paterson, F.;
Paul, S.; Pelan, D.; Pelletier, C.; Penner, K.;
Perkins, D.; Peter, J.; Peters, C.; Peterson, L.;
Picken, G.; Polley, J.; Petter, J.; Rattray, C.;
Reddy, G.; Reed, R.; Rettenbacher, V.; Richard,
K.; Riseing, E.; Rivard, J.; Roberts, C.; Robson,
T.; Rose, R.; Routledge, K.; Roy, C.; Rubia, B.;
Sandoval, M.; Sarauer, B.; Savard, M.; Savioie,
Y.; Scherger, M.; Schooner, C.; Schwartz, A.;
Sedgemore, M.; Sehra, R.; Self, D.; Selig, J.;
Singh, I.; Sklepowich, D.; Skoda, A.; Smallwood,
T.; Smart, W.; Smith, C.; Smith, P.; Smyth, T.;
Soucy, M.; Spelchan, G.; St. Pierre, R.; Stalker,
M.; Stephan, M.; Stevenson, E.; Stevenson, L.;
Stewart, A.; Stratford, J.; Streekstra, P.; Strunk,
G.; Sutton, C.; Swanson, R.; Taylor, D.; Thomas,
C.; Thompson, C.; Thompson, S.; Thomson, Shay;
Thomson, Sheri; Thorpe, E.; Thurber, J.; Tighe,
L.; Tolmie, J.; Tomson, K.; Toth, P.; Trekofski,
M.; Tremblay, J.; Tresidder, R.; Trick, T.; Tulp,
A.; Tutt, J.; Tyldesley-Gore, E.; Ulrich, M.;
Ussher, A.; Van Ryckeghem, K.; Van Stone, M.;
Vanwieren, W.; Venn, G.; Vey, D.; Walkin, B.;
Waughtal, C.; Welin, J.; West, D.; Weston, M.;
White, L.; Wiebe, M.; Wiegel, R.; Wilson, B.;
Wood, G.; Woods, S.; Young, Daniel; Young,
Douglas; Zazalak, T.

**ARMY CADET LEADER INSTRUCTOR
COURSE**
A COMPANY
08 JULY 91 - 16 AUGUST 91
Andres, Nathan; Ansorger, Earon; Avcoin, Ryan
G.; Bauer, Shaun; Becker, Jason H.; Beerwald,

Michael; Best, Carla P. (F); Bigler, Chris; Blais, Sylvain; Boucher, Curtis; Boyd, Matthew; Brerer, Todd; Briggs, Micheal A.; Burnett, Helen (F); Burridge, Craig; Carlson, James; Chafe, Frederick J.; Christensen, Lars; Clare, David; Desjarlais, Henry; Diamond, Joel; Dobson, Chris A.; Dubois, Lucien; Earle, Lisa K. (F); Edgett, Jessica Elizabeth (F); Ellenor, Jessica E. (F); Evans, Erin G. (F); Fieldhouse, Caley; Forbes, J.P.; Goss, Alan; Grimm, Jason; Guilbeault, Don; Hadley, Tami; Helzer, David; Huisca, Carlos; Jackson, Chris Martin; Jackson, Tyson; Johansen, Chris R.; Johnson, Bernard; Johnson, David P.; Johnson, Jason; Kennedy, Daniel; Kirk, John; Krol, Jeremiah T.; Lee, Adam; Lehrer, Anthony; Lelewski, Mark; Low, Kevin; Lubkiwski, Jeffrey; MacAndrew, George; Macausland, Greg S.; Marchand, Jason; Mattson, Jean L. (F); McDonnell, Lesley M. (F); McGregor, David; Meldru, Tom; Michaud, Trixie; Millroy, Kelly Anne; Moore, Kieran; Murametz, John; Morin, Robyn; Morris, Wendy; Mullin, Calvin; Naismith, Colin, Norell, Clayton; Ogden, Jessica; Olmsted, John; Parrent, Jacqui; Patrick, Kent; Patterson, Andrew P.; Perrault, Kevin J.; Plank, Adam S.; Ramsay, Lee; Read, Micheal; Richards, Patrick N.; Rosendahl, Mark P., Rowsell, Dean; Scherger, Deanna (F); Shelton, Barry; Simmons, Cory; Sinha, Richard; Spiers, Peter A.; Stapleton, Kevin; Swan, Blaine D.; Tanaka, Jazmyn (F); Townley, Tim J.; Wallace, Susan C. (F); Warner, Kris A.; Wasyliw, Amie Lynn Hope (F); Watt, Brett Donald; Wheeler, Brenton A.; Wiggins, Bill; Wilson, Lance; Winkelaar, Keri; Wright, Veronica L. (F); Zerebesri, Jeff J.

ARMY CADET RIFLE INSTRUCTOR COURSE
B COMPANY
08 JUL 91 TO 16 AUG 91
Adamkewicz, Wesely; Armstrong, Chad; Babcock, Lori (F); Baldwin, Erica (F); Bently, Scott; Bibeau, Rene; Bibeganek, Shane; Blind, Robert; Brall, Andreas; Broughton, Mathew; Callaghan, Tim; Carbary, Mike; Chapman, Brad; Clapham, Barbara (F); Collis, Ila (F); Dell, Dereck; Dickson, Amy (F); Ditchfield, Chris; Doggett, Buffy (F); Donford, Curtis; Duboura, Mark; Ehret, Crissy (F); Empey, Roger; Fell, Liam, Ferguson, Trevor; Fiessel, Chris; Fisher, Matthew; Flett, Sarah (F); Francis, Micheal; Gatz, April (F); Gionet, Daniel; Goudreault, Martin; Goulet, Catherine (F); Greaves, Chris; Guinet, Lorna (F); Hamada, Steven; Hebert, Paul; Hollick, Ken; Hrdlickz, Robert; Ingram, Brenda (F); Jack, Rennie; Jeffares, Brett; Johnson, Aaron; Kennedy, Gene; Landsman, Cameron; Logan, Amber, Logan, Gerlyn (F); Martin, Shawn, Martin, Patrick, Mason, James; Massicotte, Tammy (F); McConnell, Chad; McCrae, Scott; Mills, David; Morley, Brent; Newton, Chris; Nickel, Jason; Oram, Kelly; Oster, Jamie; Pankiewicz, Leszek; Peterson, Carrie (F); Pianidin, Mark; Pleasants, Chad; Prigione, Stephen; Porter, Jason; Rehill, Victor; Sali, Kim (F); Salmon, Ron; Samchek, Jennifer (F); Scheltgen, Teresa (F); Schinborn, Joe; Sevigny, Roberta (F); Sheeham, Shawn, Soullier, Romy (F); Strunk, Charlene (F); Surgeson, Cory; Szwaba, Sean; Tutt, Lonnie; Webber, John-Adam; Winsor, Ronald; Yanush, James.

ARMY CADET LEADER COURSE
C COMPANY
08 JULY 91 - 17 AUG 91
Airth, Clayton A.; Anastasakis, Jim; Basisky, Dustin; Bedford, Robert D.; Bell, Jonathon; Benedict, Kyla G. (F); Berns, Thomas; Bickford, Kevin M.; Borthwick, Daniel; Boudreau, Ronnie; Bradfield, Joe; Brassard, Frances D. (F); Brown, Joel; Brown, Ross Martin; Buechler, Wayne; Butler, Micheal; Burleigh, Jason; Campbell, Bernadette G. (F); Carruthers, Charmin (F); Chambers, Trevor; Channel, Allan W.; Clark, Brent; Clemens, Chris Elwin; Clemens, Curtis; Conlin, Chris; Connor, Bernard; Crane, Katherine D. (F); Cumby, Jeremy; Dalziel, Jason M.; Denes, Mike Andrew; Dent, Scott; Deschamps, Denis;

Dispatus, Danial; Dixon, Chris; Doiron, John; Duarte, Nelson; Dunlop, James; Duttenhoffer, Carla (F); Eldridge, Chris Lee; Ells, Jamie; Erickson, Alan; Escott, Sean; Evans, Jamey (F); Fisher, Jonathan A.; Fisher, Simone (F); Forgues, Dodie (F); Fox, Bill Jr.; Garceau, Krista (F); Gibbons, Roy Francis; Goovaerts, Allan; Gracie, Trevor Ernest; Grenier, Pauline P. (F); Groeger, Robert; Groome, Annie (F); Hache, Annette (F); Hall, Neil, Halliday, Steven; Hastings, Jay Ronald; Haughain, James; Hawkes, Garth; Hedlund, Cory W.; Hislop-Perraton (F); Hodges, Walter; Hoeg, Scott; Johnston, Reginald; Jones, Nadine; Jones, Tony; Jordon, Tricia (F); Kanski, Alex; Keeles, Derrick; Keller, Bernie J.; Kelly, Erin; King, Stephanie (F); Kingston, Ryan David; Kolstad, Jason; Konjolka, Jeremy; Kristoff, Ryan; Kulczycki, Angele (F); Lafleur, Jason; Lane, Roger; Larose, Tracey Kaye (F); Larson, Jef; Learmonth, Ricky William; Lecuyer, Clair (F); Lenton, David; Lentowicz, Sean; Lesniewski, Andrew; Liggs, Merle Raymon; Lug, Mike; Lyons, Michael; Maasz, Shawn; MacAuley, Lamuel; Mackay, Jerry Dean; MacKenzie, Carry (F); Maher, Ryan; Marchand, Maymi-Lynne (F); Mathews, Melissa (F); Maslanka, Clinton; Mazerolle, Craig L.; McIvor, Bruce; McAll, Steven G.; McLean, Edison; McLean, Karen (F); McLellan, James C.; Melanson, Shawn; Mercredi, Kevin; Misener, Calvin A.; Mitchell, Clifton; Moffatt, Andrea (F); Moriera, Karroll M. (F); Morin, David; Morris, Christian; Neufeld, Robert; Nisbet, Rob; Nolet, Chris C.; Ormston, Tim; Patterson, Shawn; Peoples, David Kelly; Peoples, Morris; Pettyjohn, Robert James; Pratt, Wesley M.; Provost, Nanci (F); Radl, Jennifer Anne (F); Rafuse, Timothy; Rasalan, Alex; Regier, Andy; Rienks, Christina (F); Riley, Kathlene Marie (F); Roberts, Greg; Russell, William; Rutherford, Stewart; Sacco, Adam John Craig; Sanford, Darrel; Saunders, Ryan; Schofield, Robert; Senechal, Paul; Shanahan, Michael David; Sharburne, Kevin; Sharpe, John; Skeoch, Shane; Smith, Cris; Soullier, Rene; Savoie, Monique (F); Sparks, Cicely Dannel (F); St. Coeur, Jason J.; Steeves, Cris; Stephan, Ryan; Stoppler, Lance; St. Pierre, Cesare; Surrett, James; Thistle, Scott David; Tomm, Mathew; Thomson, James; Tujik, Peter; Turner, James; Vanryckeghem, Chris Sean; Watson, Melanie (F); Widdifield, Nadine; Williamson, Ronald; Wolff, Michael, Wong, Lori Dawn; Wyville, Allen; Zubkowski, Chris; Thompson, Rhonda L. (F).

VERNON ARMY CADET CAMP
ARMY CADET LEADER COURSE
D COMPANY
08 JULY 91 TO 16 AUG 91
Abram, Callin; Ahlefeld, Crystal Dawn (F); Ainley, Greg; Alvarez, Juan Luis; Aucoin, Bertie; Audette, Daniel Joseph; Baldwin, Emery; Belanger, Phillip John; Benedict, Ryan Dennis; Bezeau, Cory; Bishop, Shawn Micheal; Bleasdale, Kristian; Bornmann, Erik; Bortnick, Lena (F); Bortnick, Terrie L. (F); Bourque, Jeremiah J.; Bowden, Thomas M.; Bray, Jason; Brett, Scott; Brittain, Jamie R.; Brodhagen, Cindy E. (F); Brown, Ryan; Brown, Terry J.; Brown, Malcolm J.; Cann, Michael P.; Castle, Gloria M. (F); Chandra, Mark; Chang, Michael J.; Charney, Jason M.; Charette, Nicole (F); Christians, Terry M.; Church, Harcourt Brian; Clinton, Brandy (F); Colborne, Janet P. (F); Crawford, Jeff W.; Delowski, Cory; Dickson, Christine (F); Dixon, Andrew; Dow, Trueman E.; Downey, Gerry W.; Dufault, Clinton A.; Enequist, Rose (F); English, Anthony Charles; Evans, Patricia (F); Faircloth, Bill; Faundex, Cesar A.; Foley, Susan Allice (F); Ford, Joseph W.; Frazer, Shawn Dewayne; Fulford, Sarah Mary (F); Fulford, Susan R. (F); Gafka, Kerri Ann (F); Galway, Roxanne (F); Gerbrandt, Trevor; Gibb, Robert W.; Gilhooly, Liam; Gillis, Patrick Micheal; Gobin, Brandon; Goodyear, Tammy; Gorak, Tarace Alexander; Grenier, Wilfred Laurent; Grenier, Tyler; Greve, Adam Daniel; Guinet, Wanda (F); Haleem, Reza; Hanna, Ross; Hart, Sheldon; Harrison, Clark Scott;

harvey, Shawn; Herbert, Trevor; Herritt, Ken; Hill, Duncan; Hipwell, Matthew J.; Hobbs, Larry William; Hoffus, Adele L. (F); Hunter, Jason; Irwin, Vaughn R.; Jackson, Russell K.; Jerez, Matilde (F); Johnson, Charles; Johnson, David J.; Johnson, Lee Allan; Johnson, Shane E.; Jones, Dave; Keddie, Kelley; Kenney, John, Kirkby, Kenny; Knoke, Alicia (F); Kolsteren, Shannon M. (F); Koski, Kevin; Kubu, Brian; Labelle, Cora-Lee (F); Lacey, Joshua Samuel; Lafontaine, Shawn; Lane, Toby Ann (F); Lee, Richard A.; Leonard, Sharron L. (F); Lukey, Steve; MacGillivray, Jason; MacKenzie, Jeremy; Martin, Brian; Martin, Robert; Maygot, Merrilee (F); McCormack, Thomas; McCorriston, Jonathon; McDonald, Bonni J. (F); McEachren, Heather (F); McKenna, Kerri (F); McLellan, Peter; Miljour, Chantal (F); Milne, Jake; Mirani, Roag; Moar, Alex Howard; Montgomery, Lance William; Moyen, Angela (F); Moyen, Kevin; Mullett, Wayne; Murray, Darry; Nash, Gordon; Neal, Robert Gordon; Nelson, Marie (F); Norell, Chris Glen; Norman, Linda (F); Novicki, Sherry (F); Nowak, Tisa (F); Ohman, Laurie (F); O'Donnell, Tommy; Opferselt, Lana (F); Pangalia, Johan; Paterno, Richard Joeseph; Patterson, Chantal (F); Pearce, Andrew Evan; Porter, Chris; Putsey, David; Rae, Clayton William; Reschny, Tonya (F); Reynolds, Shane; Rideout, Steven; Robertson, Kent; Robinson, Frank R.; Robinson, Mike; Rosenthal, Ryan; Roy, Martin R.; Ryan, Thomas; Sali, Leah (F); Sali, Taylor J.; Schingler, Josie A. (F); Seymour, Terry-Lee (F); Skillen, James A.; Sissons, Robert G.; Smith, Katrina T. (F); Smith, Marlene (F); Smyk, Jason; Thomson, Angie (F); Thompson, Derek; Toupin, Amy (F); Vandurme, Donald I.; Vince, Andrew G.; Waddell, Anthony; Warner, Leigh W.; Werners, Angel (F); Wisniowski, Bart Mack; Young, Neil H.W.; Zelimer, Jason.

ARMY CADET BASIC COURSE
G COMPANY
22 JULY 91 - 02 AUG 91

Ahlefeld, Byron; Armstrong, Ashley; Armstrong, Tyler; Beaton, Mitzi (F); Biollo, Calvin; Bohemier, Chrissy (F); Buckler, Cindy (F); Cable, Aaron; Callaghan, Matthew; Cantifio, Osvaldo; Chamberlain, Rajan; Church, Jason; Combs, Jason; Cote, Lisa (F); Dalgetty, Ryan; Desrosiers, Dave; Doleman, Jason; Duttenhoffer, Kelly (F); Dziadyk, Russell; English, Patricia (F); Fisher, Bill; Hamilton, Darren; Hancock, David; Hartley, Dave; Haynes, Mike; Heintz, Paul; Heitman, Jennifer (F); Hewett, Mike; Hinson, Bryan; Howe, Mark; Hynes, Catherine (F); Jackson, Jason; Kamel, Zsa Zsa (F); Kelly, Tina (F); Kerr, Jocelyn (F); Kilgare, Crystal (F); Kirstianson, Jason; Knight, Kandice (F); Knight, Vanessa (F); Kudlovich, James; Lamontagne, Ken; Lancashire, Sol; Larade, Jeanette (F); Lario, Jamie; Lauzon, David; Lesniewski, Chris; Lewis, Milo; Liggs, Natasha (F); Loke, Kevin; Lytle, Carla (F); MacDonald, Chris; Madge, Lyle; Martens, Kimberly (F); McIsaac, Josh; McIsaac, Matthew; McKerlie, April Dawn (F); Michaud, Jason; Michel, Gerlad; Mollet, Emily-Amanda (F); Morrisseau, Steven; Moser, Larry; Mostowchuk, Miles; Murray, Shane; Nesbitt, Robert; Nicholson, Clinton; Norris, Andrea (F); O'Connor, Riley; Papps, Melanie (F); Patterson, Steven; Pawlak, Adrian; Peoples, Peter; Phillips, Ryan; Pressey, James; Riddell, Daniel; Roenspies, Scott; Rollo, Chad; Samchek, Mike; Schindelka, Ryan; Schmidt, Jesse; Schuster, Garth; Scmeniuk, Ronnie; Seewald, Adam; Sims, Leonard; Sonneveld, Mark; Spooner, Jason; Sitt, David; Tait, Jesse; Tinga, Levi; Tomei, Tatiana (F); Tully, Kris; Waller, Judith (F); Waller, Mitch; Warnica, Bryce; Weightman, Jason; Whitecross, Shawn; Wiebe, Corla (F); Wilcox, Erik; Williams, Jason; Wolkosky, Joey.

ARMY CADET BASIC COURSE
F COMPANY
22 JULY 91 - 02 AUG 91

Allen, Curtis; Allison, John; Alves, Paul; Anderson, Mike; Bachelu, Neil; Bakke, Jared; Banick, Tyler; Biggar, Guy; Borrill, Brandon;

Borysiak, Adam; Bronson, Chris; Bruce, Ben; Bruce, Graham; Cameron, Kelly (F); Chouinard, Trent; Clark, Paul; Clark, Russell; Constantinoff, Danny; Daniels, Cheryl (F); Daniels, Michelle (F); Danvers, Michael; Desjarlais, Miranda (F); Dionne, Ryan; Dunstan, Benjamin; Elek, Trent; Fraser, Travis; Gardner, Brian; Garling, Matthew; Gray, Jeffrey; Green, Cherie (F); Haluska, Jolene (F); Harper, Brian; Hart, Robert; Hobler, Jason; Hurren, Matt; Hutchings, Tami (F); Jansen, David; Johnson, Dony; Johnson, Lee; Keach, Richard; Klapatiuk, Christopher; Knapp, Averyl (F); Kolinski, David; Kreschok, Kelly; Kuzmicz, Mark; Kwasnycia, Vicki (F); Laqui, Moises; Lauzon, Crysta (F); Leekie, Rachel (F); Lewis, Troy; Litz, Casey; Low, Rene; Maki, John; Matyjanka, Collin; McGowan, Colin; McNabb, Darren; Meister, Jeff; Mills, Nicola (F); Moar, Tracy (F); Moyen, E. (F); Murphy, Jeff; Murtegh, Cameron; Nelson, Terry; Neufeld, Marc; Nixbet, James; Nolan, Robert; Pettigrew, Anna (F); Polson, John; Redl, Grant; Reignier, Chris; Richardson, Nathan; Robinson, Lorne; Robinson, Rhonda (F); Rohrig, Brent; Schmaltz, Ericka (F); Schuitema, Richard; Schwartzenheur, Ryen; Scriven, Shawn; Sendecki, Shawn; Shank, Terry; Shannon, Patrick; Sirack, Mike; Slusaryck, Cameron; Sobchyshyn, Ryan; Soden, Erik; Spaven, Danielle (F); Stajkowski, Jeremy; Stanjek, Laura (F); Starck Jr., Dennis; Stephanson, Wade; Stoll, Lydia (F); Strid, John; Strid, Richard; Tollefson, Robert; Verge, Jolene (F); Waite, Adam; Weber, Charity (F); Wilson, Darryll; Wingert, Jyl (F); Woroschuk, Tammy (F); Wutke, Brad; Wyder, Michael; Zorn, Crystal (F).

NOMINAL ROLL
AS AT 1400 HRS 25 JUN 91

Adams, J.; Barnes, B.; Bayley, L.; Belmont, S.; Bruneau, D.; Burrows, P.; Chan, R.; Cole, R.; Connors, J.; Croze, P.; Crummey, S.; Fisher, J.; Fisher, K.; Fisher, M.; Fortin, P.; Gallant, A.; Goetz, D.; Graham, D.; Gravel, D.; Hardy, R.; Harland, A.; Hayes, L.; Henderson, R.; Homeniuk, E.; Hurtubise, M.; Ingram, L.; John, C.; Jobin, R.; Johnson, H.; Lacey, R.; Larsen, A.; Liggett, J.; Lindsay, K.; Littlemore, K.; MacDonald, J.; MacDonald, R.; MacKenzie, R.; McCoy, C.; McBain, W.; Mangat, J.; Markin, G.; Meehan, J.; Meyer, M.; Meyer, S.; Murray, W.; Neil, M.; Novak, M.; Olsen, F.; Palno, J.; Paul, S.; Peter, J.; Potter, J.; Rettenbacher, V.; Rose, R.; Savard, M.; Scherger, M.; Schooner, C.; Skoda, A.; Smith, P.; Tolmie, J.; Trekofski, M.; Trick, T.; Tyldesley-Gore, E.; Vanwieren, W.; Venn, G.; Wilson, B.; Young, D.; Arnold, K.; Coady, M.; Hawkins, L.; Larochelle, D.; Riseing, E.; Ronberg, M.; Ronberg, M.; Savoie, Y.; Self, N.; Selig, J.; Thomson, S.; Henderson, T.; White, L.; Wiegel, R.; Meyer, K.

NOMINAL ROLL
AS AS 2400 HRS 17 JUN 91

Adams, J.; Bayley, L.; Belmont, S.; Cole, R.; Connors, J.; Croze, P.; Devine, D.; Fisher, K.; Fortin, P.; Goetz, D.; Harland, A.; Hayes, L.; Henderson, R.; Ingram, L.; John, C.; Jobin, R.; Johnson, H.; Lacey, R.; Larson, A.; Littlemore, K.; MacDonald, J.; MacKenzie, R.; McBain, W.; Murray, W.; Neil, M.; Olson, F.; Rettenbacher, V.; Rose, R.; Skoda, A.; Smith, P.; Trekofski, m.; Tyldesley-Gore, E.; Venn, G.; Wright, B.; Young, D.; Chan, R.; Novak, M.; Trick, T.

NOMINAL ROLL
AS OF 2400 HRS 10 JUN 91

Adams, J.; Bayley, L.; Croze, P.; Davies, J.; Fisher, K.; Harland, A.; Hayes, L.; Henderson, R.; Ingram, L.; Instance, M.; Jobin, R.; John, C.; Johnson, H.; Lacey, R.; Larsen, A.; MacDonald, J.; MacKenzie, R.; Murray, W.; Neil, M.; Olsen, F.; Rettenbacher, V.; Rose, R.; Rousseau, D.; Skoda, A.; Tyldesley-Gore, E.; Venn, G.; Wright, B.; Young, D.; Devine, D.; Goetz, D.; Littlemore, K.; Trekofski, M.

VACC - 1992

Aak, Endel; Adamkewicz, Wesley; Adderley, Jeff;
Alguire, Michael; Allan, Cheryl; Allan, Leslie;
Allen, Shawn; Anastasakis, Gus; Armstrong,
Tony; Armstrong, Pat; Attlesey, Coley; Auclair,
Robyn; Augustine, Nola; Baldwin, Erloria;
Baldwin, ERica; Bauer, Shaun; Bayley, Larry;
Beahm, Derek; Becker, Jason; Berg, Gregg;
Biggar, Jamie; Bombay, Lyle; Botterill, Don;
Boucher, Lizane; Boucher, Michelle; Boyko, Fred;
Boytel, Patrick; Brass, Angela; Brennan, Cynthia;
Briand, Soleille; Brookes, Teresa; Broughton,
matt; Brown, Alexander; Bruce-Carter, Moira;
Burrell, Alana; Burridge, Craig; Burrows, Patricia;
Buttnor, Jacqueline; Byrne, Ronan; Cameron, Ian;
Campbell, Darren; Campbell, Grant; Campbell,
Robin; Carritt, Jason; Cawkell, Winston;
Chamberlin, Sasha; Chan, Rick, Charland, Marie;
Chartrawd, Mike; Chase, Robyn; Chow, Bing;
Christensen, Kevin; Clapham, Barbara; Clifford,
Trevor; Colborne, Janet; Colenutt, Geoffrey;
Colliss, Ila; Cooper, Trent; Creaser, Janet; Cripps,
Brenda; Dales, Amber; Danner, Yvette;
Demerchant, Chris; Denis, Lanette; Denness,
Brian; Dobmeier, Sarena; Dominie, Jennifer;
Douaire, Eric; Doyle, Brennan; Du Bourg, Marc;
Dubois, Paul; Dubuc, Carolyn; Duffill, Robert;
Dufresne, Denis; Dunford, Curtis; Dutertre, Les;
Ellenor, Jessica; Elliott, Christopher; Elliott,
Kerrie; Emde, Wayne; Engelbretson, Jason;
Erickson, Brian; Evans, Angelee; Fieldhouse,
Caley; Fiessel, Christopher; Finlayson, Phillip;
Fisher, Kevin; Flett, Sarah; Fone, Edward; Fortin,
Pauline; Francis, Mark; Francis, Michael; Fraser,
Brent; Friesen, Tony; Gafka, Travis; Gallant,
Alvin; Gee, Derrick; Geil, Douglas; Generous,
Donna; Gerow, Chuck; Gibson, Mary; Giles,
Michael; Goulet, Cathy; Graham, Ryan; Gray,
Bethany; Green, Stewart; Greissel, Murray;
Grenier, Louise; Greve, Adam; Grove, Bruce;
Guembes, Luis; Hall, Robert; Hallam, Glen;
Harland, Albert; Hart, Michael; Hasson,   ;
Haughian, Robert; Haughian, Bruce, Hawkins,
Leisa-Ann; Hayes, Lloyd; Head, Dion; Heinrich,
Dawn; Henderson, Ray; Hickey-Somerville, Julia;
Hiscock, Anthony; Holland, Joseph; Hollick,
Kenneth; Homeniuk, Ernest; Horn, Odin; Howard,
Darryl; Hsieh, Eugene; Huisca, Carlos; Humphrey,
Brett; Hunt, Christopher; Hykaway, Charlene;
Ingram, Brenda; Ingram, Lloyd; Irish, Adam;
Jacobs, Peter; Jensen, Jeremy; Jesso, Laetitia;
Jobin, Robert; Johnson, Harry; Johnson, Lyle;
Johnson, Stefan; Johnson, Jason; Johnston, David;
Juma, Hussain; Jyrkkanen, Stacey; Kelley, Jacob;
Kelly, Stephen; Kennedy, Daniel; Kereluke,
Marlon; Kidd, Dave; Kimber, Kenneth;
Kindrachuk, Tracy Lee; Knaap, Kristina; Krause,
Robert; Lacey, Russ; LaPorte, Brian; Larochelle,
Jose; Larsen, A.; Laviolette, Wayne; Leschert,
Erika; Liggett, Paul; Logan, Amber; Logan,
Gerlyn; Lubkiwski, Jeffery; MacKenzie, Richard;
Macko, Christopher; Madigan, Carson; March,
Michelle; Markin, George; Martin, Shawn; Masny,
Melanie; Massicotte, Tammy; Matsalla, Devon;
McAlley, Thomas; McDermid, John; McGinn,
Elan; McGregor, David; McIsaac, Alphonse;
McPhee, Laurie; Meehan, G.; Melanson, Shawn;
Meldrum, Tommy; Mellema, Paul; Menzies,
Richard; Meyer, Mariela; Molenkamp, April;
Morin, Sondra; Morley, Ivan; Morrison, Tammy;
Munday, Dona; Naismith, Colin; Neal, Michael;
Neil, Michael; Nickel, Jason; Noral, Chris;
Northrop, Randy; Novak, Miroslav; Novak,
Richard; O'Malley, Christopher; Obermeyer,
Charleen; Ogima, Ken; Oram, Kelly; Pankratow,
Jason; Parr, Gary; Parrent, Jacqueline; Paterson,
Elizabeth; Patterson, Taydra; Paziuk, Rae; Pearce,
Eric; Pertson, Jason; Peterson, Carrie; Picard,
Michael; Picken, George; Pillikko, Anita; Poirier,
Claude; Polley, Nicholas; Powell, Edward; Pratt,
Robert; Pratt, Robert; Primeau, Genevieve; Rae,
Maureen; Raedere, Walter; Rajotte, Richard; Read,

Michael; Reddy, Govino; Reed, Ryan; Rehill,
Brian; Reschny, Kendra; Rettenbacher, Victor;
Riseing, Ed; Robicheau, Nichalas; Rowsell, Dean;
Roy, Martin; Sadler, William; Seli, Neil; Selig,
Janice; Shelton, Barry; Shirk, Wayne; Simmons,
Karin; Sinha, Richard; Sklepowich, Derek; Smith,
Daniel; Soullier, Romy; Spence, Jennifer; Spiers,
Peter; St. Pierre, Gerald; Stalker, Mason; Stevely,
Grant; Stewart, April; Stewart, Norma; Stockley,
Robert; Stuart, Daniel; Stubbs, Neal; Sturgeon,
Ross; Thomson, Shay; Timmerman, Alisa;
Townsend, Jamie; Trick, Teena; Turgeon.
Catherine; Tutt, Barbara; Tutt, Jennifer; Tyldesley-
Gore, Eric; Vanryckeghem, Karl; Van Stone,
Melvin, Vere, Marc, Waddington, Rob; Warner,
Derrick; Wasylin, Michael; Webber, John;
Webster, RS; Weightman, Tara Ann; West, Dallas;
Whalley, Shannon; Wiley, Linden; Windsor,
David; Winkelaar, Keri Lynn; Wood, Jessica.

BASIC BAND

Bragg, Michael James; Cameron Kelly (F); De
Silva, John Paul; Devin, Sean Paul; Harrington,
Michael W.; Lee, Devon; Lulashnyk, Angele (F);
Mallek, Asaf; McBride, Stephan; McDonald, John
C.; McElrevy, Erin (F); Opaleke, Christiana S. (F);
Passmore, Adrean D.; Quartley, Sean Allan;
Reimer, Benjamin James; Shepherd, Amanda (F);
Silliker, Sarah (F); Smith, Andrew; Stubbs,
Jonathon; Thomson, Lynn (F); Toutant, Chantal
(F); Traenenberg, Ronald; Unwin, Adam; Zesko,
Sandra (F).

ARMY CADET LEADER INSTRUCTOR COURSE

Abram, Callin; Anastasakis, Jim; Bakewell,
Shawn; Bezeau, Cory; Bishop, Andy; Butler,
Mike; Butler, Tammy (F); Carruthers, Charmin
(F); Chambers, Trevor; Chandra, Mark; Chang,
Michael W.; Christian, Hardy; Clarke, Thomas;
Clinton, Brandy (F); Cole, Shawn; Corcoran,
Tanya (F); Cork, Vanessa (F); Cox, Ian Louis;
Crane, Katherine (F); Deschenes, Jean; Dickson,
Christine (F); Drover, Lori (F); Elliott, Kevin;
Fellner, Matt; Fisher, Jonathan; Fortune, Colin;
Fulford, Sarah (F); Gafka, Kerri (F); Harbour,
Michele (F); Hira, Marnie (F); Horan, Ben;
Hourihan, Jeremy; Inman, Kenneth; Johnson,
Tom; Kives, Kory; Kulczycki, Angele Roaland
(F); La Fontaine, Kirk; Lane, Toby (F); Lenton,
David; Liggs, Natasha (F); Luj, Mike; MacDonald,
John; MacDonald, Nathan; Mark, James;
Martinson, Chris; Maslanka, Clinton; McKenna,
Kerri (F); McNab, Lawrence; Milne, Jake; Moline,
Irene (F); Moreira, Karoll (F); Morin, David
Howard; Morris, Christian; Morrow, Shane;
Moyen, Kevin; Munro, Ross; Osler, Donald
Joseph; Pangalia, Sohan; Pearce, Andrew Evan;
Pearson, Chad; Peoples, David; Peterson, Joshua;
Pike, Carla (F); Prokulevich, Nicole (F); Provost,
Nanci (F); Quilty, Marshalina (F); Rae, Clayton;
Reimer, Chris; Rollo, Heather (F); Soundrers,
Ryan; Shanahan, Michael; Schwinghamer, Steve;
Sherburne, Kevin; Sigstad, Glen; Smith, Katrina
(F); Steeves, Christopher; Sweetapple, Caren (F);
Vanryckeghem, Kelly; Wennerstrom, William.

ARMY CADET LEADER INSTRUCTOR COURSE

Ahlefeld, Andy; Ahlefeld, Gary; Ainley, Greg R.;
Allegretoo, Julie (F); Audette, Daniel; Augustine,
Jeremy; Baisky, Dustin; Barter, Colette (F); Bell,
Giselle (F); Benedict, Ryan; Berns, Thomas; Best,
Tanya (F); Blyth, Richard; Bond, Angela (F);
Brohur, James; Castle, Gloria (F); Chaisson,
Colette (F); Cluney, Chris; Cheverie, Danny;
Christians, Terry; Church, Brian; Daeppen, Lucie
(F); Dauphinas, Anthony; Despatis, David; Dube,
Christian; Duguay, Christian; Eckton, Neil; Foley,
Lori Ann (F); Fulford, Susan (F); Gale, Stephanie
(F); George, Nancy (F); Gills, Seumas; Haleem,
Reza; Hammond, Matthew; Hanna, Ross C.; Hart,
Sheldon K.; Hislop-Perraton, Deborah (F);

Hodges, Walter; Koski, Kevin; LeBlanc, Richard E.; Liggs, Merle; Maher, Ryan; Maygut, Merrilee (F); McCrae, Scott; McNeilage, Timothy; Mercredi, Kevin; Miljour, Chantal (F); Morrison, Jason A.; Moyen, Angela (F); Mylonakis, Stella (F); Ogima, Dave; Porter, Chris; Puffer, Shannon (F); Rafuse, Timothy A.; Regier, Andy; Roberts, Tracy (F); Rodier, Yann; Rosenthal, Ryan; Royal, Mark; Samchek, Jennifer (F); Savoie, Monique (F); Schingler, Josy (F); Schofield, Kyle; Seymour, Terry-Lee (F); Smith, Bonnie (F); Stephanik, Jason; St. Coeur, Shawn J.; Surrett, James Chales; Thompson, Derek; Tomm, Matthew; Tremblay, Eric; Vandurme, Don; Vince, Andrew; Walsh, Harry; Waunch, Steve; Wick, Azrael (F); Wilson, Terra (F); Zubkowski, Chris.

ARMY CADET LEADER COURSE
C COMPANY
6 JUL 92 - 14 AUG 92

Allard, Lenny; Arnoth, Geza; Bachelu, Neil; Benedict, Kyla (F); Bohemier, Christiane (F); Boyd, Andrew; Boyce, Brianna (F); Brannstrom, Andrew (F); Bray, Christopher; Broadfoot, Dave; Brown, Denny; Carruthers, Lane; Chenier, Corrie (F); Copeland, David; Copeland, Scott; Cosman, Christina (F); Cuffe, Mandy-Lynn Marie (F); Cuthbertson, Donald; Degrey, Stuart; Dodds, Patrick; Farmer, Christopher; Ferdinand, Thomas; Fisher, William; Fletcher, Jon-Rae; Fournier, Brian; Fraser-Easton, Adam, Craig; Friesen, Ellery; Fromm, Andrew; Geekie, Clayton; Getten, Dwayne; Goodrich, Lindsey (F); Graham, Tom; Guenther, Kevin; Hall, Jason; Hamm, Jacob; Harrower, John; Hawkes, Garth; Meigh, Amanda (F); Hermary, Jerimy; Heward, Jason; Hilton, Crystal (F); Jackson, Jason; Jarnovin, Joseph L.; Jarvis, Kerriann (F); Jobin, Rheal; Johnson, Thomas; Karasevich, Raymond; Kerr, Jocelyn (F); Klages, Chris; Klapatiuk, Kevin; Kroetsch, Kristian (M); LaFleur, Gilles; Kusznier, Claude; Law, Eugene; Lebel, Shane; L'eheureux, Calvin; Lewis, Troy; Lloyd, Jarrett; Low, Rene; Lyons, Chris; Maure, Gordon; McClure, Angela (F); McCoshan, Mike; McGowan, Colin; McIsaac, Josh; Metamczuk, Drew; Miljour, Jacqueline (F); Miller, Angela (F); Mills, Terri (F); Mitchell, Gary; Moore, Neil; Mrowiec, Lena (F); Murray, Amy (F); Myshyniuk, Layne (F); Nelson, Terry; Nolan, Robbie; O'Conner, Riley M.J.; Peoples, Peter; Piton, Jimmy; Proctor, Darin; Rapsha, Jon; Rienks, Terry; Rollo, Chad; Samchek, Micheal; Schofield, Tim; Schuitema, Richard; Sendecki, Shawn; Skok, Jennifer (F); Sonneveld, Mark; Stajkowski, Jeremy; St John, Brian; Strid, John; Strid, Richard; Sturt, Tanya (F); Thompson, Derek; Thwaites, Jennifer (F); Tinga, Levi; Torres, Kris; Twardy, Karen (F); Welton, Malcolm (Harry); Willoughby, Chad; Yellowknee, Dwayne.

ARMY CADET LEADER COURSE
D COMPANY
6 JUL 92 - 14 AUG 92

Anderson, Natasha (F); Armstrong, Tyler; Bader, Travis; Barnes, Gary; Beam, Heather (F); Bertrand, Tina (F); Biden, Tab; Brennan, Jim; Callaghan, Matthew; Challoner, Trevor; Cehnier, Steven; Claybrook, Alice (F); Cripps, Shaun W.; Crooker, Russell; Dabrowicz, Marivsz; Darrow, Lee; Demchuk, Jenny (F); Duarte, Michael; Dufour, Dominique (F); Eley, Steve; Evans, Mitch; Fiddler, Doug; Fox, Vicki (F); Freve, Rodney; Garceau, Krista (F); Garling, Matthew; Grills, Ryan S.; Hagen, William; Hahn, Ryan; Hegedus, Lindsay (F); Heitman, Jennifer (F); Hewitt, Micheal; Horan, Christopher; Howatt, Jason; Hughes, Becky (F); Hunter, Justin; Kaludjer, Bram; Kalynuk, Colin; Kamel, Zsa Zsa (F); Keating, Ryan; Kezar, Tina (F); Kidd, Trevor; Kolisnyk, Micheal; Laird, Janine (F); Lammers, Michelle (F); Langridge, Stuart; LaPointe, Dominique; Larose, April (F); Lawhead, Eddie; Lawrence, D'arci S. (F); Litz, Casey D.; Lohman, Sheldon W.; MacDonald, Chris G.; MacLean, Alex; Maitland, Lorne (Ted); Marcq, David; Matyjanka, Collin; McKee, Steven; McMaster, Steven; McNabb, Darin; Michaud, Jason; Moser, Larry; Nagam, Darcy; Nepinak, Dwayne; Nichol,

Debra (F); Nystedt, Jason; Ostrosser, Amy (F); Parks, Christopher; Pearce, Tricia (F); Pettigrew, Anna (F); Pohjolainen, James; Potyra, Nick; Poulson, Jon; Pressey, James; Richter, Kurt; Riddell, Danny; Robinson, Travis; Rondeau, Chad; Squarebriggs, Marc; Szabla, Arthur; Todd, Ryan; Tollefson, Robert; Tomei, Tatiana (F); Turel, Rocky; Turney, Bryan; Wiebe, Corla J.; Williamson, Reginald R.; Wilson, Chris; Wilson, Corinne G.; Winders, Jefferey; Wolkosky, Joey; Yellowega, Vincent; Yorkston, Michael; Zerebeski, Richard; Zimrose, Troy.

ARMY CADET LEADER COURSE
E COMPANY
6 JULY 92 - 14 AUG 92

Anderson, Jason; Armstrong, Ashley; Baldwin, Emery; Blake, Steven; Beaton, Mitzi (F); Bronson, Chris; Bucknell, Joey; Calvert, Tom; Carey, Darren; Carey, Janine Lorilie (F); Chang, Richard; Channell, Alan; Clark, Paul Adam; Cline, Robert D.; Coisne, Douglas; Chailler, Germaine (F); Childs, Curtis; Claridge, Serena K.; Corbett, Nicolle (F); Dalgetty, Ryan; Davis, Marsha (F); Dayal, Kamlesh; Dewson, Scott; Doleman, Chris; Dudley, Erin K. (F); Dunn, Kyle P.; Dunstan, Benjamin; Finter, Clifford; Fisher, Carrie (F); Fordman, Cory; Gaffney, Peter; Godbout, Fannie (F); Gosnell, Mella (F); Hart, Robert; Henschei, Joseph; Jerrett, James Benjamin; Johnson, Donald; Johnston, James; Kemball, Greg; Kerr, Graeme; Kirkhope, Barry; Klapatiuk, Eric; Kilinski, David; Lancashire, Sol; Larose, Yves; Lecuyer, Claire (F); Leighton, Scott; Livingston, Kellie (F); MacKenzie, Jeremy A.; McDonald, Robert; McFadyen, Patricia (F); Materi, Blayne; Meister, Adriene; Miele, Carl; Mobey, Jessy; Murtagh, Cameron; Nesbitt, Robert; Neufeld, Marc; Nolan, Patrick; Noonan, Tanya (F); O'Mahony, Simon David; Papps, Melanie (F); Pinnell, Fiona (F); Plewes, Richard; Proctor, Jason; Quincey, Carrie (F); Regnier, Chris; Rhodes, Faith (F); Robinson, Rhonda (F); Rohrig, Brent; Rouse, Barry; Rumball, Jordin; Sacco, Adam; Savoie, Daniel; Schartner, David; Seguin, Julie (F); Semeniuk, Ronald J.; Sevigny, Luc; Shank, Terry; Simpson, Jenny L.; Trahan, Maxime; Turner, Cindy (F); Van Eck, Daniel A.; Waller, Mitchell; Walker, Natalie Elizabeth; Weaver, Adam; Welty, Calvin; Wenger, Sean; Wilcox, Eric; Wilson, Lance; Wutke, Bradly Donald; Young, Jason; Zimmerman, Shawn.

ARMY CADET LEADER COURSE
F COMPANY
6 JUL 92 - 14 AUG 92

Airth, Clayton; Alves, Paul; Anderson, Frank; Arnot, Josh; Bakke, Jared Wade; Ballard, Michael; Banick, Tyler; Berg, Amanda (F); Biggar, Guy; Borho, Jeremy; Brainere, Jon; Brown, Wendy (F); Buckler, Cindy C. (F); Cahoon, Danny; Champagne, Trevor S.; Church, Jason; Cruickshank, Scott; Comerford, Sean; Crush, Kevin; Deleurme, Rachelle (F); Dufault, Patrick E.; Duttenhoffer, Kelly (F); Emmett, Brendon; English, Patricia (F); Fidler, Tyler; Flevelling, Dan; Fralic, Matthew; Gillingwater, Jamie; Gladue, Gary; Grenier, Wilfrid; Griffiths, Morgan; Gulliver, Lisa (F); Hammer, Mike; Hoffman, Katie (F); Hovey, Ryan M.; Hutchings, Tami L. (F); Irwin, Wayne; Jackson, Matthew; Keddie, Kelly; Keeler, Derrick; Kennedy, Damon; Kirk, Cory; Knapp, Averyl (F); Knight, Vanessa (F); Kubu, Mike; Kubrak, Michael; Lamontagne, Ken; Larade, Jeanette (F); Levesque, Neill; Madge, Lyle Scott; Mannix, William; Martell, Rachel (F); Martell, Rebecca (F); Martens, Kim (F); Maure, Jacques; McCloy, Trevor J.; McMurtrie, Steven; Milner, Danny; Morin, Willy; Morton, James; Olsen, Tyler; Paschke, Brian; Pawluik, Matthew; Price, Jackie (F); Rastad, Yvonne (F); Redel, Chris J.; Reimer, Ryan; Renaud, Kyle; Reviczky, Josh; Rickovic, Sandra (F); Ringuette, Rob; Royle, Kristine (F); Sanocki, Luke P.; Schmidt, Jesse; Semenuik, Richard; Sikasak, Lenethong; Sinclair, Che; Smith, Jerry; Smyk, Michael; Storms, Michael, Joseph; Tait, Jesse; Todoroff, Mike; Volcz, Peter; Waller, Judith (F); Walsh, Peter;

598

Watson, Melanie (F); Watson, Rayna (F); Weightman, Jason; Wilson, Darryl D.; Wood, Brent E.; Yeremiy, Jason J.; Young, Skylar.

ARMY BASIC CADET COURSE
G COMPANY
20 JUL 92 - 31 JUL 92
Aguilar, Wiley; Awasis, Crystal (F); Axani, Christian; Barry, Allen; Beauchamp, Raymond; Blais, Rob; Blumhagen, William; Brandt, Trevor; Brass, Larry; Brennan, Justin; Brown, Kelsie; Bujan, Travis; Burrell, Derek; Cambell, Gina (F); Campeau, David S.; Challoner, Jason; Champagne, Belinda Lee (F); Chanbrinho, Frank R.; Chang, Danny; Charette, Roberta (F); Colen, Scott; Collins, John; Cross, Wonetta (F); Deacon, Mike; Dengler, Jackie (F); Dion, Debera N. (F); Dow, Tanya (F); Elliott, Dan; Ellison, Elizabeth (F); Faubert, Adam J.; Ferguson, Livia (F); Follis, Kane; Germain, Casey; Goulet, Joseph; Haleem, Razi; Haverstock, Matthew; Hayford, Lee E.; Heimbecker, Brad; Hemmingway, Michael; Henry, Gaylene (F); Hoefling, Darcy; Hunter, Ryan; Jacobs, David; Kearney, Camon; Kerr, Danial D.; Kidney, Windy (F); Kingsenamongkhol, Moy; Kirk, Eric; Kozmaniuk, Jessice (F); Larose, Tyrel; Lazorko, Charity (F); Lenio, Peter; Linxs, Matt; Leyen, Chad; Lucuk, Rhonda (F); Lucyk, Daniel; Mannix, Diane (F); Martin, Elwood; Matthews, Ryan; McCaw, Kyle; McClean, Colin; McMahon, John; Menz, Terry; Miller, John; Miotto, Geoff; Mobey, Amanda (F); Moore, Dale; Morlin, Jason; Nolette, Tanya (F); Opaleke, Dele; Ortanez, Mark L.; Ovalle, Shawn; Philippot, Andrea (F); Picco, Anne Marie (F); Pilon, Shannon (F); Puffer, Kari (F); Rankin, Christon; Reid, David; Robinson, Tyler; Rolston, Kenny; Scheller, Brent; Soczynski, Mike; Stadnyk, Natasha (F); Staven, Chris; Stewart, Jeremy Patrick; Strathdee, Sheri (F); Thompson, Joseph; Tibbett, Sabrina (F); Tomashiro, Mike; Vandenbrink, John C.; Violante, Tony M.; Wakefield, Chris W.; Watson, Denny; Weiss, Allison (F); Wells, Amanda (F); Wentz, Mark; Wilson, Delvin; York, Derek.

VERNON ARMY CADET CAMP
ARMY BASIC CADET COURSE
G COMPANY
6 JUL 92 - 17 JUL 92
Anderberg, Dan; Balcom, Erik; Barter, Dale; Beairsto, Ian J.; Beairsto, Keri Dawn (F); Beairsto, Melissa (F); Beaudoin, Wayne; Beck, Ken; Belanger, Lawrence M.; Berns, Stephen; Bjordal, Jason M.; Blakley, Jodie; Bornmann, Roy; Bouchard, Allan; Bourassa, John E.; Bromley, Sean; Burr, Brad; Cameron, Raymond P.; Carriere, Chad; Chadsey, Bill; Chandler, Brian; Copeland, Gordon; Courtoreille, Adam; Cross, Clayton; Cruickshank, James; Cullum, Andrew; Curtis, Angela (F); Daley, Isiah; Daw, Wade; Dixon, Jamie; Dodgson, Danny A.; Elliott, Robert G.; Emmett, Daniel; Fei, Ritchie; Fisher, Trevor; Fleming, Clint; Fleming, Shawna (F); Foster, Aaron; Germain, Dwayne; Gibson, Tana (F); Gigliotti, Ryan M.; Gillan, Steven; Glinski, Tom Peter; Goodrich, Carol (F); Greanya, Tina (F); Hackworthy, Regan Dale; Hamnett, Sean; Heemeryck, Christopher G.; Heimbechner, Tanya L. (F); Herzog, Alayne (F); Hildebrand, Kevin; Huck, Cliff; Hudak, David; Hughes, Timothy; Jack, Amber (F); Johnston, Josh V.; Jones, Ryan K.; Jurasek, Chris; Lalande, Lyne (F); Lange, Kylie (F); Levatte, Nicolas; Little, Taryn B. (F); Lumley, Tyler; Luron, Jeff; Lyndgren, Troy; Lystang, Shane; Macleod, Tarra (F); McClelland, Morris; McClure, Rhea (F); McLaughlin, Sheldon; Mesner, Christopher; Miller, Chad; Mills, Peter; Mitchell, Ted; Moore, Curtis; Noritz, Kirstin N. (F); Morrison, Alexandra (F); Nickerson, Billi-Jo (F); Novak, Kristy (F); Opperman, Jason; Philipp, Andrea (F); Philipp, Stephanie (F); Pierce, James; Pinnock, Michael; Plamondom, Justin; Plouffe, Micheal; Powell, Ryan; Radcliffe, Cory; Randolf, Robert; Rawluk, Ryan J.; Razzo, Cliff; Reid, Sean; Reiss, Joshua W.; Reynolds, Norman J.; Richard, Eric D.; Rochon, Terry; Rodzinski, Ryan W.; Rutledge, Ben; Sachatsky, Angie C. (F); Saffin,

Edward; Sali, Bryan E.; Schenkeveld, Sonja (F); Schmidt, Monty; Schneider, Shawna (F); Seabrook, Jennifer M. (F); Shaw, Stephanie (F); Smith, Amber (F); Tablason, John C.; Thomson, Jeffrey; Trautman, Michael; Tworek, Neil A.; Ulinder, Jon; Vailas, Angelle (F); Wallace, Sarah (F); Ward, Candace (F); Waughtal, Glen; Wilson, Sabrina (F); Woudstra, Sharon (F); Wyntjes, Rhett B.; Yurchyshun, Burton.

ARMY BASIC CADET COURSE
H COMPANY
6 JUL 92 - 17 JUL 92
Amrud, Steve; Anderson, Tevor; Bateman, Devin; Batsch, Michael; Beaulieu, April (F); Benoit, Travis; Bernier, Tanya (F); Bilawchuk, Aaron; Bindas, Remi; Blind, Chad; Blum, Brandy (F); Bolton, Leonard; Bosma, Daniel; Brauner, Teresa (F); Breton, Sonny; Broccolo, Russell; Brodt, Curtis; Button, Lea (F); Carleton, Derrick; Cloutier, Graham; Cote, Vince; Desjarlais, Stacy (F); Desmeules, Tanya (F); Donnelly, Jason; Dube, Carl; Duguay, Caroline (F); Ebel, Colin; Eley, Jamie; Ewen, Amanda (F); Fehr, Erin (F); Flannigan, Geri (F); Gagne, Allan; Germain, Trevor; German, David; Gordon, Terri (F); Graham, Jaime (F); Grant, Josh; Gray, Andrew; Grenier, Kyle; Griffiths, Cody; Guldie, Daniel; Hachey, Jeremy; Homes, Adam; Harding, David; Hesse, Alexander; Hiibner, Derrick; Hildebrandt, Crystaline (F); Hoover, Tim; Huber, Jamie; Johnson, Brian; Johnson, Chris; Johnson, Susan-Rae (F); Johnston, Spencer; Kaglea, Ryan; Klassen, Melanie (F); Krause, Brad; Kudras, Michael; Lapoint, Harlan; Larose, Thomas; Lavallee, Katherine (F); Lawhead, Jeff; Loke, Jason; Losee, Cathy (F); McDonald, Dean; McDonald, David; McKenna, Nicki (F); McRae, Tanya (F); Margiotta, Marina (F); Martin, Robert; Miskolczi, Jason; Moore, Liegh; Moss, Neal; Muise, Joey; Murata, Warren; Myers, Chris; Nicholson, Devin; Nichols, Ryan; Numada, Jonathon; Oakes, David; Pahtayken, Derek; Patching, Jesse; Pearce, Tessa (F); Perry, Phil; Peters, Jason; Pfeifer, Miranda (F); Pharis, Shep; Ricklefs, Elizabeth (F); Quince, Colin; Robinson, Philip; Rogoza, David; Ross, Theran; Rumancik, Douglas; Schindelka, Jason; Sikorski, Kristopher; Southwind, Kenward; Smockum, Edwin; St. Hilaire, Nicole (F); Thompson, Matthew; Vandersluis, Curtis; Van der Zander, Peter; Vince, Anthony; Wade, Michael; Waffle, Marvin; Wattan, Susie (F); Wiebe, Derrick; Weinschenck, Olaf; Winders, Jeremy; Woolhether, Teresa (F); Zradicka, Stephen.

ARMY BASIC CADET COURSE
H COMPANY
20 JULY 92 - 31 JUL 92
Abraham, Sheila (F); Bacho, Jayson; Bacon, Corey; Baker, Dominic; Baker, Terry; Bayly, Curt; Beaudry, Aaron; Beaudry, Ian; Bell, Luke; Benner, Paul; Bergeron, Andrea (F); Biggar, Taylor; Braun, Laurie (F); Brautigam, Christine (F); Brosinsky, Clayton; Brown, Ryan; Brugge, Adrian; Burke, Ryan; Carr, Courtney (F); Coulter, Michael; Dahl, Amanda (F); Dart, Christopher; Davis, Brad; Davis, Wesley; Delaney, Archie; Dewitt, Bruce; Dobrowski, Derrick; Dong, Quynh; Dumouchel, Yvette (F); Dushynski, Mark; Eilers, Jonathon; Ellam, Drew; Fund, Kevin; Gerow, Michelle Ann (F); Greer, David; Grimm, Charles; Gosnell, Dory (F); Guballa, David; Hamilton, Mark; Hermanson, Vanessa (F); Jackson, Bonnie (F); Jurasek, Terry; Kitto, Dan; Knoll, Brad; Lake, Matthew; Lazorko, Misty (F); Lee, Katie (F); Lightfoot, Shawn; Livingston, Ken; Madson, Chrissy (F); Mahood, Corrina (F); Martin, Ryan; Metcalfe, Andrew; Mathieson, Laura (F); May, Jeff; Millar, Ian; Morgan, Donald; Morrison, Trevor; Murray, Kimberly (F); McCullagh, Shayne; McDonald, Tyler; McGillis, Karen (F); McGregor, Ian; McInnes, Patrick; McKay, Martin; McKenzie, Rick; McPhee, Tristan; Nichol, William; Niessen, Michael; Niklas, Renee (F); Olsen, Neil; Papadopoulos, Jason; Pearson, Joanna (F); Petryshyn, Donovan; Pratt, Calvin; Richards, Donnie; Richardson, Elizabeth (F); Rowell, Adam;

Rowell, John; Scherr, Andrew; Sanderson, Cheryl (F); Sanderson, Cindy (F); Santos, Michael; Schroedter, Tracy (F); Sinasac, Mark; Speed, Daniyel; Stark, Andrew; Surgeson, Clayton; Thibodeau, Terry; Thomas, Sajiev; Tildsley, Darren; Tornyi, Joseph; Turner, Deanna (F); Traenenberg, Joey; Vincent, Holden; Weber, Walter; Whyte, Lori (F); Willerton, Troy.

ARMY BASIC CADET COURSE
H COMPANY
3 AUG 92 - 14 AUG 92
3RD INTAKE
Acompanaeo, Gene Rose; Anderson, Naomi (F); Baldeo, Gary; Ball, Jared; Bard, Jentina (F); Barnett, Cody; Barns, Shane; Baumann, Kevin; Bergman, Eric; Blocksidge, Todd Robert; Bohemier, Tiana (F); Boswell, Alline (F); Boutilier, Mike; Braun, Chad A.; Braun, Travis; Brock, Colin S.; Broere, Matt; Brooks, McKenzie (F); Carlson, Kyla (F); Christensen, Dara (F); Cockwill, Mark; Cox, Anna (F); Day, Daxton; Drinkwater, Tracy (F); Dyck, Brad; Feissel, James; Foran, Jay; Ford, Bryan; Frocklage, Clint; Galarneau, Ryan; Gauthier, Natalie (F); Gray, Cristie (F); Groome, James; Halcrow, Steven; Harden, Christina (F); Hansen, Kurt; Hanley, Eric; Hannah, David; Hansen, Cal; Hayes, Sauvol; Henry, Brett; Hlady, Kathy (F); Hope, Paul; Hope, Stewart; Huebschwerlen, Rory R.; Hutcheson, Patrick; Kalpatiuk, Allen; Kelm, Brita (F); La Greca, Nadine (F); Lane, Jason; Leicht, Jan; Lemky, Shane; Leonard, Kristy (F); Levitt, Shaun; Lima, Kirk; Lissimore, Travis; Loiselle, Nathan; Lowe, Darren; Lueke, Cindy (F); Lynem, John; Macadams, Shawn; Maleschuk, Ellys; Martin, Chris; Martin, Greg; Mason, Tara (F); Meakin, Brandy (F); Melnyk, Jamie; Morgan, Tamara (F); Morin, Glair; Morin, Eddy; Murphy, Tanya (F); Nesbitt, David; Newell, Eddie; Nicolet, Genevieve (F); Noy, Shannon (F); Oliver, Chris; Oostenbrug, John; Palmer, Colleen (F); Palmer, Christina (F); Patenaude, Leon; Perras, Krista (F); Peters, Robin; Plamondon, Kelly (F); Poier, Shelly (F); Portier, Lee-Anne (F); Powlowski, Justin; Pudlo, Jason; Radcliffe, James; Renton, Chris (F); Ricklefs, Sheri (F); Robbins, Sheldon M.; Robertson, Doug J.; Rogers, Casey; Rolle, Megan (F); Scales, Mellany (F); Schuitema, Cheryl (F); Seymour, Kenneth; Silva, Graham; Sinclair, Dallas; Smart, Chad; St. Amand, Lucy (F); Strandquist, Mike; Stringer, Cameron; Study, Chris; Sylvain, Roger; Tenveen, Danny; Townsend, Kevin; Turcotte, Lise (F); Ulrich, Karen (F); Vale, Daniel; Watson, Tyler; Westhauer, Michael; Whitehead, Eli; Zaplachinski, Darcy; Zaplachinski, Jason.

ARMY CADET RIFLE INSTRUCTORS COURSE
30 INDEPENDENT PLATOON
6 JUL 92 - 14 AUG 92
Allegretto, ; Andres, Nathan D.; Armstrong, Chad R.; Baldwin, Danielle D. (F); Blyth, ; Boucher, Curtis; Brown, Carol N. (F); Callaghan, Keri Ann (F); Carberry, Michael G.; Church, ; Cleary, Brennan J.; Clifford, ; Cox, Christopher F.; Dobson, Christopher A.; Dunlop, James Evans, Erin G. (F); Gessner, Tracey Lee (F); Hoffus, Adele (F); Jackson, Tyson Wayne; Kenneoy, Cindy Jay (F); Kivi, Tammy (F); Knoke, Alicia Dawn (F); Kolsteren, Shannon Marie (F); McLellan, Peter John; Maetche, Christopher; Mead, Travis Robert; Merrick, Daniel; Mitchell, Arlene Mary (F); Muranetz, John; Murphy, Margeret (F); Raymond, Jaymie (F); Redmond, Joseph R.; Rumpel, Philip C.; Russell, William R.; Sanford, Darryl D. RTU'D; Scherger, Deanna M. (F); Smith, Chris M. RTU'D; Smith, Keith R.; Sylvester, Claresa V. (F); Tanaka, Jazmyn (F); Trimble, Ryan; Ursulan, Keith; Walsh ; Zerbeski, Jeff J.

ARMY CADET LEADER INSTRUCTOR BAND COURSE
ARMY CADET LEADER BAND COURSE
ARMY CADET BASIC BAND COURS 93
WKS0
BAND COMPANY
6 JUL 92 - 14 AUG 92

Anderson, Jennifer (F); Anderson Lynne Marie (F); Baragar, Nathan; Bedard, Jacob; Bell, Christopher; Bothwick, Daniel; Bowie, Robert; Brassard, Timothy; Brown, Gerard; Bruce, Graham; Bundy, Noel; Cadotte, Ryan; Chor, Lisa (F); Crawford, Jeffrey; Delyea, Ann (F); Derosa, Jason; Devins, James; Dionne, Ryan; Drinkwater, Jody; Eiriksson, Jesse; Erickson, Allan; Flowers, Paul; Grainger, Samantha (F); Hastie, Candace (F); Hesser, Roy; Heugh, Brad; Holloway, Jeffrey; Howells, David; Humphrey, Farrah (F); Jeffares, Mark; Kardynal, David; King, Stephanie (F); Kiriakidis, George; Kolisnyk, Vincent; Kudlovich, James; Lauzon, Crysta (F); Lauzon, David; Lawson, Kim (F); Nelson, Sonja (F); McBride, Andrew R.; McCrae, Lisa (F); McIssac, Matthew; McLaren, David; Mills, Michelle (F); Morse, Landon; Morse, Sean (F); Musial, Martin; Pruden, Roxanne (F); Ross, Douglas; Salmon, Maureen (F); Salter, Glenda (F); Smith, Allison (F); Stephan, Ryan; Thornhill, Toby Elizabeth (F); Tritz, Daniel; Turcott, Gregory; Turner, Jay Thor; Turner, Kevin; Whitford, Terrance; Wickens, Bruce; Wong, Marco; Wyness, Twila (F); Young, Stuart; Anderson, Angie L. (F); Bigler, David; Bland, Jodi (F); Bland, Nicole E. (F); Bond, Frank; Bouteiller, Lana (F); Briggs, Alastair; Cadotte, Collin; Carlson, Jefferey; Carritt, Gina (F); Childs, Cheryl (F); Copeland, Christopher; Demmon, Clay; Dunn, Kenneth; Dunn, Skylene (F); Eiriksson, Darren; Elliott, Jeremy; Fermaniuk, April (F); Gibb, Billie-Jo (F); Hancock, David; Harris, Peter; Heal, Rachel (F); Johnson, Caylee (F); Knott, David; Lapsley, Justice; MacMain, Alexander; Marlow, Andrea (F); Marlow, Lisa (F); MacConnell, Kim (F); McPhee, Eliscia (F); Meldrum, Candace (F); Miller, Regan (F); Pantayken, Debra (F); Proctor, Blaine; Robinson, Brandon; Sabo, Lucas; Sigstad, Wade; Simard, Misty (F); Stuart, Jamie; Sundin, Dustin; Toulouse, Jason; Trotter, Clifford; Turcott, Dwight; Turcott, Melvin; Vereecken, Lars.

VACC - 1993

OFFICERS AND NCD'S – 1993
Aak, E.; Adair, P.; Adams, R.D.; Adams, R.T.; Allan, L.; Armstrong, H.; Aymont, R.; Barter, J.; Beckett, L.; Bilous, V.; Blain, D.; Blois, M.; Boucher, L.; Brookes, T.; Brown, R.; Burgoyne, D.; Byrne, R.; Cawkell, W.; Chase, R.; Chorazy, A.; Cluff, P.; Colman, P.; Cree, J.; Cummins, W.; D'Arcy, S.; Davies, J.; Delong, O.; Devine, D.; Devonshire, E.; Dominie, J.; Donley, S.; Duazo, T.; Dufresne, C.; Dufresne, D.; Dunphy, P.; Emde, W.; Fone, E.; Fraser, K.; Gamblin, V.; Gans, A.; Gee, D.; Generous, D.; Giannetta, V.; Girard, C.; Glover, P.; Goyetche, D.; Green, S.; Harland, A.; Harrison, L.; Harth, G.; Haughian, B.; Haughian, R.; Hawkins, L.; Hayes, L.; Hayter, S.; Head, N.; Henderson, R.; Henderson, T.; Heinrich, D.; Hickey-Somerville; Hildebrandt, L.; Hiscock, A.; Holland, J.; Hutchinson, C.; Inskip, K.; Jalonen, M.; Jardine, M.; Jobin, R.; Johnson, H.; Johnson, L.; Kantola, J.; Kearsey, K.; Kelly, P.; Kindrachuk, T.; Kiecker, B.; Lacey, R.; Lamothe, S.; Lacroix, M.; Langtry, J.; Larsen, A.; Macaulay, K.; MacKenzie, R.; Marsh, A.; Marshall, R.; Martin, C.; McDermid, I.; McIsaac, A.; McLaughlin, J.; McOnie, J.; McPhee, L.; Mavin, G.; Meehan, G.; Meikle, D.; Munday, D.; Nangle, W.; Neuls, H.; Novak, K.; Pangalia, D.; Pangalia, S.; Paradis, A.; Penney, M.; Penny, M.; Pertson, J.; Peterson, T.; Picard, M.; Picken, G.; Poirier, M.; Pratt, R.; Prothero-Brooks; Rajotte, R.; Reddy, G.; Redekopp, D.; Reed, R.; Roberts, C.; Rodger, D.; Ross, S.; Ryder, G.; Sadler, W.; Samplonius, M.; Schick, C.; Schooner, C.; Simmons, K.; Sly, G.; Smith, C.; Spicer, S.; Stevenson, T.; Stewart, N.; Thomson, S.; Trerice, D.; Treuer, I.; Trick, T.; Tyldesley-Gore; Venn, G.; Vey, D.; West, D.; Westover, C.; Wilding, J.; Wood, E.

NOMINAL LIST OF STAFF CADETS
Abril, Carlos; Ans, Kevin; Attlesey, Colby; Augustine, Jeremy; Ayers, Jeremy; Bahry-Abbott,

PUBLISHER'S ERRATUM

Top of page 82, please insert-
...maintain interest. "It means that..."

Top of page 89, please insert-
...her age, but she was a great piano teacher. Particularly when she hit high 'C.'"

Top of page 353, please insert-
...About thirty yards away, James noticed *all* other Alpha cadets were...

Top of page 356, please insert-
...the best lecture I've ever heard you give. But let me ask you a question. How...

Top of page 363, please insert-
...times we all have some growing up to do. Survival at Vernon is only achieved...

Top of page 369, please insert-
...Although Glenemma is a hard place to leave, hot showers and the culture of...

Theresa; Bartlett, Bryan; Bell, Giselle; Bennett, James; Berg, Amanda; Berns, Thomas; Bieganek, S.D.; Biggar, Janie; Bigler, Chris; Boden, Curtis; Bornann, Erik; Borthwick, Daniel; Boucher, Curtis; Brohm, James; Broughton, Matt; Buechler, Wayne; Burleigh, Jason; Burrell, Alana; Burridge, Craig; Butler, James; Cameron, John; Campbell, Darren; Chapman, Brad; Cheverie, Danny; Christian, Terry; Church, Harcout; Clapham, Barb; Clemens, Chris; Clifford, Kevin; Cloney, Chris; Colborne, Janet; Colliss, Ila; Cote, Tony; Crawford, Jeff; Creaser, Janet; Dales, Amber; Denis, Lanette; Dickson, Amy; Dixon, Christopher; Drover, Lisa; Dutertre, Les; Earle, Chris; Earle, Lisa; Ellenor, Jessica; Enequist, Rosemarie; Erickson, Brian; Evans, Angelee; Evans, Erin; Fenwick, Mary; Fieldhouse, Caley; Finlayson, Philip; Flett, Sarah; Fleury, Kevin; Flowers, Luke; Fraser, Brent; Fulford, Susan; Gaetz, April; Giles, Micheal; Goss, Alan; Greve, Adam; Hadley, Tamara; Hamming, Bryce; Hart, Micheal; Hay, Shawn; Helzer, David; Hira, Mamie; Horan, Benjamin; Howard, Darryl; Howells, David; Hsieh, Eugene; Huisca, Carlos; Irish, Adam; Jackson, Christopher; Jobin, Jacqueline; Johnson, Aaron; Johnston, James; Kaludjer, Bram; Keller, Bernie; Kennedy, Cindy; Kiriakidis, George; Kives, Kory; Kozloski, Trina; Kristjanson, Jon; Lane, Barry; Lawrence, Jamie; Lenton, David; Leschert, Erika; Logan, Amber; Logan, Gerlyn; Lubkiwski, Jeffery; MacDonald, David; Maher, Ryan; Malanowski, Jaroslaw; Marchant, Christopher; Marlow, Lisa; Marshall, Bree; Mason, Jim; Mathews, Melissa; McDermid, Jon; Melanson, Shawn; Merrick, Dan; Middleton, Cam; Morrow, Shane; Moyen, Kevin; Muranetz, John; Murray, Anoreena; Murray, Darcy; Neal, Micheal; Neuneyer, James; Newton, Christopher; Ogden, Jessica; Olive, Todo; Opfergelt, Lana; Parkinson, Jonathan; Paterson, Faydra; Pavia, Andrea; Pavia, Robynn; Paziuk, Rae; Pelan, Danielle; Pelan, Dionne; Perrault, Kevin; Perry, Jonathan; Porter, Jason; Prokulevich, Nicole; Reimer, Chris; Rein, Corey; Reschny, Kendra; Rickard, Matthew; Rowsell, Dean; Russell, Ken; Schofield. Kyle: Shoults. Doullas; Smith, Keith Smith, Todd; Stubbs, Neal; Sullivan, Vinessa; Surgeson, Cory; Sylvester, Claresa; Talbot, Thomas; Thompson, Derek; Thorpe, Kyle; Townley, Timothy; Turgeon, Catherine; Turner, James; Turney, Bryan; Van Berkel, Roswitha; Van Ryckeghem, Chris; Vanasse, Marie; Vandurne, Don; Vere, Marc; Villeneuve, Ashley; Wallace, Susanne; Walters, Christine; Wasyliw, Amie; Waughtal, Jennifer; Whitney, Robert; Widdifield, Nadine; Winkelaar, Keri; Wisniowski, Bartosz; Yanash, James.

ARMY CADET LEADER INSTRUCTOR – DRILL & CEREMONIAL
A COY
12 JUL 93 - 20 AUG 93

Abraham, Sheila (F); Alvarez, Juan; Anderson, Jason; Anderson, Nitasha (F); Arnoth, Geza; Bakke, Jared W.; Barrey, Kathleen (F); Beam, Heather H. (F); Beaton, Mitzi L. (F); Bedford, Robert; Brannstrom, Andrea M. (F); Brown, Denny; Bickler, Cindy (F); Budd, Jason; Caddell, Amy (F); Chaffman, Jason; Chamberlain, Rajan; Chipman, Courtenay (F); Corbett, Nicolle (F); Crush, Kevin; Cuffe, Mandy (F); Darrow, Lee S.; Dayal, Kamlesh; Doleman, Jason; Duttenhoffer, Kelly (F); Evans, Mitch; Forgues, Dodie (F); Freve, Rodney; Fromm, Andrew J.; Gillett, Charles M.; Horan, Christopher; Hunter, Richard G.; Hutchings, Tami (F); Irwin, Wayne A.; Jordan, John James; Kalynuk, Collin; Kamel, Zsa Zsa (F); Karasevich, Raymond; Kardynal, Andrew D.; Knight, Vanessa (F); Laird, Barret; Laird, Janine, (F); Lalonde, Johnathon; Langridge, Stuart H.; Law, Eugene; Lawrence, D'arci (F); Litz, Casey; MacDonald, Chris; Materi, Blayne DT.; Matyjanka, Cain; McIsaac, Joshua; McNabb, Darrin W.; Mill, Terri (F); Mitchell, Gary; Mobey, Jesse R.; Morris, Paul; Nelson, Terry; Pettigrew, Anna (F); Pinay, Brydon; Pinnell, Fiona (F); Pohjolainen, James; Riddell, Daniel Luke; Rohrig,

Brent; Royle, Dristine (F); Schroedter, Tracy (F); Sidhu, Mickey M.; Sonneveld, Mark; Todd, Ryan; Twardy, Karen Rae (F); Vandenbrink, Mark; Wallace, Cory H.; Welty, Calvin; Wright, Chris; Yellowega, Vincent; Zimmerman, Shawn; Zimrose, Roy.

ARMY CADET LEADER INSTRUCTOR – DRILL & CEREMONIAL
B COY
12 JUL 93 - 20 AUG 93

Airth, Clayton; Allard, Lenard; Arsenault, Jeremie; Asner, Samul; Beach, Patricia (F); Blundon, David; Bohemier, Christiane (F); Bray, Chris; Briggs, Peggy (F); Broadfoot, David; Brulotte, Anthony; Burrows, Fraser; Carey, Darren; Carlson, Kyla (F); Channell, Allen; Church, Jason; Cloutier, Louise (F); Comerford, Gary; Dean, Lee; Degray, Stuart; Dudley, Erin (F); Dufault, Patrick; Emmett, Brendon; Geekie, Clayton; George, Amy (F); Harrowei, John; Head, Jessica M. (F); Hewitt, Micheal; Johnson, Donny; Kenny, Lyle; Lamontagne, Ken; Liston, Jeremy; Livingston, Kellie (F); Loder, Helen (F); Marcoux, Yann; Martell, Rachel (F); Maure, Jacques; McCloy, Trevor; McDavid, Iris (F); McDonough, Eric; McIssac, Mathew; Miljour, Jacqueline (F); Moore, Neil; Neuls, Andrea (F); O'Mahony, Simon; Oxford, Rachell (F); Papps, Melanie (F); Parker, Ryan; Peterson, Danny; Redel, Chris; Renaud, Kyle; Richard, Wendy M. (F); Robinson, Rhonda (F); Rumball, Brad; Schiebelbein, Scot; Schofield, Chris; Schuitema, Richard; Sparks, Lori (F); St. Amand, Kevin; Stone, Lori (F); Tamsett, Matthew; Tarrant, Kent; Thompson, Derek L.; Tremblay, Judith (F); Turcotte, Gaetan; Turner, Cindy (F); Veillette, Sandra (F); Wells, William B.; Wessel, Nathan; Wiebe, Corla (F); Wilcox, Erik; Wilson, Dustin; Winders, Jeff; Wood, Brent; Yellowknee, Dwayne.

ARMY CADET LEADER
C COY
12 JUL 93 - 20 AUG 93

Abdon, Stephanie (F); Armstrong, Jim; Beegan, Rory Patrick; Bencit, Ryan; Bergeron, Andrea (F); Blocksidge, Todd; Boivin, Julien; Brant, Scott; Brant, Trevor; Brooks, MacKenzie L. (F); Brown, Patrick; Butlin, Chris; Carbonell, Brent; Carroll, Steve; Caughy, Michelle (F); Christensen, Dara (F); Colangelo, Anthony; Copeland, Gordon; Cross, Jeff; Dirienzo, David; Dumouchel, Yvette (F); Dutkiewicz, John; Emmett, Daniel; Erkelens-Lapointe, Tanya; Escott, Carl; Evans, Daniel; Fei, Ritchie; Fillion, Marie Eve (F); Forcier, Michele (F); Gabriel, Melisa (F); Germain, Casey; Goodridge, Darryl; Gosse, Elisabeth (F); Grimm, Charles; Hackworthy, Regan; Hesse, Alexander K.; Jurasek, Chris; Larder, Chris; Lemky, Shane; Leyen, Chad; Lima, Kirk; Lynem, John; Marshall, Carrie (F); Mayo, Tracy (F); McEvoy, Georg; Mercer, Karen (F); Mercier, Greg; Miller, Chad; Morin, Edgar; Morin, Willy; Morris, Stephanie (F); Nichol, William; Nolan, Stephen; Olson, James K.; Palmer, Christina (F); Peddle, Randy; Petryshyn, Donovan; Pettinger, Jamie; Pinsent, David; Poirier, Julie (F); Purdy, Stephanie (F); Raymond, Christa (F); Reid, David; Robinson, Philip; Ryan, George; Savard, Dominique; Scarfe, Kathleen (F); Sinasac, William M.; Smardon, Joey; Smart, Chad; Smiley, Amanda (F); Soderburg, Shane; Spurrell, Chad; Stewart, Jeremy; Surgeson, Clayton D.; Thibeault, Ron; Traenenberg, Joseh W.; Ulinder, Jonathan O.; Violante, Tony; Wattam, Suzie (F); Weatherb, Stuart; Weitzel, Shannon (F); Wentz, Mark; Whitehead, Jason; Whyte, Lori (F); Willcott, David; Williams, Dwayne; Wilson, Adam E.; Windjack, Andrew; Winchester, Marc; Wurtz, Tara (F); Yankech, Shellisa (F); Zaplashinski, Darcy; Zaplachinski, Jason.

ARMY CADET LEADER
D COY
12 JUL 93 - 20 AUG 93

Ali, Ahsen; Axani, Christian; Ball, Jared; Barry, Allen H.; Beaudoin, Wayne; Bennett, Christine (F); Blum, Brandy (F); Boymhagen, William; Braun, Travis; Brewer, Rhonda (F); Bronson,

Christopher; Brown, Kelsey; Burr, Brad; Button, Lea (F); Caron, Roxanne (F); Carriere, Chad; Chevalier, Patrick; Cockwill, Mark; Collard, Shaun; Colli, Joseph A.; Curry, Everet; Cyr, Amanda (F); Desmeules, Francois; Drapeau, Marc; Elliott, Robert; Estey, Heather M. (F); Fehr, Patrick; Flannigan, Tanya Anne (F); Follis, Kane; Frame, Heather (F); Frocklage, Clint; Gloutier, Isabelle (F); Gorman, Robert; Greanya, Tina (F); Greenslade, Stephen; Grey, Andrew; Greer, David; Hachey, Jeremy; Hamilton, Mark A.; Hamon, Bryan; Hayes, Sauvol; Hayford, Lee; Heward, Blaine; Hughes, Lisa (F); Hughes, Madeline (F); Jurasek, Terry; Kelm, Brita (F); Kidney, Windy (F); Kroetsch, Kristian; Lee, Katie (F); Leicht, Jan; Little, Taryn (F); Livingston, Kenneth N.; Lucvk, Rhonda (F); MacInnis, Amanda (F); Madsen, Christine (F); Martin, Elwood; Martin, Chris; Mason, Tara (F); May, Jeff; McAleese, Brendan; McDonald, Tyler; McEwan, Jason; McMahon, Tad; McMullen, Eric; Melnyk, Jamie; Michaud, Louis-Pierre; Milord, Frederic; Mitchell, Amy (F); Moore, Joseph; Moquin, Russell; Nielsen, Eric; Noonan, Angela (F); Oldfield, Michael; Olson, Neil; Oliver, Erin (F); Portelane, Jean-Joseph; Pratt, Calvin; Radcliffe, Corey; Radcliffe, James; Randolph, Robert; Rawluk, Ryan J.; Reynolds, John; Richard, Christian; Riley, Travis; Ryan, Leann (F); Savoie, Marc; Shillington, Thomas; Smith, Jennifer (F); St. Jacques, Riley; Stark, John; Van Den Brink, John; Vennings, Marthyn; Vincze, Anthony; Willerton, Troy; Witwicki, Lukas.

Army Cadet Leader
E Coy
12 Jul 93 - 20 Aug 93
Almasi, Karen (F); Arshad, Dean A.; Aylott, Dave E.; Baker, Dominic; Baker, Terry M.; Baldeo, Gary; Baumgartner, Lisa (F); Berns, Stephen G.; Bjarnason, Koreana (F); Brauner, Teresa (F); Brennan, Justin; Breton, Sonny; Burke, Ryan; Chambers, Tonia (F); Chang, Daniel; Collins, John; Dobrowski, Derrick; Espares, Larry; Eyestone, Russell; Fleuelling, Mike; Fontaine, Thomas; Forseth, Brian; Gerow, Michelle (F); Goodridge, Dean; Gray, Jeffrey D.; Haleem, Razi; Hanley, Eric; Harden, Christina (F); Harden, Laura (F); Hunter, Lyan S.; Hutcheson, Patrick; Jackson, Bonnie (F); Jacobs, David; Klassen, Melanie (F); Lacovetsky, Ryan; Lange, Kylie (F); Larose, Tom; Lazorko, Charidy (F); Lazorko, Misty Dawn (F); Levitt, Shaun; Lindsay, Dylan; Lissimore, William; Lussier, Christopher; Martin, Gregory H.; Martin, Joy (F); Mazurkiewicz, Michael; McInnis, Patrick D.; McKelvie, Kelly; McKenna, Nicki (F); McKenzie, Rick; Meakin, Brandy (F); Menz, Terry; Mesner, Christopher; Millar, Ian; Mills, Michelle (F); Mitchell, Ted; Moline, Sherry Lynn (F); Mollet, Emily (F); Morgan, Tamara (F); Morton, James Richard; Morton, Micheal John; Nickerson, Billi Jo; Oliver, Christopher; Palmer, Colleen (F); Perry, Bret Robert; Perry, James; Pfeifer, Miranda (F); Piechotta, Carla (F); Plamondon, Kelly Ann (F); Plouffe, Mike; Poulson, Christopher F.; Poier, Shelly L. (F); Quince, David C.; Richards, Philip; Scheller, Brent; Scheneveld, Sonja (F); Seymore, Kennith C.; Shaw, Stephanie (F); Stringer, Cameron S.; Thompson, Joey; Tibbett, Andrew; Tibbett, Sabrina (F); Tor, Sebastian; Traenenberg, Ronald S.; Tworek, Neil AS.; Vallecillo, Milton; Waffle, Marvin C.; Wallace, Sara (F); Weber, Bryan D.; Westhaven, Mike D.

Army Cadet Leader
F Coy
12 Jul 93 - 20 Aug 93
Anderbrg, Dan; Aucoin, Valerie (F); Barker, Russell; Bergman, Eric; Bernier, Tanya (F); Biglar, David; Bolton, Leonard; Bornmann, Roy; Boswell, Alline (F); Bradley, Kirk; Brass, Larry; Braun, Chad; Brock, Colin; Broere, Matt; Bromley, Sean; Camerom, Raymond; Carlson, Jeff; Chadsey, Berson; Challoner, Jason; Challoner, Trevor; Champagne, Belinda (F); Cluff, Chrissy (F); Cluff, Jennifer (F); Connolly, Michelle (F); Cox, Anna (F); Crews, Cory; Davis,

Brad; Davis, Wesley; Demman, Terri (F); Dobbie, Donald; Doerksen, Bonnie (F); Drinkwater, Tracy (F); Dube', Carl; Dyck, Brad; Ebert, Clinton; Eilers, Jon; Finter, Mary-Ellen (F); Forbes, Ronald J.; Graham, Jaime (F); Griffiths, Cody; Heft, Alfred A.; Heimbechaer, Tanya L. (F); Hlady, Katherine (F); Hourd, Ryan; Huck, Cliff; Hudak, David; Hydamaka, Dallas; Jack, Amber (F); Kaglea, Ryan; Keefer, Mike; Knight, Kandice (F); Knoll, Bradley; Lake, Mathew; Lundgren, Troy; Maleschuck, Ellys; Miller, Kerith; Milne, Dallas; Moore, Curtis; Moore, Dale; Morlin, Jason; Morris, Cory; Murata, Warren; Nesbitt, David; Nordic, Dion; Norman, Shane; Numada, Jonathan; O'Keefe, Jeff; Papps, Roxanne (F); Pearce, Tessa (F); Pearson, Micheal; Philipp, Stephanie (F); Podolas, Micheal; Powell, Ryan; Reyes, Paul; Richards, Donnie; Richards, Sherwin; Rienks, Terrance; Ripplinger, Robin; Robinson, Tyler; Rogoza, Dave; Rosebush, Michael; Rumansik, Douglas; Rutledge, Ben; Schmidt, Monte; Schuitema, Cheryl (F); Selbie, Joey; Sigstad, Wade; Sikorski, Kristopher; Silveira, Ryan; Stachowich, James; Stewart, Troy; Stubbington, Darrell; Tait, Joe; Trautman, Mike; Turczyn, Jason; Unwin, Adam; Vandersluis, Curtis; Van der Zander, Peter; Wakefield, Christopher; Walden, Vern; Waughtal, Glen; Wells, Amanda (F); Winders, Jeremy.

Basic Army Cadet - Intake 1
G Coy
12 Jul 93 - 23 Jul 93
Aparicio, Mark Antonio; Baker, Eldon Lucas; Baxter, Joseph Perry; Beauchamp, Dawn (F); Belisle, Trent M.; Bellamy, Cain; Berg, Hal; Berg, Sheldon; Bernhard, Daemien; Bohner, Cory J.; Brady, David; Bryant, Dona Marie (F); Byers, Brian J.; Chapman, Jacob; Chen, Mallory; Clements, Teresa May (F); Cobbs, Jamieson Dean; Cossette, Daniel; DeGray, Jared C.; Dobson, Kevin A.; Dufault, Martin R.; Dufault, Stephan; Duffy, Travis R.; Durr, William M.; Euston, David J.; Evans, Edward; Ewasienko, Carol (F); Ferris, Glen Arthur; Fryklund, Gordon Francis; Gale, Josh David; Gill, Noel; Glass, William Keith; Graham, Owen; Guthrie, Jennifer (F); Hamilton, Val (F); Hanssen, Michelle (F); Harding, David; Hawkins, Thomas; Hede, Daniel, David S.; Hegedus, Lori (F); Hoffman, Monty William; Holtz, Christopher; Jackson, Michael A.; Jaculak, Amanda (F); Johnson, Jeff; Johnson, Michael; Johnson, Neil; Judd, Cynthis D. (F); Kerr, Clinton; Komarychka, Tammy (F); Kozina, Kory; Lambert, Quentin L.; Lamoureux, Christopher; Lange, Kristin M. (F); Laurie, Kevin; Legarie, Cindy (F); Lockhart, Sean; MacPhee, Matthew; Mark, Bryan E.; McEachern, John D.; Mercler, Frank; Mesner, Douglas; Meyers, Angela (F); Mitchell, Jason J.; Morrison, Dana A.; Murfitt, Carl; Mushka, Arthur; Nevett, Murray D.; Nilson, Chad R.; Parr, Mike; Penfold, Christopher E.; Perkins, Andrew F.; Pilon, Philip; Robinson, Christine E. (F); Schluter, Neil; Sigurdson, Kristjan; Sikorski, Kelly E.; Sinclair, Lisa (F); Sobchuk, Matthew; Spray, Lee A.; Stone, Sonja (F); Stonechild, Barbara M. (F); Stonechild, Snowdove (F); Sullivan, Ben Allan; Taylor, Adrian James; Thorne, Amy Louise (F); Trapp, Norman Bruce; Tuchek, Jamie (F); Tuckanow, Elton; Van Moorlehem, Jada M. (F); Van Moorlehem, Jordan; Ward, Corey Nathan; Warner, Kevin; Wells, Vanessa (F); Wilson, Chris Trent; Wilson, Jonathon Floyd; Woodford, Jason; Yoner, Triston David; Zoethout, Matthew.

Basic Army Cadet-Intake 2
G Coy
26 Jul 93 - 06 Aug 93
Armstrong, Josh; Barnett, Marnie (F); Bayley, Adam; Belanger, Mike; Blades, Cory; Boreczek, Sebastian; Brand, Harald; Braun, Jennifer (F); Campbell, Craig; Challenger, Jason; Chin, Vanessa (F); Chorney, David; Cobral, Paul; Cool, Ray; Cottingham, Tana (F); Defosse, Shawn; Desjarlais, John; Dixon, Steven; Doerksen, Chris; Donald, Jason; Dunkley, Carla (F); Dunn, Mike; Dussion, Grant; Eckes, Rick; Edwards, Che; Erb, Melani (F); Evans, Joshua Dean; Fei, Victor;

602

Forsyth, Lee; Fortune, Travis; Gaignard, Dan; Gauthier, Chantal (F); Geekie, Heather (F); Gent, Don; Gibert, James; Gibert, Treasa (F); Giggie, Stanley; Gold, Crystal (F); Gordon, Carla (F); Grinsted, Robert; Haveman, Tim K.; Henderson, Damen; Higgins, Tammy (F); Holbrook, Oren; Holden, Leigh; Hunt, Brian; Huston, Robert; Hynes, Patricia (F); Jacques, Wiley; Julilen, Steve; Kennedy, Lorne; Klein, Eric; Kitsch, Michael; Kosokowsky, Brad; Kutzer, Joey; Lambert, Clinton; Lambert, John; Lardner, Ian; Leahul, David; Leyen, Ryan Daniel; Lima, Jose; Lind, Jolene (F); Loreth, Shawn; Lubinicki, Jenelle (F); Makow, Mike W.G.; Manca, Dawn (F); Mantei, Chris; Martin, Jennifer (F); McDonald, Corey; McDonald, Curtis; McFay, Jason; McKay, Tymoor; McLeod, Charles; Milo, Chad; Namon, Robert; Oakly, David; Offrey, Jessie (F); Ong, Micheal; Parcher, Richard; Parry, Janet (F); Pepper, Kenneth; Peterson, Keith; Peterson, Vincent; Plamondon, Carson; Rakose, Daen; Rivet, Ronald; Rumpel, Anthony; Schuh, Mike; Slauenwhite, Cameron; Smith, Brent; Smith, Ryan P.; Stewart, Chris; Suprun, Robin W.; Swayda, James; Symon, Greg; Taverner, Ryan T.; Van Denbrink, Ryan; Vierra, Diniz; Volk, James; Watkins, Chris; Wesa, Kristian (F); Willis, Chris; Willis, Tammy (F); Wiltse, Kim (F); Winter, Jocelyn G. (F); Wolfe, David; Wolosnick, Ryan; Woolford, Issaac; Young, Charlene (F).

Basic Army Cadet-Intake 1
H Coy
12 Jul 93 - 23 Jul 93
Amos, Paul Raymond; Awan, Aliza Marsha (F); Barber, Graeme; Battle, Mark Timothy; Beaulieu, Melvin Fred; Behm, Daniel Dale; Belanger, Adam Edward; Betz, Tobias; Bishop, Jon Alexander; Blois, Paul; Boarer, Tara (F); Bosma, Michael James; Bowman, Ben; Brown, Andrew A.; Burfield, Kirt; Cloke, Micheal A.; Cockram, Seth; Conroy, Pat; Couper, Sarah Lee (F); Crook, Lisa M. (F); Csercsics, Thomas; Danielson, Lori Lee (F); Darroch, Alfred; Davis, Mark; Desmazes, Ryan P.; Dick, Justin A.; Enequist, Eddy; Ernie, Robert J.; Ford, Tim; Fortier, Amanda (F); Friesen, Brad K.; Gilbert, Stanley I.; Gjuric, Jason; Glowacki, Lucas S.; Gordon, Kenneth J.; Graham, Robert A.; Hallett, Samantha (F); Hauer, Michael M.; Hawkes, Ross A.; Hildebrandt, Jacki (F); Hoover, Ryan J.; Johnston, Cheryl L. (F); Judge, Marc F.; Kenney, Christopher J.; Kincaid, Robert; Krol, Angelica (F); Lafreniere, Chris L.; Lafreniere, Clayton T.; Lagore, Timothy A.; Lamontagne, Jeff; Lamparski, Wojtuk B.; Larsen, Tammy D. (F); Lowe, Justin; Lunan, Ariessa A. (F); Marrington, Ryan R.; Martin, Neil; Martin, Scott Kristopher; Matthews, James Edward; McCallum, Scott; McComb, Colin Brian; McDonald, Christopher J.; McDonald, Josh; McKay, Scott; McKeddie, Bryan G.; Melburn, Bradley T.; Metzner, Raymond M.; Miconi, Jeff; Molesworth, Brent Russel; Munch, Wesley A.; Nayler, Elaine D. (F); Nelson, Karey L. (F); Palmer, Roxy (F); Patrick, Kelvin C.; Ponsford, Tannis L. (F); Ransom, Charlie; Ransom, Nicola A. (F); Reelick, Armand; Reschny, Colton G.; Rhoades, Kelly S. (F); Ristvedt, Lisa (F); Roskell, Jeremy W.; Sak, Trevor; Saunders, Jennifer L. (F); Sawkew, O.J.; Sharma, Bernice (F); Shepherd, Steve; Sinclair, Adam G.; Skipper, Jason H.; Skipper, Wayne D.; Souvie, Amanda (F); Sylvain, Gislain; Tohill, Alana; Tutkaluk, Dwight P.; Van Norman, Blake; Wallace, Matthew A.; Willshear, Leanne (F); Wood, Lindsay D. (F); Wylie, Adam; Yates, Jarritt W.; Zaharoff, Berry.

VERNON ARMY CADET CAMP
Basic Army Cadet-Intake 2
H Coy
26 Jul 93 - 06 Aug 93
Anderson, Kevin; Angus, Laura (F); Anthony, Mark; Baht, Marcel; Barnes, Cori (F); Barnes, Ian; Bauman, Tom, R.; Benard, Kirk D.; Benoit, Roger; Bielecki, Monika (F); Bielacki, Thomasz; Bingham, John; Braun, Matthew; Brickett, Timothy John; Brooker, Nikki (F); Brown, Jeremy; Brunner, Josh; Cal, Donald; Cameron,

Jacob A.; Campbell, Darren; Chartrand, Jason E.; Collins, Daniel; Conners, Tammy (F); Cramton, Aaron; Cuffe, Cassandra (F); Curran, Mathew; Dary, Curtis; Doerr, Keith Kurt; Doerr, Kim; Doucette, Michael; Flannery, Dale; Forest, Ralph George; Foster, Devin Earl; Francis, Sean Scott; Freve, Kurtis; Friese, Ryan Michael; Gainford, Ian; Glena, Peter; Griesbach, James Henry; Hamiton, Corey; Hanson, John; Harriman, Cory; Hartlen, Brian; Hastings, Sherry J. (F); Hipwell, Corrie (F); Holloway, Steven R.J.; Jenkins, Jennifer (F); John, Colin; Jure, John; Kematch, Connie J. (F); Kozak, Colin; Kozloski, Laura (F); Laffin, Steven G.; Lario, Crystal (F); Lazorko, Nathan; Lyons Thomas, Pierre; Maddison, Craig; Mapletoft, Cory Robert; Martinez, Danny; Maxwell, William E.K.; McColm, Debra (F); McDonald, Jason T.; McGonigle, Byron; McInnes, Gordon; McMenamie, Christopher; Moline, Mistie (F); Morin, Tyler; Munn, Kevin; Nicoll, Sean; Norton, Tim James; Olumolade, Gaenga; Olumolade, Toyin (F); Owen, Terence E.; Panagrot, Jonathan; Parsonage, Stephanie A. (F); Parsons, Shane; Patterson, Bradley; Paul, Christopher A.; Pearce, Jonathan; Peerce, John; Pettigrew, Michelle L. (F); Phan, Trung; Poznanski, Lucas; Quinn, Jordan Allan; Robicheau, Tennille (F); Rodriguez, Theresa Mary (F); Rattie, Jamie; Rawluk, Jason Bruce; Rivett, Stephen Paul; Scarfe, Heather (F); Sinclair, Rodd; Sliva, Garth; Smith, Dwight; Stauropoulos, Marrina (F); Stenner, Christian; Stephen, Bernadette (F); Stephen, Thomas; Sterlin, Mike; Sylvester, Jason B.; Tait, Timothy H.; Tardif, Jason W.; Tardiff, Michael; Tinord, Daniel M.J.; Trollope, Chad; Truckle, Clinton; Webb, Shelly (F); Wise, Lance; Yule, Kelly E. (F); Yuen, Jose A.; Zicba, Bart.

Army Cadet Leader Instructor
– Small Bore
I Coy
12 Jul 93 - 20 Aug 93
Baldwin, Emery; Bader, Travis; Benner, Paul; Biggar, Guy R.; Boudreau, Jeffrey; Bourdon, Alan; Boutilier, Elsa-Jean (F); Bourque, Philippe; Buczynski, Henry; Claybrook, Alice (F); Clinton, Brandy (F); Ducas, Dominique; Dauphinais, Anthony; Davidson, Andrew; Davis, Michael Rea; Ellam, Drew; Evely, Chris; Galpin, Morgan Arthur; Gray, Christie (F); Hart, Robert James; Hiltz, Derrick; Hoar, Dwayne; Holden, Patrick; Holloway, Jeffrey A.; Huberdeau, Eric; Ingraham, Maura (F); Jarvis, Kerri (F); Jenkins, Brian; Jones, Greg; Kennedy, Damon J.; Koczak, Andrew; Lalancette, Nancy (F); Laliberte, Renee (F); Le Blanc, Trevor; Lecuyer, Claire J. (F); MacLean, Alex M.; Maslanka, Clinton P.; Maure, Gordon, A.; Miljour, Chantal (F); Miller, Jon; Moyen, Angela (F); Myles, Marcia V. (F); Myshyniuk, Layna (F); Neufeld, Marc; Normore, Donald; O'Toole, Ellen (F); Paschke, Brian; Prescod, Victor; Proctor, Jason; Reid, Benjamin R.; Reid, Laurie; Rodrique, Sylvia; Sacco, Adam J.C.; Smith, Jeffery; Tait, Jesse C.; Todoroff, Michael; Viens, Sarah (F); Weatherbee, Sarah (F); Williamson, Reginald; Witton, Brock.

Army Cadet Leader Instructor
– Quartermaster
I Coy
12 Jul 93 - 20 Aug 93
Bucknell, Joey; Carney, Scott; Carruthers, Charmin (F); Dabrowicz, Marc; Dufault, Clinton A.; French, Christine F. (F); Furlong, Christine (F); Hanna, Ross; Hildebrand, Kristen; Kerr, Jocelyn (F); Kettle, Tanya (F); Kohler, Patrick; Leonard, Lisa (F); Liston, Julia L. (F); Marshall, Chris R.; McCullagh, Shane; Milne, Jake; Neal, Robert G.; Piton, Jimmy; Pollard, Ryan; Proctor, Darin M.; Radl, Jennifer (F); Reviczky, Joshua; Spiers, Peter; Spiers, William R.; Sturt, Tania (F); Willshear, Ian; Wilson, Corinne (F).

Army Cadet Advanced Band
Band Coy
12 Jul 93 - 20 Aug 93
Eiriksson, Darren; Elliott, Jeremy; Philipp, Andrea (F); Salter, Glenda (F); Tritz, Dan; Trott, Teresa (F).

Army Cadet Leader Instructor – Band
Band Coy
12 Jul 93 - 20 Aug 93
Alves, Paul; Bundy, Noel; Crane, Katherine (F); Eiriksson, Jesse J.; Flowers, Paul; Heigh, Amanda S. (F); Knott, David A.; Liggs, Natasha I. (F); Mollin, Patrick R.; Turcott, Gregory; Turner, Kevin; Turner, Jay T.; Wickens, Bruce; Bland, Jodi (F).
Army Cadet Leader - Band
Band Coy
12 Jul 93 - 20 Aug 93
Anderson, Angie (F); Beaudry, Aaron; Beaudry, Ian; Bland, Nicole (F); Brydges, Mitzi (F); Chambrinho, Frank; Childs, Cheril (F); Deacon, Michael; Dion, Debra (F); Dube, Robert; Dunn, Ken; Dunn, Skylene (F); Hiebert, Willie; Howells, Marla R. (F); Johnson, Caylee A. (F); Maguet, Lisa M. (F); Marlow, Andrea R. (F); McPhee, Eliscia M. (F); Meldrum, Cadice (F); Offerman, Dean A.; Peers, Stephen; Philipp, Andrea (F); Razzo, Cliff; Sabo, Luke; Schell, Michael A.; Simard, Misty (F); Stuart, James D.; Stubbs, Jonathon; Stubel, Amie V. (F); Stubel, Ashley L. (F); Toole, Lonnie E.; Toutant, Chantal (F); Turcott, Dwight; Turcott, Melvin; Wyness, Twila (F); Yurchyshyn, Burton; Zradicka, Stephen G.
Army Cadet Leader Instructor - Pipes and Drums
Band Coy
12 Jul 93 - 20 Aug 93
Anderson, Lynn M. (F); Cadotte, Ryan; Devin, Sean P.; Drinkwater, Jody; Eley, Steven; Harrington, Mike; Jones, Jenny (F); Kerr, Braeme; Lauzon, Crysta (F); Lauzon, David; McElrevy, Erin (F); McLaren, David; Morse, Jean (F); Neuls, Nick N.; Stephan, Ryan.
Army Cadet Leader – Pipes and Drums
Band Coy
12 Jul 93 - 20 Aug 93
Burk, Brandon; Cadotte, Collin T.J.; Cameron, Kelly (F); Da Silva, John Paul; Ferguson, David; Gibb, Billi-Jo (F); Hunter, Eric; Lane, Jason; Links, Matthew; Marcq, David Joseph; Martin, Robert; McAmmond, Amber (F); McAmmond, Kenneth L.; Quartly, Sean; Robinson, Brandon J.; Ross, Doug J.; Sheridan, Colleen (F); Sheridan, William; Sillika, Sarah M. (F); Smith, Andrew; Smith, Suzanna J. (F); Townsend, Kevin M.; Wagg, Susan (F).

Basic Army Cadet Band - Intake 1
Band Coy
12 Jul 93 - 30 Jul 93
Asress, Binyam; Bland, Jennifer (F); Bragg, Michael; Bratushesky, Colin; Courtney, Travis; Dart, Curtis; Deines, Curtis; Denny, Scott R.; Dicosimo, Raphael (F); Doerksen, Trevor; Flowers, Leila (F); Foster, Craig; Galitzine, Gloria (F); Gregorowich, Curtis; Haines, Jason S.; Hallett, Sondra Mae (F); Hamelin, David A.; Hein, April Lee; Kaczmarski, Timothy; LaLande, Monique (F); Leonard, Karen (F); Mason, Brent; Mayan, Brandy (F); Mullin, April (F); Pelletier, Tamara (F); Perkinson, David; Pinard, Bernard; Proctor, Kevin J.; Radmacher, Anita L. (F); Robinson, Kenneth; Shuter, Glenn; Stewart, Jeff; Stusrud, Tammy L. (F); Thomson, Andrea L. (F); Yurchyshyn, Cory A. (F).
Army Cadet Basic – Pipes and Drums – Intake 1
Band Coy
12 Jul 93 - 30 Jul 93
Brautigan, Christine (F); Bjordal, Jason; Glass, Patrick; Higgins, Kevin; Lane, Tracy (F); LeClaire, Lyall D.; Martin, Andrew S.; Norris, Mark; Oige, Patricia A. (F); Tennant, Clinton; Wagner, Daniel.
Basic Army Cadet Bank – Intake 2
Band Coy
02 Aug - 20 Aug 93
Barry, Kerylynna; Blakley, Jodie; Calaresu, Sheranda; Cameron, Adele; Challenger, Jennifer; Cook, Tara; Daly, Cherl; Drinkwalter, Steven; Elliott, Dan; Fritsch, Craig; Garrioch, Ryan; Gibb, Donald; Glesby, Ashley; Glousher, Adam; Grexton, N.; Heinrich, Ana; Hochkievich, Shannon; Lousier, Jennifer; Lubkiwski, Shawna; Marlow, Lora-Lee; Pagels, Matthew; Paul, Angela; Paulin, Danielle; Trowsdale, Elaine.
Army Cadet Basic – Pipes and Drums – Intake 2
Band Coy
02 Aug - 20 Aug 93
Bennie, William; Bernier, Joel; Hawkes, Robert William; Howe, Mark; LaPoint, Daris (F); Lochrie, Bobbie; MacMillan, Paula (F); MacPherson, Melena (F); McIntyre, David; Rooks, Darcey; Williams, Megan (F).

"RIGHT DRESS! STAND STILL!"
Real rifles, real bayonets and a knowledge of safety.